1 MONTH OF
FREE
READING

at

www.ForgottenBooks.com

By purchasing this book you are eligible for one month membership to ForgottenBooks.com, giving you unlimited access to our entire collection of over 1,000,000 titles via our web site and mobile apps.

To claim your free month visit:

www.forgottenbooks.com/free922353

ISBN 978-0-260-01544-0
PIBN 10922353

THE

PARLIAMENTARY DEBATES

(AUTHORISED EDITION),

EDITED BY A. KAPADIA.

FOURTH SERIES.

COMMENCING WITH THE FIFTH SESSION OF THE TWENTY-SIXTH PARLIAMENT

OF THE

UNITED KINGDOM OF GREAT BRITAIN AND IRELAND.

---

62 VICTORIÆ.

VOLUME LXVIII.

COMPRISING THE PERIOD FROM

THE SEVENTH DAY OF MARCH

TO

THE TWENTIETH DAY OF MARCH

1899.

PRINTED (FROM LINOTYPE BARS) AT THE

PARLIAMENTARY DEBATES PRINTING WORKS,

CLEMENT'S HOUSE, CLEMENT'S INN, LONDON, W.C.,

FOR

F. MOIR BUSSY,

PUBLISHER OF

"THE PARLIAMENTARY DEBATES" (AUTHORISED EDITION),

(UNDER CONTRACT WITH H.M. GOVERNMENT).

TABLE OF CONTENTS

TO

VOLUME LXVIII.

FOURTH SERIES.

LORDS: TUESDAY, 7TH MARCH 1899.

a 2

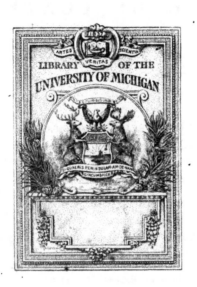

House adjourned at half-past Four of the clock.

COMMONS: TUESDAY, 7TH MARCH 1899.

PRIVATE BILLS (STANDING ORDER 62 COMPLIED WITH)—Mr. Speaker laid
upon the Table Report from one of the Examiners of Petitions for Private
Bills, that in the case of the following Bills, referred on the First
Reading thereof, Standing Order No. 62 has been complied with, viz. :—
Great Southern and Western Railway Bill; Great Southern and
Western, and Waterford, Limerick, and Western Railway Companies
Amalgamation Bill—Ordered, That the Bills be read a second time   ...   4

Brompton and Piccadilly Circus Railway Bill—Read a second time, and
committed   ...   . -   4

South Eastern Railway Bill—Read a second time, and committed   ...   5

Bexhill and Rotherfield Railway Bill—(By Order). Second Reading
deferred till Tuesday next   5

Gas Light and Coke Company Bill—(By Order). Order for Second Reading
read   5

Motion made, and Question proposed—

"That the Bill be now read a second time."

Amendment proposed—

"To leave out the word ' now,' and at the end of the Question to add the words
' upon this day six months.' "—(*Mr. Pickersgill.*)

DEBATE :—

Mr. Pickersgill (Bethnal Green, S.W.)	5	*Mr. Pickersgill*...	8
Mr. Buxton (Tower Hamlets, Poplar)	7	*Mr. Boulnois*	8
Mr. Boulnois (Marylebone, E.)	4	*Mr. Cohen (Islington, E.)* ...	9
		Mr. Bartley (Islington, N.) ...	11

Question put—

"That the word ' now ' stand part of the Question"   11

Motion agreed to.

Main Question put, and agreed to.

Bill read a second time.

Motion made—

"That the Bill be committed to a Select Committee of 15 Members, of whom
seven shall be nominated by the Committee of Selection."
"That it be an instruction to the Committee to inquire into the powers of charge
conferred by Parliament on the Metropolitan Gas Companies, and to report as to the
method in which these powers have been exercised, having regard to the differences of
price charged by the various companies, and also whether the provisions of the Acts
fixing the price of gas supplied and the rate of dividend should be reconsidered.'

HOUSES OF LORDS AND COMMONS PERMANENT STAFF, JOINT COMMITTEE.

Order read, for resuming Adjourned Debate on Question (6th March)—

" That Mr. Hanbury be a Member of the Joint Committee."

OBSERVATIONS :—

Mr. Pirie (Aberdeen, N.) ...   42   [Mr. Speaker] 42

Question put, and agreed to.

Motion made, and Question proposed—

" That Mr. James William Lowther be one other Member of the Committee."— (Mr. Anstruther.)

OBSERVATIONS :—

Mr. Swift MacNeill (Donegal, S.)   42

Question put.

The House divided :—Ayes 214 ; Noes 63. (Division List No. 31.)

Motion made, and Question proposed—

" That Mr. Wharton be one other Member of the Committee."—(Mr. Anstruther.)

OBSERVATIONS:—

Mr. Pirie (Aberdeen, N.)   47

Question put.

The House divided :—Ayes 220 ; Noes 69. (Division List No. 32).

Motion made, and Question proposed—

" That the Committee have power to send for persons, papers, and records : That Three be the quorum."—(Mr. Anstruther.)

OBSERVATIONS :—

Dr. Clark (Caithness)   ...   50   Dr. Clark   51
[Mr. Speaker]   51

Question put.

The House divided :—Ayes 230 ; Noes 63. (Division List No. 33.)

March 8.] *Page*

COMMONS: WEDNESDAY, 8TH MARCH 1899.

Amendment proposed—

" To leave out from the word 'That' to the end of the Question, in order to add the words 'this House refuses to add to the complexity of our present franchise system, which, in its opinion, can be remedied only by the adoption of a single, simple, and uniform franchise' instead thereof."—*Sir C. Dilke.*

Question put—

" That the words proposed to be left out stand part of the Question."

The House divided:—Ayes 188 ; Noes 88.—(Division List No. 35.)

Main Question put, and agreed to.

Bill read a second time, and committed for to-morrow.

Rivers Pollution Prevention Bill—Order for Second Reading read.

Motion made, and Question proposed—

" That this Bill be now read a second time."—*(Sir F. Powell.)*

Amendment proposed—

" To leave out the word 'now' and at the end of the question to add the words 'upon this day six months.'"—*(Mr. Kenyon.)*

And, it being half-past Five of the clock, the Debate stood adjourned.

Debate to be resumed to-morrow.

LORDS: THURSDAY, 9TH MARCH 1899.

House adjourned at fifty-five minutes after Four of the clock.

COMMONS: THURSDAY, 9TH MARCH 1899.

SUPPLY—NAVY ESTIMATES.

Motion made—

" That Mr. Deputy Speaker do now leave the Chair."

House adjourned at ten minutes after Twelve of the clock.

LORDS: FRIDAY, 10TH MARCH 1899.

House adjourned at half-past Four of the clock.

COMMONS: FRIDAY, 10TH MARCH 1899.

MR. SPEAKER'S INDISPOSITION—The House being met, the Clerk at the
Table informed the House of the unavoidable absence of Mr. Speaker,
owing to the continuance of his indisposition :—

Whereupon Mr. JAMES WILLIAM LOWTHER (Cumberland, Penrith, Chairman
of Ways and Means) proceeded to the Table, and, after Prayers, took
the Chair as Deputy Speaker, pursuant to the Standing Order, at Three
of the clock   428

PRIVATE BILLS (STANDING ORDER 62 COMPLIED WITH)—Mr. Deputy
Speaker laid upon the Table Report from one of the Examiners of
Petitions for Private Bills, That in the case of the following Bill,
referred on the First Reading thereof, Standing Order No. 62 has been
complied with, viz. :—Walker and Wallsend Union Gas (Electric Lighting)
Bill. Ordered, That the Bill be read a second time   429

SUPPLY—Considered in Committee.

CIVIL SERVICES AND REVENUE DEPARTMENTS (SUPPLEMENTARY ESTIMATES), 1898-99.

CLASS V.

1. £256,000, Supplementary, Uganda, Central and East Africa Protectorates, and Uganda Railway.

Debate resumed on the Question—

" That a supplementary sum not exceeding £256,000 be granted to Her Majesty to defray the charge which will come in the course of payment during the year ending 31st day of March 1899, for grants-in-aid to Uganda, British Central Africa, and British East Africa."

March 10.]   *Page*

Original Question put, and agreed to.

CLASS II.

2. £2,400, Supplementary, Colonial Office.

Motion made, and Question proposed—

"That a supplementary sum not exceeding £2,400 be granted to Her Majesty to defray the charge which will come in the course of payment during the year ending 31st March 1899, for salaries and expenses of Her Majesty's Secretary of State for the Colonies."

OBSERVATIONS :—

Sir E. Ashmead-Bartlett ...   465   [The Deputy Chairman]   ...   465

Question put, and passed.

CLASS V.

3. Motion made, and Question proposed—

"That a supplementary sum not exceeding £139,425 be granted to Her Majesty to defray the charge which will come in the course of payment during the year ending 31st day of March 1899, for sundry Colonial services, including certain grants-in-aid."

Motion made—

"That the item B, £70,000 for the Gold Coast (Grants in Aid of Northern Territories) be omitted from the proposed Vote."—(*Mr. Weir.*)

March 10.]   *Page*

House adjourned at twenty minutes after Seven of the clock.

LORDS: MONDAY, 13TH MARCH 1899.

House adjourned at forty-five minutes past Four of the clock.

QUESTIONS.

" That Her Majesty's Representative at Pekin is now supporting the demands
of Italy for a sphere of interest in Chinese territory with Samnun Bay as a naval
base, notwithstanding the Resolution passed by this House on the 1st March 1898,
' that it is of vital importance for British commerce and influence that the independence
of Chinese territory should be maintained.' "

Motion made, and Question proposed—

" That this House do now adjourn."—(*Mr. Pritchard Morgan.*)

Motion negatived.

BUSINESS OF THE HOUSE (GOVERNMENT BUSINESS)—Motion made,
and Question proposed—

"That Government Business have precedence To-morrow, and that the provisions
of Standing Order 56 be extended to that day's Sitting."—(The First Lord of the
Treasury.)

Question put—

"That the words 'Government Business' stand part of the Question   570

Agreed to.

Main Question put—

"That Government Business have precedence to-morrow, and that the provisions
of Standing Order 56 be extended to that day's sitting."—(First Lord of the
Treasury)   570

The House divided—Ayes 222 ; Noes 118. (Division List No. 39.)

House adjourned at twenty minutes after Twelve of the clock.

"That this Bill be read a second time." (The Lord Chancellor.)

OBSERVATIONS:

The Lord Chancellor (The Earl of Halsbury)   667

Question put,

Bill read a second time, and committed to a Committee of the Whole
House on Friday next.

Question put—

　　" That the word ' now ' stand part of the Question."

The House divided :—Ayes 288 ; Noes 82. (Division List No. 41.)

Main Question put, and agreed to.

Bill read a second time.

OBSERVATIONS :—

　　" Bill committed to a Committee of nine Members, five to be nominated by the House, and four by the Committee of Selection."—(*Mr. Bryce.*)

Great Southern and Western, and Waterford, Limerick, and Western Railway Companies Amalgamation Bill—Second Reading.

Amendment proposed—

　　" To leave out the word 'now,' and at the end of the Question to add the words ' upon this day six months.'"—(*Mr. J. Redmond.*)

DEBATE :—

SUPPLY [2ND ALLOTTED DAY]—

(In the Committee.)

ARMY ESTIMATES, 1899-1900—Motion made, and Question proposed—

"That a sum not exceeding £6,509,000 be granted to Her Majesty, to defray the Charge for the Pay, Allowances, and other Charges of Her Majesty's Army at Home and Abroad (exclusive of India) (General Staff, Regiments, Reserve, and Departments), which will come in course of payment during the year ending on the 31st day of March 1900."

Motion made—

"That Item I (Recruiting Expenses) be reduced by £100."—(Mr. Weir)

March 14.]   *Page*

DISCUSSION :—

Question put—

     " That Item 1 (Recruiting Expenses) be reduced by £100."—(*Mr. Weir.*)

The Committee divided :—Ayes 56 ; Noes 161. (Division List No. 42).

Original Question again proposed.

Motion made—

     " That Vote 1 be reduced by £100."

DISCUSSION :—

     Mr. Courtenay Warner (Staffordshire, Lichfield)   835

And, it being midnight, the Chairman left the Chair to make his report to the House. Committee report Progress, to sit again this day.

TUBERCULOSIS—Question as to Discussion of Motion.

Infectious Diseases (Notification) Act, 1889, Extension Bill—Second Reading.

DEBATE :—

Second Reading deferred till Monday next.

COMMONS: WEDNESDAY, 15TH MARCH 1899.

House adjourned at forty-five minutes after Five of the clock.

LORDS: THURSDAY, 16TH MARCH 1899.

South Eastern and London, Chatham, and Dover Railway Companies Bill—
  Motion made, and Question proposed—

> "That it be an Instruction to the Committee that they consider the terms and
> conditions proper to be imposed upon the said Railway Companies on the occasion of
> their amalgamation, in respect of reductions of fares, rates, tolls, and charges leviable by
> them on their local and continental traffic, and in respect of the provision of any such
> further and better facilities for the conveyance of passengers and goods as may be
> properly required from them."—(Mr Woods.)

DEBATE:—

Motion, by leave, withdrawn.

VOL. LXVIII. [FOURTH SERIES.]

March 16.]   *Page*

SUPPLY (NAVY ESTIMATES)—Debate resumed on Question [13th March]—

" That 110,640 men and boys be employed for the Sea and Coast Guard Services
for the year ending on the 31st March 1900, including 18,505 Royal Marines."

DEBATE :—

House adjourned at half-past Twelve of the clock.

LORDS: FRIDAY, 17TH MARCH 1899.

COMMONS : FRIDAY, 17TH MARCH 1899.

SUSPENSION OF TWELVE O'CLOCK RULE.

Motion made, and Question put—

       " That the Business of Supply, if under discussion at Twelve o'clock this night, be not interrupted under Standing Order Sittings of the House."—*(First Lord of the Treasury)*   1158

The House divided : Ayes 159 ; Noes 96.   (Division List No. 46.)

SUPPLY—ARMY ESTIMATES, 1899-1900.

Motion made, and Question proposed—

       " That a sum not exceeding £6,509,000 be granted to Her Majesty to defray the charge for the Pay, Allowances, and other charges, of Her Majesty's Army at Home and Abroad (exclusive of India) (General Staff, Regiments, Reserve and Departments), which will come in the course of payment during the year ending 31st day of March, 1900."

Amendment proposed—

       " That a sum; not exceeding £6,508,800, be granted for the said Service."—*(Mr. Courtenay Warner.)*

DISCUSSION :—

Mr. *Courtenay Warner* (*Stafford, Lichfield*) ... 1161	The *Under Secretary of State for War* (Mr. *G. Wyndham, Dover*) 1179
Mr. *Buchanan* (*Aberdeenshire, E.*) 1171	Mr. *Courtenay Warner* ... 1180
[*The Deputy Chairman*] ... 1173	Mr. *Wyndham*... 1180
Mr. *Buchanan* 1173	Mr *Courtenay Warner*... ... 1185
General *Goldsworthy* (*Hammersmith*) 1178	

Question put—

       " That a sum, not exceeding £6,508,800, be granted for the said Service "— *(Mr. Warner)*   1186

The Committee divided :—Ayes 79 ; Noes 170.   (Division List No 47.)

VOL. LXVIII. [FOURTH SERIES.]   *f*

DISCUSSION (Continued):—

Original Question again proposed.

Motion made—

" That a sum not exceeding £6,508,950 be granted for the said Service;"—(Mr. Pirie.)

DISCUSSION :—

Amendment, by leave, withdrawn.

Original Question again proposed.

DISCUSSION :—

f 2

Original Question again proposed.

DISCUSSION :—

Vote agreed to.

Motion made, and Question proposed—

     " That a sum not exceeding £1,555,000 be granted to Her Majesty to defray the Charge for Retired Pay, Half-Pay, and other non-effective Charges for Officers and others, which will come in course of payment during the year ending on 31st March 1900."

DISCUSSION :—

Motion made, and Question proposed—

     " That the Chairman do report Progress and ask leave to sit again."—*(Mr. Buchanan.)*

DISCUSSION :—

Motion made, and Question put—

     " That the Chairman do report Progress and ask leave to sit again."—*(Mr. Buchanan.)*

The Committee divided :—Ayes 32 ; Noes 107. (Division List No. 50.)

Original Question again proposed—

DISCUSSION :—

House adjourned at Two of the clock.

LORDS: MONDAY, 20TH MARCH 1899.

THE LORD CHANCELLOR acquainted the House that the Clerk of the Parliaments had laid upon the Table the Certificates from the Examiners that the further Standing Orders applicable to the following Bills have been complied with: Crowborough District Gas; St. David's Water and Gas. And the Certificate that no Standing Orders are applicable to the following Bill: Broughty Ferry Gas and Paving Order [H.L.]. The same were ordered to lie on the Table   1289

STANDING ORDERS COMMITTEE—Report from, That the Standing Orders not complied with in respect of the Petition for additional provision in the Mersey Docks and Harbour Board (Pilotage) Bill [H.L.] ought to be dispensed with, and leave given to the Committee on the Bill to insert the additional provision. That the Standing Orders not complied with in respect of the Petition for additional provision in the Gainsborough Urban District Council (Gas) Bill [H.L.] ought to be dispensed with, and leave given to the Committee on the Bill to insert the additional provision. That the Standing Orders not complied with in respect of the London Water (Welsh Reservoir and Works) Bill ought to be dispensed with. That the Standing Orders not complied with in respect of the Belfast Corporation Bill ought to be dispensed with, provided clause 41 be struck out of the Bill. That the Standing Orders not complied with in respect of the National Telephone Company (No. 1) Bill ought to be dispensed with, provided clause 94 be struck out of the Bill. That the Standing Orders not complied with in respect of the National Telephone Company (No. 2.) Bill ought to be dispensed with, provided clause 16 be struck out of the Bill.—Read and agreed to   1290

WORKINGTON CORPORATION WATER BILL [H.L.]—Petition for additional provision; of the Corporation of Workington; together with proposed clauses and amendments annexed thereto; read, and referred to the Examiners   1290

DUNDEE GAS, TRAMWAYS, AND EXTENSION BILL (H.L.)—A Petition of Messrs. Grahames, Currie, and Spens, of 30, Great George Street, Westminster, Parliamentary agents, praying for leave to present a petition of Captain Clayhills Henderson, praying to be heard by counsel against the Bill, although the time limited by Standing Order No. 92 for presenting such Petition has expired; read, and ordered to lie on the Table; and Standing Order No. 92 to be considered to-morrow in order to its being dispensed with in respect of the said Petition   1290

Arbroath Corporation Gas Bill [H.L.]—Committee to meet on Friday next 1291

Kirkcaldy Corporation and Tramways Bill [H.L.]—Committee to meet on Friday next 1291

COMMONS: MONDAY, 20TH MARCH 1899.

March 20.]

SUPPLY—COMMITTEE—

CIVIL SERVICES AND REVENUE DEPARTMENTS, 1899-1900 (VOTE ON ACCOUNT).

Motion made, and Question proposed—

"That a sum, not exceeding £14,781,000, be granted to Her Majesty, on account, for or towards defraying the Charges for the Civil Services and Revenue Departments for the year ending on the 31st day of March 1900."

DISCUSSION :—

Motion made, and Question proposed—

"That Item 5, Class 2 (Foreign Office) be reduced by £100."—(Mr. Joseph Walton.)

DISCUSSION :—

Amendment, by leave, withdrawn.

ANGLO-AMERICAN COMMISSION.

DISCUSSION :—

Motion for reduction withdrawn.

Original Question again proposed.

March 20.]   *Page*

LORDS: 21ST MARCH 1899.

REPRESENTATIVE PEERS FOR IRELAND—Earl of Wicklow's Claim—Report made from the Lord Chancellor that the right of Ralph Francis Earl of Wicklow to vote at the elections of Representative peers for Ireland, has been established to the satisfaction of the Lord Chancellor ; read, and ordered to lie on the Table   1497

Parish Churches (Scotland) Bill—(Committee).

Amendment proposed—

"Page 1, line 10, after ' of ' insert ' the heritors and Kirk Session of the parish and.' "—*(Lord Tweedmouth.)*

DISCUSSION :—

Amendment negatived.

Question put—

Motion agreed to.

New clause proposed—

" Page 2, after line 11, insert new clause 3—

" 3. The Court of Teinds, before making any order under this Act, for the sale of any old church or site thereof, and manse, shall satisfy itself whether there are any objects of historical or architectural interest in connection with such church, site, or manse which are worthy of being preserved and maintained, and, on being satisfied that such objects exist, to direct that such church, site, or manse shall be disposed of subject to such stipulations and conditions as the Court shall consider appropriate and sufficient to secure the proper preservation and maintenance of such objects.

" The Court of Teinds, before making any order to change the site of a parish church in a city or town, shall satisfy itself that reasonable provision is made for the care and support of the poor of the district from which said church is proposed to be removed.

" Should the Court of Teinds be of opinion that any locality from which a church or manse is proposed to be removed is in need of an open space, it may, in its discretion, sanction the removal of such church or manse on condition only that the old church or manse shall be demolished, and that the site thereof shall be cleared and left as an open space in all time coming.—*(Lord Tweedmouth.)*

DISCUSSION :—

House adjourned at Five of the clock.

COMMONS: TUESDAY, 21ST MARCH 1899.

TABLE OF CONTENTS.

And, it being Midnight, the Debate stood adjourned.

Debate to be resumed upon Thursday.

CIVIL SERVICES AND REVENUE DEPARTMENT, 1899-1900 (VOTE ON ACCOUNT).

"That a sum, not exceeding £14,781,000, be granted to Her Majesty, on account, for or towards defraying the charges for the Civil Services and Revenue Departments for the year ending on the 31st day of March 1900, viz. :—

CIVIL SERVICES.	£		£
CLASS II.		Royal Parks and Pleasure Gardens	40,000
		Miscellaneous Legal Buildings	
Colonial Office	17,500	Great Britain	18,000
		Houses of Parliament Buildings ...	12,000
CLASS I.		Art and Science Buildings, Great	
Royal Palaces and Marlborough House ... .., ...	16,400	Britain	10,000
		Diplomatic and Consular Buildings	9,000

Resolution read a second time.

Amendment proposed—

"To leave out '£14,781,000' and insert '£14,780,900' instead thereof."—
(*Mr. Havelock Wil on*)

DISCUSSION :—

Question put—

"That '£14,781,000' stand part of the Resolution.".. 1680

The House divided :—Ayes, 139 ; Noes, 31. (Division List No. 67.)

DISCUSSION (Continued) :—

Question put—

"That this House doth agree with the Committee in the said Resolution." ... 1690

House divided :—Ayes, 134 ; Noes, 32. (Division List No. 68.)

House adjourned at twenty-five minutes after Two of the clock.

BILLS DEALT WITH IN VOL. LXVIII.

THE

PARLIAMENTARY DEBATES

(AUTHORISED EDITION)

EDITED BY A. KAPADIA.

IN THE

FIFTH SESSION OF THE *TWENTY-SIXTH PARLIAMENT* OF THE
UNITED KINGDOM OF *GREAT BRITAIN* AND *IRELAND*, APPOINTED
TO MEET THE 7TH FEBRUARY 1899, IN THE 62ND YEAR OF THE
REIGN OF

HER MAJESTY QUEEN VICTORIA.

THIRD VOLUME OF SESSION 1899.

An Asterisk (*) at the commencement of a Speech indicates revision by the Member.

HOUSE OF LORDS.

Tuesday, 7th March 1899.

THE LORD CHANCELLOR took his
seat upon the Woolsack at Four of the
clock.

PRIVATE BILL BUSINESS.

WICK AND PULTENEY HARBOURS
BILL [H.L.]

A Petition of Messrs. Sherwood and
Company, of 7, Great George Street,
Westminster, Parliamentary agents,
praying for leave to present a Petition of
the Provost, Magistrates, and Town
Council of Wick, praying to be heard by
Counsel against the Bill, although the
time limited by Standing Order No. 92
for presenting such a Petition has expired; read, and ordered to lie on the
Table and Standing Order No. 92 to
be considered on Thursday next in order
to its being dispensed with in respect of
the said Petition.

VOL. LXVIII. [FOURTH SERIES.]

ABERDEEN HARBOUR BILL [H.L.]
Committee to meet on Tuesday next.

COALVILLE URBAN DISTRICT GAS BILL
[H.L.]
Committee to meet on Tuesday next.

LONDON AND SOUTH WESTERN RAIL-
WAY BILL [H.L.]
Read second time (according to order).

NORTHERN ASSURANCE COMPANY
BILL [H.L.]
Committed.

Cambridge University and Town Gas Bill
[H.L.]

South Staffordshire Tramways Bill [H.L.]

Weston-super-Mare, Clevedon, and Portishead Tramways Company (Light Railway Extensions) Bill [H.L.]

A

Oystermouth Railway or Tramroad Bill [H.L.]

Committed: The Committees to be proposed by the Committee of Selection.

St. Alban's Gas Bill [H.L.]

Oystermouth Railway or Tramroad Bill [H.L.]

Birkenhead Corporation Bill [H.L.]

Wallasey Tramways and Improvements Bill [H.L.]

Great Yarmouth Corporation Bill [H.L.]

Great Yarmouth Pier Bill [H.L.]

Loughborough and Sheepshed Railway Bill [H.L.]

Birmingham, North Warwickshire, and Stratford-upon-Avon Railway Bill [H.L.]

North Staffordshire Railway Bill [H.L.]

Report from the Committee of Selection, That the following Lords be proposed to the House to form the Select Committee for the consideration of the said Bills; (viz.),

E. Dartrey,
L. Saltoun,
L. Forester,
L. Poltimore (chairman),
L. Raglan;

agreed to; and the said Lords appointed accordingly: The Committee to meet on Tuesday next, at Eleven o'clock; and all petitions referred to the Committee with leave to the petitioners praying to be heard by Counsel against the Bills to be heard as desired, as also Counsel for the Bills.

———

NEW BILL.

———

TROUT FISHING ANNUAL CLOSE TIME (SCOTLAND) BILL [H.L.].

A Bill to provide an annual close time for trout fishing in Scotland—Was presented by the Lord Balfour; read the first time; and to be printed. (No. 18.)

BILLS ADVANCED.

———

PARISH CHURCHES (SCOTLAND) BILL [H.L.]

To be read the second time on Thursday next.

———

TELEGRAPH (CHANNEL ISLANDS) BILL [H.L.]

Read third time (according to order); an amendment made; Bill passed, and sent to the Commons.

House adjourned at half-past Four of the clock, to Thursday next, a quarter-past Four of the clock.

———

HOUSE OF COMMONS.

Tuesday, 7th March 1899.

———

MR. SPEAKER took the Chair at Three of the clock.

———

PRIVATE BILL BUSINESS.

PRIVATE BILLS (STANDING ORDER 62 COMPLIED WITH).

MR. SPEAKER laid upon the Table Report from one of the Examiners of Petitions for Private Bills, That in the case of the following Bills, referred on the First Reading thereof, Standing Order No. 62 has been complied with, viz.:—

Great Southern and Western Railway Bill.

Great Southern and Western, and Waterford, Limerick, and Western Railway Companies Amalgamation Bill.

Ordered, That the Bills be read a second time.

———

BROMPTON AND PICCADILLY CIRCUS RAILWAY BILL.

Read a second time, and committed.

SOUTH EASTERN RAILWAY BILL.
Read a second time, and committed.

BEXHILL AND ROTHERFIELD RAILWAY BILL.

(By Order). Second Reading deferred till Tuesday next.

GAS LIGHT AND COKE COMPANY BILL.

(By Order). Order for Second Reading read. •

Motion made, and Question proposed—

" That the Bill be now read a second time."

Amendment proposed—

"To leave out the word 'now,' and at the end of the Question to add the words 'upon this day six months."—(*Mr. Pickersgill.*)

MR. PICKERSGILL (Bethnal Green, S.W.): Mr. Speaker, I rise to move that this Bill be read a second time this day six months. It is a Bill promoted by a company of which the House has heard a good deal during recent years. This company has an enormous capital, amounting to nearly 12 millions sterling, and serves a very large area in the North of London. Throughout that vast area the most profound dissatisfaction exists among the consumers with the management of this company, and the results of that management, and the dissatisfaction is made all the more keen and all the more clamorous by the fact that the consumer on the north side of the Thames has to pay 3s. per thousand feet for his gas, whereas the consumer on the other side gets his gas for 2s. 3d., and will, according to an announcement which was recently made, get it for 2s. 2d. in the immediate future. This Company keeps coming to Parliament for new powers. Last year it obtained an Act enabling it to split its stock, and this year the Company has a Bill of another kind, which is now before the House. All the gas consumers of North London say, and what I desire respectfully to press upon the House is, that before these new powers are granted, some conditions ought to be imposed on this Company in the interests of the consumers. The promoters of the Bill have issued a statement in which they say that this is a most ordinary type of private Bill. That is a distinction to which I cannot give my assent. Part, and a very important part, of this Bill seems to me of an unusual, exceptional, and extraordinary character. It appears that from time to time lands have been acquired by the Company without Parliamentary powers. These lands were conveyed to the Governor of the Company and another person, and held by them as trustees for the Company, who now come to Parliament and, through this Bill, ask Parliament to legalise their position with regard to these lands. I think, Sir, that that is a demand made upon Parliament to which Parliament should be slow to respond, and certainly there is nothing in the relations of the Company with the public to induce Parliament to in any way consider and be lenient to this Company. The Company have been holding lands without legal authority, and I think this House ought to leave them to settle their position the best way they can, and not now condone their illegality. The remainder of the Bill deals with the proposed increase of stock. The House may possibly remember, from the discussion we have had on this Company and its management on previous occasions, that it is over-capitalised at present. But, notwithstanding that that is so, this Bill actually proposes to increase the capital of the company by no less a sum than three and a half millions sterling. The promoters urge that debenture stock bears a lower rate of interest than the ordinary capital. That is true, and if the new debenture stock were to take the place of the ordinary capital, the statement would be evidently true, but this debenture stock is to be created in addition to the already existing capital. Therefore, the interest to be provided on so large an amount of new capital must tend to an increase rather than to a reduction of the cost of gas. There is one other portion of this statement to which I must refer. An allusion is made to the poorer class of consumers, who make use of the penny-in-the-slot system. I am surprised that that reference should have been made, because of all the classes of consumers of the Gas Light and Coke Company, I think the poorer class, who have occasion to make use of the penny-in-the-slot system, are most harshly treated. I find that the Gas Light and Coke Company charge 1d. for every 22 cubic feet consumed, whereas the South Metropolitan Gas Company charge 1d. for every 29 cubic feet. So much for the allusion to the tender regard of the Company for the interests of the poorer class of consumers. This Bill is opposed by the Corporation of the City of London, and the fact that I am co-operating with the Corporation of the City of London in this matter—and I very seldom have the pleasure to ' be in agreement with that Corporation—is, I think, some sort of *primá-facie* argument in favour of the reasonableness of my opposition to this Bill. I ask the House, then, to reject the Bill, but if the House should be against me on that issue, I will, as an alternative, ask the House to refer this Bill to a Select Committee, so that full inquiry may be made into the management of the Company, and the operation of the Sliding Scale, and as to the justice of the existing Statutory conditions before the House departs finally with its control over this Bill. I move, Mr. Speaker, that this Bill be read a second time this day six months.

MR. BUXTON (Tower Hamlets, Poplar): Mr. Speaker, I rise to second the Amendment.

MR. BOULNOIS (Marylebone, E.): Mr. Speaker, the honourable and learned Gentleman the Member for Bethnal Green has described this as not an ordinary Bill. I maintain that it is quite ordinary in character. It is a Bill of the type which is usually sent to a Select Committee. It is promoted by the existing Company in order to raise further capital, which they cannot do unless they get the sanction of Parliament. There is no question of principle whatever involved in it; it simply asks that the Company may raise further capital in order that they may fulfil the Statutory obligations which have been imposed upon them by Parliament. It is quite impossible for this House to say whether this further capital is needed by the company or not; that is a matter for the Select Committee to inquire into in the ordinary way. As to the question of the price of gas which the honourable and learned Member has raised, I maintain that that is a question with which this House cannot deal. That is also a matter for the Select Committee. If

Mr. Pickersgill.

the company are charging too much, the Committee will deal with that, no doubt. There may be 20 reasons why the Gas Light and Coke Company charge more than do the South Metropolitan Gas Company on the other side of the water, and I have no doubt the former company could give a very good defence of their higher charge if an inquiry were made. My honourable Friend the Member for East Islington has put down a Motion to ask the House to appoint a Select Committee to inquire into the powers conferred by Parliament on the Metropolitan Gas Companies, and this Motion had been practically blocked by the honourable and learned Gentleman the Member for Bethnal Green, who will not allow the inquiry, and also refuses the company this Bill. I hope the House will free the company from the present deadlock by adopting the usual course, and letting this Bill go to a Select Committee. The honourable and learned Member for Bethnal Green said this company was continually coming to Parliament for further powers. That is not exactly correct. It is true that they came last year or the year before to Parliament in order to get permission to consolidate or make some alteration in their stock; but it is a fact that they have not been to Parliament for 23 years for powers to raise additional capital. And when one considers the enormous growth of London, and the extension of the district which this company have to supply, I think it will be agreed that it is not unreasonable that after so long a time the company should find themselves unable sufficiently to extend their works and mains in order to supply the increased population. The honourable and learned Member has referred to the claim of the company that they are supplying the increasing demand of the working population for gas on the penny-in-the-slot system. I think it is creditable to the country that they should have established that system.

MR. PICKERSGILL: Mr. Speaker, I should like to say, by way of explanation, that I do not object to the penny-in-the-slot system. What I objected to was the exorbitant charge which is made by the company.

MR. BOULNOIS: The honourable and learned Gentleman says that the Gas Light and Coke Company charge 1d. for every 22 cubic feet consumed in this way, whereas the South Metropolitan Gas Company charge 1d. for 29 feet. That is not a very great difference, and there may be many reasons why the company are obliged to charge more than the South Metropolitan Gas Company. The same thing applies to Electric Lighting Companies in London. It is quite understandable that their prices vary for many reasons. The honourable and learned Gentleman says he is allied with the Corporation of the City of London in opposition to this Bill. I should like to know whether the Corporation has given him a brief to appear for them. I should be very much surprised if the City of London were desirous of throwing out this Bill on the Second Reading, when they would have a right to appear and lodge their objections against the Bill before the Committee upstairs to which it would be sent. Moreover, the City of London have two representatives in this House who could come here and stand up for the City without the City being compelled to appeal for assistance to the honourable and learned Gentleman the Member for Bethnal Green. I am surprised at the unusual course he has adopted of asking the House to reject this Bill, and not to send it to the Committee, who could make all the necessary inquiries, examine all the witnesses, and hear all the objections which could be urged against it. This House is not the proper tribunal to deal with details, and I contend that the honourable and learned Gentleman opposite has not shown any reason why this Bill, which is urgently required by the company, should not be considered, and I hope the House will give it a Second Reading, so that it may go to Committee and be carefully considered.

MR. COHEN (Islington, E.): Mr. Speaker, I should like to say one word in support of what has fallen from my honourable Friend the Member for East Marylebone, because I have had, ever since the commencement of the Session, a Motion on the Paper, which has for its object, and which, in my opinion, would have for its result, that which the honourable Member for Bethnal Green professes to desire—namely, the appointment of a Committee to inquire into the powers of charge conferred on the Metro-

politan Gas Companies, with a view to secure uniformity of charge on the north and south sides of the Thames. It is owing to the opposition of the honourable Member for Bethnal Green that that inquiry could not be obtained. I do not see how opposition to this Measure, or to this inquiry for which I have moved, can in any way cheapen the price of gas. The effect of the honourable Gentleman's tactics is to prevent inquiry, and also to prevent our getting before the Committee upstairs the case which we believe we have to make. I do not come to this House as a supporter of the interests of the Gas Light and Coke Company. I believe they do charge unjustly, and it is because I believe that that I want to apply a remedy which will give us redress from our grievance. But I do not want to stop the company in obtaining the Measure now before the House, which, if it does anything at all, will facilitate a more efficient supply of gas on the north side of the Thames. I believe the improvement of their plant would facilitate a cheap and expeditious supply of gas throughout their district. I am sorry that the London County Council, of which body I have the honour to be a member, is also opposing this Bill, but they do so avowedly for reasons with which I have no sympathy. They are of opinion that it will enhance the value of the undertaking of the Gas Light and Coke Company. I do not know whether it will or not, but if it does it will only do so legitimately, because the company are going to add many hundred miles of additional piping. I hope the argument of the London County Council is not one which will appeal to the House. I have the honour to be one of the representatives of the City on the London County Council, and I know that the Corporation of the City of London are in sympathy with my Motion for a Committee, which the honourable Member has blocked, and I do not know, notwithstanding that I am one of their representatives, that they are at all opposed to this Measure. I, therefore, view with some suspicion the statement of the honourable and learned Member that he is opposing this Bill in association with the Corporation of the City of London. I hope the House will unanimously give the Bill a Second Reading.

MR. BARTLEY (Islington, N.): Mr. Speaker, my constituents take a great interest in this matter, and are extremely anxious to have the inquiry which my honourable Friend has suggested. I think it should be publicly stated that the reason why this inquiry cannot be held is that the honourable Member for Bethnal Green has insisted in blocking the inquiry.

Question put—

"That the word 'now' stand part of the Question."

Motion agreed to.

Main Question put, and agreed to.

Bill read a second time.

MR. PICKERSGILL: Mr. Speaker, I will now ask the House to take the alternative course to which I alluded just now, and send this Bill to a Select Committee. That is a course which, under similar circumstances, the House has often taken. There are many precedents, of which I will cite one or two, where a private Bill, having been introduced in connection with a subject relating to which an inquiry by the House was either pending or imminent, has been referred to a Select Committee with special instructions. In 1866 the City of London had a Gas Bill before this House, and the House read it a second time, and referred it to a Select Committee, at the same time directing that Committee to inquire into the operations and the results of the Metropolis Gas Act, 1860. In the following year there was the East London Thames Supply Bill, which was also committed to a Select Committee, with instructions to inquire into the operations and the results of the Metropolis Water Act, 1852. Again, in 1886, there was the London City Traffic Regulation Bill—a private Bill—which was committed to a Select Committee, with instructions to inquire as to the best means of regulating the traffic in the Metropolis. These are precedents on which I rely in asking the House to take the course which I suggest. I therefore propose to move—

"That the Bill be committed to a Select Committee of 15 Members, of whom seven shall be nominated by the Committee of Selection."

"That it be an instruction to the Committee to inquire into the powers of charge conferred by Parliament on the Metropolitan Gas Companies, and to report as to the method in which these powers have been exercised, having regard to the differences of price charged by the various companies, and also whether the provisions of the Acts fixing the price of gas supplied and the rate of dividend should be reconsidered."

*MR. SPEAKER: Perhaps it will assist the honourable Member if I tell him now that his Instruction is out of order. It proposes to refer to the Select Committee on this Bill the consideration of the affairs and position of a number of other independent companies, to which the Bill has no reference. The honourable Member will see that it is an altogether impossible Instruction upon this Bill.

MR. PICKERSGILL: Then I beg to move that this Bill be referred to a Select Committee. The object of doing this is to enable the House to keep control over the Bill until a more effectual inquiry has been made into the management of the Gas Light and Coke Company, into the results of that management, and into the statutory conditions at present existing than would be possible if this Bill was referred to an ordinary Committee.

MR. S. SMITH (Flintshire): I beg to second the Motion.

THE CHAIRMAN OF WAYS AND MEANS (Mr. J. W. LOWTHER, Cumberland, Penrith): I hope the honourable and learned Member will not persist in this Motion. After the ruling of the Speaker there can be no real object in sending this Bill to a Select Committee of 15 Members, because they would not have the power that the honourable Member intended when he put this Instruction on the Paper.

MR. PICKERSGILL: In view of your ruling, Mr. Speaker, I beg to withdraw my Motion.

Motion, by leave, withdrawn.

Bill committed.

PETITIONS.

EAST INDIA (CONTAGIOUS DISEASES).
Petition from Heywood, against State Regulations; to lie upon the Table.

EDUCATION OF CHILDREN BILL.
Petitions in favour;—From South Ashford;—Lincoln;—and Newcastle; to lie upon the Table.

JUVENILE VAGRANCY.
Petition from Sunderland, for alteration of Law; to lie upon the Table.

LOCAL AUTHORITIES SERVANTS' SUPERANNUATION BILL.
Petitions in favour;—from Gillingham;—and, Solihull; to lie upon the Table.

PRIVATE BILL LEGISLATION (MUNICIPAL TRADING).
Petitions for inquiry by a Select Committee; — From Heckmondwike;—and Sunderland; to lie upon the Table.

PUBLIC HEALTH ACTS AMENDMENT BILL.
Petition from Kidderminster, in favour; to lie upon the Table.

SALE OF INTOXICATING LIQUORS ON SUNDAY BILL.
Petitions in favour;—From Stratford (two);—Erdington;—Croydon(twelve); Thornton Heath;—Great Plumstead; —Warrington;—Hedon;—Norwood;— Higher Broughton;—St.Peter's Park;— Stratford;—Newton Abbot;—Manchester; — Sutton;—and Pontllanfraith; to lie upon the Table.

SALE OF INTOXICATING LIQUORS TO CHILDREN.
Petition from Patrington, for alteration of Law; to lie upon the Table.

VACCINATION ACT, 1898.
Petition from Gower, for repeal; to lie upon the Table.

RETURNS, REPORTS, ETC.

MUNICIPAL CORPORATIONS (REPRODUCTIVE UNDERTAKINGS).
Return (presented 6th March) to be printed. (No. 88.)

VACCINATION (RETURN OF CONSCIENTIOUS OBJECTIONS).
Return (presented 6th March) to be printed. (No. 89.)

TRADE REPORTS (MISCELLANEOUS SERIES).
Copy presented,—of Diplomatic and Consular Reports, Miscellaneous Series, No. 499 (by Command); to lie upon the Table.

GRAND JURY PRESENTMENTS (IRELAND).
Copies presented,—of Presentments made by Grand Juries in Ireland and fiated by the Court of Assize during the year 1898 (by Act); to lie upon the Table.

URBAN DISTRICT COUNCIL OF WOKING V. LONDON NECROPOLIS AND NATIONAL MAUSOLEUM COMPANY.
A petition of Robert Mossop, of Woking, for leave to the proper Officer of the House to attend a trial and produce a Document and give evidence before the Justices of Guildford.

Leave given to the proper Officer to attend accordingly.—(Dr.Farquharson.)

SCHOOLS (SCOTLAND) (NUMBER OF
SCHOLARS, ETC.).

Return ordered,

"Showing for each School in Scotland aided from the Parliamentary Grant for the year ended the 30th day of September 1897 (a) the number of Scholars on the School Register at the end of the School year; (b) the Actual Average Attendance during the School year; (c) the number of Children for whom Additional Attendances were claimed under Article 23 (b) (1) (a), and Article 23 (b) (1) (b) of the Code."—*(Captain Sinclair.)*

STANDING ORDERS.

Resolutions reported from the Committee—

"1. That in the case of the Belfast Corporation Petition, the Standing Orders ought to be dispensed with :—That the parties be permitted to proceed with their Bill, provided that Clause 41 be struck out of the Bill :—That the Commitee on the Bill do report how far such Order has been complied with.

"2. That in the case of the National Telephone Company (No. 1) Petition, the Standing Orders ought to be dispensed with :—That the parties be permitted to proceed with their Bill, provided that. clause 94 be struck out of the Bill :—That the Committee on the Bill do report how far such Order has been complied with."

"3. That, in the case of the National Telephone Company (No. 2) Petition, the Standing Orders ought to be dispensed with :—That the parties be permitted to proceed with their Bill, provided that clause 16 be struck out of the Bill :—That the Committee on the Bill do report how far such Order has been complied with."

"4. That, in the case of the Southport and Lytham Tramroad Bill [Lords], the Standing Orders ought to be dispensed with :—That the parties be permitted to proceed with their Bill, provided that the powers to construct the proposed Tramways A and B be struck out of the Bill :—That the Committee on the Bill do report how far such Order has been complied with."

"5. That in the case of the Skipton Gas Bill [Lords], the Standing Orders ought to be dispensed with :—That the parties be permitted to proceed with their Bill."

"6. That in the case of the Coatbridge and Airdrie Light Railway Petition, the Standing Orders ought not to be dispensed with."

First Five Resolutions agreed to.

Report to lie upon the Table.

BELFAST CORPORATION BILL.

Report (this day) from the Select Committee on Standing Orders read.

Bill ordered to be brought in by Mr. William Johnston, Mr. Arnold-Forster, and Sir James Haslett.

_____

NEW BILLS.

_____

GROUND VALUES (TAXATION) (SCOTLAND) BILL.

"For the Taxation for local purposes of Ground Values in Burghs in Scotland," presented, and read the first time ; to be read a second time upon Wednesday 3rd May, and to be printed. (Bill 114.)

TANCRED'S CHARITIES SCHEME CONFIRMATION BILL.

"To confirm a Scheme of the Charity Commissioners for the management of the several Charities founded by the Settlement and Will of Christopher Tancred, of Whixley, in the county of York, esquire, deceased," presented, and read the first time ; to be read a second time upon Friday 24th March, and to be printed. (Bill 115.)

_____

QUESTIONS.

_____

COUNTY COURT FEES.

SIR C. DILKE (Gloucester, Forest of Dean) : I beg to ask the Secretary to the Treasury whether there is any prospect of the reduction of fees in county court cases?

THE FINANCIAL SECRETARY TO THE TREASURY (Mr. R. W. HANBURY, Preston): I cannot, of course, go into detail in a mere reply to a printed question. The Government will be prepared to state their views fully on the Vote for the County Courts. I may say at once, however, that if any particular fees were found to press unduly on the poorer class of suitors the Treasury would be ready to consider, with the Lord Chancellor, whether any readjustment of the scale were possible which would afford relief in the items complained of.

POST OFFICE SAVINGS BANK.

MR. BARTLEY (Islington, N.): I beg to ask Mr. Chancellor of the Exchequer if he could state to the House what was the total amount due to depositors in the Post Office Savings Banks and the Trustees Savings Banks on the 31st December, 1898, and what was the par value of the Consols and other securities held against those liabilities at that date?

THE CHANCELLOR OF THE EXCHEQUER (Sir MICHAEL HICKS-BEACH, Bristol, W.): The estimated amount due to depositors in the Post Office Savings Banks at the 31st December, 1898, was £123,155,000, and the amount due to Trustees of Savings Banks at the 20th November, 1898 (the latest date on which the figures were made up) was £50,624,655. The par values of the Consols and other securities held against those liabilities at those dates were £123,494,000 and £50,423,418 respectively.

PATENT LAW.

MR. CAWLEY (Lancs., Prestwich): I beg to ask the President of the Board of Trade whether he is aware that the protection granted in Germany to a supplementary patent (Zusatz) is limited to the remaining term of the original patent, whilst in the United Kingdom it is treated as a new patent running for the full term; and that a patent originating in Germany and registered in France ceases to exist in Germany and in France simultaneously; and whether, considering that the longer duration of such patents in this country than in Germany and France is so serious a disadvantage to British manufacturers, more particularly to manufacturers of chemicals, who are precluded from using them, often for years, during which their German and French competitors are at

liberty to do so without restraint or payment of royalty, the Government would be willing to bring in a Bill during the present Session to remedy this inequality arising, not from natural causes, but from discordant legislation?

THE PRESIDENT OF THE BOARD OF TRADE (Mr. C. T. RITCHIE, Croydon): In Germany and France the duration of an ordinary patent is 15 years. For this reason patents taken out in both these countries expire simultaneously. In the United Kingdom the duration of a patent is limited to 14 years. Therefore, in the great majority of cases in which patents for the same invention are taken out in the three countries, the patent expires one year earlier in the United Kingdom than in Germany or France, and not later, as might be inferred from the honourable Member's Question. The existing law, so far from placing manufacturers in this country at a disadvantage in this respect, operates distinctly to their advantage on the whole. In the very exceptional case of patents of addition in Germany it would depend upon the date of the application for the patent whether the patent would expire earlier in Germany or in the United Kingdom. If the application were made within a year from the date of the application for the original patent, the patent would expire earlier in the United Kingdom than in Germany. If made later, the patent would expire later. I am not prepared to introduce legislation this Session.

ALLEGED MURDER OF MR. EDGAR.

SIR E. ASHMEAD-BARTLETT (Sheffield, Ecclesall) had on the Paper the following Question: To ask the Secretary of State for the Colonies whether it is a fact that the Boer policeman Jones has been acquitted on the charge of shooting Mr. Edgar, an Englishman resident in Johannesburg; and what steps Her Majesty's Government propose to take to secure justice for British residents in the Transvaal? On being being called upon, the honourable Member said he would simply inquire if the right honourable Gentleman could add anything to the answer given on his behalf on 2nd March to the honourable Member for Cumberland.

THE SECRETARY OF STATE FOR THE COLONIES (Mr. J. CHAMBERLAIN, Birmingham, W.) : I can add nothing except that I have since heard it is true the policeman was acquitted.

BARRISTERS IN THE TRANSVAAL.

SIR E. ASHMEAD-BARTLETT : I beg to ask the Secretary of State for the Colonies whether it is a fact that a special tax of £25 a year has been placed upon non-Boer barristers practising in the Transvaal ; and whether such tax is in accordance with the Conventions of 1881 and 1884 ?

THE SECRETARY OF STATE FOR THE COLONIES : The licence of £25 appears to have been in existence for many years, and, so far as I am aware, there is no differential treatment of foreigners.

SIR E. ASHMEAD-BARTLETT : Do I understand that this tax is placed on Boers as well as Uitlanders ?

THE SECRETARY OF STATE FOR THE COLONIES : Yes, Sir.

PUBLIC ROAD IN COUNTY TIPPERARY.

MR. HOGAN (Tipperary, Mid) : I beg to ask the Chief Secretary to the Lord Lieutenant of Ireland whether he has received a memorial signed by the principal ratepayers of Monard, Cullen, and Sologhead, county Tipperary, in reference to the neglected and dangerous condition of a local road in which two Roman Catholic churches and one Protestant place of worship are situated ; whether he is aware that 300 children have to use this road daily in going to their respective schools, and run serious risks in so doing ; and whether he will cause inquiry to be made as to what local authority or official is responsible for the protracted and perilous neglect into which this thoroughfare has been allowed to fall ?

THE CHIEF SECRETARY TO THE LORD LIEUTENANT OF IRELAND (Mr. GERALD W. BALFOUR, Leeds, W.) : The memorial mentioned in the first paragraph has been received. I am informed that the road referred to is in a bad state of repair, though not in a dangerous condition, as alleged in the Question. The parties responsible for the state of the road appear to be the ratepayers of the district and the Barony Presentment Sessions. The former have never applied to the Sessions for an adequate sum of money for the repair of the road, whilst, on two occasions, namely, in 1895 and 1898, the Sessions refused to pass a sufficient sum for the purpose, though urged to do so by the County Surveyor. At the Sessions in 1898, which was largely attended by associated ratepayers, the County Surveyor applied for an expenditure on the road at the rate of £80 per mile, but Sessions made a presentment for £50 a mile only. No contractor, however, has tendered for the work owing to the low price passed at the Sessions, and the Grand Jury, who are not authorised to increase the presentment, handed over the road to the County Surveyor to expend the limited sum passed.

HILLTOWN (CO. DOWN) TELEGRAPH OFFICE.

MR. M'CARTAN (Down, S.) : I beg to ask the Secretary to the Treasury, as representing the Postmaster-General, if he will state whether the guarantee required for the establishment of a telegraph office at Hilltown, county Down, was given, and the date on which same was signed by the guarantor ; also when the connecting wire with Hilltown was commenced to be laid ; what is the cause of the delay in opening the telegraph office there ; and whether he can state about what date will the office be open for the dispatch and receipt of telegrams, and from what date will the guarantee commence to run ?

MR. HANBURY : The office will be opened to-morrow, from which date the guarantee will run.

ARMY TEXT BOOKS.

Mr. LLEWELLYN (Somerset, N.): I beg to ask the Under Secretary of State for War whether his attention has been called to the fact that several of the official text books, laid down as being those to be studied by officers of Her Majesty's forces presenting themselves for examination for promotion to captain and major, have been for some considerable period, and still are, out of print and quite unobtainable; and whether he can state at what date the following books, "Field Artillery Drill," "Army Book of the British Empire," "Manual of Military Engineering," and "The Manual of Military Law," will be procurable?

The UNDER SECRETARY of STATE for WAR (Mr. G. Wyndham, Dover): It is the fact that some among the official text books are out of print. This is due, partly, to an increased demand for such works, and, partly, to the absence of a proper system of communication between the Stationery Office and War Office, by which intimation of an approaching exhaustion of stock could be given. This is now being remedied, and every effort will be made to accelerate the revised editions of the four works named. The last two have already reached the proof stage.

BRITISH NEW GUINEA.

Mr. HOGAN: I beg to ask the Secretary of State for the Colonies whether the Governments of New South Wales, Victoria, and Queensland intend continuing their annual subsidies towards the expenses of the administration of British New Guinea after the expiration of the present month; and whether there is any ground for the statement in the Colonial press, that the early conversion of British New Guinea into a Crown Colony is in contemplation?

The SECRETARY of STATE for the COLONIES: The contributing Colonies have agreed to continue the New Guinea expenditure on the present basis to the 30th of June next, pending a settlement of the Federation question. There is no ground for the statement referred to in the second Question.

SWINE FEVER ORDERS.

Mr. LLOYD MORGAN (Carmarthen, W.): I beg to ask the President of the Board of Agriculture whether, in countries where it has been deemed necessary to increase the police force owing to the operation of the swine fever order, he has any power to make a grant of public money for the purpose of defraying such expense, or whether additional cost has to be paid by the county?

The PRESIDENT of the BOARD of AGRICULTURE (Mr. W. H. Long, Liverpool, West Derby): No, Sir. It is part of the statutory duty of a police force to execute and enforce the Diseases of Animals Acts, and the Orders made thereunder, and no special contribution for the work thus arising can be made out of Imperial funds.

SCHOOL TROUBLES IN FLINT.

Mr. S. SMITH (Flintshire): I beg to ask the Secretary of State for the Home Department whether his attention has been drawn to the disturbances which took place at a meeting at Flint last Monday evening, called to protest against the conduct of the rector in refusing to the parents of children attending school there exemption from attendance when the Creed and Catechism of the Church of England were being taught; whether he is aware that this meeting was practically broken up by the conduct of persons who thus attended, and that the police who were present declined to render assistance in the preservation of order; whether after the meeting the crowd followed the speakers who had attended the meeting, threw stones at them, and struck the chairman; and whether the Government will take any necessary steps for preserving the peace?

The UNDER SECRETARY of STATE for the HOME DEPARTMENT (Mr. J. Collings, Birmingham, Bordesley): The Secretary of State has had before him a report of the meeting referred to, and it does not appear to him that the police in any way fell short of their duty, as, in his opinion, it is no part of their duty to secure a hearing for speakers at meetings of this kind or to prevent interruption.

It appears that one of the speakers, on his way home after the meeting, was struck by a stone ; the police are making every endeavour to discover who threw it. Such an occurrence obviously affords no sufficient ground for intervention on the part of the Home Office.

PRISON ADMINISTRATION.

MR. PICKERSGILL (Bethnal Green, S.W.): I beg to ask the Secretary of State for the Home Department whether he is aware that a prisoner in Walton Gaol, Liverpool, has recently been kept in irons for between 20 and 30 days, contrary to law ; and whether he will cause inquiry to be made into the case, and state the result of such inquiry to the House ?

MR. COLLINGS: The facts are as stated in the Question. The prisoner, owing to violent conduct, was handcuffed, and the officer in charge of the prison during the Governor's absence through illness, finding that the man would not promise to behave, gave directions, after obtaining the concurrence of one of the Visiting Committee, for his further restraint, which was continued owing to his persisting in threats of further violence. As soon as the matter came to the knowledge of the Prison authorities, through one of the inspectors, directions were given for the immediate release of the prisoner from restraint, and steps taken to prevent a recurrence of this unfortunate misapprehension of the law. The Secretary of State is glad to learn that no injury has resulted to the prisoner.

HOSPITAL OF ST. BARTHOLOMEW, OXFORD.

MR. MORRELL (Oxon, Woodstock): I beg to ask the Parliamentary Charity Commissioner whether he is aware that the Hospital of St. Bartholomew, Oxford, was placed under the care of Oriel College by Edward the Third for administration, and that the Commissioners in 1897 declared that before Oriel College is entitled to take any share in the profits of the hospital property it must fulfil cer-

tain obligations, *inter alia*, providing lodgings for the almamen, repairing the buildings, and providing a chaplain to officiate in the chapel ; whether, since 1897, the College has discharged these obligations, or any of them ; what is the total income arising from the hospital property, and whether the College has taken it for itself without performing the obligations ; and, if so, whether the Commissioners will lay the matter before the Attorney-General ; and whether he is aware that the buildings are now used as cattle-sheds, and no chaplain in Holy Orders maintained?

THE PARLIAMENTARY CHARITY COMMISSIONER (Mr. GRANT LAWSON, York, N.R., Thirsk): In the opinion of the Commissioners, the hospital was not placed in the care of, but granted to, the College by Edward the Third for its better administration and for the benefit of the College. The Commissioners did in 1897 give the opinion set out in the second paragraph of the Question. With the exception of doing certain repairs to the buildings, the College has not discharged the obligation specified in the Question, and the Commissioners consider that no one would benefit by their doing so, as the old method of administering the charity has fallen into desuetude and is incapable of performance. The total net income is estimated at about £105. After deducting the expense of repairs to the buildings and the amount of stipends paid either to existing almsmen or to a suspense account, the College has taken the income for itself. The Commissioners will not at present lay the matter before the Attorney-General, as they are engaged in negotiating for an arrangement. In view of the foregoing circumstances, the buildings are used as farm-buildings, and no chaplain in Holy Orders is maintained.

APPEALS UNDER THE WORKMEN'S COMPENSATION ACT.

MR. PICKERSGILL : I beg to ask the Secretary of State for the Home Department whether his attention has been called to a recent case in which a workman, who appealed from an award under the Workmen's Compensation Act, 1897, was ordered by the Court of Appeal to find security for costs; and whether, having regard to the fact that the procedure under the Workmen's Compensation Act is of a very special character, he will favourably consider a proposal to make a workman's right of appeal effective by amending the law as to requiring security for costs in proceedings under that Act?

MR. COLLINGS : The Secretary of State has seen the Report of the case referred to and also that of another important case decided yesterday. In both these cases the appellant has been ordered to find security for costs in accordance with the Rules governing the procedure of the Court of Appeal made under the Judicature Act. The Secretary of State thinks that there are grave objections to interfering with these Rules by special legislation in favour of a particular class of appeals. At the same time the effect of these Rules upon appeals under the Workmen's Compensation Act is an important question, and the Secretary of State proposes to confer with the Lord Chancellor thereon.

IRISH INDUSTRIAL SCHOOLS.

MR. DILLON (Mayo, E.) : I beg to ask the Chief Secretary to the Lord Lieutenant of Ireland whether his attention has been drawn to the meeting of the Philanthropic Reform Association held in Dublin on Tuesday last, to the speech of The O'Conor Don at that meeting, and to the extracts from letters from managers of industrial schools circulated by the Philanthropic Reform Association; and whether the Irish Executive will now consider the desirability of withdrawing or modifying the circular complained of, and so allowing the Irish Industrial Schools Act to be administered (as it has been administered for 30 years), pending any further legislation which the Irish Government may judge desirable?

MR. GERALD BALFOUR: My attention has been drawn to the proceedings at the meeting referred to in the first paragraph. It is not the intention of the Government to withdraw or modify the circular in question.

ST. CLEMENT'S CHURCH, BELFAST.

MR. DILLON : I beg to ask the Chief Secretary to the Lord Lieutenant of Ireland whether he is aware that, on the 26th February, the Reverend Mr. Peoples was followed by a large and disorderly crowd from St. Clement's Church to his own house on his return from morning and evening service; and that the crowd boohed, hissed, and threatened Mr. Peoples; and, considering that it was necessary to furnish Mr. Peoples with a large police escort, why no effective steps are taken by the Executive to put an end to such proceedings?

MR. GERALD BALFOUR: I am aware of the facts stated in the first paragraph. The only additional steps that the Executive could take beyond those already taken would be to prosecute individuals in the crowd or to disperse the crowd by force if necessary. The Executive have not hitherto thought it expedient to adopt either of these courses. Should, however, the disorder assume a more serious character, it may be necessary to take stronger action.

SOLDIERS AND CIVIL EMPLOYMENT.

CAPTAIN DONELAN (Cork, E.) : I beg to ask the Under Secretary of State for War whether he is aware that the system of utilising soldiers to execute carpentry and other skilled work required in and about barracks deprives civilian tradesmen of employment; if he can state at what rate of pay soldiers who perform this work are remunerated; and, whether it is intended still further to extend this system?

MR. WYNDHAM: In accordance with paragraph 690 of the Regulations for Engineer Services incidental repairs to War Department Buildings are executed by military labour where it is available. Soldiers so employed are paid 2d. or 1½d. an hour according to their skill. It is proposed to continue this system in the interest both of the public purse and of the soldiers, who thereby are put in a better position to obtain employment on leaving the colours.

CAPTAIN DONELAN: Will not this practice inflict injustice on civilian tradesmen? Has not the Cork Allied Trades Association adopted a Resolution complaining of the practice?

MR. WYNDHAM: I do not know, but if they had it would not interfere with the policy we are pursuing.

MR. TREW AND THE BELFAST CHURCH DISTURBANCES.

MR. YOUNG (Cavan, E.): I beg to ask the Chief Secretary to the Lord Lieutenant of Ireland whether the police authority has power to suppress, in Belfast, meetings held each Sunday for inflammatory harangues calculated to disturb the peace of the city, called in following terms: " Mr. Trew at Custom house steps. Subject, First Martyr. Come in your thousands. No surrender;" whether he is aware that all the disturbances at St. Clement's Church have arisen from the declamation of Trew on those occasions; and, will the Government take some effectual measures to maintain the peace?

MR. GERALD BALFOUR: The police authorities undoubtedly have power to suppress meetings calculated to lead directly to a breach of the peace. Whether Mr. Trew's harangues properly come under that designation, or not, is a question on which there may be possibly some difference of opinion. In any case, these matters involve considerations of degree, and what may be lawful may not always be expedient. I do not think the statement in the second paragraph is accurate; and in reply to the third paragraph the Government have taken, and will continue to take, whatever measures that they deem necessary for the preservation of the public peace.

CASTLEWELLAN BOILER EXPLOSION.

MR. McCARTAN: I beg to ask the President of the Board of Trade whether his attention has been called to the death of a man named James Canning, who was killed by the explosion of a boiler at the granite quarries near Castlewellan, county Down, on the 28th ultimo; whether he is aware that, after medical evidence, the coroner's jury found that deceased had been killed by shock and injury arising from the explosion, and the jury recommended that a sworn inquiry should be held by the Board of Trade; and, whether any such inquiry will be held; and, if so, about what date and where?

THE PRESIDENT OF THE BOARD OF TRADE: Yes, Sir, my attention has been called to the case referred to in the Question, but I have not yet received any communication with regard to the recommendation of the coroner's jury. The Board of Trade have, however, already held a preliminary inquiry under the Boiler Explosions Acts, and a formal sworn investigation will follow. It will be held as soon as possible and as near the scene of the explosion as practicable.

BOER GOVERNMENT AND THE SOUTH AFRICAN LEAGUE.

SIR E. ASHMEAD-BARTLETT: I beg to ask the Secretary of State for the Colonies whether he is aware that the Boer Government in January arrested certain members of the South African League, because they had drawn up a petition to the Queen setting forth the grievances of the Transvaal Uitlanders; and that five times the amount of bail was demanded by the Boer Court for them as was asked for the Boer policeman charged with the murder of Mr. Edgar, an Englishman; whether the meeting held in January by the Uitlanders to protest against the arrest of their leaders was deliberately broken up by armed Boers, who were at the time in Government employ and who were brought in from the country, and were organised for the purpose by Boer officials; whether he is aware that the chief of the Boer police, Commandant Van Dam, himself watched, without reproof, the violence of his men, whilst they destroyed the furniture in the Amphitheatre, where the meeting was held, and that they afterwards marched round the town assaulting individual Uitlanders; and what steps Her Majesty's Government intend to take to protect British subjects in the Transvaal from outrage and to obtain redress for the grievances of the Uitlanders?

THE SECRETARY OF STATE FOR THE COLONIES: Two members of the South African League were arrested on a charge of having committed a breach of the law regulating public meetings; their bail was at first fixed at £1,000 each, which was five times the amount of the bail originally fixed in the case of the policeman charged with the murder of Edgar, but this was subsequently withdrawn, and the policeman re-arrested. The bail for the members of the League was afterwards reduced to £500 each. The meeting held to protest against their arrest was broken up by Boers. I am not in a position to say that those persons were armed or were in Government employ, or were brought in from the country, or were organised by Boer officials. I am not aware whether the Chief of the Police was present at the meeting—some police were present, and it has been stated that they did not interfere. I am expecting a report from the High Commissioner, and am not yet in a position to say whether any action is called for on the part of Her Majesty's Government.

SIR E. ASHMEAD-BARTLETT: On a later day I shall repeat portions of the Question that have not been answered.

WASTE LAND ORDINANCE OF CEYLON.

MR. SCHWANN (Manchester, N.): I beg to ask the Secretary of State for the Colonies whether his attention has been drawn to the Waste Land Ordinance of Ceylon (No. 1 of 1897), and whether it is true that the High Court of Ceylon had held and stated that the said Ordinance was against the fundamental principles of justice; whether, notwithstanding certain decisions of the High Court of Ceylon, rendering proceedings under the said Ordinance invalid, the Government of Ceylon are enforcing its claims independently of the Courts by armed police, and what steps he proposes to take in the matter; and whether he is aware that the Government of Ceylon have passed an amended Ordinance Act, which has been, or shortly will be, submitted to the Home

Government, which is still more stringent and harsh to the claimants of land (ancestral, gardens, and uncultivated) than the Ordinance of 1897?

THE SECRETARY OF STATE FOR THE COLONIES: The Waste Lands Ordinance, No. 1 of 1897, has been under my most careful consideration. I have not seen any judgment of the Supreme Court of Ceylon to the effect referred to in the first paragraph. Allegations have been made to the effect of the second paragraph of the honourable Member's Question. I am awaiting a Report from the Governor. An Ordinance has been introduced amending the Ordinance of 1897, but I do not consider that it answers to the description conveyed by the third paragraph of the Question.

NAVAL WORKS BILL.

SIR U. KAY-SHUTTLEWORTH (Lancashire, Clitheroe): I beg to ask the Civil Lord of the Admiralty when he expects to introduce the Naval Works Bill; whether, meanwhile, he will lay upon the Table, as on 9th March, 1898, a Statement of Estimated Expenditure to 31st March, 1899, under the Naval Works Act, 1897; and, when the Annual Account for 1897-8, under the Naval Works Acts, corresponding to Paper 124 of last Session, will be in the hands of Members?

THE CIVIL LORD OF THE ADMIRALTY (Mr. A. CHAMBERLAIN, Worcestershire, E.): I cannot yet fix a date for the introduction of the Naval Works Bill, but it will not be taken before Easter. I shall be glad to lay on the Table the Return asked for. I understand that the Annual Account for 1897-8 will be issued in a few days.

ST. JAMES SCHOOL, NORTHAMPTON.

MR. CHANNING (Northampton, E.): I beg to ask the Vice-President of the Committee of Council on Education whether the accounts for St. James School, Northampton, have been submitted to the inspector at his annual visit, and sent to the Department under Form IX., for the years ending 30th November 1898, 30th November 1897, and 30th November 1896; what was the debt incurred by the managers in respect of the annual maintenance of the school up to 30th November 1896, and up to 30th November 1897, respectively; what proportion of the debt of £285, shown at the commencement of the last school year, on 30th November 1897, and carried over into the balance-sheet just issued, was incurred in the years named; and was any of that debt incurred prior to the passing of the Act of 1897?

THE VICE-PRESIDENT OF THE COMMITTEE OF COUNCIL ON EDUCATION (Sir J. GORST, Cambridge University): The answer to the first paragraph is in the affirmative. No debt was incurred by the managers for annual maintenance in either of the years referred to, since the overdraft at the end of each of those years was more than covered by the amount of Annual Grant then due from the Education Department.

MR. CHANNING: Will the right honourable Gentleman say when the debt of £285, which was paid off in this account, was incurred?

SIR J. GORST: There was no debt of £285. Although the account shows an overdraft, that was a great deal more than covered by money due from the Exchequer, which, in the course of a few weeks after, was paid in.

METROPOLIS WATER BILL.

MR. H. SAMUEL (Tower Hamlets, Limehouse): I beg to ask the President of the Local Government Board whether, in the event that the Metropolis Water Bill does not pass into Law in time to prevent a recurrence next summer of the water famine in East London, he will take temporary measures to prevent a scarcity of water in that district of the Metropolis?

THE PRESIDENT OF THE LOCAL GOVERNMENT BOARD (Mr. H. CHAPLIN, Lincolnshire, Sleaford): I do not quite understand what are the temporary measures to which the honourable Member refers, or why he should assume that the passage of the Bill may be delayed. Nothing that I am aware of except the completion of certain connections between the works of different companies, can ensure the inhabitants of East London against recurrence of scarcity, in the event of a similar drought to that of last summer, and every effort will be made to promote the passing of the Bill.

COUNCILLOR GAGEBY, OF BELFAST.

MR. McCARTAN: I beg to ask the Chief Secretary to the Lord Lieutenant of Ireland whether his attention has been called to the disqualification of Councillor Gageby, as declared at the meeting of the Belfast Town Council on Tuesday; whether he is aware that, through no fault of his own and without warning or notice of any kind, Mr. Gageby's name was omitted from the register, that he was disqualified and deprived of the franchise; whether, considering the hardship and injustice of the case, he will consider the desirability of having the Law amended so as to remedy such a defect; and, if he can say who was responsible for this disfranchisement?

MR. GERALD BALFOUR: My attention has been drawn to the disqualification of Mr. Gageby. I am not in a position definitely to say whether the omission of his name from the register arose from the default of a local official or from negligence on Mr. Gageby's own part. In any case, it is a matter with which the Executive cannot interfere. If an amendment of the Law is called for, as suggested in the Question, such an Amendment should apply to the whole of the United Kingdom, and not to Ireland alone.

LOCAL GOVERNMENT AUDIT DISTRICTS.

MR. LOUGH (Islington, W.): I beg to ask the President of the Local Government Board if he could state to the House how many audit districts there are in which the work is so heavy that temporary assistance has to be sent every year; also, how many audit districts there are in which the work is so light that it should not employ the whole of the working year of the auditor; and whether he proposes to improve the present arrangement of audit districts which appears to necessitate the employment of a larger number of assistant auditors than is actually required?

THE PRESIDENT OF THE LOCAL GOVERNMENT BOARD: The number of districts referred to in the first paragraph of the Question is 32. There are no districts of the kind mentioned in the second paragraph. The subject of a rearrangement of the audit districts was considered by the Departmental Committee which sat in 1897, and they recommended that any permanent settlement of the question should be deferred until the experience of the next three years had become available. I do not propose therefore to alter the districts at the present time, but I am not aware that the present arrangement necessitates the employment of a larger number of assistant auditors than is actually required.

CONSTABLE TOWNSHEND, OF BEDRAGH.

DR. AMBROSE (Mayo, W.): I beg to ask the Chief Secretary to the Lord Lieutenant of Ireland whether he is aware that on a recent occasion Constable Townshend, of the Bedragh police hut, near Westport, was drunk and disorderly, and that he broke into the neighbours' houses; and have any steps been taken to summon the constable in the ordinary way, or has action been taken by the police authorities to investigate his conduct; if so, with what result?

MR. GERALD BALFOUR: It is a fact that the constable named in the Question was drunk on the 29th November last and broke a pane of glass in the house of a man named Thomas Moran, near Westport, but it is not true that the constable broke into the neighbours' houses. Moran did not prosecute the constable, and stated he did not wish to take any action

in the matter. He was dealt with, however, by the Inspector-General under the rules of the force, and fined in a sum of 40s., and also warned for dismissal in the event of a repetition of any similar misconduct on his part.

CUBIC SPACE IN REGISTERED COMMON LODGING HOUSES.

MR. M'GHEE (Louth, S.): I beg to ask the President of the Local Government Board whether he can state the amount of cubic space which the local authorities for South West Ham insist upon being located to each person living in registered common lodging houses within their jurisdiction?

THE PRESIDENT OF THE LOCAL GOVERNMENT BOARD: I am informed that the amount is 300 cubic feet.

THEOLOGICAL PROFESSORS IN SCOTCH UNIVERSITIES.

DR. CLARK (Caithness): I beg to ask the Lord Advocate whether he can state the number of professors in the Theological Faculties of the Scottish Universities, and the amount paid to them for their services from fees, endowments, or grants from Parliament; and whether there is any fund for the superannuation of such professors, and its source?

THE LORD ADVOCATE (MR. A. GRAHAM MURRAY, Buteshire): As regards the first part of the Question, the honourable Member will find the information he desires in the Annual Statistical Reports, page 3, made by the University Court of each University in terms of section 30 of the Universities (Scotland) Act, 1889, and which have been laid before Parliament and circulated for the year 1896-97. As regards the second part, there is no special fund for superannuations, but Ordinances 32 and 53 deal with the granting of pensions to professors retiring from age or infirmity, and Ordinances 25, 26, 27, and 46 provide for the order of priority in which such charges fall to be met out of the general university revenue.

B

MINING IN INDIA.

MR. H. ROBERTS (Denbighshire, W.): I beg to ask the Secretary of State for India whether he will state whether it is true that a Bill to regulate mining and the exploration of minerals in India has been drafted by the Indian Government and will shortly be presented in Council; and, if so, whether, in view of the great importance of the question to British capitalists, he will lay a copy of the Bill upon the Table of the House?

THE UNDER SECRETARY OF STATE FOR FOREIGN AFFAIRS (Mr. BRODRICK, Surrey, Guildford): Perhaps I may be allowed to answer this Question. It is true that a Bill on the subject of mining has been drafted and will shortly, I believe, be brought before the Legislative Council of the Viceroy. But to lay on the Table of this House a copy of a Measure which is under discussion in that Council is contrary to the established practice, and would have the effect of transferring to the House of Commons a responsibility which by law rests, firstly, with the Legislative Council, and, secondly, with the Secretary of State, who has the power of disallowing any Measure which the Council may pass. I have already stated in this House that I do not think this would be right; and I cannot, therefore, undertake to do what the honourable Member suggests.

SCIENCE AND ART CLERKSHIPS AT SOUTH KENSINGTON.

MR. DUNCOMBE (Cumberland, Egremont): I beg to ask the Vice-President of the Committee of Council on Education whether it is proposed to fill up two of the three vacancies in the Second Division establishment at the Science and Art Department, South Kensington, by promoting a Mr. G. S. Watts, at present serving in Dublin, and a second division clerk (Ridley) at £70 per annum; whether there are several assistant clerks in the department at South Kensington of long and approved service who are eligible for promotion to these vacancies under clause 15 of the Order in Council of 29th November, 1898; and whether he would be willing to inquire into the matter in view of the fact that the assistant clerks at South Kensing-

ton have been led to expect that, when opportunities arose, they would receive priority of consideration?

SIR J. GORST: It is proposed to fill up two of the three vacancies in the Second Division staff of the Science and Art Department, South Kensington, by promoting Mr. Watts and an assistant clerk now employed in that department. The answer to the second Question is in the affirmative. Assistant clerks at South Kensington have not been led to expect that, when opportunities arose, they would receive priority of consideration.

COURSE OF BUSINESS.

MR. E. ROBERTSON (Dundee): I beg to ask the First Lord of the Treasury if he can make some further explanation of the procedure to be followed in regard to the Navy Estimates on Thursday, and, in particular, if he will state how he proposes to carry out his suggestion that, after the adjournment of the Debate on the Question that the Speaker do now leave the Chair, the House should go into Committee on the Supplementary Estimates.

THE FIRST LORD OF THE TREASURY (Mr. A. J. BALFOUR, Manchester, E.): I understand that there are some technical objections to taking the Supplementary Estimates immediately after the Motion that the Speaker do now leave the Chair on the Navy Estimates has been adjourned. That difficulty could be got over if the House permitted us to get the Speaker out of the Chair, when we could then proceed with the Supplementary Estimates. I do not know whether the House will think that course agreeable; if so, it would be convenient to the Government. If, however, that suggestion does not meet the views of the House, I certainly shall not press it. In that case, we shall go on with Government Bills. The Food and Drugs Bill will be the first order, the second will be the Water Bill, and the third the Colonial Loans Bill.

MR. E. ROBERTSON: May I ask whether, if the course suggested by the right honourable Gentleman that the

Speaker should be allowed to leave the Chair were adopted, the Amendments on the Paper would not be lost?

MR. SPEAKER: No Amendment could be moved to my leaving the Chair if I had already left it upon the Order of the House.

SIR C. CAMERON (Glasgow, Bridgeton): May I ask the right honourable Gentleman whether he is aware that the Food and Drugs Bill was only circulated last Thursday, and was only explained last night; whether those interested in it have only this morning learned the nature of its provisions; and whether, in view of that fact, he will not make the Water Bill, or some other Bill, the first order on Thursday, in case the Navy Estimates should not be proceeded with; and, further, whether he will not allow the adjournment of the Debate on the Second Reading of the Food and Drugs Bill to extend over such a reasonable time as will permit those interested in its details to learn something as to what it means?

THE FIRST LORD OF THE TREASURY: I really think the request of the honourable Gentleman rather unreasonable. We had a Debate last night, and not the slightest objection was raised of the character which the honourable Gentleman now raises. He himself, I think, supported the rejection of the Bill in a long and interesting speech. It is, therefore, rather unreasonable to ask us to defer the consideration of the Measure to a subsequent date.

THE CIRCULATION OF THE ESTIMATES.

MR. BUCHANAN (Aberdeen, E.): I beg to ask the First Lord of the Treasury whether, considering that both this year and last year the Army Estimates and the statement of the Secretary of State for War were circulated shortly after Committee of Supply was set up, and several days given before the statement was made in the House by the Under Secretary of State for War, he can state the reasons why the Navy Estimates and the Memorandum have not been circulated either this year or

last year at such a date as to enable Members to consider them before the First Lord of the Admiralty makes his statement in the House

THE FIRST LORD OF THE TREASURY: I have not discussed the question whether the procedure on the Army Estimates or the Navy Estimates is the more convenient, but, generally speaking, on the present occasion the proposed procedure with regard to the Navy Estimates is one dictated by considerations of public policy. The honourable Member will perhaps wait for further explanation on this subject until the statement of the First Lord of the Admiralty.

MR. ASQUITH (Fife, E.): Will the First Lord of the Treasury state what business he proposes to take on Friday?

THE FIRST LORD OF THE TREASURY: We shall now take the Supplementary Estimates which we had hoped to be able to take on Thursday—first the Civil Service, and then the Navy. After the Supplementary Estimates we shall take Vote 1 of the Army Estimates.

TALIENWAN.

MR. PROVAND (Glasgow, Blackfriars): I beg to ask the Under Secretary of State for Foreign Affairs if any official statement has been made by the Russian Government as to the terms on which British vessels may trade with the port of Talienwan; if it is now or will at any fixed future date be subject to the navigation laws of Russia, and if these prevent British ships from trading between Talienwan and any other Russian port; and, is the Customs tariff the same as that of the Treaty Ports in China or that of Russia?

MR. BRODRICK: The assurances given by the Russian Government with regard to Talienwan have already been published in China No. 1, 1898. We understand that a formal declaration will have to be made to the representatives of the Treaty Powers in China when the port is considered to be open to foreign commerce, which will not be until a Customs service has been established similar to that which exists at other ports opened by treaty. Her Majesty's Government were informed some time ago that steps were being taken for the organisation of a general administration and Customs establishment at Talienwan, and that duties would be collected by Russian officials for the Chinese Government according to the Chinese tariff. We are not in a position to express any opinion as to the bearing of the Russian navigation laws upon the position of the port.

PAPERS ON CHINA.

COMMANDER BETHELL (York, E.R., Holderness): I beg to ask the First Lord of the Treasury, with a view to future discussions on China, when the Papers relating to recent events in China will be presented; and whether it will be possible to include the negotiations affecting the Niu-chwang Railway?

THE FIRST LORD OF THE TREASURY: The utmost dispatch is being used in the preparation of these Papers, and it is hoped that they may be ready for presentation next Tuesday. I greatly regret that they have not been ready before. The negotiations with regard to the Niu-chwang Railway will be published subsequently in a separate Paper. Questions involving matters for diplomatic discussion are still pending, and until these are settled we cannot lay the Papers on the Table.

MUSCAT.

SIR C. DILKE: I beg to ask the Under Secretary of State for Foreign Affairs a Question of which I have given him private notice, and which, I believe, he is ready to answer—namely, whether the Government desire to make any modification in the recent statement to the House with regard to the affairs of Muscat, and whether it is the case that Her Majesty's Government have expressed to France their profound regret at recent occurrences.

MR. BRODRICK: Perhaps the House will allow me to answer this Question at some little length. The circumstances of the Muscat case are as follows:—In the middle of March of last year the French agent obtained from the Sultan of Muscat the lease or concession of a piece of land to be used as a coal depôt. On the land so ceded, which was in a small harbour, some way from Muscat, the French Government would have been at liberty to hoist its flag and to build fortifications. No hint of these proceedings reached the British Agent until this year. As soon as they were known, they were at once declared by the British Government to be contrary to the Treaty of 1862 and to the Sultan's special obligations to the British Government in respect of the assignment or alienation of any part of his territories, and the Sultan was required to cancel the lease. This he did, and the lease has been annulled. We expressed no disapproval of the action of our Agent, which, indeed, was taken under our instructions, and Lord Salisbury informed the French Ambassador more than once that, in his judgment, the British Government was absolutely right in the contention it maintained, and that it was impossible for us to recede from it. With respect to the form of the matter, the statement of Monsieur Delcassé is somewhat imperfect. He omits to mention that in November he was asked by Sir Edmund Monson whether there was any truth in the rumours of an acquisition of land on the littoral of Muscat, and he said that he had heard nothing whatever about it. He repeated the same statement a few days ago. It was therefore a case of action of the French Local Agent in excess of the instructions he had received, and in such a case it is usual to bring the question to the knowledge of the Government concerned, and secure its decision by diplomatic means, in order to avoid the publicity involved in a threat of bombardment. While on this account Lord Salisbury, as he stated to the French Ambassador, would have preferred a less public mode of action, it is clear that no blame attaches to our Agent on the spot, who was not in a position to distinguish between the responsibility of the French Agent and the Sultan of Muscat on the one side, and that of the French Government on the other, and we held his action in substance to have been absolutely right. By the Convention between

France and England of 1862 there is nothing to prohibit France from having a coal store at Muscat itself, as Great Britain has done within the terms of the Convention, provided there is no concession of territory, and it is understood that the French Government will avail itself of this power subject to the above-named limitations.

ENGLAND AND RUSSIA IN CHINA.

MR. YERBURGH (Chester): I beg to ask the Under Secretary for Foreign Affairs the following Question, of which I have given him private notice:—'Whether it is true, as stated in the "Daily Graphic" of the 4th inst., that the British Minister at Pekin has been instructed to inform the Tsung-li-Yamén that Great Britain is prepared to support China in resisting any pressure that may be brought to bear upon her to force her to repudiate her obligations to this country under the Northern Railway Extension contract; and, if so, whether that promise of support applies to all the terms and stipulations of the said contract?

MR. BRODRICK: From telegrams recently received at Pekin it appears that the Russian Minister is objecting to the employment of an English engineer and a European railway accountant, and to the charge given on the freights and earnings of the lines outside the Great Wall, as being contrary to the agreement between Russia and China. Her Majesty's Government have instructed Sir Claude Macdonald to point out that none of these points constitute foreign control of the railways or involve possession or control of such lines in the event of default on the loan. I have already stated that Her Majesty's Government regard the contract as a binding engagement on the Chinese Government.

HOUSES OF LORDS AND COMMONS PERMANENT STAFF, JOINT COMMITTEE.

Order read, for resuming Adjourned Debate on Question (6th March)—

*MR. SPEAKER: The Question is that Mr. Hanbury be a member of the Houses of Lords and Commons Permanent Staff Joint Committee.

*MR. PIRIE: (Aberdeen, N.) Upon this Question, Sir, there are two points of order upon which I wish to take your Ruling. As regards this Motion which has been made by the honourable Baronet the Member for the Tiverton Division of Devonshire, I would request to know whether it is in order in coming in upon the Paper of to-day, in view of Standing Order 16 of the House, which rules that on Monday and Thursday Motions are to be taken by Members of the Government, and on Tuesday and Friday by non-official Members of the House. Under that ruling I would venture to submit that the honourable Baronet, as a Member of the Government, took his precedence yesterday to move on Mondays and Thursdays, and, therefore, he is not entitled to bring in this Motion until the next Government day.

*MR. SPEAKER: The same point was taken last Session, and I then stated that the effect of Standing Order 16 is to enable any Member, whether a member of the Government or not, to put down Motions on Tuesdays and Fridays, and to give the Government the additional privilege of putting such Motions down on Mondays and Thursdays.

*MR. PIRIE: I would respectfully put another point of order to you, and that is whether the Motion ought not to appear at the end of Private Business, and whether it is not taking up the time of the private Members to put it in at the commencement of Private Business on a private Members' day?

*MR. SPEAKER: That appears to me to be exactly the same Question—that upon which I have just ruled.

Question put, and agreed to.

Motion made, and Question proposed—

"That Mr. James William Lowther be one other Member of the Committee."—(*Mr. Anstruther.*)

MR. SWIFT MacNEILL (Donegal, S.): I object to the honourable Gentleman being a member of the Committee; not that I object with reference to any personal qualification which the honourable Gentleman may possess, but because I think, in the case of a Committee of this kind, an Irish Member would be better. My objection is in the interest of the Prime Minister, who, as we all know, is to be on this Committee. He would understand our powers of cross-examination, and we could assure him that we could enlighten him on many abuses that take place, and we all know that it is the Irish Members who expose all these abuses and bring them into the light of day. The Prime Minister knows the right honourable Gentleman the Chairman of Committees, but he has not the privilege of knowing any of us, to his own great loss, and if he was on the Committee we should be able to make his acquaintance, and he ours. And, what is more, we know all about these offices and these dark places. It is rather a brave thing for an Irish Member to go in search of the House of Lords. The object of having an Irish Member on this Committee is that it does not look well to the public at large in cases of this kind, where abuses are being investigated—abuses which were first brought to light by Irish Members—that Irish Members should not be represented on the Committee. Of course, I am perfectly well aware that there is no ground for such a sugges-

tion, but, still, it does not look well to the public at large. I am not saying anything against the constitution of the Committee, but it is certainly clear that the preponderating influence will be all on one side. The two Radical Members on the Committee who represent this side of the House are the only two Radicals which will be on the Committee, because one could not by any possibility find a Radical in the House of Lords, however many microscopic glasses were applied to that institution. Honourable Gentlemen have come to me and asked me "for God's sake" to get an Irish Member on the Committee. Therefore, in the interest of Lord Salisbury, who does not know the Irish Members, I would ask that an Irish Member should be on the Committee. And, also, in the interests of fair play, because, as I said before, it is the Irish Members who first discovered these abuses. I therefore propose to negative the name of the right honourable Gentleman the Chairman of the Committees in order to substitute another.

Question put.

The House divided:—Ayes 214; Noes 63.—(Division List 31.)

AYES.

Aird, John	Buxton, Sydney Charles	Douglas, Rt. Hon. A. Akers-
Ambrose, William (Middlesex)	Causton,Richard Knight	Doxford, William Theodore
Arrol, Sir William	Cavendish, V. C. W.(Derbysh.)	Duncombe, Hon. Hubert V.
Asquith. Rt Hn. Herbert H.	Cecil, Evelyn (Hertford, East)	Dyke, Rt Hn Sir William Hart
Atkinson, Rt. Hon. John	Cecil, Lord Hugh (Greenwich)	Egerton, H m. A. de Tatton
Bailey James (Walworth)	Chaloner, Capt. R. G. W.	Elliot, Hon. A. Ralph Douglas
Baillie, James E.B. (Inverness)	Chamberlain, Rt.Hn.J.(Birm.)	Ellis, Thos. Ed. (Merionethsh.)
Baird. John George Alexander	Chamberlain, J. Austen (Wor.)	Ferguson, R. C. Munro (Leith)
Balcarres, Lord	Charrington, Spencer	Fergusson,Rt Hn SirJ.(Manc'r)
Baldwin, Alfred	Cochrane, Hn. Thos. H. A. E.	Finlay, Sir Robert Bannatyne
Balfour,Rt.Hn.A.J.(Manch'r)	Coghill, Douglas Harry	Fisher, William Hayes
Balfour,RtHnGeraldW.(Leeds)	Collings, Rt. Hon. Jesse	FitzGerald,Sir Robert Penrose
Banbury, Frederick George	Corbett, A. Cameron(Glasgow)	Fitzmaurice,)Lord Edmond
Barry,RtHnAH.Smith-(Hunts)	Cornwallis, Fiennes Stanley W	Fletcher, Sir Henry
Bartley, George C. T.	Courtney, Rt. Hn. Leonard H.	Flower, Ernest
Barton, Dunbar Plunket	Cranborne, Viscount	Folkestone, Viscount
Bathurst, Hn. Allen Benjamin	Cripps, Charles Alfred	Foster, Harry S. (Suffolk)
Beach,Rt.Hn.SirM.H.(Bristol)	Crombie, John William	Fowler, Rt. Hon. Sir Henry
Beach,W W.Bramston (Hants)	Cubitt, Hon. Henry	Fry, Lewis
Bethell, Commander	Curzon, Viscount	Garfit, William
Bill, Charles	Dalbiac, Colonel Philip Hugh	Giles, Charles Tyrrell
Blundell, Colonel Henry	Dalkeith, Earl of	Gilliat, John Saunders
Bonsor, Henry Cosmo Orme	Davenport, W. Bromley-	Goldsworthy, Major-General
Boscawen, Arthur Griffith	Davies, M.Vaughan-(Cardigan)	Gordon, Hon. John Edward
Bowles,T Gibson(King's Lynn)	Denny, Colonel	Gorst, Rt. Hn. Sir John Eldon
Brassey, Albert	Dilke, Rt. Hon. Sir Charles	Goschen,RtHnG.J (St G'rge's)
Brodrick, Rt.Hon. St.John	Dorington, Sir John Edward	Goschen, George J. (Sussex)
Bryce, Rt. Hon. James	Doughty, George	Gourley, Sir Edwd. Temperley

Graham, Henry Robert
Gray, Ernest (West Ham)
Greville, Hon. Ronald
Gull, Sir Cameron
Halsey, Thomas Frederick
Hanbury, Rt. Hn. Robert Wm.
Haslett, Sir James Horner
Hayne, Rt. Hon. Charles Seale
Heath, James
Heaton, John Henniker
Helder, Augustus
Hermon-Hodge, Robt. Trotter
Hoare, Ed. Brodie (Hampst'd)
Hobhouse, Henry
Hornby, Sir William Henry
Horniman, Frederick John
Howard, Joseph
Hozier, Hn. James Henry Cecil
Hubbard, Hon. Evelyn
Hutchinson, Capt. G.W.Grice-
Hutton, John (Yorks., N.R.)
Jeffreys, Arthur Frederick
Jenkins, Sir John Jones
Jessel, Capt. Herbert Merton
Johnston, William (Belfast)
Johnstone, Heywood (Sussex)
Kay-Shuttleworth,Rt Hn SirU
Kenyon, James
Kenyon-Slaney, Col. William
Kimber, Henry
King, Sir Henry Seymour
Knowles, Lees
Lafone, Alfred
Laurie, Lieut.-General
Lawrence,SirE.Durning-(Corn
Lawson, John Grant (Yorks.)
Lea, Sir Thos. (Londonderry)
Leighton, Stanley
Llewellyn, Evan H.(Somerset)
Lockwood, Lt.-Col. A. R.
Loder,Gerald Walter Erskine
Long, Rt. Hn. Walter (L'pool-)
Lopes, Henry Yarde Buller
Lowles, John

Lowther, Rt. Hn. James (Kent
Loyd, Archie Kirkman
Lucas-Shadwell, William
Macartney, W. G. Ellison
Maclean, James Mackenzie
Maclure, Sir John William
M'Calmont, H. L. B.(Cambs.)
M'Ewan, William
M'Iver, Sir Lewis (Edin.,W.)
M'Killop, James
Malcolm, Ian
Mappin, Sir Fredk. Thorpe
Mellor, Rt. Hn. J.W.(Yorks.)
Meysey-Thompson, Sir H. M.
Middlemore,Jno.Throgmorton
Milner, Sir Frederick George
Moon, Edward Robert Pacy
Moore,William (Antrim,N.)
Morgan,Hn.Fd.(Monm'thsh.)
Morgan, J. Lloyd (Carm'thn.)
Morton, Arthur H.A.(Dep'fd.)
Mount, William George
Muntz, Philip A.
Murray,Rt.Hn.A.Grah'm(Bute
Murray, Col. Wyndham (Bath)
Newdigate,Francis Alexander
Nicol, Donald Ninian
Northcote,Hn.Sir H.Stafford
Orr-Ewing, Charles Lindsay
Paulton, James Mellor
Pease, Herb.Pike(Darlington)
Percy, Earl
Pierpoint, Robert
Platt-Higgins, Frederick
Plunkett,Rt.Hn.HoraceCurzon
Powell, Sir Francis Sharp
Priestley,SirW.Overend(Edin.)
Purvis, Robert
Rasch, Major Frederic Carne
Ritchie, Rt. Hn. Chas.Thomson
Robertson, Herbert (Hackney)
Rothschild, Hn. Lionel Walter
Royds, Clement Molyneux
Russell, T. W (Tyrone)

Rutherford, John
Samuel, Harry S (Limehouse)
Sharpe, William Edward T.
Shaw, Thomas (Hawick, B.)
Shaw-Stewart, M.H.(Redfrew)
Sidebottom, Wm. (Derbyshire)
Simeon, Sir Barrington
Smith, Abel H. (Christchurch)
Smith, Hn. W. F. D (Strand)
Spencer, Ernest
Stanley, Hn. Arthur (Ormskirk,
Stanley, Henry M. (Lambeth)
Stevenson, Francis S.
Stewart, Sir M. J. M'Taggart
Stone, Sir Benjamin
Strutt, Hon. Charles Hedley
Sturt, Hon Humphry Napier
Talbot, Lord E. ((Chichester)
Thorburn, Walter
Thornton, Percy M.
Tollemache, Henry James
Tritton, Charles Ernest
Valentia, Viscount
Ward, Hn. Robert A (Crewe)
Warr, Augustus Frederick
Webster, R. G. (St. Pancras)
Webster, Sir R E (I of W)
Wentworth, Bruce C. Vernon-
Whiteley, George (Stockport)
Whitmore, Charles Algernon
Whittaker, Thomas Palmer
Williams, Jos. Powell (Birm.)
Wilson-Todd, Wm. H. (Yorks.)
Wodehouse,Rt.Hn E.R.(Bath)
Wortley, Rt. Hn. C. B. Stuart-
Wyndham, George
Wyndham-Quin, Major W. H.
Wyvill, Marmaduke D'Arcy
Yerburgh,Robert Armstrong
Young,Commander (Berks, E.)

Tellers for the Ayes—Mr.
Anstruther and Lord Stanley.

NOES.

Allan, William (Gateshead)
Allen,Wm.(Newc.under Lyme)
Allison, Robert Andrew
Ambrose, Robert (Mayo,W.)
Atherley-Jones, L.
Austin, M. (Limerick, W.)
Baker, Sir John
Bayley, Thomas (Derbyshire)
Blake, Edward
Buchanan, Thomas Ryburn
Caldwell, James
Cameron, Sir Charles (Glasgow)
Cawley, Frederick
Channing, Francis Allston
Clark,Dr.G.B.(Caithness-sh.)
Clough, Walter Owen
Dillon, John
Donelan, Captain A.
Farquharson, Dr. Robert
Goddard, Daniel Ford
Gold, Charles
Hedderwick, Thomas Chas. H.

Hogan, James Francis
Hutton, Alfred E. (Morley)
Jacoby, James Alfred
Joicey, Sir James
Kinloch, Sir John Geo. Smyth
Kitson, Sir James
Langley, Batty
Lewis, John Herbert
Lloyd-George, David
Lough, Thomas
Lowther,RtHnJ.W.(Cumblnd.)
Macaleese, Daniel
M'Cartan, Michael
M'Ghee, Richard
M'Kenna. Reginald
Maden, John Henry
Montagu, Sir S. (Whitechapel)
Moore, Count (Londonderry)
Norton, Capt. Cecil William
O'Brien, James F. X. (Cork)
O'Brien, Patrick (Kilkenny)
O'Connor, Jas. (Wicklow, W.)

O'Connor, T. P. (Liverpool)
O'Kelly, James
Oldroyd, Mark
Power, Patrick Joseph
Priestley, Briggs (Yorks)
Roberts, John H. (Denbighs.)
Schwann, Charles E.
Sinclair, Capt. J. (Forfarshire)
Smith, Samuel (Flint)
Spicer, Albert
Sullivan, Donal (Westmeath)
Thomas, Alfd. (Glamorgan, E.)
Wallace, Robert (Edinburgh)
Wilson, John (Durham, Mid.)
Wilson, John (Govan)
Wilson, J. H. (Middlesbro')
Woods, Samuel
Young,Samuel (Cavan, East)
Yoxall, James Henry

Tellers for the Noes—Mr.
MacNeill and Mr. Pirie.

Motion made, and Question proposed—

"That Mr. Wharton be one other Member of the Committee."—(*Mr. Anstruther.*)

*MR. PIRIE: I oppose the name of the honourable Gentleman upon the ground that the Committee is becoming of a more and more one-sided description. The House may not be aware of the fact that in former years Joint Committees were composed of double the number of Members from both sides of this House compared to the number of Members from the House of Lords. As the House of Lords at the present time is particularly Conservative, this brings out with greater force how the proposed composition of this Joint Committee will be of a one-sided character. That is very much in opposition of the intentions of the Government as stated last year. Last year there was a Committee of this House appointed to meet the House of Lords. The honourable Member for Dumfries was a member of it, and a few other Members

from this side of the House, and the national interests were represented, but this year it is one-sided in every way, and it is for that reason more than any other that I, as a Scotch Member, object. We in Scotland have to bear the burden—the unprofitable burden—of keeping up the House of Lords, and it is only right that we should have the power of regulating the salaries of the officials of the House of Lords in comparison with those of the salaries of this House. It is on this ground that I oppose the honourable Member whose name is before the Committee. If it was possible to increase the number of the Members of this House on the Committee I would not object so strongly, but as only five, according to the present arrangements, can be on the Committee the only redress we have is to object as much as we can.

Question put.

The House divided:—Ayes, 220; Noes, 69—(Division List No. 32.)

AYES.

Aird, John
Ambrose, William (Middlesex)
Arrol, Sir William
Asquith, Rt. Hn. Herbert H.
Atkinson, Rt. Hon. John
Bailey, James (Walworth)
Baillie, James E.B. (Inverness)
Baird, John George Alexander
Balcarres, Lord
Baldwin, Alfred
Balfour,Rt.Hn.A.J.(Manch'r)
Balfour,RtHnGeraldW.(Leeds)
Banbury, Frederick George
Barry,RtHnAH.Smith-(Hunts)
Barton, Dunbar Plunket
Bathurst, Hn. Allen Benjamin
Beach,Rt.Hn.SirM.H.(Bristol)
Beach,W.W.Bramston (Hants)
Beckett, Ernest William
Bethell, Commander
Bhownaggree, Sir M. M.
Biddulph, Michael
Bill, Charles
Blundell, Colonel Henry
Bonsor, Henry Cosmo Orme
Boscawen, Arthur Griffith
Brassey, Albert
Brodrick, Rt Hon. St.John
Brown, Alexander H.
Bryce, Rt. Hon. James
Buxton, Sydney Charles
Causton,Richard Knight
Cavendish, V C. W.(Derbysh.)
Cecil, Evelyn (Hertford, East)
Cecil, Lord Hugh (Greenwich)
Chaloner, Capt. R. G. W.

Chamberlain, Rt.Hn.J.(Birm.)
Chamberlain, J. Austen (Wor.)
Chaplin, Rt. Hon. Henry
Charrington, Spencer
Cochrane, Hn. Thos. H. A. E.
Coghill, Douglas Harry
Collings, Rt. Hon. Jesse
Corbett, A. Cameron(Glasgow)
Cornwallis, Fiennes Stanley W.
Courtney, Rt. Hn. Leonard H.
Cranborne, Viscount
Cripps, Charles Alfred
Cubitt, Hon. Henry
Currie, Sir Donald
Curzon, Viscount
Dalbiac, Colonel Philip Hugh
Dalkeith, Earl of
Davenport, W. Bromley.
Davies, M.Vaughan-(Cardigan
Denny, Colonel
Dilke, Rt. Hon. Sir Charles
Dixon-Hartland, Sir F. Dixon
Dorington, Sir John Edward
Doughty, George
Douglas, Rt. Hon. A. Akers-
Douglas-Pennant, Hon. E. S.
Doxford, William Theodore,
Duncombe, Hon. Hubert V.
Dyke, Rt.Hn.Sir William Hart
Egerton, Hon A. de Tatton
Elliot, Hon. A. Ralhp Douglas
Ellis, Thos. Ed (Merionethsh.)
Ferguson, R. C. Munro (Leith)
Finlay, Sir Robert Bannatyne
Fisher, William Hayes
FitzGerald,Sir Robert Penrose-

Fletcher, Sir Henry
Flower, Ernest
Folkestone, Viscount
Foster, Harry S. (Suffolk)
Fry, Lewis
Galloway, William Johnson
Garfit, William
Gibbons, J. Lloyd
Giles, Charles Tyrrell
Gilliat, John Sanders
Goldsworthy, Major-General
Gordon, Hon. John Edward
Gorst, Rt. Hn. Sir John Eldon
Goschen,RtHnG.J.(St.G'rge's)
Goschen, George J. (Sussex)
Gourley, Sir Edwd. Temperley
Graham, Henry Robert
Gray, Ernest (West Ham)
Greville, Hon. Ronald
Gull, Sir Cameron
Halsey, Thomas Frederick
Hanbury, Rt. Hn. Robert Wm.
Haslett, Sir James Horner
Heath, James
Heaton, John Henniker
Helder, Augustus
Hermon-Hodge, Robt. Trotter
Hickman, Sir Alfred
Hoare, Ed. Brodie (Hampst'd)
Hobhouse, Henry
Hornby, Sir William Henry
Horniman, Frederick John
Howard, Joseph
Howell, William Tudor
Hozier, Hn. James Henry Cecil
Hubbard, Hon. Evelyn

Hutchinson, Capt. G.W.Grice-
Hutton, John (Yorks., N.R.)
Jeffreys, Arthur Frederick
Jenkins, Sir John Jones
Jessel, Capt. Herbert Merton
Johnston, William (Belfast)
Johnstone, Heywood (Sussex)
Joicey, Sir James
Kay-Shuttleworth,Rt Hn SirU.
Kenyon, James
Kenyon-Slaney, Col. William
Kimber, Henry
King, Sir Henry Seymour
Kitson, Sir James
Knowles, Lees
Laurie, Lieut.-General
Lawrence,SirE.Durning-(Corn)
Lawson, John Grant (Yorks.)
Lea, Sir Thos. (Londonderry)
Leighton, Stanley
Llewellyn, Evan H.(Somerset)
Lockwood, Lt.-Col. A. R.
Loder,Gerald Walter Erskine
Long, Rt. Hn. Walter (L'pool.)
Lopes, Henry Yarde Buller
Lowles, John
Lowther, Rt. Hn. James (Kent)
Loyd, Archie Kirkman
Lucas-Shadwell, William
Macartney, W. G. Ellison
Maclean, James Mackenzie
Maclure, Sir John William
M'Calmont, H. L. B.(Cambs.)
M'Ewan, William
M'Iver, Sir Lewis (Edin.,W.)
M'Killop, James
Malcolm, Ian
Mappin, Sir Fredk. Thorpe
Mellor, Rt. Hn. J.W.(Yorks.)

Meysey-Thompson, Sir H. M.
Middlemore,Jno.Throgmorton
Milner, Sir Frederick George
Moore,William (Antrim,N.)
Morgan,Hn.Fd.(Monm'thsh.)
Morgan, J. Lloyd (Carm'thn.)
Morley, Charles Breconshire
Morton, Arthur H.A.(Dep'fd.)
Mount, William George
Muntz, Philip A.
Murray,Rt.Hn.A.Grah'm(Bute)
Murray, Col. Wyndham (Bath)
Newdigate,Francis Alexander
Nicol, Donald Ninian
Northcote,Hn.Sir H.Stafford
Orr-Ewing, Charles Lindsay
Paulton, James Mellor
Pease, Herb.Pike(Darlington)
Percy, Earl
Pierpoint, Robert
Platt-Higgins, Frederick
Plunkett,Rt.Hn.HoraceCurzon
Powell, Sir Francis Sharp
Priestley,SirW.Overend(Edin.)
Purvis, Robert
Rasch, Major Frederic Carne
Ritchie, Rt. Hn. Chas.Thomson
Robertson, Herbert (Hackney)
Rothschild, Hn. Lionel Walter
Royds, Clement Molyneux
Russell,Gen.F.S. (Cheltenham)
Russell, T. W. (Tyrone)
Rutherford, John
Samuel, Harry S (Limehouse)
Sassoon, Sir Edward Albert
Sharpe, William Edward T.
Shaw-Stewart, M.H.(Renfrew)
Sidebottom, Wm (Derbyshire)
Simeon, Sir Barrington

Smith, Abel H. (Christchurch)
Smith, Hn. W. F. D. (Strand)
Spencer, Ernest
Stanley, Hn. Arthur (Ormskirk)
Stanley, Henry M. (Lambeth)
Stewart, Sir M. J. M'Taggart
Stirling-Maxwell, Sir John M.
Stone, Sir Benjamin
Strutt, Hon. Charles Hedley
Sturt, Hon. Humphry Napier
Talbot, Lord E. (Chichester)
Thorburn, Walter
Thornton, Percy M.
Tollemache, Henry James
Tritton, Charles Ernest
Valentia, Viscount
Ward, Hn. Robert A. (Cre.vo)
Warr, Augustus Frederick
Webster, R. G. (St. Pancras)
Webster, Sir R. E. (I. of W.)
Wentworth, Brace C. Vernon-
Whiteley, George (Stockport)
Whitmore, Charles Algernon
Williams, Jos. Powell-(Birm.)
Wilson, John (Falkirk)
Wilson, John (W'cestersh.,N.)
Wilson-Todd, Wm. H. (Yorks.)
Wodehouse,Rt Hn.E.R.(Bath)
Wortley, Rt. Hn. C. B. Stuart-
Wyndham, George
Wyndham-Quin, Major W. H.
Wyvill, Marmaduke D'Arcy
Yerburgh,Robert Armstrong
Young,Commander (Berks, E.)

TELLERS FOR THE AYES—Mr.
Anstruther   and   Lord
Stanley.

NOES.

Allan, William (Gateshead)
Ambrose, Robert (Mayo,W.)
Atherley-Jones, L.
Austin, M. (Limerick, W.)
Baker, Sir John
Barlow, John Emmott
Bayley, Thomas (Derbyshire)
Blake, Edward
Buchanan, Thomas Ryburn
Caldwell, James
Cameron, Sir Charles (Glasgow)
Cawley, Frederick
Channing, Francis Allston
Clark,Dr.G.B.(Caithness-sh.)
Clough, Walter Owen
Condon, Thomas Joseph
Crombie, John William
Dillon, John
Donelan, Captain A.
Farquharson, Dr. Robert
Fitzmaurice, Lord Edmond
Goddard, Daniel Ford
Gold, Charles
Hayne, Rt. Hon. Charles Seale-

Hedderwick, Thomas Chas. H.
Hogan, James Francis
Hutton, Alfred E. (Morley)
Jacoby, James Alfred
Kinloch, Sir John Geo. Smyth
Langley, Batty
Lewis, John Herbert
Lloyd-George, David
Logan, John William
Lough, Thomas
Macaleese, Daniel
M'Cartan, Michael
M'Ghee, Richard
M'Kenna, Reginald
Maden, John Henry
Mendl, Sigismund Ferdinand
Montagu, Sir S. (Whitechapel)
Moore, Count (Londonderry)
Norton, Capt. Cecil William
O'Brien, James F. X. (Cork)
O'Brien, Patrick (Kilkenny)
O'Connor, Jas (Wicklow, W.)
O'Connor, T. P. (Liverpool)
O'Kelly, James

Oldroyd, Mark
Power, Patrick Joseph
Priestley, Briggs (Yorks)
Roberts, John H. (Denbighs.)
Schwann, Charles E.
Shaw, Thomas (Hawick B.)
Sinclair, Capt. J. (Forfarshire)
Smith, Samuel (Flint)
Spicer, Albert
Stevenson, Francis S.
Sullivan, Donal (Westmeath)
Tennant, Harold John
Thomas, Alfd. (Glamorgan, E.)
Wallace, Robert (Edinburgh)
Whittaker, Thomas Palmer
Wilson, John (Durham, Mid.)
Wilson, John (Govan)
Wilson, Jos. H. (Middlesbro')
Woods, Samuel
Young,Samuel (Cavan, East)
Yoxall, James Henry

TELLERS FOR THE NOES—Mr.
Pirie and Mr. MacNeill.

Motion made, and Question proposed—

"That the Committee have power to send for persons, papers, and records: That Three be the quorum."—(*Mr. Anstruther.*)

DR. CLARK (Caithness): I propose to leave out those words. This is a Committee that is thrust upon us, I will not say in consequence of a conspiracy of the two Whips, but it has been thrust upon us. This year there is a new departure altogether as to the principle for which we on this side of the House have fought for the last 20 years, and which we have compelled the Whips on both sides of the House to respect. Up to last year the principle of nationality was carried out, but this year it is thrown aside.

*Mr. SPEAKER: Order, order! The honourable Member must confine himself to the Motion on the paper, "That the Committee have power to send for persons, papers, and records."

Dr. CLARK: If a proper Committee, one in which the great bulk of the House had confidence had been appointed; a Committee which would have received the support of those who were not upon it, we might have been content to have allowed the Motion to pass without discussion. But, unfortunately, that is not the case. When the Report comes up we shall require to closely debate it, and under the circumstances I do not think it is worth our while to spend any money or give any power to a Committee of this kind. They have appointed a Committee, I will not say to work this matter, because they dare not do so, but they have appointed a Committee upon which a large portion of the country—not England—is not represented, and because of that I shall object and divide the House upon the matter. I beg to move the omission of those words.

*Mr. SPEAKER: The simpler course will be to negative the Motion.

Question put.

The House divided:—Ayes, 230 ? Noes, 63.—(Division List No. 33.)

AYES.

Aird, John
Ambrose, William (Middlesex)
Arrol, Sir William
Asquith, Rt. Hn. Herbert Hy.
Atkinson, Rt. Hn. John
Bailey, James (Walw rth)
Baillie, James E..B. (Inverness)
Baird, John George Alexander
Balcarres, Lord
Baldwin, Alfred
Balfour,Rt.Hn.A.J.(Manch'r.)
Balfour,Rt.Hn.G'rld W.(Leeds
Banbury, Frederick George
Barry,RtHnAH.Smith-(Hunts)
Barton, Dunbar Plunket
Bathurst. Hn. Allen Benjamin
Beach,Rt.Hn.SirM.H.(Bristol)
Beach,W.W. Bramston (Hants)
Beckett, Ernest William
Bethell, Commander
Bhownaggree, Sir M. M.
Biddulph, Michael
Bill, Charles
Blundell, Colonel Henry
Bonsor, Henry Cosmo Orme
Boscawen, Arthur Griffith
Bowles,T.Gibson(King's Lynn)
Brassey, Albert
Brodrick, Rt. Hon. St. John
Brown, Alexander H.
Bryce, Rt. Hon. James
Buxton, Sydney Charles
Causton, Richard Knight
Cavendish,V.C.W.(Derbyshire)
Cecil, Evelyn (Hertford, East)
Cecil, Lord Hugh (Greenwich)

Chaloner, Capt. R. G. W.
Chamberlain,J.Austen(Worc'r)
Chaplin, Rt. Hon. Henry
Charrington, Spencer
Cochrane, Hn. Thos. H. A. E.
Coghill, Douglas Harry
Collings, Rt. Hon. Jesse
Corbett, A. Cameron (Glasgow)
Cornwallis, Fiennes Stanley W.
Courtney, Rt. Hn. Leonard H.
Cranborne, Viscount
Cripps, Charles Alfred
Crombie, John William
Cubitt, Hon. Henry
Currie, Sir Donald
Curzon, Viscount
Dalkeith, Earl of
Davenport, W. Bromley-
Davies,M.Vaughan-(Cardigan)
Denny, Colonel
Dilke, Rt. Hon. Sir Charles
Dixon-Hartland, Sir F. Dixon
Dorington, Sir John Edward
Doughty, George
Douglas, Rt. Hn. A. Akers-
Douglas-Pennant, Hon. E. S.
Doxford, William Theodore
Duncombe, Hon. Hubert V.
Dyke, Rt. Hn. Sir Wm. Hart
Egerton, Hn. A. de Tatton
Elliot, Hn. A. Ralph Douglas
Ellis, Thos. Edw.(Merioneths.)
Ferguson, R. C. Munro (Leith)
Fergusson,Rt Hn SirJ.(Manc'r)
Finlay, Sir Robert Bannatyne
Fisher, William Hayes

FitzGerald,Sir Robert Penrose-
Fitzmaurice, Lord Edmond
Fletcher, Sir Henry
Flower, Ernest
Folkestone, Viscount
Foster, Harry S. (Suffolk)
Fowler, Rt. Hon. Sir Henry
Fry, Lewis
Galloway, William Johnson
Garfit, William
Gedge, Sydney
Gibbons, J. Lloyd
Gilliat, John Saunders
Goldsworthy, Major-General
Gordon, Hon. John Edward
Gorst,Rt.Hn.Sir John Eldon
Goschen,RtHnG J.(St.G'rge's)
Goschen, George J. (Sussex)
Gourley, Sir Edwd. Temperley
Gray, Ernest (West Ham)
Greville, Hon. Ronald
Grey, Sir Edward (Berwick)
Gull, Sir Cameron
Haldane, Richard Burdon
Halsey, Thomas Frederick
Hanbury, Rt. Hn. Robert W.
Haslett, Sir James Horner
Hayne, Rt. Hn. Charles Seale-
Heath, James
Heaton, John Henniker
Hermon-Hodge, Robert Trotter
Hickman, Sir Alfred
Hoare, Ed. Brodie (Hampst'd)
Hobhouse, Henry
Hornby, Sir William Henry

Horniman, Frederick John
Howard, Joseph
Howell, William Tudor
Hozier, Hn. James Henry Cecil
Hubbard, Hon. Evelyn
Hutchinson, Capt. G.W.Grice-
Hutton, John (Yorks., N.R.)
Jeffreys, Arthur Frederick
Jenkins, Sir John Jones
Jessel, Capt. Herbert Merton
Johnston, William (Belfast)
Johnstone, Heywood (Sussex)
Joicey, Sir James
Kennaway,Rt. Hn. Sir John H.
Kenyon, James
Kenyon-Slaney, Col. William
Kimber, Henry
King, Sir Henry Seymour
Kitson, Sir James
Knowles, Lees
Laurie, Lient.-General
Lawrence,SirE.Durning-(Corn)
Lawson, John Grant (Yorks.)
Lea, Sir Thos. (Londonderry)
Leighton, Stanley
Llewellyn, Evan H.(Somerset)
Lockwood, Lt.-Col. A. R.
Loder,Gerald Walter Erskine
Long, Rt. Hn. Walter (L'pool.)
Lopes, Henry Yarde Buller
Lowles, John
Lowther, Rt. Hn. James (Kent)
Loyd, Archie Kirkman
Lubbock, Rt. Hon. Sir John
Lucas-Shadwell, William
Macartney, W. G. Ellison
Maclure, Sir John William
M'Calmont, H. L. B.(Cambs.)
M'Ewan, William
M'Iver, Sir Lewis (Edin.,W.)
M'Killop, James
Malcolm, Ian

Mappin, Sir Frederick Thorpe
Meysey-Thompson, Sir H. M.
Middlemore,Jno.Throgmorton
Milner, Sir Frederick George
Montagu, Sir S. (Whitechapel)
Moon, Edward Robert Pacy
Moore,William (Antrim,N.)
Morgan,Hn.Fred.(Monm'thsh.)
Morgan, J. Lloyd(Carmarthen)
Morley, Charles (Breconshire)
Morton, Arthur H.A.(Dep'fd.)
Mount, William George
Muntz, Philip A.
Murray,Rt.Hn.A.Grah'm(Bute)
Murray, Col. Wyndham (Bath)
Newdigate,Francis Alexander
Nicol, Donald Ninian
Northcote,Hn.Sir H.Stafford
Oldroyd, Mark
Orr-Ewing, Charles Lindsay
Paulton, James Mellor
Pease, Herb.Pike(Darlington)
Percy, Earl
Pierpoint, Robert
Platt-Higgins, Frederick
Plunkett, Rt. Hon. Horace C.
Powell, Sir Francis Sharp
Purvis, Robert
Rasch, Major Frederic Carne
Ritchie, Rt. Hn. Chas.Thomson
Robertson, Herbert (Hackney)
Rothschild, Hn. Lionel Walter
Royds, Clement Molyneux
Russell,Gen.F.S. (Cheltenham)
Russell, T. W. (Tyrone)
Rutherford, John
Samuel, Harry S. (Limehouse)
Sassoon, Sir Edward Albert
Seton-Karr, Henry
Sharpe, William Edward T.
Shaw, Thomas (Hawick B.)
Shaw-Stewart,M.H.(Renfrew)

Sidebottom, Wm (Derbyshire)
Simeon, Sir Barrington
Smith, Abel H (Christchurch)
Smith, Hn. W. F. D. (Strand)
Spencer, Ernest
Stanley, Hn. Arthur (Ormskirk)
Stanley, Henry M. (Lambeth)
Stanley, Lord (Lancs.)
Stevenson, Francis S.
Stewart,Sir Mark J.M'Taggart
Stirling-Maxwell, Sir John M.
Stone, Sir Benjamin
Strutt, Hon. Charles Hedley
Sturt, Hon. Humphry Napier
Talbot, Lord E. (Chichester)
Thorburn, Walter
Thornton, Percy M.
Tollemache, Henry James
Tritton, Charles Ernest
Valentia, Viscount
Vincent, Col. Sir C. E. Howard
Ward, Hn. Robert A. (Crewe)
Warr, Augustus Frederick
Webster, Sir R. E. (I. of W.)
Wentworth, Bruce C. Vernon-
Whiteley, George (Stockport)
Whittaker, Thomas Palmer
Williams, Jos. Powell (Birm.)
Wilson, John (Falkirk)
Wilson, J. W. (W'cestersh.,N.)
Wilson-Todd, Wm. H. (Yorks.)
Wodehouse,Rt Hn.E.R.(Bath)
Wortley, Rt. Hn. C. B. Stuart-
Wyndham, George
Wyndham-Quin, Major W. H.
Wyvill, Marmaduke D'Arcy
Yerburgh,Robert Armstrong
Young,Commander (Berks, E.)

TELLERS FOR THE AYES—Sir
William Walrond and Mr.
Anstruther.

NOES.

Allan, William (Gateshead)
Allen,Wm.(Newc.under Lyme)
Ambrose, Robert (Mayo,W.)
Atherley-Jones, L.
Austin, M. (Limerick, W.)
Baker, Sir John
Barlow, John Emmott
Bayley, Thomas (Derbyshire)
Blake, Edward
Buchanan, Thomas Ryburn
Caldwell James
Cameron, Sir Chas. (Glasgow)
Cawley, Frederick
Channing, Francis Allston
Clough, Walter Owen
Condon, Thomas Joseph
Dillon, John
Donelan, Captain A.
Evans, Sir Fras. H. (South'ton)
Farquharson, Dr. Robert
Goddard, Daniel Ford
Gold, Charles

Hedderwick, Thomas Chas. H.
Hogan, James Francis
Hutton, Alfred E. (Morley)
Jacoby, James Alfred
Kilbride, Sir John Geo. Smyth
Langley, Batty
Lewis, John Herbert
Lloyd-George, David
Logan, John William
Macaleese, Daniel
MacNeill, John Gordon Swift
M'Cartan, Michael
M'Ghee, Richard
M'Kenna, Reginald
Maden, John Henry
Mendl, Sigismund Ferdinand
Moulton, John Fletcher
Norton, Capt. Cecil William
O'Brien, James F. X. (Cork)
O'Brien, Patrick (Kilkenny)
O'Connor, Jas. (Wicklow, W.)
O'Connor, T. P. (Liverpool)

O'Kelly, James
Power, Patrick Joseph
Priestley, Briggs (Yorks.)
Roberts, John H. (Denbighs.)
Schwann, Charles E.
Smith, Samuel (Flint)
Spicer, Albert
Sullivan, Donal (Westmeath)
Tennant, Harold John
Thomas, Abel (Carmarthen, E.)
Thomas, Alfd. (Glamorgan, E.)
Wallace, Robert (Edinburgh)
Walton, Jno Lawson (Leeds, S.)
Wilson, John (Durham, Mid.)
Wilson, John (Govan)
Wilson, Jos. H. (Middlesbro')
Woods, Samuel
Young,Samuel (Cavan, East)
Yoxall, James Henry

TELLERS FOR THE NOES—Dr.
Clark and Mr. Pirie.

ORDERS OF THE DAY.

PRIMARY EDUCATION (ENGLAND AND WALES.

Motion made, and Question proposed—

"That, in the opinion of this House, the system of Primary Education in England and Wales inflicts upon a large portion of Her Majesty's subjects a serious grievance which demands the immediate attention of Parliament."—(*Mr. Lloyd-George.*)

MR. LLOYD-GEORGE (Carnarvon, etc.): Last year I moved a Resolution, which in terms was bound to influence a very large and influential religious community with regard to Primary Education, and I also in that Resolution suggested a remedy which, to my mind, was a possible one for the state of things. The right honourable Gentleman who represented the Government on that occasion admitted the evil, though he repudiated the remedy; therefore, I am going to invite the House upon this occasion to discuss whether we are not upon common ground. Is it admitted by the right honourable Gentleman that there is an evil? If there is an evil it demands the immediate attention of the House of Commons. There is a very general agreement upon one question, and that is that there is something seriously defective in the condition of Primary Education in this country. The educational authorities must acknowledge that there is something seriously defective in the system in a good many respects. It compares very unfavourably with the Primary Education which is carried on in countries which constitute our far most formidable trade rivals. In this country children are allowed to leave school at 11 years of age, and some at 10. In hundreds of parishes of England there are very few children in school at all after they are 10 years of age. You have hundreds and thousands of children leaving school before they are 12 years of age. Our apparatus is defective, the equipment is bad, the accommodation is insufficient, and with regard to some of our Voluntary schools the condition is perfectly disgraceful. It is discreditable to this country and to civilisation, and it is certainly a disgrace to the religion in whose name all these offences are perpetrated against the children of the

land. The last Report of the Education Department goes in that direction. It points out that the direction of the qualification of our education is bad. It calls it a mechanical form of bookish instruction, which is the cheapest style of teaching. It calls for the least thought on the part of the teacher. There is too much pen and too little work, and it is because it is cheaper that our system is defective. Children leave school at an age when their education is really commencing. Up to that point they only acquire sufficient schooling in the elements to enable them to start their educational career. Not only that, their intelligence and interest in education is weakened, and worse than that, the only thing that is left is a distaste for all knowledge owing to the conditions and discipline and restraint under which they have been taught. There is no interest to counteract all that, and, so far as thousands of our school children are concerned, especially with regard to the Voluntary schools, it would be better for the children if they never entered them. I do not know whether the noble Lord who interrupted me last has read the very able articles which appeared in the "Manchester Guardian" lately. They were written by a schoolmaster, and in an exceedingly impartial style. They treat both of Voluntary schools and Board schools. His description of some of the Voluntary schools in the country districts is simply appalling. There is no ventilation, the accommodation is insufficient, and the atmosphere is mephitic. I say the worst thing that could happen to these children is that they should enter these schools at all. It would be better that they never entered them. Their minds are not improved, their physique is damaged just at the time when they are laying the foundation of their constitutions. That is the condition of education in this country, and it is sufficiently appalling. Go to other countries, and especially to our great trade rivals. There is compulsory education in Prussia up to the age of 14, and in Saxony up to the age of 15. Go to the United States, which is our most formidable trade competitor; 14 is the minimum age there. In some States it is 15, in several States it is 16, and in one State the compulsory age is 18. (Laughter.) It amuses honourable Members that all children should attend school up to the period of 18 years, but it is not so amusing when you come to discover that these children afterwards become artisans and merchants, and lead us in all the markets of the world. That is one of the reasons why we have been deprived of our trade, not merely in foreign markets, but even in our home and Colonial markets by those children when they have grown up to manhood. The question is: "How is this so?" Is it not because this country cannot afford to set up an excellent and efficient system of education? This is the wealthiest country in the world. I believe that our bill for armaments next year, for the whole of our Empire, will amount to something like 70 millions of money—30 millions more than the expenditure of any other country in the world. How is it, then, that we cannot afford to spend more money on education? As a matter of fact, we do not spend the necessary amount of money in bringing the educational system of our country up to the condition of efficiency which is comparable with that which obtains in other countries with whom we have a life struggle for commercial ascendency. I think, Mr. Speaker, there is but one answer to such a state of things. It is said that we have no money. Last year the surplus of the Chancellor of the Exchequer was so great that he did not know what to do with it; and so he produced the famous Bristol Birds-eye Budget. What is the reason, I again ask, for the existing state of things as to education? It is because we have got in this country two rival, hostile, and perfectly incompatible systems of education, the partisans of each of which do their very best to cripple the resources of the other.

Honourable Members: No, No!

Mr. LLOYG-GEORGE: I would not state a proposition like that without attempting to prove it, and that is what I propose doing now. What is the avowed policy of the Voluntary schools with regard to the Board Schools? It is this: First of all, it is to prevent any additional Board schools being planted in new districts. ●

Honourable Members: No, No!

Mr. LLOYD-GEORGE: Yes; that is the avowed policy, and if the statement is challenged, I can quote in support of it passages from the Church Extension pamphlet. And I do not think there is anything in that which, from their point of view, they need to be ashamed of. The policy is to prevent any additional Board schools being planted in the new districts. What is the effect of that? It is this: at the present moment the Voluntary schools have not sufficient funds for the purpose of keeping in decent repair the schools already existing under their control. It is quite as much as they can do to keep up the subscriptions; in fact, the subscriptions are tumbling down. While they have not sufficient resources to administer the empire they have got, they insist on further expansion. The right honourable Gentleman the Vice-President gave them good advice in his speech at Liverpool. He said, "Concentrate; you have not sufficient funds to extend the Voluntary system." Very good advice, but not identical with the opinions of those he was addressing. The right honourable Gentleman the Vice-President wants to make scholars; they want to make proselytes, and, therefore, they decline to follow his advice. Another result of this policy is that they have got to draw practically from the charity of the same donors to existing schools and to new schools. That weakens and impoverishes the schools already established, and, therefore, you have an anæmic and attenuated system throughout the land. That is not the case in regard to Board school.

Honourable Members: Hear, hear! ●

Mr. LLOYD-GEORGE: I quite understand that cheer. That is not the case with School Board schools, because they have the rates to draw upon.

Honourable Members: Hear, hear!

Mr. LLOYD-GEORGE: I am glad to see that statement accepted. The School Boards spend more, for they have the rates to draw upon. Their schools are bad enough in the rural districts; they are quite disgraceful, and a discredit to the system in some of the small areas, and I would rejoice to see these areas increased. But, bad as they are, they spend 3½ millions more a year upon educating two million children than the Voluntary schools spend in educating 2½ million children. That is not wasteful extravagance; they could do with more money. What is the result? They have better teachers, better schools, they have more abundant accommodation. That tells not merely on the physique of the children, but on their mental alertness, their power, and their energy. You cannot get children breathing foul air to give the best of their thought to the problems put before them. The School Boards, then, have got a larger staff and a better staff than the servant girl article, of which there are practically 10,000 in the Voluntary schools and two or three thousand in the Board schools. All that is bound to tell on the education in the schools of these respective systems. And it does tell. Anyone who studies the results of the examinations will see that; although I do not think that these results tell all the story, because a great deal of indulgence is shown by some of the inspectors in regard to the Voluntary schools. A manager admits that, with some inspectors, the Voluntary schools in his district have been wiped out. That is the difference between the two systems. The Board schools confer a superior education to the Voluntary schools, and that is much more clearly evident when you come to the higher standards. In the higher standards the number of grants to Board schools contrasted to grants to Voluntary schools is most marked. That means not only that the education in these higher standards is better, but it is really a test of the superiority of the education given up to that point. It becomes manifest that, when these children attain 10 or 11 years of age, their education begins to tell on their mode and manner of thought, and on their mental action. What, then, is the consequence of this policy of keeping out Board schools and planting Voluntary schools? It is, as I have stated, to keep out the better schools in order to plant inferior ones. It impoverishes the Voluntary schools, and therefore cripples them; whereas by planting Board schools you do not impede the resources of the School Boards because there is no increased source of revenue. ˜ That is not all the effect of the policy of the Voluntary schools. Not merely do they con-

spire to keep out Board schools, and to drive out superior education, but they do their best, by raising a false cry of economy, to cripple the resources of existing Board schools, and to lower and depress the standard of education there. I venture to say that at every School Board election throughout the kingdom where you hear the cry of economy raised, it is raised by the friends of the Voluntary system. What is the effect of that? It is too manifest in some of the rural School Boards. The staff is poor in quality and in numbers, and the apparatus is miserable. All this is due to the cry of economy. In every community you have a certain number of men who, whenever they can raise the cry of economy, do so. They care nothing about the object for which the rates are to be expended. What do they care about the education of children? They take sordid and selfish views on this matter. The friends of Voluntary schools have discovered that these people are a source of political power in these rural districts, and unscrupulously appeal to them, with the result that in many parts of the country the education of the children suffers. It has nothing to do with the religious education — absolutely nothing. All this crippling of education, this perpetuating of ignorance in the rural districts, is done in the name of religion, but it is really caused by the cupidity of some of the ratepayers. It is a conspiracy of greed and creed against the efficiency of the School Board schools. And the worst thing about the system is that it tends to perpetuate itself. It keeps down the standard of education, and it drives children out of the schools. Four or five millions of children are turned out of the schools without practically any education—their minds stunted, their interest in knowledge weak, and their intellect not roused. What is the result? These become the ratepayers who will elect the School Boards of the future. These are the ratepayers who will listen to the cry of economy when the education of the children is concerned. They will say, "What do we care about the education of children; they are getting as good an education as we got, and why should they have any better?" These children, too, will eventually become the electors who return Members to Parliament to vote down Board

Mr. Lloyd-George.

schools, and keep up this inefficient system of Voluntary schools. Let us look quite frankly on the other side of the case. I admit that the same thing applies when there is an appeal for any aid to Voluntary schools. When there is any proposal of a grant-in-aid to the Voluntary schools the friends of the Board schools, especially in Dissenting communities, and those who sympathise with them, by every means in their power, and by every resource, oppose these grants being made by the Government. As long as the Voluntary system inflicts an injustice on the consciences of a section of the community, they are bound to resist every grant out of the pockets of the ratepayers, which will have the effect of perpetuating the system, and of extending its operations. What does all this mean?. It means that the friends of the Voluntary schools cripple the Board schools, confine their operations, diminish their resources, and repress education. The same thing happens when there is an application made for a grant in aid of the Voluntary schools, and the result is that both classes of schools use their power and influence to depress the level and standard of education throughout country, instead of competing with each other in healthy rivalry. That is a very serious state of things, and demands the attention of Parliament, and that is all I ask for in this Resolution. What I say, therefore, is that it is impossible to effect a settlement of this question as long as the grievance remains unredressed which affects the consciences so many people. Our children are suffering, our country is suffering, our Empire is suffering, from this low rate of education. It is time we came face to face with it, and endeavoured to effect some settlement which will be satisfactory to the majority of the people of the country. And I say it is impossible to effect a settlement of the kind so long as you perpetuate the grievance which afflicts the consciences of so many millions of the people of this country. Now, what is that grievance? It is this: that you use funds, to which men of all creeds and classes contribute, for the purpose of propagating dogmas which are offensive to large bodies of the contributaries to the common fund. You have 14,000 schools in this country where the dogmas of one sect are taught at the ex-

pense of all. That is an injustice, and a grievance. But that is not all. You have 8,000 parishes in the country where you have no schools except the schools of one faith managed by the minister of one creed or denomination. The dogmas of one creed are taught in a large number of these parishes where the majority of the children belong to other denominations. There are hundreds of these schools in Wales, and I would ask the right honourable Gentleman if he can give me a list of 20 out of all these hundreds of schools where the majority of the children do not belong to another denomination, and yet where the dogmas of another faith are not taught at the expense of the community. What has rather aggravated this state of things is what has occurred recently in the Church of England. Now, I am fully alive to the fact, Mr. Speaker, that I cannot raise the question of ritualism on this Resolution.

HONOURABLE MEMBERS: Hear, hear!

MR. LLOYD-GEORGE: If the honourable Members will just listen to the end of my sentence, they will find their zeal has outrun their knowledge. I am fully alive to the fact that on this Resolution I cannot raise the question of ritualism, and the conduct of the Bishops, and all these recent controversies. But, in as far as these strange doctrines are introduced into the schools of the country and constitute a part of the grievance to which I have referred—I am not all sure that they do not constitute the greatest part of the grievance of which we complain—to that extent alone I shall refer to ritualism. I gave a case last year, and quoted from Gaze's Catechism, in which some of these new doctrines are taught in the schools. It is not a question of vestments or a question of incense—though I am not sure, from the descriptions given of some of the Voluntary schools, that a little incense would not make them all the better. It is not merely a question of incense, it is a recrudescence of the old claims of the priesthood to possess miraculous powers. These are the doctrines which are taught in the schools of the nation, maintained by the nation, and at the expense of the nation, and out of funds contributed to by Protestants. These are the new doctrines which are being taught, and I think they are most dangerous doctrines. That is a new claim put forward by the clergy, or rather an old claim which was fought against, disposed of, and overthrown in this country centuries ago. It is an attempt to exalt the vanity of a class into a creed for all in this country. This is what is taught in Brighton, and at Cardiff, and, indeed, all over the kingdom in the form of what is known as Gaze's Catechism. I observe that when I refer to the case of Brighton, and to the case of Cardiff, that the interruption is not so clearly marked. Now these are the things taught in the schools at the expense of the nation, and I say that is an injustice to the people of this country. But there is another injustice from which Nonconformists especially suffer. In 14,000 schools of the country a Nonconformist child is not allowed to become a pupil teacher. The right honourable Gentleman the Vice-President of the Council of Education shakes his head ; he has done that repeatedly when that statement has been made before. I give him a challenge. I gave it last year, and he is far more ready to shake his head than give me information. Last year, when he and the Leader of the House challenged my statement, I asked whether he is prepared to grant a Return of the Voluntary schools in the country where Nonconformists are allowed to become teachers. I know of one case in my own constituency, and have no doubt there are many other cases of that kind, where the Voluntary schools cannot be carried on without the aid of Nonconformist teachers, and these are employed as long as the head teacher is in the hands of the Anglican Church. There is only one condition, however, under which Nonconformists can become teachers, and that is to sell their creed, to become traitors to the faith of their fathers, and to join a church to which they do not belong, and to which they would not belong except for considerations which are not exactly germane to the nature, quality, and spirituality of their faith. I think we are entitled to doubt the sincerity of a conversion which is contemporaneous with the temporal advantage which would not otherwise be conferred on the applicant. These are the two great grievances from which Nonconformists suffer. But there is a third—the training colleges. Ninety per cent. of the accommodation in these col-

Mr. Lloyd-George.

leges is in the hands of the secretaries and managers of the colleges, and out of their income of £200,000 there is only £8,000 contributed by the voluntary subscriptions, the rest is the amount of the State subsidy supplemented by the fees of the students. But it is only the members of one particular faith who are allowed to enter these training colleges. Ten per cent. of the accommodation is free, it is true, but 90 per cent. is confined exclusively to these sectarian teachers, and the 10 per cent. open to Nonconformists is only open in competition with the other 90 per cent. Does the right hónourable Gentleman or any other honourable Member on the other side of the House really defend that on the grounds of justice and fair play to a large section of the community? I observe that the honourable Member for Lowestoft, who is the champion in this House of the rights of the Church, has placed an Amendment on the Paper, in which he complains of the grievances of Churchmen in this respect. I am perfectly prepared to face this question. I admit it is an important one. I say that if Churchmen suffer any grievance which is identical with or even analogous to that sustained by Nonconformists, I am ready to vote for any remedy or proposal that will redress it. I do not see why it should not be done on the basis suggested by the Majority Report of the Royal Commission—equal participation in the Parliamentary grant. That Report was signed by the present Archbishop of Canterbury, by Cardinal Manning, and all the friends of the Voluntary scheme. The proposal seems to me perfectly reasonable. They say—

" Weighing all the evidence that has been put before us, we have come to the conclusion that the State should continue to recognise Voluntary and Board schools as together forming the national provision for elementary education ; and that both ought to continue to participate on equal conditions in the Parliamentary grant."

I am perfectly prepared to vote for any grant to the Voluntary schools, but on the condition that it must be equally participated in by the Board schools. Honourable Mnbers may say, " It is true you may be suffering from grievances in the Anglican parishes, but what about the grievances of the Anglican children in the School Board districts?" I have two questions to ask as a test in regard to that. The first is, Is there a single Board school in the kingdom where any privilege, position, or advantage is given to. Nonconformist children that is not equally open to the Anglican children? My second question is this, Have honourable Members perused the Returns of the syllabus of religious instruction given in all the Board schools, obtained by the House of Lords in 1888, and subsequently in 1895. If they have not perused these Returns, then I suggest they have no right to condemn the system of religious instruction in Board schools, of which they know nothing. But assuming that honourable Members have perused that syllabus, can they point out a single item, in these carefully prepared Returns where there is anything taught that is offensive to the conscience of any Anglican parent in the land? If not, where is the grievance? And there is no Anglican school, or few Anglican schools, of which the same can be said. Well, the honourable Member doubts that. Let me put it as plainly as possible. Can it be said of Anglican schools that every privilege and position and advantage which is open to an Anglican child is equally open to a Nonconformist child; and there is nothing in the religious instruction given in the Anglican schools which is obnoxious to the conscience of the Nonconformist parent? The second point I put to him is, Is there nothing in the religious instruction conferred in these Voluntary schools which is offensive to Nonconformist parents?—it may be inoffensive to the honourable Member. Does he know his Catechism? I assume that he does. Surely he knows that the very first lesson in the Catechism—I had to learn it all myself—is one which is offensive to every Nonconformist parent throughout the country. He knows it perfectly well—the doctrine with regard to baptism and godfathers and godmothers. Though we do not wish to say anything which would in the slightest degree hurt the feelings of an Anglican Member of this House, at the same time we are bound to point out that there are doctrines taught in these schools which are, I believe, really obnoxious to the conscience of a large majority of the Nonconformists of this country, if not the whole. Very well; how then can honourable Members really say that the case of the Anglican schools and that of the Board schools is on the same basis? We are willing to adopt the recommendation of that Commission to support grants to these schools on equal conditions. Equal conditions are: First, popular control in the Voluntary schools, as you have got it in the Board schools. A second condition is that every position which is paid for by the State should be equally open to every child without setting up an inquisition to examine what his creed is. And I venture to say, Mr. Speaker, there is no other country in the world where you have got the present system. You have denominational schools on the Continent. You have sectarian doctrines taught there. But there is no country in Europe where you have got the doctrines of the minority taught at the instance of the majority and forced upon their children. You have Catholic countries where Catholic doctrines are taught in the schools. You have Protestant countries where Protestant doctrines are taught in the schools. You have got countries, it is true, where there are both Catholics and Protestants, but I ask the noble Lord to point out a single case in these countries where the Protestants may enforce Protestant doctrines upon Catholic children, or the converse, where you get a Catholic minority forcing Catholic doctrines upon Protestant children. That is really the test. What would happen in Prussia or Saxony if this had been the case? And may I point out another distinction to the noble Lord? Although you have got sectarian schools on the Continent, they are all schools under popular control. The teachers are appointed by the State or by the Commune. Will the noble Lord accept that in this country? That is the test of his sincerity upon that point. And whilst I am on this point, here is another matter. In some cases, where you have got a community split up into Catholic and Protestant, you have the teacher teaching Protestant doctrine, and then you have the priest of the parish opposing and teaching Catholic doctrine to his children. But can the noble Lord point out a case to me where a Member of any faith is excluded from the position of teachers in any State school because of his creed? Go to the Protestant district of Saxony. Are Catholics excluded from teaching there? Go to the Catholic districts. Are Protestants excluded? Not in a single case! That is why I say the system in this country has nothing which compares to it in unfairness and injustice to a large section of the community. And I ask, What would have happened in Prussia or Saxony if you had attempted to impose it there? Supposing education in Prussia had been an Imperial question; the clericals had a majority in the German Parliament; they set up Catholic schools throughout the whole of Prussia; every Lutheran teacher not allowed to teach except on condition of becoming proselytised, and then Catholic doctrines to be taught— What would have happened? There would have been insurrection there. It never would have been allowed. And yet Protestants in this country are even sneered at when they make a demand for fair and equal treatment in the case of the education of their children. But this is another country. What the honourable Members ask for is that they should have exceptional privileges in these schools. They must recognise this fact. This country is not divided between Catholics and Protestants in the sense that these great Continental countries are—one corner of the country is Methodist, and another Anglican, and another Presbyterian, and another Catholic. You have all these religious communities side by side, and you must recognise that fact and act accordingly. You cannot set up separate schools for each without damaging the State schools for all. You cannot split up schools in small parishes with a population of 500, and give four separate schools for each. You would simply ruin the schools for all. Under these conditions, every sect must accept that situation loyally, and endeavour to make the best of it. But what is done here? The Anglican Church, although a minority in the village, say, " You must pick out our faith, our doctrines, give us all the privileges, and let the others do what they please." That is no fair treatment to the rest. I say it is time—and I say it respectfully—that the Anglican Church in this country should recognise that it has failed to compass uniformity of faith in this land. It is not their fault, I admit; they have tried it for centuries, by persecution, prosecution, gibbets, bribes, doles, Voluntary schools, and it has failed. Dissent is a fact, and a great fact, in the life of this country, and it will remain so. I ask honourable

Mr. Lloyd-George.

Members to recognise that when discussing this question. And that is exactly what they have not done. You have got a country where you have a similar state of things to what you have here in the United States of America. In the United States of America you have these religious communities living side by side, and the United States of America say : We cannot give any privilege to one sect, we cannot pick out one and say we will make you the one typical standard sect, make your children teachers in the schools, make your ministers managers of them, hand the funds to you. The United States of America has recognised the impossibility of doing that, and it has said : You may teach the children in the schools, but you must not teach the doctrines of any sect, you must leave it to each individual sect to attend to its own doctrines. And what is the result? You might have imagined that Atheism and infidelity would have been rampant in these unsectarian schools of the country. But what is the state of the case there? I was very interested to see the conclusion of the right honourable Gentleman the Member for Aberdeen, in his book on this question, and I think it is a very fair test. The argument of honourable Gentlemen opposite is, If you withdraw dogmatic teaching from the schools, you will injure the character of the children, you will damage the State, you will injure, as the Report puts it, the integrity, the high standard of integrity, which Englishmen have attained, if you withdraw dogmatic teaching and substitute Bible teaching instead. What does the right honourable Gentleman say about the American system?—

" The ordinary man knows the Bible better, and takes up an allusion to it more quickly than does the ordinary Englishman."

And you come to a still more telling test. He says—

" Not only are the sums collected for all sorts of philanthropic purposes larger, relatively to the wealth of America, than in any other European country, but the amount of personal interest shown in good works, and personal effort devoted to them, seems to a European visitor to exceed what he knows at home."

Better than in the Continent of sectarian schools! And the last quotation, and I think it is a very germane one when you come to consider the question of teaching on the character of a nation, is this—

"The general impression of those who have lived long both in Protestant Europe and in America seems to be, that as respects veracity, temperance, and purity of domestic life, tenderness to children and the weak, and general kindliness of behaviour, the native Americans stand rather higher than either the English or the Germans."

And yet those are the countries of definite dogmatic teaching at the expense of the State. Now, I think that is a fair test, and I think we are entitled to ask, What is it that the friends of the Voluntary schools really ask for? If it is religious instruction, they can get it in the Board schools. They themselves admit it. The way they put their case in the majority Report of the Commission—which, after all, is a statement of their case—is, that all they ask for is that the Bible shall be taught. This is the statement of the case in the majority Report of the Commission, which, of course, is a report in favour of Voluntary schools. I will read the words—

"As we look to the Bible for instructions concerning morals, and take its words for the declaration of what is morality, so we look to the same inspired source for the sanctions by which men may be led to practise what is there taught, and for instructions concerning the help by which they may be enabled to do what they have learnt to be right."

That is their statement of the case for religious instruction, and there is nothing in it that you cannot bring within the four corners of the School Board system. Everything they ask for is taught there, and they admit it. They talk about the desirability of bringing up the standard of religious education in the Board schools of the country to the high level which obtains in some Board schools. That is not all. The right honourable Gentleman himself admitted last year that, as far as religious teaching was concerned, it is much better conferred in the Board schools than it is in the Voluntary schools. That is his own admission, and if it is not the case in the rest of the Board schools of the country, why is that so? Because the friends of Voluntary schools, instead of trying to raise the level of instruction in these schools, do their very best to cripple their resources and reduce the number of their staff and its quality. The majority

Report of the Commission admits that the general sense of the community is in favour of religious instruction, and in favour of making it efficient. If that is the case, why need they fear leaving instruction to the representatives of the people? They say the people are in favour of religious instruction. They are in favour of making it effective, and yet they will not trust the people with the religious instruction of their children. Mr. Speaker, I am afraid that it is not so much religious instruction that is asked for. The most thorough, drastic, searching religious instruction can now be given in the Board schools, and anyone who reads that syllabus I have referred to can see this, that with the exception of the Catechism, there is nothing taught in the Voluntary schools which is not quite as well taught in the Board schools of this country. And does anybody really mean to say that the Decalogue and the Sermon on the Mount are so defective and incomplete an exposition of the moral law that they require to be supplemented by something that inculcates the duty of humility to the squire of the parish? I say there is nothing in the Catechism itself, apart from what is objectionable to Nonconformists, which would not be included in the doctrine which may be given and taught in the Board schools. And what is really wanted, I fear, is, not religious instruction, not teaching the principles of the Christian faith in these schools—what is aimed at is proselytism. What is wanted is to use these schools for the purpose of proselytising the children of Nonconformists. There was abundant evidence upon that point before the Commission; all sorts of inducements given in the schools to Nonconformist children to attend Church Sunday Schools, to quit the fold in which they have been brought up—inducements of a substantial character quite irrelevant to the principles of the Catechism, and this is very manifest when you come to the case of teacherships. Their teacherships are offered to children on the express condition that they become members of the Church of England. Well, now, I ask honourable Members opposite whether that is a system they can honestly defend, whether it is a system they do not really at heart condemn in the interests of religion itself? You go to a child whose parents may be poor, and you offer to him the position which may lead him to make a livelihood, an income which will be four times that made by his father, and you say: The only conditions we ask you to accept is that you leave the associations of your childhood and become a member of the Church of England. It is a bad system. It is a bad system in the interests of the teacher himself; it is a bad system in the interests of the hundreds and thousands of children who will be eventually committed to his charge. The teacher is asked to take his conscience to the pawnbroker whenever he wants to raise funds for his own advantage. It is a rotten system, it is an immoral system; yet I say it is applied in hundreds of parishes both in Wales and in England, and I ask any friend of moral and religious instruction to get up and defend that in this House. But unfortunately, Mr. Speaker, this is what happens. A man is asked to give up his own religious faith, cut himself adrift from the early religious associations of his youth, which, after all, constitute the most valuable moral asset of any man, whatever his faith may be, for the purpose of advancing himself. It is a kind of a State-aided sheep-stealing, plundering the Nonconformist fold at the expense of the State. Mr. Speaker, the system of education in this country is defective. That will be admitted. We are suffering as a nation from those defects. Those defects will continue as long as these two rival systems are allowed to wage war with each other by cutting off each other's supplies. And there is only one obstacle that stands in the way of the benefit of the whole community, and that is the desire of the clergy to use these schools for proselytising members of the Nonconformist Churches. That system is one which aggravates, makes worse, the whole of the Voluntary system, unfair as it is. It creates religious strife and bitterness by exasperating the religious communities who suffer from its depredations, and who are compelled to contribute towards a fund which is used for raiding their own flock. It injures, demoralises its victim, teaching him to treat his religious convictions as a marketable commodity. It injures the children who are entrusted to the charge of men whose creed is a mere clause in the hiring agreement. It debases the ethical currency

Mr. Lloyd-George.

of the Christian faith in the man whose standard is sacrificed to self-seeking. It curses him that gives and him that takes; and I ask the House by this Resolution to declare that it does some amount of injury to the State, and cannot be compensated for by all the Catechisms ever devised by theologians to elucidate, or confuse, the problems of life.

*MR. A. HUTTON (York, W.R., Morley): Mr. Speaker, I rise to second the Motion which my honourable Friend has made in a speech which everybody must admit was of a very able character indeed. I can only hope to emphasise one or two points which he already has touched upon. I think, Sir, there is far too much complacency in the minds of a great many people in their attitude to the question of education. Too much is said of the marvellous progress that we have made. I myself cannot subscribe to that optimistic view of the situation. Now, Sir, although it is nearly 30 years since we had the advantage of the Education Act of 1870, we have not as yet been able to enjoy all the advantages which we might under that particular Act have expected. Still, the obstacles that are before us have been frequently and frankly stated more than once by the right honourable Gentleman the Vice-President of the Council. The obstacles are many, are various, and are some of them difficult to overcome. But, Sir, I agree with my honourable Friend that there is one chief obstacle which underlies all those which the right honourable Gentleman has been good enough to mention. Sir, I do not think it would pass the wit of the Government or the House of Commons to overcome these obstacles if we can get rid of what is commonly called the religious difficulty, but what is in reality the denominational difficulty. Sir, it is this constant denominational strife, denominational jealousy, the one of the other, the desire to capture and control public funds in the interest of one denomination or another, that makes everybody suspicious of one another, and, as a consequence, unwilling to make the grants that are necessary. I believe, Sir, that this controversy is most harmful, not only to education but to the denominations, and to religion and Christianity itself, and I think it is our duty to see if we cannot put education upon some basis which shall be independent of all denominational controversy. The right honourable Gentleman tells us that there is no religious difficulty in these schools. Well, I cannot subscribe to that. He says the only religious difficulty is on the platform and in the House of Commons. Well, Sir, I should think that the controversy which is going on in St. James' End, as I think it is called, in Northampton, might have convinced him that, after all, there is some religious difficulty in the schools. I do not refer to the "medal" question, but when you have the majority of a town saying that they do not believe that the Church of England Voluntary school is a proper school for Nonconformist children, then I think there is a very serious religious denominational question before the Department, before the Government, and before Parliament. Well, Sir, to remove this religious difficulty you must remove the irresponsible control and management, the irresponsible administration of public funds. There is no other public duty that you would discharge in the same way. There is no other branch of the public service that you administer in the same way. Take the question of the Poor Law. Why, you have even recently removed the ex-officio members of the Boards of Guardians, and handed the work over absolutely to the control of the popularly elected representatives. Sir, I should have thought that a clergyman would have been as well fitted, if not better fitted, to decide as to who were suitable recipients of out-door relief as to settle questions with regard to education. And supposing clergymen came forward and said that they were willing to subscribe one penny or twopence in the shilling of the rates, should we consent to hand over for that paltry sum the control and administration of the Poor Law of this country? Why, certainly not. Everybody in the country would hold it in the greatest contempt; and if you are to hold it in contempt with regard to the administration of the Poor Law, surely in this matter of the education of our children we should equally treat it with the utmost contempt. Well, now, the difficulty is two-fold—first of all the difficulty of irresponsible control, and, secondly, the difficulty that there are a number of places where there is only one school, and that a Church of England school, at which all children are compelled by law to attend. With regard to the second difficulty, I should just like to say a word. I put another case. Supposing in these eight or ten thousand places you had one school only, and that was a Unitarian school. Would you, would the clergyman, would the friends of the Church of England, long consent that their children should be educated in this place, be driven by law to a Unitarian school? They would be up in arms. Indignation would not be the word for it. Well, Sir, we do not need to suppose a case, because there is, as a matter of fact, a town in the south of England that has now become somewhat notorious—the town of Arundel. In that town there were two schools, one a Church of England school and the other a Roman Catholic school, and it so happens that the Church of England school has been condemned as unsuitable by the Education Department. Well, Sir, the usual cry was got up by the friends of the other school that if the Church of England school is closed there will be Board schools, there will be a school rate, and all the other bogies are held up; and so the Duke of Norfolk, as the landed proprietor, kindly comes forward and offers to enlarge his Catholic school which is already in the town, and receive all the children who have hitherto attended the Church of England. Is that calmly submitted to? Certainly not. A clergyman writes from the neighbourhood, the Rev. John Goring, and he says what we have been saying for years. He writes—

"The power of money is being lavishly used in a way that, if not compulsion, is hardly distinguishable from it, to draw away children from Church of England schools into those of another communion. It is not too much to say that it is a line of action at variance with religious liberty, and it is most certainly abhorrent to the principles, religious and political, prevalent in this country as I have known them for the last 50 years."

Well, Sir, that clergyman may have known those principles of religious liberty and equality thoroughly, but those principles have not been practised, and now he has experience, not of the principles he has held, but of methods which other people have been compelled by law to practice. Then he writes to protest against the power of money, rank, and influence being used to drive

Church of England children into Roman Catholic schools. If that could be' said in one instance, all that need be said for our position is to multiply it several thousand times over. Now we are told that this dual system is advantageous. Supposing we brought a student of systems of education to this country and tried to explain our system to him, we would have a great deal of difficulty in making him understand it. If we explained to him that there were 8,000 places in which we have only one school, and asked him whether in those places the schools should be under the National system or the denominational system, of course he would reply that where the whole of the town depended on one school, it should be under the National system. But we should then have to explain to him that the contrary was the case, and that the denominational school is the one which children are compelled by law to attend. I pass from the question of schools to the question of training colleges and teachers. We have heard a great deal said about the policy of the "open-door," which has been proclaimed with regard to another matter. What we ask in regard to our training colleges is the policy of the "open-door." At present, in the words of the noble Lord the Member for York, Nonconformists are faced by a brick wall. I think it is reasonable that this great national profession should no longer be practically a closed profession as it is at present. My honourable Friend pointed out the difficulties of Nonconformists becoming pupil teachers. I think the right honourable Gentleman, the Vice-President of the Council, will admit that the difficulty of securing pupil teachers is becoming a very serious matter to managers and school boards. They are finding it difficult to get the necessary number of pupil teachers. I think there are two reasons which explain that difficulty. I believe the religious difficulty is one reason, and that there are some parents who will not allow their children to make the sacrifice that the clergy of a great many of these schools demand they should make. Then there is another reason. The right honourable Gentleman told us last year that the pupil teachers in many of these schools are nothing more or less than drudges. He used that word. With re-

Mr. A. Hutton.

gard to this particular matter, the Education Department appointed a Committee to inquire into it, but has the right honourable Gentleman or the Education Department adopted one single recommendation of that Committee?

THE VICE-PRESIDENT OF THE COMMITTEE OF COUNCIL ON EDUCATION (Sir J. GORST, Cambridge University): Yes, Sir.

*MR. A. HUTTON: I was not aware of that, but I think it cannot be a recommendation of a far-reaching character. He told us that the National Society had raised such an outcry in favour of cheap labour and school drudges that the Education Department had to let the case of an efficient staff of teachers go by the board altogether. He was speaking of the Committee, and he said—

" I say there is little hope of mending it, because, as was mentioned by the Seconder of the Motion, a Committee was appointed of experts to consider how the position of these pupil teachers could be improved, and before the Committee had even taken their scheme into consideration, or pronounced any opinion upon it, it was denounced from all sides, even by such bodies as the National Society. It has been denounced as a scheme which, if carried out, would retard the supply of cheap child labour, by which the schools are so often rendered less valuable, and I am afraid that, under this dire necessity of having cheap teachers in the schools, in the first place, the welfare of these poor, little school drudges themselves, and, in the next place, the national interest in getting better trained and better taught teachers for the rural districts will have to go."

Now, Sir, I submit I did not travesty the words of the right honourable Gentleman, but that I stated practically his proposition in plain and simple terms. The right honourable Gentleman did not take any steps because the National Society demanded school drudges and cheap labour, and the education of the country and the Department had to stand still. This question of pupil teachers is a very serious one indeed. At the present moment the town of Leeds, which is a very progressive town with regard to education, is unable to get certificated assistant teachers. It is not a question of salary, and the managers now have to employ ex-pupil teachers against their custom, who have only passed in the third class of the Queen's Scholarship. I admit that that does not immediately touch the question of the supply of pupil teachers, but it shows that when pupil teachers are unable to get into training colleges, progressive school managers and School Boards are obliged to have resort to other classes of teachers. Indeed, Article 68 teachers have doubled in five years since 1892 from 7,000 to 14,000. A great many of them sought admission to training colleges and passed the test of the Queen's Scholarship Examination, and to the disadvantage of other teachers and of schools, and to the disadvantage of the public interest, they were obliged to be admitted as teachers untrained and uncertificated. As a matter of fact, there were according to the last return 1500 applications for admission to training colleges refused to persons who had passed the test, and 2,200 were admitted, and those admitted, scandalous to say, were not admitted in accordance with order of merit, but because of some denominational connection they might have had. A few days ago a clergyman attended a deputation which waited upon the right honourable Gentleman, and he said he had been called upon to train for confirmation a great many young men in order that they might have the privilege of entering these training colleges. He deplored that—we all deplore it. We think it is not right that these colleges, which are practically maintained out of public funds, should be closed to a large proportion of the community. Now, I would wish in conclusion to bring one case before the right honourable Gentleman. In answer to a question put by me last year with reference to the conscience clause in training colleges, he said—

"The Royal Commission recommended in effect that no conscience clause should be imposed on existing training colleges, but that no new training college should be established without one. Upon this principle successive Governments have since acted down to the present time."

"Down to the present time" has turned out to be a very significant phrase. The Bishop of Rochester has received permission from the Department to establish a training college in Lambeth, and there is to be no conscience clause with regard to residential students. This permission has been given on the condition that a certain proportion of places shall be thrown open to Nonconformists as day pupils.

Sir J. GORST: An equal number of day students with the protection of the conscience clause.

Mr. A. HUTTON: I submit that that is hardly in keeping with the principle on which the Government has hitherto acted. If we are to have a conscience clause for new colleges it should refer to residential as well as day students, and it must be obvious that in the case I have quoted Nonconformist day students are placed in a position of inferiority which is not at all pleasant. We regard this profession of teachers from the Nonconformist point of view, as one that ought to be dealt with by the Government. A profession which is trained at the expense of the State, paid by the State, and pensioned by the State, ought not to be practically a closed profession, and it is the duty of those in authority to see that these real and important grievances are removed, and that the principles of religious equality are recognised when it is a matter of the distribution of public money. I beg to second the Motion.

*Mr. CECIL (Herts, Hertford); I was greatly astonished by the speech of the honourable and learned Member for Carnarvon. It was only a year or a year and a half ago that many Members on the opposite side of the House took an active part in pushing forward the then Radical programme in the School Board elections in the metropolis, and one of the principal planks in that programme was that they were going to adhere absolutely to the Compromise of 1870. It appears to me that the speech of the honourable and learned Member was wholly and entirely directed to destroying that Compromise. He astonished me in another respect, for he rather emphasised throughout his speech the exceedingly antagonistic position of Board and Voluntary schools. For myself I have always been brought up in a school which believes that the two sets of schools act in friendly rivalry and competition, and are not actuated by that venomous desire imputed to them by the honourable and learned Member

is, I think, misconstruing the objects of Voluntary school supporters to say they are conspiring to resist Board schools in every respect. If that were so I cannot help thinking that I might justly say of the honourable and learned Member that he is prepared to assist Board schools to conspire against Voluntary schools. I quite admit that there are grievances such as the honourable and learned Member who moved this Resolution has touched upon, as, for instance, the difficulty of Nonconformist teachers securing appointments. I should not wish to allow any unfair restriction to stand in the way, but, of course, in all matters, in this as well as in others, the question of supply and demand for teachers must rule the market. But, at the same time, the honourable and learned Member can hardly suppose that he is going to get rid of Voluntary schools with the ease which perhaps he hopes. The system has many staunch and active supporters throughout England. That is proved by the fact that 2,500,000 children go to Voluntary schools in England and Wales, whereas only 2,000,000 attend Board chools. No doubt it may be said as he suggests, that in many cases children who would naturally go to Board schools are forced into Voluntary schools, but I might equally reply that many children who desire to attend Voluntary schools are forced into Board schools. But apart from any question of that kind, there is no doubt a strong feeling in the country that the Voluntary school system is economical as well as efficient. There is no doubt about its being economical; that fact is not disputed. Its economy, I regret to say, is largely due to the low salaries which the Voluntary schools are unfortunately obliged to pay their teachers. That economy, nevertheless, produces very good results, for, to judge of the efficiency of education by the return of the annual grants given to the schools, there is very little difference in the amount granted by the Government per head per year to the Board schools and to the Voluntary schools. The grant to Board schools in England last year averaged 19s. 8¾d., and to Voluntary schools 18s. 10¼d., so that the difference in the efficiency of the education in those two sets of schools was only 10¼d. In Wales the grant to Board schools was 19s. 5¼d.,

and the grant to Voluntary schools 18s. 11d., the difference between the efficiency of the two sets of schools being only 6¼d. And when we remember that in the case of Board schools the cost of maintenance in England and Wales was 12s. 8½d. more per child than in Voluntary schools, and if we take London alone, which is a more conspicuous instance, it was £1 3s. 11½d. more in Board schools than in Voluntary schools, I think we have some reason to be proud of these Voluntary schools. It is not because there is a desire on the part of Voluntary schools to bring about a lower grade of education that the Board system is objected to. I have always maintained that I wish to secure to every citizen in the country a sound elementary system of education. That was the object of the Act of 1870. That I trust is our object now. But if a grievance exists, it appears to be the fact that there is no popular control over Voluntary schools. I am inclined myself to dispute that. I have always maintained that there is already popular control over Voluntary schools through the Department of the Council of Education. That Department is a Public Department; it supervises Voluntary schools; it secures a public audit; and so far as authority is concerned it has a share in the management, inasmuch as it can stop the grant and so destroy the school, if not satisfied as to its efficiency. It is directed by a Minister who is responsible to this House, and who changes with every change of Government, and I cannot see how it can be said, in the face of those facts, that there is no public control at all over Voluntary schools. If it becomes a matter, as I think it really is, of the two kinds of religious education given in the two sets of schools, I venture to think we come to the crux of the question. It is because Voluntary schools afford security for broader and more definite religious instruction than Board schools that we have so much difficulty in settling these problems, and I wish that some arrangement could be arrived at. No one is likely to suggest that the Board school system of religious instruction is absolutely perfect. I do not know whether honourable Members opposite hold that view, but, if so, I will explain in what respect I consider it is not perfect. It is a well-known

Mr. Cecil.

fact—I have not quite the latest figures —that in Wales there are 320 School Boards, 62 of which give no religious teaching whatever. That is possible under the School Board system, and it is reasonable to object to a system where there may be no religious instruction whatever. In 118 more of these schools the Bible is taught without note or comment. It is even maintained that we cannot teach under the Board school system such a generally accepted doctrine as the Divinity of our Lord. That is, I think, a reasonable ground of complaint against Board schools. It is essential under the Board school system that teachers should be appointed without reference to their religious belief. That is a principle which is very strictly adhered to and supported by honourable Members opposite. But that necessitates that we might have teachers appointed who held the opinions of the late Mr. Bradlaugh, and if the school to which such a teacher were appointed were the only one in the district in which I lived I might have to send my children to it to be taught their religion by a teacher who held such opinions, or else I should be obliged to withdraw them altogether from school under the conscience clause. And when I inform the House that it has been recently decided by the London School Board that on the appointment of a teacher he may not be asked if he goes to any religious place of worship on Sundays, I trust honourable Members will agree there is some ground for our objection. I do not say all this in any mere antagonism to the opinions expressed on the opposite side of the House. I am perfectly willing to recognise them, and to give them an opportunity of being satisfied so far as I can. But what I urge, and urge most emphatically, is that the parent who desires that his children should have definite denominational teaching, no matter what denomination he may belong to, should be able to obtain it at the national schools. I am not speaking in the interest of any one denomination. I do not for one moment sneer at the Nonconformists, to use the honourable and learned Member's words; I speak myself from an essentially Protestant point of view, but I speak also in the interests of all denominations, and I am desirous that all parents who wish it should be able to obtain for their chil-

dren such definite religious instruction as they consider essential. It is not an impossible proposal; it is not even a new proposal; it is a proposal which has been tried in almost every quarter of the globe. It has been tried at Birmingham. So long ago as 1874, just after the passing of the Education Act, the Birmingham School Board passed this resolution, and it has worked without friction, and is still in force—

" Facilities will be afforded for the giving of religious instruction by voluntary agency in the school buildings belonging to the Board to children attending the Board schools. In every case the wish of the parents or guardians shall determine whether a child shall receive religious instruction, and whether a child shall receive any specific religious instruction that may be provided."

A similar form of specific religious instruction goes on, as honourable Members know very well, in Ireland. A similar form goes on in the British Army. A similar form goes on in Germany; and perhaps I may read to the House a note I received on the subject from a Member of the Reichstag—

"The administrative unit in Germany is the Parish (*Gemeinde*), and where the parishes are very small, they are, as in England, united into a school district. Large parishes, such as town parishes, with a numerous population of various religious persuasions, have very frequently set the example of dividing their schools according to denominations; but in parishes where this does not occur, special religious instruction is expressly attended to by the proper denominational minister.

In Austria a similar system goes on. It has been referred to by the right honourable Gentleman the Member for Dublin University in his book "Democracy and Liberty." In that he says—

"In the State schools, religious instruction must be given separately to the scholars of different denominations, by their own priests or pastors, or by lay teachers appointed by the different religious bodies."

That suggestion, I venture to think, is a most excellent one. If we could depute, as it were, lay teachers, who could be employed in the State school to give definite religious teaching if they happened to belong to the denominations which the parents desired, it would be a means of solving this problem.

MR. LLOYD-GEORGE: Would the honourable Member apply that to Voluntary schools?

*MR. CECIL: Yes, I would. In New South Wales an Act was passed in 1880 of a similar character. It is, perhaps, too long to read to the House, but it is an Act which enables various denominations to obtain, within certain limits, exactly the same complete, definite, religious instruction with which I am dealing now. So that no one can say that this arrangement has not been tried. Indeed, it is being tried in one form in London at this moment, in the case of Jews, and I do believe that if this House would devise means by which facilities could be granted in this manner to National schools for definite religious teaching, it would take away a great deal of the bitterness which exists. There is no valid objection why this system should not be tried. If there are parents who desire this system, surely it is all the stronger reason for taking away the grievance which exists in their minds. If, on the other hand, as is sometimes alleged, there are no parents who desire it, what harm is there in introducing it? Board school religion would go on just as before. I think it is very hard that the rich man should be able at this moment, when he desires definite religious teaching, to send his children to a school where he can get it, and where he has to pay for it; whereas the poor man has to send his child to a Board school—because he cannot afford to do otherwise—where he cannot get the teaching he desires. So that, virtually, under the existing system, comparing the rich and the poor man, you are making definite religious teaching a luxury which has to be paid for. Surely that is not just? I hope, as time goes on, this proposal for giving facilities for definite religious teaching in National schools may gain more ground. I am quite certain that the more it is thought over the more it will gain ground, and the more it will diminish the acerbity which is sometimes raised in these Debates.

MR. FOSTER (Suffolk, Lowestoft): The speech of my honourable Friend who has just sat down is more likly to commend itself to the favourable atten-

tion of the House than the somewhat bitter tone which characterised the speech of the honourable Member for Carnarvon. The honourable Member for Carnarvon has submitted a Resolution to the House alleging a grievance. He has not actually defined what that grievance is, except so far as we have been able to gather from his speech. The Amendment which I have put on the Paper demands much more attention than the grievance to which the honourable Gentleman calls attention. After all, is it not a fact that the Government, three years ago, brought in a very large and revolutionary Measure of educational reform, and that the very grievances to which the honourable Gentleman has called attention were remedied by those proposals? Was it not then suggested— and the suggestion has been repeated to-night by my honourable Friend behind me—that there should be full liberty of denominational and religious teaching in every one of the Primary schools of the country? Is not that the position to which we are gradually approaching, notwithstanding the Compromise of 1870? I for one, Mr. Speaker, look forward to the time when Primary schools shall be open during the interval devoted to religious instruction for such definite dogmatic teaching to be given to the children as the parents shall themselves select. If that state of things be once arrived at then the whole controversy will disappear. As matters stand at present, what is the position of disability in which the Denominational schools are placed? I suppose the honourable Gentleman will acknowledge that religious instruction to be of any value must be more or less dogmatic. There must be some dogma in it; if you take away that dogma you take away the real value of the teaching. Well, now, at the present moment those who believe in definite dogmatic teaching, whether it be Church of England, Roman Catholic, or Wesleyan, are put under severe disabilities by Parliament. That is one of the results of the Compromise of 1870. These schools are doing, I firmly believe, the same educational work as is being done in Board schools. They are inspected under precisely the same system of inspection. They have to obtain in exactly the same way the Government grant. They have to teach under exactly the same Code. They are fulfilling that which Parliament requires of them—namely, the duty of instructing in Primary Education every child of school age. Therefore, whether it be the Voluntary schools or the Board schools, so far as elementary education is concerned, apart from the question of religious instruction, they are doing exactly the same work. And they are doing it very largely with exactly the same results. The last speaker alluded to the fact that, notwithstanding the enormous pecuniary advantages in the way of money and machinery which the School Boards possess in comparison with their less favoured rivals, the result, as proved by the inspection test and the Government grant earned as the result of that test, is that the state of efficiency of the Board schools and of Voluntary schools is practically the same, the Board schools earning 19s. 9¼d. per head and the Voluntary schools 18s. 11¾d. But even that difference, so far from proving that the Board school ought to be supported in preference to Voluntary schools, from my point of view accentuates the hardships which Voluntary schools suffer. The Member for Carnarvon said, and I quite agree with him, that it is all a question of funds. He impressed upon the House, in the first part of his speech, that the whole question of efficient education was a question of funds. Very well. Now, Voluntary schools, as he himself must admit, are labouring under very serious disadvantages with regard to funds, and I submit that the very fact that the Voluntary schools have been deprived of earning something like £100,000 in comparison with the Board Schools, because of their less efficient machinery, accentuates the grievance which the Voluntary schools suffer. But that is by no means the whole of the difficulty. The Board schools are State-aided, and they are rate-aided. Their less fortunate rivals, the Voluntary schools, are State-aided but are not rate-aided, and that not only has a direct effect upon the question of results, but it also has a direct effect upon the control of the schools. My honourable Friend behind me pointed out very truly that there is a very large measure of public control over the Voluntary schools to-day through the Education Department and through the Minister of that Department, who is responsible to this House. That control is much more effective over the Voluntary schools than the Board schools. In the case of Voluntary schools, if the Department is not satisfied with the way in which the school is carried on, or with the character of the education given, it may deprive that school of its grant, and by depriving it of its grant it practically deprives it of its life. In the case of the Board schools, if the Department is not satisfied with what it is doing—if the character of the education is deficient, or the accommodation is not satisfactory, and if the Department in consequence refuses the grant—it does not, either directly or indirectly, stop the school. Not a bit of it. The only result is that members of the School Board, because they are so much short in the grant, increase the amount of the precept which they issue to the rating authorities. The deficiency is consequently made up in that way. Therefore, the Department has a much more effective control over the efficiency of Voluntary schools than it has over Board schools, because, in the latter case, what Parliament does not vote the rating authority are bound to provide. Honourable Gentlemen know that, while there are many public Acts—the Public Libraries Act and others—where there is a limit on the amount to be raised in any one year from the ratepayers, in the case of the School Board there is no such limit. Whatever the precepts may be that the Board demand, the rating authority, without appeal of any kind, has to provide. Therefore, there is little wonder that the Board schools throughout the country should be able to show somewhat better educational results than their less favoured brethren. If my honourable Friend really desires—and I am sure he must—to promote the efficiency of the education of the children, why does he favour the continuance of that pecuniary disability? He must desire that the wishes of the majority shall be carried out. Now, notwithstanding the enormous financial advantage of the Board schools during the last 26 or 27 years, it is a remarkable fact that to-day, for every four children being educated in the Board schools, five are being educated in the Voluntary schools. That shows a very remarkable preference on the part of the parents with regard to the education provided. I would venture to quote from an extract from a speech delivered in this House in 1897 by the right honourable Gentleman the Member for the Bodmin Division (Mr. Courtney). The House knows that he is no friend of the denominational system; indeed, I believe he would much prefer to see a universal system of Board schools. He has, however, said very frankly—

"He has come to recognise that they must pay deference to the wishes of parents when they were clearly expressed, and, if they were followed, it would be absolutely unjust to withhold public money from the schools."

A little later on he said—

"Looking at the permanent forces at work in support of Denominational schools, he was inclined to think that in the reasonable progress of time they would see, not perhaps the present Government, but possibly the Member for Monmouth, introducing a scheme of rate-aided support of Denominational schools."

Well, now, the disability under which Voluntary schools labour at the present moment is due to some extent to the fact that they have no support from the rates. Parliament did something a few years ago for the purpose of removing to some extent the financial disability under which Voluntary schools suffer, and, as the House knows, a grant amounting to something like £600,000 was given for the purpose of helping them out of their difficulties. Honourable Gentlemen opposite have said that this was a system of favouritism to Voluntary schools, which was not, but ought to have been, extended to Board schools. But what are the facts? So far from Voluntary schools having been favoured, I submit to the House that they had a right to a larger grant of public money, according to the public work they are doing in the education of the children, than the Board schools. I find that if they were to have received the same amount per child out of the public money that the Board schools are receiving for the education of Board school children, instead of receiving £600,000 they would have received £1,770,000. In other words, Parliament to-day is giving Board schools for the public work they are doing, either through the Imperial grant or through the local rates, £1,000,000

Mr. Foster.

more for the work that is being done *pro rata* than is being allowed to Voluntary schools. I say, therefore, that the present system ought not to be allowed to continue. It is quite true that, owing to their financial position, some of the Voluntary schools have had to be shut up. It is perfectly true also that if the educational screw continues to be turned, and if the standard is raised from year to year, as I hope and trust it will be raised, the effect must be that if these schools are to keep their heads above water we shall have to assist them, and appeals will once more be made by that body of opinion in this country which desires denominational teaching in Voluntary schools, and demands will be made for further grants. Well, in my humble judgment, that is not a satisfactory way of dealing with the matter. The time may not yet be ripe for that system under which all Elementary schools, whether Board or Denominational, will be entitled to receive, and will receive, the same recognition from the State for the same work done, but I believe that we must ultimately logically arrive at it. Something has been said, Mr. Speaker, about the hardship which Nonconformists suffer by reason of their children being sent to Church schools, and it is said, and I confess I sympathise with the statement that that difficulty is accentuated at the present moment by the crisis in the Church. Personally I regret that the honourable Member for Carnarvon should have appeared to draw such a complete line of difference between the Church of England and the Nonconformist bodies. I should have thought that he would have recognised that most Nonconformist bodies differ in a very slight respect form the Protestant Church of England. I should have hoped, particularly at this juncture, when large numbers of the Protestant Church are joined by large numbers of Nonconformists in endeavouring to preserve the Protestant character of the National Church, that he would not have chosen this time to accentuate these differences. I suppose men at all times must regard these questions from different standpoints, but these are minor differences when we come to consider the question of sacerdotal teaching. I confess frankly that if I had a child of mine in a Voluntary school I would rather submit that child to the religious instruction of the Board school than to sacerdotal teaching in a Voluntary school. So far I am entirely with the honourable Gentleman, and I must say this—and here again I believe I shall have the general assent of the House— that religious instruction is of value only in so far as it is dogmatic. Many absurd and unjust things have been said about the kind of religious instruction given in Board schools. I had the honour for some years of sitting on the London School Board, and I can state, without fear of contradiction, that the religious difficulty was completely unknown in any single school except at election times. We ask that there shall be the same liberties extended to Voluntary schools as are given to Board schools, and that the hundreds of thousands of parents who prefer definite religious instruction to be given to their children at school shall be allowed to exercise that right. We do not deny the grievance which the honourable Gentleman alleges, but it is only one of many other grievances, and, as far as I am concerned, I perfectly desire to see those grievances removed all round. I have put this Amendment on the Paper because it appeared to me that I could not vote a plain negative to the Motion of the honourable Member for Carnarvon, because I feel that there are grievances in the present system, though they are of a different character to those the honourable Member mentioned, and grievances far more pressing and urgent. If the House is to pass a Resolution that the present system is unsatisfactory, I think it should be asked to state in what respect it is unsatisfactory, so that we may know what we are voting for. For the purpose of doing that, I have put the Amendment on the Paper, which I now beg to move, and which is in these terms—

"To insert after 'Wales' the words 'under which Board schools receive a larger grant of public money than Voluntary or Denominational schools for the same educational work, carried on under the same inspection and under the same Educational Code, and under which the local burdens for National Primary Education are unequally distributed."

With regard to the inequality of local taxation for National Primary Education, to which I have not alluded, my honourable Friend who seconds the Amendment will no doubt call the attention of

the House to those inequalities. At the present time the supporters of Voluntary schools are not only called upon to contribute to the cost of those schools, but they are also, as ratepayers, called upon to pay the heavy burden imposed upon them for the support of the Board schools. I hope the House will affirm that this is a grievance which is much more important than the one to which my honourable Friend the Member for Carnarvon has called attention. I look forward with confidence to the day—it may not be in this Parliament, or in the next Parliament, but I am certain that it will be in the lifetime of many of us—when Parliament will recognise the injustice of penalising Voluntary and Denominational schools because they venture to teach doctrines, while the Board schools are allowed to have unlimited money because they teach no doctrine. The right honourable Gentleman the Leader of the House, in closing the Debate in 1896 on the Education Bill, pointed out that while dogmatic teaching was considered wrong in England, it was considered good in Scotland, and he asked those honourable Gentlemen who were going to vote against the idea of supplying money in England to any school which taught dogmatic teaching why, if this was wrong in England, it was right in Scotland. I hope that the injustice of the present state of things will soon be remedied.

*Mr. GRAY (West Ham, N.): Mr. Speaker, there is happily one thing in the Resolution with which both sides of the House will agree—that the system of Primary Education in England is unsatisfactory. But I cannot help feeling myself that much of the difficulty in finding a remedy is due to the continuous obtruding of the sectarian question. I am persuaded that speeches such as that made by the honourable Member for Carnarvon do not tend to peace and progress, but to discord and the perpetuation of the difficulties which friends of education lament. I listened to the opening sentences of the honourable Member's speech with no little interest. It left me in some doubt as to what the grievance was of which he complained, but I had very little doubt that sooner or later we should hear the sectarian question brought very prominently forward, and every other grievance glided over, apologised for, or justified. In the

earlier part of his speech he referred to a large number of difficulties in regard to staffing, buildings, and the inadequate supply of money, but he passed them all over very quickly, and elevated into a position of the usual prominence the sectarian difficulty—a difficulty which exists almost entirely on public platforms, and does not exist in practice within the schools. I was alarmed at the rapidity with which the honourable Member for Carnarvon generalised on insufficient data. This thing, he said, existed in Brighton and in Cardiff, and then came, with rapid generalisation, "and all over the country." What proof is there that such a state of things exists all over the country? Again and again one solitary expression of an injudicious person is brought forward, and upon this the House is asked to believe that the whole Voluntary school system is rotten to the core, and ought to be swept out of existence to-morrow. There are 14,000 Voluntary schools, and you are told that because one of them does so and so, the whole lot ought to go. I could not help noticing the inadequate material on which the honourable Member founded his unjustifiable accusations against the whole Voluntary system, and that, I am afraid, is not unusual with him. How can any of us on this side of the House, who have seen some of the good work done by the Voluntary schools, and who have recognised some of the evils that exist in their ranks, approach with any sympathy the consideration of claims put forward by one who puts the gibbet, persecution, prosecution, and Voluntary schools all in one breath, and goes about speaking of Voluntary school managers as if they were sheep stealers, with designs upon Nonconformist lambs. It is almost impossible to approach a plea put forward in those terms with anything like sympathy. I have recognised in and out of this House many of the difficulties with which Voluntary schools are beset, and I know there are fanatics in the Voluntary system as there are on some of the largest School Boards in the country. I think we on this side have condemned them with equal justice, with impartiality, recognising faults when they exist in both systems, and have been anxious, above all things, to secure a remedy which will benefit the children, regardless of any particular religious denomination. I find

Mr. Gray.

that, according to the honourable Member, the simple difference between Board and Voluntary schools seems to be this: that, while they both do wrong, the Board schools are justified in doing wrong. The honourable Gentleman the Member for Carnarvon, after pointing out some of the evils perpetuated by small School Boards, immediately followed it up with the sentence, "Is it surprising?" and, "Can it be wondered at?" It is not only in small School Boards that troubles arise. There is an instance, as recently as last week, in which the London School Board pursued a system of most unjustifiable harassing towards a Voluntary school in Marylebone, a system of which even Progressive members did not approve; but it would be exceedingly wrong on my part if I were to take that one illustration and immediately pronounce a speedy condemnation of the whole School Board system. I should think myself altogether unjustified in doing so on one instance alone, or even if I could secure a dozen similar instances. One cannot help feeling in this matter that there is a strong desire on the part of Nonconformists to retain a grievance. Clause 27 of the Bill of 1896 contained a proposal very similar to that outlined by the honourable Member for Carnarvon amid the cheers of his supporters, but that proposal in the Bill met with most active opposition from the other side of the House.

MR. CHANNING (Northampton, E.): And would again.

*MR. GRAY: That confirms what I said, that they want to retain a grievance rather than approach with sympathy any attempt to remove it. "We are prepared," said the honourable Member on the other side, "to grant money to these Voluntary schools to remove some of the difficulties, provided they are placed under public control." The Bill of 1896 proposed a large Measure on local control, but it was fought with all the strength the Opposition could command at that time. I suppose that, after the condemnation of Voluntary schools, I might assume that the educational work is well done in those parts where School Boards have flourished. I suppose, further, having regard to the opinions that have been promulgated by the right honourable Gentleman the Member for Carnarvon, that I would be justified in expecting a high level of efficiency in the schools in the county of Carnarvon, but when I turn to the Reports of the Education Department I find that the county of Carnarvon stands almost at the very bottom of the list. There are more schools in Wales where the religion is unsectarian, and where they have absolutely banished the Bible, than there are throughout the whole of England, and I find that the level of education is much worse in Wales than in England or in Scotland. There is one exception—the county of Monmouth, in England—which, I believe, has the unenviable notoriety of being at the very bottom of the list. It is, therefore, with regret that I find the right honourable Gentleman the Member for West Monmouth absent from this Debate. The attendance at Board schools is also lower in Wales than in England or Scotland. In Scotland the attendance stands at 84 per cent., in England at 81 per cent., but in Carnarvon the figure is only 77 per cent. Then I turn to the question of the school staffs. In the Principality of Wales, where the School Board system has flourished, and where the unsectarian Board school is seen at its brightest, the schools are more inadequately staffed than are the schools in England. A third of the teachers are pupil teachers, another third are uncertificated teachers—there being only one-third certificated teachers. That is in the Principality of Wales, where the School Board system is so flourishing. I regret that Wales occupies this low position on the list, but it leads me to suggest that some of the superfluous energies of the Welsh Members should be turned towards their own districts before they come here to criticise the Voluntary schools in England. I know something of the working of Voluntary schools, not from mere hearsay or from letters sent up by interested parties, but from actual experience, from visiting many of them, from reports, almost daily, from persons working in them, from knowing the teachers, and what the managers are doing, and I have no hesitation whatever in asserting that a large number of our Voluntary schools are doing as thorough, sound, good, and satisfactory work as any of the School Boards in the country. This wholesale condemnation cannot be justified. Some of the Voluntary schools are condemned because they are badly equipped and badly staffed, but this

is solely due, as you will find, to the poverty of the locality, and its utter inability to furnish the necessary moneys to equip the schools. This evil will never be grappled with until it is recognised that assistance should be given sufficiently to cope with it. If in those particular districts you were to change the position, and establish School Boards temporarily, you would have exactly the same evils existing, as sufficient money could not be raised in the locality. I contend that it is the duty of the nation, and not the duty of the locality, to provide the necessary funds for the maintenance of these schools. These evils of which we are complaining will never be satisfactorily grappled with until the principle is realised that, as the State fixes the curriculum, demands the level of education, inspects the schools, trains and sanctions the appointments of teachers, guides and controls local management, so of necessity the State must follow that up by making a State grant sufficient to cope with the necessities of the districts. I believe the principle is altogether wrong of demanding from the locality a subsidy towards the support of education. We have our territorial regiments, but whoever heard of demanding money from the local rates to support those territorial regiments, or of our seaport towns providing out of their local rates a contribution towards the cost of Her Majesty's Navy? Popular education is a stronger line of defence than either the Army or the Navy, and should be paid for by the State. The evil caused by the unequal distribution of the charges of national education is tenfold greater than this sectarian trouble. Can anyone justify a principle under which, if a man moves from one side of the street to the other side, which happens to be in another parish, he is compelled, if the School Board rate is higher in the parish to which he has removed, to pay more, although he may continue to send his children to the same school? The education of the country is standing still, while in other countries it is moving forward, and while we are wasting our time over this question the children are suffering. Last Wednesday we had a piece of good work transacted, and a piece of educational reform accomplished, free altogether from the squabbles of sectarianism. The House was crowded, and

the interest in the Debate was keen, and
if there need be any condemnation of
this Debate, I would call attention to
the state of the Benches around us as an
illustration of the little interest which
the House of Commons takes in such an
academic discussion as this. I can assure the House that out in the country
exactly the same attitude is adopted.
The great majority of the parents themselves who are familiar with the working of the schools—at least those who
are not fanatics—adopt exactly the same
attitude on this question. They admit,
as I admit, that on paper you can make
out a big grievance. It is all very well to
talk about those 1,000 schools, in which
Nonconformists are placed at a disadvantage. That looks very plausible, but in
actual practice it is found not to exist. It
is said that your Nonconformist child is
anxious to become a pupil teacher. I
was led to believe by the remarks of the
honourable Member for Carnarvon that
the children of Nonconformist parents
are rushing in crowds to the schools
managed by the Church of England,
anxious to become pupil teachers. Why,
the fact is, it is difficult to secure pupil
teachers, whether Nonconformists or
Churchmen. Take Birmingham, for instance. Are the Birmingham Board
schools sectarian in their character, and
are they also contaminated by this
Church influence that is so strongly deprecated? How is it that the Birmingham School Board cannot secure male
pupil teachers? It is because the children are not anxious to become pupil
teachers. It is difficult to secure them
now for the schools, and it will continue
to be difficult so long as the schools remain in their present unsatisfactory condition as to staff, appliances, buildings,
curriculum, and attendances. Now, I
wish to say a word or two, if I may, to
dispel the illusion that all the managers
of Church schools are restricted in their
action, and exclude the Nonconformist
child. All the Voluntary schools
are not under the individual management of one man, for I have been interested during the Recess in the trust
deed of a school near Wolverhampton,
where the Charity Commissioners have
given us clauses whereby the clergyman,
churchwardens, and the representatives
of the subscribers, the parents, and the
patrons of the living all unite in forming

Mr. Gray.

one board of management for this Voluntary school. At this school the diocesan
inspector does not enter, and the
religious teaching satisfies thoroughly
every Nonconformist in the district;
and I venture to say that there are
hundreds, if not thousands, of schools in
the country where the education given in
Voluntary schools is of the same liberal
character as in the case I am referring
to. It is the exception that is being
condemned here, and I protest against
the whole system being swamped in one
condemnation which should be made
against the exception, and which is made
without any differentiation between the
just and the unjust. I am not pleading
on behalf of Voluntary schools because
they are cheap, because I realise that
if the managers of the Voluntary schools
had their own way they would be quite
ready to spend more money upon them.
I am sure my honourable Friend does
not plead for cheapness in the conduct
of the schools. Well, I know something
might well be said for free management,
but I, for one, am not prepared to dispense with, in a hurry, such control, and
jump out of the frying pan into the fire
by coming under the control of one of
those small School Boards where a penny
rate produces £3, and where the last
election cost them £20. I have a list
here of the School Boards showing the
returns of the last election expenses in
the School Board elections, and I cannot
help thinking that a perpetuation of
that system is a disgrace to the country,
and we might as well take the taxpayers' money and fling it into the
gutter as waste it on these small School
Boards. The areas must be enlarged.
Now, the Bill of 1898 offered that enlargement, but it was objected to from
the other side, although it would have
given popular control. It contained a
plan for dealing with the religious or
sectarian question, but again it was objected to, and when we see some prospect of this question being approached
from an educational standpoint rather
than in a sectarian spirit, I believe there
will be a ready response from every
Churchman and from every manager of
Voluntary schools. The Voluntary
schools are not afraid of popular control,
but they are starved to death to-day,
and they hardly know how to make both
ends meet. The principle has been recognised of adding to the contribution of

the State and 'diminishing the contribution of the locality, and that principle will have to be carried out before we can expect our schools to be placed on a level with those on the Continent. I can well recollect the amazement shown by those interested in education in Munich, when I tried to explain to them some of the troubles that we are face to face with in England, such as the pupil teacher difficulty, the provision of accommodation and equipment by the locality, and small School Boards and restricted areas; for all these things it is utterly impossible for the Saxon to understand why they exist. They cannot understand why a child should leave school at 11 years of age, or why our education should be looked at grudgingly and carpingly when in their schools they look upon a sound elementary education as the finest "trade secret" that they possess. If you endeavour to persuade them that we have in England a "religious difficulty" you will find it beyond your power of explanation and beyond their power of comprehension. One thing they are convinced upon, and that is, that all their educational work shall be founded upon some religious teaching, and if Great Britain was polled to-morrow I have not a shadow of doubt that they would return by an overwhelming majority the same answer. What we want is a religious teaching which is not bigoted, and which is not dominated by fanatical bigots, but which is framed in a broad spirit, which will enable the Churchman to obtain what he considers of more value than geography, whilst at the same time giving to the Nonconformist all the freedom of the Board schools which he may well claim. This Debate leaves an impression upon my mind that it is not education which is at the bottom of this Motion, not a desire to advance education, but a desire to secure a Party victory, and to give vent to strong Party political feelings.

MR. LLOYD-GEORGE: No, no!

*MR. GRAY: Well, at any rate, that is the view I hold, and I hold it strongly, because I know what the schools are, and what they want, and because I realise that a speech of that character would have met with strong denuncia-

tion even in Wales. I have seen evidence in Wales itself of a keen desire to drop for ever this sectarian trouble, and to work together, one and all, for the benefit of the schools. In conclusion, Mr. Speaker, I cannot help expressing the hope that, whether the Amendment be carried or not, an emphatic rejection will be given to the main proposition before the House, and that we may abandon for ever sectarian complaints, and give our undivided attention to National Education.

MR. WALLACE (Edinburgh, E.): I wish to say a very few words indeed on this matter, and even these few words I should have withheld if I had not heard the opinions expressed on the religious question during this Debate. The view which I am about to express is one which is held by a very influential portion of the public outside, influential both in numbers and intelligence, and, therefore, I think it should be briefly mentioned in the course of this discussion. My intention is to vote in support of the Motion of my honourable Friend the Member for Carnarvon, and to some extent I wish to add something to the material adduced in support of his proposal, but which he omitted, and I shall not say for what reason, but I suspect it was because he was not perfectly conscious of the additional support which lay at his hand. I perfectly agree with him in all that he said upon the educational aspect of the matter. I believe that in many respects and in many quarters the state of Primary Education is in what one might almost call a lamentable condition. It is a matter for regret that the difficulty of obtaining, in small parishes, really competent School Boards exist, and the position of the teacher is one to be deplored, for he is liable to be dismissed without appeal by arrogant clerics or by ignorant school managers. I think also that the machinery for compulsion is in a most unsatisfactory position, and I believe that the curriculum is greatly open to reform, more particularly in what I may call "the fancy subjects," on which I think a good deal of time and money are wasted in view of the real necessities, industrial and educational, of the working classes. To my mind, the great educational problem of the future is the technical education of the working classes, giving to the manual labourer a thorough scientific grasp of the calling, whatever it is, by which he is to serve society and keep himself alive. I believe that if these things were properly attended to that it would be the means not only of keeping us abreast, or ahead, of our industrial rivals—although I believe it would do so, but I consider that that is almost a secondary consideration. To my mind the principal thing is making the working man intellectual in reference to his calling, so that he is lifted up into a position which I may call a cultured position, and which leaves him no longer what he is at the present time. This, to my mind, would be a political and social gain of priceless value, for at the present moment I see no encouragement, but, on the contrary, I see obstacles in the way of bringing about this state of things in the condition in which primary education is at this moment. I turn to the religious aspect of the matter as set forth by my honourable Friend the Member for Carnarvon, and there, as I have hinted already, I do not think that he was aware of all the arguments that were at his command. I think that he and my Nonconformist friends have actually doubled the grievances which he so graphically described. I think that in himself and his friends are to be found some of the very strongest reasons why Parliament should institute an inquiry into the religious grievances, and I say so because, in my opinion—and I am prepared to prove it in detail if time permitted—that he and they, by persisting in keeping the Board schools in their present dogmatic and sectarian position, are offending quite as much a portion of the taxpayers and ratepayers of this country as the body of which he forms a part, who, he alleges, are put to great inconvenience by the action of the Anglican and Catholic bodies. I say that they do so not only by continuing to support that state of things, but by refusing to accept the only solution of what I believe, and what the people outside this House believe, to be the only satisfactory solution of the problem of State proselytism, and that is by abolishing, or, at all events, doing their best to effect the absolute severance of secular and theological teaching in regard to State schools. If they would allow only secular instruction to be provided by the State.

and relegate religious instruction to the parents, the clergy, and the churches, whose proper function religious instruction is—a system which is carried out with success at the present moment in many of our colonies—they would do all that was needed to check and make impossible these aggressions of Anglican upon Nonconformist and Nonconformist upon Freethinkers which are creating all the grievances and mischief which we deplore. And why they who insist upon Disestablishment in their churches and the disestablishment of religion in churches should at the same time insist upon the permanent establishment of religion in schools is one of those things which I have never been able to comprehend, any more than I am able to understand why it should be wrong to learn arithmetic without religion, and perfectly innocent and right to learn dancing or calisthenics without accompaniments. I have never yet met a Catholic parent desiring that his child should learn the pianoforte who would object to have that child taught the piano by a Protestant professor of that instrument; nor have I ever met an Anglican parent who would object to his child learning dancing from a Dissenting dancing master. I know what their answer is. They contend that the Board schools are undogmatic and unsectarian, but between them and me there is a wide gulf fixed. To my mind the Board schools are dogmatic, permissively dogmatic, but dogmatic still; and every dogma is sectarian in its relation to all the people who do not hold it, and I never heard of any dogma that was exempted from the position of not being held by somebody. Now, the only way, indeed, for any man to be undogmatic is to be dumb, for the moment a man opens his mouth on religion, necessarily out flies a dogma, because a dogma in practice is simply a proposition in religion. I can give dogmas as well as a belief, although I do not say that they would be so universally accepted, but in their psychological nature and in their logical definition they are dogmas just as well as the dogmas of the oldest church in the world. Now, I want to ask my honourable Friends who hold the opposite view about the Board schools to really consider how the facts of the matter stand,

and when I do so I shall be compelled to use language that is not commonly used in this House; but I wish it to be understood that I do it with all reverence and with perfect seriousness, because I regard this as one of the greatest questions that can come before this assembly or any other assembly. I wish to ask what is the real state of matters in connection with the Board school religious instruction? When the management of a Board school orders, as it has a right to order, the Bible to be used as a handbook of instruction, it practically and essentially says, "This Book is the word of God." I say that cannot be denied by those who look facts in the face. But the moment that is asserted, in whatever way, two of the most stupendous dogmas have been laid down, namely, theism and revelation. Now I maintain that the School Board dogma of theism is one that is offensive to a very large class of the ratepayers and taxpayers of this country. I say that that dogma is contrary to the view of that very large class who are known as agnostics and anti-theists, who, in my opinion, are practically identical with the immense and numerous class who frequent neither church nor chapel, and I say these people have as good a right to be considered as the most pious attendants at public or other worship. Then there is another class of a totally different character to whom this School Board dogma of theism and teachings in the schools is offensive—I mean the Anglican and the Catholic inhabitants of this country. They consider—at least, I know a great many of them consider, and to my mind, not unnaturally—that the naked teaching of theism is practically the teaching of Unitarianism, or indirectly of the essence of Mahomedanism, and I must say, for my part, when it is considered profoundly, I do not see that they are very far wrong. I say, therefore, in this way the School Board exercises a sectarianising influence in respect of these two classes which I have mentioned, which, in point of fact, are as wide as the poles asunder. Then with regard to the School Board dogma of revelation. I say that that also necessarily arouses an antagonism and a controversy of a very extended and complicated description. Every man of average intelligence now knows that after the Reformation, after the position

in which Scripture was placed at the Reformation by statute and by ecclesiastical definition, there have been 200 years of advance and development of what it is the fashion to call "the higher criticism," and that as the result of that progress there is scarcely, I believe, a religious sect in this country which does not openly admit that there is what is called a human element in Scripture; and then when the question arises as to what is the human, or what is the superhuman, or whether there is any superhuman element in the matter, why, controversy of an infinitely extended character at once arises, so that the School Board dogma of revelation is one of the most sectarianising influences that can possibly be conceived. So, with regard to these School Board dogmas, I limit myself to these, which I say are incontestable. I say nothing of the thousand and one dogmas which must necessarily be propounded by the teachers, when they are giving this instruction to the pupils, which, although perhaps not recognised in any of the historical creeds, are still dogmatic in their nature. I confine myself to these two important and undeniable dogmas, and I say that my honourable Friend and those Nonconformists who support him are really, although they may be unconscious of it, quite as dogmatic and quite as sectarian in the position they take up as the Anglicans whom they attack; and, accordingly, I maintain that in the position they occupy, and in the arguments they employ, as well as in the zeal with which they push—and naturally push—their own dogmatic and sectarian propositions, they are turning the Board schools to quite as objectionable sectarian purposes as the Anglican communion turn, according to their allegations, the Voluntary schools. The fact of the matter is that my friends have left themselves in this matter very few legs to stand upon in this "pot and kettle" controversy. But while this is so the position is made all the more distinct and clear to me in settling how I have to vote, because they have doubled the material and quadrupled the reasons for my supporting my Friend the honourable Member for Carnarvon in demanding a Parliamentary inquiry into the matter. If when that Parliamentary inquiry comes—as I hope it will come and won't be long in coming—I shall look quite as sharply upon my Friend the Member for Carnarvon as he and his friends are going to look upon the Anglican and Catholic communions, and others whom they dub as dogmatists, forgetting all the time that they are no more dogmatists than themselves, although the dogmatism of one side may be different in the logical form, whatever they may be in substantial reality, from those who differ from them.

On the return of Mr. SPEAKER after the usual interval,

*MR. S. SMITH (Flintshire): The honourable Gentleman who sat down just before the adjournment of the House delighted us—as he always does—with his wit and humour, but I cannot feel that he made any really valuable contribution to this question, and the views he expressed are not the views of this country. I think this can be proved by a very simple illustration: Supposing he were to stand for the School Board in any of our large towns—would he put forward those views then? I very much doubt whether there is a single constituency in this country which would return the honourable Member if he held such views as he has expressed to-night; and that proves that the great majority of the people of this country are in favour of religious education. But the question is—What kind of religious education? It all 'turns upon that. Now, I venture to remark that up to the last 20 or 30 years there was practically no difference in this country as to what the religious education should be which was given to the children. At the time of the passing of the Education Act of 1870 was laid down the foundation upon which we have built ever since, and what the country understood by religious education was simply Biblical instruction. In that I think the Vice-President of the Council will bear me out, for he was in the House at that time, and I think he will remember the controversy which was raised upon it. It was taken for granted all over the country that religious education meant the simple teaching of the elementary truths of Scripture to young children, and that was the almost universal desire of the whole country at that time. There was no practical differ-

Mr. Wallace.

ence between the Church of England and Nonconformists then as to what constituted religious teaching in our schools, and we might say that up to 1870, in 99 out of every 100 schools in this country the religious teaching given to children was, in the main, simple Scripture teaching, and nothing else was contemplated by Mr. Forster at the time when he introduced his great Education Bill and passed it through this House. Nothing more than that was contemplated by Mr. Gladstone, who was then Leader of the Party and the Prime Minister of the country. But what is the reason why the grievances of the Nonconformists have grown so much since 1870. Why, the reason is known to everyone in this House, and to everyone in this country. It is because an entire change has passed over the conception of religion held by a large part of the Anglican Church clergy. I should like to know, for example, whether the 400 clergy who are members of the Holy Cross Society, and the 650 who are members of the Guild of All Souls, who have the control of a great number of schools in this country, are content to give simple Biblical instruction? Will the clergy who are members of the Confraternity of the Blessed Sacrament be content to limit themselves to simple Bible teaching? I will put that question to the Vice-President, and perhaps he will be able to throw some light upon it when he addresses the House. Will the clergy of the Guild of All Souls, whose main object is to introduce requiem masses for the dead, and who are, in some cases, the principal governors in rural schools—will they give simple Bible teaching to the children which either Nonconformist or Churchman wish their children to have? This is a plain question, and I put it to Members on the other side of the House. I see some Members here who defend the High Church party, and I put it to them whether they consider that the clergy who belong to these extreme sacerdotal societies are likely to give the children the kind of education which would satisfy Protestant Nonconformists, or, even, I would venture to say, the great bulk of the laity of the Church of England. This is the reason why these grievances have become so acute. One of the speakers on the other side of the House asked a question about the Catechism used in the schools which represent the views of a large section of the advanced Anglican clergy. I can hardly answer that question, although I have read through a large number of Catechisms which are very largely taught in Sunday schools.

Sir F. POWELL (Wigan): There is only one orthodox Catechism.

*Mr. S. SMITH: Now, these Catechisms represent the views of thousands of the Anglican clergy——

Sir F. POWELL: No, no!

*Mr. S. SMITH: There is no doubt whatever about it. I ask this question, Is it likely that men who from the bottom of their hearts hold those views, and who use their whole influence to teach them in the Sunday schools, when they have control of elementary day schools, and when they have half-an-hour in which they can teach whatever education they like—is it likely that they will refrain from teaching those things which they believe to be the very essence of Christianity? I do not believe it. I believe that in many cases they avoid teaching those Catechisms publicly in order to prevent the facts becoming known to the public. Discussions of this subject in this House, if they serve no other purpose, are useful because they require these advanced clergy to practice with very great care and caution a teaching which would be otherwise done openly. These discussions are of great value in this House, and I am glad to see the right honourable Gentleman the Member for Wolverhampton in his place, because I remember he made a most powerful speech in this House, in which he quoted largely from one of these Catechisms. Well, I acknowledge that this Catechism is not taught to any extent in the schools, but I see there are a large number which are equally offensive made use of by the advanced Anglicans of the Church of England. Now let us look at this point. This House knows perfectly well to what an enormous extent the old Protestant character of the National Church has been subverted; it knows perfectly well that at least half the clergy resent the name of Protestant, and teach most of the doctrines of the

Church of Rome; and we must remember that these clergy have supreme control of most of the rural education of this country. The consequence is that religious education has undergone an entire change in the last 30 or 40 years; formerly, it was mainly Bible instruction, to which Protestant Nonconformists took no exception; now it is in many cases almost Roman Catholic, and excites the vehement dislike of the Protestant population, both Church and Nonconformist. The House need not be surprised at this: it can well understand that clergy who belong to the English Church Union, whose defiant manifesto has just been published, and to the Society of the Holy Cross, the Confraternity of the Blessed Sacrament, the Guild of All Souls, and other secret or semi-secret societies pledged to introduce Catholic doctrine and ritual into the National Church, are certain to use their enormous power over the children in Church schools. I have read several of the Catechisms taught by these clergy, and I told the House not long since that they were translations or adaptations from Roman Catholic books; several of them were "Mass books for children." I am not able to prove that they are largely taught in the National schools, but I believe the substance of them is taught. The teachers are trained in colleges under the control of the clergy. I have no doubt that the same transformation is passing over the training colleges for teachers that has passed over the training colleges for clergy; these latter are now chiefly in the hands of extreme Ritualists, who are rapidly changing these training colleges from Protestant to Catholic.

Sir F. POWELL: No, no!

*Mr. S. SMITH: Does the honourable Gentleman know the text books which are used in these colleges?

Sir F. POWELL: I know nothing of the sort is used in the colleges for which I am responsible, and I utterly repudiate the honourable Member's insinuation.

*Mr. S. SMITH: I do not happen to know so much about the training colleges as I do about the theological colleges.

*.IR. SPEAKER: I must remind the honourable Member that he is going outside the scope of the Motion before the House. The question is only that of Primary Education.

*MR. S. SMITH: I will bow to your ruling, Mr. Speaker. My object is to show that our great difficulty is that the teachers and clergy alike in those schools are giving a kind of education which is not only objectionable to the Nonconformists, but also to a large proportion of the laity of the Church of England. We know how the younger clergy are trained in Romanising doctrine. Is it not morally certain that many of the teachers are educated in the same way? The National Church is fast becoming a huge machine for killing out the principles of the Reformation; is it likely that so vital a part of the work is left undone? I believe that of all the dangers that threaten the Reformed faith of England to-day, none are so great as the power which the Romanising clergy have over the education of the young. We have left nearly three millions of the children of the nation at their mercy; and I warn the House that if this system is not overthrown we shall have to fight a life and death battle for our Protestant faith in the next generation. I approach this question as one who has always been in favour of Bible instruction in the schools of the country. I think that such instruction, given in a way suited to children, would have received the assent of all classes and creeds of the country, except the Roman Catholics; it was the only religious instruction that would permanently stand. Our Education Compromise of 1870 was accepted on that understanding; it would never have been accepted had it been foreseen that Bible teaching would be substituted by Children's Eucharists, and imitations of the Roman Mass. I allege it was a gross departure from the honourable understanding on which the great Education Act was passed. Certainly Mr. Forster in 1870 never contemplated such things as are witnessed at Brighton, when at St. Bartholomew's Church the children of the Voluntary school are marched once a week at 9 a.m. to attend a Children's Eucharist which is indistinguishable from the Roman Mass. Let me quote from the account in the "Daily News" a week or two ago—

"With humble mind and contrite heart
    We come before Thy face,
Let Mary and the Saints on high
    Implore for us Thy grace.

"Upon the intoning of the Creed the children all knelt until they came to the words, 'and was incarnate by the Holy Ghost of the Virgin Mary and was made man.' At that profound passage, so eminently suitable for a children's service, in accordance with their printed instructions, they all stood up, kneeling again when the words had been uttered, and all making the sign of the Cross when the Creed concluded. "'Then follows the Act of Consecration,' said the instructions, and the sheet continued: 'When the bell rings as the Priest says, "This is My body," children bow their heads and say by themselves, "Hail! most sacred flesh of Jesus." When the bell rings again and he says, "This is My blood," children bow their heads and say "Hail! most sacred blood of Jesus." During the Consecration the children must be very quiet and reverent, and pay great attention, and, as Jesus is now present on the Altar, children must not sit after the Consecration, but either stand or kneel.' The small folk then sang the Agnus Dei, and among verses that followed, one ran:—

"I worship Thee, Lord Jesus,
    Who in .Thy love divine
Art hiding here Thy Godhead
    In forms of bread and wine.

"Confessional boxes, it need hardly be said, are among the features of this large church, and the hours for hearing confessions are posted on them. On one of the walls of the church was an exhortation to the members of the congregation of their charity to pray for the souls of certain dead, whose names were set forth in a list, and up in one corner was a large board well-stocked with leaflets and pamphlets on points of religious controversy."

SIR F. POWELL: Will the honourable Member state where that occurred?

*MR. S. SMITH: At St. Bartholomew's Church Voluntary school, Brighton, which was reported in the "Daily News." I should like to have the opinion of the right honourable Gentleman the Vice-President of the Council as to how far he considers that this is a legitimate use of the powers which the clergy have in the Voluntary schools. We need not go far from this House to witness a Children's Mass. In the Debates last year in this House the right honourable Gentleman the Member for West Monmouth brought to the notice of the

House a similar thing that happened close at hand at Clapham. He brought before the House the celebration of the Mass at Christ Church, Clapham, on the festival of Corpus Christi. I quote from the "Church Review" how this affected, the children of the school—

"The Catholic faith is taught in its fulness at this church. Catholics will be pleased to hear that the children of the schools are instructed daily in the faith of the Catholic Church, and they also attend Mass every Thursday at nine.

"The new schools of this parish will be begun as soon as the funds will allow. There are Catholics who sympathise with the Vicar in his very uphill work of teaching the Catholic faith in this very difficult parish."

*MR. SPEAKER: I must say that the honourable Member is departing from the Motion before the House, which relates to grievances in connection with education in Primary schools. The honourable Member is now discussing certain religious services attended by the children, of which he may or may not approve, but which do not seem to me to be a part of Primary School Education.

*MR. S. SMITH: I will bow to your ruling, Mr. Speaker. I was under the impression that the greatest grievance of Primary Education was just the fact that children of Nonconformists, and many Church people, to a very large extent were receiving a kind of religious education to which they offered a vehement opposition.

*MR. SPEAKER: The honourable Member misunderstands me. He is at liberty to refer to anything that takes place in the schools as part of Primary Education; but when he addresses himself to church services which are attended by the children, and to the doctrine or ritual in such churches, he is going outside the scope of the question.

*MR. S. SMITH: Then I will not further trespass upon that branch of the subject. I will venture, however, to read to the House a letter which I received last week from a teacher, to show how these questions affect the teachers in Voluntary schools. The teachers are wholly at the disposal of the parish

clergyman. Here is a specimen of the tyranny to which they are subjected—

"A relation of mine, who is a schoolmaster, had lately under him a young man as assistant master. He obtained an appointment as master. He was giving instruction to the pupils concerning the Sacraments, telling them there were two—Baptism and the Supper of the Lord. The vicar being present, said, 'There are seven.' The master said he was taught there were but two, 'so say the Articles.' 'Oh, yes, there are seven.' Subsequently he told him he must either join the Confraternity of the Blessed Sacrament or send in his resignation."

Attention having been called to the fact that there were not 40 Members present, the House was counted, when 40 Members being present—

*MR. S. SMITH (continuing): It is within the power of the vicar of a parish to dismiss a teacher if he refuses to join the confraternity of the Blessed Sacrament? I believe that the practice of marching the children of Voluntary schools in procession to attend Mass or Children's Eucharists in the Church is steadily growing, and I understand from the answer given by the right honourable Gentleman the Member for Cambridge University (Sir John Gorst) that it is no part of the duty of the Education Department to interfere. The Church of England schools may insist on the Confessional and put up images of the Virgin Mary and saints, and require veneration to be paid to them, and yet no interference can take place, so we are led to understand.

SIR. J. GORST: No.

*MR. S. SMITH: Then I understand the right honourable Gentleman to say that there is nothing illegal in it?

SIR J. GORST: I did not say that there was nothing illegal in it. I said that the Committee of Council on Education had no power to interfere.

*MR. S. SMITH: Then I do not think that the country understands the point of this question. I know of another case where the teacher is a Protestant, and he is in fear and trembling lest he be dismissed because he will not teach Catholic doctrine, and he knows that when he does his place will be taken by one who will do the bidding of the Ritualists. I said that the teaching of the Church of England is used to stamp out all sympathy with the Reformation. One of the most deadly ways of doing this is by teaching unfair, one-sided histories of the Church of England. The object of these jaundiced histories is to suggest the view that the Reformation made no real change in the Church. Two of these histories are largely used in schools. Nye's History has circulated to the extent of 550,000, and Wakeman's has also a very large circulation. That very accurate historian, J. Horace Round, states—

"The matter becomes really serious when our schools are flooded, through the agency of the clergy, under the guise of faithful history, with treatises in which notorious facts are either ignored or explained away."

Let me give specimens of the sort of teaching inculcated on the young. This is what Nye says about the Reformation—

"Nothing is more certain than the fact that the Church of England before the Reformation and the Church of England after the Reformation was the same identical Church."

Again, I quote from Wakeman—

"The vast majority of those who suffered (under Mary) were not people even of religious influence. They were illiterate fanatics, convinced that the Pope was Anti-Christ, and Transubstantiation idolatry."

"Tract XC.—Newman argued (in Tract XC.) that there was no Catholic doctrine, and hardly any theological Roman doctrine, condemned by the Articles; but only popular exaggerations and misrepresentations of Roman doctrine current at the time when the Articles were drawn up. Most men would now admit that, for the purpose which he had in hand, Newman's argument was in the main sound."

"From the point of view of history the Church revival of the present century is seen to be nothing more than the complete reaction against the Protestant movement of the sixteenth century."

I venture to say that history taught in this way is little better than poison. Surely it is an example of the maxim approved by Newman—

"He both thinks and speaks the truth, except when careful treatment is necessary, and then, as a physician for the good of his patients, he will lie, or rather utter a lie as the sophists say. . . . Nothing, however, but his neighbour's good will lead him to do this. He gives himself up for the Church."

Mr. S. Smith.

It is commonly thought that the "conscience clause" is a sufficient protection to the children of Protestant Nonconformists : let the proceedings in the town of Flint, last week, be an answer to this. Many Nonconformist children are obliged to attend the Church school, as their only choice is between it and the Roman Catholic school. Some of these children asked exemption from learning the Church Catechism. The rector of the parish read out the names from the pulpit on Sunday evening in a way that exposed them to opprobrium, and wrote letters of an offensive kind to some of the parents; he also, I am informed, called upon the stationmaster to complain of one of the men who was employed by the London and North Western Railway Company. This induced the Nonconformists to call a meeting for Monday of last week. It was virtually broken up by rowdies, who were instigated by the rector to attend and defend the Church. Allow me to quote from a letter I have received from one who was present—

"The Nonconformist ministers in leaving the hall were followed by a yelling mob, and were hooted and pelted with eggs; a desperate attempt was made to strike a blow at Mr. Hirst Hollowell in the street; the chairman (the Rev. H. Meirion Davies) was struck on the back of his head with a stone, fortunately not seriously hurt. My own house was surrounded by this ruffianly gang, and stones were thrown at my door, very nearly striking my wife, who happened to open the door to see what was going on at the time, and, as I was not in, she was, of course, very much terrified, as they could be heard swearing and cursing and threatening what they would do to me if they could only get hold of me. Of course, I have taken a prominent part in this movement, having been the first to send in a claim under the conscience clause—hence this attack. Others who have taken a prominent part were subjected to somewhat similar treatment; but the crowning part of the whole affair was that, having done all this, the crowd next assembled before the house of one of the curates (the Rev. T. Jones Roberts), and he actually came out and thanked the crowd for their manly and noble defence of the Church."

This is an extreme instance of a kind of intimidation that goes on in many villages where the Nonconformists are obliged to send their children to the Church school. In some cases the parents would lose employment if they withdrew their children under the conscience clause, and the children are often stigmatised, in a way that makes their lives miserable, if they venture to absent themselves. There is no real remedy for this cruel tyranny except the placing of Board schools within reach of the whole population. The great hindrance is the dread of the school rate; and I see no remedy for this except making the whole cost of education a national charge. Surely this rich country can afford to give its children as good an education as Germany or Switzerland; but it is utterly behind them in every way. It has the most clerical system of education of any modern civilised State, the most backward as regards the age at which children leave school, and it is the country which allows the greatest amount of child labour. I appeal to the Protestant Members of the Unionist Party to support this Motion. They are justly alarmed at the fearful spread of Romanism in the National Church. They know well the great propagandism of Catholic doctrine carried on among the young. It is in youth that the confessional and the supernatural power of the priesthood are riveted on the mind. I appeal to my Protestant friends to withdraw their support from clericalism in education. It is no longer the teaching of the Scriptures, which no one objects to, but the instilling of priestcraft in the case of thousands of clergy and thousands of schools. All modern States have to fight this battle for liberty; we are plunged into it anew in England through the arrogance of sacerdotalism; we have put our hand to the plough, and cannot draw back till the power of the priests is swept out of the public Elementary schools of this country. Now, what is the remedy we claim for this state of things? The honourable Member for Hereford made a speech to which I have listened with much interest, and I think the spirit of that speech was sound, charitable, and just, and I believe that some of the views that he put forward might form the basis of an agreement between the two sides of the House. Under the present system there is no real protection given to the conscience of the parents of the children. No doubt in many cases, by private arrangement, the Voluntary schools could be taken over and utilised for public purposes on some conditions that would be fair to the existing schools. I do not wish to say that a

great deal of good has not been done by the Voluntary schools in this country, and I believe that, if they had adhered to the arrangement made in 1870, we should never have had the differences which we have to-day. Had the religion taught in those schools been simple spiritual religion the country, as a whole, would have accepted it. There is a suitable way of teaching Scripture to children and an unsuitable one, and I am certain no man of sense would teach children of from 10 to 12 years of age extreme dogmatic religious creeds. Common religious teaching is no longer possible, owing to the fact that a large section of the National Church has entirely broken away from it, and now refuses to consider as religious teaching for children what 50 years ago it would gladly have accepted. I believe these grievances will grow greater, and will become more vexatious until a settlement is arrived at. Now, what is the main reason why we have not had universal School Boards before this? Everybody knows the reason. There is no doubt that the dread of the education rate is the great reason why School Boards are not spread universally over the country. It is not because the parents preferred Voluntary schools. I would like to see the matter tested by having put within the reach of every parent the choice of having a good Board school or a Voluntary school, and I think that the great majority of the British public would prefer to send their children to a Board school. Under the present Government every effort has been made to discourage the Board school system and to uphold that of the Voluntary schools. I maintain that the children of this country have the same right to be taught in the same way as the children of Germany, and the children of France, and the children of America are taught—at the public expense. The whole cost of education should be thrown upon public sources and placed under public control. Under those circumstances the objection to Board schools would be gone, and the schools themselves would be spread universally over the country. I do not mean that every little parish or hamlet should have a Board school, but I do think that every area containing 10,000 or 20,000 people ought to have the power, if they so desire, of

having a School Board. There
are men of intelligence, when drawn
from a large area—capable men—who
would be able to deal with this matter.
And until that is done this grievance
will continue. But I say it is a scandal,
a very great scandal, that a rich country
like this—the richest country in the
whole world—should not be able
to do for its little children what Germany
and France and other much poorer
countries can do. We have at the present moment the most backward system
of education in this country that any
advanced nation possesses. Everybody
knows that America has a universal system of public schools, and one cardinal
point of the American system is that
almost every State of the Union passed
a law that no grants of public money
should be given to any school or semi-
nary under ecclesiastical control. The
same constitutional principle was passed
by Congress. That is a fundamental
principle of the American Constitution.
Our own Colonies have also adopted
this principle of education; yet the
old mother country, the source from
which all these vigorous and continually-
growing nationalities have sprung, is
behind in this important matter. We
are fighting against the inevitable. It
must come, and we shall have universal
Board schools spread over the country.
I appeal to the honourable Members on
that side of the House, many of whom
are extremely anxious that the education
of the children of this country shall be
placed upon a more perfect basis, to
support me. There is real alarm with regard to the great change which is passing
over this country in respect of religious
education; and I know that many honourable Gentlemen upon that side of the
House feel the same as I do myself on
this subject, and I appeal to them
whether they are going to give greater
aid to the clerical party of this country,
knowing, as they do, what class of education they will give, and what these
men are sure to do. I say that the
Unionist Party of this country must
reconsider the whole of the policy
with regard to education, because
it is perfectly certain that the
time is coming when a division
will take place in the ranks of honourable Gentlemen on that side of the
House upon this question which
will be just as marked as that which

Mr. S. Smith.

has taken place now with regard to the
condition of the Established Church
of this country. I believe that if we
could poll the Conservative Party with
any accuracy that at least two-thirds of
the honourable Gentlemen who sit upon
that side of the House would be found
to be utterly opposed to the English
Church Union, and I say, for the same
reason, they should give their support
substantially and really to the suggestion
which we have made on this side of the
House.

*VISCOUNT CRANBORNE: (Rochester):
I confess that I approach this subject
with a certain amount of hesitation, because I cannot but think that the House
at the present time must be somewhat
weary of hearing the same old arguments
repeated which have formed so large a
part of our Debates during the last few
years. The honourable Gentleman who
has just sat down gave, in the course of
the remarks which he addressed to the
House, a prominent example of the use-
lessness of addressing that class of argument to ears that will not hear. He
said that he believed that in the country
districts of England thousands of parents,
if they had the opportunity of choosing
between Voluntary schools and Board
schools, would choose the Board schools.
Now, I should think that at least 20
times in the course of the Debates in
this House arguments of that kind have
been met with the obvious retort that, if
that is so, why is it that in towns where
the parents have this choice so large a
number prefer to send their children to
the Church schools? I must apologise
to the House for repeating that argument, though it appears to have no effect
whatever upon the honourable Gentleman. The honourable Gentleman, in
dealing with the subject, with which I
might say that he dealt very earnestly,
and in the manner with which the
House is so familiar, said that the
Church of England had entirely changed
its constitution in recent years, and that
the result of the change had been that,
in a very large number of schools, so I
understood him, teaching not to be
distinguished from Roman Catholic
teaching was being given to the children.
The first observation which occurs to me
on that point is this: if that is so, how
is it that we do not see a very wide use
made of the conscience clause upon this

question? Taking the country as a whole, how is it, if it is a fact that the whole attitude of the Church of England towards the religious teaching of the young is repugnant to them, that ardent Protestants like the honourable Gentlemen do not use their influence to withdraw the children from such teaching; and, if they do use their influence, how is it that the conscience clause is not made a wider use of? As a matter of fact, it is notorious that the conscience clause is not used at all. Of course, the House is aware that we have had no authentic information upon this question later than that which was given before the Royal Commission ten years ago. On that occasion, however, the whole subject was fully gone into, and, among other things, a very great deal of evidence was given with regard to the conscience clause. It was stated by witnesses that the conscience clause was very little used at all, and what is the more remarkable is that that statement came, not from the Church of England witnesses, but from the Nonconformist witnesses. An eminent Nonconformist witness stated it, and also stated what was much more remarkable—he was an eminent Nonconformist minister—he said there were a large number of parents who knew nothing about the conscience clause whatever. Speaking for himself, he said he was unwilling that people should take advantage of the clause, and that in his opinion the duty of Nonconformist ministers was not to suggest that the children should be withdrawn from religious instruction. I sincerely hope that the honourable Gentleman will carefully consider what that means. Here is a statutory right which is given by the Government to the Nonconformists to give them an opportunity to withdraw their children, and one would imagine that if these schools were permeated with these pernicious doctrines of which the honourable Gentleman has spoken so feelingly, that the Nonconformists would have withdrawn their children from this religious instruction. Yet they do not do so, and, not only do they not do so, but their very ministers do not even suggest that they ought to. This is the evidence given before the Royal Commission.

*Mr. S. SMITH: Thirteen years ago.

*Viscount CRANBORNE: If the honourable Gentleman has any more recent evidence than that, I shall be very glad to quote it. But, with the exception of these very few cases, it will be found that the Nonconformist ministers themselves did not suggest to their own people that they should avail themselves of the conscience clause.

Mr. LLOYD-GEORGE: The noble Lord does not give the reason, which is also stated in that very evidence, why they did not.

*Viscount CRANBORNE: I know it is alleged that the children are in some way damaged. Yes; but we are talking about religion, the most important thing which a human being can think of, and about ministers' religion. Does the honourable Gentleman come forward and suggest to this House that Nonconformist ministers think so little of their religion that they place some twopenny-halfpenny school treat or such like temporal advantage above it?

Mr. LLOYD-GEORGE: No, that is not the reason.

*Viscount CRANBORNE: I know perfectly well that that is not the view which the Nonconformist ministers take on this subject. If they thought the children were being damaged morally and intellectually by what is going on they would, at all costs, use their influence upon the parents to use the power which the law has placed in their hands. The honourable Member for Flintshire spoke of certain catechisms which he alleged were used in the Church of England schools. I suspect that when it comes to be analysed it will be found that, like most of the honourable Gentleman's evidence, that statement is a trifle exaggerated. It appears that he has not got evidence of this catechism being used in the day school; that this catechism that he knows of is used in the Sunday schools, which, of course, the State do not control, and to which it does not contribute one-halfpenny. He did not give an example as to the use of this catechism in Sunday schools,-but he did, as I think injudiciously, mention Gace's catechism, and I think that I ought to remind the House as to what is the history of that catechism. It was brought forward with a great flourish of trumpets at one time that Gace had authorised a catechism of the Church of England for use in a number of Voluntary schools, and that statement was used with great effect in a great variety of speeches, and upon a great variety of platforms and opportunities. But the facts came out, unfortunately, and it was stated by the publishers that at that time—before 1885—that they doubted whether as many as 10,000 copies had been sold; but that since 1885—that is to say, during the last ten years—4,000 copies only had been issued, the great bulk of them being issued in consequence of the extensive advertisement given to the pamphlet in the anti-Church papers. That in 1889—this is the evidence of the publishers, and not of sacerdotalists —that, so far as they could judge by the orders, the pamphlets were not purchased by the clergy, but for use as a Disestablishment pamphlet. The Archbishop of Canterbury—not the present Archbishop, but Archbishop Benson—entirely repudiated the catechism, and, in the course of a speech, told the following story—

"A new vicar, a friend of mine, had his breath taken away on his first appearance in the parish in which he worked by the fact that he was supposed to teach the doctrine found in this formidable book, which he had never seen nor heard of. He immediately rushed to his bookseller and procured a copy. He asked the bookseller: 'Have you sold many copies?' 'Yes.'—'In my parish?' 'Yes.'—'To the clergymen and schoolmasters?' 'No; we have sold a good many to the worshippers of the chapel.'"

That is one of the Liberationist examples of the extreme sacerdotalism which was trotted out at that time, and which was made to do duty against the Church of England. But I think I have shown that we must accept this kind of accusation with a certain amount of reserve. I should like to state, in a few words, what I believe, from information which I have been at the trouble to ascertain, is the practice of the Church. I believe that very great care is taken, in the vast majority of schools, as to what they shall put into the children's hands. Such books as Gace's Catechism have no sale at all, except amongst those who buy them for political purposes. I have made inquiries at the depository of the National Society, and as the House knows, that society is the great storehouse of ecclesiastical literature for educational purposes to which the great

Viscount Cranborne.

bodies of the National Schools come for what they require, and they say that the sale of anything except the simple text of the Catechism is very small, and constantly decreasing. Only the text of the Catechism is given to the children, except in very exceptional cases. Now I think that is probably a sober and accurate account of what takes place actually in the schools of the Church of England, and the honourable Gentleman can make his mind to a certain extent easy as to the terrible inroad that sacerdotalism is making on the minds of the future citizens of this country. Now, I should like to say in reference to the speech of the honourable Gentleman who moved the Motion just a few words. The honourable Gentleman spoke in very strong terms of the condition of the Voluntary schools at the present moment. He told us that their teachings were extremely bad, and that the children were being physically and mentally demoralised by what went on there, and that the state of things was lamentable considering its effect upon the young generation which would have to regulate the destiny of this country in the future. But though he drew a very lurid picture, the honourable Gentleman himself admitted that he was not prepared to take the only obvious step which would enable these Voluntary schools to do their work better, namely, to grant them a little more money. That is the test of the sincerity—I do not wish to use that term in any opprobrious form—of the honourable Gentleman towards these Voluntary schools. Desperate though their condition is, he would not put forward a finger or spend a shilling to assist them. As a matter of fact, like the other honourable Gentleman, he exaggerated, but how he came to make such a mistake I do not know. I remember, not so very long ago, when the right honourable Gentleman, who, I am sorry to say, is no longer in the House, Mr. Acland, presided at the Education Department, he tried by every effort in his power to bring up the Voluntary schools to what he considered to be a state of efficiency, both physically and intellectually in the standard of education. He practically brought the whole weight of his influence to bear in every part of England, and he did raise the standard both physically and intellectually of those schools. That being so, it is not fair of the honourable Gentleman to say that they fall far below the position they ought to occupy unless he says at the same time that the efforts of that Government were unavailing. As a matter of fact, the Voluntary schools are not in that desperate condition which he has alleged as to physical condition or the standard of education. It is undoubtedly true that in certain cases the condition of the children is not absolutely satisfactory from a hygienic point of view. That is a point which this House will have to very carefully consider. I am bound to say that much evidence seems to me to be brought to show that in many cases the children have been very much overworked. I do not mean to say that they are learning too much, but that too much pressure is put upon the children during the time they remain at school, and that leads me to think whether the time that these children spend at school ought not to be prolonged. I do not think that the condition of the children to which attention has been drawn is due to the insanitary condition of the buildings in which they work, but that it is due, if it exists at all, to the over-pressure which is brought to bear on their young and growing brains. And the only way in which the House can meet this difficulty, if it is found necessary to meet it, is by prolonging the time which the children spend at school. But that is a matter upon which, of course, one must reserve one's own opinion until it is proposed. But that is the direction in which the House, I am sure, must look for remedy on the whole question. We are not opposed to the improvement of education, we are perfectly willing to do our best to bring education up to the standard required. We are not bigoted upon educational or religious matters, and we are most anxious that any other denomination should share in privileges which we claim for ourselves in this matter. My honourable Friend the Member for East Hertford explained, in a very good speech which he made to the House, how he would be inclined to see that equality should be introduced into the educational system. I quite agree with every word he said, and, as a matter of fact, it has been the burden of our contention in times past. What we desire to do is to give the other religious bodies all the authority that we have

ourselves, and if they have any desire to have a clause like the 27th Clause of the Government Bill of 1896, by an means let them have it. If they desire to build Nonconformist schools to compete with the Church schools, let them build them by all means. There is nothing to prevent them; they are entitled to build a school in a Voluntary school district if they desire to do so; and if they get 30 scholars for 12 months—efficient scholars, they are entitled to a grant. I should like to see the Nonconformists build schools wherever they might desire. In every respect, we are anxious to consult the feelings, the susceptibilities, and the religious beliefs of the Nonconformist bodies. With regard to the actual Amendment before the House, I should like to make just one observation. I am afraid my honourable Friend the Member for Lowestoft was, to some extent, in difficulty, but I practically agree with him. I have always desired that a larger measure of public money should be given to the Voluntary schools, and that we have urged very often at great length; we have urged that the Voluntary schools and the board schools should be put on a more equal footing on the matter of support. But the honourable Gentleman will observe that he brings this matter before the House as one which demands the immediate attention of Parliament. But I believe that after all the Government have done on the question of elementary education in a short time, I do not think they are likely to introduce another education Bill immediately, and I think that the usual Parliamentary course may be adopted in this matter. The honourable Member for Carnarvon Boroughs drew his Motion in a very careful manner, with the intention, I suppose, of inducing those from this side of the House to vote with him, but the strategy is not likely to deceive honourable Members of this House to any large extent. He delivered a violent, strong, and a wholly indefensible attack upon the Voluntary schools, and especially upon those of the Church of England; but I have no doubt that that attack will be met by a most emphatic negative in the Lobby.

*Mr. YOXALL (Nottingham, W.): The speech of the honourable Member who has just resumed his seat is one of a.

series of speeches which have been made to-night, prompted by sincere good feeling, and filled with a spirit of compromise and an honourable desire to come to some satisfactory arrangement. If I say anything to-night it is to show the House how very little are the real differences existing between the two parties to this question. The honourable Member declared that religion was the most important thing in a man's life. That I will not take exception to. But in relation to day schools, I will venture to suggest perhaps a slight qualification. There are churches, chapels, mission halls, and Sunday schools expressly founded and carried on for the sake of developing in the human mind an earnest attention to that which the honourable Gentleman has declared to be the most important thing which man can think of in his life. But remembering how brief are the school years of a child's life, beginning very often at five years of age, but not seldom at seven, eight, nine, 10 and 11 years of age, and on the average ceasing at 12; during that brief period, I say, we must not pay too much attention to dogmatic religion, but we must rely on the teachings of the special agencies founded for that particular purpose. And I submit that the parents of the children agree with me on that point rather than with honourable Members opposite. I also agree with all that has been said in regard to the parents making use of the conscience clause. Why, that is my argument. It has been said again and again in this House by the honourable Member for West Ham, by myself, by members of school boards, by all who know the facts of the case, that there is no real religious difficulty in the schools themselves. It is true, neither among teachers, among parents, nor among children in the public elementary schools, is there any real religious or theological difficulty. I sympathise with the difficulty which the honourable Member for Flint has referred to. I recognise that a difficulty does exist, certainly in some Voluntary schools under the control of the clergy of the High Church section of the Church of England. It does exist there, but they are fortunately, even, yet, in a very small section of the Voluntary schools of this country. I know that the same difficulty was likely to have taken place in the London

School Board, and it is significant to those of us who sympathise with the protest the Protestants are making just now, that the man who lit the flame of theological hatred in the London School Board is the author of a brochure entitled, "The Hours of the Blessed Virgin Mary." We have been twitted with the fact that we refused the 27th clause of the Bill of 1896, but I beg to remind the House that that Bill contained other clauses, limiting the State and rate grants to schools, and that, if that Bill had become law, the grants under the Voluntary Schools Act could not have been given. Why should there not be some compromise on this question? There are in many parts of the country village schools that are Voluntary schools in name, but are publicly managed schools. In fact, there are Church of England schools of which the majority of the committee of management are Nonconformist, and there are Church of England schools which have on their committees of management representatives of Nonconformists and of the local authority, and it is in consequence of the condition of their permitting representatives on the management of these of Noncomformists and of the local authority that these schools receive the Voluntary rate. There are also schools which are Board schools in name, but which are Voluntary schools in fact, for, by the terms of the transfer of these schools to the School Board, the right is reserved, by special clause, of a control by the clergy of the Church of England over the religious teaching. Schools of that kind work remarkably well, and I would like to point out to the House that by having schools of that kind throughout the country you can solve the difficulty. The honourable Member for Edinburgh tells us that in Board schools dogmatic instruction is given, and it is true that in the vast majority of them the dogmas of a revelation from God to man, and the Godhead of Christ, and all that depends on that, and the commonly-accepted Christian way of salvation—that all these doctrines are taught in the Board schools by teachers who themselves have been trained in the Church of England training colleges. As I said before, there is no real difficulty in the schools, and no barrier in the way of a compromise. It is too much to hope, I suppose, that honourable Members opposite will at once accept the idea that Board schools are so dogmatic, so truly Christian in their teaching, that they can possibly be proper schools to replace the Voluntary schools in the country. Honourable Members behind me will certainly refuse to accept that idea; but, with regard to the management of Wesleyan schools and Church of England schools, I do assure this House, speaking with a full knowledge of this question, that the difficulties of a theological kind in the way are comparatively few. The Church of England Catechism and the Wesleyan Catechism are not taught in our Board schools, and it is true that the Church of England Catechism is taught in the Voluntary schools, but how is it taught? It is often taught without any commentary or gloss. I do not deal with the doctrine of godfathers and godmothers. These are slight and unimportant subjects, after all. If you take a child seven years of age and make him learn, parrot-like, by rote, inexplicable theological terms, you have given him a piece of useless intellectual lumber. But if you want to give a real foundation of goodness, and a guidance for after life, you can give it to him better by simple Bible lessons than by any definitions of theological terms expressed in technical language. Many of the School Board schools have been inspected by Diocesan inspectors. The Diocesan inspector of the See of York has gone into Sheffield Board schools and put to the children there the same kind of questions as he had put in Church schools, but not in the mere verbiage of the Catechism. He has made slight omissions, but practically the examination of the Board schools by Diocesan inspectors has been exactly the same as in the Voluntary schools, and time after time these Diocesan inspectors, who did this service without pay or reward, and who owe no allegiance or subservience to the School Boards, have said that the religious instruction given in the School Board schools is thoroughly sound and Christian. Again, I say, the partition between the two kinds of schools is very thin indeed, and I would urge that it is the duty of this House to agree to some comprehensive and impartial inquiry into the whole question of the alleged religious difficulty. We are nationally faced with all sorts of difficulties coming from the present state of education. The great difficulty is not ecclesiastical. The great difficulty the way is how to make the schools more efficient. We are assured that the most important thing in the school curriculum is the half-hour devoted to teaching the dogmas of the Church of England. But above a million and a-half of children are never at school at all. After making every allowance for justifiable causes of absence, there are about 40,000,000 hours of instruction lost to the children of the country every week. That is a great waste, and that is the great difficulty. It is a question on which the House ought to rest its attention, and this discussion is only important in so far as it deals with a barrier to the improvement of our educational system. I am anxious, no one more so, to remove this barrier. Again, I say that those who know most about this question from experience are satisfied that, with certain small exceptions, the barrier between the Voluntary schools and the Board schools is thin; it is almost diaphanous, and it could be made to almost vanish completely. A select committee of five men sitting round a table would be able speedily to come to an arrangement which would be satisfactory to most of the Members of this House. The difficulty is not between the Members of the House. The Debates of the last three years have shown that the tendency on all sides is to come to a practical compromise according to the genius of the English race. The difficulty is not in this House; it is outside. Who are the people who stand up most vehemently in support of the Voluntary system? I want to abuse no class of men. There are clergy and also laity in the Church of England who are honest and sincere in their belief of the necessity for having their own schools and their own system. But I want to point out that there is another side to the picture. The Voluntary school fund provides not only for ordinary education but for Sunday schools, for mothers' meetings, for boys' brigades, for clothing clubs, for shoe clubs, for libraries, for penny banks, for nearly all the machinery of village life, a house without rent, and fuel, lighting, and cleaning, all paid for by income received from the

State. These are the obstacles which stand in the way and which make it "pay" a church or chapel to run a Voluntary school. The time is rapidly approaching when men will refuse to allow considerations of that kind to stand in the way of improved education so much needed and on which so much depends. If you would give the children of this country as long a school life as the school life in Germany, from five to fourteen years of age, if you would give regular attendance of the children at school during these years, our educational system, with all its defects and shortcomings, need not fear competition with the schools of Germany, Switzerland, Holland, or Denmark. I come back to the important things that ought to be borne in mind. These are better attendance, a longer school life, and more efficient teaching; and this religious question is only important in so far as it stands between them and this most desirable consummation.

*Mr. CRIPPS (Gloucester, Stroud): I think the House must have noticed the striking contrast between the speech of the honourable Member who has just sat down and the far different tone and language used by the Mover of the Resolution. The honourable Member for Nottingham, W., did not take the very narrow and extreme views both of the Voluntary schools and the School Board schools which were taken by the honourable Member for Carnarvon. The latter honourable Member said that the Voluntary schools were rotten and a discredit to civilisation; and he ended up by saying that the Voluntary school system was a State-aided form of sheep-stealing. On the other hand, the honourable Member who has just spoken recognised in the most cordial spirit the advances which have been made in all the schools. When the Voluntary schools are discussed in this House it seems very often to be thought that the management of such schools is synonymous with the management by the village clergyman. Now, that is a great mistake. Voluntary schools are not managed by the village clergyman, except under conditions which I shall relate. Every Voluntary school in this country has a board of managers, selected, as a rule, from those who subscribe to the funds of the school. In

fact, the board of managers represents the subscribing body to the Voluntary schools in the same way as the elected body represents the rate-paying subscriptions which are made to the School Boards. In either case you have a representative body, representing either in the one case or the other, the body from whom the funds come. That is an important fact to remember in dealing with the Voluntary schools. It may be true that in some cases the school managers are not called on to interfere with the action of the village clergyman, but the reason of that is that in the vast majority of cases the action of the vicar or rector in particular parishes is in accord with the wishes of the parishioners at large. If that action is not in accordance with the wishes of the parishioners, the power of the board of managers becomes real, and is constantly exercised. I say this from my experience, as the manager of one of these schools myself. I cordially assent to the statement made by the honourable Gentleman who has just sat down that in a very large number of cases the managers of schools which belong to the Church of England are not themselves members of the Church of England. I know of the case of a parish where some of the managers of a Church of England School are not members of the Church of England, although 98 per cent. of the parishioners belong to the Church of England. The real truth is, as was said by the honourable Member for Nottingham West, that except for political purposes and discussion in this House, we do not find this religious difficulty in our country educational system. That is the real truth, and the sequence of the honourable Gentleman is not logical. If, as he said, the difficulty is not a real, but a somewhat invented difficulty, why should he suggest a complicated and comprehensive inquiry on this question? Why, we might create by this inquiry the very difficulty which, according to the honourable Member's own admission, does not exist at the present moment. The noble Lord the Member for Rochester has referred to the attitude taken by certain Liberationist Members of this House; and, if you enter upon an inquiry on a subject which wants no inquiry, you might create the very difficulty which on both sides of the House we seek to avoid. In regard to the religious difficulty, as it has been presented to the House to-night, I believe that, so far as educational efficiency is concerned, it has not come to the front at all. We have had the religious question presented to us in two very different aspects. I believe that religion is the most vital element in the educational system, not only of the Anglican schools, but of the Wesleyan and Catholic schools. There ought to be, I firmly believe, definite religious instruction given to all children whose parents ask for it. What I mean by definite religious instruction is, to my mind, only that form of instruction which a child's mind is ready to grasp. The honourable Member who represents East Edinburgh brought forward the frankly Secularist view, and he argued, with great logical power, that if we were really sincere in our desire to get rid of the religious difficulty we ought to keep religion out of both the School Board system and the Voluntary school system. The only question to my mind is this: Is it true that the honourable Member for East Edinburgh is supported by any very large number of the people of the country at large? If it is true, no greater argument could be urged for the absolute necessity of preserving every safeguard which we have at the present moment. I very much doubt whether that statement of the honourable Member for East Edinburgh is accurate. In 1870 when the question of education was brought to the front there was a very important division in this House on the religious question, and a large minority supported the view that education ought to be given on an entirely secular basis. I believe if such a Motion were to be made at the present time it would hardly have any support at all. The view of a purely secularist education has gone infinitely back since the discussions of the Bill of 1870, and I am convinced that the honourable Member who spoke on this subject is entirely inaccurate, entirely mis-informed, if he thinks that the parents of the country want their children brought up under merely secular conditions. Let me deal with the other side of the question, with the point brought forward by the honourable Member who introduced the Resolution. He protested against a formal dogmatic teaching, and so do I.

I ask him, if he had the choice, whether he would like dogmatic teaching in accordance with the religion to which he is attached, or teaching of an indefinite, general kind. I believe if you put that same question to any Member who complains of the religious difficulty, the answer would be that his desire would be for definite teaching in accordance with the religion to which he is attached rather than for teaching of merely colourless principles. That is all we contend for. Let me say one word on another topic. I do not wish to carry it very far, for I would be repeating the arguments put more forcibly by other speakers. But, in answer to the honourable Member who moved the resolution, I may say that I do not think there would be any great difficulty in providing that nearly every parent in this country should have the choice of his children being taught the definite form of religion to which he is earnestly and sincerely attached. That is the true direction in which educational reform ought to go. Where I join issue with the honourable Member who moved the Resolution is on this point. If he had the direction of the educational policy of the country he would put an end as much as possible to all true definite religious teaching. My answer to that is, that true reform lies not in putting an end to definite religious teaching, but in extending it in every possible direction. I can conceive nothing more selfish or intolerant in the advocates of religious teaching than to say that they would deprive other sects and bodies of the same opportunity and chances which they themselves consider vital in the interests of their own children, and I have no doubt that a compromise might be found upon some terms of this kind if it were not for the spirit which seeks to make, not only political capital, but political difficulty in the country out of this topic. I welcome what was said by the honourable Member for West Nottingham, more especially coming as it did from the other side of the House, that we should try and get rid of this religious difficulty, and devote our undivided attention to education. That is the true keynote to strike. But I would remind the House that there are two

F

ways of getting rid of it. You may get rid of it by having no definite religious teaching at all. To get rid of it in that way would lead to nothing but misfortune. The other way is to extend this definite religious teaching in favour of all sects and all bodies alike. I believe that that is the true way, and that there are means to carry out a proposal of this kind. The religious difficulty would then come to an end, and we could devote our attention to what is of far greater importance upon the mere educational question, that is, the question of increased educational efficiency and advantages. There are one or two other points on matters of principle which I should like to urge in answer to the honourable Gentleman who moved the Resolution. Surely he is quite wrong when he argues that local control should be given over State-aided Voluntary schools. It has been recognised ever since 1870 that, so far as State aid is concerned, it is not a question of local control at all. Has anyone ever suggested that from 1870 up to the present time, so far as State aid is concerned, it has not been a constitutional principle that this House should keep the control, and that the Education Department should be responsible to this House, as regards education? And when the honourable Member talked about money being given by the State without any corresponding measure of local control, he is merely stating a truism, that you do not have local control in connection with Imperial or State aid. As regards that, you have the control of this House, which is to be exercised in this educational matter, as also in all other matters, and there is no new principle. One often hears the mistake made; one often hears the wrong argument used upon this point. What is the true argument? That the people who find the money are to control the expenditure. If it is a case of Imperial funds, we are responsible for finding the money, and we are responsible for the way in which the money is spent. I am not objecting, of course, to popular control from an educational point of view; but I want to take what the honourable Mover of this Resolution has said on the question of principle, and I want to know what principle of local control is there when you give State aid—control

Mr. Cripps.

in this case is exercised, and properly exercised, through the medium of this House? Now, Sir, the only other question, I think, with which the honourable Gentleman dealt was that of the character of the education given in the Voluntary schools as against that given by the School Boards. Now, upon that I only want to make two remarks. First of all, as has been pointed out, the grants show that there is no great difference in efficiency between the education given under one system and the other. But what is far more important than that, and what is so often over-looked in these discussions, is this, that the Voluntary schools often provide education under the most difficult conditions. You have poor and isolated districts, and it is particularly in these districts that the Voluntary schools are doing an excellent and admirable work. But you cannot expect—nobody expects—that in poor and isolated country districts you can possibly give the same educational advantages as you give in our great industrial centres. No one can suppose that for an instant. So that when you compare on the basis of grants, that is not even a fair comparison, so far as the Voluntary schools are concerned, because they are carrying out a great work in the very poorest districts, doing the work of education under the most difficult circumstances, and under conditions which ought to give rise to the gratitude of everyone who really wants a good educational system in all parts of this country.

MR. LLOYD-GEORGE: Take the cases of Liverpool and Manchester.

*MR. CRIPPS: The honourable and learned Gentleman refers me to Liverpool and Manchester. I cannot speak from my own knowledge of either Liverpool or Manchester.

MR. LLOYD-GEORGE: There are the statistics in the Returns.

*MR. CRIPPS: I have not got the Returns here. I join issue with him so far as London is concerned. I do not know what is his personal experience of London. Of course, London is a very large place, and I am bound to admit that my own experience is limited to the district of Kensington. That is all I know about it, and it is exceedingly difficult in this matter to make general statements. And, as regards the Voluntary schools which I know in London, I join issue with the honourable Member altogether. I am not led away by these isolated cases; I am not led away by a mere example here and there. Has the honourable Member got the statistics of London showing the difference in grants as between the Voluntary schools and the Board schools?

*Mr. FOSTER: The Board schools earn 8d. per head more.

*Mr. CRIPPS: Does that show a very great difference?

Mr. LLOYD-GEORGE: Certainly, for the attendances has to be taken out.

*Mr. CRIPPS: I will not argue that further. I entirely join issue with the honourable Member upon that. But what I was going to point out is this, that so far as there is any difference between the two systems of education, I believe myself it is indisputable that the Board schools, being better off, are enabled to command a better staff. I have no doubt about that, and I have often said myself that the true answer to that should be this, that the several districts in this country, whether poor or rich, or whatever the local conditions may be, ought to be entitled to the same staff for educational purposes, to be found in the same way in proportion to the number of the children, and that is the true solution of our educational difficulty. Education is not a local matter. It is a matter of great national concern with which we have to deal. I think the honourable Member agrees with me in that. When we are dealing with a great matter of national concern, the nation itself, or we as the representatives of the nation, ought to see that a similar amount of educational efficiency is, as far as possible, obtained in all districts, whether rich or poor.

Mr. LLOYD-GEORGE: On equal conditions.

*Mr. CRIPPS: And how can we do that? There is one way, and one way only—that is that we can insist on all these schools, wherever they are, having an equally efficient staff, and, as

VOL. LXVIII. [Fourth Series.]

I think, we must find the money to pay for that, that is, in my mind, the true solution, the true and ultimate solution of this educational difficulty. Now, Sir, I am afraid I have detained the House longer than I had intended upon this point, but surely this educational question, after all, is of the greatest moment, and we ought to keep it in accordance with true principle, and I am satisfied myself that if anyone who went to the country were to be guided by the view expressed on the Benches opposite, and to ask for a universal School Board system, he would get a very decided vote in the negative.

*Mr. SPICER (Monmouth Boroughs): I do not think that we ought to complain, or that anyone ought to complain, of the evening being given to perhaps the most important subject that the House of Commons can discuss, and I do not think that anyone can have listened to nearly the whole of the Debate, as I have done, without feeling almost amused at the different views that have been expressed with regard to the so-called religious difficulty. We have been constantly told that there is no religious difficulty, and yet there is hardly a speaker who has spoken to-night who, before he has finished his speech, has not referred himself to this religious difficulty. I do not think that the honourable and learned Member who last spoke was quite fair to those who take what my honourable and learned Friend the Member for East Edinburgh calls the secularist view. I have a very keen recollection of the Debates in connection with the 1870 Bill, because they formed some of the first conflicts I had in public life. Those who asked for that system were those who were most keenly interested in the religious education of the children of this country. It was not that they wanted secular education, but they said that, because the State was going to give these grants to the day schools, all religion should be kept out of these schools, and the religious teaching should be left to the churches and to the Sunday schools. I am bound to say that I still adhere to that position as the logical position. But we are not a logical nation, and those of us who held that view were simply beaten by the force of circumstances. We arrived at the London School Board compromise

F

of simple Bible teaching, and though our friends in the early days of the first Birmingham School Board accepted the plan of no religious teaching in the schools, allowing, of course, others to come and teach religion before the ordinary school hours, the London School Board compromise was practically accepted as a satisfactory solution, and became the accepted doctrine of the Board schools of the country. But, after all, there are 8,000 parishes in this country where all the children of the parish must go to the one school—and let me say that we do not want to set up schools, and I, as a Nonconformist, should be very adverse to starting any scheme which should mean setting up a second school in these parishes. We all know that small schools are bound to be poor schools. You cannot classify small schools in the same way as you can large schools, and I maintain that anyone who attempted to induce Nonconformists, although they are often now in the majority in many of the rural parishes, to set up separate schools would be an enemy to education. But I say that, so long as there are 8,000 parishes where all the children are compelled to go to the one school, and where, whilst the State bears five-sixths of the expense, the whole management is really—I admit, of course, there are exceptions—in the hands of one Party, and where also, in a large majority of cases, no Nonconformist young man or woman can enter the educational profession, I say there is a religious difficulty which you cannot shut your eyes to. And what is the effect of this religious difficulty? I want to look at this matter, not as a Nonconformist, but purely from the citizen's point of view, and I say that, so long as this religious difficulty exists, you are lowering the whole standard of educational efficiency in this country, and you are placing this country in a very dangerous position in competition with other nations. And I think that lately, Mr. Speaker, we have had an object lesson on this question. For some time, apart from the Reports in the Education Blue Books, we have had no accurate account of the actual condition of education in these rural parishes, and though the Blue Books are extremely interesting, of course they are but partial, and you cannot from these Blue Books get any very accurate account of the

full position of education in these districts. Well, I have no doubt many Members of this House have seen, thanks to the enterprise of the proprietors of the "Manchester Guardian," a series of articles which have been appearing in that newspaper, and are the result of a visit paid by a commissioner sent to the rural districts in five counties, viz., Kent, Middlesex, Buckinghamshire, Lincolnshire, and Cornwall—and I hope that if right honourable Members have not seen the pamphlet which now contains the series of articles they will do so, because I think that that pamphlet presents about as truthful an account of the position of education in these rural parishes as has been presented to the country for a long time, and I do not think anyone can read that pamphlet without feeling that it is fair in every way. It is not at all complimentary to some of my Nonconformist friends in many of the rural parishes, but I think it states accurately and honestly the true facts of the case. But what is, after all, the general impression which you gain from the pamphlet? It is that in the rural districts of England at the present time there is an enormous amount of educational indifference. The people are willing at all costs, whether they belong to one side or the other, to accept anything so long as it is cheap. They are against Board schools because Board schools are dear. They do not like many of the conditions of the Voluntary schools, but they accept them because they are cheap. There is an absence of leadership on educational matters. I do not say that this is always the case. There are some cases where clergymen—and it is to their credit—sometimes stand alone as educational leaders. In other cases there are earnest Nonconformists who are equally keen on this subject, but, speaking broadly, there is throughout these districts, which he describes in the pamphlet, an immense amount of educational indifference. In these schools they are content with Article 68 teachers, as is proved by the fact that whilst Voluntary schools have 8,970 certified masters, they have also 8,970 Article 68 teachers, women of perfectly good character, but who have had no educational training. And why are they satisfied with Article 68 teachers? Because the managers get

Mr. Spicer.

the wives thrown in with the husbands
for a comparatively small salary. It is
simply a question of cheapness, and, consequently, whilst the wife ought to be
at home looking after her family, she
is, without any training, simply trying
to do her best in the school. Well
then, as a necessary sequence, there is
no leadership in education, and there
is no stimulus amongst the better-edu-
cated people to induce parents to keep
their children at school. Consequently,
in a school of 120 or 130, there are,
perhaps, three, five, or seven who are
over 12, but all the rest go out to
work at 11 years of age. Now,
that is, I believe, a perfectly true
picture, and I do not think anyone
can read that pamphlet without feeling it is true. It is not written by
a man who wanted to make out a
case all one side. I take it he is a
schoolmaster, and he is himself keenly
interested in all the interests of the
schools, but it is a true picture of the
state of education in our rural districts.
And now, what about our towns? A
return has recently been issued to this
House on the different classes of employment to which boys and girls attending elementary schools in England and
Wales went on leaving school during
one complete year. I have been examining the figures in that return, and I
have been looking at the percentage
of boys who, on leaving school, go into
different kinds of employment. I have
chosen the cases where the Educational
Department have been able to obtain
the largest percentage of population. I
will now turn to the classification of
employment. I have picked out three
special classes, which I think will show
the point on which I lay stress—those
who go as errand boys on leaving school,
as hawkers, and as newsboys, and I find
that in some towns the percentage is no
less than 40 per cent. We always know
that these three departments of labour
constitute what is often called "the
little place." It is the easiest to
get, and, practically, leads nowhere. As
errand boys, or hawkers, or newsboys,
they can learn nothing, and their occupation fits them for no other employment. This is a great temptation to
a very large number of the working
classes, and especially those who have
left school early, for they have not any
outlook, they have formed no idea as

to what employment they would like
to go into, and there is no stimulus
from home or from any friends. They
choose this employment, and from
errand boys or like occupation they drift
into other unskilled employment, the
result being that they can earn better
wages during the first 10 or perhaps
eight years of their career, as unskilled
labourers, than they could if they went
into any skilled employment, because,
of course, they would, so to speak, be
learning their trade. The consequence
is, that in that class, you have a set
of men who come to their highest wage-
earning capacity when they are about
22 to 25. I know well enough from
my experience in the East of London
the crowds we have of this particular
class. With the least lapse in character,
or even the last lapse in health, they very
often begin to find themselves on the
downward grade about 25, so that in
the poor parts of our large towns, when
they reach 35 or 40 you will find a
huge crowd of men being supported by
the earnings of their own children.
And it is this residuum which we are
creating at the present time, and which
is such a huge danger to our towns.
I believe it is very largely owing to
the fact that public opinion with regard to true elementary education is
so comparatively low, and that there is
no stimulus put before the minds of
the children to look out for some skilled
employment. After all, we come back
to the religious difficulty which divides
us all in this country as regards elementary education, and which is very largely
responsible for this low standard of
efficiency. What do we gain by it? It
is said that the Church of England is
very anxious to keep this power in her
hands, that the schools are a nursery
for the Church. Do the facts really
justify this statement? I believe that
the Sunday school is a nursery for the
Church, and I think when you consider
the very large proportion of children
being educated in Voluntary schools the
figures with regard to Sunday schools
bear out my contention. What are
those figures? They show that whilst
you have in the Anglican church
219,159 Sunday school teachers and
2,393,000 scholars, you have in the
Evangelical free churches 381,000
teachers and 3,284,960 children, showing, as a matter of fact, that where

F 2

they go on a week-day does not influence where they go on a Sunday. That is the gist of the Report of the Commissioner who has been round these five rural districts. He gives case after case where there is only one school, and that a Church school, but where there is a majority of Nonconformists, and yet in some cases where there is only a Church day-school there is not even a Church Sunday school—all the children are in Nonconformist Sunday schools. I say, therefore, that any attempt to make day schools a nursery for the Church is a huge failure. I think there are a good many clergymen who are beginning to feel that this is the case. There was remarkable testimony given the other day by a clergyman at Upper Edmonton—the Rev. Lucius G. Fry—and, with the permission of the House, I will read what he says—

"He has come to the conclusion that Church day schools do not feed the Established Church. A census of his own boys' and girls' schools show the following results: —Out of 542 scholars 213 attend Church Sunday Schools, 211 Nonconformist Sunday schools, and 118 attend no Sunday school at all. More than half Mr. Fry's Sunday school children go to Board schools. He has come to the conclusion that poor parishes should no longer have to bear such 'a sickening burden' as a Church day school. This is his conclusion— 'After 20 years of hard struggle I am utterly sick and tired to death of Church day schools, and, wherever I go, I find that clergy placed with day schools, as I am, say the same; those who have directed our educational policy in the Church, through the National Society and the Diocesan Board of Education, have made a most awful mistake, and the sooner it is realised and acknowledged the better. It is the Sunday school, not the day school, which feeds the Church.'"

But I do not want to argue on that point. I want to argue it on the ground that the present religious difficulty which is dividing the people of this country with regard to elementary education is a tremendous drawback to the educational efficiency of the country. I am glad, therefore, that this evening has been devoted to the consideration of this question, and, if it has made us understand one another's position better, I think it may have proved of some advantage.

Mr. ABEL THOMAS (Carmarthen, E.): Mr. Speaker, I think there can be no doubt that there is a religious difficulty. A child between six and 12 years

Mr. Spicer.

of age does not, I suppose, care what particular sect or doctrine is taught in its school; but that there is a difficulty amongst the parents where there is a Voluntary or Church school only, there cannot be the slightest doubt. We hear a good deal about the conscience clause, and it has been suggested by an honourable Member that parents should take advantage of it. Well, how in the world is a parent to take advantage of it in certain places? Imagine the position in a district which I have in my mind in Wales—and the same thing happens in many districts in England and Wales—where the clergyman and the squire, who are Churchmen, are the chief and, indeed, the only subscribers to the Voluntary school. I know that there are districts where the school committee have admitted Roman Catholics and Nonconformists to the governing body, even when there were only 3 or 4 per cent. of Nonconformist children in the school, but there are hundreds of districts in Wales, where the children, in a very large majority, at any rate, are the sons or daughters of Nonconformist parents, whilst every manager of those schools is a Churchman. To say that there is no religious difficulty under those circumstances is to imagine that you cannot see what everybody else can see. It is a matter of common knowledge that the doctrines taught by the Church of England are not believed in by the Nonconformists. They say that not only are they wrong, but that they will do anything in the world to prevent their children being taught those doctrines. Where that position exists, you are bound to have a religious difficulty. It is no use shutting one's eyes to the plain facts of the case. There is the religious difficulty, and it is the chief difficulty in making our education in this country a really satisfactory education for the children at large. It has been said, "Why don't you try, under the conscience clause, to have these children excluded?" The objection is that most of us are not martyrs. I do not know that my fellow-countrymen are any more martyrs than anybody else in England or Scotland. It very often happens that the Nonconformist father and mother depend upon the squire or the clergyman for their livelihood, and it is ridiculous to suppose, under these circumstances, that they would incur the risk which the conscience clause in such a case would involve. Parents feel that they are not being treated properly in being compelled—because it is compulsion as far as they are concerned—to send their children to what are distinctly Church schools. It really does seem to me that when honourable Members on the other side of the House, and, indeed, some on our own side, make a distinction between the religious difficulty in the schools and religious difficulties, as they call them, in politics, that they are disregarding the main point. The real point is that a child does not care one scrap one way or the other. But the parent does care. Then it has been seriously suggested, not by one, but by a very great number of honourable Members upon the other side of the House, that we have popular control at the present moment in the Voluntary schools of this country. Well, Mr. Speaker, what is the meaning of popular control? If it means that the Education Department shall decide for each particular district what the particular doctrine they wish to be taught in any district in England or Wales is to be, then we have popular control; but that is not the meaning of popular control. What is meant, I imagine, by popular control is that the ratepayer and the parents of the children shall themselves decide what kind of education they want the children to have. It may be said that they do not contribute towards the Voluntary schools. They do not pay towards the Voluntary schools in rates, it is true, but they contribute towards the grant. It does not make the least difference whether the money comes through the local authority or the rates. It is the parents of the children who pay finally for the education. It is simply putting the matter one degree further off whether you call it a grant or whether you call it a rate. I cannot understand the mind of the man who suggests that there is a total distinction between the education of a child by rate and the education of a child by grant. When one hears—I do not like to call it nonsense, Mr. Speaker, but it sounds very much like it—that there is popular control of Voluntary schools, I really do think that honourable Members on the other side of the House should try and define what they mean by popular control, because it really cannot be popular control, I am afraid, at the present mo-

ment. The man who pays the educational rate should have the opportunity of selecting the way in which religious education is to be applied to the children. The fact is, that the body of persons who are conducting these schools bring up the children who are taught in those schools in the religion in which the managers themselves believe. I cannot help thinking that the position now is very different from what it was 20 or 25 years ago—30 years ago, at any rate. We then had as managers of these Voluntary schools clergyman of the old sort. They were men who, I have no doubt, strongly believed in their own religious tenets, but they had regard for the feelings of other people, and they were not proselytisers, except in very few instances. Is it possible to say that at the present moment of many managers of the schools in this country? I am not going to say one word against the High Church Party, because, in my opinion, they are the most earnest division of the Church of England; they are doing the most good in the lowest urban districts as well as in some of the poorest agricultural districts. They are passionately earnest, and that is the very reason why they are also trying to convert everybody to their own views. It is no use to shut one's eyes to the fact, it is to be seen on all sides amongst men who believe in doctrines which are not the doctrines of the Protestant Church of England. Wherever you get one of those men who is very passionately earnest, he is forced to become a proselytiser—he cannot help himself; and when one goes to Brighton, Cardiff, and other places, one sees what is happening at the present moment. At the same time, if I were a sacerdotal clergyman and manager of a school, it would be utterly impossible for me, doing my duty to the Higher Power which I should worship, to do other than to convert everybody into my way of thinking. It would be wicked of me not to do so. But so far as we in England and Wales are concerned, we—most of us, at any rate—are Protestant people. It has been said, not once, but many times, that there are 14,000 Voluntary schools at the present moment where it is practically impossible for a Nonconformist to become a teacher. Then, in addition to that, you have 8,000 parishes where there is no Board school, and every Nonconformist, or

... ... man who believes ... ... compelled to send his ... ... church school. I venture ... ... a gross injustice to the ... ... under those circumstances ... with all my heart the Motion ... arable Friend.

Mr J. GORST: The honourable Member who has just sat down addressed the House in that conciliatory and philosophic tone which has prevailed during the latter part of this Debate at all events; but he really came back to the same position taken up by the honourable Member for Carnarvon, who moved this Motion. That honourable Member invites the House to affirm that there is a serious grievance in our educational system, that that serious grievance is what is generally known as the religious difficulty, and that the attention of Parliament should be forthwith directed to it, to the exclusion of any other subject connected with our educational system, in order to remove it, as the greatest obstacle to educational progress. Now, the first thing the House ought to consider is whether there is really this religious grievance, which has been so graphically depicted. The honourable and learned Member, in a speech of very great sincerity and fervour, worked himself and his friends in the House up to a kind of imagination of a state of things existing in the rural parts of this country, where the labourers, whose children frequent the elementary schools, are divided into very sincere and earnest Churchmen on the one side and very sincere and earnest Nonconformists on the other, each extremely anxious about the education of their children in their particular dogmas and tenets, and most aggrieved and oppressed if the realisation of that wish is interfered with. But really, is there such a state of things existing in the country? Why, everybody knows that the greater part of the agricultural labourers are absolutely indifferent as to what is the teaching of their children in either secular or religious subjects, that the greater part of them never go either to church or chapel. Yet, even the religious part of the rural population is extremely indifferent upon the subject of church or chapel. They usually themselves from the one to the other upon very slight, very insufficient grounds. Some of them, and not by an ...

W. ... (A.) ... ...

means the worst, make a practice of attending on the same Sunday the church in the morning, and the chapel in the evening, or *vice versâ*—a proceeding which a former Bishop of London (Bishop Blomfield) used to stigmatise as "dodging the devil." The honourable Member for Carnarvon has asked the House to consider the grievances of the Nonconformist population in three distinct particulars, and I will address myself briefly to each. First of all, he says there are 8,000 parishes in which there is nothing but a Church school, and that practically Nonconformists, who form in some cases the majority of the population, and in others a large minority, have no choice but to send their children to the Church schools. Well, if that is sound in theory, it is a very serious grievance; but what remedy is suggested by honourable Members in this House? The honourable Member for Monmouth District made an extremely valuable speech on this subject. He said nothing would induce him to have two schools in his parish. In some of these villages, he said, the one school was too small, and if you split up the population between a Church school and a Nonconformist school you would have two schools still more inefficient. The honourable Member for Flintshire seemed to think that the true remedy was the assumption by the Education Department of a sort of Episcopal conscience, and their interference in the kind of religious instruction given. If the Education Department or any Minister responsible to this House were to take upon themselves to interfere in the kind of religious instruction given, it would certainly not lessen the religious difficulty. The true attitude the Department has always assumed is one of complete impartiality in connection with religious instruction. The whole attitude of the Department is to see that no child whose parents object to the particular religious instruction given in a school is compelled to attend it, and there its right of interference with religious instruction begins and ends. Then there is the remedy of the school board. A school board the people in the village will not have. They prefer the Church school, with its catechism and its clerical tyranny, to a school board. They would rather their children were taught anything ... they should have to pay a rate. The honourable Member for Monmouth referred to some description of rural education which appeared recently in the "Manchester Guardian," and I think he will bear me out in saying that one of the most striking portions of that picture was the total indifference of the rural population, even in such a county as Cornwall, where the vast majority of the people are Nonconformists, for this religious difficulty. So far from burning to be free from the tyranny of the few Church schools in Cornwall, the testimony was that they were more anxious it should continue, because they would rather their children were taught the Church catechism than have to pay a school board rate.

Mr. LLOYD-GEORGE: Most of the schools in Cornwall are Board schools.

Sir J. GORST: That is exactly what I am saying; but so far as the Church schools that survive in Cornwall are concerned, the Nonconformists are anxious to keep them up, because they prefer their children to be taught the Church catechism than that they should have to pay a school board rate. Then there is the conscience clause. That is the remedy Parliament has provided, and that remedy I believe on the whole to be a very fair one. I think the conscience clause is very seldom used in any school unless it is stirred up from the outside. Of that, recent Debates in the House have given evidence. The case referred to by the honourable Member for Flintshire as having occurred in the town of Flint is a very remarkable instance of this. That, however, is a matter which is still under inquiry. I have only heard one side of the case from the honourable Member, and therefore I should not like to speak positively about it. But so far as the evidence before me goes, it appears that in this parish there is an extremely popular Church of England clergyman, who is very much liked both by Churchmen and by Nonconformists, and there has never been any difficulty in the school for years in connection with the conscience clause. Then comes an emissary—an emissary, I believe, of the honourable Member himself. I am sure the honourable Member himself would not intimidate anybody, though he may have induced some of the Nonconformists of the parish to withdraw their children under the conscience clause.

*Mr. S. SMITH: No, that is not so.

Sir J. GORST: Well, I know the managers of the school have settled the matter. The parishioners have not withdrawn their children from all religious teaching, but only from a part of it. What the honourable Member complains of is that this gentleman, instead of receiving this rebuff as, I suppose, any charitable clergyman ought to receive any rebuff, appears to have made a denunciation in the pulpit of these people. That is a matter with which I cannot interfere, because it is obviously an episcopal affair altogether, and he has in two cases appealed to the employers of those who had taken their children away from school to exercise their influence upon them. That proceeding, if it were true —about which I cannot express any opinion—would be most reprehensible. I am bound to say that we in this House know a good deal about meetings and how meetings are broken up, and I will just give the House one short quotation from a speech which was made at that meeting, as it is reported in the "Flintshire Observer" for 2nd March, 1899, and I do not think the House will be surprised at the meeting being broken up. Remember that this was undoubtedly a popular clergyman, who was arraigned at this meeting by a gentleman—an orator from Lancashire—who had nothing whatever to do with the town of Flint. This is what he said in his speech—

"I am here to denounce the rector of Flint as one of the greatest cowards I have ever met with. I see gentlemen of the Press here, and I ask them to enter on their note-books my statement that the conduct of the rector of Flint is that of the greatest coward I have ever met with in public life."

I appeal to gentlemen who have had experience of public meetings, whether a speech of that kind was not certain to result in the breaking up of the meeting. Now, I have never concealed from the House my dissatisfaction with the existing conscience clause, and the Government, of which I am an humble Member, made an attempt two years ago to propose to this House a conscience clause, which would not only have allowed people to withdraw their children from that religious instruction which they did not like, but would have secured to every one that in every school in the country every effort should be made to give his children that religious instruction which he did like. What did the honourable and learned Member for Carnarvon and his friends do upon that occasion? They denounced this particular clause as if it were the invention of some religious persecutors, and would not even discuss it. I think that the honourable Member said that if the clause was reintroduced he would act in the same manner now. But the real state of affairs in the country is not at all what has been described. In most places the people have any religious instruction they like. In nearly all these Church schools the instruction given on four days out of the five on which the school is open is identical with that given in the Board schools, and consists of lessons chiefly from the New Testament—lessons on Scriptural history, which are adapted to children of immature age. It is only on one day in the week, as a general rule, that any catechism is taught at all, and I venture to say that in the great majority of Church schools in the rural district that catechism is only taught to the children whose parents acquiesce in it, and if any conscientious or religious-minded Dissenter were to say he did not wish his children to be taught the Church catechism, his children would have Bible lessons during the time the other children were learning the Church catechism, and his children would never be required to learn it at all. Therefore, though the grievance of the honourable Member sounds a very serious one, yet I quite agree with what was said by his colleague, the honourable Member for Nottingham, who has had considerable experience in this matter, and who, I believe, is a perfectly staunch and respected Liberal, and who tells us that there is really no religious difficulty in the schools at all, and if you do not have outside influence—orators from Lancashire and others—in the schools, the teachers and parents and the children will get on perfectly comfortably together. Now the next grievance which has been spoken of by many Members here, is that in all these rural schools Nonconformist children are absolutely debarred from entering the teachers' profession. I confess that if

Sir J. Gorst.

that were so I should be very indignant —not as a Nonconformist, but as a Minister of Education looking out most anxiously for all the teaching staff that can possibly be procured in the country. But it is not so. I took some trouble to ascertain what the facts were about this. I have two letters from Welsh inspectors. One is from Mr. L. J. Roberts, an inspector at Denbigh. He is a Churchman, and he says—

"Though I have a pretty wide knowledge of my district, in which small Church schools abound, not a single case of hardship endured by a Nonconformist aspirant for pupil teachership has come under my notice. Of late a growing desire seems to have been shown to accept Nonconformist boys and girls as pupil teachers in Church schools. At the opening of a new school at Prestatyn about a year ago the Bishop of St. Asaph made a speech in which he strongly urged the clergy to give equality of opportunity as candidates for pupil teachers to Nonconformist as well as Church children. I know that there are a good many Nonconformists employed at present in the Church schools in this district. But, despite all this, there are parishes, doubtless, where a Nonconformist child has little chance of being brought up to the teaching profession if there are eligible Church of England candidates. The exclusion of Nonconformist children is no doubt a real grievance in some parishes, though I have no definite instance to give."

The second report is from Mr. Darlington, of Aberystwith, a Nonconformist, and a gentleman with large experience in Wales, having been a lecturer there before he became one of Her Majesty's inspectors. He says—

"The great majority of my Voluntary schools are not large enough to need to employ pupil teachers. Where they do employ them I should say that Nonconformists would stand a greater chance of being selected than would be the case in England, for the simple reason that it would frequently happen here that most of the eligible candidates, even in Voluntary schools, would be Nonconformists. I have never made any inquiries on the subject, nor has it ever been mentioned to me by managers or others in my district, but I happen to know of at least two cases in which Nonconformist pupil teachers have been employed in Church schools."

I have made inquiries also in Lincolnshire, and the inspectors have never heard of a case where a Nonconformist child had been refused admission to a pupil teachership in consequence of his religion.

Mr. LLOYD-GEORGE: Will the right honourable Gentleman grant a Return?

Sir J. GORST: I cannot give a Return, because I have no knowledge. I inquired last Session all over the country, and I have not been able to find a single instance of a child refused to be made a pupil teacher in consequence of the religious tenets of his parents. I should like the honourable Member to give me a Return of a single instance, and I will have it inquired into, but so unwilling are the managers of country schools, who have no means of training pupil teachers, to take them in at all that I am afraid, unless some fresh plan is adopted, the country teacher will soon become a thing of the past. I understand that in Wales there are a great many pupil teachers now taken from the Secondary schools, and I believe that is the real source from which the young teacher of the future will have to be derived. The last grievance is the question of training college accommodation. No doubt it is greatly too small. But the State has not taken on itself the practical duty of training teachers; it has subsidised bodies who do, and if the Nonconformists have a difficulty in finding colleges to go to it is because the Nonconformists have established fewer training colleges than the Church of England. The true remedy for that state of things would be for Nonconformists to imitate the other side, and to establish training colleges in sufficient numbers. I do not see how you can force the conscience clause on the managers of the existing training colleges, and if you wish Nonconformist residential colleges the true remedy would be to adopt the day training college system, in which the pupils can have the benefit of the conscience clause, and can be received into the college. I hope the House will see that at present there is no such practical religious grievance as demands the immediate attention of Parliament to the exclusion of much more important matters. Therefore, I hope that the House will negative the Resolution. With regard to the Amendment, it sets up another grievance as that to which the attention of Parliament must be directed. It is the grievance of the different financial position of Voluntary and Board schools. I quite agree with the honourable Member who moved the Amendment that the financial position of the managers of Board and Voluntary schools is very different, and greatly to the disadvantage of the latter; and it is to the interest of the nation at large that such financial arrangements should be made as would put the managers of Voluntary schools in a satisfactory and proper position. But I do not think that we can ask the attention of Parliament immediately to it. Two years ago a Bill was passed which gave a large sum of money to the managers of Voluntary schools, and naturally Parliament will wait and see the effect of that Bill, which, as far as I know, has been, from an educational point of view, very useful, and has enabled a great number of Voluntary schools to be placed in a much more efficient position, to obtain more numerous and better teachers and better apparatus. But we can hardly ask that the attention of Parliament should be again immediately directed to the subject. I hope that the honourable Member will consent to withdraw his Amendment, so that we can take the vote on the Motion of the honourable Member for Carnarvon. Those who really believe that the progress of education in the country is stopped by this religious difficulty will vote for the Motion. Those who think that, after all, although this religious question is logically a difficulty it is not really a practical obstacle to education will vote to negative the Motion, in order that the attention of Parliament may be directed to matters which really are much more urgent and essential to the progress of education.

*Sir H. FOWLER (Wolverhampton, E.): The House always listens with interest to the speeches of the Vice-President, and his speech to-night has not been wanting in any of those characteristics of novelty and surprise which we always expect, and of which the right honourable Gentleman never disappoints us. He is a very accomplished Minister of Education, he is a very brilliant debater, and he is a very formidable antagonist to any Party opposed to him. But of one thing he is profoundly ignorant, and that is the state of the Nonconforming residents of the rural parishes in England. I do not hesitate to say that the description which he has drawn this evening of the rural Nonconformists and their indifference to religion is a libel on them.

SIR J. GORST: I never said indifference to religion. I said indifference to the differences between the Church and Nonconformity.

*SIR H. FOWLER: The right honourable Gentleman spoke of their indifference to affording their children any religious education whatever. There is another portion of the right honourable Gentleman's speech to which I will call attention at once. He has treated this Motion as dealing purely with the religious grievance and with nothing else; and he has made no reply to the remarks of honourable Members on both sides with reference to the system of Primary Education which the Resolution says "Inflicts upon a large portion of Her Majesty's subjects a serious grievance." The religious grievance to which he has directed the whole of his remarks is but one section of that grievance. The noble Lord the Member for Rochester says that he is wearied of these educational discussions. He will have to undergo a great deal more of that weariness.

*VISCOUNT CRANBORNE: I said that the House was weary of them.

*SIR H. FOWLER : The House has enjoyed the noble Lord's speech, and when he addresses the House as pleasantly as he has done to-night, the House will always enjoy the speeches of the noble Lord. But we have in this country the most expensive, the most inefficient, and insufficient system of education in Europe. We have now on the register of the public elementary schools five-and-a-half millions of scholars, and we have only four-and-a-half millions in average attendance. That system costs the country in grants from taxes and in local rates nearly £12,000,000 of public money, totally excluding the subscriptions of the friends of Denominational schools. The right honourable Gentleman knows better than I do that we have not 20 per cent. of the children in average attendance who are above the Fourth Standard. That is the first grievance —that the education is bad, is insufficient, and is putting this country to a serious disadvantage from a commercial, from a manufacturing, and from a national point of view. Every

honourable Member who has spoken to-night has dwelt upon some disadvantage or other ; no one has got up and said the present system is perfect. No one has indulged in the optimism of the right honourable Gentleman. Even those who thought that the views expressed on this side of the House with reference to the religious grievance were exaggerated, and possibly unfair, have a religious grievance of their own. They put the case of the Board schools, and they maintain, with great force, as is maintained on this side, that this system is defective. In a sentence or two, I should like to put before the House the real difficulty that arises. It has been seen in to-night's Debate that we are apt to consider our educational system as one system, dealing with one class of the population, and under one system of administration. That is not the case. Our system of education in the towns and our system of education in the country are essentially different. The same conditions cannot apply to both ; yet, where a difficulty is raised with reference to the education in towns, the answer to it is given by illustrations drawn from the rural districts, and where, as was the case in the majority of the speeches to-night, the difficulties of the rural districts are raised, the answer is given as to what prevails in the towns. The honourable Member for Hertfordshire, who made a very powerful contribution to our Debates to-night, and who certainly dealt with this question both as a practical educationist and in a statesmanlike manner, said that what was wanted was a friendly rivalry between the two systems—the Voluntary Denominational and the Board schools. Where can there be a rivalry in the rural districts? There are 8,000 districts where there is but one school ; there can be no rivalry there. And then he also went on to show that the people of this country had indicated their preference for the Denominational system over the Board school system by quoting the large number of scholars who were to be found in the one class of school as contrasted with the other class of school. In 8,000 districts they have no choice whatever, no opportunity of saying which they prefer. Again, with reference to the suggestion that was made very fairly by the honourable Member that provision might be made for the giving in the respective Board schools of religious education— and he frankly admitted he was willing to extend that to Voluntary schools also —by the various preachers of the religious denominations whose children might be found in those schools, that might be practicable in the towns, where you have an organised staff of Nonconforming ministers, in the same manner as the Church of England has, but it is absolutely impossible in a rural village. There are no such resident ministers there. Nonconformity in a rural village is taught in the main, even on Sunday, by a minister who comes from a distance, or by a lay preacher who works hard for his living every day of the week—that man cannot go into a school on a week day and give religious education. The thing is impracticable; it has broken down in Birmingham, where it was commenced under very favourable auspices, and I know no place where it has been a success. For the moment I am simply pointing out that whereas one class of circumstances may be dealt with in the town satisfactorily you have a different class of circumstances in the country. There is another point. The Department which the right honourable Gentleman is pleased to call the Committee of the Council I prefer to call, in what I think is true Parliamentary language, the Administration of the Lord President of the Council, the Duke of Devonshire, and I think it would be far better if in our discussions on educational matters we got rid of the joke of the right honourable Gentleman about the Committee of Council and dealt with the Education Department, as we deal with the Foreign Office, the Colonial Office, and the Home Office—dealt with the Minister who is responsible to Parliament for the administration. We have a grievance there, and a large portion of Her Majesty's subjects have a grievance with reference to the administration of the Education Department, and I will tell the right honourable Gentleman why. Because we say that Department is not impartial, because its administration is adverse to Board schools and favourable to Denominational schools.

AN HONOURABLE MEMBER: The last Government.

*SIR H. FOWLER: The last Government! I frankly say that it was not so unfavourable to Board schools. I am not for a moment denying that. I glory in it. I think it was very much to the honour of Mr. Acland that he did deal with the system which had grown up of unfairness to Board schools, and endeavoured to correct it. We know, for we have had those cases again and again before us, that wherever there is a chance of preventing the establishment of a Board school, and welcoming the establishment of a Denominational school, the force of the Department at present is thrown into the scale in favour of the Denominational school. The right honourable Gentleman has dealt with three branches of the various questions raised to-night. I will deal with one. He is so anxious to have statistics about pupil teachers; he has told us, on the testimony of two inspectors who have never heard of the case of a pupil teacher being deprived of the opportunity of learning his profession on account of his religious opinions, that he does not believe such cases exist. It is a very singular thing that the various organised representative bodies of the Nonconformists should have again and again pressed this matter upon successive Governments. The Wesleyan Committee on Education determined to have this grievance investigated. They have heard the denials of the right honourable Gentleman that these cases existed, and I will read to you what was the result. I will give the right honourable Gentleman the cases for which he asked. This is the result of the Committee appointed by the Wesleyan Conference—

"Out of 946 towns and villages, in regard to which the Committee of the Wesleyan Conference made inquiry, it was found that there were only 88 cases in which candidates were admitted to become pupil teachers without any act of conformity to the Church of England, and 858 cases in which either confirmation or attendance at service of the Church of England was required as a condition of pupil teachership."

And yet the Minister for Education gets up and tells the House there is no such class. There is a large class—one half of the population of this country living in the rural districts—to whom it is an ambition in life that their children should go into the teaching profession, the one opportunity they have of raising their condition; and these children are prevented on account of their religious creed from pursuing that course. Great as Nonconformist grievances are in relation to educational matters, there is no grievance more keenly felt than the shutting out from the profession of teaching—which is kept up out of the taxation of the country—of children of a large class of Her Majesty's subjects. What is the real difficulty in reference to the control and management of schools? The honourable Member for the Stroud Division drew a picture of boards of managers, and informed us there was an election by subscribers. He did not tell us who elected when there were no subscribers. There is a general impression that it is a nominated body, but, undoubtedly, after what the honourable and learned Member has said, that impression appears to be not the correct one. He went on to say that in some favoured parishes Nonconformists were permitted to become members of the managing body, and he said there was no difficulty in that example being followed. I should like to ask him whether it is not one of the conditions of the model deed of the schools of the National Society that the managers shall all be communicants of the Church of England. I have a strong impression that that is so—that the manager of a Church school must be a Churchman. I have also an impression that I have heard again and again in this House the statement made, when we were pressing for popular control or a voice in the management of the schools, that we should be met with this insuperable difficulty of the deed on which the National Schools were founded. The next point in dealing with this question of control is that, in the overwhelming bulk of these parishes, you have practically no lay managers. Does the honourable and learned Member say it is because the laymen who are nominated are satisfied with the management of the school by the clergyman? Then he admits this: that you have an institution which, in the main, is supported by public money, controlled by one individual who has no responsibility. The very phraseology in use by the clergy,

Sir H. Fowler.

"my school," and "my schoolmaster" shows that. Then we have the supplementary work, which, to the discredit of the teaching profession, is imposed on the teacher, playing the organ, training the choir, and of being, so to speak, a man-of-all-work in the village. We know that is 'a real grievance. Then, Sir, the honourable and learned Member asked what was the difference between popular control and public control, and said that, Parliament being the body that voted money for these various grants, we had in Parliament, through the Minister responsible to the House, effective control over this expenditure. I have two remarks to make in reply. The first is, that it is a radical defect of our present educational administration that it is centralised. We want it to be decentralised. We do not believe that even with the great powers of my right honourable Friend opposite, or of the Duke of Devonshire, that the Education Department can satisfactorily deal with 20,000 schools, and we know, from answers that are given in this House, that the varied grievances of which localities complain—which we know would not exist if there were anything approaching a system of popular control in the neighbourhood—cannot be redressed. I give another answer to the honourable and learned Member. He said this was really public money dispensed by the British Parliament, and that the responsible Minister is responsible to the House for the administration of public money, and in that way Parliament preserves control. Will he tell me what is done with the grants to the Local Taxation Fund? Many millions of money are voted in this House, are paid out of the Consolidated Fund to the Local Taxation Account, are distributed to the local authorities, and are spent by the local authorities. The local authorities are alone responsible for that expenditure to their constituents, and Parliament has nothing whatever to do with it. Will he tell me where is the difference between money voted for educational purposes and money voted for sanitary purposes and money voted for police purposes? I cannot see any distinction which admits of popular control in the one case and will not admit of it in the other. I only wish to detain the House for a moment more, and that is to refer to what is called the religious grievance. The right honourable Gentleman may smile, even my honourable friend the Member for Nottingham may say it is an imaginary grievance—but you have only got to state the plain facts of the case, and no man has admitted these more clearly and decisively than the right honourable Gentleman the First Lord of the Treasury. There are 8,000 parishes in this country in which the children are compelled to go to one school. If the children do not go to that school their fathers will be sent to prison; and in that school the children will be compelled to have religious teaching from which their fathers may dissent. (Ministerial cries of "No.") Oh, I am not forgetting the conscience clause. But I am perfectly well aware, not of its value, but of its worthlessness. There are two reasons why it is not used. The first, given by my honourable and learned Friend, is that the parents of little children do not want their little children made martyrs of, and do not want to be martyrs themselves, and I think the parents are right in objecting to have that stigma placed upon them. A short time ago I was talking to a lady on this question. She told me that her husband was giving a treat, of which she was the administratrix, to the school children of the parish, and that the clergyman of the parish proposed to her, almost as a matter of course, that those children who went to the Nonconformist Sunday school were to have no part in it. The right honourable Gentleman may call that a twopenny-halfpenny matter. But, happily, the squire was an Englishman and his wife was an English lady, and they would not allow anything of the sort. Those are little things; but I will tell the House what is a greater grievance, and why the conscience clause is not used. It is because Nonconformist parents of children in these rural parishes attach very great importance to the religious teaching of their children, and they will not avail themselves of the conscience clause because they wish their children to have the benefit of the Bible lessons which are given in the schools. The typical rural Nonconformist has not that attitude of hostility towards the Church of England which many honourable Members oppo-

site think. He strongly prefers his chapel, not upon political grounds, or because of the alliance between Church and State, but because the chapel is associated with his own religious life, because he prefers a more elastic worship and additional services, and because he prefers the simpler teaching of men in his own rank of life. But he has no animosity against the Church as the Church; the fathers and mothers are quite willing that their children should have the advantages of the teaching of the Bible in the schools, even at the risk of the children being taught something else from which they dissent. But I have been speaking of the past. That is not the state of things to-day. A new school of clergymen has arisen; a new class of teaching is being taught. The noble Lord told us that statements about Gace's Catechism had been exaggerated, but he did not tell us about Mr. Gace's own interview in the "Westminster Gazette," in which he said that by teaching his catechism to teachers he would get the teaching without the Catechism even into the Board schools. I do not attach any great importance to Gace's Catechism. The Catechism is offensive to Dissenters, but Dissenters will endure that! But what we have to deal with to-day is that throughout the length and breadth of the country new doctrines are being taught to the children of Nonconformists, from which their fathers most earnestly dissent. I am not talking of Ritualism. Personally, I attach very little importance to Ritualism. But there are two points to which, whether rightly or wrongly, the Nonconformists, and, I believe, large numbers of Churchmen, attach vital importance. One is the doctrine of the Mass, and the other is the practice of Confession. That doctrine and that practice are being taught to children, are being taught to girls in a large number of schools. (Ministerial cries of "Where?") Oh, I am perfectly aware with that mode' of interruption. I say these doctrines are taught in the schools controlled by the 4,000 clergy who are members of that disloyal society, the English Church Union. That is the question. I tell honourable Members opposite it is no smiling matter. We do not intend to allow it to rest as a smiling matter. We are not willing to submit to this teaching in schools, five-sixths of the cost of which is paid out of public money. (Ministerial cries of "No.") I say "Yes." Of every shilling of the cost 10d. comes from the public purse, and 2d. is provided from other sources. I put it to the House, totally irrespective of Church, of Dissent, and of Voluntary schools and Board schools, and I ask, is it fair, is it right, is it just, that these children should be compelled to learn these lessons to which their parents so strongly object? You may ask, "What is your remedy?" This Resolution does not specify the remedy, but it says the matter deserves the attention of Parliament. There is a remedy, but I have not time to go into it now. I am satisfied, if we had proper local control of education—not education in small parishes and scattered areas, but in larger districts—we should get rid of all these cobwebs which are doing so much injury to the cause of education, and let in a freer atmosphere into the whole administration of our Primary Education. I shall vote for the Resolution, not because it is dealing with any one question alone, but because I believe the whole of our system of Primary Education is bad, and because I believe it inflicts on a large portion of Her Majesty's subjects, whether Nonconformists or not, a serious grievance. I know we shall be beaten by your large battalions, but we believe this matter involves the whole principle of civil and religious liberty; we consider those principles are at stake, and this matter will be fought on until a clear and definite issue has been decided by the people.

THE FIRST LORD OF THE TREASURY (Mr. A. J. BALFOUR, Manchester, E.) : If the question before the House was whether in our parochial schools what the right honourable Gentleman has described as the doctrine of Confession and the practice of the Mass was to be taught either to Nonconformist children or to any children except the children of Roman Catholics, I believe the House would be absolutely and unanimously in agreement with the right honourable Gentleman. But that is not the question before the House, and I get up now, not to argue for or to speak against any of the views so ably laid before the House, but simply

Sir H. Fowler.

to state what I believe is the question upon which we are now going to vote. There is a Resolution before the House, and also an Amendment. Both of them state that the time of Parliament ought to be immediately devoted to legislation on educational matters. I think it is absolutely impossible for the Government, under any circumstances, to grant such time. Our legislative programme for the Session is already before the House, and, unless my forecast is very incomplete, the time of the Session will be quite adequately occupied. While it is impossible for us either to accept the Amendment or the Resolution, I hope my honourable Friend will withdraw his Amendment to the Resolution in order that the House may vote distinctly against the Motion as interpreted by the speech of the Mover. The question is not whether our system of education is a perfect system or not. We all admit that it is not. I have myself on more than one occasion expressed my own views as to some of the grievances from which both Nonconformists and Churchmen suffer. But what we are going to vote upon is quite different. It is as to whether the Voluntary schools system in this country is to be maintained or abandoned. That issue is, indeed, not clear upon the face of the Resolution—the studiedly ambiguous Resolution moved by the honourable and learned Member for Carnarvon Borough this evening—but while the Resolution of the honourable Member is ambiguous, his speech was not an ambiguous speech. Unless we clearly show to-night that the Resolution as interpreted by the speech of the honourable Member for Carnarvon is one which does not meet the approbation of the House of Commons, we shall be open to the suggestion that we are prepared to abandon the system of Voluntary combined with Board schools, which has been adopted in this country since 1870, and which, unless some great modification in the existing Board system is carried in this House, must remain the system of this country if the religious views of the great majority of the population are to be considered. Therefore, I venture to hope that my honourable Friend will withdraw his Amendment, and that we shall vote against the Resolution of the honourable Member for Carnarvon Borough, regarding that Resolution as a distinct challenge to the Voluntary schools, and the vote we now give as a distinct statement on our part that that system is one that has our uncompromising adhesion.

the House if I ask leave to withdraw my Amendment.

Amendment, by leave, withdrawn.

Main question put.

*MR. FOSTER: I shall probably consult the convenience of both sides of

The House divided:—Ayes, 81; Noes, 204.—(Division List No. 34.)

AYES.

Abraham, William (Rhondda)
Allison, Robert Andrew
Asquith, Rt. Hn. Herbert H.
Baker, Sir John
Barlow, John Emmott
Bayley, Thomas (Derbyshire)
Beaumont, Wentworth C. B.
Birrell, Augustine
Bolton, Thomas Dolling
Bryce, Rt. Hon. James
Buchanan, Thomas Ryburn
Buxton, Sydney Charles
Caldwell, James
Cawley, Frederick
Channing, Francis Allston
Clark, Dr. G. B. (Caithness-sh.)
Clough, Walter Owen
Colville, John
Davies, M. Vaughan(Cardigan)
Denny, Colonel
Dilke, Rt. Hon. Sir Charles
Evans, Sir Francis H.(South'ton)
Farquharson, Dr. Robert
Ferguson, R. C. Munro (Leith)
Fitzmaurice, Lord Edmond
Foster, Sir Walter (Derby Co.)
Fowler, Rt. Hon. Sir Henry
Goddard, Daniel Ford
Gold, Charles

Gourley, Sir Edwd. Temperley
Grey, Sir Edward (Berwick)
Haldane, Richard Burdon
Hayne, Rt. Hn. Charles Seale-
Hedderwick, Thomas Chas. H.
Horniman, Frederick John
Hutton, Alfred E. (Morley)
Jacoby, James Alfred
Joicey, Sir James
Kay-Shuttleworth, Rt Hn SirU.
Kearley, Hudson E.
Kitson, Sir James
Labouchere, Henry
Langley, Batty
Leuty, Thomas Richmond
Lewis, John Herbert
Lloyd-George, David
Logan, John William
Lough, Thomas
M'Laren, Charles Benjamin
Maden, John Henry
Mendl, Sigismund Ferdinand
Morgan, J. Lloyd (Carm'thn.)
Morley, Charles (Breconshire)
Moulton, John Fletcher
Norton, Capt. Cecil William
Oldroyd, Mark
Paulton, James Mellor
Perks, Robert William

Philipps, John Wynford
Pickard, Benjamin
Priestley, Briggs (Yorks)
Randell, David
Roberts, John H. (Denbighs.)
Robson, William Snowden
Schwann, Charles E.
Shaw, Charles Edw. (Stafford)
Shaw, Thomas (Hawick B.)
Sinclair, Capt. J. (Forfarshire)
Smith, Samuel (Flint)
Spicer, Albert
Stevenson, Francis, S.
Tennant, Harold John
Thomas, Abel(Carmarthen, E.)
Thomas, Alfd. (Glamorgan, E.)
Thomas, David Alfd. (Merthyr)
Wallace, Robert (Perth)
Walton, J. Lawson (Leeds, S.)
Whittaker, Thomas Palmer
Wilson, John (Durham, Mid)
Wilson, John (Govan)
Woods, Samuel

TELLERS FOR THE AYES.—Mr. Thomas Ellis and Mr. Causton.

NOES.

Allhusen, Augustus Henry Eden
Arrol, Sir William
Atkinson, Rt. Hon. John
Bagot, Capt. Josceline FitzRoy
Bailey, James (Walworth)
Balcarres, Lord
Baldwin, Alfred
Balfour, Rt. Hn. A. J. (Manch'r)
Balfour, Rt Hn Gerald W.(Leeds)
Banbury, Frederick George
Bartley, George C. T.
Barton, Dunbar Plunket
Bathurst, Hn. Allen Benjamin
Beach, Rt. Hn. Sir M.H.(Bristol)
Beckett, Ernest William
Bemrose, Sir Henry Howe
Bentinck, Lord Henry C.
Bethell, Commander
Bigwood, James
Bill, Charles
Blundell, Colonel Henry
Bond, Edward
Boscawen, Arthur Griffith-
Brassey, Albert
Brodrick, Rt. Hon. St. John

Burdett-Coutts, W.
Butcher, John George
Cavendish, V.C.W. (Derbysh.)
Cecil, Evelyn (Hertford, East)
Cecil, Lord Hugh (Greenwich)
Chaloner, Capt. R. G. W.
Chamberlain, J. Austen(Worc'r)
Chaplin, Rt. Hon. Henry
Charrington, Spencer
Cochrane, Hn. Thos. H. A. E.
Coghill, Douglas Harry
Cohen, Benjamin Louis
Collings, Rt. Hon. Jesse
Colston, Charles E. H. A.
Compton, Lord Alwyne
Condon, Thomas Joseph
Cook, Fred. Lucas (Lambeth)
Cornwallis, Fiennes Stanley W.
Cranborne, Viscount
Cripps, Charles Alfred
Curzon, Viscount
Dalkeith, Earl of
Davenport, W. Bromley-
Dickson-Poynder, Sir John P.
Disraeli, Coningsby Ralph

Doughty, George
Douglas, Rt. Hon. A. Akers-
Douglas-Pennant, Hon. E. S.
Doxford, William Theodore
Duncombe, Hn. Hubert V.
Egerton, Hon. A. de Tatton
Fergusson, Rt Hn. Sir J.(Manc'r)
Field, Admiral (Eastbourne)
Finch, George H.
Finlay, Sir Robert Bannatyne
Fisher, William Hayes
FitzGerald, Sir Robt. Penrose-
Flannery, Sir Fortescue
Folkestone, Viscount
Forster, Henry William
Foster, Harry S. (Suffolk)
Fry, Lewis
Garfit, William
Gedge, Sydney
Gibbons, J. Lloyd
Gibbs, Hn A.G.H.(City of Lond.)
Gilliat, John Saunders
Godson, Sir Augustus Fredk.
Goldsworthy, Major General
Gordon, Hon. John Edward

Gorst, Rt. Hn. Sir John Eldon
Gray, Ernest (West Ham)
Gretton, John
Greville, Hon. Ronald
Gull, Sir Cameron
Halsey, Thomas Frederick
Hanbury, Rt Hn. Robt. Wm.
Hatch, Ernest Frederick Geo.
Heath, James
Helder, Augustus
Hermon-Hodge, Robert Trotter
Hickman, Sir Alfred
Hoare, Ed. Brodie (Hampst'd.)
Hobhouse, Henry
Hornby, Sir William Henry
Hubbard, Hon. Evelyn
Hutchinson, Capt. G.W.Grice-
Hutton, John (Yorks., N.R.)
Jebb, Richard Claverhouse
Jenkins, Sir John Jones
Johnston, William (Belfast)
Johnstone, Heywood (Sussex)
Jolliffe, Hon. H. George
Kemp, George
Kenyon, James
Kilbride, Denis
Knowles, Lees
Lafone, Alfred
Laurie, Lieut.-General
Lawrence,SirE.Durning-(Corn)
Lawson, John Grant (Yorks.)
Lees, Sir Elliott (Birkenhead)
Leigh-Bennett, Henry Currie
Leighton, Stanley
Loder, Gerald Walter Erskine
Long, Rt. Hn. Walter (L'pool)
Lopes, Henry Yarde Buller
Lorne, Marquess of
Lowe, Francis William
Lowles, John
Loyd, Archie Kirkman
Lucas-Shadwell, William
Lyttelton, Hon. Alfred
Macaleese, Daniel
Macartney, W. G. Ellison

Macdona, John Cumming
MacIver, David (Liverpool)
Maclure, Sir John William
M'Arthur, Charles (Liverpool)
M'Calmont, H. L. B. (Cambs.)
M'Iver, Sir Lewis (Edin., W.)
M'Killop, James
Malcolm, Ian
Middlemore, John Throgmorton
Mildmay, Francis Bingham
Molloy, Bernard Charles
Moon, Edward Robert Pacy
Moore, Count (Londonderry)
Moore, William (Antrim, N.)
More, Robt. Jasper (Shropsh.)
Morgan, Hn. F. (Monm'thsh.)
Morrison, Walter
Morton, Arthur H. A. (Deptf'd)
Mount, William George
Muntz, Philip A.
Murray,Rt Hn.A.Graham(Bute)
Murray, Charles J. (Coventry)
Newdigate, Francis Alexander
Nicholson, William Graham
Nicol, Donald Ninian
Northcote, Hn. Sir H. Stafford
O'Brien, Patrick (Kilkenny)
O'Connor, Arthur (Donegal)
Orr-Ewing, Chas. Lindsay
Pease, Herbert Pike(Drlngtn.)
Pierpoint, Robert
Platt-Higgins, Frederick
Plunkett,Rt.Hn.HoraceCurzon
Powell, Sir Francis Sharp
Pretyman, Ernest George
Priestley,SirW.Overend(Edin.)
Pryce-Jones, Lt.-Col. Edward
Purvis, Robert
Pym, C. Guy
Ritchie,Rt.Hn.Chas.Thomson
Robertson, Herbert (Hackney)
Rothschild,Hn.Lionel Walter
Round, James
Royds, Clement Molyneux
Russell,Gen.F.S. (Cheltenham)

Russell, T. W. (Tyrone)
Sassoon, Sir Edward Albert
Savory, Sir Joseph
Scott,Sir S.(Marylebone,W.)
Seton-Karr, Henry
Sharpe, William Edward T.
Sidebottom, Wm. (Derbyshire)
Simeon, Sir Barrington
Sinclair, Louis (Romford)
Smith, Abel H. (Christchurch)
Smith, Hn. W. F. D. (Strand)
Stanley, Edwd. Jas. (Somerset)
Stanley, Lord (Lancs.)
Stewart, Sir Mark J.M'Taggart
Strutt, Hon. Charles Hedley
Sturt, Hon. Humphry Napier
Sullivan, Donal (Westmeath)
Talbot, Lord E. (Chichester)
Talbot,RtHnJ.G.(Oxf'dUniv.)
Thornton, Percy M.
Tritton, Charles Ernest
Valentia, Viscount
Ward, Hn. Robt. A. (Crewe)
Warde, Lt.-Col. C. E. (Kent)
Webster, R. G. (St. Pancras)
Webster, Sir R. E. (I. of W.)
Welby, Lieut.-Col. A. C. E.
Wentworth, Bruce C. Vernon
Whitmore, Charles Algernon
Williams, Jos. Powell (Birm.)
Willox, Sir John Archibald
Wilson, John (Falkirk)
Wilson-Todd,Wm.H.(Yorks.)
Wodehouse,Rt.Hn.E.R.(Bath)
Wortley, Rt. Hn. C. B.Stuart-
Wylie, Alexander
Wyndham, George
Wyndham-Quin, Major W. H.
Young,Commander(Berks,E.)

WILD BIRDS PROTECTION BILL.

Second Reading deferred till Tuesday next.

SHOPS (EARLY CLOSING) BILL.

Second Reading deferred till Tuesday next.

SHOPS BILL.

Adjourned Debate on Second Reading (21st February) further adjourned till Tuesday next.

PLACES OF WORSHIP (LEASEHOLD ENFRANCHISEMENT) BILL.

Second Reading deferred till Tuesday next.

SALE OF INTOXICATING LIQUORS ON SUNDAY BILL.

Second Reading deferred till Monday next.

SEATS FOR SHOP ASSISTANTS (SCOTLAND) BILL.

Second Reading deferred till Tuesday next.

PARISH COUNCILLORS (TENURE OF OFFICE) BILL.

Committee deferred till this day.

House adjourned at ten minutes after Twelve of the clock.

ERRATUM. — Division List No. 27 (pp. 1207-8).

Friday, 3rd March 1899.

General Power Distributing Company (Suspended) Bill [H.L.] (By Order).

In the Noes, leave out Johnston, William (Belfast).

HOUSE OF COMMONS.

Wednesday, 8th March 1899.

MR. SPEAKER took the Chair at Twelve of the clock.

PRIVATE BILL BUSINESS.

FISHGUARD AND ROSSLARE RAIL-
WAYS AND HARBOURS BILL.
Read a second time, and committed.

VALE OF GLAMORGAN RAILWAY BILL.
Read a second time, and committed.

NATIONAL TELEPHONE COMPANY
(No. 1).
Report (7th March) from the Select Committee on Standing Orders read.

Bill ordered to be brought in by Sir John Lubbock, Colonel Denny, Mr. David MacIver, and Mr. Perks.

NATIONAL TELEPHONE COMPANY
(No. 2).
Report (7th March) from the Select Committee on Standing Orders read.

Bill ordered to be brought in by Sir John Lubbock, Colonel Denny, Mr. David MacIver, and Mr. Perks.

PETITIONS.

CHURCH DISCIPLINE BILL.
Petition of the Scottish Women's Protestant Union, in favour; to lie upon the Table.

EDUCATION OF CHILDREN BILL.
Petition from Newport (Mon.), in favour; to lie upon the Table.

VOL. LXVIII. [FOURTH SERIES.]

GROUND RENTS (TAXATION BY LOCAL AUTHORITIES).
Petition from Llanguicke, in favour; to lie upon the Table.

LOCAL AUTHORITIES SERVANTS' SUPERANNUATION BILL.
Petitions in favour;—From Beckenham;—Birkenhead;—and Ham; to lie upon the Table.

PARLIAMENTARY FRANCHISE.
Petition from West Kensington, for extension to Women; to lie upon the Table.

POOR LAW RELIEF (DISFRANCHISE-
MENT).
Petition from Daventry, for alteration of Law; to lie upon the Table.

PUBLIC HEALTH ACTS AMENDMENT BILL.
Petitions in favour;—From Liverpool;—and Blackburn; to lie upon the Table.

ROMAN CATHOLIC UNIVERSITY IN IRELAND.
Petition from Poplar, against establishment; to lie upon the Table.

SALE OF INTOXICATING LIQUORS ON SUNDAY BILL.
Petitions in favour;—From Lingdale;—Gloucester (three);—Linton;—York (three);—Colyton;—Bedford;—Everton;—and East Barnet; to lie upon the Table.

SUPERANNUATION (METROPOLIS) BILL.
Petition from Islington, in favour; to lie upon the Table.

G

VACCINATION ACT, 1898.

Petition from Axminster, for alteration of Law ; to lie upon the Table.

Petition from St. Thomas, for repeal ; to lie upon the Table.

RETURNS, REPORTS, ETC.

ARMY (OFFICERS' SERVICE).

Return presented,—relative thereto (Address 23rd February ; *Sir Seymour King*) ; to lie upon the Table, and to be printed. (No. 90.)

NAVAL WORKS ACTS, 1895, 1896, AND 1897.

Account presented,—showing the amount of Money issued out of the Consolidated Fund ; the amount and nature of the Securities created in respect thereof ; the amount of the surplus of Income over Expenditure for the financial year ended 31st March 1896, and the amount of Money expended in pursuance of the Acts during the year ended the 31st March 1898 ; together with the Report of the Comptroller and Auditor-General thereon (by Act) ; to lie upon the Table, and to be printed. (No. 91.)

HIGH SHERIFFS (IRELAND) (EXPENSES OF OFFICE).

Copy presented,—of Circular addressed by the Lord Lieutenant to High Sheriffs with regard to the expenses of their Office, together with a Copy of the Letter of 2nd November 1898 from Her Majesty's Treasury upon which the Circular was based (by Command) ; to lie upon the Table.

CIVIL SERVICES (ADDITIONAL ESTIMATE, 1898-9).

Additional Estimate presented,—of the amount required in the year ending the 31st March 1899 for a Grant in Aid of the Expenses of the Royal Commission for the British Section at the Paris International Exhibition, 1900 (by Command) ; Referred to the Committee of Supply, and to be printed. (No. 92.)

PAPERS LAID UPON THE TABLE BY THE CLERK OF THE HOUSE.

---

1. Charitable Endowments (London),—Further Return relative thereto (ordered 2nd August 1894 ; *Mr. Francis Stevenson*) ; to be printed. (No. 93.)

2. Charity Commissioners' Reports, and Swansea County Borough (Inquiry into Charities) and Cardiff County Borough (Inquiry into Charities),—Further Return relative thereto (ordered 17th February 1896 and 31st July 1897 ; *Mr. Grant Lawson*) ; to be printed. (No. 94.)

3. Charitable Endowments (Anglesey) (Inquiries Held),—Further Return relative thereto (ordered 17th March 1896 ; *Mr. Grant Lawson*) ; to be printed. (No. 95.)

4. Endowed Charities (County of Norfolk),—Return relative thereto (ordered 16th February ; *Mr. Grant Lawson*) ; to be printed. (No. 96.)

FIRE BRIGADES.

Return ordered,

"Showing (1) the names of the Town Councils, Urban District Councils, Rural District Councils, Parish Councils, and Lighting Inspectors, who, as shown by the Local Taxation Returns, incurred expenditure in the year ended March 1898, in respect of Fire Brigades ; (2) the names of such Brigades ; (3) the total strength of each Brigade ; and (4) whether the Brigade is supported wholly or only partly out of the rates."—(*Mr. Pym.*)

ORDERS OF THE DAY.

SERVICE FRANCHISE BILL.

Order for Second Reading read.

Motion made, and Question proposed—

" That the Bill be now read a second time."

*Sir J. BLUNDELL MAPLE (Camberwell, Dulwich) : I rise to move the Second Reading of this Bill, the object of which is to prevent large classes of persons, such as the majority of the police in all districts, assistants in shops, warders and attendants in asylums, hospitals, workhouses, and other public establishments, stablemen, grooms, gardeners, and caretakers, being deprived of the franchise by reason of the restricted interpretation put on certain provisions of the Representation of the People Acts in a recent decision of the Court. Now, Sir, this is a very important Bill, because it does not only apply to London and all the large provincial towns, but it also applies throughout the whole of the United Kingdom to people such as gardeners, stablemen, grooms, and caretakers, and the other classes I have mentioned who are resident on the premises. It is necessary, perhaps, that I should explain why it has become necessary to pass this Bill. It is necessary because of the recent decision of the Court of Appeal, given in 1896. In 1884 the Representation of the People Act was passed, I think, by Mr. Gladstone, and from that time for about 10 years these different persons whom I have described were put on the registers, and they were allowed to vote on the Service Franchise. In 1895 an action was tried which is known as Clutterbuck v. Taylor, and then it was held by two judges in the Court of Appeal that a person occupying a cubicle in a room was not separately occupying a dwelling-house. Lord Justice Rigby, however, took a very different view altogether from his brother judges, and it is to maintain his opinion that this Bill is brought forward. If we go back to the time when this new Service Franchise was brought forward, Mr. Gladstone, very wisely I contend, recognised that there was a very large community of the people who were thoroughly entitled to the exercise of this franchise—who are, in fact, by their education and their position in society, better qualified to pass a judgment upon the affairs of the State than the agricultural labourer—and he, therefore, introduced what he was pleased to call the Service Franchise. Now, in that speech he said—

"This Service Franchise is a far-reaching franchise. It goes to men of high class who inhabit valuable houses as the officers of great institutions. It descends to men of humble class who are servants of the gentry or servants of the farmer, or the servants of some other employer of labour, who are neither owners nor tenants, and who, in many cases, cannot be held as tenants in connection with the essential conditions intended to be realised through their labours."

That clearly points to the fact that Mr. Gladstone recognised that what was necessary was simply that these men who were otherwise entitled to the franchise were not to be disqualified because they had in pursuing their employment to live on the premises. We all know in regard to policemen that it is necessary that they should live in barracks in connection with the police station, which is a very wise provision. It is also necessary that in establishments such as large business houses, where the employer does not live upon the premises, that some of the employees should live there; and those of us who are in the habit of employing a large number of this class of people know very well that it is much better and much more healthier that these men should live in large rooms—it is better for their morals, and they are quieter and better conducted when living in cubicles than when living two or three in a room together. We find this system goes on better, and so in country houses now it is being generally recognised. I know gentlemen in the country who lately have been building stables, and they have adopted this cubicle system for all their grooms, and they find it very much better than having them in rooms. Therefore, these cubicles are things to be encouraged. When you come to consider the number of these men, I believe myself that there are something like 100,000 of them at the present time who would be entitled to vote under the Service Franchise, but who, through the decision of the Court of Appeal in the case of Clutterbuck v. Taylor, are now unable to record their vote. Well, Sir, I think it will be well for me to review the whole of that case which was set out in a very clear way by Lord Justice Rigby. Those who have studied the Franchise Bill will see that in section 5 of the Parliamentary and Municipal Registration Act of 1878 a "dwelling-house" is defined as follows—

"In and for the purposes of the Representation of the People Act, 1867, the term 'dwelling-house' shall include any part of a house where that part is separately occupied as a dwelling-house."

The preceding paragraph of the same

section 5 of the Act of 1878 also defines the £10 business occupation franchise as—

"House, warehouse, counting-house, shop, or other building,"

including any part of a house where that part is separately occupied for the purpose of any trade, business, or occupation. It will be observed that both for the £10 business occupation franchise and the dwelling-house occupation franchise the definition given in section 5 is the same, namely—

"Any part of a house where that part is separately occupied."

Then, again, this seems an anomaly, more especially when the two paragraphs defining the occupation of a dwelling-house and of business premises are summed up by a third paragraph of the same section as follows—

"For the purposes of any Act referred to in this section, where an occupier is entitled to the sole and exclusive use of any part of a house, that part shall not be deemed to be occupied otherwise than separately by reason only that the occupier is entitled to the joint use of some other part."

This Bill is a very simple one. It does not create a new franchise, and if you turn to the Bill you will see that it is very simple and, in fact, a one-clause Bill. Clause 1 provides—

"Where a man himself inhabits any dwelling-house by virtue of any office, service, or employment, and the dwelling-house is not inhabited by any person under whom such man serves in such office, service, or employment, he shall be deemed for the purposes of the Representation of the People Acts to be an inhabitant-occupier of such dwelling-house as a tenant, and shall be entitled as such to be registered and to vote, notwithstanding that the dwelling-house which he occupies is merely a compartment of a room, and notwithstanding any control, restrictions, conditions, or disabilities whatsoever imposed on the occupation."

In the decision given by Lord Esher and Lord Justice Lopes, they say that nobody can apply for the franchise under the Service Franchise because in all cases there are some restrictions placed upon the people who have rooms given to them to live in in connection with their service. They are not allowed to have whom they like in these rooms, and they are not allowed to smoke in

Sir J. Blundell Maple.

them. They are supposed to go to bed at a certain time, so as not to disturb the neighbours. According to this decision all such restrictions as these would invalidate a person being entitled to the Service Franchise. Now, Lord Justice Rigby in his decision reviewed the case most thoroughly, and I would like the House to permit me to read his decision. In the course of his judgment in the case of Clutterbuck v. Taylor, he said—

"The question raised is, whether the appellant was an inhabitant occupier of a dwelling-house within the meaning of section 3 of the Representation of the People Act, 1884. He was, as I understood the statement made in the case, allowed, as a matter of fact, to occupy the cubicle during the whole of the qualifying period without interference. He had the key of the cubicle, and I gather that, when he was on night duty, he did, in fact, use it for sleeping in during the day, and, when he was on day duty, he used it for sleeping in at night. He used it, therefore, for sleeping in as occasion required; and it appears also that he was, in fact, allowed to take meals in it if he liked. Section 3 of the Representation of the People Act, 1884, says that 'where a man himself inhabits any dwelling-house by virtue of any office, service, or employment, he shall be deemed, for the purposes of this Act, to be an inhabitant occupier of such dwelling-house as a tenant.' In this case it cannot be said that the cubicle was inhabited by any superior under whom the appellant served. Assuming for the moment that cubicle was a 'dwelling-house' for the purposes of the Act, it appears to me that the appellant was an inhabitant occupier during the qualifying period. I cannot see that the existence of a power in the Chief Constable to make regulations or restrictions with regard to the use of the dwelling-house by the appellant has anything to do with the franchise given by the section, provided that he did in fact inhabit. The section says nothing about the nature of the inhabitancy, or as to how far it may or may not be subject to restrictions; and I think we ought to be very slow to insert limitations which the Legislature has not expressly mentioned. There are, we know, cases of large establishments where a great number of persons are employed who inhabit parts of a house by virtue of their employment, and who, in so inhabiting, must be subject to such directions as their masters choose to give. I cannot see that such directions, if actually given, could affect the existence of the franchise given by the section; and the mere fact that there was power to give directions which were not given appears to me to be quite beside the question. The truth is that the Service Franchise is essentially different from the other occupation franchises."

That is just what Mr. Gladstone said. Lord Justice Rigby goes on to say—

"It is not given in respect of any property in or right in respect of the place occupied.

It is assumed by the section that there is no such right. The person who occupies by virtue of his employment is not even in the position of a tenant at will. He is not a tenant at all, but simply a person who is permitted by his master to occupy, subject to such regulations, if any, as may be made by his master. Then, was the appellant the inhabitant occupier of a 'dwelling-house'? At first sight one would be disposed to say that this cubicle was a very different thing from a dwelling-house. But it is obvious that the extraordinary sense in which the term 'dwelling-house' is used in the Acts relating to the franchise includes things that are totally different from anything which would, in the ordinary use of language, be called a dwelling-house, because any part of the house will suffice if occupied as required by the Act. It need not be any particular part of a house, and it does not matter how small it may be. The extent or nature of the part occupied is immaterial so long as it is occupied separately as a dwelling. This cubicle was none the less part of the whole police barrack because it was part of a room in it. Whether it was what would ordinarily be called a dwelling-house is not the question. It was said that it shared the air and light common to the whole room. The Legislature appears to me to have dealt with that very consideration in section 5 of the Parliamentary and Municipal .Registration Act, 1878, which provides that, 'For the purpose of any of the Acts referred to in this section where an occupier is entitled to the sole and exclusive use of any part of a house, that part shall not be deemed to be occupied otherwise than separately, by reason only that the occupier is entitled to a joint use of some other part.' I can see no reason for cutting down the generality of those words, which appear to me to meet the contention based upon the enjoyment by the appellant of air and light common to the room of which his cubicle formed a part. In this case the appellant had the key of his cubicle without any interference during the whole of the qualifying period. It is true that, if occasion had arisen, his superior officer might have insisted on going into his cubicle for any purpose; but, as a matter of fact, he appears never to have done so. So that, if the appellant occupied this cubicle at all—and it appears to me clear that he did—his occupation was, in fact separate. Then, did he occupy it as a dwelling? I cannot find anything in the section which provides that, in order to come within it, the occupier must occupy with all the powers which a person would have in respect of a dwelling-house in the ordinary sense."

That is a very important statement, I think, and the House should bear it in mind. Continuing, Lord Justice Rigby says—

"The test, as it appears to me, is the nature of the occupation which has in fact taken place, not whether the occupier might have been ordered to occupy in a different manner. Considerable light is thrown on this question by the previous part of section

5, which provides that 'in and for the purposes of the Reform Act, 1832, and the Municipal Corporations Act, the terms 'house, warehouse counting-house, shop, or other building' shall include any part of a house where that part is separately occupied for the purpose of any trade, business, or profession.' If part of a house is, in fact, separately occupied for the purpose of a trade, business, or profession, the section says that part of a house is to be deemed to be a house. I think the term 'dwelling' is used in the section as an antithesis to 'trade, business, or profession.' I concede that there appears to have been an extensive power of interference with the use by the appellant of this cubicle. But in order that a man may be an inhabitant occupier he is not bound to show a title to occupy. He may have been a trespasser, or a tenant at will, or merely on sufferance. The only question is, did he in fact occupy as an inhabitant? With regard to that question whether the subject matter of the occupation was a dwelling-house, I concede, again, that the appellant had not the same rights as persons would have in the case of ordinary dwelling-houses. But the question appears to me to be not whether he had such rights, but whether he separately occupied part of a house as a dwelling. It seems to me that, whatever the powers of the Chief Constable may have been, these cubicles were the dwellings of these policemen, who occupied them by sleeping in them from day to day throughout the qualifying period. I cannot see that using them as sleeping places is anything else but occupying them as dwellings, although the occupants may not have been entitled to use them for other purposes for which people ordinarily use their dwellings. So far as it goes, I think sleeping in a place is using it as a dwelling. In point of fact, these policemen appear to have been allowed, if they liked, to take meals in their cubicles, and not to have been interfered with in the use of them in any way. There was, no doubt, the power of interfering with them; but I do not think that the existence of such a power is made by the Legislature the test. In my opinion, the question is whether they did in fact occupy part of a house as a dwelling, not whether they had a right to occupy in the same manner as ·that in which a person occupies a 'dwelling-house' in the ordinary sense of the term."

I am sorry to have detained the House so long in reading that judgment, but it seems to me to be very important. It is very ably argued, and it is to support the argument of Lord Justice Rigby and his position that this Bill has been brought forward. We look upon the House of Commons at all times as a House of justice, and the House of Commons has decided to accept this Service Franchise, which gives these men the right to vote; but there is no other appeal from the Court of Appeal to restore these men to their citizenship except in the House of Commons. The right honourable Baronet the Member for the Forest of Dean, who we all know is a man of advanced ideas, has often expressed himself that he wished that everybody should have the franchise given to them. I know that those are his sentiments, and they are the sentiments of other honourable Gentlemen on that side of the House, and also of honourable Gentlemen on this side of the House. Although we should not go so far as to say that everybody should have a vote, still we should like to see the Service Franchise altered. I contend that the right honourable Baronet ought not to try to obstruct this Bill in the way that he is doing by moving this Amendment, because this Measure goes towards simplifying the question, and does not tend to make it more confused. This Bill, I say, goes to simplify it, and I will explain why. Now, it is extremely difficult to have the franchise carried out properly because of the technicalities to which I have referred as regards the restrictions placed upon these men. [Laughter.] The right honourable Baronet laughs at that, but I would ask him to see my side of the question, and my side is this: at the present time if any restrictions whatever are placed upon the men by the masters in respect of the lodgings, even for stopping a man from smoking, or restricting him from going in and out of his habitation, after a certain time that man would not be allowed to be put on the register. That was the decision of Lord Esher and Lord Justice Lopes, if the right honourable Baronet will turn it up and examine it. No doubt the right honourable Baronet by-and-by will have an opportunity to criticise the remarks which I have made. The object of this Bill is not only to allow a man who occupies a cubicle which is to be considered as a dwelling-house to vote, but it also removes those restrictions which are placed upon him by his master, and whatever restrictions, conditions, or disabilities are imposed on the occupation. This is a very important thing, because I know there are in England at the present time, and in Scotland and Wales, and also in Ireland, a large number of men who are entitled to the Service Franchise who are put upon the register at the present moment, but who, I believe, after this

Sir J. Blundell Maple.

decision of Clutterbuck v. Taylor will have to come off if the law is not altered. It may be thought that it is an extraordinary thing that a Measure like this should have come from this side of the House, and that it ought to have come from the other side. I should have thought that the right honourable Baronet opposite and his friends on the Front Bench on the other side would have welcomed this extension of the franchise, which is simply carrying out or repairing, so to speak, the Representation of the People Act of 1884, which was not thoroughly carried out, and the wording of which was not such that the judges have been able to interpret as meaning what was the general intention when the Act was passed, and that was that the right should be given to these men to vote. I am convinced from conversations which I have had with Members of the Cabinet that the whole of those who sit on the Front Bench will support this Measure; for although we recognise that it will be a Measure which will put a large number of new electors on the list of opposite views to ourselves, at the same time it will put on a very large number of those who hold the same view as we do. It is not so much a question of what Party it affects, as it is the great question that these men are really qualified to use the suffrage; and to say that these men are not to have the vote, but are to wait until this millennium arrives which the right honourable Baronet may wish for is absurd. If ever Gentlemen opposite come back into power within the next ten years—and I doubt whether they will come back to power during that period—they would not be able to bring in a really new Bill giving universal suffrage, or even going so far as to repair the mistakes, the errors, or inequalities which exist at present. I acknowledge that the Representation of the People Act of 1894 has inequalities, and I should be the first to help other Members in trying to get those inequalities and other things readjusted. The question of the registration of votes wants to be inquired into, but here is one matter which I think can be satisfactorily settled by this Measure, for it will give to a large number of men who are thoroughly able and thoroughly qualified to express an opinion on the affairs which interest all

Englishmen the right to vote. I think, Sir, that this House will do well to accept the Bill. I do not say when we come to the Committee stage that it may not be necessary to alter some of the words. That question I do not deal with at the present moment. I do think that one of the Instructions put down by my honourable Friend on this side of the House may be, perhaps, considered out of order, and that is the question of Female Suffrage. But that is not a question which touches this Bill, because females generally have not votes. If the vote is given to them by-and-bye no doubt they would be equally entitled to a vote under the Service Franchise after this Bill is passed; but to suggest that this Bill should be hung up waiting for that to come about and waiting for the other questions with which my honourable Friends on the other side of the House would like to deal, I think would be a great injustice to a large and important body of men. I look upon the policemen of England as men who ought to be allowed to have some interest in the affairs of the State. We had a Bill passed some few years ago to enfranchise the policemen, but in consequence of the action that has been decided, unless you pass this Bill you give them with one hand the franchise and with the other hand you take it away from them by compelling policemen to live at the police station. It seems to me inconsistent and not at all right that you should do so. I know that the right honourable Baronet opposite, the year before last, in 1897, said that this question did not affect a very large number of policemen. Well, I have made inquiries, and I believe I am right in saying that half the policemen of England live in connection with the barracks in some shape or form.

*SIR C. DILKE (Gloucester, Forest of Dean): No, that is not so.

*SIR J. BLUNDELL MAPLE: I may be wrong, but it is a question I have made inquiries about, and that is what I have been informed. I do not know that I need detain the House any longer on this subject. It is a subject which we have heard of before in this House, for last year it was introduced by my honourable

Friend below me, but a few honourable Members on the other side of the House never neglect an opportunity of preventing this Bill from passing. I do not know why they should do so unless they fear that their own constituencies will be affected, and that their seat might become unsafe. As regards my constituency, I have no fear either one way or the other, because there are not such a large number of people in my Division under the Service Franchise. But this Bill was thoroughly discussed in 1897, and then my right honourable Friend the Member for the Forest of Dean brought forward the same Amendment as he brings forward now; but after we had discussed the question at some length, he withdrew his Amendment, and the Bill was read a second time. I trust that that may occur again, and that honourable Gentlemen will not, by their opposition, necessitate a Division, because I cannot see that either they themselves personally or their Party would gain anything by trying to prevent a large and important portion of the community to which I have already referred from being entitled to take part in the affairs of this great Empire. I beg to move the Second Reading of this Bill.

Amendment proposed—

"To leave out from the word 'That,' to the end of the Question, in order to add the words 'this House refuses to add to the complexity of our present franchise system, which, in its opinion, can be remedied only by the adoption of a single, simple, and uniform franchise' instead thereof."—(*Sir C. Dilke.*)

*SIR C. DILKE: The honourable Baronet, remarked, in the course of his speech, that the object of this Bill was contained in the terms of the Memorandum of the Bill itself, and I cannot, I think, do better than begin my remarks by calling attention to the terms of that Memorandum. Now, the terms of the Memorandum published on a Private Member's Bill are supposed to be under the authority of the Chair. Of course, it was impossible that you, Mr. Speaker, or anyone else acting on your behalf, could be responsible for the statements of facts contained in those Memoranda, and they must be taken on the responsibility of the Members who put them forward, unless some obvious

mis-statement is made in the Memorandum. Now, I do not think that I shall be saying anything disrespectful to the Chair when I say that some of the words in this Memorandum to the Bill before the House are not in the least justified by the actual condition of affairs, and I allude to the last matter mentioned by the honourable Baronet in the portion of the Memorandum which states that this Bill affects large classes of persons—"such as the majority of police in all districts." Now, I have to give the most unqualified denial to that statement. I have inquired into the case of my own constituency, and I find there that not one single constable is affected by this Bill. The Memorandum suggests that most of the police-constables who possessed the franchise after the passing of the Act of 1884, and who enjoyed the right to vote down to the year 1896, have had that right taken away from them by the judgment which was given in the Court of Appeal in that year. Well, not a single constable in my Division, who has not been moved too frequently, and who possessed the franchise from 1884, has lost the franchise by the decision of the Court of Appeal, and there is no reason whatever to apprehend that they are going to lose it, and I have no reason to believe that my Division is peculiar in that respect. Now, Sir, I may add, with regard to what the honourable Member said about the effect of the Bill on the seats of honourable Members on this side of the House, who are opposed to this Measure on principle, that I may extend the observations which I have just made with regard to voters generally. Not one single service voter lost the franchise in 1897 through the decision of the Court of Appeal in my Division, and I have no reason to think that this is an exceptional state of things; and I am sure that this decision has not had any such far-reaching effects as the honourable Baronet has suggested to the House. The honourable Member has given us the history of the Service Franchise, and I should like the opportunity of saying a word or two with regard to that question, because it so happens that I had something to do with this Service Franchise when it was adopted. It was suggested by Sir George Trevelyan during the preliminary discussion on the Bill of 1884, in order

Sir C. Dilke.

to meet the case of the Scotch shepherds, because it was supposed that in Scotland there were a number of people in the same position as the agricultural labourers, who were enfranchised by that Bill, but who for technical reasons would not receive the franchise unless this provision was put in. The practical effect of this clause was to enfranchise in some constituencies a considerable number of those shepherds, but its principal effect was to enfranchise a great number of coachmen and a certain number of shop assistants and policemen under orders of the kind described. The honourable Member has assumed that the judgment of the Court of Appeal, if carried into effect, will disfranchise the service voters under the restrictions mentioned in his Bill, but I do not read it in that manner. I confess, after having read that judgment carefully more than once, that it appears to me that the structural nature of the term "dwelling-house" was the main ground of the judgment given in the Court of Appeal. Then there is the clause taken from the Parliamentary and Municipal Registration Act of 1878, which I had the honour of conducting through this House. That clause was intended not to alter the law, but merely to state the law, although some persons were under the impression that this clause actually changed the law. But whether it did or not it was intended to carry out Mr. Goschen's Act in Amendment of Mr. Disraeli's Reform Act. Dwelling-house was made to include "any part of a house separately occupied as a dwelling," while, separately was defined to mean that "the occupier was entitled to the sole and exclusive use of his part," but was "not disqualified by the fact of being entitled to the joint use of any part." If the House wishes to extend the term "dwelling-house" in such a way as to include the compartments which are mentioned in this Bill, I suggest to the House that the proper way to do it would be by altering the definition of dwelling-house; but here the whole thing is governed by the title and scope of the Bill, which extends the term to servants only but refuses and denies it to all those persons who are not servants. That is to say, that a man who pays rent and who is his own master, and who is not under any of these restrictions, but who lives in exactly similar cubicles to those mentioned by the honourable Baronet, will not have the franchise if this Bill passes. You cannot cure this defect, because the title and scope of the Bill make it so clearly an amendment of the Service Franchise that no Instruction to extend the Bill in this way to admit the large self-governing class of persons who are in the same position as the persons to whom the Bill applies would be in order. Now, Sir, many of us on this side of the House are willing to give the franchise to anybody, or, at all events, to establish it on a very wide and simple basis; but our complaint against the honourable Baronet is that this Measure will introduce a complicated element into the Service Franchise, and add to our franchises of which I believe there are 18 already. He has begun to tamper with this question by a proposal affecting one small class only, namely, those under certain conditions of service. Of course, if this Bill passes thousands of heads of families in exactly the same position will be excluded from the franchise, while this particular class of servants alone will be included. Let the House consider for a moment what the effect of this will be to a certain class—take the ordinary case of a workman in such a constituency as I represent. Those who are not freeholders, but occupiers, live, as a rule, two families in one house. The head of one of these families is without the franchise, and the head of the other is enfranchised, almost accidentally as compared with the other, and this state of things will continue under this Bill. Now, that man cannot get on as a lodger because he does not pay £10 a year, nor can he get on as a joint tenant because the house is not of sufficient value to come up to £20 a year, which is necessary to be divided by two in order to put two heads of families on the register for one house. Think how unfair that would be to those people to pick out a class of people, who are generally unmarried, who live under the restrictions prescribed for in this Bill, and leave all these tremendous restrictions excluding all those heads of families in this country from the franchise altogether. Now, with regard to the actual terms of the Bill itself, the honourable Gentleman has referred to the technicalities of the law, and he says that, by his

Bill, he is simplifying the law. Now, my honourable and learned Friend who is sitting above the Gangway (Mr. R. Wallace, Perth) has been a revising barrister, and I should like to ask his judgment as to whether this Bill will simplify the law. It is the great object of many of us to simplify the law, because the complaints from both sides of the House and from voters throughout the country as to the complexity of the Registration laws, are not really complaints against the Registration Acts or against registration officials and the revising barristers. It is the fault of Parliament, by the complexity of its franchises, that has made all this enormous expenditure on registration necessary by super-posing one franchise upon another. This Bill goes very far in that direction. It intends to apply to the case of cubicles, but it does not go to the root of the question. Persons who inhabit cubicles which go up to the ceilings of the room have the franchise, but the Court of Appeal has decided that persons whose cubicles do not go to the ceiling and have common light, and where the cubicle is formed by a small partition, do not separately inhabit a dwelling-house. The honourable Member tries to get over that difficulty in this way. His Bill says that where a man inhabits any dwelling-house, and that dwelling-house is not a dwelling-house but a compartment, then, if he is a servant, but not otherwise, he shall vote. He tries to get over the difficulty by introducing a new word—" compartment "; but, of course, he does not define that word ; in fact, he leaves it to the Courts ; and we shall have this going to the Court, and to the Court of Appeal, to decide what is a compartment within the meaning of this Act if it passes. The Bill goes on to enact that the franchise shall be given

"Notwithstanding that the dwelling-house which he occupies is merely a compartment of a room, and notwithstanding any control, restrictions, conditions, or disabilities whatsoever imposed on the occupation."

That is a very strong phrase, and the words are absolutely sweeping in their effect. We desire to enfranchise everybody, but we do object to specially picking out for extraordinarily favoured treatment the particular class of servants who are under the strict conditions and limitations of employment. Just consider how this Bill, if it comes into effect, will work. Take some of the rural districts with which I· am acquainted, where the farmers employ a good class of labourers living in the farm house, and a less good class who are provided with accommodation in barns. Why, it will be absolutely at the discretion of the farmer to pick and choose among these people, and enfranchise those whom he desires should have a vote and refuse the franchise to others. The man has got to be in the occupation of this separate dwelling-house, which is now to be called a compartment, and he has got to be in occupation of that separate dwelling-house from July to July before he can be placed upon the register which comes in force on 1st January after. The farmer has only got to break the occupation of that man by sending him upon a job; the honourable Member or any employer of labour of this kind has only to send a man to another job to prevent him getting on the register for two and a half years. A man sent on a job in August and breaking his occupation cannot get on the list again for two and a half years. Then, again, it will be a matter of the greatest difficulty to give evidence as to the moving of these people during the qualifying period from July to July, and it will also be a matter of the greatest difficulty and the greatest cost to those who have to take part in the registration work. Now, with a simple extension of the franchise to all these classes none of these difficulties would arise, while this Measure is creating enormous difficulties and opening the door to fraud. This Bill, of course, can be best considered by those who can bring to bear upon it lawyer-like knowledge of its construction in the way it was considered a few years ago by the late Attorney-General, who, in his speech upon that occasion, subjected a similar Bill to this to a severe criticism, and showed the reason why, in his opinion, it should not be passed into law. But you cannot cure the defect of the Bi'l, for it enfranchises these persons at the sole will of the employer, who can give the franchise to those whom he chooses, and not give it to those whom he desires to refuse the vote. If the honourable Members whose names are on the back of this Bill desire to do that which the shop assistant class desire—and I believe

Sir C. Dilke.

the mover of this Bill is greatly interested in shop assistants—they will find upon inquiry among the shop assistants that what they desire is not this Bill, but a wide and simple franchise from which that class has more to gain than any other class, because they are the least represented class of all persons in this country from the peculiar conditions of their employment. They do not like these conditions and restrictions which are laid down in the Bill, for they dislike the living-in system altogether. Now, surely, if the franchise is to be dealt with at all, it clearly ought to be dealt with on the responsibility of the Government, and should be dealt with in the most intelligible way. We have, I think I said before, 18 franchises, and of those 18 franchises we have 11 which are in common operation. There are five included in the ownership list. There are two occupation ordinary franchises, the £10 occupation and ordinary occupation; there is the service franchise, the lodger franchise, the parochial franchise, and the municipal franchise. There are 11 of these 18 franchises in common and active operation, and all of them have their own peculiar incidence and technicalities. Our contention is that the time has come when the Government must face the difficulty of these franchises. You cannot deal with them by disfranchising any class. The country will not tolerate a retrograde movement of that description, and you can only deal with the matter by a universal or manhood franchise ; by franchise on a simple basis. This would get rid of the whole difficulty, and I believe that no Party would suffer in any way from the simplification of the franchise. Under the present franchises a great number of the very best people in the country are excluded from a vote, and the time has come when the simplification of the franchise is necessary. Whether you should go to universal or only to manhood suffrage is a question upon which I should not be in order in discussing details ; but, as a first step, the simplification of the franchise among men is a matter which we must deal with, and it is useless to deal with this matter by frittering Bills of this description. The time has come when we must sweep away all these artificial distinctions, and deal with this question in a broad and intelligent manner.

*CAPTAIN NORTON (Newington, W.):
In support of the Motion of my right
honourable Friend the Member for the
Forest of Dean, I desire to bring one
point prominently before the attention
of the House, and that is this: the proposal before the House evidently seeks to
depart from the great principle upon
which all our franchises in the past were
granted. It strikes at the root of the
great principle of property qualification.
Now, we who sit upon this side of the
House are not in favour of property qualification. I myself am not only in favour
of manhood suffrage; but I am in favour
of adult suffrage, for the simple reason
that when you come to deal with all
these anomalies, you will have to go to
adult suffrage for the remedy. At the
present time you have women's suffrage
in parochial affairs. But I do not wish to
deal with that aspect of the question; I
merely wish to point out to the House
that anything short of a simple uniform
suffrage only multiplies the difficulties
and intricacies which surround this important question. Now, the last great
Measure, the Representation of the
People Act of 1884, upon which our
present franchise is based, never attempted to touch the question of
property qualification. The honourable
Baronet who introduced this Bill has attempted to show the House that the Service Franchises had nothing as to any
property qualification in them.

*SIR J. BLUNDELL MAPLE: I only
quoted Mr. Gladstone.

*CAPTAIN NORTON: Whether that is
the opinion of Mr. Gladstone or whether
it is the opinion of the honourable
Baronet himself I do not know,
but I maintain that the object
of Service Franchise was this, to
give to that man who was a servant
that right which he would have had
if he had not been a servant. The
man who had an occupation—a £10
occupation, and would have had the
franchise as a householder, had he not
by accident lived under these conditions.
Even that franchise is based on the question of rateable value. The object with
which the Service Franchise was given
was, in a great measure to obviate fraud
and also to secure identification, and if
you cannot secure identification, and that
is the object of the rateable value, you

immediately open the door to a new
fraud—a fraud, let me point out to the
House, which, in its turn, will generate a
whole family of other frauds. Now, the
House knows to what extent that occurred with reference to the franchise
after this Bill of 1884 was passed.
Certain registration agents belonging to
both Parties, smart registration agents,
sought, as all agents will do, to do the
best they could do for their employers.
They attempted, as it were, to make this
Act elastic. I will not say that they attempted to drive a coach and four
through it, but they endeavoured to place
upon the register every man who, by
hook or by crook, could be placed upon
it. That is to say, they attempted to
place upon the register those who
it was never intended by this Act should
be placed upon it. And, in the end, a
conflict having arisen, they appealed to
the Courts and obtained certain judgments, and at length a great legal lumin-
ary, who was also a Member of this
House, though honourable Members will
admit that he must have shone to a
greater extent in courts than he did here,
decided in favour of the registration
agent's contention. And this is a Bill to
uphold the decision of Lord Justice
Rigby, as against the judgments of Lord
Justice Lopes and Lord Esher. It is a
Bill to uphold the judgment of one particular judge of the Court of Appeal. As
regards the object of the Bill, the object,
as I understand it, is to extend the franchise, not to a particular class, but to a
particular section of a particular class.
It is to extend the franchise, not to shop
assistants as a whole, but to a portion of
shop assistants. It is scarcely worth
while to deal with the question of the
police. We know that throughout the
country the rural police all have a vote
at the present moment, as the right honourable Baronet the Member for the
Forest of Dean has shown, and so far as
London is concerned—I have a large
number of constables in my constituency,
over 400, and I know that of those 400
not more than 10 or 12 are deprived of
the vote in the manner suggested, and
that out of the 14,000 police in the
county of London not more than
say some three per cent. are deprived of
their vote in consequence of the
law which it is now proposed to
change. There are other classes, such as
grooms and so forth, but the number of

those who lose their votes in consequence of the present law is infinitesimally small. This is an artificial franchise, to deal with a favoured few to the exclusion of the working classes throughout the kingdom, and it operates most adversely so far as London is concerned, inasmuch as one of the features of London labour life is the migration of the people. People migrate at a rate of some 30 per cent. per annum, and the working men in consequence are constantly deprived of their franchise. With all this in view, I consider that a Bill which favours a small section of a class, but which leaves these people out of the list, will manifestly do a great injustice to the working classes. The Bill would add confusion to the perplexities of the present system, and would generate fraud and create bad distinctions, and would lead to a vast amount of litigation. When lawyers attempted to define the meaning of the term dwelling-house it was certainly difficult enough, but when you come to define the meaning of compartment it is to base the franchise on a board partition, or a paper partition, or a curtain which extends to the ceiling. Why not carry that argument out *ad infinitum* to its logical conclusion, and make it a chalk mark on the floor. If you do that, the whole thing is reduced to a state of absurdity. If you deal with it in that way, you arrive at the solution, and the proper solution, of a simple and uniform franchise, with manhood suffrage. This Bill again appears to place the whole power in the hands of the employers, because the overseer is bound to accept the list handed to him by the employer. The registration agents and the revising barristers are equally in the dark, and the agents can make no inquiry as regards the occupation of these men, and still less can they make inquiries as to whether they have been a sufficient time in occupation or not. We all know what a smart registration agent can do for his employer, and I venture to assert that a smart registration agent going into 40 out of the 60 constituencies in the area of the county of London for one or two years prior to an election— provided he had sufficient funds at his disposal for registration and organisation —could get the great bulk of the voters upon his side of the register. I say, without the slightest hesitation, that where the parties are supposed to be equally

Captain Norton.

divided he could, even as the law at present stands, make the register so favourable towards one particular candidate as to carry the election in his favour.

AN HONOURABLE MEMBER : No, no.

*CAPTAIN NORTON : I have a great deal of practical knowledge of this question, more so than a good many Members of this House, and I venture to assert that, not only can that be done, but that it is done in many constituencies of the present day. I think this Bill would enlarge the field for fraud to a degree which cannot by any means now be appreciated. I will give point to my case. First of all, the list of objections to the claims which are made by voters will be something enormous, and will involve the candidates in considerable expense. It would not be possible without large funds to successfully oppose all these claims, and in that case you would put the poor candidate at the mercy of the rich candidate. If this Bill is brought in, you make the Corrupt Practices Act very much less operative than it is at the present time, and you will enable a man who has money to go down to the constituency of a poor candidate and beat him right out of the field. That is something which the working men of London will bitterly resent. Take a case in point: there is nothing to prevent a registration agent going down to a working-class district in London within a year or two of an election. There is nothing to prevent a smart agent co-operating with the owners of tenements of houses, with publicans, and with owners of refreshment houses, and so on, and with employers who employ a large number of shop assistants and getting these men to create votes. It may be thought that that would be a difficult matter, because there is the qualification period to be considered, but we all know the gross frauds in that particular which take place now with regard to lodgers' qualification. It will be easier to do that when this Measure is passed than it is now. Then there is another thing of which I can give an example. If this Measure is passed you will have young men who happen to be shop assistants —living in a cubicle, the value of which is from 1s. to 2s., roughly speaking, and which they get as part payment of their wages—upon the register. Now, some of these young men, having obtained slightly higher wages, become married men or wish for greater comfort, and they go out into the cheap suburbs in London, and obtain lodgings, for which they pay 3s. to 4s., and by so doing they are not entitled to vote, which they previously exercised; but their younger brothers, paying a small sum for living in these cubicles, are entitled to their vote. This is to give the franchise to the less experienced and younger men, and men who are controlled by their employers, in preference to those uncontrolled and independent men who by the same means you deprive of the franchise. There is another point to which I might allude. My right honourable Friend the Member for the Forest of Dean says that you have 11 forms of franchise in common operation, and you add to this a 12th, in order to make confusion worse confounded; but apart from this you place a very great power in the hands of the employer. Take a large employer in London who employs hundreds of shop assistants, there is nothing to prevent him from forming two houses, one of his own political complexion in which he puts these cubicles, and the other of a different political complexion in which he does not, so that he could come at times of election and claim the franchise with regard to one building and disfranchise entirely the other class. I may be told that no employer is likely to do this. That may be so, but at the same time it is not right and proper that such a power should be placed in the hands of any man. This is in effect a class enfranchisement Bill; and a Bill which will do some small measure of justice to a small class, but will do a very great injustice to a class, not 10, but 40, 60 times as large—inasmuch as the political power in the country is lessened for the one class as the other is increased. These men will be deprived of the vote, because they do not happen to live under the control of their employers, and it is being brought in to give political power to a large number of shopkeepers and other employers who hold a large number of votes in their own hands, and may make use of that power at the time of any election. I beg leave to second the Motion of my honourable Friend.

Amendment proposed:—To leave out all after "That," in order to insert—

"This House refuses to add to the complexiy of our present franchise system, which can only be remedied by the simple and uniform franchise."

Question put:—That the words proposed to be left out stand part of the Question.

*MR. MARKS (Tower Hamlets, St. George's): I am happy to find myself in agreement with the honourable and gallant Member who has just spoken upon this one point. I agree that the Bill will do a small measure of justice. That is all we claim for it. It is not the idea of the promoters of this Bill that it will set right all the wrongs of the present system of the franchise. It is not denied by the promoters of the Bill that great difficulties and inequalities and some conspicuous injustice exist in the present system, and I have no doubt that there would be found on this side of the House a strong desire to support honourable Gentlemen on the other side if they had been disposed at any time to introduce a Measure to do away with these inequalities and rectify this injustice. But we have not to deal with the general question of franchise to-day, though one might suppose so from the speeches that have been made. It is not proposed by this Bill that we should enter into that large controversy which has been opened up by the right honourable Baronet the Member for the Forest of Dean upon this subject, because this Bill is said to extend favourable treatment to a certain class. It has been said that it deals only with servants. It has been said that it is a Measure to benefit the few to the detriment of the many. Sir, the fact has been entirely lost sight of that this Bill is only introduced for the purpose of restoring a right which has recently been taken away—a right which existed and which was practised and practically unquestioned for some 12 years—from 1884 down to the time of the decision of the Court of Appeal—a decision, by the way, which was not unanimous in 1896. The people who are to benefit by this Bill actually did benefit; they had the right which this Bill seeks to restore, not to confer upon them, of exercising the franchise, and it seems, therefore, hardly fair that the Bill should be debated as-if it were being introduced for the purposes of conferring a new franchise. So far as the right honourable Baronet the Member for the Forest of Dean is concerned, we hear from him that no one has lost a vote in his constituency by reason of the decision of the Court of Appeal, and we can, therefore, understand that he does not sympathise very much with this Bill; and the honourable Gentleman the Member for Newington Division said that a very few votes had been lost in his constituency, therefore we cannot expect any very warm support from him in this matter; but his assertion that by this Bill fraud will be rendered ten times more easy than it is at present suggests that the number of votes actually affected in his constituency must be considerable. Now, as to the question of fraud, it seems to me that the House of Commons seldom passes a Bill—that the Legislature seldom enacts a law which does not create an opportunity for a new illegality to be practised. You may make your statutes as strict as you will, and your laws as biting as you can, but you will inevitably find in every case evil-disposed persons to take unfair advantage of the law when it is enacted. If the Legislature is to limit its operations to the passing of Acts which cannot by any means be evaded, then the law-making business of this House will be very materially reduced. I do not say that that would be a very regrettable thing; but it is a matter to be contemplated. It is true that this Bill does only deal with servants, because servants were the only people affected by the decision of the Court of Appeal which has made this Bill necessary. I quite understand that this Measure affords an opportunity for honourable Gentlemen who sit upon the other side of the House to come forward with new proposals with regard to universal suffrage, or uniform suffrage—an opportunity which has not been lost, but the arguments adduced to-day in favour of universal suffrage are somewhat weakened by the suggestion that if this Bill is passed there would not be any means of identifying the voters. So far, honourable Gentlemen who have advocated universal suffrage have not pointed out how they propose to identify the voters under that system.

Mr. Marks.

The fact that the promoters of this Bill do not attempt to remedy all the wrongs which now exist is no reason why we should not do what we can to restore a right recently taken away, and which was up to 1896 enjoyed by these people under the Act. The objection has been taken with regard to this Bill that it gives power to employers to enfranchise or disfranchise, or, as an honourable Gentleman on the other side has said, to pick and choose. I venture to suggest that that is possible now. The employer can turn his bedrooms into cubicles, or cubicles into separate rooms, as defined by the Court of Appeal, to suit himself. But it is equally true that unscrupulous landlords may renew, or may refuse to renew, terminable leases, in view of an election that is going to take place, and so take away from their tenants the right to vote at that election. You cannot by this or by any other Measure make a man honest by Act of Parliament, and it seems to me it is a very weak argument to say that you will not restore the right to the service voter because by restoring that right you may put the power into the hands of his employer to do something which is dishonest. It has also been said that the effect of the passage of the Bill would be to place in the hands of a very large number of people who have no stake, no interest in the country, a right to vote. That argument does not come with much force from the advocates of manhood suffrage. Those who benefit under this Bill would certainly not have less interest in the country than the majority of voters under a system of universal suffrage. The 12 months' occupation would be extended to them just as it is to other classes. The Act of 1884 lays down that this particular class of voters shall have the right to vote. That right it was the intention of Parliament to confer upon them—that right was conferred upon them, and it was exercised for the most part unchallenged, and in cases where it was challenged the right was upheld until this decision came in 1896. All the Bill asks the House to do is to restore the practice upset by that decision, to give effect to the plain and obvious intention of the House when it passed that Act, and to remedy the wrong which has fallen upon these people, not by the action of this

House, and not by the deliberate intention of this House, but by the mere accidental interpretation of a technical point in the law in the case of Clutterbuck v. Taylor.

MR. WALLACE (Perth): I think everyone must recognise the grievance which this Bill is intended to deal with, and having had a good deal of practical experience upon this subject, I venture to ask the House to allow me to say a few words upon it. For some 10 years I have had practical experience as a revising barrister for London and Middlesex, and I do not agree with the honourable Baronet the Member for the Forest of Dean as to the operation of the change itself. He assumes that it will affect a very small class of the community. I can say from practical experience that it will involve thousands of those in London and Middlesex. The honourable Gentleman who supported him said that no policemen in his district were disfranchised by the operation of the law. Now, it was my unfortunate duty to strike off year after year thousands of policemen in different districts. I make these observations because I think we ought to approach this subject with accurate information as to the circumstances of the case. I will go even further than that, and say that under the Act many of the policemen and other classes were put upon the roll of voters, and many of them since the decision of the Court of Appeal in 1896 have lost their votes. That is the position of things, as has been related by the honourable Gentleman who moved this Bill, and I believe that thousands of voters have been struck off the roll by the decision of Clutterbuck v. Taylor. They have not, as the honourable Gentleman who has just spoken said, lost any right which legislation conferred upon them, but they have lost a privilege which the revising barristers allowed, which they exercised for many years until the decision of the Court of Appeal. That is the first position which I wish to take up before this House. There is sometimes a great deal of loose description as to what the Service Franchise was, as it was originally understood by those who interpreted the Act. It was to give the franchise to those who were residing by reason of their employment on the premises of their employers,

after a certain period of occupation. Now I am bound to say this, that I think most revising barristers, in their desire to extend so far as possible the rights of citizenship to the inhabitants of a district, carried as far as they could the interpretation of the clause, and perhaps ventured to carry it a little further than the Act intended. The opinion was very strongly expressed that where you had got a cubicle in the definite occupation of a particular individual it was exclusively occupied by him; that under the definition which had been given as to what was a dwelling-house it became, in fact, a dwelling-house, and it did not depend in any way on the height of the partition, whether it was a foot from the ground or 10 feet from the ground. Carrying that view out to its logical conclusion, many of us held that if you could find the adequate space in a room in the exclusive possession of one person, whether it was partitioned off or whether it was marked out with a permanent chalk line, it became a dwelling-house within the meaning of the Act, and I, for one, see no objection to that view being taken in any shape or form. I very well remember being in communication with the police authorities, and I pointed out to them the effect of the existing system, that in large dormitories, without putting up a partition or marking a permanent mark to the space occupied by each man, they were disfranchising hundreds of policemen in London. I do not know for what reason, whether on the ground of ventilation, or sanitation, or any other reason, but they declined in many cases to erect these partitions, and as a result in many districts the police were not placed upon the roll. In other districts the police authorities, in their desire to see that their men had their political rights, did erect these partitions and make these distinctions, and as a result thousands of policemen and thousands of other men were placed upon the roll of voters. Now I say, in the face of what was decided by the Court of Appeal, that in what we have done we were all wrong, and that, therefore, these men have not lost a right which they were entitled to exercise, though they have lost, by the decision of the Court of Appeal, a privilege which they had exercised without objection for years. In consequence of that decision they lost that which they supposed to be a right. Take the case of the Greenwich pensioner as an instance. He had been for years placed upon the roll, but last year my Friend, who acts as revising barrister in that district, found himself compelled to strike all these men off the roll. I say at once that while I recognise this grievance, I do not follow my right honourable Friend the Member for the Forest of Dean in what he has said. I speak from practical experience, and I say that the class to which he referred is a very small class compared with the hundreds of thousands who are excluded, by the operation of our law, from exercising that right to which they are clearly entitled. Now I notice this in connection with this Bill, that the honourable Gentleman does not provide in his Bill a clause that the employer shall be non-resident. I think he can scarcely understand what the effect of that is. If he is resident on the premises it will disfranchise many of those who are resident there. Might I tell the House the practice in these matters? It is a very common thing to find manufacturers and warehousemen who are on the roll by reason of the £10 occupation clause disfranchised because they happen to reside beyond the seven-mile limit. Under the recent Act and all the other Acts they are obliged to reside within seven miles from London. This Bill will not affect in any way those thousands; they will still be disfranchised, and they will find themselves, under this Bill, through no fault of their own, in the same position.

*Sir J. BLUNDELL MAPLE: I will at once tell my honourable Friend that I will endeavour to alter that part of the Bill after we have got the Second Reading.

Mr. WALLACE (Perth): I take the Bill as it stands for the purpose of showing how it operates; and may I ask my honourable Friend how he proposes to carry out the Amendment he suggests? In many parts of London you have resident employers—I do not speak merely of those business men who live in the country and keep a bed-room in their premises in the City—but men who have one or two employees in the occupation of a portion of their employer's dwelling. These men are just as respectable and

Mr. Wallace (Perth).

just as entitled to the franchise as the class which the honourable Baronet wishes to enfranchise. Will the honourable Baronet make his Amendment so wide as to include all these? I want to invite an expression of opinion, for I shall point out to him what practical difficulties will immediately stare him in the face. If he does not respond to the invitation it is not necessary for me to go further on that point. I am certain that the honourable Baronet is desirous of seeing the large class of persons in whom he is interested enfranchised, but I would like to believe that he is equally anxious that the other classes of men to whom I refer, and who by the operation of the existing Registration law, have no votes, should also be placed on the electoral roll. Permit me to give an illustration, to let the House understand that we are only dealing with the fringe of a large question by this Bill. Any one who knows anything of the central districts of London, knows that there is a class of men who are known as house-farmers. These men take several houses and let them out room by room to different families. The house-farmer resides in one of these houses, occupying the basement for the purpose of carrying on some trade or business, and where he sleeps. I ask the honourable Baronet is it fair or right, where there are two houses side by side, owned by the same house-farmer, in which the same class of people are resident, that every occupant of rooms in the house in which the landlord resides should be disfranchised while every occupant of a room in the house next door is placed on the electoral roll? But I would go further, and point out one of the most extraordinary anomalies in our electoral law I have ever known. If a house-farmer occupies number 1 house to-day and in the middle of the year changes his occupation and moves into number 2 and resides in the basement there, the lodgers and occupiers alike in both houses are disfranchised. Now, does the honourable Baronet think that is a just or a fair system?

*Sir J. BLUNDELL MAPLE: No, I do not.

Mr. WALLACE (Perth): The honourable Baronet does not think it right or fair. Well, does he think it fair and right that. if a lodger by the improvement of his circumstances is enabled to acquire the occupation of the entire house instead of only one room in it, the revising barrister has no option in the existing state of the law but to strike him off the register simply because he has increased the number of rooms he occupies? I am quite certain that the honourable Baronet will agree that as a man grows in prosperity he grows in wisdom; but here is the case of a man who increases in prosperity to such an extent that he not only keeps on the original room which he occupied and for which he had a vote, but takes the occupation of the whole house, and the result is that he cannot get a certificate of occupation as a lodger and is struck off the register. I have no desire to intrude at any length on the attention of the House, but I could give illustration after illustration showing that under the existing system of our Registration laws, not hundreds, nor even thousands, but tens of thousands of these people are disfranchised all over London.

An HONOURABLE MEMBER: No injustice is done to them.

MR. WALLACE (Perth): No injustice done to them! Is it not an injustice that of two men living side by side, under exactly the same conditions—you are to enfranchise the one and refuse enfranchisement to the other? That is an injustice against which we are protesting. It is not an injustice to a few poor people, but a gross injustice to tens of thousands of people who ought to be on the electoral roll. I have the strongest sympathy with the honourable Baronet and his Bill, but I wish exceedingly that he could have seen his way to go much further. From the position he holds, he, in common with his friends, might have brought influence to bear on the Government which we on this side of the House cannot pretend to do, and have pointed out to them that not merely in this respect, but in many others, the Registration laws should be so altered as to make a very valuable reform. If the honourable Baronet were to do so I am sure he would have the enthusiastic support of every man on this side of the House. It is because you are picking out a few hundreds here and there to grant them the franchise and excluding hundreds of thousands who are equally entitled to the franchise, that I find myself in the posi-

VOL. LXVIII. [FOURTH SERIES.]

tion of being compelled to vote for the Amendment.

*MR. FAITHFULL BEGG (Glasgow, St. Rollox): I rise to speak in opposition to this Bill, not because I have any real hostility to the object which my honourable Friend the Mover of it seeks to attain, but because from a special and particular point of view I desire,that there should not be any legislation of any kind whatever in connection with the franchise in this country until the particular change in that franchise in which I take an interest has been brought about. I have much sympathy with the object of my honourable Friend, and I think that it is a hardship that the very deserving class of persons, who are described in the Memorandum attached to the Bill, should be excluded, as they are at present, from the electoral franchise. But this injustice, if it is an injustice, is very small in comparison with the great and crying injustice to which I have alluded. In consequence of the forms of the House I shall not have an opportunity of moving the Amendment I have put on the paper, and therefore I should like, in a very few brief sentences, to speak from the special point of view I have already indicated. Any addition to the scope of the electoral franchise in this country will only add to the disparity which already exists in regard to the basis on which the franchise at the present moment rests. I do not wish to speak disrespectfully in any sense of those on whose behalf my honourable Friend has pleaded this afternoon; but it is evident that among those for whom I am speaking there are many who are more responsible as taxpayers and rate-payers, who are equally intelligent, who are equally educated, and in various ways equally qualified to vote as are those on behalf of whom this plea is made. I think that, speaking generally, it is unfortunate that I cannot in the least degree agree with the honourable Gentleman opposite. The tendency in this country appears to be to reduce the value attachable to the claims of those who by contributions in the shape of rates and taxes or by their intelligence and education are admitted to the franchise at the present moment. I think we appear to be going further in that direction than we were —leaving sex alone as a bar to the exercise of electoral privilege in connec.

H

tion with the membership of this House. I quite believe that I shall be accused of advocating a very selfish policy in regard to this Bill, but I am content to rest under that imputation. It may be urged that selfishness in matters of this sort is not a proper line to be taken. But whatever view one may take of that from the point of view of the strictly orthodox canon—when you treat a large class of the population in a selfish manner, I do not think that they should be blamed if they retaliate in a similar manner. It would not do for me to appeal to the honourable Baronet to support me in the reform I have referred to, for his views are well known on the subject. I have not even the resource of saying to the honourable Baronet "If you support me, then I will do the best I can to support you." I am forced into the position of advocating what he will no doubt call a dog-in-the-manger policy. But I am fortified by the opinion of the House——

*MR. SPEAKER: The honourable Member may give his reasons for opposing the Bill, but he must not make this an opportunity for an argument in favour of woman's suffrage.

*MR. FAITHFULL BEGG: Then I will merely say that I shall do everything in my power to advocate the particular point which I have briefly discussed and that I oppose the Bill, not on its merits but as a protest against the continuance of the crying injustice under which a large section of Her Majesty's subjects labour at the present moment, and I shall continue to do so until that grievance is remedied.

CAPTAIN JESSEL (St. Pancras S.): I am astonished that the honourable Gentleman opposite has, while expressing approval of this Measure intimated that he does not intend to go into the lobby with us who are promoting this Bill. I can assure him that many of the objections he has to the anomalies in the present registration laws, which he has so ably indicated, are shared by honourable Members on this side of the House as well as by those who sit on the other side of the House, and we would be delighted to see a great many of them done away with altogether. But I fail, for my part, to see why, because other objections exist, honourable Members on the other side of the House should not

Mr. Faithfull Begg.

help us to obtain the removal of the grievances of those whose cause we are at present advocating. I would like to deal with one other remark the honourable Gentleman made, and to point out the discrepancy between what he says and what the honourable and gallant Member for West Newington says. The honourable Member for Perth says that this question involves the question of the votes of hundreds of policemen. Well, the honourable and gallant Member for West Newington, who has professed to be the champion of the police in this House, said it was scarcely worth while to deal with a question which only affected a few policemen. He told us that not three per cent. of the whole police force in London were affected by the decision in the case of Clutterbuck v. Taylor. I have made considerable inquiry into this subject—I have gone to almost the highest authority—and I am informed that no fewer than 1,100 policemen out of 14,000 in London live in cubicles. That is rather a large number and I cannot congratulate the honourable and gallant Member for West Newington on his researches on this point. I come to another point—that is the shop assistants, of whom there is a large number in my constituency and in other constituencies. The shop assistants have a grievance in this matter, and I am very specially interested in the removal of that grievance. With the permission of the House, I will read a letter written to me some little time ago. That letter is as follows—

"SIR,—At a recent meeting of the Executive Committee of Shop Assistants at 55, Chancery Lane, they considered the decision of the Revising Barrister in St. Pancras to strike off 170 shop assistants from the list of voters. The reason was technical, that in sleeping-rooms the partitions between beds did not quite reach the ceiling. My Committee consider that some alteration of the law is urgently needed, and I am instructed to ask if you are prepared to take any action in the next Session of Parliament to put an end to the absurdity that a few more inches of wood would qualify the shop assistants to exercise their privileges as citizens. (Signed) JAS. MACPHERSON."

Well, sir, I maintain that this class of citizens are, by the judgment given in the case of Clutterbuck v. Taylor, put to a considerable disadvantage and that they suffer from a real grievance. I know that we will be told that there are other people who suffer from grievances, and that it is a great grievance that a man in a similar position, but who does not happen to be a servant, should not have the vote because he sleeps in a cubicle. I should like to point out that at present it would be very difficult to deprive a man of his vote, for the qualification is so very low in some parts of London. A man who occupies furnished apartments for which he pays four shillings a week, and in some cases five shillings a week, is given a vote. I must say that in my opinion, even if a man who is not a servant, if he occupies an apartment by himself, could reach a qualification of four shillings or five shillings a week. My honourable Friend and those who are supporting this Measure are quite agreeable to any Amendment on the Bill which does not strike at the root of the Bill. We should be only too anxious to join with those—if the Bill gets into Committee—who desire to obviate any chance of fraud; to see, for instance, that measures are taken to make the claims for the Service franchise in the same way as for the Lodger franchise, and so to prevent owners from disfranchising their employees. If such a proposal were made in Committee it is very probable that it would be accepted. I wish to point out that we do not wish to tinker with the Constitution in any way. We do not wish to flood the electorate with faggot votes. We only wish to restore the franchise to a very intelligent and deserving class of the population. We may also be told that this is piecemeal legislation, but I maintain that most of the legislation passed by this House is piecemeal. We cannot deal with all these questions at once, and we cannot possibly hope for the removal of every grievance. If it were not for piecemeal legislation, I think that the occupation of the Opposition would be gone, and I am sure honourable Gentlemen opposite would be very sorry if we brought in a Measure dealing with the whole subject of registration at the same time, for they would have then nothing to agitate about. I maintain that there is no question of class legislation in this matter, but simply an effort to get rid of a class grievance.

Mr. LUCAS-SHADWELL (Hastings): After the interesting remarks of the honourable Member opposite, I am some. what surprised to find those who advocate manhood suffrage opposing the extension of the franchise on this occasion to a respectable and deserving class of people. I am not desirous of gaining the attention of the House for more than a moment or two, because I did not rise specially to state my intention to support this Bill. I rose, briefly, to humbly protest against the speech of the honourable Member for St. Rollox Division of Glasgow, who is a well-known supporter of female suffrage. I know I should be entirely out of order if I went into the subject of female suffrage, but I only wish to place myself right with my constituents and others, for I am myself in favour of the extension of the suffrage to women. I am sorry my honourable Friend is not here now, but I would appeal to him not to oppose this Measure, because he cannot advance the interests of female suffrage by opposing the extension of the franchise to those who are in every way justly entitled to possess it. It is quite open to the honourable Member on a future occasion to advocate female suffrage, and by voting for this Bill he can in no way hinder the extension of the franchise to the class in whom he is so much interested. I have great pleasure in supporting the Bill of the honourable Baronet near me, and I hope it will receive the approval of the House of Commons.

On the return of Mr. Speaker after the usual interval,

Mr. ASCROFT (Oldham): Mr. Speaker, I think that, on behalf of honourable Members on this side of the House interested in the Second Reading of this Bill, I may congratulate the honourable Member on the spirit in which he addressed the House, and the valuable personal information he furnished. I do not quite agree with the grounds upon which the honourable Member pressed this Bill on the House for Second Reading, by maintaining the opinions of Lord Justice Rigby. I think he was in a minority on the occasion when the decision was given, and all the members of the legal profession do not go so far as to support his view. I therefore support this Bill on higher ground, on what I hold and maintain to have been the opinion of Parliament in 1884, when the Franchise Bill was passed. The question seems to me to be an exceedingly simple one, if we are to deal with it in a just and fair spirit.

What was the intention of Parliament in 1884? Was it intended that servants who occupy——

Attention having been called to the fact that there were hot 40 Members present, the House was counted, when 40 Members being present—

MR. ASHCROFT (continuing) : The question, as I have said, Mr. Speaker, was, What was the intention of Parliament in 1884 when the Service Vote was given? Well, in proof of it, we had a thousand people placed on the Register by the revising barristers—men of great experience, men who had considered the Act to the best of their ability, who took no part in politics, and were entirely independent. And that went on until the year 1896. In 1896 the decision was given of which we have heard so much this morning, and the result was that, without any fault of their own, a great number of respectable voters who in 1884 were placed upon the Register ceased to have any voice in the government of the country. That, everyone must agree, is a grievance. Parliament, I submit, has no greater duty to perform than that of redressing grievances, and if there is a grievance, then it is the duty of the House to redress it, more especially where a number of people are affected, not through their own fault, but through the fault of the draftsmen of the Bill—through the way in which the Bill was drawn. It has been said that in some constituencies only a very small minority is affected. That, I think, ought to have no weight whatever with Members in this House. There is a grievance. No matter how small it is, that grievance, if it can be remedied, ought to be remedied at the earliest possible moment. It has also been said by the right honourable Baronet the Member for the Forest of Dean that it is unfair to pick out a particular class. What I wish to submit is this, that if the House had agreed in 1884 to place these men on the register, it was the House which picked them out, and not we who pick them out to-day. It has also been said that it is unfair to a large · number of other people in a similar class of life that they have not the same opportunity of voting. That is not our fault to-day. That is the fault of the Legislature in 1884. It then picked out those whom it was thought had a

Mr. Ashcroft.

fairly reasonable right to be placed on the Register, and if any grievance exists it exists against the honourable Members who formed a majority of the House in that year. A good deal has been said in respect to registration. The registration laws are not only condemned on the opposite side: they are condemned on this side. There is no greater scandal existing at the present day than to give men votes and make them fight, year after year, at considerable expense and loss of time, and great trouble and annoyance, for the purpose of being put on the register, because some active agent, of whom we have heard from the honourable Member for Newington, takes opportunity of constantly objecting to them; and I do not hesitate to say that if this Parliament is allowed to close without the Government dealing with the Registration Laws, simplifying them, making them easily understood, appointing proper officers to deal with them, and throwing responsibility on somebody, I hope and trust that when the next election comes the Government will be on the opposite side of the House, and not on this side. Now, Sir, the right honourable Baronet the Member for the Forest of Dean has made a pretty similar speech to what he made last year. We all know that he is very anxious that everyone should be placed on the register. We know that he is very anxious that the franchise should be given to all classes. Well, we shall be prepared to do that when the proper time comes, but it would be utterly impossible, utterly unjust and useless, to attempt to deal with all these questions at the present moment. What we are attempting to do is simply to scratch out a blot in the Act of Parliament, and to do justice to a number of people. In 1901 it is possible that these questions which the right honourable Gentleman refers to may be dealt with. I expect that will be the year of the millenium, when we shall have redistribution of seats, simplification of the franchise, new registration laws, all Members of Parliament to be paid salaries, all their expenses to be paid, and they will be able to send free telegrams from this House and post letters without putting stamps upon them, and we shall not be allowed to be directors of companies—I do not know whether we shall be allowed to acquire shares in a company, or to have any money at all. However, that is the time when the right honourable Gentleman's speech will be appropriate. The honourable Member for Newington objects that great powers will be left in the hands of the employers. We know perfectly well that the owner of a great number of cottage houses could disfranchise every man living in them if he wanted to by refusing to pay the poor rate. We know by accident it has sometimes been done; but we ought to have something more than mere assertions, we ought to have proof. We have not been able to get one single case; and I think we may congratulate ourselves on both sides of the House that since 1884 there has never been any attempt made either by Liberal or Conservative employers to throw any difficulty in the way of their men being placed upon the register. The fault lies upon those active agents who have been active in the interests of Members of this House, and are determined to get as good a state of the register for their side as they possibly can. Then we were told by the honourable Member for Newington—and I was astonished, because I thought I knew something about registration—that a smart registration agent, with a few thousand shekels of gold, can keep 40 out of 60 away from the poll. It is somewhat astonishing. I was not aware that there were any possible means of winning an election, or getting over those who were going to vote against a man, save by sending them off by steamboat or train, or putting them on the Big Wheel during the time of the poll. That is not an objection to this Bill. The chief objection seems to be that a number of other people who ought to be on the register are not to be put upon it. That is not a sufficient reason why this House should not render the justice which is asked. We are told that there are already 11 forms of franchise. We are not increasing the number. The Service Franchise already exists; and we ask that this House, in fairness to those who have been deprived by a mere technicality of their votes, to allow this Bill to be read a second time, and I hope and trust that will be done.

*Mr. HEDDERWICK: Mr. Speaker, I find myself in the unusual position of being on this question somewhat at variance with my honourable Friends on this side of the House. I mean to support the Second Reading of this Bill, for reasons which I am afraid will scarcely commend themselves to the honourable Baronet who moved the Second Reading, but which I think must commend themselves to the right honourable Baronet who moved the Amendment. All my political life I have been in favour of manhood suffrage, and I have upon nearly every political platform on which I have appeared con-stantly advocated an extension of the suffrage. Well, here we have a Measure which does, to some extent, endeavour to widen the franchise. It is a small step it is true, a miserably small step, but still it is a step in that direction, and, therefore, I feel, unless there are adequate reasons offered which commend themselves to my judgment, that I should be doing something in opposition to those principles which I have always advocated if I were not to support this Measure. Now, what are the objections advanced against it. It is said that if this Bill were passed it would be a means of effecting political jobbery. That is always possible, no doubt. Take as a specific example the great upholsterers of London, who nightly stow away an army of employees in cubicles like catacombs; it is quite conceivable that if these employers were determined to create faggot votes they might have a weapon formed to their hands under this Bill. But that is a risk which I think we must take. I certainly would be the last man to deny a right which certain persons in the community ought to have, because of a possibility of that sort. Then it is said that if this Measure were passed it would add to the already almost intolerable mass of enfranchising enactments. That is true; but I for one would not be sorry for that, because I believe the more intolerable we make these enactments the more likely we are to obtain something in the nature of the real reform which I should like to see. Then it is said that the present proposal is an unfair proposal, because it picks and chooses—these' are the words of the right honourable Baronet the Member for the Forest of Dean—among ser-vants; that is to say, it would enfran-chise a small section of servants while at the same time it would deny the franchise to a much greater number. That, I think, is also true, but am I to deny the privilege of voting to a certain section of servants because the honourable Baronet who introduced this Measure did not bring within its purview all possible servants? I think that would be absurd, especially when, in addition, I believe that the very unfairness of this Measure will act as a lever to create such an intolerable situation among the other unenfranchised servants that we will before long be compelled to pass a much wider Act than the present Measure. The only other objection worth while noticing is that of the right honourable Baronet the Member for the Forest of Dean. He objects to the Bill on the ground that it has been brought forward by a private Member and not by a responsible Government. My answer to that is very short. I do not personally care a straw whether a reform be brought forward by a private Member or by a responsible Government; if it be a good Measure or a Measure going some distance, however short, in the direction of justice, it will have my support; and I think it is to the credit of a private Member, when a responsible Government refuses to move in the direction of reform, that he should take upon himself the burthen of introducing into this House a Measure in itself to be commended. Without attempting to go into the technicalities of the subject I beg to give the Bill before the House my support.

MR. LOGAN (Leicester, Harborough): Like the honourable Gentleman who has just sat down, I find myself under the painful necessity of differing on this matter from some of my honourable Friends on this side of the House. I intend to support the Second Reading of this Bill, because it enfranchises somebody, and God knows there are enough of people in this country who are disfranchised. I do not care whether the persons proposed to be enfranchised by this Bill are likely to be political friends or foes. That makes no difference to me, and so long as I am assured they are good citizens I cannot feel myself justified in offering any opposition to their being enabled to exercise the franchise. Of course, we have heard that

Mr. Hedderwick.

this is piecemeal legislation. During the short time I have been in this House I have come to the conclusion that most of the legislation proposed is piecemeal legislation, and if this Bill can fairly be called piecemeal it is only in accordance with our usual custom. My experience is that it takes a considerable amount of mental bracing on the part of Members of this House to agree to give the people of the country the power they are entitled to have. This Measure does not go anything like as far as it ought to go, and in supporting it I do so largely because I believe that the honourable Baronet who introduced it, who has told us that he desires to see the franchise extended to all classes generally who do not now possess it, will, should the Bill get to another stage, extend its powers, which he can do in a very simple and easy manner, in order to bring within its purview certain other servants who are every bit as much entitled to exercise the franchise as are the servants for whom he now pleads. This he can do by the insertion of four or five simple words. For instance, in our towns, and I am sure in our villages throughout the length and breadth of the country, there are a large number of young men who remain unmarried because they desire to support their widowed mothers. Under the Bill as it now stands these deserving young men cannot exercise the franchise. They live at home because they are anxious to do the best they can for their mothers, and the old ladies are naturally anxious to keep possession of their houses in their own names, and the sons, although they practically defray most of the expenses, are not entitled to vote. Then there is another class also very numerous. I mean young men who, working in villages and towns, live at home with their parents. Now, I ask the honourable Baronet why in drafting this Bill he should have excluded those young men from the benefit of the franchise. Why should he deprive them of the right to vote? They pay for their rooms and for the expense of their living, but they are not eligible to exercise the franchise because the rooms they occupy are not of the necessary value. If the honourable Baronet will take this matter into consideration he will see that by adding the four or five words I have suggested, and striking out something, he will bring within the purview of this

Bill a large number of servants quite as qualified to exercise the Franchise as the limited few for whom he so eloquently pleads. If the Bill goes to another stage I hope I will have an opportunity of moving an Amendment which will have the effect of including the two classes to which I have referred. At any rate, because this Bill proposes to enfranchise somebody I do not find myself able to vote against it, and having placed before the House my suggestion to amend the Bill and to redress a further wrong, I shall be very pleased to support the Second Reading.

Mr. WEBSTER (St. Pancras, E): I most heartily support this Measure. I think when we consider the Bill we will acknowledge after all is said and done that it is a most useful Measure. The Legislature no doubt intended that the persons whom my honourable Friend now wishes to be enfranchised should be enfranchised. For 12 years they enjoyed the franchise, but by a technical mistake in the drafting of this particular Act of Parliament they were disfranchised. Honourable Members who have spoken against this Measure say it is a small Measure, and that it does not enfranchise a number of persons whom they would like to see enfranchised. But let us look at the Bill from the present position of affairs. At present if the large employers of London decided to house their servants in small rooms, each with a window, at the top of the house they would all enjoy the franchise. But if, on the other hand, the employees slept in cubicles—which are very much better on sanitary grounds than small rooms— an honourable Member called cubicles catacombs, but small rooms are much more like catacombs than are cubicles on the dormitory system—they would be disfranchised. The right honourable Baronet the Member for the Forest of Dean states that in his constituency there was no reason for the Bill at all, and that the police did not require it. That may be the case, but the right honourable Baronet represents a rural constituency, and probably the police are very few and far between, and every policeman has probably a separate house to himself, and has the franchise. But in this vast metropolis the police have to be put into barracks, and under the present law, as has been pointed out by the honourable and gallant Member for South St. Pancras, they are disfranchised. This Bill will enfranchise a large number of very intelligent and intellectual people: first the police, then those connected with shops as assistants—and no man can be an important assistant in a shop who cannot read and write, and has not a knowledge of arithmetic; and lastly attendants in hospitals and asylums. In some parts of the world there is an education franchise, and why should we disfranchise educated people in this country because of a technical mistake? The honourable Member for Newington had a great many objections to this Measure. I cannot for one moment believe that this Bill would lead to fraud or that employers of labour would move into various buildings owned by them in order to disfranchise a large number of people just before an election; but an Amendment could be added to prevent any such thing. Surely the danger of fraud would be greater if the qualifying period, instead of being a year or a year and a half, were reduced to a quarter of a year. I had the honour of moving the rejection of the Bill introduced by the right honourable Gentleman the Member for Wolverhampton. I think it was carried to a Second Reading, but for some reason or another which I could not understand, whether the Liberal country Members objected to some provisions and the town Liberal Members objected to others, the Bill, which was nothing more nor less than a Reform Bill, was dropped. The honourable Baronet the Member for Dulwich is now bringing in a useful Measure, and I venture to believe that if it is passed it will be very advantageous. Again, I would advocate this Bill because it gives the franchise to people who have a definite stake in the country. I must confess I hold with the old Conservative doctrine that the rights of property should be respected, and that the electoral franchise should be accompanied by some property qualification. I disagree entirely with the suggestion of the right honourable Baronet the Member for the Forest of Dean that we should have universal suffrage in this country. I think with a country so thickly populated as ours it would lead to very grave danger. I believe we should throw into the hands of the migratory population the full political power of this country, and I am therefore strongly opposed to universal suffrage. There is one other point on which I should like to touch. I think at the present time the franchise should not be altered in any material way, but I agree with the honourable Member who said that the method with which we collect our votes and our entire registration system ought to be thoroughly amended. At the present time there is a vast expenditure associated with it. There are paid officials to register the electors, and revising-barristers and overseers, though in some districts the work is done, and done well, by town clerks and vestry clerks. I would advocate that we appoint permanent officials to register the electors of the country, and that political parties should not be put to the ridiculously heavy and unnecessary expense they now have to bear. At present a great deal of energy is devoted to registration which might be wisely used in other ways. I do not think we are ready for universal suffrage, and I do not think it would work well for one moment.

*MR. SPEAKER: The honourable Member is not in order in discussing payment of election expenses or universal suffrage now.

MR. WEBSTER: But I will not touch on the question any further than to say that I believe the Bill my honourable Friend the Member for Dulwich has brought in would be a very useful and very desirable amendment of the law, and I believe it would enfranchise a vast number of very deserving people.

MR. DILLON (Mayo, E.): I should like to say a few words with regard to this Bill. It seems to me to belong to a most objectionable class of measure, for it proposes to deal piecemeal with the suffrage, Sir, I do not know what would be the political effect of this Bill if it were passed into law, but I venture to say that those who have supported it on the opposite side have a certain view as to what the effect would be, and that is the reason why the Bill is introduced. I hold that the question of registration or the suffrage ought to be approached in some general, broad measure which would

Mr. Webster.

be free from the suspicion of a desire to admit some limited and well-defined section of the population to the franchise. Now, Sir, the honourable Member who has just spoken has used as an argument in favour of the Bill that it is only proposed to enfranchise a set of individuals who have been disfranchised by some technical construction of the complicated registration laws. Sir, this is not the only outcome of the constructions placed upon the Bill. Hardly a year passes without some fresh judgment, either admitting or excluding various sections of the community to the franchise, being given upon the registration laws. But what I maintain is that if it is considered desirable—and I believe it to be extremely desirable—to simplify and improve the registration system of this country it ought to be done by some general Bill dealing with the whole subject, and not by a Bill introduced by a private Member on behalf of one particular section of the population. I think it would have been very desirable if the Government had introduced such a Bill and given us the opportunity, now that there is a strong Tory Government in office, to deal with this question as a Government Measure. Everybody who has heard the discussions during the last few years on the registration law must admit that it is very bad, and, in fact, indefensible. But, of course, the difficulty is to agree upon a general measure of reform. I think it would be a very reasonable thing for the Government to introduce a general measure simplifying and reforming the registration laws, for which I venture to say there is not a parallel for complication and expense in the whole civilised world. Now, Sir, the honourable Member who spoke last said this Bill would be a "small and useful Measure," and would admit to the suffrage an intellectual and intelligent body of men—I suppose he means by that a body of men who would vote Tory. It is a small and useful Bill to the Tory Party, but that is not the principle upon which the question ought to be dealt with. These "small and useful measures" lead to a system absolutely destructive of all good principles in dealing with this question. One honourable Member on this side of the House alluded to the case of sons of widowed women who live at home and postpone their marriage from the very laudable motive of contributing to the support of their mothers. Sir, I should like very much to bring in a " small and useful Measure" which would enfranchise all the sons of widow landowners in Ireland who are kept off the rent-roll by the Irish landlords, and who have as great a right, morally speaking, to vote as any other electors in the whole of the United Kingdom. But I should like to know what would be said of such a " small and useful Measure " on the opposite side of the House. No doubt it would remedy a great wrong, and if I thought it was the slightest use to draft a Bill on such lines I would joyfully bring it in. But we know perfectly well the Tory Party would rise in revolt against such a " one-sided " Measure. I could make out a stronger case in favour of such a Measure than honourable Members opposite have done in the case of this Bill to-day. I only mention this to show the absurdity of the arguments of honourable Gentlemen opposite. If you are going to deal piecemeal with these anomalies and injustices you will have not one " small and useful Measure," but a dozen. That is not the way in which this House can, with any sense of self-respect, deal with this great question of registration and the franchise. You must deal with it in some general Measure, which can be defended on general principles. What I would like to see would be a Measure admitting fearlessly to the franchise—and there must be such a Measure before many years are passed—every grown man who is free from the taint of crime and has contributed to the wealth of this great country ; so that without the intervention of lawyers—or with as little intervention as possible—and without the intervention of the agents of political Parties, all shall be placed upon the Register of this country.

MR. W. MOORE (Antrim, N.): I regret, Sir, that on the present occasion in rising to address this House I am unable to find myself entirely in accord with the honourable Irish Member who has joined in this Debate. He has objected to piecemeal legislation on the one hand and on the other he denounces the extension of the franchise to a most deserving class. I have no doubt that in his zeal to extend the suffrage to the sons of widows in Ireland he will have no objection to do now what he and his Party have for years refused to do, namely, give equal

rights to the Royal Irish Constabulary with the English Police. I venture to hope that as they are grown men, and as the English Constabulary already have the privilege, he will not raise objection if a Bill is brought forward by Colonel Saunderson, or any other Unionist Member for Ireland, to admit them to the privileges of the franchise.

MR. DILLON : Not if the Bill gave universal suffrage to every grown man.

Mr. W. MOORE : It seems to me that the question we are discussing is, if I may say so, not really an extension of the franchise : we are discussing the privileges which have been kept from a body of men who, *de facto*, if not *de jure*, were entitled to those privileges for a considerable time, and who, in the opinion of many competent authorities, namely, the revising barristers, who are constituted the franchise tribunals through the country, came within the scope and intendment of the original Act. It is only by a recent decision of the Court of Appeal, which, of course, everyone must treat with the greatest respect, that these men have been found to be no longer entitled to the franchise. If this House now sees fit to restore them their privileges which the Court took from them, though *de jure* it will be an extension, *de facto* it will not. Now, Mr. Speaker, I have been concerned as a stranger to this House—and, I am afraid, also to its privileges—during the three Debates it has been my privilege to hear at the vast amount of fraud there seems to be amongst the English people. As a simple Irish Member I had not suspected it. But I listened with interest on the first night of my arrival to a Debate on margarine, and I heard honourable Gentlemen say that they objected to legislation in the proposed direction because it would lead to fraud. Last night, in the Debate upon Education, we were told that the existing Act, which dealt with the control of Primary schools, was being beset by fraud again. To-day the same argument is again being made use of—that if the House passes this piece of legislation the unfortunate people who are supposed to benefit by it will once more be defrauded. Mr. Speaker, I am sure the honourable Member for East Mayo will bear me out when I say that that argument will not hold water across

St. George's Channel. But there is another point to which I would draw attention; the objection is put forward that the Bill does not go far enough. Is that any ground for refusing what is now offered? Half a loaf is better than no bread. The Bill is the half loaf. Why refuse it? Oliver Twist asked for more. He did not get it, but he stuck to what he had got. A Bill is now brought in to extend the franchise to a certain number, but I cannot see why, because others are not included in it, that that is any logical ground for honourable Members opposite objecting to it. The honourable Member for East Mayo has brought forward the objection that this is merely piecemeal legislation. Mr. Speaker, it is not the first time in the history of this House during the past 25 years that Parliament has been obliged to pass piecemeal legislation to get over a particular decision in a particular case in a Court of Appeal, and I understand that it is fully admitted on both sides that it is simply by a recent decision of a Court of Appeal that this legislation has become necessary. The anomalies of the Franchise Act have been discussed. Any one who has had experience of the Registration Courts must be aware of those anomalies. I have had a certain amount of experience in this respect, for I have been a revising barrister on more than one occasion. I remember on one occasion a clergyman claimed to be entitled to vote as a householder, and he proved to my satisfaction that although his landlord lived under the same roof as he himself did, he nevertheless had an entirely separate part of the house, coming out of his own door, having his own rooms, his own latch-key, and all the other necessaries of a householder. I was about to allow the claim, when the agent on the other side said, as an after-thought, that the reverend gentleman originally decided to put in a claim to be a lodger. I have not the least doubt that there was not the suggestion of fraud in this case, but that the reverend gentleman left himself entirely in the hands of the agent of the party to which he belonged. There is nothing in the Bill, however, which will affect these anomalies, which must always arise under the existing election law, because they arise as mixed questions of law and fact so frequently. On the ground that this is not really an extension of the franchise, and that it is legislation in the interests

Mr. W. Moore.

of a very large class of men who make their living by the sweat of their brows —police, warders, and people in honourable service—I ask the House to support the Bill.

MR. McKENNA (Monmouth, N.): Mr. Speaker, those who have supported the Second Reading of this Bill have done so on two grounds—either that the Bill merely corrects a technical mistake in the existing law—a mistake so technical that it was only discovered in 1896, 12 years after the passing of the Act — or that it is a desirable extension in the direction of manhood suffrage. Now, Sir, upon the question of whether or not this is a mere technical correction of the law I have a few words to say. One honourable Member has said that the Bill proposes to give effect to the plain and obvious intention of this House as expressed in the Representation of the People Act. Another honourable Member said that it corrects a mere technical mistake in drafting, and similar expressions were cheered by the Attorney-General sitting opposite. If we are to understand that this is a mere correction of a technical error in drafting, I suppose there is no better authority to go to than the author of this Act, and we must consider, therefore, the words of Mr. Gladstone when he introduced the Representation of the People Act in 1884. I find that Mr. Gladstone, speaking of the Service Franchise, said—

"Our object is to provide a franchise for those inhabitants who are neither owners nor tenants; but they must be householders in this sense—either, in the first place, that they are actual inhabitants; or, in the second place, that there is no other inhabitant with them, superseding them, or standing in the same position with them; and, in the third place, they must either be inhabitants of an integral house, or else of that separate part of a house which at any rate has already been declared to be a house for electoral purposes. Honourable Gentlemen are aware of the general reasons which may be pleaded in favour of this enlargement. It is an enlargement absolutely required by the principle of this Bill, because the principal and central idea of this Bill is to give every householder a vote. The householder is just as much a householder and has just as much the responsibility of a householder, whether he is in the eye of the law an owner or a tenant, or whether he is not, provided he is an inhabitant in the sense I have described. And this Service franchise is a far-reaching franchise. It goes to men of high class, who inhabit valuable houses, as the officers of great institutions. It descends to men of humble class, who are the servants of the gentry, or the servants of the farmer, or the servants of some other employer of labour, who are neither owners nor tenants, and who, in many cases, cannot be held as tenants, in consequence of the essential conditions intended to be realised through their labours, but who fully fulfil the idea of responsible inhabitant householders."

Now, Sir, upon these words of Mr. Gladstone, the really responsible person for this Act, I think it cannot be any longer contended that the Bill before the House merely corrects a technical error in drafting. But if the words of Mr. Gladstone are not sufficient, let me remind the House of the opinion of the then Attorney-General, now Lord James, as expressed shortly afterwards. He said, speaking of the Service franchise, that " the franchise voter must be *dominus* of the house and able to keep others out of it." That is what the intention of the Service franchise was—namely, that the person going on the register under the Service franchise should be the *dominus* of his house and be able to keep others out. Now, Sir, after the authority of Mr. Gladstone, and the interpretation at the time put upon it by the Attorney-General, I trust that we shall not hear anything more in this House that this Bill is merely correcting an error in the drafting of the Representation of the People Act. The fact is that the Service franchise voter has all the essential characteristics of an occupier in the eyes of the law, except that he does not pay rates. Sir, it is very surprising that honourable Members opposite should now be taking opposite views to those taken by their Party when the Representation of the People Act was passed. On the clause relating to the Service franchise, Mr. Warton, a prominent Conservative Member of those days, made use of the following somewhat interesting remarks—

" Had it escaped the attention of the Prime Minister that under this section it was possible for a farmer to arrange any large shed in such a way as would give the vote to each of a large number of persons whom he might allow to occupy it; that is to say, if it was divided into compartments like the stalls for oxen? "

That, Sir, is exactly what this Bill proposes to do. Were it part of a general Bill dealing with manhood suffrage I should have nothing to say against it, but it is an extension of the franchise wholly against every principle in the existing franchise-law, in order to secure what Mr. Warton rightly said would be the result, if such a Measure as the honourable

Baronet has introduced were passed. Now, Sir, existing franchises, although very numerous, are all based upon some clear principle. We have got the Ownership franchise, the Ancient franchise, the Household franchise, the Service franchise, and the Lodger franchise, so that the alteration now proposed is not a mere extension of the existing principles of our electoral qualifications, but is the adoption of an entirely new principle. It is proposed practically to give manhood suffrage to a particular class of persons. And what is the single definition or limitation of that particular class of persons? It is that they should be under the orders of somebody else. That is your new qualification for the vote. If you once put a man under the control or authority or orders of somebody else, you qualify him immediately for manhood suffrage. Sir, as has been said by an honourable Member, the ramifications of our franchise admit of the greatest variety of amendment. It surely is unwise that a temptation should be put in the way of private Members to poke about in the dusty corners of the Constitution to see if they can find something of advantage to themselves in a Party sense. Yet that is the inevitable condition which will occur if this Bill is allowed to pass. In extending the franchise hitherto we have always endeavoured to secure the representation of some class other than those already represented. Nothing of this sort, however, will be done by this Bill. You will only enfranchise persons just according to whether their employers wish them to be enfranchised or otherwise. That, Sir, I take it, is absolutely clear from the Bill. The admission and disqualification equally depend upon the employer's good will. I know it has been said that already landlords can disqualify their tenants. I admit that there are evils under our existing system, but there is no such completeness of control as is proposed under this Bill. Under this Bill, if a master sends away a man for a week, he disqualifies him for the vote. (An honourable Member: No.) Yes, he will break the occupation. If he goes out of employment for a single day he breaks the Service occupation. He is, therefore, absolutely under the control of the employer. But, Sir, in order that there should be no doubt upon this point the authors have put words into the Bill rendering the meaning absolutely clear. The words are—

"A person shall be entitled to be registered notwithstanding that the dwelling house which he occupies is merely a compartment of a room."

They have introduced a new word, "Compartment." If their intention under this Bill had not been so much directed in the way I cannot help thinking it has been, they might very well have used the words—

"The occupier of the dwelling house shall be entitled as such to be registered, notwithstanding that the dwelling-house which he occupies is not separately occupied by him."

With words of that kind, everybody, whether the employer liked it or not, would have become entitled to a vote under this Bill. It has been said in the course of this discussion that the mere drawing of a chalk line might constitute a compartment. Is that the intention of honourable Gentlemen opposite? As to that they leave us absolutely in the dark; not a word has been said as to the meaning they propose to put on the word "compartment." It has been said, too, that this is piecemeal legislation. It is true that it is so, and I hope that if this Bill passes its Second Reading it will not be allowed to go to Committee unless accompanied by an Instruction giving the Committee power to extend its scope so as to provide for the appointment of a registration officer, who shall inquire into and report to the revising barrister on the case of every person registered under the Bill, and who shall further make provision for placing on the register every person who ought to be placed there. I hope, too, that one other reform may be effected, and that we shall introduce the principle of "One man one vote." I would suggest that, as we are dealing with great electoral reforms in a piecemeal and tinkering fashion, with a tinkering and piecemeal Bill, we should amend the Measure by an Instruction or Amendment in Committee to secure that persons qualified to vote under this Bill shall be strictly limited to that vote, and shall not be qualified in any other constituency. The opportunity ought not to be denied us of making the changes I have suggested on this Bill, and I trust we shall discuss the desirability of reforming our

Mr. W. Moore.

registration laws by the appointment of a registration official and by securing the adoption of the principle of "One man one vote."

THE SOLICITOR-GENERAL (Sir R. FINLAY, Inverness Burghs): I listened with interest to the speech last delivered, in which the honourable Member announced his intention, if the Bill were read a second time, to move an Instruction which will so enlarge its scope as to amount to "One man one vote," or "One vote one man." My honourable and learned Friend quoted the Debate which took place in the year 1884, on which occasion Mr. Gladstone spoke of the extension of the franchise to householders who, for technical reasons, could not be considered to be tenants, and, therefore, did not enjoy the franchise. But the question of whether a compartment can be deemed to be a dwelling house within the meaning of the Act of 1878 has never arisen, and never can arise, with reference to any person who comes under the Service franchise. I wish all honourable Members now in the House had been present earlier in the day to hear the most interesting speech of the honourable Member for Perth, who traversed the whole ground with complete knowledge. And although I do not quite agree with all the conclusions of the honourable Member, I think that he has ably dealt with nearly all the objections which have been raised to the Bill. He has done so in a manner in which very few in this House are qualified to do it. He effectively disposed of the objection put in the forefront by the right honourable Baronet the Member for the Forest of Dean when he said that the Bill was a small one because there was not a single policeman in his constituency who did not enjoy the franchise without it, while it was not the intention of the Act of 1884 to deal with these cases. But, as the honourable Member for Perth has pointed out, the Forest of Dean is not a constituency which fairly represents such large urban constituencies as are found, for instance, in London. I understand that as many as 1,100 or 1,400 policemen in London— a very considerable proportion indeed of the whole force—have been deprived of the franchise owing to the view which was taken by revising barristers of the law in 1895, and confirmed by the Court of Appeal in 1896. The right honourable Baronet also said the Bill was very objectionable because it dealt only with the Service franchise, and did not deal with cases where several people were in occupation of the same house, and he put a case in his own experience, where several miners occupied a .small house together. This Bill, he said, would not confer the franchise on them. My answer to that is, that if they occupy several parts of the house they have the franchise already, and do not want the Bill. If they have not, it is because their occupation is a joint one. It has also been said by the right honourable Baronet that the Bill will give power to the employer or the officer in command of the police, if he chooses to exercise it, to break the period of occupation of the men occupying cubicles, and thus increase the facilities for fraud, for undue interference with the right to vote, and for the creation of faggot votes. If there is anything in that objection it cuts at the root of the Service franchise altogether. The one objection which my honourable and learned Friend the Member for Monmouth has brought forward to the Bill is that it is intended to help classes under the dominion of other people. Would my honourable Friend be so consistent as to repeal the Service franchise altogether?

*MR. McKENNA: My objection was that the Bill would enable employers to say which servants should go and which servants should not go to the poll, but I do not object at all to servants having votes.

SIR R. FINLAY: If that objection is good for anything it goes a great deal further. It is really an objection to the Service franchise altogether. The honourable Member for Newington drew a dismal picture of the frauds which might be perpetrated in some constituency by a clever electioneering agent by which an enormous number of bogus voters might be created. Looked at in the light of common-sense it will be at once seen that that picture is a pure figment of the imagination. In the first place, in order to create these votes there must be houses in which the men are to live, employers who, wanting the men in their employment, give them cubicles ; and there must also be resi-

dence for the required period. Is it conceivable that an electioneering agent would have recourse to so clumsy and extensive a fraud as that? With regard to the question of the merits of the Bill I ask the House to remember that the Measure is intended to give effect to the judgment of that eminent lawyer and distinguished judge Lord Justice Rigby. I think the House will feel that there can be nothing very revolutionary in any Measure which is intended to carry out views which come to us under such sanction. There are two provisions in the Bill. One is to remove the difficulty in regard to the partition of a room which does not go up to the ceiling. It appears to me that if there is a partition which cuts off effectively one part of a room from the other, it creates distinct dwellings just as much as if the partition were carried up to the ceiling. Yet some honourable Members are fighting this as if it affects the British Constitution. Surely the distinct dwelling is just as effectually created by a partition which does not go quite up to the ceiling as by one which does and thus makes the ventilation not quite so good. It is said that air is common to all, and we breathe the same air whether the partition goes up to the roof or not. In any house there is a community of air, and I cannot understand the enormous importance which is attached to the question of the height of the partition. The other part of the Bill is intended to prevent servants losing the franchise because of some restrictions in the terms in which they occupy the premises given them because of their service. There must always be some restrictions of service ; but why should that affect the right to vote of the servant who had occupied the premises for the qualifying period? It seems to me that if a servant has the qualifying period of residence he has got all that is wanted for the purposes of the franchise. It has been said that whatever may be the merits of the Measure in itself—and not much has been said against it from that point of view—we ought not to read the Bill a second time, because there are a number of other grievances which the Bill does not profess to redress. That view was expressed in the crudest way by the honourable Member for the St. Rollox Division of

Glasgow, who said he was extremely anxious that women should have votes, and until they got them he did not intend that anybody else should have them. Had the honourable Member been present I would have put it to him whether that attitude is calculated to promote the cause he has so much at heart. My honourable and learned Friend the Member for Perth gave it as a reason for not being able to support the Measure that there are other anomalies which this Bill in its present form could not redress, and a matter upon which he laid particular stress was the fact that if an employer came to reside for a time during the year at the premises where the men are accommodated in cubicles they will be disqualified. In the first place, I understand that objection hardly could arise with reference to the police at all, and in a great many cases with reference to the shop assistants it would not arise, because the buildings are altogether separate, and are laid out entirely for the occupation of shop assistants. But I would point out to my honourable and learned Friend and to the House that that difficulty does not arise from the words in the Act of 1884—provided the employer does not occupy any part of the dwelling-house—because if a dwelling-house is a room or portion of a room occupied by a servant the employer never occupies that. The difficulty arises from the general law as to whether a man is occupier or merely a lodger. As a good working test great importance is attached to the residence of the owner of the house on the premises, and, practically speaking, from the fact that the owner resides on the pre-premises his tenants there are very often considered to be lodgers, but I would point out to my honourable and learned Friend that it is hardly a good reason for not voting for a Measure which in every, respect is pronounced to be excellent to say that it does 'not deal with such a tremendous difficulty as the question of the distinction between tenant and lodger. The whole question of the

Sir R. Finlay.

Lodger franchise is one of great difficulty, but I am sure those who have such a complete knowledge of the subject as my honourable and learned Friend will be the first to recognise the extraordinary difficulty there would be in dealing with this subject by legislation. Wider considerations are opened up by the honourable Member for East Mayo, who objects entirely to the Bill as dealing with but a small part of a large subject, and urges that the House ought not to deal with any part of the subject unless it is prepared to have a complete reform of the laws in relation to registration and to introduce manhood suffrage. Of course observations of that kind open up a very wide field. But I would ask the House to consider the way in which matters of this kind have been usually dealt with in this country. It has sometimes been said it is a good thing for England that she is not governed by logic. We have not been always perfectly logical or always consistent. One great feature of English history is that England has not always insisted on pushing any principle to the bitter end. She has proceeded on the basis of redressing grievances as they have arisen and been brought to notice. If we are to wait until we have a complete code dealing with subjects of such enormous importance as those which the honourable Member for East Mayo has referred to, we shall, indeed, have to wait a long time. Under these circumstances I cannot help thinking it would be well if the House were to grant a Second Reading to this Measure, which is not unimportant, which does restore to a number of people the privilege which for a great many years they enjoyed, and which will not in any way impair any subsequent reform, if such should be proposed.

Question put—

"That the words proposed to be left out stand part of the Question."

The House divided:—Ayes, 188; Noes, 88.—(Division List No. 35.)

AYES.

Aird, John
Allhusen, Augustus H. Eden
Ambrose, Wm. (Middlesex)
Anstruther. H. T.
Archdale, Edward Mervyn
Arrol, Sir William
Ascroft, Robert
Atkinson, Rt. Hon. John
Baldwin, Alfred
Balfour, Rt. Hn. A.J. (Manc'r)
Balfour, Rt Hn Gerald W. (Leeds)
Banbury, Frederick George
Barry, Rt Hn A H. Smith (Hunts)
Bartley, George C. T.
Barton, Dunbar Plunket
Bathurst, Hn. Allen Benjamin
Beach, W. W. Bramston (Hants)
Beckett, Ernest William
Bemrose, Sir Henry Howe
Bentinck, Lord Henry C.
Bethell, Commander
Bhownaggree, Sir M. M.
Biddulph, Michael
Bill, Charles
Boscawen, Arthur Griffith-
Boulnois, Edmund
Powles, T Gibson (King's Lynn)
Burdett-Coutts, W.
Butcher, John George
Cavendish. V. C. W. (Derbysh.)
Cecil, Evelyn (Hertford, East)
Chaloner, Capt. R. G. W.
Chamberlain, Rt. Hn. J (Birm.)
Chamberlain, J. Austen (Wor.)
Channing, Francis Allston
Chaplin, Rt. Hon. Henry
Charrington, Spencer
Collings, Rt. Hon. Jesse
Cook, Fred. Lucas (Lambeth)
Cornwallis, Fiennes Stanley W.
Cubitt, Hon. Henry
Curzon, Viscount
Dalbiac, Colonel Philip Hugh
Dalkeith, Earl of
Dalrymple, Sir Charles
Davenport, W. Bromley-
Doughty, George
Doxford, William Theodore
Drucker, A.
Duncombe, Hon. Hubert V.
Dyke, Rt Hn. Sir William Hart
Egerton, Hon. A. de Tatton
Fardell, Sir T. George
Finch, George H.
Finlay, Sir Robert Bannatyne
Fisher, William Hayes
Fitzgerald, Sir Robert Penrose-
Fletcher, Sir Henry
Flower, Ernest
Folkestone, Viscount
Forster, Henry William
Fry, Lewis
Garfit, William
Gibbons, J. Lloyd

Giles, Charles Tyrrell
Godson, Sir Augustus Frederick
Goldsworthy, Major-General
Gordon, Hon. John Edward
Gorst, Rt Hn. Sir John Eldon
Graham, Henry Robert
Gray, Ernest (West Ham)
Green, Walford D. (Wednsbry.)
Greville, Hon. Ronald
Gull, Sir Cameron
Halsey, Thomas Frederick
Hanbury, Rt. Hn. Robert Wm.
Haslett, Sir James Horner
Heath, James
Hedderwick. Thomas Chas. H.
Hickman, Sir Alfred
Hill, Sir Edward S. (Bristol)
Hoare, Edw. B. (Hampstead)
Howell, William Tudor
Hozier, Hon. James H. Cecil
Hutchinson, Capt. G. W. Grice-
Jeffreys, Arthur Frederick
Jenkins, Sir John Jones
Jessel, Capt. Herbert Morton
Johnson-Ferguson, Jabez Edw.
Johnstone, Heywood (Sussex)
Jolliffe, Hon. H. George
Kenyon, James
Knowles, Lees
Lafone, Alfred
Lawrence, Sir E. Durning-(Corn)
Lawrence, Wm F. (Liverpool)
Lawson, John Grant (Yorks.)
Lees, Sir Elliott (Birkenhead)
Leigh Bennett, Henry Currie
Llewellyn, Evan H. (Somerset)
Lockwood, Lt.-Col. A. R.
Loder, Gerald Walter Erskine
Logan, John William
Long, Rt. Hn. Walter (L'pool)
Lopes, Henry Yarde Buller
Lowther, Rt. Hon. Jas. (Kent)
Loyd, Archie Kirkman
Lucas-Shadwell, William
Macartney, W. G. Ellison
Macdona, John Cumming
MacIver, David (Liverpool)
M'Arthur, Charles (Liverpool)
M'Iver, Sir Lewis (Edin., W.)
M'Killop, James
Malcolm, Ian
Melville, Beresford Valentine
Middlemore, John Throgmorton
Mildmay, Francis Bingham
Milner, Sir Frederick George
Monk, Charles James
Moore, William (Antrim, N.)
More, Robt. J. (Shropshire)
Morgan, Hn. F. (M'nm'thsh.)
Morrison, Walter
Morton, A. H. A. (Deptford)
Murray, Rt. Hn. A. G (Bute)
Murray, Col. Wyndham (Bath)
Newdigate, Francis Alexander

Nicholson, William Graham
Nicol, Donald Ninian
Northcote, Hon. Sir H. S.
O'Brien, Patrick (Kilkenny)
O'Connor, Arthur (Donegal)
Orr-Ewing, Charles Lindsay
Parkes, Ebenezer
Percy, Earl
Powell, Sir Francis Sharp
Pretyman, Ernest George
Priestley, Sir W. O. (Edinb'h)
Purvis, Robert
Rentoul, James Alexander
Ritchie, Rt. Hon. Chas. T.
Rothschild, Hon. Lionel W.
Royds, Clement Molyneux
Russell, Gen. F. S. (Chelt'nh'm)
Russell, T. W. (Tyrone)
Rutherford, John
Ryder, John Herbert Dudley
Samuel, Harry S. (Limehouse
Sassoon, Sir Edward Albert
Savory, Sir Joseph
Scott, Sir S. (Marylebone, W.)
Seely, Charles Hilton
Sharpe, William Edward T.
Shaw, Charles E. (Stafford)
Sidebottom, Wm. (Derbyshire)
Sinclair, Louis (Romford)
Smith, Abel H. (Christchurch)
Smith, Hon. W. F. D. (Strand)
Stanley, Hon. A. (Ormskirk)
Stanley, Edwd. Jas. (Somerset)
Stanley, Henry M. (Lambeth)
Stanley, Lord (Lancashire)
Stock, James Henry
Stone, Sir Benjamin
Strutt, Hon. Charles Hedley
Talbot, Lord E. (Chichester)
Thorburn, Walter
Thornton, Percy M.
Tollemache, Henry James
Tritton, Charles Ernest
Usborne, Thomas
Walrond, Rt. Hon. Sir W. H.
Ward, Hon. Robt. A. (Crewe)
Warde, Lieut.-Col. C.E. (Kent)
Webster, R. G. (St. Pancras)
Webster, Sir R. E. (I. of Wight
Wentworth, Bruce C. Vernon-
Whiteley, H. (Asht'n-under-L.
Whitmore, Charles Algernon
Willox, Sir John Archibald
Wilson, John (Falkirk)
Wilson-Todd, W. H. (Yorks.)
Wodehouse, Rt.Hn.E.R.(Bath)
Wylie, Alexander
Wyndham-Quin, Major W. H.
Wyvill, Marmaduke D'Arcy
Young, Commander (Berks, E.)

TELLERS FOR THE AYES—Sir
    J. Blundell Maple and Mr.
    Marks.

NOES.

Abraham, Wm. (Cork, N.E.)
Abraham, William (Rhondda)
Allan, William (Gateshead)
Allison, Robert Andrew
Asquith, Rt. Hn. Herbert Hy.

Austin. M. (Limerick, W.)
Barlow, John Emmott
Bayley, Thomas (Derbyshire)
Beaumont, Wentworth C. B.
Blake, Edward

Buchanan, Thomas Ryburn
Burns, John
Burt, Thomas
Buxton, Sydney Charles
Caldwell, James

Cameron, Sir Chas. (Glasgow)
Cameron, Robert (Durham)
Cawley, Frederick
Colville, John
Condon, Thomas Joseph
Crombie, John William
Davies,M.Vaughan- (Cardigan)
Dillon, John
Donelan, Captain A.
Dunn, Sir William
Ellis, Thos. Ed. (Merionethsh.)
Evans,SirFrancisH.(South'ton)
Farquharson, Dr. Robert
Ferguson, R. C. Munro (Leith)
Foster, Sir Walter (Derby Co.)
• Gladstone, Rt. Hn. Herbert J.
Goddard, Daniel Ford
Gold, Charles
Gourley, Sir Edward Temperley
Haldane, Richard Burdon
Hayne, Rt. Hn. Charles Seale-
Horniman, Fredrick John
Hutton, Alfred E. (Morley)
Jacoby, James Alfred
Joicey, Sir James
Jones, William (Carnarvonsh.)

Kay-Shuttleworth,R;Hn Sir U.
Kilbride, Denis
Kinloch, Sir John Geo Smyth
Labouchere, Henry
Langley, batty
Leuty, Thomas Richmond
Lough, Thomas
Macaleese, Daniel
MacDonnell,Dr.M.A.(Qn's.Co.)
MacNeill, John Gordon Swift
M'Ghee, Richard
M'Kenna, Reginald
Maden, John Henry
Mappin, Sir Frederick Thorpe
Molloy, Bernard Charles
Moore, Arthur (Londonderry)
Morgan,J.Lloyd (Crmrthn.)
Morgan,W.Pritchard (Merchyr)
O'Brien, James F. X. (Cork)
Oldroyd, Mark
Power, Patrick Joseph
Price, Robert John
Randell, David
Reid, Sir Robert Threshie
Roberts, John H. (Denbighs.)
Schwann, Charles E.

Soames, Arthur Wellesley
Spicer, Albert
Stanhope, Hon. Philip J.
Stevenson, Francis S.
Sullivan, Donal (Westmeath)
Tanner, Charles Kearns
Tennant, Harold John
Thomas, Abel (Carmarthen, E.
Thomas, Alfred (Glamorgan, E.
Thomas, David A. (Merthyr)
Wallace, Robert (Perth)
Walton, John L. (Leeds, S.)
Whittaker, Thomas Palmer
Wills, Sir William Henry
Wilson, John (Durham, Mid.)
Wilson, John (Govan)
Wilson, J. W. (Wor'stersh. N.)
Wilson, J. H. (Middlesbrough)
Woods, Samuel
Young, Samuel (Cavan, E.)
Yoxall, James Henry

TELLERS FOR THE NOES—Sir
Charles Dilke and Captain
Norton.

Main Question put, and agreed to.

Bill read a second time, and committed for to-morrow.

RIVERS POLLUTION PREVENTION
BILL.

Order for Second Reading read.

Motion made and Question proposed—

" That this Bill be now read a second time."
—(Sir F. Powell.)

*SIR F. POWELL (Wigan): I have waited six years to get the opportunity of making this statement with regard to the Bill which I am now asking the House to read a second time. I do not introduce it on my own initiative, but at the request, and on behalf, of the County Councils Association, whose members come from all parts of the country; and I venture to submit that a Bill introduced under such conditions deserves the careful attention of the House of Commons. This question of the pollution of our rivers is not a new question. It has attracted the attention of successive Governments. There have been Commissions appointed to consider it, and their reports fill many volumes. It has also had the attention of Committees of both Houses of Parliament. These inquiries resulted in the passing of the Rivers Pollution Act of 1876, but that Act has been found to be so

full of technicalities, and so much encumbered by restrictions, that it has proved inoperative in practice. The pollution of our rivers still continues to such an extent that it is a disgrace, in my judgment, to the civilisation of this country. I believe that in many instances the present state of things is injurious to public health, and it is fatal to the amenity of the surroundings of the houses inhabited by many of the working classes, to whose comfort, I am sure, every section of this House desires to minister. While Parliament has been slow as regards Public Bill Legislation, local authorities have been active. There was passed some years ago a Bill called the Mersey and Irwell Act, which was followed a year after by the West Riding of Yorkshire Rivers Board Act. There was another decision of Parliament in the course of last Session, which was of even more importance than the Acts to which I have referred. I allude to the Middlesex County Council Act dealing with the River Brent. The provisions of that Act are far more stringent than those of the Mersey and Irwell Act, or the West Riding of Yorkshire Rivers Board Act. The working of these Acts has been found to be most effective and salutary. Mr. Littler, a well known and distinguished parliamentary counsel, who is chairman of the Middlesex County Council, speaks in the most emphatic terms of the good results which have followed that legislation. I think I shall more clearly explain this Bill by comparing the provisions of it, in the first instance, with those of the Act of 1876. The first part of the Act of 1876 deals with solids—solids of an offensive character and solids that are not offensive, but which block the stream and prevent the flow of the water. The Act of 1876, as regards solids, only prohibits when they either prevent the flow of the water or pollute the stream. Now, it is not easy to find a proof in many cases of one or the other. In any case the finding of the proof leads to delay, involves additional expense, and in many cases makes the issue doubtful. The first clause of this Bill proposes that the mere act of putting solids into the stream should of itself be prevented. Many people will by design place a mass of cinders in the bed of a stream. The mass will remain there until the flood comes, and the flood then carries the cinders down the stream until they settle where the flow becomes less rapid. They there cause an obstruction, and very often a morass occurs, to the great injury of the locality. I have an illustration here, taken from the Report of the Mersey and Irwell Conservancy Board of 1898. They make this remark with regard to solids—

" The improvement with respect of pollution from solid matters has been well maintained, and the bed of the river in its upper reaches is now practically free from cinders and other refuse."

Now, Sir, what has been done in Lancashire I desire to do for the whole country. Provision, however, is made in this Bill for those who have a legal right to place solids in a stream for weirs, foundations, and the like. The next part of the Bill deals with liquid sewage. The Act of 1876 seems to me to be of an extraordinary character, because it gave a right to discharge liquid sewage into a stream by persons who were in the habit of doing so at the time of the passing of the Act. My opinion is that this right has lasted so long that it has now become a wrong, and ought to be done away with. There is really no difficulty whatever in keeping liquid sewage out of a stream. The accumulation of this liquid sewage is most injurious to the stream, and becomes most pestilential in its effect. It may be said that the sanitary authority has in some cases discharged raw sewage, as it is called,

into a stream, and there is no doubt a difficulty in at once curing this evil, but provision is taken in the Bill to give local authorities time to remedy this mischief. On the application of any sanitary authority which at the passing of this Bill is committing any offence, the Local Government Board may—if, having regard to all the circumstances of the case, they think necessary—by order, grant time to such authority for executing any works or doing any acts necessary to prevent the commission of the offence, and during the time specified in the order, which may be extended by a subsequent order, no proceedings are to be taken by any person against the authority. The object is to move one step at a time, so that the work may be proceeded with continuously, and that the authority may not be burdened by an excessive expenditure. We now come to a far more difficult part of the Bill—liquid manufacturing and other pollution. We have had many deputations from those engaged in manufacture in various parts of the country on this subject, but I think this Bill will sufficiently guard manufacturers. First of all, the authority which sets in motion this part of the Bill is of a different character from that of the authority which deals with the first and second parts of the Bill. The authority which would deal with this would be either the joint committee appointed under the Act of 1888, or the committee appointed under some local Act, or the council of the administrative county. That concession was made to meet the views of municipal corporations with whom we have had many consultations, and I believe they are satisfied with the proposal. Then there is a further restriction, one, I think, which gentlemen engaged in trade must surely feel to be most valuable: that proceedings cannot be taken under this part of the Bill without the consent of the Local Government Board. Not only is that consent required under this Bill, but the latter part of clause 8 expressly provides that the Local Government Board shall not give their consent to such proceedings unless they are satisfied, after local inquiry, and having regard to the reasonableness of the cost, and the effect on the industry or trade in question, that means for rendering harmless the poisonous, noxious, or polluting liquid are reasonably practicable and available under all the circumstances of the case. I think this provides security for manufacturers. I represent a manufacturing district, and all my interests, or nearly all of them, are associated intimately with these districts, and naturally I should not be a party to bring in a Bill in this House which would prove injurious to trade. Then we get to another provision dealing with the storm waters. We have received a deputation from municipal corporations on this point, and the clause in this Bill provides that where a sanitary authority have their sewers and sewage works so constructed, maintained, and used as efficiently to prevent the fall or flow of sewage into any stream at all times, except during or immediately after an unusual rainfall, an offence shall not be deemed to be committed under this Bill in the case of an overflow from those sewers or works containing polluted matter, if it is shown to the satisfaction of the court that such overflow was caused by the unusual rainfall. It will be seen, therefore, that the case of storm waters is wholly met, and the difficulties which took place in our preliminary discussions are now, I hope, entirely removed. We now come to the question of penalties and procedure. Objection has been taken to proceedings in respect of offences coming before the county court. There are many reasons why a county court is not a satisfactory tribunal, but it has been found in some cases in Lancashire that resort to the county court has been desirable. This Bill provides that proceedings may be taken either before a court of summary jurisdiction or a county court. Alternative procedure is not in itself always satisfactory, but there has been such a desire on the part of some to have the county court, and on the part of others to have a court of summary jurisdiction, that we have given the alternative in this Bill.

Attention having been called to the fact that there were not 40 Members present, the House was counted, when 40 Members being present—

*Sir F. POWELL (continuing): I have stated what I may describe as the operative part of this Bill. I do not think I need delay the House by going fully into the machinery which is provided, and

Sir F. Powell.

which, I hope, is suited to the occasion. We have met, as far as we can, every suggestion. We have seen, and have had interviews with municipal corporations, and with those who are concerned in the different industries, and so far as I know, every objection and every difficulty has been met. There has been some difficulty in the cases where there are Local Acts, and in this Bill we have left untouched Local Acts, which have been passed within recent years, and to the benefits of which we feel those who have passed them are entitled. These are the main features of the Bill, and I hope they will commend themselves to the House of Commons. It is possible that some expense may arise as we are proceeding, but that is no new question. We have had to deal in the past with many difficulties in connection with legislation concerning dangerous trades; but they have been removed by a firm hand, and I am sure no one ever regrets the passing of the Acts to which I refer. I am sure that the placing on the Statute Book of the Bill, the Second Reading of which I have the honour to move, would prove of great benefit to the districts affected. I think this is one of those Measures eminently fitted for discussion by a Standing Committee on Law. The Measure contains many details, some of which may not commend themselves to honourable Members who are not able to accept the Bill in its entirety, and it is possible also that the machinery may be improved. The Standing Committee is, I think, the proper tribunal to make these investigations, and if I succeed in obtaining a Second Reading for this Bill, I shall move that it be referred to the Standing Committee on Law.

MR. WILSON-TODD (York, N.R., Howdenshire): I beg to formally second the Motion.

Amendment proposed—

"To leave out the word 'now,' and at the end of the Question to add the words 'upon this day six months.'"—(*Mr. Kenyon*).

MR. KENYON (Bury, Lancashire): I have listened carefully to the speech of the honourable Baronet, and I must express my surprise at hearing him say that the bulk of the people—I think those were his words—approved of the Mersey and Irwell Act of 1892. I contend, Mr. Speaker, that if the people in those districts were polled on the question you would find an enormous majority of them against that Act. I believe it has been one of the most troublesome, most irritating, most annoying, and most expensive Acts of Parliament which has ever been brought into force in this country, and I am astonished that the honourable Member should not have had more and better information on the subject. Last Session I took the same course that I am taking to-day, and opposed the honourable Baronet's Motion, and I shall be glad to give him some information as to the great expense and annoyance which this Act has been to Lancashire. I am also surprised that the honourable Member should introduce this Bill without waiting for the Report of the Royal Commission on Sewage which is now sitting, and the reference to which covers all these points. I certainly think the honourable Baronet might have postponed this matter until the Report of that Commission was received. The object of the Bill which is now before the House is to extend to county councils, to joint committees, and to rivers boards, the many provisions of the Mersey and Irwell Act of 1892, and I shall not only be very sorry indeed for the manufacturers, but also for the ratepayers, if the Bill passes. I have heard many times in this House expressions of opinion that the local rates in this country were growing very considerably, and the Chancellor of the Exchequer has viewed with alarm the increase of local indebtedness. This Bill is one of those Measures which will tend more to raise the rates throughout the country than any other Measure which could be brought forward. It is a most expensive process that the honourable Baronet the Member for Wigan is seeking to get the House to adopt, and the results from the other Bills have proved very doubtful indeed. No standard of purity is fixed, and a locality would be absolutely at the mercy of the inspector and the few faddists on a joint committee or county council. If the inspector's liver was not in good order, he might complain, and as there is no standard of purity fixed manufacturers are put to a great deal of annoyance and irritation. That is so under the Mersey and Irwell Act, and would be so under this Bill, as

there is nothing in it to remedy that state of things. I had the misfortune, some years ago, to be concerned in a law suit, and, and, to show honourable Members what some people's ideas of pollution or deterioration of water may be, I may say that the learned judge who tried the action gave it as his opinion that water which had been boiled and passed through the condenser of a steam engine was deteriorated. Of course, honourable Members will understand that my feelings, on hearing the learned judge give that opinion, were more like iced water going down my back than hot water or condensed water. I mention this to show the House the different opinions which may be held, perfectly conscientiously, and by the most honourable people in the world, as to what constitutes deterioration of water. When you have well-educated people like our judges, who have great experience in all matters, and particularly in these matters of water rights, expressing such opinions as the one I have quoted, what may you expect from the ordinary joint committee, county council, magistrates, county courts, or quarter sessions, whoever may be called upon to judge in this matter? Under this Bill you place manufacturers and the local authority in a most unfair position, and in a position which I do not think they ought to be placed. Then there is another most important matter in regard to the Mersey and Irwell Act, and in regard also to the Bill the Second Reading of which the honourable Baronet has just moved. The majority of manufacturing works are placed at a low level, so that the water supply may gravitate down to the works, and the effect of such a Measure as this would be that all the polluted water would have to be lifted to a considerable height in order to prevent it getting into the tributaries. The great bulk of manufacturers are not unwilling to provide some simple settling beds, but to require them to filter and purify the water, making it as clear as when it was taken from the stream, is to make a most unreasonable demand. Allow me to relate a few experiences of the Mersey and Irwell Act. The county borough which I have the honour to represent, which has a population of 60,000 people, was compelled, in order to meet the requirements of this Act, to alter the levels of their drains. They have put down very large sewage works to treat this sewage, and they have gone to a considerable expense in many ways. The total cost of these works, up to the present time, is £130,000, and before they are finished and got to work I expect the cost will be another £30,000, or about £2 10s. per head of the population, for this precious fad of the Mersey and Irwell Committee. I do not think it has done five shillings' worth of good in regard to improving the state of the stream, or in improving the health of the people. The upper reaches of the river, I admit, are improved slightly, but near Victoria Station at Manchester the river remains a sewer, as it always has been. I do not think I am exaggerating when I say that the Mersey and Irwell Act has cost Lancashire over two millions sterling, and I repeat that I do not think it has done five shillings' worth of good. I do not think expenditure under any Act has been so foolishly wasted as the expenditure which has been incurred under the Mersey and Irwell Act. As regards the Bill now before the House, I should like to call attention to one or two clauses. Clause 9 provides that—

"Where a sanitary authority have their sewers and sewage works so constructed, maintained, and used, as efficiently to prevent the fall or flow of sewage into any stream at all times, except during or immediately after an unusual rainfall, an offence shall not be deemed to be committed under this Act in the case of an overflow from those sewers or works containing polluted matter, if it is shown to the satisfaction of the Court that such overflow was caused by the unusual rainfall."

Surely the honourable Member, with his experience of the North of England, will know that this very clause would be sufficient to cause no end of litigation in proving whether there was an unusual rainfall or not. There would be the temptation to let go the sewer when a rainfall came, especially when it was an unusual one. Clause 18 provides that—

"For the better enforcement of the provisions of this Act it shall be lawful for any officer of or other person authorised by local authority to enter at any reasonable time on any land, manufactory, or other work or building, for the purpose of taking and carrying away samples of any effluent at the point where it passes into the stream. Such officer or person shall leave under seal a duplicate of every sample taken by him with the owner or occupier of the premises whence the effluent flows."

Mr. Kenyon.

The manufacturer would, therefore, be subject to the annoyance of an inspector coming to demand samples at any hour of the day or night. Work is carried on both day and night in many of the factories, and this system of inspection would, I am afraid, be carried on in a very objectionable manner. The inspectors in Lancashire have, in their zeal, inquired as to which was the worst machine, and where the dirtiest water and the most polluted water was turned out, and, when they have obtained this information, samples have been taken from the very worst point in the works. These samples have been presented to the committee and spoken of as if such water was constantly coming from the works, and it has required considerable persuasion on the part of the manufacturer to get the committee to believe that water of the kind that had been taken by the inspector was not always being turned out. The manufacturers of the whole country are, as I have already said, quite willing to clear their effluent to a certain extent, but they do not wish to be put to the enormous expenditure which such Acts as the Mersey and Irwell Act imposed. And when one talks of expenditure, it is just as well to bear in mind that this is another factor which has to be taken into account when we consider the question of competition with our friends abroad. I have travelled a good many miles in the United States, and I have never heard anything said about the pollution of the rivers. The manufacturers there do just as we did in the old days. The same thing obtains in Germany and in many other countries. I must ask honourable Members to consider the question of foreign competition in regard to this Bill. Under this Bill small manufactories will be handicapped by an additional expenditure of quite £400 a year to carry out the provisions of this Bill, if passed, and I am sure in some works where they use a large quantity of water, such as bleaching works, dyeing works, and paper works, the expenditure would be much higher. If you handicap manufacturers in this country with all these expenses you must remember that you are handicapping them in their competition with foreign countries. We have frequently heard during the last 12 months that the British manufacturers cannot do this, and cannot make that, at the price which foreign countries are able to. We in England are not afraid of any competition so long as we are treated fairly and reasonably. We can make the goods, and we can compete with the foreigner, and give quite as long credit if we are not interfered with. I appeal to honourable Members, before they sanction such a Measure as this, to consider the expense which it would throw on the British manufacturers. These are matters deserving of the most careful attention of this House, and I sincerely trust the House will reject the Second Reading of the Bill, and leave manufacturers free from such burdens as this Bill would impose. The Bill will cost a great deal of money, and will confer but little benefit, if any. I beg to move that this Bill be Read a Second time this day six months.

Captain GREVILLE (Bradford, E.): I beg to Second the Amendment.

Mr. CAWLEY (Lancashire, Prestwich): Mr. Speaker, as I have had to go to considerable expense in purifying my effluent, I am in a position to say something on this matter. I do not agree with my honourable Friend, that if the people of Lancashire were polled they would vote against the Mersey and Irwell Act, but I do say that manufacturers in Lancashire consider that they have a very great grievance, inasmuch as they are compelled to spend large sums of money in purifying their sewage, whereas other manufacturers throughout the country are not compelled to do so. What we want is that all parts of the kingdom should be placed on a level in this matter, and I shall vote for this Bill, not because I consider it a perfect Bill, but because I think it may be so altered in Committee, after the experience of the Mersey and Irwell Act, as to be made a good Bill. I think the other Acts ought to be repealed, and this Bill, as amended, made the law of the country. When the Mersey and Irwell Act was brought in a friend of mine, a large manufacturer spoke to me in a very aggrieved tone. He had been for years in the habit of throwing into the river tons of cinders, and he was aggrieved because he would not be able to put them into the river in future. It is gentlemen like this whom we wish to catch, and I think if a Bill was

brought in applying to the whole country, and not to Lancashire alone, it would be of considerable advantage. Competition is not always between England and foreign countries. It is sometimes between manufacturers in one part of England and manufacturers in another part, and I do think paper-makers, for instance, in Lancashire have a very great grievance when they are compelled to spend thousands of pounds under the Mersey and Irwell Act, while their competitors in other parts of the country have had to spend nothing, and are, therefore, able to under-sell them. That seems to me a real grievance in Lancashire. My honourable Friend mentioned the town of Bury, and other towns which had had to purify their sewage. It is not right that large towns with 60,000 inhabitants should be allowed to turn their sewage unpurified into the river. I think an Act which prevents large towns on the upper reaches of the Irwell sending undiluted sewage into the river will commend itself to this House. I sympathise with the manufacturers who have had to spend so much money on their works, but I think that a very great number of them, notwithstanding that they have had to spend this money, would not go back to the old state of affairs, because it must be remembered that bleachers and dyers, if they can have a stream purified above their works, sometimes get compensation for any outlay they may make by being able to obtain purer water out of the river. I should like this Bill to go to a Standing Committee and be made a little less drastic than it is, but I should be very sorry to see it rejected.

Sir W. FOSTER (Derbyshire, Ilkeston): This Bill has been before the House on many occasions. It is one on which I hope we shall receive an expression of opinion from the Government, and I trust that that expression of opinion will be favourable to the general principle of the Bill. I have been grieved to hear the Member for Bury defend that barbaric ignorance by which the pollution of the rivers all over the country has been allowed. To have allowed this to go on so long is one of the greatest mistakes this country has ever made. The honourable Member who has just spoken, and who has gone through the process of purifying his effluent, says that he desires that in this matter manufacturers in all parts of the kingdom should be treated alike. I believe that in the end that would be an economic process. If the pollution of rivers had not been allowed, we should have had much less difficulty in obtaining pure water supplies, and great communities would not have to spend millions, and even tens of millions sterling. in order to provide pure water for their people. Although the immediate effect of the passing of this Bill may be a temporary, and perhaps permanent, slight increase in the rates, I believe it will be good economy that that slight increase should be made, because it will have the effect of improving the health of the people, and of giving them closer to their doors a large amount of pure water. I hope the Government will support this Bill, and send it to a Grand Committee on Law.

THE PRESIDENT OF THE LOCAL GOVERNMENT BOARD (Mr. CHAPLIN, Lincolnshire, Sleaford): Whatever views may be held by honourable Members with regard to this Bill, I think we shall all agree with my honourable Friend behind me that the question of the pollution, of the prevention of the pollution of our rivers is one of the very first public importance. At the same time, it is quite evident that there are rather sharp differences of opinion in the House upon the particular merits and the machinery of the Bill which is before us this afternoon. My honourable Friend has explained its provisions very fully and very clearly. What the Bill does, in a word, is to extend to county councils, to joint committees, to river boards, and to town councils throughout the country the provisions of the Mersey and Irwell Act, and what is known as the West Riding Act. My honourable Friend the Mover of the Amendment, the Member for Bury, spoke in terms of the severest condemnation of the operation of the Mersey and Irwell Act, and declared that not only had it been futile and useless in effecting its purpose, but that in its operation it had been enormously expensive, entailing upon the people of

Sir W. Foster.

Lancashire a cost of something like two millions sterling. I wish to guard myself against being supposed to endorse the statements made with regard to the operation of that Act, but I refer to these statements in order to show that there are many matters in connection with these questions which undoubtedly do deserve most careful consideration. The honourable Member entertained the greatest apprehension that if this Bill were passed in its present state its operation would tend to enormously raise the rates in Lancashire. We all agree, I think, that, as far as it is possible to effect it, our rivers ought to be free from the pollution which affects many of them. The general conclusion I have arrived at is that I hope the House will be disposed to agree to the Second Reading upon condition that the Measure should be referred, not to a Standing Committee on Law, but to a Select Committee, by whom it should be considered in detail. Subject to that condition, I, on behalf of the Government, will be quite ready to assent to the Second Reading.

MR. JACKSON (Leeds, N.): I am sorry to say that I entirely disapprove of the course which the right honourable Gentleman proposes to take in regard to this Bill. I have had some experience in dealing with this difficult question, and I think the Mover of the Second Reading of the Bill himself will hardly claim for it that it satisfies even him with regard to its machinery, and in many other respects. I do not hesitate to say that a Bill of this importance, applying, as it does, to the whole country, and affecting, as it would, to a large extent the manufacturing industries of this country, ought not to be dealt with on a Wednesday afternoon. I endorse a great deal of what has been said by the honourable Member for Bury as to the great expense which the Acts now in force on this matter have involved. As I understand it, the honourable Member who moved the Second Reading of this Bill proposes to exempt all districts where they have local Acts already. Therefore, the result of the passing of this Bill would be that we should have one law in one part of the country and another law in another part of the country. I entirely agree with the honourable Member opposite who said that there is such a thing as competition between manufacturers in this country, and I am strongly of opinion that a Bill of this importance ought not to be passed by the House except after the most careful consideration of the Government. The West Riding Act has created a great deal of friction and a great deal of expense, and while I have heard a great many objections raised to it, I have never heard one word in its favour. I know one man who is at the present moment being prosecuted by the West Riding Rivers Board. I express no opinion on the merits of the case, but I do say this, of my own personal knowledge, that he has told me that if the West Riding Rivers Board are successful in their prosecution, he will be compelled to close his works. That, surely, is a very important question.

*SIR F. POWELL rose in his place, and claimed to move "That the Question be now put," but Mr. SPEAKER withheld his assent, and declined then to put the Question.

MR. JACKSON: My honourable Friend the Mover of this Bill has, I think, large interests in Yorkshire, and I wonder what his friends would say with regard to this Bill. I should be surprised if they supported it. I have an interest in a business which is a source of great pollution. We have been trying for years to deal with it; we have had chemists to assist us in endeavouring to try a remedy, and we have made considerable progress; but, after all we have done, we have failed to satisfy the West Riding Rivers Board, and we have appealed to the local authority —the Corporation of Leeds—to help us out of our difficulty by allowing us to turn our effluent into their sewer. We

have had a little help from the Local Government Board in that direction, but we are now met with another difficulty. A navigation company claim to have certain water rights in the stream into which the effluent went, and they now threaten us with legal proceedings to compel us to turn the effluent back again into the stream.

And, it being half-past Five of the clock, the Debate stood adjourned.

Debate to be resumed To-morrow.

———

RIVERS POLLUTION PREVENTION
(No. 2) BILL.

Order for Second Reading read, and discharged:—Bill withdrawn.

WATER SUPPLY BILL.

Second Reading deferred till Monday next.

POOR LAW OFFICERS' SUPERANNUA-
TION ACT (1896) AMENDMENT BILL.

Second Reading deferred till Tuesday next.

REGISTRATION OF FIRMS BILL.

Second Reading deferred till Wednesday 26th April.

WORKMEN'S HOUSES TENURE BILL.

Second Reading deferred till Wednesday next.

CONSTRUCTIVE MURDER LAW AMEND-
MENT BILL.

Second Reading deferred till Wednesday next.

MERCHANDISE MARKS ACT (1887) AMENDMENT BILL.
Second Reading deferred till Wednesday next.

WORKING MEN'S DWELLINGS BILL.
Second Reading deferred till Wednesday next.

SCHOOL BOARD ELECTORATE (SCOTLAND) BILL.
Second Reading deferred till Friday.

BUILDING FEUS AND LEASES (SCOTLAND) BILL.
Second Reading deferred till Wednesday next.

CHEAP TRAINS BILL.
Second Reading deferred till Thursday 16th March.

VACCINATION (CONSCIENTIOUS OBJECTORS) BILL.
Second Reading deferred till Wednesday 22nd March.

CROFTERS' HOLDINGS (SCOTLAND) ACT (1886) AMENDMENT BILL.
Second Reading deferred till Thursday 16th March.

OCCUPYING TENANTS ENFRANCHISEMENT BILL.
Second Reading deferred till Wednesday 12th April.

CROWN CASES BILL.
Second Reading deferred till Tuesday next.

SUPPLY.
Committee deferred till to-morrow.

SUPPLY (3RD MARCH).
Report deferred till to-morrow.

WAYS AND MEANS.
Committee deferred till Friday.

PARISH COUNCILLORS (TENURE OF OFFICE) BILL.
Committee deferred till Friday.

————

NEW BILLS.

———

INDICTMENTS BILL.
" To amend the Law with regard to Indictments," presented, and read the first time ; to be read a second time upon Monday 1st May, and to be printed. (Bill 116.)

SALMON FISHERIES (IRELAND) ACTS AMENDMENT BILL.
" To amend the Salmon Fisheries (Ireland) Acts," presented, and read the first time ; to be read a second time upon Wednesday 3rd May, and to be printed. (Bill 117.)

———

REPORTS.

PUBLIC ACCOUNTS COMMITTEE.
First Report from the Select Committee brought up, and read ; Report to lie upon the Table, and to be printed. (No. 97.)

PUBLIC PETITIONS COMMITTEE.
First Report brought up, and read ; Report to lie upon the Table, and to be printed.

House adjourned at thirty-one minutes after Five of the clock.

HOUSE OF LORDS.

Thursday, 9th March 1899.

THE LORD CHANCELLOR took his seat upon the Woolsack at fifteen minutes past Four of the clock.

NEW PEER.

The Earl of Strafford—Sat first in Parliament after the death of his brother.

PRIVATE BILL BUSINESS.

THE LORD CHANCELLOR acquainted the House that the Clerk of the Parliaments had laid upon the Table the Certificate from the Examiners that the Standing Orders applicable to the following Bill have been complied with—

Watermen's and Lightermen's Acts Acts Amendment.

The same was ordered to lie on the Table.

BRISTOL FLOODS PREVENTION BILL [H.L.]

Committee to meet on Thursday next.

NORTHERN ASSURANCE COMPANY BILL [H.L.]

Committee to meet on Tuesday next.

LIVERPOOL OVERHEAD RAILWAY BILL [H.L.]

Committed.

SOUTH HANTS WATER BILL [H.L.]

Committed: The Committee to be proposed by the Committee of Selection.

VOL. LXVIII. [FOURTH SERIES.]

KNOTT END RAILWAY BILL [H.L.]

THE CHAIRMAN OF COMMITTEES informed the House, that the promoters do not intend to proceed further with the Bill: Ordered that the Bill be not further proceeded with.

Cromer Protection Bill [H.L.]
Glastonbury Water Bill [H.L.]
Yeadon and Guiseley Gas Bill [H.L.]
Bristol Gas Bill [H.L.]
Lea Bridge District Gas Bill [H.L.]
Queen's Ferry Bridge Bill [H.L.]
Nene Valley Water Bill [H.L.]
St. Neot's Water Bill [H.L.]

Report from the Committee of Selection that the Earl of Stamford and the Lord Wimborne be proposed to the House as members of the Select Committee on the said Bills in the place of the Earl of Radnor and the Lord Carew; read, and agreed to.

WICK AND PULTENEY HARBOURS BILL [H.L.]

Standing Order No. 92 considered (according to order), and dispensed with, with respect to a Petition of the Provost, Magistrates, and Town Council of Wick; Leave given to present the said Petition.

CATHCART'S DIVORCE BILL [H.L.].

House in Committee (according to order): An Amendment made: Standing Committee negatived: the Report of Amendment to be received to-morrow.

PRIVATE AND PROVISIONAL ORDER CONFIRMATION BILLS.

Ordered—

That no Private Bill brought from the House of Commons shall be read a second time after Tuesday the 27th day of June next.

That no Provisional Order Confirmation Bill originating in this House shall be read a first time after Tuesday the 2nd day of May next.

K

That no Provisional Order Confirmation Bill brought from the House of Commons shall be read a second time after Tuesday the 27th day of June next.

That when a Bill shall have passed this House with Amendments these orders shall not apply to any new Bill sent up from the House of Commons which the Chairman of Committees shall report to the House is substantially the same as the Bill so amended.

That this House will not receive any petition for a Private Bill later than Tuesday the 25th day of April next, unless such Private Bill shall have been approved by the High Court of Justice; nor any petition for a Private Bill approved by the High Court of Justice after Friday the 5th day of May next.

That this House will not receive any Report from the Judges upon petitions presented to this House for Private Bills after Friday the 5th day of May next.

Ordered, That the said orders be printed and published, and affixed on the ·doors of this House and Westminster Hall. (No. 21.)

STANDING COMMITTEE.

To meet on Tuesday next, at a quarter before Four of the clock.

HOUSES OF LORDS AND COMMONS PERMANENT STAFF.

Message from the Commons to acquaint this House that they have appointed a Select Committee of Five Members to join with the Select Committee appointed by this House, as mentioned in their Lordships' message of the 27th of February last, to consider and report on the subject of the Houses of Lords and Commons Permanent Staff.

RETURNS, REPORTS, ETC.

TRADE REPORTS—MISCELLANEOUS SERIES: No. 499.

Suggestions for development of British trade with Italy.

Presented (by Command) and ordered to lie on the Table.

HIGH SHERIFFS (IRELAND) (EXPENSES OF OFFICE).

Circular addressed by the Lord Lieutenant to High Sheriffs with regard to the expenses of their office; together with letter of 2nd November 1898 from Her Majesty's Treasury upon which the circular was based.

Presented (by Command) and ordered to lie on the Table.

CHURCH ESTATES COMMISSION.

Forty-eighth Report from the Church Estates Commissioners.

Presented (by Command) and ordered to lie on the Table.

COMMERCIAL, No. 1 (1899).

Reports respecting the telephone service in various foreign countries.

Presented (by Command) and ordered to lie on the Table.

GRAND JURY PRESENTMENTS (IRELAND).

Presentments made by grand juries in Ireland and flatted by the Court of Assize during the year 1898: Laid before the House (pursuant to Act), and ordered to lie on the Table.

PETITIONS.

INTOXICATING LIQUORS.

Petitions against the sale of, on Sundays; of Inhabitants of Chatteris—Linton—Lister Hills—Bradford—Newhaven—and Sheerness—Read, and ordered to lie on the Table.

NEW BILL.

LINCOLNSHIRE CORONERS BILL [H.L.]

A Bill to constitute the divisions of Lincolnshire separate counties for all the purposes of the Coroners Acts—was presented by the Lord Heneage; read the first time; to be printed; and to be read a second time on Monday the 20th instant. (No. 20.)

PUBLIC BUSINESS.

PARTRIDGE SHOOTING (IRELAND) BILL.

Brought form the Commons; read the first time; and to be printed. (No. 19.)

MONEY-LENDING BILL [H.L.].

To be read second time on **Thursday next.**

PARISH CHURCHES (SCOTLAND) BILL.

Order for Second Reading read.

Motion made and Question proposed—

" That this Bill be read a second time."—(*Lord Balfour of Burleigh.*)

THE SECRETARY FOR SCOTLAND (Lord BALFOUR of BURLEIGH) : My Lords, I rise to move the Second Reading of this Bill, which is practically the same Measure that passed your Lordships' House during last Session, but failed to become law mainly owing to the pressure of business at the conclusion of the Session in another place. The principal object of the Bill is to adapt the ecclesiastical arrangements of the Church of Scotland in certain parishes to the present needs both of those parishes and of the Church. As your Lordships are aware, towns and cities have extended their boundaries, and the population have migrated from one district to another, and are consequently, in many places, now dwelling at an inconvenient distance from the sites of the old parish churches which they attend. The Bill in its structure is entirely domestic to the Church of Scotland, and is not intended as an attack upon any other religious community. We have this year carefully revised it, and have done so with a view of meeting many of the objections which were raised by political friends of the noble Lord opposite. The noble Lord (Lord Tweedmouth) warned me last year most courteously that this was a Bill which would probably be opposed in another place, and that, my Lords, is one of those prophecies which those associated with the noble Lord are, of course, able to fulfil. I have carefully studied the report of the discussion on this Bill in

another place, and, as I say, we have endeavoured to meet all the objections which we possibly could. I am afraid we shall never be able to meet the objection of some of those who took part in the discussion and who said that nothing would satisfy them except the disestablishment of the Church altogether. But, my Lords, apart from objections of that class, I think your Lordships will see, and those who take an interest in the Bill in another place will see, that every effort has been made to give effect to the objections which were then made. We largely, but by no means exclusively, rested the case for this Bill upon the present state of matters in the City of Edinburgh, and it was alleged that so far as Edinburgh was concerned the case for the Bill had entirely broken down. Statistics were produced showing that in all the city churches there was such a large number of communicants that it was ridiculous to suggest that the site of any one of the churches could be changed with advantage. Now, my Lords, that was not an objection which it was easy beforehand to anticipate, but the explanation is simple in the extreme. There is no doubt that there are communicants upon the rolls of these churches. But the explanation is this, that only an infinitesimal minority of those communicants reside within the bounds of the parishes and districts attached to the various parish churches. I do not wish to go at length into the figures, but the whole of that branch of the subject has been carefully examined, and with this result. Taking the eight city churches of the old town of Edinburgh, it is the case that there are on the rolls of those churches 6,500 communicants. That does not give an average of 1,200, which was stated last year, but it gives an average of 806 communicants to each church. But out of the whole of those 6,500 communicants there are only 193 resident in the districts attached to the respective churches That is an average of about 24 to each, or about 3 per cent. of the whole. The object of this Bill is to give power, on proper cause shown, and on a proper consideration in detail of the circumstances of any one of those churches which it might be thought desirable to remove, to consider the cause and to give a power which does not now exist to remove the church to a district which would be more convenient for the population,

K 2

I should be the last to suggest that all, or even a majority, of those churches should be removed. But surely this is a power which ought to be possessed, and one which is for the benefit not only of the churches, but of the population of the City of Edinburgh. One clause to which some exception was taken last year was the clause dealing with the endowments of *quoad sacra* churches. These churches are omitted from this Bill. I do not say this is not a power which, in some cases, it would be desirable to have, but it is not nearly so urgent as the other matter, and as objection has been taken to it I have omitted that clause in the hope that it will diminish the opposition to the Bill. There are some minor changes in drafting of the Bill, but I should not allude to them in detail at this stage. In case the noble Lord on the Front Bench opposite (Lord Tweedmouth) thinks I have broken faith with him in regard to one amendment I excepted last year, I will point out that the drafting of the clause has been changed, and the heritors, whose cause the noble Lord championed, are now included in the general term "persons interested." That term will not only include heritors, but magistrates and town councils. For the sake of simplifying the Bill we have deleted the detailed description of persons interested, and have described them in the one term, "persons interested," which is wide enough to cover both classes to which I have referred. There are one or two other changes in the Bill, but I hope it will be more for the convenience of the House that any detailed explanation of them should be delayed till a further stage, and explanation be asked for. I now beg to move that this Bill be read a second time.

LORD TWEEDMOUTH: My Lords, I must say that the noble Lord who has just spoken has made a gratuitous attack upon myself. I stirred up no opposition to this Bill. I told him I thought opposition might arise in another place, but I can assure him I was in no way responsible for it. On the contrary, with the object of this Bill I am entirely in sympathy. Whilst I frankly confess that I think the Church is much better untrammelled by the State, and that the State is much better relieved from the responsibility of the Church, at the same

time I have never been one of those who attempted to frustrate legislative effort to improve the condition of the Established Church. As a matter of fact, I have always thought that as long as we have an Established Church it is our duty to make that Church as valuable an instrument for the benefit of religion and the people as possible. I thoroughly support this Bill, which is to give power in certain circumstances to move churches from one place to another within the same presbytery, to give power to sell the sites of the churches for the benefit of the new churches that are to be erected, and to alter the bounds of parishes. But I would ask your Lordships to consider whether in this Bill the interests of the different parishes are sufficiently safeguarded. There are three bodies who are principally inter-concerned in the churches of Scotland. There are the heritors, there is the congregation, and there are the poor of the parish. Now, last year the noble Lord was good enough, at my instigation, to accept an Amendment on the Bill which made the heritors the consenting party to any change proposed under the Bill. Not only was the consent of the presbytery of the bounds necessary, but also the consent of the heritors. The heritors are, as your Lordships know, the persons in whom are vested the property both of the church and the manse, and the land on which those fabrics stand. They are also the persons who provide the tiends for the support of the church. They are the defenders of the interests of the lay portion of the parish, and I do think that they should be consulted, and that they should give their consent to any proposal to change the site of a church or to apply the proceeds from the sale of the site of a church to a church in another part of the parish. Then there comes the question of the congregation. The noble Lord last year pointed out that in the eight city churches in Edinburgh, and in the five churches in Glasgow, the congregations were very small. He, himself, to-day has admitted that the congregations are very large in the Edinburgh churches, and that they have an average of 806 communicants. A church that has a congregation of so large a number of communicants has a very much larger congregation than 806 people, so that these churches are, therefore, used by a considerable number of people. Since the passing of the Patronage Act the congregations have become more important than they were before, for they have assigned to them now the right of choosing a minister, and I do say the congregations of these churches should have the opportunity of being consulted and of putting forward their case and their views before such a question as this is decided, whether it be done through the votes of the congregation, or by the Kirk-Session of the congregation consisting of the elders and the minister of the particular church. I now come to the question of the poor of the parish. The poor have always been considered in Scotland to be especially the care of the Established Church. It has always been recognised that one of the first duties of the Established Church was to take care of the poor of the parish, whether they belong to the congregation or not; and whatever may be said about these parishes in the great cities of Scotland one thing is practically certain. There has been no such denudation of population in the great cities of Scotland as there has been in certain areas within, say, the City of London. We should carefully consider if sufficient attention has been given to the poor persons who dwell within the limits of the parishes to be affected by this Bill, whether they belong to the congregation of the Church of Scotland or not. In either case they should be under the care of the minister of the Established Church. Then, my Lords, there are other matters to which I do not think any attention has been paid. What, for instance, are you going to do with the site of the church and the manse when you have pulled the buildings down? These churches and manses are within crowded parts of the city. Are you to allow the sites to be used for any purpose whatever? Are they to be put up and sold to the highest bidder, and used for the purpose of warehouses, manufactories, and so on? Are not open spaces greatly needed in these crowded districts? And are the claims for open spaces to be thoroughly set aside in this matter? No provision is made in this Bill with regard to this question at all. Then there comes the question of the preservation of the architectural beauties and historical interests connected with these important churches. Are any provisions to be made for securing that these interests shall be cared for and preserved for the benefit of the inhabitants of the city? I have no doubt the noble Lord will say that all these are matters which will be dealt with by the Court of Tiends. Well, that to me is not sufficient! It seems to me that the questions which I have raised should be dealt with by Parliament itself, and not be left to anybody outside the Houses of Parliament. I have not got the least intention to oppose the Second Reading of this Bill, but I do most earnestly hope that the noble Lord will give his attention to the points I have raised, and himself endeavour to amend the Bill in the direction I have indicated in Committee.

THE SECRETARY FOR SCOTLAND: If I gave the noble Lord the impression that I had intended to make any attack upon him, I must say that I expressed myself very badly. I certainly had no such intention, and I hope that when he sees my words in print, as possibly he may, he will see that there was no real attack made.

LORD TWEEDMOUTH: The noble Lord said that the prophecy I made was one which I and my friends could secure the fulfilment of in another place. I deny having done anything to secure the fulfilment of that prophecy.

THE SECRETARY FOR SCOTLAND: The noble Lord has stated that the interests of the poor populations in these parishes have not been sufficiently present in my mind. I think it is sufficient to remind him that even if one or two of these churches were removed the population would not have far to go, and that the districts would not be too large for the care of the ministers that would remain. There is not one of these eight city churches which is half a mile away from any other, and it is a fact that there have been large changes of population in Edinburgh, notably by the reconstruction of the Waverley Station, and by the number of buildings which were formerly dwelling-houses, but which are now warehouses in the central part of the city. I will carefully consider the points which my noble Friend has raised, but I can hold out no hope of meeting his suggestions. I will certainly do my best to meet those of them for which I think a reasonable case can be advanced.

Question put, and agreed to.

Bill read a second time, and committed to a Committee of the Whole House.

IRISH LAND COMMISSION DECISIONS.

VISCOUNT TEMPLETOWN : My Lords, in accordance with the notice which I have placed on the Paper, I beg to ask Her Majesty's Government—(1) Whether Patrick Markey purchased in 1889, for £180, which included auction fees, the tenancy in a farm of 10A. 0R. 10P. held under the Earl of Gosford at the yearly rent of £9 4s. 8d., the Poor Law valuation being £9 10s. ; and whether in 1897 the Irish Land Commission on re-hearing reduced the rent to £6 10s. ; (2) Whether Mr. Justice Bewley in announcing this decision laid it down as the law that a deduction should be made on account of what he described as " the occupation interest " of the tenant, although the two other members of the court who had heard the case, one of whom, though a barrister, has no legal status as a member of the court, and the other is a layman, dissented from the decision of the Judicial Commissioner, but concurred with him as to the amount of reduction ; (3) Whether it has been recently decided by the Court of Appeal in Ireland in other cases, that Mr. Justice Bewley's view of the law, as decided in Markey's case, was erroneous, and that any deduction for " occupation interest " is illegal ; and having regard to the fact that Markey purchased the holding so recently for £180, and that it is assessed for income tax under Schedules A. and B. at the annual value of £12 13s. 4d., will not Her Majesty's Government take the matter into their consideration ; (4) Whether any and what steps are intended to be taken as to the illegal deductions that have been made by the Land Commission in the past, and to prevent such a possibility in the future.

THE EARL OF DENBIGH : My Lords, in reply to the Question which has been put down by the noble Viscount, I have to inform him that it appears to be the fact that Patrick Markey purchased the farm in question in 1888 or 1889 for £175. The Land Commission, on re-hearing, by order of 31st May 1897, unanimously fixed the fair rent of the holding at the sum of £6 10s. It is not, however, the fact that no improvements were claimed by the tenant or allowed by the court. One of the grounds of appeal stated in the landlord's notice of re-hearing was that the deduction made by the Sub-Commissioners in respect of im-provements was excessive. The Land Commission confirmed the finding of the Sub-Commission that all the buildings and fences upon the holding were tenants' improvements, but reduced the allowance made by the Sub-Commission in respect thereof.

VISCOUNT TEMPLETOWN : The noble Earl will see that in the Question, as it appears on the Paper to-day, the reference to improvements has been omitted.

THE EARL OF DENBIGH : With regard to the second Question, the judgments of Mr. Justice Bewley and the other members of the court on the question of " occupation interest " are reported in the Irish Law Times Reports, Vol. 31, p. 97. The Irish Land Commission is a judicial tribunal established and constituted pursuant to the Land Act of 1881, which Act. defines the *status* of the judicial and other Commissioners. The majority of the Commissioners who heard the case, although they concurred as to the amount of fair rent, dissented from the view of Mr. Justice Bewley as to the " occupation interest," and the present Judicial Commissioner has expressed his concurrence with and acted upon the decision of the majority. The Commissioners do not know to what particular decision or decisions of the Court of Appeal the third paragraph refers. There is no reported decision to the effect indicated, but individual members of the Court of Appeal, in the course of their judgments, have expressed approval of the views so expressed by the majority of the Land Commission, and it is not considered that there is anything in the matter calling for the consideration of Her Majesty's Government.

VISCOUNT TEMPLETOWN : Does the noble Earl give any answer to the fourth Question?

THE EARL OF DENBIGH : If the noble Viscount presses for an answer to the fourth Question, I am bound to say I think the suggestion contained in the Question is open to almost as much objection as the suggestion which was contained in the Questions first of all put down by the noble Viscount, and upon which I remarked the other day ; and I can only tell him that no admission at all can be made by Her Majesty's Government, and that suitors must proceed as they may be advised in reference to litigation in which they may happen to be involved.

VISCOUNT TEMPLETOWN: The noble Earl referred me last Session to the Irish Law Times Reports, which I had then examined, and which I have since carefully gone through, but I have failed to find the information which I require. Further, I am informed that there are no public published Reports which will give the information. With reference to Question four, there was no intention on my part, or on the part of those who requested me to put this Question, to ask anything improper of Her Majesty's Government. I express no opinion upon the answers which have been given by the noble Earl on behalf of Her Majesty's Government, because I feel they require very careful consideration.

House adjourned at fifty-five minutes after Four of the clock.

HOUSE OF COMMONS.

Thursday, 9th March 1899.

MR. SPEAKER'S INDISPOSITION.

The House being met, the Clerk at the Table informed the House of the unavoidable absence of Mr. Speaker, owing to indisposition—

Whereupon MR. JAMES WILLIAM LOWTHER (Cumberland, Penrith, CHAIRMAN OF WAYS and MEANS), proceeded to the Table, and after Prayers, took the Chair as Deputy Speaker, pursuant to the Standing Order, at Three of the clock.

PRIVATE BILL BUSINESS.

PRIVATE BILLS (STANDING ORDER 62 COMPLIED WITH).

Mr. Speaker laid upon the Table Report from one of the Examiners of Petitions for Private Bills,—That, in the case of the following Bills, referred

on the First Reading thereof, Standing Order No. 62 has been complied with, namely—

London, Brighton, and South Coast Railway (Various Powers) Bill.

Tenderton Railway Bill.

Woodhouse and Conisbrough Railway (Abandonment) Bill.

Ordered, that the Bills be read a second time.

PRIVATE BILLS (LORDS).

Mr. Speaker laid upon the Table Report from the Examiners of Petitions for Private Bills, That, in respect of the Bills comprised in the List reported by the Chairman of Ways and Means as intended to originate in the House of Lords, they have certified that the Standing Orders have been complied with in the following case, namely—

Watermen's and Lightermen's Acts Amendment.

LONDON COUNTY COUNCIL (GENERAL POWERS) BILL.

On the Order for the Second Reading of the London County Council (General Powers) Bill,

*MR. CECIL (Herts, Hertford): I think it would simplify matters, so far as the Instruction which stands in my name on the Paper is concerned, if at this stage I made a statement with regard to this Question in its present aspect in view of a resolution passed by the Lea Conservancy Board. The Lea Conservancy Board, since this matter was previously before the House, have passed this resolution—

"That if the clauses relating to the Lea Conservancy be withdrawn from the present Bill, the Lea Conservancy Board will themselves promote a Bill in the next or following Session of Parliament for the reconstitution of the Board in such a manner as to make it representative of all the interests of the River Lea."

The Hertfordshire and Bedfordshire Members, who are specially concerned in this question, have also come to the decision that it would be desirable that the

Lea Conservancy Board should be allowed to promote such a Bill next year on condition that the present clauses relating to the constitution of the Lea Conservancy Board are withdrawn. I am given to understand that as the Lea Board have a bonâ fide intention of promoting this Bill, and as it is also the desire of Hertfordshire, which I particularly represent, that such a Bill should be promoted, the London County Council will withdraw the clauses.

MR. STUART (Shoreditch, Hoxton): I may as well reply at once to the statement that has been made by the honourable Gentleman. In the Bill itself there are a large number of clauses to which no objection has been taken. The whole question centres round that portion of the Bill which refers to the reconstruction of the Board of the Conservancy of the River Lea. Now, Sir, I regret that there should be opposition to these clauses, or to something being done even in the present year in this matter, because the preamble of the Bill fairly states, I believe, the position of things. By reason of the large abstraction of water, the condition of the River Lea below a certain point is offensive to the inhabitants residing in or near thereto, and if anyone looks at the present constitution of the Board of Conservators they will see that it is not a Board of the present day, nor one that can be continued. Indeed, the interests of the River Lea are those of the sanitary authorities which surround that river, and their interests, from a sanitary point of view, are pre-eminently the interests of the population represented by the London County Council. The matter has been pressed upon the London County Council by the various local sanitary authorities. It is also a matter that has been before the House. It may be within the remembrance of some honourable Gentlemen that the present Lord Chief Justice, then Sir Charles Russell, in 1886 secured the appointment of a Committee to investigate the offensive condition of the River Lea. That Committee sat and took a great deal of evidence, the whole of which clearly pointed to the absolute necessity of re-organising the Conservancy Board, and of making it much more representative in character. That Committee did not conclude its labours by the end of the

Mr. Cecil.

then Session, and, owing to Parliamentary circumstances, the Committee was not at the time reappointed, but I venture to think that if anyone peruses the report of the evidence given before that Committee they will see that the report could scarcely have stated other than that the condition of the Lea was offensive, and that some reconstitution of the Lea Conservancy Board was necessary. I will not detain the House longer, but it is necessary for me to lay these facts before you in taking the course I am about to take. As to the present Conservancy Board, I should like to read a couple of extracts from the evidence taken the day before yesterday by the Royal Commission. Here is a question put by Mr. Pember to the Chairman of the Commission, Lord Llandaff—

"I do not know," said Mr. Pember, "whether you have had the constitution of the Lea Conservancy Board referred to. We may as well have it."

The Chairman replied—

"We have had it many times, I think. I do not want to say anything against the integrity or impartiality of the Lea Conservancy Board, but it is obvious that they are dependent on the water companies. They could not live without them."

Mr. Pope added—

"If the water companies did not pay, the Conservancy Board would have to shut up."

Let me now show the House, from another quotation, what occurred before Lord Balfour of Burleigh's Commission on the Water Supply of London. A certain gentleman was called as a witness for the East London Water Company, and he was asked by the Chairman of the Commission—

"Will you explain to the Commission why it is that you come to speak as a witness for the East London Water Company and not for the Conservancy Board?"

That witness was the special adviser, the consulting sanitary engineer, who looked after the purification of the river, and whose duty it was to see that the companies did not take more water from the river than they were entitled to; but he appeared before that Commission to speak on behalf of the water company, by whom he was retained, instead of on behalf of the Conservancy Board. I think the few facts which I have brought before the House will show the very difficult position in which the River Lea is placed, and the necessity for the reorganisation of the Conservancy Board upon some basis which shall be adequately representative of the population concerned. I observe that the resolution which has been passed by the Lea Conservancy Board states that they will bring in their Bill next year or the following year, and that the Hertfordshire County Council, or the Hertfordshire representatives, have urged that it should be brought in next year. I would venture to say that this Bill ought not to lie over till the year following next, but ought to be brought in next year. I have no doubt that that is what the Lea Conservancy Board intend to do, but, should they not bring in a Bill next year, I must hold the hands of the London County Council open to reintroduce a Bill dealing with the matter, and I must at the same time also hold the hands of the London County Council perfectly open to deal with the Measure which may be brought forward by the Lea Conservancy Board—either to oppose it or support it in accordance with the way in which it answers the ideas which the London County Council may form of an adequate and proper representation. With these restrictions I accept the pledge which is now given in the House, on behalf of the Lea Conservancy Board, and am prepared, on behalf of the London County Council, to withdraw the clauses which are referred to.

MR. PYM (Bedford): I think it is only just and fair to say that my honourable Friend the Member for Hertford would have spoken at greater length if he had known that the Member for Hoxton was going so fully into this matter. The Lea Conservancy Board consider that the proposal of the County Council, which desires to change the whole character of the Board, is a most unjustifiable one. The County Council propose to change the Board into one which should be entirely representative of the majority of the County Council members, and this is a proposal which, in justice to the great interests which are concerned, the Lea Conservancy

Board felt they ought to oppose in every way possible.

MR. BUXTON (Tower Hamlets, Poplar): As to what has been said by the honourable Member for Bedford, I think it was absolutely necessary that the honourable Member for Hoxton, in withdrawing these clauses, should give his reasons for so doing, and explain why the County Council originally introduced the clauses. The animadversion of my honourable Friend is therefore unmerited. I hope this Bill which the Lea Conservancy Board are to introduce will be brought in next Session, and not postponed for two or three years, and, in the second place, that the representation will be adequate and proper.

Bill read a Second time, and committed.

SOUTH EASTERN AND LONDON, CHATHAM, AND DOVER RAILWAY COMPANIES (NEW LINES) BILL (BY ORDER).

Second Reading deferred till Tuesday next.

NATIONAL TELEPHONE COMPANY (No. 1) BILL.

" To provide for dissolving the National Telephone Company (Limited), and for reincorporating the Company and defining its objects, capital, and powers; and for other purposes," read the first time; and referred to the Examiners of Petitions for Private Bills.

NATIONAL TELEPHONE COMPANY (No. 2) BILL.

" For conferring powers on the National Telephone Company (Limited)," read the first time; and referred to the Examiners of Petitions for Private Bills.

BELFAST CORPORATION BILL.

" To empower the Lord Mayor, Aldermen, and Citizens of the City of Belfast to make works and to purchase lands for cemetery purposes; to amend several of the Local Acts in force in Belfast; and to confer various powers on the Corporation," read the first time; to be read a second time.

PETITIONS.

PARLIAMENTARY FRANCHISE.

Petition from Barnet, for extension to women; to lie upon the Table.

PRIVATE BILL LEGISLATION (MUNICIPAL TRADING).

Petition from Leeds, for inquiry by a Select Committee; to lie upon the Table.

SALE OF INTOXICATING LIQUORS ON SUNDAY BILL.

Petitions in favour;—From Truro;—Gloucester;—Liverpool;—and, Redbank (two); to lie upon the Table.

RETURNS, REPORTS, ETC.

CHURCH ESTATES COMMISSION.

Copy presented,—of Forty-eighth Report from the Church Estates Commissioners for the year preceding 1st March 1899 (by Command); to lie upon the Table.

ARMY (ORDNANCE FACTORIES) (EXCESS), 1897-8.

Copy presented,—of Statement of the Sum required to be voted in order to make good the Excess on the Grant for the Expense of the Ordnance Factories for the year ended 31st March 1898 (by Command); referred to the Committee of Supply, and to be printed. (No. 98.)

TELEPHONE SERVICE (FOREIGN COUNTRIES) (COMMERCIAL, No. 1, 1899).

Copy presented,—of Reports respecting the Telephone Service in various Foreign Countries (by Command); to lie upon the Table.

BANKRUPTCY COURTS (IRELAND).

Annual Returns presented,—of the Official Assignees of the Court of Bankruptcy in Ireland and the Local Courts, Belfast and Cork, for the year 1898 (by Act); to lie upon the Table.

CIVIL SERVICES (EXCESS), 1897-8.

Copy presented,—of Statement of the Sum required to be voted in order to make good an Excess on the Grant for the Public Record Office for the year ended on the 31st March 1898 (by Command); referred to the Committee of Supply, and to be printed. (No. 99.)

NAVAL WORKS.

Copy presented,—of Statement of Estimated Expenditure to 31st March 1899, under the Naval Works Act, 1897 (by Command); to lie upon the Table.

CIVIL SERVICES (ADDITIONAL ESTIMATE, 1898-9).

Order (8th March), That the said Estimate be referred to the Committee of Supply, and be printed, read, and discharged; Estimate withdrawn.—*(Mr. Hanbury.)*

SANITARY INSPECTORS' EXAMINATION BOARD.

Return ordered, ·

"Of Copies of the Memorandum and Articles of Association of the Sanitary Inspectors' Examination Board (formed by the Sanitary Institute and other bodies) and of the Licence granted by the Board of Trade pursuant to section 23 of the Companies Act, 1867.—*(Mr. Hobhouse.)*

PAUPERISM (ENGLAND AND WALES).

Return ordered,

"Of monthly comparative statements of the number of Paupers of all classes (except lunatics in asylums, registered hospitals, and licensed houses, and vagrants) in receipt of relief in England and Wales on the last day of every week in each month of the several years from 1857 to 1899, both inclusive; and Statements of the number of Paupers (lunatics and vagrants included), distinguishing the number of adult able-bodied Paupers relieved on the 1st day of January 1899, and the 1st day of July 1899, respectively."—*(Mr. T. W. Russell.)*

Return presented accordingly; to lie upon the Table, and to be printed. (No. 100.)

STANDING COMMITTEES.

Ordered,—That all Standing Committees have leave to print and circulate with the Votes the Minutes of their Proceedings, and any amended Clauses of Bills committed to them.—*(Mr. Stuart Wortley.)*

MESSAGE FROM THE LORDS.

That they have passed a Bill, intituled, " An Act to amend the Telegraph Acts, 1863 to 1897, and the Post Office Acts in relation to the Channel Islands." (Telegraph (Channel Islands) Bill (Lords.)

QUESTIONS.

TEACHERS' SUPERANNUATION IN SCOTLAND.

Mr. NICOL (Argyll): I beg to ask the Lord Advocate whether, in view of the hardship which would otherwise be caused to teachers who cannot in all respects fulfil the conditions of the Superannuation Act, it would be possible to continue for a few years the pensions now offered under the Code; and whether, seeing that in Scotland the principle of the Revised Code of 1862 was not adopted until after the passing of the Scottish Education Act and seeing that the date fixed in the Code before which teachers must have served in order to be qualified for a Code pension, namely, 9th May 1862, was fixed by the introduction of that Code, it might in the case of Scotland be altered to the year 1872, the date of the passing of the Education Act?

The LORD ADVOCATE (Mr. A. GRAHAM MURRAY, Buteshire): In reply to the honourable Member, I have to say that the Department recognises the hardships which might arise were the pensions offered under the Code to be immediately withdrawn, and they have obtained the consent of the Treasury to the maintenance of these pensions for the present. They also recognise that the difference in the date at which the principle of the Revised Code was applied to Scotland does constitute a valid claim for a difference in the period from which a teacher should have served in order to become qualified for a pension; and on their representation to the Treasury has agreed that the date should be altered accordingly to the 6th August 1872, when the Education Act was passed. A Minute will be placed on the Table accordingly.

BLOOD MONEY FOR WOUNDED BRITISH OFFICERS.

COLONEL KENYON-SLANEY (Shropshire, Newport): I beg to ask the Under Secretary of State for War whether it is the fact that blood money on the authorised scale has been granted to British officers wounded on service while employed in the Egyptian Army; and whether it is intended to extend similar treatment to those wounded in recent operations; if not, could he explain the reason; and, if so, when will such payments be commenced?

The UNDER SECRETARY OF STATE FOR WAR (Mr. GEORGE WYNDHAM, Dover): The whole question is still under consideration, and I am not yet in a position to give a reply.

SHEEP STEALING IN THE ISLE OF MAN.

Mr. HOZIER (Lanark, S.): I beg to ask the Secretary of State for the Home Department why John Dickson, an ex-policeman, who was sentenced on the 8th of July last to five years' penal servitude for sheep stealing in the Isle of Man, was released on the 8th of August, after undergoing only one month of his sentence; and whether sheep stealing is very prevalent in the Isle of Man?

The UNDER SECRETARY OF STATE FOR THE HOME DEPARTMENT (Mr. JESSE COLLINGS, Birmingham, Bordesley): After careful consideration of all the facts of the case the Secretary of State came to the conclusion that the verdict could not be upheld, and advised the grant of a free pardon. He has no information as to the prevalence of sheep stealing in the Isle of Man, but has no reason to suppose that it is more prevalent there than the other parts of the country where sheep farming is conducted under similar conditions.

TELEGRAPH CLERKS' INCREMENTS.

COLONEL DALBIAC (Camberwell, N.): I beg to ask the Secretary to the Treasury, as representing the Postmaster-General, whether the Post Office decline to grant increments for technical knowledge to telegraph clerks who possess a first-class certificate for technical telegraphy and have passed in electricity and magnetism (Science and Art Department), but do not possess a certificate for the latter; and whether the South Kensington authorities have consented to place their official list at the service of the Post Office; if this is so, will the Postmaster-General accept the information thus supplied as a sufficient proof of the applicant for the increment having passed the examination?

THE FINANCIAL SECRETARY TO THE TREASURY (Mr. R. W. HANBURY, Preston): Yes, Sir. Mere passing is not enough. The Science and Art Department grants certificates only to those who pass in the first class. Telegraphists who do not attain this class cannot be allowed the double increment.

PRISONERS' EARNINGS.

MR. FLOWER (Bradford, W.): I beg to ask the Secretary of State for the Home Department whether it is intended to carry out the recommendations of the Departmental Committee on Prisoners that prisoners should be able to earn something continuously during their sentences?

MR. COLLINGS: The suggestion made by the Committee has not been lost sight of, and is still under the consideration of the Prisons Commissioners, but the financial question, of course, presents considerable difficulty.

PRISON SCHOOLMASTER-WARDERS.

MR. FLOWER: I beg to ask the Secretary of State for the Home Department whether it is a fact that schoolmaster-warders are only allowed the same extent of annual leave of absence as ordinary warders; and if the hours of duty of schoolmaster-warders are considerably longer than the hours of duty of other prison schoolmasters?

MR. COLLINGS: The answer to the first paragraph is in the affirmative. This matter was inquired into by the Departmental Committee of which Lord de Ramsey was Chairman, and which reported that the evidence did not support the demand for alteration in the terms of the service of the schoolmaster-warders. The answer to the second paragraph is also in the affirmative. The schoolmaster-warders are discipline officers who have satisfied the Chief Inspector of the Education Department that they are qualified to teach. They are disappearing as a class, and are being replaced by the new clerk and schoolmaster-warder class. The maximum number of hours given to teaching is the same in all cases, namely, six a day.

BREAD SUPPLY TO MANCHESTER GAOL.

MR. FLOWER: I beg to ask the Secretary of State for the Home Department, with reference to the statement contained in the last annual Report of the Visiting Justices of Manchester Prison, to the effect that the bread provided during part of last year was of an inferior quality, being tasteless and chaffy, and its ultimate effect prejudicial to the health of the prisoners; if the contractor for such bread has been notified by the Prison Commissioners that his contract must be determined; and, if so, whether the declaration on page 314 of the last annual Report of the Prison Commissioners that the diet of Manchester has not been sufficient and of good quality is, in respect of the bread supplied, well-founded or not?

MR. COLLINGS: The Secretary of State is not aware what is the report referred to. In the Visiting Committee's Report for 1898 they stated that the provisions were of good quality. It appears that in 1897 they had occasion to call attention to the bad quality of wheat supplied to the prison, and steps were at once taken to put the matter right.

MR. FLOWER: But is it not the fact that the Visiting Justices did complain of the quality of the bread?

MR. COLLINGS: That was in the Report for the year 1897. In 1898 it was said in the Report that the provisions were of good quality.

PRISON LABOUR.

MR. FLOWER: I beg to ask the Secretary of State for the Home Department if he can state the number of cranks and treadwheels at present in use in local prisons?

MR. COLLINGS: There are 33 treadwheels and 11 cranks now in use. All these are used for productive or useful prison purposes, e.g., grinding wheat, sawing wood, or pumping water.

MR. FLOWER: Is there any intention of gradually doing away with these cranks and treadwheels?

MR. COLLINGS: That I cannot say.

ITALY IN CHINA.

MR. PRITCHARD MORGAN (Merthyr Tydfil): I beg to ask the Under Secretary of State for Foreign Affairs whether the Chinese Government has refused to concede to the demands of the Italian Government for a sphere of influence with a lease of Sammun Bay as a Naval base, and that the Tsung-li-Yamen has received a note from the British Minister at Pekin supporting the demands of Italy; and whether the Liquin dues of the Province of Che-Kiang (in which Sammun is situated) have been pledged by the Chinese Government as security for the repayment of the loan for 16 millions sterling?

THE UNDER SECRETARY OF STATE FOR FOREIGN AFFAIRS (Mr. ST. JOHN BRODRICK, Surrey, Guildford): We understand that the matter is still under the consideration of the Chinese Government. We have expressed our sympathy with the desire of Italy to obtain a coaling station, but have always recognised that it is one which it is for the Chinese Government to consider whether they shall accept or not. The Likin dues of a portion of the Province of Che-Kiang are understood to have been pledged to the bondholders, but, no doubt, in any arrangements made by the Chinese Government, these interests will be safeguarded.

MR. PRITCHARD MORGAN: Are the English Government advocating the demands of Italy?

[No Reply.]

CONNEMARA POLICE HUT.

MR. O'MALLEY (Galway, Connemara): I beg to ask the Chief Secretary to the Lord Lieutenant of Ireland whether, in view of the peaceable condition of the district, he will abolish the police hut at Maam Cross Roads, Connemara, occupied by a sergeant and four policemen, which was established there in 1882 when the the country was in a disturbed condition?

THE CHIEF SECRETARY TO THE LORD LIEUTENANT OF IRELAND (Mr. GERALD W. BALFOUR, Leeds Central): The hut at Maam Cross was established in 1891 as an ordinary police station, and not for special protection purposes. It is the only police station on the direct road between Oughterarde and Clifden, a distance of 32 miles, and in the opinion of the responsible authorities, there are no sufficient grounds for disestablishing it.

MR. KILBRIDE (Galway, N.): What was the reason for the increase of the establishment in 1891?

MR. GERALD BALFOUR: I have not the facts. If the honourable Member wishes further information, perhaps he will put down a Question.

Mr. PATRICK O'BRIEN (Kilkenny): What is the cost for extra police to the country in connection with this hut?

Mr. GERALD BALFOUR: There is no charge for extra police.

Mr. PATRICK O'BRIEN: Where does the money come from that is required to keep it up?

Mr. SWIFT MacNEILL (Donegal, S.): Out of the Chief Secretary's salary, perhaps.

TELEGRAPH WAY-LEAVES IN BELFAST.

Mr. ARNOLD-FORSTER (Belfast, W.): I beg to ask the Secretary to the Treasury, as representing the Postmaster-General, if he is aware that serious public inconvenience is being caused by the great delay, and in many cases the refusal of the Post Office to give consent to the carrying of wires across railways over which the Postmaster-General possesses exclusive way-leave rights for telegraphs; and whether he is aware that business firms in Belfast are thus deprived of the telephone service; and whether the refusal of these way-leaves will be persisted in in view of the Treasury Minute on Telephones approved by Parliament in 1892?

Mr. HANBURY: The right of the Postmaster-General to refuse such way-leaves was specially reserved by the agreement of 1896. In places where there is no competition, such as Belfast, they will continue to be granted, subject, of course, to revocation at short notice in order to place the Company and the municipality, so far as possible, on equal terms in this respect, should there be two competing systems.

COAL FOR THE NAVY.

Sir C. DILKE (Gloucester, Forest of Dean): I beg to ask the First Lord of the Admiralty what is the explanation of the diminution of the Supplementary Estimate for coal from £316,000 to £140,000?

THE SECRETARY TO THE ADMIRALTY (Mr. MACARTNEY, Antrim, S.): The explanation is that the balance has been met by saving on other items of the Vote.

Sir C. DILKE: Then that amount has been spent on coal?

Mr. MACARTNEY: Yes, certainly.

CHINESE AGREEMENTS.

Mr. MOON (St. Pancras, N.): I beg to ask the Under Secretary of State for Foreign Affairs whether the Agreement concluded on the 27th August (8th September), 1896, by the Imperial Chinese Government with the Russo-Chinese Bank is more or less comprehensive than the Statutes of the Eastern Chinese Railway Company, which were imperially confirmed on 4-16 December, 1896, and presented in an abridged translation to this House in March, 1898 [C. 8777], and whether he will obtain and supply to Members translations of the following sections of the Statutes of the Eastern Chinese Railway Company, namely, (18) Functions of Board of Management; (19) Constitution of the Board; (21) General meetings of shareholders, and the subjects that shall come under their notice; (23) Conditions under which general meetings shall be recognised as legally held; (24) Participation of shareholders in proceedings of general meetings; (25) Local management of works of construction; (26) Local management of railway when in working order; (27) Questions to be submitted for confirmation by Russian Minister of Finances; and (28) Committee of audit; and whether he will consider the question of appointing a British Consul at Vladivostock where there are already United States, French, Belgian, and German Consuls or Commercial Agents?

Mr. BRODRICK: We have not seen the Agreement of August 27th (September 8th), 1896. Her Majesty's Ambassador at St. Petersburg will be requested to send home translations of the sections referred to, and his dispatch will be included in any further correspondence respecting China which may be presented to Parliament after its receipt. The question of the possible appointment of a British Commercial Agent at Vladivostock has been suggested, but no decision has yet been arrived at.

EASTERN CHINESE RAILWAY COMPANY.

MR. MOON: I beg to ask the Under Secretary of State for Foreign Affairs whether he will ascertain and state to this House how much bond capital has up to this date been issued under section 11 of the Statutes of the Eastern Chinese Railway Company; whether any annual reports have been presented under section 16 of the same Statutes to the general meeting of shareholders in respect of the years ending 4-16 December, 1897 and 4-16 December, 1898, respectively, and whether he will supply translations of such reports, if they exist, to Members; what are the names of the chairman, vice-chairman, and the other seven members of the board of management of the company; and whether, under section 19, the chairman is appointed by the Chinese Government from among the nine members elected by the shareholders, or independently?

MR. BRODRICK: The information which the honourable Member desires to obtain is not in the possession of Her Majesty's Government, but if he attaches importance to it, Her Majesty's Ambassador at St. Petersburg will be asked whether any documents giving the particulars are available to the public.

TELEGRAPH FACILITIES AT BELFAST.

MR. YOUNG (Cavan, E.): On behalf of the honourable Member for South Down, I beg to ask the Secretary to the Treasury, as representing the Postmaster-General, with reference to the desired establishment of a telegraph office at the post office beside the Grand Metropole Hotel, Donegal Street, Belfast, whether any further representations have been made to the Postmaster of the City of Belfast on the matter; and whether, considering the urgent necessity for same, he will favourably consider the establishment of a telegraph office there without unnecessary delay?

MR. HANBURY: It is the fact that further representations have been made to the Postmaster of Belfast with reference to the establishment of a telegraph office in Donegal Street, Belfast. As promised on the 20th ultimo, a further report has been called for on this subject, and as soon as it is received, no time shall be lost in communicating with the honourable Member.

DUNDRUM BAY FISHERIES.

MR. YOUNG: On behalf of the honourable Member for South Down, I beg to ask the Chief Secretary to the Lord Lieutenant of Ireland whether he has received a petition from the women of Newcastle, county Down, directing his attention to the injury and threatened ruin caused to them and their families by steam trawlers without lights trawling in Dundrum Bay; whether the petitioners complain that a number of the poor fishermen of Newcastle are now being prosecuted for alleged carrying away of gear belonging to one of these trawlers, while the owners of the trawlers, notwithstanding their destruction of fish, have been allowed to escape; and whether he will, in the interest of these poor fishermen, cause full inquiry to be made into the matter.

MR. GERALD BALFOUR: The answer to the first and second paragraphs is in the affirmative. With regard to the proceedings now pending against a number of fishermen at Newcastle, I am informed that the case will be investigated by the magistrates at the next petty sessions to be held on the 17th instant. Under these circumstances, it is undesirable, at the present stage, to make any statement respecting the action of the fishermen which led to their prosecution for malicious injury.

KENSINGTON PALACE.

MR. SINCLAIR (Essex, Romford): I beg to ask the First Commissioner of Works whether, in view of the fact that a sum of £23,000 is being expended on the restoration of the State Rooms and Banqueting House of Kensington Palace, will he state if arrangements can be made for this Palace, or part of it, to be opened during certain hours to the public?

THE FIRST COMMISSIONER OF WORKS (Mr. AKERS DOUGLAS, Kent, St. Augustine's): I thought I had made it sufficiently clear, both last year and again on the Supplementary Estimate, that the sum expended on Kensington Palace was voted by the House in consequence of Her Majesty having more than a year ago signified her intention of throwing open the State Rooms of Kensington Palace to the public during her pleasure.

BALLINTOY AND PORTBALLINTRAE HARBOURS.

MR. W. MOORE (Antrim): I beg to ask the Chief Secretary to the Lord Lieutenant of Ireland if he will endeavour to secure for the Antrim coast some allocation of the moneys now being spent in harbour and pier accommodation in the west of Ireland, and to have same expended in scouring out and rendering reasonably safe the harbours at Ballintoy and Portballintrae, so as to enable the fishermen of those districts to pursue their calling; and if his attention has been called to the present dangerous condition of those harbours for want of the necessary expenditure, and of the strong local demand for same?

MR. GERALD BALFOUR: I am afraid the two harbours mentioned in this Question cannot be considered as possessing claims for special consideration by Government. If the expenditure referred to in the Question is that provided for out of the funds of the Congested Districts Board, the answer is that it would obviously be impossible to apply the funds of that Board to a non-congested district. My attention has been called to the condition of one, if not both of these harbours, by a Question put to me on the 17th ultimo by the honourable Member for Galway, and I would refer my honourable Friend to the reply given by me to that Question.

MILITIA TRANSPORT.

MR. PATRICK O'BRIEN: I beg to ask the Under Secretary of State for War whether the attention of the Secretary of State for War has been directed to the Militia being without a transport service, and, in view of the absolute necessity of having the Militia provided with its own transport, will he issue an authority to each unit of Militia to detail an officer and a limited number of non-commissioned officers and men during the approaching preliminary drill and training to go through a course of instruction in transport duties?

MR. WYNDHAM: In the event of war the majority of the Militia regiments will be posted in garrisons, where transport will not be required. Transport is allotted to those regiments which will form part of the Field Army.

MILITIA O.R.C.S.

MR. PATRICK O'BRIEN: I beg to ask the Under Secretary of State for War whether it is proposed to remedy the grievance under which the Militia O.R.C.S. of all branches of the service at present labour, namely, being deprived of all chances of advancement higher than the rank of sergeant by virtue of the position they hold; and whether, prior to the publication of Army Order 294 in 1890, the position of Militia orderly room clerk carried a progressive rank, and other inducements were offered for suitable non-commissioned officers to undertake the work without destroying their prospects of future advancement?

MR. WYNDHAM: Before the publication of Army Order 294 of 1890 orderly room sergeants were on the permanent staff of Militia regiments. In 1890 these appointments were abolished and it was decided to substitute orderly room clerks on the depôt staff. These clerks are eligible for promotion to the post of orderly room sergeants of the depôt when a vacancy occurs. They can also obtain promotion in the ordinary way in their service units.

IRISH MILITIA TRAININGS.

MR. PATRICK O'BRIEN: I beg to ask the Secretary of State for War if it has been decided not to have any Irish Militia trained at Salisbury Plain this year; and whether, as they would therefore be deprived of the advantages of an extended period of training 34 days which is to be granted to the English and Scotch regiments training at Salisbury Plain, will he extend the period of training in the Irish Militia brigade camps to 34 days?

MR. WYNDHAM: No Irish Militia will be trained at Salisbury Plain this year. The regular period of training is 28 days, and it is not desirable to extend it in ordinary cases.

IRISH TRAINING COLLEGES.

MR. M'GHEE (Louth, S.): I beg to ask the Chief Secretary to the Lord Lieutenant of Ireland if he can state what number of monitresses in their fifth year of service and girls for entrance to training colleges presented themselves for examination at the different centres in Ireland last Easter week; and whether monitresses were examined three months previous to the termination of the monitorial engagement, although in former years the examination was held in the month of July; whether, considering that a number of new subjects were added to the programme and for the first time made compulsory, he will explain on what grounds young girls having given five years' faithful service as monitresses should be dismissed the service upon failure in needlework only; and if the whole matter will be taken into consideration in the interest of the service?

MR. GERALD BALFOUR: 1,163 candidates of the class mentioned presented themselves at the Easter examination of 1898. Of these 550 were monitresses and 613 training candidates. The examination took place in July in previous years, but due notice of the change was given. Only one additional subject was included in the new programme. Monitresses who failed to qualify in needle-

VOL. LXVIII.   [FOURTH SERIES.]

work and who made sufficient answering on the whole, were not denied classification, but obtained it provisionally on condition of passing needlework at the Easter examination of 1899, to which they will be summoned. There were only 15 such cases. The Commissioners consider that it is for the interest of the service that this arrangement should be continued.

ABERDEEN RAILWAY STATION.

MR. BRYCE (Aberdeen, S.): I beg to ask the President of the Board of Trade whether the attention of the Board of Trade has been called to the scheme of the Caledonian Railway Company and Great North of Scotland Railway Company for making a new station at Aberdeen, and to the omission in that scheme to make provision for a public access on each side of the station (which will be a long one), and to make adequate provision for the very large and increasing traffic in fish; whether the Board is aware that a strong and general feeling exists in Aberdeen that the plans for the new station are seriously defective in both the above respects; and whether the Board will take the matter into consideration, and will, if satisfied that the facts are as above stated, represent to the two railway companies the propriety of so amending their scheme as to make due provision for securing the above objects, and generally for the convenience and safety of the public using the station?

THE FIRST COMMISSIONER OF WORKS (for the PRESIDENT of the BOARD of TRADE): My right honourable Friend requests me to state that he has received a letter from the Caledonian Company which he will be happy to show to the right honourable Gentleman. The company are, he believes, conducting negotiations with regard to the improvement of the station, and are consulting the local authority with reference thereto. Until those negotiations are further advanced he is not able to say what their effect will be.

L

BELGIUM AND CHINA.

MR. MOON: I beg to ask the Under Secretary of State for Foreign Affairs whether the Belgian Minister at Pekin stated to the Tsung-li-Yamên that that Minister's application for a concession at Han-kau for the Lu-han railway terminus is supported by England?

' MR. BRODRICK: We have not heard that any such statement has been made, and it would be incorrect.

MILITARY FUNERALS FOR VOLUN-TEERS.

CAPTAIN NORTON (Newington, W.): I beg to ask the Under Secretary of State for War whether it has been brought to his notice that, in connection with the recent death of a non-commissioned officer of the 4th Volunteer Battalion (the Queen's) Royal West Surrey Regiment, application was made for leave for a military funeral, and whether the application was not acceded to on the ground that no authority could be found for such a ceremonial in relation to Volunteers; and whether, if that be the case, the Secretary of State for War will cause the Volunteer Regulations to be so amended as to permit in future of Military honours being paid at the funeral of any officer, non-commissioned officer, or private serving in the Volunteer force at the time of his death, provided such Military funeral is desired by relatives or others concerned?

MR. WYNDHAM: The application for a Military funeral was refused by the officer commanding the battalion on the grounds referred to in the question. The suggestion of amending the regulations to provide for such funerals will be carefully considered by the Secretary of State for War.

SECOND DIVISION CLERKS.

MR. ALLAN (Gateshead): I beg to ask the Secretary to the Treasury whether he is able to give a reply to the memorandum presented last Session on behalf of the second division clerks of Her Majesty's Civil Service; and whether, before filling up all the vacancies in the first division by direct appointment, the Lords of the Treasury will cause careful inquiry to be made whether there are meritorious and deserving second division clerks of over eight years' service in the Admiralty, War Office, Board of Trade, Board of Agriculture, Local Government Board, and Inland Revenue Departments, who are, under the terms of the Orders in Council, eligible for consideration for advancement in accordance with the recommendations of the Playfair and White-Ridley Commissions?

MR. HANBURY: The Treasury have had under consideration a series of petitions from clerks of the second division relating to their pay, prospects of promotion, and annual leave. The arguments in these petitions and in the memorandum handed to me by the honourable Member in the course of last Session included nothing which had not been considered and dealt with in former Minutes of the Board of Treasury; and the petitioners were so informed by a circular letter of 24th December 1898. It is not the duty of the Treasury to take the initiative with regard to the exceptional promotion of second division clerks to posts in the upper division. But whenever a second division clerk is recommended for such special promotion by the head of his department on the ground of "exceptional fitness" or "very exceptional ability, merit, and diligence"—which are the words used by the Ridley Commission—his case always receives the most careful consideration at the hands of the Treasury.

RAILWAYS ON THE GOLD COAST.

MR. ALLAN: I beg to ask the Secretary of State for the Colonies whether he is able to state the present condition of the railways now in progress in the Colony and Protectorate of the Gold Coast, and when it is proposed to open the first section of the line for traffic; and what steps have been taken, or will be taken, to ensure the erection of suitable piers and landing stages for commerce at Accra, Cape Coast Castle, Axum, Winnebah, Addah, Chamah, and Quittah?

THE SECRETARY OF STATE FOR THE COLONIES (MR. J. CHAMBERLAIN, Birmingham, W.): The railway from Sokondi to Tarquah is making good progress, and it is anticipated that, if the seasons are not unfavourable, this line will be open for traffic early next year. Surveys of certain other routes have also been made, including a flying survey for a line to Coomassie. The construction of piers and landing stages on the West Coast is impracticable, in most cases, without very costly protective works against the heavy surf which constantly prevails. The question of carrying out such works at the places which may eventually be selected as the coast termini of the different railways is receiving careful consideration.

IRISH SUB-POSTMASTERS AS COUNTY COUNCILLORS.

MR. PATRICK O'BRIEN: On behalf of the honourable Member for South Roscommon, I beg to ask the Secretary to the Treasury, as representing the Postmaster-General, whether the postal authorities in Ireland have issued an order forbidding sub-postmasters becoming candidates for the position of county councillor; whether this applies to the office of district councillor; and, if not, what is the reason for the discrimination between the two councils; whether the postal authorities intend to treat a salary of about £6 per annum (as in many cases) to a rural sub-postmaster as a disqualification for filling an important public position at the call of the electors; and, in case this order, if made, be disregarded, what action it is proposed to take against the offender?

MR. HANBURY: The reply to the first Question is in the affirmative. On the introduction of the Irish Local Government Act post office servants were reminded that they were forbidden to become candidates for the county councils. This prohibition, which was laid down by the Government in 1888 for the whole Civil Service, was not extended to district councils or parish councils, for the reason that attendance at meetings of district or parish councils would not, it was considered, be calculated to interfere with post office servants' official duty so

much as attendance at meetings of county councils which might take place at a considerable distance from their offices. The permission to become candidates for district or parish councils was given to post office servants in 1894 on the understanding that in any case in which the duties of the council were found to conflict with those of the post office the Postmaster-General reserved to himself the right to require the officer to retire from the council. As regards the third Question, the Postmaster-General could not undertake to make any distinction between officers with small salaries and those more highly paid. The reply to the fourth Question is that disregard of the rule relating to county councils would in all probability lead to the severance of the officer's connection with the Service.

MR. PATRICK O'BRIEN: Is there any reason why sub-postmasters whose salary is less than £5 per year should be prohibited, while inland revenue officers are not? Is the right honourable Gentleman aware that an inland revenue officer has already been elected a county councillor?

MR. HANBURY: I believe the prohibition is the same in all cases, but I will inquire.

LABOUR IMMIGRATION INTO ASSAM.

MR. SCHWANN (Manchester, N.): I beg to ask the Secretary of State for India if he can lay upon the Table of the House the Triennial Report on Labour Immigration into Assam, which should have appeared at the end of the year 1895, or thereabouts, and which was not produced when last asked for because it was said that the last Viceroy had not been able to consider it owing to the grave events in India—war and famine.

THE SECRETARY OF STATE FOR INDIA (Lord GEORGE HAMILTON, Middlesex, Ealing): On the 9th of May last I explained, in reply to a Question from the honourable Member, how the matter stood: the Report in question was sent home in March, 1897, but the Government of India had not arrived at a conclusion in regard to certain changes

L 2

of system recommended by the Lieutenant-Governor of Bengal. These recommendations are still under their consideration. but I learn from a dispatch of February last that I may expect to receive their conclusions at an early date.

GAME LICENCES.

MR. SCHWANN: I beg to ask the Secretary to the Treasury whether it is illegal for game dealers in the United Kingdom, either wholesale or retail, to sell English game after 10th February which has been killed and bought before the close time (1st February) and consigned to cold-air stores in this kingdom, in view of the fact that foreign game can be sold all the year round; and, in the affirmative case, would he consider whether it would be possible to allow game dealers in this country to sell British and Irish game after close time on production, when challenged, of the cold-air stores delivery notes; and what proof is at present given that so-called foreign game exposed for sale after 10th February is what it professes to be?

MR. HANBURY: This Question should be addressed to the Home Office.

OLDHAM ROAD GOODS YARD FATALITY.

MR. SCHWANN: I beg to ask the President of the Board of Trade whether he has now inquired into the case of J. Cavanagh, who lost his life in December last at the Oldham Road Goods Yard of the Lancashire and Yorkshire Railway Company in Manchester; whether he will ascertain if any, and what, improvements can be made in the working of the capstans by applying treadles, better lighting, or otherwise, with a view of lessening the loss of life in that yard; and would he inquire how many accidents have happened in that goods yard during the last five years, and the nature and cause of each accident?

THE FIRST COMMISSIONER OF WORKS (for the PRESIDENT of the BOARD

of TRADE): My right honourable Friend has been in communication with the company on the subject referred to by the honourable Member, but has not yet received their reply. Until he does it is not possible for him to say what steps (if any) can be taken in the matter.

DELAGOA RAILWAY ARBITRATION.

MR. HENNIKER HEATON (Canterbury): I beg to ask the Under Secretary of State for Foreign Affairs whether nine years have elapsed since the Delagoa Railway case was sent to a tribunal for arbitration, and that the final decision was promised before last autumn; whether there is any prospect of the decision being promulgated within a reasonable time; and whether the lease by Portugal of Delagoa Bay for a term of years to the British Government is awaiting the decision of the experts in the Railway case?

MR. BRODRICK: The answer to the first portion of the Question is in the affirmative, but no promise as to the date of the final decision appears to have been given. Her Majesty's Government trust that the decision on this question will not now be much further prolonged, but we have no power to accelerate it. The answer to the last paragraph of the Question is in the negative.

DISTURBANCES IN ST. CLEMENT'S CHURCH, BELFAST.

MR. McCARTAN (Down, S.): I beg to ask the Chief Secretary to the Lord Lieutenant of Ireland whether he is aware that on Sunday last there was a repetition of the disturbances in St. Clement's Church, Belfast, and that the constabulary had to be called in to remove or order out the disturbers from the church; whether he is aware that a most disorderly mob pursued the Rev. Mr. Peoples on his way from the church to his residence, and that a stone fired from the crowd went through a window of his residence and seriously injured in the face a young lady who was in the room: and whether some steps will be taken to protect this clergyman from the disorderly rabble in the performance of his duties?

MR. DILLON (Mayo, E.): At the same time may I ask the Chief Secretary to the Lord Lieutenant of Ireland whether he is aware that on Sunday last a stone was thrown through a window in the house of the Rev. Mr. Peoples, in Belfast, and that the stone struck a lady who was sitting in the house; and whether the offender has been brought to justice?

MR. GERALD BALFOUR: The facts are generally as stated in the two Questions of the honourable Members for South Down and East Mayo. A large force of police is employed in protecting Mr. Peoples, and the authorities will continue to afford him every necessary protection. The person who threw the stone that struck one of the inmates of the house has not yet been made amenable.

MR. DILLON: Does the right honourable Gentleman think there was the necessary protection when a lady was struck in the face with a stone?

[No Reply.]

MR. SWIFT MacNEILL: Oh, they are Orangemen.

PROMOTION IN THE ROYAL IRISH CONSTABULARY.

MR. MACALEESE (Monaghan, N.): I beg to ask the Chief Secretary to the Lord Lieutenant of Ireland is he aware that the system called the "P Examination is causing much discontent in the ranks of the Royal Irish Constabulary through practically abolishing promotion by seniority, and lifting constables of a few years' service over the heads of old and experienced officers; whether experience shows that the "P. Examination is detrimental to the efficiency of the constabulary, since young constables, studying for it, neglect to perfect themselves in a thorough knowledge of police duties; and, if this be so, will he devise some means by which a remedy may be applied to this grievance?

MR. GERALD BALFOUR: I am not aware that the system of examination referred to is causing discontent, as suggested in the first paragraph. It is not correct to say that promotion by seniority is practically abolished. Out of 186 promotions made in the past year as many as 156 were made from amongst deserving senior men. The reply to the second paragraph is in the negative; the result of experience shows that men who have been successful at the examinations in question generally make excellent sergeants. It is not proposed to alter the present system.

DURHAM TERRITORIAL REGIMENT.

MR. ELLIOT (Durham): I beg to ask the Under Secretary of State for War if he will consider the advisability of bringing the city and county of Durham into close connection with the territorial regiment, by establishing barracks at at the city of Durham which might contain the depôts of the Durham Light Infantry and the permanent staff of one or both Militia battalions?

MR. WYNDHAM: The Durham Light Infantry and the Northumberland Fusiliers now have a double depôt at Newcastle, which would have to be broken up if effect were given to the suggestion of the honourable Member. In view of the advantages afforded by double as compared with single depôts the Secretary of State cannot assent to a proposal which would involve the breaking up of a double depôt.

BELFAST CUSTOM HOUSE STEPS.

MR. MACALEESE: I beg to ask the Chief Secretary to the Lord Lieutenant of Ireland if he is aware that the Custom House steps in Belfast are being used as a platform by itinerant preachers and others on Sundays for haranguing gatherings of disorderly persons, to the prejudice of the public peace; and will he take steps to enclose this Crown property in such a way as will prevent those persons from making the steps a platform for their mischievous addresses?

MR. GERALD BALFOUR: It is the fact that the steps of the Custom House in Belfast are being used, and have been used for many years, as a platform by persons representing various sects and religious denominations? The expediency of enclosing the steps is doubtful.

MR. SWIFT MacNEILL: Will the Government consider the propriety of proclaiming these meetings?

[No Reply.]

ORKNEY LAND TAX.

MR. HEDDERWICK (Wick Burghs): I beg to ask the Lord Advocate whether a double land tax is levied in Orkney; and, if so, upon what grounds the imposition is justified?

MR. GRAHAM MURRAY: I am informed by the Office of Woods and Forests that a double land tax is not levied in Orkney. The Skatt in Orkney appears to be the equivalent of the Feu-duties imposed on lands in other parts of Scotland, where the land tax is paid in addition to the Feu-duties.

WATERVILLE POST OFFICE.

MR. KILBRIDE: I beg to ask the Secretary to the Treasury, as representing the Postmaster-General, whether his attention has been directed to the great inconvenience to tourists and others staying at the hotels in Waterville, county Kerry, owing to the fact that there is no telegraph office attached to the Post Office at Waterville; whether they are obliged to make use of the Cable Company's Offices, situate more than half a mile from the hotels, causing loss of revenue to the Post Office and inconvenience to the visitors; and whether, in consideration of the increasing importance of Waterville as a favourite fishing place and health resort, he will provide telegraph facilities in connection with the present Post Office?

MR. HANBURY: No representations appear to have been made to the Postmaster-General in regard to the alleged inconvenience of the existing telegraph arrangements at Waterville. An offer to extend the telegraphs to the Post Office under guarantee which was made some years ago did not meet with acceptance, and but for the arrangement under which the Commercial Cable Company undertook to accept telegrams at their Cable Station, on behalf of the Postmaster-General, the locality would have been without telegraphic facilities. The extension to the Post Office would involve considerable expense, but the Postmaster-General will be happy to look into the matter, and will communicate with the honourable Member.

MR. KILBRIDE: Is the right honourable Gentleman aware that the local postmaster is willing to give the guarantee?

MR. HANBURY: The honourable Member must be well aware that that is not the sort of guarantee that we require.

FLEET PAYMASTERS.

CAPTAIN DONELAN (Cork, E.): I beg to ask the Secretary to the Admiralty if he can state how many Fleet Paymasters over 55 years of age have been refused retirement; and whether steps will be taken to augment the entries of assistant clerks in order that the list of paymasters may be brought up to the number sanctioned by the Queen's Regulations?

MR. MACARTNEY: Optional retirement has been temporarily suspended in the case of six Fleet Paymasters, owing to the exigencies of the Service. Care is taken that the entry of assistant clerks is sufficient to meet requirements.

CAPTAIN DONELAN: May I ask whether it is not the fact that the list of paymasters is at present 20 short?

MR. MACARTNEY: I am not aware of that.

POSTCARDS.

CAPTAIN DONELAN: I beg to ask the Secretary to the Treasury, as representing the Postmaster-General, whether any decision has yet been arrived at relative to the provision of large sized postcards; and, if it has been decided to provide them, when will they be issued?

MR. HANBURY: No decision has yet been arrived at.

LONGFORD COUNTY CESS COLLECTOR.

MR. KILBRIDE: On behalf of the honourable Member for East Galway I beg to ask the Chief Secretary to the Lord Lieutenant of Ireland whether he is aware that Mr. G. Sherritt Golding, county cess collector for the barony of Longford, county Galway, had about 200 notices served between the 1st and 3rd of February on the cesspayers in the Killimore district; and whether, although they paid on the next day the collector visited the district, he was entitled to charge each of them 6d. costs?

MR. GERALD BALFOUR: The facts, I understand, are as stated in the first paragraph. The cost of serving the notices was stated, on each of the forms, to be 6d. The proceedings in these cases were taken under the Grand Jury Acts, which are administered by the Grand Juries, and it is not for the Government to express any opinion as to the legality of the charges to which reference is made in the Question.

LICENCES ON HEARSES AND WHEEL BIERS.

MR. H. D. GREENE (Shrewsbury): I beg to ask Mr. Chancellor of the Exchequer, whether a parish council or churchwardens keeping, for the use of parishioners, a hearse or wheel bier adapted for being drawn by one or more horses is exempt by statute from taking out a licence in respect of it; and whether, if there is no such exemption in the Statute, Her Majesty's Government will introduce such an exemption.

THE CHANCELLOR OF THE EXCHEQUER (SIR MICHAEL HICKS BEACH, Bristol, W.): I do not think the suggestion of my honourable Friend is necessary. I understand that a licence is not required in such a case.

BRAWLING IN BELFAST.

MR. DILLON: I beg to ask the Chief Secretary to the Lord Lieutenant of Ireland whether it is true that a man who gave evidence against Johnson, who was sentenced to two months' imprisonment for brawling in St. Clement's Church, was brutally assaulted on last Friday in the yard of Messrs. Workman and Clarke, in Belfast; whether he is aware that the witness was knocked down, kicked whilst on the ground, and obliged to fly amidst a volley of stones; and what action the Executive propose to take?

MR. YOUNG: I beg also to ask the Chief Secretary to the Lord Lieutenant of Ireland whether his attention has been drawn to a scene at the shipbuilding yard at Messrs. Workman and Clarke, Belfast, in which a witness, on returning to work, who had given evidence in the prosecution of Johnson for brawling and disturbing the congregation at St. Clement's on 2nd March, was stoned, kicked, and barely escaped with his life, and deprived of his livelihood; and whether any steps will be taken to investigate the nature of this outrage, with the view of bringing its perpetrators to justice?

MR. GERALD BALFOUR: It is the fact that a man named John Moore, who was a witness for the prosecution in the case brought by a churchwarden of St. Clement's Church against a man named Johnson for brawling in the church was assaulted on the 3rd instant. Moore received some kicks, and was struck with a stone on the back of the neck. He gave the name of two of his assailants to the police, and stated he would prosecute them; but I am informed this morning that he will not now issue a summons against his assailants. Under these circumstances the case will be taken by the Crown, and directions have been issued to the police accordingly.

RUSSIAN PROTEST AT PEKIN.

SIR E. ASHMEAD-BARTLETT (Sheffield, Ecclesall): I beg to ask the Under Secretary of State for Foreign Affairs whether the Russian Minister at Pekin has renewed his protest against the conditions of the Chinese North Eastern Railway Extension Loan; and whether the Russians have 20,000 soldiers near Kirin, the capital of Manchuria, and are everywhere acting as if they were owners of the country?

MR. BRODRICK: So far as we are aware, the protest of the Russian Minister has not been renewed. It is understood that his representations to the Chinese Government were made with the object of calling their attention to the tendency which it appeared to the Russian Government had been displayed in the Loan Agreement of not keeping to their prior engagements with Russia; and not with the object of opposing the conclusion of a loan in England for the construction of the railway. The information in our possession does not lead us to believe that there are 20,000 Russian troops at Kirin.

SIR E. ASHMEAD-BARTLETT: Do I understand that the protest referred exclusively to matters within the Russian sphere of influence?

[No Reply.] .

SIR E. ASHMEAD-BARTLETT: I wish to ask either the Under Secretary for War or the First Lord of the Treasury whether we are to understand from the reply that the Russian Government have withdrawn their objection to the conditions of the Northern Railway Extension in the two principal details—namely, the objections to a British engineer and to a chartered accountant.

MR. BRODRICK: I must ask my honourable Friend to give notice of the Question.

MUSCAT.

SIR E. ASHMEAD-BARTLETT: I beg to ask the Under Secretary of State for Foreign Affairs on what part of the Muscat coast it is proposed to place the French coaling depôt; whether the

French Government have clearly renounced all territorial and political rights over the site where the depôt is to be placed; and whether the Russian Government have also applied for a coaling depôt on the Persian Gulf?

MR. BRODRICK: The site of the proposed French coaling depôt has not yet been actually fixed, but the Sultan will be advised only to grant a depôt at Muscat itself. The French Government have now accepted our view of the Treaty of 1862, that it precludes either Government from accepting any cession or lease of Muscat territory, and in lieu of their former concession have agreed to accept a coal depôt on exactly the same terms as our own. We have received no information to the effect stated in the third paragraph of the Question.

EAST HAM POLICE FORCE.

MR. SINCLAIR : I beg to ask the Secretary of State for the Home Department whether his attention has been called to the limited number of police in East Ham; and, having regard to the immense growth of this district, and to the fact that a little girl has been most brutally murdered lately, whether he will cause inquiry to be made and see that the police force is adequate to protect life and property in that part?

MR. COLLINGS: The Secretary of State is not aware of any ground for supposing the strength of the police in East Ham to be inadequate for the requirements of the place, but will make inquiry in the matter.

POSTAGE ON TYPE-WRITTEN CIRCULARS.

MR. COLVILLE (Lanark, N.E.): I beg to ask the Secretary to the Treasury, as representing the Postmaster-General, whether circulars which have been typewritten are subject to be charged at the letter rate, while the same circulars, if printed, would only be charged a halfpenny each!

MR. HANBURY: The reply to the honourable Member's Question is in the affirmative. Written or type-written circulars rank with letters, and are liable to letter postage; while printed circulars, like other printed matter, are transmissible at the book or halfpenny rate of postage. I should add that copies not less in number than 20, produced by some mechanical process, can be sent by book post.

to compulsory rotation duties, which was forwarded through the proper official channel in September last, and which was stated by the Controller to be under consideration in December last, has now been dealt with; and when the petitioners may hope for a reply?

MR. HANBURY: The reply will be sent very shortly.

MUSCAT.

SIR C. DILKE : I beg to ask the Under Secretary of State for Foreign Affairs whether, if the Muscat incident is at an end, Her Majesty's Government will at once lay upon the Table the Papers which explain it?

MR. BRODRICK : Though the question is settled in principle, the details are still under discussion, and it would not be expedient at this stage to lay any Papers on the subject.

TELEGRAPH CONSTRUCTION ON THE GOLD COAST.

MR. BUCHANAN (Aberdeenshire, E.): I beg to ask the Secretary of State for the Colonies what are the branches of special expenditure, other than telegraph construction, in the northern territories of the Gold Coast for which a Supplementary Estimate for £70,000 is asked?

THE SECRETARY OF STATE FOR THE COLONIES: Of the £70,000 £20,000 is for telegraph construction, and the remaining £50,000 is for the cost of maintaining a force in the Hinterland to protect the inhabitants, with whom we have made treaties, and to secure the peace and good government of these territories for which we are now responsible.

COMPULSORY ROTATION SORTING DUTIES.

CAPTAIN NORTON: I beg to ask the Secretary to the Treasury, as representing the Postmaster-General, whether the petition from the postal sorting force in the East Central district, with reference

GREAT BRITAIN'S PLEDGES TO CHINA.

MR. YERBURGH (Chester): I beg to ask the Under Secretary of State for Foreign Affairs whether the instructions given to Sir Claude Macdonald on the 22nd of July last, namely, that he was to inform the Yamen that Her Majesty's Government would support the Chinese Government against any Power which committed an act of aggression upon China because China had granted to a British subject permission to make or support any railway or similar public work, have been cancelled or in any way modified; and, if not, whether the said promise of support applies to the case of the Northern Railway Extension contract?

MR. GIBSON BOWLES (Lynn Regis): I desire to ask the right honourable Gentleman a Supplemental Question, of which I have given him private notice—namely, whether, in referring to this statement on behalf of Her Majesty's Government, he will include in his answer a reference to the statement made by Lord Salisbury in the House of Lords, which somewhat differs from this? Lord Salisbury said that Sir Claude Macdonald was instructed to inform the Yamen that Her Majesty's Government would support the Chinese Government in resisting (not " against ") any Power which had committed an act of aggression on China because China had granted to a British subject permission to make or support any railway or public work. In Lord Salisbury's statement the word " similar " is left out.

MR. BRODRICK : There has been no modification of the undertaking announced in the House of Commons by Mr. Curzon on 2nd August 1898, but it is not anticipated that any question regarding it will arise in respect to the Northern Railway Extension.

MUSCAT.

MR. LABOUCHERE (Northampton): I beg to ask the Under Secretary of State for Foreign Affairs whether the concession which the Sultan of Muscat had granted to France in regard to a coaling depôt included the right to fly the French flag on the depôt, and to fortify it; and what is the nature of the concession now granted?

MR. BRODRICK: A piece of land was granted in one of the coves dependent on Muscat as a mark of favour and respect to the French Government. There was no stipulation in the grant to preclude the hoisting of the French flag or the erection of fortifications. It is now proposed that the French Government shall have the use of a coal-shed in exactly the same manner as the British Government have, and probably in the same place; but there will be no lease or cession of any kind.

FASHODA.

MR. LABOUCHERE: I beg to ask the First Lord of the Admiralty whether any portion of the sum demanded in the Navy Supplementary Estimates is due to expenditure in regard to preparations and demonstrations connected with the Fashoda incident; and, if so, under which sub-heads such expenditure is to be found?

MR. MACARTNEY: The answer is in the negative.

MR. LABOUCHERE: Do I understand that those thousands of pounds which the Chancellor of the Exchequer said had been spent in preparations and demonstrations are not included in the Supplementary Estimates?

MR. MACARTNEY: I am not aware that the Chancellor of the Exchequer ever made such a statement.

MR. LABOUCHERE: He certainly did.

ECCLESIASTICAL COURTS.

MR. MELLOR (York, W.R., Sowerby): I beg to ask Mr. Attorney-General if he can state by what authority the Archbishop of Canterbury is about to hold a Court with the Archbishop of York as assessor; whether such Court is a legal Court; if not, would the Archbishops in such a Court be bound by the decisions of the Privy Council; will all parties be heard; and how is it proposed that the decisions of the Court shall be enforced?

THE ATTORNEY-GENERAL (Sir R. WEBSTER, Isle of Wight): The question of the right honourable Gentleman is founded on a misapprehension. The hearing proposed to be held by his Grace the Archbishop of Canterbury will not be a Court, but will depend, as other similar tribunals, upon the consent of the parties who appear before him. None of the subsidiary questions which the right honourable Gentleman has raised apply to such a tribunal.

MR. SWIFT MacNEILL: Does consent give jurisdiction?

SIR R. WEBSTER: Yes, certainly.

RELIGIOUS INSTRUCTION IN ELEMENTARY SCHOOLS.

MR. HUBBARD (Lambeth, Brixton): I beg to ask the First Lord of the Treasury whether, in view of the admittedly unsatisfactory working of the Conscience Clause, the Government will, in the interests of religious liberty, bring in a Short Bill at an early date to amend the Education Act, 1870, and provide that any child withdrawn from religious teaching at an elementary school under the Conscience Clause may be also withdrawn from the school during such period for the *bonâ fide* purpose of obtaining religious instruction elsewhere?

THE FIRST LORD OF THE TREASURY (Mr. A. J. BALFOUR, Manchester, E.): I agree with my honourable Friend that there are cases in which the Conscience Clause does not work satisfactorily. Perhaps they are not so great as is sometimes supposed, although they undoubtedly exist. If I understand my honourable Friend's proposal right, it is very much on the lines of a clause we introduced in the Bill of 1896, and, therefore, naturally, I am disposed to look at it with sympathy and favour. I cannot, however, promise legislation on the subject. It is impossible in the present state of legislation to add to our programme, and though no doubt it might be in our power to bring in a short Bill, I can hardly guarantee on that Bill that the discussions would be equally short.

PRIVATE LEGISLATION PROCEDURE (SCOTLAND) BILL.

MR. THORBURN (Peebles and Selkirk): I beg to ask the First Lord of the Treasury if he can name an early day when the Second Reading of the Private Legislation Procedure (Scotland) Bill will be taken?

THE FIRST LORD OF THE TREASURY: I hope to be able to take the Second Reading of this Bill before Easter, but in the present state of Supply I cannot give any definite pledge on the subject.

ST. DOGMAEL'S BATTERY, NEAR CARDIGAN.

MR. PHILIPPS (Pembroke): I beg to ask the First Lord of the Admiralty whether a contract for work to be done at St. Dogmael's Battery, near Cardigan, was given to a London tradesman; whether a local tradesman wrote to the Admiralty for specifications, and got no reply till after the contract had been given; and why this work was handed over to a contractor in London when it could have been done as efficiently and more cheaply in the locality?

THE CIVIL LORD OF THE ADMIRALTY (Mr. A. CHAMBERLAIN, Worcestershire, E.): The local tradesman referred to did not apply for specifications till four days after the tenders had been opened. The contract was given to a London firm whose tender was the lowest received.

MR. PHILIPPS: Was it known locally that tenders were to be invited?

MR. A. CHAMBERLAIN: I cannot say whether it was in this case. The work required was of a peculiar class, and I very much doubt if any local contractor could have executed it. We always try to get local tenders if possible.

MR. PHILIPPS: On another occasion will the Admiralty let it be known locally that specifications are to be given out?

MR. A. CHAMBERLAIN: I cannot undertake to advertise on every occasion. But we always call for local tenders when possible.

CLOGHER BOARD OF GUARDIANS.

MR. JOHNSTON (Belfast, S.): I beg to ask the Chief Secretary to the Lord Lieutenant of Ireland whether his attention has been called to the meeting of the reinstated Board of Guardians of the Clogher Union, held on the 11th February, at which Mr. Cuthbertson, the rate collector appointed by the Local Government Board, reported having collected and lodged about £22, out of £254, in Monaghan divisions of the union; whether he is acting by deputy, which Miss Magill would not be allowed to do; and what reply has been given to the resolution passed by the Clogher Board requesting the Local Government Board to dispense with the services of Mr. Cuthbertson, and to appoint Miss Magill to complete the collection?

MR. GERALD BALFOUR: The Guardians' resolution of the 11th ultimo called attention to the unsatisfactory state of the collection in Collector Cuthbertson's district, and pointed out that they believed that the only way to bring the collection to a close before the 25th of March was the immediate issue of a sealed Order of the Local Government Board dispensing with Mr. Cuthbertson's services, and directing Miss Magill to complete the collection. The Local Government Board were unable to regard this suggestion as made in good faith, the Guardians being fully aware of the Board's ruling as to the necessary qualifications of poor rate collectors; and as the Board had local information· to show that the only effect of the Guardians' resolution had been to induce the people to further withhold the payment of rates, their reply to the Guardians was to the effect that instead of passing resolutions which placed obstacles in the way of the collection, the Guardians should call upon the people of the district to pay their rates. The Board also pointed out in answer to the alleged unsatisfactory progress ·made by the collector, that if his collection was backward they could only regard it as the natural consequence of the letter written by the present chairman of the Board at the outset of the dispute, advocating the non-payment of rates to the collector appointed by the Local Government Board. I am informed that the collector has, as a matter of fact, lodged £288 in this district. The Board understand that he is not acting by deputy, but owing to the opposition to payment of rates (prompted very possibly by the chairman's letter), he has to make many seizures for rates, and is obliged to employ persons to assist him in this work.

Mr SWIFT MacNEILL: Is it not the fact that the Board was dissolvd because it appointed a woman rate collector, and insisted on retaining her against the direction of the Local Government Board?

Mr. GERALD BALFOUR: It was dissolved because it would not appoint a proper rate collector.

ST. CLEMENT'S CHURCH, BELFAST.

Mr. DILLON: I beg to ask the Chief Secretary to the Lord Lieutenant of Ireland whether, on or about Friday, 24th February last, a number of hymn books, the property of the church, were carried off from St. Clement's Church, Belfast; and whether the police have taken any steps to bring the offenders to justice?

Mr. GERALD BALFOUR: The reply to the first paragraph is in the affirmative. On the matter being brought under the notice of the police inquiries were at once made, and every endeavour made to trace the books as well as the person, or persons, by whom they were removed from the church, but so far without result.

DISPATCH OF IRISH MAILS FROM THE HOUSE OF COMMONS.

Mr. M'GHEE: I beg to ask the Secretary to the Treasury, as representing the Postmaster-General, with reference to the posting of letters from the House of Commons to Ireland, whether he is aware that the latest hour for posting with an extra stamp is 8 p.m., and whether this was exactly the latest time for posting such letters when the mails left Euston considerably earlier than they do now; and whether he will consider the matter with the view of extending the time for posting letters addressed to Ireland?

Mr. HANBURY: The facts are as stated by the honourable Member. The late letters from the House of Commons for the Irish night mail—dispatched from Euston at 8.45 p.m.—are sent to Euston with the late letters for the Scotch mail, which is dispatched at 8.30 p.m.

ARMENIAN ORPHANAGE.

Mr. S. SMITH (Flintshire): I beg to ask the Under Secretary of State for Foreign Affairs whether the Government have yet received any information regarding the closing of the Choonkoosh Orphanage; whether the man who rented the house for the orphans and one of the house fathers has been thrown into prison; whether the orphanage at Palu has been closed; and whether the German Orphanage at Diarbekir has also been closed?

Mr. BRODRICK: I gave on Monday last all the information which Her Majesty's Government have as to the closing of these orphanages. Her Majesty's Government have received no information as to the imprisonment of persons connected with the orphanages.

DISEASE AMONG THE TROOPS IN INDIA.

Major RASCH (Essex, S.E.): I beg to ask the Secretary of State for India whether, in view of the facts stated in the Army Medical Report of 1897, that the number of admissions to hospital for venereal disease per 1,000 was 507, only three per cent. less than in 1896, and that the number invalided to England in 1897 was 662, an increase of 183 over the previous year, the Government will consider the advisability of permitting the Indian Government to take such measures as they may think fit for the detection of diseased persons of both sexes, and to detain such perons in hospital until cured; and whether the Government has received any Reports as to the effectiveness or otherwise of the new cantonment rules enforced in 1899?

THE SECRETARY OF STATE FOR INDIA: The statement quoted by my honourable and gallant Friend relates to troops in cantonments only. Including those on field service, the admission rate for venereal disease was 485 per 1,000 in 1897, against 511 in 1896, a reduction of 26 per 1,000. The new cantonment rules were not brought into operation until towards the end of 1897, and could not be expected to have much effect in lowering the ratio for the whole year. No Report has yet been received as to their effectiveness or otherwise, and until the results of their working have been ascertained I do not propose to take any further action. The Returns for 1898 so far as they are known are very encouraging, and show a considerable further decrease.

CASE OF GEORGE JOHNSON AT LIVERPOOL ASSIZES.

MR. M'GHEE: I beg to ask the Secretary of State for the Home Department whether his attention has been drawn to the case of George Johnson, who was tried at the recent assize held at Liverpool, and sentenced to six months' imprisonment with hard labour and to be flogged three times, receiving 15 lashes on each occasion; and whether he will consider the revision of such sentence with a view to remitting the flogging?

MR. COLLINGS: The Secretary of State's attention has been called to this case, and he is making inquiries into the matter.

LASCARS ON BRITISH VESSELS.

MR. M'GHEE: I beg to ask the President of the Board of Trade when he expects to be in possession of the opinion of the Solicitors to the Board of Trade as to whether the provisions of the Merchant Shipping Act, 1894, are applicable to Lascars in like manner with other seamen employed on British registered vessels regardless of the port of engagement?

THE FIRST COMMISSIONER OF WORKS (for the PRESIDENT of the BOARD of TRADE): A case upon the point mentioned in the Question has been prepared for submission to the Law Officers of the Crown, upon which an opinion will be obtained in due course.

NAVAL QUESTIONS.

SIR FORTESCUE FLANNERY (Yorks, Shipley): I beg to ask the First Lord of the Admiralty whether the number of engineer students to be entered into the Royal Navy in the financial year has been determined by the Admiralty, with a view to rendering possible the option of retirement of Fleet engineers of 50 years of age; and whether the system of such retirement, which was temporarily suspended seven years ago, will be again resumed?

MR. MACARTNEY: The answer to the first paragraph is in the negative, and to the second, not at present

SIR FORTESCUE FLANNERY: I beg to ask the First Lord of the Admiralty if he could state to the House what facilities, if any, are afforded to the senior engineer officers of the Royal Navy to enable them to attend the valuable lectures on the progress of marine engineering given at the Royal Naval College, Greenwich, and how far such facilities, if any, compare with those afforded to the senior officers of other branches in the Fleet; and whether the senior engineer officers are precluded from attending the engineering lectures owing to the paucity of their numbers?

MR. MACARTNEY: The lectures on marine engineering at the college are equally open to engineer officers of the Royal Navy as to other branches of the Service when they are not otherwise employed. The exceptional requirements of the Service did not admit of these officers attending last year, but the lectures given on the last occasion were printed and issued to the Fleet.

SIR FORTESCUE FLANNERY: I beg to ask the First Lord of the Admiralty if he could state to the House what was the actual sea-going engine-room complement of H.M.S. "Argonaut" and "Ariadne" at the time of their official trials, exclusive of the party for taking records; and what numbers of engine-room ratings were drafted from the Medway Reserve to make up such complement?

MR. MACARTNEY: The drafts of engine-room ratings employed on the trials of the "Argonaut" and "Ariadne" numbered 207, and all the ratings were provided from the Medway Reserve, to which the vessels belong.

SIR FORTESCUE FLANNERY: I beg to ask the First Lord of the Admiralty whether it is the intention of the Admiralty to carry into effect the recommendation of the Committee presided over by Admiral Sir A. Cooper Key 22 years ago, that engineer officers in the Royal Navy should have executive control in their own department?

MR. MACARTNEY: The answer is in the negative.

MR. ALLEN (Newcastle-under-Lyme): Why has not the recommendation of the Committee been carried out with regard to the engineer officers of the Royal Navy?

MR. MACARTNEY: The honourable Member had better give notice.

SIR FORTESCUE FLANNERY: I beg to ask the First Lord of the Admiralty whether large additions are to be made to the executive ranks of admirals, captains, commanders, and lieutenants in the Navy; and whether any increase is contemplated, and, if so, to what extent, in the number of engineer officers of the various grades to meet the growing requirements of the Fleet?

MR. MACARTNEY: Certain additions will be made to the executive ranks and to the lists of engineer officers.

SIR FORTESCUE FLANNERY: When will it be made known?

MR. MACARTNEY: The honourable Gentleman had better wait for the First Lord's statement.

CLERKS TO SURVEYORS OF TAXES.

MR. HEYWOOD JOHNSTONE (Sussex, Horsham): I beg to ask the Secretary to the Treasury who has the appointment and dismissal of clerks (other than assistant surveyors) employed in the offices of the surveyors of taxes, and if any standard of qualification is required, or any examination has to be passed by them; and whether these men, who in the ordinary course of their duties become possessed of information of a confidential and private nature, are employed under an agreement terminable at a week's notice at wages varying from 8s. to £2 a week, and without any claim to a pension or to allowance in case of prolonged illness?

MR. HANBURY: The clerks in the offices of the surveyors of taxes are appointed and dismissed by the surveyors themselves. They are not required to pass any examination in order to qualify for the employment. It is a fact that these clerks are liable to dismissal at a week's notice. The large majority of them are in receipt of wages varying from £1 to £2 10s. a week, but 16 receive less than 10s. They are not entitled to pension or sick pay.

POINT OF PROCEDURE.

MR. BUCHANAN : With regard to the Orders of the Day I desire to ask the Deputy-Speaker's ruling on a point of procedure—whether there is any precedent for the course which the Government propose to pursue, and, if there is no precedent, whether it is in order to move the Deputy-Speaker out of the Chair in order to go into Committee on the Navy Estimates when the Navy Estimates have not yet been placed in the hands of Members?

MR. DEPUTY-SPEAKER: I believe there are two precedents, in 1896 and 1897, when the same course was pursued as is proposed to be followed to-day.

MR. BUCHANAN: Do I understand that in 1896 and 1897 a Motion was made to move the Speaker out of the Chair on the Navy Estimates, or any other Estimates, without those Estimates having been circulated?

MR. DEPUTY-SPEAKER: The honourable Member only gave me a very few moments' notice, but during the interval I have ascertained so far as I have been able that precisely the same course is being followed to-day as on those two occasions.

"THE TIMES" AND THE NAVY ESTIMATES.

MR. DILLON: I beg to ask the First Lord of the Admiralty whether he can explain how it is that "The Times" has been enabled to make some important statements as regards the Navy Estimates which are not known by Members of this House?

THE FIRST LORD OF THE ADMIRALTY (Mr G. J. GOSCHEN, St. George's, Hanover Square): I have absolutely no idea how "The Times" could have got any information whatever. Absolute secrecy has been preserved with regard to every newspaper and every individual. I can give a guarantee for the truth of that assertion.

ORDERS OF THE DAY.

SUPPLY.

NAVY ESTIMATES.

THE FIRST LORD OF THE ADMIRALTY'S STATEMENT.

Order for Committee read.

Motion made, and Question proposed—

"That Mr. Deputy Speaker do now leave the Chair."—(*Mr. Goschen.*)

*THE FIRST LORD OF THE ADMIRALTY (Mr. G. J. GOSCHEN, St. George's, Hanover Square): The Navy Estimates have never, perhaps, been introduced under more singular circumstances in some respects than to-day. Before us we have the proposed Conference on International Disarmament. Behind us we have the troubled months of October and November last, when comparisons as to the relative strength of the naval forces were in everyone's mouth. Memories are short, but I think that everyone will be able to recall the striking confidence which the people of this country showed at those critical moments in the naval forces of this country and in their preparedness to meet any emergency. That confidence, I humbly submit to the House, is the reward and the result of past expenditure. It was the result and the reward of the liberality of the House of Commons and of the nation as regards the Navy Estimates. We were ready. We had to make no feverish purchases, no sudden enrolments; we had not to come down to the House for a Vote from the Treasury. It was possible to conduct everthing with calmness and quietude. Now, I know that a different opinion prevailed in some quarters. The public rather likes headlines in newspapers, and it likes sensational statements, and many sensational statements were made at that time. It was said that we were spending millions. If we had spent such a large sum we should have had a large Supplementary Estimate to propose. On one occasion it was said we had made a gigantic purchase of coal. We had purchased 200,000 tons of coal, it is true, but the occasion of that purchase was not our preparations, but the fact that the strike had come to a conclusion, and that we had to replenish our stores in the ordinary course. Then it was said that officers were being recalled from leave in haste. It was entirely a mistake. One officer at one dockyard had left a ship on leave, and was wanted back for some particular duty. That was the whole of the ground for that particular statement. We had some small expenditure, and I can reply now to the honourable Member for Northampton. I made inquiry into the amount of money spent in the dockyards during the months of October and November, at the time when headlines in the Press were largest. The approximate total addition to the sum for wages in the dockyards during the eight weeks in question, including overtime, the cost of docking and cleaning the bottoms of many of the Fleet reserve ships, repairing and refitting the Fleet, and repairing ships in commission and reserve, was £13,600. That is all that we spent in labour on ships in order to produce mobilisation. Of course, we took steps at once to examine any weakness in our joints. We took the opportunity of seeing where we could improve our defences. There were constant conferences with the War Office, but only to adjust particular points. One weakness we found and remedied. That was, that in the mobilisation scheme in general, kits had not been prepared for the Naval Reserve men, if they should be suddenly called out. We asked for kits for 10,000 men, and they were produced at once. That is the main expenditure connected with the so-called mobilisation, and it is an expenditure that ought to have been made before. It was not made in order to strengthen us at that moment, but because we ought at all times to be in a position to put our reserve men into fighting condition if they are required. The result of our past expenditure has been this, for instance, that we have had to purchase no ammunition, we have given no new orders. There is an item in the Supplementary Estimates of £100,000 under Vote 9. That is not in respect of mobilisation; it represents the commencement of the guns to arm the ships to be built under the supplementary programme which was sanctioned by the

First Lord of the Admiralty.

House in August last. This was not taken to increase our resources at the moment. It was no menace of any kind; it was simply providing guns in advance for ships which will not be ready for two or three years to come. I think the Estimates of last year were justified by the tranquillity of the country. Under the conditions which then existed, if we had not had a Navy ready and prepared, should we not have lost many more millions than have been spent on the increase of the Navy, in the fall of securities, in the general disorganisation of trade, and in the general feeling of disquietude which would have taken place, besides the credit which we might have lost by timid counsels prevailing in place of the attitude which the country took, and was entitled to take, during those troubled months? The Continental Powers were somewhat disturbed by the allegation that we were arming so greatly. I am glad to have had the opportunity of making this statement, because I do not know that it has been made before, in order to remove the impression that we were either arming unnecessarily, or were arming for any particular purpose, or for any aggressive action. It was the belief in many Continental countries; in fact, we had reports from almost every capital in Europe to that effect. There was a deeply ingrained idea in the Chancelleries of Europe that England had some plan of attack for which she thought her opportunity had come, and that, having regard to the greatness of her naval forces, she would take care to seize that favourable opportunity. I need not assure this House—it would be absurd almost to do so—that such an idea never entered into the mind of the Government of this country. I know that people abroad are incredulous, but they ought to know that such a war undertaken in such a spirit would have been against the whole traditions of this country, and would have been against the whole moral sense of this country. [Laughter from the IRISH MEMBERS.] Both sides of the House are agreed on that subject, and I do not see the point of honourable

Members' merriment. That being so, foreign countries may be assured that while we have the country behind us in maintaining our rights and in the justice of our cause which affects our honour or our interests, I do not believe that we should have the country behind us in the case of what I may call an Opportunist War. I have spoken, Mr. Deputy-Speaker, of the slight preparations which were made in consequence of the incidents of last autumn. I now pass to the ordinary work of the present financial year before I deal with the Estimates for the future year. The shipbuilding work has been more satisfactory than in the preceding year, but there are still short deliveries of armour and machinery. In the year before, the course of business, the course of construction, was interrupted by the strike, but the effects of that strike did not cease with the cessation of the labour troubles. The effects were felt during the present year, and they were felt in this way : there was a boom generally in mercantile shipbuilding. All the ships the construction of which had been arrested, and tho machinery of which could not be completed, had to be taken in hand, and the consequence was that the contractors found very great difficulty in keeping up to their dates. And indeed they had not the matter entirely in their own hands, for their sub-contractors were dilatory in their deliveries of many of the materials which they require for construction. The House may recollect the controversy as to the output of armour. In the course of the present financial year the output of armour has increased, but the Admiralty were so far justified by the provision they had made, that the output has not been, in fact, what it was expected to be, and which was hoped by the manufacturers to be possible. There was a short delivery of armour and machinery of £800,000 on Vote 8. The "Cressy" class of cruisers has been delayed in consequence, and there has been some delay in the completion of the "Canopus" class, but in the dockyards new construction has proceeded most satisfactorily. The dates for laying down the new battleships have been anticipated. We have been able to begin these battleships before we expected when I made my statement to the House last year. Let me recapitulate the new

programme of construction of the present year. There were three battleships under the original programme, and four battleships under the supplementary programme. There were four cruisers under the original programme, and four cruisers under the supplementary programme. The House will remember the cause of that supplementary programme. It was due to the celebrated ukase of the Emperor of Russia, when 90 millions of roubles—that is to say, £9,000,000 sterling—were assigned to the Minister of Marine out of a special fund. The Government held, and the country supported them in their view, that an effort like that must be met by some corresponding effort on our part ; and the consequence was, much against the grain, and regretting as much as anyone could regret the increased burden thus put upon this country, we were nevertheless compelled to commit ourselves to the construction of four battleships and four cruisers. Of the three battleships, two were of the "Canopus" and "Formidable" class, and each of these two classes now forms a complete and homogenous group of six ships. The chief features of the new battleships I am able to submit to the House. They do not differ greatly from the ships which have been already designed. The following are the principal features of the battleships : I may say that we propose to name the four ships the "Duncan" class, i.e., the "Duncan," "Exmouth," "Cornwallis," and "Russell" —all great historical naval names. The following are the measurements of these vessels : Length 405ft., breadth 75ft., mean draught 26ft., displacement 14,000 tons, indicated horse power 18,000. Their chief armament will be four 12-inch breechloading guns in barbettes, 12 6-inch quick-firing guns in casemates, and 12 12-pounders. Stability and buoyancy will be secured by vertical side armour 7 inches thick, extending over a considerable portion of the length, and continued in a gradually reduced thickness to the bow. The barbettes for the 12-inch guns will have 11-inch armour, and the casemates for the 6-inch guns 6-inch armour. The speed of 19 knots with natural draught exceeds that of the preceding battleships in the Royal Navy, and is to be obtained on an eighthours' trial with natural draught in the

M

stoke-holes. I may say that these battleships are of a similar class to the "Formidable." With reference to the four cruisers on the original programme, two, as stated by me last year, are of the "Cressy" class, and two are of a type equal to that of the "Powerful" class, so far as armour protection is concerned. We propose to name these the "Francis Drake" class. The principal features of these ships are: Length between perpendiculars 500ft., extreme breadth 71ft., mean draught 26ft., displacement 14,100 tons, indicated horse power 30,000, speed with natural draught 23 knots. The armament is two 9.2-inch guns with armour shields, 16 6-inch quick-firing guns in casemates, 14 12-pounder quick-firing guns, three 3-pounders. The 9.2-inch and the 6-inch guns will be of the latest and most powerful types, with armour protection equal to that of the "Powerful" class. Buoyancy and stability will be secured by vertical side armour about six inches thick, associated with strong steel decks, as in the "Canopus" and "Cressy" classes, and the bows of the new vessels will be most strongly protected. I may say generally that these ships will be the most powerful cruisers afloat in any Navy in the world. It is a necessity for us. I do not want to make any special comparison with foreign ships, but I may say we have been driven to construct these ships after a careful review of the new designs of the ships of various other Powers; and we hope that these designs will secure to us that we shall have four ships stronger than any cruisers which are now building by any other country.

SIR F. EVANS (Southampton): Are they capable of going through the Suez Canal?

*THE FIRST LORD OF THE ADMIRALTY: Yes certainly. The draught is 26ft., and the speed 23 knots. I may say generally that what we aim at now in these new ships and in all our cruisers is speed. That is the governing factor in all the cruisers which we are building. Besides these new cruisers, there are two which are of a smaller class, and will be built with special reference to a great rate of speed. Sir William White has endeavoured, in his designs, to solve the

First Lord of the Adm·

problem of armoured cruisers of a very high rate of speed and of moderate dimensions. Again I say that this design has been carefully considered with reference to the ships which they may have to meet. Their length is 240ft., extreme breadth 66ft., mean draught 24½ft., displacement 9,800 tons. Their speed with natural draught will be 23 knots, and the indicated horse power 22,000. They are to have 14 6-inch quick-firing guns, four in turrets and 10 in casemates, 10 12-pounder quick-firing guns, and three 3-pounder, and two torpedo tubes. The 6-inch guns will be of the latest type, and will be protected by armour about four inches thick. Vertical side armour of the same thickness will be carried over a considerable portion of the length, with thinner armour on their bows. In laying down these ships we have been simply following a plan, which I have indicated throughout, of not exceeding the standard which I consider we ought to maintain to meet what is being done by the other Powers. I am still dealing with the programme of the present year, and am not speaking of the coming financial year. The two cruisers I have last mentioned are not yet ordered, although the tenders for them have been issued, and they do not belong to the programme of the coming year; they belong to the supplementary programme. If there has been some delay it has been in order to see how this problem can be met—i.e., the combination of armour, of high speed, and of small displacement—and the delay has been well worth the result which we hope to attain. I have said that under Vote 9 there is an increase of £100,000, but it is in respect of guns which have been ordered for these new ships. I now turn to inform the House how we have fared as regards the *personnel* in the present year. The number of men and boys voted will be secured without any difficulty by the 1st April. The recruiting, of course, is spread over 12 months, and for the 10 months past we have secured the full proportion. There has been no difficulty in obtaining the necessary number of recruits. With regard to the Reserve, I may say that the experiment which has been tried of insisting that all Reserve men within a certain time should go to sea, has been completely successful. Many Members of the House will remember the object we had in view —that the Reserve should not be a paper Reserve, that they should not simply be trained at our batteries, but that we should have the security that a large number of men had actually been trained in a man-o'-war at sea. Well, we have made that experiment, and I am glad to say that in the present financial year 1,800 Reserve men will have been embarked on Her Majesty's ships, many of them in the Channel Squadron, some of them in the Mediterranean Squadron, and some of them in the guard-ships; and in all respects we have heard a satisfactory account of them. They take great interest in their work, and the officers take great interest in them. There has been perfect good feeling between these Reserve men and the ordinary crews of the ships, and I am very glad that such a link has been established—a very valuable link, I think I may say—between the Mercantile Marine and Her Majesty's Navy. Now, if I may sum up briefly the results of the last financial year. We shall have secured all the men we wanted; we shall have succeeded in our Reserve scheme; we shall have perfected our mobilisation arrangements; we shall have strengthened the stores in our naval bases; and we shall have secured all the guns and all the ammunition for the guns which was necessary. I may say that every ship has not only got its guns and ammunition ready, but that the reserve of guns for the ships and the reserve of ammunition for these guns were all ready on the 1st January last. We have commenced seven battleships; we have anticipated the programme in the dockyards in the dates of laying down three of these new ships; we have commenced six new first class armoured cruisers, besides two the tenders for which have been invited. The only drawback I see in the year's work has been the short deliveries of armour and machinery by the contractors. The total cost of all this is enormous, but if we have enrolled the men, if we have got the ships ready, if our bases have been strengthened—if in all these respects we have been able to place the Navy in a position of preparedness, I think that the taxpayer has his reward in the serene tranquillity with which the nation is able to face any dangerous crisis that

may arise. Before I pass to the Estimates of the coming financial year there are two topics upon which the House would probably like me to touch. One is Wei-Hai-Wei, and the other is the Naval Works Bill. With reference to Wei-Hai-Wei there has been some expenditure on account of some purchase of land in the island in the present financial year, and some money has been taken for Wei-Hai-Wei in the coming financial year. What we propose to do is to make it what I may call a secondary naval base, to fortify it sufficiently against a raid, to have coal stores and small repairing shops, and, above all, to secure a good anchorage by dredging. A dredger has been sent out for the purpose, and if honourable Members thought that the anchorage at Wei-Hai-Wei was an unsatisfactory anchorage generally, I can assure them that the captains of our ships, after considerable experience during the past year, have come to the conclusion that it is one of the most valuable anchorages that we have in the East, and that it will be of great importance to us in any operations we may engage in in the China seas. The climate is good, and in every respect we are able to give a good account of the place. The other point is the Naval Works Bill. I shall leave that this year, as I have left it in past years, to be expounded to the House by my honourable Friend the Civil Lord, but in order that the total expenditure may be gauged by the House, which I know they are all anxious to do, I may say that the expenditure of the present financial year under the Naval Works Act will reach about £1,300,000, and that in the coming financial year we expect that the expenditure will be a little over 1½ millions. I pass now to the coming financial year, and I will deal briefly in the first instance with the other Votes, leaving the shipbuilding Vote, which is the most important, to the last. As regards the *personnel*, we propose an increase of 4,250 men and boys, which will bring up the *personnel* to 110,640, including 6,500 boys under training. Here again we see, and we cannot but feel, the result of the necessity for our supplemental programme. I had hoped to have been able to have stopped at the point which we reached last year. 1 indicated such a possibility in my statement last year, but our hopes have been falsified, not by any desire that we should expand our armaments, but simply because we had to take corresponding action to that taken by other Powers. Let me remind the House of the drawback under which we are in any comparison of international expenditure by the fact that we have a recruited Navy as we have a recruited Army, and that the cost of that Navy is, of course, naturally very largely in excess, in proportion, of that of any other country. Again, we have to give heavy retainers to our Reserve, and our system of pension, gratuities, and retired pay, necessary as it is, and fitting in with the whole system of our recruited Navy, also adds to the vast proportions of the total cost of the Navy. Perhaps it would be wise for me to say that this increase of men was settled in August last before the Fashoda incident. It was settled then in the ordinary way, by the study of the Manning Committee as to the number of men necessary for the Fleet, and it had no reference whatever to any subsequent difficulties which we may have had. It is the extension which we considered necessary in ordinary times. Honourable Members of the House who do not care for the study of the Estimates may not know the great proportion which the pay of the men and officers of the entire *personnel* bears to the whole. It amounts to £5,242,000 in this coming Estimate, besides half-pay and gratuities to the amount of £2,232,000. The total pay for the *personnel* which goes into their pocket, apart from victualling and clothing and all that appertains to the general fitting out of the Fleet—the actual pay, pensions and gratuities amounts to £7,474,000. France pays £3,000,000 under that item, and as to Russia—I cannot understand how it can be—but a study of their estimates only reveals an item of £445,000 for the pay of the entire Russian navy. I say again, that in any international examination of the Estimates, the different position which we occupy would have most seriously to be taken into account. The increase in the amount for the *personnel*, taking all the Votes together is £46,000. Then, of course, when there are more men they need more clothing, more

First Lord of the Admiralty.

rifles, more guns, generally more ammunition, more hospital accommodation, and more barrack accommodation. Many increases are hidden away in other Votes, and, therefore, not taken into account generally, although due exclusively to the *personnel*, when the cost of the *personnel* is being discussed. Here I would ask, is there any Party in the country, is there any body of men in the country who would wish to see the *personnel* decreased, or are they prepared to pay, and to pay cheerfully, for that large *personnel*? These great numbers which we have successfully enrolled during past years were enrolled not spasmodically, but by a steady calculation of what was necessary; and in that way we have added 27,000 men to the Fleet since 1894-95. I doubt whether there are many people in the country who would condemn that portion of these large Estimates which I have to submit to the House. Under Vote 9 for Armaments, I have to ask for an increase of £161,000, chiefly due to the construction of guns, but partly due also to the increased need of ammunition for firing practice. The House knows the enormous importance which has been really attached to gunnery. That is a matter which has commanded our special attention. All the events which have taken place of late show that the firing of guns and the practice of the gunners are matters to which too much attention cannot possibly be given. We have increased the number of guns and ammunition, but we are also anxious to provide for sufficient ammunition at all events, to give them the necessary practice with their guns in time of peace. I have to add £161,600 increase on Vote 9 to the increase which we have before for *personnel* of £462,000. That gives an increase on *personnel* and gunnery of £623,600. There remain outside Vote 8, Vote 10, and miscellaneous Votes. Vote 10 is for works, and we have had to increase the accommodation of hospitals, to improve the accommodation of hospitals in order to meet the modern necessities of hospital treatment. It has been for some years difficult to secure sufficient money for the development of our hospitals, but it has been absolutely necessary; and we have not considered it possible, even in a year of such great expenditure as this, to refrain from a certain addition to the Vote in respect of hospital accommodation. There are other items which go to swell the total. The increase of Vote 10 is £145,000, and there is an increase in miscellaneous Votes of £31,500. Adding to that the previous sum of £623,600 for the *personnel* and for the gunnery we get a total excess over this year's Estimates of £800,100. This excess is exclusive of the Ship Building Vote. In what respect can we diminish these Estimates? I can see none. They are the natural corrollary of what has been done as regards *personnel*, the natural corrollary of the position which both sides of the House have always desired their respective Governments to take up. I now come to the Ship Building Vote, the most important Vote of all. We propose to provide for about the same number of men who are now in the dockyards, which is a slightly larger number of men than those taken for the Labour Vote last year. The increased cost of £199,000 for labour over the original Vote of last year is distributed over the various headings of the Vote with which I shall presently have to deal. Now, let me remind the House that the amount of this Vote is determined by four factors —first, the liabilities which are carried over from the previous year, that is to say, the necessary provision for the continuance of the building of the ships under construction on 1st April; secondly, the necessary provision for the commencement of such further ships as it may be necessary to lay down; thirdly, the necessary provision for such repairs and reconstruction as may have to be undertaken—work on ships already built, work for the maintenance of the Fleet; and, fourthly, the necessary provision for coal, sea stores, yard services, and a number of miscellaneous items. In order that I may deal undisturbed by any parentheses with the ship building proper part of this Vote, that part with which naval policy is mostly concerned, let me clear off the minor but still very considerable remaining items grouped under this Vote. I am met in the forefront by a formidable item for coal. Last year we asked for £660,000 for coal; practically, we spent £920,000. £200,000 of that sum was due to the enhanced prices caused by the strike; the remainder was due to increased use, the necessity of further steaming, and

purposes of that kind. We propose to take in the coming year £135,000 more than we asked for in the present year. that is to say, £765,000, which is less than the cost of the coal for this year, but which has been burdened by the excessive cost due, I am sorry to say, to the strike. I am also sorry to say that the present prices still remain higher than the normal prices, and we have been obliged to include in our Estimate for coal, consequently, an allowance for a somewhat higher price. I am not going to detain you with any details about stores or matters of that kind, but I will say at once that we ask £78,000 more for stores, and £75,000 for yard machinery. The construction of the new ships, the constant necessity of repairs on old ships, and the greater amount of work thrown on the dockyards, makes it absolutely necessary, and, of course, economical, to keep up the machinery in the yard to the best condition of efficiency that is possible. It would be false economy to strike out from these Estimates such necessary improvements in the yards as are required for the purposes of the work to be turned out. Then, we are unfortunate in this coming year in that we do not secure the benefit of £100,000 which the Vote has had in the present year. The present financial year was relieved to the extent of £100,000 by purchases made in anticipation in previous year. We have no similar benefit, and consequently the Vote appears to that extent to be £100,000 more than that of last year. Putting these items together I get a total of £438,000. Well, then, as regards repairs, we ask for £411,000 more than in the present year—more than was asked for, but not very much more than we spent last year. A portion of the short earnings by contractors for armour and machinery has been with the consent of the Treasury applied to other work in the dockyard, work that otherwise would have probably involved a Supplementary Estimate. We wish in this coming year, if possible, to avoid a Supplementary Estimate. I think my right honourable Friend opposite knows that scarcely any First Lord has ever succeeded in keeping below his estimate for repairs in the dockyards. It is an item that is habitually under-estimated. I wish on the occasion of these vast Estimates to be entirely frank with the taxpayers, and that is why I have gone perhaps more fully into the details of this Vote than has been usual in a statement of this kind. I do not wish to gloss over items and muddle up totals; I am anxious that the country should thoroughly understand these Estimates. £438,000 more is asked for machinery, sea stores, coal, yard services, and purposes of that kind, and £411,000 more for repairs. I am afraid than in my anxiety to make everything as clear as possible I have taken the House through a considerable number of details.

HONOURABLE MEMBERS : No, no.

*THE FIRST LORD OF THE ADMIRALTY: I now approach the question of new construction, and that is under two heads, namely, the continuance of the ships under construction, and the new Programme of such ships as we may think the occasion may require us to lay down. We are faced, in the first instance, by the inexorable claims of the work begun. There are the liabilities of the Original Programme and the liabilities of the Supplementary Programme, which altogether form an item of £8,255,000. Of that two millions is represented by the liabilities of the Supplementary Programme. The liabilities of the original Programme would have been £6,225,000, but it has been raised by two millions through the action we were forced to take in August last year. Then the liabilities of the Original Programme are somewhat swollen by the short deliveries during the past two years of armour and machinery. These have not been so great as we anticipated in the present financial year, and a certain portion of that will fall on the coming financial year. This is included in the £6.225,000. Let me recall the facts of the Supplemental Programme. We must remember that 90 million roubles, or nine millions sterling were to be spent by Russia over a course of years, and if I take it that that course of years is five years, which is a moderate estimate, it means an additional expenditure of two millions a year. If the Chancellor of the Exchequer had had a windfall like the fortunate Minister of Marine in Russia, and had been able to place a corresponding sum of eight or nine millions at the disposal of the Admiralty,

First Lord of the Admiralty.

our liabilities this year would have been less by two millions, and we could have shown no increase on Vote 8 at all. I hope I have made myself clear. If our liabilities have been swollen to the extent of two millions in the present year— I need not enumerate all the ships that will be under construction—these liabilities represent a formidable amount of work. And now the question arises, that being the situation, what ought to be our course as regards the laying down of new ships? I have to survey the position from three points of view. I have had to frame a Programme on the examination of the Estimates and Programmes of other nations; on the examination of how these Programmes bear on the distinct mandate of the British people, as I understand it to be, as to the relative position in Naval strength which this country ought to hold; and lastly, I have examined the position from the point of view of the near approach of a Conference for International Disarmament. Thus far I have seen no reference to the approaching Conference in the Naval or Military Estimates or Programme of any of the great Powers of Europe. But that is no reason why, representing a Government which has accepted the invitation of the Tsar, I should refrain from considering the position which has been created by means of that Conference. I have stated that I have examined the Programmes of other countries as they stand. It would be affectation to pretend that it would be possible to frame our Programme without examining those of other countries. I have studied the Programmes of other nations, and that study has not been very reassuring. It is not only the Powers who may be our possible opponents, but there has been an immense increase in shipbuilding on the part of other nations, which of late years have only begun to enter into what I may call the naval competition. I have caused to be added up the amount of warships under construction by the six chief Naval Powers, and I find there are 685,000 tons of men-of-war under construction besides 225,000 tons which are projected.

MR. DILLON (Mayo, E.): What are the names of the Powers?

The FIRST LORD of the ADMIRALTY: France, Russia, the United States, Japan, Italy, and Germany. Well now, looking at the ships building all over the world, and looking, on the other hand, at our position, I want to call the attention of the House to this question. Is it fair to say our increased Estimates—an increase which we are compelled to propose—are the result of the aggressive policy of any particular Government of this country? Are these Estimates framed in any aggressive spirit? Does not the House see that they are forced upon us by the action of other countries? We have not taken the lead in any excessive steps. We have not endeavoured to raise the standard of the number of ships on which we are working. We have gone forward steadily, keeping that standard in view. I believe that it is going to be said in certain quarters that these Estimates are the Estimates of extravagance. [Some Opposition cheers]. I am glad to hear that that cheer comes from a very small 'Party in the House. I make the remark not for any political purpose; not to draw any contrast between one Government and another. What I want to do is to point out to the public, and, if possible, to Europe, that these Estimates cannot in any way be considered the Estimates of aggression. For that reason I was anxious that these Estimates should not be published before I made my statement.

Mr. DILLON: Will the right honourable Gentleman tell us at the same time whether he can give us any explanation why the figures appeared in the "Times" this morning?

The FIRST LORD of the ADMIRALTY: I do not know what the honourable Member means. I have already said that the Admiralty have no knowledge of the matter. It must have been some breach of trust in some quarter or other. I think the honourable Gentleman ought not to have interrupted me at this important stage of my statement. Why I was anxious to make this statement before the Estimates were in the hands of honourable Members was because I did not wish the amounts of these Estimates to go forth to the world without the explanation which I was able to give of the motives which underlie them and the circumstances in which they are framed. It is perfectly possible that if these Estimates had been in the hands of the public it might have been telegraphed all over Europe that we had made an immense increase in our Estimates, indicative of aggressive purposes, and of some design hostile to the general peace which we know the country desires, and which no Government ever desired more than we desire ourselves. I have spoken of the general increase in shipbuilding all over the world, but I must look to one case in particular. I look to the Estimates of the two most powerful nations—France and Russia. The increase in the French Estimate for naval construction is very small. In the case of Russia it is very different. They have increased their ordinary Estimate for ship construction by £1,500,000, and if you add to that a proportion of the £9,000,000 which was placed at their disposal they would be able to spend this year between £3,000,000 and £3,500,000 more than they have been able to spend in former years. If, therefore, on Vote 8 there should be an increase of £2,000,000, let it not be thought that we have gone one jot beyond the circumstances as they stand now before the Conference is held. Looking at the Estimates and Programmes of other countries now before us—looking, I say, at the general situation and the known Programmes of other nations—I have come to the conclusion to lay down the following new ships:—Two ironclads, the construction of which will be in strict accordance with the principle we have followed throughout; two armoured cruisers of the displacement of 9,800 tons; and three smaller cruisers of a design not yet settled, which are to be very fast, and much smaller than the others in order to meet a special purpose. I want to call the attention of the House very briefly to the fact that some of our rivals are practically giving up the idea that they would be able to meet us in the open sea, or, if they were able to meet us in the open sea, that at all events the better policy would be to endeavour to wear out the patience of this country by prolonged attacks upon our commerce, our food supply, and our sources of production. They think that while our battleships would be lying opposite their ports, they would be able to

sweep down upon our commerce, until this country tired of the uncertainty and the injury inflicted upon us, and of the flag being transferred to other nations. It has been avowed in the most distinct terms. Scientific and professional writers and politicians and statesmen have all commended this plan, and, what is more, they have acted upon it. The plan now is to build very fast cruisers which shall prey upon our commerce and which shall inflict that damage upon us which I have attempted to describe. We cannot sit still in the face of the construction of cruisers intended for that purpose. We know that purpose, and it is our bounden duty to defeat it. It is in consequence of this that our Programme for the present year has been proposed. It is in pursuance of this policy, which I am sure honourable Members opposite would pursue if they were in the place of the present Government, that we have made our plans, and it is for that purpose we lay down in the coming year these five cruisers which I have described. It is scarcely necessary to speak of a couple of sloops which are to take the place of older ships. The money required for this new Programme in the coming financial year will be £550,000. The two large cruisers are to be commenced late in the year. The money we have taken is £550,000, besides the sum of £80,000 for some smaller craft and steamboats. Adding this sum of £630,000 to the £8,225,000 at which the liabilities of new construction from former years stood, you get a total of £8,855,000, an increase of £1,167,000 for the coming year. Adding the other items under Vote 8, the total Vote rises to £12,817,000, being an increase of £2,016,000 over the Vote for the present year. Those are the Estimates as they stand, looking to the present situation. But an International Conference is to be assembled. Will the deliberations of that Conference—will the actions of other nations resulting from that Conference—make it possible for us to diminish or modify our Programme for new construction, while, of course maintaining our standard and not altering our relative position? We have been compelled to increase our expenditure as other nations have increased theirs, not taking the lead, not pressing on more than they. As they have in-
First Lord of the Admiralty.

creased, so we have increased. I have now to state on behalf of Her Majesty's Government that similarly, if the other great Naval Powers should be prepared to diminish their Programme of shipbuilding, we should be prepared on our side to meet such a procedure by modifying ours. The difficulties of adjustment are no doubt immense, but our desire that the Conference should succeed in lightening the tremendous burdens which now weigh down all European nations is sincere. But if Europe comes to no agreement, and if the hopes entertained by the Tsar should not be realised, the Programme which I have submitted to the House must stand. It is constructed on the basis on which the House itself has always expected us to rest it. It is the lowest which can be justified by the existing expenditure on shipbuilding of other countries; it is the lowest by which we can secure the object which the people expect of the Navy. The increase in Vote 8 is £2,016,000. I have arrived at £850,000 as the increase in the *personnel* and other Votes, and thus we arrive at an increase of £2,866,000. The total estimates will be £26,594,000. The right honourable Gentleman the Member for Montrose (Mr. Morley) said the other day that our expenditure at that time of £24,000,000 was an expenditure in a time of profound peace. I do not know whether the House, bearing in mind the agitating time of the autumn, will think that the state of Europe was a state of profound peace. I should rather say it was at that time a state of precarious peace. I see now that the expenditure of the country is about to be attacked. I shall wish to know how far under the general cover of the reduction of expenditure those who embark in that campaign intend to attack the figures of the Navy Estimates. I do not care whether they denounce the Government, but do not let them attempt to dissuade the people from bearing such taxation and bearing such burdens as may be necessary to carry on the duties of Empire. If they wish to reduce, let us know in what they wish to reduce. Let them come out into the open; let us know where we are. The moment has come, perhaps, when the nation may be put to the test as to paying for this great expenditure. I believe the nation will be prepared to bear it. I do not believe that the nation, which was satisfied with its position last year, I do not believe that honourable Members who last year went from platform to platform sincerely and patriotically, as we believe, speaking of our naval predominance—I do not think they, under the guise of denouncing expenditure in general and resisting the imposition of taxation, would wish that the result of their action should be in the slightest degree to diminish the efforts which we must make if we intend to hold our own. It depends on how you look at it. If you think that a war is simply an absurd impossibility, if you think you can have peace without power, if you believe in the sweet reasonableness of Europe in arms, then I admit that these Estimates are a crime. If, on the other hand, it is not so, then these Estimates are a necessity, and they are simply the embodiment of the will of a peace-loving, but a determined people.

On the Question that the Motion to go into a Committee of Supply be withdrawn,

MR. ASQUITH (Fife, E.): I think that the peculiar position in which we are placed should not be allowed to pass in silence. The right honourable Gentleman has made, as he always does, a lucid and powerful statement, but in listening to that statement the House has been deprived of the advantage which, until the present Administration came into power, it uniformly enjoyed of having had before it the Estimates in print. Owing, however, to the position in which we are placed, it is impossible intelligently to follow the statement of the right honourable Gentleman, and to adequately appreciate the situation. I am bound to say, speaking for myself, and speaking, I believe, the opinion of a very large number of Members on both sides of the House, that the reason which the right honourable Gentleman has given for a departure from the usual practice is wholly inadequate. The only reason he has stated is that if he circulated these Estimates in advance foreign nations might have been so alarmed at the apparently extravagant figures that they would have imputed to this country aggressive designs. Is that an adequate or satisfactory reason for depriving the House of Commons of its constitutional right to know beforehand exactly what the Ministers of the Crown have to submit? For my part, I do not think we should be justified in allowing this opportunity to pass without a strong and emphatic protest against the course adopted, which is an entire departure from the uniform practice of the past, and which, if persisted in, will to a large extent, in these introductory statements which are so important, deprive the House of a privilege and indeed disable it from performing the duty of effective criticism. I wish to ask the First Lord of the Treasury when he proposes that this Debate should be resumed. In the circumstances in which we are placed I would suggest that at any rate a reasonable delay should take place in order that we may have the opportunity of comparing the right honourable Gentleman's statement with the figures which we have seen for the first time in print.

ADMIRAL FIELD (Sussex, Eastbourne): Are we to be favoured with a Memorandum, or are we to depend on the First Lord's speech?

MR. DILLON: When I previously directed the attention of the right honourable Gentleman to this subject, the only reason which he gave for withholding the Estimates and the Memorandum until the close of Questions was that, if he had allowed the figures to become public property without being accompanied with his explanations, the facts might have been telegraphed all over Europe; and, having heard the figures, I am not surprised that he believed Europe would interpret them as a menace and a threat. But, Sir, how could such an argument for a moment justify the withholding of the Estimates or the Memorandum during this forenoon? Does the right honourable Gentleman imagine that if the Estimates and Memorandum had been placed in the Vote Office this morning, or at two or three o'clock this afternoon—as we were led to expect they would be from the answer of the right honourable Gentleman the Leader of the House—or even yesterday, that they would have been immediately communicated to Europe and produced the international results feared? Now, Sir, I think I am entitled to draw the attention of the

House to one of the inevitable evils which always spring from such attempts to keep the House in darkness. The newspapers are active, and some of them unscrupulous in endeavouring to get information that is interesting. And what is the result? "The Times" this morning gives a *résumé* of the right honourable Gentleman's figures which were denied to the House of Commons. When I asked the right honourable Gentleman to explain the fact that these formidable and startling figures were published in "The Times," to the exclusion of the other papers—because it is generally understood that the words "We understand" are used by such papers as "The Times" to introduce a semi-official *communiqué* —he said that the utmost secrecy had been maintained. How is it that the newspapers fail to get hold of the Budget figures? Why cannot the Admiralty maintain the secrecy of their office as well as the Chancellor of the Exchequer? When I pressed the question, the right honourable Gentleman said all he could say was that there must have been a very great breach of official duty and a betrayal of trust. Well, Sir, this is only another example of the rule which I think has a universal application— namely, that unless, as in the case of the Budget, there is an overwhelming and overmastering public necessity for maintaining secrecy, all these attempts to keep the House in the dark are always productive of great evil and ought to be avoided. The general result is to be seen in the scandalous publication, as I do not hesitate to call it, in "The Times." As a private Member, I must say that I think the practice of the present Government of introducing the Navy Estimates in this way, without previously giving the Opposition an opportunity of seeing them, is a very bad one. I do not see why the introduction of the Navy Estimates should not be preceded with the same publicity as the Army Estimates.

*THE FIRST LORD OF THE ADMIRALTY: I tell the honourable Member that no one can regret more than the Admiralty do that by some means or other, which I have called a gross breach of trust, or some piece of carelessness, those figures should have become known. I would apologise to the House if it *Mr. Dillon.*

were necessary, or if it thought it had been treated by a want of courtesy through the non-circulation of the Estimates. I must remind the House, however, that the same practice as is now condemned was followed two years ago by common consent of the House, and I understand that it was considered to be a convenient method. [" No."] It was at that time. If serious remonstrances had been made at that time the practice would not have been followed now. I regret now that I have taken the course which I have taken. I wish to be entirely frank with the House, and to give honourable Members every possible convenience in studying the Estimates. The present method was adopted in the full belief that the House would find it to be as convenient now as I believe it found it to be convenient in 1896.

*MR. BUCHANAN (Aberdeenshire, E.): After the statement and expression of regret made by the right honourable Gentleman, I think it would be invidious to persist in the complaints we have been making during the past few days. I should, however, like to point out that our complaint is not of any want of courtesy on the part of the right honourable Gentleman, but that the Government have deprived the House of its constitutional opportunity of seeing the Estimates before the speech and Motion made by the right honourable Gentleman. Since the right honourable Gentleman the First Lord of the Treasury made a statement in answer to the Question which I put to him on Tuesday, I have made investigations, and desire to take this opportunity of pointing out the course pursued in 1896 and 1897. I find that in 1897 the Motion for the Speaker leaving the chair was taken on Friday, 5th March, and the Estimates were circulated on Wednesday 3rd March. In 1896 a Motion was made on the Speaker leaving the Chair on the 2nd March. The Estimates were not circulated to Members until the morning of the 3rd March, but I am informed in the Vote Office that to Members who inquired for them the Estimates and the Memorandum of the First Lord of the Admiralty were in the Vote Office for the use of Members at the moment that the First Lord of the Admiralty made his speech. So I venture to say that the course of proceedings to-night by the First Lord of the Admiralty has been a distinct departure from all former precedents, or, at any rate, a very large extension of the bad precedent of two years ago. Now, I appeal to the First Lord that he should go back to the old practice of the House, and that Members of the House of Commons should be safeguarded in the maintenance of their privilege in having an opportunity of seeing these Estimates in detail, and the Memorandum of the Minister responsible for them, before they are called upon to hear his elaborate and detailed statement, which otherwise they cannot fully comprehend. And I venture to submit, Sir, that in so doing he would be returning to a good practice, which has proved acceptable and useful, at any rate, until two years ago, and which apparently, by the proceedings of to-night, there is no sound or substantial reason for departing from to-day.

MR. COURTNEY (Cornwall, Bodmin): I wish to ask, Sir, whether if any Member continues the Debate now, he will be debarred from joining in the Debate when it is resumed?

*THE DEPUTY SPEAKER: If the House now grants permission to withdraw the Motion, he would not be debarred. Of course, if the House does not do so, discussion will have to go on, and then every Member who has already taken part in the Debate would be debarred from taking further part in the Debate upon the Motion.

MR. SWIFT MACNEILL (Donegal, S.): I take my chance of being debarred and I have got up now to ask a simple question, for which I desire an answer from someone in a responsible position on the Treasury Bench. I wish to know whether there will be an inquiry in the Admiralty Office as to how this special information was furnished to " The Times?" Now, there is a precedent for that. In 1878, when the Schouvaloff-Salisbury Memorandum was published, I believe in the " Globe" newspaper, an inquiry was held—but the " Globe" is not " The Times": it is not the more-favoured journal. When that Schouvaloff- Salisbury Memorandum was

published two days before Lord Salisbury denied all about it, there was an inquiry at the Foreign Office, and then three or four officials were dismissed. It can be easily found out who gave this information if it is wished to do so. If the Government refuse an inquiry, we will still believe that this information reached " The Times" through some authorised source.

MR. BARTLEY (Islington, N.): No doubt it may be by a little technical irregularity that we should not have had the Estimates; but it does seem to me somewhat strange that those honourable Members who are making so much about the increasing desire for peace throughout the world should forget that the reason the Government has given us is that they thought that this might tend to aggravate the feeling of Europe, and that the Estimates have been withdrawn until this very reasonable Statement could be put forward. It seems to me that those of us who really wish to promote peace ought to support the Government in this, because the reason given by the First Lord of the Admiralty seems to me to be a most pacific one, and one likely to tend rather to the welfare of the world than the reverse.

MR. ASQUITH: Would the right honourable Gentleman now answer my question?

THE FIRST LORD OF THE TREASURY (Mr. A. J. BALFOUR, Manchester, E.): On Monday.

Motion, by leave, withdrawn.

SALE OF FOOD AND DRUGS BILL.

Order read, for resuming Adjourned Debate on Amendment proposed to Question (6th March)— .

" That the Bill be now read a second time:"— .

And which Amendment was—

" To leave out the word 'now,' and at the end of the Question to add the words 'upon this day six months.' "—(*Mr. Lough*.)

Question again proposed—

" That the word 'now' stand part of the Question."

MR. PHILIPPS (Pembroke): The feature of the opening Debate on this Bill, when it was introduced by the

President of the Board of Agriculture, was, I think, that the Bill was not warmly received in any quarter of the House. Now, Sir, I think the reason of that is very simple. The Bill is not a Bill that can create any enthusiasm among those who wish to strengthen the position of the consumer, as against the adulteration of food, and the Bill is not one that can create any enthusiasm from the friends of the farming industry. Now, Sir, the President of the Board of Agriculture, when he was introducing this Bill, said that even if this Bill was passed as it stood, the law of the land as so amended would not be nearly as drastic on the subject of adulteration as were the laws of other countries. I can well believe it, because this Bill, if it became law, would do exceedingly little to make the law more drastic. All through his speech in introducing this Bill the President of the Board of Agriculture was talking of fraud, and there is no doubt—it is admitted on all hands, on both sides of the House—that the sale of margarine, as it is conducted at present, does undoubtedly lend itself largely to fraud, and it is used largely for the purpose of fraud. And in respect of that fact the President of the Board of Agriculture, in introducing the Bill, used mild phrases about being very reluctant to hinder trade: he would not stop the colouring of margarine for fear of hindering an innocent trade that supplied a most wholesome and excellent food. But, Sir, I should like the President of the Board of Agriculture to remember this, that when he is introducing a Bill like this he is defending the interests of two great classes. He is defending the interests of the consumers, and he is defending the interests of the farmers, and I must say I wish the right honourable Gentleman had taken in his speech some bolder tone. It was said by the honourable Member, sitting on this side of the House, who represents a Division of Glasgow that this Bill aimed at securing agricultural produce a monopoly. Well, Sir, I do not think it does, but what it aims at, although I do not think it effects its purpose—what it purports to do, is to secure agricultural produce a monopoly of sale as agricultural produce, and I do not see how any Member of this House can say that agricultural produce is not

Mr. Philipps.

entitled in justice to be the only thing sold to the consumer as agricultural produce. Now, to turn to the Bill itself. My contention is that this Bill is a very weak thing, that is going to do very little good to anybody. I turn to Clause 1 of the Bill. Clause 1 says that if margarine or margarine cheese is imported, except in packages marked as margarine or margarine cheese, or, being adulterated or impoverished before, is imported, except in packages showing what is contained therein, or if condensed, separated, or skimmed milk is imported in tins or other receptacles not bearing the words "separated" or "skimmed" milk—then in any of these cases the importer is to be fined. How much is he to be fined? For the first offence, a fine not exceeding £20— this, Sir, not being a fine of £20, but to be a fine not exceeding £20; it may be as low as you like, but it must not be more than £20. For the second offence, it may not be more than £50, and for every subsequent offence it may not be more than £100. Now, it is admitted on all hands that if margarine is sold as butter the profit is very large indeed, and it is admitted that mixtures of margarine and butter cost something like 6d. a pound and largely sell at 1s. 2d. a pound. Well, a man who is fraudulently selling stuff he gets for 6d. for 1s. 2d., and doing that every day of the week, is making such profits that if once or twice in a year he is fined £100 it will mean very little out of his pocket. He could well go on repeating the offence. It is well known that men who commit fraud of this kind are detected, not every time they commit it, but only once in very many times. What I submit to the Government is this: Let them, after the first and second offence, at any rate, do away with fines; let them sentence a fraudulent importer to imprisonment instead of fine. If some of these respectable people who defraud the poor were sent to prison instead of being fined, then I think it would be a very fine example, and would be doing a great deal to keep trade pure. That is not done in this Bill. Well then, Sir, I turn to another clause, Clause 7 of the Bill. In that clause it is proposed to compel a manufacturer of margarine, or a wholesale dealer in margarine, to keep a register with certain particulars, and if he fraudulently omits to enter any particular—and I should like the House to remember it is not a case of mere careless action—which this Bill orders him to enter, what is to be done with him? He is to be fined, and the fine is not to be more than £10. That is from the Government which is strengthening the law against fraud, and in this particular case there is no punishment more than a maximum fine of £10. I ask, What is that going to do to stop fraud? Then take clause 11, which is perhaps the weakest clause in a weak Bill. By clause 11 it is enacted that every tin or other receptacle containing condensed, separated, or skimmed milk. must bear a label on which the words "separated" or "skimmed" milk are printed in large type, and if any person otherwise sells or offers for sale condensed or skimmed milk—what is he to be fined? A fine not exceeding £2. Well, Sir, it may be said you stop a poor milkman in the street when he is selling skimmed milk once in a way, and it is quite enough to fine him £2; but we all know that the man who sells skimmed milk for real milk is not found out every time, is not detected every time. It is only once, perhaps, in one hundred times that he is detected. I venture to say this is one of the cruellest frauds that can be committed. There are numbers of ignorant people in the country who do not know that milk from which the cream has been extracted is not enough to support the life of children, and numbers of children in this country are fed, or rather starved, on milk from which the natural fat has been removed. And yet this form of cheating, which is one of the cruellest forms of cheating you can have, is by this bold Government proposed to be punished by a maximum fine of £2. Why, it ought to be punished with imprisonment. Then I want to call the attention of the Government to another matter, to clause 2 of the Bill. . By clause 2 of the Bill the Government may, in relation to any matter appearing to the Board of Agriculture to affect the general interests of agriculture in the United Kingdom, direct an officer of the Board to procure for analysis samples of any article of food, and thereupon the officer shall have all the powers of procuring samples conferred by the Sale of Food and Drugs Acts. Well, Sir, the President of the Board of Agriculture, when he introduced this Bill, complained—and it is quite true that all over the country, or, at any rate, in many parts of the country—that the Acts against adulteration are very badly enforced. The local authorities do not take action, and so he proposed to give the Board of Agriculture power. But, Sir, why should not other people have the power? Why should you confine it to officials of the Board of Agriculture? Why not give the general public the power of protecting themselves? I do not quite see why the Board of Agriculture is to have this special power. I wish the President of the Board of Agriculture would explain why this special power under his Bill should be confined to the officials of the Board of Agriculture. Then, Sir, as to the working of this Bill. It is true the Government by this Bill propose that packages should be marked, but we all know that is a provision that it is almost impossible to enforce. Men in shops may put margarine into paper marked "margarine," or they may not. It is very difficult to detect frauds of this kind, especially when children and ignorant people are acting as purchasers. But there is one way in which fraud as regards margarine can be stopped, and everybody knows it, and that is by preventing margarine being coloured like butter. Sir, it is not the first purchaser only who ought to be protected. Most of us may be able, in buying butter for consumption in our own houses, to deal with tradesmen we know, and we may get butter; but, after all, people in all positions in life eat stuff in hotels and restaurants which may have been sold to the hotel-keeper or restaurant keeper as margarine, but it may be retailed by the hotel-keeper or restaurant keeper as butter to his customers, and who is going to stop these frauds? There is only one way, and that is to have margarine coloured differently to butter. And, Sir, you can see what may happen now. A man may go into an hotel, eat some nasty stuff believing it to be butter, whereas it is margarine, and then he may say, "What an ignorant person the British farmer is. He does not know his business. How superior the Danish butter is. How far superior the butter from Normandy." Yes, because butter from Normandy and Danish butter is butter, and half the time the stuff you are eating in hotels and restaurants may

not be butter at all, but margarine.
Now, Sir, the President of the Board of
Agriculture, when introducing the Bill,
said you could not stop the colouring of
margarine without stopping the colouring of butter. For my part, I do not
quite see why you should not, because
I think it would be easy to differentiate
between the colour of butter and of margarine. If you colour a light butter
yellow, after all it is butter. It is being
sold as butter. But if you colour margarine you are colouring a thing which
is not butter in order to have it sold as
butter. But if it is necessary, as the
President of the Board of Agriculture
says, that if you forbid colouring in the
one case you should forbid it in the
other, I, for my part, should be quite
ready to accept that alternative, and to
see colouring forbidden altogether,
whether the stuff coloured was margarine or butter. I know the President of
the Board of Agriculture complained that
some people in the House would insist
upon margarine being coloured something
different altogether. I do not think
there would be anything very outrageous
in that. An honourable Member talked
the other day as if yellow was a sort of
sacred colour in food, and nobody could
reasonably be expected to eat any food
which was not yellow. I do not know
why we should set up margarine on a
pinnacle in that way. After all, there is
plenty of good food in the country which
is not yellow. You cannot say that
yellow is general. Jam is not bad, but
it is not yellow. I have never heard that
pâte de fois gras was a nasty thing; I
have never heard that caviare has a nasty
look about it. But the President of the
Board of Agriculture says that anybody
who tries to stop margarine from being
coloured yellow wishes to stop the margarine industry. Well, Sir, I do not
pretend to know what effect the prevention of margarine being coloured yellow
would have upon it. He said that that
would be the result. I do not know
what the result would be, but we all
admit that margarine when it is coloured
yellow lends itself to fraud, and if it
would destroy the trade were we to say
that it shall not be coloured yellow, it
only tends to show that the margarine
trade is largely fraudulent, and that
margarine is largely sold because it is
yellow and because it imitates butter,
and for no other reason. Now, somebody

Mr. Philipps.

on this side of the House said the other
day that to prevent the colouring of
margarine yellow would be a Protective
measure. In one way it is. It is protective against fraud. I say I shall
never be ready, I hope, to vote for the
protection of the produce producer
against competition, but I do say the
British producer has an absolute right to
be protected against fraud. And this
trade is largely a fraudulent trade. That
is admitted on all hands. I say that we
understand——["No!"] It is admitted
——["No!"] Well, almost everybody
who spoke the other night spoke
of cases of fraud in connection
with the trade, and I venture to say
that the Report of the Committee that
sat upon this question showed endless
cases of fraud, and the correspondence
that has been appearing in the papers in
the last few days from country grocers
and others show that this fraud is a very
common one, and not only injures the
consumer and injures the purchaser, but
injures honest tradesmen as well, who
have to suffer from the competition of
unscrupulous rivals. Well now, Sir, the
President of the Board of Agriculture
made a statement the other night that
rather surprised me. He said that it
would be unwise of the farmer to stop
colouring altogether. I do not know
why. I do not suppose the President of
the Board of Agriculture holds the belief
that margarine is such a good food that
if people knew it was margarine and not
butter——

THE PRESIDENT OF THE BOARD OF
AGRICULTURE (Mr. LONG, Liverpool,
West Derby): If the honourable Member quotes me I must ask him to quote
me accurately. I did not say it would
be unwise of the farmer, I said it would
be a very great change which I thought
the farmer would have to make. I did
not express an opinion whether it was a
good or a bad one.

MR. PHILIPPS: I am sorry if
I misinterpreted the right honourable
Gentleman, for it was far from my intention to do so. I think the farmers
whom I have the honour to represent
would take the risk, and would be quite
prepared to welcome the change and see
margarine coloured something which was
not yellow. But I must say that, from
my point of view, the Bill is a disappoint-

ing one. The Bill does one thing—I do not say that it was intended to do it: flatters the farmer with the idea that his interests are being looked after. The Government will be able to go to the country, to the agricultural constituencies, at the next Election and say, "We have done something to prevent the fraudulent sale of margarine." But before this Bill comes into law some of us on this side of the House will give the Government one more chance. We will put down Amendments that will make the Bill a real Bill, Amendments that shall prevent margarine from being sold as butter, shall prevent margarine from being coloured yellow. We will put down Amendments so that fraudulent salesmen may be sent to prison instead of being fined; and if these Amendments are carried, and if they are passed into law, I venture to say that the Bill will be a real Bill, and will be a thousand times more effectual against fraud than in the milk-and-water form in which the Government has introduced it.

*MR. GRANT LAWSON (York, N.R., Thirsk): I am sure the President of the Board of Agriculture must have listened with great pleasure to the speech that we have just heard, because last Monday night we heard nothing but denunciations of this Bill as hampering trade, harassing manufacturers, and ruining retail traders. Then, up gets the honourable Gentleman on the same side and says, on the contrary, it will do nothing: it is a milk-and-water Bill and will have no effect whatever. Now, Sir, the honourable Gentleman commenced his speech by saying that no one has risen to say that this is a good Bill. Sir, I do not think there has ever been introduced into this House any Bill which those who spoke on the occasion of its introduction have declared to be so good that they could not themselves make it better. What the honourable Member means is that one speaker after another has risen and pointed out how in detail he could have made it a better Bill if he had had the drafting of the Bill. No doubt honourable Members could—or think they could—have made it a better Bill. But the real position is this. We are not discussing these details, which we may be enabled to do in Committee, but the general principle of the Bill. No doubt the general principle of

this Bill is that adulteration should be put an end to by process of closer inspection of articles than is now given to these articles. We desire—and under this Bill it is done—to make the inspection at the ports, which is at present spasmodic, regular, and real, and energetic; and as for the inspection at home, we desire that where the local authorities are inactive they shall be galvanised into action by the central authority. Two honourable Members have been found in this House, carrying out what is said to be one of the functions—of the principal functions—of an Opposition, to oppose this Bill—the honourable Members for West Islington and for the Bridgeton Division of Glasgow. But their attacks upon this Bill show that, though they might agree in the ultimate end of their speeches, their ways of looking at the Bill were totally divergent. The honourable Member for West Islington opposed the Bill because, although he has no objection to the second part, he could not swallow the first part of it. His seconder seconded, as he told us, not because he had any objection to the first part, but because he could not swallow the second part. And between the two of them they moved the rejection of this Measure altogether. Now when those two honourable Gentlemen did agree they seemed to show that their agreement was on this point—that though they loved adulteration little, they loved agriculture less. They belonged, both of them to a section of this House who are always in fear of Protection. They must know that Protection is dead.

COLONEL SIR HOWARD VINCENT (Sheffield, Central): No.

*MR. GRANT LAWSON: Yes, with respect to the honourable Member, I say that they know—though perhaps my honourable Friend behind me does not know it—that Protection is dead, and yet they are always conjuring up its spirit in the most unlikely places. Why, Sir, the honourable Member for West Islington in his speech said that this was a Bill to exclude foreign food. I wonder under what section of the Bill he considers that foreign food is excluded. A far more damaging criticism of the Bill has come from another speaker on that side, who complained not only that the Bill would not stop the introduction of foreign food when adulterated, but does not even detain it in transit. Under the Bill the consignments, although adulterated, are to go forward to their destination, with the sleuth-hounds of the Board of Agriculture let loose upon their track, under sub-section 6 of the first clause. That clause provides that when articles come to this country adulterated, they are to be clearly branded with a conspicuous mark that they have fallen from the state of purity; and adulteration is defined in a way which really answers the whole speech made by the honourable Member for South Somerset. The honourable Member for South Somerset complained that any quantity of acids, of which he gave us the names, might be put into milk, and into butter, and yet that would not be stopped by this Bill. Sir, they would be stopped under the last words of clause 1. As I have said, the principle of this Bill is close inspection. The Customs are to take samples. It may be said that the Customs have the power now to take samples under the Customs Consolidation Act of 1876. That is so in law: but what is the fact? The Chairman of the Board of Customs came before the Committee and he said this—

"As a matter of fact, under the existing law we do very little, I may almost say nothing, except in respect of tea."

Well, the object of this Bill is that the Board of Customs should do something, acting under instructions which they are sure to receive, at any rate, from the present Chancellor of the Exchequer and the present Minister of Agriculture. Sir, I hope myself that the analysis of these samples when taken will be sufficient to detect the presence of microbes. I believe that this tubercle bacillus, of which we are so much afraid at the present moment, is very often a foreign immigrant, and that matter should be looked into at the ports before we endeavour to cast out these particular microbes from our homes by the very strong measures now before this House promoted by private individuals. The sample having been taken, and the adulteration detected, these articles go forward to their destination. When they get there the recipients can consume them if they like; if these articles contain matters which are injurious to

Mr. Grant Lawson.

health he may not sell them under the present law, if they contain certain adulterations which are calculated to deceive he may not sell them so as to deceive. That is the law at present, so that it is perfectly obvious that the law, if properly administered, is strong enough to catch the offenders. The arm of the law was strong enough originally, but in many cases it was paralysed because it was to be wielded by the local authorities, and in many cases they did not wield it. Evidence was given before the Committee that in the years 1895 and 1896 the Board of Agriculture called the attention of the local authorities to 70 cases of adulterated articles, a trade in which was going on in their jurisdiction, and not a single prosecution followed. Now this Bill will enable the Board of Agriculture to see that the law which was intended to reach the offender shall reach him, a result which has not been found to be the case in the past. The honourable Gentleman the Member for the Ilkeston Division is tremendously jealous of the honour of a Department with which he himself has been connected, and he said that the Board of Agriculture was not a proper Department to perform this function. Now, the Bill expressly confines the first part of its operation to matters affecting the general interests of agriculture. If the Board of Agriculture cannot look after the general interests of agriculture I should very much like to know what Department has a better claim. The honourable Gentleman himself saw the weakness of his own case, because he said if the Local Board fixed a standard of purity the feed and breed of cattle might make a great difference. Who is the best judge of the breed of cattle, the Board of Agriculture or the Local Government Board? Now I want to say a word or two upon the subject of colouring, which has been dealt with by the honourable Member who has just sat down. I think if anything has been done by this discussion, what has been done has been to show the consumers of this country that the natural colour of margarine is so odious that a man has to shut his eyes before he opens his mouth to take it in its natural colour. Supposing we boldly said that colour was not to be added, the ingenuity of of the margarine manufacturer would produce a compound the natural colour of which would be that of butter, and then we should have to amend our Act in order to make that colour some other colour. It is not fair to say that the colour of margarine is always put in for the purposes of fraud, because a large amount of margarine is sold openly as margarine. There is, of course, some colouring done for the purpose of fraud. Margarine is apparently always sold coloured. In this discussion the prevention of colouring has been discussed as if that was the end at which the agricultural interest has been aiming. That is not so; it is not the end, it is only one means to the end. The end in view being to prevent margarine being sold as butter. My right honourable Friend has found that if he adopts the most obvious means of stopping the sale of margarine as butter that course would be too dangerous to contemplate. He has to find some other road to the same goal. All I can say is that if my right honourable Friend finds a way to the common object that we all have in view which is practicable—a way in which it is possible for us at once to travel—we, so long as he reaches his object, should not complain about leaving the route to him. The very mildest provision in an Act of Parliament is more valuable than the strongest provision in a Bill that remains a Bill. My opinion is that half a loaf is better than no bread. The route by which my right honourable Friend has elected to reach his destination is by way of inspection, detection, and punishment. The route has many advantages; in the first place, it places inconvenience on the dishonest seller without touching the consumer. Secondly, it follows a route which has led to success often before with regard to other articles; and it has a third advantage, that it does not introduce a new principle into our laws. I do not think there is an article, certainly no compound article, which is sold in its natural colour. I do not think that any honourable Gentleman in this House, for instance, can tell me what the natural colour of his boots is. Then, again, the natural colour of ginger ale is not the same as that of beer; yet the teetotaler colours it to be the same as beer, no doubt for the purpose of deceiving himself, and nobody objects to his doing so. The law has not to interfere with colour-

ing; the law has to be very careful not to do so. If it did, what would happen to all traders in artificial articles? Ladies would have to do without sealskins that never clothed a seal, and without ostrich feathers that never grew on an ostrich. Then take the case of jewellery, you take a bit of glass and colour it and it looks like a ruby or a pearl. We do not grudge the poor man his eighteen-penny ruby, and the law does not step in. Take another illustration, that of a knife or spoon or fork; by silver plating those articles assume the colour of silver, but nobody says they ought to be allowed to stop it, that a spoon or a fork ought to be left in the natural colour of its baser metal. I think that I have shown that it would be a very strong thing indeed if my right honourable Friend had attempted to make a law on the subject of colouring; it would be far better for us to concentrate our efforts on other methods of preventing these fraudulent sales. Some methods are mentioned in the Bill, but there are many matters which had better be left to the consideration of the Committee. I am myself in favour of what the honourable Member for Pembroke proposed, namely, prison fare for the adulterators of food. I am also in favour of publishing their names. These are questions for Committee. Those who oppose the Second Reading have to show one of three things—first, that there has been no adulteration to speak of. That was completely contradicted by the evidence given before the Committee. Or, secondly, to show that if this is not the best way to stop adulteration that there is an alternative, and you have got to show the alternative. No one has attempted to suggest the alternative course. Thirdly, you may attempt to show that adulteration ought not to be stopped; that the people ought to be allowed to remain under this system of robbery, for fear that some profit should come to the interest of the dealer in genuine articles. The honourable Gentleman who has just sat down said that we were considering the consumer and the farmer; there is a third person who has to be considered, and that is the honest trader, who does not wish to sell adulterated articles, but who must sell them or he would be undersold by his fraudulent neighbours. I think that this will lead to meeting a great evil, and for that reason I shall support the Bill.

*Mr. KEARLEY (Devonport): What-ever may be the opinions of honourable Members on either side of the House as to the merits or demerits of that Bill no one has ventured to gainsay that an enormous amount of adulteration has been carried on in this country, and that it has been injurious to the principles of honest trade. I think that the criticism to which the Government has been subjected, and the suggestion that they meant wholly to benefit the agricultural interest by this Bill, arises from the language which has been employed by them in drafting the Bill. Personally, myself, I have no hesitation in saying that the day has gone by when any Government could set up any protective Measure which would interfere with the free flow of the supply of food products into this country. But it is perhaps a little unfortunate that the Government in this Bill should appear to be influenced, to some extent at all events, in the direction of protection. As the practice of adulteration extends to articles of almost every description there should not, in my opinion, be a preference given to agriculture; but the Bill should be a comprehensive one dealing with all articles of food in which adulteration exists at present, or in which it might exist. The last speaker who addressed the House commented upon some of the alarming statements that were made the other evening, and I certainly do not believe that this Bill will raise prices, or deal in any way with the fair competition of foreign food supplies, or interfere in any manner with their importation into this country. I will go further, and say that agriculture is as much entitled to protection against unfair competition as any other trade. And though some agriculturists may hold the impression that this Measure will diminish competition, the chances of its doing so are so remote that, in my opinion, they are bound to be disappointed. Now, the right honourable Gentleman in introducing the Bill, made a statement to the effect that it 'was based upon the recommendations of the Select Committee; technically, of course, that is true, because some of the provisions of the Bill were made in view of the recommendations of the Select Committee,

but in the main I assert, and my first complaint is, that it does not follow the recommendations of the Select Committee to their full extent. Out of the 23 recommendations of that Committee the Government in this Measure have ignored all but 10, and some of those which they have ignored contain some of the provisions which would have proved most beneficial, if they had been incorporated in this Bill. Therefore, I am prepared to regard this Bill as a mere instalment of the legislation necessary to give us effective protection against adulteration. But that is no reason why I should offer the Bill uncompromising opposition. I prefer to regard it as a framework into which we must endeavour to work our wishes by Amendments which may result in a very useful Measure. Before I sit down I shall mention some of the matters which I think we should criticise, so that on further consideration the Bill may be amended in those particulars. In Committee, of course, we shall have an opportunity to make many suggestions for amending the provisions of the Bill, and I do not think that the Second Reading should be made the occasion for moving the rejection of the Bill. Now the most serious omission from the Bill, in my opinion, is the recommendation of the Select Committee, carried with absolute unanimity, that there should be set up an independent court or body of reference to deal with the technical and scientific questions which will have to be considered in connection with the adulteration of food products. The Board of Agriculture proposes to set up a body presenting some of the characteristics recommended by the Select Committee, but I am confident that the body which it is proposed to set up by this Bill will not possess the confidence of this country. The Board of Agriculture is not in such a position to command the best technical and scientific knowledge as would be a Board that had a perfectly independent existence. Under the proposals of the Board of Agriculture is not in such a Board of Agriculture to set up these Boards they propose to take enormous powers. In the first place, they intend to establish standards of purity for milk.

HONOURABLE MEMBERS: No; no!

Mr. Grant Lawson.

MR. KEARLEY: If you will allow me to state it in my own way first, when I have stated it you can correct me. I say that they propose, if they propose to do anything at all, to establish standards of purity for milk and butter, and they propose to set up a standard of preservatives and colouring that may be legitimately introduced into these products. Now, the right honourable Gentleman, in reply to a Question, said that the Board of Agriculture was not prepared to fix a definite standard. Are you prepared to fix an indefinite standard, because if you are that appears to me to give point to the objection of the Irish representatives? At the present moment the one thing which the Irish butter producers complain most bitterly of is that there is no definite standard, and they want to know what the standard will be. If you have a low standard of purity fixed for milk the milk producers of this country will be able to water down their milk to the standard, and the vicious effect of that will be as great as it is now at the present moment. While I am upon the question of standards, I notice that there is one which you do not propose to deal with at all, and that is the percentage of water that shall be permissible in butter. We have heard from all the speakers who have addressed the House upon this subject of the adulteration of butter with margarine, but I venture to suggest that there is just as much adulteration of butter by dishonest persons by the addition of water as there is by the addition of margarine; but there is no proposal at all in this Bill to deal with that. Now, Mr. Speaker, it was pointed out the other night that in order to make legislation effective it is necessary that the law should be enforced. I agree with that, and I go beyond, and say that in addition to enforcing the law deterrent penalties must also be enforced. At the present time not only is the law not enforced as it should be, but the penalties which are inflicted are not sufficiently deterrent. One of the speakers said that the law at present in existence was efficient if it was properly administered; I think to a large extent that is so. The proposal of the right honourable Gentleman is that the Board of Agriculture shall have power to enforce the administration of the law, but it is only where the interests of agriculture are affected that the Board of Agriculture proposes to step in. It is stated in the Bill that where the law is not enforced, and the interests of agriculture are found to be affected, the Board of Agriculture is to compel the local boards to take action. I should strongly advise the Government to delete all language from this Bill which pre-supposes a predilection in favour of agriculture. These references carry no substance with them, whilst they are great disfigurement to the Bill, and they will give rise to accusations against the Department which it would be better to avoid altogether. I strongly advise the Government to get rid of these words; they can only prejudice the Board of Agriculture, because so long as that Department has the adimnistration of this Act there will be an opening for the enemy to say that it is worked in the interests of agriculture. I do not suggest that that is so myself, but I do think that it is a pity, considering that the Local Government Board is the recognised central authority for dealing with local boards, to transfer these powers to the Board of Agriculture. The Local Government Board is the most fitting authority to set local authorities in motion. I could give reasons why the Local Government Board is the most appropriate body to have the power to enforce the Act where local authorities fail to enforce it. In the first place, they would not be subject to the suspicion which is attached to the Board of Agriculture. The Local Government Board is a national body, and so is the Board of Agriculture, but the Local Government Board is not the servant of any particular interest in this House, while the Board of Agriculture is the servant of the agricultural representatives in this House. Even if I had listened to the speech of my honourable Friend the Member for Pembrokeshire with my eyes shut I should have known that he was an agricultural representative by the tone of his argument, and that is the spirit that permeates the whole of the agricultural interest in this House. Of course, they want to do the best they can for their own interest, and they are quite right too. So long as the Board of Agriculture has the administration of this Act there is always an opening for the enemies of this Measure to say, " It is worked in the interests of agriculture." I do not allege that myself, but I do say that considering that the Local Government Board is the recognised central authority for dealing with local bodies, it seems to me to be improper to transfer these powers to the Board of Agriculture. The local Government Board already deals with the local authorities when they are in default in respect of proper water supplies or drainage. If they refuse, the Board have power to apply for a mandamus to compel them to act. Surely the question of a power of this nature in regard to food is as important as the power with regard to the water supply; and as the Local Government Board is the body for securing to the public pure water, I contend that it should be the body to secure by its administration pure food supplies for the people. Now I want to deal with one or two points that have already been referred to in connection with some provisions under this Bill. There is a general agreement, I think, that the penalties which are already imposed are inadequate. On the Select Committee we passed a unanimous decision that the penalties were altogether inadequate, and that they ought to be strengthened and increased. That Committee recommended that for the second offence there should be a minimum fine of £5. Under this Bill you propose to increase the fine which is leviable for the second offence, but you make no minimum fine, and magistrates are so prone to regard these offences leniently, that unless you lay down by Statute that for the second offence the fine shall be a substantial one, I am sure there will be a repetition of these one shilling or two shilling fines which have been so common in the past. That was what the Select Committee recommended ; and perhaps I may be allowed to say that I took an active part in inducing them to come to that decision. Now, for the third and subsequent offences, I think it should be within the power of the magistrate to send a man to prison who is found guilty of adulteration. Of course, I know that it would be a very drastic proposition that a man brought up for a third offence and convicted should be imprisoned, but it certainly should be left to the discretion of the magistrate to take that step if he thought fit and proper. I will cite a

Mr. Kearley.

case brought to my notice some little time ago in regard to the operations of a particular gang. There is a gang working in the poor parts of London, who have shops, known as the Welsh Gang, but I hope this will not be taken as a bad compliment by the Welsh Members of this House. It is called the Welsh Gang because the name of the founder, I believe, is Morgan. Well, these people have been prosecuted time after time and convicted. They appeared at the Clerkenwell Police Court a few months ago, and were fined £70 with £21 costs, but the very next week the same men for the same offence appeared at the same Police Court, but before a different magistrate, and were fined £1. That will give the House an idea as to the manner in which some magistrates regard these offences. Now, I do think that people of this description should be sentenced to a term of imprisonment, and more especially so because they find it sufficiently profitable to continue their evil ways and pay the fines. Of course, I do not allege this against traders as a whole, but there seems to be almost a criminal class in this respect who cannot resist the temptation of stealing—for it is nothing else but stealing—and defrauding the public, and they persevere in their evil deeds, although they are fined from time to time.

MR. A. MOORE (Londonderry) : The fines are paid by an association.

*MR. KEARLEY : Well, that is not within my knowledge. I wish to press upon the Government the necessity of carrying out the recommendation of the Select Committee, that the magistrates should have it in their power on the third conviction to send a man to prison, and that is not asking for an extraordinary power, because the power to imprison people already exists for far less serious offences. Take for example an Act in which the agricultural Members are particularly interested, namely the Contagious Diseases (Animals) Act. For a second offence under that Act in the same year a man is liable to a month's imprisonment. As to the nature of the offence, there can be no comparison between the offences committed under the Contagious Diseases (Animals) Act and defrauding the public by forcing upon the consumer an article which is not what it is represented to be. Similar powers of sending people to prison for smaller offences than those of adulterating food exist under the Merchandise Marks Act and the Licensing Laws. I hope, therefore, that the Government will take a strong attitude upon this question of minimum fines and imprisonment, because, if they do not, they will very much mar the prospects of their Bill being successful. If the Government will be firm, I think 99 per cent. of the adulteration will disappear, that is providing that you make the local authorities do their work. If you imprison the rogues and the thieves I am sure that you will have no great amount of adulteration existing in this country. Now, I want to say a word or two about the provision of this Bill dealing with goods at the port of entry. The Government propose to continue their operation of taking samples, but that will not prevent adulterated articles from circulating in this country, and it will be impossible, by the time they have finished their investigation, to enable any of these adulterated articles to be recalled, and the sale of them checked. I have spoken before upon this matter, and I repeat that falsified goods coming into this country should be detained pending an analysis. Well, of course, the answer will be made, "How are you to tell that these goods are falsified? You cannot tell until they are analysed." That is so, but there are always merchants who are prepared to give to the Customs authorities information as to the practices of certain shippers. The leading importers in this country take the precaution of having the opinion of an eminent analyst, and they can find out by that means, from time to time, whether certain shippers' goods are dishonest. I maintain that if you take powers, as you should do, in this Bill which will enable you to detain goods which are falsely described, you may, when the information is supplied to you from time to time, detain such goods pending analysis, and if you find them to be falsified you can confiscate them. That was done in connection with butter some years ago. A certain merchant had reason to suspect that a shipper was sending him adulterated produce, and he stated his case to the Customs authorities, but they said they could not inter-

fere. He then went to the present Chancellor of the Exchequer, and the right honourable Gentleman only agreed to interfere after this importer had entered into a very heavy bond. Well, the goods were investigated and analysed and found to be adulterated, and they were confiscated. Now I want the Government to obtain this security against falsified goods in this Bill. It may not be necessary to put it in force very frequently, but I think it would have a deterrent effect if the authorities had this power. It would be a great pity to forego and to lose the opportunity which is now offered of putting in a clause of this description. When we have done with this piece of legislation, it will be 20 years at least before the House will again listen to any more proposals to deal with the adulteration of food products, so that now is the time to try and make this Bill as strong as we can in every particular. Now, the other points that I will refer to briefly are those affecting the admixture of butter and margarine. My honourable Friend said the other night, "Why interfere? Why not let butter be mixed with margarine?" That seems a very simple question to put, but I will give a reason why. The reason why it should not be allowed to manufacture mixtures is this—that they are intended to be sold not as what they really are, because if that was the case they would have to be sold as margarine, but they are intended to be sold as butter. If the present law was properly administered we should not now be advocating this Measure, and I will give you a convincing argument against these mixtures. Honourable Members know that the system of joint stock enterprise in connection with distributing agencies has enormously increased of late years, and there are now in this country well-recognised distributors whose turnover amounts to several millions a year. I have made inquiries amongst some of these distributors, and many other firms who represent in this trade a net turnover of no less a sum than ten millions a year. Now ten millions a year is a large sum of money to be taken from the public. I have made inquiries from these distributors as to whether any of them sell these mixtures, and not a single one of these firms, who are merchants of the highest eminence, admit that they sell mixtures, but on the contrary, they deny it altogether. They say that the demand for margarine is a definite demand, confined to a certain class by its low price, and between that price and the price of butter there is a large margin. These distributors inform me that if they were to sell mixtures at a price intermediate between margarine prices and butter prices the public would not buy them at all. It seems to me absolutely conclusive that there is no demand for this particular class of article if it is sold for what it really is, but if it is sold to represent butter there is no question that it commands a large sale. Therefore I am strongly in favour of denying the right of manufacturers of margarine to mix butter with margarine at all. The Government have seen fit to give power to admix to the extent of 10 per cent., but I suggest that that is too high, and I am supported in my contention by the authoritative declaration of a large manufacturer in this country of high repute, and who is well known. I asked him what was the percentage of butter fat that should be present in margarine, and he replied that butter fat in margarine would not exceed 3 per cent., and would, as a rule, be about 2 per cent. I hope I have made it clear that when an article is intended to be sold as margarine, 3 per cent. is the outside percentage of butter fat which should be present. Now, the right honourable Gentleman proposes to make it legal at 10 per cent., but I think he has an open mind on that question, and perhaps he may be able to come down to 5 per cent., which would be about fair. The question of colouring to my mind is very simple, and if you are going to prohibit it in one direction, you should prohibit it in all. Now I come to the question of warranty, and I think the right honourable Gentleman, before he has done with this Bill, will probably find that this will be the issue round which most of the conflict will be raised. At the present moment, under the Food and Drugs Act, section 25, a warranty is not valid unless it is a written warranty, but under the Margarine Act, passed 12 years later, an invoice is a warranty, so that it has been felt that an invoice should be a warranty in all cases. Some of us maintain that if a tradesman orders from his merchant certain articles, whatever they may be—take butter for in-

Mr. Kearley.

stance: if the invoice states that it is butter, without expressly saying "guaranteed pure butter," the invoice itself should be the warranty, and it should be producible against the man who gave the warranty. Now I think that should be the position of a merchant. If he invoices so many packages as "butter," that certainly should be a warranty, and it should not be left to a buyer to say, "the law will not recognise your statement without you put on the invoice "absolutely pure," or "guaranteed pure." The right honourable Gentleman will be wise, I think, if he gives way on this point, for there appears to be already a great amount of anxiety upon it in the country that this should be recognised. But I will ask him this question—if he refuses to recognise an invoice as a warranty under the Sale of Food and Drugs Act, does he propose to retain the power under the Margarine Act, which does recognise the invoice as a warranty? Here, under the Margarine Act, section 5, as I have before stated, the invoice is a warranty, and that was provided for in an Act passed 12 years after the Sale of Food and Drugs Act. Now, under the latter Act an invoice is not a warranty, and I ask the right honourable Gentleman whether he proposes to repeal what appears to be an anomaly in the case of the Margarine Act?

*THE SECRETARY OF THE LOCAL GOVERNMENT BOARD (Mr. RUSSELL, Tyrone, S.): No.

*MR. KEARLEY: The right honourable Gentleman says "No," but it seems to me incomprehensible that you should admit an invoice as a warranty under one Act and not admit it under the other. Then there is a smaller point, which is that of claiming exemption when the tradesman can prove that he has exercised due diligence to have the article sold for what it really was, and that his employee was the offender. He should then be able to produce the defaulting employee, and let him bear the consequences of his dereliction of duty. Now here is an Act which again has a different bearing on this question. Under the Sale of Food and Drugs Act there is no exemption for the act of the servant, but under section 7 of the Margarine Act an employer is exempted if he can prove that he has exercised due diligence. I would ask the right honourable Gentleman to consider the claim of a tradesman to be exempted if he can prove that he has exercised due diligence, and that the adulteration is owing to the negligence of his assistants. Under one Act an employer can claim exemption, and under another he cannot, and I believe the magistrate is perfectly able to discriminate whether the defence when set up is a genuine one or not. If the right honourable Gentleman is anticipating that this will open a wide door to fraud, I do not think he need have any apprehensions in that direction, for I think the magistrate will be able to determine whether the defence is legitimate or otherwise. I have now criticised the various clauses in this Bill which I consider to be weak. There is one other defect which I will mention in a word. I think legislation would be more effective if there had been a consolidation and strengthening of the existing law. I would have liked to have seen every law upon this subject repealed, and a thoroughly good adulteration Act passed, framed on broad lines, so as to comprehend all the forms of adulteration that exist. What we want is really a consolidation, because this piecemeal legislation is only confusing to those who have to abide by the Act. There is one proposal in this very Bill which shows that the right honourable Gentleman who introduced it is not acquainted with its effect. Section 11 of this Bill makes provision for "skimmed" or "separated" milk, and for the contravention of this section a fine not exceeding £2 may be imposed. But this offence is already contemplated under the Food and Drugs Act, section 9, under which a penalty of £20 can be imposed, and I have known a case in which a fine of £10 has been inflicted. I think that that proves that the right honourable Gentleman is not acquainted with the multiplicity of details connected with these two Acts. It would be better, I think, to have had a consolidation Bill put before Parliament. However, we must take events as we find them, and I believe that although this Bill is defective in many respects, if the Government really mean business in this matter, and will afford an opportunity in Committee to honourable Members of giving them the benefit of their experience, I think

we shall be able to amend the Bill and alter it to such an extent that it will be acceptable to the country.

MR. RUSSELL: Apart from the speeches of the two honourable Members who moved the rejection of the Bill, I do not think the Government have any right to complain of the reception accorded to their proposals. Most of those who have spoken have, indeed, criticised the proposals of the Bill. But it is sins of omission rather than of commission that have been charged against the Government. We have been told that we have erred in not following the precedents set as regards several matters in the Margarine Act of 1887, and that we have been guilty of grievous default in setting aside several of the recommendations of the Select Committee. But whilst this is the case the general tenour of the Debate has been that, so far as it goes, the Bill is a good Bill, and more than one speaker found to his satisfaction as the Debate proceeded that the Bill went further than he thought it did. Before, however, I proceed to answer the criticism upon detailed points, let me refer for a moment to the main objection urged by the honourable Member for West Islington as a reason why the Bill should be rejected. He declared, in so many words, that it was a Bill designed to protect the agricultural community, and to raise prices. This assertion was met, as it deserved to be, by the derisive cheers of honourable Gentlemen who sat immediately around him. It is true, indeed, that the Bill does propose to put difficulties in the way of the foreign merchant who sends adulterated or impoverished articles of food into this country. But I do not know that even the most ardent member of the Cobden Club would claim a right for the foreigner which is not conceded to the home trader. It has been left for the honourable Gentleman to say of a Bill that proposes most reasonably to prevent fraud by a foreign trader that it is a mere Measure of protection and calculated to raise prices. I am satisfied, and indeed my honourable Friend opposite the Member for Ilkeston agreed— that clause 1 is a most valuable provision. He has a right to speak on this question, because he shared with me the labour of presiding over the Committee upstairs. I come now to other speakers. It was urged by my honourable Friend the Member for the Bridgeton Division of Glasgow, and repeated with emphasis to-night by the honourable Member for Devonport, that if the Bill was to be worth anything, the retail trader should be allowed to treat a mere invoice as the legal equivalent of a written warranty. He said that this was lawful under the Margarine and the Fertilizers Acts, and he pointed out that this constituted one of the recommendations of the Select Committee which the Government had rejected. The honourable Baronet is entirely right in saying all this, and the only question remaining is as to the decision of the Government. Is it right or wrong? Is it defensible or indefensible? Let us see how the case stands. Almost every speaker has admitted that one of the main difficulties in connection with this whole question is the lax administration of the law. Local authorities, in many cases, and for reasons that were made plain to the Committee, administer the various Acts in the most perfunctory manner. That is admitted on both sides of the House. Now, assuming the contention of honourable Members to be correct, and that a mere invoice should be equivalent in law to a written warranty, see what would happen. In every case the retail shopkeeper who had sold the adulterated article would produce his invoice, and the responsibility would be at once shifted to the wholesale dealer. This trader may carry on business in Ireland, in Scotland, or at a place hundreds of miles from where the summons is heard. When he is brought into Court what is to happen? He has, no doubt, an invoice from the manufacturer of the goods. Is he to plead this invoice and walk out of Court, shifting the responsibility on to the manufacturer? If not, why not? And, should the manufacturer reside outside the jurisdiction, what then? Nobody in that case could be made amenable, and you would be placing the home trader, who can be made amenable, at a great disadvantage with the foreign merchant who cannot be reached. But I ask what would the effect of all this be on the careless and unwilling local authority? They would probably say: "We have gone to great

Mr. Russell.

expense in an attempt to carry out the law; the only result being that we have been driven from post to pillar, finding ourselves in the last resort unable to reach the original offender." Is it wise, I ask, to run the risk of bringing the administration of the law to this pass? And all the while, be it remembered, the retail trader can enforce a warranty from the wholesale dealer, which will be a valid defence, if he chooses to do so. If he does not do it he ought to take the responsibility for the character of the goods he sells. I think that to make this change in the law would be to run the gravest risk of bringing the law into disrepute, and that the only safe method of procedure is to make the actual purveyor to the public responsible for what he sells. Then we have been told that we ought to have followed the precedent of the Margarine Act, and made the assistant responsible where the actual trader had taken all necessary and reasonable precautions against fraud. That was urged very strongly by the honourable Member for Devonport. There are traders, it is said, with scores of shops. How can a trader, it is asked, be responsible under such circumstances? This line of argument, if pursued, may carry us very far. And I hold that the owner of these places of business ought to be responsible for the goods he sells. If he chooses to have 100 shops in different parts of the country, there is nothing in the law to say him nay. But it is a wholly different thing for him to say you must frame the law so that I shall not be responsible for the acts of those I employ.

*Mr. KEARLEY: The demand comes from the individual shopkeeper.

*Mr. RUSSELL: And, assume the law to be changed, what would happen? A young man in one of these shops is brought up instead of his employer. The employer has taken all reasonable precautions, and let me say, by the way, that it is now in the power of the magistrates to acquit an employer if he is found to have taken all reasonable precautions. The young assistant may be a totally irresponsible person, sleeping, perhaps, in one of the cubicles we heard so much about yesterday. What about the penalties? How are they to be recovered in such a case? To enact a provision of this kind would be to place such difficulties in the way of administration as to seriously imperil the working of the Act. A good deal has been said, and I am not surprised at it, about the regulation in the clause as regards the quantity of butter fat that may be used in the manufacture of margarine. It is a point of some importance, and I propose to examine into it with some care. What are the facts now? First, you have pure butter, which sells at 10d., 1s., 1s. 2d., or 1s. 4d. per lb., or even more. This article is not affected at all. It is butter, and is sold as such. Then, we have margarine of the ordinary type—which fetches in some of our great towns 5d., 6d., and up to 8d. per lb. Provided this is sold for what it is, namely, margarine, nobody objects. But it is in regard to the third article the difficulty arises. This article consists of a mixture of pure margarine and inferior butter. Now, under the Margarine Act this mixture ought to be sold as margarine. It is at this point the whole difficulty arises. This mixture is not usually sold as margarine. It is not even sold as a mixture. It is very generally sold as tenpenny butter. It is sold for what it is not, and up to the present it has been exceedingly difficult to deal with the fraud. Now, what the Government had to consider was how this fraud could be best prevented? The Select Committee considered the matter carefully. It came to a decision contrary to the view I had submitted in my Draft Report as Chairman. It decided that the mixture should be prohibited by law. My own view put before the Committee was simply this—that so long as no injury was done to the public health, and that the public were duly and fully apprised as to the nature of the article they were purchasing, these mixtures ought to be allowed. I was over-ruled. Now, after giving the fullest consideration to the point, my right honourable Friend has taken a line between the view I expressed and the view taken by the Committee. It is quite impossible to prevent the mixing of butter fat with margarine altogether, for the very good reason given before the Committee by experts—that it could not be detected up to 5 or 6 per cent. My right honourable Friend practically says

in the Bill to the manufacturer of this article—

"Fraud frequently follows this practice of mixing. The fraud is not yours. But we must prevent it if we can. In future, margarine must be sold as margarine and not as butter. By using 10 per cent. of butter fat it will not be possible for those who sell the article to sell it as butter, and therefore we fix that limit."

The aim of the clause is to have two legitimate articles—butter and margarine—and to exclude from the market those mixtures that ought by law to be sold as margarine, but are in fact largely sold as butter. There is nothing sacred in 10 per cent., and it is a reasonable question for discussion in Committee. The next question of importance is that of food standards. The Committee gave great attention to the matter, and I am not quite sure that the House exactly realises how much is done by the Bill in the direction favoured by the Committee. As the proposal emerged from the Committee it involved the setting up of a Standing Committee of Experts, called a Board of Reference, to determine the question of what was and what was not food adulteration. The proposal covered every article that came under the definition of food as defined in the Sale of Food and Drugs Act, 1875. The necessity for some action of this kind was clearly shown by the conflicts between Somerset House and various public analysts throughout the country, the result being that the Courts were often at a total loss to know what was and what was not adulteration.

DR. CLARK (Caithness): The Courts have now determined that the standard must be put in the report of each analyst.

*MR. RUSSELL: I think it is very inconvenient that there should be different and conflicting standards all over the country. Now, in view of the determination of the Committee, I ask the House to examine clause 4. It is true that the clause does not set up a fixed standard for anything. It is true that what is proposed to be done covers only three articles. True; but looking at the enormous difficulty in fixing exact standards was it not wiser to arrange for a decision of experts that would establish a presumption as to purity, leaving a certain elasticity to cover different cases? And was it not wiser to confine this delicate and difficult operation to three great staple articles of food—namely, milk, butter, and cheese? Entirely agreeing with the complaints of those who declared that the Courts were often puzzled by the conflicting testimony of analysts, I believe that clause 4 gives the thing contended for by the Committee in a safer and more effective form. Under that clause the undue admixture of water with butter is as much an adulteration as if the butter were adulterated with margarine.

*Mr. KEARLEY: Is it definitely decided in that clause that the question of water will be dealt with?

*Mr. RUSSELL: I quite agree. What the Committee suggested was the setting up of standards in respect of all classes of food, which I think would be almost impossible and might act unfairly. This clause covers all the necessities of the case. The honourable Member for Somerset said a good deal about the use of preservatives and colouring matters, and other honourable Members have dwelt upon the necessity of stopping the colouring of margarine to imitate butter. As to the first point, it must be remembered that the Committee arrived at no conclusion as to the use of preservatives. They were not satisfied, after hearing all the evidence, that these articles were prejudicial to health, and they certainly did not believe them to be used in a fraudulent sense. Why, then, should their use be prohibited? I entirely agree with my honourable Friend the Member for the Horsham Division of Sussex, who said that he would not like to say that a farmer sending milk from the South of England to London on a July or August day should be prohibited from using a preservative that would ensure its delivery in a state fit to be used. I know what is said. There are people who enter into minute and elaborate calculations as to the quantity of boracic acid and other articles of the kind we consume by reason of the use of these preservatives and colouring matters. We had it all out upstairs. I rose from the inquiry quite convinced that if we are going to eat and drink by rules of this kind we should end in eating nothing. I don't believe these preservatives used in

Mr. Russell.

moderation do appreciable harm. I believe they are useful in carrying on legitimate trade, and we have seen no reason for prohibiting their use. Of course, if they are injurious to health, they come under the present law and can be dealt with. Then as to colouring. I admit that here, again, I was over-ruled on the Committee. My agricultural Friends behind me, aided by the agricultural Members on the other side, and backed by the Irish Nationalists, left me with a small band of supporters representing as I thought, and still think, the common-sense of the matter. I am of the same opinion still. You cannot stop the artificial colouring of butter. Most, if not the whole, of the foreign butter in the English market, and that is most of the butter used in this country, is artificially coloured. Can you prevent it? Ought you to prevent it? The colouring matter is not injurious to health. It is not used fraudulently. To attempt to prevent the colouring of butter would raise a storm of opposition, and would be most unfair. But if butter is to be coloured at will by the producer—you cannot make a different law for the producer of margarine. Both are legitimate articles of commerce. And so long as the colouring does not injure public health and is not fraudulent, the producer is entitled to make the article he produces as attractive as it can be made. The honourable Member for Pembrokeshire complained at some length that the penalties of this Bill were not sufficient, and the honourable Member for Devonport has reinforced that opinion. It is quite true that the Committee upstairs decided to recommend that for the second offence there should be a minimum penalty of £5, and that the magistrates might at their discretion imprison for a third offence. Now, I confess that this doctrine of a minimum penalty is exceedingly difficult. You complain—and properly complain—that magistrates will not now act and that they inflict totally inadequate penalties. But, supposing a person comes before a bench of magistrates who now hesitate about moderate penalties, and a hard and fast line is laid down that if you convict on the second occasion you must inflict a penalty of £5. the chances are that these unwilling magistrates will dismiss the case. That is certain to happen. I think the Government have exercised a wise discretion in not fixing a minimum penalty. The same observation applies to the question of imprisonment. If you cannot get magistrates to enforce the law now and exact the present penalties, how can you get them to send people to gaol? Every speaker has referred to the difficulty of getting these penalties enforced, moderate as they are, and I do not see that by putting into an Act of Parliament a stronger penalty you will succeed in enforcing it. But so far as the question of penalties is concerned, I think it is a perfectly reasonable matter for the Committee to discuss. I am perfectly sure my right honourable Friend will keep an open mind upon all these questions of detail, and if the House chooses to take the responsibility of adding imprisonment for a third or a specially bad offence I say that that can be discussed upstairs with perfect freedom. The House will take the responsibility for it, but undoubtedly the Government have not seen their way to put stronger penalties into the Bill. With reference to detention of goods at the port of entry, the whole difficulty is that much of the goods are perishable, and you run the risk of detaining perishable goods that may be perfectly pure, but by the time your analysis is complete they may be injured or destroyed. I think clause 1 really meets the difficulty in question.

MR. G. WHITELEY (Stockport): Are we to understand that this question of 10 per cent., which we thought was a fundamental part of the Bill, is to be subject of Debate upstairs? Is the Government going to adhere to it?

*MR. RUSSELL: Everything will be subject to debate upstairs. These are really matters for Committee, and not for Second Reading. The last thing I have to say is this. It was complained on the first night of this Debate that this was not heroic legislation. Why should it be? I never knew a question on which there was less room for heroics. All the speakers have declared that the present Acts are good Acts if they could only be tightened up and enforced a little better. The object of the Government has not been to produce heroic legislation. The

object has been, in the first place, to protect the public from adulteration; in the second place, not to interfere with legitimate commerce; and, in the third place, not to harass or annoy the honest trader. I believe the Bill clearly carries out that design, and I hope the House will consent to read it a second time.

MR. BRYCE (Aberdeenshire, S.): Mr. Speaker, the honourable Member who has just sat down, in his elaborate defence of the Bill, commented on the fact that only two Members have asked the House to reject it altogether; but, on the other hand, he has not been able to cite a single Member on the other side of the House who has expressed satisfaction with the Bill. One honourable Member, sitting for a Yorkshire constituency, did recommend the House to take it as the best they could get at present, but even he thought it a very unsatisfactory instalment of what was desired. It is a remarkable fact that the Bill has been criticised from so many points of view. Some have said that it does not go far enough. That complaint is made not only by agriculturists, who desire a much more severe restriction, and more stringent penalties, but it comes also from those who, like my honourable Friend the Member for Devonport, desire to see the whole subject of adulteration dealt with. I think there was great force in the observation of my honourable Friend, and it would be a great deal easier to administer the law and have a higher measure of certainty if the whole question of adulteration were put upon the same lines, without any privileges being given to agricultural produce. On the other side, it is said that the Bill itself is objectionable in many respects. Some Members have remarked that it is vexatious, and that particularly with regard to the registration clause, which has, I hear, excited very considerable annoyance in the country. And others again, like my honourable Friend the Member for Islington, scent in it a certain Measure of protection. We are always told when these Bills come up that there is danger of their being protective Measures. But I do not think there is very much of the element of protection in this particular Bill. It is not altogether unnatural, however, that that element should be suspected, because there was something in the language of the President of the Board of Agriculture which tended to give that impression. He talked in his introductory speech not in the way I should have expected him to talk, about the desirability of preventing fraud and deceit, but he spoke of the importance of securing honest competition. Well, we are not here for the purpose of securing fair competition. We are here for the purpose of preventing deceit and detecting frauds upon consumers. If the right honourable Gentleman the President of the Board of Agriculture had based his arguments upon the interests of the consumer, and. had not thrown out this suggestion to his agricultural friends that this was a Measure intended for their special benefit, he would have done a good deal to disarm the suspicion with which the Measure was received by severe and stringent Free Traders of the type of the honourable Member for Islington. I cannot help regarding with great suspicion the words in clause 2 with regard to the functions of the Board of Agriculture. The clause says that—

"the Board of Agriculture may, in relation to any matter appearing to it to affect the general interests of agriculture in the United Kingdom,"

take samples of agricultural produce. Now, if the Bill is simply a Bill to prevent adulteration, these words are not in the least necessary. It would be sufficient to say that the Board should interfere to prevent fraud. The right honourable Gentleman said that they were only intended to define the scope of the action of the Board. For that purpose also I say that they are not necessary. It would have been sufficient to say that the Board may interfere in the case of food products such as milk, butter, and cheese, but the words "general interests of agriculture" seem to suggest a motive and reason for intervention which is entirely apart from the interests of the consumer, which it ought to be the business of the Bill to protect. Furthermore, we have the ringing into this Bill of the Board of Agriculture instead of the Local Government Board. That is a very important change in the law, and it is a change which neither the right honourable Gentleman nor the Secretary to the Local Government Board have justified.

Mr. Bryce.

I have not heard in this Debate, and I have listened to it from the beginning, a single word to justify the substitution of a new Board for the Board which is in possession of the field, and which is not alleged in any way to have neglected its duties. I can only suppose either that the Board of Agriculture wishes to ingratiate itself with its agricultural supporters, or else it is an underworked Department, and is so anxious for fresh work that it has determined to take over this function, and thus to relieve the Local Government Board. The matter is really one of some importance. The Local Government Board is already the authority which is properly charged with the administration of the Adulteration Laws. It will retain its general administration of those laws after the passing of this Bill, if it passes, and it will remain the authority which spurs on and supervises the action of local authorities for every kind of adulteration except that referring to these particular three forms of food products. Is it not, then, very inconvenient and anomalous that, while the Local Government Board retains its general power, this particular duty should be entrusted to a new Board altogether. The mischief does not stop there. The reason why the Local Government Board has control of the matter is this : that the administration of these Acts rests in the hands of the local authorities. These local authorities appoint analysts, and these analysts have to be approved by the Local Government Board. The Local Government Board, therefore, is ultimately the master of the local authorities and of the analysts. It is not proposed to take away the approval of the appointment of analysts from the Local Government Board and give it to the Board of Agriculture. Why, then, introduce the Board of Agriculture at all ? Surely all the arguments, both on the ground of symmetry and of convenience, are in favour of keeping those who have to execute the law under the control of those who have appointed them, and those who supervise their action in every other branch of their work. I think if the Government were going to give, as they have given in many respects, a laboured answer upon the criticisms on this Bill, they ought to have dealt with this, which is a change at first sight, and, so far as we have heard, quite contrary to principle, and quite without justification on any ground of practical convenience. Now I have little to say with regard to the main provisions of this Bill. So far as they go to prevent fraud, we are heartily in favour of them. There is no relation at all between free trade and fraud, and our maxims ought to be " everything against fraud," and " nothing against freedom." There is no contradiction between the two, and nobody can say that legislation against fraud can in any way interfere with free trade. But I do think it is extremely desirable, when we are endeavouring to protect the consumer and to prevent fraud, that we should introduce any provision which can even be suspected of a different design. There is one provision which seems to have a design, as to which I am not satisfied with the explanations given by the Secretary of the Local Government Board, and that is the provision with regard to the manufacture of margarine containing more than 10 per cent. of butter fat. The defence made for this provision I understand to be this : that all butter which is not perfect and genuine butter, but which is in the main margarine, is prohibited by law, and it is an offence against the Adulteration Act to sell it.

*Mr. RUSSELL : It must be sold as margarine.

Mr. BRYCE : It must not _be misdescribed ; it must be sold for that which it is. I understand there is a good deal of stuff which is neither pure butter nor margarine, but it is a mixture between the two. That is one of the things which I have learned in the course of this discussion. I have learned also that this mixed substance is practically indistinguishable from inferior kinds of butter, and that one might have it served up at his table without knowing the difference. It would appear that already it is an offence to sell this article unless it is labelled margarine, and the present Bill contains a provision requiring the mark to be more complete and unmistakable than it now necessarily is. The Government say that, in spite of this provision of the law, the sale of this mixed stuff will go on, and that it will be sold for butter even if it is described as margarine, and they think

it is necessary for that purpose to stop the sale of it altogether. Surely the answer to that is, that you ought to enforce the law more strictly, and, if the law prohibits the sale of the article except as margarine, make it as stringent as you like. By why debar people who wish to pay 10d. for something which is much better than ordinary margarine, although it is not as good as perfect butter, from indulging in that wish?

*The PRESIDENT of the BOARD of AGRICULTURE : That is exactly where we do not agree. We say there is no merit in any mixture of margarine and butter, destined to be sold as margarine, over the best natural margarine produced under this limit of 10 per cent. We are assured by the best information we can get, such as that given by the honourable Member for Devonport, who is largely interested in this trade, as well as by other experts, that the very best margarine, so far as quality goes, can be produced within the limit of 10 per cent. Therefore, you do not gain anything, so far as margarine is concerned, by allowing any greater amount of butter to be mixed with the margarine.

Mr. BRYCE : I am much obliged to the right honourable Gentleman for his explanation. I have been told that this considerable mixture of butter with margarine confers a more general flavour of the character of butter, and that, therefore, it is preferable. I understand it is not so, and that in point of fact this butter atmosphere, this persuasion that one is really eating butter, is attainable with something less than 10 per cent. of butter fat, and that, therefore, the consumer will not be in any way prejudiced, because he has a palatable and edible article under the law as formerly. If that is so, it to some extent removes my objection, but it is an additional piece of knowledge which this Debate has given me. Still I cannot help thinking that where you have a law in force which should be enough, you go dangerously near interference with trade if you prohibit an article when your law, if enforced, ought to be a sufficient protection to the consumer. I now come to the question of invoices, and here I desire to clear up one preliminary difficulty. The invoice question, upon which so much has been said, arises upon clause 17, which provides that a warranty or invoice shall not be available as a defence in any proceedings under this Act unless the defendant gives seven days' notice of his intention to plead it. It appears to me that these words make an invoice substantially a warranty. I do not understand how it can be contended that it is not a substantial warranty if the clause provides that under certain circumstances it shall be a defence. Perhaps the right honourable Gentleman will explain that.

*THE PRESIDENT OF THE BOARD OF AGRICULTURE: The explanation is this: Clause 17 must be read with clause 23 of the Food and Drugs Act. If the right honourable Gentleman will look, he will see that that Act is to be read with the Margarine Act, 1887. Under the Margarine Act the invoice is a warranty, and, therefore, this clause merely provides that, where the defendant intends to claim the right to produce a warranty or invoice as a defence, he must give certain notice. This leaves the law with regard to the position of a warranty or invoice exactly as it is now, and this Bill only indicates that where it is produced and pleaded as a defence due notice shall be given of the intention to adopt that course.

MR. BRYCE: I understand that. It seems to me to be the natural explanation of the words. But I do not see why the right honourable Gentleman said that an invoice was not intended to operate as a warranty.

*THE PRESIDENT OF THE BOARD OF AGRICULTURE: Because under the Food and Drugs Act an invoice is not a warranty, whereas under the Margarine Act it is, and the Government propose to leave the law exactly as it is. It does not repeal the section of the Margarine Act nor change the law under the Food and Drugs Act.

MR. BRYCE: This is an admirable illustration of the extraordinary difficulty caused by incorporating other Acts in such a Bill as this. I think, if you read the Acts, it is doubtful whether you will get that construction out of them. Not only is it in the highest degree doubtful, but nothing can be

Mr. Bryce.

conceived more likely to give rise to litigation and to cause great difficulty in the administration of the Act. I earnestly hope that if this Bill goes to Committee that we shall amend clause 17 so as to make it mean what it says and say what it means. That brings me to a question dealt with by the last speaker, as to whether invoices should or should not be accepted as a defence. One honourable Member said that it would be necessary if they were accepted as a defence to go against the foreign producer, but surely he omitted to notice the second part of section 17, which provides expressly for the case of the foreign producer. I should have thought when he spoke of the difficulty of securing a conviction that he would have remembered that in these cases the person one chiefly wanted to get at is the manufacturer or wholesale dealer. It is far more important to strike at him than at the local trader.

*MR. RUSSELL: May I point out that there is this difficulty in the matter? The question that would arise is whether the goods supplied to the public by the retail dealer were in the same condition as when they left the manufacturer. My contention was that the courts and the local authorities would be so discouraged that prosecutions would cease altogether.

MR. BRYCE: I should have thought that in that case the *onus probandi* of showing that there had been any change in the goods would rest upon the manufacturer, and that difficulty would be completely met in this way. I should also have thought that in those cases which are tested by analysis any change in the character of goods not likely to be caused by lapse of time would not be a change which affected the analysis. However, that is a highly technical question on which I, as a layman, will not dwell. In this case it is better to get at the large men—at the manufacturer or wholesale dealer—for by such means you secure more effective protection for the public. One difficulty in getting a conviction against the local dealer arises from the fact that in many cases, even if he is called upon to show that the article was pure, there is sympathy with him on the part of the court trying the case, and there is a disposition to let him off because he could not have known that he had been imposed upon by the large dealer—a sympathy which would not exist if the large dealer himself were before the court. Therefore, the latter person is the better one to strike at. I cannot acquiesce as a matter of policy in the view stated by the Government that it is better to prosecute the retailer that the wholesale dealer. I think it is much better to get at the wholesale dealer if you can. These are the chief points in the Bill upon which I wish to remark. But I must say I think it is rather a pity that the Government should have brought forward the Bill so soon after it was printed. I have heard that there is a great deal of feeling in the country, and a great desire has been aroused to make representations in regard to the Measure, and it seems rather a pity, therefore, that the Government did not bring forward their Agricultural Holdings Bill first, and let this Bill come second, although the First Lord of the Treasury said, a few days ago, that he believed the agricultural community were more anxious to have this Bill first. I saw to-day a letter from the Secretary to the Scottish Chambers of Agriculture, expressing a strong desire that the Agricultural Holdings Bill should come before this Bill. I make this observation for the sake of suggesting to the Government that they ought not to send this Bill to the Committee at once, but should give full and ample time for representations regarding it to be received from the country. It touches a great many trades, and excites a good deal of interest, and it would be a mistake, I think, to hurry it forward until the feeling of the country was well ascertained as to the course which should be taken on the Bill. I must say, I think it rather a defective Measure, containing many points very much open to question. On the other hand, I cannot find that even the ingenuity of the honourable Members for Islington and Glasgow has succeeded in convincing me it is so bad that it ought not be read a second time. But it will require careful consideration, and I hope we shall be able, as suggested by the honourable Member for Devonport, to screw it up a little more tightly, and make it a more complete protection against fraud than it appears to be at present.

Mr. LOPES (Grantham): I think the right honourable Gentleman the President of the Board of Agriculture may fairly congratulate himself upon the reception which the Bill has met with at the hands of the House, for, although there has been a considerable amount of criticism, everybody approves the principle contained in the Measure. For my own part, I believe the Bill is essentially a useful and practical one. It is an honest endeavour on the part of the Government, not merely to put an end to the unfair competition between adulterated produce and really genuine articles, but to put down, as far as possible, the whole system of adulteration which is so prevalent, and has done so much injury to the interests of the whole community. The adulteration of food has been reduced almost to an exact science, and it is owing to the blissful ignorance of the people as to the gross frauds to which they are subjected that they have in the past been so extremely apathetic and indifferent on this matter. I confess I was surprised to find any honourable Gentleman, even with the very keenest scent for the taint of protection, getting up in this House and suggesting he has been able to discover it in a Bill of this kind. But it was left to the honourable Member for Islington to make this somewhat startling and surprising discovery. He moved the rejection of this Bill mainly upon the ground that it was a protective Measure in the interests of agriculture. If it is a protective Measure at all, it is protection, not only in the interests of agriculturists, but also of the trader and general consumer. The producer of an article has a right to know that what he exposes for sale is not subjected to unfair competition, and, if that is conceded, then the consumer has an equal right to know that what he buys is a really genuine article, and something which is not prejudicial to his health. The honourable Member went on to say that the effect of this Bill would be to force the people of this country to consume bad butter made at home, instead of good butter imported from Normandy. But this Bill only subjects butter imported from abroad to the same analysis as the butter which we produce in this country, and if it is fair, right, and reasonable that home-produced butter should be subjected to inspection, surely it is also just and reasonable that butter imported from abroad should be inspected. If I may pass for a few moments to the more serious criticisms upon this Bill, I should like to point out that while some Members have said that it is not drastic enough, others have remarked that it is far too drastic, and I venture, therefore, to think that the reasonable presumption is that my right honourable Friend has been very wise in steering a middle course between the two extremes. He has in that way avoided many pitfalls and many difficulties, and I think he has taken the course which is most likely to secure the best result. While the Bill has taken every reasonable precaution that the trade of this country shall be conducted upon sound, honest, and upright principles, it does not unduly harass any legitimate interest, nor does it put an end to any lawful trade. Another criticism brought against this Bill is that the Board of Agriculture is not the proper authority for dealing with these matters. Why, Sir, there is no shifting of responsibility from the Local Government Board to the Board of Agriculture of any of the powers which the Local Government Board has hitherto exercised. I agree with my honourable Friend near me that in a Bill of this kind, which deals absolutely and solely with agricultural matters, we naturally look to the Board of Agriculture to safeguard those interests, and not to the Local Government Board. The farmers, I think, would naturally expect that the Minister of Agriculture should be the controlling authority, and I believe the consumer would be quite as ready to put his interests in the hands of my right honourable Friend. Now, Sir, there comes the question of margarine. To have heard many of the speeches, one would almost imagine that the Bill was intended to deal with margarine only. I know that there are many honourable Friends of mine sitting on this side of the House who may be naturally disappointed that the colouring of margarine has not been prohibited. I believe also that there is a strong feeling in this direction in the agricultural community, but when my right honourable Friend comes down to this House and tells us that, after the most careful examination, and after consulting expert authority, he is perfectly convinced that to prohibit the colouring of margarine

would destroy the margarine trade, I ask this House seriously whether it is prepared to take such a responsibility on its shoulders. I, for my part, would not associate myself with legislation of that kind. I believe it would be most unfair, most unwise, and most impolitic if we were to put down the legitimate trade in margarine, which, if it is not so nutritious as butter, is still wholesome and palatable, and does contain certain valuable nutritive properties, and is largely bought and consumed by the poorer part of the community. One honourable Member said that colouring meant fraud. I advise him to preach that doctrine to his agricultural Friends. I am perfectly convinced of this, that if you are to permit the farmers to colour their butter, which they simply do in order to make it more saleable, more palatable, and more acceptable to the common taste, then it is impossible to prohibit the colouring of margarine. Some honourable Members seem to think that margarine competes with butter, and that if you were to destroy the trade in it you would very much enhance the sale of butter. I believe that that is an entire fallacy. I do not believe that margarine is competing against butter to-day. The price of butter as compared with margarine is so prohibitive that if you were to do away with the margarine trade to-morrow you would not increase the sale of butter, but you would simply take away from the poorer classes of the community a valuable commodity which they consume in very large quantities. One honourable Member on the other side said he regretted that the Bill had made no definite provision prohibiting the putting into milk of anything injurious to health. But I would remind him that at the present time, if it is shown that any preservatives are put into milk which are injurious to health, the case can be dealt with under the Sale of Foods Act, 1875. Not only that, the Act has done something to prevent the adulteration of these articles by very largely increasing the penalties under the Bill, and I confess that I, for one, should have no objection to see in it an additional penalty allowing imprisonment to be imposed in some cases. It is perfectly true that the Bill does not set up Courts of Reference in order to establish a fixed standard of purity. I believe it would be almost impossible to establish such a fixed standard for every article. The composition of commodities which are sold under one and the same name varies so considerably. We know that the substance and quality of milk varies in different seasons, and it would be almost impossible to fix any definite standard so as to say where purity ends and where adulteration begins. There would be this additional danger, that there would be a tendency on the part of the manufacturer to level down his produce to the point which would satisfy the standard, and thus you might have levelling down instead of levelling up. The Bill goes a very long way indeed towards satisfying the requirements of agriculturists on this matter, because it authorises the Board of Agriculture to determine what deficiency or addition to milk would raise a fair presumption that the article was adulterated. Now, Sir, this Bill deals with articles which are very largely consumed, and which, I believe, are adulterated more than any other, and by shifting the responsibility of the proof of purity upon the seller, I think you are doing something which will act as a strong deterrent, and you are going very far to meet the wishes of agriculturists, as well as to safeguard the interests of consumers. So much for the criticisms which have been passed with respect to the Bill. I believe myself that this Measure has far more prospect of being a success than any other Bill owing to the power which the Board of Agriculture have taken to initiate proceedings themselves, and to take samples all over the country, as well as to exercise authority over defaulting local authorities. We know very well that the success of a Measure depends far more upon the spirit in which it is carried out than upon the actual measure of the law. Where these Acts have been properly administered, they have been proved to be most beneficial; in fact, instances were given before the Committee in which many forms of adulteration had altogether disappeared. We know that some authorities have for different reasons been extremely adverse to taking proceedings under these Acts, but I do think that the extra power which has been given to the Board of Agriculture to force local authorities to take action will prove extremely bene-

ficial and satisfactory in its results. I have only to thank the House for the patience with which it has listened to me, and to say that I support the Bill because I believe it is an honest, practical, and genuine attempt on the part of the Government to put down adulteration. It does not unduly harass or vex any industry, it is not class legislation, but it is legislation in the interests of the whole community.

MR. G. WHITELEY (Stockport): While I have taken for many years great interest in this matter, as a Member of the Committee upstairs, which has been so often referred to, I desire to say a few words upon this Bill. I came down to the House to-day with the full intention to bless the Bill, and I desire to congratulate the President of the Board of Agriculture on the fact that under circumstances most difficult, and amid a variety of conflicting interests, some of which are almost irreconcilable, he has evolved a Bill which is an honest and fair attempt to steer an even keel between all interests surrounding this matter. But I am bound to say that I do look upon several phrases which fell from the Secretary to the Local Government Board with great alarm. An honourable Member on the other side of the House described this Bill as class legislation, and I believe he hinted that it was tinged with protection. Nobody in this House is more opposed to anything savouring of class legislation than I am, and I confess I cannot see in what sense or by what twist or turn of the imagination this Bill can be described as class legislation. It seems to me it may be better described as omnibus legislation—it is intended for all and to reconcile the differences of all. I have regarded this Bill throughout as a compromise—a compromise in which all the interests affected by it has had to surrender something in order to contribute to the solution of the difficulty. I have looked upon the essential and fundamental parts of this compromise as these: Firstly, that the agricultural interest fail to obtain what they are striving for, namely, the prohibition of the colouring of margarine; whilst, secondly, the distributing and consuming classes has had taken from them the possibility of obtaining margarine of a better quality than that

O

which contains not more than 10 per cent. of butter fat. It seems to me that there are three interests affected. There is the agricultural—the butter producing interest, who have undoubtedly sought for years to obtain the prohibition of the colouring of margarine and the admixture of butter with it. My right honourable Friend has not gone to that extent, and, therefore, that is their contribution to the solution of this difficulty. Then I come to the distributing interest. This, perhaps, is best represented by the Federation of Grocers' Associations, which represents the whole of the grocers of England, and possibly of Great Britain. From that Federation I have from time to time introduced deputations to my right honourable Friend, as well as to the President of the Local Government Board. And, connected with these, are the margarine producers, and these two classes are naturally very much disappointed with the restriction as to the amount of butter fat to be allowed in margarine in the future. Gentlemen connected with the margarine trade, who have possibly a greater stake in this matter than any others, tell us that this Bill will cut off those higher classes of margarine which have been produced, and which have been sold by the distributors at a greater profit than that is obtained for the lower classes. Some manufacturers say that it will seriously hamper their business. They have for years been accustomed to producing the better classes of margarine; they have built up a trade which is now to be destroyed, and they will practically have to begin business over again. But, while the Bill cuts off the production of the higher classes of margarine, I am assured by others that it will permit of their producing still an excellent and valuable article of food. I do not agree with the right honourable Gentleman that the higher classes of margarine which have contained 20 per cent. or 25 per cent. of butter fat are not superior to those containing 10 per cent. I think the right · honourable Gentleman has been misinformed on that point. I possibly have met as many margarine producers lately as he has. But I would ask him why has the public been willing to pay the higher price? The contribution of the distributing and margarine producing section to the compromise is that they

Mr. G. Whiteley.

are prohibited from producing the higher class of margarine and can only produce a quality, which is undoubtedly a lower quality, although at the same time it is an excellent class of food. This I look upon as a fundamental part of the compromise, and if the Government were to propose to depart from it I should have to vote against them. I think it would be, if not a breach of faith, at least unkind treatment, on the part of the Government towards many of us who have taken a great deal of trouble to persuade those with whom we have been associated to accept the Bill. There are other points I had intended to speak upon, but I think they have been laboured sufficiently. With regard to the question of an invoice being a warranty, I do not think it would pass the wit of man to devise in Committee some superscription or foot note which would make an invoice equivalent to a warranty, and thus the difficulty could be disposed of without opening the door to fraud in any degree. It is merely a matter of machinery. I need not press that further. And then there is the consuming interest. The consuming class is not merely the poor class—it is the very poorest of the poor. Nobody buys margarine when he can purchase butter. Necessity is the mother of margarine, as much as she is the mother of invention. Are they to be prohibited from enjoying the better class of margarine? Is the House or the Committee going to take the very grave decision that the only class of margarine they shall be enabled to purchase is one which is as low as can be manufactured, and that the consumer must be content with that? Surely it would be a monstrous thing that the quality of margarine should be ground down to the lowest possible point, and that the poor should be told that they must have that or none. I want to press that strongly home to my right honourable Friend. Then there is the question of the colouring of margarine. Its prohibition has been suggested, and, had it been received with favour by the Committee, it would have been recommended. One honourable Member—above all, a Radical and Liberal Member—has suggested that it ought to be coloured blue. and that the working classes of the country, if they cannot buy butter at 10d., 1s., or 1s. 2d. per lb., should be compelled, as an alternative, to have their bread spread with this blue mixture. I can only suggest that the honourable Member who suggests that should himself have to eat blue butter. I am delighted that the right honourable Gentleman has taken a broad and statesmanlike view in refusing to lend an ear to any of these absurd suggestions that have been made. I believe that if he had acceded to the desire to prohibit the colouring of margarine or to enforce its colouring in any other shade, he would have raised a storm of indignation in the country. It would have been a most dangerous proceeding, and I am sure that many of us in this House would have vehemently and vigorously opposed it. Many of us who have taken an interest in this matter, and have recognised, or have thought we recognised, agricultural leanings on the part of the Government, have looked forward to the production of this Bill with some anxiety. I myself, a supporter of the Government, have done so with some degree of fear and perturbation. I am rejoiced and relieved, therefore, to find, now it has been produced, that it is an honest and fair attempt to reconcile all our differences. I hope that it will pass in the state practically in which it has been introduced. May I press this upon the House, that it should be looked upon as an honourable compromise, and that it is essential that the fundamental parts of that compromise should be retained in it. Speaking as I do for a large industrial population, and knowing as I do the feeling of the industrial classes, I am sure that if it is passed in the form in which it is now introduced, it will remove from the sphere of contention topics and matters which have agitated men's minds for many years past.

On the return of Mr. DEPUTY-SPEAKER after the usual interval,

*MR. A. MOORE: Before this Debate ends I desire to say a few words upon this subject, having had the honour of seconding the first Resolution dealing with this subject 18 years ago. I find that since then we have had several changes on the question. At that time oleo, that is the crude oil from which margarine is made, was not distinguished from butter, and the whole of these oils and all the butter imports were imported into this country without any dis-

tinction being made in the Customs returns. We had to be thankful in those days for very small mercies, and after a good deal of pressure the Government granted us the concession that these oleo margarine oils should be distinguished from butter. We had the greatest difficulty in getting that concession, notwithstanding the fact that almost every Government in Europe had taken action, and very strong action, upon this question. I have heard Members here to-night speaking in praise of Normandy butter, and recommending it to the consumers in this country. Well, Sir, I would recommend honourable Members who entertain this view to read the reports of the Debates in the French Assembly, and there they will learn how great were the difficulties, and how rife corruption and fraud was in France which necessitated legislation of a stringent character in later years. We have been told that this is legislation in favour of a particular class. I would, however, remind the House and the public of the fact that we paid during the year 1898 16 millions sterling to foreigners for our butter imports. Now, if we take the returns of the analyses made by the Board of Customs, we find that in one out of every nine of those cases a conviction was obtained for fraud, and this gives us some idea of the amount of possible fraud that may exist in connection with our imports. Therefore, I say we are contending here not only for fair play to the agriculturists, but also to the citizens of all your populous districts, and I have now the honour myself to sit here as the representative of a large working class constituency. In addition to the 16 millions that you import from abroad, we send you from seven to nine millions from Ireland every year: but for all that I do not want to spare the Irish butter maker, because I want to bring him up to the full level and height of his duty. I have had the honour for some years to be connected with my right honourable Friend opposite in the noble efforts he has made on behalf of the Irish agriculturists, and I say that it is the desire of all intelligent men who have examined this question to raise the standard of the imports of Irish butter, and we do not want to spare fraud any more at home than we do abroad. I come now, Sir, to the question of the administration of this Act, and I find that there is one extremely weak point in this Bill. We have had an exhaustive discussion—in fact a very prolonged and minute discussion—and I think much of what has been said might very well have been said on the Committee Stage of the Bill. Minute details have been closely investigated, but there seems to me to be one point which has entirely escaped the notice of every speaker who has preceded me, and that is the question of registration. Now, this question is not altered by the present Bill, for registration under this Act goes back to clause 9 of the Act of 1887, which provides that the factories for the manufacture of margarine should be registered by the local authority, and the local authority is defined as being the authority which has the power to appoint an analyst. I must say that we never have had a thorough system of registration of factories, and we never shall have, unless some strong measures be taken to enforce this clause. This is part of the principle of your Bill, and if you shut one door and exclude fraudulent butter substitutes, by means of the Customs authorities, from coming into the country, you ought not to leave the door of the manufacturer open and allow him to put any amount that suits his convenience of fraudulent butter substitutes upon the market. If you adopt no means of detecting such practices, then your Bill, while it deals severely with the foreigner, allows the home manufacturer to go practically unpunished. This point, I think, requires to be very carefully considered. You must have some efficient system of registration, because it is useless to expect that the local authorities can be relied upon for carrying out this registration work. When the Committee were investigating this subject upstairs what were we told had taken place in London? We were told that an officer had initiated several prosecutions under the Act of 1887, but for doing that he was had up before the local authority and severely reprimanded; therefore I say that you cannot rely upon the local authorities in this matter. It must be remembered that you are dealing with a very profitable trade, which does not scruple to spend very large sums of money in its own defence. It is a trade which has been making from one time to another during the last 18 years profits varying from 50 to 100 per cent.

Mr. A. Moore.

Under such circumstances to talk of fines is absurd, and I was astonished to find that the honourable Member for Devonport did not know that these fines were paid by an association. Therefore, fines in these cases are useless, because if the retailer is condemned to pay a fine it is paid by the association out of a joint fund, and this fact is perfectly notorious. Therefore, I emphasise the point that fines are perfectly useless in such a profitable business; and it is hopeless to expect the local authority to put this law vigorously into force, because some of the members of those local bodies may be engaged in this profitable business themselves.

*MR. RUSSELL: I may point out that clause 3 provides that where a local authority fails to carry out the Act the Board of Agriculture can carry it out for them.

*MR. A. MOORE: This interruption, like most interruptions, recoils upon the interrupter. The fact is that the central authority may do this when the local authority is in default, but if the right honourable Gentleman will turn back to the Act of 1887 he will find that the local authority, and that authority only, has the power to register these manufactories. No doubt the right honourable Gentleman and the Minister for Agriculture would never have allowed things to come to this pass but for the fact that their hands have been tied. You cannot move against a manufacturer unless he is declared to be one, and he cannot be declared to be one and known unless he is registered as such. My experience has been this—that I have known these factories to exist, and I have gone to the Government authorities and searched the records of the Board of Trade, and yet I have been unable to find any record whatever of these factories which I have known myself to exist. I need not say that it is absolutely illogical to put heavy pressure upon the foreigner through the Board of Customs if you are not going to close the door by which these fraudulent butter substitutes might come from the manufacturers in this country. I want to ask also is this Act going to be enforced? Is it going to be worked? If anybody will take the trouble to read the Act of 1887 they will find that there is a perfect army of officials under that Act, and what is the reason why none of them have done anything? What guarantee have we that this Act is going to be worked? As regards these officials to whom I have referred, there are no less than five classes, numbering many thousands of officers. In the first place, you have all the officers of the Board of Inland Revenue; secondly, you have all the Customs officials; thirdly, the medical officers of health; fourthly, you have the inspectors of nuisances; and, fifthly, you have the police constables, authorised under the Food and Drugs Act of 1875. Now, how is it that with all these officials nothing has been done under the Act of 1887, and what guarantee have we got that this Act will not be such a lamentable failure as the Act which has preceded it? Then I come to another point—and it has been alluded to by many other honourable Members; it is, however, one of extreme importance, and that is the power which the Board of Agriculture takes, for the first time, to fix standards. The feeling of the country is rather that this sweeping power should be delegated to a board of scientific experts. I am not, however, opposed to this provision, although it is one of very great importance, and will require very careful examination in Committee. Under this clause, however, it might be possible to do us a very great injury indeed in our Irish butter trade. Some honourable Members who have spoken alluded to the question of water in butter. Now, in the high-class fresh butter we have no reason to object to any standard which you may choose to fix, no matter how high you may fix it; but there is also the salt butter trade, so very well known in past years, and which is peculiar to Ireland, that is the system of producing and conserving butter which preserves all its high qualities and delicate aroma right into the early months of spring. I have tasted this sort of butter myself, five or six months after it has been made, and found that it possessed all the aroma and flavour of the finest butter. That was a special Irish trade in the days before the advent of steamers and before there were any refrigerators. I believe that in the north of England there is still a demand for that butter; therefore, speaking on behalf of the producers, I say that this butter cannot be made without added water, and that this is a matter which will

have to be very carefully considered. I should just like to say one or two words about preservatives, for I think it a most serious thing that this country should tolerate the putting of these powerful drugs into butter and óther produce, and by this means forcing them down the throats of the people twice and three times a day. These are very strong and potent drugs, and the question is, do you wish to have them forced upon you and upon your children at every meal. It seems to me that this is a question which requires immediate attention, and although the Board of Agriculture are taking upon themselves under this Bill very heavy responsibilities, I for one do not object, because we shall be able to control and follow their action in this House. I must say that I think it is very ill-timed to hear all these gibes and jeers on this side of the House directed against the Board of Agriculture. The whole of Europe is far in advance of this country. Only the other day a young man asked me where he could get a thorough agricultural training. I am sorry that I had to state that there was no thoroughly scientific agricultural education to be had in this country, and was obliged to advise him to go to Louvain, and now that you have established a Board of Agriculture I think that we ought to support it, and try and make it what it ought to be—a thoroughly efficient department. I was glad to hear the right honourable Gentleman on the Treasury Bench, and several others on this side, speak in favour of imprisonment as a penalty under this Bill, although I know that it is a serious matter. I do not wish to take any extreme action on this question, as the representative of the producers, but I wish to say that many of the fines which are now imposed are neither here nor there, and they are absolutely useless. As I said at the beginning of this Debate, it is well known that margarine producers have an association which guarantees to see any shopkeeper through who gets into trouble through selling margarine. We should all deplore to see such a power used unnecessarily, but I do think such a provision ought to be inserted in the Bill, and I hope the right honourable Gentleman will be prepared to strengthen the Measure on the point in accordance with the recommendations suggested from this side of the House.

MR, ASCROFT (Oldham): In making the few remarks which I shall now address to the House I am not speaking in the interests of manufacturers, but in favour of protecting the health of the people of this country. The object of this Bill is, first of all, to stop the introduction into this country of adulterated produce, and that will be quite useless unless action is to be taken at the port of entry. If that is to be effectively achieved, you must strengthen your Bill in this way—that where analysis has been taken and where adulteration has been discovered you must have the power of detaining those goods until judgment has been delivered, and then if adulteration is proved let us have a confiscation of the whole goods. Then there are other points upon which I should like a distinct and clear understanding. I differ with the Secretary of the Local Government Board in the view which he takes as to how the Bill will affect the retailer. He tells us that he has studied the question, but I am perfectly certain that he is wrong. He tells us that the only way to stamp out adulteration is to punish the small retail shopkeepers. But that is not the way to do it. I have heard it said that if you want to get rid of thieves, the best way to do it is to get rid of the receivers. If you wish to get rid of this evil you must first get rid of these great syndicates who send over their filthy stuff into this country. It is almost impossible for small shopkeepers to have these things analysed, but if the law is altered, when the shopkeeper who is summoned hands to the court his invoice, the court will then know who to proceed against, and it will probably be the merchant over in Manchester or Liverpool. In scores of cases the merchant knows perfectly well when those goods are sent out that they are not goods of the quality which they ought to be, and that the invoice is a misrepresentation. The Under Secretary said that we can achieve this with the present Act, but in my experience that is not so. Thousands of these little shopkeepers in the country go to the merchant and ask him to trust them with the goods, and when the merchant knows that he will have to wait for the money the shopkeepers are in his hands, and it is utterly impossible for them to

force from him the guarantee which is provided for under this Act. Therefore, I say this is the greatest blot on this Act, and you are taking the wrong course if you only stop this practice in this country. If the merchant was made responsible he would soon give the foreigner notice that he would have no more of his rotten goods. Why is it that prosecutions under this Act are to be taken under the Food and Drugs Act? Margarine prosecutions are taken under the Margarine Act of 1887, and why should there be any alteration, because margarine and butter adulteration is pretty nearly the same? That is another ground of objection to this Bill. Then there is another point. In the Margarine Act of 1883, in the Factory Act, and in many other Acts which I could name, provision is made that where an employer can show that he has taken every precaution to prevent adulteration, and that those around him in authority have disobeyed his orders, then he is able to bring that servant before the court, the employer is released, and the servant is fined. Now, why was this left out of the present Act? There must be some reason for it. If you had this provision that the assistants in shops would be liable, they would constitute one of the greatest checks to prevent fraud, because it would turn every shopman all over the country into a sort of amateur policeman. You would have the shopman saying to his employer—

"Here I am liable to this penalty, and I cannot afford to pay it; therefore I decline to sell these adulterated goods, and you must get your goods from some place where they are not adulterated."

You would thus have a system of amateur police all over the country who would do very much to assist in carrying out the object of this Bill. I may say that I am speaking not only on behalf of my constituents, but also in accordance with the representations and request of an association which comprises nearly all the grocers and provision dealers in my own constituency, who welcome this Bill, which will do much to put a stop to fraud and adulteration. The shopkeepers are not able to protect themselves, and so we ask them to assist us in stamping out this fraudulent system which has been going on so long, and we say that the only way in which it can be done effectually is in the way we suggest. You should be able in the easiest possible way to get at the man who is guilty of the fraud and who knows of it. How can a poor shopkeeper know, because he is entirely in the hands of the dealer? But if you will make him one of your friends he will be ready to help you to put an end to the fraud. Now on those three points I should like to have a little information from the right honourable Gentleman. First of all, in respect of the invoice as a warranty; secondly, as to the section by which the assistant who disobeys his employer's orders can be made liable as under the Margarine Act. That certainly ought not to be left out unless it has proved to be a failure. Can the right honourable Gentleman tell us of any case where a young man has set his employer at defiance and by that means evaded the Act or made the Act a nullity. We say that you have no right, unless you have good cause, to prosecute under the Food and Drugs Act when you have already an Act which deals with that particular question and meets the case, and which is perfectly strong enough to meet this case if the Act is only put in force. There is no other point of any importance which I wish to detain the House upon. I am anxious and willing to support the Bill, and I welcome it. I believe that the Bill may be made strong enough if the instances I have alluded to can be inserted; and if I can have some assurance upon these points I shall feel that the Government are prepared to go to the Committee with an open mind, ready to discuss the matter fully and to do what is thought best in the interests of the whole country. Unless they are prepared to do this I shall be unfortunately compelled to go into the Lobby against the Bill.

CAPTAIN DONELAN (Cork, E.): This Bill has been so deeply thrashed out and criticised by high authorities on both sides of the House that I only intend to occupy the time of the House for a very brief space. But as the representative of the very great butter producing province of Munster, I desire to say that I support this Bill, not because I consider that it is by any means a heroic Measure, but because I think that it is better to obtain an instalment of justice than to obtain no justice at all. Probably no country is more deeply interested in the prevention of adulteration and spurious imitations of articles of food than Ireland, because—thanks chiefly, I regret to say, to what ought to have been the blessings of British rule —the production of articles of food is practically the only industry left in Ireland. Therefore, this Bill will certainly be regarded as a step in the right direction by the Irish people, although in their opinion, as in mine, it certainly does not go nearly far enough. Most of the objections which I have to the Bill have been already made. For instance, I consider that the punishment provided is altogether inadequate. The French system, I think, imprisons a man upon the second conviction, and I think that system should be adopted in this Bill. As has been already said, the wholesale dealers and manufacturers of fraudulent margarine can snap their fingers at the fines which are to be inflicted under this Bill, for they can pay the largest fine imposed, because, as the honourable Member for Londonderry has stated, the association pays the fines. A good deal has been said in reference to the fixing of the standard of water in butter, and my honourable friend the Member for Devonport implied that Irish butter contained rather an undue proportion of water. That may be the case or may not be, but I know that the Cork butter market have strict rules on the subject, and they do not permit butter in their market that contains over 18 per cent. of water. But be that as it may, I know that it is the general desire in Ireland that a water standard should be fixed, and I sincerely trust that something in that way may be done in Committee. Another blot in the Bill which has been pointed out in this Debate is the fact that no steps have been taken to prevent the colouring of margarine so as to imitate butter. It has been said that if prevention was made in that direction we should also require that the same laws must necessarily apply to butter. As far as I am concerned I really cannot see that there is any great analogy in the two cases. Butter is coloured simply because it is the custom and because it suits the present taste, and it is not coloured for the purpose of deception. Now, I venture to say that margarine in nine cases out of ten is coloured for the purpose of deception. I think that the colouring of butter might be very well compared to the addition of a little rouge to improve a lady's complexion; the colouring of margarine might be very well compared to putting on a mask to hide the face. The whole aim of margarine manufacture, in my humble judgment, .is to endeavour to produce as exact an imitation of butter as they possibly can, and when margarine is coloured to imitate rich grass-fed butter people are naturally inclined to buy it; they consume it, and if they are not poisoned altogether they are apparently satisfied. I think this Bill should also compel spurious imitations to be called by their proper names. Even if margarine is the palatable and the toothsome substance that some honourable Gentlemen have declared it to be, although I have very considerable doubts as to whether those honourable Gentlemen are able to speak from experience as to what the taste of margarine really is—in fact one honourable Gentleman was kind enough to admit, while speaking favourably of margarine, that he had always avoided inflicting such an injustice upon his system as tasting it—it should be described as margarine. It is hard enough for Irish farmers to struggle against honest competition without having to fight against fraud. Therefore, Sir, the more stringent the provisions of the Bill are made in the direction of preventing adulteration or obvious imitation, the better Irish farmers will be pleased. The other reason why Irish farmers require protection is that they have not only to fight against fraud. but the whims of fashion. I suppose that Ireland is too near home to be fashionable, and therefore fashionable, but more especially would-be fashionable people must go to Denmark and Normandy for their butter, just as they go to Norway for their scenery, although they might find a far superior quality of both the one and the other in Ireland. But notwithstanding this drawback, Irish farmers can very well hold their own if they get fair play. All they ask is fair play and no favour. For that reason I desire to support this Bill, and I have reason to hope, from what the honourable Member for Tyrone, South, says, the Bill will be improved in Committee.

Captain Donelan.

MAJOR RASCH (Essex, S.E.): The honourable Member for Aberdeen, East, has very severely criticised the Bill, as well as other honourable Members on the other side of the House. But he has probably forgotten that when he sat on this side of the House the Board of Agriculture never did anything in this matter. I did not rise, however. to bring recriminations before the House, but simply to support, from an agricultural point of view, the Second Reading of the Bill. I think the Minister of Agriculture is entitled to the utmost consideration from the agricultural interest for having brought in this Bill, and for having done what he has done on this extremely difficult subject. It is the best Bill which has been laid on the Table of the House ever since I have been here. I do not go so far as to say that they are perfectly satisfied with it. Neither am I. As to the margarine question, my friends would have wished that margarine had been left in its natural state, or else coloured blue, black, or green. I think the Minister of Agriculture sees also that it is practically impossible to do this, for if it were done it would practically kill the margarine trade. That is not what we want to do at all. The margarine trade is a very large trade in this country. Margarine itself is eaten by a very considerable section of the population, and practically there is very little harm in it. If we allow the people to drink what they are pleased to call British port and British sherry, to eat " fill " cheese, or drink milk fortified with boracic acid, it would be hard to penalise people who desired to eat margarine as a cheap substitute for butter. and one which does no harm to health. I think the agricultural interest should be generous in this matter, and for two reasons: first, if you allow margarine to be rouged, as an honourable Member opposite suggested, I hardly see what the butter producers can do, for you would have to prevent them also from colouring their products. In the second place. if you kill the margarine trade—for this margarine sells at present at the rate of 4½d. to 7d. per lb.—I do not see how it would help the agricultural interests, because a very large class of the people who are at present able to buy margarine could not afford to buy pure butter. Under all these circumstances it is better to reserve any of these details for the Committee upstairs. I would advise my agricultural friends in East Anglia to thankfully accept this Bill as a very considerable half loaf which the Minister of Agriculture has given them, and which is a good deal better than no bread at all.

CAPTAIN SINCLAIR (Forfar) : The speech of the honourable Gentleman who has just sat down, coupled with many other speeches delivered in the course of the Debate, must have left on the House the impression that a large section of the House supports this Bill as a Measure intended to aid the agricultural industry. It seems to me that the first blot on the Bill is that it is so stamped with the Board of Agriculture. The Bill starts under very great disadvantages, as was pointed out early in the Debate by the honourable Gentleman who sits on this side of the House. The honourable Member for Londonderry reproached Members on this side of the House for taking no interest in agriculture. I do not think that is a fair reproach. There is work which the Board of Agriculture has to do in connection with agriculture, but it should have nothing to do with the province of administration, and no justification has been laid before the House for the departure from the proposals made the year before last. The administration of all previous Adulteration Acts has always lain with the Local Government Board, and it was from the Reports of the Local Government Board that we could judge of the progress made in checking adulteration.

*THE PRESIDENT OF THE BOARD OF AGRICULTURE : I beg the honourable and gallant Member's pardon. The work which it is proposed that the Board of Agriculture should do under this Bill is work which it has done for several years, and which was commenced at the instance of the right honourable Member for Monmouth West, when he was Chancellor of the Exchequer.

CAPTAIN SINCLAIR : That is not so very long ago. The Board of Agriculture has been established since the last Adulteration Act was passed, and if you want to look at the progress of this country in checking adulteration it is to the Reports of the Local Government Board that you have to go. In Scotland

the administration of the Adulteration Acts is not with the Board of Agriculture, but with the Local Government Board. Everyone who approves of this Bill has done so from the point of view that it is a protective Measure. Even the honourable Gentleman behind me, before he sat down, said that Irish Agriculture badly needs protection, and that Irish farmers badly want protection.

CAPTAIN DONELAN : Only from adulteration.

CAPTAIN SINCLAIR : There is no mention in this Bill except protection from fraud. I do not want to take advantage of the honourable and gallant Member's extreme sensitiveness on the question of protection. The Bill is a Measure designed chiefly for securing protection from fraud. But let me suggest that in regard to protection from fraud this Bill is an entire departure from previous Adulteration Acts. It is perfectly true that if a substance—a compound substance—was found to be injurious, it was ipso facto a criminal act to sell it ; but if the article was not injurious to health, all that the previous Acts insisted upon was that such a substance should be labelled what it is, so that the man who buys it shall know what he is getting. In this Bill you go a great deal further in laying down that the sale of a substance which can be consumed without injury to health shall be prohibited. It should be remembered that we are legislating, not only for the present, but for the future, and how do you know that scientific research and chemical experiment may not bring a much fuller knowledge in regard to foods than we possess now ? Now, a great deal has been said about margarine. Well, there are lots of people—there are even some in this House, who have eaten margarine, and there is no one who will maintain for a moment that margarine is injurious to health. I cannot for the life of me see how the Government is justified, no matter what knowledge they may have on the subject, in taking this departure from the lines adopted in previous legislation on adulteration. Will the right honourable Gentleman explain ?

*THE PRESIDENT OF THE BOARD OF AGRICULTURE : What we propose doing now in regard to imported milk, etc., is what has already been done by the Board of Agriculture, but only doing it in a somewhat different way. The honourable and gallant Member is also mistaken in saying that we propose in the future to follow a different course in Scotland than in the past.

CAPTAIN SINCLAIR: I hold the view very strongly that the clause dealing with the 10 per cent. addition of butter to margarine is a bad clause, and a departure from the principles of previous Adulteration Acts. The first principle was that if an article of food was injurious to health it was *ipso facto* a criminal act to sell that article. And the second principle was that if the article was not injurious to health and was sold, it should only be labelled with a description of what it really was. This Bill goes beyond both these principles. The Government conceive themselves justified in doing so, but I cannot agree with them. They do not limit themselves to saying that it shall be labelled margarine, but that it shall not contain more than 10 per cent. of butter fat. The Secretary of the Local Government Board says that he bases his figures on information given him by manufacturers of margarine, and that the ground of their taking this step was that it is impossible if you mix butter with margarine to prevent fraud. In fact, they wish to shut the door against all trade in a mixture of butter with margarine, which is perfectly wholesome, because they say there will be no guarantee that it had been manufactured as margarine and not as butter. That is limiting the supply of what is a valuable food of the people without sufficient reason. They tell us that they wish to protect against fraud, but I say that if you would have behind you the sympathy of the people the protection must be reasonable, and I maintain that it is not reasonable for the Legislature to step in and prevent the sale of an article which is perfectly wholesome, and which is really wanted by hundreds of thousands of poor families throughout the country. I hope we shall have more information from the Government as to the three points mentioned in his speech by the honourable Member for Oldham, namely, the question of warranty, the question of the shop assistants, and the question of the prosecutions being made under the Margarine Act. Another objection which I have to this Bill is that it makes a

President of Board of

very serious interference with the work of the local authorities. I agree with the honourable Member for Devonport, that by good administration you could cure 90 per cent. of the evils now complained of, but that would not be done at all under this Bill. How are you going to get good administration if you propose to carry out what was deliberately rejected by the Committee which sat on this question, namely, the constitution of a great central authority to over-ride the local authorities. I quite agree that the local authorities may have been apathetic and slow in the administration of the existing Adulteration Acts. But local authorities have been apathetic about the administration of other Acts. The figures which the President of the Board of Agriculture gave us last night seemed to show that in London, at any rate, the administration of the local authorities had very largely diminished the evils. Then as to the examinations at ports, it is said that these were diminishing. But is not that an indication to the Government that they should not, without further consideration, enact the provisions giving them a title to over-ride the local authorities? It is said that this is a very short cut towards improvement in a matter like this, but probably it will be found to be the longest way round in the end. Local authorities have been apathetic hitherto in administration in regard to education, but I do not see that that affords ground for this House acting in such a way as will inevitably paralyse altogether the action of the local authorities. You have got two courses open. You should provide better information on the subject of adulteration to the local authorities in all parts of the country, when they would assuredly recognise their responsibilities in the matter, and work more actively to repress adulteration. You cannot expect people to move unless they feel what is complained of. The evils are far more acute in the large towns, where the catering for the necessities of life are in the hands of large contractors, than in the country districts, and I therefore deplore altogether the very stringent proposals of the Bill giving power to the central authority to over-ride the local authorities. It deprives the local authorities of responsibility, and centralises the administration to a degree that is not justifiable. As a matter of fact, the country does not know what the provisions of the Bill really mean. The Bill was only introduced on Monday last, and discussed for the first time on Thursday. The great number of telegrams which have been received by a large number of Members on both sides of the House in regard to many of the provisions in the Bill is sufficient proof that traders, manufacturers, and retail dealers have not yet realised what the provisions of the Bill really mean. There is great misapprehension as to the Clause dealing with warranty, and in regard to that and many other points there is a great want of information and knowledge. I must confess that if the President of the Board of Agriculture is satisfied with the reception given to the Bill he must be a very sanguine man, for there is no Member of the House who has not taken one objection or another to its provisions. I am certain if my honourable Friend who moved the rejection of the Bill has not a large following, he, at any rate, has the sympathy of many honourable Members on both sides of the House. I object to the proposed over-riding of the local authorities to the Clause which prevents the mixing of butter with margarine, and also to the fact that the Bill from first to last is a Bill dealing with the interests of agriculture and not with the interests of the general consumer—as all previous Adulteration Acts have done—and the general consumer, it should be remembered, includes the agriculturist.

*General LAURIE (Pembroke and Haverfordwest): I think that the object of the Bill was very aptly described by the honourable Member for the Thirsk Division of Yorkshire. The policy of the Bill, he said, was inspection, detection, and punishment. In regard to the first two of these—inspection and detection— I think that the local authorities have distinctly their work to do. And the question is whether they have fairly done it or not. Now, I have in my hand a return from the whole of the local authorities in London, showing how they have tried to put the Adulteration Acts in force and how utterly impossible it has been for them to do so satisfactorily owing to their inability to obtain the

fruits of the third object of the Acts— namely, the punishment. Local authority after local authority has spent large sums in obtaining convictions, but the penalties inflicted were trifling. Take the case of Rotherhithe. They spent £124 in prosecutions but only obtained £31 in penalties. St. Mary's, Newington, spent £250 besides analyst's fees, and only obtained penalties of £134. It is absolutely impossible for local authorities to carry out the provisions of the Acts if the magistrates inflict such small fines. The vestry in which I have the honour of a seat carried case after case into court at an average cost of £5 each, and in many cases they only obtained a 5s. fine against the adulterator. In my experience it is not merely a question of margarine, it is not merely a question of dealing with imported articles, it is a question of adulteration producer and get into the hands of the after the goods leave the hands of the distributors. Some honourable Members have taken up the case of the shopkeepers, and some the case of the farmers. I take up the case of the consumer. It is the consumer that ought to be protected, and not until we are able to get the laws enforced—it may be by the strength of the public opinion— shall we get the magistrates to inflict adequate penalties. From 1893 to 1895 it is true the fines have increased occasionally above 5s., but they have often been much less. It is absurd to ask a local body to go into court and spend £5 in obtaining a judgment if the magistrate only inflicts a fine of 1s. or even 5s. Why, in one case where it was proved that the so-called butter was adulterated with 60 per cent. of margarine, the fine imposed was only 1s., while the solicitor's costs alone were £2 10s., without reckoning all the other costs. If the local bodies are not enabled to obtain support from the magistrates they will, after a time, give up attempting to enforce the law. After the charges brought against the local authorities in this House I felt that it was only right that I should, on their behalf, show that they had done the best in their power to attempt to enforce the law, and that the failure in the successful enforcement of the law has not been on their side, but has rested

Q

on the magistrates over whom they have no control whatever. I am very doubtful in regard to the Clause with regard to the warranty. Action must be taken within 28 days. By the time the sample is taken, and the analysis is made, and action is taken against the original seller, a week has passed probably. Within seven days the seller has the right of pleading that the warranty is a sufficient defence. You then have to go, in the case of milk, to the shipper out in the country, and serve notice on him. He has again seven days privilege before he produces the warranty of the original seller, and, in fact, the 28 days are gone and the local authority is left absolutely helpless. This warranty Clause should be changed, and the person who sells the adulterated article should be held responsible. And the remedy should be against the person who has given the warranty. I hope that the warranty Clause will be amended in Committee.

THE FIRST LORD OF THE TREASURY: I appeal to the House to bring the discussion to a close. I have followed this Debate, and I gather the general impression that the view of the House, whatever the opinion of the honourable Members may be as to the particular Clauses, is strongly in favour of the Second Reading of the Bill. Of all the speeches made I have heard not one which has been directed against the main principle of the Measure, unless I except the speech of the honourable Member for one of the divisions of Glasgow. Under these circumstances, I think it is not unreasonable that the Debate, which has been carried on for the best part of two nights, should be brought to a close, and the Bill read a Second Time, and allowed to go to the Grand Committee.

HONOURABLE MEMBERS: No, No!

THE FIRST LORD OF THE TREASURY: I do not prejudge that now; but to go to Committee. An appeal was made by the honourable Member for Aberdeen, who said, with great force, that it was only right that the country should have a chance of seeing what the provisions of the Bill are. Sympathising with the full strength of that feeling the Government are willing that the Committee stage—whether in Grand Committee or Committee of the whole House—should not be unduly pressed; but I think that it is generally agreed that the Second Reading of the Bill should now be taken. But inasmuch as after all the objections that have been raised to this Bill there seems to be a general desire upon the part of the House that it should be proceeded with, I ask you now to allow us to proceed with an important, though not a very controversial, Measure, by letting us get the Second Reading of the Bill.

MR. DILLON: This Bill is one which I confess I am certainly in favour of myself, though I do not think it goes far enough. It is a contentious Bill, and one upon which I certainly do think a great many of the Members of the Committee would like to have a say, both those in favour and those who are opposed to it.

THE FIRST LORD OF THE TREASURY: That is a matter for the Committee.

MR. DILLON: Yes, no doubt, but then we may not be upon the Committee. But I do not intend to delay the progress of the Bill, because, as I have before remarked, I am myself in favour of it. I only rise for the purpose of pointing out to the House two, in my opinion, important points. The first point is as to the objection to the colouring which is put into margarine in order to make it look like butter. I perfectly agree with the honourable Gentleman the Member for Cork in the views he put forward to the House upon this particular point. The real point is whether margarine should be allowed to be coloured to look like butter for the purposes of fraud. There is nothing æsthetic or particularly beautiful in the colour of butter, and red or pink or blue are just as good as the colour of butter. Then, why should people who sell margarine desire to colour it like butter. It is in order that they should sell it under the fraudulent name of butter. We do not object to their colouring margarine in any way which they think will be æsthetic or beautiful in itself, and which is not distasteful to those who purchase it, but we do object to their colouring it in such a way as to enable them to sell it at a larger price and in a fraudulent manner. But when it is said that if you prohibit the colouring of margarine you must also prohibit the colouring of butter, that is an argument which, I confess, I do not follow. Butter is not coloured to conceal its real essence; it is butter, and it is sold as butter. But margarine is so coloured as to be sold as butter, which it really is not. Now, there is another point to which we in Ireland attach very great importance, which, in my opinion, is not fully or satisfactorily dealt with in this Bill, and that is the question of adulteration by water. Of course, everybody knows there is a class of butter coming from Ireland, largely sold in this country, and particularly in the North of England, which is butter of a very excellent quality, and owing to the diverse opinions of the magistrates upon the law it has been condemned in some districts, whilst in others it has been approved by those magistrates who take a different view. This Irish salt butter, as it is called, is a well-known article of commerce; but in addition to salt, it contains a large proportion of water. But everybody knows that, and this butter is bought upon its merits. Now, what we in Ireland want to know is, how much water will be allowed in butter? and then we shall be prepared to meet the standard laid down by the statute. It certainly does seem to me to be a very great injustice to the people of Ireland that they should be called upon to send their butter over to England, not knowing if it is going to be condemned in Manchester and approved in Liverpool. If there is to be allowed so much water in butter—and it must be larger in salt butter than in fresh—the Irish people can meet that fact accordingly. That is a point which, in the opinion of the Irish representatives in this House, ought to be attended to. I do not desire to increase the difficulties of the promoters of this Bill, but what I do earnestly press upon the Government is this—that it is most desirable that this Bill should be referred to a Grand Committee. Now, if they do send it to a Grand Committee, they ought to add to the Committee a full representation of the classes interested in this very important matter.

Mr. ALLEN (Newcastle-under-Lyme): This is a Bill which very greatly affects the wholesale manufacturers of margarine, and therefore I would ask the House to allow me to say just a few words upon a Measure which so much affects that interest. In the first place, I wish most emphatically to protest against the wholesale allegations of fraud that have been levelled at the manufacturers of margarine by honourable Gentlemen who have spoken upon this subject from both sides of the House. The manufacturers take every possible precaution to insure that this article shall be sold for nothing else but what it is, and if it is sold in a fraudulent way, as butter or anything else, they always very strongly condemn and resent it. Now, I do not believe that the House really knows what a very great industry it will kill if it passes the 8th Clause of this Bill, which provides that margarine can only be sold with 10 per cent. of butter in it. A very large quantity of margarine sold in this country contains 20 per cent. and 25 per cent. of butter in it, and the company with which I am connected opened a large margarine manufactory in Yorks, and all the margarine manufactured in the manufactory contains a very much larger amount of butter than 10 per cent. The margarine brought to England from abroad contains less than 10 per cent. So that if this Bill is passed; the English industry of margarine is destroyed. It will be killed, whilst the foreign manufacture of margarine will be fostered and encouraged. What you are going to do by this Bill, if it becomes law, is to encourage the manufacture of the poorer class of margarine and kill the better class article altogether. We have heard from honourable Gentlemen in various parts of the House that butter is very much more nutritious and wholesome than margarine, and if that is the case we are going, by this Bill, to prevent people who cannot always afford to buy butter from buying good margarine which contains 40 or 50 per cent. of the more nutritious and wholesome article, butter, in it. There are three classes of people in this country. There are the rich, who wholly confine themselves to butter; the artisan class, who cannot always afford to buy butter in the dearer seasons of the year, and who buy the better class margarine—they cannot always afford butter, but they can always afford margarine of the better grade at 10d. a pound; and there are the poorer classes, who buy inferior margarine. Now, by this Bill, you are going to allow us to sell this poor class of margarine, and going to prevent us from selling the better class article altogether. You are going, if this Bill passes into law, to destroy a very great industry, in which in this country a very large amount of capital is invested. And if I can find anybody to tell with me, I shall certainly divide the House upon this question, and oppose the Bill so far as lies in my power.

*Sir J. LENG (Dundee): Having sat on the Committee which inquired into this matter upstairs, and having taken some interest in the proceedings, I should now like, if I might trespass upon the patience of the House for a short time, to say a few words upon this subject. My doing so might be avoided if there were an understanding arrived at that a Bill of this great importance should be considered by a Committee of the whole House. The observation made recently by the honourable Gentleman the Member for Mayo that there was a distinct grievance upon a very important point forms the crux of the whole question. How is margarine to be dealt with? In the Committee upstairs an effort was made—and to some extent the idea was adopted in the Report of the Committee, very much against the views of a strong minority of the Committee —that margarine, which it was admitted was a nutritious, wholesome, and useful article of food, should be either entirely discoloured and sold in the same way as lard, or it should be coloured in some distinctive manner so as to distinguish it from anything else, and be coloured pink or blue. We have even heard during the discussion to-night proposals which in some respects may be thought to be of a loyal character that we should have it coloured red, white, and blue. The idea of all these proposals is to make this nutritious article of food distasteful in appearance ; in fact, to rule it out as an article of food altogether. The only justification that there can possibly be for introducing any Measure of this kind is that it shall protect the public health and that it shall enforce individual honesty. Now, none of those who sit upon this side of the House wish the public, and especially the poor, either to be poisoned or robbed. We are in favour of honest dealing, and we will support any Measure for which necessity can be shown to secure the honest dealing. But many of us think that, under the Margarine Act as it exists, very ample protection is secured

for the poor in this matter. Margarine can only be sold in parcels which have upon the package the word Margarine printed in large letters, and it has been admitted during the Debate that the fault is not so much in the state of the law that at present exists as it is in the administration of it, and a very large number of us would be very glad to support any Measure which would give more power to the agents of the authorities to enforce the law. I must say, with regard to Scotland, with which I am more particularly familiar, that if an attempt were made to override and coerce the local authorities, it would be stoutly resisted. The proposed limitation as to the colouring of margarine and butter, as has been pointed out in the course of the Debate, is an innovation in our legislation. There is no precedent which I know of and upon which it can be based. You are under these proposals about to interfere with the carrying on of a legitimate business. Why do you not attempt the same thing in other directions? Why do you not apply it to beer? Will the right honourable Gentleman the President of the Board of Agriculture venture to introduce any Measure fixing the proportion of hops and malt to be used in the manufacture of beer? Much less will he attempt to prevent other admixtures, though some of them are known to be manifestly injurious and deleterious. If you adopt this proposal you will establish a precedent for all kinds of mischievous and meddlesome interference with the carrying on of legitimate businesses. As far as regards the admixture of margarine and butter is concerned, I think at present any such admixture can be sold as margarine providing you give notice to the purchaser. The poor can frequently have the means to purchase an honest and fair mixture of these two articles when they could not afford the means to purchase butter itself. No doubt, in many cases the love of cheapness comes into play : in some respects that is a curse. But you have to deal with human nature as you find it, and many prefer a cheap article if they can get it, and so long as it is not harmful and mischievous they are entitled to purchase it. We know how women especially love to purchase a bargain, and you have no right to interfere with them in doing so. It is for the persons themselves to exercise their own judgment as to what they shall purchase. I must congratulate the honourable Gentleman who introduced this Bill, in so far that it is a much less mischievous and meddlesome Measure than I was prepared to expect, and I am very thankful for small mercies. It is a comparatively small Measure, and is neither complicated nor intricate; but it contains elements of great importance, and we are entitled, as there appears to be a great divergence of opinion on the different sides of the House, to discuss it in Committee of the whole House, and not to send it to a Committee where we shall lose all control over it in the future. Therefore, unless the right honourable

Gentleman is prepared to signify his willingneśs that it shall be discussed in the manner in which I suggest, I shall certainly oppose it.

THE FIRST LORD OF THE TREASURY: I move that the Question be now put.

MR. CALDWELL, (Lanark, Mid): Upon a point of order, may I ask whether the Question can be put, having regard to the fact that the Deputy Speaker is in the Chair.

Question put—

"That the Question be now put."

The House divided:—Ayes, 164: Noes, 55.—(Division List No. 36.)

AYES.

Acland-Hood, Capt. Sir A. F
Allhusen, Augustus Henry E.
Allsopp, Hon. George
Archdale Edward Mervyn
Arnold-Forster, Hugh O.
Atkinson, Rt. Hon. John
Balcarres, Lord
Balfour, Rt. Hn. A. J. (Manc'r
Balfour,RtHn GeraldW.(Leeds
Banbury, Frederick George
Barton, Dunbar Plunket
Bathurst, Hon. Allen Benjamin
Beach,Rt.Hn.Sir M.H.(Brstl.)
Beckett, Ernest William
Bemrose, Sir Henry Howe
Bentinck, Lord Henry C.
Bethell, Commander
Bigwood, James
Bill, Charles
Blundell, Colonel Henry
Boulnois, Edmund
Bowles, T. G. (King's Lynn)
Brodrick, Rt. Hon. St. John
Cavendish, V.C.W. (Derbysh.)
Cecil, Evelyn (Hertford, East
Cecil, Lord Hugh (Greenwich
Chaloner, Captain R. G. W.
Chamberlain, J. A. (Worc'r)
Chaplin, Rt. Hon. Henry
Cohen, Benjamin Louis
Collings, Rt. Hon. Jesse
Colston, Charles E. H. Athol
Corbett, A. Cameron (Glasgow
Cranborne, Viscount
Curzon, Viscount
Dalbiac, Colonel Philip Hugh
Dalkeith, Earl of
Dalrymple, Sir Charles
Denny, Colonel
Dixon-Hartland, Sir Fred. D
Doughty, George
Douglas, Rt. Hon. A. Akers-
Dyke, Rt.Hn. Sir William Hart
Fergusson,Rt.Hn SirJ.(Manc'r
Field, Admiral (Eastbourne)
Finch, George H.
Finlay, Sir Robert Bannatyne
Fisher, William Hayes
Fletcher, Sir Henry

Flower, Ernest
Fry, Lewis
Garfit, William
Gibbs, Hn.A.G.H.(City of Lon.
Giles, Charles Tyrrell
Godson, Sir Augustus Fred.
Goldsworthy, Major-General
Gordon, Hon. John Edward
Gorst, Rt. Hon. Sir John E.
Goschen, George J. (Sussex)
Graham, Henry Robert
Gray, Ernest (West Ham)
Gretton, John
Greville, Hon. Ronald
Gull, Sir Cameron
Hanbury, Rt. Hon. Robt. W
Hardy, Laurence
Hare, Thomas Leigh
Haslett, Sir James Horner
Heath, James
Helder, Augustus
Hill, Sir Edw. Stock (Bristol
Houston, R. P.
Howell, William Tudor
Hubbard, Hon. Evelyn
Hudson, George Bickersteth
Hutton, John (Yorks. N.R.)
Jeffreys, Arthur Frederick
Johnston, William (Belfast)
Johnstone, Heywood (Sussex
Kennaway, Rt. Hon. Sir J. H
Kenyon, James
Keswick, William
Kimber, Henry
Kinloch, Sir John Geo. Smyth
Lafone, Alfred
Laurie, Lieut.-General
Lawrence.SirE.Durning·(Corn
Lawson, John Grant (Yorks.)
Lea, Sir Thos. (Londonderry)
Lees, Sir Elliott (Birkenhead)
Leigh Bennett, Henry Currie
Lockwood, Lt.-Col. A. R.
Loder, Gerald Walter Erskine
Long, Col. Chas. W.(Evesham)
Long, Rt. Hon. W. (Liverpool)
Lopes, Henry Yarde Buller
Lowe, Francis William
Lucas-Shadwell, William

Macartney, W. G. Ellison
Macdona, John Cumming
Maclure, Sir John William
M'Arthur, Charles (Liverpool
M'Killop, James
Maple, Sir John Blundell
Meysey-Thompson, Sir H. M.
Middlemore, John T.
Monk, Charles James
Moore, Arthur (Londonderry
Moore, William (Antrim, N.)
More, Robt. J. (Shropshire)
Morrell, George Herbert
Morton, A. H. A. (Deptford
Murray, Rt. Hon. A. G. (Bute)
Myers, William Henry
Newark, Viscount
Newdigate, Francis Alexander
Nicholson, William Graham
Nicol, Donald Ninian
Northcote, Hon. Sir H.Stafford
O'Brien, Patrick (Kilkenny)
O'Connor Arthur (Donegal)
O'Kelly, James
Orr-Ewing, Charles Lindsay
Parkes, Ebenezer
Phillpotts, Captain Arthur
Pierpoint, Robert
Platt-Higgins, Frederick
Pretyman, Ernest George
Pryce-Jones, Lt.-Col. Edward
Purvis, Robert
Pym, C. Guy
Rasch, Major Frederic Carne
Bentoul, James Alexander
Ritchie, Rt.Hn.Chas. Thomson
Robertson, Herbert (Hackney)
Round, James
Royds, Clement Molyneux
Russell, T. W. (Tyrone)
Sandys, Lt.-Col. Thos. Myles
Seely, Charles Hilton
Sidebottom,William (Derbysh.
Skewes-Cox, Thomas
Smith, Abel H (Christchurch)
Smith, Hon. W. F. D. (Strand)
Stanley, Edwd. Jas (Somerset'
Stanley, Lord (Lancs.)
Stewart, Sir M. J. M'Taggart

Strauss, Arthur
Sturt, Hon. Humphry Napier
Talbot. Lord E. (Chichester)
Thorburn, Walter
Valentia, Viscount
Wanklyn, James Leslie
Ward, Hon. Robert A. (Crewe)

Webster, Sir R. E (I. of W.)
Whiteley, George (Stockport)
Whitmore, Charles Algernon
Williams, Jos. Powell- (Birm.)
Willox, Sir John Archibald
Wilson, John (Falkirk)
Wilson-Todd, Wm. H. (Yorks.)

Wodehouse, Rt.Hn.E.R.(Bath
Wylie, Alexander
Wyndham-Quin, Major W. H.

TELLERS FOR THE AYES—
Sir William Walrond and
Mr. Anstruther.

NOES.

Allen, W. (Newc.-under-Lyme)
Ascroft, Robert
Ashton, Thomas Gair
Barlow, John Emmott
Bilson. Alfred
Bryce, Rt. Hon. James
Burt, Thomas
Buxton, Sydney Charles
Cameron, Robert (Durham)
Clough, Walter Owen
Colville, John
Davies,M.Vaughan-(Cardigan
Douglas, Charles M. (Lanark)
Ellis, Thos. Ed. (Merionethsh.
Farquharson, Dr. Robert
Fenwick, Charles
Foster, Sir Walter (Derby Co.
Harwood, George
Hedderwick, Thomas Chas. H.
Johnson-Ferguson, Jabez Edw

Jones, Wm. (Carnarvonshire)
Lambert, George
Leng, Sir John
Lewis, John Herbert
Lough, Thomas
Macaleese, Daniel
M'Arthur, William (Cornwall)
Maddison, Fred.
Mendl, Sigismund Ferdinand
Molloy, Bernard Charles
Montagu. Sir S. (Whitechapel)
Morton, Ed. J. C. (Devonport)
Moulton, John Fletcher
O'Connor, T. P. (Liverpool)
Oldroyd, Mark
Palmer, George W. (Reading
Pearson, Sir Weetman D.
Philipps, John Wynford
Pickersgill, Edward Hare
Pirie, Duncan V.

Power, Patrick Joseph
Randall, David
Roberts. John Bryn (Eifion)
Spicer, Albert
Stuart, James (Shoreditch)
Sullivan, Donal (Westmeath)
Tanner, Charles Kearns
Thomas, Alfd. (Glamorgan, E.)
Thomas, David Alf. (Merthyr
Walton, Joseph (Barnsley)
Warner, Thomas Courtenay
Whittaker, Thomas Palmer
Wilson, John (Govan)
Woods, Samuel
Yoxall, James Henry

TELLERS FOR THE NOES—Mr
Caldwell and Sir Charles
Cameron.

Question put accordingly—
"That the word 'now' stand part of the
Question."

The House divided:—Ayes, 212;
Noes, 18.—(Division List No. 37.)

AYES.

Acland-Hood, Capt. Sir A. F
Allhusen, Augustus H. Eden
Allsopp, Hon. George
Archdale, Edward Mervyn
Arnold-Forster, Hugh O.
Ashton, Thomas Gair
Atkinson, Rt. Hon. John
Austin, M. (Limerick, W.)
Balcarres, Lord
Balfour, Rt.Hon.A.J.(Manch'
Balfour, Rt.Hon.G.W.(Leeds
Banbury, Frederick George
Barlow, John Emmott
Barton, Dunbar Plunket
Bathurst, Hon. Allen Benj.
Beach,Rt.Hn.SirM.H.(Bristl.)
Beckett, Ernest William
Bentinck, Lord Henry C.
Bethell, Commander
Bigwood, James
Bill, Charles
Billson, Alfred
Blundell, Colonel Henry
Boulnois, Edmund
Bowles, T. Gibson(King's Lyn
Brodrick, Rt. Hon. St. John
Burt, Thomas
Cameron, Robert (Durham)
Cavendish, V.C.W. (Derbysh
Cecil, Evelyn (Hertford, East
Cecil, Lord Hugh (Greenwich
Chaloner, Captain R. G. W.
Chamberlain, J. A. (Worc'r
Chaplin, Rt. Hon. Henry
Coghill' Douglas Harry
Cohen, Benjamin Louis
Collings, Rt. Hon. Jesse

Colston, Chas. E. H. Athole
Corbett, A. Cameron (Glasgow
Cranborne, Viscount
Crilly, Daniel
Curzon, Viscount
Dalbiac, Colonel Philip Hugh
Dalkeith, Earl of
Dalrymple, Sir Charles
Davies, M.Vaughan-(Cardigan
Denny, Colonel
Dillon, John
Dixon-Hartland, Sir Fred. D
Donelan, Captain A.
Doughty, George
Douglas, Rt. Hon. A. Akers-
Douglas, Chas. M. (Lanark)
Dyke, Rt. Hon. Sir Wm. H.
Elliot, Hon. A. Ralph Douglas
Evans, Samuel T. (Glamorgan
Farquharson, Dr. Robert
Fenwick, Charles
Fergusson,Rt.Hn.SirJ.(Manc'r
Field, Admiral (Eastbourne)
Finch, George H.
Finlay, Sir Robert Bannatyne
Fisher, William Hayes
FitzGerald, Sir Robt. Penrose
Fletcher, Sir Henry
Flower, Ernest
Foster, Sir Walter (Derby Co
Fry, Lewis
Garfit, William
Gedge, Sydney
Gibbs,Hn.A.G.H.(City of Lon
Giles, Charles Tyrrell
Godson, Sir Augustus Fredk.
Goldsworthy, Major-General

Gordon, Hon. John Edward
Gorst, Rt. Hon. Sir John E.
Goschen, George J. (Sussex)
Graham, Henry Robert
Gretton, John
Greville, Hon. Ronald
Gull, Sir Cameron
Halsey, Thomas Frederick
Hanbury, Rt. Hon. Robert W
Hardy, Laurence
Hare, Thomas Leigh
Haslett, Sir James Horner
Heath, James
Hedderwick, Thomas Chas. H.
Helder, Augustus
Hill, Sir Edward S.(Bristol)
Houston, R. P.
Howell, William Tudor
Hubbard, Hon. Evelyn
Hudson, George Bickersteth
Hutton, John (Yorks. N.R.)
Jeffreys, Arthur Frederick
Johnson-Ferguson, Jabez E.
Johnston, William (Belfast)
Johnstone, Heywood (Sussex
Kearley, Hudson E.
Kennaway, Rt. Hon. Sir J. H
Kenyon, James
Keswick, William
Kilbride, Denis
Kimber, Henry
Kinloch, Sir John Geo. Smyth
Lafone, Alfred
Lambert, George
Laurie, Lieut.-General
Lawrence,SirE.Duruing-(Corn
Lawson, John Grant (Yorks.)

Lea, Sir Thomas (Londonderry)
Lees, Sir Elliott (Birkenhead)
Leigh-Bennett, Henry Currie
Leng, Sir John
Lockwood, Lieut.Col. A. R.
Loder, Gerald Walter Erskine
Long, Col. C. W. (Evesham)
Long, Rt. Hn. W. (Liverpool)
Lopes, Henry Yarde Buller
Lowe, Francis William
Lowles, John
Lucas-Shadwell, William
Macaleese, Daniel
Macartney, W. G. Ellison
Macdona, John Cumming
Maclure, Sir John William
MacNeill, John Gordon Swift
M'Arthur, Charles (Liverpool)
M'Arthur, William (Cornwall)
M'Kenna, Reginald
M'Killop, James
Maddison, Fred. .
Maple, Sir John Blundell
Massey-Mainwaring, Hn.W.F.
Mendl, Sigismund Ferdinand
Meysey-Thompson, Sir H. M.
Middlemore, John T.
Molloy, Bernard Charles
Monk, Charles James
Montagu, Sir S. (Whitechapel)
Moore, Arthur (Londonderry)
Moore, William (Antrim, N.)
More, Robt. Jasper (Shropsh.)
Morrell, George Herbert
Morton, A. H. A. (Deptford)

Moulton, John Fletcher
Murray, Rt. Hon. A. G. (Bute)
Murray, Charles J. (Coventry)
Myers, William Henry
Newark, Viscount
Newdigate, Francis Alexander
Nicholson, William Graham
Nicol, Donald Ninian
Northcote, Hon.Sir H.Stafford
O'Brien, Patrick (Kilkenny)
O'Connor, T. P. (Liverpool)
O'Kelly, James
O'Malley, William
Orr-Ewing, Charles Lindsay
Palmer, Geo. Wm. (Reading)
Parkes, Ebenezer
Pearson, Sir Weetman D.
Philipps, John Wynford
Fhillpotts, Captain Arthur
Pierpoint, Robert
Pirie, Duncan V.
Platt-Higgins, Frederick
Power, Patrick Joseph
Pretyman, Ernest George
Pryce-Jones, Lt.-Col. Edward
Purvis, Robert
Pym, C. Guy
Randell, David
Rasch, Major Frederic Carne
Rentoul, James Alexander
Ritchie, Rt. Hn. Chas.Thomson
Robertson, Herbert (Hackney)
Round James
Royds, Clement Molyneux
Russell, T. W. (Tyrone)

Sandys, Lt.-Col. Thos Myles
Seely, Charles Hilton
Sidebottom,William(Derbysh.)
Skewes-Cox, Thomas
Smith, Abel H. (Christchurch)
Smith,'Hon. W. F. D. (Strand)
Stanley, Ed. Jas. (Somerset)
Stanley, Lord (Lancs.)
Stewart, Sir M. J. M'Taggart
Strauss, Arthur
Stuart, James (Shoreditch)
Sturt, Hn. Humphry Napier
Talbot, Lord E. (Chichester)
Tanner, Charles Kearns
Thorburn, Walter
Valentia, Viscount
Walton, Joseph (Barnsley)
Ward, Hon. Robert A. (Crewe)
Warner, Thos. Courtenay T.
Webster, Sir R.E.(I. ofWight)
Whiteley, George (Stockport)
Whitmore, Charles Algernon
Williams, Jos. Powell (Birm.)
Willox, Sir John Archibald
Wilson, John (Falkirk)
Wilson-Todd, Wm. H. (Yorks.
Wodehouse, Rt.Hn.E.R.(Bath)
Woods, Samuel
Wylie, Alexander
Wyndham, George
Wyndham-Quin, Major W. H.

Tellers for the Ayes—Sir ·
  William Walrond and Mr.
  Anstruther.

NOES.

Allen, W. (Newc.-under-Lyme)
Ascroft, Robert
Caldwell, James
Clough, Walter Owen
Colville, John
Harwood, George
Lewis, John Herbert

Oldroyd, Mark
Pickersgill, Edward Hare
Roberts, John Bryn (Eifion)
Spicer, Albert
Sullivan, Donal (Westmeath)
Thomas,Alfred(Glamorgan,E.)
Thomas,David Alfd.(Merthyr)

Wallace, Robert (Edinburgh)
Whittaker, Thomas Palmer
Wilson, John (Govan)
Yoxall, James Henry

Tellers for the Noes—Mr.
  Lough and Sir C. Cameron.

Main Question put, and agreed to.

Bill read a second time.

Motion made, and Question proposed—

"That the Bill be committed to the Standing Committee on Trade, etc."

Debate adjourned till Monday next.

METROPOLITAN WATER COMPANIES BILL.

On the Motion—

"That this Bill be now read a Second time,"

Mr. STUART (Shoreditch, Hoxton): When this Bill was introduced I refrained from making any remarks upon it, feeling that we should know exactly the details of the Bill before we should trust ourselves to comment upon it. I must to some extent complain, Sir, that this Bill should be brought forward so late in the evening as this, when it affects

such very large interests as this Bill undoubtedly does affect. More particularly I wish to make complaint of the bringing forward of the Bill now, because of the way in which the Bill has been brought before the House. The House will observe that at the top of the Bill are the words, "To be substituted for the Bill previously delivered."

The PRESIDENT of the LOCAL GOVERNMENT BOARD (Mr. Chaplin, Lincolnshire, Sleaford): The honourable Member is perfectly right, and perhaps he will allow me to make an explanation. It is perfectly true that on the top of the Bill are the words, "To be substituted for the Bill previously delivered." The substitution occurs in the sub-section of clause 2, in a proviso. What I have to say is this. As the Bill left my hands, as authorised to go to the printer, it contained that proviso, and the mistake is entirely the printers. How it has arisen I do not know. That proviso embodies a recommendation of the Royal Commission, and, though I am speaking from memory only, I am pretty certain I am right when I say that that proviso has been in every draft of the Bill from the first time it was drawn.

MR. STUART: Of course, as a private Member of the House I cannot be aware what was the case in the previous drafts, but let me say that I thoroughly accept the explanation of the origin of this paragraph that the right honourable Gentleman gives. But, while that is the explanation, which I frankly accept, of the origin of this paragraph, yet, it does not diminish the effect of the paragraph, and the enormous difference to the whole Bill that is made by the introduction of this paragraph. As the Bill was first printed, I obtained early copies of it, as many other Members of this House must have done. I took my copy and I looked at it with some of my Friends, and, when I looked down to clause 2, which anyone acquainted with the London Water Question would immediately see was a very important clause in the Bill, and read that clause, I said, "I do not think there is any further need to discuss the Bill, because the Sinking Fund is in it." Now, Sir, you may imagine my surprise or discomfiture—I entirely clear the right honourable Gentleman of any of the fault in the matter—when, after having taken that decision, I found that there was a clause which excluded the operation of the Sinking Fund. Now, Sir, departing for a moment from the entrance of this particular clause, I may say that the whole Bill in its progress through this House up till now has been somewhat unfortunate, because its introduction as a public Bill, without due notice, helped it to pass through the Standing Orders Committee, and the Standing Orders Committee clearly by their decision were not satisfied with the steps which had been taken in the promotion of the Bill; and, as the House knows, an order was made that certain steps should be taken, or else the Bill should not be proceeded with. The House knows that in connection with a Bill affecting private interests notice would have to be given to those private interests concerned, and that that notice has not been given in respect to this Bill. I am sorry that the Government had not known what they were to do in this

matter at an earlier date, but, at the same time, I must admit that they probably did not receive in time to give this notice the Report of the Royal Commission upon which this Bill is founded, but all that proves is that that method of legislation whereby the Government refers to a Royal Commission a vital and important point, and does not itself make up its mind upon that point, is not a method of legislation which is conducive to the good order of proceedings in this House. As I have raised that question of the paragraph on the Sinking Fund, let me ask the House for a moment to look at what that matter means. Now, Sir, it would be quite impossible to discuss the Sinking Fund in the House itself or in a full Committee of this House. Everybody who is connected with, and who has been acquainted with, the extremely complicated conditions of the Sinking Fund, which have been established by degrees and gradually made clear and intelligible to the expert— everybody who knows the conditions and circumstances of that Sinking Fund must know this, that it is impossible for it to be properly considered, and it is impossible for the bearings of its inclusion or its omission from this Bill to be properly considered, without referring this Bill to a Select Committee, and I trust I may hope that that Select Committee will be one which can call for persons and documents, and hear counsel as in the form of an ordinary Private Bill.

THE PRESIDENT OF THE LOCAL GOVERNMENT BOARD: Yes.

MR. STUART: I am glad to hear that, and so far that will be an orderly and proper proceeding. I will not, therefore, endeavour for one moment to delay the House by any exposition of what the Sinking Fund is, but I will point out this, that for many years every Bill that has been passed into an Act connected with the London Water Companies has had introduced into it a clause which practically makes the public of London sharers in the profits which arise in connection with the new capital raised. That is the effect of the Sinking Fund, and that has never been excluded, in the end, from any Bill which has become an Act of late years, and I cannot see on what ground it can be excluded from the present Bill, excepting that the Royal Commission seems to have made a statement about it. Well, but I have followed, as no doubt Members on the other side of the House have done, the proceedings of the Royal Commission with very great care and attention, and I cannot say that they have at any point investigated the bearings of the Sinking Fund upon any such Measure as this. Now, they have not gone into the Sinking Fund at any length at all. The consequence is that, however that portion of the Report may have come to be made, it has never been based upon an inquiry into the effect of that fund, and the clauses connected with it. Now, before I pass from that point of the Bill, which I venture to say is an extremely important point of the Bill, let me say this, that the water companies have in many instances, and in all the instances in the present year before the House, introduced their Bills without the Sinking Fund, and when they complain of opposition to these Bills, and to expense incurred thereby, let me remind them, and remind the House, that a large portion of the expense which they have had to incur has been because they have not introduced that Sinking Fund clause, which has invariably been introduced by Committees before whom the Bills were contested. Well, now, it seems to me that this Bill bears the same character as the Bills which of late have been introduced by the water companies, and I should hope that before a Select Committee this question of the Sinking Fund would bear the same fate. But look a little earlier into the clause ; look at the last wording of this clause. That refers to this very matter before the Sinking Fund itself is excluded. There is a provision which says—clause 2, about line 25—" That they shall make it a condition of their assent." That is, the Local Government Board should make it a condition of their assent

" that the stock be raised in accordance with the provisions contained in the most recent Acts for the time being with reference to the issue of debenture stock by a metropolitan water company."

What are the most recent Acts for the time being, since these Acts differ amongst themselves? Is it to be the most recent Act, because then we could understand it ; or is it to be any definite Act? That clause, which is the most vital clause in the Bill, seems to me not only to have been essentially altered from its first appearance, but it also appears to me to be exceedingly loose

in its conception. Passing from that question, I want to look for one moment —and I can assure the House that I shall not delay them long, but this matter is very important for those for whom I speak—at the general spirit of the Bill. What is to be done by this Bill? Connections are to be made under the authority and direction of the Local Government Board between the various water companies for the purpose of supplying temporary deficiencies. Well, Sir, look at what one of the most immediate results of that is. It is that in respect to the vast water famine that may occur in London, the responsibility will attach to the Local Government Board, and not to the water companies. Now, I must say that I think that the right honourable Gentleman is adopting a responsibility for his Department which he will be sorry some day at having adopted, and I do say that he is liberating the companies, who have the right and are bound to supply the districts which they do supply, or part of the districts which they do supply—he is liberating them from a very proper responsibility. It is not that they do not come to Parliament for many facilities. They come to Parliament for many facilities, and they generally get those facilities. Now, as to connections of all these companies. There is only one company about which there has been any real difficulty in this matter, that is to say, the East London Water Company ; and the East London Water Company has already, largely by the assistance of the London County Council, which gave it leave to take the first supplies from the Blackwall Tunnel—I presume this from what their reports say—got as much water as its directors believe they require. Well, if you look at the evidence upon which this Bill is founded, you will see the most diverse views of the various water companies as to what should be done, and what is necessary to be done ; but at the same time, generally, you will see this expression on their behalf before the Royal Commission, that what they would do on this account would only be to meet the demands of public opinion, rather than the demands of any essential public necessity. Well, what is the principle upon which this Bill proceeds? It proceeds on the principle of supplying the East London Water Company—for that is what you must focus your eyes upon—with water which is to be given to it from other water companies. Now, what I want to know, in the first place, is, if those water companies are to be allowed to draw more water than they are at present drawing from the Thames, or what sanction is to be given to them? Is the sanction given in this Bill, or is it not? Well, it will be obvious that it is open to contention, and is contended——

AN HONOURABLE MEMBER: No!

MR. STUART: Stop a moment; you do not know what I am going to say. And is contended that the water companies, although having, some of them, statutory rights to draw a certain amount, are yet not at liberty to draw those amounts unless it is for their own requirements. Now, if that be so, where is the surplus that they can legally give the one to the other? I want an answer to that question, because it is upon the proposition that they have a surplus which they can supply that this Bill is founded. Now, in the claim that was made by the water companies, and is made, I believe, in the Bill which they are introducing, if I am not mistaken—they claim to have an absolute right to draw from the Thames for any purposes a certain statutory amount—or an amount claimed to be statutory—which they at present, in many instances, fall short of. I say again that this is not a clear matter at all—that they have a right to draw any water at all more than they need, each for its own requirements. But passing from that, I want to point out that I believe this Bill has taken up a wholly erroneous method of putting the matter right. The East London Water Company has too little water to serve those people whom it at present supplies, but it is at present supplying no fewer than a quarter of a million of persons who, if they did not supply them, could call upon the New River Company to supply them. That is so. There is a district in East London—as indeed is the case in almost all the areas served by the water companies—wherein these two water companies, the New River and the East London, overlap, and in which the inhabitants, if not supplied by the one, could be supplied by the other. The House must know very well that almost every area in London —almost every area—is within the limits of supply of at least two, in some cases three, and in one case four, water companies. If in the case where there are two water companies one was not supplying them, the inhabitants would have the right to call upon the other to supply them. The water companies, as I understand the matter, after looking into their origin, were established for the most part—at any rate the more recent ones were established—as competitive undertakings against the older ones, and they were therefore placed in areas which overlapped those of the older ones. But the House will observe that in the course of years they have come to terms with one another, each retiring within a more limited district than that which they had the power to serve. But which has retired? The company in all cases has retired which was at liberty to charge rates which had a less maximum than the other, and the company which has been left to supply the district is the company which has leave to charge the highest maximum; and then the consequence is that that area of London which might be supplied by the New River Company, or might be supplied by the East London Company, is now wholly supplied by the East London Company, and a quarter of a million of persons are being supplied by the East London Water Company who, if it did not supply them, would have leave to call upon the New River Company. And what is the result? The result is that a quarter of a million of persons pay £11,000 a year at the present moment more for their water than they would have if they had been allowed to be supplied by the New River Company— nay, more, they get a much worse water, because everybody knows that the New River Company is one of the very best companies in London—it is probably the best in London. It is a very fine undertaking, supplying good water, and treating its customers exceedingly well; and in a very large number of cases it is not reaching or levying the highest rate of charge that it might levy, although, as far as I know, the East London Water Company does so in practically every instance. I know very few other instances of water companies in London who are either so good in their supply or are so generous in their charges as the New River Company.

COLONEL LOCKWOOD (Essex, Epping): Does the honourable Member say that the East London Water Company supplies bad water? MR. STUART: The people in this large area are prevented from having the advantage of the New River Company's supply; and I think anybody who has the choice of getting the New River supply or the East London supply, even leaving the charges out of account, would not hesitate as to which he would take. COLONEL LOCKWOOD: Why? MR. STUART: That is my opinion. The consumer gets better treatment: Now, Sir, what are we going to do by this Bill? The East London Water Company, having taken on its back the quarter of a million persons who might be supplied by the New River Company, what does it now do? It goes to the New River Company, and it gets New River Company's water under this arrangement to supply indirect to these persons, and it supplies it at a higher price than that at which the New River Company would supply it direct. And what does this Bill do? This Bill stereotypes that position. The proper method of dealing with this matter would have been to confine the area which the East London Water Company supplies within the limit of the powers of that company to supply, and if these portions which might be supplied by the New River Company were cut off from the East London Company it would be a far better and more sensible and more just method of procedure. Then take the case of this Bill—for this Bill, as I pointed out, accepts the position that the East London Water Company shall supply people in areas which the New River Company would have to supply if the East London Water Company were not there, and then it arranges for the New River Company to supply the water, which it might supply direct, to the East London Company, and thereby charges the inhabitants £11,000 a year more than would be charged if they got that water direct. I say, therefore, that the whole idea of this Bill in dealing with this temporary difficulty is wrong— that the idea should not be to supply water from a cheap company to a company which can charge dear for it, and can collect more from the inhabitants, but it should be to rectify the boundaries of these various water companies' areas of supply, limiting them in their own areas to those districts which they can supply with their water, and not permitting them to go into other areas where a cheaper supply might be given direct. After having first pointed out in this Bill the immense question of the Sinking Fund, I have now pointed out what I believe to be the fundamental error in the whole Bill. But there is a point in the Bill where it says that—

" If the undertaking of any of the Metropolitan Water Companies is purchased within seven years from the passing of this Act, otherwise than by agreement, by any public body or trustee, nothing in this Act shall authorise the company to bring into account or make any claim in respect of any advantages conferred upon it by, or resulting from, the passing of this Act."

Well, that is, in other words, to prevent this Act increasing the saleable value of these companies. But, Sir, I remember very well when, two years ago, the Southwark and Vauxhall Water Company brought in a Bill which was introduced in this House for gaining access to larger supplies of water, I pointed out that that would increase their saleable value, and when I pointed that out it was stated that a clause of this kind would be introduced, and I pointed out then to the House that, even in respect of that clause, there would be a very large increase in the purchasable value of the company. I pointed out at that time that if the clause was not introduced there would be something like a million of money added to the value of the shares of that company. I found that, of course, that clause had had some effect in reducing that large sum, but whereas the shares of the Southwark and Vauxhall Water Company stood at something like 166 before that Act was passed, they stand at something like 200 at the present time. In other words, more than £300,000 has been added to the value of the shares of that company in the market by that procedure. Now, although that may, perhaps, enable any purchasing body to plead that the market value in these shares is in no sense a sign of what their purchasable or saleable value ought to be, still it is quite clear that the public believe in purchasing these shares, that the value of that company has permanently increased, and I venture to say that, even with this clause, such a Measure as this will raise the purchasable price of these companies. Sir, that is only one of the many proofs that we have had in the last few years of the extraordinary disadvantage to the ratepayers of London that the delays in the carrying through of a purchase scheme have created. As we have pointed out, if the water supply of London was in one hand, then all that this Bill contains would be done, and perfectly easily done, without the necessity of an Act of Parliament. This Bill is an endeavour to ride two horses at once ; in the one case, to continue the authorities that at present exist—namely, the water companies, for the supply of London ; and, in the other case, to introduce some system of unity or amalgamation. Sir, you have before you only two methods really of dealing with the water supply of London. One is amalgamation, and the other is purchase. So far as this Bill goes, it is an effort in the direction of amalgamation. I have endeavoured to show that it is faulty in the most important details, and that it is wrong entirely in the conception of how to remedy the difficulty.

*SIR F. DIXON-HARTLAND (Middlesex, Uxbridge): Sir, the honourable Gentleman who has spoken last has entirely missed the grand principle of this Bill. It is a Bill which it is difficult to attack by the special pleading to which he has given expression. The Bill is one which has been most carefully considered by the Thames Conservancy: it affects them very closely, and it is one to which they have given their most urgent attention. I can only say that the principle of this Bill is not to increase the powers of the water companies, but only to amalgamate them. Last year I brought in a Bill myself in this House which had a similar clause to the Government Bill—to allow the various companies to amalgamate during a certain time. That Bill was killed by the London County Council, which objected to it because they said that it did not agree with the Standing Orders. I am only too delighted to see this Bill brought before Parliament this year by the Government. The real object of this Bill is this: We are to take a step which is to make it impossible in future that a water famine should occur in any part of London, such as has existed, unfortunately, of late in East London. But if we look back upon the question of water famines in East London, we cannot forget this one point, that the East London Water Company applied—in

1893 I think it was—for leave to increase their storage capacity, and that Bill was thrown out at the instance of the London County Council, and if that storage had been allowed that year the water famine which has lately existed in the East London district, if it had existed at all, would have been very much curtailed to what it has been lately, and which we all so much deplore. I do think that this Bill is a grand Bill in this way, that it will prevent in future any feeling that one company which has more storage than another is unable to help the other company that wants water. I have no hesitation in saying that in the Thames there is enough water to supply London for a great number of years to come, if only it is taken in the proper way—that is, in the way of storage. What we object to is that the river should be run low in dry times. What we want is that navigation shall not be interfered with—as that is the primary interest and duty of the Conservancy—by having water drawn off when the river is at its lowest point, but that all the companies should take into large reservoirs the water which is running away to waste at other times of the year, and that those reservoirs should be used in times of drought, so as to supply London without diminishing the water required for the navigation of the River Thames. This Bill certainly has that effect. Enormous loss was incurred in East London in consequence of the water famine last year, but that loss would not again be incurred if this Bill became law, because the companies would have the power of helping one another. We think that this is a Bill which thoroughly deserves the attention of the House of Commons, and we understand that the rights of the Thames Conservancy are not in any way interfered with. These companies have a right to draw 130,000,000 gallons a day out of the Thames, but some of them draw considerably less than they are allowed to. The difference can be utilised in the way suggested, and if this Bill passes there is no doubt it would be used in that way, to the great benefit of London generally. What the London County Council think about the matter is nothing to us. We do not care two straws whether the passing of this Bill would increase the purchase value of the companies or not. What we have to look to is the benefit of London, and to see that there is no recurrence of the recent water famine. It has been proved before the Royal Commission that the Thames water is the finest water that can be supplied by any means whatever to this city, and there is no doubt that if this Bill is passed every part of London will have the advantage of that water. On behalf of the Conservancy, I strongly support this Bill, and I hope it will be passed into law.

THE PRESIDENT OF THE LOCAL GOVERNMENT BOARD: I apologise to the House for rising so early in the Debate, but the object of this Bill is so simple, time is of so much importance, the question is of such considerable urgency, and, moreover, the scope of the Bill is so strictly limited to one branch, and one branch alone, of what is called the London Water Question, that I shall not detain the House except at very short length. I hope, therefore, the House will allow me to make an appeal to them to pass a Second Reading of this Bill. My honourable Friend opposite, who spoke first in this Debate, complained, in the first place, that we should take this Bill at so late an hour. We are obliged to cut our coat according to our cloth, and it was not within my power to do what I should have liked to have done—namely, to have taken the Bill earlier. The honourable Member said the Bill was introduced without the due notices that ought to have been given with regard to a Bill of this kind. I frankly acknowledge that that is true, but it was impossible for the Government to give the necessary notice on this occasion, and for this reason—which I think the honourable Member will admit is conclusive—that the Bill is founded and based upon the Report and recommendations of the Royal Commission, and the Report of the Royal Commission was not issued until a period after the date on which these notices ought to have been delivered. It was, therefore, absolutely impossible for me to comply with that rule which usually holds good in these cases. Then the honourable Member complained of that provision in the Bill which exempts the companies for these particular works from the operation of what is known as

the provisions with regard to the Sinking Fund. The honourable Member said—

"Every Bill of late years has contained a clause which makes the public sharers in the profits which are to be provided by this investment of capital."

But in this particular case, so far as I have been able to ascertain, there are going to be no profits in which the public can share. The honourable Member threw some doubt upon the opinions of the Royal Commission, but still the Royal Commission has had the opportunity of hearing everything that can be said for and against this particular provision, and the conclusion which they came to was a very simple one. It was this—

"It was contended before us, on behalf of the companies, that, inasmuch as the money raised by the issue of debenture stock could not yield revenue or profit to the companies, the Sinking Fund clauses, which are founded on the assumption that the debenture capital is expended so as to produce revenue and profit, were not applicable in this case. We think that there is force in this contention, and that this debenture stock might be exempted from the application of the sinking fund clauses."

On this point it is really a question between the opinion of the honourable Member opposite and the opinion of the Royal Commission. Though I value the opinion of the honourable Member, I prefer, without any disrespect to him, to rely upon the information of the Royal Commission. Then the honourable Member said the Local Government Board were taking a very great responsibility upon themselves. Well, Sir, that may be the case, and if it is so I am quite ready to take it, having regard to the great object which we have in view. What is that object? That object is to prevent, so far as it is possible for us to do so, any recurrence of the curtailment of the water supply in the East End of London, which inflicted so much hardship and suffering during the prolonged summer upon thousands of the poorer inhabitants. Nobody who has witnessed the results of water famine in the East End of London, as I have done myself, can fail to sympathise strongly with the objects of this Bill. The honourable Member also asks whether the Bill sanctions the taking of more water from the Thames, and he contends that without that provision the Bill would be practically useless. There is no provision of the kind in the Bill, and I am of opinion that it would be improper for me to introduce it into a Measure of this description. But theré is surplus water available at the present time, and the purpose of this Bill is to establish connection between the works of the different companies, so as to enable the surplus water of one company to supply the deficiency of the other. There is nothing, I think, very surprising in a proposal of this kind being made. The honourable Gentleman says he finds some difficulty in respect to the price to be charged for a supply of water by the New River Company, whose charge is lower than that of the East London Water Company. On that ground he takes some objection to the Measure, but that question will depend entirely upon the price which the New River Company may demand from the East London Company. If there is any difference of opinion between them, it is provided that the whole question shall be settled by arbitration. The consumers will pay no more than they do at present, because the price which the consumers in East London have to pay is settled by Statute. Therefore, their interests will not be prejudiced in the least, but by the passing of this Bill the position of these people in East London will be improved, and the short supply of water to which they are now constantly liable will become a thing of the past. The honourable Member has contended that what is wanted is to rectify the boundaries of the different companies, and then to allow each to supply its own district. But if that were done, the position of affairs would be no better than it is at the present moment, for there is not water enough within the resources of the East London Water Company to supply their customers during a period of drought like that of last year, while there would be no water famine if this Bill passes. This really is a matter of very considerable urgency. The object of the Bill is to prevent the poor people of East London from again enduring all the troubles, hardships, and difficulties they have undergone in the past, and there are no other means, in my opinion, of accomplishing this object than those proposed in the Bill. The Bill in no way affects the larger questions of the future water authority of London, the purchasing value, or the interests of ratepayers and consumers. The question of the water authority is

President of Local Government Board.

left absolutely untouched by this Bill. On that question I preserve an entirely open mind until the Report of the Royal Commission is furnished, when it will be my duty, if I am still a Member of Her Majesty's Government, to come to a decision upon it. With regard to the second question, the purchase value, there is a special clause in the Bill which provides that it shall not in any way authorise the companies to bring into account, or make any claim in respect to, any advantages conferred by or resulting from the passing of this Measure. Upon the third point, the object and the effect of the Bill is quite certain to be an improved water supply. Honourable Gentlemen need be under no fear whatever on these grounds. With regard to the fourth point, I think I have said enough to show that it is directly to the interest of the ratepayers, and of consumers in particular, that this Bill should be passed. The details to which honourable Members may take exception can be threshed out before the Committee, and, in the interests of the hundreds of thousands of the poorer classes in East London, I appeal to the House to allow this Bill to be read a second time, so that it may proceed on its course, and become law at the earliest possible moment.

MR. BUXTON (Tower Hamlets, Poplar): I certainly am not going to oppose the Second Reading of this Bill nor to talk it out, but I should like an assurance from the right honourable Gentleman that, so far as this particular Measure is concerned, he looks upon it as temporary, and that it will not be allowed to prejudice the question of the best means of inter-communication between all the companies. This Bill, as I understand the explanation of the right honourable Gentleman, is only intended for an emergency. I cordially sympathise with the object the right honourable Gentleman has in view, and I think he can be trusted to see that the Bill will not be allowed to prejudice the question of the best means of inter-communication between the companies.

*MR SINCLAIR (Essex, Romford): Mr. Lowther—Sir, representing, as I do, a very large constituency, portions of which suffered very much indeed in consequence of the very limited supply of water afforded by the East London Water Company, I hope, at this very late hour, I may be allowed to say a few words on the subject in question. I first of all wish to assure the House that it is not my intention to talk this Debate out. I see that I have exactly seven minutes before me, and in that short time I hope I may express my satisfaction that this matter has been found of such importance that it has moved the Government to adopt some Measure to remedy the great evil occasioned by the drought and the non-fulfilment by Water Company of its obligations. I would like to point out that I do not think the Bill adequate enough for the needs of the case, but it is a step in the right direction, and that is the reason that I will not throw any impediment in the way of the Second Reading, and will reserve to myself, on a future occasion, the privilege of going into the various and many grievances my constituents underwent through the want of that most necessary article to our very existence. I will only mention one point, and that is that the East London Company said that the suffering, in a great measure, resulted from the action of consumers in not having cisterns to store their water. Now, Mr. Lowther, I wish to point out that it is not the duty of consumers to store the Company's water. It is the duty of a water company to give a good and ample supply to the persons who pay for it, and I hold that these cisterns which they advocate have been proved to be a source of the greatest danger to those who have them. They are death traps to those who do not have them cleaned frequently, and in small houses, often inhabited by a number of people, it is most important that the water should be pure, and that they should have enough of it. I am glad, Sir, for more reasons than those I have time to show, that the Government is alive to the exigencies of the case, and shall hope that the sufferings of many of my constituents have endured will, thanks to this Bill, be greatly mitigated in the future.

Question put.

Bill read a second time and referred to a Select Committee.

COLONIAL LOANS FUND BILL.

Second Reading deferred till Monday next.

TELEPHONIC COMMUNICATION (CONSOLIDATED FUND).

Resolution reported—

"That it is expedient—(A) To authorise the issue out of the Consolidated Fund of a sum not exceeding £2,000,000 for making further provision for the improvement of telephonic communication ; (B) to enable local authorities to raise or apply money for telephonic purposes."

Resolution agreed to :—Bill ordered to be brought in by Mr. Hanbury and Mr. Chancellor of the Exchequer.

TELEGRAPHS (TELEPHONIC COMMUNICATION, ETC.) BILL.

"To make further provision for the improvement of Telephonic Communication, and otherwise with respect to Telegraphs," presented accordingly, and read the first time ; to be read a second time upon Thursday next, and to be printed. (Bill 118.)

SUPPLY (3rd March).

Report deferred till Monday next.

LONDON GOVERNMENT BILL.

Second Reading deferred till Thursday next.

CHARITABLE LOANS (IRELAND) BILL.

Second Reading deferred till Thursday next.

INEBRIATES ACT (1898) AMENDMENT BILL.

Second Reading deferred till Thursday next.

IMPROVEMENT OF LAND BILL.

Second Reading deferred till Thursday next.

UNIVERSITIES (SCOTLAND) ACTS AMENDMENT BILL.

Order for Second Reading read.

Motion made, and Question proposed—

" That the Bill be now read a second time."

MR. J. CALDWELL (Lanark, Mid.) : I protest that a Bill of this importance should be brought forward at this time.

And, it being Midnight, the Debate stood adjourned.

Debate to be resumed upon Monday next.

LICENSING EXEMPTION (HOUSES OF PARLIAMENT) BILL.

Adjourned Debate on Second Reading (23rd February) further adjourned till Monday next.

METROPOLITAN GAS COMPANIES.

Order read for resuming Adjourned Debate on Question (20th February)—

" That a Select Committee be appointed to inquire into the powers of charge conferred by Parliament on the Metropolitan Gas Companies, and to report as to the method in which those powers have been exercised, having regard to the differences of price charged by the various companies."—(*Mr. Cohen.*)

*MR. PICKERSGILL (Bethnal Green, S.W.) : I heartily welcome this inquiry. Indeed, I first suggested to the House a Committee, and the honourable Member for East Islington has annexed my suggestion, but has, unfortunately, spoilt it in the terms of his Motion. It is clear that the value of such an inquiry depends upon the terms of the reference, and I desire, in addition to the terms of reference which the honourable Member has placed on the Paper, that the Committee should inquire whether or not the statutory conditions with regard to the price of gas and the dividend should be reconsidered. The Government, however, the other night objected to my Amendment, and as it is clear that I have no possible chance of carrying it, in these circumstances I shall not press my Amendment, but shall throw upon the Government the responsibility of declining to take such steps as would have made the inquiry really beneficial.

SIR W. WALROND (Devon, Tiverton) : As I was the Member of the Government who objected to the terms

of the reference of my honourable Friend the Member for Bethnal Green, I desire to say that I did so because I believed the reference in the Motion of the honourable Member for East Islington was quite wide enough for the purpose, and I am glad to hear that the honourable Member for Bethnal Green has withdrawn his Amendment.

Question put, and agreed to.

Ordered—

" That a Select Committee be appointed to inquire into the powers of charge conferred by Parliament on the Metropolitan Gas Companies, and to report as to the method in which those powers have been exercised, having regard to the differences of price charged by the various companies."

SERVICE FRANCHISE BILL.

Considered in Committee :—

(In the Committee.)

Clause 1—Committee report progress ; to sit again upon Wednesday 7th June.

RIVERS POLLUTION PREVENTION BILL.

Adjourned Debate on Amendment to Second Reading (8th March) further adjourned till Wednesday next.

PALATINE COURT OF DURHAM BILL [H.L.].

Read the first time ; to be read a second time upon Thursday next, and to be printed. (Bill 119.)

SOLICITORS BILL [H.L.l.

Read the first time ; to be read a second time upon Thursday next, and to be printed. (Bill 120.)

NAVY ESTIMATES.

MR. E. J. C. MORTON (Devonport) : I should like to ask the right honourable Gentleman the First Lord of the Treasury whether the Navy Estimates will be taken on Monday, and whether he contemplates getting any Votes on that day.

THE FIRST LORD OF THE TREASURY : The discussion on the Navy Estimates will occupy Monday's Sitting, and I hope Vote A will be agreed to.

House adjourned at ten minutes after Twelve of the clock.

An Asterisk (*) at the commencement of a Speech indicates revision by the Member.

HOUSE OF LORDS.

Friday, 10th March 1899.

THE LORD CHANCELLOR took his seat upon the Woolsack at Four of the clock.

PETITION—CLAIM TO VOTE.

Earl of Wicklow—Petition of Ralph Francis Earl of Wicklow claiming a right to vote at the election of Representative Peers for Ireland; read, and referred to the Lord Chancellor to consider and report thereupon to the House.

PRIVATE BILL BUSINESS.

THE LORD CHANCELLOR acquainted the House that the Clerk of Parliaments had laid upon the Table the Certificate from the Examiners that the further Standing Orders applicable to the following Bill have been complied with:—

Surrey Commercial Docks [H.L.]

The same was ordered to lie on the Table.

ABERDEEN CORPORATION BILL [H.L]

A Petition of John Kennedy, writer to the signet, praying for leave to present a petition of Malcolm Vivian Hay and his curators, praying to be heard by counsel against the Bill, although the time limited by Standing Order No. 92 for presenting such petition has expired; read, and ordered to lie on the Table; and Standing Order No. 92 to be considered on Monday next in order to its being dispensed with in respect of the said petition.

VOL. LXVIII.   [FOURTH SERIES.]

WESTON-SUPER-MARE GRAND PIER BILL [H.L.]
Committed.

HULL, BARNSLEY, AND WEST RIDING JUNCTION RAILWAY AND DOCK BILL [H.L.]
Committed.

Southport Tramways Bill [H.L.]

North Eastern and Hull and Barnsley Railways (Joint Dock) Bill [H.L.]

Furness Water Bill [H.L.]

Totland Water Bill [H.L.]

Great Grimsby Street Tramways Bill [H.L.]

Committed: The Committees to be proposed by the Committee of Selection.

LANARKSHIRE (MIDDLE WARD DISTRICT) WATER BILL [H.L.]
THE CHAIRMAN OF COMMITTEES informed the House that the opposition to the Bill was withdrawn; The orders made on the 27th of February and on Monday last discharged; and Bill committed for Tuesday next.

KIRKCALDY CORPORATION AND TRAMWAYS BILL [H.L.]
THE CHAIRMAN OF COMMITTEES informed the House that the opposition to the Bill was withdrawn: The orders made on the 27th of February and on Monday last discharged; and Bill committed.

Belfast Corporation Bill

National Telephone Company (No. 1) Bill

National Telephone Company (No. 2) Bill

Mersey Docks and Harbour Board (Pilotage) Bill [H.L.] (Petition for additional Provision)

Gainsborough Urban District Council (Gas) Bill [H.L.] (Petition for additional Provision)

Examiner's Certificates of non-compliance with the Standing Orders referred to the Standing Orders Committee on Thursday next.

R

RETURNS, REPORTS, ETC.

MERCHANT SHIPPING ACT, 1894.
Order in Council of 7th March 18$_{99}$, respecting the load line of ships registerd in the Colony of Victoria.

Laid before the House (pursuant to Act), and ordered to lie on the Table.

ASSIZE ACTS, 1876 AND 1879.
Two Orders in Council of 7th March 1899, under the Spring Assizes Act, 1879, for the Spring Assize Counties, Nos. 2 and 3.

Laid before the House (pursuant to Act), and ordered to lie on the Table.

BANKRUPTCY COURTS (IRELAND).
Returns of the official assignees of the Court of Bankruptcy in Ireland, and the local courts Belfast and Cork, for the year 1898.

Laid before the House (pursuant to Act), and ordered to lie on the Table.

EDUCATION DEPARTMENT PROVISIONAL ORDER CONFIRMATION (SWANSEA) BILL [H.L.]
To be read second time on Monday next.

CATHCART'S DIVORCE BILL [H.L]
Amendment reported (according to order), and Bill to be read third time on Monday next.

Aberdeen Corporation Bill [H.L.]
Dumbarton Burgh Bill [H.L.]
Greenock and Port Glasgow Tramways Bill [H.L.]
Perth Water, Police, and Gas Bill [H.L.]
West Highland Railway Bill [H.L.]
Airdrie and Coatbridge Water Bill [H.L.]
Wishaw Water Bill [H.L.]

The meeting of the Select Committee, which stands appointed for Tuesday next at Eleven o'clock, put off to Wednesday next at Eleven o'clock.

Cromer Protection Bill [H.L.]
Glastonbury Water Bill [H.L.]
Yeadon and Guiseley Gas Bill [H.L.]
Bristol Gas Bill [H.L.]
Lea Bridge District Gas Bill [H.L.]
Queen's Ferry Bridge Bill [H.L.]
Nene Valley Water Bill [H.L.]
St. Neot's Water Bill [H.L.]

Report from the Committee of Selection that the Lord Pirbright be proposed to the House as a member of the Select Committee in the place of the Lord Rookwood; and that the Lord Pirbright be Chairman of the said Committee; read, and agreed to.

HOUSE OF LORDS AND COMMONS PERMANENT STAFF JOINT COMMITTEE.
A message ordered to be sent to the House of Commons to propose that the Joint Committee do meet in Committee Room A on Friday next, at Twelve o'clock.

House adjourned at half-past Four of the clock, to Monday next, a quarter past Four of the clock.

HOUSE OF COMMONS.

Friday, 10th March 1899.

MR. SPEAKER'S INDISPOSITION.
The House being met, the Clerk at the Table informed the House of the unavoidable absence of Mr. Speaker, owing to the continuance of his indisposition:—

Whereupon Mr. JAMES WILLIAM LOWTHER (Cumberland, Penrith, CHAIRMAN of WAYS and MEANS), proceeded to the Table, and, after Prayers, took the Chair as Deputy Speaker, pursuant to the Standing Order, at Three of the clock.   •

PRIVATE BILL BUSINESS.

PRIVATE BILLS (STANDING ORDER 62
COMPLIED WITH).

Mr. DEPUTY SPEAKER laid upon the
Table Report from one of the Examiners
of Petitions for Private Bills, That in
the case of the following Bill, referred on
the First Reading thereof, Standing
Order No. 62 has been complied with,
viz.:—

Walker and Wallsend Union Gas (Electric Lighting) Bill.

Ordered, That the Bill be read a
second time.

PRIVATE BILLS (STANDING ORDER 63
COMPLIED WITH).

Mr. DEPUTY SPEAKER laid upon
the Table report from one of the
Examiners of Petitions for Private Bills,
That, in the case of the following Bill,
referred on the first reading thereof,
Standing Order No. 63 has been complied with, viz.:—

MENSTONE WATER BILL.

Ordered that the Bill be read a second
time.

CROWBOROUGH DISTRICT GAS BILL.

As amended, considered; to be read
the third time.

ST. DAVID'S WATER AND GAS BILL.

As amended, considered; to be read
the third time.

PETITIONS.

EDUCATION OF CHILDREN BILL.
Petition from Keighley, in favour; to
lie upon the Table.

LOCAL AUTHORITIES SERVANTS'
SUPERANNUATION BILL.
Petitions in favour;—From Dorking;
and Crick; to lie upon the Table.

PARLIAMENTARY FRANCHISE.
Petition of Mona Caird and others,
for extension to women; to lie upon the
Table.

PRIVATE LEGISLATION PROCEDURE
(SCOTLAND) BILL.
Petitions in favour;—From Scottish
Trade Protection Society; — and,
Greenock; to lie upon the Table.

PUBLIC HEALTH ACTS AMENDMENT
BILL
Petitions in favour;—From Black-
pool;—and Reading; to lie upon the
Table.

REGISTRATION OF FIRMS BILLS.
Petition from Birmingham, in favour;
to lie upon the Table.

SALE OF INTOXICATING LIQUORS ON
SUNDAY BILL.
Petitions in favour;—From Ledbury;
—Bradford;—Sister Hills;—Hungate;
— Monmouth; — Middlesbrough; —
Brandon; — Bristol; —and, Cochester
(four); to iie upon the Table.

SCIENCE AND ART GRANTS.
Petition from York, for alteration of
Law; to lie upon the Table.

STEAM TRAWLERS (ENCROACHMENT).
Petitions for protection of fishermen;
—From Newbiggin by the Sea (two);—
Cambois;—and, Newton by the Sea; to
lie upon the Table.

RETURNS, REPORTS, ETC.

ASSIZE ACTS, 1876 AND 1879.
Copies presented,—of two Orders in
Council of 7th March 1899, relating to
Spring Assize Counties, Nos. 2 and 3
(by Act), to lie upon the Table.

R 2

MERCHANT SHIPPING ACT, 1894.

Copy presented,—of Order in Council, of the 7th March 1899, respecting the Load-line of Ships registered in the Colony of Victoria (by Act), to lie upon the Table.

PAPERS LAID ON THE TABLE BY THE CLERK OF THE HOUSE.

---

1. Charitable Endowments (London), —Further Return relative thereto [ordered 2nd August 1894; *Mr. Francis Stevenson*]; to be printed. (No. 101.)

2. Inquiry into Charities (County of Lancaster),—Further Return relative thereto [ordered 8th August 1898; *Mr. Grant Lawson*]; to be printed. (No.102.)

BILL REPORTED.

CROWBOROUGH DISTRICT WATER BILL.

Reported; Reports to lie upon the Table.

FISHGUARD WATER AND GAS BILL.

Reported; Reports to lie upon the Table.

PUBLIC LIBRARIES (SCOTLAND) ACTS AMENDMENT BILL.

Reported, without Amendment, from the Standing Committee on Law, etc.

Report to lie upon the Table, and to be printed. (No. 103.)

Minutes of Proceedings to be printed. (No. 103.)

Bill to be read the third time upon Wednesday next.

STANDING ORDERS.

Resolutions reported from the Committee:—

"1. That, in the case of the Dublin Corporation (Markets) Bill, Petition of 'Messieurs Sewell, Son, and Simpson' for dispensing with Standing Order 129 in the case of their Petition against the Bill, the said Standing Order ought to be dispensed with."

"2. That, in the case of the London Water (Welsh Reservoirs and Works) Petition, the Standing Orders ought to be dispensed with. That the parties to be permitted to proceed with their Bill."

Resolutions agreed to.

LONDON WATER (WELSH RESERVOIRS AND WORKS) BILL.

Report [this day] from the Select Committee on Standing Orders read.

Bill ordered to be brought in by Mr. James Stuart, Mr. Sydney Buxton, and Mr. Moulton.

SHOPS BILL.

Adjourned Debate on Second Reading [21st February] deferred from Tuesday next till Tuesday 21st March.

MESSAGE FROM THE LORDS.

Houses of Lords and Commons Permanent Staff,—That they propose that the Joint Committee appointed to consider and report on the subject of the Houses of Lords and Commons Permanent Staff do meet in Committee Room A on Friday next, at Twelve o'clock.

Lords Message considered.

Ordered, That the Committee of this House do meet the Lords Committee as proposed by their Lordships.

Message to the Lords to acquaint them therewith.—*(Sir William Walrond.)*

NEW BILLS.

FINE OR IMPRISONMENT (SCOTLAND AND IRELAND) BILL.

"To assimilate the Law of Scotland and of Ireland as to Imprisonment on default of payment of Fines to that of England," presented, and read the first time; to be read a second time upon Wednesday next, and to be printed. (Bill 121.)

WINE AND BEERHOUSE ACTS AMENDMENT BILL.

"To amend the Law relating to the Licensing of Beerhouses and Places for the Sale of Cider and Wine by retail in England and Wales," presented, and read the first time; to be read a second time upon Wednesday next, and to be printed. (Bill 122.)

QUESTIONS.

CANADIAN TARIFFS.

COLONEL SIR HOWARD VINCENT (Sheffield, Central): I beg to ask the Secretary of State for the Colonies if he can inform the House what has been the result, as regards British goods, of the first six months operation of the preferential terms granted on 1st August, 1898, by the Dominion of Canada to imports from the United Kingdom, India, the West Indies, and other parts of the British Empire; and, if the Governments of Australasia and South Africa or of any Crown Colonies have already or are likely, in the near future, to adopt the same system?

THE SECRETARY OF STATE FOR THE COLONIES (Mr. J. CHAMBERLAIN, Birmingham West): The United Kingdom Trade Returns for the six months ended the 31st January 1899, show in respect of the exports to Canada of the chief enumerated articles an increase of a little over 1 per cent. over the figures for the period ended 31st January, 1898. If, however, the exports during the month of July last, the greater part of which would have arrived in Canada under the preferential tariff, are taken into account, the increase would be a little over 6 per cent. The period is, however, too short, even if complete statistics were available, to form an accurate judgment of the effect of the preferential tariff on the trade between the United Kingdom and Canada. As regards other parts of the Empire to which the preferential tariff extends, statistics are available only for India, and these show a slight decrease, but the trade between Canada and India is so small and the period is so short that it is impossible to draw any conclusion from the figures. No other Colonial Government has as yet adopted the same system. As regards the future, I have nothing to add to the answer which I gave to a similar Question by the honourable Member on the 29th July last.

COUNCILLOR GAGEBY, OF BELFAST.

MR. MADDISON (Sheffield, Bright side): I beg to ask Mr. Attorney-General for Ireland whether he is aware that Councillor Gageby, of Belfast, has been deprived of his seat on the Belfast Corporation by reason of his name being been omitted from the register of voters after it had appeared on the revising barrister's list; whether he will cause an inquiry to be held to ascertain how this irregularity occurred; and, whether he will take the necessary steps to restore Mr. Gageby's name to the register?

THE ATTORNEY-GENERAL FOR IRELAND (Mr. ATKINSON, Londonderry, N.): A similar Question was addressed on Tuesday last to my right honourable Friend the Chief Secretary by the honourable Member for South Down. To the reply given to that Question, to which I beg to refer the honourable Member, I have nothing to add.

MR. MADDISON: If it can be proved that the name had appeared in the town clerk's list, would that fact in any way alter the answer?

MR. ATKINSON: It is entirely a matter for the local authorities.

LONDON AND NORTH WESTERN RAIL-
WAY COMPANY'S SERVANTS.

MR. MADDISON : I beg to ask the
President of the Board of Trade, whether
he will make a further appeal to the London and North Western Railway Company to adopt the recommendation made
in the Board of Trade Circular respecting
the hours of flagmen and watchmen employed in tunnels, that company being
the only one which has refused to adopt
the eight-hour spell of duty ?

MR. SWIFT MacNEILL (Donegal,
S.): May I ask the right honourable
Gentleman a Question, of which I have
given him private notice, namely, will the
right honourable Gentleman make a
further appeal to the directors of this
company, through the Secretary to the
Admiralty, who has become a director of
the company since he became a Member
of this House ?

THE PRESIDENT OF THE BOARD
OF TRADE (Mr. C. T. RITCHIE, Croydon): No, Sir ; any appeal I make must
be through the Secretary to the Board
and not through the Secretary to the
Admiralty. I have communicated again
with the London and North Western, and
the general manager informs the Board
of Trade that

"This company has no objection to such a
general rule so long as it is not made a hard and
fast regulation."

HYDE PARK.

COLONEL WELBY (Taunton): I beg
to ask the First Commissioner of Works
whether his attention has been drawn to
the number of persons of evil character
who haunt Hyde Park and Green Park
during and after nightfall ; and, whether
he can see his way to a better supervision
of these parks in the evening ?

THE FIRST COMMISSIONER OF
WORKS (Mr. A. AKERS DOUGLAS, Kent,
St. Augustine's): Disorderly conduct in
Hyde Park has of course been brought
to my notice from time to time ; but the
matter is properly one for the action of
the police authorities, and they are, I
believe, fully alive to it.

EX-LORD CHANCELLORS' PENSIONS.

MR. COGHILL (Stoke-on-Trent): I beg
to ask Mr. Chancellor of the Exchequer
whether he will take advantage of there
being no ex-Lord Chancellor alive to
alter the amount of pension paid to ex-
Lord Chancellors, and to reduce it to
the same amount that is given, when
claimed, to other Cabinet Ministers?

THE CHANCELLOR OF THE EX-
CHEQUER (Sir M. HICKS BEACH, Bristol,
W.): I do not think there is any analogy
between the office of Lord Chancellor and
that of any other Cabinet Minister with
regard to a claim to pension. When anyone is appointed Lord Chancellor he
necessarily gives up a lucrative practice
at the Bar, and cannot return to his
profession on resignation of office, which
he may hold for a very short time. Ex-
Lord Chancellors sit regularly as Judges
of Appeal, so that the more proper comparison would be with the pensions of
judges. Regarded from these points of
view, the pension of a Lord Chancellor
does not appear to me to be too high.

MR. SWIFT MacNEILL: Is the right
honourable Gentleman aware that
the honourable Member who asked
the Question is wrong in saying
there is no ex-Lord Chancellor alive ?
The Right Honourable Samuel Walker,
ex-Lord Chancellor of Ireland, one of
the best judges we ever had, is still in
the land of the living.

THE CHANCELLOR OF THE EX-
CHEQUER: I understood the honourable Gentleman to refer to England.

TELEGRAM ADDRESSES.

MR. SIDEBOTHAM (Cheshire, Hyde):
I beg to ask the Secretary to
the Treasury, as representing the Postmaster-General, why the Post Office is
giving notice of its intention to refuse
to deliver all telegrams which have for
an address merely the surname of the
addressee and the post town in which
he lives; whether in cases in which
there is only one person of the name
living in the district, and that person
has only one residence, and that residence is perfectly well known, the requirements of the Post Office that the address

should contain the necessary particulars to insure delivery without difficulty and without inquiries or references to directories are not complied with, why, in such cases, the registration of the address and the payment of a fee of one guinea should be demanded; and whether the Post Office is not bound to deliver a telegram in cases where there can be no doubt as to the person for whom it is intended?

THE FINANCIAL SECRETARY TO THE TREASURY (Mr. R. W. HANBURY, Preston): The Post Office has not recently issued any general notice on the subject to which the honourable Member refers. Probably he has in view some particular case, and if he will bring it to the Postmaster-General's notice inquiry will be made into the circumstances. The Telegraph Regulations require that the address of a telegram shall be sufficient to enable delivery to be effected without difficulty or delay, and unless the Regulations are complied with the Postmaster-General is not bound to deliver a telegram.

INNISKEEN RAILWAY ACCIDENT.

MR. MACALEESE (Monaghan, N.): I beg to ask the President of the Board of Trade, can he state the extent of the damage caused by the derailing of a cattle train some days ago at Inniskeen on the Great Northern Railway of Ireland, when, as reported in the Press, several dealers were seriously hurt, and a large number of cattle killed and many shockingly injured; were many of the cattle, in all degrees of mutilation, turned into a field and allowed to lie there in agony for many hours, as the railway management would not undertake the liability of directing their slaughter; and, if so, will a prosecution be ordered; and has the cause of the accident been ascertained; if so, will he state it to the House?

THE PRESIDENT OF THE BOARD OF TRADE: The Board of Trade have ordered an inquiry into the causes of this accident.

MR. MACALEESE: Can the right honourable Gentleman say when it will be held?

THE PRESIDENT OF THE BOARD OF TRADE: No, Sir, I cannot.

LORD PENZANCE.

MR. COGHILL: I beg to ask Mr. Chancellor of the Exchequer if he could state what was the yearly sum paid to Lord Penzance as Judge of the Court of Arches; and whether he had any duties to perform in connection with his office?

THE CHANCELLOR OF THE EXCHEQUER: Nothing was paid to Lord Penzance as Judge of the Court of Arches out of public funds. The duties are described in the Public Worship Regulation Act, 1874.

MR. COGHILL: Did he not receive a sum of £5,000 a year?

THE CHANCELLOR OF THE EXCHEQUER:: No, Sir. He received a pension for his service as Judge, but nothing as Judge of the High Court of Arches.

UNCLAIMED DEBTORS' ESTATES.

MR. HAZELL (Leicester): I beg to ask the President of the Board of Trade whether trustees administering estates under deeds of arrangement are often left with unclaimed sums which it is not the duty of any Government Department to accept from them, as is done in similar cases where proceedings have been taken in bankruptcy; whether he has any means of knowing what amount the sums so held reach, and how long they have been in the present hands; and whether it is proposed to take any steps to relieve such trustees in the future from this difficulty?

THE PRESIDENT OF THE BOARD OF TRADE: The answer to the first part of the Question is in the affirmative. I am not at present in a position to state the amount of unclaimed funds in the hands of trustees under deeds of arrangement, nor can I promise legislation on the subject.

RESIDENT ENGINEER TO THE HOUSES OF PARLIAMENT.

MR. HAZELL: I beg to ask the Secretary to the Treasury whether the Resident Engineer at the Houses of Parliament, who is also Consulting Engineer to the Trustees of the British Museum, is also the Engineer to the Royal Courts of Justice; and, if so, why that fact is not noted in the Estimates on the Votes for his salary; and whether there is any reason why his salary as Resident Engineer at the Houses of Parliament, which is stated to be £250 per annum, rising by £7 10s. per annum to £300, should be again raised to £308 in the Estimates for next year?

MR. HANBURY: The Resident Engineer to the Houses of Parliament is not Engineer to the Royal Courts of Justice. He vacated that post on his appointment to his present position. The statement in the Estimates that his salary for 1889-1900 will be £308 is due to a clerical error. The amount should, of course, be given as £300.

TREASURY VALUER.

MR. HAZELL: I beg to ask the Secretary to the Treasury whether he has observed that, according to the Estimates, Class I., it is proposed to appoint a new Treasury Valuer and Inspector of Rates at the same salary, namely, £1,000 rising by £50 annually to £1,200, as paid to the present holder of the office, in spite of the fact that the salary has been starred in the Estimates for many years, and a note appended that it would be revised on a vacancy; and whether he can say by whose authority this appointment is proposed to be made on such terms, and who is responsible for the omission of the footnote referred to from this year's Estimates?

MR. HANBURY: Yes, Sir. The facts of the case are as follows:—A Treasury Minute, dated 28th June, 1892, fixed the salary of Mr. Griffiths, who then held the post of Treasury Valuer and Inspector of Rates, at £1,200 a year, with the proviso that this rate would not be continued to his successor. A note was in-serted in the Estimates for the years 1893-4 to 1898-9 embodying this proviso, and the salary of the post has accordingly been reduced from a fixed amount of £1,200 to £1,000, rising by annual increments of £20 to £1,200. This reduction was effected in spite of the fact that in recent years circumstances have recently led to a considerable increase in the work of valuation. The omission of the footnote, for which I am responsible, was necessary and proper.

ELECTRIC LIGHTING.

MR. BAYLEY (Derbyshire, Chesterfield): I beg to ask the President of the Board of Trade if he can state the number of local authorities that have obtained and are holding Provisional Orders for electric lighting without doing anything to carry their powers into practical effect?

THE PRESIDENT OF THE BOARD OF TRADE: There are 30 local authorities who have obtained Provisional Orders for electric lighting who have taken no steps to give effect to their Orders within the time prescribed for the execution of compulsory works. Besides these there are 63 local authorities who obtained Orders in 1897 and 1898 and have apparently done no work, but the time prescribed by their Orders has not yet expired. I may mention that the Board of Trade have lately been calling the attention of local authorities who are not exercising their powers to the matter, and have intimated that the Board propose to consider the question of revoking the Orders. In nearly all of these cases the local authorities have replied that they are now taking steps to carry their Orders into execution.

MR. GIBSON BOWLES (Lynn Regis): Can the right honourable Gentleman say how many authorities who have obtained powers are exercising them?

THE PRESIDENT OF THE BOARD OF TRADE: I am afraid I cannot answer that Question.

BAILIEBOROUGH UNION NURSE.

MR. YOUNG (Cavan, E.): I beg to ask the Chief Secretary to the Lord Lieutenant of Ireland whether he is aware that a trained nurse, Miss Widdess, was appointed by the Bailieborough (county Cavan) Board of Guardians last year, and that the appointment was approved and confirmed by the Local Government Board; whether Miss Widdess has discharged her duties to the entire satisfaction of the medical officer; and why the Local Government Board seeks, after sanctioning the appointment, to surcharge the lady's salary, and thus compel the guardians to inflict great injury on the competent nurse referred to?

THE CHIEF SECRETARY TO THE LORD LIEUTENANT OF IRELAND (Mr. GERALD W. BALFOUR, Leeds Central): The appointment of Miss Widdess as infirmary nurse of the Bailieborough Workhouse was sanctioned by the Local Government Board two years ago. The reply to the second paragraph is in the affirmative. Under section 58, subsection 2 of the Local Government (Ireland) Act, it was obligatory on the Board to prescribe the qualifications necessary in the case of any person claiming to be a trained nurse for the purpose of obtaining recoupment under the section. Miss Widdess does not possess the necessary qualification. There is no question of surcharging the salary of this lady. The repayment of half the salary of a trained nurse will not apply until the financial year commencing the 1st April. The Board have, in cases like that of Miss Widdess, where the existing nurse is approved by the medical officer, decided to allow the guardians to give leave of absence to the nurse for such a period as will enable her to complete the training necessary to place her on the board's register of trained nurses, the only condition being that the Guardians shall appoint a qualified person to act as her *locum tenens*. A Circular Letter to this effect is about to be issued to boards of guardians.

NEWFOUNDLAND AND THE REID CONTRACT.

SIR F. EVANS (Southampton): I beg to ask the Secretary of State for the Colonies whether it is within the competence of a future Parliament in Newfoundland to disaffirm the Reid contract by statute, having regard to the circumstances under which it was obtained?

THE SECRETARY OF STATE FOR THE COLONIES: It would be competent to a future Parliament to pass an Act annulling a contract ratified by an Act passed by the present Parliament, but I must not be understood to express any opinion on the circumstances attending the making of the contract referred to in the Question.

CANADIAN FISHERIES.

GENERAL LAURIE (Pembroke and Haverfordwest): I beg to ask the Secretary of State for the Colonies what has been the result of the negotiations with Portugal with the object of obtaining the most favoured nation clause, thus removing the disabilities under which the Newfoundland and Canadian fisheries are placed in competition with the Norwegian fisheries, which were mentioned by the Secretary of State for the Colonies to a deputation on the subject on the 29th April, 1897, and stated in a letter from the Colonial Office to the London Chamber of Commerce to be still in progress on the 31st January, 1898.

THE UNDER SECRETARY OF STATE FOR FOREIGN AFFAIRS (Mr. ST. JOHN BRODRICK, Surrey, Guildford): The negotiations between Great Britain and Portugal with the object of securing a most-favoured-nation clause have not as yet led to any satisfactory result, so that I cannot make any statement on the question.

CASE OF M. LE MESURIER.

MR. STEVENSON (Suffolk, Eye): On behalf of the honourable Member for North Manchester, I beg to ask the Secretary of State for the Colonies whether he is aware that M. C. J. R. Le Mesurier, on refusing to leave his own property in Ceylon without an order of Court, was violently assaulted by Government officials who were afterwards sentenced to three months' imprisonment by the High Court, and that in this case the Government prosecuting department appeared for the accused, by special order from the Attorney-General of Ceylon, although it is this very department that has to give the instructions for the commitment of and the prosecution of the accused in the Supreme Court; whether these same officials, after serving their term of imprisonment, are now to be reinstated by the Government; and whether he has communicated by telegraph with the Governor of Ceylon, instructing him to prevent any further police raids?

THE SECRETARY OF STATE FOR THE COLONIES: I have received memorials from M. Le Mesurier, complaining of his treatment by the Government of Ceylon, one of which contains allegations to the effect of the honourable Member's first Question. An early report has been promised by the Governor on the subject of these memorials, and pending the receipt of this report, I have not telegraphed, and do not propose to telegraph any special instructions as to the course to be adopted by the Ceylon Government in the case of M. Le Mesurier.

INDIA AND BOUNTY-FED SUGAR.

COLONEL SIR HOWARD VINCENT: I beg to ask the Secretary of State for India if the Government of India has with his approval determined to levy a countervailing duty on the importation of Foreign bounty-fed sugar?

THE SECRETARY OF STATE FOR INDIA (Lord G. HAMILTON, Middlesex, Ealing): A Bill, under which countervailing duties will be imposed upon all bounty-fed sugar imported into India, has, I believe, been introduced to-day, with my approval, into the Legislative Council at Calcutta.

MR. MACLEAN (Cardiff): May I ask the noble Lord whether this Bill has been introduced with his assent?

THE SECRETARY OF STATE FOR INDIA: I have already said so.

MR. MACLEAN: Does the noble Lord intend to submit this change of policy to the House of Commons before it is carried into effect?

THE SECRETARY OF STATE FOR INDIA: I have more than once told my honourable Friend I have no intention of interfering with the independence of the local Legislature.

MR. MACLEAN: Does the noble Lord remember how he interfered with that independence in the case of the cotton duties?

MR. DEPUTY SPEAKER: Order, order!

WATER GAS.

MR. ASCROFT (Oldham): I beg to ask the Secretary of State for the Home Department whether his attention has been called to the report of the Departmental Committee appointed to inquire into the manufacture and use of water gas and other gases containing a large proportion of carbonic oxide, and to the dangers that are likely to arise to the public safety unless restrictions are placed upon the manufacture, as recommended by such Committee; and whether it is the intention of the Government to introduce a Bill dealing with the question?

THE UNDER SECRETARY OF STATE FOR THE HOME DEPARTMENT (Mr. J. COLLINGS, Birmingham, Bordesley): The Report of the Departmental Committee was made to the Secretary of State, and it was by him that it was laid upon the Table of the House. He is now consulting his colleagues the Presidents of the Board of Trade and of the Local Government Board, who were represented on the Committee, as to the recommendations; but it has not yet been decided what action should be taken.

IRELAND AND THE PARIS EXHIBITION.

MR. CAREW (Dublin, College Green) : I beg to ask the Secretary to the Treasury whether it is true that the funds set apart for the Irish Committee in connection with the Royal Commission on the Paris Exhibition have been cut off; whether the Irish Committee and Sub-Committee are about to be dissolved; and whether, if this is so, any steps are to be taken to facilitate intending Irish exhibitors at the Exhibition of 1900?

Mr. HANBURY: I understand that the correspondence which has passed between the Royal Commission in London and the Lord Lieutenant of Ireland will be published in the Irish newspapers to-morrow morning, together with the report of the proceedings of the Irish Committee up to date. I should be glad, therefore, if the honourable Member would postpone his Question till Monday.

CHINESE NORTHERN RAILWAY EXTENSION LOAN.

SIR E. ASHMEAD-BARTLETT (Sheffield, Ecclesall): I beg to ask the Under Secretary of State for Foreign Affairs whether the Russian Government, or the Russian Minister at Pekin, have withdrawn their protest against the conditions of the Chinese Northern Railway Extension Loan, and especially the protest against the appointment of an English railway engineer and of an English accountant to supervise the work of the railway?

Mr. BRODRICK: We have not heard that the Russian Minister has actually withdrawn his protest, which was made verbally. But so far as we are aware it has not been confirmed by any written communication, and we have reason to believe that it will not be renewed. The object of the protest was indicated in the answer given yesterday.

SIR E. ASHMEAD-BARTLETT: Are we to understand that the Russian Government have not supported the demand of their Minister at Pekin?

Mr. BRODRICK: I cannot add anything to what I have said.

SALES OF CROWN ESTATES IN SCOTLAND.

Mr. WEIR (Ross and Cromarty): I beg to ask the Secretary to the Treasury if he will state whether any of the £44 969 8s. 5d. received from the sales

of estates, as recorded in the Woods, Forests, and Land Revenue Abstract Accounts 1897-8, has been derived from estates in Scotland; and, if so, will he give the names of the estates?

Mr. HANBURY: Out of the £44,969 mentioned by the honourable Member £1 10s. 0d. was received from estates in Scotland for the sale of a piece of ground adjoining Fortrose Cathedral Churchyard.

SALES OF OBSOLETE VESSELS.

Mr. WEIR: I beg to ask the First Lord of the Admiralty if he will state the respective sums received from the sale during the financial year 1898-9, of torpedo boats Nos. 68, 88, and 98, also the ships " Victor Emmanuel," " Indus," " Resistance," and " Nelson"?

THE SECRETARY TO THE ADMIRALTY (Mr. W. E. MACARTNEY, Antrim, S.): I have already informed the honourable Member that it is not usual to give the prices realised.

PROVOST MUNGALL OF COWDENBEATH.

Mr. WEIR: I beg to ask the President of the Board of Trade whether he is aware that the Provost of Cowdenbeath, Fifeshire, Provost Mungall, is also manager of the Fife Coal Company at Cowdenbeath, and that the Provost, as representing the local authority, has declined to take any steps to require the Company to provide protection for the public at their railway level crossing which passes across High Street, Cowdenbeath; and, having regard to the fact that the county council, in respect of its road administration, is not responsible to any Government Department, will he consider the expediency of introducing legislation so that a local authority which happens to be under the control of a private company may be compelled to see that suitable provision is made for the public safety?

THE PRESIDENT OF THE BOARD OF TRADE: No, Sir; this is a matter within the discretion of the Road Authority, and I am not prepared to introduce legislation to interfere with that discretion.

AUTOMATIC RAILWAY COUPLINGS.

MR. GEDGE (Walsall): I beg to ask the President of the Board of Trade on what expert evidence he relied as to accidents on railways and sidings in Great Britain and Ireland caused by coupling and uncoupling trucks, and as to the effect of the American system, when he introduced the Bill for the Regulation of Railways, and whether that evidence was based on oral or written reports, and who gave it; and whether he will lay upon the Table all such reports?

THE PRESIDENT OF THE BOARD OF TRADE: My honourable Friend invites me to take a very inconvenient course—namely, to make a Second Reading speech in answer to a Question. I must reserve what I have to say on the matter until the Second Reading of the Bill.

MR. BAYLEY: Will the right honourable Gentleman place a model of the American couplings in the Tea-room?

THE PRESIDENT OF THE BOARD OF TRADE: I do not propose to exhibit any model. The Measure I have introduced into the House does not set up any coupling, American or otherwise; and I should be very sorry to become godfather to all the various inventions which are in existence in regard to couplings.

MR. COGHILL: Is the right honourable Gentleman aware that in the only place in which these couplings have l een tried in this country they have been condemned in the most unqualified manner by the workmen?

THE PRESIDENT OF THE BOARD OF TRADE: I am not aware of anything of the kind. I am aware that yesterday I saw an entire train at the Great Central terminus fitted with the American automatic couplings.

MR. GEDGE: Can we see the reports?

THE PRESIDENT OF THE BOARD OF TRADE: If my honourable Friend will inform me what reports he requires I will consider the Question. I have already laid on the Table the report of the Assistant Secretary to the Board of Trade dealing with the information he obtained on his visit to America.

ARMY ESTIMATES.

SIR C. DILKE (Gloucester, Forest of Dean): I wish to ask the First Lord of the Treasury whether he is aware that notice was not given in the Blue Order Paper issued to Members this morning of the fact that the Army Estimates were to be taken to-night, and that, in consequence, some honourable Members on both sides of the House who take the greatest interest in the Army Estimates and had put Amendments down to some of the Votes, have left town? I do not know whether I should be in order in putting to you, Mr. Deputy Speaker, the point of order. I prefer at present simply to raise it as a question of public convenience.

THE FIRST LORD OF THE TREASURY (Mr. A. J. BALFOUR, Manchester, E.): It is perfectly true that there was a printer's error in the Blue Order Paper, but it is corrected in the White Paper. I made the statement in the House more than once that the Army Estimates would be taken to-night; and I do not think there can be any misconception in any part of the House as to the intentions of the Government.

SIR C. DILKE: The right honourable Gentleman made such a statement some days ago, but he did not mention it yesterday, and many Members have thought there was a change in the intentions of the Government.

THE FIRST LORD OF THE TREASURY: As far as Government time is concerned it is a matter of indifference to us whether we take the Army Votes to-night or not, but if not to-night, it will be necessary to take them on Tuesday. I am only thinking of the convenience of private Members.

SIR C. DILKE: On a Question of Order, may I ask you, Mr. Deputy Speaker, whether a public notice some days ago by a Minister, that he intended to take a particular Vote on a particular day without any subsequent reference to it, is sufficient as against the order mentioned in the Blue Paper? On the 8th March 1898, there was a similar case in regard to Supply, and on that occasion complaint was made that the Blue Paper, which was effective notice to Members, had been circulated without the item of effective Supply, which had, however, been put on the White Paper. The Secretary to the

Treasury apologised to the House, and Mr. Speaker subsequently said a mistake had evidently been made, and the notice of effective Supply was insufficient. I am aware that there is a precedent of public notice having been given definitely where it was held to overrule this decision, but I want to ask if the somewhat vague public notice of Tuesday last is sufficient under the circumstances that in the meantime there has been no further reference?

Mr. DEPUTY SPEAKER: At a date subsequent to that quoted by the right honourable Baronet an almost identical thing occurred. A precisely similar point was raised on 21st June, 1889. Owing to a printer's error certain Votes did not appear on the Blue Paper, but the error was corrected and the Votes did appear on the White Paper. On that occasion also public notice had been given that the Votes in question would be taken, and Mr. Speaker ruled in consequence that notwithstanding the printer's error the Votes could be taken, and they were taken. I feel bound to follow that precedent.

Mr. CALDWELL (Lanark, Mid.): On Tuesday the notice was that Vote 1 would be taken. Now there are two Army Votes down.

Mr. DEPUTY SPEAKER: I do not think the Government can take more than the one Vote.

Mr. PIRIE (Aberdeen, N.): I appeal to the Government not to take the Army Votes to-night. I, for one, wish to raise an important question as to recruiting.

THE FIRST LORD OF THE TREASURY: I will not go behind appeals of this sort, sincerely made, as I am sure they are, by honourable Members, and I will not take the Army Votes to-night. Therefore, on Monday I shall move to take Tuesday.

COURSE OF BUSINESS.

Mr. McKENNA (Monmouth, N.): What will be the business next Thursday?

THE FIRST LORD OF THE TREASURY: I hope to be able to take the Navy Estimates.

Mr. McKENNA: And on Friday?

THE FIRST LORD OF THE TREASURY: That depends on the progress made on Thursday.

TELEPHONIC COMMUNICATION BILL.

SIR J. FERGUSSON (Manchester, N.E.): I beg to ask the First Lord of the Treasury whether he will postpone the Second Reading of the Telephone Communication Bill, which is down for Thursday next, for another week, as the Bill is not yet printed, and being of great importance requires time for consideration?

THE FIRST LORD OF THE TREASURY: Yes, Sir; I am quite willing to enter into an engagement not to take the Bill for at least a fortnight.

ORDERS OF THE DAY.

SUPPLY.

Considered in Committee.

Mr. JOHN ELLIS (Nottingham, Rushcliffe) in the Chair.

(In the Committee.)

CIVIL SERVICES AND REVENUE DEPARTMENTS (SUPPLEMENTARY ESTIMATES), 1898-99.

CLASS V.

1. £256,000, Supplementary, Uganda, Central and East Africa Protectorates, and Uganda Railway.

Debate resumed on the Question—

"That a supplementary sum not exceeding £256,000 be granted to Her Majesty to defray the charge which will come in the course of payment during the year ending 31st day of March 1899 for grants-in-aid to Uganda, British Central Africa, and British East Africa."

*SIR C. DILKE (Gloucester, Forest of Dean): I had rather anticipated that the Colonial Office Vote would have been taken first, but as we are going to finish the Vote on Uganda I should like to put two questions to the right honourable Gentleman the Under Secretary for Foreign Affairs. Since the discussion which occurred on this Vote a few days ago we have heard from the ordinary sources of information of the return from Lake Rudolph of the expedition under Colonel Macdonald, which started in the autumn. I am sure the House will be glad to obtain any information which the right honourable Gentleman can give us in regard to that expedition, and whether it is intended to abandon the further prosecution of the expedition. The right honourable Gentleman led us to understand that the main object of Major Macdonald's expedition was to explore the neighbourhood of Lake Rudolph, and then to pass on to the sources of the Juba. The very large expense involved in sending the expedition hundreds of miles further than Lake Rudolph has evidently led to its being entirely abandoned ; but, as we understand it, the expedition did leave some small stations in the neighbourhood of that lake which, however, had been previously partially surveyed by two private expeditions. Any information the right honourable Gentleman can give us will be grateful to the House. While I am on this question, I may refer to the slight indignation which the right honourable Gentleman showed at our pressing for information on the case of the Mombasa fugitive slaves. He told this House that it ought to be content with the statement that communication had been made with the Colonial authorities, but that great difficulty was experienced in reaching them. I ask the right honourable Gentleman when these communications with the Colonial authorities took place. Surely the right honourable Gentleman knows quite well that inquiries were made in regard to the matter last Session, and if communication had been made at once to the Colonial authorities the information might have been obtained shortly after the House adjourned last Session ! If the right honourable Gentleman waited till this year before he called for a Report, you cannot wonder at the delay in obtaining the information. I want to ask when the communications were made with the Colonial authorities, and when he expects to receive a Report ?

THE UNDER SECRETARY OF STATE FOR FOREIGN AFFAIRS (Mr. St. J. BRODRICK, Surrey, Guildford): I am sorry that the right honourable Baronet is under the impression that on a previous occasion I had showed indignation in connection with this subject. If there was any, it was not against the right honourable Baronet personally, but only against an expression which was used by another honourable Member, and which seemed to me to be uncalled for. I objected to the expression that we appeared to be purposely withholding information from the public. I have looked into this matter as regards the actual date when communication was made with the Colonial authorities as to the Mombasa fugitive slaves, and I find that there was some little delay at the Foreign Office in making the inquiries. A pledge was given last Session by Mr. Curzon (now Lord Curzon) the day before he was taken ill to make inquiries ; but his illness intervening the matter was not taken up again until he was able to attend to business at the end of August, and there was some delay in sending out instructions to the Protectorate authorities. Had I known that this question would be raised I would have obtained the particulars as to the date when these inquiries were made. As yet we have no information from Mombasa, but it ought to be here in about a fortnight from this date. We are using every power we have in order to accelerate its arrival, and we shall have it before the House when we come to discuss this matter again. With regard to Colonel Macdonald's expedition, it is quite true that since we discussed the Vote last week Colonel Macdonald has actually returned to Mombasa, and is now in telegraphic touch with England. That, however, does not enable me to give the Committee any material information beyond that which I gave to the House a few nights ago. But I may say that Colonel Macdonald has returned to Mombasa from Juba, he having carried out to a considerable extent the work which it was intended he should do, and that his mission has now terminated. I understand that the Colonel, as the result of his expedition, has obtained important and valuable information, but we must now wait the arrival of the mail in order to get the details. As I have said, we have only telegraphic information that Colonel Macdonald has actually reached the coast, and is now on his way to England. When he returns the Government will be prepared to lay on the Table of the House whatever Papers we can that show the results of his expedition. It is to be clearly understood, however, that Colonel Macdonald has carried out his original instructions, and that his expedition has now terminated. The expedition of Colonel Martyr, which is now going on up the Nile, is under separate instructions.

Mr. GIBSON BOWLES (Lynn Regis): The first item in the Estimates of Uganda states that the original Estimate of the grant-in-aid was £142,000, and that the additional sum required is £197,000, so that the so-called Supplementary Estimate is much larger than the original. I wish to raise this point because it is a question of the manner of keeping the public accounts. Supplementary Estimates are intended for items which cannot possibly be foreseen, and they are intended to apply to absolutely nothing else; for, however small they may be, they are always a disturbing element in the public accounts. This year we have two millions of Supplementary Estimates, and these two millions will have to be provided for out of next year's receipts, although sometimes Supplementary Estimates are provided out of the previous year's receipts. I am not sure that a surplus is to be anticipated this time. My point is that a Supplementary Estimate should be capable of being explained as an expenditure that could not have been foreseen at the time the original Estimates were made up. I am, therefore, justified in asking the right honourable Gentleman to give me some answer to the question how it is that when this Estimate for Uganda of £142,000 was made up he did not foresee such a large additional expenditure as £197,000 would be required.

Sir E. ASHMEAD-BARTLETT (Sheffield, Ecclesall): Will the right honourable Gentleman at the same time inform us to what point on the Nile the expedition of Colonel Martyr has reached?

*Mr. BRODRICK: I stated the other night that Colonel Martyr had reached a point on the Nile, the exact name of which I forget. We have had no direct information from him since his expedition left Dufile. There was a rumour that he has not yet reached Lado. As to the honourable Member for King's Lynn, I always welcome him when he appears in the particular rôle of financial purist. When I sat on the other side of the House with him I humbly assisted him in that rôle as far as I could. I think his Question is a perfectly fair one, but I also think I answered it the other night. Of the £197,000, which is the addition to the original Estimate of which he complains, no less a sum than £175,000 was due to the necessity of bringing to Uganda an Indian regiment, and taking it up country at an enormous cost for transport and supplies. Now, the Indian regiment was brought after the original Estimate was framed, and the difficulties of transport in the conditions of the country at the time rendered it impossible to make any estimate of what the expense would be. I may remind the Committee that the bringing of the Indian regiment was absolutely necessary at the time in order to secure the quelling of the mutiny, in which they did such excellent service. I believe I can assure the Committee that there is not a single item in that £197,000 which could have been foreseen at the time the Estimate was prepared. It was entirely due to the mutiny and the bringing of the Indian regiment to Uganda, with the exception of the sum for the new steam launch ordered for the Lake.

*Mr. McKENNA (Monmouth, N.): I do not think the right honourable Gentleman is altogether right in regard to the exceptional expenditure of £197,000 if he compares last year's Estimates with those of 1899-1900. I maintain that had the proper Estimate been taken for Uganda last year we should not have been met now by this extraordinary Supplementary Estimate—so much larger than the original Estimate. Did I understand the right honourable Gentleman to say that Colonel Macdonald's instructions have been fully carried out when he stated that Colonel Macdonald's expedition was completed?

*MR. BRODRICK: The expression I used was that Colonel Macdonald's instructions had been largely carried out. These instructions were that he was to make an exploration of the sources of the Juba, and to map out the whole country. What he attempted to carry out he has carried out—the most difficult part of his instructions. As regards the particular Estimates for Uganda, it must be remembered that they have to be given in some time in November, and that it was absolutely impossible early in November to estimate what would be required in the disturbed state of the country for the following year. Moreover, in the matter of the Uganda Estimates considerable difficulty was experienced because of the lateness with which certain of the accounts were presented or the information with regard to them was received.

CAPTAIN NORTON (Newington, W.): Mr. Deputy Speaker, perhaps the right honourable Gentleman will give us some information with reference to the details of this excess sum of £197,000? Surely there must have been some basis to go on for the original Estimate of £142,000! It seems to me that £197,000 is an enormous sum to take this expedition from Mombasa to Juba and back.

MR. BUCHANAN (Aberdeenshire, E.): Speaking from my experience, and from what has come within my own knowledge as a member of the Public Accounts Committee, I can corroborate the statement of the right honourable Gentleman that the Uganda administration is very much behindhand in rendering its accounts. The Auditor-General has not yet got these accounts later than 31st December 1896. If these accounts were rendered up to date accurately it would be possible to make the Estimates more accurate in future. And I trust that the Colonial authorities in Uganda will be stimulated to render their accounts hereafter more regularly. I should like to ask the right honourable Gentleman as to the second item in the Vote for British Central Africa, of £5,000 for the Sikhs, whether that is in any way connected with the reorganisation of the regiment which was brought up to quell the mutiny, or with those Sikhs who were going back to India after their te·   ·ne had expired/

*SIR C. DILKE : The honourable Gentleman the Member for East Aberdeen seems to be under the impression, as a member of the Public Accounts Committee, that there is some fault on the part of the local administration of Uganda in rendering their accounts at a late date. But if he refers to Mr. Berkeley's report, he will see that the mutiny of the Soudanese was caused by the delay in the preparation of the Estimates for their payment, for the purpose of laying them before the House of Commons. We cannot fix the blame on the local authorities. The fault was with the Foreign Office.

MR. LABOUCHERE (Northampton): My complaint is that we have not got the exact dates in regard to the Mombasa slave case. The right honourable Gentleman does not tell us when he received the information on which he decided to act. Did he learn it from the newspapers, or from reports made outside this House, or from some official source? The girl Kombo, who had been for 10 years under the protection of missionaries at Ribe, was handed over to a former master, Salehe Bin Husein, last July, and the right honourable Gentleman must have had some information on the subject which will enable him to give us any information we require. In all these cases we are put off from time to time. When atrocities take place we are told someone must be written to; and then, long afterwards, we find that the right honourable Gentleman responsible in this House is unable to give us any information at all, and puts it off to some future occasion. In regard to Colonel Macdonald's expedition, it appears to me to be one of the most absurd and eminently silly expeditions ever dreamt of by the mind of man. Colonel Macdonald appears to have been sent on a wild goose expedition to look for the sources of the Juba, and he seems to have come to the conclusion that they did not exist, and were not to be found. The right honourable Gentleman told us, in regard to the Juba river, that the Government had entered into an agreement to make it the frontier between the Italian sphere of influence and our sphere of influence, and he pleaded, as a reason for Colonel Macdonald's expedition, that, having entered into that agreement, we ought to know where the river was. I believe it was known before where the river is, and that steamers have gone up it. There was, therefore, no earthly object in sending an expedition to find where the Juba was. Was Colonel Macdonald recalled, or did he himself come to the conclusion that, as he had spent a large amount of money, he ought to come back? Why, when it was quite well known that there might be trouble in Uganda, and that the people were not well affected to our rule, should you have taken a large number of the Soudanese garrison, which had been raised in order to keep down the Ugandese, and have sent them off to the Juba river? I pointed out the other night that the expedition started with a large number of women and children, who were afterwards sent back. These Soudanese were angry because they understood when they were enlisted in our service that they were to be employed in the Soudan, and to live there with their women and children. When they were ordered to the Juba, they got a vague idea into their heads that you wanted to conquer some other country, to raise the British flag, and declare it part of the British Empire, or some nonsense like that. These Soudanese, who seem an exceedingly intelligent body of men, were not to be caught by such nonsense, and therefore they mutinied. Now, we are told that Colonel Martyr, for whom the main part of the Vote is put down, has gone off on another expedition. I want to understand what Colonel Martyr is really doing. Is he confining himself to the waterway with his gunboats, or is he in any sort of way taking steps to establish posts in order to administer the vast extent of country that lies between Uganda and Omdurman, or wherever the Egyptian frontier is at the present moment? Are you, at the present moment, engaged in any expedition with the view of practically bringing under the British Protectorate those large tracts of country which you say are within our sphere of influence? I have not yet understood why the right honourable Gentleman puts down this large expenditure to the necessity of moving an Indian regiment up to Uganda. He says, perfectly truly, that it is an exceedingly expensive operation, but he should have

thought of that before he entered into that expedition. I take it that that regiment of Indians consists of 1,000 men. Do I understand that the whole of that £150,000 was expended in sending these Indians up to Uganda? There is another point I should like to ask. When you send a regiment up country, you have to take porters from the coast. Is the way of getting these porters a system of slavery? Do you make an arrangement with the owners of the porters and pay them for their services; and are these porters actually and positively obliged to go, whether they like it or not? Is it not the case that they are naturally subject to the discipline of slaves; and although they receive a small amount of money themselves, does not the largest amount of the money paid for their services go to their owners? Again, does the right honourable Gentleman say that there are at present a sufficient number of troops in Uganda, or are we to anticipate further reinforcements of troops being sent there? The fact is, that this Uganda is a perfect sink for the money of England. Nobody did suppose when that country was taken over in the vague way we generally do these things, that we should go on spending money as we are spending it at the present time. The right honourable Gentleman says that he does not contemplate administering the country until the railway is built. But that will take many years. The right honourable Gentleman himself says it will take three years. Are we to go on perpetuating this enormous expenditure of money for years to come? Here you have a huge country, with a large population; you are attempting to rule it on the cheap, because you hope when you have a railway you will get more money to administer it. All this is an entire mistake. What we should have done was to have withdrawn these troops, and to have had nothing to do with Soudanese regiments or Indian regiments. A certain number of missionaries were there, and they got on very well before you went there; but ever since you have been there, there has been a long series of wars. You are never satisfied with the frontiers you have. Take the case of Unyora: it is perfectly understood that that country was not in any way connected with Uganda. We were told that the King of Unyora—King Kaba-rega—was a very wicked man, and he was sent out of his country, and Unyora was annexed to Uganda. This is all the more preposterous because, first of all, you sent a force to attack King Kabarega, as he occupied regions which belonged to Egypt, and that you said you wanted to establish Egyptian rule there. Is the Egyptian flag flying in Unyora, or is the English flag? or, under the system of the partnership of the lion and the lamb, are the English and the Egyptian flags flying there? So far as I know, we have declared our Protectorate over Unyora, but what earthly right had we, if the country belonged to Egypt, to conquer that country and lay hold of it for ourselves?

*MR. BRODRICK: So far as I have been able to follow the remarks of the honourable Gentleman, I think he made them, and that I answered them, on the last occasion on which this Vote was discussed. We had also a Division on it. Item C (grant-in-aid of British East Africa) was discussed separately. I wish to know, Mr. Ellis, if the honourable Gentleman is in order in discussing this question?

THE DEPUTY CHAIRMAN: I think the honourable Member is in order. If he had not been, I would have called him to order at once.

SIR E. ASHMEAD-BARTLETT: Can the right honourable Gentleman the Under Secretary for Foreign Affairs give us any further information as to the real character of the Soudanese troops? On the last occasion on which the honourable Member for Northampton addressed the Committee, he described these Soudanese troops as the most horrible set of brutes that had ever existed. To-night he describes them as a highly intelligent set of men.

MR. LABOUCHERE: There is such a thing as an intelligent brute.

SIR E. ASHMEAD-BARTLETT: One other question I should like to ask. The honourable Member for Northampton informed us that the missionaries had a very happy time of it before our arrival in Uganda. I want to know whether

Mr. Labouchere.

that happy time was illustrated by the murder of Bishop Hannington?

*MR. BRODRICK: My honourable Friend has asked me questions to which he obviously does not wish a reply. He must know by long experience, if he has watched the honourable Member for Northampton closely enough, that that honourable Member always supplies in one speech the answers to the statements he has made in another. The honourable Gentleman always finds out that what he has written has been more or less discredited by someone, and he never returns to the charge a second time. More especially is this the case with regard to Uganda. When the honourable Member for Northampton desires to treat a subject seriously he is always comic, and when he endeavours to treat a subject from a comic point of view it is really tragic. He is anxious that I should explain why it is that in six months I have not obtained information regarding the Mombasa fugitive slaves. I have already explained that there was some delay on account of Lord Curzon's illness, and I cannot go beyond that, because the details have not passed through my hands. The honourable Gentleman also made a point in regard to the expeditions of Colonel Macdonald and Colonel Martyr. Now, I stated the other night very clearly what the intentions of the Government are as to the administration of Uganda. I told the Committee that Lord Salisbury proposed to continue the administration of those districts over which we have established control, but that he did not intend, until the railway was further advanced, to extend our borders and attempt to establish administrative posts further than was necessary. The one exception was the expedition under Colonel Martyr. That expedition was meant to join hands with Lord Kitchener on the Nile. But in making that statement I could not give a pledge at the time that Colonel Martyr would do more than establish such posts as are necessary to maintain communications. At these posts such administration as is necessary will, of course, be carried out. Beyond that, it is not proposed to involve the House, in regard to the administration of Uganda, until the railway is completed and we can send up supplies. I have been asked to give the items of the expenditure on Colonel Macdonald's expedition. The main items are: Rations, which are of an especial kind for Indian troops, £110,000; transport, £17,500; mules and saddles, £15,000; stores, £35,000; making altogether, £175,000. So far as I know no money was thrown away, or unnecessary expense incurred. We have done all that was asked us by the military authorities on the spot, and we have done all that was asked us by the military authorities at home. We believe that the time is coming when the Indian regiment can be dispensed with and be brought down to the coast. Lastly, in regard to the Soudanese, the honourable Gentleman has answered himself. There is no doubt that the original body of Soudanese enlisted were a good set of men; but they had been influenced by other men who came over the border, and who had already given trouble of which we were not aware. We have had the very highest accounts of the Soudanese troops and their present officers, and we shall avoid as far as possible in the future the constant changes of officers, which were formerly a source of trouble.

Mr. LABOUCHERE: What is the condition of the porters?

*Mr. BRODRICK: I do not know what their particular condition is at the present moment; but there is no difficulty in getting a supply of porters.

Mr. LABOUCHERE: In former expeditions up to Uganda porters were employed who were obtained from their owners, on the condition that the owners should receive certain sums of money for their services. I wish to know whether the porters employed on this expedition were of this class of slaves?

*Mr. BRODRICK: There have been various changes in regard to porters. Last year, with the enormous increase of the forces going up country, there was necessarily a great increase in the number of porters employed. There were considerable difficulties in connection with the demand for porters on account of the extension of the railway at the same moment. The question, however, was carefully considered on the spot; and ultimately the Protectorate authorities

succeeded in establishing a proper service.

Mr. LABOUCHERE: I only ask a plain answer to my plain question. What was the status of these porters? Were they slaves or were they not?

*Mr. BRODRICK: I never heard any suggestion that they were slaves. I believe that some question arose in the early days as to whether some of the men who were employed as porters were supposed to have been forced. But, so far as I am aware, there was no question of slavery in regard to the Uganda porters. I believe, as a matter of fact, that a certain number of them had escaped from slavery; but they were taken on as free labourers.

Sir R. REID (Dumfries Burghs): This point about slavery is a very serious one. Some of us entirely objected to the propriety of our going to Uganda at all, and we pointed out that one of the methods formerly adopted there was that slaves which were publicly employed had been hired from their masters, and that masters let out slaves to different people. What we ask is whether or not the organised system of hiring slaves is going to be continued. The right honourable Gentleman does not appear to recollect that circumstance. Can he tell us now whether that is the system by which the railway is being built, and whether stores are being taken up country by the organised employment of slaves from their masters by the British Government? Can the right honourable Gentleman tell us whether that is the case or not? If he cannot tell us I think he will see that it is proper that he should obtain the information as soon as he can, so that the House may know that there is no direct encouragement or recognition of the employment by this country of slaves, as such, in the building of the railway. A second point I wish to make is this. There is a rather ominous observation made by the right honourable Gentleman in regard to the intention of the Government in extending the boundaries of British possessions in Uganda. I think that the right honourable Gentleman said twice that until the railway is completed there was no intention of extending the boundaries. Are we to understand from that that there is any fixed intention of extending the boundaries in these territories at any time?

*Mr. BRODRICK: In 'regard to the last point, the question of extending the boundaries, it is not a question of extending the boundaries of the Protectorate, but of establishing posts at points where we may come into conflict with the natives. In that enormous territory you may have a few points at which our influence is not felt, and where trade would not consequently follow. But as time goes on we may make an extension of administrative posts. In regard to the first portion of the right honourable Gentleman's remarks, as far as I recollect it, from reading the Blue Book, the question which arose was that certain tribes should furnish a certain amount of labour on a general claim, for pay; which was interpreted here to mean a claim by the masters for the services so rendered by their tribesmen. That was long before my time. I cannot say from memory when that system was established, but if it ever existed it was put a stop to. I can assure the Committee that so far as I am aware the whole of the labour now employed, either on the railway or in porterage, in Uganda is free labour, for which the men themselves are paid wages at so much a head.

*Mr. McKENNA: I wish to ask the right honourable Gentleman whether the men employed were hired from Zanzibar masters at Zanzibar; and whether Colonel Macdonald was recalled from his expedition to Juba, or whether he came back of his own motion. I rather gathered that he has been recalled, and if that be so, how much of the expenses in the Supplementary Estimates were in consequence of Colonel Macdonald's expedition.

*Mr. BRODRICK : I cannot go into details until the accounts come in. Colonel Macdonald was not recalled. He returned having carried out the trust committed to him. As to the Zanzibar masters, I gave an answer just now. There never was any case of a contract so far as I know in which the wages were paid to masters; but if there was, *Sir R. Reid.*

it is not so now. The men are paid individually.

Captain NORTON: Can the right honourable Gentleman state on whose recommendation an Indian regiment was sent to Uganda for this work? The right honourable Gentleman says that the cost of the rations was £110,000, but surely a very large proportion of that must have been for camels, and there must have been a very heavy loss of these camels. The amount of impedimenta must have been enormous. Is it not the custom to take Somali men and train them on the spot for this work, as they are far more effective than other native troops? On whose recommendation were these Indian troops sent, and what was the cost of the Indian regiment as compared with the cost of Somalis, had they been employed?

Mr. BAYLEY (Derbyshire, Chesterfield): I would like to ask the right honourable Gentleman whether the money we are voting to-day is for free labour or whether it is for slave labour? That is the real question. Are these men employed on the railway free men, or are they slaves? Will the right honourable Gentleman make inquiry if he does not know the facts?

*Mr. BRODRICK: I really must apologise to the Committee. It seems impossible for me to make myself understood or to convey my meaning to the honourable Member. I have answered this question twice, and I do not think I should convince the honourable Gentleman if I answered it again.

*Mr. WEIR (Ross and Cromarty): I do not rise to discuss this question of slavery, but only to ask what is the cost of the new steam launch provided for the lake.

*Mr. BRODRICK: I believe that the actual cost of the launch on delivery would be £10,000.

Mr. BRYN ROBERTS (Carnarvonshire, Eifion): I should like to know with whom the contracts of the men employed on the railway are made; whether they are made with the individual workmen, or whether they are made with some agent, who assures the Government that he has some power over the workmen to make them work—in other words, whether there is a contract with each individual labourer or a general contract with an agent? In the second place, I would ask what are the terms of the contract? Is it a contract day by day, or for a fixed term; and if for a fixed term, for how long? I would ask, also, is there a payment made to anybody besides the individual workman?

*MR. HEDDERWICK (Wick Burghs): I understand the staple article of food among Indian troops is rice. If so, are we to suppose that this Indian regiment consume £110,000 worth of rice, or does the term "rations" include other items than food?

Original Question put and passed.

CLASS II.

2. £2,400, Supplementary, Colonial Office.

Motion made and Question proposed—

"That a supplementary sum not exceeding £2,400 be granted to Her Majesty to defray the charge which will come in the course of payment during the year ending 31st March 1899, for salaries and expenses of Her Majesty's Secretary of State for the Colonies."

SIR E. ASHMEAD-BARTLETT: I would like to ask whether I should be in order on this Vote, which includes £750 for salaries, wages, and allowances, in discussing the position of affairs in the Transvaal?

THE DEPUTY CHAIRMAN: No, I think the honourable Member would not be in order.

Question put and passed.

CLASS V.

3. Motion made, and Question proposed—

"That a supplementary sum not exceeding £139,425 be granted to Her Majesty to defray the charge which will come in the course of payment during the year ending 31st day of March 1899, for sundry Colonial services, including certain grants-in-aid."

Motion made—

"That the item B, £70,000 for the Gold Coast (grants in aid of Northern Territories) be omitted from the proposed Vote."—(*Mr. Weir.*)

*MR. WEIR: The Motion I have put down is in respect of £70,000 for a grant in aid of the Northern Territories of the Gold Coast. The original estimate was £25,000, and a sudden jump up has been made to £95,000. On page 20 of the Estimates it is stated that the additional sum of £70,000 is required because the original Estimate was based on incomplete information supplied from the Colony. Now, I think we are entitled to know who is responsible for giving this inaccurate information to the Colonial Office. I also notice that in a second note under this item it is stated that so much of this expenditure as is found to be due to the cost of telegraph construction, which is believed to be from £25,000 to £30,000, is to be treated as a loan to be repaid by the Colony. I think we are entitled to know whether it is the intention to make the Colony pay interest on the balance of that amount, for in the last Report dealing with the Gold Coast Colony, dated 1896, it is stated that the Colony has no public debt. If we are to give money in this way to a Colony which has no public debt, without a return, I think it is most unfair to the taxpayers of this country. For what purpose is this money required? I find a reference in the Estimates that it is for the construction of roads. But surely that is a duty obligatory on the chiefs of the tribes. It appears to me that we are going to supply this £70,000 for the purpose of maintaining a number of idle native chiefs and their men. Why should they not do the work themselves, and why should a Colony without any public debt move the Colonial Office to ask this House to provide this sum of £70,000? I am not going to enter into the subject of the difficulty of getting money for the Highlands of Scotland, but I am satisfied that if the Secretary for Scotland had asked for £70,000 to do some good work, not for idle chiefs, but for an industrious people, he would have got very little encouragement from the Chancellor of the Exchequer; and yet the Colonial Secretary comes down here and boldly asks us for this £70,000.

I protest against this system of providing large sums of money for a Colony which has no public debt. I beg to move the Motion which stands in my name. I hope, however, the right honourable Gentleman the Secretary for the Colonies will give the Committee such information on the point as will afford me an opportunity of withdrawing my Motion.

MR. LABOUCHERE: My honourable Friend has made some most pertinent remarks, and has asked for certain information, which is undoubtedly required before we can pass the Vote for this money. And I am surprised that the right honourable Gentleman the Secretary for the Colonies does nothing but sit there on the Treasury Bench nodding his head and smiling. I would have thought that the right honourable Gentleman would have bounded up to answer the honourable Member for Ross and Cromarty. As it is, the honourable Member's statement appears to me to stand undisputed by the Colonial Secretary. Does the right honourable Gentleman imagine that he can get vast sums of money in Supplementary Estimates from the House without explanation? Perhaps the right honourable Gentleman will get up afterwards and give us a very clear and satisfactory account of this expenditure. The fact is, we are really spending far too much on these African ventures; and all this money is wasted and squandered in a desperate attempt to get a species of bastard Empire within the tropics of Africa. What I understand is, that this money is to be given to the Colony of the Gold Coast, which is actually in funds and has no public debt. If that be the case, the Colony itself ought to pay for its own public works. There is one reason why we should not give any money to the Gold Coast Colony, and that is the mode in which it gets its revenue. Last year the revenue amounted to £237,857, and of this amount it is stated that £162,847 was obtained from the duties on spirits, tobacco, and guns. We may deduct the duties on tobacco and guns, and presume that £150,000 was obtained from the duty on spirits. We are always boasting of our civilising mission in the world. The Colonial

Mr. Weir.

Secretary told us lately that we have a mission from Heaven to civilise these tropical countries. And this is how we do it! In 1896 no fewer than 126,000 gallons of spirits were imported into the Gold Coast. In 1897 the amount was increased to 127,000 gallons of spirits, or an increase of 43,000 gallons. They were not even British spirits. I have no particular sympathy with the British distiller. Still, if we go into this poisonous business, we ought to give the benefit of it to the poisoners of this country instead of the poisoners of Germany. It is perfectly monstrous to levy the greatest part of the revenue of the Colony by sending vile spirits to its most unfortunate people, and to call that a mode of civilising them. We are told that we are now going to give freer access to the country, and are going to spend £70,000 in telegraphic communications. The telegraphs will be used, I suppose, to wire that the spirits have arrived, and their price. If the honourable Member for Ross and Cromarty goes to a Division, I will support him. But if the right honourable Gentleman the Colonial Secretary says that we don't want to extend our territory any further, and that we do not consider that we have a right to obtain the best part of our revenue from spirits, I shall be inclined to vote for him. But he tells us, practically, in these Estimates that we are going to increase the revenue from spirits, and therefore I think the House ought to go against the Vote as a protest against the money being spent in telegraphic communications with the Colony. There are many uses for the money in England, and it would be a boon if the poisonous spirits were excluded altogether from the Colony.

THE SECRETARY OF STATE FOR THE COLONIES (Mr. J. CHAMBERLAIN, Birmingham, W.): The speech of the honourable Member for Northampton seems to me not to be relevant to the Vote, nor does it seem pertinent to the discussion of the number of the troops necessary to preserve order throughout the northern territories of the Gold Coast to raise the whole question of the consumption of spirits in West Africa. There is no intention of putting on the taxpayer of this country a single farthing of the expenditure for telegraphic communications in West Africa. It is only in consequence of the forms of the Treasury that we have to put this temporary loan which we have asked for on the Estimates. Every penny of it will be repaid by the Colony. So far as ·he telegraphic expenditure is concerned, I am informed that it will amount to between £25,000 and £30,000, and not a penny of it will be placed as a charge either for principal or interest, on the taxpayers of this country. The honourable Member for Northampton having referred to the question of the consumption of spirits, might have, I think, recognised the fact that I have taken more trouble since I came into office than anyone else in order to deal with this matter, and to reduce, if possible, the consumption of spirits in these native States. It is always extremely difficult —I do not say it is absolutely impossible—for us to raise our duty upon spirits above the duties which foreign countries continue to levy. If we do so it is said, with some show of reason, that we should lose not only the trade in spirits, but other legitimate trade which goes with the trade in spirits. Therefore, our action in this matter has been determined really, to a large extent, by the action of other Powers. A Conference, however, has been called at Brussels to deal with the question, and the instructions to the British representative set forth that we are prepared to raise the duties to any level to which foreign countries are agreed to go, that we should prefer a high level of duty, and that there is no level of duty which is too high for us. I may say in regard to the special case of the Gold Coast that I have recently authorised an Ordinance by which the duty on spirits is to be raised 1s. per gallon. I have taken the step, unusual as I feel it to be, in spite of the fact that up to the present time the duties of the neighbouring countries have not been altered. Now, I come to the point, to the particular point raised by the honourable Member for Ross and Cromarty, who asked why it was there had been such a large increase in the Vote. I am afraid that owing to my indisposition I did not see the exact words of the Estimate which were put on the Paper. I admit the honourable Gentleman was justified in thinking that as these words stand they seem to imply some blame to the officials of the Gold Coast Territories. It is

quite true that the Estimates were incomplete, but the Colonial officials are not to blame. In the circumstances, it was perfectly impossible for them to make a better Estimate or to anticipate what has actually occurred. You must remember what the state of things was a year or two ago. It was this: Our neighbours, both French and German, were rapidly over-running our Hinterland both of the Gold Coast and Lagos. No preparation whatever had been made to meet that, and I think it is very much to be regretted, but not to be wondered at. We had no troops at our disposal, and the chance was that the whole of our territories would be rushed before we had any troops on the spot. The Government, however, did the best they could. We called for a West India regiment, and began to raise, as quickly as we could, a Native regiment. All this took time, but meanwhile the progress of the French expedition particularly was continuing. They were most active and energetic, and we soon found that more considerable operations on our part than we had originally contemplated would be necessary if we were to preserve these territories. And so we had to bring another regiment from the West Indies, and to incur great expense which was not anticipated at the time these Estimates were prepared. Let me point out why these operations are so expensive. The principal town which we occupy at the extreme end of the Yambada territory is about 500 miles from the coast. It takes 36 days to send an officer on leave down to the coast, and the cost of his journey with his necessary luggage and porters is £54. The carriage of goods, the same distance costs £135 per ton. It is perfectly evident that as long as that continues the cost of a movable force in that country must be exceedingly great. That large expenditure put upon us is not due in any way to the policy of the Gold Coast Colony, but has been forced upon us for international reasons, and owing to the energetic action of our French and German neighbours. It seems to me, therefore, to be very unfair to put the whole of the cost on the Colony. The Colony undertook the payment of the whole cost of the Ashanti war, and a balance remains, it is true, but it is being rapidly paid off, and before long it will be wholly repaid. In the same way it is my intention that the Colony shall take on its own shoulders and ultimately repay every expenditure intended for the development of these territories. The Committee may think I have been too sanguine in the past, but I am more confident than ever that these Colonies will turn out to be a most valuable possession, and I am acting in that belief. I am placing on the Colony a certain burden in the shape of debt with the fullest confidence that before very long it will be able to repay it. I base that confidence not on the consumption of spirits, but on the general increase of the general trade which is taking place, and which I anticipate will develop to an extraordinary degree as soon as we get railway communication. This railway service has already been commenced for a certain distance. I base my confidence still more upon prospects of the gold industry of the country, which I profess I do not wish to boom at this time, but which, from all the information I have obtained from many different quarters, is going to be a most solid, valuable, and profitable industry in the Gold Coast Colony. I think the House, therefore, need have no fear that this expenditure will recur for any lengthened period of years. And I am quite convinced that it will be recouped, directly or indirectly, before very long. I will just say in passing that my hopes of the trade of the Gold Coast Colony, independent of the gold industry, are greatly confirmed by the improvement which is taking place in the trade of the other West African Colonies. In Sierra Leone, for instance, and Lagos. The improvement is very remarkable in the case of Lagos, where the British imports amount to nearly a million sterling. That is a very considerable increase, and there is every probability that that increase will be continued. I hope I have now explained satisfactorily the difficulty caused by the irregularity in the Estimate, and how that irregularity occurred; and I trust that the honourable Member for Ross and Cromarty will withdraw his Amendment.

MR. BUXTON (Tower Hamlets, Poplar): I viewed this enormous expenditure with some alarm. It is a very large expenditure for such a small Colony. But I am bound to say,

Secretary of State for the Colonies.

after having heard what the right honourable Gentleman has said in support of the proposal he has made to this Committee, that this particular Vote is not an unreasonable one. I understand the right honourable Gentleman practically admits that the bulk of this expenditure was due to the international difficulties which, unfortunately, we had got into with the French nation as to the boundaries of the northern territories of Gold Coast Colony. If we were to maintain our position at all in connection with the Gold Coast and Lagos, if we were not to allow ourselves to be squeezed out of the Hinterland of these Colonies, it was essential that the Imperial Government and the Colonial Government should take action in the matter. No doubt, £100,000 seems to be a considerable amount, but as the right honourable Gentleman has explained, many of the troops and the officers had to be sent up country, and the cost of their transport was very heavy, and could scarcely have been conducted on a more economic basis. I understand from what the right honourable Gentleman has said that a considerable amount of the expenditure will ultimately be borne by the Colony itself. I do not think, therefore, that under these circumstances this particular Vote is an unreasonable one. I was glad to hear what the right honourable Gentleman said in regard to the future of the Gold Coast, Lagos, and of the Niger Territory. We have not had the opportunity of judging completely the possibilities as regards these three Colonies until now; but I consider that there is a considerable future before them, more esepcially the Gold Coast, when the railway shall have been completed. There is little doubt that that Colony will be able, not only to pay its way in the future as it has done in the past, but that it will form a very valuable asset of the British Empire. The right honourable Gentleman has made it clear that in regard to the Gold Coast there is no intention of developing that Colony at the expense of the British taxpayer. In regard to the question of railways, telegraphs, and other items, these will be of great advantage to the trade of the Colony and of the mother country, and the whole expense of them will be borne ultimately by the Colony itself. This particular item appears to me to be one on a totally different basis from the other Votes we discussed this evening. It is founded on a policy which has largely actuated our relations with our Colonies, namely, that they should be as far as possible self-supporting. Under the circumstances explained by the right honourable Gentleman, I shall support this Vote. I should like to say, if the right honourable Gentleman will allow me to do so, that I cordially congratulate him upon the steps he has taken in regard to the question of the spirit duties on the West Coast of Africa. It has been recognised that the right honourable Gentleman has done a great deal by his action there, and by endeavouring to call together the Conference at Brussels, to diminish the evils of the drink traffic referred to. I shall be glad of any information as to the likelihood of the date being fixed for the Brussels Conference. If active steps are being taken to bring about that Conference, it will give the greatest satisfaction to all of us.

*SIR C. DILKE: So far as the charge is explained by the necessity of sending for another West Indian regiment, the right honourable Gentleman will have my support, but I wish to say a word or two on the subject of a separate Colonial army if it is relevant to the present Vote.

THE SECRETARY OF STATE FOR THE COLONIES: I think my right honourable Friend will find it more convenient to discuss the question referred to in connection with the more important Vote which will appear on the general Estimates of the year. In answer to the honourable Gentleman opposite, I may be allowed to say that the Vote for a Native force is not entirely a new Vote, but rather takes the place of a different expenditure. Hitherto, what has happened is this. Wherever there has been a disturbance, whether it was at Sierra Leone, or the Gold Coast, or at Lagos, we have had to make a demand at once on the West India Regiment. Now the West India Regiment is an extremely admirable fighting force; at the same time, it is an extremely expensive force. Although they are men of colour, the climate does not seem to agree with them very well, and they require attendance in the shape of porters, transport, stores, and so forth, which make them very much more expensive than the Native regiments would be which we propose to substitute for them. Of course, as soon as the Native regiments are finally established, I hope we shall never again see a West Indian regiment in a West African colony. Of course, that will probably lead to a reduction in the cost of the West India Regiment, and this saving will compensate for any increase in the Colonial Vote.

*SIR C. DILKE: The right honourable Gentleman has alluded to the West African Regiment apart from the West African frontier force. I think it would be desirable to give the House some information in the form of a Return—I do not say to-day—as to the new departure which has been taken in this matter. Everyone will agree that there must be a force of armed police under the Colonial Office; but a regimental force which goes through regimental drill ought to be under the control of the War Office, so as to ensure unity of command. It will, no doubt, be very difficult to draw an exact line between a Native military police force and the force it would be necessary to employ regimentally in time of war. Hitherto, there has been great clashing of the various authorities, the troops under the War Office and the troops under the Colonial Office and Foreign Office being employed together. The Under Secretary for War told us the other day that 21,000 Foreign Office and Colonial Office troops are now being employed in Africa at a cost of a million a year, and as the expenditure is becoming larger and larger, the matter is one as to which we ought to have full information. I will not press the point further, but would ask the right honourable Gentleman the Under Secretary of State for the Colonies to take some steps to keep us fully informed in the matter.

THE SECRETARY OF STATE FOR THE COLONIES: I can give the information at once. We intend to have two battalions of the West African frontier force, amounting together to 2,600 men. It is further intended to have one battalion of something under 1,000 men for the Gold Coast. Their permanent headquarters will be on the Gold Coast, and on the Niger, respectively, but, if necessary, I hope it will be quite possible to make these forces interchangeable, so that they may be used for a common purpose.

*SIR C. DILKE: That does not exceed what we were told last year. What we were beginning to get alarmed ' at was the very large sum mentioned by the Under Secretary of State for War, namely, one million a year.

THE SECRETARY OF STATE FOR THE COLONIES: As this Colonial force gets into working order, which it is doing very rapidly indeed, I hope the constabulary or police will become more and more a civil force. We shall then reduce its numbers, and use it simply as a police force for the preservation of order.

MR. BUXTON: Will the right honourable Gentleman say whether the Colony will contribute something to the expense of the new force?

THE SECRETARY OF STATE FOR THE COLONIES: I am ready to give every information. By way of illustration, I will take the case of Lagos. We have in the Hinterland there the new West African frontier force, 2,600 strong. That force, we hope, will be quite sufficient for preserving order for preventing slave raiding, for stopping war between the tribes—all operations of a military character which, up to this time, have always been more or less undertaken by the constabulary. If in future those duties are undertaken by the West African force, the constabulary will not be required for the purpose, and we shall then reduce their numbers, and, as I say, make them more of a civil character. I see no reason why the same thing should not take place on the Gold Coast. For some years to come, it is clear that a considerable proportion, if not the whole, of this cost must be laid on Imperial revenue, because it is the result, I will not say of the Imperial policy, but of Imperial Government. I do not call it Imperial policy, because it was not our policy. Our policy was to allow these Hinterlands a much slower development. We have been forced into the position of taking up that policy, and having taken it up, we have,

Secretary of State for the Colonies.

of course, to carry it on. But if we had had our way—if our hands had not been forced by other Powers—there is no doubt it would have been a considerable time before it would have been necessary to take up the development of the Hinterland; but it is my conviction— I do not pledge myself as to the exact period—that before very long, not only the whole of the Gold Coast force, but the whole of the West African frontier force will be paid for by the West African Colony ut of local resources.

MR. LABOUCHERE: The right honourable Gentleman has expressed the opinion that the loan is likely to be repaid. I venture to say that there is no evidence before us of any such financial probability. The right honourable Gentleman suggests that gold may be found in the country, and that this may produce a great deal of money. Well, I imagine the climate there is so extremely bad that, even if the gold were found, it would be very ' doubtful whether, as it could not be carried into another world, it would benefit anybody. There is no evidence of any kind, apart from the sanguine mind of the right honourable Gentleman, to warrant any confidence that this loan is likely to be repaid, or even the interest upon it met. We have already had considerable experience of the granting of loans to the West Indies. We are perpetually asked to give doles and grants and loans to the Indians, and we know perfectly well what a curse our Colonial possessions often are in this matter. The right honourable Gentleman has drawn a glowing picture of the future of these Colonies. For my part, I prefer to rely upon facts, and take existing facts as they stand. I am perfectly certain that if the loan had to be advanced on the guarantee of the Colony alone, you would not find any business man ready to make it. The right honourable Gentleman quoted Lagos, and said that all these gold Colonies are likely to increase in value. I hold in my hand the last Report with which we are favoured, the annual Report for 1897. And what do I find? Not only have the exports fallen off, but the imports have fallen off during the year to the amount of £131,000. Surely, in the face of these figures, it cannot be said that Lagos is thriving and extending—it has fallen back. Then the right honourable Gentleman said that he proposed to deal with the liquor question by raising the duty upon imported spirits. This will not reduce the amount of liquor consumed. The natives may, perhaps, do a little more work to get their liquor, but liquor they will have so long as you are prepared to provide it. It seems to me that it would be infinitely more reasonable to propose at the Brussels Conference that no liquor should be imported into any of these African Colonies.

THE DEPUTY CHAIRMAN: Order, order! I do not think the honourable Member is justified in discussing the liquor question at this stage.

MR. LABOUCHERE: It appears that a portion of this money is to be expended on the army which is to be raised in these Colonies. I believe it to be a doubtful policy to embody an army of negroes in order to employ them against other savages. Lord Chatham, in referring to our use of Red Indians in America, described them as "the hell hounds of savage war," and I am certainly inclined to agree with the description in this case because these black troops cannot be kept under control. In the event of any difficulties occurring, the force will have to be strengthened by the use of British troops. You cannot absolutely depend upon these men, because at any time they may turn against you. The right honourable Gentleman tells us that he hopes the

time will come when the Colony will pay for the troops itself. It is not likely that such a time will ever come. The right honourable Gentleman proposes, in addition to the huge increase in the Army and Navy, to augment the burden on the British taxpayer by increasing the Colonial army by 2,600 men, in order to extend our territories in the interior of Africa. Now, Sir, I am opposed to the extension of territory in the interior of Africa. I think the less we have to do with the interior of Africa the better, and I should be exceedingly glad to see any other nation snap up what remains of the interior of Africa, and so fortify and defend it that we should be prevented from going further in acquiring possession in the interior of that God-forsaken country. Under these circumstances, I should certainly divide the House upon the Vote.

*MR. WEIR: I object most strongly to the granting of the proposed sum to the Colony, on the ground that the taxpayers of this country are bound to lose by it, and that we ought not to make gifts of money to people who do nothing to help themselves.

Question put—

"That Item B. £70,000, for the Gold Coast (Grant in Aid of Northern Territories), be omitted from the proposed Vote."—(*Mr. Weir.*)

The Committee divided:—Ayes, 49; Noes, 226.—(Division List No. 38.)

AYES

Abraham, Wm. (Cork, N.E.)
Allen, W. (Newc.-under-Lyme)
Allison, Robert Andrew
Ambrose, Robert (Mayo, W.)
Austin, M. (Limerick, W.)
Bainbridge, Emerson
Burns, John
Caldwell, James
Cameron, Sir Charles (Glasgow)
Cameron, Robert (Durham)
Channing, Francis Allston
Clark, Dr. G. B. (Caithness-sh.)
Condon, Thomas Joseph
Crilly, Daniel
Curran, Thomas B. (Donegal)
Dillon, John
Donelan, Captain A.
Duckworth, James

Fenwick, Charles
Jacoby, James Alfred
Kilbride, Denis
Lambert, George
Lawson, Sir Wilfrid (Cumbrlnd.)
Leng, Sir John
Lewis, John Herbert
Macaleese, Daniel
MacNeill, John Gordon Swift
M'Ghee, Richard
M'Kenna, Reginald
Maddison, Fred.
Mendl, Sigismund Ferdinand
Moore, Arthur (Londonderry)
O'Brien, James F. X. (Cork)
O'Brien, Patrick (Kilkenny)
O'Kelly, James
Power, Patrick Joseph

Price, Robert John
Randell, David
Roberts, John Bryn (Eifion)
Roberts, John H. (Denbighs.)
Souttar, Robinson
Stanhope, Hon. Philip J
Sullivan, Donal (Westmeath)
Tanner, Charles Kearns
Wedderburn, Sir William
Whittaker, Thomas Palmer
Williams, John Carvell (Notts.)
Wilson, Henry J. (York, W.R.)
Wilson, John (Govan)

TELLERS FOR THE AYES—
Mr. Weir and Mr. Labouchere.

NOES.

Acland-Hood, Capt.Sir Alex.F.
Allan, William (Gateshead)
Allhusen, Augustus HenryEden
Allsopp, Hon. George
Archdale, Edward Mervyn
Ascroft, Robert
Ashmead-Bartlett, Sir Ellis
Atkinson, Rt. Hon. John
Bailey, James (Walworth)
Baillie, James E. B. (Inverness)
Balfour, Rt. Hn. A. J. (Manc'r)
Balfour,RtHn GeraldW.(Leeds)
Banbury, Frederick George
Barry,RtHnAH.Smith.(Hunts)
Barry, Sir Francis T. (Windsor)
Bartley, George C. T.
Barton, Dunbar Plunket
Bathurst, Hon. Allen Benjamin
Beach,Rt.Hn.Sir M.H.(Bristol)
Beckett, Ernest William
Bentinck, Lord Henry C.
Bethell, Commander
Bhownaggree, Sir M. M.
Bill, Charles
Blundell, Colonel Henry
Boscawen, Arthur Griffith-
Bowles,T.Gibson (King's Lynn)
Brodrick, Rt. Hon. St. John
Brunner, Sir John Tomlinson
Buchanan, Thomas Ryburn
Burdett-Coutts, W.
Burt, Thomas
Buxton, Sydney Charles
Causton, Richard Knight
Cavendish, V. C. W. (Derbysh.)
Cecil, Evelyn (Hertford, East)
Chaloner, Captain R. G. W.
Chamberlain, Rt.Hn.J. (Birm.)
Chamberlain, J. Austen (Wor.)
Chaplin, Rt. Hon. Henry
Clough, Walter Owen
Cochrane, Hon. Thos. H. A. E.
Coghill, Douglas Harry
Cohen, Benamin Louis
Collings, Rt. Hon. Jesse
Colville, John
Compton, Lord Alwyne
Corbett, A. Cameron (Glasgow)
Cranborne, Viscount
Cripps, Charles Alfred
Crombie, John William
Cross, Alexander (Glasgow)
Cross, Herb. Shepherd (Bolton)
Cubitt, Hon. Henry
Currie, Sir Donald
Curzon, Viscount
Dalkeith, Earl of
Dalrymple, Sir Charles
Davenport, W. Bromley-
Davies, M.Vaughan- (Cardigan)
Denny, Colonel
Dickson-Poynder, Sir John P.
Dixon-Hartland, Sir F. Dixon
Donkin, Richard Sim
Doughty, George
Douglas, Rt. Hon. A. Akers-
Doxford, William Theodore
Drucker, A.

Duncombe, Hon. Hubert V.
Dunn, Sir William
Egerton, Hon. A. de Tatton
Elliot, Hon. A. Ralph Douglas
Fardell, Sir T. George
Farquharson, Dr. Robert
Fergusson, Rt.Hn. Sir J.(Man.)
Finch, George H.
Finlay, Sir Robert Bannatyne
Firbank, Joseph Thomas
Fisher, William Hayes
Fison, Frederick William
Fitzmaurice, Lord Edmond
FitzWygram, General Sir F.
Flannery, Sir Fortescue
Flower, Ernest
Folkestone, Viscount
Foster, Sir Walter (Derby Co.)
Fry, Lewis
Garfit, William
Gibbs,HnA.G.H.(Cty.of Lond.
Giles, Charles Tyrrell
Gilliat, John Saunders
Goldsworthy, Major-General
Gordon, Hon. John Edward
Gorst, Rt. Hon. Sir John Eldor
Goschen,Rt HnG.J.(St.G'rge's)
Goschen, George J. (Sussex)
Goulding, Edward Alfred
Gray, Ernest (West Ham)
Green,WalfordD.(Wednesbury
Greville, Hon. Ronald
Gull, Sir Cameron
Haldane, Richard Burdon
Hamilton, Rt. Hn. Lord Georg.
Hanbury, Rt. Hn. Robert Wm.
Hare, Thomas Leigh
Harwood, George
Hayne, Rt. Hn. Charles Seale-
Heath, James
Heaton, John Henniker
Hedderwick, Thos. Chas. H
Helder, Augustus
Hill, Sir Edwd. Stock (Bristol)
Holland, Wm. H. (York, W.R.
Howard, Joseph
Howell, William Tudor
Hozier, Hn. James Henry Cecil
Jeffreys, Arthur Frederick
Jessel, Capt. Herbert Merton
Johnston William (Belfast)
Johnstone, Heywood (Sussex)
Jones, David Brynmor (S'nsea)
Kemp, George
Kenyon, James
Kimber, Henry
Kinloch, Sir John Geo. Smyth
Knowles, Lees
Lafone, Alfred
Laurie, Lieut.-General
Lawrence,SirE.Durning-(Corn)
Lawrence, Wm. F. (Liverpool)
Lea, Sir Thomas (Londonderry)
Lees, Sir Elliott (Birkenhead)
Leighton, Stanley
Long, Rt. Hon. Walter (L'pool)
Lopes, Henry Yarde Buller
Lorne, Marquess of

Lowles, John
Loyd, Archie Kirkman
Lubbock, Rt. Hon. Sir John
Lucas-Shadwell, William
Macartney, W. G. Ellison
Macdona, John Cumming
Maclure, Sir John William
M'Arthur, Charles (Liverpool)
M'Arthur, Wiliam (Cornwall)
M'Calmont, H. L. B. (Cambs.)-
M'Ewan, William
M'Hugh, E. (Armagh, S.)
M'Killop, James
Malcolm, Ian
Mappin, Sir Frederick Thorpe
Marks, Henry Hananel
Middlemore,John Throgmorton
Milner, Sir Frederick George
Monk, Charles James
Moon, Edward Robert Pacy
Moore, William (Antrim, N.)
More, Robt Jasper (Shropsh.)
Morgan, J. Lloyd (Carmarthen)
Morgan,W.Pritchard(Merthyr)
Morrell, George Herbert
Morton, Arthur H. A. (Deptf'd)
Moulton, John Fletcher
Mount, William George
Murray,RtHnA.Graham(Bute)
Murray, Col. Wyndham (Bath)
Myers, William Henry
Nicholson, William Graham
Nicol, Donald Ninian
Northcote, Hn. Sir H. Stafford
Norton, Capt. Cecil William
Orr-Ewing, Charles Lindsay
Paulton, James Mellor
Perks, Robert William
Phillpotts, Captain Arthur
Pirie, Duncan V.
Plunkett,Rt.Hn.Horace Curzon
Powell, Sir Francis Sharpe
Pryce-Jones, Lt.-Col. Edward
Purvis, Robert
Reid, Sir Robert Threshie
Rentoul, James Alexander
Ritchie, Rt. Hn. Chas.Thomson
Robertson, Herbert (Hackney)
Rothschild, Hon. Lionel Walter
Royds, Clement Molyneux
Russell,Gen.F.S.(Cheltenham)
Russell, T. W. (Tyrone)
Ryder, John Herbert Dudley
Samuel, Harry S. (Limehouse)
Seton-Karr, Henry
Sharpe, William Edward T.
Sidebottom,William (Derbysh.)
Simeon, Sir Barrington
Sinclair, Capt. J. (Forfarshire)
Spencer, Ernest
Spicer, Albert
Stanley, Hn.Arthur (Ormskirk)
Stanley,Edward Jas.(Somerset)
Stanley, Henry M. (Lambeth)
Stanley, Lord (Lancs.)
Stevenson, Francis S.
Strutt, Hon. Charles Hedley
Sturt, Hon. Humphry Napier

Talbot,Rt HnG.J.(Oxf'd Univ.)
Tennant, Harold John
Thorburn, Walter
Thornton, Percy M.
Tritton, Charles Ernest
Valentia, Viscount
Wallace, Robert (Edinburgh)
Wallace, Robert (Perth)
Walton,John Lawson(Leeds,S.)

Walton, Joseph (Barnsley)
Warner, Thomas Courtney T.
Webster, Sir R. E. (I. of W.)
Welby, Lieut.-Col. A. C. E.
Williams, Jos. Powell-(Birm.)
Wodehouse, Rt.Hn.E.R. (Bath)
Wortley, Rt. Hn. C. B. Stuart-
Wyndham, George
Wyndham-Quin, Major W. H.

Wyvill, Marmaduke D'Arcy
Young, Commander (Berks, E.)
Yoxall, James Henry

TELLERS FOR THE NOES—
Sir William Walrond and
Mr. Anstruther.

MR. BUXTON: I wish to ask the right honourable Gentleman a question respecting the Report of the Commission for Sierra Leone. I should like to know when he expects to have that Report, or whether he has already received it, and, if so, when he will have it printed and placed in our hands? I do not propose at the present moment to go into the question of the Hut Tax, or of the rising which took place in Sierra Leone, or rather the causes which created that rising, because that is a matter which has been referred to the Commissioner, and we cannot deal with it until we have his Report before us. But I want to ask the right honourable Gentleman a question as to what recently occurred. When we last discussed this question—it was in the course of the Debate my honourable Friend the Member for Mayo raised on the question of Adjournment—we understood from the right honourable Gentleman in the first place, that the operations which had taken place had been suspended, that, in the second place, a Royal Commission would be appointed to inquire into the matter, and in the third place, that with regard to the Hut Tax, he would maintain an open mind for the time. Not so very long after, we saw in the newspapers that there had been further operations in the same directions and in regard to the same matter, against the chief called Bey Burai, which seem to have been successful in his capture. What I want to ask the right honourable Gentleman is: What caused this suddenly renewed activity in military operations, when we understood that the question of further military operations was to stand over until after the Report of the Royal Commission had been received, and the right honourable Gentleman was in a position to judge whether or not he intended to retain the Hut Tax, which was the alleged cause—I do not say it was the real cause—of the troubles?

THE DEPUTY CHAIRMAN: Order, order! I do not think it would be in order to discuss those questions in connection with this Vote. All that can be discussed is the policy of the inquiry.

MR. BUXTON: Well, Mr. Ellis, I will ask the right honourable Gentleman this question when we get to the general Colonial Vote, because as regards the Commission itself and the cost of it, I have no objection to it, because we were all very glad that the right honourable Gentleman was sending out such an admirable Commission to make inquiries into this matter.

THE SECRETARY OF STATE FOR THE COLONIES: I think the honourable Gentleman cannot have seen my replies to Questions on the same subject. My first reply was to the effect that I had now received the official Report. It will be printed and distributed very shortly.

*SIR C. DILKE: I wish to ask the right honourable Gentleman a question as to the Newfoundland shore. I wish to know whether, pending the reception of the Commissioner's Report, the instructions which have been sent in previous years to Naval officers in regard to what should be done pending the settlement of this shore question have been sent as usual before the fishery, which begins in May. The right honourable Gentleman knows the extremely difficult question that has arisen. The right honourable Gentleman has admitted, year after year, that the action of the Naval officers is beyond all law in fixing the price of bait on the shore—fixing a different price for purchasers according to their nationality. I want to know whether the ordinary instructions——

THE DEPUTY CHAIRMAN: Order! I do not think that question arises on this Vote.

U 2

Mr. GIBSON BOWLES: I also wish to ask a question of the right honourable Gentleman with reference to the Newfoundland shore, and the Royal Commission which has been sent out. I shall not refer to the actual state of facts in Newfoundland, and the action of the Naval officers there, whch the right honourable Baronet has already referred to. No doubt the Newfoundlanders are difficult to handle. What I wish to say is this: The right honourable Gentleman, of course, in negotiating with France with regard to this question is obliged to act through the Foreign Office, and, therefore, he cannot himself, no doubt, give me a direct reply as to the present state of the negotiations with France. Well, I am assured that in the months of December and January last the French Government were thoroughly prepared to entertain any reasonable proposals in this matter. I hope to get from the right honourable Gentleman an assurance that that opportunity was taken advantage of by the Foreign Office, and that negotiations were then opened and are now proceeding. If that be so, I am perfectly certain that a proper settlement may be looked for. If it be not so, then I am afraid that neither this Commission nor anything else will enable us to win the ground that has been lost.

Lord E. FITZMAURICE (Wilts, Cricklade): I wish to ask the right honourable Gentleman if the terms of reference to this Royal Commission have already been communicated to the House—I think not—and if not, whether they will shortly be communicated, because naturally it is a matter of very great interest to the Committee and the House to know precisely what it is that this Royal Commission is inquiring into, and what it is going to report upon. I always myself regretted that certain very important documents dating from the last century, bearing upon this question, had not been put before the House; and, possibly, if this Royal Commission is inquiring into the whole matter it will be a good opportunity of so doing. It is quite true that Lord Salisbury's very full dispatch —a very important, and, if I may say so, in its way a most complete dispatch —is to be found in the Blue Book of, I think, five years ago. It summarises all these very interesting and important documents; but as this is really a matter depending upon the interpretation of documents of the year 1783, I always thought these discussions both in Parliament and outside Parliament have been conducted at considerable disadvantage, owing to the public not being in possession of the actual facts. When I was at the Foreign Office I took a very active part in the examination of these papers, and I have always contended, both in this House and elsewhere, in answer to the point that the French raise upon this question, that the more the documents are examined the stronger will be our case. Now, if this Royal Commission is going to be the means of communicating to the House and the public at large this information, all I can say is that I think Her Majesty's Government will have earned the gratitude of this House and of the country. But at this moment we really do not know what this Royal Commission has been doing, or what it was proposed to do. I do not want to trespass upon your ruling, Sir, in any way. If the right honourable Gentleman can give us any information, or can communicate what the terms of reference to the Royal Commission are, I think the Committee will be glad to have it.

Mr. BUXTON: Do I understand, Sir, that in regard to the new item of payment of this Royal Commission which is to inquire into a specific matter, we are not entitled to discuss the policy of the appointment of that Commission? We cannot, of course, discuss that without discussing the situation which led to the appointment of that Commission. Do I understand that we are excluded from discussing anything in regard to the position of Newfoundland arising on this item?

*Sir C. DILKE: On the same point of order, Sir, I wish to make clear the matter as to which I was asking information from the right honourable Gentleman. The Commission is to "inquire into the state of matters on the Treaty Shore." Now, Sir, a very dangerous state of things on the Treaty Shore has been caused by the action of the naval officers there, under orders communicated by the Admiralty, and of which the Colonial Office are aware. We do not know what the Commission has been doing, but we imagine that it has been inquiring all along the Treaty Shore into these grievances of the population in regard to the action of the Naval officers ordered from here, and I should imagine that we should be in order in asking a Question upon that.

THE DEPUTY CHAIRMAN: As to the causes which may have led to the appointment of the Commission, I think it would be open to make inquiries, but as to the present state of the negotiations with France in regard to this matter, òr as to the policy of this country in attempting to settle the matter, I do not think it can be raised. - The policy of the appointment of the Commission, of course, is open to discussion.

SIR C. DILKE: The questions I was desirous of putting were exactly within the limits of your ruling, Sir. The evidence that has been taken upon and along the Treaty Shore has been as to the relations between the naval officers and the population caused by the French rights. That question is one which has been pressed year after year upon the attention of the Colonial Secretary in this House. In May each year, when the fishing begins, certain regulations are made affecting the sale of bait, and a different rate of price is fixed for the French fishermen and fishermen of other nationalities, for which the Colonial Secretary has stated there is no legal authority. Sir, those regulations are probably being issued now for the present year. I want to know whether the action of the Commission, and of the Government in appointing the Commission which is to consider this matter, has led to any difference in the instructions given to the naval officers upon this point.

THE SECRETARY OF STATE FOR THE COLONIES: In reply to the right honourable Baronet, I must say that I do not agree with his views as to the character and effect of the regulations on the French shore. I do not agree at all that they are in any way the cause of the troubles on that shore. I think it will be shown that they are perfectly satisfactory, and, on the whole, working extremely well. In answer to the question whether there is any alteration now proposed in the regulations, I have to

say that no alteration is proposed in consequence of the appointment of the Commission. We are waiting for the Report of the Commission, and when we get that Report, and are able to found our conclusions upon it, we shall consider what other regulations it may be advisable to make, and issue them in the usual way. The Commission has practically completed its work, the Report is in type, and it will be in the hands of Members very shortly. Of course, if the noble Lord opposite is unwilling to wait for that, and desires to see the terms of reference beforehand, I shall be glad to assist him, but I imagine that he will be satisfied, as the Report certainly will not be long delayed.

DR. CLARK (Caithness) drew attention to a Vote for the Dreadnought Hospital, in connection with a new school which it was proposed to found for the study of tropical diseases. He did not desire to oppose the Vote, but he thought the Committee would be glad if the right honourable Gentleman would give them some information upon it.

THE SECRETARY OF STATE FOR THE COLONIES: I attach the very greatest importance to this Vote, and I am glad the honourable Member does not propose to oppose it. Of course, it is well known that all these Colonies, and especially the West African Colonies, are subject to peculiar diseases of a most distressing and often very dangerous character. I do not know anything which has given more pain and anxiety to me in connection with my tenure at the Colonial Office than the constant reports of deaths of very promising officers in consequence of these diseases. I have endeavoured to see what can be done to make this state of things better. I am not at all hopeless about it, because it is very interesting to observe that the same sort of thing was said of other Colonies which now are, at all events, very fairly healthy. For instance, exactly the same thing happened at the time of our first occupation of Calcutta, and the description given of Calcutta in the early days might be almost word for word the description which I should be inclined to give now to some of the worst of our West African stations. In the same way

Hong Kong was called "The White Man's Grave," and Lord Grey, I think, expressed regret that it had ever been taken over, although he felt that under the circumstances, as we had occupied it so long, it was impossible to give it up. In fact, the view taken in these discussions about Colonies like Calcutta and Hong Kong was very much the same view that the honourable Member for Northampton now takes, from very inaccurate information, in regard to the West African Colonies. I hope, in fact, to do for our West African Colonies very much the same as has been done for Calcutta and Hong Kong. Without being able to say that we are going to make a sanitorium of places of this kind, we at least hope we may reduce the unnecessary mortality which I believe goes on in consequence of preventable causes. Now these preventable causes are numerous, and all of them have had the most careful attention. One cause is insufficient and improper nursing, and the remedy, I am happy to say, now being undertaken by a private association called the Colonial Nursing Association, which is sending out to all these Colonies trained European nurses to attend cases which require their attention. Then a second difficulty has been the difficulty of finding doctors who were acquainted beforehand with these peculiar diseases; the diseases themselves are very peculiar, and it has been almost impossible to give clinical instruction to doctors who were going out to the Coast in these particular diseases. It has been suggested to me by the very able and well-known medical gentleman who is the Colonial Office adviser in all these cases, Dr. Manson, that we should establish a graduates' class, and that just in the same way as we have a School of Musketry at Hythe, to which military men are sent for a month's or a couple of months' training before they go to these foreign stations, so we should have a school of tropical medicine somewhere established in this country, to which all the doctors who are sent out to these tropical countries could go for two months' tuition before leaving, and in which they could receive clinical and practical instruction in the cure of these particular diseases. Dr. Manson considers that the Dreadnought Hospital is the best place for dealing with these matters, because so many sailors go there who come home from the Colonies suf-

Secretary of State for the Colonies

fering from these diseases, and there are more opportunities for efficient study provided there than at any other hospital. We have considered very carefully the alternative advantages of Netley and Haslar, and we think it would be very much better to take advantage of the opportunities afforded by the Dreadnought Hospital, and accordingly arrangements have been made for erecting the necessary buildings for the accommodation of the doctors who will go through this probationary course, and we hope also in a short time to give accommodation for nurses, who equally require a similar training. That will cost a considerable sum annually, and a considerable sum for the first expenditure. That sum will be provided, partly by private subscription in this country, partly by contributions from the Colonies, and partly by this small grant—for it is really a small grant—which the Chancellor of the Exchequer has been good enough to give me for the purpose. I would like to say that up to the time we made this proposal, I do not think it had been made by anybody else, but the moment it was made there was some disturbance in the minds of the medical officers connected with different institutions, who all thought that their institutions ought to have been selected, or might have been selected, instead of the one actually selected. But I believe that we have satisfied these gentlemen, so far, at all events, as we have seen their complaints, by assuring them that in such cases, for instance, as King's Hospital or the Liverpool School, or other places at which special training in tropical diseases is given, we will give a preference in the selection of officers for these Colonies; but we do not intend to give up the further security that after the gentlemen have been selected they shall undergo this probationary course of two months at Dreadnought Hospital before they leave. I hope this proposal will satisfy the House.

Mr. BUXTON: I am glad the honourable Member for Caithness does not object in any way to this Vote. I am bound to say, as far as I am concerned, I think it is the best item of the whole of the Supplementary Estimate we are dealing with this afternoon. The right honourable Gentleman based his arguments on the ground of humanity and mortality, and I think every Member of the Committee entirely agrees with the right honourable Gentleman. But I want to place it also on the ground of efficiency and economy, because one of the greatest difficulties which exist in the way of our administration of our tropical Colonies is, that our officers, unfortunately, are compelled to spend a very large proportion of their time at home on leave, and home on leave in a very large number of cases because of some small illness they have contracted abroad, but for which they have been unable to be treated in the Colony. They have to come home, and they get out of touch with their Colony, and in a very large number of cases I believe their absence from their post might be prevented. I only hope that the right honourable Gentleman will be able to receive the assistance from voluntary sources which he has alluded to, and also the valued assistance of the different institutions of the medical profession to which he has alluded.

Mr. LABOUCHERE: The right honourable Gentleman has said something about my inaccuracy. I do not quite know how the right honourable Gentleman has managed to drag me in. I can only hope that he will not himself——

The SECRETARY of STATE for the COLONIES: The honourable Gentleman said that he did not believe that my views about the future prosperity of the Gold Coast .were correct, because everybody who went out there died.

Mr. LABOUCHERE: I only spoke in general terms. I can assure the right honourable Gentleman that a great many do die. I can only say that I hope that the right honourable Gentleman will not carry his views as to the salubrity of this charming region so far as to go there himself, because the right honourable Gentleman, if he came back, would not come back so healthy as when he went. I am going to read an extract—it is not a question of my inaccuracy or accuracy—as to the climates of these places, to show that all endeavours have already been made that are possible by doctors, and without success. This is from the Report of the Niger Coast Protectorate—

"The total number of cases treated was 1078 "—   .

which means that every European was treated by the doctor about six times a year.

"The deaths amounted to 15, a death rate of 72 per 1,000 of the population. Fifty-eight Europeans were invalided, this being a percentage of 281 per 1,000. Although every effort was made throughout the Protectorate by medical authorities during the year in the direction of sanitation generally, and by using every means which experience teaches are necessary for preserving the lives of Europeans in a climate like this, the above figures are not at all encouraging. The acting principal medical officer in his report calls special attention to the unhealthiness of Suppel."

Now, there is no Colonial station in the district better situated than is this place. It is situated on high ground, 50 miles from the river, the water being clear and fresh. The death rate for the year amounted to 226 per 1000, and the number of cases of men invalided amounted to the extraordinary proportion of 1509 to the 1000 European inhabitants. In this station, with a population of 13 white inhabitants, no fewer than 133 cases were treated, showing that each European had been in the doctor's hands 10 times a year.

"The acting principal medical officer remarks that the unhealthiness of Suppel demonstrates the fact that the most swampy regions are not always the most fever-stricken."

Then this acting principal medical officer goes on to suggest—

"Whereas young men are now sent out for three years, they had better in future be only sent out for eighteen months, because no young man can possibly stand the climate without his constitution being thoroughly destroyed, if he remains there more than eighteen months."

I hope the right honourable Gentleman will find that his views as to improving the sanitary conditions of the tropical Colonies will work out right, but I confess, looking at the facts as they are, that I very much doubt whether his hopes will be justified by the event.

Dr. FARQUHARSON (Aberdeenshire, W.): I should like to add one word of congratulation to the right honourable Gentleman upon this new departure he has made in starting a school of tropical medicine. I am not so hopeless as is the honourable Member for Northampton about the possibility of, if not stamping out altogether, at all events diminishing, these diseases which are so little understood now by the ordinary doctor, and for the study of which so very insufficient arrangements are now made in our general hospitals. I think the arrangement with regard to the Dreadnought Hospital for study there of these tropical diseases by men who are going out to tropical countries can only lead to good results, and I congratulate the right honourable Gentleman on having had the opportunity of calling to his counsel such a very able medical man as Dr. Manson, whose connection with the study of these diseases is well known. I hope this new departure will be the means of saving life, and be the means of carrying out the views of my honourable Friend, which lead him to believe that these tropical countries may be made to be much better adapted to Europeans than they are now. The only means by which it is to be done is to instruct young medical men as to the incidence of these particular diseases, so that they may be, so to speak, immune from these tropical diseases. I am sure the right honourable Gentleman has done a good thing for medical men and has done a good thing for medicine as well. Might I ask the right honourable Gentleman if this Vote is to be an annual one?

THE SECRETARY OF STATE FOR THE COLONIES: I forgot to say that among other things which we are doing in the same direction is inquiring into the cause and cure of malaria. I have been in communication with the Royal Society, and the Royal Society has made a grant, which the Government propose to supplement. A Commission has been appointed by the Royal Society to examine into the question of the cause and cure of malaria. That Commission will visit Egypt in order to study the experiments that are being made there, and it will then go to India. They will afterwards in all probability go to Nyassaland, where they will have a permanent station, to make examinations on that

Dr. Farquharson.

spot, and they will finally wind up in West Africa.

GENERAL RUSSELL (Cheltenham): As one of the few honourable Members who have experience of the Gold Coast, I desire to modify the statements of the honourable Gentleman the Member for Northampton. I am alive myself, and I must congratulate the right honourable Gentleman the Colonial Secretary on this new departure. After my return from East India I suffered greatly from West African fever, or malaria, and, although I found the medical officers over there were acquainted with malaria, scarcely a doctor in London knew anything about it. I had a very great deal of difficulty in finding any medical officer in this country with any knowledge of the subject. Only those military doctors who had been out in the country knew. I may say I consulted the most celebrated physicians in London, and I might also say that a fellow-officer of mine has had a similar experience. I think the step that has been taken by the right honourable Gentleman is an admirable one, and I am only surprised that it has never been adopted before this. I hope the House will join me in congratulating the right honourable Gentleman.

DR. CLARK: I have got all the information that I was desirous of obtaining, but, before the Vote is given, I think a Paper should be circulated, giving us all the information required. You cannot get the special material you want at the Colonial Office, because all you get there are the chronic cases, the serious cases are duplicated; and in ordinary schools, under ordinary circumstances, they ought to pay attention to the special class. It is also very desirable that civil surgeons should go out and should have special facilities, as the military surgeons have. The only doubt in my mind is whether you ought not to have it altogether—whether it would not be worth while to pay a definite sum to inquire into it? This is a very small sum, and the experiment can be tried, and then by-and-bye we can have a permanent Estimate. But before it comes before us permanently we must have all the information. This question affects the Army, Navy, and Civil

Service, and I think that we ought to have a proper method of inquiring into it. I am afraid that the money will be frittered away by there being two or three men doing the same thing. However, I congratulate the right honourable Gentleman upon this departure.

MR. GIBSON BOWLES: Let me suggest that some of these Gentlemen may be sent to Jamaica, which is so little visited, but which is so beautifully situated for this purpose. Jamaica is the very hotbed of yellow fever, and I think that medical science would obtain more knowledge there than elsewhere. The support that the honourable Gentleman the Member for Northampton has given to this Vote is most remarkable, and there can be no greater reason than that suggested by him for introducing such institutions as is proposed. The honourable Member for Cheltenham has also said that medical men are not well instructed in this disease. Where should they learn it if not at Jamaica? We all remember the old sailors' rhyme, "The bight of Benin, the bight of Benin, few come out, tho' many go in"; and I certainly do think that this extremely small sum is the only sum in the Estimates which will be well spent. I see a small sum is destined for the Royal Society, and the right honourable Gentleman is going to do for an extremely small sum of money a work which, I venture to say, will be associated with his name and office so long as hospitals and fever exist.

*MR. LAWRENCE (Liverpool, Abercromby): I emphatically object to the statement of the honourable Gentleman who has just sat down that Jamaica is the very best place for the study of yellow fever. Three years ago I became acquainted with the House Surgeon at Kingston Hospital, who told me that for 16 years he had not seen one case of yellow fever, excepting in one instance, when four or five people were hit by it. It is a calumny upon the climate of Jamaica to have such a statement made upon the floor of this House. I have heard that in days gone by the climate of the West Indies was thought to be equally as unhealthy as that of the West Coast of Africa, and therefore I believe that what has happened there,

where there has been so much improvement, will happen here, and that the time will come when the Colonial Secretary will find his statements correct. I would only say, before I sit down, that I regret that the city of Liverpool, which has a large interest—which is concerned with at least half of the trade of the West Coast of Africa—is not to have the benefit of such a grant as this. The trade of the West Coast is handled by Liverpool, and the city of Liverpool did hope that the Government would see its way to have a school situated in the heart of that important trade centre. I trust that the right honourable Gentleman will give the matter his consideration, and, even if on this occasion he does not see fit to vote a sum to Liverpool to assist in the study of these diseases, that on a future occasion, as the matter becomes more important, it may be thought proper, on the part of the Government, that if there should be two hospitals in this country for the study of this very important disease, one shall be at Liverpool. I did not rise specially to touch on this matter of hospitals for tropical diseases, but rather to allude to the other Votes, which I understand the House is now prepared to consider. I do not wish to stand in the way of those who wish to continue the discussion upon the hospitals, but I was under the impression that no other honourable Member was willing to deal with that subject. I rose really to ask the right honourable Gentleman the Secretary of State for the Colonies if he can tell us what is the principle on which the Vote of the special subsidies in the matter of the hurricane is going to be expended; whether the right honourable Gentleman himself has given instructions as to how they ought to be expended in the Colonies; why it is that the island of St. Lucia does not figure in the list; and why has St. Vincent, which has been hardest hit, the lowest grant, and the island of Barbados the largest? There is one other matter which I should like to allude to. Since the matter of the West Indies was discussed in this House last Session, one of the most terrible hurricanes of the century has passed over the islands. That hurricane has thrown a great deal of light upon the question as to how these islands should be dealt with in future, especially by the Home Government. The Royal Commission dealt especially with this question, and strongly recommended the cultivation of sugar.

THE DEPUTY CHAIRMAN: Order, order! The question does not arise on this Vote. The honourable Member must confine himself strictly to items arising out of this Vote.

*MR. LAWRENCE: What I desire to point out is, that under this hurricane, which is an abstract lesson as to the way in which these West Indian questions should be treated, we have learnt, as all the reports of the island showed, where the hurricane completely destroyed the fruit trees root and branch, when it came across the fields of sugar, théy, after having been for a fortnight laid flat, rose up, and there was still a crop to be reaped. I venture to remind the House of one single consideration, that whereas the Royal Commission laid great store on fruit cultivation we have this hurricane to show that if the inhabitants had put their trust in the cultivation of fruit they would have suffered more than they did through continuing to cultivate sugar. In order to inform the House how frequent these hurricanes are, I hold in my hand a list of the hurricanes which have visited the island of Jamaica, which is not, I might state, in the direct line of hurricanes. During the last century there were no less than 11 hurricanes, and during the present century there have been 14 hurricanes, up to the present year, which have actually hit the island. There were six or eight other hurricanes which visited the neighbourhood, and although this island is not in the line of hurricanes, as I said before, it is a very risky district in which to grow fruit. It seems to me that this is a very important matter, and these hurricanes supply us with a good deal of information, because they show us how the Mother Country is to treat its West Indian Colonies. And if it does that, it will not altogether have been an unmitigated evil. We shall have learned a lesson from these hurricanes, which will thus have made for the good of the people out there; but if we do not learn that lesson we shall spend our money in vain.

Mr. Lawrence.

MR. LABOUCHERE: It appears to me that if the honourable Gentleman who has just spoken was going into the question of the West Indies he might go a little further than he has done, showing that in his view they ought not to build houses in the West Indies, but that they ought to put them in the grant, on the ground that not only fruit trees were destroyed but houses as well. Now, my honourable Friend the Member for Islington intended to bring in an Amendment upon the question of Barbados, but, unfortunately, he is not at present in the House. He asked me last evening if I could bring it on for him, and I consented to do so. Now, my honourable Friend collected a vast amount of information, which he was to give to me yesterday, and which I, having mastered, was to give to the House; and I am sure that the House will share my regret that my honourable Friend the Member for Islington has forgotten to provide me with that information, and he is not here to give it himself. Now, I doubt whether these grants are altogether useful. There was in 1897 a grant of £160,000 for the West Indies, and in 1898 a further large grant was made for the same purpose. I am, of course, quite aware that these amounts had been expended through the Colonial Audits. These grants, no doubt, have been added to by private subscriptions. When the last disaster occurred we had a fund started by the Mansion House. That fund produced £50,000, and there is no evidence that that was not sufficient to meet the immediate distress in those islands. Sir, it strikes me very forcibly that the damage, as is generally the case, was very greatly exaggerated in the newspapers. Whenever we hear of any disaster taking place in Barbados, we are always told that 10,000 houses are destroyed, and 100,000 people are rendered homeless, and, in point of fact, that everything is destroyed. Now, if you heard in England of 10,000 houses being destroyed by a hurricane you would stand aghast. But the honourable Gentleman who has just sat down will bear me out when I say that the houses in Barbados are simply bamboo huts.

MR. LAWRENCE: I saw in the papers that the houses destroyed were 4,000.

MR. LABOUCHERE: I can only say that my honourable Friend the Member for Islington saw in the papers that the houses destroyed were 10,000. But perhaps my honourable Friend the Member for Islington reads newspapers of a more sensational character than the honourable Gentleman opposite. No doubt a great deal of injury has been done, but it is only of a temporary character, because these huts which have been destroyed can be built again for £1 or £2, and when we talk of people being rendered homeless I have myself been homeless in the sense of sometimes sleeping under a tree, when I slept just as well as I could have done in a house. What I should like to know from the Colonial Secretary is whether this money is to be expended solely for the necessities of the poor people. Take the Mansion House Fund of £50,000. That will provide 50,000 persons with 5 shillings a week for four weeks, by which time the immediate distress of the people would be over, because by that time they would get their bananas and other foods to grow up, and the £50,000 could hardly be exhausted during that time in buying food; but it is well observed in the newspapers that the property in the island of St. Vincent, property of the Church of England, was destroyed to the extent of something like £213,000. It is also observed that the loss to the Wesleyan community for injuries to their chapels is £6,000, while the Roman Catholic Church will not repair their churches for less than £3,000. Now, of course, the great body of the people of the islands had a very good claim for the immediate relief of their necessities, but I doubt whether the West Indies have a right to claim that we should make them a going concern in consequence of the loss which they have sustained by the hurricane. I should like to know whether any of this money is to be expended on the property of the religious communities or upon the planters' sugar houses. I saw myself in the papers that the sugar industry had been destroyed, that the industry had been so damaged that they had no means to carry on their business. Now, we have trouble enough in England. Take the case of Essex, which, as we know, has some of the best wheat-growing land in the country, but it has depreciated till the land in Essex is now absolutely worthless; but it is never suggested that we should compensate the labourer, the tenant, or the owner of the land in Essex; and it seems to me that when any planter has a sugar house, or any religious community has a church or a chapel, that they ought to insure it. Now, the honourable Gentleman who has just sat down said that there were 13 hurricanes in Jamaica during the last few years. My honourable Friend the Member for Islington has apparently gone very much more deeply into this subject, because he says that during the last 300 years there have been 355 hurricanes passing over the country, which is an average of one and a half hurricanes in each year. But in any case there is no doubt that hurricanes are of frequent occurrence there during August and September, and anybody who lives in the West Indies and puts up his sugar factories must accept the fact that if he does not insure them he runs a great risk of being injured by any hurricane which comes along. Might I ask the right honourable Gentleman to give a full explanation to the Committee of the mode in which the money was expended, how much has been expended, and how much remains, because I see a note that the amount shall be paid over as a whole, and no part remaining unpaid after the 31st of March shall be paid. The West Indies have got over the effect of their hurricane now. Nobody is now being starved because of the hurricane, or are without houses. £50,000 was, I think, enough to give food and necessaries of life to the people who were suffering from the climate. That does not seem to be the case here; in view of the cases that I have seen in the newspapers as to the Wesleyan, the Church of England, and the Roman Catholic communities. The view that I take of the Estimates is that all the money has not been expended, and that it is being kept for a nest egg. I will not move my Amendment now because the right honourable Gentleman proposes, I believe, to give an explanation of what has occurred. If that explanation, however, is not satisfactory I reserve to myself the right to move an Amendment.

THE SECRETARY OF STATE FOR THE COLONIES: I do not think that the House of Commons will envy the honourable Gentleman in the task he has taken over from the honourable Member for Islington. After all it is not a very gracious matter to make bad jokes about a calamity which is the greatest national calamity that has happened in the West India Islands within our recollection. Hurricanes are, according to the honourable Gentleman, common in the West Indies, and he stated that there had been 355 hurricanes in 300 years. That may be so, but there has not been a great hurricane such as that which has recently taken place, which has caused so much calamity since 1831. On that occasion Lord Althorpe came down to the House —apparently the country was not so rich then as it is now—and proposed a grant of £100,000, in addition to a loan of one million sterling. Curiously enough I find, on looking through the Debate that took place upon that occasion, that he was warmly supported in his proposal by Mr. Labouchere. The honourable Member makes light of the sufferings of these poor people on this recent occasion, and he does so on the ground that he has seen statements in the newspapers which are greatly exaggerated. Well, that is not an uncommon thing, for statements in newspapers are often exaggerated. But we have made this proposal not upon the statements in the newspapers, but upon the Official Reports which we have received ourselves from the governors and officials on the spot. Now let me read what is said by one who was, at all events, an impartial witness, in the person of the captain of Her Majesty's ship " Intrepid," who was there at the time. This officer states that—

" The whole islands, including St. Vincent, had the appearance of having been fired through, and utter desolation prevailed everywhere. There was hardly a green spot where before all was verdant and beautiful to look upon. Towns and villages, viewed from the sea had the appearance of having been bombarded. In St. Vincent 200 lives were lost, and out of a total population of 41,000, some 20,000 were shelterless and without the means of subsistence, and three-fourths of the population were only kept from starvation by receiving daily rations. In Barbados, 112 persons lost their lives, and the total loss to property was £283,000. The number of labourers' houses destroyed was 11,426, and the number damaged 4,984."

In addition to this damage, Government public works, and State-aided schools suffered enormously. To meet that damage we have asked—in addition to the private subscriptions, which amount to something like £45,000, raised by the Mansion House Fund—for a free grant of £40,000 for Barbados, a free grant of £2,000 for St. Vincent, and for a loan in each of these islands of £50,000. The grants from the Mansion House Fund, which were very early distributed, were given entirely in the shape of relief, and the free grants which we ask for now have been expended to cover the expenses of relief, to assist the people in re-housing themselves, and in repairs to public works, because we have to consider, in the condition in which these islands are now placed, the question of restoring these public works, some of which have been destroyed. I must confess that I think this demand is an extremely moderate one, and it has been made after the most careful consideration and conference with Governor Hay, and upon the written reports which we have received from the islands. Certainly there is no idea of making a nest-egg, and the whole of this money will be required and will be spent for the benefit of the population. I do not know why the honourable Gentleman introduced this tale about Wesleyan chapels and churches, for there is not, and never has been, the slightest intention of making grants out of the public funds for the repair of those institutions, no matter to what denomination they belong. No doubt these people have suffered seriously, but we have not made any grants towards the repair of their property, and the honourable Gentleman has no ground for suggesting that any grants will be made for this purpose. My honourable Friend asked why a grant was not made to St. Lucia. Well, in the first place, the damage there was not so great, and we had reason to believe that the grant was not so necessary in that district, although we have taken care that St. Lucia has had a liberal contribution from the Mansion House Fund. St. Lucia is not quite in the same position as the other islands, because, owing to the arrangement made by the Admiralty, it is now a naval station, and enjoys a larger measure of prosperity. With regard to what my honourable Friend said in reference to the sugar-cane industry as contrasted with fruit, I think he is inclined to argue against the Report of the Royal Commission, but it seems to me that there is room for both. I have no desire to see the destruction of the sugar industry, and I am perfectly convinced that any such violent change as the honourable Gentleman behind me has suggested would be disastrous to the interests of the West Indies. On the other hand, I cordially agree myself with the recommendations of the Commissioners that we should endeavour to aid other industries, so that those Islands might not be dependent upon the one industry of sugar. I hope that the House will think that I have made out a case for this moderate grant in what I have said, and I am quite sure that the benevolence which has been already anticipated by some of our Colonies, such as Canada, Natal, Lagos, Mauritius, and the Straits Settlements, will be thoroughly appreciated.

MR. BUXTON: I only need to trouble the Committee with a very few words upon this Vote, because it is totally different, and is not affected except indirectly by what we have already voted, or what the right honourable Gentleman may offer to do in the future. This is simply a Vote to give—as we have frequently given—the Government of the day funds to meet the damage which has occurred, and which has caused such disastrous results that if relief were not given there would have been such distress that perhaps starvation would have taken place in a large number of cases, and the Government have come down and asked us to assist in relieving that distress. Therefore, this is purely a matter of relief. The right honourable Gentleman has explained that every sixpence of this grant will go to the relief of those unfortunate people in Barbadoes and St. Vincent, and this money has not been asked for with the motives which seem to have actuated the honourable Member for Northampton that we were going to a great expenditure to benefit the sugar industry, for the repair of religious institutions, or any other way. That is as far as I understand the right honourable Gentleman. Therefore, I shall give a cordial support to this Vote, and I trust that the right honourable Gentleman will do all that is

possible to relieve this great distress which has occurred in the West Indian Islands.

MR. LABOUCHERE: I understand from what the right honourable Gentleman the Secretary for the Colonies has stated that nothing out of this grant is to go to any of these religious sects to which I have referred. My honourable Friend who has just spoken said he understood that nothing was to go to assist the sugar industry.

THE SECRETARY OF STATE FOR THE COLONIES: What I meant was that in this grant we are asking for nothing in connection with the policy of assisting the sugar industries, for which we have had Votes already and for which we may have other Votes. I do not say that this grant may not indirectly benefit the sugar industry, because it will assist the natives in a large number of cases to carry on their industry.

MR. LABOUCHERE: My honourable Friend and I agree that the right honourable Gentleman does not wish this money to be spent in assisting the owners of sugar industries, although they may have suffered loss, but he wants the money to be spent upon the direct and absolute necessities of the poor inhabitants of the country. Do I understand from the right honourable Gentleman's statement that that is so?

THE SECRETARY OF STATE FOR THE COLONIES: All grants that are made are expected to assist the sugar industry. I do not think, however, that any part of the free grant will be given to assist directly the sugar industry, for a large portion, if not the whole, of the loans will be devoted to that express purpose. The object of this grant is to enable those estates which have been temporarily thrown out of cultivation to resume cultivation, and in that way this assistance will be of the greatest possible advantage to the population.

MR. LABOUCHERE: What about the Loans Bill?

THE SECRETARY OF STATE FOR THE COLONIES: Perhaps I have given the honourable Gentleman more infor-

mation than I should have done. It is
a large question, and I would rather
argue it when the Estimates for the
year come on. This is only a preliminary to the carrying out of that
scheme.

Vote agreed to.

CLASS VI.

4. £517, Supplementary, Pauper
Lunatics, Ireland.

Vote agreed to.

CIVIL SERVICES (EXCESS), 1897-8.

5. £1 5s. 1d., Public Record Office.

Vote agreed to.

NAVY (SUPPLEMENTARY), 1898-9.

6. £350,000, Supplementary, Navy.

*SIR U. KAY SHUTTLEWORTH (Lan-
cashire, Clitheroe): I desire to ask for
an explanation as to the substitution of
the Supplementary Estimate now before
the Committee in place of that first issued
to Members. The Supplementary Estimate
introduced earlier in the Session and
then withdrawn was for £450,000, but
the Estimate now before the Committee
has been revised, and is £100,000 less
than the original Estimate asked for.
Not only is this Estimate considerably
different to the total amount, but the
details are also different. I find some
new items in the Estimate produced on
the 1st of March which did not appear
in the original Supplementary Estimate.
I find that there is an entirely
new item under Vote 9, Naval
Armaments, for which £100,000 is
asked. I think, for these reasons,
the Committee may fairly ask for more
information than that which is given in
the Supplementary Estimate. I gathered
from the statement of the First Lord
of the Admiralty that some of this expenditure on guns was needed in connection with the Supplementary Naval Programme, and I should like to know
whether that money is to be spent at
Woolwich. Then, with respect to coal, an
answer was given yesterday which leads
me to think that £316,000, in addition to
what was taken in the Estimates of last
year, has been expended on coal. That

is rather a large amount. I should like
some further explanation on that point,
especially as it is a very large excess.
The total amount which was voted in
the original Estimate was £605,000, so
that it looks as if more than half as
much again had been spent in coal
during the current year than was provided for in the original Estimate. There
is one further question I would like to
ask, and that is: Whether there is anything in this Estimate in relief of the
Estimates of 1899-1900? We have had
an Army Supplementary Estimate before the House, in which a large amount
of the sum asked for was in relief of
the Estimate of next year. In other
words, the Estimate was framed and
the money was asked for in order that
the Estimates for the coming year might
be reduced. I will not go into details
on this question, but I should like to
know if there is anything in this Estimate of that character, because if there
is, some remarks should be made by
way of protest against this growing
practice. I hope serious notice will be
taken by the authorities in this House
of the growing practice of introducing
Supplementary Estimates, not with the
object of providing for some additional
expenditure incurred within the year, but
for items which really belong to the
expenditure of another financial year. I
do not think I need trouble the House
further except to ask for these details
of information, which I have no doubt
the Secretary to the Admiralty will be
able to furnish.

*THE SECRETARY TO THE ADMI-
RALTY (Mr. MACARTNEY, Antrim, S.): I
can assure the right honourable Gentleman that not one penny is taken
in this Supplementary Estimate in relief of the Estimates for this year. The
money we are asking for entirely applies
to the expenditure for the current year.
The right honourable Gentleman has
asked me to explain the reasons which
led to the substitution of the present
Supplementary Estimate for the one
previously laid before the House. In the
first Supplementary Estimate the
amounts were prepared from the information which was then at our disposal with regard to the earnings of the
contractors, but subsequent to that Supplementary Vote having been prepared,
we were informed that the earnings of

the contractors during the present financial year would fall short by £100,000. Under these circumstances, I will say at once that it would have been not only inexpedient, but improper, to ask Parliament to give its sanction to a Supplementary Estimate so largely in excess of what we had reason to believe would be required. With regard to the new items, alluded to by the right honourable Gentleman, which did not appear in the original Estimate, I may say that these sums have been put down as the amount which we shall require to make up the total of £350,000, and there was no special design in the substitution of these particular items. The reason Vote 9 was taken was that I desired to make use of the Appropriation in Aid. It would not have been quite a proper course of procedure from the accountant's point of view, to utilise the Appropriation in Aid in relation to a Vote which was not in the Supplementary Estimate. For this reason I took £100,000 on Vote 9. With regard to coal, the expenditure for the current year would be, roughly, £900,000. Of that total, £140,000 represents the demand made very early in the financial year, in the month of May, at a time when we could not expect to have any savings, and this expenditure was for the North American station, the ships in Chinese waters, and the Cape station, the details of which are £97,000 for Chinese waters, £16,000 for the Cape station, £17,000 for the North American station, and £10,000 for other stations.

SIR H. CAMPBELL-BANNERMAN: I am not quite sure that the honourable Gentleman has made it clear to the ordinary intelligence why this second edition of the Supplementary Estimate was required. There is such a material discrepancy between the two successive editions, that it makes one wonder upon what principle the Supplementary Estimates are framed at all, and it gives rise to all sorts of natural suspicions of somewhat careless financing. I think the right honourable Gentleman opposite will admit that we do want a little more explanation on this subject. The right honourable Gentleman said something with regard to the guns, but there was no item of guns at all in the first edition, and here there is an item of £100,000; and in

order to explain it, the honourable Gentleman says that there was a miscalculation with regard to the earnings of contractors. That only amounted to £20,000, therefore there was a discrepancy of £80,000 suddenly discovered.

*MR. MACARTNEY: I desired to utilise the Appropriation in Aid.

SIR H. CAMPBELL-BANNERMAN (Stirling Burghs): That would justify the Vote for £20,000; but there is a large margin of £80,000 for guns. I daresay this is all necessary and required, but if that was found to be the case, and found to be true when this second edition of the Supplementary Estimate was issued, why was it not known when the first edition was issued a few days before? That is the point as to which we express some surprise. We seem to be providing now in this Estimate for something which has been known for weeks and months before, and what has not been made clear to us is that there was a Supplementary Estimate issued by the Admiralty and circulated amongst Members of the House of Commons, and then a few days later a totally different Estimate with different figures and new items is circulated. It may be all right, but it looks as if there has been an amount of carelessness of a haphazard character about it which I think deserves a little more explanation than we have yet reached.

THE FIRST LORD OF THE ADMIRALTY (Mr. GOSCHEN, St. George's, Hanover Square: The point is this, that the first Supplementary Estimate was withdrawn and another substituted in its place because we found that the contractors could earn by £100,000 the amount which we asked for in the Supplementary Estimate.

SIR H. CAMPBELL-BANNERMAN: And that was discovered in this short interval of time?

THE FIRST LORD OF THE ADMIRALTY: That is so. I am sure that the right honourable Gentleman will see that over these vast sums we cannot know exactly what will be earned, and it does not seem desirable if we did not want £450,000, to ask the House of Commons for it. These guns were ordered and instalments paid upon them, and during the previous months we knew all about it. But originally these guns were paid for out of the savings of the Supplementary Estimate. There has been no miscalculation except so far as this £100,000 is concerned, as to which we are dependent upon the information of the contractors.

*Sir C. DILKE: The right honourable Gentleman has not alluded to the point of coal to which his attention was called, and as to which I do not understand the reply of the Secretary to the Admiralty. As I understood him, there has been a large additional expenditure in coal over the normal expenditure, and that has not arisen, I understand, in consequence of the mobilisation of the Reserve Squadron, but has arisen on the China, South African, and North American stations. Therefore, I cannot myself quite understand how so large an additional expenditure on coal can have arisen at stations like those I have mentioned.

*Mr. MACARTNEY: I think I explained that the sum of £140,000 only went to these stations, but that does not account for the whole of this expenditure, and as the right honourable Gentleman is aware, large sums are spent upon other important stations. We are now asking the consent of the House to the sum which was specifically allocated to the Fleet in those waters on the 24th of May.

Mr. LABOUCHERE: I must congratulate the Admiralty on having done a very clever thing. They do not wish to have an item appearing in the Supplementary Estimates which will give us the opportunity of raising a discussion on the Soudan and Fashoda policy in connection with this Vote. But as a matter of fact the Admiralty are asking for a considerable amount for coals. These coals were consumed during that time, and yet we are assured that these were not the particular coals that the right honourable Gentleman is asking for, and for which an excess Vote is required. The Secretary to the Admiralty gave a list of the stations where they were consumed, and then it suddenly struck him that there was still a little more coal to be accounted for, and he simply waved his hand and said, "The Committee will understand that the balance has been expended in other

stations." I should have liked to raise the whole question, and I regret that the right honourable Gentlemen on the Treasury Bench have not given us some clear explanation in regard to these coals. At the same time, I am bound to say that I think they do not want to discuss this matter.

Vote agreed to.

ARMY (ORDNANCE FACTORIES) EXCESS, 1897-8.

7. £100, Army (Ordnance Factories).

Vote agreed to.

Resolutions to be reported upon Monday next; Committee to sit again upon Monday next.

MOTION FOR ADJOURNMENT.

THE FIRST LORD OF THE TREASURY: I beg leave to move—"That the House do now adjourn." I hope no objection will be taken to this course, for as the House is aware, we have now obtained the amount of Supply we desired up to this point. An arrangement has been made that the Army Votes shall not be proceeded with now, and, by a long-standing rule, it is not usual to take Bills on Fridays when Supply is set down.

Question put.

Motion agreed to.

WAYS AND MEANS.

Committee deferred till Monday next.

ADULTERATION (FOOD PRODUCTS) BILL.

Second Reading deferred till Monday next.

House adjourned at twenty minutes after Seven of the clock.

An Asterisk (*) at the commencement of a Speech indicates revision by the Member.

HOUSE OF LORDS.

Monday, 13th March 1899.

THE LORD CHANCELLOR took his seat upon the Woolsack at Four of the clock.

PRIVATE BILL BUSINESS.

WATERMEN'S AND LIGHTERMEN'S ACTS AMENDMENT BILL [H.L.]
Presented, and read the first time.

GREAT YARMOUTH PIER BILL [H.L.]
A witness ordered to attend the Select Committee.

Belfast Corporation Bill,

National Telephone Company (No. 1) Bill,

National Telephone Company (No. 2) Bill,

Mersey Docks and Harbour Board (Pilotage) Bill [H.L.] (Petition for Additional Provision),

Gainsborough Urban District Council (Gas) Bill [H.L.] (Petition for Additional Provision),

The meeting of the Standing Orders Committee (which stands appointed for Thursday next) put off to Monday next.

NORTHERN ASSURANCE COMPANY BILL [H.L.]
Committee (which stands appointed for To-morrow) put off *sine die.*

LANARKSHIRE (MIDDLE WARD DISTRICT) WATER BILL [H.L.]
Committee (which stands appointed for To-morrow) put off to Thursday.

WOLVERHAMPTON TRAMWAYS BILL [H.L.]
Committed: The Committee to be proposed by the Committee of Selection.

VOL. LXVIII. [FOURTH SERIES.]

LONDON HOSPITAL BILL [H.L.]
Committed.

GREAT GRIMSBY STREET TRAMWAYS BILL [H.L.]
The Chairman of Committees informed the House that the opposition to the Bill was withdrawn : The order made on Friday last discharged ; and Bill committed.

DUMBARTON BURGH BILL [H.L.]
The Chairman of Committees informed the House that the opposition to the Bill was withdrawn : The orders made on the 27th of February and on Monday last, discharged ; and Bill committed for Thursday next.

NORTH STAFFORDSHIRE RAILWAY BILL [H.L.]
The order made on Monday last appointing certain Lords the Select Committee to consider the Bill, discharged.

TRANSVAAL MORTGAGE LOAN AND FINANCE COMPANY BILL [H.L.]
Read second time (according to order).

SURREY COMMERCIAL DOCKS BILL [H.L.]
Read second time (according to order).

ABERDEEN CORPORATION BILL [H.L.]
Standing Order No. 92 considered (according to order), and dispensed with, with respect to a Petition of Malcolm Vivian Hay and his curators : Leave given to present the said Petition.

BODIES CORPORATE (JOINT TENANCY) BILL [H.L.]
To be read second time To-morrow.

PARTRIDGE SHOOTING (IRELAND) BILL.
To be read second time To-morrow. [The Lord de Vesci (V. de Vesci)].

X

EDUCATION DEPARTMENT PROVISIONAL ORDER CONFIRMATION (SWANSEA) BILL [H.L.]

Read second time (according to order).

CATHCART'S DIVORCE BILL [H.L.]

Motion made and Question proposed—

"That this Bill be read a third time."—
(The Lord Chancellor.)

THE LORD CHANCELLOR (The Earl of HALSBURY): My Lords, I beg to move that this Bill be read a third time, and in doing so I desire to explain some observations I made on this Bill which appear to have been misunderstood. As your Lordships are aware, certain official documents have to be authenticated and made evidence by an official stamp, and the tribunal which receives these documents has to be satisfied that the stamp is such as is required by the Act of Parliament. I stated in regard to the certificate in this case, which was issued under the Seal of the General Registry Office, Dublin, that it was not properly stamped. I now find that it is stamped, but that the stamp is so faint that it can only be seen by holding the document up to the light, and could, with a little moisture, be erased altogether. I think those who are responsible for the issue of these documents should in future take care to make the authentication in a more distinct form, which will prevent similar mistakes again occurring.

Question put.

Bill read a third time, passed, and sent to the Commons.

Cromer Protection Bill [H.L.]
Glastonbury Water Bill [H.L.]
Yeadon and Guiseley Water Bill [H.L.]
Bristol Gas Bill [H.L.]
Lea Bridge District Gas Bill [H.L.]
Queen's Ferry Bridge Bill [H.L.]
Nene Valley Water Bill [H.L.]
St. Neot's Water Bill [H.L.]

Report from the Committee of Selection that the Earl of Derby be proposed to the House as a member of the Select Committee in the place of the Lord Pirbright; and that the Earl of Derby be Chairman of the said Committee; read, and agreed to.

Aberdeen Corporation Bill [H.L.]

Greenock and Port Glasgow Tramways Bill [H.L.]

Perth Water, Police, and Gas Bill [H.L.]

West Highland Railway Bill [H.L.]

Airdrie and Coatbridge Water Bill [H.L.]

Wishaw Water Bill [H.L.]

Report from the Committee of Selection that the Earl of Northbrook be proposed to the House as a member of the Select Committee in the place of the Earl of Derby; and that the Earl of Northbrook be Chairman of the said Committee; read, and agreed to.

RETURNS, REPORTS, ETC.

TRADE REPORTS (1899).
Annual Series: No. 2209. Havre and district.

Presented (by Command), and ordered to lie on the Table.

CHINA, No. 1 (1899).
Correspondence respecting the affairs of China.

Presented (by Command), and ordered to lie on the Table.

LIGHT RAILWAYS ACT, 1896.
Report of the proceedings of the Board of Trade under the Light Railways Act, 1896, during the year 1898; and of the proceedings of the Light Railway Commissioners during the period from 22nd November 1897 to 1st December 1898.

MUNICIPAL CORPORATIONS (INCOR-
PORATION OF HOVE).

Charter of Incorporation of the
Borough of Hove, dated 8th August
1898.

———

HOUSES OF LORDS AND COMMONS
PERMANENT STAFF.

Message from the Commons that they
have ordered the Select Committee
appointed by them to join with a Committee of this House on the House of
Lords and Commons Permanent Staff,
do meet the Committee appointed by
their Lordships in Committee Room A.,
on Friday next, at Twelve o'clock, as
proposed by this House.

———

PETITION.

———

MUNICIPAL TRADING.

Petition that a Committee be appointed to define the extent to which
municipal trading should be sanctioned
by Parliament; of the Leeds Federation
of Engineering Employers; read, and
ordered to lie on the Table.

———

BROUGHTY FERRY GAS AND PAVING
ORDER BILL [H.L.]

A Bill to confirm a Provisional Order
under the Burgh Police (Scotland) Act,
1892, relating to Broughty Ferry Gas
Supply and paving—Was presented by
the Earl Waldegrave (for the Lord Balfour); read the first time; to be
printed; and referred to the Examiners.
(No. 22.)

———

NEW BILL.

———

LAND BANKS (IRELAND) BILL [H.L.]

A Bill to authorise the establishment
of Land Banks in Ireland—Was presented by the Earl of Camperdown (for
the Lord Castletown); read the first
time; and to be printed. (No. 23.)

House adjourned at forty-five
minutes past Four of the clock.

HOUSE OF COMMONS.

Monday, 13th March 1899.

———

Mr. SPEAKER took the Chair at
Three of the clock.

———

PRIVATE BILL BUSINESS.

———

BAKER STREET AND WATERLOO
RAILWAY BILL.

To be read a second time upon Monday 27th March.

———

GREAT SOUTHERN AND WESTERN,
AND WATERFORD, LIMERICK, AND
WESTERN RAILWAY COMPANIES
AMALGAMATION BILL.

To be read a second time To-morrow.

———

GREAT SOUTHERN AND WESTERN
RAILWAY BILL.

To be read a second time To-morrow.

———

REDDITCH GAS BILL.

Read a second time, and committed.

———

WOKING WATER AND GAS BILL.

To be read a second time upon Thursday.

———

GLASGOW CORPORATION TELEPHONES
BILL.

(By Order.) Second Reading deferred
till Thursday 20th April.

———

LONDON WATER (WELSH RESERVOIRS
AND WORKS) BILL.

"To authorise the construction of
reservoirs and works in Wales for the
supply of water to London and neighbourhood; and for other purposes,"
read the first time; to be read a second
time.

X 2

PETITIONS.

EDUCATION OF CHILDREN BILL.
Petitions in favour;—From Womb-well;—Leeds;—and London; to lie upon the Table.

LOCAL AUTHORITIES SERVANTS' SUPERANNUATION BILL.
Petitions in favour;—From Wimbledon; — West Ham; — Worcester;—and, Bradford-on-Avon; to lie upon the Table.

PRIVATE LEGISLATION PROCEDURE (SCOTLAND) BILL.
Petitions in favour;—From Edinburgh; — Irvine; — and, Dundee; to lie upon the Table.

PUBLIC HEALTH ACTS AMENDMENT BILL.
Petitions in favour; — From St. Helen's; — Lichfield; — Wisbech;—and, Worcester; to lie upon the Table.

SALE OF INTOXICATING LIQUORS ON SUNDAY BILL.
Petitions in favour;—From Great Ormesby; — Galston; — Brich; — Wavendon;—and, Fenton; to lie upon the Table.

SUPERANNUATION (METROPOLIS) BILL.
Petition from St. George-in-the-East, in favour; to lie upon the Table.

VACCINATION ACT, 1898.
Petition from Ashbourne, for repeal; to lie upon the Table.

RETURNS, REPORTS, ETC.

NAVAL WORKS.
Paper [presented 9th March] to be printed. (No. 104.)

MUNICIPAL CORPORATIONS (NEW CHARTERS) (HOVE).
Copy presented,—of Charter of Incorporation of the Borough of Hove, dated 8th August 1898 (by Act); to lie upon the Table.

LIGHT RAILWAYS ACT, 1896.
Copy presented,—of Report of the Proceedings of the Board of Trade during the year 1898, and of the proceedings of the Light Railway Commissioners during the period ending 31st December 1898 (by Act); to lie upon the Table, and to be printed. (No. 105.)

CHINA (No. 1, 1899).
Copy presented,—of Correspondence respecting the affairs of China (by Command); to lie upon the Table.

TRADE REPORTS (ANNUAL SERIES).
Copy presented,—of Diplomatic and Consular Reports, Annual Series, No. 2209 (by Command); to lie upon the Table.

TELEGRAPH (CHANNEL ISLANDS) BILL [LORDS].
Read the first time; to be read a second time upon Thursday, and to be printed. (Bill 123.)

NEW MEMBER SWORN.
Charles Philips Trevelyan, esquire, for the Northern Part of the West Riding (Elland Division).

QUESTIONS.

MORAY FIRTH FISHERIES.

MR. PIRIE (Aberdeen, N.): ·I beg to ask the Lord Advocate whether his attention has been called to a public statement made by Mr. A. Jamieson, a member of the Fishery Board for Scotland, on the 21st ultimo, which was reported as follows—

"It was the Moray Firth line fishermen themselves who had been the means of getting the Firth closed, and whenever they got the Moray Firth fishermen to go in for trawlers and trawling then they would get the Firth opened. The Fishery Board was looking after the interests of the fishing trade, and they knew better almost than any other what the fish trade of Scotland needed";

whether such a statement is authoritative; and whether, in view of the fact of Aberdeen being the largest centre of the fishing industry in Scotland, and that neither its interests as regards line or trawl fishing are represented by any member of the Board, the Government proposes taking any steps to more fully carry out the intentions of the Sea Fisheries Regulation Act of 1895, which provides that the Fishery Board shall be representative of the various sea fishing interests of Scotland, by appointing one Member of the Board to directly represent Aberdeen fishing interests, and so rectify the present one-sided representation?

THE LORD ADVOCATE (Mr. A. G. MURRAY, Buteshire): I am informed by the Fishery Board that the remarks referred to were made by Mr. Jamieson at the annual meeting of the Edinburgh and Leith Fish Trade Association, of which body he is honorary secretary, but that he did not claim to speak for anybody but himself. As to the statement in the Question that Aberdeen is the largest centre of the fishing industry in Scotland it may be stated that the quantity of fish landed at Fraserburgh in 1898 was greater than that landed at Aberdeen. The Aberdeen line and trawl fishing interests do not differ from those of other parts of Scotland, and are fully represented on the Fishery Board. It is not thought desirable that any one having a direct interest in either of the conflicting methods of fishing should have control of an industry which must be carried on in the interests of the public good as a whole.

MR. PIRIE: May I ask if the Secretary of State approves of a member of the Fishery Board making such a statement as that?

MR. GRAHAM MURRAY: It is not for him to consider whether he approves or not what a member says in his private capacity.

MR. PIRIE: Is it possible to assume that Mr. Jamieson was on this occasion acting in his private capacity?

MR. SPEAKER: Order, order!

FOREIGN TRAWLERS IN THE MORAY FIRTH.

MR. PIRIE: I beg to ask the Lord Advocate if he is aware of the presence of upwards of 20 foreign trawlers fishing in the protected waters of the Moray Firth at the present time; and how long this state of affairs, so injurious to the national fishing interests of Scotland, will be allowed to continue?

MR. GRAHAM MURRAY: I am informed by the Fishery Board that the greatest number of foreign trawlers observed by superintending vessels working in the Moray Firth in one day recently has not exceeded 10. During the fortnight ended 7th instant 10 different vessels have been reported as fishing in the Firth.

MR. PIRIE: Is the right honourable Gentleman aware of the fact that since I put the Question down it has been stated there are upwards of 50 foreign trawlers now fishing in Moray Firth?

BRITISH EXPENDITURE IN AFRICA.

MR. J. ELLIS (Nottingham, Rushcliffe): I beg to ask the Under Secretary of State for Foreign Affairs what have been the total sums voted (including the purchase of the interests of any chartered company) or to be voted, up to

31st March 1899, in respect of the British Central African, East African, and Uganda Protectorates since their establishment; and what is the total sum advanced up to the 31st December 1898 in respect of any railways or other public works in these Protectorates, and on what terms as regards interest and repayment?

THE UNDER SECRETARY OF STATE FOR FOREIGN AFFAIRS (Mr. St. J. BRODRICK, Surrey, Guildford): The grants-in-aid of the revenues of the Uganda Protectorate, including the Supplementary Vote before Parliament to the 31st of March 1899, amount to £621,000; for British East Africa, £406,675; for British Central Africa, £147,200; grant to British East Africa Company for surrender of its charter, and of the sale and cession of its property, assets and rights in East Africa, £50,000; Uganda Railway to 31st December 1898, £1,690,404. The terms as regards interest and repayment of sums borrowed are fixed by the Treasury under section 2 of the Uganda Railway Act 1896.

MATRONS AT METROPOLITAN POLICE STATIONS.

MR. TALBOT (Oxford University): I beg to ask the Secretary of State for the Home Department whether he can state to the House what progress has been made in the provision of matrons for the police stations of the metropolis; and whether he can hold out an assurance that arrangements shall be made for insuring that female prisoners shall not be detained without the supervision of persons of their own sex?

THE UNDER SECRETARY OF STATE FOR THE HOME DEPARTMENT (Mr. COLLINGS, Birmingham, Bordesley): Arrangements have been made for the practically continuous attendance of matrons at some of the principal stations of the inner or Town Divisions of the Metropolitan Police District, where female prisoners are most frequently received. These women attend upon all female prisoners, and the system appears to have worked with sufficient advantage to justify its extension whenever circum-

stances require it. At stations where the reception of female prisoners is comparatively infrequent the services of a respectable female—either the wife or widow of a police officer living near—are invariably secured whenever a female prisoner is brought in and detained.

ANTRIM DISTRICT COUNCIL.

MR. JOHNSTON (Belfast, S.): On behalf of the honourable Member for East Antrim I beg to ask the Chief Secretary to the Lord Lieutenant of Ireland whether he is aware that, in regard to the district council of Antrim, that township and its rural electors, numbering 810 voters, are to have six representatives, while the town and rural electors of Ballyclare, in the same district council, numbering 925 voters, are to have but two representatives; and whether he will direct the attention of the Local Government Board to the matter, so that the anomaly may be amended?

THE CHIEF SECRETARY TO THE LORD LIEUTENANT OF IRELAND (Mr. GERALD W. BALFOUR, Leeds, Central): In fixing the number of councillors for towns under section 23 of the Act of last year, the general principle followed was to give the towns as nearly as possible the same representation on the district councils, in proportion to the total number of councillors, as they had on the board of guardians. When the number of district councillors in a rural electoral division was made two instead of one by an Amendment carried in the House of Lords, the number of councillors assigned to the electoral division of Antrim, which previously had three guardians, was also doubled, in order to keep the proportion the same. Of the six councillors thus assigned to the original electoral division of Antrim, four were assigned to Antrim Urban, and the other two, in accordance with the Act, to Antrim Rural. Ballyclare is a purely rural division. No dissatisfaction was expressed at the number of councillors to be returned for it until the Orders of the Local Government Board had been issued, and the question of adding to its representation was not considered. There are, undoubtedly, anomalies in connection with the population and representation of different electoral divisions in many cases throughout Ireland, but, as I have already explained, it would have been impossible to have remedied this state of things without carefully examining the circumstances of some 4,000 constituencies.

ALLOTMENTS.

DR. TANNER (Cork County, Mid.): I beg to ask the Chief Secretary to the Lord Lieutenant of Ireland if the allotments system in force in England will be extended to Ireland; and, if so, when may it be expected?

MR. GERALD BALFOUR: In answer to this Question, I would refer the honourable Member to my reply to a somewhat similar Question put to me on the 8th February 1897 by the honourable Member for South Mayo. The circumstances of Ireland as compared with those of England are not identical, and I am not prepared to give any undertaking on the subject.

DR. TANNER: If a Bill is brought in by our Party, will the right honourable Gentleman afford facilities for it?

MR. GERALD BALFOUR: I cannot promise that.

KILLINARDRISH POSTAL ARRANGEMENTS.

DR. TANNER: I beg to ask the Secretary to the Treasury, as representing the Postmaster-General, if any difficulty has of late been experienced and complained of in the house-to-house delivery of letters in the district of Killinardrish, in Mid Cork; and what steps will be taken to remedy this alleged grievance?

THE FINANCIAL SECRETARY TO THE TREASURY (Mr. R. W. HANBURY, Preston): No complaints have been brought to the notice of the Postmaster-General, but proposals for extending the house-to-house delivery in the parts of the Killinardrish district, where it is not yet established, are being framed, and will be carried out as soon as possible.

SLIPS FOR NEW BATTLESHIPS.

SIR C. DILKE (Gloucester, Forest of Dean): I beg to ask the First Lord of the Admiralty by what launches, at what dates, he proposes to free slips for the construction of the two battleships of the 1899-1900 Programme; and whether he can now make his promised explanation as to additional slips?

THE SECRETARY TO THE ADMIRALTY (Mr. W. E. MACARTNEY, Antrim, S.): The "Venerable," which will be launched at Chatham about September next, and the "Bulwark," which will be launched at Devonport in October or November, will free two slips on which the new battleships can be laid down. Provision has been made for commencing an additional building slip at Chatham in 1899-1900, and for making preparations for commencing one at Devonport. Provision has also been made for lengthening a building slip at Portsmouth, and another at Pembroke.

CONVICTIONS FOR ILLEGAL TRAWLING IN SCOTTISH WATERS.

MR. WEIR (Ross and Cromarty): I beg to ask the Lord Advocate if he will state how many convictions were obtained in the year 1898 against persons engaged in illegal trawling in Scottish waters, and in how many instances there was a repetition of this offence by the same master; will he state in how many cases the men elected to go to prison rather than pay the fines imposed; and whether in all cases the trawling gear of convicted trawlers was confiscated?

MR. GRAHAM MURRAY: I am informed by the Fishery Board that there were five prosecutions for illegal trawling in Scottish waters undertaken in 1898, and convictions were obtained in four of them; in the remaining case, that of a foreign trawler, the verdict was "Not proven." In none of the four instances was there a repetition of the offence by the same master. In two cases the men chose the alternative of imprisonment. The gear belonging to two of the trawlers implicated was seized and forfeited.

MR. PIRIE: Is not the present state of affairs a direct incentive to the breaking of the law——

MR. SPEAKER: Order, order! That is a matter of opinion.

OFFICE OF WOODS AND FORESTS.

MR. WEIR: I beg to ask the Secretary to the Treasury if he will state the sum received annually during the last 10 years from the unimprovable rents sold by the Office of Woods and Forests in the year ending 31st March 1898 for £11,564 9s. 4d.?

MR. HANBURY: The sums received annually during the last 10 years in respect of the unimprovable rents sold in the year ending 31st March 1898 are approximately as follows:—England, Wales, and Ireland, £432 19s. 9d.; Scotland, £8 15s. 1d.; Island of Man, £24 0s. 5d.; total, £465 15s. 3d.

FOREIGN TRAWLERS IN THE MORAY FIRTH.

MR. WEIR: I beg to ask the Lord Advocate if he will state the names and nationality of foreign trawlers observed by the Fishery Board cruisers in the Moray Firth during the year ending 31st December, 1898?

MR. GRAHAM MURRAY: I am informed by the Fishery Board that trawlers of the following nationalities were observed by their cruisers in the Moray Firth during the year 1898:—Four Dutch, 10 German, four French, nine Belgian, and five Danish. If the honourable Member desires the names of the vessels, he can have them on applying to the Scottish Office.

RATHFARNHAM POLICE BARRACK.

MR. J. O'CONNOR (Wicklow, W.): I beg to ask the Chief Secretary to the Lord Lieutenant of Ireland whether he is aware that the day roo Rathfarnham barrack, wher arrested for drunkenness i offences are in future to be d the place in which the police meals; an arrangement which convenient to the police; whet

tions are made from the pay of the police towards the rent of the barrack in which they are stationed; and, whether, considering that four or five years ago a sum of £250 appeared on the Estimates for the purpose of procuring a more suitable barrack for the police stationed at Rathfarnham, he will state whether the money has been so applied.

MR. GERALD BALFOUR: I am informed that three unmarried constables at this station have taken their meals in the day room. There is no objection to their using another room for the purpose. The statutory deduction of one shilling per week for barrack accommodation is made from the pay of each of the men at Rathfarnham, as elsewhere. The reply to the third paragraph is in the negative. It appears that the vendor's title was not sound enough to justify the purchase, and the sum voted was accordingly surrendered to the Exchequer.

REGISTRATION IN IRELAND.

DR. TANNER: I beg to ask the Chief Secretary to the Lord Lieutenant of Ireland if his attention has been called to the cases of Betty Riordan, of Millstreet, County Cork, who died on 15th October, and John Riordan, of the same place, who died on 2nd November, both being insured in the Prudential Insurance Society; if, the poor claimants, being next-of-kin, asked the local registrar eight times to register their deaths; if he is aware that the poor claimants buried the aged couple, and, despite the non-production of the certificates from the registrar, humanely paid their claims unconditionally on 23rd January; and, whether some steps will be taken to improve the existing condition of the Law of registration in Ireland?

MR. GERALD BALFOUR: In the two cases mentioned in the first paragraph, it is a fact that the registrar refused to register the deaths at the ages dered, namely 67 in the case of the le, and 71 in the case of the male. ‌ears that the registrar, who was ‌e medical attendant of the de- ‌ersons, had reason to believe ‌ements they made to him ‌ir illnesses, that both were considerably older than was represented, and an examination of the census records showed that the woman was 87 years of age at her death, and that the man was 84 when he died. This information was communicated to the parties by the registrar, who also acquainted them he would register the deaths if the certified ages were given. The lives of the deceased were insured, but I am unable to answer the third paragraph. The suggestion in the last paragraph seems to have been made under a misconception of the actual facts.

Dr. TANNER: May I ask if it is not a fact that the action taken was calculated to deprive these poor children of the right of inheritance? I will put another question on this.

RECRUITING.

Major RASCH (Essex, S.E.): I beg to ask the Under Secretary of State for War whether his attention has been called to the fact that, before Sir George Kekewich and a bench of magistrates at the petty sessions, Sunbury, Edward Wainwright, aged 19, charged with stealing, was remanded to give him an opportunity to enlist; that he had not done so, and was remanded to Holloway, where a recruiting officer was to visit him; and whether he will take steps to stop the degradation brought upon the Army by such a practice?

The UNDER SECRETARY of STATE for WAR (Mr. G. Wyndham, Dover): This youth was remanded at Sunbury "on condition that he enlisted," and the recruiting staff officer at St. George's Barracks was so informed by a missionary. The recruiting officer immediately informed the magistrates that "under no circumstances whatever would we accept a recruit while in custody, or in any way make enlistment an alternative to imprisonment." The lad was discharged by the magistrates, and subsequently presented himself for enlistment. Wainwright produced a good character extending over nine years

from the missionary, and he had a brother serving in the Army. The recruiting officer enlisted him and sent him to join his brother's regiment. I may add that Sir George Kekewich is not chairman of the Bench, and did not deal with the case.

ROYAL ARTILLERY FIELD BATTERIES.

Major RASCH: I beg to ask the Under Secretary of State for War if he can state whether the 10 new field batteries will be formed by reducing the 20 six-gun batteries to a strength of four guns?

Mr. WYNDHAM: There are 59 field batteries on the six-gun establishment —46 abroad and 13 at home. None of these will be reduced in order to form the four-gun batteries.

EDUCATION IN RURAL DISTRICTS.

Sir CAMERON GULL (Devon, Barnstaple): I beg to ask the Vice-President of the Committee of Council on Education whether, having regard to the unsatisfactory state of elementary education in rural districts, Her Majesty's Government will propose legislation with a view to improve the existing law; and whether, pending any such legislation, he can by regulations in the Education Code encourage local school authorities so to arrange the school vacations as to enable children to obtain suitable employment during periods of exceptional agricultural activity, while maintaining a high standard of attendance when the school is open?

The VICE-PRESIDENT of the COMMITTEE of COUNCIL on EDUCATION (Sir J. Gorst, Cambridge University): There is no prospect of such legislation during the present Session. The Committee of Council will consider how far alterations in the Code are necessary or possible to carry out the suggestion in the second paragraph.

CARBOLIC ACID.

Dr. FARQUHARSON (Aberdeenshire, W.): I beg to ask the Secretary of State for the Home Department whether, considering the frequency of accidental poisoning by carbolic acid, the Government will now consent to the addition of this substance to the schedule of poisons within the meaning of the Pharmacy Act, 1868, thus making it subject to the poison regulations recently adopted by the Pharmaceutical Society of Great Britain, in accordance with Act, which require that all lotions containing poison shall be sent out in bottles readily distinguishable by touch from ordinary medicine bottles?

Mr. COLLINGS: The Secretary of State understands that the Privy Council, while not thinking it expedient to include carbolic acid in the schedule to the Pharmacy Act, are of opinion that regulations should be made with regard to its sale, and have prepared a Bill for that purpose. It is, however, impossible to say whether the state of public business will permit of the Bill being introduced this Session.

MILITARY MARCHING TOURS.

Mr. PIRIE: I beg to ask the Under Secretary of State for War if he will state what marching tours of battalions and detachments through their territorial districts for recruiting purposes took place during 1898 beyond the five instances in the Annual Report of the Inspector-General of Recruiting of that year; the number of recruits enlisted whilst the march was taking place, and during the four weeks immediately succeeding its termination in each of the experiments mentioned in the Report; and also the number of miles and time occupied by each march, and the additional expenditure entailed in each instance?

Mr. WYNDHAM: There were no marches for recruiting purposes other than the five referred to in the Annual Report of the Inspector-General of Recruiting. The detailed information for which the honourable Member asked is too lengthy to read to the House, but I shall be glad to supply him with it privately.

Mr. PIRIE: How is it the Inspector-General of Recruiting in his Report mentions these five cases "among others" which took place if there were no others?

Mr. WYNDHAM: I am informed no others took place.

EXPENDITURE ON BARRACKS.

Mr. PIRIE: I beg to ask the Under Secretary of State for War if he could state to the House what was the total expenditure on the provision of barrack accommodation, excluding maintenance, in England, Scotland, and Ireland respectively during the years 1887-97, and what were the sums allowed each country for last year and for this year respectively?

Mr. WYNDHAM: The sums are as follows:—Total expenditure from 1887-8 to 1896-7 inclusive: England, £3,182,495; Scotland, £73,399; Ireland, £903,372. The sums expended in 1897-98 were:—England, £231,789; Scotland, £11,893; Ireland, £136,131. The sums provided for 1898-99 were:—England, £330,851; Scotland, £23,262; Ireland, £148,498.

BOUNTY-FED SUGAR IN INDIA.

Mr. HERBERT ROBERTS (Denbighshire, W.): I beg to ask the Secretary of State for India whether he will lay upon the Table of the House a copy of the Bill introduced on Friday, the 10th instant, in the Legislative Council of India, imposing a countervailing duty on bounty-fed sugar?

The SECRETARY OF STATE FOR INDIA (Lord G. HAMILTON, Middlesex, Ealing): On Tuesday last my right honourable Friend the Under Secretary of State for Foreign Affairs stated, on my behalf, in reply to a Question, that the responsibility for Indian legislation is thrown by the law, firstly, upon the Legislative Council, and, secondly, upon the Secretary of State for India, on whose advice any Bill may, if he thinks fit, be disallowed, and that to lay a copy of an Indian Bill during its passage through the Council upon the Table of this House would involve a transference of responsibility to which I am not prepared to agree. It is hardly necessary for me to add that I am responsible to this House for the advice which I may give on each case; and I shall be perfectly ready, if this Bill is passed, to lay a copy of it on the Table, and, if necessary, to justify the course which I have taken.

ST. CLEMENT'S CHURCH, BELFAST.

MR. YOUNG (Cavan, East): I beg to ask the Chief Secretary to the Lord Lieutenant of Ireland whether instructions can be given to the police authorities at Belfast to place a sufficient number of policemen in plain clothes each Sunday in St. Clement's Church, with directions to arrest and prosecute any one attempting to interfere with the service?

MR. GERALD BALFOUR: The proposal to place policemen in plain clothes in the church for the purpose of identifying and proceeding against persons making the disturbance has already been considered by the Government, who, however, are of opinion that disturbers of the services should be brought into a court of law by the churchwardens rather than by the police. The police are prepared to assist the churchwardens to prevent persons entering the church, if the churchwardens are empowered by the bishop or the rector to exercise this authority.

MARGARINE FACTORIES.

MR. A. MOORE (Londonderry): I beg to ask the President of the Board of Agriculture what knowledge, if any, the Board of Agriculture has of the registration of margarine factories; whether the local authorities are the bodies charged with the duty of registering margarine factories; and whether they are bound to communicate the names of factories so registered to any department of Government; and, if not, whether he will

provide for this contingency in the Bill at present before Parliament for the Sale of Food and Drugs?

THE PRESIDENT OF THE BOARD OF AGRICULTURE (Mr. W. H. LONG, Liverpool, West Derby): As my honourable Friend is aware, section 9 of the Margarine Act provides for the registration of margarine manufactories with the local authority, and sub-section (4) of clause 7 of the Sale of Food and Drugs Bill requires the local authority to notify such registration to the Board of Agriculture. We shall therefore, I think, have no difficulty in obtaining the information we require for the exercise of the powers proposed to be conferred upon us by the clause in question.

CAPTAIN DONELAN (Cork, E.): Are these margarine factories open to periodical inspection?

THE PRESIDENT OF THE BOARD OF AGRICULTURE: That I cannot say.

ERYTHREA.

SIR E. ASHMEAD-BARTLETT (Sheffield, Ecclesall): I beg to ask the Under Secretary of State for Foreign Affairs whether there is any foundation for the report that Italy is about to cede Erythrea, or any portion of it, to Great Britian?

MR. BRODRICK: No, Sir; the answer is in the negative.

PREMATURE ANNOUNCEMENT AS TO THE NAVY ESTIMATES.

MR. J. ELLIS: I beg to ask the First Lord of the Admiralty whether any investigation has been made by him as to the breach of trust of some one in his Department, by which information respecting the Navy Estimates, intentionally withheld from the House of Commons, was supplied to a particular newspaper; and, if so, with what result?

MR. D. A. THOMAS (Merthyr Tydvil): I see that the Question refers to a "particular newspaper." May I ask the right honourable Gentleman whether it is nót the case that one provincial newspaper, as well as a London newspaper, also had the information referred to in the Question—namely, the "Birmingham Daily Post"?

MR. MACARTNEY: I have no personal knowledge of that. I am aware that in several newspapers guesses were made as to the Naval Estimates, some of which were much nearer than that which was given in the paragraph to which thé honourable Gentleman refers. As regards the Question on the Paper, I am desired by the First Lord of the Admiralty to say that he demurs to the statement that a breach of trust necessarily occurred within the Department. The case is not one of the abstraction of documents which might be traced. The several figures given were known to scores of men, and I see no means by which any clue could be arrived at as to information which was probably verbally given.

MR. McKENNA (Monmouth, N.): Can the honourable Gentleman name any newspaper that contained a more accurate forecast than the "Birmingham Daily Post" except the "Times"?

MR. MACARTNEY: Yes, the "Daily Telegraph."

MR. D. A. THOMAS: May I ask the honourable Gentleman whether the First Lord of the Admiralty did not speak of it as a breach of trust?

MR. MACARTNEY: I have been asked by the First Lord of the Admiralty to ask that any further question may be deferred until he is in his place in the House.

DOG LICENCE EXEMPTIONS.

MR. WEIR: I beg to ask the Secretary to the Treasury whether he is aware that the dog kept by Ann Mackay, Drynie Park, Muir of Ord, for the purpose of tending cattle on her croft, is of precisely the same breed as a dog kept by her next-door neighbour, Peter Mac-Lennan, to whom a certificate of ex-

emption from dog tax has been granted; and with regard to the report of the supervisor that Ann Mackay's dog is of no use for tending cattle, will he state what particular section of the Customs and Inland Revenue Act, 1878, empowers the Board of Inland Revenue to determine what particular breed of dog shall be kept by a crofter for tending sheep or cattle in order to secure a certificate of exemption from dog tax?

MR. HANBURY: There is no such section as that to which reference is made in the second paragraph of the Question. In granting certificates of exemption the Board of Inland Revenue consider all the qualities of the dog, not merely its breed.

MR. VESEY STONEY.

DR. AMBROSE (Mayo, W.): I beg to ask the Chief Secretary to the Lord Lieutenant of Ireland whether he is aware that Mr. Vesey Stoney, who was allowed to serve on the last grand jury for the county of Mayo, was dismissed from the deputy lieutenancy, the magistracy, and the managership of a national school, on the ground of repeated misconduct in swindling the Government of emigration grants and being guilty of notorious acts of immorality; whether Mr. Stoney has again been summoned to act on the grand jury for the Spring Assizes; who has jurisdiction over the sheriff with reference to the selection of persons as grand jurors; and will the Government convey to the proper quarter their disapprobation of the summoning a person with such a record as a county grand juror?

MR. GERALD BALFOUR: I am not aware whether Mr. Stoney was summoned to act on the grand jury at the Spring Assizes. Grand juries are appointed by the high sheriffs at each assizes, and the Executive Government exercises no control whatever over a high sheriff in the selection of persons to serve on a grand jury. This being so, it does not appear to me that I am called upon to make any observations in reply to the first paragraph of the Question.

CASTLEBAR POST OFFICE.

Dr. AMBROSE: I beg to ask the Financial Secretary to the Treasury, as representing the Postmaster-General, whether he is aware of the inconvenience caused to the Post Office officials in Castlebar, county Mayo, by the want of space in, and the insanitary condition of, the present Post Office; and have any steps been taken to remedy this state of things?

Mr. HANBURY: An advertisement has been issued for a suitable site for a new building. Several offers have been received and examined, but only in one case, that of a property opposite to Christ Church, is the price such as the amount of the business would warrant. The owner has been asked to make an amended offer with a rather wider frontage.

MR. GARVEY OF MURRISK.

Dr. AMBROSE: I beg to ask the Chief Secretary to the Lord Lieutenant of Ireland whether he is aware that Mr. Garvey, of Murrisk, county Mayo, was dismissed from the Royal Navy and sentenced to two years' imprisonment with hard labour for stealing the money of a brother Naval Officer, and that he was subsequently employed as petty sessions clerk at Louisburgh, county Mayo, but had to be called on to resign in consequence of defalcations in his accounts; and, if so, whether, under the circumstances, Mr. Garvey will be continued in his present position, in which he is entrusted with the distribution of the funds of the Congested Districts Board in connection with the improvement of the breed of farm stock and poultry?

Mr. GERALD BALFOUR: A similar Question was put to me by the honourable Member on Monday last, containing reference to a claim by Mr. Garvey for compensation, which it was suggested was of a fraudulent character. I then requested the honourable Member to postpone the Question until after the Assizes, which open on Saturday next, in order to avoid any risk of prejudicing the case when it

comes before the judge at the Assizes. Under the circumstances, I must request the honourable Member to be good enough to postpone the present Question also for the same reason.

Mr. SWIFT MacNEILL (Donegal, S.): Is Mr. Garvey still discharging his duties, or is he suspended temporarily?

[No Reply.]

EMPLOYEES OF PARLIAMENT.

Captain NORTON (Newington, W.): I beg to ask the First Commissioner of Works whether the position as regards wages and working hours of the employees in the Lighting, Heating, and Ventilating Department of the Houses of Parliament has been brought to his notice; and whether he will consider the advisability of improving that position, seeing the general improvement that has taken place in recent years throughout the Metropolis in respect of wages and working hours?

The FIRST COMMISSIONER of WORKS (Mr. Akers Douglas, Kent, St. Augustine's): I informed the honourable Member for Stepney on the 28th ultimo of the improvements which I had decided to introduce into this Department, as regards hours, and I promised to give further consideration to the rates of pay —a promise which has not been lost sight of.

ARMY NURSES.

Captain NORTON: I beg to ask the Under Secretary of State for War whether he can state the exact training in months and years of the Army nursing sister and of the Army orderly respectively; and whether the men of the Medical Staff Corps are employed in many other duties besides nursing, such as cooking, gardening, clerking, and general cleaning work?

Mr. WYNDHAM: An Army nursing sister is required to have had three years' training in a civil hospital and six months' probation in the Army Nursing

Service before her appointment is confirmed. A private of the Royal Army Medical Corps receives theoretical and practical instruction at the depôt at Aldershot for about five months. He is then attached as a supernumerary to a large military hospital to learn practical nursing and ward work, and he remains there until he is considered efficient. His education, however, is systematically continued throughout his service with the colours. That it is sound may be inferred from the fact that many on leaving the colours obtain employment at good salaries as nurses in institutions and for private cases. The Royal Army Medical Corps is responsible for all hospital duties, including those mentioned in the second paragraph, but all the men are available for nursing duties, and perform them in turn. Where there is gardening to be done pensioners are as far as possible employed.

IRELAND AND THE PARIS EXHIBITION.

Mr. CAREW (Dublin, College Green): I beg to ask the Secretary to the Treasury whether it is true that the funds set apart for the Irish Committee in connection with the Royal Commission on the Paris Exhibition have been cut off; whether the Irish Committee and Sub-Committee are about to be dissolved; and whether, if this is so, any steps are to be taken to facilitate intending Irish exhibitors at the Exhibition of 1900?

Mr. HANBURY: The Treasury is under no responsibility for the details of the Commission's expenditure, but I understand that the facts are as follows: The Royal Commission placed the sum of £800 at the disposal of its Irish Committee for the current financial year to cover all the expenses of the Committee and its Sub-Committees. On the 24th of February last, however, they pointed out to the Lord-Lieutenant, as Chairman of the Irish Committee, that the allotment of space to exhibitors would shortly be completed, and that any communications which it might then be necessary to make to Irish exhibitors would be sent equally to them and to

exhibitors from other parts of the United Kingdom from the central office of the Royal Commission. They, therefore, expressed the hope that it would not be necessary to extend the appointment of the Secretary or to provide funds for the use of the Committee beyond the end of the financial year. The Irish Committee thereupon considered that its duties had ceased, and resolved to discontinue its functions on the 31st of March next. The same facilities will, of course, be given by the Royal Commission to Irish exhibitors as to the exhibitors from other parts of the United Kingdom.

PURCHASE OF WORKMEN'S DWELLINGS.

COLONEL SIR HOWARD VINCENT (Sheffield, Central): I beg to ask the First Lord of the Treasury if he can say when the Bill announced in Her Majesty's Most Gracious Speech, for enabling local authorities to assist the occupiers of small dwellings in the purchase of their houses, will be introduced by Her Majesty's Government?

THE FIRST LORD OF THE TREASURY (Mr. A. J. BALFOUR, Manchester, E.): My honourable Friend will see by the Paper that my right honourable Friend the Secretary for the Colonies proposes to introduce the Bill on Tuesday.

SIR H. CAMPBELL-BANNERMAN (Stirling Burghs): May I ask the right honourable Gentleman if we are to understand that it is seriously intended that this Bill, which must be one of the most important Bills of the Session, is to be introduced under such circumstances that there cannot be a discussion upon it?

THE FIRST LORD OF THE TREASURY: The Bill is an important one, but I should not think that it will be a very controversial one, and I am not aware that there is any reason why it should not be introduced under the Ten Minutes Rule.

MADRAS LAND REVENUE.

Mr. S. SMITH (Flintshire): I beg to ask the Secretary of State for India whether the Government have yet received the answer to the further dispatch stated to have been sent to the Government of Madras last year, on the subject of land revenue defaulters and the general administration of land revenue in that Presidency; and, if so, whether he is now prepared to lay upon the Table of the House the correspondence on the subject as promised in his answer last Session?

The SECRETARY of STATE for INDIA: I am unable to trace, in the reports of the answers given by me last Session, any promise of the kind referred to in the honourable Member's Question, but I find that I offered to furnish the honourable Member with copies of the Madras Land Revenue Reports for 1894-5 and 1895-6, adding that I did not propose to lay them on the Table. I am now in a position to supply him with the Report for 1896-7, if he wishes it; but I do not see any sufficient reason for presenting papers on the subject.

INLAND REVENUE OFFICIALS AND IRISH LOCAL GOVERNMENT.

Mr. PATRICK O'BRIEN (Kilkenny): I beg to ask Mr. Cnancellor of the Exchequer whether he is yet in a position to say whether officers of the Inland Revenue in Ireland are allowed by the rules of the service to become candidates for, and, if elected, to sit on county councils, urban district councils, and town commissions created under the Local Government (Ireland) Act; is he aware that an Inland Revenue officer on the staff is at present a member of one of those bodies in the west of Ireland; and what is proposed to be done in his case?

The CHANCELLOR of the EXCHEQUER (Sir M. Hicks Beach, Bristol, W.): By a Treasury Minute in 1894, it was laid down with regard to Great Britain that members of the Civil Service are not allowed to undertake outside work of any description which is incompatible with the devotion of their whole official time to the public, and that they cannot, therefore, serve on county councils, nor on any district council, the meetings of which are held during hours required for official duty, but that it is within the discretion of the head of a department to allow a civil servant to serve on a parish council, if the necessary attendance does not interfere with his official duties. This Rule will now apply to Inland Revenue officers in Ireland. Under it, members of the Civil Service will be expected to inform the heads of their departments before they allow themselves to be nominated for a district council. An Inland Revenue officer at Loughrea was recently elected a town commissioner without having given such notice, and the Board of Inland Revenue have stated that they will not object to his serving for the term for which he has been elected, but that he must not offer himself for re-election.

DEPARTMENT OF AGRICULTURE FOR IRELAND.

Captain SINCLAIR (Forfar): I beg to ask the Chief Secretary to the Lord Lieutenant of Ireland whether the Government have any intention of introducing during this Session any proposals for the establishment of a Ministry or Department of Agriculture and Industries in Ireland; and, if so, at what date?

Mr. GERALD BALFOUR: I have already stated it is the intention of the Government to introduce a Bill this Session for the purpose mentioned. I am not yet able to say on what date the Bill will be introduced.

LONDON GOVERNMENT BILL.

Mr. BARTLEY (Islington, N.): I beg to ask the First Lord of the Treasury if we are to take it for granted that the London Government Bill would not be brought in before Easter?

The FIRST LORD of the TREASURY: I hope my honourable Friend will take it for granted that it will be taken before Easter.

WAR OFFICE.

SIR H. CAMPBELL-BANNERMAN: I wish to ask the Under Secretary for War a Question of which I have given him private notice—namely, whether the Order in Council published in the newspapers on Saturday relating to the distribution of duties among the chief officers of the War Department can be laid on the Table of the House, together with the Order in Council which it supersedes, so that the alteration may be apparent?

THE FINANCIAL SECRETARY TO THE WAR OFFICE (Mr. J. POWELL WILLIAMS, Birmingham, S.): Yes, Sir, they will be laid on the Table of the House.

LORD KITCHENER.

MR. SWIFT MACNEILL: May I ask the First Lord of the Treasury whether the Bill relating to Lord Kitchener will be introduced before Easter?

THE FIRST LORD OF THE TREASURY: No, Sir, it will not be introduced before Easter.

———

ADJOURNMENT.

———

CHINESE TERRITORY (DEMANDS OF ITALY).

MOTION FOR ADJOURNMENT.

MR. PRITCHARD MORGAN (Merthyr Tydvil) rose in his place, and asked leave to move the Adjournment of the House for the purpose of discussing a matter of urgent public importance, viz.,

"That Her Majesty's Representative at Pekin is now supporting the demands of Italy for a sphere of interest in Chinese territory with Sammun Bay as a naval base, notwithstanding the Resolution passed by this House on the 1st March 1898, 'that it is of vital importance for British commerce and influence that the independence of Chinese territory should be maintained.'"

Motion made, and Question proposed—

"That this House do now adjourn."—(*Mr. Pritchard Morgan.*)

MR. PRITCHARD MORGAN: Mr. Speaker, in rising to make a few observations in regard to what I consider to be a matter of urgent public importance, I desire to say that I do not do so from any Party feeling, nor with any desire whatever to embarrass Her Majesty's Government. /I have for a period of three years taken an interest in the development of this great empire, and until this week, I have never even pronounced the name of China in this House, so that no one, I think, can charge me with any desire either to embarrass the Government or in any way make it a Party matter. I look upon this Question, Sir, from a purely commercial point of view. I think it is due to the House that it should have at least a knowledge of some of the facts which have come to my notice during the last two and a half years. England has had a first-rate opportunity during the last three years to build the Pekin-Hankow Railway. That opportunity was allowed to slip. I do not know whether it was in consequence of our having, as the noble Lord the Member for York (Lord Charles Beresford) said in China, a bad horse or a bad rider; still the fact remains that in this race in China we have been left far behind. The next opportunity which England had, and it was, to my mind, the greatest, to increase our trade and commerce in China, was when the Chinese Government requested the English Government to assist them with regard to a loan of 16 millions, intended, as the House well knows, for the purpose of paying off the Japanese indemnity. If England had taken this opportunity, China would have been saved an immense sum in interest, and England would not have run the least possible risk.

*MR. SPEAKER: Order, order! The honourable Member must confine himself to the terms of his leave.

MR. PRITCHARD MORGAN: Of course, Mr. Speaker, I bow to your ruling, and I will not attempt to travel outside the four corners of the Resolution. I only desired to show the House that an opportunity has been lost, and that the time has arrived when we should certainly not throw away any more opportunities for our protection in that great Empire. Now, Sir, I will at once, under your ruling, come to the question of Italy. Italy is claiming to-day a sphere of interest, or influence, or whatever it may be called—because I really do not know what either term means—and if we are going to support Italy in her demand, then Belgium, Austria, and other countries will necessarily claim to be entitled to spheres of interest or influence also. And where is this partitioning of this great Empire to stop? What is the use of this House passing a Resolution that we should maintain the integrity of China if, within twelve months, we support the claims of another country for a special sphere of influence? I submit that we are not only acting in violation of that Resolution, but that we are acting in a most dangerous manner, because if we have all the Powers of Europe occupying various parts of China and we become, as it were, next-door neighbours, irritation must necessarily be created, jealousies must necessarily exist, with the one and only result that the occupying Powers will ultimately be at war with regard to this broken-up China. Now, Sir, I submit that it is the duty of this House to be bound by the Resolution passed last year, and to see that we do not allow any further Power to acquire any interest in China. What, I ask, does a naval base mean if it does not mean that it will entitle those on the coast to the *Hinterland*, and thus inevitably, in the opinion of those who have studied the question, prove dangerous to peace. I am not going, Mr. Speaker, to take up a great deal of the time of the House by referring to authorities, but the Blackburn Commission has definitely and distinctly laid down the opinion that this sphere of interest, or influence, or whatever it may be called, ought not to exist, but that the policy of the "open-door" should be fully observed in this great Empire. I would like to explain to the House the effect of one incident which has lately transpired. A great bar which existed in China has been removed by the admission of foreigners of all nationalities, and, that being so, the reason is far greater why the integrity of China should be maintained, now that those in authority, and especially the present Powers, have made up their minds that the time has arrived for this great, this vast, this enormously rich, Empire to be broken up for the development of the trade of

the world. Now, Sir, what does America desire with regard to China? What does Japan desire with regard to China? What does England profess to desire with regard to China? Expansion of trade and commerce. That seems to be the universal desire of the world, and if that can be accomplished by the simple means of preserving the integrity of this country, instead of allowing this policy of partitioning to go on, then, Sir, I say we shall have all we desire. Now, Mr. Speaker, I do not wish to travel outside the terms of the Resolution in any way, but I should like to explain to the House that it is my opinion that so far as Russia is concerned we have in Russia a friend. We ought not to look upon her in any way as an enemy. Russia has in Manchuria——

*Mr. SPEAKER: Order, order! I must again remind the honourable Member that he is branching into a general question, which is not open to discussion. He must keep within the four corners of his Notice.

Mr. PRITCHARD MORGAN: I was endeavouring to point out to the House the benefit to be derived from the policy of the "open-door" as distinguished from the policy of partition. I say that this House should again necessarily express an opinion as to what that policy should be.

*Mr. SPEAKER: Order, order! That is not the question before the House. What the honourable Member has proposed to discuss is not the policy of the "open-door," but the policy of the Government in supporting Italy.

Mr. PRITCHARD MORGAN: Now, Sir, I will not further detain the House, I would, however, venture to submit that we could not possibly make a greater mistake than by continuing to support Italy or any other country in taking possession of this vast Empire. Our opportunities for trade there, with the "open-door" will more than counterbalance the advantages which the Government may think they are going to derive from having Italy as a friendly neighbour in proximity to the Yang-tsze-kiang. It is nothing but the nervousness, the weakness, and the short-sightedness of Her Majesty's Government which justifies them in allowing Italy to come anywhere near our sphere of influence. All we had to do was to deal with Russia with a firm hand, and at the same time in the most friendly way, by saying "Thus far shalt thou go and no farther," instead of allowing, as the Government did, British ships to leave Port Arthur. Mr. Speaker, I beg to move the Resolution standing in my name.

*SIR E. ASHMEAD-BARTLETT (Sheffield, Ecclesall): Sir, although I do not agree with the honourable Gentleman who has just spoken in the conclusion at which he has arrived with regard to the support by this country of the interposition of Italy in China, I do agree with a good deal that he has said upon China. If the honourable Gentleman had made this Motion two years ago, or even a year ago, before these incursions upon the Chinese Coast had taken place on the part of Russia and Germany, a great deal might have been said for his Motion. But the position we are now in with regard to——

*MR. SPEAKER: Order, order! I thought the honourable Member rose to second the Motion.

*SIR E. ASHMEAD-BARTLETT: I will second *pro forma*, although it is not a Motion I would have made myself. It is, however, by no means unusual for a Motion of this kind to be seconded *pro forma*. Had it not been for the fact that Russia has not only obtained a great naval port and arsenal on the Yellow Sea, but a great hold upon Chinese territory, and that Germany has got Kiao-Chau, and that we have occupied Wei-hai-Wei, I should have supported the Motion of the honourable Gentleman with regard to Italy. But we are in the presence of accomplished facts. Three great countries, including our own, have already established positions on the Chinese Coast, with certain spheres of influence or interest, and the question which the Government have to deal with now is, Will the arrival of Italy upon the scene of operations in China be of advantage or disadvantage to this country? Italy is well-known to be one of our oldest and most reliable friends in Europe.

Mr. Pritchard Morgan.

Indeed, I doubt if any other country in Europe can be said to be bound to England by such strong historical and traditional ties, as well as by ties of national interest and naval necessity, as the Italian nation. Therefore, assuming that the objects of Italy in China are the same as our own, namely, opposition to the acquisition and seizure of territory, I should be disposed rather to welcome the arrival of Italy. If difficulties should arise we should find Italy our friend rather than our enemy. Italian interests are not really opposed to ours, and the Italian fleet is likely to be of decided advantage to the fleet of Great Britain should active operations ever become necessary. I think my honourable Friend opposite has been rather misled by what he himself publicly said was his want of information upon the meaning of the words "sphere of interest" and "sphere of influence." I admit that a great deal does depend upon the meaning of those words. Now, Sir, we have had various meanings attached to those words, and it would be well to have some definition arrived at. In a previous Debate, two honourable Friends of mine on this side of the House, the Member for Chester and another, treated "spheres of influence" as if they had practically meant the "partition" of China. They assumed to speak on behalf of a Committee which I believe is known as the Chinese Committee, though I very much doubt whether they represented that Committee in this particular view, because I do not believe that that organisation is pledged to the partitioning of China in the sense that they represented it to be. Now, Sir, as the honourable Member opposite very correctly said, the only policy with regard to China is the policy of maintaining its territorial integrity. In that I thoroughly agree with him. If the arrival of Italy upon the scene of operations, or of any other Power, meant the partitioning of China, I should most strongly oppose it. The partitioning of China, as the honourable Gentleman said, is the most deadly policy which this country could follow, because it may mean not only the breaking up of that great Empire, with all the attendant disasters both to the people of China and to ourselves, but that other Powers rather than

Great Britain will get control of the greater part of that Empire. I do not, however, think that Italy's interposition will tend to partition. In a previous Debate my honourable Friend the Member for King's Lynn (Mr. Gibson Bowles) and the right honourable Gentleman the Under Secretary of State for Foreign Affairs defined the sense in which this House might accept the meaning of "sphere of influence," or, at all events, "sphere of interest." I am not misinterpreting my right honourable Friend the Under Secretary of State for Foreign Affairs when I say that he told the House that by "sphere of interest," i.e., the policy which Her Majesty's Government have been pursuing in China, they meant, not the acquisition of any political or military control, but the establishment of certain spheres, as to which the Powers possessing them had a primary claim to commercial concessions. Commercial concessions are very different things from political interests or political or military control. That is a policy to which no one, however much he may desire the territorial integrity of China, should take exception, and I doubt whether the honourable Gentleman opposite who moved this Resolution would object to certain spheres being assigned to the great Powers, if those Powers merely had the first claim on the commercial advantages of the territory in question.

MR. PRITCHARD MORGAN: I regard anything in the shape of spheres of interest and naval bases as an interference with the integrity of China.

*SIR E. ASHMEAD-BARTLETT: There are already three naval bases existing belonging to Russia, Germany, and England, and I do not think the establishment of a fourth will do any serious harm to China.

MR. PRITCHARD MORGAN: I should like to ask the honourable Gentleman whether he thinks two or three robberies justify a fourth!

*SIR E. ASHMEAD-BARTLETT: Well, Sir, that is rather a bald way of putting it. Does not the honourable Gentleman think that, as there are already three Powers established in China, the establishment of a fourth may be a balance to the others, and may help to prevent any one of the others from getting possession of Chinese territory? I cannot believe for one moment that the Government would either advocate a policy of partition in China, which the honourable Gentleman seems to fear, or that they would refuse to give their friendly support to a country which is so well established and so useful an ally of Great Britain as Italy. I sincerely hope that nothing will be done tending to the partition of China, which I should regard not only as a great crime but as a blunder, as it would cause the loss by us of the support of the United States and of Japan in our Eastern policy. On the other hand, I regard the approach of Italy to Chinese waters, and the acquisition by her of a base there as not likely to injure China, and as certainly likely to be of advantage to this country.

*THE UNDER SECRETARY OF STATE FOR FOREIGN AFFAIRS (Mr. BRODRICK, Surrey, Guildford): I fear I am in rather a peculiar position in replying to this Motion, for up to the present the Debate has consisted of disputes between the proposer and the seconder, and the seconder has not left me much to say in reply to the proposer. I do not object to the demands for information, but I think it is an inconvenient course to attempt, on a Motion of this kind, to raise all the questions incidental to China which have occupied us during the last few years. To the issues specially raised in the Motion the honourable Member devoted only two or three sentences, which carried with them their own refutation. He is never tired of urging publicly and privately that the British Government should assume as much authority as possible in China, and should create spheres of interest or influence over the provinces in which he himself takes an interest. But now he demands from us not only that we shall safeguard our interests, but that we shall take care that no other Power safeguards hers.

MR. PRITCHARD MORGAN: I beg the right honourable Gentleman's pardon. Does he represent me as saying that England should assume responsibility throughout China?

MR. BRODRICK The remark made by the honourable Member—it was, perhaps, entirely haphazard, as most of his remarks were—the remark made by him with some emphasis was that we should not allow any Power whatever to have any interest in China. We are to declare, according to the honourable Member, that we alone have any right in China; and it is our business to prevent any other Power from establishing any interest there. These observations are really too crude for it to be necessary for me to reply to them. In this particular case, as regards Italy, I can make this statement to the House. The position which Italy has taken in this matter has been entirely taken on her own initiative. The Italian Government has desired to secure a sphere of interest or influence in China. The honourable Member says that we ought to have met that step with a negative. I do not know what title we have to negative·any negotiations.

MR. PRITCHARD MORGAN: The words of my Motion refer to " support."

MR. BRODRICK: The honourable Member, by several sentences in his speech, showed that he wished Italy to be practically elbowed out altogether. That was the gist of his speech. The position which the Government has taken is the only proper position under the circumstances. Italy is a friendly Power. For many years she has been an ally of Great Britain. She is anxious for certain advantages in China. In regard to that desire we have shown a friendly attitude, but our attitude has been strictly limited—and our approval, as · far as given, has been strictly limited—to diplomatic negotiations. As far as we are concerned, if the Italian Government by diplomatic negotiations can get China to make concessions to her, we shall welcome her success. I do not think it is necessary that I should advert to what has fallen from the honourable Member as to this attitude having been taken from nervousness or shortsightedness. In these matters there is nothing which is more unwise than to go beyond what is your proper province, and our proper province at present is to safeguard our own interests. As far as these are not threatened we do not

assist them by standing in the way of other friendly Powers who wish to safeguard their interests. That is the whole case of the Government; and in the case of Italy we wish well to her negotiations, and, as far as we are concerned, by diplomatic means we are willing to support them.

MR. COURTNEY (Cornwall, Bodmin): In interposing for a few moments in this Debate I feel compelled to say that the speech of the Under Secretary has a little disappointed me. I had hoped that the right honourable Gentleman was going to say that the attitude of this country had been misunderstood, and that, in respect of the Italian application we maintained a strict neutrality, neither favouring it nor doing anything against it. The right honourable Gentleman said that we had done nothing against it, and, so far, the Government will have the support of the House and the country. But the right honourable Gentleman also said that we are giving our diplomatic support to the action of Italy. Well, Sir, in the interests of Italy itself, as well as of this country, I confess that that action is most unfortunate. The honourable Member for Sheffield has spoken of Italy as our ancient and traditional friend—as the friend, not only of years, but of generations—

*SIR E. ASHMEAD-BARTLETT: I did not say so.

MR. COURTNEY: The word "traditional" does not mean much if it does not cover more than a generation. I am old enough to remember quite well the beginning of the Italian nation, and how it was regarded at the time. And there are those now who are doing their best to lure Italy to her destruction. Italy first was to go to Africa, and we all know what came of it. Now, she is to have our diplomatic support in establishing a naval base or sphere of influence in China. It is urged that the step will be in our interests. But in the interests of Italy herself, every one who knows her condition must desire that Italian ambition and energies shall be restricted to affairs at home, and that these foreign ambitions ought not to be encouraged. If the Italian Government take this action, we cannot restrain them. But in advising them to do it, in countenancing it, in saying something to the Chinese Government in support of it, we are not acting in the interests of Italy. Sir, I submit this act cannot stand alone. Italy is following the lead of England, Germany, and Russia, and Austria-Hungary and Holland may follow the example of Italy. In the interest of ourselves, as well as in the interests of China, I altogether deprecate the action which Her Majesty's Government seem to have taken. No well-wisher of Italy can desire her to embark upon these adventures, and it is not for us to encourage the dream of the recovery of the ancient Roman Empire for Italy which is exemplified in the Italian Chamber of Deputies by a display of a map showing what that empire once was. I sincerely regret that the action of Her Majesty's Government has not been one of the strictest neutrality.

SIR E. GREY (Berwick-on-Tweed): I should not have intervened in the Debate, but I think the speech to which we have just listened may leave a rather false impression as to the position in which the House has been left by the speech of the Under Secretary of State for Foreign Affairs. Sir, the questions which have been causing us anxiety with regard to China, and about which we should most like to speak, or about which I should most like to speak, would not be in order on this Resolution. But I listened to the speech of the Under Secretary for Foreign Affairs, and did not receive from it the impression which it seems to have conveyed to my honourable Friend the Member for Bodmin. I understood the Under Secretary for Foreign Affairs to say that the attitude of the Government with regard to Italy had not been one of spurring her on or encouraging or instigating her. But, Sir, I think the impression we shall get by reading the speech of the right honourable Member for Bodmin is that the Government have taken a more active part in this matter than has been the case. Well, Sir, I am not surprised that this Motion should have been raised, because the Government did accept last year a definition of what they meant by protecting our own interests in China which went far beyond the scope of the speech of the right honourable Gentleman the Under Secretary. When they

accepted the Resolution of an honourable Member last year, they undoubtedly were understood to pledge themselves to maintain the integrity of China, and they are undoubtedly open to the charge of inconsistency, not merely in supporting this demand which Italy has put forward, but also in not resenting it. But we on this side of the House have always maintained that the Government undertook far too much in that Resolution. It was not intended to be taken too literally. In any case, a great deal has happened since. Matters have gone very far. Spheres of interest have matured in China—more than one—and I do say that the Government would be placed in a great difficulty if Italy came forward on her own motive and impulse, acting in accordance with what she believed to be her own interests, and demanded that she should have something like that sphere of interest which has been gained by other Powers. I do not see how the Government could possibly have resented that after what has passed. Then the right honourable Member for Bodmin would say that the Government should have stood entirely on one side. I am sure even he would feel that the Government could not offer to Italy the advice he has offered to her this evening.

MR. COURTNEY: There are many ways of offering advice.

SIR E. GREY: Yes, Sir; and there are many kinds of advice. I think it would tax all the resources of diplomatic ingenuity for one Government to put into a friendly form, or a form which would be received as friendly by another, the advice my right honourable Friend has offered.

MR. COURTNEY: It would not be written at all.

SIR E. GREY: I did not say it would be written. But I should be very sorry to be charged with the delicate task of conveying it, because if conveyed verbally it would still be placed on record; but, to return to my point—whether Government ought to have left the matter entirely alone. If they had, would other Powers have left it alone? Would there have been no intervention from anyone? The moral to be drawn from what has happened in China is that it is impossible for us to stand aside from what is taking place and confine our actions solely to representations to the Chinese Government without communicating with other European Powers. Isolation is becoming more and more impossible, and what we wish to see is constant communication and constant touch between Her Majesty's Government, and, not merely Italy, but also the other European Governments interested in the matter; because we know that if constant touch is not maintained we and other Powers run a risk of drifting apart, and we believe, therefore, it is necessary there should be constant communication and touch in order that friendly relations may be preserved in this matter with Italy and the other Powers interested.

MR. BRYN ROBERTS (Carnarvonshire, Eifion): In reply to the remarks by the honourable Baronet the Member for Berwick, that there is no diplomatic method by which the Government could have tendered to the Government of Italy advice of the nature suggested by the right honourable Member for Bodmin, I would venture to point out that the right honourable Baronet has himself furnished a precedent showing how informal but important communications from one Government to another can be made on the floor of this House when he made his unfortunate " unfriendly act " speech, which had such important results. A Member of Her Majesty's Government can, therefore, in a speech at the Table, give to another Power advice which cannot diplomatically be given direct.

CAPTAIN BETHELL (York, W.R., Holderness): Though last year I argued that it was not a disadvantage to have several great Powers in China, I doubt whether we ought, even diplomatically, to assist Italy in gaining what she requires. I think it would be better if, instead of assisting her, we stood entirely aside and let Italy fight her own battles in China for herself. I do not believe it is true or sound policy to make arrangements with other Powers of Europe for the partition of China.

*MR. MARKS (Tower Hamlets, St. George's): There is one aspect of this question to which I would venture, in a

Sir E. Grey.

word or two, to call the attention of the House. When we were discussing our position in China last year, and when accusations were brought against the Government that we had been left behind in the search for commercial and other advantages, it was stated in this House by the First Lord of the Treasury that amongst other advantages gained were very important mining and railway concessions in Shang-si which had been granted to an English syndicate; and a similar statement was made by the present Under Secretary of State for War at the same time. Well, Sir, it must not be forgotten that these concessions were granted largely in consequence of the influence brought to bear by the Italian Minister in Pekin. That fact was made manifest in the negotiations between Sir Claude Macdonald and the representative of the Chinese Government at the time. We have not had hitherto so many friends in China that we can afford to dispense even with one friend, and, considering the good turn which Italian diplomacy did us at the time when we were in need of assistance, and considering what has been said of the results of that diplomacy by one of the best authorities in this House, it does seem to me that if it be possible without detriment to our interests to make a good return for that service it is in the highest degree desirable and expedient that we should do so.

MR. GIBSON BOWLES (Lynn Regis): I desire in a very few words to point out that not only is Germany established in China, and Russia, and England, but also France. There are already four European Powers in China, and with what countenance can Her Majesty's Government protest against the arrival under similar circumstances of a fifth? It seems to me that that is an important consideration. The right honourable Member for Bodmin seems to think we ought to go to the Italian Government and tell them that what they want is all wrong, that their people are all wrong, and that we understand their interests better than they do themselves. On the 1st March of last year we were told that Her Majesty's Government would maintain, not merely the integrity but also the independence of China. Meanwhile Italy has gone to China. I am sorry to see France, Germany, Russia, and now Italy gnawing coaling stations out of China, but since France, Germany, and Russia have done it, it is quite impossible for Her Majesty's Government to offer any resistance to its being done by Italy.

Motion negatived.

BUSINESS OF THE HOUSE (GOVERNMENT BUSINESS).

Motion made, and Question proposed—

"That Government Business have precedence To-morrow, and that the provisions of Standing Order 56 be extended to that day's Sitting."—*(The First Lord of the Treasury.)*

THE FIRST LORD OF THE TREASURY (Mr. A. J. BALFOUR, Manchester, E.): I do not know that it is necessary I should remind the House in general of what took place last Friday, because probably most of the honourable Gentlemen whom I am now addressing were present on that occasion; but the honourable Member for Northampton, who is interested in the business to-morrow, appears not to have been here on Friday, and in the complete ignorance in which he was with regard to what took place on that occasion he has written a letter to the newspapers, which has been brought to my notice, in which he accuses the Government of not having been fair and straightforward in their management of the proceedings of the House, and in which he further states that it was owing to some error on my part that the business of the Army Estimates was not placed on the Paper for Friday.

*MR. CHANNING (Northampton, E.): In the letter I did not in the least attribute anything like want of straightforwardness with regard to not putting the notice on the Paper.

THE FIRST LORD OF THE TREASURY: The phrase I referred to was—

"I submit, not as a question of personal claim, or of the specific Motions on the Paper, but as a question of ordinary fair and straightforward procedure, that Mr. Balfour's proposal should be withdrawn."

I do not think that is a very happy phrase. Let us hope it does not accurately represent the views of the honourable Member who penned it. But with regard to the other statement— namely, that I was to blame for not putting the Votes on the Paper—had he been present, or made any inquiries of any Gentleman who was present, he would have known it was not an error made by me or by my honourable Friends, but an error made elsewhere, and by other persons.

*MR. CHANNING: Hear, hear!

THE FIRST LORD OF THE TREASURY: I am glad he assents; but that is directly contrary to what he states in his letter, as I understand it. What actually did take place on Friday was that objection was first taken by the right honourable Baronet the Member for the Forest of Dean. He stated, I think, that he and some honourable Gentlemen on this side had formed the conclusion, on receiving the Blue Papers on Friday morning, that these Estimates were not to be taken on Friday evening, and that the honourable Members, therefore, made arrangements which would prevent them from being here.

SIR C. DILKE (Gloucestershire, Forest of Dean): I made that statement on behalf of other Members of the House, not on my own.

THE FIRST LORD OF THE TREASURY: In answer to the right honourable Baronet, I said it made very little difference to the Government; that if the actual objection taken was held to be sufficient, we should be driven to the alternative course of taking Tuesday. The House had some few minutes to consider that alternative proposal, and the Debate went on for some time after I made that statement, and then the honourable and gallant Member for Aberdeen got up and pressed me very strongly, in the interest of himself and other persons interested, not to insist that the Army Estimates should be proceeded with. Under the circumstances, I felt driven to take the alternative course. I then informed the House I should be compelled to take it if we did not proceed with the Army Estimates. The House has a right to know why it is that, in the interest of Supply, it is necessary we should either have had last Friday or have to-morrow. The case as regards Supply before Easter stands thus: We have to get the First Reading of the Appropriation Bill not later than Tuesday the 21st, in order that we may take the Second Reading on Wednesday the 22nd, get through Committee on Thursday the 23rd, and take the Third Reading on Friday the 24th. That leaves us to-day, and to-morrow, and Thursday, Friday, and Monday to finish our work in Committee of the whole House. Of those days we propose that to-day, Thursday, and Friday should be devoted to the Navy Estimates, to-morrow to the Army Votes, and next Monday to the Vote on Account. I do not know that it is possible to narrow down the time I have allocated to these necessary Services to any smaller length than that which I have assigned to them. We are driven, in the interests of public business, to take to-morrow, and to devote Thursday, Friday, and Monday entirely to the work of Supply. I hope that justification of the policy of the Government will be deemed sufficient, and that, without further curtailment of time, the House will grant the privilege I now ask.

SIR H. CAMPBELL-BANNERMAN (Stirling Burghs): In the course of this Parliament we have witnessed some extraordinary demands made upon the House of Commons, but I cannot help thinking that this is one of the most unjustifiable that have ever been submitted to the House by a responsible Minister. I can assure the right honourable Gentleman that, so far as time is necessary to proceed with the requisite financial business of the current year, he will receive every assistance from every part of the House. I am not in a position to either acquiesce in or controvert the programme he has drawn up of the necessary manner of spending the time available for that purpose, but I demur altogether to the view he has communicated to the House of what occurred on Friday, and I would carry my glance a little bit further, and invite the House to consider the progress of business last week. If there is this great necessity to have so many days devoted to the voting of Supply before the Finance Bill is introduced, the necessity existed a week ago or more just as strongly as it does now. But I will deal first with the case of Friday last. The right honourable Gentleman speaks as if he were an aggrieved person because he was not allowed to pro-

First Lord of the Treasury.

ceed with the discussion of the Army Estimates on Friday last. Whether it be his fault, or the fault of some person under him——

THE FIRST LORD OF THE TREASURY: Not under me.

SIR H. CAMPBELL-BANNERMAN: Matters not to us, because, after all, whatever may have been said of the intentions of the Government as to business on a certain day, the latest word that Members receive, the latest information, and therefore the most accurate information, of the intentions of the Government for any particular day is usually contained in what is known as the Blue Paper, which is circulated in the morning. The right honourable Gentleman had said, no doubt, that it was intended to take the Army Estimates on Friday, but when an honourable Member received his Blue Paper, and did not find the Army Estimates down, he naturally concluded that the Government had changed their minds, and that for some reason known only to themselves they were postponing the consideration of the Army Estimates to another day. I have nothing but praise for the courtesy and consideration with which the right honourable Gentleman at once accepted the situation on Friday last. Whether it was his own, or some one's acting on his instructions, or whether it was the convenient printer's, it was somebody's error, and for that somebody's error I am afraid the right honourable Gentleman must be held responsible.

HONOURABLE MEMBERS. Oh, oh!

SIR H. CAMPBELL-BANNERMAN: Surely he is responsible in the result—not in the intention. But I go further back than last Friday. With this great pressure of financial business before them, what were the Government doing on Monday and Thursday last? They occupied those days with a Bill which, so far from being urgent, was taken prematurely, was taken before the country had had an opportunity of considering it, and the right honourable Gentleman himself acknowledges that it was in a rather premature condition, because at the moment the Second Reading was taken he promised to allow a considerable interval to elapse before he asked the House to go into Committee on the Bill, on the very ground that it was not long since the Bill had been printed and was in the hands of those interested in it. Both of the days of last week which were devoted to the Food and Drugs Bill might have been devoted to that financial business, as to which there was urgent pressure of time; so that the right honourable Gentleman has nobody but himself to blame for the position in which he finds himself. Finding himself in that position, the right honourable Gentleman proposes to take Tuesday from my honourable Friend the Member for Northamptonshire. I know that on these occasions any honourable Member who has a Motion upon the Paper can always make out a very strong case, so far as that particular Motion is concerned, for extreme urgency, but it does not seem to me that in this case there is really a strong case, as was pointed out in the letter to which the right honourable Gentleman has referred. The honourable Gentleman the Member for Northampton is going to bring forward a Motion of the deepest interest to all those who are connected with or interested in the agricultural industries of the country; the question of tuberculosis. That Motion, if not absolutely necessary, is most desirable, in order to clear the air and point the way with regard to certain private Bills that have to be dealt with on Thursday next. That is the point. Certain private Bills of great importance, both to towns and the agricultural community throughout the country, are to be brought forward on Thursday, and with that view, it is, if not absolutely necessary, highly expedient that we should know the views of the Government upon the Question, and that opportunity will be forfeited by my honourable Friend if he is unable to bring on his Motion on Tuesday. But I base my opposition to the proposals of the right honourable Gentleman, not upon that, but on the facts previously deduced, which show that if the Government had exercised reasonable precaution and looked a little ahead some 10 days ago they would have absorbed the time at their command in such a manner as would have prevented there being any necessity for trespassing at this early period of the Session upon the time of the private Members of this House in a manner which makes it ridiculous to set up the right of private Members to Tuesdays at all. I would

not press the rights of private Members too far, but they are, after all, human beings, and they have certain rights which have been in the most cold-blooded manner infringed. So far as we are concerned, the right honourable Gentleman may be sure, as I commenced by saying, so far as the financial business of the year is concerned, we shall give him every assistance, but we cannot be parties to proceeding in this way, which seems so much to trespass upon the time of the private Members.

*MR. CHANNING: The right honourable Gentleman the leader of the Oposition has really said all that I might have wished to say upon this question. The right honourable Gentleman the First Lord of the Treasury, in dealing with this question, appeared to consider that the letter which I sent to the " Times " newspaper in some way reflected upon his honour and fairness in the conduct of the business of this House. I want to relieve him from any feeling of that kind which he may have in his mind. But what I do wish to insist upon is this: that throwing away four or five hours of Government time, which he was at perfect liberty to occupy by the ruling of the Chair, and then taking Tuesday for the Government business, does constitute a wholly novel and a very dangerous precedent in the taking away of the time of private Members. I think it is a very serious thing indeed to have a precedent of that kind introduced into the procedure of the House. The ruling of the Deputy Speaker was perfectly clear, and, as a matter of fact, there was a similar ruling given some years ago under the same circumstances. But the right honourable Gentleman, acting apparently out of the impulsive generosity of his heart, on the appeal of one or two Members on this side of the House, deliberately threw away four or five hours of the time of the House on Friday last which the Chairman told him were perfectly at his disposal. That is a fact that the right honourable Gentleman the Leader of the Opposition did not touch upon. I am always perfectly ready, and I think that private Members generally are ready, to make any sacrifice that may be necessary for the promotion of the genuine business of the House, in the stress of public affairs, or when there are great arrears of Votes which have to be cleared off. But that is not so here. The right honourable Gentleman has stated his case as to the position of Supply in such strong terms to-day that it seems to me absolutely inconceivable that he could not have seen the force of his own arguments on Friday, and instead of allowing the whole of this time on Friday to be wasted, that he should not have used it for the purpose of carrying a great number of Votes, as he might easily have done in the temper of the House that night. Now, with regard to the Motion which stands in my name for to-morrow, the essential point raised by that Motion —I should be out of order in attempting to-day to discuss the details—the essential point raised is to obtain some statement from the Government as to their general policy on a question of the most urgent interest to public health. It is of the utmost importance to the consumers of milk, and to the local authorities who represent their interests all over the country, as it is of the utmost importance to agriculturists to know whether the Government is going to deal with this question of tuberculosis on a uniform plan, with uniform machinery, and with compensation where necessary all over the country. The course adopted by the right honourable Gentleman is injurious to the interests of these great towns which are promoting Bills on this subject, one of which is Manchester, and another of which is Leeds. I think that the interests of these communities and these towns have been very greatly prejudiced by the action taken in this matter by the right honourable Gentleman. I think that he has given us no reason whatever, nor has he given us any precedent for deliberately throwing away four or five hours of the time of this House, which it was perfectly open to him to occupy, and then to calmly appropriate the time of the private Members. That is a practice which up to now has been utterly unknown to Parliamentary history. It is adopted now to the prejudice of the interests of agriculture, and to the loss of all those who are interested in the urgent Question which I proposed to bring forward to-morrow.

Mr. Channing.

MR. HOBHOUSE (Somerset, E.): I think that the private Members of this House ought to second the gallant efforts which have been made on their behalf by the right honourable Gentleman the Leader of the Opposition by saying a word or two upon their own rights. This is an occasion upon which private Members are suffering through their not having committed any fault of their own. They are suffering, in the opinion of my honourable Friend opposite, by having the most convenient day for the discussion of an extremely important agricultural question, and at the same time an extremely important question with regard to public health, taken away from them without any compensation being offered to them. If it so happens that this discussion on tuberculosis cannot be proceeded with next Tuesday, the Government, I sincerely hope, will attempt to provide some other convenient opportunity for the discussion of that very important question. We know that after Easter the Government propose to take every Tuesday from the private Members, and therefore, if no effort is made by them, we shall have no opportunity at all of discussing what in my opinion is one of the most important questions of the day. Under those circumstances, it is surely not too much to hope that some time at least will be left to my honourable Friend opposite next Tuesday, if the Army Members of this House will confine their remarks within reasonable limits. Do I understand my right honourable Friend the First Lord of the Treasury to say that the only Government business for which he asks precedence, and the only business which he will place upon the Paper next Tuesday, is the remaining Army Votes?

THE FIRST LORD OF THE TREASURY: Only the Army Vote.

MR. HOBHOUSE: Very well; if that be so, then I think there is a reasonable chance of getting a discussion upon the question of tuberculosis after that business is concluded; but if that discussion does not take place, then I really do think the Government, in all fairness to the private Members of the House, should find some other opportunity for the discussion of this very important subject, and I hope that they will do their best to do so.

*SIR J. LUBBOCK (London University): I am one of those who always support the private Members when the Government proposes to take away their time, but upon this occasion I cannot quite agree with my honourable Friend the Member for Northamptonshire. But I do feel that there is some force in the remarks made by the right honourable Gentleman the Leader of the Opposition, that the Government might have taken these Votes at an earlier period of the Session. At the same time, we have now to consider the state of things in which we find ourselves to-day, and the days being so few before the period at which these Votes must be taken, I confess that it appears to me that my right honourable Friend the First Lord of the Treasury has made out an unanswerable case. Much as I regret his taking away the time of private Members I cannot but admit that upon this occasion a good case has certainly been made out. At the same time, it was the practice in other days that when the Government found themselves compelled by the nature of their business to take away a private Member's night they always felt they were under some obligation to him on that account, and they always gave him some other opportunity to bring his Question forward. I am very glad to hear from the right honourable Gentleman the Leader of the House that if there is any time on Tuesday night after taking the Army Votes that my honourable Friend opposite will be able to bring forward his Motion on the question of tuberculosis, and further, I would make an urgent appeal to the Government that, if it so happens that they occupy the whole · of the time on Tuesday, that they will place my honourable Friend in the position he would otherwise have occupied by giving him another opportunity of bringing this ╱matter forward.

MR. SWIFT MACNEILL (Donegal, S.): I am very sorry to hear the right honourable Baronet the Member for the London University say that the right honourable Gentleman the First Lord of the Treasury has made out a good case for appropriating the time of the private Members of this House. Believe me when I say I will not follow the most pernicious example of the right honourable Gentleman the First Lord in wasting the time of the House, to which I only intend to address a very few words. And I am speaking really more in sorrow than in anger when I say that the right honourable Gentleman deliberately and wantonly wasted on Friday evening four or five hours of military time, and now desires to curtail the rights of the private Members to the time of the House to-morrow night. What is his excuse for acting in this manner? He simply relies on a printer's error, and he performs a miracle, a miracle which the right honourable Gentleman only is capable of preforming—that is, he converts a " printer's devil " into a Parliamentary Statement. No other honourable Member would ever dream of doing that. I really believe that a Motion of this kind is calculated to very much weaken all Parliamentary institution. This Parliament is old ; it is the mother of all Parliaments, and is, I believe, 700 years old ; then why does the right honourable Gentleman the First Lord of the Treasury, who I have always understood loves all old institutions, and respects them, try to weaken one of the oldest institutions of this country. But in this particular case I have a personal grievance against the right honourable Gentleman the First Lord of the Treasury. I, on Friday night, was prepared to speak at some length upon the Army Votes, and had prepared all my information, and, so to speak, got all my ammunition ready for the conflict. But what was my surprise when I found that the right honourable Gentleman, without any reason whatsoever, merely intimated that he would adjourn the Army Estimates and take the time on Tuesday for the discussion of them. I was prepared to do this ; I was prepared to respect the rights of the honourable Gentlemen who had various motions for reduction down upon the Paper, and when I brought forward my own points —I knew from experience, having heard some of their speeches three times over —I was prepared, when I brought forward my points, to move the reductions and to say what the honourable Gentlemen would be likely to say. The Gentlemen who debate upon the Army Estimates may be divided into two classes. There is the military class, and there are the civilian experts. Now, in order to assist the Government in getting these Votes through, I was prepared, after my own speech was over, to make a speech upon the general details of the Votes, and then I was prepared to make what might be termed a military speech, which, embracing all the views of the military Members, would tend to shorten the discussion, but, instead of giving us that opportunity, the right honourable Gentleman allowed his night to go by, and now has attached ours. On Friday he sent us away early from this House to our own homes, where we were not expected, possibly to the great inconvenience of our families, and now proposes to appropriate our time. There is one other point which ought to be mentioned in this connection. Perhaps honourable Gentlemen may not have noticed it, but there is another Motion which is down to come on on Tuesday. After the subject of tuberculosis had been discussed, we were to discuss the position of the Right Honourable Cecil Rhodes as a Privy Councillor. Is that to be burked in order to allow this Vote to be taken? I rather suspect that that is the true inwardness of the Government's desire to take Tuesday. I don't know whether that is so or not, but all I can say is that I cannot fail to have that impression. [Cries of "Divide, divide!"] Honourable Gentlemen on the other side of the House are crying out "Divide!" It is the only opportunity that many of them have of speaking, and it is the only speech that they can make or have ever made in this House. The right honourable Gentleman must recollect this—that this Moton gives him no promise that the Army Estimates will be discussed shortly when they do come on.

SIR W. FOSTER (Derby, Ilkeston): I should like, before this discussion comes to an end, to make some appeal to the generosity of the right honourable Gentleman the First Lord of the Treasury in reference to the time of private Members. The point which is to come under discussion on Tuesday is of the greatest interest to a very large section of the people outside this House, as well as to a large number of Members here, and the loss of an opportunity to discuss so serious a question,

Mr. Swift MacNeill.

which conflicts with so many interests, is very greatly felt under these circumstances; and, as I think that we are rather hardly treated in this matter, I would earnestly appeal to the right honourable Gentleman to try and make some way for this discussion to come on. I think if he limited the Government efforts on Tuesday to the carrying of Vote 1 of Army Estimates there would be no objection to that, and the rest of the day might then be devoted to a discussion on the very important subject of tuberculosis. Vote 1 would give him enough money to go on with for some months, and I think that the carrying of the Vote, and the discussion of it, might be concluded within the limits of a morning sitting on Tuesday. Under those circumstances, we might afterwards ventilate what is of the greatest interest to those interested in the public health, and, not only that, but that which is of the first importance to all those who have any regard for the agricultural interest of this country. I do hope that the right honourable Gentleman will take such a course as to do away with what seems to be ungenerous and hard lines meted out to the private Members of this House in preventing the discussion on so important a matter as that of tuberculosis.

MR. COURTNEY: The honourable Member for the Ilkeston Division has made one very practical suggestion, and I rise to make one of another character, though it leads to exactly the same result. The Leader of the House has promised to give such time as remains after the Army Estimates have been disposed of to the consideration of this question. He has stated that he will confine himself to the passing of the Army Votes on Tuesday, and after that the subject of tuberculosis can be discussed. Of course, if the discussion of the Army Estimates goes on it will be very doubtful whether there will be any time left for that purpose. My honourable Friend has just suggested that Vote 1 only should be taken, and that should be taken at a morning sitting. Now, if that is practicable, that will solve the difficulty. The right honourable Baronet the Member for the London University also has pointed out that he remembers the time when these matters were the subject of an arrangement between the Government and the private Members, and that the Government gave compensation for whatever time they took. Now, I am going to suggest that the method of compensation should be adopted. I do not say anything about Tuesday. But what about Thursday the 23rd? The right honourable Gentleman proposes to bring in the Financial Appropriations Bill on Tuesday the 21st; to be read a second time on Wednesday the 22nd; and on Thursday the 23rd, it is to go into Committee. Now, the Committee stage, as we all know, cannot take any time, as no Amendments can be moved. Now, why should not the Government give Thursday the 23rd, after the Committee stage of the Financial Appropriations Bill is over to the discussion of tuberculosis? No doubt it might be taken in that manner. But it is possible that the London Bill will be taken on that night. I do not think it is probable, because there are so many honourable Members who are interested in it that you could not get rid of it in one sitting; therefore I do not think that the right honourable Gentleman would make a very great sacrifice if on the 23rd, after the Committee stage of the Financial Appropriations Bill is disposed of, he gave up the rest of the time to the private Members of the House.

*Sir M. STEWART (Kirkcudbright): Although this is a question that greatly affects the interest of agriculture, it is certainly a question which affects the interest of boroughs and towns quite as much as it does the country, and, upon that ground, I do earnestly press my right honourable Friend the First Lord of the Treasury to allow us to have some facility for bringing on this Motion to deal with the question of tuberculosis. It is so very important, in order that we might know what the Government are going to do in regard to the matter. If you are not going to have a Debate upon the question, it is likely to be very much misunderstood. I speak from great experience of the importance of this matter, and I do hope that some time will be given to us for this discussion. The right honourable Gentleman who has just sat down has talked with regard to a day which the Government

might place at our disposal, but if the Government could see their way to giving us a day before the Easter Recess, we should raise no difficulty in the discussion of the Army Estimates tomorrow.

Mr. BUCHANAN (Aberdeenshire, E.): So far as I can recollect, last Tuesday the First Lord of the Treasury made a statement as to the business that he intended to take on the following Friday; in the course of that statement he said that he proposed to take the Vote on the Army Estimates. And that was the Vote which we expected to take, but which we did not see upon the Blue Papers, and which, consequently, was understood was not to be taken then. Now, I apprehend that the right honourable Gentleman has made some promise as to what he will take to-morrow. He has said that he will simply take the Army Estimates, and that, after the Army Estimates are disposed of, he will take nothing more. I think he might be induced to take only Vote 1 of the Army Estimates. I beg to move an Amendment—

"To omit the words 'Government Business,' in order to insert the words 'the proceedings on Army Estimates, Vote 1.'"

The FIRST LORD of the TREASURY: The honourable Gentleman opposite has enforced, in the form of an Amendment, the appeal that has been made to me on this occasion, from other parts of the House. I cannot go the length which the honourable Gentleman desires me to go, but I should be prepared to go on with Vote 1 and the three non-effective Votes, and, if the House will give me those, I should be perfectly willing to put down no further Supply to-morrow. I do not think that I can accede to the appeal of my honourable Friend behind me with regard to Thursday week, because he has based his claim to further Government time upon some error which he supposes I have committed. But I do not admit that I have committed any error at all, and, therefore, I do not think it is possible for me to respond to his suggestion, on that ground, at all events. The honourable Member for Northampton, East, attacks me for not having accepted the ruling of Mr. Deputy Speaker, and insisting upon going on with Vote 1 on Friday last, but there he is in direct opposition with his own Leader, who told the House that I could have done nothing less than yield, as I did yield, to the appeal made to me from the other side on Friday last. But surely, when the right honourable Gentleman himself says that I should have arranged the business of last Thursday and last Monday so as to have got Supply in such a condition that no claim could be made on Tuesday, the right honourable Gentleman has given me credit for a gift of prophecy which I assure him I do not possess. If I could have foreseen that there would be this mistake in the Blue Paper last Friday, I should have made all necessary arrangements for that particular contingency; but, as I could not foresee it, and as I did not foresee it, I did not make the necessary arrangements, and we are obliged, therefore, in order to get through the necessary business of the year, to ask private Members to make this sacrifice which we now ask. If they will consent to give us Vote 1, which is on the third day of the discussion of Army Estimates already, and the non-controversial Votes to which I have referred, I will undertake that there shall be no further Government business taken on Thursday.

SIR H. CAMPBELL-BANNERMAN: I acknowledge the spirit in which the right honourable Gentleman has spoken, but I wish to put in a little addition to that speech. If the Government obtains Vote 1 and the non-effective Votes, they obtain a very large sum of money; and, therefore, the further consideration in Committee of Supply of the Army Estimates may be put off to a very advanced time in the Session. Now, if the right honourable Gentleman will agree that we shall have a good night—a good effective night—or two nights, not in the decaying days of the Session, to discuss the Army Estimates, at a more convenient time to the House, then I think his offer might be accepted. If we were to take his offer without some such provision, we might be in the woful plight of having all the Army Estimates put off until the month of August. I feel sure, however, that

First Lord of the Treasury.

that is not the intention of the right honourable Gentleman. This year the sum to be granted is especially large, and if the right honourable Gentleman would give us a full opportunity for the discussion of this money question I shall be ready to accept the offer he has made.

THE FIRST LORD OF THE TREASURY: The right honourable Gentleman knows, and probably has present in his mind, that any privileges which I grant in respect of the Army Votes must be necessarily carved out of the time at the disposal of the House to discuss the other Votes. Therefore, it would not be fair that in respect of those other Votes the House should dwell too long a time in discussing the Army Votes. If, however, the right honourable Gentleman will make an appeal to me with regard to any special Friday on which he would like the Army Estimates to be considered, that appeal will certainly be met by me.

MR. DILLON (Mayo, E.): With reference to the question of the Army Votes being taken on Tuesday, I assume that it is the intention of those who are entering into this arrangement that it shall be taken at a reasonably early hour of the evening that will allow of some discussion. That, of course, depends upon the number of military speeches to which we shall be called upon to listen. There is a very important question connected with the Army which we desire to bring forward, and which may lead to a long discussion unless a favourable answer is received from the Under Secretary of State for War. I do not rise for the purpose of prolonging this discussion, and I only do so in order to say that we are no parties to this arrangement, and we shall claim our right, to the best of our ability, to demand a fair hearing on Vote 1 in the Army Estimates, for I feel sure that upon that occasion both sides of the House will agree when they have heard what we have got to say—that the question is one demanding the attention of the House.

MR. LABOUCHERE (Northampton): I understand that in this arrangement the right honourable Gentleman has not assumed that he may find it necessary to move the Closure at any particular hour of the night with regard to Vote 1 of the Army Estimates. For my part I am not anxious that the right honourable Gentleman should get his Votes for the Army at all, and I think the less he gets, and the longer the time it takes him to get them, the better it will be for the community. We do not enter into any bargain on this side of the House that we are going to arrest the flow of eloquence with regard to the Army. Under this arrangement the Leader of the House is really trying to get an advantage for himself out of the mistake of this unfortunate printer, and he hopes to be able to get these Votes in a few hours instead of the ordinary time generally occupied on that Vote. I have simply risen to say that while it may be that the Vote will be taken at an hour at which tuberculosis can be brought in, we enter into no sort of pledge, after a certain hour of the night, not to move any Amendment.

Mr. HEYWOOD JOHNSTONE (Sussex, Horsham): I do hope that the Government will be able to give us some definite suggestion as to when an opportunity will be given in which this subject of tuberculosis can be discussed. It is a very important question, and one upon which we desire to learn the opinion of the Leaders of the House. I think we ought to be grateful to the Government for giving the House an early opportunity of recognising and defining the position of the private Member. It seems to me that the private Member has become an anachronism, and I think the sooner his Parliamentary impotence is recognised the better. Many of us come here to try and do the business of the nation, and we find that two-thirds of the time of the House is taken up by the Orders of the House with these cheap philanthropic discussions, or by those fireworks on Tuesday which result, as all fireworks do, in empty squib cases, and we are kept here listening to this class of oratory. What I wish to ask the right honourable Gentleman is, whether he could not manage in the next Session of Parliament to arrange for the private Members one clear uninterrupted week for themselves in which to deal with Private Bill Legislation?

Mr. LLOYD-GEORGE (Carnarvon Boroughs): I should like to ask one Question, and that is, whether tomorrow will be counted as one of the days allotted to Supply under the Standing Order, and whether it will be a whole day?

The FIRST LORD of the TREASURY: Yes.

Question put—

"That the words 'Government Business' stand part of the Question."

Agreed to.

Main Question put—

"That Government Business have Precedence to-morrow, and that the provisions of Standing Order 56 be extended to that day's sitting."— *(First Lord of the Treasury.)*

The House divided—Ayes, 222 ; Noes, 118.—(Division List No. 39.)

AYES.

Acland-Hood, Capt. Sir Alex. F.
Aird, John
Allhusen, Augustus Henry Eden
Allsopp, Hon. George
Arnold, Alfred
Arnold-Forster, Hugh O.
Ascroft, Robert
Ashmead-Bartlett, Sir Ellis
Atkinson, Rt. Hon. John
Bagot, Capt. Josceline FitzRoy
Bailey, James (Walworth)
Baillie, James E. B. (Inverness)
Baird, John George Alexander
Baldwin, Alfred
Balfour, Rt. Hn. A. J. (Manc'r)
Balfour, Rt Hn Gerald W. (Leeds
Banbury, Frederick George
Barry, Sir Francis T. (Windsor)

Bartley, George C. T.
Barton, Dunbar Plunket
Beach, Rt. Hn. Sir M. H. (Bristol)
Beckett, Ernest William
Begg, Ferdinand Faithfull
Bemrose, Sir Henry Howe
Bentinck, Lord Henry C.
Bethell, Commander
Bhownaggree, Sir M. M.
Biddulph, Michael
Bill, Charles
Blundell, Colonel Henry
Bonsor, Henry Cosmo Orme
Boscawen, Arthur Griffith-
Boulnois, Edmund
Bowles, T. Gibson (King's Lynn)
Brodrick, Rt. Hn. St. John
Brown, Alexander H.

Butcher, John George
Cecil, Evelyn (Hertford, E.)
Cecil, Lord Hugh (Greenwich)
Chaloner, Captain R. G. W.
Chamberlain, J. Austen (Worc'r
Charrington, Spencer
Cochrane, Hn. Thos. H. A. E.
Coddington, Sir William
Coghill, Douglas Harry
Cohen, Benjamin Louis
Collings, Rt. Hn. Jesse
Colomb, Sir John Chas. Ready
Colston, Chas. Edw. H. Athole
Compton, Lord Alwyne
Cooke, C. W. Radcliffe (Heref'd)
Corbett, A Cameron (Glasgow)
Cornwallis, Fiennes Stanley W.
Courtney, Rt. Hn. Leonard H.

Cranborne, Viscount
Cripps, Charles Alfred
Cross, Alexander (Glasgow)
Cross, Herb. Shepherd (Bolton)
Currie, Sir Donald
Curzon, Viscount
Dalkeith, Earl of
Dalrymple, Sir Charles
Davenport, W. Bromley-
Dickson-Poynder, Sir John P.
Dixon-Hartland,SirFred.Dixon
Dorington, Sir John Edward
Doughty, George
Douglas, Rt. Hon. A. Akers-
Doxford, William Theodore
Drucker, A.
Duncombe, Hon. Hubert V.
Egerton, Hon. A. de Tatton
Elliot, Hn. A. Ralph Douglas
Fardell, Sir T. George
Fergusson,Rt.Hn.SirJ.(Manc'r
Field, Admiral (Eastbourne)
Finch, George H.
Finlay, Sir Robert Bannatyne
Firbank, Joseph Thomas
Fisher, William Hayes
Fison, Frederick William
Folkestone, Viscount
Forster, Henry William
Foster, Colonel (Lancaster)
Garfit, William
Gedge, Sydney
Giles, Charles Tyrrell
Gilliat, John Saunders
Goldsworthy, Major-General
Gordon, Hon. John Edward
Gorst, Rt. Hon. Sir John Eldon
Goschen, George J. (Sussex)
Graham, Henry Robert
Gray, Ernest (West Ham)
Green,WalfordD.(Wednesbury)
Greville, Hon. Ronald
Gull, Sir Cameron
Halsey, Thomas Frederick
Hamilton, Rt. Hn. Lord George
Hanbury, Rt. Hn. Robert Wm.
Hardy, Laurence
Hare, Thomas Leigh
Hatch, Ernest Frederick Geo.
Heath, James
Heaton, John Henniker
Helder, Augustus
Hermon-Hodge, Robt. Trotter
Holland, Hn. Lionel R. (Bow)
Hornby, Sir William Henry
Houston, R. P.
Howard, Joseph
Hozier,Hn.James Henry Cecil

Hubbard, Hon. Evelyn
Hutchinson,Capt.G.W.Grice-
Hutton, John (Yorks., N.R.)
Jackson, Rt. Hn. Wm. Lawies
Jeffreys, Arthur Frederick
Jessel, Capt. Herbert Merton
Johnston, William (Belfast)
Johnstone, Heywood (Sussex)
Jolliffe, Hon. H. George
Kemp, George
Kenyon, James
Keswick, William
Kimber, Henry
King, Sir Henry Seymour
Knowles, Lees
Lafone, Alfred
Lawrence,Sir E.Durning(Corn
Lawrence, Wm. F. (L'pool.)
Lecky, Rt. Hn. Wm. Edw. H.
Leighton, Stanley
Llewellyn, Evan H.(Somerset
Loder, Gerald Walter Erskine
Long, Col. Chas. W.(Evesham)
Long, Rt. Hn. Walter (L'pool)
Lopes, Henry Yarde Buller
Lorne, Marquess of
Loyd, Archie Kirkman
Lubbock,Rt. Hon. Sir John
Macartney, W. G. Ellison
Macdona, John Cumming
Maclean, James Mackenzie
Maclure, Sir John William
McCalmont, H. L. B. (Cambs.)
Maple, Sir John Blundell
Marks, Henry Hananel
Martin, Richard Biddulph
Massey-Mainwaring,Hn. W. F.
Maxwell,Rt.Hn Sir Herbert E.
Meysey-Thompson, Sir H. M.
Middlemore, John Throgmorton
Milbank,SirPowlett Chas.John
Monk, Charles James
More, Robt. Jasper (Shropsh.)
Morrell, George Herbert
Morton, Arthur H. A. (Deptf'd)
Mount, William George
Muntz, Philip A.
Murray,RtHnA.Graham(Bute)
Murray, Charles J. (Coventry)
Murray, Col. Wyndham (Bath)
Myers, William Henry
Nicholson, William Graham
Nicol, Donald Ninian
Northcote, Hn. Sir H. Stafford
Orr-Ewing, Charles Lindsay
Pease, Herbert Pike (Drlngtn.)
Penn, John
Phillpotts, Captain Arthur

Pilkington, Richard
Platt-Higgins, Frederick
Purvis, Robert
Rasch, Major Frederic Carne
Ritchie, Rt. Hn. Chas.Thomson
Robertson, Herbert (Hackney)
Rothschild, Hn. Lionel Walter
Round, James
Royds, Clement Molyneux
Russell, Gen F.S.(Cheltenham)
Russell, T. W. (Tyrone)
Ryder, John Herbert Dudley
Samuel, Harry S. (Limehouse)
Setou-Karr, Henry
Sharpe, William Edward T.
Simeon, Sir Barrington
Sinclair, Louis (Romford)
Smith, Abel H. (Christchurch)
Spencer, Ernest
Stanley, Hn.Arthur (Ormskirk
Stanley, Edwd. Jas (Somerset
Stanley, Henry M. (Lambeth)
Stanley. Lord (Lancs.)
Stewart, Sir M. J. M'Taggart
Stirling-Maxwell, Sir John M.
Stone, Sir Benjamin
Strauss, Arthur
Strutt, Hon. Charles Hedley
Sturt, Hon. Humphry Napier
Talbot, Lord E. (Chichester)
Talbot,RtHnJ.G.(Oxf'd Univ.
Thorburn, Walter
Thornton, Percy M.
Tollemache, Henry James
Tritton, Charles Ernest
Usborne, Thomas
Valentia, Viscount
Ward, Hn. Robt. A. (Crewe)
Warr, Augustus Frederick
Webster, R. G. (St. Pancras)
Webster, Sir R. E. (I. of W.)
Welby, Lieut.-Col. A. C. E.
Wentworth, Bruce C. Vernon-
Whiteley, George (Stockport)
Whitmore, Charles Algernon
Williams, J. Powell- (Birm.)
Wodehouse, Rt.Hn.E.R.(Bath
Wylie, Alexander
Wyndham, George
Wyndham-Quin, Major W. H.
Wyvill, Marmaduke D'Arcy
Young, Commander (Berks, E.

TELLERS FOR THE AYES—
Sir William Walrond and
Mr. Anstruther

NOES.

Abraham, William (Cork,N.E.
Allan, William (Gateshead)
Allison, Robert Andrew
Ambrose, Robert (Mayo,W.)
Asquith, Rt. Hn. Herb. Henry
Austin, Sir John (Yorkshire)
Austin, M. (Limerick, W.)
Baker, Sir John
Barlow, John Emmott
Billson, Alfred
Birrell, Augustine
Brunner, Sir John Tomlinson

Buchanan, Thomas Ryburn
Burt, Thomas
Caldwell, James
Cameron, Sir Chas. (Glasgow)
Cameron, Robert (Durham)
Campbell-Bannerman, Sir H.
Causton, Richard Knight
Channing, Francis Allston
Crilly, Daniel
Crombie, John William
Curran, Thomas (Sligo, S.)
Dalziel, James Henry

Davies,M.Vaughan-(Cardigan)
Dilke, Rt. Hn. Sir Charles
Dillon, John
Donelan, Captain A.
Douglas, Chas. M. (Lanark)
Duckworth, James
Dunn, Sir William
Ellis, John Edward (Notts.)
Ellis,Thos.Edw.(Merionethsh.
Evans, Sir F. H. (South'ton.
Farquharson, Dr. Robert
Fenwick, Charles

Ferguson, R. C. Munro (Leith)
Fitzmaurice, Lord Edmond
Foster,Sir Walter(Derby Co.)
Gladstone, Rt. Hn. Herb.John
Goddard, Daniel Ford
Gold, Charles
Gourley,Sir Edward Temperley
Grey, Sir Edward (Berwick)
Haldane, Richard Burdon
Harwood, George
Hayne, Rt. Hn. Chas. Seale-
Healy, Timothy M. (N. Louth)
Hedderwick, Thos. Charles H.
Hobhouse, Henry
Holland, Wm. H. (York,W.R.
Humphreys-Owen, Arthur C.
Jacoby, James Alfred
Jones, Wm. (Carnarvonshire)
Kay-Shuttleworth,RtHnSir U
Kearley, Hudson E.
Kilbride, Denis
Kinloch,Sir Jno.Geo. Smythe
Lawson,SirWilfrid(Cum'land)
Leese, Sir Jos. F.(Accrington)
Leng, Sir John
Lewis, John Herbert
Lloyd-George, David
Lough, Thomas
Macaleese, Daniel

MacNeill, John Gordon Swift
M'Arthur, Wm. (Cornwall)
M'Ewan, William
M'Kenna, Reginald
Mendl, Sigismund Ferdinand
Molloy, Bernard Charles
Montagu,Sir S.(Whitechapel)
Moore, Arthur (Londonderry)
Morgan,W.Pritchard(Merthyr
Moulton, John Fletcher
Nussey, Thomas Wilians
O'Brien, James F. X. (Cork)
O'Brien, Patrick (Kilkenny)
O'Connor,James(Wicklow,W.)
Palmer, Sir Chas. M. (Durham
Paulton, James Mellor
Perks, Robert William
Pickersgill, Edward Hare
Pirie, Duncan V.
Power, Patrick Joseph
Provand, Andrew Dryburgh
Reid, Sir Robert Threshie
Rickett, J. Compton
Roberts, John Bryn (Eifion)
Roberts, John H. (Denbighs.)
Robertson, Edmund (Dundee)
Robson, William Snowdon
Schwann, Charles E.
Sinclair, Capt. John (Forfarsh.

Smith, Samuel (Flint)
Souttar, Robinson
Spicer, Albert
Stanhope, Hon. Philip J.
Steadman, William Charles
Sullivan, Donal (Westmeath)
Tanner, Charles Kearns
Tennant, Harold John
Thomas, David Alfd.(Merthyr)
Trevelyan, Charles Philips
Wallace, Robert (Edinburgh)
Wallace, Robert (Perth)
Walton,John Lawson(Leeds,S.
Walton, Joseph (Barnsley)
Wedderburn, Sir William
Weir, James Galloway
Whittaker, Thomas Palmer
Williams, John Carvell (Notts.
Wills, Sir William Henry
Wilson, Henry J.(Yorks,W.R.
Wilson, John (Govan)
Wilson, Jos. H. (Middlesbro')
Woods, Samuel
Yoxall, James Henry

TELLERS FOR THE NOES—
Mr. Labouchere and Mr
Warner.

Ordered, That Government Business have precedence To-morrow, and that the provisions of Standing Order 56 be extended to that day's Sitting.

ORDERS OF THE DAY.

SUPPLY.

NAVY ESTIMATES, 1899-1900.

Order for Committee read.

Motion made, and Question proposed—

"That Mr. Speaker do now leave the Chair."

*SIR U. KAY-SHUTTLEWORTH (Lancashire, Clitheroe): I think I shall——

*MR. KEARLEY (Devonport): I rise to a point of order, and I desire to ask whether a Member who secures priority by ballot, and who puts his notice on the Paper, is not entitled to priority.

*MR. SPEAKER: The honourable Member has not got an Amendment down on the Paper.

VOL. LXVIII.   [FOURTH SERIES.]

*MR. KEARLEY: May I ask if that is the reason why I am not entitled to priority?

*MR. SPEAKER: I could not give the honourable Member priority over other Amendments, because all he has done is to put a notice on the Paper that he will call attention to a particular matter. In a general discussion I call upon the honourable Member who catches my eye first.

*MR. WEBSTER (St. Pancras, E.): I have also an Amendment down on the Paper, which I intend to move. So far as the practice in this matter is concerned, it seems to me that we are in the position of "Alice in Wonderland."

*MR. SPEAKER: Order, order! I must ask the honourable Member to address himself at once to the point of order, if he has one.

*MR. WEBSTER: I should like to ask whether, on going into Committee of Supply, we are to have only set Debates between the Front Benches?

*MR. SPEAKER: Order, order! The honourable Member is not raising any point of order.

Z

*MR. WEBSTER: My point is that I wish to ask permission to move a Resolution if I have the right to move it, and I wish to know if I have any priority?

*MR. SPEAKER: The honourable Member is in error in supposing he has given notice of any Amendment. He has only given notice that he will put down a Resolution, and that he has not done.

*SIR U. KAY-SHUTTLEWORTH: I think I shall be expressing the general feeling of the House when. I say how much we regret to observe the absence of the right honourable Gentleman the First Lord of the Admiralty, and especially when we are informed of its cause. I am the more sorry that the right honourable Gentleman is absent, because I shall naturally have to refer several times to the speech which he addressed to us on Thursday last. In moving the Navy Estimates last year the First Lord of the Admiralty said that he was asking the House to grant a colossal sum, and the sum which he then referred to, including certain expenditure under the Naval Works Act, amounted to 25½ millions. Making a similar addition for the money to be expended this year under the Naval Works Act, the sum which the right honourable Gentleman is proposing that the Admiralty should administer within the year which is about to open is no less than 28 millions of money. That is almost double the sum with which the Admiralty had to deal at the time when the late Government entered office in 1892. The Estimates then were 14¼ millions. To that, in fairness, ought to be added, £1,150,000 issued under the Naval Defence Act, and therefore the actual Naval expenditure for that year was about 15½ millions. Perhaps I ought not to leave out of the account the other parts of our naval and military expenditure in order to show how vastly the whole of our naval and military expenditure has grown. Going

back for seven years, in the year 1892 the amount spent, as a charge against the revenue, for the Navy and the Army was not quite 33½ millions. To that an addition of two millions has to be made on account of money spent under various Acts of Parliament from various loan funds, giving a total of under 35½ millions, and I calculate from such information as we have now before us that the corresponding sum for the year which is now about to open will be no less than 50 millions of money. Under the circumstances, I do not think that the epithet "colossal" seems to be exaggerated. Last year the right honourable Gentleman evidently thought that his large proposals were likely to be popular. I am not quite sure that I did not observe somewhat of a difference of tone in the right honourable Gentleman's speech on introducing the Estimates this year. When the Government have before them a prospective deficit, naturally the tone which they assume in announcing any large proposals of expenditure to the House will be somewhat different. They further realise that the British public are now under the influence of the hopes aroused by the Rescript of the Emperor of Russia, and that also I think had a proper and natural effect upon the spirit in which the right honourable Gentleman presented his proposals to the House. But in view of this enormous expenditure of 50 millions, I venture to express an opinion that the question of how much more the British public will calmly stand is becoming acute, and the question arises whether we cannot find means either in our policy or in our administration, or by an agreement with the other Powers of Europe—who have to endure a still heavier burden than this country, especially on account of a ruthless system of conscription—to check this expenditure, or at least to put a limit to its further growth, and prepare the way for reducing this great military and naval outlay in the future. It is not for me in this Debate to enter upon the discussion of the hopes raised by the proposal of the Tsar and the Conference which is to take place, but it has aroused hopes in this country of which the Government should take note. There may be a cynical scepticism as to its practical results in certain quarters in London, but if Her Majesty's Government should fail to offer every assistance in promoting the object of the Tsar of Russia the country will be of opinion that a great opportunity has been lost. I think our hopes would have been much brighter but for these gigantic Estimates, and this increase of nearly three millions. However, we must fasten upon the words in which the First Lord expressed the readiness of the Government to modify their programme of shipbuilding if the other great Naval Powers are prepared to diminish their programmes also. I pass from this topic to the opening statement of the First Lord's speech on Thursday in which he expressed legitimate satisfaction at the striking confidence shown by the country last autumn, and at the fact that there was no need to ask for a Vote of Credit. I warmly share that feeling of satisfaction. There has been nothing more unsatisfactory in our expenditure in past years than the great waste which has taken place under various Votes of Credit, not for the purpose of really increasing the naval and military strength of this country, but for the purpose of a mere demonstration. I have had before me in years past a good many details of the mode in which one, at least, of these Votes of Credit was expended, and I am perfectly prepared to admit with the right honourable Gentleman that it is much more economical to spend money by means of the Estimates on a real addition to the naval strength of the country than, on a sudden spurt in a moment of alarm, to waste a quantity of money upon some mere demonstration, and upon purchases in a hurry which turn out to have no permanent value at all. The First Lord of the Admiralty went on to make some very sarcastic remarks about the exaggerated ideas of the public as to the expenditure in the dockyards last autumn. He referred to the impression that officers' leave had been stopped; he referred to the head-lines in the newspapers, and to their sensational statements. Well, Sir, when the Chancellor of the Exchequer came to speak a little later in the autumn, he told us, as the right honourable Gentleman told us on

Thursday last, that, after all, the expenditure had only been a few thousands. But why did not the First Lord of the Admiralty allay all this excitement and neutralise all these head-lines in the newspapers? Why did he not promptly allay the perturbation of the public mind and correct the evil effects of all these rumours by a statement of an official character? I will go further when asking that question, and remind the House and the Government of a certain letter from the First Lord himself, excusing himself from attending the Cutlers' Feast at Sheffield—a letter that must have delighted the honourable Member for the Ecclesall Division of Sheffield, but which did more than all these head-lines to disturb the public mind, and to give currency to the rumours to which he has referred. Well, Sir, in referring to the satisfaction which we must feel at the comparative calmness of public feeling in the country last autumn, and to the fact that there was no need to come before Parliament and ask for a Vote of Credit, I think I may justly say that more than one or two Boards of Admiralty may take some credit for that state of the public mind. The advance of our naval strength, the arrangements for mobilisation, our readiness to victual the Fleet, to clothe our men, to coal our ships, and supply them with the necessary ammunition, and to equip them with officers and men, have not been the work of only one Board of Admiralty, but have been the work of two or three successive Boards at least. Another point which is extremely satisfactory now as compared with a good many years ago, is the efficient condition of our ships in the Reserve, of which we have had ample demonstration on more than one occasion in the last two or three years. And what has been the consequence of this? First, we have had tranquillity amongst the best-informed portion of the public; secondly, it has not been necessary to have recourse to those methods to which I have already referred, to remedy the omissions of Admiralty administration by sudden and hasty steps and a scrambling outlay of millions. Now, Sir, before I leave that subject, perhaps I may be allowed, though I shall do it, I hope, with due modesty and diffidence, to utter a note of warning. It is nearly seven years since

I became intimately acquainted with Admiralty administration, and at that time the Dockyards and certain Departments of the Admiralty seemed to me to be very heavily weighted with work and responsibility, and I would refer especially to two officers, members of the Board of Admiralty, who seemed to me to be burdened with an enormous amount of work—I mean the First Sea Lord and the Controller. Consider how that work has increased. If you compare the number of men of all kinds, officers, blue-jackets, boys, marines, in the Navy at that time and those which are proposed in these Estimates, you will find that now there are half as many again. If you take the Controller's Vote, Vote A, the figures for new construction, including all the Naval Defence Act expenditure in 1893, were £4,400,000. Now they are close upon £8,900,000. Therefore, the figures for new construction which have to be administered from the Controller's Department have more than doubled. If you take the Armaments Vote for guns and ammunition, torpedoes, and the like, it has increased by 77 per cent. The net Estimates plus the expenditure of the year under the Naval Defence Act and the Works Acts has not very far from doubled. Now, Sir, the burdens of administration are not the only objection, nor the most serious objection, to be put in the balance and weighed against the arguments for these huge Estimates. When we pride ourselves on the admirable state of preparation last autumn, we may reflect that we have put so greatly increased a burden on our administrators that the time may have come when, on the one hand, the brake should be applied to further increase, and on the other, some attention should be paid to internal organisation, in order that we may guard against any break-down of administrative machinery, any over-weighting of the individual officers who have presided with such great success over these growing and now almost unwieldy Departments. I do not propose to deal at the present moment with the question of manning; but there was one omission from the speech of the right honourable Gentleman in introducing these Estimates which I hope will be supplied by and by. Turning to the explanation of Vote A, we see that the whole of the additional

Sir U. Kay-Shuttleworth.

numbers proposed for the year are 4,250. But while the increases proposed this year for the seaman class of men, engine-room ratings, and so on, boys, and Royal Marines are considerably less than they were last year, there is a very considerable increase in the number of officers. This year, an addition of 173 commissioned officers is proposed instead of 111, and an increase of 119 subordinate officers instead of 39 increase, and an increase of 171 warrant officers in place of an increase of 50 last year. I hope also that some explanation more than is given on page 4 of the First Lord's Memorandum will be afforded to the House as to the proposed permanent increases in the several lists of officers, and that we shall be told how this large increase in the officers will affect the results of the inquiry which was conducted by an Inter-Departmental Committee, in which Admiral Sir A. Hoskins, Lord Welby, Captain Bourke, and others took part some four or five years ago. I would rather deal with that subject after the explanations have been offered, and therefore I pass from it to the question of new construction. Sir, there is an omission this year in the Memorandum of the First Lord of a paragraph which for many years has regularly appeared, showing, on page 10, for example, of the Memorandum of each of the last two years, the number of ships actually under construction of each class. Well, now, I have done my best to supply this omission for myself, and I will give the results to the House. During the year which is now coming to an end, a very large number of ships were to be under construction, according to the statement of the First Lord in March last. I will give in each case the figures as I make them out now. There were 12 battleships under construction during the current year, 18 in the next year. First-class cruisers, 16 this year, 22 next year. Other cruisers, 16 this year, and 19 next year. Torpedo boat destroyers, 41 increased to 58. Thus we shall have six more battleships and nine more cruisers under construction apparently in the coming year than have been under construction during the present year, and we shall have 17 more torpedo-boat destroyers also under construction than in 1898-99. This, Sir, is a larger number of battleships and of first-class cruisers and of torpedo-boat destroyers than has been under construction in any former year. And I need not dwell upon the enormous size or the enormous cost of them, for the House is probably already aware of it. The battleships range from 13,000 tons to 15,000 tons, whilst the cruisers range from 9,800 tons up to 14,000 tons—that is, first-class cruisers. As to the cost, we have not got the figures before us, but we may infer what it is if we bear in mind that the "Royal Sovereign" class cost from £840,000 to £900,000 apiece; "Majestics" from £850,000 to £900,000 a piece; and that "Formidables" are calculated to cost £997,000 to a million a piece. And coming to first-class cruisers, the "Powerful" and "Terrible" cost £700,000 each, and the "Cressy" class about £720,000. Sir, I stated that in seven years our expenditure on new construction has more than doubled, and that our expenditure on naval armaments has increased by 77 per cent. I may be told—"Look abroad and see the expenditure which is going on there." Well, Sir, it is very difficult to compare with some foreign countries, because the information is not available, at all events to an independent Member. But there is one country with which we can compare—that is France. I will therefore take France. France is usually the first referred to in these comparisons, because it has the second largest fleet and naval expenditure, coming after ourselves. I find, on referring to the Report of the Reporter of the Budget Committee of the French Chamber, M. De la Porte, that the new construction in 1892 amounted to 70½ millions of francs. In 1899 it is 92½ millions of francs. It has not doubled like ours, but has increased by about 31½ per cent. French armaments in 1892 cost 32½ millions of francs; in 1899 the cost is 28¾ millions of francs—that is, the Armament Vote has not increased by 77 per cent., but diminished by nearly one-eighth. I am bound to admit that there seems to be an extraordinary fluctuation in the French expenditure upon armaments from year to year. But still the increase, if increase there has been in recent years, has not been at all the same as in our case. The cost of the navy to France altogether seems to have increased in these

seven years by about 20 per cent. Well, it may fairly be argued—Why cannot we afford to wait and watch a little under these circumstances of France's expenditure? There are great advantages in waiting. It is astonishing in naval constructive science what great strides and advances have been made within recent years: sometimes even in a few months immense strides in advance are taken, not only with respect to guns and other instruments of attack, but also with respect to protective armour, in which we have seen enormous changes within a few years, and with respect to the speed which can be attained by vessels of each size and each description. Moreover, this country has still, comparatively, an immense advantage in the speed of naval construction and completion of our ships. No doubt last year we grumbled at the delays which took place in consequence of a great trade dispute, and there were serious failures to expend the money which Parliament had voted. But those delays are relatively unimportant if you make a comparison between the delays in this country and the delays which occur in France. Let us look for a moment at what are the results obtained by shipbuilding in this country I will take two instances of which we have evidence in this day's newspapers. The "Implacable," which was launched on Saturday at one of the dockyards, was commenced in July 1898. The "Glory," which was commenced in December 1896, was floated out on Saturday, and is to be delivered in August or September 1899, because she has been floated out in a very advanced condition, with a great deal of her structure completed. I need not remind the House of the records obtained in the building of the "Majestic" and "Magnificent," one of which was finished and put in commission within 22 months after the laying of the keel, and the other within 24 months. Let us turn from that to the facts about France. I have here the statement of the Reporter of the French Budget Committee, M. De la Porte, and referring to the facts which he sets forth, I will briefly summarise them to the House. I will take first the cruisers, as he does. These are the results both at arsenals and private yards. The "Jeanne d'Arc" is a first-class cruiser of over 11,000 tons. She was talked of in 1895 or sooner; she was not put on the slip until October 1896; she is not to be completed until the end of 1901. So that she will have been more than five years under construction. Take the "Dupleix" next; she was ordered in December 1897, in January 1899 she was not yet laid down; she is not likely to be finished by the beginning of 1902 at the earliest. These are official facts stated in this Report. For the "Desaix," the "Kleber," and the "Chateau-renault," three years and four months, three years and six months, and three years and nine months respectively, are asked by the contractors—the "Chateau-renault" being one of the commerce-destroyers of which we hear so much. For the "d'Entrecasteaux," four years were asked, and it is found that five years will be needed before she will go through her trials. Now, I come to the battleships. The "Charlemagne" was begun on the 30th September 1893. Her gunnery trials took place on the 15th October 1897, but the vessel will not be complete for some months; while the "Gaulois" is not yet complete, though begun on the 22nd of January 1895. And then there is the case of the "Saint Louis." The "Saint Louis" was laid down in 1894; she will begin her trials in April of this year, but she must wait for the delivery of her turrets until June 1900. It seems that in respect to turrets, not only this ship, but at least one, perhaps two, other battleships of the French Navy have been greatly delayed because of a discussion which has gone on as to the nature of the turrets to be placed on these battleships. That discussion ultimately resulted in the original design being adhered to, but the result is that the ships are delayed for those long periods that I have mentioned to the House. The Reporter of the Budget Committee calls these "afflicting statements." He devotes four quarto pages to a lament over "the excessive slowness of shipbuilding" in France. I venture to ask the House again whether we should not be gainers by waiting and watching a little. We can overtake new foreign ships that are being constructed with more modern designs and with the latest improvements. And then there is another fact which I have kept for the end, because, after all,

Sir U. Kay-Shuttleworth.

it is perhaps the one we ought to consider most seriously; and that is, that France is slackening in building battleships. No doubt this is the effect of the policy which has been pursued by, as I have said, not only one Board of Admiralty, but by two or three successive Boards of Admiralty. France has come to the conclusion that this is a race in which she cannot profitably persevere. I do not propose to trouble the House with more than two quotations, but if they will permit me I will read a few passages from this Report of M. De la Porte, because I think it is important that the House and the country should know what is the present feeling of the French with regard to battleships, and what has been the effect of the policy which we have pursued in recent years. This is what he says—

"Thanks to the vigorous and costly effort made during these last years, our Fleet will have been augmented by 12 battleships in the decennial period from 1890 to 1899 inclusive."

The House will remember that: 12 battleships in 10 years—

"Can we flatter ourselves that by continuing that effort we shall some day see our battleships rival in number those of England? It is enough to consult a table showing the composition of the English squadrons . . . to convince oneself that they comprise in point of fact 21 battleships launched between 1891 and 1896."

Well, Sir, I do not think M. De la Porte is quite accurate in his facts with respect to England. If he had stated 20 battleships completed between 1891 and 1897 I think he would have been correct; so we may compare 20 battleships within eight years to 12 battleships within a period of 10 years. He enumerates the stations of our ships, and then goes on to say—

"If our battleships are, and must remain, whatever we do, inferior in number to those of England, she distances us even more in the matter of cruisers."

And then he points out that the tonnage of English cruisers is 528,415 tons, and the tonnage of French cruisers 136,690 tons, giving a difference in favour of England of 391,725 tons. He adds—

"Our inferiority in battleships is 287,815 tons. We are therefore short, as compared with England, of 100,000 tons more in cruisers than in battleships."

Well, Sir, perhaps I may there interject one remark. I think M. De la Porte overlooks in that argument the fact that we have immensely greater duties to perform in time of peace all over the world in respect of our commerce, and in respect of our Colonies, than any other nation in the world, and I do not think our preponderance of cruisers must be only on the two-nation basis, as undoubtedly, even in time of peace, we require far more cruisers than any other nation. Interjecting that remark, lest I should be accused of overlooking an important point, I will again refer to M. De la Porte, who says—" We are not on the eve of regaining the lost time." And he ends by approving

"without reserve the decision of the Minister of Marine to suspend for 1899 the ordering of a new battleship, so as to concentrate all available resources on cruisers, torpedo boats, and submarine vessels."

I think I am not mistaken in saying that a similar course was adopted in the previous year; so there is to be a reduction of from two battleships projected, to one started in the present year, and there has been a reduction from three to one in the past year. Well, Sir, I do not think I need detain the House in pointing out our strength in battleships. We have a total of 29 first-class battleships built and at this moment in commission, and in addition to that we are building six of the "Canopus" class, six "Formidables," and four "Duncans," making a total of 45, without the addition of two which are proposed in the Estimates now before us, which will make a total of 47 in all. Then there is the question raised by a great naval authority—Admiral Colomb. In an article which he published lately he referred to_ the "Cressy" class of cruisers, with their powerful armour, and he maintained that these cruisers could be counted as battleships. Under all these circumstances, I think we may be very easy on the subject of our strength in battleships. I turn for a moment to the question of cruisers. We hear a great deal outside, and we heard something in the speech of the right honourable Gentleman on the subject of cruisers as commerce destroyers, and of the hopes of some foreign nations which

seem to be based on the idea that if they cannot beat us in line of battle or destroy our squadrons, at least they can destroy our commerce. Well, that must be taken into account no doubt; but if any honourable Member of this House, or any person who reads these Debates, is disposed to regard that system of naval warfare, that system of commerce destruction, as one that is likely to do us fatal harm, I would advise him to look at the treatment of that subject—and the very thorough treatment of it—in the great historical works of Captain Mahan. I am sure the House will forgive me if I read a sentence or two from that distinguished naval authority. He deals with the question in a scientific and complete fashion in his great works, "The Influence of Sea Power in History," and the other specially dealing with the period of the French Revolution. At page 137 of the former book Captain Mahan, dealing with this very question of commerce destroyers, says—" We need not expect to see the feats of these ships " (the "Alabama," the "Sumter," and their consorts, to which he had been referring) "repeated in the face of a great sea Power." Again, on page 138, he says—" Such injuries, unaccompanied by others, are more irritating than weakening." Sir, unless the command of the sea is acquired by an enemy by the defeat of our Fleets in battle, little more than temporary annoyance would be caused to this country by commerce destroyers. The temporary annoyance to commerce might be serious if we had no fast cruisers, or had an insufficient number of them, but if our Fleets were undefeated our sea power and our national safety would remain. Returning to the question of battleships, I do not think that the right honourable Gentleman the First Lord gave us sufficient grounds or sufficient argument to justify the building of two more battleships in the face of the strength of this country in battleships to which I have alluded, and also in the face of the change of policy which is being pursued in France. But, at the same time, I think it would be most unwise if anyone speaking on this side of the House were to dogmatise on a subject of this sort. The Government may be in possession of information which is not accessible to us; but that information needs to be more fully communicated to the House. The right honourable Gentleman the First Lord admitted as regards France that the increase on the French Estimates was very small. He has not given us sufficient facts in regard to Russia, and these we cannot obtain for ourselves. But I think before the House is asked to vote these enormous sums of money, augmented as they will be this year and in future years by the addition of two more battleships to the great strength which we already possess, we are entitled to more exact information as to the grounds upon which the Government bases this increase. We, on this side of the House, at any rate, advocate a policy of good understanding between England and Russia, and that good understanding may affect what we may have to do in the way of building ships. It is not my province to dwell fully on the subject, but I do venture to suggest that, unless the case is very overwhelming and is far stronger than was stated by the right honourable Gentleman the First Lord, we should pause before we agree to the necessity of building these two battleships. I once more, in conclusion, express the hope that the Peace Conference will prepare the way for the abatement of this enormous outlay and a relief to the burdens weighing not only on the rich and prosperous, but on the poor and struggling masses of the people, on whom taxation falls with crushing effect.

Sir J. COLOMB (Great Yarmouth): The right honourable Gentleman who has just sat down stated that he was arguing from past experience; but I think that it is very unsafe to dogmatise as to what would be the effect of operations against commerce 'under modern conditions, which have so wholly changed during the past few years. It is not the actual damage that would be done by an enemy of inferior power to our commerce, but the moral effect on those manifold and delicate transactions of commerce which would result from any interference with it. No man is entitled to dogmatise as to what the effect would be. I am not going to enter into questions relating to the *personnel* or the material of the Navy, because I think that time will be saved by de-

Sir U. Kay-Shuttleworth.

ferring observations on any of these points until we get into Committee. But there are two main points connected with the broad Question of the Naval policy of this country on which I wish to offer a few observations. One is a statement contained in the First Lord's admirable and statesmanlike speech, the other is an omission from that speech. In regard to the speech of the First Lord, he stated on behalf of Her Majesty's Government—

"That similarly if the other great naval Powers should be prepared to diminish their programmes of shipbuilding we should be prepared, on our side, to meet such a procedure by modifying ours."

Then the First Lord went on to say—

"But if Europe comes to no agreement the programme must stand."

No one will deny that that is a statement of immense gravity; and I think I need not apologise to the House for examining it for a few minutes. I venture to think that an official intimation of readiness to determine the extent of our naval force by reference to the wishes of a selected number of European maritime nations is a regrettably new departure in British policy. I object to allowing our naval policy to be saddled with any conditions laid down at any conference, only representing certain maritime powers, and not all. My reason for that is that there is no parallel at all in the British position and in the position of any other nation in the world. Geographically we are absolutely distinct from these other nations. Russia, for example, is a self-contained Power. And if you take France, which is the nearest neighbour to us, she has a Colonial Empire next in importance to ours. But if you look at the French position and at our position, you at once see that there is no parallel between them. The geographical facts are that the outlying areas of France are nothing to the outlying areas of Great Britain. From an economic point of view the two nations cannot be compared in any shape whatever. Why, the aggregate trade of the outlying portions of the British Empire alone, from year to year, exceed in annual value the aggregate imports and exports of France, Russia, Germany, and Italy all put together. And that shows this, that the main difference between us and any other Powers I have mentioned, is, that the internal communications of our world-wide Empire are our sea communications, and that is not the case with any other Powers. Then, I come to the next point—the point of the standard of measurement. The only standard that can be relied on of the required naval strength is the standard based on a careful review not merely of the forces of the other Powers, but on a survey of the whole position and of the geographical distribution of their ports. We are told that the standard we are now acting upon is that if we have a Fleet equal to a combination of the fleets of any other two nations which could be brought against our Fleet, we are perfectly safe. I do not know where that standard came from, Sir. I agree that it is a very useful standard, but it is a rule-of-thumb standard, and mainly political. It is not a scientific standard, and you cannot base comparisons of naval strength simply on the abstract number of ships. The standard now adopted and acted upon is a wholly theoretical standard, an entirely untested standard. Even if it is based on the fact that in war our Fleet will be equal to the two most powerful fleets of other Powers, it means that you allow no margin whatever for the accidents of maritime war, no margin for a combination against us of more than two Powers. And you allow no margin for the result of errors of judgment in a commander. In these days these are very important factors. At most it leaves this Empire with its vast communications at the mercy of a third Power. While agreeing, therefore, that that standard, from a political point of view, is a reasonable rule of thumb standard, it is not, in my opinion, a standard to pin ourselves to abide by in judging of our relative superiority over other nations. The conditions and requirements our Fleet has to fulfil must vary with the quarter from which war comes. The question is one of the geographical distribution of the enemy's ports. That is the main factor in the problem. The further these ports are from this island the greater will be our difficulties, and the greater must be the numerical preponderance which we require to produce

equality. Certain people, of whom I believe the noble Lord the Member for York is one, think that in war we must abandon the Mediterranean; and one reason for that is the distribution of foreign war ports in one sea. I wholly disagree with that programme, but it is the natural corrollary of the fallacy of a rule of thumb standard of abstract equality of one Fleet to two. Our standard must be, I think, to provide and to maintain equality at least in every sea and off every coast and under all circumstances, and not equality of numbers merely on paper. Our numbers must be sufficient to do that. For these reasons, Sir, I object to our going into a Conference with the assumption that the standard, that the rule of thumb standard, is a thoroughly reliable one, and that if certain other European Powers reduce their Fleets, then we are to reduce ours. I protest against that. I think the idea is dangerous. My right honourable Friend says that if Europe comes to no agreement, our programme must stand. So we are to understand that if Europe, in the Peace Conference, does come to an agreement we will modify our rule of thumb standard. I venture to ask: What about the United States, and what about Japan? We cannot deal with this question of our relative strength of our Fleet, and of European Fleets, and be bound by a proposal for a reduction of our Fleet, if any portion of the great maritime Powers is left out of account. Therefore, I must say, I look on the statement which the First Lord deliberately made on behalf of the Government as containing elements of great danger. Who can say, for example, that circumstances may not arise at no very distant period which may bring about in the North Pacific a combination between the United States and Japan and Russia? All of them are North Pacific Powers, and have local ports. Their aims may be similar, and the objects of their policy may be similar, and these aims and these objects it will be their interest and their duty to enforce. In such an event, and in view of the naval developments of these Powers in the North Pacific which is now plainly visible, the difficulties of our two islands in the north-east corner of the Atlantic to assert supremacy in the North Pacific are too obvious to need my enlarging upon them. They strike one at once. My belief is it could not be done except by so weakening our Fleet in European waters, in order to produce equality in the North Pacific, as to imperil our own maritime position in this hemisphere. In my humble judgment, therefore, I submit that all the maritime Powers in the world must agree to modify their naval armaments before we can seriously consider any suggestion to modify ours. We are an Oceanic Power, and not a European Power pure and simple. And we cannot tie up our hands because, not all the Oceanic Powers, but a certain select number of European nations, think we ought to do so. Now, every sensible man wishes that the Conference at the Hague will make for peace; but no sensible man can really believe that the reduction of British naval power, which would make British supremacy at sea doubtful, would make for peace at all. All history is against that idea. It was not until the supremacy of the seas fell into our hands, 94 years ago, that there was any prolonged peace at all. And if I read history aright, that is because the undoubted supremacy of the sea has been for 94 years in the hands of the greatest traders in the world, who have the greatest interest in maintaining peace. British naval supremacy of the seas is, therefore, the best guarantee of peace. It is because I desire to see peace that I do not wish to see tampering with the Navy whatever. That brings me to the next point I want to make, and that is, the omission from the speech of my right honourable Friend the First Lord, to which I have referred. It is, to my mind, a very remarkable omission, and I am puzzled to understand it. In the Queen's Speech we had a paragraph pronouncing satisfaction that the Cape Parliament had recognised the principle of a common responsibility of the Colony, and had made a contribution to the British Navy. The First Lord, in a long speech he delivered the other night, never touched upon that important fact once. I do not think that, looking at the facts of the British position with regard to the great Colonies, that great event—for great it is—should be passed over practically in silence by the First Lord. Here you have a new departure, a recognition on the part of an outlying portion of the Empire, of the duties and responsibilities attaching

Sir J. Colomb.

to it for the naval defence of the Empire, passed over in silence by the First Lord, and hardly alluded to by any other honourable Member in the Debates in the House. Now, I regard this as an unfortunate omission. Looking at the thing fairly in the face, you are trying to carry on the maintenance and the defence of the Empire, spread over the whole world, out of the resources of two over-crowded islands in the north-east of the Atlantic. That is what you are trying to do. It appears to me that that is a programme which the British people cannot regard with satisfaction. I will endeavour to make one or two points, which will establish my position. We are paying no heed to the broad fact that the potentialities of British strength are shifting; the centre of gravity of the sources of British power is changing, and the time is at hand when a recognition of that fact cannot be ignored. It is somewhat strange that the practical recognition of that fact does not come from Her Majesty's Government or from the Leaders of the Opposition, but comes from the Cape Colony, which spontaneously makes a permanent annual contribution to our Fleet, and Members in the House, and indeed the House itself, takes it quite as a matter of course. Surely this is a melancholy proof of the apathetic disregard of the problem that lies before the British people. The problem lying before us is this: How to combine the resources of all parts of the Empire for the defence of common interests and the security of common rights. The common interest and the common right is the security of the sea. I would like to justify that statement of the shifting of the potentialities of British strength during the Queen's reign. For example, at the Accession of the Queen the population of the whole British Empire was 126 millions; it is now over 400 millions—more than treb'e. The aggregate revenue was 78 millions; now over 400 millions—more than treble. The sea trade, which was at the Queen's Accession only 210 millions, is now nearly 1,400 millions—about sevenfold. Now, let us look at the relative growth of the United Kingdom and of our Empire over sea since 1837. The population of the United Kingdom has only increased by 15 millions; the over-sea population has increased by 260 millions. The aggregate revenue of the United

Kingdom has not doubled; the aggregate revenue of British possessions over sea has increased sixfold. The sea trade of the United Kingdom has not quadrupled; the sea trade of the over-sea portion of the Empire has increased by 500 millions, or sixfold, and that is going on more rapidly every year. Such facts as these cannot be ignored. With an Empire with a revenue of 257 millions and with common interest, surely it cannot be expected that only a small part of that revenue should bear for ever the whole charge of its defence. When you come to face the problem of how you are going to combine these forces, you are met with this fact, that you cannot force your self-governing Colonies to contribute to the common defence. You gave them self-government without any reservation, and you must abide in honour by that. But th: question is: Are we quite right in ignoring these growths, and not paying a little more attention to what lies before us? It strikes me as very remarkable that the First Lord, with his vast knowledge and his statesmanlike grasp o. this question, did not see the opportunity and seize it to draw the attention of the public in this country and in our Colonies to the fact of the Cape contribution, and to the fact that that is the beginning of a policy which must be pursued if the Empire is to survive. The growth of the self-governing Colonies has been very rapid, and is really astonishing. These self-governing states beyond the sea have now an aggregate sea trade nearly double what the sea trade of the United States was at the time of the "Alabama." The aggregate revenue of the self-governing Colonies is now five times the revenue of the United States when the Queen came to the Throne; and the population of the Colonies is now about equal to that of the United States at the time of the Queen's Accession. You have one outlying province, British North America, owning a mercantile marine equal to the mercantile marine of the United States, and yet you have to protect that trade alone. Surely the time must come for drawing the attention of Canada to the fact that were circumstances to change in the United Kingdom, their trade might be imperilled, simply because the people of the United Kingdom had got a cold fit about the Navy. I think, therefore, I am not unreasonable in expressing my regret that my right honourable Friend the First Lord did not take so fitting an opportunity of looking at this question from a proper statesmanlike point of view, and did not seize the opportunity of bringing the broad facts of the case before the people at home and abroad. My belief is that if you go on as you are going, the time is not far distant when you will have to choose between imperilling the Empire by reducing the Navy or increasing the taxation on the people of this country only to a very serious extent. If then it is discovered, and it will be discovered before long, by the people of this country that they alone are paying for the protection of a trade exceeding in value the total sea trade of France— a trade that never comes to nor goes from the United Kingdom, you will have this question raised in a hostile spirit, which will be disastrous to the Colonies and to ourselves. But by degrees we are getting to recognise the actual state of the case, viz., that these armaments are necessary for the defence of the Empire, the whole weight of which has to be supported by the hundred millions of revenue raised by the public in this Kingdom.

*MR. KEARLEY: Mr. Speaker, during the last ten years we have been increasing the *personnel* of the Navy at the average rate of 4,000 per annum. In 1890 the total *personnel* amounted to 65,000, whereas last year it was 106,000, and for the coming financial year we are voting over 110,000 men. I presume the *personnel* will go on increasing for some considerable time, but the moment must arrive when it will be almost impossible for it to increase to a greater extent, because a limit will be reached when it will be impossible to keep employed a larger number of men, and we know the effect on the *personnel* if it is not always kept employed; it tends to deteriorate, and that difficulty will occur if we go on largely augmenting our Navy. All those in favour of the extension of the Navy will admit that it is impossible to keep the *personnel* of the Navy up to war requirements. That is not the habit or practice of any country. All countries without exception have to fall back in war time on a substantial Navy Reserve. Already the expenses in connection with the *personnel* amount to nine millions a year, and if we continue largely increasing the *personnel*, the burthen will, I think, become much greater than the country will be prepared to bear. It is, therefore, of importance that we should consider our position in regard to our reserve of seamen in time of war. I think it is a sound proposition that our Naval Reserve, to be reliable, must be well organised, well equipped and well drilled, which means it should be built up now, so that when the day arrives when we want it, it will not be found lacking. That brings me to consider what is our present position as regards the strength of the Royal Naval Reserve. In the last nine years we have increased the *personnel* of the Navy by 40,000 men, and during that period we have only increased the *personnel* of the Royal Naval Reserve from 19,000 to something less than 27,000. But the number at the present moment in no way represents the probable requirements of the Naval Reserve when it is called upon to make up the waste and loss which happen in time of war, and if we judge from previous experience as to the probable requirement of the Reserve, we find that in all our great wars in the last 150 years the number in many cases required was four times the number borne on the Navy. Of course the number that would be required would very much depend on the duration of the war. There is a prevalent idea that a naval war, whenever it comes, will be a short war. That was the idea held by many in the autumn. I, myself, happened to be in Gibraltar during the time the Channel Fleet was there awaiting the outcome of the Fashoda incident, and I had considerable conversation with naval men, and they all seemed to be under the impression that if war broke out it would be rapidly brought to a termination. That is really a matter of opinion. But I think all are agreed on one point; that whether the war be short or long the present number of the Royal Naval Reserve is altogether inadequate. There are naval experts of repute, notably the noble Lord the Member for York, who have stated the minimum number that should be borne on the Naval Reserve. The noble Lord has fixed the figure at 75,000, and accepting that as a basis, we find we have

Mr. Kearley.

a shortage of no less than 50,000. The question I want to discuss is, how are these men to be obtained? There are two schemes that are considered with a view to bringing about an increase in the Reserve. The first scheme has many supporters, especially among naval men. It is that the Navy should create and train its own Reserve. That would, of course, necessitate a system of short service, a system at variance with that which has proved effective in building up the admirable body of men now manning the Fleet. There are many distinguished advocates of that system, including the noble Lord the Member for York. I remember some time ago reading a speech he delivered at the Liverpool Chamber of Commerce on the subject. He went fully into details as to how the proposed short service should be established for the purpose of building up the Reserve. That system would, of course, have many advantages over the existing system, such as prolonged training afloat, and it would turn out a more finished article and a more trained man than is possible under the present system. The First Lord pointed out to us the other night that a large body of men have been serving six months afloat, but that is not to be compared to the benefits derived by a man who is permanently in the Navy for five years. I am not an advocate of the short-service system. I think a serious objection to it is that it would tend to jeopardise the long-service system, which has done so much for the Navy. In my judgment it would be altogether impossible to have the two systems running side by side. There would be an option open to every boy entering the Navy to adopt either term of service, and he would probably go in for short service, because if he liked the Navy there would be no difficulty in serving a longer term. That, I think, would be a tremendous danger, because it would prevent men definitely committing themselves as at present to a minimum of 12 years' service. Under the present long-service system, as far as blue-jackets are concerned, when a boy enters, he enters the Service definitely for about 14 or 15 years. There would be another difficulty—namely, to find an opportunity for training these short-service men. We are gradually approaching the point when, with the regular requirements of the Navy, it will be difficult to train larger numbers, Now I come to the other proposal, that we should develop the Royal Naval Reserve from the Mercantile Marine on more improved lines than at present. I think that the step taken in 1897 has proved advantageous and the re-organisation of the training and regulations under which Royal Naval Reserve men are engaged has, no doubt, had a beneficial effect, and has brought them into closer touch with the Navy. But the great difficulty, when we propose to increase the Royal Naval Reserve, is the decline of British seamen in the British Mercantile Marine. That decline is rapid, and the fact remains, that owing to it we are not producing material requisite for the Naval Reserve. Indeed, the most serious aspect of this question is that the greatest falling off has taken place among young men. In the Return published in 1897 the greatest falling off took place between the ages of 15 and 25, and, of course, that decrease is being supplied by foreign seamen. To give an idea, I will quote a few figures : We find that the number of British seamen in 1890 was 168,722 and that the number of foreign seamen and Lascars was 49,961. In 1897 the number of British seamen had fallen to 160,126, and the number of foreign seamen and Lascars had increased to 65,387. That shows that in seven years British seamen had decreased by nearly 9,000, and foreign seamen and Lascars had increased by 15,000. And during that time British tonnage had largely augmented. Prior to 1850, when the Navigation Laws were repealed, we were able to regulate the supply of seamen in this country by compulsory legislation. There was a time in the thirties when the supply of British seamen showed a falling off. Legislation was at once undertaken, with the result that in 1848 the total of indentured apprentices was no less than 28,000.

*MR. SPEAKER: The honourable Member appears to be entering on a subject rather remote from the Estimates. He cannot go into the full question of the Navigation Laws.

*MR. KEARLEY: I had no intention of doing that, Mr. Speaker, and I accept your ruling. I must content myself by pointing out what the remedy is to be if, in view of this decline, we are to secure for the Royal Naval Reserve a sufficient supply of men. In the first place, it will be necessary to interest the shipowners of this country, and that can be done no doubt by a Conference. I believe last year a suggestion was thrown out in this House when the question of building up the Reserve was discussed by shipowners in connection with Light Dues remission that they would be pleased to meet the Admiralty to consider what steps should be taken by them to assist in this matter. But apart from that altogether, there is something to be done by the Government itself. The Government might establish around the coast a number of depôt ships, into which a number of boys should be received every year. There are now what are called stationary training ships, but the majority of the boys in them are reformatory boys, and everyone knows that the Navy will not take boys except they are of respectable parentage. If we could get hold of these boys for the Reserve it would be necessary to bind them down, for, say, four years. The first year should be spent on the depôt ship, and then, by a satisfactory arrangement with the shipowners, they should be drafted into the Mercantile Marine on agreement that they would join the Naval Reserve. That is a system which, I believe, the shipowners are open to consider. It resolves itself into a question whether the Government is prepared to come to such terms as would be considered satisfactory. There is one other point, which has already been raised in this House by the First Lord of the Admiralty, to which I wish to refer. That is the question of enlisting into the Royal Naval Reserve men in the Colonies. It was stated last year by a prominent Member of the Canadian Government that there were as many as 76,000 eligible men in Canada well suited to join the Reserve. A deputation was received by the First Lord on this question last year, and he very properly insisted that if entries were to be received from the Colonies for the Reserve that the men should be as well trained as ours, and that they should undertake to go through the same training, put in the same drill, and go afloat for six months. He also offered that if the Canadian Government would pay the expenses of training these men that this country would pay their retainer. I understand that instructions have been sent to commanders of all naval stations abroad, asking them to put before the Governments of the Colonies our regulations with regard to the Naval Reserve, and I should be glad if the honourable Gentleman who replies to this discussion would tell us what has been the effect, and whether the Colonial Governments are inclined to entertain the idea, because it has an important bearing on this question. I hope that no step will be left untried that will bring about an increase in the number of the Naval Reserve. We believe that it is at present inadequate, and that we want 50,000 more men. It would be cheaper and to the national advantage if we could build up from our Mercantile Marine the Reserve to an adequate number, and train them properly; and in support of this ideal I hope we shall hear something to-night as to what steps are being taken by the Admiralty to induce men in the Colonies to join the Reserve.

MR. GIBSON BOWLES: The honourable Member who has just sat down has, I think, overlooked the fact that only a small proportion of Reserve men could be employed in a man-of-war. I think also, that he overstated the number required, or that could be usefully employed. We cannot have an equal number of Reserve men and Navy men. We must have a larger proportion of the latter. Now, Sir, I was much interested in the speech of the right honourable Gentleman the Member for North-East Lancashire, especially that part of it with reference to the French Navy, regarding which I will have a word to say later on. It is very much to the credit of the First Lord that no Member has been found to move an Amendment to the Motion before the House. Even the honourable Member who spoke last sat down without moving any Amendment at all. These are large Estimates. They amount to 28 millions, and include an increase of three millions. They propose to spend two millions more on ships and a half million more on men. Is this large increase necessary? I think it has been clearly shown that the Great Powers are increasing their armaments. Even the Tsar, as we have been reminded by the

First Lord of the Admiralty, has allocated nine millions of money for his Navy, in addition to which it is impossible to overlook the fact that he has an army double the British Army, and that he is adding to it 60 new regiments of Cavalry. All the Powers of Europe are really increasing their strength, and, to my mind, that which the right honourable the First Lord seems to regard as a promise of peace—the Disarmament Conference—is the most menacing sign of all. What are you to suppose when a man comes to you with words of peace on his lips while he is engaged in putting on all the panoply of war? No increase in our Navy can really be regarded as aggressive. We are not going to invade France or Russia or Germany with our Navy, not that a Navy cannot be used with effect on land, but our Navy, in its nature, is not aggressive, and, therefore, I cannot conceive how any increase could be, or would be, construed by any Power in Europe as a menace. Well then, Sir, the importance of these Estimates, and the very large increase which arises from them, is undoubtedly that they must be the result of the deliberations and consultations of that most important body of the Cabinet—the Defence Committee. Looking at the matter from the point of view of the state of Europe at the present moment, and the possibilities of the near future, why the increase is so large, coming as it does on the increases of previous years, I do not know, but I cannot but suppose that the Cabinet Defence Committee conceive that there is at least a possibility of war. Perhaps it has another opinion, which I will touch upon later. But the justification, after all, for these Estimates is to be found in the fact that they are approved, not only in this country, but also by some foreign Powers. Everyone has expressed approval of the great increase in our naval Estimates. No doubt an increase of some sort was necessary. But what are the conditions upon which you settle the amount of your naval force. I think it is quite clear that some considerations may be put forward which are not always apparent in a discussion of this sort. There is, for instance, the two other European Powers combined. Then there is the All Europe theory, which assumes that our Navy should be equal

Mr. Kearley.

to the whole of the navies of Europe. But how is strength to be measured, and how is a common denominator to be obtained? How are we to judge of the relative strength of the navies? This is far more difficult than most people suppose. You cannot take tonnage, for that would be no guide at all, and still less can you take the number of ships, for the basis of comparison, unless they are equal in speed, armament, and crews. Then, again, the number of men and guns will not do, as in these days so much depends, not merely on speed, but on the handling of the vessels and the practice and traditions of the Navy. The first and foremost advantage that England has over all other countries is that for over 300 years we have gone on adding to our naval traditions, until at last we have an absolutely complete Service code, and what are called rules of the Service, which cover almost everything affecting the welfare of the Navy. I will give an instance which shows the value of these traditions. It will be in the memory of honourable Members how Her Majesty's ship "Calliope" was the only vessel which escaped from foundering in a hurricane off Samoa. She was not a better ship, nor were her crew and engines superior to those of the German vessel which foundered, but her escape was undoubtedly due to the traditions of the British Navy. Then, again, take the case of Crete. There a Russian vessel joined in the bombardment, and a terrible accident happened in consequence of a tremendous explosion through the breach of one of her guns. Her armament was not worse than ours, and her crew were equally brave with ours, but it was the long experience which we had gained which has taught our men how little matters, unless carefully watched, may lead to serious disasters. I could mention other instances to show the real importance to the Navy of these traditions. You cannot compare the English Navy with any foreign navy, nor can you compare foreign navies with one another, because their traditions vary so much. But I am certain of this, that the British Navy is superior in its rules and traditions to any of them. Another advantage which we possess, and it is a tremendous one, is in our geographical position. We are sometimes told by honourable Gen-

tlemen that we run the risk of being blockaded, and of having our food supplies cut off. But I venture to say that the whole of the navies of the world could not blockade these islands, which, especially on the western side, are so open, while if we were at war with enemies in the North and South of Europe, we are so situated as to be able to prevent their fleets joining hands. We have a station at Gibraltar which practically enables us to divide the Mediterranean from the West of Europe and to prevent the junction of any Mediterranean force with any Atlantic force. Take the case of a naval war between England and France and Russia. The fleets of those countries could be kept so divided that instead of one large force, there would be three scattered forces. I should like in this connection to quote some observations by Captain Mahan in his book, "The Influence of Sea Power upon History." He says—

"The geographical position may be such as of itself to promote a concentration, or to necessitate a dispersion, of the naval forces. Here, again, the British Islands have an advantage over France. The position of the latter, touching the Mediterranean as well as the ocean, while it has its advantages, is on the whole a source of military weakness at sea. The Eastern and Western French fleets have only been able to unite after passing through the Straits of Gibraltar, in attempting which they have often risked, and sometimes suffered loss."

And here is another quotation, showing how we do really divide the North and South of Europe. Captain Mahan writes—

"The geographical position of a country may not only favour the concentration of its forces, but give the further strategic advantage of a central position, and a good base for hostile operations against its probable enemies. This, again, is the case with England; on the one hand, she faces Holland and the Northern Powers, on the other, France and the Atlantic. When threatened with a coalition between France and the Naval Powers of the North Sea and the Baltic, as she at times was, her Fleets in the Downs and in the Channel, and even that of Brest, occupied interior positions, and thus were readily able to interpose their united forces against either one of the enemies which should seek to pass through the Channel to effect a junction with its ally."

I think that that shows that in the opinion of a most eminent authority on the naval strategy of the present day we have an extraordinary advantage in our geographical position. This, therefore, must also be taken into account in estimating the naval strength of England, and in comparing that strength, you must allow a good many ships and a good many men for that geographical advantage. There is another thing to be taken into account. Every possible naval adversary of England has formally given up the idea of meeting England in line of battle on the high seas. France has expressly and absolutely renounced the idea of so competing with us, and no other country in Europe is likely now to entertain it. But what does France propose to substitute for it? She intends to carry on a war of commerce destroying, and as to that, Captain Mahan has well pointed out that a war carried on by cruisers against commerce means that the cruisers must always remain near their own coast. Therefore, if it should so happen that we should be at war with France, which God forbid, her commerce destroyers could never go far from her own coast, and consequently their action would not affect the final result of the war. When I think of all these advantages, I confess that I am not only satisfied with the amount and extent of the Naval Estimates, but I am more than satisfied, and I indeed feel some misgiving as to whether we are not exaggerating the naval panic, and pushing our expenditure a little too far. As to that, however, I must accept what the Government say, and, above all, I must take into account what they know and do not say. If it be as I suppose, that the Defence Committee of the Cabinet have reason to believe that there is an approximate possibility of war, I, for one, cannot quarrel with the amount of the Estimates. Still, I have some special misgiving with regard to new construction. We can build a battleship in from 20 to 24 months, and send her to sea. The French take twice as long, and, therefore, you can give them two years start, and still be even with them before the battleships go to sea. That is an enormous advantage, and, therefore, our object should be not to build as soon as we can, but rather as late as we can, as by doing that we shall be able to introduce into our ships all the latest improvements. Assuming, then, that you begin two years later than France, you will be able to gain the

Mr. Gibson Bowles.

advantage of all naval improvements which may arise during that period. That is a tremendous advantage, and that is the reason why I have some misgivings with regard to new construction. I am glad of one thing. This increase in the naval Estimates, as compared with those of the Army, much more truly represents the proper relative position in this country of the Army and Navy. It more truly recognises the undoubted fact that this country's battles in the future will be fought by the sailor rather than by the soldier. In 1893, Lord Playfair said in the other House that Great Britain needs no supremacy at sea. We do not agree with him. That was said at the time when the naval Estimates amounted to 14½ millions, as compared with 18 millions asked for the Army. Now the Army Estimates have gone up to 28 millions. That is something stupendous. In little more than five years we have nearly doubled the Navy Estimates, and now they have reached a sum which was not in 1893 even dreamed of. We are now considering how we are to provide an extra three millions for the Navy. I do not know where it is to come from, but it certainly must come out of new resources, and that is one of the main features of these Estimates. The most remarkable point about them is the absolute and complete conversion of the Treasury from its old theories and practices. It has departed from its practices of former days, and has adopted what I may call the most modern, up-to-date theories of finance. The Chancellor of the Exchequer used to be considered a sort of hard-fisted personage, whose only object was to reduce debt and diminish taxation, and he sat upon his money bags refusing the Departments the common necessaries of life. That is all changed now, and we see the Chancellor of the Exchequer is no longer a curmudgeon, but a debonnair, open-handed gentleman. He goes to the relief of the agricultural taxpayer and the tobacco manufacturer; nobody appeals to him in vain, and he is an ideal Chancellor of the Exchequer. It is, indeed, an encouraging feature of the Estimates that the right honourable Gentleman has at last been converted to the importance of finding money for these purposes. It must be regarded with intense satisfaction, and I think we may congratulate the First Lord of the Admiralty that at last he has been able to find a Chancellor of the Exchequer so generously disposed. The Estimates have very greatly increased, and I must believe the Government have such knowledge as to justify them in making the increase. I believe they will commend the acquiescence of all, both at home and abroad, and it only remains for us to go through the important function of finding the money to pay for them.

On the return of Mr. SPEAKER, after the usual interval—

SIR J. BAKER (Portsmouth): Mr. Speaker, I think it must be very satisfactory to the Government that their scheme has met with such general satisfaction. Speaking on behalf of a large number of men and officers of the Service, I feel bound to tender to the Government a meed of praise for their programme. There are, however, one or two details and omissions to which I should like to call attention. I, with other honourable Members, who sit for naval ports, have for some years past represented to the Admiralty the necessities of the Navy as viewed by the representatives of those ports. I desire to acknowledge the fact that the First Lord of the Admiralty very kindly received the representatives of the Dockyards and the Navy, and, with great patience and pains, went through with them the claims they presented for consideration. There has, however been practically no reference to the sub ject in the statement of the First Lord except the comparatively small one to which I shall presently refer. The House will remember that the First Lord gave that conference consequent upon the procedure of the House not enabling the representatives to fairly put their representations before the Admiralty in the House of Commons Of course, these men, being under martial law, must have some method or means of presenting claims they think reasonable and just. The fact is incontestable that, whilst almost every class in the Army has been dealt with in a spirit of generosity which no one be grudges, there has practically been for many years no change whatever in regard to the great body of men in the

Navy. They remain year after year, both as to pay, as to rations, and as to pensions, practically in the same position that they were in 10 or 20 years ago. The Admiralty, however, have made one change, affecting about 10,000 men. It was decided to increase the pay of the Marines on shore about 2d. a day. That is a very fair and reasonable change, but it is justifiable. Whilst, however, the Admiralty, year after year, made these several changes in the increase of pay, they kept the payment of seamen the same, with slight alteration, and this is a question which I hope the Admiralty will not omit to give some consideration to. Then the question arises, what is the cause of the dearth in naval shipwrights? The simple cause is that the Admiralty has refused to give them, either in pay, conditions, or rank, sufficient temptation or inducement to enter the Service. Even now the Admiralty does not offer to apprentices sufficient inducements to enter, and at Portsmouth the number of those who enter for competition every year is infinitesimally small. I think five will be found to be the average number. The shipwrights, both in the Dockyards and on Her Majesty's ships, are alike in opinion as to the inadequacy of the present arrangements. The Admiralty have reduced the period of apprenticeship to four years, but practical men all say that that is not sufficient, and that six years should be the shortest period of service, having regard to the highly responsible duties the shipwright has to perform. Then, on the other hand, not the slightest reference has been made to the claims of the chief class of men which have been made from time to time. Again, the Government want a large number of additional stokers. It is a matter of common knowledge in the Service that, though the Admiralty cast their net all over the land to get stokers, they do not get hold of trained and efficient men. They get men who have helped anywhere and everywhere, who are accustomed to fire, and who have had, perhaps, two or three months' training on board ship. The position, however, is one of great responsibility, and the duties connected with it should be properly paid for. There is, however, no stimulus whatever afforded to this particular class of men, and in civil service the same class get nearly double the amount the Admiralty offers to induce them to enter the Navy. In factories and gasworks stokers receive from 37s. to 42s. a week. In face of this condition of things, what temptation is offered to a man to pass the miserable existence the stoker passes on board a battleship? Now, I think that is a sufficient reason why the Admiralty should give special attention to this department of labour. With regard to other positions in the Service, again and again have promises been held out—they have not, perhaps, been absolutely given in a way that would bind the Admiralty—that some claim was about to be recognised in a way which would satisfy partially, if not wholly, the demands of the men. Unless, however, the First Lord of the Admiralty can give some information that some response will be made to the continuous claims presented by the men on whose behalf I speak it will be a matter of bitter disappointment to them, because it must always be remembered that if the chief and petty officers are discontented, that discontent goes down to every boy in the Service, since all look forward, not unnaturally, to some day occupying these positions. I wish most strongly to impress upon the Admiralty the fact that the best men in the Service are bitterly disappointed at the prolongation of the delay in responding to the claims with which the Admiralty is as familiar as I am, and which relate to every class in the Service. I have only typified three or four of the grievances which have been presented from time to time but I do think it is of vast importance since we are increasing the strength of the Navy by leaps and bounds that the men in this Service should be treated relativel on the same conditions as the men in the Army. We do not ask for any more. The Army have succeeded in obtaining it, but this grievance has been going on for some 10 or 12 years with no response whatever being made by the Admiralty. I know of no instance in which a response has been made, except on one occasion when some slight improvement was made in the case of the engine-room artificers, and some 50 of them were promoted in rank; but that is all. It does seem hard that these men should be in the

Sir J. Baker.

same position now, when the wealth of the country is so prodigious that millions are being scattered like snow flakes, as they were in times past. And I certainly do think it is time that the Admiralty should consider this matter, and not ignore it as it has done for so long.

*ADMIRAL FIELD (Sussex, Eastbourne):
I could have wished, Sir, that the House could have gone into Committee upon these Estimates before this, but there are certain reasons why we should go on with the discussion here, otherwise we should be shut out, by reason of the unfortunate Amendment which has gone down upon the Paper from all discussion. Now, I desire, in the first place, to thank the honourable Member for Portsmouth for the appeals which he has made on behalf of the rank and file in the Service. I know perfectly well that there are long standing grievances on the part of the rank and file, and so do my brother officers, and we have brought the matter before the Admiralty constantly for the last 10 or 12 years. The case is well nigh hopeless, professional men are not listened to by Lords of the Admiralty, but I certainly hope the honourable Members representing important dockyard boroughs may be more successful in their attempts to redress those grievances than we have been. But though I desire to thank the honourable Gentleman for the efforts that he has made, I do not quite agree with all that he has said, and I will deal with one or two points upon which I do not agree with him. He appeals for the reconsideration of the whole of the claims of the rank and file of the Service. Now, all naval men are in favour of giving extra pay for extra qualifications, and the seamen class have very advantageous openings offered to all of them in the way of obtaining higher pay for extra qualifications, in the shape of trained men, torpedo men, and gunnery men, and other classes, and men with good conduct badges. So that the case really is not so bad as the honourable Member might have been led to believe by those who have waited upon him in this matter. With regard to the stokers, I certainly agree with what he said about their case being a hard one, but we have represented their case before this House

for the last 10 years. We did at last appeal to the Admiralty, through the First Lord, to make a second class rate for the leading stokers; that was something, and we obtained that nearly five years ago. We quite agree with what has been said by the honourable Member upon this point. We quite agree that the stokers have grievances; and we know perfectly well that the Admiralty is aware of it, and have been for years. and there is not a man amongst us who would not like to see them remedied. But the unfortunate part of the whole business is that the Secretary to the Admiralty is the finance minister, the connecting link—I should like to break it—not him—with the Treasury. It is an unfortunate state of things. When money is voted to the Navy the Admiralty ought to be allowed to administer it, but we are not, and thus it is that the expenses are cut down. We are very glad to see the honourable Gentleman the Secretary to the Admiralty in his place, and we much regret the circumstance which necessitates the absence of the First Lord upon an occasion like this. The re-engagement money for stokers for 10 or 12 years is a very great grievance that ought to be remedied. The seaman class have an extra 2d. a day at the end of 12 years, because it is recognised that at that time they are better men, and I certainly think that the stokers should be put on the same level. I am perfectly well aware of the cold-blooded argument that, so far as the stokers are concerned, the market is full, and that you can always get men when you want them. I can only say I do not like that argument, and I would direct the attention of the honourable Gentleman the Member for Portsmouth to his own side of the House, who are also responsible in this matter, and if ever that Party comes into power again, though God forbid that it ever should, I would ask him to appeal to the First Lord of the Admiralty of that Government and urge upon him the same arguments that we have urged upon him from time to time for the remedy of these grievances. We may talk about these grievances for 10 or 20 years, but there is no remedy, whatever Government may be in power. I hold in my hand a copy of the petition which the coastguard men sent to me, and which I presented to Lord Spencer, the First Lord of the Admiralty of that time. I not only did that, but I got it backed up by over 50 Members of this House—Members of both sides—and was particular to obtain as many as I could from that side. There is the cruel sinner sitting there who would not allow any attention to be paid to these poor men, and so the sin goes on from Government to Government, and I suppose it will be a very long time before Parliament gives absolution to either one side or the other. We almost had a promise from the Gentleman who was Secretary to the Admiralty, but who is now Secretary of State for India, to redress these grievances, and it would have been done, I believe, by giving another step in rank to warrant officers, but for certain circumstances. We have Fleet Paymasters and Fleet Surgeons; and there is no reason, except the stubborn opinion of the Admiralty, why these officers should not have this step. But the fact is that here it is the Treasury steps in. The Secretary to the Treasury knows it quite well. I believe the Admiralty of the day, when the right honourable Gentleman the Secretary of State for India was First Lord, offered a scheme, but it was blocked by the finance minister, the Secretary to the Admiralty, the connecting link with the Treasury. I hope the honourable Member for Portsmouth will do his best to obtain redress for these grievances. Now I pass away from that subject, and come to the First Lord's Memorandum, and I would ask the House to allow me to refer to that as I think it would be much more convenient to deal with the First Lord's Memorandum and discuss it as we go along than to make a long general speech upon the subject. Now, first of all, I am thankful to see that the Admiralty realises the necessity of largely increasing the officer class, the executive class, and, in fact, all the classes. I rejoice to see the increase of warrant rank; the chief boatswains and gunners are to be increased by 20, whilst boatswains and gunners are to be increased by 230. There will be two chief carpenters and 36 carpenters. Now, all these ranks will be highly valued, and it is a step which is thoroughly deserved, but which, in my opinion, has been much too long delayed. Now, the honourable Member for Portsmouth seems to challenge the Admiralty for not giving sufficient wages for the shipwright class. He says, what are you doing? You are training up a lot of boys to do this work, and not paying the wages which you are entitled to do. Now, I think the expedient that has been hit upon by the Admiralty is one of the best schemes that were ever invented; it delivers us from the absolute tyranny of the trades unions, which have too long used their power and have prevented good men coming to us. In my opinion it is time that the Admiralty emancipated themselves from this system of constructive tyranny. We train our forces in this way; then why on earth should we not train artificers, and so render the Admiralty independent of the tyranny of the trades unions? Now, as to the Royal Marines, I am very glad to see that they are to be increased by 500. And now I come to the class which, in my opinion, have been very hardly treated. The Admiralty gives them an extra two-pence a day. I do not thank the Admiralty for that at all. It is only a tardy recognition that there was some claim to be satisfied. No one will convince me, when their Lordships have been aware, year after year, for the last 20 years, of these grievances, which were pressing and of long standing and ought to have been redressed time after time, that they could not have been redressed before. Ex-Sea Lords acknowledged the grievance and sought to redress it, but did not, owing to the pressure of work. This grievance ought to have been redressed in 1873, when the free ration was given to the Army. Deferred pay was given to them in 1876, and when the First Lord of the Admiralty sitting on that side of the House, and Mr. Shaw Lefevre, challenged the Admiralty to give similar treatment to the Marines Mr. Cardwell said that the want of free rations in the Army was a serious want. There was a similar want so far as the Marines were concerned. The Marines, when they are afloat, are taken care of by us, but when they come ashore they are under military rules and regulations, and we thought it was only right that when the Army got free rations that they should get them too; but they did not. Now, Sir, my honourable Friend knows perfectly well that I am

Admiral Field.

thoroughly satisfied that the Naval Lords have never of themselves been parties to the making of a proposition of this kind—unless, of course, the honourable Gentleman in reply tells me that this was formulated by them. I do not think he will tell me so. The remedy for this grievance ought to be a free ration of fourpence halfpenny a day. The beer money ought to have been given up, which would have left the men three-pence halfpenny a day. The beer money was given up, but the men only got two-pence a day. Now, I thank the Admiralty for that very little indeed, and I do not thank it for dealing with these matters in such a flimsy and, if I may say so without offence, such a mean manner. Then, with regard to the Marines, I notice further down——

*MR. SPEAKER: Order, Order! The honourable Gentleman appears to me to be dealing with matters which would be more properly dealt with upon the Votes themselves.

*ADMIRAL FIELD: It was with great diffidence that I have ventured to point out to the House that I should have been only too glad to assist the Speaker out of the Chair by moving; but after your remarks, Sir, I will not trouble the House further now, and will not say another word until we get into Committee.

*SIR C. DILKE: Before I come to the interesting speech of the honourable Gentleman the Member for Devonport, and the important speech of the right honourable Gentleman the Member for Clitheroe, there are two matters of policy arising on the Estimates to which I should like to make a very brief reference. The first one is in regard to the great delay in the supply of armour, a matter to which in the three previous years several of us upon both sides of the House have called the attention of the Admiralty, notably the Member for York. Previously, as we have said, the supply of armour was not in a very satisfactory condition. The Government depend upon private firms for the supply of armour, and we pointed out last year that some of the firms supplying Government were supplying armour more rapidly for ships being built for a foreign Government— the Japanese Government—than they were supplying it to Her Majesty's Government. The question of remedy was discussed at some length, and the First Lord of the Admiralty, in his speech last year, though he considered it of value, on the whole rejected the idea that it would be well for the Government to have plant of its own and manufacture armour to some extent. But he considered the alternative suggestion more favourably that the Government should guarantee work at a scale of payment and at certain times to four firms which he named. But there has been a considerable delay, a considerable retardation, of naval programme because of the retardation in the supply of armour. That is a matter in which the remedy is more difficult than the remedy for the other evil, to which I shall shortly allude. Last year I ventured to call the attention of the First Lord of the Admiralty to the question of slips, and there can be no doubt that we have got into a very curious position in the last three years with regard to our Naval Programme. We have got into the curious position of beginning our programme each year at the extreme end of the financial year. The programme of the year before last was begun at the extreme end of the financial year; and last year it was the same, and only to-day at the earliest can one of the last-year ships be laid down, owing to the fact of the slip not being free before. Now, that is a very curious state of things, and during the last three years it appears to have become permanent; the two battleships, as to the building of which objection is to be taken by the Opposition, would only be begun, if at all, if the Peace Conference does not stop them, at the extreme end of this financial year. The promises as to the exact time when the ships will be laid down have not been always kept. We are told precisely the same thing each year. We were told the programme of this year would be begun in December or January, which is not the case, because, as I have already said, one battleship is not laid down to-day; the ship has been waiting for the slip to be freed by the launch of a battleship which only took place on Saturday. Having mentioned the matter of slips, it is not a very difficult matter to suggest to the Admiralty a remedy. I have to admit

that we have to-day heard that there is to be some increase in slip accommodation. There is, however, no mention of the new slip at Devonport in the Statement of the First Lord of the Admiralty, and it is only by an answer to a Question asked to-day that we have become officially aware that there is to be a new slip at Devonport. There is now to be this increase of slip accommodation in the dockyards, and some of us think that the armour difficulty might have been dealt with in the past as this slip difficulty might have been dealt with, in the same way; and we might have got into a more businesslike way of beginning to build our ships in the beginning or the middle of the financial year, and not putting them off until the extreme end. For all practical purposes it does not matter whether the. two battleships of this year's programme are begun in this year at all; but there is some trifling amount of money to be expended on those ships in the present year, the promise of which has not been kept with regard to other ships in the last year and the year before. The speech of the right honourable Member for the Clitheroe division about the two battleships of this year's programme was rather a declaration as to a policy of 1900-1901, than a present menace. My honourable Friend the Member for Devonport was called to order when he got into the discussion of the details of the Board of Trade scheme for manning. Now, it is a very difficult thing to discuss the Navy without going into the Board of Trade Votes, or to discuss the Board of Trade Votes without drifting into the Navy. But what my honourable Friend did show in that portion of his speech which was in order was that there was a stationary character about the number of the Naval Reserve, as compared with the great increase in the number of active Service men in the Fleet, and that if the proportion selected some years ago was a fair one, that proportion was a declining proportion. Now, presumably, when this matter was looked into some years ago, a fair proportion was arrived at. Anybody, who knows anything about it, knows that whilst there is diminution in the proportion of Reserve men, that is not the question: the question is whether in the case of rapid mobilisation in the case of war, it will be possible to satisfactorily get the Reserve men, in their right proportion, into the various ships. It is a very difficult thing to properly apportion the Reserve men to the various ships, so as not to be left with an undue number of Reserve men in this country for the ships that would be fitted out after a declaration of war. But my honourable Friend pointed out that there was a decline in the number of those who could be taken for a Reserve. The honourable Member for King's Lynn denies that statement. But my honourable Friend is right in saying that there is a marked decline in the number of boys, and he put forward a remedy to meet that state of things. The honourable Member for Devonport also told the House that upon the sudden breaking out of the war and consequent rapid mobilisation, you could not count upon rapidly getting anything like the total number of Reserve men; the men who are now in the Reserve at the present moment. What is the view of the Government now as to the number of the Reserve men which they would be able to embark in the ships if necessary; last year they thought it was 12,000 men? That was the number which the First Lord of the Admiralty thought he could draw from the Reserve at the beginning of a war for immediate embarkation. I notice from the Estimates that precautions have been taken to keep ready at hand 10,000 kits, and that with the 2,000 men who are now on active service would bring up the figure to 12,000 which the First Lord of the Admiralty expects to be able to embark in the event of an outbreak of war. It shows the Administration count upon obtaining very rapidly from the Reserve 12,000 men, but it does seem to me to be a very small proportion, compared with 110,600 men, which are now to be taken on Vote A. The time, in my opinion, has come when you ought to look to all possible sources of supply, with the view of increasing the number of the Reserves. Now, my honourable Friend and another honourable Member who spoke to-night mentioned the reserve of officers, and the increase of officers was also mentioned by the right honourable Baronet. Now, that is a matter which also ought to be taken into consideration in connection with the Naval Reserve. We have been informed that

Sir C. Dilke.

there is to be a very great increase in the number of officers, and the Government have issued documents, by which they show that they expect to make an increase of 500 lieutenants in the course of time. But no statement has been made to show how the rapid increase taking place this year in the lieutenants' list is to be accomplished. This increase, when completed, will still leave us very short of the number of the lieutenants which we require, as compared with the proportion of lieutenants of the French navy. The French navy is a smaller navy than ours; it is only half the size, but it has the same number of lieutenants as we have at the present moment. Of course, unless you go into the respective duties of the lieutenants in the two services, you cannot make an exhaustive examination of the facts. There may be duties in the French service which are performed by commissioned officers, which in our Service are carried out by officers of warrant rank. But I confess I am as little satisfied with regard to the number of Reserve officers as I am with regard to the number of men. There can be no doubt whatever that in the event of an outbreak of war you would require a much greater number of lieutenants than you actually possess, and though you are increasing the number of the lieutenants you are not showing us how they are going to be rapidly obtained. And you will have either to fall back on the Reserve lieutenants, or adopt the alternative suggestion put forward by the honourable Member for York, and draw upon a certain class of the warrant officers in the Navy for promotion. Now, Sir, for a minute or two I turn to the speech of the right honourable Baronet, the Member for Clitheroe, who has made a speech which, unless explained, is likely to be misinterpreted, and in as few words as I can I should like to put the view which occurs to me before the House. The right honourable Baronet has used words which I say are likely to be misinterpreted. He spoke of the enormous, gigantic, and huge expenditure, and he used those words as leading up to a declaration, as I understood it, that he did not see his way to support the building of the two battleships which are in the programme of the present year. He has spoken of it as a question of how much the public will stand, and he has asked whether the time has not come to apply the brake. The right honourable Gentleman the Member for Clitheroe has also indulged, at some length, in a comparison of our Navy with that of France, and I could not help thinking that in doing so he was giving very great and practical support to the Motion which is going to be made to-night by my honourable Friend the Member for Northampton, who intends proposing a resolution for the reduction of the number of men and the amount of money. Now my honourable Friend the Member for Northampton is logical and consistent, but if we supported him on this side of the House many of us would not be either logical or consistent. The speech of the honourable Member for Dundee last year was entirely different in tone to the speech made by the right honourable Gentleman to-night. The Estimates of this year are merely a carrying out of the second programme of last year, and every single figure this year might have been anticipated and foreseen. It is a programme nearly to the end of the year, and these battleships will make no difference at all in the present year. But from the manner in which this statement has been made I am afraid that his words, unless they are explained, will be misunderstood, and we shall find the honourable Member for Northampton taunting those who vote against him with supplying him with arguments in favour of his Motion and then voting against him in the Lobby. The right honourable Gentleman said it was impossible to take Russia into account, because we did not sufficiently know the facts. But the case put forward by these large Estimates is not put forward now, but was put forward in July last. The Estimates of this year are simply the programme of last year—that is, the second programme. That programme involved the whole of these Estimates, and if we agreed to the policy of last July we ought to agree to pay the money now. The grounds put forward for the programme of last year were the Russian grounds, and this year they consist of a repetition of what we were told in July last. The right honourable Gentleman the Member for Clitheroe says that we should watch and wait. I am quite aware of all that can be said in favour of watching and waiting for the construction of ships abroad, because with

the rapidity of construction in this country we can catch them up. That argument has always been put forward against those who advocated a larger programme, but as I understood the First Lord of the Admiralty, he has taken this view that they have watched and waited, and only at the last moment, noticing the increasing strength of the navies of other Powers, have they decided to strengthen our own Navy. I understand that the defence of the Board of Admiralty is that they have watched, and that they have now put forward a programme which is not, perhaps, quite sufficient to keep up our strength to the standard generally adopted, but which is, nevertheless, sufficient, taking into consideration the rapidity of construction in this country. I cannot help thinking that when the right honourable Gentleman spoke at the beginning of his speech of this enormous, gigantic and huge expenditure he was lumping together, to some extent, military and naval expenditure. I do not think that he distinctly committed himself to the view that the naval expenditure of this country of itself was too large, but I cannot help thinking that his speech somewhat smacked of the old heresy that it is possible to separate the expenditure of the Army and Navy, and to make increases in both when the country is prosperous, and reductions when the country is less prosperous. No one realises more than I do the enormous weight of our military expenditure, and I have pointed it out time after time. Some of us have always argued that you cannot separate the two questions of Army and Navy expenditure, and you must take into account the relative importance of those two Services. If the time has come when, to use the right honourable Gentleman's words, we must apply the brake, you must apply that brake not necessarily to both Services equally, but to the more costly Service, and the branch of the Service which is less vital to our interests. This Empire is an Empire of the seas, and the Navy is vital to our existence, but our Army is not. Our Indian Army is vital to our possession of India, but India pays the full cost of it, and perhaps rather more. But although our Army at home is of immense value, because with it you can rapidly bring a war to an end, yet it is an immensely costly Army as compared with the Navy, and it is not so absolutely vital to our existence as our Navy is. Now, when my right honourable Friend talks about the time having come to apply the brake, I will submit this view to the House : if the constituencies of this country will not stand the present enormous expenditure, and if you cannot induce the Colonies to contribute—as my honourable Friend opposite has argued with theoretical skill that they ought to contribute—towards the cost of the Navy, must you not then first make up your mind whether or not your naval expenditure is a necessity and a vital policy of the country? Now I have said that this is an Empire of the seas. It is a certain fact that it is our Navy which makes us feared, and which is likely to secure for us peace, for our Army is not thought much of by foreign Powers. It is to the Navy that we owe our military power in the world, and yet we spend vastly more upon our Army than upon our Naval Service. Our military standing in the world is produced by our Navy, and yet our Navy does not cost anything like half of our total military expenditure. I calculate that our military and naval expenditure in the Empire will be 71 millions sterling in the coming financial year. Now out of that 71 millions sterling the expenditure on the Navy will be 29 millions, and upon the Army and fixed defences the expenditure will be 42 millions. Of course, I know that some of the expenditure of the Army is really naval expenditure, and that must be admitted. There is the expenditure to which the Leader of the Opposition pointed in his speech last year on the Army Estimates. There is a portion of that expenditure for naval bases, and for coaling stations, which falls upon the Army Estimates; but if you take a large amount for that, and take off two millions sterling—which is my computation—you will find that even then only 31 millions out of 71 millions is utilised for the Navy or for naval bases, and 40 millions is spent upon the Army and fixed defences. Now, I do confess that it does seem to me that if the time has come to take a review of the whole financial situation in connection with your military and naval expenditure—if it is true that the people will not stand a further increase in that expenditure—the line of wisdom is not to attack both the Army and Navy together, for that is the old Treasury heresy ; it is

Sir C. Dilke.

not wise to say that we must knock so much off the Army and so much off the Navy, but we must consider both of them together and see which is most vital to our position. We must see whether the Army cannot be altered in its nature and maintained more efficiently, or just as efficiently, for less expenditure of money rather than fall upon these unfortunate Naval Estimates and say that something must come off these as well. Now I return for one moment to the general position which I ventured to take up. I believe that the most optimist writer on the Navy who writes with a real knowledge of the subject is Mr. Brassey, of the "Navy Annual." Mr. Brassey has always supported the policy of the Board of Admiralty, but in the 1898 "Naval Annual" he declares, for the first time without hesitation, that the number of men for the Navy is insufficient. With that view I agree, and I urge it in support of my honourable Friend the Member for Devonport. I believe our numbers are insufficient in this respect for our present purpose, and I believe the programme of ships, as proposed, is as necessary for the defence of our country as the First Lord of the Admiralty believes, for the Navy is vital to our position in the world. If it is true that the time has come when the constituencies cannot any longer support our enormous military expenditure ; and if it is true that we are hopeless of obtaining that relief from the Colonies which the honourable and gallant Gentleman has pointed out, I would once more urge that we should not make up our minds to reduce our naval expenditure, but support the Government in regard to their naval expenditure, and if it is necessary, make a reduction in the expenditure of the Army.

*MR. WEBSTER : In rising to say a few words in regard to the Naval Estimates, I will not follow the ground covered by the right honourable Baronet the Member for the Forest of Dean, whose observations I entirely re-echo. I would rather try to point out to the House that I most cordially and heartily support the proposals which fell from the honourable Member who spoke earlier in this Debate—I allude to the honourable Member for Devonport. He advocated —and I think the House should very carefully consider what he put before us —an increase in the *personnel* of the reserves of the Fleet. Now we must consider the facts. We are building year by year, and the House cordially votes from time to time, a great increase in the ships, and we equally increase the number of men serving in the Fleet. I believe I am stating the facts accurately when I say that a few years back—only about eight or ten years back—we had only 65,000 men. Now we are going to vote for an increase of men to be on the ships, I believe, to 110,000 men. This is a very important fact, and we must recollect that, whilst increasing the *personnel* of the fleet, we should seriously consider if we ever have to go to war whether we have an adequate and sufficient Naval Reserve to go behind that Fleet. Now, Sir, the honourable Member for Devonport, in a very excellent speech, points out to the House a very grave fact in reference to the decrease in our Mercantile Marine. Why I refer to the Mercantile Marine in this connection is because the Royal Naval Reserve must be recruited, and ought to be recruited, from the Mercantile Marine, and I do not believe you can recruit from any other source. The honourable Member points out, and I again emphasise it, that whilst in 1851 there were only 6,000 foreigners in our Fleet who did not belong to the British nation, yet at the present moment there are no less than 55,000. Now our present Mercantile Marine, roughly speaking, consists of 220,000 men, and in that connection—although there are only about 160,000 of them who are British subjects — if you could get those men to serve it would be a very great advantage to this country to have them as a reserve to our Fleet. Now, what are they ? In the first place, on our ocean lines of steamers they are handy men; they are accustomed to machinery, and to all kinds of work in that respect. Therefore, I venture to say that if we are to have a really efficient Naval Reserve we ought to do everything in our power to secure the assistance of the Mercantile Marine. I think I shall be in order if I mention the fact that we passed a Bill in this House which the shipowners did not seem to care very much about, and which comes into operation on a very remarkable and rather an ominous day for a new Measure—namely, the 1st of April. Now I have letters from shipowners in Hull and Newcastle, and from all over the country, and they

state that they are quite willing and desirous of employing a larger number of British sailors on their ships if sufficient inducements can be given for them to have those men. We acknowledge the fact that probably when many of these men come on board they come from these crimps' houses, and I am sorry to say that the English Mercantile Marine sailors are not quite as steady as some of the foreigners are. It has been stated that these foreigners are not reliable.

*MR. SPEAKER : The honourable Member will not be in order in discussing the manning of the Mercantile Marine.

*MR. WEBSTER : Then I will leave that question in accordance with your ruling. I want to advocate a stronger Naval Reserve. The honourable and gallant Member for York unfortunately is not in his place, but he could do that with greater force than I can, for he told us in this House, and he has stated to me and many other Members, that he advocates an addition to the Naval Reserve of at least 40,000 men, but we do not find this addition in this Vote. I would point out to the House that upon all the Reserve in the Navy you only spend annually £271,000, and I would especially point this out to the Secretary to the Admiralty, whom I see in his place, whilst on the Reserve of the Army you spend nearly two millions per annum. Therefore, I would advocate very strongly that you should do everything in your power to encourage boys to enter the Navy, but that they should first enter the Mercantile Marine. At the present time these are the real recruits of the Reserve of the Navy, and therefore, you must have sufficient boys enter the Mercantile Marine if you desire to keep an efficient Naval Reserve. I am afraid that I am right in stating that many of the boys who enter the Mercantile Marine either come from workhouses or reformatories, and that, I venture to state in this House, is a wrong system ; and a large proportion of them are trained for the sea, but never make it a profession—that is a waste of money. There are vast numbers of boys all over the country, who would be very glad and very willing to enter the Mercantile Marine who are most respectable and honourable boys, and, therefore, I think that we should do everything in our power as has been pointed out by the honourable Member for Devonport, to have more training ships to assist us in training boys for our ships, and I would advocate that we have more training ships at the various ports, and re-name for that purpose some of the old cruisers that are out of date by the names of various towns, not necessarily all seaport towns, such as H.M.S. "Sheffield," H.M.S. "Birmingham," H.M.S "York," and of course others named after the various ports—Liverpool, Glasgow, Portsmouth, Cardiff, Hull, Bristol, Plymouth, Belfast, Cork, &c., and that the boys from those places should go on board these vessels and thus create a local interest in the future welfare of the British Navy and also the Mercantile Marine. Well, Sir, I will not weary the House by emphasising the figures which have been pointed out by my honourable Friend the Member for Devonport. In the past, in times of difficulty and danger, we have been able to draw largely upon our Mercantile Marine. The French Naval Reserves number no less than 135,000 men, but we have only 25,000 in our Naval Reserve. I do not deny that you have also 7,000 or 8,000 naval pensioners, but I have never been able to get from my honourable Friend the Secretary to the Admiralty, who has forwarded me figures, with which I will not trouble the House, the fact that a sufficient number of men, after they leave the Service, join the ranks of the Naval Pensioners Reserve. My honourable Friend told me that every sailor who leaves the Fleet after 21 years' service is liable for active service, but that is not, in my mind, enough. He would have an occasional training at sea. We are told that it is necessary for the men who join the Reserve to have had a short experience. I would strenuously point out to the Admiralty that it is no use building ships, and having a first-rate line of defence consisting of 110,000 men if you do not look to the question of increasing your Naval Reserve, either by recruiting or offering inducements to honourable boys from the various towns in the country to join training ships, or give inducements to your sailors after serving in the Mercantile Marine to go into the Reserve, and thus become useful to the country.

Mr. Webster.

*MR. ALLAN (Gateshead): Ever since I had the honour of sitting in this House I have always consistently voted for the Navy Estimates, whatever they are. I have voted for the increases that have been put down both by the late Government and by the present Government, and I must say that it pained me very much indeed to-night to hear the late Secretary to the Admiralty speak in the manner he did in relation to the two battleships which it is proposed to build, and when he used the phrase that it was "time to put on the brake," and that this country would not stand any further increase in our military expenditure. Now, I am at a loss to understand such sentiments and such phrases coming from that quarter. Does the right honourable Gentleman know that I supported him in reference to the increases proposed by him? I think it is only fair to the Party with which I am identified that the right honourable Gentleman should take a Vote on his sentiments, and then we shall know where we are. I have listened with a great deal of pleasure to the speeches made on the general question of the Navy. So far as the programme of the First Lord is concerned I have no fault to find with it personally. To my way of thinking it is modest—and when I use the word modest I may be asked, "Why do you say so?" Well, I have never yet had a clear definition of what ought to be the magnitude or the extent of a nation's Fleet. The general concensus of opinion in all commercial circles with which I am acquainted is that the Fleet ought to be commensurate with the Mercantile Marine. Now the Mercantile Marine under the British flag amounts to somewhere about thirteen-and-a-half million tons, whereas the mercantile marine under the French flag is about one-and-a-half million tons. If, therefore, the proportion of fleets or the number of ships is to be in accordance with the mercantile marine, it naturally follows that our Fleet is too small in proportion to the fleets of other nations in comparison to their mercantile marine. The mercantile marine of Russia is practically *nil*, and yet she has a very powerful fleet. Therefore, I am not opposed at all, in any shape or form, to the modest increase which the First Lord has put down in his Statement. There are some points in connection with the general question of the Navy which I think demand—and ought to command—attention. They have been alluded to to-night by the various speakers who have taken part in this Debate, and I will not take up the time of the House long by expressing my views on certain points. The other day I received an answer to a Question which I put to the right honourable Gentleman the Secretary to the Admiralty, and he told me that a much larger amount of coal has been used, accounting for no less an increase in the present Estimates than the sum of £316,000. Now, I would like to draw the right honourable Gentleman's attention to one fact, which would save the nation a great deal of money, and that is the condition of the coals which you have stored in the various harbours. Go to Portsmouth, or any of our great coaling stations abroad, and there you will find the coals stored in the open, and they decrease in value through being exposed to the weather, and the result is that they lose a great deal of their carboniferous value, and consequently more has to be consumed to produce the same quantity of steam. I saw thousands of tons of coal at Portsmouth stored when I was there.

MR. MACARTNEY dissented.

*MR. ALLAN: Oh, don't shake your head, Sir. The honourable Member for Yarmouth spoke about the First Lord omitting to mention the action of the Colonies.

*SIR J. COLOMB: Only the Cape.

*MR. ALLAN: Then I will take the case of the Cape. I think the authorities there would be well advised if they abandoned this idea and substituted for their war-ship large floating docks capable of letting in for repairs any of our ships of the Fleet which may arrive damaged into the station, instead of building a war-ship. At present the dock accommodation there is practically *nil*, and I would therefore suggest to the right honourable Gentleman the Secretary to the Admiralty that he might put that suggestion before the Cape authorities, and they might contribute the money as a warranty of their good faith, and then they might erect a grand floating dock there which would take any of our ships which may be damaged. The honourable Member for Devonport spoke about the want of Reserves. I am

entirely at one with him in his speech. I am afraid he did not go far enough. It is a well-known fact—and there is no use in blinking the matter—and there is no use in the First Lord of the Admiralty trying to throw dust in our eyes—that we have not sufficient Reserves. I would ask the Secretary to the Admiralty how many Reserve firemen, engineers, and stokers have we got? You have not as many engineers as would practically man a couple of men-of-war. Take the case of stokers. What are the words used in the advertisements of the provincial newspapers? That "no previous experience is necessary." Now, do you mean to tell me that you can take a man from the plough-tail and make him into a stoker with two, three, or even six months' training? You have not the men and you cannot get them; you have not enough of artificers either. That is a patent fact. I shall tell the right honourable Gentleman why he cannot get the men. It is simply from the fact that the accommodation provided for them in the ships is very poor, and that the treatment of the men is anything but right. And now, when you are driven into a corner in order to get artificers you are going to lower the common standard of examination—a standard which was low enough before. That is your true position, so far as the Reserve is concerned. I would impress in as friendly a way as possible upon the right honourable Gentleman that it is time to take this question of the Reserve in the spirit it ought to be taken, and which ought to be in conformity with the wishes of the nation as to the efficiency of the Fleet. I come to the cause why you do not obtain Reserves. It is entirely a question of money. You do not give the money and you will not get the men. There is no getting out of that. You do not pay them well enough, and you do not treat them well enough—either sailor-men, stokers, or artificers. I do not think I would be trespassing too much on the time of the House if I read an extract from a letter which I received here the other day from a man in one of the first-class cruisers, which have been so much lauded in the House. It shows the necessity of firemen being required. I shall not read the whole of the letter, for it contains other information which I shall have the opportunity to give to the House on another occasion. My correspondent says—

"The first-class stokers are not men who have the necessary experience in looking after the engines, and if they had, there is not enough of them. Another point I have not mentioned is that there were fifty bluejackets acting below as stokers during over two hours last trial trip. They had not the men, and the trial trip was a failure, and the ship had to put back to Portsmouth to repair the damage caused during our last run. And we were detained for a month for the purpose."

I am giving perfectly true information to the House because it is a national question. The reason why we have so many abject failures in our trial trips is that the ships are insufficiently manned, and not by the right class of men. I challenge every official in the Admiralty to deny it or to disprove it. I say you would get the right class of men if you paid them better. Why don't you add £50,000 on the Estimates to improve the pay of these men? The country would give it at once,

HONOURABLE MEMBERS: Hear, hear!

*MR. ALLAN: All the honourable Members round about me and on both sides of the House are cheering that except the late Secretary to the Admiralty. I listened to the honourable Member for King's Lynn with a great degree of pleasure. I always do so—he is so interesting and so patriotic upon the Navy. He said that we should delay ship building for two years. That is to say, that after designing the vessels, and making many arrangements and fixing up the details, we are to stop for two years. I may tell the honourable Member that the building of a man-of-war is totally different from the building of a yacht. The work is not to be gone on with, the drawings are to be pigeon-holed and we are to wait for two years! Why, we would never get the work done in that way. The way to do our work is to make the drawings and then go on with the building. The right honourable Baronet the Member for Forest of Dean spoke of the delay in obtaining the armour. Now, I happen to know something of the manufacture of armour, and I would like to inform the right honourable Gentleman that the manufacture of modern armour is one of the most difficult and ticklish operations that you can perform in the rolling mill. The

Mr. Allan.

armour takes a long time to prepare; it has to be Harveyised and to be nickelised, and to be tested properly, and all these processes take a long time. It is different altogether from the protective armour shield for the three-inch guns, which would not suit our battleships. There must be allowances for delay in the manufacture of this armour. Something has been said about slips. I have spoken in this House many times on the necessity for more slips. The reason why we do not lay our ships down when the House votes the money for them is that we have not the room for them. The Governments are all alike, and will not put the slips down on which to build the ships, and the consequence is that the money is voted for certain vessels from one year to another before a start is made with building them, and all because there is no room for them on the existing slips. I say, therefore, that all these matters ought to be very carefully looked after by the Admiralty officials. Well, Mr. Speaker, I do think that when the Naval Estimates come before the House they ought to receive the thorough support, the patriotic support, of every Member of this House.

AN HONOURABLE MEMBER: No, no!

*MR. ALLAN: The right honourable Gentleman says, "No, no!" I will allow him to differ; but I am a patriot before I am a partisan.

HONOURABLE MEMBERS: Hear, hear.

*MR. ALLAN: And I say again that it pained me very much indeed to hear the late Secretary to the Admiralty practically condemning this Programme, seeing I supported him when he was in office whenever he wanted money for ships. I would challenge him to take a vote on his remarks and we should see who would win.

MR. ARNOLD-FORSTER (Belfast, W.): Some of us have been engaged in criticising not unfrequently during the past few years the administration of the Admiralty. We were most anxious to see some improvement introduced into that administration, and we spared no pains in enforcing our opinions. I feel that it would be ungracious for us who were so engaged to appear to be absolutely indifferent to the enormous advance that has been made of late years. Feeling, as I do now, that the present is in some sense a critical moment—a moment when the Government will require in this day of large expenditure, the full support of the public—I think it is permissible for those who have worked as I have worked to pay a tribute to the work which has been done, and is being done, by the present Admiralty, and of which an example is given in the Estimates now on the Table of the House. The commendations that come from the outside also are simply inevitable. I do not say this because I attach importance to what is in the Estimates, but because I have seen perhaps more of Her Majesty's ships in and out of dock than is generally the case with Members of this House. I know that these Estimates represent actual facts; and that what they represent as having been done, has been done, and that what is contemplated as about to be done, will be done. There is hardly a month passes when I do not revive my recollections of the Royal Navy, and when I do not strive to acquaint myself with what is being done in the Dockyards. I can inform the House that the progress that is being made is almost miraculous to anyone who remembers the condition of the yards and the ships 12 years ago. I say that the House and the country does owe an enormous debt to the present First Lord in regard to the Navy Estimates, and I wish that the example which he has set had been more frequently followed. I believe that there is no Minister who has ever presided at the Admiralty who has done more for, or who has identified himself more with the spirit of the Navy—which is the most important thing after all—than the present First Lord. I happened to be in Gibraltar last year when the First Lord came out in a man-of-war to inspect the fortress, and I must say—in the first place—that I believe that the precedent he set by embarking alone on a man-of-war and seeing for himself the interior economy of the ship was a precedent which might be followed with great advantage. Having gone over the fortress of Gibraltar step

by step after the right honourable Gentleman, I was made the recipient of opinions which had been formed in regard to that visit. The opinions were absolutely uniform—that the interest the First Lord had shown in every detail, and in what was taking place there—the intelligent and active interest—delighted all. They became aware of the fact that he had passed over nothing, and that in spite of his advanced age he had spared no effort to acquaint himself with what was going on, and to encourage those who were at work. I do think that it is permissible, and that it is almost obligatory, on those who have for many years criticised the way in which the Admiralty was administered, to state now how differently things are managed. Probably there will be a certain amount of feeling in the country in regard to the large amount of money asked for in these Estimates; but I think it will be the opinion of everyone who has studied year after year the development of the programme of the Admiralty that these Estimates are but the normal outcome of a definite plan—not exaggerated, not overstated; and that they represent, in fact, the *minimum* rather than the *maximum* programme which is necessary from the movement of opinion in the House and the country. That being so, I am glad that the Estimates have met on the whole with a very cordial reception from the House. I am glad they have the support of the honourable Members opposite. I entirely associate myself with the honourable Member for Gateshead in his regret that an official representative of the Opposition should have taken exception to any portion of the Estimates, and, with him, I agree that if a vote of the House were taken a majority would be found in favour of the Estimates, because anyone who knows anything at all about the Navy and its past administration must acknowledge that these Estimates are the necessary outcome of the programme approved by the House and the country.

MR. HARWOOD (Bolton): I do not intend to engage in a discussion in regard to the programme before us. So far as I can see, I have no fault to with it. But it seems to me that se naval questions are too much ated in this House as the property of admirals and the captains and the embers for seaport towns, and that the avy is regarded too much as a preserve f the seaport towns. I would suggest o the Admiralty that it would be wise, s well as fair, to take systematic means to popularise the Navy among the population of the large manufacturing towns in the north of England. I think the Admiralty cannot be aware how extremely ignorant the population of these towns are as to the means by which they or their sons can enter the Royal Navy. I am frequently consulted by boys and the parents of boys as to how they can get into the Navy. If youths want to go into the Army proper and useful means are taken to afford the information as to how they can go about it. But there are no such means taken in regard to the Navy. The consequence is that these youths are discouraged, and they have not a fair chance of entering on a career which ought to be open to the whole nation. I am quite aware that there is much advantage in habit, in family association, and in inherited liking for the sea. I quite allow that the population of the seaboard towns are more likely to make good sailors than the population of the manufacturing towns. But there are other considerations that ought to weigh in the matter. The love of the sea is not a mere matter of habit, a mere tradition, but a matter of temperament. In the great manufacturing towns many youths are moved by the thirst for the salt sea, which is a saving grace of our nation; and this love of the sea runs not only in the blood of boys bred by the sea, but runs in the blood of the youths in our manufacturing towns. It is part of the burden of our naval supremacy. Therefore, it would be wise if our naval authorities were to give an opening to those young men who are inspired by a passion for the sea, and who we ought to encourage to join the Navy. Another matter of importance is this: We all know that the conditions of the naval occupation have changed much within the last 50 years. Our ships have become more and more huge masses of machinery, and

Mr. Harwood.

less and less merely white-winged galleons, on board which opportunities are afforded for the display of heroism and the inherited qualities of seamanship. On that ground I beg to call the attention of the authorities to the fact that in the town which I represent there are thousands of the most skilled engineers in the world, and if their sons have not inherited the capacity for seamanship, they have inherited a capacity for workmanship; and it is that capacity which is more and more required in the Navy. If you offered an opening in the Navy to these young men, you would have, as a consequence, a much larger selection from which to pick your engineers and artificers. You may think that you get enough at present, but I hold there is a question of right and of fairness in filling up the Navy. I suggest that the Admiralty should take more systematic methods to make known in all the large centres of population the means which should be employed in securing an entrance into the Navy. It should be as easy for men to ascertain how they can get their sons into the Navy as to get their sons into the Army. It may seem a vulgar suggestion, but you might make use of a naval visit to the manufacturing towns. To increase the recruiting, you send the ships to the seaports, and the sight of the Fleet stirs the patriotism of the young men. We have a canal up to Manchester, but I do not suppose you would send a fleet of men-of-war up that Ship Canal. But you might take the opportunity of sending a company of sailors to march through the streets of the manufacturing towns. There is no more stirring sight in the world than a company of British bluejackets marching in their picturesque uniforms. You must learn to teach the people not merely by written language, but also by appealing to their sense of the dramatic. There is a French saying that a career should be open to all the talents. In the manufacturing towns in the North of England we pay a fair share—indeed, a large proportion—of the expense of the Navy, and we have a right that our sons should have as free access to the Navy as anyone else. And I say that that is not so now, and that it is quite unusual for the sons of manufacturers to go into the Navy. I have been the means of introducing a few, but I found it extremely difficult, because I did not know how to go about it. I hope the authorities will take my suggestion seriously into consideration, and I do so from another motive than that I have alluded to. I believe that you would be wise to encourage more heartily the feeling of attachment to the Navy in the nation. We may want that feeling soon. My own grandfather was press-ganged into the Fleet, and the time may come when you may want to appeal to the national enthusiasm for the Fleet again. It is, therefore, wise and truly patriotic to do everything you can to strengthen the attachment of the nation to the Fleet.

THE SECRETARY TO THE TREASURY (Mr. MACARTNEY, Antrim, S.): My honourable and gallant Friend the Member for Eastbourne has alluded to two or three things of detail which would be more germane to discussion in Committee than in a discussion of this description. My honourable and gallant Friend will pardon me if, without any disrespect to him, I postpone my reply to him on one or two points to a future occasion. The House will agree with me that any cold-blooded arguments may not correspond to his rather vehement rhetoric. The question just alluded to by the honourable Gentleman who preceded me is one, I admit, of great importance. The methods by which the Navy may be popularised in the large manufacturing districts are constantly before the Admiralty. They are at the present moment being examined by a Committee, and I trust that the experiences we are collecting from the Northern districts of the country will be of benefit in securing additions to the Services, especially of artisans and of the higher mechanical ratings, which are so desirable. Of course, it is impossible, as he admits, to make a naval demonstration on land to attract the inland population by the same means as we can secure recruits along the sea coast, but every effort that can be made will be made by the Admiralty and by the present administration to enlarge the methods by which we disseminate the information as to the means of joining the Navy. Now, Mr. Speaker, the De-

bates so far have been unanimous in approval of the programme that has been laid before the House, that it would have been hardly necessary for me to intervene at this stage if it had not been for some questions put by right honourable and honourable Gentlemen opposite. The right honourable Gentleman in his interesting speech, lamented, as I understand, the increase in the Estimates for this year. I understand\him to admit the necessity for them to a greater degree than some other honourable Gentlemen in the House, and I do not know that he desired to question that necessity underlay the dimensions of the Estimates. But he asked for some information as to the reasons upon which our shipbuilding programme was founded. I trust that before I sit down I shall be able to show him that this programme, large though it is, even in comparison with last year—and the expenditure involved by the programme, though greater than that of last year—is one justified by necessity, and by necessity only. And it is because it is necessary that it is presented to the House. Before I come to the question of the programme, I will refer to a question the right honourable Gentleman put as to whether I could give some further explanation than was contained in the First Lord's printed statement as to the reasons for the large increase in the number of officers we are providing for. Sir, that increase is caused, first of all, by the increased number of ships now in commission; and secondly, by the fact that the ships in the Reserve, being older ships, are gradually being replaced by modern ships, with more elaborate machinery and more scientific armaments. This necessitates that in the event of mobilisation we should have at disposal a sufficient number of officers from the active Services to command those ships, and for those reasons we deem it advisable to have the numbers indicated in the First Lord's statement, which will be reached gradually in a certain number of years. The right honourable Baronet asks me how we propose to arrive at the increase in the list of lieutenants. Sir, we propose to reach the numbers indicated in the First Lord's statement with regard to lieu-

find with it. But it seems to me that these naval questions are too much treated in this House as the property of the admirals and the captains and the Members for seaport towns, and that the Navy is regarded too much as a preserve of the seaport towns. I would suggest to the Admiralty that it would be wise, as well as fair, to take systematic means to popularise the Navy among the population of the large manufacturing towns in the north of England. I think the Admiralty cannot be aware how extremely ignorant the population of these towns are as to the means by which they or their sons can enter the Royal Navy. I am frequently consulted by boys and the parents of boys as to how they can get into the Navy. If youths want to go into the Army proper and useful means are taken to afford the information as to how they can go about it. But there are no such means taken in regard to the Navy. The consequence is that these youths are discouraged, and they have not a fair chance of entering on a career which ought to be open to the whole nation. I am quite aware that there is much advantage in habit, in family association, and in inherited liking for the sea. I quite allow that the population of the seaboard towns are more likely to make good sailors than the population of the manufacturing towns. But there are other considerations that ought to weigh in the matter. The love of the sea is not a mere matter of habit, not a mere tradition, but a matter of temperament. In the great manufacturing towns many youths are moved by the thirst for the salt sea, which is a saving grace of our nation: and this love of the sea runs not only in the blood of boys bred by the sea, but runs in the blood of the youths in our manufacturing towns. It is part of the burden of our naval supremacy. Therefore, it would be wise if our naval authorities were to give an opening to those young men who are inspired by a passion for the sea, and who we ought to encourage to join the Navy. Another matter of importance is this: We all know that the conditions of the naval occupation have changed much within the last 50 years. Our ships have become more and more huge masses of machinery, and

Mr. Harwood.

less and less merely white-winged galleons, on board which opportunities are afforded for the display of heroism and the inherited qualities of seamanship. On that ground I beg to call the attention of the authorities to the fact that in the town which I represent there are thousands of the most skilled engineers in the world, and if their sons have not inherited the capacity for seamanship, they have inherited a capacity for workmanship; and it is that capacity which is more and more required in the Navy. If you offered an opening in the Navy to these young men, you would have, as a consequence, a much larger selection from which to pick your engineers and artificers. You may think that you get enough at present, but I hold there is a question of right and of fairness in filling up the Navy. I suggest that the Admiralty should take more systematic methods to make known in all the large centres of population the means which should be employed in securing an entrance into the Navy. It should be as easy for men to ascertain how they can get their sons into the Navy as to get their sons into the Army. It may seem a vulgar suggestion, but you might make use of a naval visit to the manufacturing towns. To increase the recruiting, you send the ships to the seaports, and the sight of the Fleet stirs the patriotism of the young men. We have a canal up to Manchester, but I do not suppose you would send a fleet of men-of-war up that Ship Canal. But you might take the opportunity of sending a company of sailors to march through the streets of the manufacturing towns. There is no more stirring sight in the world than a company of British bluejackets marching in their picturesque uniforms. You must learn to teach the people not merely by written language, but also by appealing to their sense of the dramatic. There is a French saying that a career should be open to all the talents. In the manufacturing towns in the North of England we pay a fair share—indeed, a large proportion—of the expense of the Navy, and we have a right that our sons should have as free access to the Navy as anyone else. And I say that that is not so now, and that it is quite unusual for the sons of manufacturers to go into the Navy. I have been the means of introducing a few, but I found it extremely difficult, because I did not know how to go about it. I hope the authorities will take my suggestion seriously into consideration, and I do so from another motive than that I have alluded to. I believe that you would be wise to encourage more heartily the feeling of attachment to the Navy in the nation. We may want that feeling soon. My own grandfather was press-ganged into the Fleet, and the time may come when you may want to appeal to the national enthusiasm for the Fleet again. It is, therefore, wise and truly patriotic to do everything you can to strengthen the attachment of the nation to the Fleet.

THE SECRETARY TO THE TREASURY (Mr. MACARTNEY, Antrim, S.): My honourable and gallant Friend the Member for Eastbourne has alluded to two or three things of detail which would be more germane to discussion in Committee than in a discussion of this description. My honourable and gallant Friend will pardon me if, without any disrespect to him, I postpone my reply to him on one or two points to a future occasion. The House will agree with me that any cold-blooded arguments may not correspond to his rather vehement rhetoric. The question just alluded to by the honourable Gentleman who preceded me is one, I admit, of great importance. The methods by which the Navy may be popularised in the large manufacturing districts are constantly before the Admiralty. They are at the present moment being examined by a Committee, and I trust that the experiences we are collecting from the Northern districts of the country will be of benefit in securing additions to the Services, especially of artisans and of the higher mechanical ratings, which are so desirable. Of course, it is impossible, as he admits, to make a naval demonstration on land to attract the inland population by the same means as we can secure recruits along the sea coast, but every effort that can be made will be made by the Admiralty and by the present administration to enlarge the methods by which we disseminate the information as to the means of joining the Navy. Now, Mr. Speaker, the De-

VOL. LXVIII.   [FOURTH SERIES.]

bates so far have been unanimous in approval of the programme that has been laid before the House, that it would have been hardly necessary for me to intervene at this stage if it had not been for some questions put by right honourable and honourable Gentlemen opposite. The right honourable Gentleman in his interesting speech, lamented, as I understand, the increase in the Estimates for this year. I understand him to admit the necessity for them to a greater degree than some other honourable Gentlemen in the House, and I do not know that he desired to question that necessity underlay the dimensions of the Estimates. But he asked for some information as to the reasons upon which our shipbuilding programme was founded. I trust that before I sit down I shall be able to show him that this programme, large though it is, even in comparison with last year—and the expenditure involved by the programme, though greater than that of last year—is one justified by necessity, and by necessity only. And it is because it is necessary that it is presented to the House. Before I come to the question of the programme, I will refer to a question the right honourable Gentleman put as to whether I could give some further explanation than was contained in the First Lord's printed statement as to the reasons for the large increase in the number of officers we are providing for. Sir, that increase is caused, first of all, by the increased number of ships now in commission; and secondly, by the fact that the ships in the Reserve, being older ships, are gradually being replaced by modern ships, with more elaborate machinery and more scientific armaments. This necessitates that in the event of mobilisation we should have at disposal a sufficient number of officers from the active Services to command those ships, and for those reasons we deem it advisable to have the numbers indicated in the First Lord's statement, which will be reached gradually in a certain number of years. The right honourable Baronet asks me how we propose to arrive at the increase in the list of lieutenants. Sir, we propose to reach the numbers indicated in the First Lord's statement with regard to lieu.

2 D

tenants by an annual entry three times a year of 65 cadets. This annual entry will supply 195 every year, and entries to that number will be kept up until the year 1904. It will then be possible to reduce the entries to the figure of 126, either by three small annual entries or two annual entries of 63. That number will suffice to give us the total number of lieutenants that it is proposed to get into the Service. Now, Sir, the right honourable Gentleman has asked us whether, in framing our programme for the total new construction for 1899-1900 we have before our view the fact of the slackening off of the French in the construction of battleships, the fact that the rate of building in France is somewhat lower than our own, and the fact that there has been put before Europe the Tsar's proposal with regard to peace. It is hardly necessary for me to assure the House that these facts have been under the consideration of the Admiralty, and that they have materially affected the programme that has been laid before the House ; but I would point out to the right honourable Gentleman that it is not possible for us to regard France and the rate of French contribution only. We have to deal with the condition of things in other countries, with the progress in construction made by them, and we feel ourselves more or less bound—in fact, entirely bound—by the principle of naval construction and the development of naval affairs which was accepted, I believe, by the Administration of which he was a Member, and which has been accepted by the Administration which is now at the Admiralty, and which has been accepted by the House, and, I may say, consistently acted upon in various naval programmes which have been lately placed before the country. Therefore, with regard to the battleship portion of our programme, that has been based upon our knowledge of what has been proposed by other countries. We are perfectly aware of the fact to which he has made allusion, that the French have slackened their building, but, as I have said, consideration of the facts relating to the building of battleships in other countries, and the general feeling which has actuated, not only this Administration, but

Mr. Macartney.

previous Administrations, have led us to consider it necessary for maintaining that position of comparative security, as against the combined strength of two other Powers, to make the proposals with regard to battleships which are contained in the First Lord's statement. The right honourable Gentleman has said, Can we not pause?—a sentiment, a principle of action, which has been objected to by the right honourable Baronet below the gangway. He has pointed out to the right honourable Gentleman that, in fact, we have paused, not once, but twice, in the proposals that we have made with regard to construction. We have adopted the attitude which, I understand, the right honourable Gentleman desired, and pressed upon us ; we have waited, not upon one occasion, but twice, until we had the fullest information with regard to the proposals of other countries, and we have shaped our constructive programme according to the designs which they had laid down. Now, Sir, my honourable and gallant Friend the Member for Yarmouth complained of a passage in the speech of the First Lord of the Admiralty, in which he seemed to think that my right honourable Friend had committed himself to a statement which involved the reduction of the naval power of this country in the event of an agreement of the European Powers without regard to the responsibilities of the Empire at large. My honourable and gallant Friend, I think, misunderstood the words of the First Lord of the Admiralty, and certainly he has attempted to deduce from what my right honourable Friend said an inference which I do not think it properly bears. My right honourable Friend said, " If Europe does not agree, the programme must stand." The honourable and · gallant Member for Yarmouth attempted to infer from that that the converse followed, and that the converse of that proportion was contained in the statement of the First Lord of the Admiralty. Sir, I myself do not believe that my right honourable Friend meant for one moment that such a converse should be deducted from his statement. In fact, if my honourable and gallant Friend will carefully re-read the speech of the First Lord of the Admiralty, he will see that while he attributed great importance to the decision of the European Conference, at the same time he took great pains to point out that the conditions which the Naval Service of this country has to meet, and the responsibilities which fall upon that Service, are totally distinct, and must be considered distinct, from the responsibilities and the conditions which the naval services of other countries are designed to meet. Now, the right honourable Baronet drew attention to the conditions of our armour supply. We pointed out that that supply was not so unsatisfactory this year as it was last year, but still it cannot be considered to be in a satisfactory condition. I regret that I have to agree with him upon that point. The output of the manufacturers has not come up to what is expected from their reputation, but we hope, and we have considerable reason for believing, that in the financial year which is coming on, the result may be much more satisfactory. The armour manufacturers have been able to make considerable strides in the laying down of their plant. I understand that they believe that the output of armour plates will be very largely increased in the early portions of the next financial year. The right honourable Gentleman has alluded to the question of slips, and has hinted that, perhaps, the fact that there were no slips vacant in the early part of the financial year has had some effect upon our programme for new construction for 1899-1900. I do not think that suspicion of the right honourable Gentleman is justified. The retardation in the laying down of two battleships was another example of that desire to pause to see what had been done, what definite action would be taken in the future, by foreign countries before we took any steps ourselves: it is in accordance with our uniform action to maintain an equality without any desire to outship the fleets of other countries. The right honourable Gentleman also drew attention to the progress made in the Naval Reserves, and he has assumed that the number of 12,000 men is the number of the Naval Reserve

available for early mobilisation. That is true to this extent, that we believe that number will be available within 48 hours, and we have made this new provision in order to meet the requirements that may come up within 48 hours, and to relieve the pressure which otherwise would undoubtedly take place in the various ports. He must not take it to mean that that number terminates or concludes the numbers of the Royal Naval Reserve who, we believe, are available for very early service. It is no indication of those whom we are confident are available for service within a week or 10 days. The honourable Member for Gateshead drew attention to one or two other minor points, which, I think, may be dealt with more effectively in Supply, and I have only to assure the House that the Admiralty is as much alive as he is to the necessity for the protection of our coal, and the necessity for constructing docks in other parts of the world than the home waters. These questions are being dealt with now, and in the Estimates which are now before the House he will find that very considerable sums of money are taken both for the establishment of protection for our coal depôts and also for the improvement of the docks that are in existence, and preparations for other docks we have need of. I hope the House will not think that I am making an undue demand upon their generosity if I would ask them now to desire you, Sir, to leave the Chair. All those who are interested in these matters well know that this does not terminate the opportunity of honourable Members for a general discussion, and I think that this afternoon honourable Gentlemen who are interested in the Estimates have had an ample opportunity of bringing forward those questions which are germane to this portion of the Debate, and it would be for the convenience, of Naval experts in the House and of the House generally if we were now permitted to go into Committee, and to deal there with other questions, not, perhaps, of the same importance, but which deserve attention.

*MR. CHANNING: I do not mean to stand for more than a few minutes between the House and the Committee of Supply, but I do think that the statement which has fallen from the right honourable Gentleman the Secretary to the Admiralty is of sufficient importance to be noted at once from this side of the House. The interpretation, apparently, which has been placed upon the speech of the First Lord of the Admiralty, that this enormous increase of the Estimates of practically £3,000,000 was, to a certain extent, conditional on the action which the European Powers might arrive at in consequence of the Conference initiated by the Tsar—that inference from his speech is apparently disowned by his present representative in this Debate. We were told that if Europe does not agree the programme must stand, but we are not to infer the converse of that proposition, that if Europe does agree to disarmament there shall be a reduction of these enormous Estimates. Now, I submit, Mr. Speaker, that that is a very serious modification of the important and very weighty speech of the First Lord of the Admiralty, which created so deep an impression on the Press and on the country the other day. It is so important that I think honourable Members on this side of the House are justified in protesting against the attitude of Her Majesty's Government as formulated by the Secretary to the Admiralty in his present speech. It practically amounts to this, that we are committed to go ahead full steam in this principle of expansion of the Navy, that this policy has practically no limits whatsoever. Now, Sir, I was reminded this afternoon of the history of this question of the expansion of the Estimates. It will be familiar to many of those who have followed these proposals, that in the years 1887 and 1888 the noble Lord who now is Secretary for India, and whose administration of the Admiralty I always look back to with great admiration, for it was under his administration that the shortening of the time of shipbuilding and the cheapening of production of our great ships was developed, and therefore a net sum saved to the country, and the efficiency of the Navy greatly increased—I say that though I admire these features of his administration in

Mr. Channing.

those years, I have always thought that the policy which he was led into, perhaps by others, in 1889, of displaying an enormous programme—21 millions of money and 70 or 80 ships suddenly thrown in the face of every Power in the world—that was a serious blunder in the tactics of dealing with this great question. Now, Sir, the policy of this country with regard to naval shipbuilding, the policy of this country with regard to maintaining the supremacy of England upon the seas, and guarding the seas all over, and enabling trade and commerce and food to reach this country in any quantity—that is a policy which will always receive the warmest support on this side of the House. But it is a policy which can be most effectively carried out, not by these vast programmes and by these enormous sums of money thrown in the face of other Powers, not by provocative proposals which only result in enormous programmes and immense outlay by other Powers—the principle of our policy should be wise self-control in these matters. Well, these matters should be considered seriously and prudently, and the man who suddenly flaunts enormous programmes in the face of those with whom he wishes to be at peace, programmes provocative and aggressive against those Powers, is not adopting the surest and most certain way of achieving his result with the lowest expenditure in men and resources, and of placing himself in a stronger position than his opponents. Sir Robert Peel, whose "Letters" are now in the Library, in reply to the alarmist suggestions which were made to him in the time of his great Administration, deprecated this policy of enormous and constant preparations in the face of the enemy; he thought that it was likely to provoke similar aggressions on the other side. "It appears to me," he replied to the Duke of Wellington, "that the proper way of maintaining our relative ascendency over other Powers is to be quietly and unostentatiously doing what is necessary," instead of making a display of all these vast and gigantic preparations. Ever since the great blunder which was committed in 1889 of that gigantic programme which was then instituted, in every country throughout the world this tendency to these enormous schemes of armaments has been developed, copying the fatal example of this country. On account of the rapidity with which ships can be turned out, and the effectiveness of the designs of this country, we have the whip hand of every country in the world with regard to the building of ships, and with regard to the types of fighting ships; and therefore the true policy would be not to fill out these bad and these gigantic and preposterous Estimates, but to quietly, year after year, go on building such ships as are necessary without these programmes. I am not sure that this aspect of the question has been discussed on the floor of the House, but I have often wished that this duty might be committed to half a dozen Members of both Front Benches of the House who are thoroughly versed in this subject, and who might be given *carte blanche* to build ships that are necessary, without this flaunting of our strength in the face of Europe and these discussions on the floor of the House. The speech of the First Lord of the Admiralty the other day seemed to foreshadow that we were not only to keep up an equality with two Powers—France and Russia—but in his calculations were introduced for the first time the forces which six Powers could place upon the seas, and apparently that is to be the new standard or measure of honourable Members opposite with regard to the responsibilities of this country. The honourable Member who spoke from this side of the House spoke about popularising the Navy, and I am sure I heartily agree with him. I think the Navy cannot be too popular in this country. I represent an inland Division, and I venture to say the Navy is as popular there as in any seaport town. But, at the same time, I do not think the Navy is likely to be popularised if it is carried on in this extravagant and over-lavish manner, and I think the wisest plan would be not to carry such extravagant Estimates as we have this year, but slowly and quietly to just keep ahead, as we easily can with our ship-building plant, of other Powers, and not to go on with these foolish and provocative programmes any more.

Question put—

"That Mr. Speaker do now leave the Chair.".

Agreed to.

Navy Estimates, 1899-1900.
Considered in Committee.

[Mr. A. O'CONNOR (Donegal, E.) in the Chair.]

(In the Committee.)

Motion made, and Question proposed—

"That 110,640 men and boys be employed for the Sea and Coast Guard Services for the year ending on the 31st day of March 1900, including 18,505 Royal Marines."

Motion made, and Question proposed—

"That 106,640 men and boys be employed for the said Service."—(*Mr. Labouchere.*)

MR. LABOUCHERE (Northampton): Mr. O'Connor, I regret that the First Lord of the Admiralty is not here. I regret it on the general ground that I understand he is not well, and on the particular ground that I have a great belief in the right honourable Gentleman as a financier, and I think I should be able to convert him, were he here, into a doctrine of very different expenditure in regard to the Navy. Now, Sir, in 1850 Lord Palmerston was Prime Minister. At that time a Resolution was brought in the House and passed to the following effect—

"That he has maintained the honour and dignity of the country in times of unexampled difficulty."

Lord Russell spoke in that Debate, which was the Pacific Debate, and he said that Lord Palmerston was not a Minister of Austria, or France, or Russia, but that he was Minister of England. And the only reason Sir R. Peel said that he would not vote in favour of the Resolution was that he considered it would be some slur, if he did so, on Lord Aberdeen, who had been Sir Robert Peel's Foreign Secretary, and, therefore, he declined to vote for it. I mention this in order to show that Lord Palmerston was what would be called at the present time an exceedingly strong Jingo. What was the amount of our expenditure upon armaments in the year 1850? The Army cost £8,600,000; the Navy, £6,900,000; the total was £15,500,000. Sir, at that time the Navy had calls upon it precisely as large as at the present time. We considered that we were defended against all probabities of invasion, that we were safe in regard to our carrying trade, that we could maintain our communications with our Colonies and India—and, moreover, a very large amount of this £6,900,000 was spent upon the Slave Squadron, which the abolition of slavery at present on the high sea has rendered unnecessary. By 1884 the Navy had run up to £10,000,000. In the years before 1884 the average cost of the Navy was from £8,000,000 to £9,000,000 and £10,000,000. In 1884 there was a naval craze, for these naval crazes are recurring crazes, and in 1887 the cost of the Navy had gone up from this £9,000,000 or £10,000,000 to £13,200,000. Well, Sir, the present First Lord of the Admiralty was then in the Ministry, and he expressed his views upon the matter. He said—

"I have reason to hope"—

this was in 1887, after the rise from £10,000,000 to £13,000,000 in three years—

"I have reason to hope that the time is not far distant when the Naval Estimates will not require to be swollen by exceptional items such as those which have fallen so heavily upon the taxpayers during the last two or three years."

Sir, this anticipation has not been verified. At that time there were alarmists, just as there are at the present time, and from 1887 to 1894 the Navy averaged £15,000,000 sterling. Since 1894 it has gone up by leaps and bounds, and we are now spending—taking the Estimates for the coming year, and including the naval works which we are called upon to provide—£28,000,000 upon the Navy, an increase over 1895— I am only taking so late as 1895—of £7,500,000, and an increase upon the past year, when we complained that we thought the Naval Estimates were unduly swollen, of £2,816,000. Taking the Supplementary Estimates which, no doubt, will be proposed, I do not question that the Navy next year will cost us £29,000,000. Sir, the right honourable Gentleman the First Lord of the Admiralty did not, as he did in 1887, express the hope or the belief that the cost of the Navy would go down. On the contrary, he hinted—and I think he was

Mr. Labouchere.

perfectly right, in the present policy that he has adopted—that the cost of the Navy would go up. Now, Sir, what is the main plea upon which this portentous and enormous increase is justified? The right honourable Gentleman now the Secretary for India, when he was First Lord of the Admiralty, said that we must be on an equality with any two Powers. We have gone very far beyond that at the present time. But we are very often told that one of the reasons why we ought to expend money is because France and Russia are expending money, and at least we ought to be on an equality with France and Russia combined. I wonder if honourable Gentlemen on either of these two Benches have ever taken the trouble to look into the real cost of the navies of France and Russia. In 1884 the cost of the French navy was £7,500,000. At the present time it is £12,000,000. The cost of the Russian navy in 1884 was £3,500,000. The cost at the present time is £7,000,000. That is to say, whilst since 1884 we have increased expenditure on our Navy by £18,000,000, the united increase of the navies of France and Russia has only been £8,000,000.

*SIR E. ASHMEAD-BARTLETT: Will the honourable Member give us the percentage?

MR. LABOUCHERE: I do not know what the honourable Member means. I seldom do know what he means. It was argued at the commencement of this naval craze that we had been obliged to increase our Navy owing to the increase on the part of Russia, but, as a matter of fact, their increases have been due to our increases. We are putting the cart before the horse when we say that our increases have been due to theirs. I was looking recently at the "Navy Annual" of Lord Brassey, in which he gives a relative statement of the number of ships that have been built by France and this country. Anyone who studies that statement will see that invariably our increase has preceded the increase on the part of France. Take any two or three years, and you will see that that is so. You will see that the increases in the navies of France and Russia have been entirely due to our increases and not *vice versa*. With regard to the recent contemplated increase by Russia, on which the First Lord of the Admiralty dwelt so long, that has followed the very great increase which has taken place during the past four years in our Navy, and it must be remembered that the increase is not necessarily in any sort of way against us. Russia in the last year or two has obtained a port on the Pacific. Russia is faced by Japan, which has become a great naval Power, and it is easy to understand that under these circumstances Russia considers it necessary to have a certain number of ships in that quarter of the world able to cope with Japan, and to prevent Japan entirely having her own way. When we come to the men, the relations between the two countries are still more remarkable. In France, since 1884, the number has been 38,000, and that number has remained stationary. In 1888 Russia had 29,000 men, and now she has 37,100. In 1889 we had 64,405 men, and in the coming year we shall have 110,000 men. It must be remembered, too, that the Reserve force, which amounts to 37,000 men, is not included in Vote A. Not more than 2,000 of these are employed in the Navy, and therefore we always have this Reserve force to fall back upon in addition to the sailors we have in active service. The increase in regard to men of France and Russia since 1888 has been 8,000, while our increase has been 45,000. In order that the Committee may clearly realise what the increase has been since we have had the honour of having the present First Lord of the Admiralty in office, I may point out that our increase in ships since 1895, taking the ships employed on our Foreign Squadron, and in the Channel Squadron, has been 50 per cent., and our increase in tonnage has been 100 per cent. Last year there was an increase of about 5,000 men to the Navy, but taking the last few years the average increase has been about 4,000. At present we are asked to vote a further increase of 4,000. Now, the Committee must remember that the real cost of the Navy consists to a very great extent in the payments to the men, and the expense of feeding them, and so on, and eventually pensioning them. The right honourable Gentleman the First Lord of the Admiralty admits himself at the present time that we are not seeking to be superior to any two Powers, because one of the pleas put forward by him for the increase he asks us to allow was that the six Great Powers are now building a very large tonnage of ships. What does this amount to? It comes to this, that we are competing in men and ships against the entire world. To-day it will be Russia which will build ships, to-morrow it may be France, the next day Japan, and then the United States, and we are actually engaged in the impossible task of seeking to outbuild the entire world. (Cheers.) Honourable Members, in cheering this statement, are giving themselves away and confirming me in my opinion. I say that is an impossible task, and one which spells ruin. It is very often said that we are richer than any other nation. As a matter of fact, we are not richer than the United States. We are not richer than France and Russia combined. As the Leader of the Opposition very well said the other day, we go about jingling our money in the faces of other people and defying them. I call this policy of swagger a most foolish and insane policy. The navy of each Power is not excessive for the requirements of that Power, but when you take the navies of all the six Powers naturally they are larger than our own Navy, and yet, because these Powers build ships in accordance with their own requirements, we are called upon to outbuild them. I should like to know why it is that we are asked to play this insane game of " beggar-my-neighbour " against the world. One of the reasons for this policy is the protection of our carrying trade. We are really under the impression that we can carry it on in war as in peace, if we have a sufficiently large Navy. I contend that that is perfectly impossible, and has never occurred under any circumstances in the world's history when two Powers have been at war. The vast proportion of the carrying trade is carried by neutrals and not by belligerents. We are told that we are only paying a modest little insurance to insure the carrying trade against injury, but what are the facts? In the last 25 years the insurance has gone up 100 per cent., while our imports and exports have only gone up 50 per cent. Then it is said that if we have not the mastery of the sea we should be starved, but Lord Wolseley, who is a practical man of war, has said, speaking at the Royal United Service Institute in 1896, that it is absolutely impossible to cut this country off from the supplies of wheat it requires, even if the Fleets of the entire world were to endeavour to do so. On that point the expert opinion of Lord Wolseley is good enough for me. It is further said that it is absolutely necessary to keep up communication between our Colonies and this country, and between this country and the East. Undoubtedly that is so, but no one will tell me that in order to effect that it is necessary to have such an enormous Fleet as we have at the present time. All these are mere pleas and excuses in order to have a large Navy. The real object is to obtain absolute supremacy over the sea, and to annex to the British Empire the entire oceans of the world. We seem to have the idea that the sea belongs absolutely to us. Foreign countries have colonies, and I presume they are anxious to maintain communication with the colonies, and that their trade, though it may be smaller than ours, should not be put an end to; yet they hold their trade and their colonies entirely at our good will. Europe at the present moment is a great factory, and sells its goods to all the nations of the earth; and I ask the Committee, is it likely that all the nations will agree to this doctrine of our being absolute masters of the sea? I ask whether we should agree to it if it were put forward by France, Russia, or Germany? We have always shown ourselves against the domination of any one Power. Half the wars in which we have been engaged have been to maintain a balance of power, and the Under Secretary of State for Foreign Affairs, in addressing a meeting on Saturday last, said that the policy of Her Majesty's Government was to

Mr. Labouchere.

maintain a balance of power. It is not a balance of power when you are absolute masters of the world. We warred with Spain to prevent her having absolute mastery of the sea; we warred with France because we did not wish France to be dominant, and we were for a time at war with Napoleon. But what was the dream of Napoleon compared with the dream of Her Majesty's Government? Napoleon simply wanted to be master in Europe, and the countries united against him and put an end to his object; but at the present time we want to be masters, not only in Europe, but over the whole world. We appear to be under the impression that foreign Powers are almost criminal if they protest against this doctrine. I do not think it likely the Government will obtain the assent of the Powers at the Disarmament Conference to the condition announced by the First Lord of the Treasury, because such assent would amount to a recognition and admission of the existing state of things which give us the mastery of the ocean. The right honourable Gentleman alluded to what had recently happened in regard to Fashoda. The country, indeed, was calm about Fashoda, not for the reason alleged by the First Lord of the Treasury—the preparedness of the Navy—but because the country was perfectly convinced that when it came to the real point two great civilised nations were not going to war over a miserable, swampy bog somewhere in the middle of Africa. The right honourable Gentleman illustrated the advantages of these large Estimates by saying that there was no fall in securities. Timorous capital is at the bottom of all this, and the country is called upon to pay this enormous sum for precautions in order that these people may not lose any of their money. The right honourable Gentleman the First Lord of the Admiralty said, practically, that it was a good thing for the country to have a war expenditure in time of peace. As my honourable Friend behind me said just now, Sir Robert Peel always combatted that view. There were alarmists in those days, and Sir Robert Peel always repudiated the doctrine that if you wish peace you must prepare for war. He did not allow himself, like the present Government, to be led away by jingoes. Again, what did Mr. Gladstone do? He despised all these taunts, and simply took off taxes, which is far better than to swell Naval and Army Estimates. Great armaments tend to war and produce the military spirit. What caused the trouble with reference to Fashoda? It was caused by our declining discussion and arbitration, and insisting upon an ultimatum. The incident of Fashoda must be an object lesson to the world as to the use we make of our naval supremacy in telling other Powers that they must accept the law as it is imposed upon them. - It will be said, are we to accept the possible risks of combinations of great naval Powers against us? I say we are to accept those risks, most unquestionably. We always have, and, what is more, all nations have. Take the case of the Continental Powers of Europe. Each Continental Power has a large army, but, supposing each country were to say that, although they had an army equal to any one Power, yet they might be attacked by two or three Powers, and it was, therefore, necessary to have an army sufficiently large to compete with the combined armies of two or three Powers, what would be the result? Why, neither country would get an advantage over the other. This is precisely what we are doing in regard to our naval armaments. I confess I am surprised that a man of the financial intelligence and ability of the First Lord of the Admiralty can ever lend himself to carry out a scheme which is in itself absurd, ridiculous, and ruinous. In 1874 the right honourable Gentleman the present First Lord of the Admiralty held the same appointment in the Government of that day, and it certainly must surprise him to think that the expenditure of the Navy has been doubled since then. What would the right honourable Gentleman have said if anyone had told him then that the day would come when, instead of sitting as the colleague of Mr. Gladstone on the Liberal Front Bench, he would sit as a Minister on the Conservative Front Bench, and would propose Estimates amounting to

Mr. Labouchere.

£29,000,000? In the words of a Hebrew king when taunted he would have replied, "Is thy servant a dog that he should do these things"? The Navy, I admit, is popular. I myself am in favour of a good strong Navy, but when we have these perpetual increases, and when we are told that millions more must be added, I think the time has arrived when we who represent the taxpayers of this country should raise our voice in protest, all the more as the principle on which these increases are based must in the nature of things lead to further increases. Honourable Members on this side have protested outside the House against the enormous cost of armaments. Surely we ought not to protest outside only, but ought to fight the question inside. If we do not oppose this expenditure now we shall be told, when the Budget is brought forward, that we voted for this expenditure, and that as money does not fall from Heaven we must pay for it out of our own pockets. We do not wish for a reduction of home expenditure. We rather desire that it should be increased. We want sums to be voted for pensions, and in many ways for the betterment of the condition of the working classes. The Education Vote has gone up by £7,000,000. No doubt we object to the incidence in regard to the collection of the Education Rate, but I do not think there is one honourable Member who would rise in his place in this House and say that he desires the sum total expended on education to be reduced. The Telegraphs and the Post Office have caused a further large expenditure, but we would rather see that increased than decreased, because a large portion of the increase has been due to fair salaries being paid to working men. We are now asked for a further increase of expenditure on armaments, and it is perfectly well known that we have come to the end of our tether. The Chancellor of the Exchequer has seized everything he can lay his hands on, and is going to ask the House for further taxes for increased expenditure on the Navy. I, for my part, am a logical person. I have always been against increases in the Army and Navy, and have voted against whether my vote was popular or not. When the Army Estimates came on this year I moved a reduction; when the Uganda Vote came up I voted for a reduction; when the Vote came up with regard to the West Coast of Africa I voted against it. No one can say, therefore, that I am not logical, and I intend to be logical now. I am not asking the House to vote for a reduction in the enormous Estimates of the present year. I am simply asking them to say that the expenditure of this year is sufficient for our requirements, that we want the money for other matters, and to vote against the increased expenditure proposed for the coming year. In 1895 Mr. Gladstone wrote a letter protesting against the expenditure on the Navy and the Army, and urging that every man who had the true interests of the country at heart should do his best to effect a reduction in the amount. What did the Estimates amount to then? The total was £17,000,000 in that year; now it has gone up to £28,000,000. Surely if we believe in the principles laid down by Mr. Gladstone, if we admire Mr. Gladstone as one of the greatest Ministers and financiers of the age, we ought, when the expenditure has risen in four years to so great an amount, to declare by our votes that we will not sanction the proposed further increase, and will not go one farthing beyond the expenditure of the present year. I beg to move the reduction standing in my name. In order to make round figures I will move the reduction of Vote A by £4,000.

Mr. DILLON: I rise for the purpose of supporting the reduction moved by the honourable Member for Northampton. I share to the fullest degree the views he has expressed, and I entirely agree that it will be idle for us to oppose, as I trust we shall oppose, any proposal for increased taxation, unless we vote against the Estimates on which the increase of taxation will be based. I listened with very great interest to the speech which was made by the First Lord of the Admiralty when he was unfolding the naval programme, and he used one very extraordinary expression, which I confess I could not

Mr. Labouchere.

thoroughly understand. Although he admitted that these Estimates were gigantic, he said the Government were only carrying out what they believed, and knew, to be the mandate of the British nation. He then went on to explain what he conceived to be the mandate of the British nation, but he did not make his meaning clear. He said these Estimates were based upon a careful survey of the shipbuilding programme of six Great Powers. I recollect when this mad campaign commenced of building in avowed competition with certain Foreign Powers, that the formula which we heard laid down over and over again *ad nauseam* was that the safety of England depended upon keeping the Navy up to a standard superior to any possible combination between two Great Powers. That was what we then understood to be the mandate of the Conservative Government and of those who went in for the recent great increases in the British fleet. Then I noticed in succeeding years that certain individuals, not the responsible Ministers, began to talk about the necessity of being equal to the possible combiation of three Great Powers. But this year the First Lord of the Admiralty, in his statement, declared, for the first time, that he had in view the policy of six Great Powers. I asked the right honourable Gentleman to mention the names of the six Powers whose naval programme he had taken into consideration when framing the Estimates. The first Power he mentioned was the United States. What, then, has become of the Anglo-American alliance? The second Power he mentioned was Japan, and we are, forsooth, in this wild career, now brought to this position, that we are called upon to base the shipbuilding programme of this country on the naval programme of the United States of America, Japan, and the four great European naval countries. That, to my mind, is the language of insanity, and when I hear, for the first time in the House of Commons, a responsible Minister deliberately allude to the shipbuilding of the United States as an element which must be seriously taken into consideration in framing the Naval Estimates of this country, I cannot help expressing the greatest astonishment. I think the day will come when British statesmen will regret that they have ever induced the United States to enter into the mad policy of competing armaments, for the United States have the resources to equip in a few years, if they chose, a navy far superior to the Navy of this country. The First Lord of the Admiralty was extremely emphatic in saying that England was in no way to blame for these increases which were forced upon us by the action of other Great Powers. Well, Sir, that is not the result of my observations. It is far more true to say that the increases of Russia and France were forced upon them by the increase of this country. This enormous development of naval armaments had its origin in Great Britain, and when the statement of the honourable Member for Northampton, that England now claimed to be the mistress of the sea as against the whole world, is loudly cheered in the House of Commons, I think that shows that a species of madness has taken hold of honourable Members on the other side of this House. I cannot conceive anything more likely to bring misery and suffering on the people of this country than that a challenge of that kind should be thrown out in the face of the world, and that the taxpayers should be intolerably burdened in making good that challenge. It is not only an impossible task, but it is an outrage in view of your expressed desire to take part in the Disarmament Conference; it is an outrage on the whole of civilised humanity that such a spirit should be avowed and openly boasted of in a country that professes to love peace. We are told by the First Lord of the Treasury that these naval armaments have nothing whatever to do with the Foreign Policy of this country. He stated the other day that while he was prepared to admit that the increase in the Army might be accounted for, at least to a large extent, by the seizure of the Soudan and the extension of the Empire in Africa and elsewhere, the naval armaments could in nowise be shown to depend upon the Foreign Policy of this country. That is a doctrine which I think flies in the face of the facts of the situation. Any country which adopts an attitude of aggression towards other nations, any country which places itself in the position which England has taken up in regard to the seizing and grabbing of all the good portions of the earth, and then deliberately throws down a challenge to the rest of the world and declares herself mistress of the sea, cannot say with any truth—and it is idle for any Minister who is a party to such a policy to declare—that the necessity of these enormously increased Estimates has no reference to the Foreign Policy of this country. So long as Ministers responsible for the policy of England adopt an attitude of aggression, and go about the country bragging that England is quite independent of the rest of the world, and means to be mistress of the sea, the inevitable consequence is this terrible increase of expenditure, which I shall be prepared to take every opportunity to oppose. It is a most absurd and preposterous doctrine to say that the more you increase the Army and the Navy the more you take safeguards for peace. That is against the established experience of mankind. It is against all the teaching of history. The universal teaching of history is that large armies and large navies have a tendency to drag nations into war. Therefore, I am convinced that these enormous Votes of money, and these great increases of men for the Army and Navy, are not making for peace, but are making in reality for war. For these reasons I am determined to oppose every single increase in the Estimates of the Army and Navy. If I did not oppose them on the general ground of policy, I should oppose them as an Irish Member, because I think it is useless for us to raise the question of the over-taxation of our country if we do not make an attack on the enormous expenditure on the Navy and Army, from which we obtain no sort of benefit whatever. We have little or no share in your trade, and none of this money is spent in our country. Therefore these Votes are specially Votes which we are bound to oppose, because they increase enormously the difficulty of giving to Ireland that financial relief which, later on, we shall be claiming, and because they are Votes for a Service which does not do one atom of good for Ireland.

THE FIRST LORD OF THE TREASURY: 1 gather that the honourable Gentleman who has just sat down conceived himself to be making a reply to some statements which he assumed had been made by my right honourable Friend the First Lord of the Admiralty. It is evident, from the remarks of the honourable Gentleman, that he did not carefully listen to that speech, or else he only imperfectly understood it, because he informed the House that the conclusion he had drawn from my right honourable Friend's statement was that we were now desiring to raise the scale of our naval expenditure so as to meet any six Powers of the world that might be selected ; and in especial that we had in view the meeting of the growing naval power of the United States. I do not know whether the honourable Gentleman seriously believes that any .such programme was ever issued by my right honourable Friend, or that any Government—either the present Government or any of its predecessors, or any of its conceivable successors—could ever put out so insane a policy. The honourable Gentleman must know perfectly well that my right honourable Friend deliberately based the policy which he asked the House to accept upon the accepted principle that the naval power of this country should not be less than that which is necessary to meet two Powers, and not the six Powers to which the honourable Gentleman alluded.

MR. DILLON: The right honourable Gentleman stated that this programme was based on a careful consideration of the building by the six Great Powers.

THE FIRST LORD OF THE TREASURY: Certainly ; and what Naval Lord would not carefully consider the naval programme of every Great Power which concerns itself with building fleets? But the honourable Gentleman, if he meant serious criticism, must have known perfectly well that the naval programme proposed by the Government had no such insane object as that which he states, and was not

Mr. Dillon.

framed on the frantic scale of expenditure which he would ;suggest. Our schemes and our ambitions are far more modest. They are the same schemes and the same ambitions, based on the same principles, as animated ourselves in previous years and our predecessors before we came into office. There are critics— the right honourable Baronet opposite among them—who think we ought to aim at a higher standard than to deal with the possible combination of two navies. But, at all events, we, who are far more modest than the right honourable Baronet, have not laid ourselves open to the reproach which the honourable Gentleman, for reasons which I am perfectly unable to conjecture, has thought fit to launch against us. I believe that in this matter there is really no difference of opinion in the House, and I do not think that any Gentleman is prepared to get up in his place and say we ought to arrange our programme upon a scale which would make us unable to meet the combined attack of any two Powers. If that be so, and if I have rightly gauged the opinion of all quarters of the House, including, I may even hope, the honourable Gentleman who has just sat down, I trust that this Debate, which is essentially upon that principle, will not be unnecessarily prolonged, and that, if we are agreed upon the *minimum*, at all events, of what our Navy should be, we should be permitted to proceed to the discussion of details, and that we should be allowed to take a Division on the honourable Gentleman's Motion before we separate to-night.

*MR. KEARLEY: I do not desire to prolong the Debate. I only wish to ask the right honourable Gentleman if, after this Vote is taken, the discussion will be permitted to be general again?

THE FIRST LORD OF THE TREASURY: Yes.

*MR. WEIR (Ross and Cromarty): I have always been in favour of maintaining the Navy in the highest state of efficiency, and I have hitherto voted with the Government; but I think matters have now arrived at such a pass when we must cry "Halt!" I do not desire to give a silent vote on this question, and I merely rise to lodge a most emphatic protest against the continued increase in the expenditure on armaments.

Question put—

"That 106,640 men and boys be employed for the said Service."—*(Mr. Labouchere.)*

The Committee divided—Ayes, 19; Noes, 147.—(Division List No. 40.)

AYES.

Allison, Robert Andrew
Barlow, John Emmott
Burt, Thomas
Caldwell, James
Channing, Francis Allston
Donelan, Captain A.
Healy, Timothy M. (N. Louth)
Hedderwick, Thomas Chas. H.

Kilbride, Denis
Lawson, Sir Wilfrid (Cumbrlnd.)
Macaleese, Daniel
Roberts, John Bryn (Eifion)
Sullivan, Donal (Westmeath)
Tanner, Charles Kearns
Wallace, Robert (Edinburgh)
Weir, James Galloway

Whittaker, Thomas Palmer
Williams, John Carvell (Notts.)
Wilson, Henry J. (York, W.R.)

TELLERS FOR THE AYES—
    Mr. Labouchere and Mr.
    Dillon.

NOES.

Acland-Hood, Capt. Sir Alex. F.
Allan, William (Gateshead)
Allhusen, Augustus Henry Eden
Atkinson, Rt. Hon. John
Baker, Sir John
Balfour, Rt. Hn. A. J. (Manc'r.)
Balfour, Rt Hn Gerald W. (Leeds)
Banbury, Frederick George
Bartley, George C. T.
Barton, Dunbar Plunket
Beach, Rt. Hn. Sir M. H. (Bristol)
Beaumont, Wentworth C. B.
Bemrose, Sir Henry Howe
Bentinck, Lord Henry C.
Bethell, Commander
Bigwood, James
Bill, Charles
Blundell, Colonel Henry
Bond, Edward
Bowles, T. Gibson (King's Lynn)
Brodrick, Rt. Hon. St. John
Burdett-Coutts, W.
Butcher, John George
Cecil, Lord Hugh (Greenwich)
Chaloner, Captain R. G. W.
Chamberlain, J. Austen (Worc.)
Chaplin, Rt. Hon. Henry
Charrington, Spencer
Clough, Walter Owen
Coghill, Douglas Harry
Collings, Rt. Hon. Jesse
Colomb, Sir John Chas. Ready
Colston, Chas. Edw. H. Athole
Colville, John
Compton, Lord Alwyne
Cook, Fred Lucas (Lambeth)
Cornwallis, Fiennes Stanley W.
Cubitt, Hon. Henry
Curzon, Viscount
Dalkeith, Earl of
Dalrymple, Sir Charles
Davenport, W. Bromley-
Dilke, Rt. Hon. Sir Charles
Disraeli, Coningsby Ralph
Dorington, Sir John Edward
Douglas, Rt. Hon. A. Akers-
Douglas, Charles M. (Lanark)
Doxford, William Theodore
Duncombe, Hon. Hubert V.
Egerton, Hon. A. de Tatton

Fardell, Sir T. George
Field, Admiral (Eastbourne)
Finch, George H.
Finlay, Sir Robert Bannatyne
Fisher, William Hayes
Fison, Frederick William
Folkestone, Viscount
Foster, Colonel (Lancaster)
Garfit, William
Gedge, Sydney
Goldsworthy, Major-General
Gordon, Hon. John Edward
Gorst, Rt. Hn. Sir John Eldon
Goschen, George J. (Sussex)
Gray, Ernest (West Ham)
Green, Walford D. (Wedn'bry.)
Gretton, John
Greville, Hon. Ronald
Gull, Sir Cameron
Hanbury, Rt. Hn. Robert Wm.
Hare, Thomas Leigh
Heath, James
Helder, Augustus
Hermon-Hodge, Robt. Trotter
Hill, Sir Edwd. Stock (Bristol)
Hubbard, Hon. Evelyn
Hutchinson, Capt. G.W. Grice-
Johnston, William (Belfast)
Johnstone, Heywood (Sussex)
Kearley, Hudson E.
Kemp, George
Kennaway, Rt. Hn. Sir John H.
Kenyon, James
King, Sir Henry Seymour
Lafone, Alfred
Lawrence, Sir E. Durning-(Corn.
Lees, Sir Elliott (Birkenhead)
Leigh-Bennett, Henry Currie
Llewellyn, Evan H. (Somerset)
Long, Rt. Hn. Walter (L'pool)
Lopes, Henry Yarde Buller
Loyd, Archie Kirkman
Macartney, W. G. Ellison
Macdona, John Cumming
Maclure, Sir John William
Malcolm, Ian
Middlemore, Jno. Throgmorton
More, Robt. Jasper (Shropshire)
Morley, Charles (Breconshire)
Morrell, George Herbert

Muntz, Philip A.
Murray, Rt. Hn A. Graham (Bute
Myers, William Henry
Nicholson, William Graham
Nicol, Donald Ninian
Nussey, Thomas Willans
Orr-Ewing, Charles Lindsay
Parkes, Ebenezer
Pearson, Sir Weetman D.
Pease, Herb. Pike (Darlington)
Penn, John
Phillpotts, Captain Arthur
Pirie, Duncan V.
Platt-Higgins, Frederick
Powell, Sir Francis Sharp
Provand, Andrew Dryburgh
Purvis, Robert
Richardson, Sir Thos. (Hartlep'l)
Ritchie, Rt. Hn. Chas. Thomson
Rothschild, Hn. Lionel Walter
Royds, Clement Molyneux
Russell, T. W. (Tyrone)
Ryder, John Herbert Dudley
Simeon, Sir Barrington
Smith, Hn. W. F. D. (Strand)
Stanley, Edw. Jas. (Somerset)
Stanley, Lord (Lancs.)
Stock, James Henry
Strauss, Arthur
Strutt, Hn. Charles Hedley
Talbot, Lord E. (Chichester)
Talbot, Rt. Hn. J.G. (Oxf. Univ.)
Thomas, David Alf. (Merthyr)
Thornton, Percy M.
Tollemache, Henry James
Ure, Alexander
Valentia, Viscount
Webster, Sir R. E. (I. of W.)
Whitmore, Charles Algernon
Williams, Jos. Powell (Birm.)
Willox, Sir John Archibald
Wodehouse, Rt. Hn. E.R. (Bath)
Woodhouse, Sir J.T. (Huddersf'd
Wortley, Rt. Hn. C. B. Stuart-
Wylie, Alexander
Wyvill, Marmaduke D'Arcy
Young, Commander (Berks, E.)

TELLERS FOR THE NOES—
    Sir William Walrond and
    Mr. Anstruther.

Original Question again proposed.

And, it being after Midnight, and objection being taken to Further Proceeding, the Chairman left the Chair to make his Report to the House.

Committee report Progress; to sit again this day.

———

REPORT OF SUPPLY.

———

SUPPLY [10TH MARCH].

Resolutions reported—

CIVIL SERVICES AND REVENUE DEPARTMENTS (SUPPLEMENTARY ESTIMATES), 1898-9.

CLASS V.

"1. That a Supplementary sum, not exceeding £256,000, be granted to Her Majesty, to defray the Charge which will come in course of payment during the year ending on the 31st day of March 1899, for a Grant in Aid of the Expenses of the British Protectorates in Uganda and in Central and East Africa."

CLASS II.

"2. That a Supplementary sum, not exceeding £2,400, be granted to Her Majesty, to defray the Charge which will come in course of payment during the year ending on the 31st day of March 1899, for the Salaries and Expenses of the Department of Her Majesty's Secretary of State for the Colonies."

CLASS V.

"3. That a Supplementary sum, not exceeding £139,425, be granted to Her Majesty, to defray the Charge which will come in course of payment during the year ending on the 31st day of March 1899, for sundry Colonial Services, including certain Grants in Aid."

CLASS VI.

"4. That a Supplementary sum, not exceeding £517, be granted to Her Majesty, to defray the Charge which will come in course of payment during the year ending on the 31st day of March 1899, for a Grant in Aid of the local cost of maintenance of Pauper Lunatics, Ireland."

CIVIL SERVICES (EXCESS), 1897-8.

"5. That a sum, not exceeding £1 5s. 1d., be granted to Her Majesty, to make good an Excess on the Grant for the Public Record Office for the year ended on the 31st day of March 1898."

NAVY (SUPPLEMENTARY).

"6. That a Supplementary sum, not exceeding £350,000, be granted to Her Majesty, to defray the Charge which will come in course of payment during the year ending on the 31st day of March, 1899, for additional Expenditure on the following Navy Services, viz.:—

	£
Vote 2. Victualling and Clothing for the Navy...	144,000
Vote 8. Shipbuilding, Repairs, Maintenance, etc.:—Sec. 2. Materiel	128,000
Vote 9. Naval Armaments ...	78,000
Total ... ...£350,000 "	

ARMY (ORDNANCE FACTORIES) (EXCESS), 1897-8.

"7. That a sum, not exceeding £100, be granted to Her Majesty, to make good the Excess on the Grant for the Expense of the Ordnance Factories, for the year ended on the 31st day of March 1898."

Resolutions agreed to.

———

BILLS DEFERRED.

SALE OF FOOD AND DRUGS BILL.

Adjourned Debate on Motion for Committal to Standing Committee on Trade, etc [9th March] further adjourned till Thursday.

COLONIAL LOANS FUND BILL.

Second Reading deferred till Thursday.

METROPOLITAN STREETS ACT (1867)
AMENDMENT BILL.

Second Reading deferred till Monday next.

SUPPLY [3RD MARCH].

Report deferred till Thursday.

UNIVERSITIES (SCOTLAND) ACTS
AMENDMENT BILL.

Adjourned Debate on Second Reading [9th March] further adjourned till Thursday.

LICENSING EXEMPTION (HOUSES OF
PARLIAMENT) BILL.

Adjourned Debate on Second Reading [23rd February] further adjourned till Thursday.

ELECTRIC LIGHTING (CLAUSES) BILL.

Second Reading deferred till Thursday.

ANCHORS AND CHAIN CABLES BILL.

Second Reading deferred till Thursday.

PRIVATE LEGISLATION PROCEDURE
(SCOTLAND) BILL.

Second Reading deferred till Thursday.

WAYS AND MEANS.

Committee deferred till Wednesday.

LOCAL GOVERNMENT ACT (1888)
AMENDMENT BILL.

Second Reading deferred till this day.

SCHOOL BOARD CONFERENCES (SCOTLAND) BILL.

Second Reading deferred till Thursday.

INFECTIOUS DISEASES. (NOTIFICATION) ACT (1889) EXTENSION BILL.

Second Reading deferred till this day.

SUMMARY JURISDICTION ACT (1879)
AMENDMENT BILL.

Considered in Committee

(In the Committee.)

CLAUSE 1.

Committee report Progress; to sit again this day.

COLONIAL SOLICITORS BILL.

Second Reading deferred till Monday next.

SALE OF INTOXICATING LIQUORS ON
SUNDAY BILL.

Second Reading deferred till Monday next.

WATER SUPPLY BILL.

Second Reading deferred till this day.

SHOP HOURS ACT INSPECTORS.

Address for—

"Return showing the counties and boroughs in which Inspectors have been appointed under the Shop Hours Act, 1892, and number of Inspectors appointed, in the following form :—

1.	2.	3.	4.
Counties and Boroughs in which Inspectors have been appointed.	Total number of Inspectors appointed.	Inspectors giving their whole time to duties under the Shop Hours Act.	Inspectors performing duties under the Shop Hours Act in conjunction with other public duties.

(in continuation of Parliamentary Paper, No. 285, of Session 1896)."—*(Mr. Provand.)*

ADULTERATION (FOOD PRODUCTS) BILL.

Second Reading deferred till Monday next.

CORONERS' INQUESTS (RAILWAY FATALITIES) BILL.

Second Reading deferred till Wednesday.

SCHOOL BOARD ELECTORATE (SCOTLAND) BILL.

Second Reading deferred till Wednesday.

PARISH COUNCILLORS (TENURE OF OFFICE) BILL.

Committee deferred till this day.

ESTATE DUTY.

Return ordered, " of the Net Receipt of Estate Duty from each class of Estates in the year ended the 31st day of March 1898."—*(Mr. Hanbury.)*

Return presented accordingly ; to lie upon the Table, and to be printed. (No. 106.)

NEW BILL.

PERMISSIVE LICENSING POWERS (SCOTLAND) BILL.

" To amend the Public Houses Hours of Closing (Scotland) Act, 1887," presented, and read the first time ; to be read a second time upon Wednesday 22nd March, and to be printed. (Bill 124.)

House adjourned at Twenty minutes after Twelve of the clock.

ERRATUM.

Friday, 10th March 1899.

SUPPLY.—Division List No. 38 (pp. 481-2).

In the Noes, leave out Talbot, Rt. Hon. J. G. (Oxford Univ.) and insert. Talbot, Lord E. (Chichester).

HOUSE OF LORDS.

Tuesday, 14th March 1899.

THE LORD CHANCELLOR took his seat upon the Woolsack at Four of the clock.

PRIVATE BILL BUSINESS.

LONDON WATER (WELSH RESERVOIRS AND WORKS) BILL
Examiner's Certificate of non-compliance with the Standing Orders referred to the Standing Orders Committee on Monday next.

GLASGOW DISTRICT SUBWAY BILL [H.L.]
Reported with amendments.

RUSHDEN AND HIGHAM FERRERS DISTRICT GAS BILL [H.L.]
Reported with amendments.

ABERDEEN HARBOUR BILL [H.L.]
Reported with amendments.

LONDON AND SOUTH WESTERN RAILWAY BILL [H.L.]
Committed: The Committee to be proposed by the Committee of Selection.

BRISTOL FLOODS PREVENTION BILL [H.L.]
Committee (which stands appointed for Thursday next) put off to Friday next.

VOL. LXVIII.   [FOURTH SERIES.]

DUMBARTON BURGH BILL [H.L.]
Committee (which stands appointed for Thursday next) put off to Friday next.

LANARKSHIRE (MIDDLE WARD DISTRICT) WATER BILL [H.L.]
Committee (which stands appointed for Thursday next) put off to Friday next.

WISHAW WATER BILL.
The order made on the 16th instant appointing certain Lords the Select Committee to consider the Bill, discharged.

ST. ALBAN'S GAS BILL [H.L.]
Report from the Select Committee, That the Committee had not proceeded with the consideration of the Bill, no parties having appeared in opposition thereto; read, and ordered to lie on the Table: The orders made on the 2nd instant and Tuesday last discharged; and the Bill committed.

OYSTERMOUTH RAILWAY OR TRAM-ROAD BILL [H.L.]
Reported from the Select Committee with amendments.

METROPOLIS MANAGEMENT ACTS AMENDMENT BY-LAWS BILL [H.L.]
Reported from the Standing Committee with further amendments: The Report of the amendments made in Committee of the Whole House and by the Standing Committee to be received on Thursday next; and Bill to be printed as amended. (No. 24.)

2 E

RETURNS, REPORTS, ETC.

TRADE REPORTS.

Annual Series: No. 2210. Trade of Texas for the year 1898.

Presented (by Command), and ordered to lie on the Table.

FRIENDLY SOCIETIES (SHOP CLUBS).

Report to the Secretary of State for the Home Department by a Departmental Committee appointed to consider the complaints made by certain friendly societies; together with the minutes of evidence.

Presented (by Command), and ordered to lie on the Table.

PUBLIC BILLS.

BODIES CORPORATE (JOINT TENANCY) BILL.

Motion made, and Question proposed—

"That this Bill be read a second time."— (*The Lord Chancellor.*)

THE LORD CHANCELLOR (The Earl of HALSBURY): My Lords, in moving the Second Reading of this Bill I may explain that the effect of it will be to enable bodies corporate to acquire and hold real or personal property as joint tenants. That is the only object of the Bill, and I do not think there can be any objection to it.

Question put.

Bill read a second time, and committed to a Committee of the Whole House on Friday next.

PARTRIDGE SHOOTING (IRELAND) BILL.

Motion made, and Question proposed—

"That this Bill be read a second time."— (*Lord de Vesci.*)

LORD DE VESCI: My Lords, this is a small Bill which I understand has passed through all its stages in the other House without opposition. Under the present law, the shooting season in Ireland for partridges begins on September 20, and ends on January 10. This Bill provides that the season shall run from 1st September to 1st February, the same as in England.

Question put.

Bill read a second time, and committed to a Committee of the Whole House on Friday next.

BOARD OF EDUCATION BILL [H.L.]
FIRST READING.

THE LORD PRESIDENT OF THE COUNCIL (the Duke of DEVONSHIRE): My Lords, at the close of last Session, in gringing in two Bills, the principal one of which was for the constitution of a Board of Education, I made a general statement of the views of the Government with regard to a reform of Secondary Education in this country, which I do not think it is necessary that I should repeat on this occasion. I circulated the speech which I then made to Members of both Houses of Parliament; and no doub* that speech has been seen by, or is accessible for reference to, any of your Lordships who may take an interest in the subject; but it may be convenient that in re-introducing one of those Bills I should recapitulate, without going into detail, the main points of the statement I then made. I gave some account of a provision which already exists for Secondary Education from public, local, and private sources, and of the departments and authorities by which that provision is controlled, and by which the expenditure upon it is regulated. I stated that we had no intention of bringing Secondary Education under any centralised control, such as that which has been found necessary in regard to Elementary Education, and that, holding this view, we recognised that the creation of local authorities with adequate powers to make provision, or to control the provision already made, for Secondary Education within their own areas, was a most important, and, indeed, essential point in any complete Measure dealing with this subject. I said, however, that in our opinion the creation of such local authorities ought to be preceded by the constitution of a central authority, not for the purpose of unduly controlling the action of such local authorities, but mainly for the purpose of giving them such information, such advice and guidance as they would not be in a position to obtain from the isolated and detached central Departments which at present exist. I further indicated the nature of the central authority which we proposed to create, and that it would concentrate within one department the powers and duties now exercised by the Educational Departments and the Science and Art Department, and I stated the relations which we proposed should exist between this reconstituted Department and the Charity and Endowed Schools Commissioners. I further pointed out the manner in which we thought it would be possible to obtain for the new Department the assistance of expert and professional advice through the constitution of a Consultative Committee. My Lords, I invited the fullest discussion and criticism upon the Bills which I then introduced. The time was, perhaps, not altogether propitious for obtaining this criticism, inasmuch as those who are perhaps best qualified to offer valuable opinions upon the subject are those who are more or less directly connected with the teaching profession; and the time at which this statement was made and these Bills were introduced, was just about the commencement of the ordinary vacation in all educational institutions. A considerable time, therefore, elapsed before much discussion took place upon these Measures, but during the late autumn and the winter and up to a very recent date, I am glad to say that the subject has been very extensively discussed both by associations of county authorities, and by a very large number of associations of educational authorities. I have no reason to be dissatisfied on the whole with the reception which these Measures have met with. They have been exposed to some obvious criticism —criticism which I think I may say has proceeded more from political than from educational quarters, or quarters associated with local government—upon the limited scope and imperfect character of these Measures, but I think very few of those who have been qualified to discuss this subject with full knowledge, either of the conditions of the present organisation of Local Government, or the present organisation or Education, have seriously questioned the contention

which I then made that the preliminary organisation of the central authority ought properly to precede the further Measure which we admit to be equally, if not still more, important, of creating competent local authorities; and from all I have heard, I am more convinced even than I was last year that the course which we have taken in this respect has been the right one, and will in the end be probably the most expeditious one. I referred last year, to some extent, to the difficulties which I still foresee in arriving at any general agreement as to the constitution of the local authorities, and I am not prepared to say that these difficulties have altogether disappeared; but I very gladly recognise that there appears to be some progress towards agreement. The question has been pretty fully discussed between the Associations of County Councils, of County Borough Councils, and of Borough Councils, and I do not see any insuperable difficulties which have still to be got over in coming to an agreement between those bodies. I still have to make some reservation as to School Boards. From causes over which they were not responsible, School Boards have been constrained to enter to so considerable an extent upon the field of Secondary Education that many of them are naturally most unwilling to surrender the position which they now occupy. Though I conceive that very few of them would contend that the School Board as now constituted would be the proper Secondary Educational authority for the future, yet I think I still apprehend that many of them will be disposed to claim a larger share of representation on, and influence over, these local bodies to be constituted in the future than it may be possible for us to concede to them. But, under any circumstances, even if all difficulties as to the constitution of the local authorities had entirely disappeared, I still think it would have been a mistake to create those local bodies and to call upon them to undertake the important duties which it is proposed to assign to them in the absence of any central organisation, which would be in a position to give them all the information, advice, and assistance which they will have a right to expect. This part of the question is, I think, in some degree illustrated by the proceedings which have taken place under the Local Taxation Acts and the Technical Education Acts. A great deal of admirable work has been done by county councils, by county borough councils, and by borough councils in disposing of the funds which have been entrusted to them by Parliament for the purpose of assisting Technical Education, but there can, I think, be no doubt that the administration by the county councils of very large grants, without any experience or without much guidance from any central authority, has, in many cases, led to some waste in the application of those funds. Their application, therefore, has not been as efficient as it might have been. The dual administration under the Education Department and the Science and Art Department has not been, in all respects, satisfactory, and some cases have come under my observation in which, I think, schools and classes have been recognised and aided by Government subventions by one department without full knowledge of what was being done by the other department, and this has led, in some cases, to unnecessary competition and undue expenditure both of public and local funds, and consequently to some loss of efficiency. When it has been announced that it is the intention of the Government to reorganise these departments, and when the office of Secretary of the Science and Art Department is about to become vacant, which will not, of course, for the present be filled up, there must ensue a period of transition, in which the defects of this dual administration will necessarily, for a time, be accentuated. I hold, therefore, my Lords, still more strongly than I did last year, that it is necessary that we should make an attempt to put our own house in order before we try to introduce order and a better system into the local administration of education. My Lords, I think that on this occasion I may confine myself to some explanation of the points in which the Bill which I am asking leave to introduce differs from that of last year. The constitution of the Board of Education provided in the Bill of last Session has been criticised, I think not without some justice, as being somewhat awkward and clumsy. It provided in certain cases for the retention as a member of the Board of the Vice-

Lord President of the Council.

President of the Council. In other contingencies there would have been no Vice-President. We propose in the present Bill to constitute a Board of the same character as the Board of Trade or the Board of Agriculture. Like the Board of Trade, and unlike the Board of Agriculture, it will have a Parliamentary Secretary as well as a President, but the office of Vice-President will cease to exist. We have, however, following the precedent of the Board of Trade Act of 1867, introduced a temporary provision providing that during the present tenure of office of the Vice-President of the Council, he will continue to be a member of the Board. In justice to the Vice-President, I think I ought to state that this provision has not been introduced in any way on his initiative, and that he himself entertains doubts as to its expediency. We have, however, considered that the experience and knowledge of the subject which is possessed by the Vice-President will be of great value, not only in the conduct of this Bill through the other House of Parliament, but in organising the Department if Parliament should sanction this Measure. We have, therefore, thought it desirable to follow exactly the precedent of the course which was taken in the Board of Trade Act of 1867. The present Bill will give more elastic powers of transfer of the educational functions of the Charity Commissioners to the new Department. It will give power to the Queen in Council, by Order, to transfer to the Education Board such powers as may appear to relate to education. The question of whether a trust is of an educational or other character, and the apportioning of the endowments for educational or other purposes will, however, as in the Bill of last year, be reserved to the Charity Commissioners. Our intention is that this transfer should only gradually come into operation, and the only power which at present will be transferred from the Charity Commissioners to the Board of Education will be that of the inspection of schools now under schemes framed by the Endowed Schools Commissioners. The future transfer of these educational powers from the Charity Commissioners will be facilitated by a change which has recently taken place in the composition of the Commission. One of the Commissioners has recently been appointed to the office of Registrar to the Judicial Committee. His place will not, at all events for the present, be filled up, and the educational duties which have hitherto almost entirely occupied the time of the Commissioner appointed under the Endowed Schools Act, and the Commissioner whose time has hitherto been entirely occupied by educational duties, will now take his share in the ordinary duties of the Board; and the Commissioners have been informed that, in view of pending changes which are in contemplation, it will not be necessary, or, in the opinion of the Government, desirable, that they should push on the work of framing new educational schemes except in such cases as, for local reasons or under special circumstances, appear urgently necessary. The question of inspection and examination of schools by the new Board is one of such importance that it will be dealt with in the present Bill in a separate clause instead of in a sub-section of a clause, as in the former Bill. That sub-section was found to confer considerably larger powers of inspection than were intended by us, or than, I think, we generally understood, and I am advised that under the Bill introduced last year all Public Schools would have been liable to inspection except Eton and Winchester, which are in a separate category by themselves. I have endeavoured to ascertain from the governing bodies and headmasters of Public Schools how far they are of opinion that it is desirable that the inspection of Public Schools by an Educational Board should be general, and how far they would themselves be willing to come under it. The result of these inquiries has been to me somewhat unexpected, and I think in a sense eminently satisfactory. Most of them, the largest and most important Public Schools of the country included, have, through their headmasters, expressed the opinion that they are so impressed with the public advantage of a general inspection of Secondary Schools by some competent authority, that they would be willing on certain conditions, although they might have little or nothing to gain by it themselves, to come under such a system of inspection. But some of the conditions which they very properly lay down are conditions which at present it would be very difficult adequately to satisfy. The headmasters indicate a great dread on their part of anything in the nature of bureaucratic interference, or any attempt to impose upon them uniformity of instruction or curriculum. They therefore attach great importance to the permanent existence of a Consultative Committee, in which they see a guarantee against any such attempt on the part of a Government Department. They also require that University inspection should be recognised as an alternative to State inspection. These are conditions which might be satisfied without great difficulty, but there are others which will be less easily met. They attach the greatest importance to the selection for this duty of inspectors whose competence for such responsible and difficult duties would be generally recognised. I need not say that such men do not exist in very great numbers, that such men cannot easily be found, and that, if they can be found, their services will have to be very highly remunerated. And they further generally express the opinion that, if inspection by the State were to be made compulsory, it ought also to be gratuitous. The form in which the inquiries have been made has, perhaps, led to some misapprehension as to the scope and intention of the Bill, and I fear that some disappointment may be felt when the extremely limited proposals of the Government on the subject are explained. It is very satisfactory to note the willingness with which the masters of the most important schools have welcomed the idea of inspection, not as required for themselves, but for the purpose of raising the character of schools which may be less efficient; but until the Department is far more organised than it is likely to be for some considerable period, it would be impossible, in my opinion, for it to undertake anything like what many of these gentlemen appear to have in their minds in the nature of a State inspection of the national provision for Secondary Education. Our present aim is limited to the better organisation of the provision for local Secondary Education on the lines indicated in the Report of the Royal Commission, and although the terms of the clause of the present Bill may be wider and may admit of something very much larger in extent in the future, all that we have at present in view is such an inspection of local schools as may assist the local authorities hereafter to be constituted, to bring the Endowed, Municipal, and Private Proprietary schools within their areas into some common local scheme. It would be impossible to draw an exact line of demarcation between those schools in which it would be desirable that inspection should be compulsory and those in which it should be optional, and therefore we propose that inspection in all cases should be optional, except in the case of those schools which are being conducted under schemes of the Endowed School Commissioners, in whose case the new Department will inherit the powers of inspection which are already possessed by the Charity Commissioners. But I believe that the advantages of recognition by the local authority will be a strong inducement to a greater number of the non-local schools to place themselves under inspection and thus to obtain a guarantee of efficiency which will enable them to be recognised as part of the local provision for education, and I trust that the assent which has been given by the higher educational authority to the principle of inspection will tend to remove any apprehension which up to the present time may have been felt by the smaller local schools. We recognise that the conditions which will be required for the higher and more important schools ought, in their due degree, to be applied to the case of the smaller local public schools, and that, in the first place, no attempt should be made to impose upon them anything like uniformity in their course of instruction; that the inspection should be conducted on the advice of, and in consultation with, the Consultative Committee to be formed under the Bill; that due care should be taken in the selection of the inspectors; that University or other competent organisations shall be admitted as equivalent to Government inspection; and, though we are unable to ask Parliament to devote funds to provide for the inspection of schools which are mainly for the benefit of the upper or middle classes, we recognise that in the case of the poorer schools the cost of inspection may properly form a charge upon funds placed at the disposal of the counties for educational purposes. The registration of teachers was provided for last year in a separate Measure. We now consider

Lord President of the Council.

that this is unnecessary. We consider that the registers of both Elementary and Secondary teachers may be most properly kept by the Department itself, and we provide that the regulations under which these registers are formed shall be framed in consultation with and on the advice of the Consultative Committee. The composition of that Committee will not be stereotyped by the terms of the Bill further than it will be provided that it shall be as to two-thirds representative of the Universities or other teaching bodies; and endowed, as it will be, with the permanent functions to which I have referred, I hope that any doubt which has been felt as to the intention of the Government to make the Consultative Committee a permanent institution under the Board will be removed. Following the precedents of similar legislation, the Bill will provide that Parliament shall retain control over the proceedings under this Act, by a clause which will make it necessary that all Orders proposed to be made under the Act shall be laid upon the Tables of both Houses before they are submitted to the Queen in Council. Not the least important part of the policy of which this Bill is only a portion will be the reorganisation of the Departments of the Government themselves. I stated last year that certain changes might be necessary in the Educational Departments. The Science and Art Department has grown up, as I pointed out last year, almost imperceptibly, from very small beginnings, so that it is probable that in its case a very searching and complete examination will be necessary. The Department has a character distinct and differing from anything which exists in the State, and, I think, differing from anything which exists in any other country. Through its colleges of science and schools of art, it is itself a teaching institution. It distributes a large sum in aid of instruction in certain subjects, and, therefore, it exercises a considerable control over the course of study throughout the country. It is also an examining body, whose certificates possess a value of the same character as that of a University degree. It also directs great museums in South Kensington, Bethnal Green, Edinburgh, and Dublin. Its internal arrangements are also of a peculiar character, having, as it has, directors of science and art who possess no executive authority, and whose functions and responsibilities I have always found it rather difficult to understand. The intention expressed in the Bill of making this Department a branch of a larger Educational Department, and also the pending vacancy in the Secretaryship of the Science and Art Department, will obviously make a thorough revision of this Department necessary. That revision will naturally be undertaken by a Departmental Committee, and as soon as the principle of amalgamation of the two Departments has been approved by Parliament that Committee will be appointed and the revision commenced. It will extend to both the science and art sides of the Department and also to the administration of the museums. It is an inquiry which must necessarily occupy a certain amount of time and entail a great deal of labour, and we therefore propose that the Bill shall not come into force until the 1st April next year, which will certainly not allow more than the necessary time for conducting this very difficult inquiry. I have now explained the principal provisions of the Bill, which I ask leave to introduce. It differs in some of its minor details from that which we brought in last year, but we have seen no reason to depart from the principle of that Measure, or to extend its limited scope. We fully admit that it is only a part of a more complete Measure, but we believe that it is a necessary and indispensable step towards a complete Measure. Our present proposals are limited, not because we shrink through timidity from dealing with the subject in a larger spirit, but because we are deliberately of opinion that the procedure which we recommend is the soundest and the most logical procedure, and in the end will be the most expeditious and the most efficient. I ask leave to introduce the Bill.

*LORD NORTON: Perhaps I may venture to make one or two remarks with reference to this Bill, which deals with a subject to which I have devoted the greater part of my life. I desire to express my gratitude to the noble Duke, the Lord President of the Council, for having so earnestly and thoroughly grappled with the important part of the subject to which this Bill refers—namely,

the concentration and organisation of the numerous central Departments which deal with education. This reform will, I am sure, obviate the great waste and expense which now takes place by a multiplicity of offices. At first one feels confused as to what the objects of this Bill are. We have all looked for a Bill dealing with Secondary Education, but this Bill is no such thing. There is nothing in it specially referring to Secondary Education. The phrase does not occur in the Bill, which is for the purpose of consolidating the authorities which deal with both Elementary and Secondary Education and Technical Instruction in this country. Secondary Education will merely be a branch of the general subject to be dealt with by a Board of Education. I know that there can be no distinct line drawn between Elementary and Secondary Education. One is the foundation and the other the continuation of education, but at the same time it was admitted by the noble Duke, in the speech he made last year, that the Board will deal with each in a different way and by different officials, and I hope they will do so in many ways in a totally different manner. It is, in my opinion, a misfortune that Elementary Education was made free, because what costs nothing is regarded as worthless, but that the Secondary Education of the sons of rich manufacturers should be supported by the public would have a most injurious effect. There is not the slightest doubt that the making of Elementary instruction gratuitous has lowered it in the estimation of the country. I know at this moment that the municipal institutions for Secondary and Technical Education in our great towns are used not so much by the children of artisans as by those of tradesmen and manufacturers. I think that is a misfortune, and I hope the higher work of the Board of Education will be self-supported as by scholarships for the poor. The constitution of this Board strikes me as rather questionable. It is a similar constitution to that of the Board of Trade and the Board of Agriculture. I have had to serve in two Departments under a Board constituted in the same way, and I can only say that I remember but one single instance in which the Board was called together or consulted in any way. It is a mere sham. The Board of Education will be merely nominal, and the Minister, with a Consultative Committee, will really conduct the business. The Consultative Committee also seems to me to be rather questionable. I hardly like to express an opinion on this subject. I have no doubt the noble Duke has more material to form an opinion upon than I have, but he cannot deny that there is some danger in making a Consultative Committee independent of the Minister. Surely it relieves the Minister of a sense of responsibility to a great extent, and it hampers and impedes his free action. It seems to me it would be much wiser, if the assistance of experts is required, that they should be inside the Board, and not outside. What is the use of a Parliamentary Secretary but to give the Minister all he wants to carry on the business of the office? Surely the Minister himself is the man who should have full responsibility! The proposal seems to me a dangerous one. I was very glad to hear that the headmasters of our great Public Schools had attached conditions to their willingness to receive inspection from this Board, which, if I understand the noble Duke correctly, would be, at all events for the present, insuperable. I do not wish, in any degree whatever, that our great Public Schools should be under this Board of Education or connected through it with the Government. This Bill is formed avowedly upon the Report of the Royal Commission of 1895. That Report was largely drawn up, I believe, by the Chairman, Mr. Bryce. It abjures altogether any idea of a State system of education, and says that nothing they recommend shall be intended to introduce a control of the State over the education of the country, but merely supervision. The Commissioners said that, I think, very wisely, but their recommendations do not quite carry out their proposition. I hope the noble Duke intends the provisions of this Bill to be for the benefit of the industrial classes, and not for the upper classes, who go to our great Public Schools. This is a very important question. A little book was published in Paris recently ably maintaining that the education of England was so infinitely superior to that of France that it fully accounted for the more prominent position England had taken in the affairs of the world. I really feel that I have been almost presumptuous in venturing to make these remarks, but I hope the noble Duke will consider them as the remarks of one who is very fully interested in his work. I desire to express my gratitude, which I believe will be widely shared in the country, to the noble Duke for having so earnestly undertaken this great improvement.

Question put.

Bill read a first time, and to be printed. (No. 25.)

House adjourned at half-past Five of the clock.

Lord Norton.

HOUSE OF COMMONS.

Tuesday, 14th March 1899.

MR. SPEAKER took the Chair at Three of the clock.

PRIVATE BILL BUSINESS.

CROWBOROUGH DISTRICT GAS BILL.
Read the third time, and passed.

ST. DAVID'S WATER AND GAS BILL.
Read the third time, and passed.

TENTERDEN RAILWAY BILL.
Read a second time, and committed.

WOODHOUSE AND CONISBROUGH RAILWAY (ABANDONMENT) BILL.
Read a second time, and committed.

BRADFORD TRAMWAYS AND IMPROVEMENT BILL.

SECOND READING.

*SIR C. DILKE (Gloucester, Forest of Dean): I do not wish to stop this Bill, but I wish to ask for a statement with regard to the understanding which I am told has been privately come to. I have received a telegram just now asking me to oppose this Bill, but I am informed that an arrangement has been come to to prevent the diminution of open spaces, by an undertaking on the part of the Corporation to leave aside 50 acres, which is the subject of dispute. I believe the honourable and gallant Member for East Bradford has come to some understanding with one Member upon this matter, but I believe those opposing the Bill have not been informed of it, although one Member has been told of it. If the honourable and gallant Member can state this definitely I shall not oppose the Bill.

*CAPTAIN GREVILLE (Bradford, E.): I may say that, having informed the honourable Baronet the Member for Northwich division that the Corporation of Bradford withdrew their claim to the 50 acres in question, he has agreed to withdraw his notice of opposition to the Bill.

Question put.

Bill read a second time, and committed.

BEXHILL AND ROTHERFIELD RAILWAY BILL.

(By Order.) Second Reading deferred till Tuesday next.

SOUTH EASTERN AND LONDON, CHATHAM, AND DOVER RAILWAY COMPANIES (NEW LINES) BILL.

(By Order.) Read a second time, and committed.

SOUTH EASTERN AND LONDON, CHATHAM AND DOVER RAILWAY COMPANIES BILL

SECOND READING.

(By Order.)—Order for Second Reading read.

Motion made, and Question proposed—

" That the Bill be now read a second time."

Amendment proposed—

" To leave out the word 'now,' and at the end of the Question to add the words 'upon this day six months.' "—(*Mr. Pickersgill.*)

*MR. PICKERSGILL (Bethnal Green, S.W.): I rise, Sir, to move the

rejection of this Bill. Whatever view the House may take of this Measure the amalgamation which it proposes is a subject which does concern not only the whole of the county of Kent, but it is also one which all of us must consider upon national grounds. The case which I desire to put before the House in moving the rejection of this Bill is shortly this: that it is a matter of national, almost international, importance that the short sea routes between England and the Continent should not be under the control of a monopoly. Now, the conduct of the promoters of this Bill has not been such as is likely to conciliate Parliament. Their conduct is not respectful to Parliament, for they have attempted to force the hand of Parliament in a manner which I hope this House will resent. They have not waited for the decision of Parliament, but they have anticipated that decision. And now, when these two companies are practically already amalgamated, they come to this House and ask Parliament to legalise an arrangement which is already in operation, and to condone the gross evasion of the intention of Parliament of which they have been guilty. Since January last a joint board has been managing all the traffic of these two companies, but the promoters, in the preamble of the Bill, admit that their Parliamentary powers beyond the Continental agreement only enable them to make agreements in respect of competitive traffic. Now, what is their defence? They say that by each company merely giving to the other running powers over the whole of its lines, they have made all their traffic competitive, and subject to the control of the joint board. Now, I do not hesitate to say that this is a mere quibble, and it is a contention which will not bear a moment's serious consideration. To suggest that by a mere stroke of the pen, or by a mere paper concession, you can make traffic competitive within the meaning of the Act of Parliament which is not really competitive seems to me to be childish. If it is seriously intended, then I say the prospect which is opened to Parliament and the country is alarming enough, and alarming for this reason: very many of the railway companies of this country have Parliamentary powers to make agreements among themselves with regard to competitive traffic, and if the action of the promoters of this Bill is to be allowed to pass unchallenged, the logical conclusion would be that half of the railway companies of England would be able to make "working unions," to employ the new phrase, which are practically amalgamations, and to make those amalgamations behind the back of Parliament. This is not a straightforward amalgamation. The Bill proposes to establish a "working union" between the two companies for all purposes. Now, working agreements between companies for certain purposes are familiar enough, and we know what amalgamation is, but a "working union" for all purposes I think I may say is a new departure in railway legislation. So far as the public is concerned, this undoubtedly is an amalgamation, because it is provided that the two undertakings are to be worked, maintained, managed, used, and improved as one undertaking; but, at the same time, the companies desire to retain the advantage of separate existences in their relations with each other. In other words, the companies propose to be at once amalgamated and not amalgamated. I say that they are not entitled to have it both ways, for such an arrangement is a novelty, and I think it is decidedly detrimental to the public interest. Then, in the third place, this Bill runs counter to public policy, for Parliament in previous years has opposed amalgamations which were unfavourable to competition, and the promoters have recognised this feeling in the country, and this tendency on the part of Parliament, and have endeavoured to meet it. I do not think, however, that they have met it in a satisfactory way. There 'is, in my opinion, a fatal inconsistency in the attitude adopted by the promoters upon this point. They say that the action of Parliament in relation to these two companies has been such as to preclude competition between them, and yet, at the same time, the very object of this Bill is to prevent competition. The honourable Gentleman the Member for Wimbledon made a speech in July last, of which he has been already, I believe, reminded, and of which probably he will be reminded again and again before this matter is concluded, in which he

said that under the arrangement prior to the formation of this company competition must ensue. As a matter of fact, this statement that the arrangement made by Parliament absolutely precluded competition is altogether contradicted by the recent history—the comparatively recent history—of the two companies. Now, what is that history only three or four years ago? In 1895 the late Sir George Russell became the Chairman of the South Eastern Railway Company, and then there was an outbreak of energy and a change of policy. A new service was established by the South Eastern Railway Company from Liverpool and Birmingham by way of Reading and Folkestone, and the London, Chatham, and Dover Railway Company immediately responded by establishing a through service, by an arrangement with the London and North Western Railway Company, by way of Willesden and Dover. The South Eastern Company started an afternoon train by way of Folkestone, and the Chatham and Dover Company responded by establishing an afternoon service by way of Dover. The Chatham and Dover Company got a newspaper train to Dover by 8.15 in the morning, and then the South Eastern Company discovered that they could get a newspaper train to Dover at the same hour. The Chatham and Dover Company found that they could do the journey in two and a half hours, and, therefore, the South Eastern attempted to do the same thing. These facts are sufficient to show that under the old system sanctioned by Parliament competition was not only practical, but that competition was on precisely the same lines as exists in other parts of the country, and such competition was actually established. Now, the promoters of this Bill have started a new theory of competition. They draw a distinction between competition in the county of Kent and competition with the county of Kent. They say that other ports will still compete with Folkestone and Dover for the Continental traffic, and of course that is true. This is a certain amount of protection, and it will always prevent any monopolist company in the South of England raising those Continental rates beyond a certain point. But that is not adequate protection, for this reason: the South

Mr. Pickersgill.

Eastern Company, or any company in a similar position, start with this enormous advantage over all other ports—that it controls the gateway of the shortest sea routes to the Continent. It must, therefore, always have a very great advantage over the other ports to which the promoters of this Bill refer. It has been suggested that there is an alternative, and that it is not necessary to reject this Bill or to refuse permission to amalgamate. It is put forward that there is the alternative of imposing conditions upon the amalgamated company. No doubt, if the House, in its wisdom, should sanction amalgamation, a determined effort should be made to take such security in the interests of the public, and an effort must be made, for instance, to bind the company down to provide a reasonable and adequate service of workmen's trains. Some effort should also be made to bind the company down with regard to the rates which they charge for agricultural produce grown in our own country. It is said that in giving preferential rates to foreigners the London, Chatham, and Dover and the South Eastern Railway Companies do not stand alone, and that is perfectly true. I do think, however, that they are among the worst offenders in respect of granting these preferential rates to foreigners; and if the House should be disposed to permit them to amalgamate, the opportunity of binding them down in some special way ought not to be lost. What I think is this: I do not place much reliance upon the so-called safeguards which the promoters of this Measure have introduced into this Bill. A safeguard in a Bill creating a monopoly is always largely nugatory and illusive. In the first place, you can only provide, at the best, for present circumstances. As the House well knows, circumstances rapidly change and new conditions arise, for it has happened in the past, and I think it will happen again in the future—that the best intended agreement at the time may, after a while, become absolutely a barrier in the pathway of progress. Parliament has recognised that in its general legislation with regard to railways by the provision that, where it gives power to railway companies to make arrangements with other com-

panies, those agreements are revisable by the Board of Trade at the end of a period of 10 years. Now, what are the safeguards which are suggested? Under pressure from the right honourable Gentleman whom I see opposite, the company has expressed its willingness to introduce a new scale of maxima fares into the Bill. I question whether the scale of maxima rates has ever conferred any real advantage or protection on the public, and such a scale of rates certainly has not protected London in the case of the London water companies, and we may expect the same result with regard to the railways, for this reason—that the scale is always fixed—and I presume must always be fixed—too high to be any real protection, whilst, at the same time, there is a constant tendency to work up to the limit thus provided. Now, what is the concession which we are promised? As I understand it, the promoters of this Bill propose to introduce a scale in regard to first, second, and third-class fares of threepence, twopence, and one penny per mile. I do not regard that as much of a concession, for it compares very unfavourably with the scales imposed upon neighbouring companies, like the London, Brighton, and South Coast Railway, on the one hand, and the scale of the Tilbury and Southend Company on the other. And, further, it does not touch the main grievances at all of which passengers complain—namely, it does not touch the exclusion of third-class passengers from so many of the trains; neither does it touch the failure to give a reduction upon return fares, which is a great grievance of the passengers in connection with these companies. Now, I do say that the least that Parliament can exact from these companies in return for amalgamation would be a provision that the company shall carry third-class passengers by every train. Then the arguments on behalf of the promoters of the Bill substantially come to this —and it is not very complimentary—is true, to the companies concerned—that the two companies have served the public so badly in the past that any change must be a change for the better. That, I think, is a short-sighted policy, and it is an argument which has not prevailed in similar cases of the proposed amalgamation of railway companies. It did not prevail in 1868, when there was a proposal made to amalgamate the London and Brighton and South Coast Company, and the South Eastern Company. Precisely the same arguments were used then, for it was said that the London, Brighton, and South Coast Railway Company was in a bad financial condition, which is just the same thing that is said now with regard to the London, Chatham, and Dover Company. The result was that the two companies were not amalgamated, and I think most people will certainly say now that it was very well that they were not amalgamated. Similar arguments were used in 1872 when a proposal was made to amalgamate the London and North Western Railway Company with another company, but such arguments did not prevail in 1872 in Parliament, and I hope they will not prevail now. But there is an alternative to this amalgamation. If the London, Chatham, and Dover Company does not almagamate with the South Eastern Company as is proposed by this Bill, something will certainly be done to improve the position of the London, Chatham, and Dover Company; and what I should like to see, and what would probably result if the House rejected this Bill, would be that we should find one of the great railway companies running north out of London would take over the London, Chatham and Dover line, and thus you would have the South of England linked up with a northern railway system, and this would develop traffic with the South of England to a degree which would not only maintain the new line, but would also improve the prospects of the South Eastern Railway itself. I think the House must recognise that this would probably be the result of rejecting this amalgamation. An active canvass has been made on behalf of this Bill, and I notice on the back of the Bill the name of a Cabinet Minister, the right honourable Member for St. Augustine's Division of Kent; and also another Minister, the right honourable Gentleman the Member for Dover. Now both these Ministers are directors of the South Eastern Railway Company. I think it is very inconvenient, not to use a stronger word, that

Mr. Pickersgill.

the names of two Members of the Government should appear on the back of a Bill in regard to which one of their colleagues will be expected to advise the House. The President of the Board of Trade will presently have to advise the House on this Bill, and whether he will bless or ban the Bill I do not know, but certainly the right honourable Gentleman is placed in an invidious position in either event by the fact that the names of his two colleagues . appear on the back of the Measure. This, I think, is an object lesson in the disadvantages of the present system of Minister directorships. Whatever this House may think, and it appears to think lightly of Ministers of the Crown occupying directorships of railway companies, there is a growing feeling outside this House that the position of a Minister of the Crown is incompatible with that of a director of a company; and whatever this present House may do or say, I feel sure that the next House will insist that Members of the Cabinet must choose between serving the public and serving shareholders.

Mr. WOODS: (Essex, Walthamstow): I rise for the purpose of joining my honourable Friend the Member for Bethnal Green in opposing the Second Reading of this Bill. I do so because there are three primary reasons upon which I base my opposition. The first is, because from the terms of the Bill, from the first word to the last, it may, with propriety and without exaggeration be called a Railway Dividend Bill. In the second place, in substance this Bill asks the House to give its permission and protection to the railway company without giving any counterbalancing benefit to the community. In and third place, after a careful examination of the provisions of the Bill, I cannot find either a sentence or a hint in any of its provisions that the people of this country are going to be any better off after the passing into law of this Measure. I think that for the last 50 years this House has set itself against the amalgamation of railway companies, and it has done that, I presume, with the object of preventing the creation of unnecessary monopolies. In 1846 a Committee of the House fully considered that question of railway amalgamation. They recommended—

"In all instances in which railway companies propose to take powers of amalgamation, the rates and tolls of the amalgamated companies should be subject to revision."

Now, I have carefully examined the provisions of this Bill, especially clause 10, which deals with the rates and charges proposed under this Measure, and there is not a sentence which indicates that there is to be any public or popular control over the charges that are to be made in connection with this railway company. But there are other reasons on which I base my objection to this Measure. First of all—and I believe honourable Members will agree with me in this—from a public point of view it is much easier to deal with a single or in-individual company than with a large corporation such as it is proposed to create under this Measure. In the second place, I think, if this Measure passes it will kill the very spirit of healthy competition which is so essential and so necessary to the common weal. Then, again, in the third place, we may take an example by looking at the railways running north of London, where there is healthy, free competition, and where there is no amalgamation, and I think that that fact in itself has proved a boon and an unmixed blessing to the trade and travelling public of this country both in regard to tariffs and railway passes. Then I find that schemes for the amalgamation of other railways on many occasions have been rejected by this House, although in those schemes of amalgamation the same advantages were offered and precisely the same provisions inserted as in this case. In all those previous Measures the same promises and the same conditions which are now put in this Bill were given as the reason why those amalgamations should be passed into law. Then, Sir, I find another significant omission in this Bill, and that is that it proposes no reduction of tariffs. The tariffs have to remain the same, and I question whether any honourable Member can see one atom of good that will result from the passing of this Measure into law. There is a suggestion put forward by the promoters of this Bill that in their present condition neither of the companies can offer any reduction in rates, fares, tariffs, or

charges. That, I think, is an ignoble suggestion, and it is not only ignoble, but it is contrary to the fact and to precedent. Then, I find that this railway company, along with other railway companies, have granted unto them large remissions of taxation, and yet they offer no cheap workmen's trains from many of the suburbs. I venture to say that there is scarcely another railway company which runs into this City that offers less facilities and less advantages to the travelling public than the two railways which it is now proposed should be amalgamated. Let me give to the House a few facts. There is Croydon, which the right honourable Gentleman opposite, who will, no doubt, reply to this Debate, has the distinguished honour of representing in this House. That town is 10 miles from London, and the return fare from Croydon, with a population of 102,000 is 1s. 6d. third class. Then there is Bromley, which is 10½ miles from London, and the single fare is 11d. There is Addiscombe Road, which is the same distance from London as Croydon, and the return fare is 1s. 6d. In the case of Beckenham, which is 10 miles from London, and has a population of 20,000, the return fare is 1s. 3d. Then, I find that on these two companies there are no cheap workmen's at all from Bickley, Clockhouse, Kenthouse, Lower Sydenham, Catford, Ladywell, Lee, Hither Green, and Shortlands. There is not a single workmen's train, I am informed, from any of these important districts. Then the fares in the Lewisham district are very excessive, and cost the working classes about 2s. 6d. per week. Now, I would ask this House whether that is a state of things which ought to act as an inducement for honourable Members to vote for the amalgamation of these two companies, when they have refused all applications made to them to bring about a system of cheap trains. Of course, we shall be told that they do run certain cheap trains. I believe on the South Eastern Railway the total number of workmen's trains is 13, while the total on the London, Chatham, and Dover line is 25. Then I am informed that the South Eastern Railway Company is the only company which runs into the City who refuse to give a statement of their workmen's fares to the Board of Trade. It is also stated, and I am informed, that the facilities and the conveniences afforded on these lines are the very worst of any company which runs into this City. Now, what is the object for which these powers are given to railway companies? The primary object of railways is not to make dividends, but to afford facilities and conveniences to the travelling and trading public of this country, but this Bill achieves neither of these objects. Therefore, I say that the House, considering all these questions, ought to reject the Bill, and I shall give my adherence to the attempt which is being made in this House to-day to defeat the Second Reading of this Bill, and I trust that honourable Members, until they get further concessions from the companies who propose to be amamalgated, will refuse to give a Second Reading to this important Measure. I have great pleasure in seconding the proposal of my honourable Friend.

Mr. HARDY (Kent, Ashford): I hope this House will hesitate before it accepts the arguments addressed to it with reference to this Bill. I understand that the first argument is that this is not a Kent question, but a question for the world; but I think that is taking the matter rather wide and far afield. I say that there is no doubt that the general public have a great interest in the Continental traffic, but that traffic is not concerned by the present Bill, for it is already safeguarded by statutory enactments, which I believe are in perpetuity, and which neither company can possibly vary; therefore, the Continental traffic is to be almost entirely taken out of this Bill. If we exclude that matter, then we have to consider primarily the wants of the district, and if it is found that the county of Kent, into which these two railways run, is almost practically unanimous in favour of this working union then I think it would be a very strong Measure indeed for this House to reject the Bill on the Second Reading instead of sending it to the usual Committee upstairs. The last speaker suggested that it was a question in which there were three primary arguments against it, and one was that this was a "Railway Dividends Bill," and that was rather emphasised by the Mover of the Amendment, who called the attention of the House to the fact that certain Ministers were interested in

Mr. Woods

one of the companies. Now, I am absolutely indifferent to that argument, for I hold no shares in either company. I have had the good fortune to know the facilities offered by these companies, and I fear that I should suffer rather than benefit by this amalgamation. But I have satisfied myself on this point—and I am glad to find that the constituency which I represent is also satisfied—that this working union will be for the benefit of the district. In reference to this I would say that, notwithstanding the somewhat irresponsible opposition which has been started in a certain daily newspaper, I have only had two representations from my constituency in reference to this Bill —one of them from the largest urban district council in my constituency unanimously in favour of the Second Reading of this Bill, and the other from a small rural parish council opposing the Bill. I may add that the one which supports the working union represents a town which has had the benefit of competition from the two lines, while the rural council represents a district which has never known what competition has been in reference to this matter. I do not think that we are concerned to-day with the past history of these two railway companies. It might be summed up in this way—that they have done a great many things which they ought not to have done, and left undone a great many things which they ought to have done. It is necessary that we should clear out these Augean stables, and I think we have something approaching a modern Hercules in the honourable Member for Bethnal Green. At all events, I can assure the House that the districts concerned, whether they be the urban districts or the rural districts, feel that the only chance of the reforms which we have been pressing for a very long time is in this working union which has at last come before this House for its sanction. We are satisfied that there are many difficulties in the way of these reforms until we have obtained this working union. We believe that there is a genuine desire on the part of those responsible for this working union to grant these reforms; and they have given strong pledges, which I believe they are willing to renew in this House. Therefore, I would urge this House to accept the Second Reading of the Bill, and send it in the usual course to the Committee upstairs, for I believe it is a Measure which will be for the benefit of the constituency which I represent.

*MR. GRIFFITH BOSCAWEN (Kent, Tunbridge): Like my honourable Friend who has just sat down, I speak as a resident in Kent, and I represent a Kentish constituency, and I may say that my constituents are very nearly unanimous in favour of this Bill. Like my honourable Friend, I am rather astonished at the character of the opposition, which seems to me to be largely factitious, and is made up by a certain newspaper which I need not mention, but the absurdity of which I could show from one little quotation. This newspaper wrote the other day that the people of Tunbridge Wells were dismayed at the prospect of less competition. Now, inasmuch as the London, Chatham, and Dover Railway never came to Tunbridge Wells, it is obvious that there cannot be less competition under this Bill than there was before. The main reason why I support this Bill is this—I do not in the least support monopolies as a rule, and if I thought this Bill was going to create a dangerous monopoly, I would oppose it. But, as a matter of fact, if there be a monopoly, it already exists. The two railways are working together now, and nothing can, as I understand it, stop them working together. They are working together now under statutory powers, and no competition exists in Kent at the present moment, and all this Bill seeks to do is to enable the two companies to borrow money to give additional facilities to the public, which, I agree with honourable Members opposite, are very much needed. This Bill does not create a monopoly, and I may say that, from what I know of the history of railways in Kent, there never was any effective competition existing there as exists in the North of England. All that we have had in Kent has been two weak railways, neither of them too rich or strong, who, by a system of rivalry, were cutting each others throats, not by granting additional facilities to the public, but by building competing lines, which nearly ruined their shareholders by their having to pay an interest on such an enormous capital. So you often had duplicate trains where

they were not wanted, but if you wanted to get from one part of Kent to another it was often easier to come up to London, change stations, and then come down again. The joint companies under this Bill intend to build certain junctions at Chislehurst and Whitstable, which, I do not hesitate to say, will be a very great advantage to the public. A certain amount of these advantages have already been secured by making use of the line between the two stations at Sevenoaks, and there is no necessity now to change stations, which involved great delay and additional cost. If there is any monopoly, I say it already exists, and the non-passing of this Bill will not put an end to it, nor will it stop these two companies from working together, because I believe their present action is perfectly legal. They are working under powers granted by certain Acts of Parliament passed in 1893 and 1894, and you cannot make them go back on the powers which have been granted them. Therefore, I say you will not put an end to this monopoly by refusing to pass this Bill, but you will clearly prevent the two companies from raising capital and carrying out necessary improvements. Therefore, I see no reason why this House should take the very strong step of refusing to allow this Bill to go to a Committee upstairs, so that we may get certain clauses inserted which, I think, will be of very great advantage to the public. And I would further point this out—you talk a great deal about monopoly, and so on, but, after all, if the whole of Kent is under one company or one joint board, the whole district so served will not be nearly so large as the whole of Norfolk, Suffolk, and Essex, which are at the present time well served by one company. Nor will it be so large as the district at present served alone by the North Eastern Company. What I do say is, that it would be very much better both for the travelling company, traders, and agriculturists in Kent to have one strong company to deal with instead of two weak companies, who in the past devoted all their money and all their energies to try and cut each others throats, without serving the public at the same time. I do not think this is an occasion to make a long speech, and all I wish to say is, that I do not associate myself in the least with the opposition to this Bill, which comes chiefly from London, and, as a Kent Member, I shall support the Second Reading of this Measure.

*Mr. CHANNING (Northampton, E.): I can assure the honourable Member who has just sat down that such knowledge as I have of the question respecting the proposals of this Bill is not in any way due to the newspaper to which he has referred, or to any of the issues which have been raised in the sensational press. My acquaintance with the subject is due to representations made at Conferences called by the Mansion House Association, which deals with railway rates, and in connection with the Central and Associated Chambers of Agriculture. I do not deny in the least the force of the arguments of the honourable Members for Tunbridge and for Ashford, which should have their weight with the House in dealing with this question. It is perfectly obvious that some benefits may be obtained by the amalgamation of two weak railways, and those companies may, by being placed in a stronger financial position, be enabled to provide advantages of a very considerable character for the benefit of traders and agriculturists in Kent. But the honourable Member for Tunbridge said the position of these two railways place them in a sort of cut-throat competition which has forced them to raise their rates and charges. I would ask him whether he has carefully considered the provisions of this Bill, and whether he does not think that the Bill as it stands, instead of giving any guarantee to the agriculturists and traders that there will be an adequate reduction of the rates and charges, which the honourable Member argued had to be raised in consequence of the unhealthy competition between these two railways—is there any guarantee that those rates and charges will be reduced to reasonable limits by this Bill? I have here a statement of the promoters of this Bill, which says that some sort of guarantee has been given to the Board of Trade that there will be some such reduction of rates and charges to the traders and agriculturists if this Bill is allowed to proceed further. But I must say that, having read that paragraph, I do not think that it is any guarantee whatso-

Mr. Griffith Boscawen.

ever to this House to justify them at the present moment in passing the Second Reading of this Bill, and giving these enormous powers which the Measure does give by the amalgamation of the companies, which would really place the passengers and agriculturists and traders of the Southern counties at the mercy of some joint board of directors. Now, I venture to say that these companies do not come before the House with entirely clean hands in this matter. Of course, their case is that there has been a series of agreements sanctioned by Parliament which have foreshadowed and logically led up to this present proposed amalgamation. I admit that at once, for all the circumstances point in that direction; but how have they used the powers obtained under those agreements? In the Bill of 1894, a clause was slipped in of which the companies promptly availed themselves to raise their third-class fares, and, therefore, the House must recognise due caution in extending further powers to these companies. My honourable Friend the Member for Bethnal Green has referred to the fact that this Bill has not been dealt with in an open and straightforward way by these companies. They have practically gone on with the process of amalgamation without Parliamentary powers, and have thereby tried to force the hand of the Board of Trade and to force the hand of Parliament. The present Bills give them ample authority to exercise to the full the advantages of a monopoly, and at the same time give them an opportunity of giving no guarantees to the traders, passengers, and others who use their lines that they will be protected in these matters. It seems to me that there is no real obligation, and unless the honourable Member for Wimbledon. or some other representative of the company, can give us some definite guarantee as to the proposals which will be introduced into this Bill, I think my honourable Friend will be quite justified in dividing the House against it. The 10th clause in this Bill, viewed in connection with the 3rd clause of the Bill shows absolutely that the proposals of the Bill are not straightforward proposals of amalgamation. There will be a joint board of these two companies, and the result will be that it will be perfectly possible to raise the rates of the other company concerned where one is higher than the other. That is taking all the advantages of a monopoly, and giving no advantages in return to the traders and others concerned in the operations of the companies. I read to-day the speech the Chairman of the South Eastern Railway Company, the Member for Wimbledon, delivered yesterday in reply to certain traders who then met him and the Board. His reply gave no guarantee whatever as to the change of rates or charges. His reply was to the effect that this Bill was amount of capital to be expended by these companies in order to carry out certain improvements and expansions of the railway systems; but there was not in the whole of that speech any indication whatsoever that this larger capital would be so utilised that it would go to reduce the rates and charges now being made against traders, agriculturists, and others who are using these railways. Now, it is perfectly well known that the whole of the rates of these companies were raised in 1893, and it is as equally well known that many of these increased rates have not subsequently been reduced. One of the conditions which ought to be laid down by this House is, that unless these increased rates are reduced to the old level, this Bill should not be allowed to go through. There is another question also in connection with the question of rates that ought to be brought to the attention of the House. The most creditable feature in the dealings of these companies has been the very high preferential rates which have been given to foreign agricultural products, as against our own agricultural products. For instance, in the case of apples and pears, the through rate which is charged to foreigners is 15s., at owner's risk. Now, when the over-sea rate has been deducted from that 15s. rate, it only leaves a rate of 1s. 8d. for the carriage of these goods into London. Now, the rate for English produce from Dover to London is not less than 12s. 6d., so that there is a very great discrepancy between the rates which are enforced for foreign and for English produce. The same remark applies to the case of onions; the rate from Dover for foreign produce, after deducting the over-sea charges, is 1s. 1d., and the rate for English produce is not less than 10s. 6d.

There again is a very heavy difference in favour of the foreign producer. With regard to the maximum rate, it is claimed that there will be some sort of a reduction so far as the maximum rates are concerned in this Bill. I certainly do think that we are entitled to know what sort of reduction is contemplated. I have here a statement of the London, Chatham, and Dover and the South-Eastern Railways' maxima, and a statement of the maxima of the Northern Railway lines, and I find that the maxima of the London, Chatham, and Dover and the South Eastern Railways greatly exceed those of the North Western Railway and others. Now, I venture to say that when we have these three facts, that there are these increased rates which ought to be cut down, that we have also a very great proportion of preferential rates in favour of foreign produce, and that we have a higher standard of maxima of rates upon these two lines already than that which is prevalent on the North Western and Great Western and other lines of this country, I do not think that these companies are entitled to have any further powers conferred upon them before we have some guarantees that these abuses shall be removed before the amalgamating Act be granted. Now, I am opposed on general principles to the policy of amalgamation of railway companies. It gives an increase of power to those companies, and I think we may be creating a dangerous precedent if we assent to this amalgamation taking place. The only instance that we have of an amalgamation between two companies being granted is in the case of the Great Western and the Bristol and Exeter line—that was the only great amalgamation which has taken place; but in that case that was an amalgamation between two companies which practically divided the continuation of a trunk line. The proposed amalgamations of the London and North Western and Lancashire and Yorkshire Railways in 1872 and of the South Eastern and Brighton Lines in 1868, which were similar to this, were both rejected by Parliament. I think that it is very unwise and very impolitic that this amalgamation should be granted at all, and still more impolitic and unwise that it should be granted without the fullest guarantee being given as to the advantages that may be derived from such a scheme by the agriculturists, traders, passengers, and more especially the working-class passengers, who should be protected, and under those circumstances, unless those guarantees are forthcoming, I think my honourable Friend will be fully justified in dividing the House against the Motion that this Bill should be read a second time.

*Sir W. DYKE (Kent, Dartford): I rise to trespass upon the attention of the House in order to bring it back to the real matter before us, and though I wish to deal lightly, and even carelessly, with the opposition that has been brought to bear against this Bill both within and without these walls, it does seem to me, as an old campaigner both within and without this House——whether it is by accident or not, I do not stop to inquire—that the force of the opposition which has been promulgated both inside this House and elsewhere, having regard to the interests which are involved, is the most peculiar that I have ever known. But what we want to arrive at here is business, and therefore, I put on one side altogether the points that have been made by honourable Members opposite, from whom this opposition comes—with the excepton of one silly blunder, which shows the ignoranco of one honourable Gentleman with regard to this matter, when he said the companies had ignored Parliament by having entered into the Continental agreement, whereas the Act for the purpose was passed in 1876.

*Mr. PICKERSGILL: I did not say that. I think the right honourable Gentleman was referring to me, and, if he was, he has grossly misrepresented me. I never referred to the Continental agreement at all. I said that the two companies were now claiming to work all their traffic together, and that their only powers outside the Continental agreement were to deal with competitive traffic.

*Sir W. DYKE: I wish to treat the honourable Gentleman with strict fairness, and I certainly thought he said that his chief objection was against Continental traffic. But, of course, I take his explanation. But however that may

Mr. Channing.

be, the issue before this House is one of supreme importance to the county of Kent, and also, of course, to those who are engaged in the Continental traffic, and to all foreigners who come to our shores. And I venture to urge this much: Out of a long experience of the unfortunate state of things we have endured as regards railway mismanagement in the county of Kent, that a blunder made by this House to-day will be absolutely irretrievable in our day and for generations to come. So far as I am concerned, I am absolutely free, beyond the vested interest which I, in common with other English people, have of the privilege of grumbling at railway mismanagement. I have no interest in either of these companies, but as a resident landowner and a representative of one of the constituencies in the county, I have a vital interest in the proposals now before the House, and in that interest I wish to make my views known, and give the House the very fullest information in my power. The question that has been raised in this House to-day out of doors is a question of competition on the one hand and possible monopoly on the other. Now, really, Sir, competition, in the strict sense and meaning of the word, has never been obtainable as regards railways in the county of Kent. In the earlier efforts of the South Eastern Railway to obtain a Continental route, they were compelled by Parliament to run for 10 miles over another railway, and that prevented them from preserving their independence with their own traffic, and running on true competitive lines. I can understand the competition of great trunk lines, but as I understand that competition, it is between two railways whose lines run through different districts, who compete for the public patronage by lowness of fares, punctuality of trains, and cheapness of goods traffic. That is competition, no doubt, and proper competition; but in that sense these two companies have never competed at all. From 1836 to 1839—from that time to this—Parliament has given statutory sanction to schemes in the county of Kent between these two lines of railway, which has made competition, so far as it is of any benefit to the public, absolutely impossible. Sir, for years past, ever since the London, Chatham, and Dover Railway was first connected, this constant intermingling of traffic has gone on, and for years past, not only has competition not been possible, but there has always been entanglement, owing to mutual responsibilities which have been imposed upon the companies by this system ; and so long as this state of things exists in the county, competition will be absolutely impossible. But what about this cry of monopoly? Monopolies themselves are not good things, but in this case we have to consider the outcome of a position which is more disastrous than any which has occurred in any other part of the kingdom as regards rates and fares and the treatment of the traders and agriculturists and passengers of these lines. What really has happened is, that while there has been no competition between these lines there has been a race and rivalry for the Continental traffic which has proved most disastrous, not only to the companies and the shareholders, but to the passengers and the goods traffic of the line. As regards this race for the Continental traffic, I am sorry to say that some ancestors of mine are somewhat responsible for it. In 1846, the South Eastern Company of that day offered an ancestor of mine a bonus of £40,000 if he would allow them to go through his property. He refused to allow them to go through his property, with the result that the South Eastern Railway was driven miles away, through the Weald of Kent by the Tunbridge route. When the London, Chatham, and Dover railway came along years after and brought a line close to my own home, and obtained a more direct route to the Continent, then the South Eastern Railway again comes in and claims a direct route through Sevenoaks and Tunbridge. During that time money flowed in the struggle between these two Companies in the Committee-rooms of this House like water. Not only has this rivalry been maintained with most disastrous results, but ever since that time there has been rivalry and litigation going on to an enormous extent, and the result has been swollen capital in the case of the South Eastern, and so far as the London, Chatham, and Dover Railway is concerned, the result has been very low dividends and very high fares and charges. I really ask this House to forgive me for

mentioning this little history as to the way in which this disastrous rivalry has been arrived at and its results. It has been arrived at entirely in that way. In what position do we find ourselves to-day? For some years past a common understanding or union has been arrived at, as I believe under Parliamentary sanction, and it is therefore legal. The question is whether Parliament is ready now to send this Bill upstairs to a Committee, and make this union effective or not? That is the whole point. That is the question we have to decide ; but in all cases of difficulty there may be an alternative. What is the alternative? The alternative is to throw these companies back into the wretched state of entanglement in which they were placed before. We see, on the one hand, a strong company anxious to help a weaker company ; willing to make this union. Are we, with our eyes open, going to prevent it ; because to prevent it is to make it absolutely impossible for the London, Chatham, and Dover Railway Company to raise any further capital to carry out its effective working. If this Bill is passed it will result in the expenditure of a million of money for the improvement of the traffic arrangement of these lines in the first year. Are we going to throw away such a chance as that? The feeling which I have upon the matter is, that Parliament should assist us out of the difficulty in which we find ourselves ; and that the only possible outcome is to support this Measure for the carrying out of these vast improvements which will not only benefit the Continental passengers, but will bring about a state of things which will enable these companies to reduce their rates on goods and agricultural products. I see much in the proposals before us, and before I sit down I think it is only right to say, that in dealing with this Bill as we are going to do, that the House, dealing as it is perhaps with a monopoly, would naturally ask what safeguards are to be provided on the question of fares, traffic, and rates. Those are very important matters, and I think before this Debate is closed, that my honourable Friend who is in charge of the Measure will show that, so far as the passengers and all rates are concerned, the promoters of this Bill will place themselves without the least reserve in the hands of the Board of Trade, and will say that no fares or rates shall be raised or dealt with without their sanction. I believe that if the House will give their assent to a union like this to help us out of our present entanglement, that under new control and new management the first outcome would be the breaking up of these old rivalries, and that working under a new system, the result would be a considerable relief to our agriculturists, to our fruit growers, and others, as regards the rates which they now pay. I thank the House for listening to me at this length, but of this I am assured, having given the utmost attention to this question, and knowing all these circumstances from my earliest years, though I have known Parliament, sometimes in ignorance, sometimes under pressure, do a hard thing to a private Bill, I would urge that this Parliament, at all events, cannot do a more cruel thing, not only to the passengers, but also to the through passengers to the Continent and the traders and agriculturists and others interested in the workings of these lines, than to refuse the passage of this Bill upstairs.

MR. BRYCE (Aberdeen, S.): The right honourable Gentleman who has just sat down has endeavoured to deny that there ever was any competition between these two companies in Kent. If I could take up the time of the House, I could show him that there was, but he went on and said that he thought that a monopoly was best.

*SIR W. DYKE: I think I must dispute that altogether; the suggestion that I made was that the only way out of the present state of affairs was by an amalgamation of these two companies.

MR. BRYCE: I am glad that the right honourable Gentleman has repudiated that suggestion; but he will not deny that the effect of this Bill, if it passes into law, will be to hand over the whole of the south-eastern corner of Britain to the operations of one company; that it will leave it in the control of a single company. That is a matter of very great importance, because it raises a question of policy. I shall only indicate this question of

Sir W. Dyke.

policy, and remind the House that there has not been for many years past any case in which such a proposal has been made to us and allowed. In 1872, the amalgamation of the Lancashire and Yorkshire Railway Company with the London and North-Western Railway was proposed, but was rejected. The Lancashire and Yorkshire Company was a weak company, and could not give a proper and effective service, and the stronger company proposed to help them. Since then that company has become a strong company, and is able to compete with the London and North-Western Railway. In the same manner the proposed amalgamation between the North British Railway and another adjacent railway was also rejected. The case presented to our consideration to-day is of special importance, for this reason: in the case of these two lines, the South-Eastern Railway and the London, Chatham, and Dover Railway, in the main, the traffic is passenger traffic; it is three-fourths passenger and one-fourth goods traffic; whereas, on the Great Northern lines, it is three-fourths goods and one-fourth passenger traffic. Now, the House will recognise that traders are far more able to combine among themselves, where it is a case in which their goods are concerned, and to organise themselves into a far more effective body than passengers, who are at the best scattered creatures. Therefore, a railway company whose profit is mainly derived from passenger traffic requires a very much greater amount of care at the hands of this House, and the passenger requires a great deal more protection than in the case of the trader, because they cannot protect themselves. Now, the two companies with which we are dealing, hold what is practically a monopoly of Continental traffic, but the honourable Gentlemen who have spoken upon this Debate have all spoken about Kent, as though they looked upon this matter as concerning Kent alone. But it concerns us all; it concerns London, which contributes a larger amount of traffic than Kent itself; it also concerns the Continental routes; and the fact that these two railways hold the two great Continental routes is in itself quite sufficient for this Measure to be considered by this House in a special manner. The Bill therefore comes before the House with a *prima facie* case against it, and no one will say that either company has so good a record that they ought to be indulged. The honourable Gentleman the Member for Ashford went further than I should go, when he likened these companies to the Augean stables. I will not recapitulate what has been said by my honourable Friend on this side of the House, but will come at once to the pith of the case made by the right honourable Gentleman who has just sat down. He said that competition, so far as we have had it, has not been a success; that Kent and Sussex have been very badly served, that rates are high and that passenger fares are very high; that the service is bad, and therefore there must be a strong case to meet them. His case is, that as competition has failed, and that it is impossible to meet it by a small expenditure of capital, that by a union of the companies a much better service, lower fares, and lower rates, would be obtained, and that the House may be fairly asked to take this step and to make a new departure and intervene to obtain by monopoly what competition has been unable to do. I think there is a great deal of force in that case, and I am inclined, therefore, despite the arguments that have been brought to bear against the Bill with great force, to think that this Bill should go before a Committee; but if it goes before a Committee certain conditions should be attached to it. The Committee should be an exceedingly strong Committee, and this Committee should have much freedom in its methods. It should not be restricted by the ordinary rules of procedure which govern the Railway Committee, but should be allowed to conduct its deliberations into this question as if it was, what it really is, a question of great public policy. I hope before the end of the Debate we shall receive some assurance from the Board of Trade and those responsible for the Bill that no objection will be raised to two proposals, namely, that the Committee shall be one of exceptional strength, and shall have a perfectly free hand in inquiring into all the questions which they may deem necessary to investigate for the purpose of solving this difficulty. I would further suggest that the Committee should have power to impose very stringent conditions as to the price of this Act of Parliament—to

require the reduction of rates and fares, and the giving of additional facilities to the travelling public, especially in connection with workmen's trains. The Committee should also have power to consider whether some proviso should not be added dealing with a future revision of rates and charges, and enabling, if the scheme be not successful, some other company to come into the district. Those who are inclined to oppose the Second Reading will not part with all their powers over the Bill by sending it to a Committee. If their demands are not satisfied, questions can still be raised on the Third Reading, and, if necessary, the Bill can be rejected. I hope and trust, however, that that step will not be necessary; but it will depend upon the view which the Committee takes, and the freedom which it is allowed.

THE PRESIDENT OF THE BOARD OF TRADE (Mr. RITCHIE, Croydon): Sir, the right honourable Gentleman who has just sat down has arrived at a conclusion to which I was the first to ask the House to come, namely, that the Bill be read a second time, and then referred to a Committee. No doubt, an amalgamation of the kind proposed is one of large public interest, and no one can be surprised that Parliament has been asked to consider the important principle involved in the Measure. The service of the two companies concerned has been such as has not hitherto proved very satisfactory to the travelling public. But that is not an argument, in my opinion, against the Second Reading, but is one altogether in favour of it. The alternatives before the House are two. The one is whether or not, by rejecting the Bill, you are to allow the present unsatisfactory state of things to continue without taking some steps to remedy it; and the other is, whether you will give assent to the continuance of a private arrangement between the two companies, instead of an amalgamation on terms which may be examined by a Committee of the House that can insist, if it chooses, as a condition of amalgamation, that certain privileges shall be given. To reject this proposal for amalgamation on some shadowy idea that, in the remote future, some northern company might purchase the London, Chatham, and Dover Railway would be a course not in accord with the public interest. I must here repudiate, on my own behalf and on that of my right honourable Friend, the statement of the honourable Member opposite (Mr. Pickersgill) to the effect that the name of the Member for East Kent (Mr. Akers Douglas) appearing on the back of the Bill has in the smallest degree, either intentionally by him or with regard to myself, had any influence on any proceeding——

*Mr. PICKERSGILL: I never suggested anything of the kind.

The PRESIDENT of the BOARD of TRADE: The honourable Gentleman did not say so, but he suggested it. Why did he mention the fact at all, then, if it was not to convey some reflection on my right honourable Friend? Such reflections are much worse than actual statements. My right honourable Friend has never mentioned the subject —neither of the two right honourable Gentlemen whose names appear on the back of the Bill, nor any colleague interested in railways has made any representations to me either for or against any proposals connected with railways which have been under my consideration since I have been President of the Board of Trade. The Board of Trade have, as the House knows, had some communications in the public interest with the railway companies in regard to some proposals in the Bill, and the railway companies concerned have shown the greatest inclination to meet the views which the Board of Trade have placed before them, and to make such alterations in their Bill as will, in our opinion, protect the public interest. The Board of Trade have insisted on the reduction of the maximum charges in the Bill; in this instance those charges may be reduced, and I do not suppose the public will express any keen regret if that course be adopted. But that is not any reason why the Bill should not go before a Committee. There is one fear to which the public are justified in giving expression. Where at present there are competitive rates, in the amalgamation care shall be taken that there is no power, on their own initiative, to increase those competitive rates; and we have secured a clause in the Bill providing that at all competitive points there shall be no increase of passenger

President Board of Trade.

charges without the consent of the Railway Commission—a provision which adequately protects the public—and so with regard to goods. The Board of Trade will have to make a Report to Parliament on the Bill, and I hope when that Report is made we may have more concessions to record; but we shall, in any case, take care to consider any points where we think the public may be more efficiently protected than under the Bill. If passed, I believe the Bill will have the effect which my right honourable Friend the Member for Kent desires—it will place in the hands of the London, Chatham, and Dover Railway Company a sum of money which they could not by any other means obtain for the purpose of improving their rolling stock, and for giving facilities to the public which they have long been demanding in vain. I believe the Bill will give great facilities to the public not at present existing for travelling between one system and the other. I look to the Committee to take such securities as shall prevent the amalgamation from being prejudicial to the public interest. I agree that the Bill should go before a Hybrid Committee. An ordinary Committee would, no doubt, deal satisfactorily with the question, but, having regard to the general interests expressed with reference to that question, it would be wise for the House, when the proper time comes, to refer the Bill to a strong Hybrid Committee. As to reducing fares and rates, insisting on workmen's trains, and other matters of that kind, my conviction is that without any instruction from the House the Committee would have full power to consider all such proposals. I am bound to say, with regard to workmen's trains, these companies have been more liberal than any other company running to London. In this connection, I think I am right in pointing out that these companies propose to give workmen tickets by every train up to eight o'clock in the morning. Sir, I hope the honourable Gentleman will not divide the House on this occasion, for I am certain that the general sense of the House is in favour of the Second Reading, all of us hoping that the Bill may emerge from the Committee in a condition which will be acceptable to all concerned.

Mr. BURNS (Battersea): Mr. Speaker, some criticisms were made by a number of Members on the other side as to the character and the legality of the opposition against the Second Reading of this Bill. Well, Sir, the right honourable Baronet the Member for Kent cannot direct such criticism against myself. I have the misfortune to ride in the railway carriages of one of the companies mentioned in this Bill, and I represent a district that has the greater misfortune of having one of these railways running through it. Consequently, my *locus standi* in this Debate is certainly as good as that of the provincial Gentlemen who represent Kent, and who look upon London simply as a means of providing the working expenses of a railway. Now, Sir, I want to say that I am extremely dissatisfied with the speech of the President of the Board of Trade. He has talked about public safeguards, and certain changes in the Bill, and indicated that the Chatham and Dover and South Eastern Railway Companies will give the 3d., 2d., and 1d. scale. Well, upon that I say, " Thank you for nothing," because nearly every other railway gives that, and considerably more already, and, consequently, the concession is hardly worth taking. I believe, Sir, that the President of the Board of Trade might have gone further and said that this company had no power to increase competitive rates, and neither would the Board of Trade allow it. What about the reduction of existing competitive rates? What about rates and fares that ought to be gradually reduced to follow the prospective reductions that other companies are sure to make, and which many companies carry out at the present moment? I believe that much good has been done to Kent and London by the Motion to reject this Bill, because without this discussion we should not have heard the highly interesting reminiscences of the right honourable Baronet the Member for Dartford, who told us that 40 or 50 years ago, or at some archaic date, an ancestor of his made a blunder in opposing the Chatham and Dover Bill. Well, Sir, what guarantee have we that his grandson 50 years hence in the House of Commons will not say a similar thing about the honourable Baronet supporting this Motion in his present unconditional manner? I have

no desire, however, to go into the ancient history of the right honourable Baronet's family and the prospective decision of his grandson. I prefer to take the business-like attitude of a London Member, and say that so far the President of the Board of Trade has neither pledged, promised, or guaranteed conditions that will satisfy the great railway traffic of London. And what is more, Sir, I have only got to go to Kent to prove my argument. The honourable Member who first spoke in support of the Bill was under the impression that London Members were trespassing upon this Tom Tiddler's ground that they represent, but he ought to know that of the 75 per cent. of the traffic of these two railways (i.e., passenger traffic) over 60 per cent is practically dependent upon London, and 50 per cent. of that 60 per cent. is London traffic pure and simple. You cannot, therefore, talk of the Chatham and Dover or South Eastern Railway Companies and leave London out of consideration. The honourable Member also said Continental traffic had been safeguarded. Yes, on present charges that may be so ; but what we want is to regulate the Continental rates that produce-growers in the beautiful county of Kent will not have to pay from 5s. to 10s. 6d. for onions, carrots, and turnips, as against 1s. 3d. or 1s. 6d. charged on these articles from Belgium and Germany. But that concession cannot be granted so long as we have Conservative Members theoretically looking after agriculture but taking the side of a railway company that has not considered the interests of Kent to anything like the extent it should have done. Then we are twitted with being irresponsible. Well, Sir, I am prepared to admit that my interest in this Bill is not dividends, and my concern in it is not directors' fees, and in that sense we are both irresponsible and independent. Honourable Members from Kent have talked about this being a local matter, and said that London Members should not intervene. But I venture to say that we suffer considerably by the blundering of these two companies, and our past expérience of them is no guarantee that we shall not be similarly treated in the future unless the President of the Board of Trade and the Committee go further in the direction of keeping these companies under popular and effective control.   An honourable Member has also said that practically there has been no effective competition, and that effective competition had never existed in Kent. Sir, where is the pledge of the honourable Member for Wimbledon? where is the pledge of the President of the Board of Trade?—that these two theoretical rival companies, who, in their desire to get Continental traffic, have ignored London and shamefully treated agriculturists in Kent, will do in the future any better than they have done in the past? Not one word in this Debate to lead us to form that view. Then we are told that concessions are being made. Well, what is the kind of concession? I have heard of one. The London, Chatham, and Dover Company have knocked off the 9.5 p.m. train from Victoria to Dover, and also the 3.45 a.m. Dover to Victoria, and, as a " concession," they substitute for these two trains, one starting at 10.30 from Victoria, going through Tunbridge Wells, and thence on the other line to Hastings and Sevenoaks, where no one wants to go or could go by the previous train. Well, if that is the kind of concession they are going to give, the fewer we have of them the better. I have received from season ticket holders representations to vote against the Second Reading of this Bill. I intend to do so simply because there has been no promise, pledge, or guarantee worthy the name from any supporter of the Bill. Now, Sir, I know from season ticket holders that the accommodation is bad, the time tables worse, and punctuality very indifferent. But there is one section of this traffic which I am much interested in, namely, workmen's train accommodation. The President of the Board of Trade has never ridden from Victoria to Ludgate Hill by the 4.30 or 5.30 on the London, Chatham, and Dover Railway. If he had he would have been reminded of what the Via Dolorosa is. But I will give the President of the Board of Trade an illustration: 12 to 16 workmen in a compartment to hold 10 on a foggy morning in November, with half of them smoking, and overcrowded to the most scandalous extent. Minor accidents frequently happen, although the Chatham and Dover, we are told, is an exceedingly good line. Well, as one who has travelled on this system, I cannot appreciate the eulogy pronounced by the President of the Board of Trade. It is

Mr. Burns.

not true. I do not believe it myself, and I believe the rest of London agree with me upon that point. With regard to the South Eastern, the company only run 13 workmen's trains, and this is the way in which some of the workmen employed by the Government at Woolwich Arsenal are treated—in consequence of having only short spells of work many of them are unable to leave London to permanently live at Woolwich, and very frequently these men have to pay 6s. or 7s. a week to go from Charing Cross to Woolwich and back out of 35s. and 38s. a week, the fares on the South Eastern being 1s. 2d. from Woolwich to Charing Cross, and 1s. 1d. from Woolwich to Spa Road. Well, Sir, I do believe that London will never be able to solve the housing problem, to destroy one-room tenements, and to mitigate the frightful poverty which exists in this large city, until Parliament compels the suburban and metropolitan railways to help the local authorities in London by a big system of cheap and frequent workmen's trains. The contribution towards the housing problem by the South Eastern Railway is practically nil. The contribution of the London, Chatham, and Dover Railway Company is not worth anything. Their general treatment of the second-class and first-class passenger is equally shabby and disreputable, and it is to the credit of the workmen that the prevalent overcrowding has not been carried further. But with regard to rates on produce, with regard to workmen's fares, either in number or price, not a word from a responsible person in this Debate. As representing one of the South London constituencies which is served by both of these two railways, I trust that the House will not be influenced by the proposed safeguards of the President of the Board of Trade. I want to see them before we vote for the Second Reading. I sincerely trust that Members on this side will not be too much influenced by the suggestion that the appointment of a Committee is the right way to dispose of this Bill. I believe that the best thing that could happen both to the Chatham and Dover and South Eastern Railway Companies is for this Second Reading to be rejected by an overwhelming majority. If that were done it would teach the directors, and especially the embryonic Hercules who is going to clear out this Augean stable, that to carry out this tremendous task they must have a stronger, sounder public opinion behind them than at present exists. If this House rejects the Second Reading of this Bill the directors of both companies would come together, and they would submit to the London public and to the Kent district a scheme of fares, rates, and tariffs, with suggestions for improvements that would be popular beyond doubt, and then they would get a Second Reading with practically no opposition at all. The only way in which you can convert the South Eastern is to apply the toe of the boot. The only way in which the Chatham and Dover Company can be influenced is for the House of.Commons to say, " Too long they mismanaged the public duty that Parliament entrusted them with years and years ago." I believe that the best thing in the interests of these two companies—I ought really, Sir, to receive a substantial solatium for making these excellent suggestions—is for the House of Commons to put its foot down and say—" We have stood your blundering and plundering too long; you must know what you are going to do, and must be certain of it, the public must be satisfied as to your capacity to discharge your obligations, and Parliament will then devise means by which it can be done. It is about time that is done. I trust the House of Commons will defeat this Bill, and turn it out, as it deserves, by a large majority.

Mr. COSMO BONSOR (Surrey, Wimbledon): Perhaps the honourable Gentleman who has just spoken is right in saying that the blundering policy of the South Eastern Railway in the past has reached its climax. I thought for a moment that he was going to suggest that he should be the general manager of the company in future, because he seemed to be absolutely conversant with all the facts of the case. He seemed to know the rates for agricultural produce, the fares of passengers, and the allowances made to foreigners. I felt he had studied the subject so thoroughly that he was prepared to suggest that possibly he might be general manager, or, perhaps, that the London County Council should take over the railways. Well, Mr. Speaker, I do not intend to enter into the details of this Debate, because I am perfectly well aware that anyone who is considered to have been, or is about to be, connected with the policy of a Private Bill is not supposed to use his influence or his vote for or against that Bill. But I do not think the House should divide on this occasion on anything like false representations. My right honourable Friend the Member for Aberdeen laid out a policy for the guidance of the proposed Committee, which I for one, speaking in behalf of the shareholders of the South Eastern Company, cannot for one moment accept. I wish this House to thoroughly understand that I cannot agree to the reference which the right honourable Gentleman wished to make to the Committee to which the Bill will be sent. I would rather lose the Bill. There is nothing in the present Bill which is exceptional. But there is this to be said, that no Private Bill has come before the House of Commons upon which greater publicity has been thrown. Everyone interested in the matter knows that for quite nine months the policy of the two companies was to be proposed in Parliament, and that policy has been before the country and before the passengers and customers of these companies, and with all that publicity there have been only seven petitions presented against the Bill. Two out of those seven petitions were presented by great railway companies, who naturally did not oppose the principle of the Measure, but merely opposed it on the ground that they have already agreements with one of the two companies, and they wish these agreements to be protected in the Bill. One petition was from the commercial travellers of Great Britain. Another petition was from the town and corporation of Canterbury, possibly the only representative authority, the only local authority, or county council or district council in the district which we serve which has petitioned against the Bill. And since I came into the House I have been informed that that petition has been withdrawn. Beyond that petition there is absolutely nothing left except the petition of the London County Council. The promoters of the Bill were advised that they might have objected to the appearance of the London County Council before the Committee of this House on the ground that the London County Council had no *locus standi.* But I think we were well advised in saying that the policy we proposed was a big policy, and that we should shut out no one from the discussion of the provisions we were going to place in our Act. We, therefore, welcomed the London County Council as the protective genius of the various bodies and authorities who wished to protest against the Bill, or who wished to get advantage from it. I do not know whether the right honourable Gentleman intends to move for the Committee which he has selected, but in the interests of shareholders, if he does, I shall oppose it. I feel as confident as possible that this Bill is really in the interests of the public first, and in the interests of the shareholders afterwards; and I am perfectly confident that the clauses which have been agreed to with the Board of Trade will be an absolute protection against any undue use of the monopoly we possess. We bind ourselves absolutely not to increase any rate, fare, or charge which is at present in existence. And we go one step further, and say that it is our absolute intention to go through the whole of the tariff of charges, fares, and the rates, and to remove anomalies, and do our best to make the interests of the company and the interests of our customers identical as they ought to be.

MR. J. LOWTHER (Kent, Isle of Thanet): As representative of a constituency which is more closely interested in this question than that of any other Member of the House, I would like to say a few words. I did not gather from my honourable Friend behind me whether he accepted the suggestion made by the President of the Board of Trade. I understand my Friend accepts the modification of the proposal of the right honourable Gentleman opposite.

MR. COSMO BONSOR: Yes.

MR. J. LOWTHER: I would like to say this, that my constituents, until a few days ago, afforded me no indication whatever of what their opinions were. But during the last 10 days I have had a great many representations on this subject. Those representations differed very widely one from the other; but among those who favoured me with representations I did not find that enthusiasm in favour of the Bill which my Friend indicated. On the other hand, I did not find any important section of

Mr. Bonsor.

them who were prepared to suggest that the Bill should be rejected. What I found was suggested was that all local interests should have a fair opportunity of being heard before the Committee— not a rambling inquiry on the part of persons who had no business whatever in the locality—but that all local interests should be fairly heard. There was one opinion which I found largely prevailed: that was that if there had been any hope or chance of getting one of the Northern lines to acquire one of these companies in order to come into Kent that would have been welcomed with open arms. But when it was found that that was impossible the present Bill was acquiesced in by them as a disagreeable alternative. I feel bound to say this, as I told my constituents yesterday, because the whole of England for railway purposes is already parcelled out very much in the same way as China is just now by the European Powers. It has been divided into spheres of interest and influence. But unlike the European Powers in China, the railway companies agree not to encroach upon each other's provinces. This is done by a *bonâ fide* agreement which makes it impossible for any of the Northern lines to invade Kent. My honourable Friend near me says it is not so; but all I can say is that hitherto none of the Northern lines have come forward to fill the void. I, for one, cannot take upon myself the responsibility of opposing the Second Reading of the Bill. I fully accept the promises of my honourable Friend behind me. I feel sure that which he has promised to carry out he will see carried out. Under these circumstances I trust the House will accept the reference of the Bill to a Hybrid Committee, so that all interested in it may be heard.

MR. LOUGH (Islington, W.): Do I understand that the suggestion that has been thrown out by the right honourable Gentleman the Member for Aberdeen has been accepted by the President of the Board of Trade?

THE PRESIDENT OF THE BOARD OF TRADE: I propose a reference to a Hybrid Committee.

MR. LOUGH: I do not understand the position taken up by the honourable Member for Wimbledon. He says that he agrees with the President of the

Board of Trade, but does not accept the position taken up by the right honourable Member for Aberdeen.

Mr. COSMO BONSOR: I willingly accept a Hybrid Committee, and the stronger it is made the better I will be pleased. But I accept it with the limitations imposed on it by the President of the Board of Trade.

Mr. LOUGH: There is no great difference, to my mind. The President of the Board of Trade has made it clear why he recommends that Committee. The object I have in rising is not to discuss the provisions of the Bill. As far as I can understand, all have admitted that we have had a wretched state of affairs on these two lines, and that something must be done to mend it. My honourable Friend who moved the rejection of the Bill has not been able to put into very practical shape before the House the reforms he wishes introduced. The honourable Member for Battersea has said that the best thing that could happen to the Bill would be its rejection by a great majority, and that then the companies should state the concessions they are prepared to make, and make these the basis of a Bill which would be passed next year unanimously. That sounds very well, but it is not practical. I do not think that next Session the House would be willing to pass a Bill which it has unanimously rejected this year. I have a little information which I wish to give to the House. The action of the honourable Member for Battersea, like the action of the London County Council as far as London is concerned, was almost confined to the question of workmen's trains. I happened last year to have something to do with these two lines, as well as with other lines with which I have relations; and I am bound to state that these companies, from whatever motive, have adopted the very suggestions which the honourable Gentleman has thrown out in regard to workmen's trains.

*Mr. BURNS: When?

Mr. LOUGH: They have taken the means of making public larger facilities for workmen's trains than have ever been given by any other lines coming into London.

Honourable Members: No, no!

Mr. LOUGH: They made it public five weeks ago, but I knew it over three months ago, when I had occasion to approach the two companies as president of a society with which I am connected. And I hold in my hand the advertisements announcing these new arrangements in regard to workmen's trains. The question is whether these new arrangements are of a satisfactory nature. I do not wish to enter into details; I will only say that we were told by the honourable Member for Walthamstow that the Chatham and Dover Company ran only 13 workmen's trains, and the South-Eastern only 25. It was pointed out to the society with which I am connected that the reason why more workmen's trains were not given was because of the physical difficulty of getting in and out of the termini of the lines. But the company said that, to meet this difficulty, they would allow workmen to travel by any train on their system and give tickets at greatly reduced fares, even after eight o'clock in the morning. These companies have done more, I think, to carry into effect the provisions of the Cheap Trains Act than any other company coming into London. I do not say that this is all that ought to be given. My honourable Friend has mentioned—and I thought he had a good right to do so in the interest of those he represents—certain stations, eight or nine in number, where the workmen's trains did not stop. But the companies have been approached, and I think it is not impossible that the Board of Trade will get some reasonable arrangement made for these stations. But the new concession I have mentioned is not the only one to which public attention has been drawn. There have been concessions in regard to Continental traffic and other matters. In fact, the very course recommended by the honourable

Member for Battersea has been, to a large extent, adopted. I believe the President of the Board of Trade has been in communication with the companies, and that many further concessions have been promised. The question is, what we have got to do at the present moment. We have received very good advice from the right honourable Member for Aberdeen, and no one can say that that right honourable Gentleman's criticism, both of the companies and of the Bill, was not sufficiently severe. He was not, however, opposed to the Second Reading of the Bill, but demanded that it be remitted to a strong Committee, and that that Committee should get every concession it possibly could from the companies before the Bill was passed. I have not detected any note of hostility in this House to the principle of the Bill, and I think that, after all, the best course which we could adopt is to pass the Second Reading of the Bill, and refer it to a strong Hybrid Committee.

Question put—

"That the word 'now' stand part of the Question."

The House divided:—Ayes 288; Noes 82.—(Division List No. 41.)

AYES.

Acland-Hood, Capt. Sir A F.
Aird, John
Allen, W. (Newc. under Lyme)
Allison, Robert Andrew
Ambrose, William (Middlesex)
Anstruther, H. T.
Arrol, Sir William
Ascroft, Robert
Ashmead-Bartlett, Sir Ellis
Asquith, Rt. Hon. Herbert H.
Atkinson, Rt. Hon. John
Bagot, Capt. Josceline FitzRoy
Baillie, James E. B. (Inverness)
Baird, John George Alexander
Baldwin, Alfred
Balfour, Rt. Hn. A J.(Manc'r)
Banbury, Frederick George
Bartley, George C. T.
Beach,Rt.Hn.Sir M.H (Bristol)
Beach,W.W.Bramston (Hants)
Beckett, Ernest William
Begg, Ferdinand Faithfull
Bemrose, Sir Henry Howe
Bethell, Commander
Bhownaggree, Sir M M.
Biddulph, Michael
Blundell, Colonel Henry
Boscawen, Arthur Griffith-
Boulnois, Edmund
Bowles,T.Gibson(King's Lynn)
Brassey, Albert
Brodrick, Rt. Hon. St. John
Brown, Alexander H.
Bryce, Rt. Hon. James
Burdett-Coutts, W.
Campbell-Bannerman, Sir H.
Carlile, William Walter
Carson, Rt. Hon. Edward
Causton, Richard Knight
Cavendish, R. F. (N. Lancs.)
Cawley, Frederick
Cecil, Evelyn (Hertford, East)
Cecil, Lord Hugh (Greenwich)
Chaloner, Capt. R. G. W.
Chamberlain, Rt.Hn.J. (Birm.)
Chamberlain, J. Austen (Wor.)
Cochrane, Hon. Thos. H. A. E.
Coddington, Sir William

Mr. Lough.

Coghill, Douglas Harry
Cohen, Benjamin Louis
Collings, Rt Hon Jesse
Colomb, Sir John Chas. Ready
Colston, Chas. Edw. H. Athole
Compton. Lord Alwyne
Cooke, C.W.Radcliffe (Heref'd)
Corbett, A. Cameron (Glasgow)
Cotton-Jodrell, Col. Ed. T. D.
Courtney, Rt. Hn. Leonard H.
Cranborne, Viscount
Cripps, Charles Alfred
Crombie, John William
Cross, Herb. Shepherd (Bolton)
Cruddas, William Donaldson
Cubitt, Hon. Henry
Curran, Thomas B. (Donegal)
Currie, Sir Donald
Curzon, Viscount
Dalkeith, Earl of
Davenport, W. Bromley-
Denny, Colonel
Dickson-Poynder, Sir John P.
Dorington, Sir John Edward
Doughty, George
Douglas, Charles M. (Lanark)
Doxford, William Theodore
Drucker, A.
Duncombe, Hon. Hubert V.
Dyke, Rt.Hn. Sir William Hart
Egerton, Hon. A. de Tatton
Elliot, Hon. A. Ralph Douglas
Ellis, John Edward (Notts.)
Evans,SirFrancisH.(S'thmptn.
Fardell, Sir T. George
Farquharson, Dr. Robert
Fergusson,Rt Hn SirJ.(Manc'r)
Ffrench, Peter
Finch, George H.
Finlay, Sir Robert Bannatyne
Firbank, Joseph Thomas
Fisher, William Hayes
Fison, Frederick William
Fitzmaurice, Lord Edmond
Flower, Ernest
Folkestone, Viscount
Foster, Colonel (Lancaster)
Foster, Harry S. (Suffolk)

Foster, Sir Walter (Derby Co.)
Fry, Lewis
Galloway, William Johnson
Gedge, Sydney
Gibbons, J. Lloyd
Gibbs, HnA.G.H.(City of Lon.)
Gilliat, John Saunders
Gladstone,Rt. Hn. Herbert J.
Godson,Sir Augustus Frederick
Gold, Charles
Goldsworthy, Major-General
Gordon, Hon. John Edward
Goschen, George J. (Sussex)
Goulding, Edward Alfred
Gray, Ernest (West Ham)
Green,WalfordD.(Wednesbury)
Greville, Hon. Ronald
Grey, Sir Edward (Berwick)
Gunter, Colonel
Haldane, Richard Burdon
Hanbury, Rt. Hn. Robert Wm.
Hardy, Laurence
Hare, Thomas Leigh
Hatch, Ernest Frederick Geo.
Hayne, Rt. Hn. Charles Seale-
Healy, Maurice (Cork)
Healy, Thomas J. (Wexford)
Healy, Timothy M. (N. Louth)
Heath, James
Heaton, John Henniker
Helder, Augustus
Hermon-Hodge, Robert Trotter
Hickman, Sir Alfred
Hill, Sir Edwd. Stock (Bristol)
Hoare, Edw. Brodie (Hampst'd)
Hobhouse, Henry
Holden, Sir Angus
Hornby, Sir William Henry
Hozier, Hn. James Henry Cecil
Hubbard, Hon. Evelyn
Humphreys-Owen, Arthur C.
Jackson, Rt. Hn. Wm. Lawies
Jeffreys, Arthur Frederick
Jenkins, Sir John Jones
Jessel, Capt. Herbert Merton
Johnston, William (Belfast)
Jolliffe, Hon. H. George
Kay-Shuttleworth,RtHnSirU.

Kearley, Hudson E.
Kennaway, Rt.Hn. Sir John H
Kenyon, James
Kenyon-Slaney, Colonel Wm.
Kilbride, Denis
Kimber, Henry
King, Sir Henry Seymour
Kitson, Sir James
Knowles, Lees
Labouchere, Henry
Lafone, Alfred
Lawrence, Wm. F. (Liverpool)
Lecky, Rt. Hn. William Ed. H.
Leigh-Bennett, Henry Currie
Llewellyn, Evan H. (Somerset)
Loder, Gerald Walter Erskine
Long, Col. Chas. W. (Evesham)
Lopes, Henry Yarde Buller
Lough, Thomas
Lowles, John
Lowther, Rt. Hn. James (Kent)
Loyd, Archie Kirkman
Lucas-Shadwell, William
Macartney, W. G. Ellison
Macdona, John Cumming
MacIver, David (Liverpool)
Maclean, James Mackenzie
Maclure, Sir John William
M'Arthur, Charles (Liverpool)
M'Arthur, William (Cornwall)
M'Ewan, William
M'Iver, Sir Lewis (Edin., W.)
M'Killop, James
M'Laren, Charles Benjamin
Maple, Sir John Blundell
Mappin, Sir Fredk. Thorpe
Marks, Henry Hananel
Massey-Mainwaring, Hn. W. F.
Maxwell, Rt.Hn.Sir Herbert E.
Mendl, Sigismund Ferdinand
Meysey-Thompson, Sir H. M.
Milbank, SirPowlettChas. Jno.
Middlemore, John T.
Monk, Charles James
Moon, Edward Robert Pacy
More, Robt.Jasper(Shropshire)
Morley, Charles (Breconshire)
Morrell, George Herbert
Morris, Samuel

Morton, Arth.H.A.(Deptford)
Moulton, John Fletcher
Mount, William George
Murray,RtHn.A.Graham(Bute
Murray, Charles J. (Coventry)
Murray, Col. Wyndham (Bath)
Myers, William Henry
Newdigate, Francis Alexander
Nicholson, William Graham
Nicol, Donald Ninian
O'Malley, William
Orr-Ewing, Charles Lindsay
Palmer, Sir Chas. M. (Durham)
Palmer, George Wm.(Reading)
Paulton, James Mellor
Pearson, Sir Weetman D.
Percy, Earl
Philpotts, Captain Arthur
Platt-Higgins, Frederick
Powell, Sir Francis Sharp
Pretyman, Ernest George
Priestley, Briggs (Yorks.)
Purvis, Robert
Rentoul, James Alexander
Richards, Henry Charles
Richardson,SirThos.(Hartlep'l)
Rickett, J. Compton
Ritchie, Rt. Hn.Chas.Thomson
Robinson, Brooke
Roche, Hn. Jas. (East Kerry)
Rothschild,Hn.Lionel Walter
Royds, Clement Molyneux
Russell,Gen.F.S.(Cheltenham)
Russell, T. W. (Tyrone)
Ryder, John Herbert Dudley
Samuel, Harry S.(Limehouse)
Sassoon, Sir Edward Albert
Savory, Sir Joseph
Schwann, Charles E.
Seton-Karr, Henry
Sharpe,William Edward T.
Sidebotham, J.W.(Cheshire)
Simeon, Sir Barrington
Sinclair,Capt.Jno.(Forfarshire)
Sinclair, Louis (Romford)
Skewes-Cox, Thomas
Smith,Abel H.(Christchurch)
Smith, Jas. Parker (Lanarks.)
Smith, Hn. W. F. D.(Strand,

Spencer, Ernest
Stanley, Hn.Arthur(Ormskirk)
Stanley,Edward Jas.(Somerset)
Stanley, Henry M.(Lambeth)
Stanley, Lord (Lancs.)
Stephens, Henry Charles
Stewart,SirMark J.M'Taggart.
Stirling-Maxwell, Sir John M.
Stock, James Henry
Stone, Sir Benjamin
Strutt, Hn. Charles Hedley
Sturt, Hn. Humphry Napier
Talbot, Lord E. (Chichester)
Talbot,RtHnJ.G.(Oxf'dUniv.)
Tennant, Harold John
Thomas, Alfred(Glamorgan,E.)
Thorburn, Walter
Thornton, Percy M.
Tollemache, Henry James
Tritton, Charles Ernest
Usborne, Thomas
Valentia, Viscount
Vincent, Col. Sir C.E. Howard
Walrond, Rt. Hn. Sir Wm. H.
Walton, Jno.Lawson (Leeds,S.,
Wanklyn, James Leslie
Warde, Lt.-Col. C. E. (Kent)
Warr, Augustus Frederick
Webster, R. G. (St. Pancras)
Webster, Sir R. E. (I. of W.)
Welby, Lieut.-Col. A. C. E.
Wentworth, Bruce C. Vernon-
Whiteley, George (Stockport)
Whitmore, Charles Algernon
Whittaker, Thomas Palmer
Williams,Joseph Powell (Birm),
Willox, Sir John Archibald
Wills, Sir William Henry
Wilson-Todd,Wm. H.(Yorks.)
Wodehouse,Rt.Hn.E.R.(Bath)
Wortley, Rt. Hn. C. B.Stuart-
Wylie, Alexander
Wyndham-Quin, Major W. H.
Wyville, Marmaduke D'Arcy
Young, Commander (Berks, E.)

Tellers for the Ayes—
Mr. Henry Forster and Mr.
Cornwallis.

NOES.

Allan, William (Gateshead)
Ambrose, Robt. (Mayo, W.)
Arnold, Alfred
Austin, Sir John (Yorkshire)
Austin, M. (Limerick, W.)
Baker, Sir John
Barlow, John Emmott
Billson, Alfred
Buchanan, Thomas Ryburn
Burns, John
Burt, Thomas
Buxton, Sydney Charles
Caldwell, James
Cameron, Sir Chas. (Glasgow)
Cameron, Robert (Durham)
Channing, Francis Allston
Clough, Walter Owen
Colville, John
Curran, Thomas (Sligo, S.)
Davies, M.Vaughan(Cardigan)
Dilke, Rt. Hn. Sir Charles

Duckworth, James
Ellis,Thos.Edw.(Merionethsh.)
Fenwick, Charles
Ferguson, R. C. Munro (Leith)
Field, William (Dublin)
Goddard, Daniel Ford
Gourley, Sir Edw. Temperley
Gull, Sir Cameron
Harwood, George
Hazell, Walter
Hedderwick, Thos. Chas. H.
Hogan, James Francis
Hughes, Colonel Edwin
Jacoby, James Alfred
Johnstone, Heywood (Sussex
Jones, Wm. (Carnarvonshire)
Kinloch, Sir Jno.Geo.Smyth
Lawson,Sir Wilfrid(Cumb'lnd)
Leng, Sir John
Lewis, John Herbert
Lloyd-George, David

Macaleese, Daniel
MacNeill, Jno. Gordon Swift
Maddison, Fred.
Maden, John Henry
Molloy, Bernard Charles
Moore, Arthur (Londonderry)
Norton, Capt. Cecil William
O'Brien, James F. X. (Cork)
O'Brien, Patrick (Kilkenny)
O'Connor, Arthur (Donegal)
O'Keeffe, Francis Arthur
O'Kelly, James
Pease,Herb.Pike (Darlington)
Philipps, John Wynford
Pirie, Duncan V.
Power, Patrick Joseph
Provand, Andrew Dryburgh
Rasch, Major Frederic Carne
Redmond, Jno. E. (Waterford)
Roberts, John H.(Denbighs.)
Robertson, Edmund (Dundee)

Smith, Samuel (Flint)
Souttar, Robinson
Spicer, Albert
Steadman, William Charles
Sullivan, Donal (Westmeath)
Tanner, Charles Kearns
Thomas, David Alf. (Merthyr)
Trevelyan, Charles Philips

Wallace, Robert (Perth)
Walton, Joseph (Barnsley)
Warner, Thos. Courtenay T.
Wedderburn, Sir William
Weir, James Galloway
Williams, Jno. Carvell(Notts.)
Wilson, Henry J.(York,W.R.)
Wilson, John (Govan)

Wilson, Jos. H. (Mid'brough.)
Woodhouse, Sir J.T.(Hud'fd.)
Young, Samuel (Cavan, East)

TELLERS FOR THE NOES—
Mr. Pickersgill and Mr. Woods.

Main Question put, and agreed to.

Bill read a second time.

MR. BRYCE: Mr. Speaker, I understand that, as a matter of order, any part of the Motion which I have here that the Bill be referred to a Select Committee which is opposed cannot be taken to-day, but I hope that will not preclude me from moving, at any rate, the first part, and I suppose I may move that now, though the latter part is opposed by the Amendment in the name of the right honourable Gentleman opposite.

Question put—

"That the Bill be committed to a Committee of nine Members, five to be nominated by the House, and four by the Committee of Selection."—(*Mr. Bryce.*)

GREAT SOUTHERN AND WESTERN, AND WATERFORD, LIMERICK, AND WESTERN RAILWAY COMPANIES AMALGAMATION BILL.

SECOND READING.

(By Order.)—Order for Second Reading read.

Motion made, and Question, proposed—

"That the Bill be now read a second time."

Amendment proposed—

"To leave out the word now, and at the end of the Question to add the words upon this day six months."—(*Mr. J. Redmond.*)

MR. J. REDMOND (Waterford): Sir, I hope the fact that the House has been engaged now for some time on the consideration of private business will not prevent the House giving its attention to the question which now comes before it upon this Bill. I would have hesitated to intervene in this matter at all upon this occasion were it not that this Bill raises issues of the widest possible character affecting the public in Ireland —issues so large and wide that I feel it is the duty of Irish Members to have them discussed and considered on Second Reading. I suppose the majority of Members who are in the House probably know little or nothing about this matter, but I would ask their permission to state in a few words what exactly it is that the Bill proposes. Sir, this is a Measure for placing in the hands of one railway company in Ireland—namely, the Great Southern and Western Railway Company—practically speaking, all the railway lines in the south of Ireland. Although this scheme does not touch the Dublin, Wicklow, and Wexford, or some small lines west of Cork, it can broadly be said that this Measure will put into the hands of one railway company all the railways south of a line drawn from Dublin to Galway. The Measure proposes to enable the Great Southern and Western Railway to amalgamate the Waterford and Limerick Railway, the Central Ireland Railway, the Tuam and Claremorris Railway, Claremorris and Swinford Railway, Swinford and Collooney Railway, and the Limerick, Kerry, and Thurles Railway, and by the Act of last Session the Great Southern and Western Railway has obtained possession of the Waterford, Dungarvan, and Fermoy Railway, and, in conjunction with the Great Western Railway of England, the new railway to be built from Rosslare to Waterford, and thence on through Mayo to Cork. So, Sir, I say that this Bill is, so far as Ireland is concerned, of far more importance than the Bill we have just been discussing was with regard to England. Under this Bill, every railway line coming into the city of Waterford, every railway line coming into the city of Limerick, practically every railway line coming into the city of Cork, if you except these little West Cork lines which cannot compete, every line of railway coming into the city of Ennis, every line of railway coming into the town of

Tralee, and every line coming into the city of Kilkenny, will in the future be all in the hands of one railway, and this railway will have, in this way, complete control of the ports of Waterford, Cork, Limerick, and Tralee. Mr. Speaker, to show how wide a Measure this is, 13 counties are affected by it—the counties of West Meath, King's County, Queen's County, Galway, Waterford, Cork, Tipperary, Limerick, Kerry, Mayo, Galway, Roscommon, and Sligo. I mention this fact in order to try and press upon the House that this is indeed an enormous proposal, one that for good or ill will affect the future of Ireland, and, therefore, a proposal that the House of Commons ought most carefully to consider upon every side. The first question, Mr. Speaker, which would, I think, be asked is—what do the inhabitants of these 13 counties and these cities that I have mentioned say about this Bill? I do not believe any Private Bill was ever more vigorously opposed, or so nearly unanimously opposed, by the people concerned as this Measure. Some little time ago a deputation waited upon the Secretary to the Treasury and the Chief Secretary to the Lord Lieutenant of Ireland upon this question. That deputation certainly was one of the most representative that ever waited upon an English Minister in this country. I think that every one of the 13 counties was represented in that deputation. The Mayors of all the chief cities concerned were there—the Mayors of Waterford, Limerick, Kilkenny, and Sligo, the Town Commissions from all the towns in this area were present; and altogether, as was admitted by the Chief Secretary when speaking in answer to the deputation, it was a gathering most representative of the populations affected by this Bill.   Sir, I do not know exactly what course the Debate will take here, but I may express my own opinion. Unless, perhaps, the Members for Mayo support this Measure, I do not believe that the Members for any of the other thirteen counties affected are likely to do so. Certainly, as for the counties of West Meath and Queen's County, Kilkenny, Waterford, Tipperary, and Limerick, the counties which are most concerned, and Kerry also, no single representative of theirs, I venture to say, will be found supporting this Bill. Sir, may I advert for one

moment from this question to the possibility of the Members for Mayo supporting this Bill. I think they are supporting the Bill from the narrow Mayo point of view. If they support the Bill, it will be for the same reasons that we oppose it, because they desire that there should be competition in their county, that the Great Southern and Western should come in there and be in competition with the Midland. That is a most reasonable view, and that, Mr. Speaker, is exactly the view that influences the other counties in opposing the Bill. Now, what is the reason of this almost unanimous opposition from the counties affected? The reason is perfectly plain. It is a dread on the part of the cities and counties of a monopoly in the hands of the Great Southern and Western Railway Company, whose history in the past makes it feared and disliked in Ireland. At present the lines that under this amalgamation scheme are to be bought up by the Great Southern and Western are in active competition with it, and I am the first to admit that that competition, as it stands, is altogether inadequate; but still, the result of that competition has been extraordinary. I have a statement here which was circulated among Members of the House this morning, showing what the result of that inadequate competition has been in the past, and I find that where competition sprung up to the Great Southern and Western Railway, either by the Claremorris extension, or the Waterford and Limerick, or by the Southern Railway from Clonmel to Thurles—in all these cases the reduction has been enormous. The rates from Limerick to Claremorris on grain and food stuffs were reduced by competition on the Great Southern and the Claremorris extension from 12s. 6d. a ton to 7s. From Limerick to Tuam the rates were reduced from 12s. to 6s.; from Limerick to Thurles, 12s. to 5s.; from Limerick to Tralee, 12s. 6d. to 6s.; from Tipperary, 4s. 6d. to 3s. The Limerick and Fergus brought the rates from 30s. a ton to 16s. 8d.; flour from 20s. to 14s., fruit from 40s. to 23s. 6d. per ton, and so on; so that the competition which has been in existence, inadequate as it undoubtedly is, has had the result of reducing the freight of grain and food stuffs about one half, and the inhabitants of these districts, who, before these competing lines came into existence, had to pay the larger freights, naturally enough look forward with dread to amalgamation which will put them absolutely in the power of the Great Southern and Western Railway once again. No one need wonder under these circumstances that the people of these counties view the passage of this Act with dread. Last year there was a Hybrid Committee appointed to consider the Rosslare and Fishguard line, and the House of Commons directed that Hybrid Committee to inquire into the whole question of competition among the railway systems in the South of Ireland. This question of amalgamation, which is now before Parliament in this Bill, and which then was the subject of a grievance between the companies, came under consideration. Now, on this question, let me say a word. I have heard it stated as a reason why this Bill should be allowed to pass that if this amalgamation be not carried the Great Western Railway of England, which is concerned with the Great Southern and the Rosslare scheme of last year, would in some way back out of its engagements, and the Rosslare and Fishguard scheme would be in danger. That has been very freely stated in Ireland, and if it were believed, Mr. Speaker, I think we could quite understand many men's minds being influenced by it, because there are many people in Ireland who are entirely against this proposed amalgamation, but who desire to see the Rosslare and Fishguard line, as sanctioned last year, carried out. I took the trouble to-day to look over the Report of the evidence before the Hybrid Committee upon this point, because it is a most serious one, and I know these threats have been used towards men in Ireland who are hostile to this amalgamation, and I find that the Committee unanimously submitted to the promoters of the Bill two questions upon this point, and after taking a night to consider their answer, on the following day their leading counsel said—

"Before the Committee resumes its labours, I desire to state that I am now in a position, with the authority of the Boards of the two companies, to reply distinctly to the questions."

And his reply was as follows—

"Whether the amalgamation of the Waterford and Limerick and Central Ireland Railways be ultimately sanctioned by Parliament

Mr. J. Redmond.

at any future time or not, this scheme will be *bond fide* persisted with, in the spirit in which it has been introduced, and whether this next year, or any subsequent year, Parliament does or does not sanction the amalgamation of the Waterford and Limerick, this scheme will be persisted with perfectly *bond fide*, independent of any such result."

So that, I think, disposes altogether of this argument which has been freely used in some quarters. It has been used in many quarters; it has been used even with myself. Therefore that may be left entirely out of the question. The Great Western Railway are bound by solemn pledges, whatever happens, not to attempt to recede from their position with regard to the Rosslare and Fishguard Railway. The Hybrid Committee to which I referred had this instruction given to them—

"That it be an instruction to the Committee that they do inquire and report whether the adoption of ary or all the proposals would prevent or prejudice adequate competition in the railway systems of the South of Ireland."

And in pursuance of that instruction the Hybrid Committee, having considered the matter, unanimously—and it was a very representative Committee, representing the whole of the South of Ireland —declared as follows—

"Although Parliament cannot in the present Session deal finally with the two proposed amalgamations, because they are not yet embodied in a Bill, your Committee are unable, after the evidence they have heard, to withhold the expression of their unanimous opinion that in the interests of the South of Ireland they will regard with grave apprehension the absorption of these two companies' undertakings by the Great Southern and Western Railway Company; and should either of these two companies become too weak to stand alone, an amalgamation with some railway system other than the Great Southern and Western would be preferable in the interests of such competition."

Now, Sir, I say that in the face of that declaration, that unanimous declaration by the Hybrid Committee of last year, it is a strong order to expect that Parliament will pass this Amalgamation Bill into law. The concluding paragraph which I have read contemplates the possibility of these small railway companies becoming too weak to stand alone, and it says that in that case they ought to be amalgamated with some other system rather than the Great Southern. Well, now, I do not know—

I have yet to hear it established, at any rate—that these companies are too weak to stand alone. I do not profess to know much about the position of the Waterford and Limerick Railway Company, but I am within the truth, I think, when I say that they have improved their position of late; their lines have improved, their rolling stock has improved, their income has increased, and so far as their capital is concerned, by paying four or five per cent. to their debenture holders and to their preference shareholders they have actually paid away ever since they have been in existence, or for a great number of years at any rate, a sum annually which would amount to about three per cent. on their entire capital. If that be so, certainly one would think that the Waterford and Limerick Railway was not so bad a concern as it is represented to be, or that it is impossible for it to stand alone. But, Mr. Speaker, even if it were established that the Waterford and Limerick Railway Company could not stand alone, then the position which I and others take up on this matter is this. There are other combinations which were clearly hinted at in the Report of the Hybrid Committee last year—there are other combinations which would enable the Waterford and Limerick Railway to be amalgamated with a stronger company, and yet not introduce a monopoly into the railway system of the South of Ireland, and to leave it with some sort of adequate competition. I do not think that I am called upon to say what these other combinations may be, but one of them has appeared recently in the public newspapers, because the Midland of Ireland, through their general manager, declared in a published letter the other day that if this amalgamation scheme fell through his company would be prepared to make an offer for the purchase of a part of the whole of the Waterford and Limerick system.

THE CHIEF SECRETARY TO THE LORD LIEUTENANT OF IRELAND (Mr. GERALD BALFOUR, Leeds, Central): Would you read that letter?

MR. J. REDMOND: Yes. It is dated the 16th February this year, and it is a letter in which Mr. Tatlow said—

"In the event of the proposed amalgamation scheme not being carried, and an amalgamation of the Waterford and Limerick Company with

any other company becoming necessary, this company would favourably consider any proposal for the acquisition of a part of or the entire system by agreement with the Great Western Railway."

MR. GERALD BALFOUR: That is a very different thing from making an offer.

MR. J. REDMOND: No doubt no offer has been made, but——

MR. GERALD BALFOUR: May I point out there is a great deal of difference in a railway company undertaking to follow the offers of others and making an offer itself.

MR. J. REDMOND: I am only quoting that to show that other combinations are possible. Surely I am not pushing my argument beyond that. I am not prepared to say whether that would be the best solution or not, but I quote that as an indication that there is at least one other combination possible, and that is with the Midland. There are other combinations which are freely mentioned.

MR. CARSON (Dublin University): Will the honourable Member say what combination is possible for the Waterford and Central Ireland?

MR. J. REDMOND: The Midland also. There are other companies besides the Midland which have been mentioned more than once. I read a most interesting article on the whole railway system of Ireland, written evidently by a skilled expert, in which it was suggested, as a possible combination of the future, a combination of the Dublin, Wicklow, and Wexford. This is only separated from the Waterford and Limerick by 14 miles between New Ross and Waterford, a connection which ought to have been made long ago, and which I hope will soon be made. There are other combinations possible, and these combinations were clearly in the mind of the Hybrid Committee when last year they unanimously declared that if it became necessary for the Waterford and Limerick to amalgamate with a stronger company, it should be an amalgamation with some other system rather than the Great Southern and Western. Now, Mr. Speaker, my honourable and learned Friend opposite referred to the Central Ireland Railway. There is a point connected with the Central Ireland Railway of great importance in this connection. That railway ends at present at Mount Mellick. Powers were obtained by the company to extend their line to Mullingar, and then, by running powers over existing lines from Cavan, they can get direct running to Belfast, and in this way there would be direct communication between the north and south of Ireland through the centre of the island, instead of at present only communication round by Dublin. Admittedly this scheme of amalgamation does not contemplate anything of the kind, and the witnesses that we had before us in the Hybrid Committee last year distinctly declined to give any undertaking that if an amalgamation were carried this line would be extended. I believe myself that if this amalgamation scheme as it now stands be carried into law, all possibility will be at an end of this connection being made between the north and south of Ireland through the centre of the island. There are two other considerations which I would like to address to the House—considerations of distinctly Second Reading importance. The first is this: There are very many people in Ireland who believe that this railway problem can only be finally and satisfactorily settled by something in the nature of State control or State purchase. There are differences of opinion upon that point, but there is a large volume of opinion in Ireland of that view. Well, it seems to me that if that is a possibility of the future, it ought to be carefully considered by the Government before the passage of a Measure of amalgamation such as this. I believe that Measures of this kind would render more difficult and more costly by far any such change in the general railway system of Ireland in the future, and the suggestion has been made that the whole of this railway problem ought again to be submitted to a Royal Commission before the passage of any further amalgamation Bills of this kind, and that suggestion is one which certainly has my approval. But, Sir, there is a second consideration of a general character which ought, I think, to be absolutely fatal in the House of Commons to the passage of the Second Reading of this Bill. I have said that there are 13 counties intimately concerned in this matter. Last year the

Mr. J. Redmond.

Local Government Act conferred on the county councils of Ireland the right of petitioning and appearing in opposition to Bills of this character. The county councils have not yet been elected. The ime for petitioning is past, and they cannot appear, and in this way, if this Bill goes through, the county councils of these 13 counties will be deprived of all voice. Mr. Speaker, the case is even stronger than that, because there are four or five of these counties that have actually guaranteed about half a million of money towards the creation of some of these small lines that are going to be amalgamated. And is it not a monstrous thing to say that they shall be deprived of voice in this matter after right to appear has been conferred upon them by Act of Parliament. The suggestion has been made, I am aware, that this matter should be postponed until some convenient date, until the county councils have come into existence, and that the time for petitioning should be extended, so as to enable them to appear. Well, Sir, the county councils will have a good deal of business to do when they come into existence, and I say it is unfair and absurd to suppose that these county councils, the moment they are created, will be able to investigate this matter fully, and to come to a determination as to what course they shall take in opposition to this Bill, and to instruct counsel, and so on. It would be impossible for that to be done in the course of a few weeks, and I say the proper course for the House of Commons to take would be to say that, under these circumstances, even apart altogether from the merits which the scheme might have—which are matters for the Committee—they will refuse to sanction the Second Reading of a Bill which deprives the county councils of a proper opportunity of appearing and making their voice known. In conclusion, I will make an appeal to the Irish Government and to the House. Whatever view the Chief Secretary individually may take about the merits of this Bill, he must recognise that this is a matter upon which the persons concerned and their representatives have a right to speak and to have their views carefully weighed. It would be a very strong thing for the right honourable Gentleman, even in his individual capacity, to go against the almost unanimous voice of these 13 counties. I say it would be a much stronger thing, and, if I may be allowed to use the word, a most improper thing if he were to use his position in the Government to make this a Government question, and, therefore, to call upon his followers, not upon the merits, but simply because he made it a Government question, to go and vote in his favour. I therefore appeal to him respectfully to leave this matter free to the House of Commons, and the free and unbiassed and independent judgment of those Members who may have taken an interest in it, and I appeal to the House generally to decide this matter not upon Party lines, but upon their judgment of the merits of the case, and if they do that, I am quite convinced that they will defeat the Second Reading of the Bill. Sir, I beg to move that this Bill be read a second time this day six months.

Mr. A. MOORE (Londonderry): Mr. Speaker, I rise to second the Motion which has just been moved. It is now proposed to rush this Bill through the House before the local authorities created under the Act of last year have had time to take up the business which has fallen from the hands of the Grand Juries, and without affording them any proper opportunity of explaining their views. That seems to me an argument which is simply unanswerable. Then I come to the question of the wishes of the people who live in the districts affected. I believe the House will be addressed by Members of great weight, and with their usual ability and knowledge, in favour of this Bill, but I would remind the House that nothing is cheaper than good advice, except, perhaps, disinterested advice. The House will receive plenty of that this evening. But I am here, living as I do in the district, to represent those towns on the Waterford and Limerick Railway which will be affected by this Bill, and I say that the feeling is very strong in Tipperary, in Clonmel, in Waterford, and all the principal towns on that line, against it. The reason is that the people dread that you are going to establish a gigantic monopoly—a perfect millenium of monopoly. The scheme contemplates the absorption of almost the whole of the railway system of the South of Ireland, as well as that

passing along to the North. It includes no less than six ports, four of great importance and two of minor importance, and it is a serious thing if the House is going to prevent a man sending his produce by any route he pleases. I would also ask the House to consider in whose favour they are about to take this most exceptional step—a step which I believe is contrary to the traditions of Parliament. The House is asked to take it in favour of a company which has pursued a grasping, unsympathetic course. The business of the Great Southern and Western Railway has been increasing in spite of itself, and in spite of the policy of its directors. We have never received from the company any consideration of our views with reference to the transit of produce. We approached them, and complained to them regarding the state in which our butter arrived at market, while Danish butter came into the Manchester market in perfect condition. It is a serious matter that butter producers should have no proper care taken of their butter in transit. When we brought our views before the company they always turned a deaf ear to us; and this is the railway to whom we are asked to extend exceptional facilities! I now come to a larger question. You have been lowering rents and taking steps in one direction or another to benefit the cultivators of the soil in Ireland. Are you now going to pile up shilling by shilling in railway rates what you have taken off the rents? That seems to me to be a question of the greatest importance. A friend of mine, perhaps the greatest financial authority in Ireland, made a careful examination of railway rates in Canada, and he found that the rates had been lowered to a farthing per ton per mile, whereas the average rate in Ireland is no less than five farthings per ton per mile, and in towns on the Great Southern and Western Railway which have no option or competition the rates are as much as $3\frac{1}{4}$d., and even 5d. per mile. I think that is a matter which ought to receive the most careful consideration of the House. With reference to the guaranteed lines, interest is guaranteed in two ways. Under recent legislation the Treasury has to pay 2 per cent., and the local authorities have to pay either

2 per cent. or 3 per cent., making it 4 per cent. or 5 per cent. altogether. There is such a thing as giving these local lines fair play, but you cannot expect a board of directors to be angels, and they, having no interest in them, will show them neither mercy nor fair play, and the Treasury and the guaranteeing districts will be bound to make good the interest. That is a very strong point, well worthy the attention of the House. Again, I would ask why it is proposed to refer this Bill to a Hybrid Committee. That would mean a great deal of additional expense. I have not been here long enough to know much about Parliamentary tactics, but it strikes me as most objectionable to appoint a Hybrid Committee——

*Mr. SPEAKER: The honourable Member cannot discuss the Committee on the Second Reading.

Mr. A. MOORE: If the Government take no exceptional line as to this Bill, but leave it to the ordinary consideration of the House, a proper and cautious line will be taken, in view of the recommendations of last year. The only object in sending the Bill to another Committee is to obtain sufficient authority to override those recommendations. This is all I wish to say. What I ask the House to do is to refuse to consent to this amalgamation, unless there is a total revision of rates throughout the South of Ireland. If that were done we might fairly support the Bill.

Mr. CARSON: Mr. Speaker, I do not intend to follow the honourable Member who has just addressed the House, or the honourable and learned Member who has moved the rejection of this Bill, into questions which properly belong to the Committee stage, in whatever way that may be brought about. But, Sir, I think that the honourable and learned Member who brought forward the Motion to reject the Bill and who asked the House to take the exceptional course of rejecting it on the Second Reading might at least have informed the House that the promoters of this Bill have brought it forward in pursuance of a pledge they gave to the Hybrid Committee on the passage of the Fishguard and Rosslare Railway Bill last year. What is more,

not only for reasons which I shall shortly state, why this Bill should be promoted, but so careful were the Committee that it should be promoted that they put that pledge into a section of the Act of Parliament relating to the Fishguard and Rosslare scheme. And what the House is now solemnly asked to do is—although an Act of Parliament passed last year expressly enacts that this Bill should be introduced this Session—to reject it on Second Reading. Any such proceeding on the part of the House would be really stultifying the whole proceeding which took place last year. It would really render it impossible for promoters to know how they could possibly conduct their business if they are put under terms by Act of Parliament to do a certain thing, and, having gone to expense, are not to be given an opportunity of having their scheme inquired into.

Mr. J. REDMOND: The honourable and learned Member must be aware that what the Committee desired to do was to prevent these companies carrying out the object of an amalgamation without a Bill by a pooling arrangement. They pledged the companies, they compelled them by inserting a provision in the Act of Parliament not to attempt an amalgamation without introducing a Bill. In that way they did direct them to introduce the proposal, with a declaration that they were unanimously against it.

Mr. CARSON: I think the Committee of which the honourable and learned Member was a distinguished ornament had a great deal more common sense than he gives them credit for. I can hardly imagine that they had solemnly inserted in an Act of Parliament a provision that this Bill was to be introduced into this House, for the purpose of turning it out. That is the character he gives to the Committee, but I think I can satisfy the House in a few minutes that the honourable and learned Member is under a misapprehension of what is really the effect of what the Committee did. He says that the Committee introduced this clause to prevent what would really be an amalgamation by agreement or a pooling arrangement.

Yes, Sir; but for how long? For one year, until this Bill could be brought in. What the honourable and learned Member says, in effect, is—"Let the House reject this Bill, and then, under the Act of Parliament which my Committee enacted last year, the companies will be able to effect a practical amalgamation which will bring about practically the same results." Really, an argument of that kind has only to be stated to show its absurdity. How did this matter stand, as I understand it, with reference to the Fishguard and Rosslare Railway? The Waterford and Limerick Railway were, under an Act passed in 1886, enabled to enter into a working arrangement with the Great Southern and Western, the present promoters, and the Great Western of England, and the result of the investigation last year was that it was evident to the Committee that those arrangements must come to an end. One result was that the Great Western of England would withdraw a rebate they pay for an interchange of traffic with the Waterford and Limerick Railway Company, which last year amounted to £10,000 or £12,000. In that event the Great Southern and Western Railway would no longer be dependent to the same extent on the Waterford and Limerick. They would modify their arrangements, and the Waterford and Limerick would then become too weak to stand on its own legs. It specially provided in the section to which I have referred that neither the Great Western of England nor the Great Southern and Western should in any way modify the arrangements with the Waterford and Limerick Railway for fear it should become so weak that it would be unable to supply the public with a service, so they were put upon terms to carry out their existing arrangement with the Waterford and Limerick until they could get the sanction of that company to the present Bill. Now, let us face this question. What will happen if we reject this Bill? The whole arrangement made by the Hybrid Committee of last year falls to the ground. The Great Western Railway will have a perfect right to terminate their arrangement by which they gave £10,000 or £12,000 a year to the Waterford and Limerick, and the Great Southern, which now wants to amalgamate, will have the power to enter into the working arrangement which the Committee did not wish them to have. They would have a virtual amalgamation without the responsibility for it. In other words, the Waterford and Limerick would in reality be worked by the Great Southern and Western, whereas the Great Southern and Western would not be at liberty to improve the rolling stock or the stations, or to do the other things which the capital at their command would enable them to do. Apart altogether from the evidence that may be given, it seems to me that it is an argument in favour of passing the Second Reading that, while the Committee were opposed to the amalgamation if they could see any better scheme, they thought it necessary and proper to put the promoters under the necessity and expense of introducing this Bill. All we ask is that the Bill should be inquired into before a Committee. A great deal has been said about the amalgamation of these small lines, many of which probably some Members have never heard of. My own individual opinion is that, so far as the management of railway companies in Ireland is concerned, it is a great pity there is not a great deal more amalgamation. I was very much struck with one fact mentioned by the honourable Member for Dublin, namely, that while they had about 3,000 miles of railways in Ireland they had about 300 directors, or about one director for every ten miles, and that at any time we propose to amalgamate with the great companies, such as the Great Southern and Western, we are told that we are going to build up monopolies, and, as a result, the interests of the country will be ruined. It is not the interests of the country that would be ruined, but the interests of a few directors. Another argument of the honourable and learned Member for Waterford is that he hopes that the Government will in the future purchase the Irish railways. But does he think because some of these small railways have been amalgamated with larger ones that that is any the less reason why the Government should be induced to purchase? One other matter was mentioned by the honourable Member for Derry. He stated that it was an unanswerable argument against the Second

Reading that the county councils, which have not yet been called into existence, have not had an opportunity of expressing their views on this Measure. As I understand, there is at the present moment upon the Paper a Motion by my right honourable Friend the Chief Secretary to the Lord Lieutenant which provides that the county councils shall have the fullest opportunity of appearing before the Committee, and, therefore, the argument of the honourable Member for Derry falls to the ground. Of course, everybody knows that the country ought to get a hearing. It is said that this Bill is being rushed through the House. One would think we were on the Third Reading. We are not asking anything of the kind. All we ask for is that a Bill which has been brought forward in pursuance of a statutory obligation should be sent to a Committee to investigate it. Let the matter be so arranged as regards time that the county councils shall have the fullest opportunity of appearing, and let the Bill, if it be rejected at all, be rejected only after the fullest consideration.

*Mr. M. HEALY (Cork): Mr. Speaker, I do not know whether the honourable and learned Member for Waterford intends to press his Motion to a division. For my part I trust that he does not, and I entertain that hope principally in the interest of the very district whose rights he takes upon himself to champion and protect. In making that observation I do not at all suggest that the Debate which the honourable and learned Member has originated is other than quite proper and necessary. It would be little to the credit of Irish Members if they let a Measure of this kind pass without a full and ample discussion. I agree with every word that has been said as regards the importance of this Bill, as regards the large nature of its proposals, and as regards the vital manner in which it may, if carried into law, ultimately affect many districts in Ireland. But while admitting its importance, and having no quarrel with a great deal that the honourable and learned Member for Waterford has said, I ask the House to take the opposite course to that proposed by him. I can conceive that the Committee which would consider this Bill might for good reasons reject it. I can conceive also that the

Mr. Carson.

Committee might for good reasons entertain the Bill and pass it into law; but one course I cannot conceive, and that is that this House should refuse to consider it when it is put forward in the manner in which it is now submitted. That is all we are asking the House to do in proposing that it be read a second time, and that is all I will contend for in the speech I am about to make. I am not here as a partisan of the Great Southern and Western Railway. The honourable and learned Member for Waterford has said some strong things in condemnation of that railway, and in that line of comment he has been followed by the honourable Member for Derry. With what they have said I cannot bring myself publicly to dissent. I took myself last year some small part in a railway struggle in which that company was interested, and I have no doubt that in the course of that contest I said about the Great Southern and Western many things quite as severe as have been said by either of the honourable Members who have spoken; and I was glad to read the other day a remark of the Chief Secretary which I trust the directors will take to heart, reminding them that the fierce opposition which they have encountered in the railway discussions of the last two years was the inevitable Nemesis overtaking them for the narrow policy they have pursued in the past. That observation was perfectly justified. I will not say that what the honourable and learned Member for Waterford has said here to-night is not also perfectly justified, and I trust the directors of that line will learn by the experience of the last two years that by the course of conduct they have pursued in the past they have not served either the interests of the company or of the shareholders. But I refuse to consider this Bill as if it were to be finally judged by the conduct of the Great Southern and Western Railway in the past. Be the action of the directors right or wrong in the past, the company now comes before us to put forward a large scheme affecting Irish interests for good or evil in an important manner, and I say they are entitled to claim from us, and we are bound to give them, a consideration of their scheme on its merits. A great deal has been said about monopoly, and justly; but when we have exhausted that topic, and painted in the most vivid colours all the evils which monopoly brings in its train, we have not said the last word to be said on this Bill or on the question of railway interests and railway development in Ireland. It is quite true that monopoly is objectionable. It is also quite true that if this Bill is carried it will confer a monopoly on the Great Southern and Western Railway. It is also quite true that if there is any means open to Parliament of securing the object to be secured by this Bill which will not create a monopoly at the same time, Parliament should take that course, but those who are best acquainted with railway matters in Ireland and those who have taken some humble part in those railway struggles in the past know, unfortunately, that in Ireland it is not possible to combat monopoly by the same means which can be employed for the purpose in England or any other country. How do you combat monopoly in England? You combat it by competition, and if in Ireland it were possible to combat monopoly by competition I would be a warm opponent of these Bills. But, unfortunately, Ireland is not rich enough to support two efficient rival systems between any two important points. We cannot support two lines between Dublin and Cork, Dublin and Belfast, or Dublin and Galway. I challenge anyone to say that it is possible to get in Ireland competition by means of two trunk lines between any two even of the most important centres such as those I have mentioned. Now, of course, between Waterford and Limerick two competitive lines exist, but the honourable Member for Waterford frankly admitted that the service which that competition gave was an inadequate one, and the issue now arises whether it can continue to exist at all. It is not, therefore, enough to pronounce the word " monopoly " in order to decide the question. It is necessary to go a step further and tell the House and the country how it is possible to get rid of the evils which monopoly create. We last year made a desperate fight with a view to create a great competitive trunk system between Cork and the South of England, but in that struggle we were beaten. The force of circumstances was too strong for us,

and we were ultimately obliged to take the Great Western and Southern Railway as partners in a scheme which was intended to create a rival system, and that will be the history of railway enterprise in Ireland so long as Ireland remains a poor country without the resources necessary to create two rival railway systems. For us in Ireland, therefore, I am forced with regret to the conclusion that the remedy for the evils of railway monopoly is not competition, which we can hardly hope for, but the effective and continuous interference of the State in the management and control of Irish railways to prevent abuse of the great privileges conferred on railway companies. Will the House allow me to say a single word as regards the history of the project which is now before the House? How does it come that we are to-day discussing this proposal? The honourable Member for Waterford has confined himself to describing in strong language the desperate things which would happen if this scheme passes into law. I wish he had addressed himself to the question—what is to happen if the Bill is rejected? I undertake to say that none of the evils predicted will follow from the passing of the Bill, and that all the evils prophesied will occur if the Bill is rejected. Last year the House witnessed a very important development in the history of the Irish railway world. Hitherto Ireland had practically only one port of communication with England—namely, the City of Dublin—and all effective traffic between the two countries, whether from Belfast in the north, Galway in the west, or Cork in the south, had to pass through the port of Dublin; but last year, for the first time, the Great Western made a bold bid for some of the Irish traffic, and it proposed to set up in the South of Ireland a line of through communication between the two countries, which would do for the South of Ireland that which had hitherto been done only through Dublin. It joined hands, as counsel used to say, with a strong railway company, the Great Southern and Western, and invited that company to come into the port of Waterford and open through that port a system of railway communication which would be an effective rival to the Dublin route. It succeeded in that project, and induced the Great Southern and Western of Ireland to come to Waterford, and then the struggle originated which eventuated in an alternative route being established, having as its port not Waterford, but Rosslare, in county Wexford. Until this new movement in the Irish railway system the companies sending traffic to the Great Western of England were solely the Waterford and Limerick and the Central Ireland lines. Both were weak lines with single rails nearly throughout their whole length, without through express trains, and unable to give a through and effective route from Ireland to England. Such, however, as their through traffic was, it was worth the while of the Great Western of England to pay them a handsome subsidy for it. The Waterford and Limerick received £10,000 a year, and the Central a subsidy less in amount but equal in importance. The effect of the combination between the Great Southern of Ireland and the Great Western of England is that the interest of the Great Western in paying these subsidies has come entirely to an end. It is under no sort of obligation to continue them, and the evidence taken before the Hybrid Committee last year went to show that it was in the power of the Great Western to terminate its arrangement with the Waterford and Limerick in 12 months. Now, what I want to ask is this: Has the honourable Member for Waterford faced the situation which would arise in the South of Ireland if this Bill is rejected, and if the Great Southern and Western of England withdrew that subsidy from the Waterford and Limerick? If that happened it would be impossible for the Waterford and Limerick to pay dividends even on its preference shares, and it has never lately paid dividends on its ordinary shares. If the subsidy is withdrawn all dividends will disappear. The same observation applies to the Central Ireland, and I ask the honourable Member for Waterford to face the problem which will arise if this Bill is rejected, and tell us what he considers will then happen to those lines. The only suggestion which he has to make throwing light on that contingency is a letter from the Midland Company of Ireland which suggests that they might, under certain conditions and contingencies, buy up the Waterford and Limerick line. Now, the

South of Ireland, taking it as a whole, would not welcome the Midland as a purchaser in preference to the Great Southern and Western, in spite of the hard things which have been said of the latter company, and if it had to choose, would not accept it in preference. But I do not believe that the Midland Company is a possible purchaser for the whole line. The Great Southern of Ireland, taken as a whole, is the richest railway company in Ireland. It has the largest mileage of lines, the largest receipts, and, though not paying quite the largest dividends, is the strongest railway company in the whole of Ireland. Now, what has been the effect upon that company of this proposed amalgamation? Its shares fell in value to the extent of half a million. The general manager of the Midland and Great Western, therefore, may, for the purpose of this controversy, and without engaging his company in any real responsibility, write in a jaunty strain about the purchase of those two lines, but the day that his directors dare to make such a proposal in the face of the shareholders would, I venture to say, be the last day that they would hold their position as directors. I do not, therefore, believe that if this Bill is rejected some other company would undertake that purchase. No company will buy the Waterford and Limerick or the Central Ireland Railway. They will remain in their present position, absolutely depending upon the Great Western of England, and as that company is now in alliance with the Great Southern of Ireland, these unhappy companies will be surrounded by a ring of fire, so to speak, and will be driven to do by a pooling arrangement what they are trying to do by amalgamation. Where, then, is the assurance that the rejection of this Bill will secure to Limerick and the other competitive points the competitive rates which they at present enjoy? A pooling arrangement which can be effected without Parliamentary sanction will most certainly deprive them of them. An amalgamation with proper safeguards can as certainly secure them to them. It is not, then, the interests of all the districts concerned to send this Bill to a Committee, which can hear their case and decide upon what terms the Bill can be allowed to pass? If I find, when this Bill returns

Mr. M. Healy.

to the House, that by this amalgamation the districts interested will be deprived of the low rates which competition has given them ; if I find that the Committee have not taken precautions to preserve on all competitive points the rights which the public have hitherto enjoyed, I will reserve to myself perfect freedom as to my future action. If, however, the Bill is now rejected, the competitive rates will not remain for a day beyond the good pleasure of the Great Western and the Great Southern. That is the explanation of the clause in the Report of the Hybrid Committee on the Rosslare Bill to which reference has been made. That Committee did view with apprehension the possibility of amalgamation, and for that reason the clause referred to was introduced, I believe, at the instance of the honourable Member for Waterford. It was the honourable Member for Waterford who last year was apprehensive that what the present Bill proposes would be effected outside the walls of Parliament by a pooling arrangement, and it was he who suggested that the amalgamation scheme should be submitted to Parliament. I regret to have troubled the House at such length, but we are under the difficulty of having to deal with this most important Irish matter in an English House of Parliament. This is a Measure dealing with vital interests for our country, which we are compelled to discuss as a petty Private Bill, when, if it were debated in an Irish Parliament, the fate of a Government might depend upon the decision on the Measure. I do not believe that the opposition to this Bill is universal, as stated by the honourable Member for Waterford.

MR. J. REDMOND: I did not say the Bill was universally opposed. What I said was that I did not think more than one or two of the Members for the localities concerned would support it.

*MR. M. MEALY: I do not know how that is. At any rate I speak for Cork, which favours the scheme, though no doubt its interests are not so nearly concerned as those of the other localities concerned. Two public bodies, representing the trade and commerce of Cork —namely, the Harbour Board and the Chamber of Shipping and Commerce, have declared in favour of the Bill.

I consider this is not a case for a summary rejection on Second Reading. I consider this to be a case for inquiry and examination. Last year we had a Bill before us which excited most conflicting views in Ireland. It brought forward opponents from all parts. It was referred to the Hybrid Committee, and that Committee, after hearing all the interests concerned, were able to come to a unanimous conclusion. The history of that Bill is a good augury of the possibilities before this Bill. A similar course is now proposed by the Government. I invite the House to take that course, and I must say that in my opinion the honourable Member for Waterford will be imperilling the very interests which he wishes to defend, and which I am sure he has at heart, if he presses his Motion to a Division.

*COLONEL BLUNDELL (Lancashire, Ince): I was a member of last year's Committee—we found that there was no competitive route from Cork to Dublin, though one could easily be made—the Committee put a clause into the Bill to prevent any amalgamation of the companies without the consent of the House of Commons. Speaking for myself, I venture to say that unless all competition in the South of Ireland is to be done away with this Bill should be opposed.

MR. DILLON (Mayo, E.): I do not intend to follow honourable Members who have already addressed the House into large questions touching the interests of the South of Ireland involved in the Measure. I speak only for my own constituency in the county of Mayo. My constituents have requested me to give expression to their feelings, and to voice their interests in connection with this Bill. From that point of view I appeal to the House to read the Bill a second time, and send it to a Select Committee. The honourable Member for Waterford, knowing what the feeling of Mavo is, alluded to the fact that the Members for Mayo would probably take up that position. I do not express any opinion as to the effect of this Bill on the traffic of the South of Ireland. That question has been studied by the honourable Members for Waterford and Cork with a thoroughness to which I can lay no claim. On the contrary, I abstained from attempting to get upon the Hybrid Committee last year, or from suggesting that any Member from the West should go upon it, because I did not consider that the West of Ireland was so closely concerned in the matter. But in the proposal now before the House the county of Mayo, and, indeed, the province of Connaught, is deeply concerned, because, while it is true that this Bill affects the traffic of the South, it is a large Measure concerning the interests of Connaught as well as those of the South and Centre, if in a less degree. I would direct the attention of the Chief Secretary to the letter of the manager of the Midland and Great Western, which has already been referred to by the honourable Member for Waterford, because, so far as I am instructed by my constituents, it is mainly because of this suggested alternative scheme that they are prepared to support this Bill. The Midland and Great Western would probably absorb the portion of the Limerick and Waterford line if the present system fell through. What our people are afraid of is that if this scheme is defeated by Parliament, the Waterford and Limerick system will collapse, and portions of it will be picked up by other companies, and that the portion between Athenry and Sligo will come into the hands of the Midland and Great Western. That would be a great disaster to the people of Mayo and Connaught generally, who now have the means of having their produce brought down to Waterford in competition with the Southern and Great Western. In this instance one is compelled to speak frankly. I am speaking simply for my constituents. This is a question of great perplexity and difficulty, but I hope the Bill will be referred to a Select Committee, and that a representative of the province of Connaught will have a seat upon the Committee. I agree with the honourable Member for Cork that it is necessary that there should be proper protection afforded the public against any increase in the fares and goods rates, and, in the belief that this can be done, I support the Second Reading of the Bill.

Mr. FIELD (Dublin, St. Patrick's): At this late hour of the evening I have no desire to intervene at any great length in this Debate. I have

Mr. Dillon.

always interested myself in railway affairs generally, while the general disposition of honourable Members is to take a personal, a narrow, or a constituents' view of any railway scheme brought before the House. It appears to me that the proposed amalgamation means practical ruin to trade in the South-west of Ireland. When amalgamation of railway lines is proposed in England there is the Board of Trade to protect trade interests. But there is no branch of the Board of Trade in Ireland. The Railway Commissioners also protect the English public, but the name of the Railway Commission is almost unknown in Ireland, and Ireland has not the same safeguards against the railway rates and charges with respect to amalgamation which exist, and which are easily obtainable, in England. To my mind any process of amalgamation which is granted in Ireland will make it more difficult to obtain what is really the cure for the situation, and that is the nationalisation of the Irish railways. In Ireland the state of the railway system is absolutely exceptional, for they are neither State-owned nor State-managed, nor is there any competition. We are in a different position economically to that of the railways in England, and I entirely agree with what the honourable Member for Cork said, that there is no room for two parallel lines of railways from one city to another. But if this amalgamation is passed our position will be worse than it was before. The right honourable Member for the University said the Great Southern and Western were paying from £7,000 to £10,000 a year for the sake of keeping up a second railway. Will any Gentleman tell me, if this amalgamation takes place, that this process of giving a certain amount of money to obtain traffic will cease? I think, as far as I am acquainted with the commercial ways of the English people, they never give away anything without they are paid for it; and I do not think these companies will give anything to the Irish people unless they have a *quid pro quo*. I hold no narrow view upon this question from my constituents, but what I want is to have this railway question brought before public opinion, and public attention focussed upon it, and if the course suggested by the honourable Member for

Mayo is correct, then I have no objection whatever. This idea of the amalgamation of railways in Ireland should be closely watched, because our experience of Irish railways is that they are the most expensive, the worst managed, and the dearest to travel upon in the world. Under these circumstances, I would beseech this House to be very careful in any amalgamation scheme which is introduced, and it must be remembered that we have no competition in Ireland. There has been a good deal said in the course of this Debate with respect to the different districts through which these railways pass. The honourable Member for Cork, who represents a very large amount of public opinion, expressed certain views, and I am not in a position to differ from his assertion; but I do say that the vast majority of this House are against railway amalgamation. I have myself received letters from various merchants in different parts of Ireland, and I do say unhesitatingly, and without fear of contradiction, that unless this amalgamation is carried out in a proper way we ought to vote against it. If we are to have amalgamation, it should be public, and it should be responsible, and it should not be left to the Great Southern and Western Railway Company alone, but public opinion should have some share in the management. I want to know from the Chief Secretary for Ireland, or from those promoting this Bill, are we going to establish a system of trusts, monopolies, and "corners" such as exist in America? In America they have competition, but in Ireland you have no such thing. If you go to any of the great cities in America you find parallel lines, brought five or six times over, from one great city to another. The result is that there is a very keen competition. Of course, I know that in Ireland you must accommodate yourself to circumstances that exist, and we do not want in Ireland either "railway kings" or great corporations in the shape of trusts, which can squeeze the vitals out of the commerce altogether in the districts through which these railways run. I do not wish to detain the House, but I think this is a matter which should be discussed at greater length than the House can afford time at present; but I would appeal to those honourable Members who are so much in favour of amalgamation to remember the different circumstances which exist in Ireland to what exist in England. As I have said before, we have no competition, and there is very little State control, and if the powerful Irish railway company gets hold of these 13 counties in the 32 counties in Ireland, when the benefits promised come to be analysed they will be found to be very different. I have had a great deal of experience in my capacity as president of a large trading association of the Irish railways, and I know how they treat that branch of the trade with which I am connected. And now I would address myself more particularly to the Chief Secretary for Ireland. I know that the right honourable Gentleman is doing his best, but if he places too much reliance upon railway directors and grants them amalgamation, without having proper guarantees, the condition of things will be made worse than it is. There are only two ways of managing railways, and they are either by amalgamation or competition. Now we have no competition, and, if we are to have amalgamation, there must be certain conditions introduced with regard to the reduction of rates. Some honourable Members may say that this new company will not be allowed to raise the rates. Well, the rates are too high now, and we want a reduction of rates and proper facilities for carrying it out. We want the trains, and especially the third-class carriage accommodation, improved. I have drawn attention to this matter before in this House, and I take this opportunity of again appealing to honourable Members, and I say that there is no country in Europe where the accommodation provided for third-class passengers is so wretched as in Ireland. I travelled up to-day from Liverpool to London in a third-class carriage, and——

*MR. SPEAKER: I would remind the honourable Member that the condition of Irish and English railway carriages is not the subject of this Debate.

MR. FIELD: Then I will obey your ruling, Mr. Speaker. In conclusion,

I would impress upon the right honourable Gentleman the Chief Secretary for Ireland, if he intends to press his Motion, to be very careful about the manner in which this amalgamation is brought about, because, as I said before, if amalgamation is to be carried out, it must be public, and it must be responsible. It must study the community, and not give too much power to the railway companies, and, until I have heard what the right honourable Gentleman has to say, and what he proposes to exact in the way of security, I cannot say at the present time how I shall vote. I am, at the same time, entirely opposed to amalgamation, because I think it makes it more difficult to accomplish the nationalisation of the Irish railways, which is the only real cure for the disease which exists in Ireland.

*Sir J. COLOMB (Great Yarmouth): This question was raised in an indirect way last year, and I do not, therefore, propose to go over the whole ground. In view of the action of the Hybrid Committee in reference to the Great Southern and Western Railway, I could not agree that we should throw out this Bill. For there was a clause inserted in the Bill which made it a condition that, until Parliament had disposed of their application for this Bill, the state of things which this Measure was introduced to deal with was to continue in the meantime. Therefore, I do not see that we should be justified in rejecting the Bill, but, on the other hand, I see no reason why we should not postpone it. It has been suggested, and will be suggested, that arrangements can be made by which the matter might be postponed till a later period of this Session, when the county councils will have met; but anybody who knows Ireland knows that it will be perfectly impossible for the county councils—which have only just been called into being, and which meet for the first time on the 1st of April— to be in a position for months to come to deal with such a difficult and critical matter. And, therefore, it all comes to this—that, while I agree with my right honourable and learned Friend that it is desirable that this Bill should go upstairs to a Committee where all

Mr. Field.

matters can be inquired into, my contention is that, under the circumstances, until the county councils have come into existence in April next, you cannot have the matter thoroughly inquired into this Session upstairs, because the county councils cannot arrange to consider it before. We must remember that this Bill affects 13 counties out of 32 in Ireland where the ratepayers are under an obligation to pay guarantees out of rates, and I do not think Parliament will be right in sending this Bill to a Committee to be inquired into until the county councils are in full working order and are able to give the matter full consideration. The county councils meet, I believe, on the 6th of April, and they have to elect their chairmen, their officers, and form their committees, and settle down to business of which they have had no experience whatever. Now, if anything is likely to upset the fair start of the Local Government Bill in Ireland, it will be, I think, for the House now to send this Bill upstairs to be dealt with just as the county councils have assembled, for that would be like putting a bombshell amongst them. Anybody who understands the condition of Ireland at the present time, and remembers the fact that these new bodies have had no experience at all, will see that this proposal will be putting upon them an unfair burden. In my opinion the proper course to pursue will be simply to adjourn this Debate.

*Sir U. KAY-SHUTTLEWORTH (Lancashire, Clitheroe): I think, on a Bill of this kind, the House should generally be very much guided by the advice and the opinions of the Members of this House who represent the districts which are specially affected by the Bill, and, therefore, the views of the Members from Ireland ought to have very great weight. But not only have the Members from Ireland spoken with a divided voice, but Members who formed the Committee over which I presided last Session on the Rosslare and Fishguard Railway have also spoken with an uncertain voice upon this question. Under these circumstances I shall detain the House a few moments, because I have had occasion to consider this matter in all its parts during the last Session of Parliament, and, therefore, I may be permitted to say a very few words. I still hold the view which the Committee expressed last Session—namely, that this proposed amalgamation of the railways in the South of Ireland should be regarded with grave apprehension. What the Committee did was this: we had an instruction from the House which obliged us to consider carefully the whole question of competition, of adequate competition, in the railway system in the South of Ireland, and almost immediately after the Committee commenced its sittings we were made aware of this agreement between the Great Southern and Western Railway Company, who were one of the promoters of the Bill, and the Waterford, Limerick, and Western Railway Company. There was this agreement to enter into amalgamation, and we were bound to consider what would be its effect upon the condition of the South of Ireland. After a very careful consideration of the matter, we came to the conclusion which has already been quoted to the House—

"Your Committee are unable, after the evidence which they have heard, to withhold an expression of their unanimous opinion that, in the interests of the South of Ireland, they would regard with grave apprehension the absorption of these two companies' undertakings by the Great Southern and Western Railway."

Well, we were unable to deal effectively with the question, because the Bill now before the House was not then before the Committee, but the intention was to introduce it. It was pointed out, and brought to our notice, that what has been done in the South-east of England in the way of virtual amalgamation, without the consent of Parliament, might be done in the South of Ireland, and that, without coming to Parliament, those companies might amalgamate; and I believe the Committee did the right thing, and took the only course open to them, when they bound the companies not to pool or amalgamate, or alter their rates against the interests of the public, until Parliament had disposed of their Bill, and that Bill is now before the House. Something has been said as to what·members of the Committee ought to do and ought not to do under these circumstances. I will, however, venture to give my opinion. I think members of the Committee are perfectly at liberty to dispose of the Bill on the Second Reading, or, if they prefer it, to send the Bill up to the Committee, so that it may be further considered. If the second course were taken, it would still be open to Members on the Third Reading of the Bill to deal with it. I will venture to give my own individual opinion to the House, and it is this: It seems to me that a Committee is absolutely necessary unless that is to happen which the Committee of last Session carefully guarded against. What is there to prevent the Great Southern and Western Railway Company from entering into an arrangement which will be a virtual amalgamation if this Bill is disposed of by its rejection upon the Second Reading, and thus the companies would be released from the binding effect of clause 72, which was introduced by us last year in the Fishguard and Rosslare Railway Bill? Under these circumstances, I would suggest that the Bill be sent to a Committee, and I hope that that Committee will most carefully consider, supposing they are inclined to reject the Bill, whether some special report should not be made to Parliament to enable the House again to guard against the danger of an amalgamation which is not desired by that Committee, by an agreement between the companies resulting in an amalgamation behind the back of Parliament. My honourable Friend the Member for Cork, whose valuable assistance on that Committee I should be very ungrateful if I did not acknowledge, argued just now that competition was practically impossible in Ireland, and said that you could not have two competing lines between Limerick and Waterford.

*Mr. M. HEALY: What I meant to say was, between the three principal lines in Ireland.

*Sir U. KAY-SHUTTLEWORTH: I was quite sure the honourable Member had made a slip of the tongue, but let me just take that point. What is the existing state of things between Limerick and Waterford? There is a direct line, and another indirect line, in the hands of the Great Southern and Western Railway, and what is the effect of their existence? In those parts of the country where this competition exists the rates give great satisfaction to the agriculturists and others, and they would be very sorry indeed to have amalgamation take place unless their interests were properly safeguarded. It is absolutely necessary, either by this Bill or by some general legislation in the interests of those parts of Ireland which now enjoy the benefits of competition, low rates, and extended facilities, that those benefits should be safeguarded. If the Committee should make some such interim report as that which I have suggested, whilst the companies are still bound by the undertaking given to Parliament and by the clause existing in the present Act, Parliament would intervene, the Government would legislate, and steps would be taken to safeguard the interests of the public. That leads me to say just one word upon the general question of amalgamation. I was very much impressed during the inquiry to which I have referred by the fact that the Irish railway system is too much divided among different companies, some of them very small indeed, and the Report of the Commission of 1888 draws attention to that fact. But there is a very great danger if you allow amalgamation to take place that certain districts will be deprived of that competition to which I have already alluded; and the precautions which should be taken by Parliament were pointed out by the Royal Commission. One of them is that there should be some external controlling authority, with powers to inquire into and remedy grievances. For various reasons the Railway Commissioners are not often appealed to from Ireland, and there is a great need of some authority to which the traders and those interested can easily have access, and before which they can place their grievances. Another necessary precaution would be that clauses should be introduced, preserving the existing privileges of such districts as I have mentioned. There is one other point. Allusion has already been made to the necessity for the county councils considering this matter. In a few days we shall have the election of these Irish county councils, and I would strongly urge that it is of immense importance that sufficient time should be given

Sir U. Kay-Shuttleworth.

to enable the county councils to thoroughly consider the Bill before the House and to be heard by the Committee.

MR. GERALD BALFOUR: The House will no doubt expect me to say a few words before this discussion comes to a close. First of all, I may respond to the appeal of the honourable Member for Waterford, by saying that it is not my intention to make this in any sense a Party question. I have formed an opinion, but it is my desire not to bring any Party pressure to bear on this side of the House, and I would rather leave honourable Members perfectly free to judge this Measure upon its merits. The honourable Member for Waterford described it as an enormous proposal, and said it was a proposal which Parliament should most carefully consider at every stage. Well, I have no occasion to quarrel with an argument of that description. This is a proposal with momentous issues, and it is undoubtedly the largest amalgamation proposal which has ever been made in Ireland; but I observed that when the right honourable Member went on to say that because this is so enormous a proposal Parliament should most carefully consider it at every stage, if the Motion which the honourable Member has now made were carried, there would be no further stage at which it would be open to the House to consider it at all. Now, what is the question which lies before us at the present time? It is not whether this scheme of railway amalgamation should be passed by Parliament, but the question is whether it should be summarily and unceremoniously rejected, without any opportunity being given for that examination and consideration which it would receive from a Committee upstairs. There is this difference between a private Bill and a public Bill—when the House passes a public Bill it accepts the principle; but when it passes the Second Reading of a private Bill it does not exactly accept the principle, but it lays down that there is a *prima facie* case for inquiry, and therefore the adoption of the Second Reading of this Measure is not exactly an acceptation of its principle. I shall certainly vote myself for the Second Reading of this Bill, and I claim, as strongly as was claimed by the honourable Member for Cork, full freedom in my action with regard to any proposals in the Bill which do not seem to pay full regard to public interests in Ireland. Therefore, what the House is now called upon to decide is whether there is a *prima facie* case for inquiry. Personally, I think there is a *prima facie* case, and a very strong one. I will not go at length into the arguments which have been so ably set forth by previous speakers, but I would just like to say what I think their case consisted of. In the first place, I do not think it would be altogether fair to the companies concerned if this Bill was summarily rejected upon the Second Reading; for, as he has pointed out by my right honourable Friend the Member for Dublin University, this Bill was introduced under statutory compulsion, and the company had no choice in the matter. With regard to what the honourable Member for Waterford has said upon this point, so far as the company is concerned, it only makes their case much stronger still. The two companies are not only bound by statute to bring in this Bill, but coupled with that obligation there are conditions imposed upon them that in the meantime they are not to do things which might be to their advantage, and if under the circumstances Parliament was to summarily reject this Bill without going to the length of considering it by a Committee it would not only be prejudicial to the public, but it might be also somewhat hard upon the companies. That is one reason why I think this Bill should go before the Committee. But, in addition to that, I think it is in the interest of the railway companies in Ireland also that the Second Reading should be adopted, because, as the honourable Member for Cork has justly pointed out, we have to consider what will be the result in this respect if the Bill is rejected. The first result will be that the hands of the Great Southern and Western Railway and the Waterford, Limerick, and Western Railway Company will be free, and they will be able to enter into a traffic arrangement which may be very prejudicial to the interests of the public without any of the advantages which might accompany amalgamation. My honourable Friend the Member for Great Yarmouth suggested that we should get over this difficulty

by adjourning the Debate, and in that way we should not come in opposition to the Bill. I cannot help saying that that would be an evasion of the intention of Parliament, and I think if we are to deprive the company of this power we should not do it by resorting to a device of this kind, because that really is equivalent in effect, though not in form, to a rejection of the Bill, if by an adjournment it means that it should never come on again. That course would practically be considering the Bill this day six months, and I do not think that that is a proposal which the House ought to sanction. But, supposing no traffic arrangement is arrived at between the Great Southern and Western and the Waterford, Limerick, and Western Railway Companies in consequence of the rejection of this Bill on the Second Reading, even then the position would still be a most unsatisfactory one. The honourable Member for Cork has pointed out with great force that in the event of this Bill being rejected the natural position of one of the companies will still further be weakened, because they have already received notice that their arrangement with the other company will be brought to a conclusion on the completion of the Rosslare and Fishguard line, and that will still further damage the financial position of the Waterford and Limerick lines. The Waterford and Limerick lines at present suffer from insufficiency of capital, and if some change is not made it would be impossible for this company to maintain its present condition, and the last state of affairs would be worse than the first. There is a third reason which occurs to me why the House should pass the Second Reading of this Bill, and it is this: that the House up to the present to a very large extent has been working in the dark. We have only got the Bill before us in the form in which it is printed, but we do not know in what form it will emerge from the Committee, if, indeed, it emerges at all; but we may be quite sure that it will not emerge from the Committee without the introduction of a great many safeguards. Do not let the House imagine that it will not be in the power of the Hybrid Committee, should this Bill be sent to one, to introduce changes of a wide and far-reaching character. If any honourable Member is prepared to look at the changes made in the Rosslare Bill by the Hybrid Committee, they will at once see how great the power of such a Committee really is. I should just like to say one word in reference to the point which has been referred to by several speakers, and by the right honourable Gentleman opposite. It has been said that the county councils will not have an adequate opportunity of expressing their views should this Bill be sent to a Committee during the present year. I understand that the promoters of the Bill are ready to consent to the postponement of the Committee stage, and to agree that it should not be taken before the 15th of May. That arrangement would give the county councils a whole month to consider what action they would take. It has been said that a month is too little, but I do not think it is too little for county councils to take such action as county councils should take in matters of this kind. I do not think it would be wise that county councils should expend their money in fighting subjects of this kind. It appears to me that they would be doing a very foolish thing if they were to take upon themselves at the present time a burden which is being undertaken for them. But, in addition to this, I am bound to say that I do not think any expression of opinion which the county councils may make will affect my judgment as to whether this Bill should or should not be read a second time. It might affect my judgment as to what should be ultimately done, but not as to whether it should be read a second time or not, for this reason: the county council can only judge of the Bill as it has been presented to us, for it cannot be expected to go into questions of a hybrid, difficult, and complex character, and they cannot be expected to be in a position to consider the various changes which it is possible to introduce, and they will certainly not be in a position to adequately judge as to the full effects of such changes which may be made by the

Mr. Gerald Balfour.

Committee. In any case, I am sure of this, that I must feel more or less in the dark as to what my ultimate judgment may be. It requires a considerable amount of study, and I do not think the judgment of any county council is likely in their present condition of enlightenment upon this question to be very much better than my own. My opinion is that in order to have a final judgment on the Bill that it is desirable that it should be referred to a Committee, for I can hardly think that the county councils can be expected to form a judgment without the assistance which is only to be derived from an inquiry before the Committee. And just one word more. The honourable Member for the St. Patrick's Division of Dublin referred strongly to the necessity of adopting safeguards, but I am not in a position to say what safeguards may be considered wise to introduce, because that is a matter for the Committee upstairs. Therefore, to sum up—although I do not wish to make it in any sense a Party question—my own private view is that it would be most unwise and most inexpedient that the House should not pass the Second Reading of this Bill.

Mr. TIMOTHY HEALY (Louth, N.): I should just like to ask whether it is proposed to send this Bill to the Select Committee which is already appointed, many members of which have already pronounced an opinion against the principle of amalgamation. It appears to me that it is absolutely essential that this Bill should go to an absolutely new Committee, the members of which have not pronounced their opinion upon the question. The honourable Gentleman opposite is a member of that Committee, but although I have the greatest possible respect for him I should very strongly object to any Committee on which he sat considering this question if I were one of the promoters of this Bill, because I should be inclined to say, "You have already pronounced against this amalgamation."

*MR. SPEAKER: The honourable Member is now dealing with the nomination of the Committee—a question which is not before the House.

MR. TIMOTHY HEALY: I understand that with regard to the exclusion of a gentleman who sat last year on this Committee it might be invidious to move such a Motion, although I think it would be competent to do so. I would suggest that we should have some expression of opinion from the Government as to the manner in which this Committee is to be formed. I have no opinion as to how it should be formed, but all I desire is that it should be a fair Committee to consider the interests of the country as well as the interests of the railway company. My right honourable Friend, who was chairman of the Committee last year, and who sacrificed so much time in the interests of Ireland, I, for one, should not object to.

MR. DILLON: There is just one point I should like to impress upon the Chief Secretary, and it is this—I trust that he will not take the same course with regard to the appointing of this Committee as was the case in the House of Lords with regard to the questions that might arise, for I really think that it would not be fair to this House.

MR. GERALD BALFOUR: As regards the members of this Committee I can only say that my object and aim as far as I am concerned will be to get that Committee as fair and equal as possible, and my own feeling in the matter is this: The Committee that sat on the Rosslare and Fishguard line was a Committee of great ability and competence, and I would ask the honourable Member whether we should commit ourselves to a proposition at this moment that the honourable Member for Cork and the honourable Member for Waterford should be shut out.

MR. TIMOTHY HEALY: I should propose both.

MR. J. REDMOND: If the honourable Member will only enter into communication with the various sections of the House there will be no difficulty. There was no difficulty last year, and there will be no difficulty this year. I agree that it would be better to have no members of the old Committee, and certainly, as a member of that Committee, I distinctly object to serve.

Question put—

"That the word 'new' stand part of the Question."

Agreed to.

Main Question put, and agreed to.

Bill read a second time.

GREAT SOUTHERN AND WESTERN RAILWAY BILL.

(By Order.) Read a second time.

GREAT SOUTHERN AND WESTERN, AND WATERFORD, LIMERICK, AND WESTERN RAILWAY COMPANIES AMALGAMATION AND GREAT SOUTHERN AND WESTERN RAILWAY BILLS.

Ordered, That the Great Southern and Western, and Waterford, Limerick, and Western Railway Companies Amalgamation Bill, and the Great Southern and Western Railway Bill be committed to a Select Committee of Nine Members, Five to be nominated by the House, and Four by the Committee of Selection.

Ordered, That, subject to the Rules, Orders, and Proceedings of this House, all Petitions against the Bills be referred to the Committee, except in the case of the County Councils, under the provisions of the Local Government (Ireland) Act, 1898, and that all such Petitions of the said County Councils shall not be subject to the Rules, Orders, and Proceedings of this House, but may be presented. seven clear days before the meeting of the Committee, and shall be referred to the Committee, and that such of the Petitioners as pray to be heard by themselves, their Counsel, Agent, or Witnesses be heard on their Petitions against the Bills, if they think fit, and Counsel heard in support of the Bills against such Petitions.

Ordered, That the Committee have power to send for persons, papers, and records.

Ordered, That Five be the quorum.

Ordered, That it be an Instruction to the Committee that they do inquire and report whether the adoption of any or all of the proposals contained in the Bills would, without adequate compensating advantages, prevent or prejudice adequate competition in the railway system of the South and West of Ireland, or in the system of communication between that country and England and Wales.—*(Mr. Gerald Balfour.)*

RETURNS, REPORTS, ETC.

PAWNBROKERS' RETURNS (IRELAND).

Copy presented,—of Returns from the City Marshal of Dublin for the year ended 31st December 1898 (by Act); to lie upon the Table.

FISHINGS AND FORESHORES (SCOTLAND).

Return presented, — relative thereto [ordered 21st February; *Mr. Weir*]; to lie upon the Table, and to be printed. (No. 107.)

SUPERANNUATIONS.

Copy presented,—of Treasury Minute, dated 7th March 1899, declaring that for the due and efficient discharge of the duties of the office of Assistant for Chan-

cery and Charity business in the Department of the Treasury Solicitor, professional or other peculiar qualifications not ordinarily to be acquired in the public service are required (by Act); to lie upon the Table.

SUPERANNUATION ACT, 1884.

Copy presented,—of Treasury Minute, dated 6th March 1899, declaring that Louis Pedreschi, porter, National Gallery, Ireland, was appointed without a Civil Service certificate, through inadvertence on the part of the head of his Department (by Act); to lie upon the Table.

FRIENDLY SOCIETIES (SHOP CLUBS) (DEPARTMENTAL COMMITTEE).

Copy presented, — of Report to the Secretary of State for the Home Department by a Departmental Committee appointed to consider the complaints made by certain Friendly Societies, that men are compelled by their employers as a condition of employment to join shop clubs; together with Minutes of Evidence (by Command); to lie upon the Table.

TRADE REPORTS (ANNUAL SERIES).

Copy presented,—of Diplomatic and Consular Reports, Annual Series, No. 2210 (by Command); to lie upon the Table.

PRIVATE BILLS (GROUP C).

Mr. Schwann reported from the Committee on Group C of Private Bills, That the parties promoting the Ilford Urban District Council Gas Bill had stated that the evidence of Mr. W. D. Herd was essential to their case; and it having been proved that his attendance could not be procured without the intervention of the House, he had been instructed to move that the said Mr. W. D. Herd do attend the said Committee To-morrow, at Twelve of the clock.

Ordered, That Mr. W. D. Herd do attend the Committee on Group C of Private Bills To-morrow, at Twelve of the clock.

PRIVATE BILLS (GROUP C).

Mr. Schwann reported from the Committee on Group C of Private Bills, That the parties promoting the Ilford Urban District Council Gas Bill had stated that the evidence of Mr. W. J. Kendall-Moore, of Oakfield, High Street, Ilford, was essential to their case, and it having been proved that his attendance could not be procured without the intervention of the House, he had been instructed to move that the said Mr. W. J. Kendall-Moore do attend the said Committee To-morrow, at Twelve of the clock.

Ordered, That Mr. W. J. Kendall-Moore do attend the Committee on Group C of Private Bills To-morrow, at Twelve of the clock.

PRIVATE BILLS (GROUP A).

Mr. Baldwin reported from the Committee on Group A of Private Bills, That at the meeting of the Committee this day a letter was received from Mr. Strachey, one of the Members of the said Committee, stating that he was unable, on account of indisposition, to attend the Committee this day.

Report to lie upon the Table.

RAILWAY BILLS (GROUP 1).

Mr. Hobhouse reported from the Committee on Group 1 of Railway Bills, That Mr. Hedderwick, one of the Members of the said Committee, was not present during the sitting of the Committee this day.

Report to lie upon the Table.

STANDING ORDERS.

Resolutions reported from the Committee—

" 1. That, in the case of the Newhaven and Seaford Water Board Bill [Lords], the Standing Orders ought to be dispensed with :— That the parties be permitted to proceed with their Bill, provided that Clauses 45 and 53 be struck out of the Bill :—That the Committee on the Bill do report how far such Orders have been complied with."

" 2. That, in the case of the South Eastern Railway Bill, Petition of ' Beckenham Urban District Council ' for dispensing with Standing Order 129 in the case of their Petition against the Bill, the said Standing Order ought to be dispensed with."

Resolutions agreed to.

———

NEW BILLS.

———

SMALL HOUSES (ACQUISITION OF OWNERSHIP).

Bill to empower Local Authorities to advance money for enabling persons to acquire the ownership of Small Houses in which they reside, ordered to be brought in by Mr. Secretary Chamberlain and Mr. Attorney-General.

SMALL HOUSES (ACQUISITION OF OWNERSHIP) BILL.

" To empower Local Authorities to advance money for enabling persons to acquire the Ownership of Small Houses in which they reside," presented, and read the first time to be read a second time upon Monday next, and to be printed. (Bill 125.)

LOCAL GOVERNMENT ACT (1894) AMENDMENT BILL.

" To amend the Local Government Act, 1894," presented, and read the first time ; to be read a second time upon Wednesday 24th May, and to be printed. (Bill 126.)

QUESTIONS.

CHANNEL FLEET.

Mr. CROMBIE (Kincardineshire): On behalf of the honourable Member for Dundee (Sir John Leng), I beg to ask the First Lord of the Admiralty whether the Channel Fleet will rendezvous this year at any stations on the East Coast of Scotland; and, if so, could he state where and when?

The SECRETARY to the ADMIRALTY (Mr. W. E. Macartney, Antrim, S.): The further movements of the Channel Squadron after return to England at the end of May cannot be determined so long beforehand.

LOCAL RATING.

Mr. COGHILL (Stoke-upon-Trent): I beg to ask the President of the Local Government Board whether he will consider the advisability of amending section 133 of the Lands Clauses Consolidation Act, 1845, so that local authorities shall in future be entitled to be recouped the whole of the local rates, instead of only the poor rate, in respect of any property acquired by railway or other companies for new works until the new works come into rating?

The PRESIDENT of the LOCAL GOVERNMENT BOARD (Mr. H. Chaplin, Lincs., Sleaford): The honourable Member is no doubt aware that a Royal Commission is investigating the whole question of local taxation. Subject to their Report and to the evidence taken by them, I shall be quite ready to consider the suggestion of the honourable Member.

CONTAMINATED OYSTERS.

Mr. LODER (Brighton): I beg to ask the President of the Local Government Board whether he can now state when he hopes to be able to introduce a Bill dealing with the subject of contaminated oysters?

The PRESIDENT of the LOCAL GOVERNMENT BOARD: I am not in a position to state the precise day, but I hope to introduce it at an early date.

LONDON SCHOOL BOARD VISITORS.

Mr. LOWLES (Shoreditch, Haggerston): I beg to ask the Vice-President of the Committee of Council on Education whether his attention has been called to the case of Joseph Bigwood, a school visitor, who recently died in Islington Workhouse Infirmary; whether he is aware that, when he retired in May 1897, Bigwood had served the London Board faithfully for 24 years, and from March 1888 till his retirement had paid two per cent. of his salary into the Board's pension fund; whether, under the contract which he signed with the Board upon the introduction of the pension scheme, he was entitled at his retirement to a pension of £48 a year, but by its actuary's advice the Board could not afford to allow Bigwood more than £6 14s. per annum; and, whether steps will be taken to prevent similar hardship to school visitors compulsorily retired under like circumstances?

The VICE-PRESIDENT of the COMMITTEE of COUNCIL on EDUCATION (Sir John Gorst, Cambridge University): The Committee of Council have no information upon the case referred to, and have no control over the administration of School Board pension schemes.

HANWELL AND SOUTHALL SCHOOLS.

Sir H. BEMROSE (Derby): I beg to ask the President of the Local Government Board whether he is aware that the City of London and St. Saviour's Guardians are proposing to increase their buildings at the Hanwell Schools at a cost of £6,545, and that the Marylebone Guardians propose to spend an estimated sum of £12,000 on the enlargement of the premises at the Southall Schools; and, whether, in view of his statement on 1st February 1897, that the Local Government Board are declining to sanction proposals which would have the effect of extending the large schools, he will take steps to prevent the above-named expenditure?

THE PRESIDENT OF THE LOCAL GOVERNMENT BOARD: I am aware of the proposals referred to in the first paragraph of the Question. The object of the new buildings at Hanwell is to afford improved school-room accommodation for infants who are in the schools, and before sanctioning the plans the Local Government Board informed the managers that it must be distinctly understood that no additional dormitory accommodation was to be provided, and that no increase would be allowed in the number of children which the school would accommodate. The buildings to be erected at Southall will provide a new infirmary for the children in the school and separate blocks of Probationary Wards. But they will not add to the number of children certified for the school. The school in question is not one of the larger schools, and there is nothing that I am aware of in these proposals which is inconsistent with my statements in 1897.

TRADE DEPOTS IN CHINA.

MR. YERBURGH (Chester): I beg to ask the Under Secretary of State for Foreign Affairs whether foreigners in China have any right of residence for purposes of trade except at the Treaty Ports; if not, whether, in view of the promised throwing open of inland waterways in China to foreign vessels, and of the necessity for up-country stations and depôts being established for the storage and delivery of goods, if this concession is to be of any real value, the Government will secure for our merchants and their agents the right of establishing and residing at such stations and depôts?

THE UNDER SECRETARY OF STATE FOR FOREIGN AFFAIRS (Mr. ST. JOHN BRODRICK, Surrey, Guildford): There is no express Treaty provision enabling foreigners, other than missionaries, to acquire and hold property beyond the Treaty Ports of China. The object which the honourable Member desires to obtain will not be lost sight of by Her Majesty's Government.

HYDE AND GREEN PARKS.

COLONEL WELBY (Taunton): I beg to ask the Secretary of State for the Home Department whether his attention has been called to the number of persons of evil life frequenting Hyde Park and Green Park in the evenings; and whether he can see his way to a more complete system of police supervision of these parks, especially of the portions of them adjacent to Bayswater Road and Piccadilly?

THE UNDER SECRETARY OF STATE FOR THE HOME DEPARTMENT (Mr. J. COLLINGS, Birmingham, Bordesley): The police have no charge over and do not patrol the Green Park. In Hyde Park they act up to the full extent of their powers in dealing with offenders, and the special action initiated in 1898 has resulted in a considerable increase in the number of convictions against offenders and also in deterring many objectionable characters from frequenting the Park.

SUGAR REFINERIES IN INDIA.

MR. MACLEAN (Cardiff): I beg to ask the Secretary of State for India if he could state to the House what number of sugar refineries have been closed in India on account of the competition of imported sugar from countries granting bounties on sugar production; what was the annual production of sugar from these refineries; what amount of capital was invested in them, and whether it was held by Europeans or Natives; and what amount of revenue the Bill for the imposition of countervailing duties is estimated to yield?

THE SECRETARY OF STATE FOR INDIA (Lord G. HAMILTON, Middlesex, Ealing): Complaints have been received by the Government from various quarters of the inability of the Native sugar refiners to compete with the bounty-fed sugars, and many small refineries have in consequence been closed, but I have not their exact numbers, nor have I any statement of the amount of capital invested in them. It is difficult to estimate what the yield of any countervailing duty will be, but I do not think that under any circumstances the yield of this duty will be over £50,000 a year.

LIMERICK TELEPHONE SERVICE.

Mr. O'KEEFFE (Limerick): I beg to ask the Secretary to the Treasury, as representing the Postmaster-General, if, in accordance with the resolutions of the Limerick Harbour Commissioners recently sent to him, he will recommend the extension of the trunk telephone system to Ennis and Kilrush from Limerick; and if he will similarly extend the same service to Kilkee, county Clare?

The FINANCIAL SECRETARY to the TREASURY (Mr. R. W. Hanbury, Preston): There is no exchange either at Kilrush or Kilkee, and it is, therefore, premature to provide a trunk wire. At Ennis there is an exchange, and the Postmaster-General has offered to provide a trunk wire under a guarantee from the Telephone Company, who, however, do not see their way to give it. The number of subscribers are so small that a trunk wire to that place could not be given without guarantee.

MARGARINE FACTORIES.

Captain DONELAN (Cork, N.E.): I beg to ask the President of the Board of Trade whether margarine factories are subject to periodical inspection?

The PRESIDENT of the BOARD of TRADE (Mr. C. T. Ritchie, Croydon): No, Sir.

Captain DONELAN: Will this Question be considered in the Bill now before Parliament?

The PRESIDENT of the BOARD of TRADE: If an Amendment is proposed, of course it will.

PROVOST MUNGALL, OF COWDEN-BEATH.

Mr. WEIR (Ross and Cromarty): I beg to ask the Lord Advocate whether he is aware that the Provost of Cowdenbeath, Fifeshire, Provost Mungall, is also manager of the Fife Coal Company at Cowdenbeath, and that the Provost, as representing the local authority, has de-

clined to take any steps to require the company to provide protection for the public at their railway level crossing which passes across High Street, Cowdenbeath; and, having regard to the fact that the county council, in respect of its road administration, is not responsible to any Government Department, will he consider the expediency of introducing legislation so that a local authority which happens to be under the control of a private company may be compelled to see that suitable provision is made for the public safety?

The LORD ADVOCATE (Mr. A. G. Murray, Buteshire): This matter has already been twice explained by me to the honourable Member, and the identical Question has been answered by my right honourable Friend the President of the Board of Trade. I have nothing to add to his Answer.

Mr. WEIR: Is the right honourable Gentleman aware that the Member for Ross and Cromarty was nearly killed at this crossing?

Mr. SPEAKER: Order, order!

NAVIGATION ON CHINESE INLAND WATERS.

Mr. ASCROFT (Oldham): I beg to ask the Under Secretary of State for Foreign Affairs whether Her Majesty's Government is aware that the Chinese Government has placed the following restrictions on the freedom of navigation by foreign craft over the inland waters of the Chinese Empire: that a steamer plying between two Treaty ports may not trade at places on the way; and that a steamer engaged in the inland waters trade may not ply other than within a certain radius, nor may such steamer go beyond the next Treaty port; and whether Her Majesty's Government will take such steps, either independently or in conjunction with other Powers interested, as may be necessary to get such restrictions removed?

Mr. BRODRICK: No such restrictions as those referred to are contained in the Regulations for the navigation of the inland waters of China as received from

Her Majesty's Minister at Pekin, published in the Blue Book to be issued to-day. In accordance with the Treaties, trade can only be carried on by Europeans at the open ports. The whole Question is receiving careful consideration.

SCOTCH BANK HOLIDAYS.

MR. PIRIE (Aberdeen, N.): I beg to ask the Secretary to the Treasury, as representing the Postmaster-General, whether, in view of the Aberdeen post and telegraph employees being entitled to six bank holidays per annum, it is intended that the three days' continuous leave given during winter months shall be considered as equivalent to a day's holiday on each of the four bank or local holidays as these occur; and, if so, whether he is aware that in a number of large offices this decision has been overruled; and whether it is intended that Aberdeen postal and telegraph employees shall have the full benefit of six bank holidays, consisting of New Year's Day and Christmas Day with four other holidays, free from any condition, so that the Aberdeen staff may receive similar treatment to that given to New-castle and Edinburgh Post Offices?

MR. HANBURY: The answer to the first paragraph of the honourable Member's Question as affecting Aberdeen is in the negative, and to the second paragraph in the affirmative.

LATE CAPTAIN FINLAYSON.

MR. PIRIE: I beg to ask the Under Secretary of State for War, with reference to the case of the late Veterinary Captain Finlayson, whether, in coming to the decision that this officer should retire from the Service, the fact that he would thereby receive a sum of £800 on complying with this decision, formed an essential element of such decision; and if he can state by whom the Secretary of State's instructions that he would be required to send in his papers were given to this officer, and whether those instructions were complied with; if so, what was the date on which Captain Finlayson's resignation was received by his superior officer?

THE UNDER SECRETARY OF STATE FOR WAR (Mr. G. WYNDHAM, Dover): The Question whether or not Captain Finlayson would be entitled to any gratuity or retiring allowance did not affect the decision arrived at with regard to him. The instructions to him to send in his papers were given by the Field Marshal commanding the Forces in Ireland, and were complied with by the 28th January 1898. The Field Marshal forwarded the papers to the War Office on the 29th January 1898.

MR. PIRIE: Who conveyed the instructions to this officer?

MR. WYNDHAM: They were conveyed through the usual channels.

RECRUITS' PAY.

MR. PIRIE: I beg to ask the Under Secretary of State for War if he can state how many of the recruits obtained since the new enlistment regulations came into force have produced, in order to benefit by the increased pay given when efficient, on their satisfying the authorities that they are really 19 years of age, definite proof by birth certificate or otherwise of their actual age on enlistment; and the percentage which this number bears to the total enlisted?

MR. WYNDHAM: Under the Royal Warrant a recruit who claims the Messing Allowance, after fulfilling the conditions of military efficiency, is not required to produce a birth certificate. The allowance is granted on a certificate from the officer commanding and the medical officer that they are satisfied that he is at least 19 years of age.

LAND QUESTION IN CEYLON.

DR. TANNER (Cork Co., Mid.): I beg to ask the Secretary of State for the Colonies whether his attention has been called to the present state of the land question in Ceylon, as administered by

General West Ridgeway; and whether he will endeavour to secure that the Estimates for the expenses of that Colony are brought forward at a time which will give honourable Members a convenient opportunity to discuss this subject?

THE SECRETARY OF STATE FOR THE COLONIES (Mr. J. CHAMBERLAIN, Birmingham, W.): Questions relating to the recent Land Ordinance in Ceylon have been and are under my consideration. There are no such Estimates— Ceylon receives no grant-in-aid from Imperial funds.

DR. TANNER: Is not the salary of the Governor voted by this House?

THE SECRETARY OF STATE FOR THE COLONIES: No, Sir.

ST. CLEMENT'S CHURCH, BELFAST.

MR. YOUNG (Cavan, E.): I beg to ask the Chief Secretary to the Lord Lieutenant of Ireland whether he is aware that under the Act 23 and 24 Vict., c. 32, secs. 2 and 3 (the words are): Any one guilty of riotous, violent, or indecent behaviour in any church or chapel, churchyard or burying ground, or who shall molest any preacher or clergyman ministering therein, may be arrested by any policeman or churchwarden, and, if convicted, fined £5, or imprisoned for two months; and whether there is any reason why this Act should not be enforced in the Church of St. Clement, Belfast, where rioting is permitted to proceed in the presence of the police?

THE CHIEF SECRETARY TO THE LORD LIEUTENANT OF IRELAND (Mr. GERALD W. BALFOUR, Leeds, Central): I am aware of the provisions of the Act mentioned in the Question. As regards the second paragraph, I would refer to my reply to the similar inquiry addressed to me yesterday by the honourable Member, in which I stated that Government are of opinion that disturbers of the Services in St. Clement's Church should be brought into a court of law by the churchwardens rather than by the police, but that the police are prepared to assist the churchwardens to prevent persons entering the church, if the churchwardens are empowered by the bishop, or the rector, to exercise this authority.

TRADES UNIONS AND THE POST OFFICE SAVINGS BANK.

MR. MARKS (Tower Hamlets, St. George's): I beg to ask the Secretary to the Treasury, as representing the Postmaster-General, what portion of the total deposits in the Post Office Savings Banks belong to Trades Unions?

MR. HANBURY: It is estimated that the deposits of Trades Unions in the Post Office Savings Bank on the 31st December last amounted to £500,000, out of total deposits amounting to £123,155,000.

TOWN TENANTS IN IRELAND.

MR. FIELD (Dublin, St. Patrick's): I beg to ask the Chief Secretary to the Lord Lieutenant of Ireland whether it is the intention of the Government to introduce legislation for the purpose of securing town tenants in Ireland in their tenure and improvements, or whether he will have any inquiries made into the subject, or appoint a committee to report thereon?

MR. GERALD BALFOUR: The question of town holdings in Great Britain and Ireland was inquired into by a Select Committee of the House some years ago, and the Report of the Committee, together with the minutes of evidence taken before it, have been laid on the Table. [See Parliamentary Paper, No. 251, of the Session of 1889.] The question of legislation, or of further inquiry by a committee, or otherwise, are matters which could only be considered in their application to the United Kingdom as a whole, and I am not prepared either to introduce legislation dealing with Ireland alone or to recommend any further inquiries as suggested.

EXPENDITURE UNDER THE MILITARY WORKS ACT.

Mr. BUCHANAN (Aberdeenshire, E.): I beg to ask the Under Secretary of State for War whether he will state, as the First Lord of the Admiralty has done with regard to the Naval Works Act, the amount of expenditure during the current year under the Military Works Act?

Mr. WYNDHAM: The amount will probably be about £800,000.

TELEPHONE BILL.

Sir J. FERGUSSON (Manchester, N.E.): I beg to ask the Secretary to the Treasury whether it is intended to issue a Treasury Minute embodying the whole scheme of telephone development, whereof only a part is provided for in the Telegraphs (Telephonic Communications) Bill, as was done in 1898; and whether such Minute will be laid upon the Table before the Second Reading of the Bill?

Mr. HANBURY: It is evident that the House should be possessed of adequate information as to the proposed mode of giving effect to clause 2 of the Telegraph Bill when it comes on for a Second Reading, and probably the best method of giving this information will be by a Treasury Minute.

IRISH WORKHOUSE HOSPITAL NURSES.

Dr. TANNER: I beg to ask the Chief Secretary to the Lord Lieutenant of Ireland if he is aware that by a new rule the Irish Local Government Board insist upon workhouse hospital nurses having in all cases a minimum hospital training of three years, which rule is retrospective; is it intended this rule shall apply to the present nurses, although these were supplied by local intelligence and private charity; and will their case be considered, since they were possessed of one year's hospital training and subsequent private nursing?

Mr. GERALD BALFOUR: There is no rule or regulation of the Local Government Board to the effect stated in the first paragraph. But there is a rule which provides that if there is one nurse in each workhouse with two years' training in a recognised hospital one-half of her salary will be recouped to the Guardians under Section 58 of the Local Government Act. This rule does not affect the position of existing nurses who do not possess the qualification mentioned; their salary will be wholly paid by the Guardians as heretofore. Where the existing infirmary nurse of a workhouse has received training, though not sufficient to comply with the Board's regulation, the Guardians are authorised to allow her, if approved of by the medical officer, leave of absence for such a period as will enable her to complete the training necessary to place her on the Board's Register of trained nurses.

BRITISH TRADE IN MADAGASCAR.

Mr. PIRIE: On behalf of the honourable Member for Dundee I beg to ask the Under Secretary for Foreign Affairs whether any representations are being made to the Government of France on the continuance of the unequal treatment of British goods which, after being charged far higher rates than similar French goods, the natives are forbidden to buy, and of the higher dues imposed on British ships, such treatment being an infraction of the promise made to the British Government when Madagascar became a French protectorate?

Mr. BRODRICK: I regret to say that no reply has yet been received from the French Government to the representations addressed to them as to the unequal treatment of British goods in Madagascar.

ARMY CANTEENS.

Mr. PIRIE: I beg to ask the Under Secretary of State for War whether it is intended to appoint a Committee by the War Office to inquire into the commission system so injuriously prevalent in the supply and sale of liquor to Army canteens; and, if so, what will be its composition and the terms of reference appointing it?

MR. WYNDHAM: A Committee, composed of a general officer as president and of two commanding officers as members, is now sitting at Aldershot to inquire into the respective merits of garrison and regimental canteens. The question of preventing the acceptance of commissions will no doubt be considered by the Committee.

MUSCAT POST OFFICE.

SIR SEYMOUR KING (Hull, Central): I beg to ask the Secretary of State for India whether the Post Office at Muscat is a branch of the Indian Post Office; and why the boon of penny postage has not been granted to British residents there?

THE SECRETARY OF STATE FOR INDIA: It is true that the Post Office at Muscat is worked as a branch of the Indian Post Office, but the Imperial penny postage scheme is intended for correspondence between the various portions of the British Empire, among which Muscat cannot be included.

HIGHLAND DEER FORESTS.

MR. WEIR: I beg to ask the Lord Advocate if the Secretary for Scotland will grant a Return giving the name of each deer forest in the six Highland crofting counties, amount of its assessment, and the increase or decrease in the acreage of each forest as compared with 1883?

MR. GRAHAM MURRAY: Yes, Sir.

TAIN COURT HOUSE.

MR. WEIR: I beg to ask the Lord Advocate if the Secretary for Scotland will consider the expediency of bestowing the vacant post of keeper of the court house at Tain, value £25 per annum, on an Army pensioner?

MR. GRAHAM MURRAY: The appointment in question is not made by the Secretary for Scotland, nor by myself.

MR. WEIR: By whom is it made?

MR. GRAHAM MURRAY: I do not know.

SCOTCH RAILWAY STATION WATER SUPPLIES.

MR. WEIR: I beg to ask the President of the Board of Trade whether the Highland Railway Company's stations at Nigg, Fearn, and Strathcarron have now been provided with a suitable supply of potable water?

THE PRESIDENT OF THE BOARD OF TRADE: I have communicated with the Highland Railway, and the General Manager informs the Board of Trade that there is a supply of potable water at Strathcarron and Fearn Stations, and that Nigg Station is situated within the Barbaraville special water supply district now being formed by the County Council of Ross-shire.

TIUMPAN HEAD LIGHTHOUSE.

MR. WEIR: I beg to ask the President of the Board of Trade if he will state what progress has been made with the construction of the lighthouse on Tiumpan Head, Island of Lewis?

THE PRESIDENT OF THE BOARD OF TRADE: I am informed by the Commissioners of Northern Lighthouses that part of the Tiumpan Head lighthouse tower has been erected, and that the construction of the lantern and lighting apparatus is in process. It is expected that the light will be exhibited early next year.

APPRENTICES IN THE MERCANTILE MARINE.

SIR E. GOURLEY (Sunderland): I beg to ask the President of the Board of Trade whether any ship-owning firms have availed themselves of clause 6 of the Merchant Shipping (Mercantile

Marine Fund) Act of 1898, for the employment of apprentices for the Naval Reserves; if not, whether it is the intention of the Board of Trade to ask the Treasury to concur in the adoption of a scale of allowance sufficient to indemnify ship owners from pecuniary loss who may agree to engage apprentices in accordance with the Act; and whether he can state the nature of the regulations intended to be issued regarding their housing and education?

THE PRESIDENT OF THE BOARD OF TRADE: The Act to which the honourable Member refers does not come into operation until the 1st April next, and some time must necessarily elapse before it can be known to what extent shipowners will avail themselves of the provisions of section 6. The scale and regulations which the Board of Trade are empowered to make will be issued at once, and I hope that the scheme may lead to a considerable increase in the number of British boy sailors in our Merchant Navy. The honourable Gentleman's Question implies that the object of the Government is to secure apprentices for the Royal Naval Reserve. This is a misapprehension. The main object of the scheme is to secure an increased supply of British seamen for the Mercantile Marine. I do not think it is incumbent on the Government to indemnify shipowners for present pecuniary loss (if any) which they may sustain in carrying out a scheme which will be for their future advantage.

LASCARS ON P. AND O. BOATS.

MR. HAVELOCK WILSON (Middlesbrough): I beg to ask the President of the Board of Trade if he can state the number of lascars employed as sailors, firemen, coal trimmers, boys, and assistant cooks on board the Peninsular and Oriental steamship "Rome" on her last voyage; whether he will give such statement from the list supplied to the officers of Customs under section 125, sub-section 4, of the Merchant Shipping Act; and whether he can state how many cubic feet of space were provided for each lascar seaman employed on this vessel on her last voyage?

THE PRESIDENT OF THE BOARD OF TRADE: I am informed that the number of lascars employed on the Peninsular and Oriental steamship "Rome" on her latest voyage, in the capacities of sailors, firemen, coal trimmers, boys, and assistant cooks, as taken from the list supplied to officers of Customs, was 112. The space in cubic feet provided for each lascar was 80.3, which, as the honourable Member is aware, is in excess of the requirements of both the Indian and the Imperial Acts.

MR. HAVELOCK WILSON: When will the Report of the Solicitors to the Board of Trade on this subject be read?

THE PRESIDENT OF THE BOARD OF TRADE: I am unable to say. I am not consulting the Solicitors, but the Law Officers of the Crown—the Attorney-General and Solicitor-General.

REVISED STATUTES.

MR. MARKS: I beg to ask Mr. Attorney-General when the new edition of the Revised Statutes up to 1887 will be completed and ready for issue; and whether he will see that in any re-issue of the 13 volumes already issued, and in those subsequently issued to complete the set, the revisions up to date of issue are included in each volume?

THE ATTORNEY-GENERAL (Sir R. WEBSTER, Isle of Wight): I am informed that Vol. XIV., which brings the work down to 1880, is in the press, and will shortly be published. Vol. XV., which completes the work down to 1887, has only recently been sent to the printers, and it is not possible at present to say when it will be published. I am not able to give the honourable Member any information as to the last paragraph of his Question.

ANGLO-AMERICAN COMMISSION.

MR. LOWLES: I beg to ask the First Lord of the Treasury whether he is able to give the name of the probable successor to the late Lord Herschell on the Anglo-American Commission?

THE FIRST LORD OF THE TREA-
SURY (Mr. A. J. BALFOUR, Manchester,
E.): I have to say that the Joint Commission has adjourned until August 2nd
next. No steps have yet been taken in
the appointment of Lord Herschell's successor.

—

LAY TITHE RENT CHARGE IN IRELAND.

MR. STOCK (Liverpool, Walton): I
beg to ask the Chief Secretary to the
Lord Lieutenant of Ireland whether his
attention has been drawn to a recent decision affecting the revision of the lay
tithe rent charge in Ireland, by which it
was set down that owing to the failure
of the " Dublin Gazette " to publish the
market prices of such commodities as
the tithes were estimated on, all reductions obtained since the cessation of
such publication were illegal, and the
tithe rent payer is in future prevented
from applying to the court for revision
of his tithes ; and whether the Government will take steps to remedy such an
injustice ?

MR. GERALD BALFOUR: I am aware
of the decision referred to in the Question. The matter is under the consideration of Government, and I hope
to be able to deal with it in the course
of the present Session.

GAME LAWS.

MR. SCHWANN (Manchester, N.): I
beg to ask the Secretary of State for
the Home Department whether it is
illegal for game dealers in the United
Kingdom, either wholesale or retail, to
sell English game after 10th February
which has been killed and bought before the close time (1st February) and
consigned to cold-air stores in this Kingdom, in view of the fact that foreign
game can be sold all the year round ;
and, in the affirmative case, would he
consider whether it would be possible to
allow game dealers in this country to sell
British and Irish game after close time
on production, when challenged, of the
cold-air stores delivery notes ; and what
proof is at present given that so-called
foreign game exposed for sale after
10th February is what it professes to be ?

MR. COLLINGS: The main question
is one of law, which the Secretary
of State has no authority to decide ;
and he is not aware that there is any
binding decision of a court of law on the
point. With regard to the last paragraph of the Question, the Secretary of
State is not aware that there is anything in this matter to require a particular kind of evidence. The foreign origin
of game would have to be proved, like
any other fact, by the person on whom
the burden lay.

S.S. "ELLINGTON" AND S.S. "SPRING-
HILL."

MR. HAVELOCK WILSON: I beg to
ask the President of the Board of Trade
whether he can state the number of able
seamen carried as deck hands on the s.s.
" Ellington " and s.s. " Springhill," now
employed trading between West Hartlepool and Cowes, Isle of Wight ; whether
he can state the respective tonnage of
these vessels ; and whether they are
complying with the Board of Trade regulations respecting the manning of ships ;
and, if not, whether he will take steps
to enforce such regulations ?

THE PRESIDENT OF THE BOARD OF
TRADE : I am informed that the s.s.
" Ellington " carries master, one mate, a
boatswain, and three A.B.'s, and that the
s.s " Springhill'' carries master, two-
mates, a boatswain, and three A.B.'s.
The gross tonnage of the " Ellington "
is 703, and that of the " Springhill " 674.
Both vessels are engaged in the coasting
trade, with respect to which the Board
of Trade have laid down no specific regulations, but I am advised that they are
not insufficiently manned for the coasting trade in which they are engaged.

MR. HAVELOCK WILSON: Is it not
necessary to have the proper complement
of men ?

MR. SPEAKER: Order, order! The
honourable Member is asking as to a
matter of opinion.

MR. HAVELOCK WILSON: I will
put another Question on this.

SMALL HOUSES (ACQUISITION OF OWNERSHIP) BILL.

FIRST. READING.

THE SECRETARY OF STATE FOR THE COLONIES (Mr. J. CHAMBERLAIN, Birmingham, W.): In asking leave to introduce " a Bill to empower local authorities to advance money for enabling persons to acquire the ownership of small houses in which they reside," I should perhaps take notice of an observation made in my absence by the Leader of the Opposition, who, in stating that this Bill was one of the most important in the programme of the Government, maintained that we did not give the House what is called an opportunity for a full-dress Debate at this stage of our proceedings. I think the right honourable Gentleman could not have made that observation if he had followed the course of proceedings in this matter, and had been aware of the nature of the Bill I propose to introduce. The subject of the Bill, and, generally speaking, its provisions, have been again and again before the House, they have been discussed and approved in the House of Commons, and the Measure certainly cannot be called one of Party controversy. In 1893 a Bill similar in its object was introduced to the House of Commons by Mr. Wrightson, then Member for Stockton-on-Tees. On that occasion the principle of the Bill was approved by the colleague of the right honourable Gentleman opposite—the right honourable Member for East Wolverhampton, and the Second Reading was carried by a very large majority. In 1896, and again in 1898, similar Bills were introduced to this House by my honourable Friends the Members for Central Sheffield and West Wolverhampton; and on these occasions also—altogether three times—the principle of the Bill has received the assent of the House of Commons. In the House of Lords a similar Bill has been introduced by Lord Londonderry, and there it passed through all its stages, including a reference to a Standing Committee, both in 1896 and 1898, and on these occasions the Bill was warmly approved by Lord Rosebery and Lord Kimberley. Under such circumstances, it can hardly be expected we should think it necessary to trouble the House with a special discussion at this early and formal stage of the proceedings. Now the present Bill has exactly the same objects as

those Bills to which I have referred. It is intended to extend to the occupiers of small houses the same facility to be come the owners of their houses that has already been extended by legislation to the owners of small farms in Ireland and to small holders of tenancies in this country; and we believe that legislation of this kind is equally applicable to the towns and to the occupation of houses as it is to the country and to the occupation of land, and that to assist occupiers to become owners will have a tendency to make them better citizens, to give them a larger stake in the country, and to provide for them a popular and favourite form of thrift, and will, in addition, do, perhaps, more than any other legislation, if it is largely availed of, to secure healthy and comfortable homes, because it is perfectly clear that the working classes and people who live in these houses cannot be expected to take a great interest in their condition or expend money or give time and labour to improve them as long as they are working only for the benefit of their landlords, and because the class of persons who now own these small properties are not men from whom you can expect any lavish expenditure in improving the houses. We believe this result will follow, that if this Bill is taken advantage of to any considerable extent the occupiers of small dwellings will become the owners of them. The provisions are substantially the same as those of the Bills to which I have referred. The Bill is a voluntary one. It is voluntary upon the working man whether he will offer to become the owner of his house, it is voluntary upon the present landlord r owner of the house whether he will sell, and it is voluntary upon the local authority whether or not they will advance the money. But, subject to those assents, which we believe it will not be difficult to obtain in a great number of cases, the operation of the Bill will proceed upon the lines of the Bills to which I have already referred. In the Debates which took place on those Bills certain practical objections were made to the details. I do not think there was much objection taken in any quarter of the House to the principle of the Measures, but certain objections were made to points of detail, and those objections we have endeavoured to meet. In the first place it was said the Bills had too limited an application, and only a very small section of the population would be able to take advantage of the facilities. We have endeavoured to extend very largely the operation of the Bill by certain changes. In the first place, we have altered the definition of the persons to be benefited. In the previous Bills it was intended that the operation of the Measures should be extended chiefly to artigans. We do not define those who are to take advantage of this Measure by any reference to their class or employment; the fact of them occupying a house below a certain value will bring them within the purview of the Bill whatever be their occupation or position in life. We have increased the value of the house, which is to be a qualifying condition, from £200 to £300, and thereby we hope to include practically the working classes and others who occupy small houses of the kind we desire to deal with in the suburbs of London and other large towns.

*MR. WEIR (Ross and Cromarty): Scotland?

THE SECRETARY OF STATE FOR THE COLONIES: Certainly; it applies exactly to Scotland as to England. Then we have also increased the limit of advance which may be made by the local authority from three-fourths to four-fifths, so that the *maximum* amount which may be advanced will be £240 upon a house of the value of £300; and, lastly, with the same object, we have made a change in the limit which has hitherto been placed upon the operations of the local authorities. Personally, I think it is unnecessary in cases where the action of the local authority is voluntary to put any limit at all on their discretion. I think they would be perfectly well able to take care of themselves and their constituents. At the same time, as there is always a fear that legislation of this kind will add largely to the rates, the Government have come to the conclusion that some limitation should be imposed. The limitation proposed in Mr. Wrightson's Bill was one-eighth of the rateable value, and it was pointed out that in many cases that would only allow a very small number of applicants to be provided for in particular localities. We have thought that the proper limit is the limit of expense and not of rateable value. It does not matter how much money is

Secretary of State for the

advanced provided no cost is put on. the rates, and the limit we propose a that whenever the expense under the Bill rises to above a rate of 1d. in the pound the operation of the Bill shall cease until such time as the expense sinks below that limit. In my opinion that will leave a wide field for the operation of the Bill, because we do not anticipate that any expense, or any but the most trivial expense, will be thrown on the local authorities, as we believe the terms on which they lend and the securities they will hold will be quite sufficient to ensure them from loss. There is. another point to which we have directed attention in the hope of improving the character of the Bill. It was said that the Bill would interfere with what is called the mobility of labour. My belief is that the mobility of labour has been considerably exaggerated by those who have spoken on the subject. My experience of a large manufacturing town is that a large number—indeed, probably by far the larger proportion—of the working classes are not more mobile than other classes. On the other hand, it is perfectly true there are certain trades which change in their situation, and the workmen have to follow them. Although, as I say, the difficulty is exaggerated, we feel that it is desirable that a workman who becomes the owner of his house should be able to transfer his holding with the greatest possible ease and facility, and we have done what we can to make it more possible for him to do so. In the first place, we propose that ownership of this kind should be specially registered by the local authority, and that transfer shall be freely made upon payment of a fee which in no case shall exceed 10s. The owner of a dwelling will have full power to transfer, and we have provided that, in cases in which an owner of a property ceases to reside in it, as he may in consequence of change of situation, and where he is himself unable to transfer, the local authority may take over the dwelling at a price to be fixed by arbitration, the abitration to be carried out by the county court judge or by an arbitrator appointed by him. Of course, in cases in which the other statutory conditions are violated—that is to say, the condition that a man shall pay his instalments regularly, that he shall keep the house insured, and keep it in proper condition—if those conditions are violated, then the local authority has power to at once enter upon possession of the house and to sell it, paying to the workman anything that may accrue from the sale over and above the debt. But we have thought a forced sale entailing possibly some sacrifice would be too hard a condition in cases in which the workman has only given up residence, and, therefore, in these cases we have made it much easier for him to obtain the value of his house by an arrangement which will give him the appreciation in value of the house, if it has appreciated in the course of his occupancy, while the local authority will be secured from loss by paying only fair value if it happens that the house has depreciated. I have only to add that there are provisions in the Bill for applying it to Ireland and to Scotland, and I hope that when it comes before the House on a Second Reading it may receive, at all events, as favourable a reception from all sides of the House as has been given to those other Measures to which I have referred.

*Mr. McKENNA (Monmouth, N.): The right honourable Gentleman must be congratulated on having assumed responsibility for this Measure, of which he has given us a lucid explanation, but I think he cannot have been aware of the facts when he says that previous Bills of this character had not been objected to. ₁ think the moment is most inopportune for the introduction of this Bill, seeing that the Royal Commission on Local Taxation is now sitting, and has had before it a vast body of evidence dealing with the question of the taxation of ground values. If it should report in favour of such taxation the prospects of this Bill would be seriously affected, and it would lose the charm it now possesses for possible purchasers. A fatal objection to the Bill is that the local rates, which press so hardly upon the poorest of the poor and the struggling tradesmen, are to be used for the purpose of creating freeholds for the benefit of particular classes who have already shown themselves fully capable through building societies of providing for their own needs. If the freehold increases in value, the gain will go to the individual; if it declines, the loss will fall upon the ratepayers. The Bill will only affect a small and limited class, and the burden will largely fall on the very poorest of the community. For these reasons, which I think go to the principle of the Bill—because it is inopportune and partial—I hope it will not be given a First Reading.

Leave was then given to bring in the Bill, and it was read a first time; to be read a second time upon Monday next, and to be printed. (Bill 125.)

ORDERS OF THE DAY.

SUPPLY [2ND ALLOTTED DAY].

Considered in Committee.

[Mr. A. O'CONNOR (Donegal, E.) in the Chair.]

(In the Committee.)

ARMY ESTIMATES, 1899-1900.

Motion made, and Question proposed—

"That a sum not exceeding £6,509,000 be granted to Her Majesty, to defray the Charge for the Pay, Allowances, and other Charges of Her Majesty's Army at Home and Abroad (exclusive of India) (General Staff, Regiments, Reserve, and Departments), which will come in course of payment during the year ending on the 31st day of March 1900."

Motion made—

"That Item I (Recruiting Expenses) be reduced by £100."—(Mr. Weir.)

*Mr. WEIR: The Motion which stands in my name, is with regard to the recruiting expenses on the Army Estimates, Vote 1, Sub-head 1. I desire to call attention to the increased sum which is to be expended this year in connection with the recruiting expenses. Last year the amount for this purpose was £22,100, and this year—1899—it is to be £28,000, which is an increase upon the amount of last year of £5,900. Now, I say that this is an excessive increase, and I only regret that I did not put a Motion down to reduce the whole amount. This would have been better than to propose, as I have done, to reduce the Vote by £100. I have no desire to put the House through the Division Lobbies upon this question. Therefore I hope the honourable Gentleman the Under Secretary to the War Office will be able to give some satisfactory reply to the two questions which I shall put to him. The first point to which I wish to draw attention is the system of marching. The cost of obtaining recruits in the Highlands and Islands of Scotland a few years ago was nearly £100 each recruit, the result of marching detachments of Highland regiments through these districts. Now it does seem to me to be the greatest piece of absurdity that could ever be conceived to send 60 or 70 men through the Highland glens of Scotland, where there is little or no population. I consider it is a wicked waste of public money, and that the system is one which ought to be stopped. Send your recruiting officers to places where there is population, but do not send them where there is not a single shieling. Shielings exist no more in the Highlands, because the people have been cleared out, and the glens are in the possession of deer and sheep. Recruiting in Scotland for the Militia is going down; last year the decrease was 1,285. In 1897 the number of recruits obtained was 13,281; in 1898 the number of recruits obtained was 11,996; and yet you continue to spend large sums of money, as was pointed out the other night. Then I see that the recruiting officers presented 65,501 recruits for medical inspection, and out of that number 23,287 were rejected. The honourable Gentleman will find that on page 4 of the Recruiting Officers' Report. When they were brought before the medical officer he rejected that number. Now, there must have been very great incompetence on the part of the recruiting officers, and there ought to be some arrangement to give them fuller instructions. It is a very serious matter indeed to bring these men forward at such a great expense, and then to find this large number rejected. The other point to which I wish to call the attention of the House is the want of consideration for the Ross-shire Militia, a very fine body of men, who have been for years past drilled in the month of April. Now, the majority of these men go to the fishing industry in the summer time, and I am informed that the commanding

Mr. Weir.

officer of the Militia, who lives in London, and who goes down to Scotland presumably to enjoy himself during the fine weather, has so arranged that the training of these men shall take place in the month of July this year. I am also informed that this commanding officer has only one more year to remain in service, and then he will have to retire. Is he to be allowed to arrange matters to suit his own convenience in fixing the time of the training of these Militiamen, drawn from the fishing population? I have already communicated privately with the honourable Gentleman.

THE DEPUTY CHAIRMAN: Order, order! I have no desire to interrupt the honourable Gentleman, but he cannot go into that question on this Vote.

*MR. WEIR: If by your ruling, Sir, I am not to be allowed to deal with that question upon this Vote, I must find some other opportunity for bringing it before the attention of the House. The honourable Gentleman knows the facts, and I still hope that I shall have some opportunity of going into the matter. With regard to the Vote itself, there is the recruiting rewards, for which a sum of £8,000 is set aside in the list for recruiting officers. Now, are these recruiting officers paid by commission? Are they paid so much for each recruit they obtain, or how are they paid? Then there is contingent allowances for recruiting, £1,450. What is that for? Is it for beer, or whisky, or what? I submit that we are entitled to have full information upon this subject. If it is for beer and whisky, I, for one, object to it very strongly. Then there are gratuities to men on transfer, etc., £3,050. Is that an extra? Then, paid to 180 non-commissioned recruiting officers £9,950. It does appear to me that there should not be this large number of men presented for medical inspection, and that these immense sums should not be paid for bringing them up. If the officers are paid by commission for all the men whom they bring along, then I can perfectly well understand that they will bring along as many as possible, whether suitable or unsuitable. Since I am not able to deal with the question of the Ross-shire Militia at the present stage, I should like to know from the right honourable Gentleman what steps he intends to take to stop this great cost of marching detachments of Highland soldiers through depopulated Highland glens. I do hope that he will stop this wilful, wicked waste of public money, and with that hope I beg to move the Motion which stands in my name.

THE DEPUTY CHAIRMAN: The question that I had to put was that £6,509,000 be granted to Her Majesty to defray the expenses of the pay allowances, etc., of the Army (general staff, regiments, reserves, and departments). Since then an Amendment has been moved to reduce the amount for recruiting expenses by £100. The question which I have to put now is, that that Vote be reduced by £100.

MR. CALDWELL (Lanark, Mid): There can be no doubt that the expense of the Queen's Army mainly depends upon the requirements of the Government. Now, there are certain facts with regard to the recruiting of the Army which admit of no difference of opinion whatever. There is, first of all, a deficiency in the number of recruits; then the Army has to be kept up to a certain standard of men, but lately it has been found necessary, in order to keep the Army up to that standard, to draw on the reserves, and we can plainly see that there is a deficiency in number so far as the recruits are concerned, to keep the Army up to a state which is efficient. Another fact connected with recruiting is that the physique of the recruits that are selected are very much under the proper standard. For instance I find that in 1896 the number of men under the standard—under the standard of height and measurement—amounted to 18 per thousand. That number had largely increased in 1898. There has undoubtedly been a great diminution in the physique and standard of the recruits in the Army. Another point in which the recruits are deficient is the number of men who are returned as well-educated. I find that the number of men returned as well-educated has fallen from 69 per thousand in 1896 to 49 per thousand in 1898. Therefore we have a deficiency in number, we have a deficiency in physique, and we have a deficiency in well-educated recruits. All that is a matter of very considerable

importance in the way in which it affects the efficiency of the Army. Then, to account for how this arises, I find there was an extraordinary effort to obtain recruits in the year 1898. The extra number of recruits obtained by that effort was 5,000. Of that extra number, I find that England produced 4,000, Scotland produced 400, and Ireland produced 296. Now, curiously enough, the greater number of recruits from England has been the cause of the lowering of the standard so far as physique is concerned, and so far as the number of well-educated recruits are concerned. Now, everyone knows perfectly well that Scotch recruits, as a rule, especially those who come from the Highlands of Scotland, have a very much finer physique than any other persons in the United Kingdom ; but, singularly enough, the Scotch recruit is a particularly well-educated man. There is one remark which I should like to make about the Highlands of Scotland. There is a great deal of poverty about them, but there is this very important feature: I venture to say that, as a class, they are better educated, as a whole, taking Scotland all over ; than, than any other of their country-men, and they are certainly very much better educated than anyone in England, taking England all over. Now, recruiting is always considerably stimulated and promoted when, as recently, you add some glory to the Army. It has the effect of stimulating recruiting to a very great extent. Well, it did not seem to have so much effect in Scotland or Ireland ; the great effect was more in England, and particularly in London ; and the class of men you get principally in England—in London and elsewhere—are a class of men who are driven into the Army by dullness in trade. There are men driven into the Army from two causes : in the one case they are stimulated by the glory of the Army, but there are a certain amount who are driven to the Army on account of the dullness in trade. So far as Scotland and Ireland are concerned, there has not been any dullness in trade. There is shipbuilding going on in Scotland, and there is shipbuilding and other industries going on in the North of Ireland, and that accounts probably for the proportion of the recruits which have been obtained from those two countries being rather small ; and it is also probably the reason why you have had to draw on London and England for the greater number of the recruits that you have got. Now, I do not wish in any way to make any invidious comparisons between the population of different portions of the United Kingdom, but it is an undoubted fact that, so far as the Highlands of Scotland are concerned, as everyone knows, you are dealing with a population who are a particularly warlike population, and who take to the Army as to a profession. The military enterprises that this country has engaged in are matters of peculiar interest to the population of the Highlands; because wherever there is a hard piece of work to do, whether it is in a small or a great war, you generally find that that hard piece of work is entrusted to a Highland regiment—with the result, of course, that you can hardly have any enterprise going on, whether in Africa, or in India, without it becomes a matter of special interest to the people of the Highlands, because they have some connections or acquaintances who are naturally engaged in all the different enterprises. The result of that is that you have got a military race, as it were—the Highland race—who are not tempted by profit, and who are not driven by idleness of trade into the Army, but who, from choice, being a military race, take to the British Army as a profession. Now, of course, the Scotch recruit is everything that you want as regards recruits. You want a man of a certain standard with a certain physique, and you get him, and anyone who goes to Scotland and goes through Glasgow will find that the policemen of Glasgow are a particularly handsome body of men as regards their physique; they are tall and strong, and 75 per cent. of those men come from the Highlands. It is an undoubted fact, and every officer in the Army will admit it, that in the case of the Highlanders you have got men of grand physique, men who take to the Army as a profession, men loyal to serve for their Queen and country, and reliable when you want any piece of hard work to be done; and as I have also pointed out, educated men. I remember on one occasion a gentleman, when he was in the Highlands, found men there among the gillies who were very well educated, one in particular that he could

Mr. Caldwell.

talk Greek to. If you know anything about the Highlands you will know that they have got secondary education in every Board school in the Highlands, so that as a rule you have a well-educated man in place of an illiterate one. Now, obviously the Highlands of Scotland is the very best recruiting ground that you have. If there is one thing we stand in need of now more than anything it is having a strong Army. The strength of your Army depends very much upon your policy. If you are going to have a policy which means a forward policy in India; which means a policy of expansion of the Empire in Africa, and which means an active policy in China, and if you are going to dangle your Fleet before the eyes of other nations, you may depend upon it that those other nations will meet you upon your weak point. That weak point will be your Army. Now, given that policy, it is absolutely essential, as the result of that policy, that you should have a strong Army, and have it as efficient as possible. Given a different kind of policy, a less forward and less expansive policy, the necessity for a strong Army does not in the same way arise. Now what has been the policy of the Unionist Government heretofore as regards cultivating the Highlander as a recruit for the Army. Your policy has always been an adverse policy in that direction so far as these Highlanders are concerned. It is not so long ago that it was thought that the best kind of way to deal with the destitution of these men was to emigrate them, to send them away to Canada, and a great amount of money was expended on that scheme, to emigrate these very men who form the backbone of the nation and of the Army. And what is your policy now; what do you do to encourage these men up in the Highlands to enlist in your Army. Why, by nature these men live on the land and the fishing, and they are a race who are naturally attached to their native soil. They wish to remain in their native glens, and they wish the population of their native glens to go forward and join in every undertaking in which this country may be engaged. For instance, there is a man in the Highlands just now; he is a surgeon who has retired from the Army himself, but he has produced six sons who will all join the Army in their turn. Obviously, then, this is a race of men who are not only willing but anxious to take to military enterprise, and, from your own selfish point of view, it is surely to your interest to take as much care of these men as you possibly can. It is quite another question whether these men are right in joining your Army and fighting your battles or not, but in your own selfish interests it is to your own advantage to take care of them. But you do not give these men any opportunity for living and developing in the Highlands, in their native lands. They are of great importance; their physique is kept up because they are living in the open, and they are certainly much better for recruits for the Army than men who are taken from the large towns, who have not the same amount of education, and who have not the same physique. Now, when you want to induce recruits to join the Army you hold out certain inducements to do so. Grants may be given not exceeding £12, that is one mode of inducement. Another inducement that you hold out to the recruits is that these men, after they have retired from the Army, may occupy certain positions. You offer certain posts to them in the Civil Service, and otherwise give them a preferential claim to Civil Service employment over the civil population. Now, that suits, and suits very well, the man who has been recruited from the town, and who, when his period of service is over, wishes to be employed in the town; but obviously an inducement of that kind is no inducement to men from the Highlands who do not live in the town, who do not wish to be employed in the town, but who wish for some occupation in their own glens, and who go back for the purpose of ending their days in agricultural and fishing pursuits. They wish to live upon their native land and breathe their native air, and to rear up families to go into the Army in their turn. Obviously the inducements which you hold out are not inducements to appeal to these men; and if you take the case of the High-lander—we hear a good deal of what the Highlanders did at Dargai—these men having done their work in India, having served their country and fought their battles, naturally wish to go back to their native homes; they find their parents there, and wish to assist them in their old age, and wish in their native

air to recover that constitution which has been wasted and destroyed in India, and Africa, and other places, where these soldiers have served their country. They return to their Highland homes, and what do they find? They find they have no opportunity of settling down there, and they are forced against their inclinations and their wishes to migrate to the towns. They have no opportunity of settling down in their native place. Look at the position. These men are asked to go all over the world to keep an open door so far as trade and commerce are concerned, and they return to the Highlands to find a closed door to their native lands, and that they cannot get a single acre which they can till, and upon which they can peacefully end their days. They find there is a man there who never did anything for his country and who never would, who refuses to give them a single acre of land, notwithstanding the fact that these men have served their country and fought her battles, and are come back home to receive the gratitude of their country. One advantage of having these men settled upon the land, to a certain extent, is this—these men will not desert the Army, because they do not wish to go anywhere else except to their native land, and the result is that if you want to find a man for your Reserve you would always be able to find him on the land. So far as these Highlanders are concerned, we have appealed on various occasions to the Government on economical grounds. We have appealed on the plea of humanity that this population should be given some means of earning their own living. We now give this opportunity which presents itself to the Government, who have not been moved by any plea of humanity, and we ask—will they move in the case of their own selfish interest when your Army is becoming a more important matter for the welfare and prestige of this country? Will a consideration of this kind not move you to do that which you ought to do, and settle these men upon the land? I see from a Return made to this House that you have 1,750,000 acres of land available which might be utilised for the purposes of these men who retire from the Army. I think they should have an opportunity of living in their own native land, following some peaceable pursuit, and if you wish to make the Army popular the best popularity you can give it is, that when these men return from Africa, with enfeebled constitutions, a grateful country should enable them to have an opportunity of living upon the land. We do not ask for doles and charity, for you give that to the landlords. You insist upon an open door for your trade and commerce, but you have a closed door for the land, and it is in the interests of these men 'that this door should be opened.

GENERAL RUSSELL (Cheltenham): I desire to say that I fully appreciate the immense strides which have been made in the efficiency of the Army under the present Government. From a very careful study of the Annual Report of the Inspector-General of Recruiting for the year 1898, and of the very clear and lucid statement made by his able deputy in this House when he introduced the Army Estimates, I feel that all those who have the efficiency of the Army at heart must fully appreciate the labours of Lord Lansdowne and the comparative success which has so far attended them. There is, however, one point to which I think it only right to call the attention of the Committee and the public—the weak point, if I may say so, of the whole Report—and that is the subject of recruiting, which is, after all, the ground-work on which our system is based, and which always has been the great difficulty in connection with the British Army. We may vote money for fortifications, and soldiers, and ammunition, and we may educate our officers up to the higher point of proficiency and excellency, but without the men we are absolutely powerless. Without efficient and healthy men, and without men of intelligence, if we ever have to meet the forces of a Continental army, we shall be at a fearful disadvantage. We have a very serious fact to consider, and it is this—that no less than 23,287 men who desired to enter the Army were rejected for various ailments and want of development. As far as I can gather, from what has been said in this Debate, some honourable Members appear to imagine that each recruiting agent gets a certain reward for every man he brings up to the recruiting officer.

Mr. Caldwell.

That, however, is an entire misapprehension, because no "smart" money is given unless a man is accepted and passed by the recruiting officer, and therefore the honourable Gentleman opposite cannot base his argument upon that. Then, the honourable Member for Lanarkshire fell into a still' more extraordinary error, for he stated that only 34 per 1,000 of these men this year were under the standard. Well, he stated the case far too favourably, for the Returns for the recruiting this year show that the total was 34 per cent., and not 34 per 1,000; therefore, the honourable Member for Lanarkshire could not have read that Report. I think, Sir, that this matter of recruiting is a national question entirely, and I am glad to see an addition to the recruiting expenses of the Army of £5,900 this year. I hope I shall not be accused of throwing stones at the Administration if I call the attention of the Committee to some statistics in connection with recruiting. It appears that, although in 1898 we had 40,729 recruits as compared with 35,015 in 1897, there were 34 per cent. under the standard in 1898, and only 29 per cent. in 1897. There is another still more serious matter which the honourable Member for Caithness referred to, and that is the fact that 23,287 men out of a total of 66,000 men who offered themselves as recruits were rejected. I think that shows very clearly that there is something radically wrong in our system of education, and it points clearly and distinctly to the fact that some system of physical training ought to be given to our school children. It is a very serious matter that out of a total of 66,000 men and boys who offered themselves as recruits, even at a. very low standard, 34 per cent. of them will never be fit for the Army. It will be remembered that the honourable Gentleman the Under Secretary of State for War stated that a great many of these rejections were in consequence of bad teeth. There is another point, which is also a national question, and that is that according to the Report only 49 per thousand of the men were well educated. This shows clearly and distinctly how desirable it is that the Government should carry out the recommendations of the two Committees of this House as to the throwing open of more appointments in civil life for discharged soldiers. If you will turn to the Report of the Inspector-General of Recruiting you will find he speaks very strongly on the question of Government employment for discharged soldiers. The Postmaster-General has done his best to assist the Government by stating that he hopes

"that the Army candidates will soon obtain the full 50 per cent. of the situations intended to be reserved for them."

It also states that—

"The Postmaster-General has also suggested to the Treasury that the wages attached to the position of assistant postman be increased by 2s. a week when such situations are given to ex-soldiers, and, on reference to the War Office, the Treasury were urged to sanction the request."

I have put down a Question for next Friday upon this subject, and perhaps the honourable Gentleman the Under Secretary of State for War will have obtained by that time the information, and then we shall know what answer the Treasury will give on this point. Then, again, it is strongly recommended—

"That all boys entering the Postal Service as telegraph messengers will be required to enter the Army on reaching 18 years of age, the Postmaster-General reserving to himself the right of selecting as many as he may require to keep up the establishment of postmen—namely, 50 per cent. of the total number, and, of the remainder, those who enlist to have places as postmen reserved for them on completing their colour service, provided their characters in the Army have been satisfactory. It has been decided to assemble a Committee to consider this proposal."

I have also put down a Question asking whether this Committee has assembled yet, and who will be on it. Then it appears in this Report—which I hope honourable Members will read and study, for it is a very important one— that there were a large number of Government offices that have not yet given employment to ex-soldiers—namely, the British Museum, Charity Commission, House of Commons, Foreign Office, Home Office, Friendly Societies' Registry, Inland Revenue, Land Registry Office, Local Government Board, London University, House of Lords, Lunacy Commission, National Debt Office, Patent Office, Privy Council Office, Public Works Loan Board, Science and

Art Department, and Supreme Court of Judicature. There is scarcely any Government Office in Scotland that has given any employment for soldiers, and scarcely any in Ireland. This is a distinct disregard of the recommendations of the Committee of this House. I should like very much to know what steps the Government intend to take to carry out these recommendations, and to hold out to the Army the prospect of future employment in after-life. I maintain that, unless we can hold out some inducement as to permanent employment to ex-soldiers as a sufficient competency after they are discharged from the Army, we shall never induce intelligent men of high character to enter the Army, for 49 per 1,000 of educated men is a very small percentage. The Government have done much in this way to promote the efficiency of the Army, but I regret that they have not done more in this direction. They have established a registry at the War Office to supply pensioners of good character with employment. This is the first time that such a register has been established at the War Office, and I am informed on credible authority that the greatest possible care is taken to inquire into the character of the men, and no soldier of bad character is recommended. I am very glad, also, to see that another Memorandum has been issued from the War Office, decentralising the system of recruiting all over the country. I earnestly hope that the Secretary of State will be able to give us before the end of this Debate some assurances that the recommendations that these Committees of the House of Commons have made will not in future be neglected, and that we may look forward to more men of a good stamp and better education being drafted into the Service. With regard to the suggestion of the honourable Member for Lanarkshire, of planting down these men in the Highlands, no doubt his idea is a most benevolent one, but he must remember when a man comes back from the Army he has not much capital, and if he is planted down on a farm we should have to supply him with capital, or otherwise he would be an absolute pauper. Therefore, with all due respect to the good intentions of the honourable Member, I scarcely think the proposal is a practical one. In conclusion, I congratulate the Government upon what they have already done. I had hoped that they would have been able to do more, and I trust the Under Secretary of State will be able to tell us that these old soldiers will be put on a more satisfactory basis.

SIR A. ACLAND-HOOD (Somerset, Wellington): I am surprised to find that the honourable Member for Lanark has advocated a system of military colonisation such as that which I believe was the ruin of the Roman Empire. I am glad to find that we have in the Under Secretary of State for War a man who knows a soldier from a recruit. He does not, like many Ministers, look upon everybody with a red coat and a rifle, which he may or may not be able to handle, as a soldier. From his training in the Army he knows the difference between a soldier and a recruit. There are two questions which I have risen for the purpose of putting to my honourable and gallant Friend. In the first place, I should like to know whether it is, or is not, the fact that any Reserve men who, under the Act of Parliament passed by this House last year, would have been re-enlisted in the new battalions of the line, were rejected as medically unfit for service, but are still drawing pay as members of the Reserve. If that is the case I think some change should be made. If a Reserve man is not fit for active service, he is not fit for service in the Reserve. He should be paid a lump sum down, discharged from the Reserve, and sent back to civil life. The other question I desire to put is with regard to recruiting. I do not wish to raise the question of the Guards over again, but I do not think that my honourable and gallant Friend the Under Secretary can view with satisfaction the state of that regiment of which he was once so smart and efficient an officer, nor the fact that of the battalion now at Gibraltar more than one half is under two years' service. It was also stated last week that in the second battalion at home there are about 300 under two years' service. This is a matter which should not be allowed to pass unobserved.

MR. DILLON (Mayo, E.): There are one or two points in connection with *General Russell.*

this question of recruiting to which I am very anxious to draw the attention of the Committee. It appears to me that we ought to have some more detailed information as to the class from which the recruits are drawn. I see from page 11 of the Annual Report of the Inspector-General of Recruiting that during the past year the number of recruits whose occupations are described as labourers, servants, husbandmen, etc., was 657; the number of manufacturing artisans, 139; of mechanics, 92; of shopmen and clerks, 72; and I should like to know what proportion of the 657 are the sons of labourers in this country and what proportion are the sons of small farmers. That is an extremely important question. I·think we ought to be informed as to what proportion of these classes is drawn from England, Ireland, Scotland, and Wales respectively. It seems to me that by far the most momentous fact contained in the Report is that alluded to by the honourable Gentleman who has just spoken. He pointed out that 66,500 recruits had been medically inspected, 23,287 of whom were rejected as medically unfit. When we remember that that rejection is determined upon a lower standard— a standard which really. reduces the British Army to a ridiculous point—it is a most striking and formidable fact that such a large number should have been rejected as radically and hopelessly unfit for service. Of the 23,000 rejected, 13,900 were rejected for various ailments, and 9,318 for want of physical development. The physical development required by the British Army is, according to this Report, exceedingly slight, and the rejection of such a formidable number discloses a terrible falling off in the physique of the people of the country. In the second place, I should like very much to know—and I have been looking over this Report from the general point of view, as apart from the military point of view—to what class of the population this terrible falling off is to be traced. Now, I see on page 16 of the Report that the recruits are classified according to nationalities. I am not quite clear whether this classification has reference to active service or to the Militia—I think it must only refer to the Militia— but I have not been able to find from the Report which part of the United

Kingdom shows the greatest deterioration. This is a matter I have brought before the House previously, because, although I am not an enthusiastic lover of the British Army, I hold that every-one is interested in putting an end to whatever causes are responsible for the ills which are wearing down the class of small agriculturists who are really the material upon which in times past the Government had to rely for filling up the gaps in the Army. Sir, I maintain that this terrible deterioration of physique will be found to be traceable to the deterioration in the physique of the British agriculturist. It is only within the last 10 years that I have travelled through the country districts in England, and for the first time I have had the opportunity of seeing the children of British agriculturists and labourers. I confess that I have been accustomed from my youth up to go about the country parts of Ireland, and to see the more healthy children and young people of the poor in the West of Ireland; and nothing has struck me more forcibly than to see the offspring of those who are described in the Report as "agriculturists, labourers, and husbandmen," in England, and to observe how unfavourably they compare with the children of five and ten-acre farmers in Ireland. I venture to say that regiments composed of such material as it seems is most available, cannot be expected to stand against such men as formerly filled the Army, and it is incumbent on the country to see what are the causes in operation which are destroying the agricultural population in physique, and driving you to resort either to the class of poor agricultural labourers or to the population of the towns for your recruits, with the consequence that the physique of the Army has steadily but irresistibly degenerated. And, now, Sir, in view of the enormous development of Empire, which in spite of the feeble protests of the small minority in this House, Her Majesty's Government, and, I am bound to say, the majority of the people of this country, seem to be committed to, you are obliged to increase your Army. But you are only beginning to increase it at the present moment. You will have to make great additions to the Army to garrison those vast possessions which have been recently added to the Empire. Where are you going to look for these recruits? Do you expect the poor recruits now enlisted to stand the hardships of garrisoning your possessions in the Soudan, or West Africa, or East Africa? Sir, the fact is, you have allowed to be crushed out of existence that population upon which, from their physique, and the hardihood arising from the circumstances of their life, you had been accustomed to rely. I would venture to ask the Under Secretary for War to allow the further classification I have suggested to be given in the Report next year, so that we may know how many recruits are the sons of small farmers; secondly, I would ask him to give us a fuller classification of the different nationalities which the recruits represent; and, thirdly and lastly, I would ask him—and to this I attach special importance—to let us know the percentage of recruits rejected in England, Scotland, and Ireland respectively, on account of physical disability. By doing that he will be giving us some valuable data with regard to a question which is now engaging the attention of medical and scientific men, namely, the extent to which the population has deteriorated by the destruction of the class of small farmers and by the creation of populations in towns. Now, there are a few other points which I desire to mention. First of all, I desire to say a word on the question of reserving Government posts for discharged soldiers. I hold a strong opinion that this growing practice is an injustice and outrage upon the civil population. Let the soldier be dealt with as he deserves, let the Service be made attractive by favourable conditions, but not at the expense of the ordinary population seeking to earn a living. Reserving posts in the Post Office and other Departments for discharged soldiers is unjust to civilians, and has created the greatest possible discontent amongst men who have a right to expect promotion. These posts are all reserved for discharged soldiers, and you will find in time that the system will inevitably result in a very strong feeling against the spirit of militarism. I should like also to have some explanation from the right honourable Gentleman of how recruiting money is expended. I see that during the past year there has been a very considerable increase in this amount. I should like to know whether it is the fact, as I have heard it stated—I have no knowledge of my own on the subject—that money is spent in drink. If any of this money is spent in giving men drinks at public-houses in order to induce them to recruit, it is a state of things against which we ought to set our faces, and I should be inclined to vote for a reduction in the Vote. There is one other point that is mentioned in the Report to which I desire to refer. An allusion is made to the enlistment of a Chinese force at Wei-hai-Wei. Now, Sir, I think we are entitled to a full explanation from the Secretary of State as to the nature of this force. The Chancellor of the Exchequer some time ago, in a very remarkable speech, which we all read with great interest, warned this country against any expansion of the system of buttressing up the Empire by the employment of mercenary troops. He pointed out the great evil of that system, and said he thought it would be a most dangerous one to embark in. Soudanese . and Haussas have, of course, been employed, but this is a totally new departure. We have had mercenaries of various kinds, but, as far as I am aware, those mercenaries have up to the present been mainly subjects of Her Majesty or claim to be subjects of Her Majesty. Under what military law are these Chinese troops to be kept at Wei-hai-Wei? Are they to be subjects of the Chinese Empire or of the British Empire? I understood from the statements made in this House that the people at Wei-hai-Wei and the Chinese generally in the neighbourhood are to remain subjects of the Empire of China, and that there is no sovereignty given by the lease to Her Majesty the Queen. Are you now going to start a Chinese Army, composed of men who are not subjects of the Queen, and, if so, under what law, and where is this kind of enterprise going to stop. It is not amiss to remind the House that when the conduct of black troops was recently criticised, the reply was made that it was not always possible to control troops of semi-savage races; and we know perfectly well that savage races in the heat of victory will revert to customs which are peculiar to them. The Chinese are not savages, but they are one of the

Mr. Dillon.

cruellest races which the world has ever seen.

*MR. PIRIE (Aberdeen, N.): I think the most important subject which the Committee has discussed in connection with the Army is that of recruiting. I agree with a great number of the points which have been emphasised by the gallant Members on the other side, but in view of this I cannot quite come to the same conclusion, namely, that the Report is eminently satisfactory. I would draw attention to the last paragraph but one in the Report, in which the Inspector says that—

" Considering the prosperous condition of the labour market and the large demands of the Navy the results of recruiting during the year may be deemed satisfactory."

The Inspector fails to mention the increased advantages which he has had during the same year in being able to offer greater attractions to recruits, as well as the increased means at his disposal to obtain them. But what is the result? You have the most serious results which this country has yet had to face. The percentage of the well-educated recruit, the enlistment of whom this country was trying to obtain, and made immense sacrifice to secure, has fallen off as it has never fallen off before. The physique qualification has diminished to an enormous extent, whilst desertion has not yet diminished to an appreciable extent, if at all, and the increase of purchase of discharge is likewise on the upward grade. Therefore I cannot see that the Report can be deemed satisfactory. To my mind, it is really a case of robbing Peter to pay Paul, and of painting the whole thing in unfairly favourable colours. I think it would have been much more satisfactory if the Inspector - General of Recruiting had placed the plain facts of the case before the country and allowed the Committee to know what they had to deal with. Most important points have been already touched upon, and I will therefore only allude to a point about which I asked a question of the Under Secretary of State for War yesterday, namely, the marching tours for the purpose of getting recruits. As to the extra expense incurred upon the country by these marching experiments I learn from the Return that an additional expense of £600 was incurred by marching a detachment of the Northumberland Fusiliers through Northumberland, and that the number of recruits enlisted through that march was only five. I also asked for the number of recruits during a period of four weeks, and I got a total of 30, thus giving an expenditure of £20 a head. Take the next case. The march of the King's Own Borderers cost an additional £310 for 19 recruits, giving an average of £16 a man. But most striking of all was the march of the Argyll and Sutherland Highlanders through Argyllshire and the West Highlands, which cost £250 for an addition to the strength of the Army of one man obtained during the march. From my own point of view, I told the House last year that I did not consider the nation was getting its money's worth for what it spent on the Army, but that as I could not take upon myself the responsibility of voting against the sums which the Government, who are responsible to the country for its Army, deemed necessary to ask, I should abstain from voting either for or against the grant. This year, however, matters have gone further forward; more money than ever is being asked for, and, in my opinion, less value is being obtained for it by the country, and I would not be doing my duty to my constituents if I refrained from protesting and voting against the enormously increased expenditure on the Army. There is one other point on which I wish to dwell for a moment. Those who have the interests of the Army at heart want to obtain some information as to the actual age of the recruits enlisted. We were told last year that that would be shown to a certain extent satisfactorily when the men became entitled to the extra threepence a day on attaining 19 years of age. The predecessor of the honourable and gallant Gentleman the Under Secretary for War distinctly stated that we, who are interested in the age of recruits, would have our demand somewhat satisfied by the new arrangements that were to be made; and yet the honourable and gallant Gentleman who answered my Question on this matter said that no birth certificate could be taken, and no

statement could be given as to the age of the recruits. In addition to the further details which the honourable Member for East Mayo asked for as to the nationalities of the recruits, I do hope that the Returns next year will contain a table stating the real, proved age of the recruits, so that the system which prevails—I hope prevails less than formerly, by which boys of 14 or 15 years of age can be enlisted as of 18 or 19 years of age, will be no longer possible, or, if it is possible, that its evils can be exposed.

*THE UNDER SECRETARY OF STATE FOR WAR (Mr. GEORGE WYNDHAM, Dover): We have listened to a good many speeches on recruiting, and it may not be inconvenient for me to reply before we pass to another topic. The honourable and gallant Member for Cheltenham begged all of us to " read, learn, and inwardly digest" the report of the Inspector-General of Recruiting. I am bound to say that everyone seems to have taken that advice, for nearly all the speeches that have been made—and the speeches that have been made by I myself am an offender—have been based very largely on that very interesting and full report. That very fact makes it difficult for me to add anything material to the information which has been given upon the subject of recruiting. And, if I may be permitted to say so, I think honourable Members of the Committee have found the same difficulty, for although they have quoted long extracts from the Report, and followed the lines of thought suggested by that Report, very few have been able to make practical suggestions which go beyond the practical suggestions made by the Inspector-General of Recruiting. And therefore, though this Report is most interesting, I doubt very much whether, as the result of all that has been said, we are likely to make any material advance towards securing more recruits. The last honourable Member who spoke—the Member for North Aberdeen—referred to a subject which has already been brought before the notice of the Committee by the honourable Member for Ross and Cromarty—namely, the apparently disappointing results of certain recruiting marches through various districts of Scotland. He takes the Inspector-General to task for having given a somewhat rosy picture throughout the whole of the Report of the result of these marches. The honourable and gallant Member for Aberdeen North based his speech on the information which I gave him yesterday, but I am afraid that that only bears out the view I took before, that the more information we give honourable Members, the longer we talk without adding anything material to the subject matter of debate. I can add very little to the information I gave the honourable and gallant Gentleman yesterday; but I can say this, that I do not think the four weeks' limit which he gave is sufficient. I do not think that you can judge of the result of a march through a district by the number of recruits who join the regiment within four weeks of that march. I have in my hand a Report from one of the districts in Scotland— Berwick-on-Tweed—dealing with the march of the 1st Battalion Scottish Borderers through that district. It states that—

"The march has been a great success, and has helped to break down many of the prejudices against a soldier's life. Recruiting was very brisk two months afterwards."

And then he goes on to state that certain economic causes led to a slackening of recruiting after these two months, but he confidently anticipates that when the economic causes are removed, and when less work is being done, the breaking down of the prejudices would lead again to more men joining. I am afraid I cannot add any more to that subject. The honourable Member who spoke first in the Debate did recommend that we should discontinue these marches.

*Mr. WEIR: In the Highlands and islands of Scotland.

*Mr. WYNDHAM: That is the only negative criticism that has been passed during this Debate. So far as I recollect, the only positive advice we received in the course of the Debate came

Mr. Wyndham.

from the honourable Member for Lanarkshire, who suggested that we should plant out all Highlanders who leave the colours upon crofts in the Highlands, and that, therefore, we should return to the policy of ancient Rome. I do not think that that is a suggestion which this or any other Government is likely to entertain. The honourable Member for East Mayo asked for a good deal of information to be added to the next Report on recruits. He wishes to know the proportion of the recruits which comes from the several nationalities in the United Kingdom. That is information I am unable to give him. I think the proportion of men serving in the Army will probably give us a fair indication of the proportion of the recruits. The proportion this year of the troops in the British Army, excluding those in the Colonial forces, was 77.7 per cent. English, 13 per cent. Irish, 8 per cent. Scottish, and 1.5 per cent. of other nationalities. I am bound to say that from these figures I gather that Ireland does rather better than honourable Members who have spoken for Scotland led me to believe; and no case has been made out for giving preferential treatment to recruits who come from Scotland as against those who come from Ireland.

Mr. LLOYD-GEORGE (Carnarvon, etc.): Do these figures include Wales?

*Mr. WYNDHAM: Yes.

Mr. DILLON: The point I asked for information on was this—not the number of recruits of the various nationalities, but how many of the recruits who were medically examined were rejected, and also what proportion of the recruits of each country belong to the class of small farmers.

*Mr. WYNDHAM: The first point is in the Report of the Inspector-General of Recruiting. As to the second, I really must deprecate the practice of turning the War Office into an office of statistical investigation. That kind of work can only be undertaken by special statisticians. It is hardly part of our duty, while discussing the Army

Estimates, to go into the recondite and abstruse investigations as to the physical characteristics of the various races represented in the British Army. My honourable and gallant Friend the Member for Somerset West said that some of the Reserve men who rejoined the colours were rejected as being medically unfit. I have no official information on that point; but I happen to know, unofficially, that certain numbers were rejected in one district as being medically unfit. That is a matter which is well deserving of consideration. Then, he touched on the question of recruiting for the Guards, and he held out to me the prospect of giving me longer rope in order to the dislocation of my official neck next year. Perhaps I shall take advantage of it when next year comes. I really think, Mr. O'Connor, that it is impossible for me to add further information to that contained in this Report.

Mr. DILLON: Another Question which I asked the honourable Gentleman the Under Secretary for War was, whether any of the money to be voted for recruiting in Ireland is now spent in drink? I also asked another Question about the Chinese regiment which is being recruited at Wei-hai-Wei. Under which law are these Chinese troops to be raised? And I desire to know whether they are subjects of Her Majesty's Government or subjects of the Emperor of China?

*Mr. WYNDHAM: As to the first Question of the honourable Gentleman the Member for East Mayo, broadly speaking, that is certainly not the case. I cannot undertake to say that nobody ever drinks a glass of beer in making a bargain. I often observe that honourable Members themselves, after retiring from the business of the House, partake of some refreshment. But I maintain that our system of recruiting is in no sense based on the practice of inveigling men to join the Service by means of treats of drink. It would be quite untrue to say that this House votes money which is spent in treating. To that I give my most unqualified denial. The honourable Member asked me as to the

new Chinese corps which is being raised Wei-hai-Wei. That is a matter which, I think, has less relation to the War Office than to some other Department of State. So far as I know, there is no objection to our recruiting at Wei-hai-Wei, but I have really no further information to give on the point.

Captain SINCLAIR (Forfar): I cannot understand the difficulty of giving particulars in regard to recruiting of this regiment for Wei-hai-Wei. That regiment is to be paid for by the War Office, and is on the Army Estimates. And why should we not also reasonably ask the honourable Gentleman the Under Secretary for War for information in regard to other regiments raised under the Foreign Office? The fact is that, in discussing this question of recruiting and the increase of our military forces, we have to consider not only the raising of the new regiment at Wei-hai-Wei, but regiments in East Africa, Central Africa, West Africa, and five or six different portions of the globe. I would point out the great disadvantage we re under in discussing military expenditure from year to year, that we have not all the military expenditure grouped under one head. Some troops are under the War Office, some are under the Foreign Office, and some are under the Colonial Office; and it is extremely misleading not to be able to see at one glance or one comprehensive survey the whole of the military expenditure which the policy of the Government has brought on the country. I ask the honourable Gentleman the Under Secretary of War whether he has not somewhat mistaken the purport of the Question which the honourable Member for East Mayo has put in regard to the return for recruiting, and as to the physical condition of recruits of different nationalities I cannot conceive why that information, were it afforded, might not be used most beneficially. The honourable Member for East Mayo pointed out that if the recruits for the Army in every district of the country were analysed, a very valuable test of the physical progress of the population of the country in various districts would be afforded. These statistics were, no doubt, at the disposal of the War Office, and should be divulged. Every recruit, when he joins his regiment, must state his occupation, where he comes from, and what kind of life he has led; and in country districts especially it is quite easy to identify the life history of these recruits. We ought, therefore, to obtain these statistics which have been asked for. On another point I wish to press for information from the Under Secretary for War. It was brought before him by the honourable Member for East Mayo on the last occasion we discussed this matter. In his last Report the Inspector-General of Recruiting touched upon the question of the civil employment of soldiers after leaving the Army, and he pressed it to a greater degree than had ever been done by any of his predecessors. That is an important departure from former policy; and I ask the honourable Gentleman the Under Secretary for War to make us some reply on this point. The Inspector-General of Recruiting recommends that all posts under the Government should be ear-marked for discharged soldiers. I ask the honourable Gentleman the Under Secretary for War whether the War Office endorses that recommendation. For myself, I agree with the honourable Member for East Mayo, that it is a very serious policy, and that it is likely to provoke a reaction, and to strike a blow at the popularity of the Army. You may over-do it in your zeal for recruits. The Report of the Inspector-General of Recruiting shows that soldiers when they leave the Army have no difficulty, so long as they have a good character, in obtaining civil employment. This was illustrated by the fact that the men who were recently brought back from the Reserve— so far as three-fourths were concerned — were in civil employment. Everything goes to show that if these Army men have a good character, their liability to serve in the Reserve is no bar to civil employment. That is a very important fact. But this Report of the Inspector-General of Recruiting goes further than any previous Report on the subject. The

Mr. Wyndham.

Inspector-General proposes that every subordinate post for which these discharged Army men are qualified, in the Government service, shall be ear-marked for them. I object most strongly to this, both in the interest of the Army and in the interest of the civil population generally. It is not desirable to make such a distinction between the Army and the civil population; and I think that the Inspector-General of Recruiting, as well as others, has shown a very unwise zeal in this matter.

COLONEL DENNY (Kilmarnock Burghs): I only want to say a few words to the Under Secretary for War in regard to the question of recruiting, and the position in which officers commanding Volunteer battalions are placed. It may not be quite within the knowledge of the honourable Gentleman that regulations have been made by the War Office and directions issued requiring the permanent staffs of the Volunteer regiments to expend a large portion of their time in obtaining recruits for the Army. I, as a commanding officer of a Volunteer battalion, strongly object to my permanent staff being diverted from their proper work. When I find my staff working in terror of their lives to secure recruits for the regular Army I think a stop ought to be put to it. I find this is by direction of the War Office. The general commanding the district, when appealed to, has no option in the matter; and the colonel commanding under him has no option. I know one or two cases which have been brought under my notice in which an extension of the terms of service of the permanent staff has been refused because, unhappily, they have not obtained a proper complement of recruits for the regular Army. In scattered battalions, like my own, where we have many detachments 40 or 50 miles from headquarters, it is impossible for the sergeant-instructors to do their duty by the Volunteer battalions and to look after recruits for the regular Army. This duty laid upon the permanent Volunteer staff has also a bad effect on the strength of the Volunteer corps, because parents will not permit their sons to join the Volunteer corps when they know that the permanent staff are employed in recruiting for the Army. That is a consideration for me, because the financial soundness of my corps depends on the number of men in my regiment. There is ample work for the sergeant-instructors and the adjutant to do in connection with our Volunteer regiments; and if you have recruiting sergeants and recruiting depôts to take up this work of recruiting for the Army, there is no necessity for placing recruiting duty on the shoulders of the permanent staff of Volunteer battalions. I hope the rule will soon be relaxed.

MR. JEFFREYS (Hants, N.): I take a great interest in discharged soldiers and sailors, and am glad to know that the Post Office authorities have offered places in the Post Office to be given to these men. That is very liberal on the part of the Post Office authorities. But I would urge on the Under Secretary for War that lists of the various posts in the Post Office which old soldiers and sailors can fill should be kept at the various branch post offices throughout the kingdom. I feel quite sure that the majority of old soldiers who reside in the country know nothing about these posts which are open to them; and it would be convenient if the lists I have referred to were posted up at each post office so that old soldiers might find what they are entitled to. I also think that some more technical education should be given to soldiers while they are with the Colours. In an ordinary Line regiment the men are not taught anything at all; and therefore when they leave the service and come into the country they are unable to obtain employment. I have often heard employers, especially in the agricultural districts, say that they could not take into their employment old soldiers because they were not suited for any particular line of work. The honourable Member for East Mayo asked why it is that the sons of small farmers do not join the Army. I live in the county of Hampshire, and I know that farmers' sons do not join the Army because they somehow think and believe, truly enough sometimes, that the recruits who join the regiments are generally not of a sufficiently good character for them to mix with. I think that if the honourable Gentleman the Under Secretary for War were to inquire into this matter he would find that, in a general way, no question is asked by recruiting officers as to the character of the men whom they are enlisting. All that the recruiting officer cares for is as to the height of the recruit and his chest measurement. I have often thought that it is a great mistake of the recruiting officer to do so. I know of many instances where fathers have bought their sons out of the Army because they thought their sons had degraded themselves by joining it. I am sure we should like to see changes made in recruiting, so that a better class of men may be induced to join our Army; and I believe if recruiting officers were more careful they would get a better class of men.

COLONEL WELBY (Taunton): I do not know that there is any more natural centre round which our discussions can take place in regard to recruiting for the Army than the Report which has been placed in our hands. That Report of the Inspector-General of Recruiting may be said to focus the facts regarding recruiting at the present time. There are two matters mentioned in that Report to which I hope the House will give some consideration. One of these is, that although we have enlisted a greater number of recruits last year than in any year since 1892, we have 1,169 men below our establishment; and at the same time the new battalions have not been raised to anything like their proper numbers. There are two points connected with this matter. There is the very great number of men who purchase their discharge at the present time. It will be seen that the number of men who purchase their discharge for £10, which represents men who have been less than three months in the Service, has very greatly increased. The percentage of those who purchase at

£18 has decreased, but I am afraid the moral to be drawn from that is that the men who enlist in the Army find out sooner than they used to do that it is not the Service that they wished to be in. Another point is the number of desertions which have taken place; and I would ask the Under Secretary if he would say whether the desertions which appear in this Return are the desertions of recruits only, and if they are the desertions of recruits, whether he would say what his definition in these Returns of a recruit is—whether it is the man who has served for one year who is technically known as a recruit—it is on page 13, the last table. All these facts which are shown in this Report go to prove that there is something radically wrong with regard to the recruiting of our Army. We have not got men enough, and I do not think we have got the right stamp of men. The cause which I believe underlies this difficulty in obtaining recruits for the Army is that men on entering the Army see that it will not be a life-long profession, that it will not lead to steady employment in the after years of their life. I am not one of those who wish to see long service returned to in the Army, but there is this to be said for long service, that men who enlisted in the Army looked upon it as a life-long profession, with a pension at the end of it; and there is no doubt that made the Army much more popular in those days than it is at the present time. But the difficulty of making it a life-long profession is this, that during the time that a man serves in the Army it is very difficult for him to learn a trade. The honourable Member has referred to technical instruction in the Army, but everybody acquainted with the inner working of the Army knows how little time there really is for a man to take advantage of increased technical education. The regular duties in garrison, and especially in regiments where there are a great number of recruits and very few long-service men, affords very little time indeed for a man to devote to technical instruction of his kind. The result of that is

Colonel Welby.

that, although a man learns a smattering of a trade, when he goes back to civil life he finds that he is in no way a worthy competitor with the man who has been able to give up the whole of his time to learning any particular trade. Not only is that a difficulty in the way, but in spite of what has been said this evening I believe there is a very great prejudice in the minds of many employers of labour against employing men who belong to the Army Reserve. They have got a feeling that these men may be called out at any time and taken away from their employment. Not only is there that difficulty, but I know from my experience in East London that there is a prejudice among his fellow workmen against an Army Reservist, because they believe that these men of the Army Reserve, who are drawing Government pay, can undersell them in the labour market, and they can, if they choose, do this same work for less money than what the others who have not Reserve money to fall back upon can do. Whatever may be the cause of it, there is no doubt at the present time that we are very much in want of recruits, and in want of the right sort. I do not believe for a moment that it is the want of martial spirit in the country, because the moment that there is active service, whether it be for the regular Army or for irregular forces such as those which are raised by the Chartered Company in South Africa, or similar forces in other parts of this great Empire, there are always men to come forward and enlist. Therefore the difficulty seems to be that the men who enlist merely to make it a peace-time profession, with the possibility of going to war, find that they cannot learn during their service the technical instruction which they require, and when they leave the Army and go into civilian life they find that they are handicapped. The honourable and gallant Member for Chelmsford has drawn attention to the employment of men in Government Departments. I am sure that point cannot be too strongly urged upon the Committee and upon the House. I am very sorry to see in the Report of the Inspector-General of Recruiting that the House of Commons has employed no old soldiers during the past year. It may have been that there were no vacancies to fill; but there is a way in which a certain amount of employment could be provided in these Houses of Parliament. We know that the police guard us with the greatest attention and care, but would it not have been more in conformity with the dignity of this Imperial Parliament that we should be protected by a corps of our own? A corps might be composed of men who have served in the Army and the Navy. The police have to deal with the criminal class. Why should we be put under their protection? Why should we not have our own corps, and let it be, as I said, composed entirely of those who have served their country in the Army and Navy? The honourable Member for Mayo has referred to the possibility of keeping so many appointments open to the Army and the Navy. I do not think that, if it is placed before the civilians of this country that the men who belong to the Army and Navy are the protectors of the country, that they are liable at a moment's notice to be placed in the forefront in a campaign in any battle that may be fought, they would for a moment grudge the inducements that are being held out to enlist in the Army by giving employment in large works. It is simply misrepresentation when this is called the spirit of militarism—which, I am afraid, is a phase which is very popular on the other side of the House. That is misleading. It is not a question of militarism. We must have a certain number of soldiers and a certain number of sailors to protect this Empire. Then we have to consider as long as we have a voluntary Army how we are going to enlist them, and how we are going to get numbers enough. If honourable Members opposite are prepared to see a compulsory Army such as exists on the Continent of Europe, then there is no difficulty about it, no necessity to keep these places open for men, but if they are in favour, as I am myself, of voluntary service, then

they must hold out to these men some career which they can look forward to when they leave the Army. There are plenty of public authorities here in London; and I am afraid that the House of Commons is not the only great public place which has not employed any men during the past year: there has been the Home Office, the Local Government Board Office and a number of others. I say that I think in all Government Departments these places ought to be wholly or very nearly wholly reserved for the Army and the Navy. I know what the difficulty is. I know that the difficulty is not altogether, as the honourable Member for East Mayo says, one of prejudice, but there is a question of patronage. Reference has been made to the Post Office, and to the objections to the boys being compelled to go into the Army and serve their time before they can become men. Surely that all points to the argument that men going into the Army cannot look forward to a private career, a career in after years, and the result of it is that parents in the country look upon the Army simply as a refuge for ne'er-do-wells, and not as a career, as they ought to do. Unless you can open these employments in the great public Departments, in these Departments over which this House has control, direct or indirect, you never will set that standard so necessary to our great employers of labour throughout the country. The railways are employing these men, and a great many employers of labour also employ old soldiers. We want that extended, to get rid of this system of enlisting every man into the Army whatever his character may be, and making it a refuge for the men who have come down in the social scale. We want to get rid of them, to get the civilian element all through the country to see that the Army is an honourable profession for men as well as for officers; and not only that, but in these practical days, when a young man who is entering upon life looks forward to the days which are coming, when he is getting towards middle age, we must be able to show him that if he conducts himself and does well in the Army and serves his country well, he will be looked after and, as far as possible, employed after he leaves the Service.

THE FIRST LORD OF THE TREASURY (Mr. A. J. BALFOUR, Manchester, E.): The discussion on the Army Estimates, Vote A and Vote 1, has now gone over a considerable time—has gone on longer this year than for many years past, and though it is very interesting, I think that honourable and gallant Gentlemen ought to remember that there is work which is put down for Committee of Supply. I venture to make an earnest appeal to them to let us have this Vote, and the uncontentious Vote which is also put down, and I base that appeal upon this fact: A certain number of Votes have actually to be got before we can start on the Vote on Account next Monday. I should be reluctant—and I think honourable Gentlemen themselves would feel the inconvenience—that we should have to sit late on Thursday and Friday, with the possibility of a Saturday sitting. But the work has to be done, and I think it would be for the general convenience of the House if honourable Members would maintain some proportion in the length of time devoted to the topics under discussion. I hope honourable Gentlemen will feel that we have discussed this enough, or nearly enough, that we have surveyed the ground——

SEVERAL HONOURABLE MEMBERS: No.

MR. SWIFT MACNEILL (Donegal, S.): Seven of your friends have been speaking upon this Motion, against four on this side.

THE FIRST LORD OF THE TREASURY: My appeal is not specially to the honourable Gentleman, nor is it especially to honourable Gentlemen on either side of the House. I appeal to the House as a whole. I make no accusation against the Opposition, nor against my honourable Friends upon this side of the House. I make an appeal to the House as a whole to maintain some proportion in the length of time they

Colonel Welby.

give to the various topics that are to be dealt with by the House before next Monday, and as the inconvenience is not only to the Government, but to private Members as well, I would ask them to give us this Vote to-night, and to enable us to get the uncontroversial Votes which we hope to get before we start the Naval Estimates on Thursday.

*MR. WEIR: Who has occupied the time? It has been occupied by honourable and gallant Gentlemen sitting behind the right honourable Gentleman the Leader of the House, and not by Members on this side of the House; and instead of the First Lord addressing himself to this side of the House, he should address himself to the other side. I am always anxious to facilitate the business of the House. I got up to ask for some information with regard to the increase of £5,900, and I am still without it. Whose fault is that? It is the fault of the Under Secretary of State for War. If he had furnished that information, I should be in a position to withdraw my Amendment, and the Debate would have dropped on this item. I protest against the silence of honourable and right honourable Gentlemen on the Treasury Bench. My honourable Friend the Member for East Mayo asked whether beer and whisky were supplied, and the Under Secretary said, "Broadly, no." What does he mean by "Broadly, no"? My honourable Friend the Member for East Mayo also asked whether the nationality of recruits would be given in future. The Return gives a great number of figures, but we want the figure asked for by the honourable Member for East Mayo in addition. I want to know whether the Under Secretary for War is prepared to give that information? I also asked whether recruiting officers are paid by commission on the number of recruits they secure, but I have got no information. If replies were given to Questions, what an immense amount of time would be saved, and we would not have the First Lord getting up and talking to us as he has done to-night. Again, detachments of Scottish Highlanders have been marched through the Highlands and islands of Scotland, and, as the result of an expenditure of nearly £250, only one recruit was enrolled. The Under Secretary called attention to the Report of the Registrar-General for Recruiting, with reference to Berwickshire, but that is a very thickly populated district as compared with the Highlands and islands of Scotland. I want to know whether the system of spending money by sending detachments of soldiers through the Highlands, where there are only deer and sheep to listen to the skirl of the pipes, is to be stopped in the future?

MR. GIBSON BOWLES (Lynn Regis): I feel loath to add to the extensive catechism of the honourable Member who has just sat down, but there is one question I would ask. Perhaps the most interesting point in the Estimates is that they represent an entirely new departure. White, brown, and black troops have worn the Queen's uniform, but this is the first time Her Majesty's forces are to be added to by a regiment of yellow troops. The Under Secretary said the question on this subject should be addressed to another Department. I think it is to his Department it should be addressed, because his Department asks for the money for this Chinese regiment. I understood him to say it was a legal question as to whether these troops became subjects of the Queen. That is not the point. What I want to know is this: What is the purpose of those troops? Are they to be employed in the defence of Wei-hai-Wei, or in the general services of the Queen? If for the service of Wei-hai-Wei, I think they will be inadequate for the purpose. We know that Wei-hai-Wei, according to the First Lord of the Admiralty, is to be made what is known as a second-class naval station. We also know that without troops it cannot be maintained, for there are the remains of four Chinese ironclads lying in the harbour, and there is testimony that some of them were sunk from the land, though no doubt some of them were sunk by torpedoes also. It is therefore clear that what is required is a land force, and there is no doubt why this regiment has been enrolled. But will one regiment suffice? I imagine not. One of the questions I wish to ask is this: Is this the beginning of a large Chinese force, or is it to be the first and final regiment, or are we to have 10, or 20, or 100 regiments? If there is only to be this one alone, I am afraid it will have to be supplemented by English troops. One other point. I rather gather from the Under Secretary that he did not think his Department was concerned with this. I wish to ask whether those troops are to be under the War Office or under the Navy? At any rate, they are not to be under the Foreign Office. These are the questions I wish to ask: Whether there is to be one final Chinese regiment, or whether it is proposed to extend it? Is it to be employed in the defence of Wei-hai-Wei, or whether it can be withdrawn from Wei-hai-Wei for the general Services of the Queen?

MR. DILLON: The Under Secretary has distinctly refused to give me any information in regard to these Chinese troops. I asked him a number of very simple questions, to which I think the Committee are entitled to have an answer. He said those questions should be addressed to another Department. I asked to what Department they should be addressed, and received no answer. If he will turn to Appendix No. 2, page 159, of the Army Estimates, he will find that there is a Vote of £21,000 asked for these troops, and I insist that the Under Secretary for War, on behalf of the War Office, is bound to explain and defend that Vote. We are entitled to know what the character of the force will be, the laws under which it is going to be enrolled, whether the Chinese soldiers will be subjects of the Queen or subjects of the Emperor of China, whether they will have to take the oath of allegiance to the Queen, and under what law is discipline to be maintained. The honourable Gentleman is not entitled to refer me to another Department for an answer. This is a question of military law.

SIR J. COLOMB: I rise to ask a question with regard to Wei-hai-Wei, and which refers to the distribution of the

British regiments, and the system under which they are distributed.

THE DEPUTY-CHAIRMAN: I am afraid the honourable Member is not in order in referring to that matter.

*MR. WYNDHAM: I should like to answer the questions put by the honourable Member for East Mayo. He seems to think I was wanting in courtesy towards him in not having previously answered his question. I can assure him that it was not my intention to be discourteous, and if I did not give him the information he asked for it was because I misapprehended his question. The honourable Member for East Mayo asked me whether the Chinese troops that were being raised at Wei-hai-Wei were subjects of the Queen. In asking that question I think the honourable Member has raised a legal point which is not really germane to the Vote. There is no novelty, for we have other troops—the Goorkhas and the Soudanese, for instance—in the same situation. As to their exact status in the eyes of international law, I do not venture to express an opinion which would be worth the while of the Committee to listen to. When I am asked what the policy is to be in respect of this Chinese regiment, I have to say, on behalf of the War Office, that we draw no distinction between it and either of the other Colonial corps we are raising in Central and West Africa. Three Colonial corps are being raised. We are going on raising them where we can most conveniently do so, in order to relieve the strain which is otherwise thrown on the British battalions. As things are, 79 battalions are abroad, and only 66 battalions at home. Every position being occupied which can be occupied conveniently and economically with an efficient force, and wherever we thus relieve one British battalion it gives us a gain, so to speak, of two battalions at home. I would repeat that there is no novelty in this policy. Already there are 6,000 troops under the Foreign Office. In these Estimates we are asking for a sum of £83,000 in order to raise about 3,000 men; we are asking for £20,000 for the Chinese battalion; £42,000 for the West African regiment, and £21,000 for raising a Central African regiment. No distinc-

Sir J. Colomb.

tion is drawn as to the three regiments, which are raised for similar purposes.

*MR. J. WILSON (Durham, Mid):
I have not much to say, Mr. O'Connor, about the recruiting of troops, because I am one of those who believe that recruiting should be abolished, and some other means adopted. If anyone will go to Trafalgar Square, on any day of the week, he will see young men about 18 or 20 years of age annoyed by a troop of recruiting sergeants, and approached with an eagerness which, if devoted to establishing peace between the nations, would, I think, be better for the country. I have not risen for the purpose of questioning the character of the recruits, although I may say that, in my opinion, very few men who enter our Army do so from the impulse of patriotism; they do it as a means of earning a living. I rise to enter my protest as a working man against preference being given to soldiers for civil offices under the Government, and I want to ask why these preferences should be given. If anyone in authority will give an answer I shall be obliged. Why should soldiers have this preference? Is it on account of their usefulness? Will anyone assert that a soldier—I do not say this disparagingly—is more useful than a working man. Some honourable Members say "Yes," but I should like them to show me how they are more useful. There is not a single working man in the industries of this country who is not as useful to the prestige of this country as a soldier. Then as to the danger; there is more danger and more lives lost in the mines than on the battle-field. Whether this provision will assist recruiting or not, I submit that the Civil offices of this country should be left open to artisans as well as soldiers. Take the case of a young man of 16 or 17 years of age, who enters one of our Civil Departments. When he arrives at the age of 21 or 22 he will find his occupation gone, and a man who has served for five years in the Army engaged in preference, and the young man is thrown out of work. I speak here for the working men, and I claim that the country should know why this preference is given. I am sure there are very few honourable Members in this House who would advocate

on a public platform, at election time, that this preference should be given. I am afraid if they did they would not be returned again. I would suggest to the honourable Gentleman the Under Secretary for War that he should give us some authoritative statement on this subject.

*Mr. PIRIE: I must ask the Under Secretary for an answer to my question as to why recruits are often taken when they are not of full age.

*Mr. WYNDHAM: The fact is, the ages are not always known, and you cannot get birth certificates from all recruits.

Captain PHILLPOTTS (Devon, Torquay): I do not desire to detain the Committee, but I rise to tell the honourable Member for Durham why a preference should be given to soldiers and seamen. It is because they have been trained under discipline and under those who have the interests of the country at heart, and have not taken their tone from demagogues. I hear sounds of dissent. Well, I have heard sounds in the tropical forests of Africa very similar and just as coherent. The policy which has been adopted of giving a preference to our soldiers and sailors for civil employment after they retire from the Service, is a thoroughly sound one, and one which should be followed up.

Captain SINCLAIR: I must ask for an answer to the question I put to the Under Secretary with regard to the appointment of ex-soldiers to civil positions.   *

*Mr. WYNDHAM: I have given my views upon the question at great length. I understand perfectly well that the honourable Member does not agree with me, but my view is that the more civil employment we can give to retired soldiers, the better. The honourable Member does not think so, but I cannot alter my conviction in order to please the honourable Member.

Mr. MADDISON (Sheffield, Brightside): I desire to ask the Under Secre-

tary whether the War Office is going to carry out the recommendation of the Inspector-General of Recruiting, that in future all civil posts should be given to retired soldiers. Surely that question is worthy of a definite reply, and one which does not begin with "Broadly speaking." We want something definite. The statement of the Inspector-General is definite. We know exactly what he means, and I should like to ask the Under Secretary whether his Department is going to carry out that recommendation. Are the working men of England to understand distinctly that this Government is going to carry out a recommendation of that kind, and that in future, in order that a man may serve the State in civil employment, he must go through the Army? My honourable Friend the Member for Mid Durham gave some reasons, which I thought very fair, why this should not be, and he was replied to by the honourable Member—I think I have to call him gallant as well—for Torquay, who compared some of us to animals whom he discovered in the tropical forests of Africa. Well, that remark may be Parliamentary, but it is not gentlemanly, and I think we should receive some answer on that point from the Government. It must not be thought that you are going to increase the number of recruits by holding out inducements that if a man joins the Army he is sure of promotion to some position under the State when he leaves the Army. The great mass of the working men of this country, who contribute to its wealth, have a perfect right to receive consideration in this matter. I wish to be candid. I do not wish to exclude soldiers because they are soldiers. What I do contend is that no preference should be given. How is it that private employers are not so ready to employ your old soldiers? The explanation is that you take little, if any, care to test the character of the men you enlist. You are very wise in not doing so, otherwise you would not have half the men you now possess. I think I am entitled to a definite reply to my question.

*Mr. WYNDHAM: I think honourable Members are labouring under a misapprehension. They seem to think that the Inspector-General of Recruiting recommends that the War Office should fill up all the posts in all other Departments with old soldiers. That, I need hardly, say, is not the recommendation of General Kenny. The Inspector-General specifies Departments which have not offered any appointments as messengers to soldiers through the War Office. He says—

"In some of these offices, particularly those with small establishments, there may have been no vacancies, and, in others, employment may have been given to soldiers without reference to the War Office. It is, however, very desirable that all such appointments should be filled by the War Office register, as they are elsewhere through the Regimental District or other authorised agencies, as if men whose character have not been sufficiently inquired into are accepted, and subsequently prove unworthy, discredit is cast upon the whole body, and much harm done to the prospects of really good pensioners who are desirous of employment."

CAPTAIN SINCLAIR: That was the general recommendation, but there are four specific recommendations in the Report of the Inspector-General of Recruiting on which I think the House are entitled to have some information from the War Office. The Inspector-General says that as regards the class of situations offered to ex-soldiers, it had been arranged with the General Post Office that no posts of less value than 14s. a week (except in London) were to be offered to ex-soldiers, whereas they are to be offered to civilians. The second recommendation is that the wages attached to the position of assistant postman be increased by 2s. a week when such situations are given to ex-soldiers. The third recommendation is that the rule giving one half of the vacancies to ex-soldiers might be suspended, or higher wages given to telegraph messengers, as the inability to assure the latter of permanent employment had caused the supply of suitable boys to fall below Post Office requirements. In the Report of the Inspector-General it is stated that a further scheme has been since put forward, under which all boys entering the Postal Service as telegraph messengers will be required to enter the Army on reaching 18 years of age, the Postmaster-General reserving to himself the right of select-

Mr. Wyndham.

ing as many as he may require to keep up the establishment of postmen, namely, 50 per cent. of the total number, and, of the remainder, those who enlist to have places as postmen reserved for them on completing their Colour service, provided their characters in the Army have been satisfactory. I do not think it is asking too much to suggest that the Committee should have some information as to the present position of these important recommendations.

THE FIRST LORD OF THE TREASURY: I can tell the honourable Gentleman that the recommendations as to the Post Office have nothing to do with the administration of the War Office. Certain recommendations of the Postmaster-General are mentioned in the Report of the Inspector-General of Recruiting, but the recommendations of the Post Office are not under consideration now, and cannot be dealt with by the War Office alone.

MR. MADDISON: As the First Lord of the Treasury has so kindly spoken on behalf of the Government, which is exactly what we wanted, may I refer him to the latter half of paragraph 93 of the Report of the Inspector-General of Recruiting? The paragraph says—

"These are among the reasons which urged me to impress upon the Government the necessity of reserving its own employment for those who have already served it as soldiers, and thereby to raise the profession in the estimation of private employers."

paragraphs, seems to make it quite clear paragraphs, seem to make it quite clear that the Inspector-General of Recruiting means to recommend that all State posts should be reserved for soldiers. I ask the right honourable Gentleman the First Lord of the Treasury if he will say definitely whether the Government intend to carry that recommendation out?

THE FIRST LORD OF THE TREASURY: What has been laid before the House are the personal views, as I understand it, of the general who has charge of recruiting. With the general principles of those views we may have sympathy or we may not, but I am certainly not in a position to say that the Government are prepared to carry out the views which have been expressed by the general in question.

*Mr. PIRIE: I desire to ask a question in order to know whether the House ought to be divided?

*Mr. WEIR: It is my Motion, Mr. O'Connor.

*Mr. PIRIE: I wish to ask why it is impossible to require birth certificates from recruits; how is it possible that recruits must be taken without definite proof of age, when definite proof of age must be produced by every child in a factory, every postal and telegraph employee, and every workman in a Government Dockyard or Arsenal?

*Mr. WEIR: I have waited long and patiently, Mr. O'Connor, for the information I have asked for from the Under Secretary for War.

THE DEPUTY CHAIRMAN: The honourable Member has repeated over and over again the same arguments. The Minister has answered—whether sufficiently or not is not for me to say. But I would remind the honourable Member that the constant repetition of the same arguments is out of order, and that there is a rule on that point.

Question put—

"That Item 1 (Recruiting Expenses) be reduced by £100."—(*Mr. Weir.*)

The Committee divided:—Ayes 56; Noes 161.—(Division List No. 42.)

AYES.

Allen, W. (Newc.-under-Lyme)
Allison, Robert Andrew
Asquith, Rt. Hn. Herb.Henry
Barlow, John Emmott
Beaumont, Wentworth, C. B.
Billson, Alfred
Bolton, Thomas Dolling
Buchanan, Thomas Ryburn
Burt, Thomas
Caldwell, James
Causton, Richard Knight
Cawley, Frederick
Channing, Francis Allston
Colville, John
Douglas, Chas. M. (Lanark)
Duckworth, James
Ellis,Thos.Edw.(Merionethsh.)
Ffrench, Peter
Foster, Sir Walter(Derby Co.)
Goddard, Daniel Ford

Gourley, Sir Edw.Temperley
Hayne, Rt. Hn. Charles Seale-
Hedderwick, Thos. Chas. H.
Jones, Wm. (Carnarvonshire)
Kilbride, Denis
Langley, Batty
Lawson,Sir Wilfrid(Cumb'ld.)
Lough, Thomas
Macaleese, Daniel
MacNeill, John Gordon Swift
Maddison, Fred.
Morgan,W.Pritchard(Merthyr)
Moulton, John Fletcher
Norton, Capt. Cecil William
O'Brien, Patrick (Kilkenny)
O'Connor, T. P. (Liverpool)
O'Malley, William
Pearson, Sir Weetman D.
Pirie, Duncan V.
Provand, Andrew Dryburgh

Richardson, J. (Durham)
Roberts, John Bryn (Eifion)
Shaw, Charles Edw. (Stafford)
Sinclair, Capt. J. (Forfarshire):
Soames, Arthur Wellesley
Souttar, Robinson
Sullivan, Donal (Westmeath)·
Tanner, Charles Kearns
Thomas,David Alf.(Merthyr)
Trevelyan, Charles Philips
Walton, Joseph (Barnsley)
Warner, Thos. Courtenay T.
Wedderburn, Sir William
Williams, Jno. Carvell(Notts)
Wilson, Henry J. (York,W.R.)·
Wilson, J. (Durham, Mid)

TELLERS FOR THE AYES—.
Mr. Weir and Mr. Dillon.

NOES.

Acland-Hood,Capt.Sir Alex.F.
Allhusen.Augustus HenryEden
Arrol, Sir William
Ashmead-Bartlett, Sir Ellis
Atkinson, Rt. Hon. John
Bagot, Capt.Josceline FitzRoy
Balfour,Rt.Hn.A.J.(Manch'r)
Balfour,RtHnGeraldW.(Leeds)
Banbury, Frederick George
Barton, Dunbar Plunket
Beach,RtHnSir M.H.(Bristol)
Beckett, Ernest William
Bemrose, Sir Henry Howe
Bethell, Commander
Blundell, Colonel Henry

Bond, Edward
Boscawen, Arthur Griffith-
Brassey, Albert
Brodrick, Rt. Hon. St. John
Butcher, John George
Carlile, William Walter
Cavendish, V. C.W. (Derbysh.)
Cecil, Evelyn (Hertford, East)
Chaloner, Capt. R. G. W.
Chamberlain, Rt.Hn.J. (Birm.)
Chamberlain, J. Austen (Wor.)
Chaplin, Rt. Hon. Henry
Charrington, Spencer
Clare, Octavius Leigh
Cochrane, Hon. Thos. H. A. E.

Coghill, Douglas Harry
Cohen, Benjamin Louis
Collings, Rt. Hon. Jesse
Colomb, Sir John Chas. Ready·
Compton, Lord Alwyne
Cook, Fred. Lucas (Lambeth)
Cornwallis. Fiennes Stanley W..
Cotton-Jodrell, Col. Ed. T. D.
Cranborne, Viscount
Curzon. Viscount
Dalkeith, Earl of
Dalrymple, Sir Charles
Davenport, W. Bromley-
Denny, Colonel
Disraeli, Coningsby Ralph

Douglas, Rt. Hon. A. Akers
Duncombe, Hon. Hubert V.
Egerton, Hon. A. de Tatton
Fergusson,Rt HnSir J.(Manc'r)
Finlay, Sir Robert Bannatyne
Fisher, William Hayes
FitzWygram, General Sir F.
Fletcher, Sir Henry
Folkestone, Viscount
Foster, Colonel (Lancaster)
Foster, Harry S. (Suffolk)
Gedge, Sydney
Gibbons, J. Lloyd
Godson,Sir Augustus Frederick
Goldsworthy, Major-General
Gordon, Hon. John Edward
Gorst, Rt. Hn. Sir John Eldon
Gray, Ernest (West Ham)
Green,WalfordD.(Wednesbury)
Gretton, John
Greville, Hon. Ronald
Gull, Sir Cameron
Gunter, Colonel
Hamilton, Rt. Hn. Lord George
Hanbury, Rt. Hn. Robert Wm.
Hardy, Laurence
Hermon-Hodge, Robert Trotter
Jeffreys, Arthur Frederick
Jenkins, Sir John Jones
Jessel, Capt. Herbt. Merton
Johnston, William (Belfast)
Johnstone, Heywood (Sussex)
Jolliffe, Hon. H. George
Kemp, George
Kennaway, Rt.Hn. Sir John H.
Kenyon, James
Keswick, William
Lafone, Alfred
Lawrence,SirE.Durning-(Corn)
Lea, Sir Thos. (Londonderry)

Lecky, Rt. Hn. William Ed. H.
Lees, Sir Elliott (Birkenhead)
Leigh-Bennett, Henry Currie
Loder, Gerald Walter Erskine
Long, Col. Chas. W. (Evesham)
Long, Rt. Hn. Walter (L'pool)
Loyd, Archie Kirkman
Macartney, W. G. Ellison
Macdona, John Cumming
MacIver, David (Liverpool)
M'Calmont, H. L. B. (Cambs.)
M'Iver, Sir Lewis (Edin., W.)
M'Killop, James
Malcolm, Ian
Massey-Mainwaring, Hn.W. F.
Middlemore,JohnThrogmorton
Mildmay, Francis Bingham
Montagu, Hn. J. Scott (Hants)
More, Robt. Jasper (Shropsh.)
Morrell, George Herbert
Morton, Arthur H. A. (Deptf'd)
Murray,Rt HnA.Graham(Bute)
Murray, Charles J. (Coventry)
Myers, William Henry
Newdigate, Francis Aexander
Nicholson, William Graham
Nicol, Donald Ninian
Parkes, Ebenezer
Pease, Herbert Pike (Drlngtn.)
Phillpotts, Captain Arthur
Platt-Higgins, Frederick
Powell, Sir Francis Sharp
Pryce-Jones, Lt.-Col. Edward
Purvis, Robert
Rankin, Sir James
Rasch, Major Frederic Carne
Rentoul, James Alexander
Richardson, Sir T. (Hartlepool)
Rickett, J. Compton
Ritchie, Rt. Hn. Chas.Thomson

Rothschild, Hn. Lionel Walter
Royds, Clement Molyneux
Russell, Gen.F.S. (Cheltenham)
Russell, T. W. (Tyrone)
Ryder, John Herbert Dudley
Sassoon, Sir Edward Albert
Sidebotham, J. W. (Cheshire)
Smith, Abel H. (Christchurch)
Smith, Hon. W. F. D. (Strand)
Stanley, Hn.Arthur (Ormskirk)
Stanley, Edwd. Jas. (Somerset)
Stanley, Lord (Lancs.)
Stewart, Sir M. J. M'Taggart
Stirling-Maxwell, Sir John M.
Stock, James Henry
Strauss, Arthur
Strutt, Hon. Charles Hedley
Sturt, Hon. Humphry Napier
Talbot, Lord E. (Chichester)
Thornton, Percy M.
Ure, Alexander
Valentia, Viscount
Wanklyn, James Leslie
Warde, Lt.-Col. C. E. (Kent)
Webster, Sir R. E. (I. of W.)
Welby, Lt.-Col. A. C. E.
Wentworth, Bruce C. Vernon-
Whiteley, George (Stockport)
Whitmore, Charles Algernon
Williams, Jos. Powell- (Birm.)
Willox, Sir John Archibald
Wilson ,J.W. (Worcestersh.N.)
Wylie, Alexander
Wyndham, George
Wyndham-Quin, Major W. H.
Young, Commander (Berks, E.)

TELLERS FOR THE NOES—
Sir William Walrond and
Mr. Anstruther.

Original Question again proposed—

Motion made—

"That Vote 1 be reduced by £100."—*(Mr. Courtenay Warner.)*

MR. COURTENAY WARNER (Staffordshire, Lichfield): I regret that it has been impossible to move this reduction at an earlier period. This is, I think, one of the largest Votes we have to make, and it is specially important. We have an enormous increase in the expenditure on armaments, and although most of us, on both sides of the House, are quite agreed that it is absolutely impossible to reduce the Naval Estimates, many of us feel that something must be done to reduce the general expenditure of armaments. I do not wish to see the Army reduced by one man, but I do wish to see some reform in the extravagant expenditure and the means that have been taken to keep up the Army as it is. I do not wish to ask the War Office to tie themselves down to any one method of reducing expenditure. There are many ways in which the present extravagance can be reduced by the War Office, and they have been advocated both inside the House and outside. The present expenditure is very considerable, and is bound, in a year or two, to further increase. Everybody is aware of the fact that these large annexations which the Empire is making throughout the world will require additional troops to garrison them. The Army will have to be increased, but this country will never be able to stand a further increase in the Army Estimates. Therefore, I protest against the present system, and I hope that something will be done in the direction of economy. I will only deal with the one Department with which I am most acquainted, namely, the Line Regiments at home. I believe there are other Members who will speak of the great waste which takes place in the War Office administration generally. Line Regiments at home are put down in these Estimates as if they were going to have 800 privates in them. If they had this strength the present number f officers and sergeants would not be too great. But, as a matter of fact, Line Regiments nominally of this strength are actually a strength of half that number, yet, by an extravagant system of having more officers than are necessary, officers and sergeants are only reduced one-sixth. The necessary part of the battalion for fighting power, however, is reduced by one-half. The answer will be given, no doubt, that this is a skeleton which will be filled up by Reserve men. Yes, but you have Reserve officers. There is an obvious reason for reducing subalterns. They will not be of very much use, because, by the time war breaks out, they will have grown up to a higher grade. I note, also, that we have a large Reserve of senior officers to draw from, so that there is no question of having any difficulty in filling the requisite strength so far as officers are concerned. I should like to know why this extravagant system of keeping more officers than are necessary is continued when the number can be reduced. You practically have twice as many officers to the same number of men as you would have on war strength, and it must be remembered that even on war strength the number ·f our officers in comparison with the number of men exceeds those of any other Army in the world. German battalions, either in war time or peace, have nearly twice as many men to each officer as we have, even if our battalions are up to their full strength. At the depôt you have practically one sergeant for every private, and one officer for every six privates.

And, it being Midnight, the Chairman left the Chair to make his Report to the House.

Committee report Progress; to sit again this day.

TUBERCULOSIS.

MR. CHANNING (Northampton, E.): I beg to ask the First Lord of the Treasury whether an opportunity will be given to discuss the Motion I have on the Paper on the subject of Turberculosis. The subject is a very important one, and a large number of Members on his own side of the House desire that a reasonable period of time should be given for its discussion?

THE FIRST LORD OF THE TREASURY: I heartily sympathise with th） honourable Member, but I am sorry that to-night, from my own point of view, has been barren, and may result in having longer sittings than we may desire on Thursday and Friday, and possibly a sitting on Saturday. These are fearful suggestions to make, but I hope they will not be fulfilled. I mention them in order to show that time is just as much needed for Government business. I am afraid I am not in a position to offer facilities for the Motion.

INFECTIOUS DISEASES (NOTIFICATION) ACT, 1889, EXTENSION BILL.

SIR F. POWELL (Wigan): I beg to move that this Bill be read a second time. The present Government and the late Government support it, and as only one honourable Member objects, I hope he will see his way to withdraw his objection.

DR. TANNER (Cork Co., Mid): The Bill contains many objectionable provisions, otherwise I would withdraw my opposition.

Second Reading deferred till Monday next.

PROGRESS OF BUSINESS.

On the Motion for the adjournment of the House,

MR. SWIFT MacNEILL: On the adjournment I desire to appeal to the First Lord of ·the Treasury, who is always kind and considerate in any matter of a personal nature, to afford me a convenient opportunity of calling attention to the death of a young soldier while in prison on a charge of shamming sickness. The question is of extreme importance, and the right honourable Gentleman will remember some weeks ago I gave up, at his request, an opportunity I had of calling attention to the subject. I think the right honourable Gentleman might give me an undertaking that he will allow the matter to be brought on before midnight. The War Office would, no doubt, like to make some answer, and I do not think this would be a proper question for discussion between the hours of two and three in the morning.

The FIRST LORD or the TREA-SURY: I am sure the honourable Member cannot appeal to anyone who is more in sympathy with him than I am, but I regret that I am unable to make any better arrangements. I hope that the honourable Member will get his opportunity on Friday.

METROPOLITAN WATER COMPANIES [GOVERNMENT] BILL.

Mr. Chaplin, Mr. Cripps, and Mr. James Stuart nominated Members of the Select Committee on the Metropolitan Water Companies (Government) Bill, with Four to be added by the Committee of Selection.—*(Sir William Walrond.)*

ELEMENTARY EDUCATION (NEW BY-LAWS) BILL.

Adjourned Debate on Second Reading [28th February] further adjourned till Friday.

SUMMARY JURISDICTION ACT (1879) AMENDMENT BILL.

Considered in Committee, and reported, without Amendment ; to be read the third time upon Friday.

BILLS DEFERRED.

WILD BIRDS PROTECTION BILL.

Second Reading deferred till Tuesday next.

SHOPS (EARLY CLOSING) BILL.

Second Reading deferred till Tuesday 18th April.

Mr. Swift MacNeill.

PLACES OF WORSHIP (LEASEHOLD ENFRANCHISEMENT) BILL.

Second Reading deferred till Tuesday next.

SEATS FOR SHOP ASSISTANTS (SCOT-LAND) BILL.

Second Reading deferred till Tuesday next.

POOR LAW OFFICERS' SUPERANNUA-TION ACT (1896) AMENDMENT BILL.

Second Reading deferred till Monday next.

CROWN CASES BILL.

Second Reading deferred till Wednes-day 22nd March.

OYSTERS BILL.

Second Reading deferred till Monday next.

LOCAL GOVERNMENT ACT (1888) AMENDMENT BILL.

Second Reading deferred till Tuesday next.

INFECTIOUS DISEASES (NOTIFICA-TION ACT (1889) EXTENSION BILL.

Second Reading deferred till Monday next.

WATER SUPPLY BILL.

Second Reading deferred till Tuesday next.

PARISH COUNCILLORS (TENURE OF OFFICE) BILL.

Committee deferred till Thursday.

TRUCK ACTS AMENDMENT BILL.

Second Reading deferred from Wednesday 29th March till Wednesday 19th April.

House adjourned at fifteen minutes after Twelve of the clock.

An Asterisk (*) at the commencement of a Speech indicates revision by the Member.

HOUSE OF COMMONS.

Wednesday, 15th March 1899.

MR. SPEAKER took the Chair at Twelve of the clock.

PRIVATE BILL BUSINESS.

BELFAST CORPORATION BILL.
Read a second time, and committed.

LONDON, BRIGHTON, AND SOUTH COAST RAILWAY (VARIOUS POWERS) BILL
Read a second time, and committed.

WALKER AND WALLSEND UNION GAS (ELECTRIC LIGHTING) BILL.
To be read a second time upon Thursday 23rd March.

LONDON AND NORTH WESTERN RAILWAY (ADDITIONAL POWERS) BILL.
Petition for additional Provision; referred to the Examiners of Petitions for Private Bills.

PETITIONS.

EDUCATION OF CHILDREN BILL.
Petitions in favour,—from Ipswich; —Syston; — Leicester; — and Melton Mowbray; to lie upon the Table.

LIQUOR TRAFFIC (LOCAL VETO) (SCOTLAND) BILL.
Petition from Glasgow, in favour; to lie upon the Table.

LOCAL AUTHORITIES' SERVANTS' SUPERANNUATION BILL.
Petition from Brighouse, against; to lie upon the Table.

LOCAL AUTHORITIES' SERVANTS' SUPERANNUATION BILL.
Petitions in favour,—from Guildford; —Stockton-on-Tees; — and, Shardlow; to lie upon the Table.

LONDON GOVERNMENT BILL.
Petition from Westminster, in favour; to lie upon the Table.

PARLIAMENTARY FRANCHISE.
Petitions for Extension to Women;— From York;—and, Weston-near-Bath; to lie upon the Table.

PRIVATE LEGISLATION PROCEDURE (SCOTLAND) BILL.
Petitions in favour,—From Hawick; —Ayr;—and, Elgin; to lie upon the Table.

PUBLIC HEALTH ACTS AMENDMENT BILL.
Petitions in favour,—From Barrow-in-Furness; — Cheltenham; — Huddersfield; — Burnley; — and, Dudley; to lie upon the Table.

SALE OF INTOXICATING LIQUORS ON SUNDAY BILL.
Petitions in favour,—From Swindon; —Beechamwell; — Clapham; — Lozells; — Leytonstone; — Broughton; —Battersea; — Paddington;—Millom; —Rusholme; — East Manchester;—Chorlton-upon-Medlock; — Burythorpe; —York (three);—and, Cookley; to lie upon the Table.

RETURNS, REPORTS, ETC.

JUDICIAL STATISTICS (ENGLAND AND WALES).

Copy presented,—of Judicial Statistics for England and Wales, 1897, Part II. (Civil Judicial Statistics), edited by John Macdonell, esquire, C.B., LL.D., Master of the Supreme Court (by Command); to lie upon the Table.

UGANDA RAILWAY ACT, 1896.

Account presented, — showing the Money issued from the Consolidated Fund under the provisions of the Uganda Railway Act, 1896 (59 and 60 Vic., c. 38), and of the Money expended and borrowed, and Securities created under the said Act, to 31st March 1898; together with the Report of the Comptroller and Auditor-General thereon (by Act); to lie upon the Table, and to be printed. (No. 108.)

TREATY SERIES (No. 6, 1899).

Copy presented,—of additional Convention to the Convention of 1st December 1897, between the United Kingdom and France, for the exchange of Postal Parcels between Australia and France (by Command); to lie upon the Table.

PAPERS LAID ON THE TABLE BY THE CLERK OF THE HOUSE.

1. Soane's Museum,—Copy of Statement of the Funds of the Museum of the late Sir John Soane on 5th January 1898 (by Act).

2. Bridlington Piers and Harbour,—Copy of Abstract of the General Annual Account for the year ending 26th July 1897 (by Act).

HARBOUR, ETC., BILLS.

Copy ordered, "of the Report of the Board of Trade upon the following Harbour, etc., Bills:—

Humber Conservancy Bill [Lords];
Glasgow and South Western Railway Bill [Lords];
Southport and Lytham Tramroad Bill [Lords]."—(*Mr. Ritchie.*)

Copy presented accordingly; to lie upon the Table, and to be printed. (No. 109.)

ORDERS OF THE DAY.

PETROLEUM BILL.

Order for Second Reading read.

Motion made, and Question proposed—

"That the Bill be now read a second time."

*Mr. H. J. RECKITT (Lincolnshire, Brigg): I rise to move the Second Reading of this Bill, and I only wish that this task had been in the hands of one more able than myself to deal with it. It is a subject which is undoubtedly difficult and complicated, but I will endeavour to lay the matter before the House in a manner free from prejudice. I hope the House will bear with me while I do my best to lay before Parliament this extremely complicated question of petroleum, which has been brought before the attention of a large number of Members of this House by means of literature of a varied character, and by means of a number of petitions from those interested in the trade, and these things have tended to make my burden heavier. Now, what is the character of this literature which has been circulated in favour of the Bill? It has been, without exception, signed by those who give authority for their statements, whilst with few exceptions the literature against the Bill has been circulated without any signature, and it has been impossible to find out who are responsible for the misstatements contained in that literature. It has been most unfortunate that the trade interests on the one hand and upon the other should have tended to introduce an amount of prejudice into the consideration of this subject, of which I hope this House, out of consideration for the importance of the question, will divest its mind: for I say that the question of the safety of the lives of the people of this country is not one which ought to be confounded with the trade interests either of America or of Scotland or Russia. This, to my mind, is the position which Members of the House should take up in dealing with a subject of this character. I sincerely hope that any remarks of mine will be free from what I consider to be a blot on the outside criticisms which have been made on this matter. The Committee which reported last Session to this House sat for a period of nearly four years, and dealt with about 85 witnesses of varying character. Many of those witnesses were expert chemists, many of them were those interested and connected with the lamp trade, and many others held official positions either in London or the provinces who had to deal with the question of the Petroleum Acts. After hearing this evidence that Committee which was appointed by this House presented a Report which is of a very interesting character because of the varied nature of its recommendations. Up to about page 9 of that Report it can be described as almost of a homogeneous character, but after that, apparently, there arises a large number of inconsistencies in the subject matter which is dealt with, and which appears in that Report. It may be interesting to the House to know how, after having come to the conclusion that the flash point of petroleum oil should be raised to 100, that Report proceeds almost immediately, in many cases, to insert clauses which entirely take away the advantage of having come to that conclusion. I must say that those of us who formed the majority of that Committee when the question of the flash point of 100 was determined, after a Debate which took the larger portion of from two to three sittings, in which every question and every phase of the subject of raising the flash point to 100 degs.; in which the question of lamps, of cost, and the question as to whether accidents had increased were

fully dealt with in that Debate—it did appear to me and to the Members forming the majority of that Committee to be almost unreasonable, to say the least of it, for Members of that Committee who had been defeated upon that matter in the Division to proceed, when they found themselves in a temporary majority, to insert clauses in that Report in opposition to the determination of the majority of the Committee which had been arrived at after a very lengthy Debate. That, to my mind, accounts to a very large extent for many of the clauses which appear to take away from the determination of the Committee, and from the reasons which actuated the majority of the Committee in coming to the conclusion that the flash point should be raised to 100 degs. In dealing with this point, I might also point out that if you read through the detailed proceedings contained in the Report of that Committee you will see that there were two Members who voted against raising the flash point to 100, who had already tabled Amendments in favour of raising the flash point either to 85 or to 90; so that in connection with the statements which have been made by some who have more or less authority that it was only by a bare majority that the Committee were in favour of raising the flash point, it should be borne in mind that there were at least two who were in favour of raising the flash point somewhat, and that makes 10 to 11 Members of the Committee who were in favour of raising the flash point above the present point of 73. The House has so far received no information officially as to the intentions of the Government with regard to the Report of that Committee, but through the Press we have received from time to time some information; in fact, upon the morning after I had given notice of my intention to bring in this Bill "The Times" newspaper was able to inform the country that the Government were going to introduce a Bill to deal with those recommendations of the Committee which had received a substantial majority. Now I should have thought that under the circumstances the question of the flash point should have also been included amongst those recommendations which would receive attention in any Government Bill. It is because those of us who have backed this particular Bill are not aware, except from the Reports of deputations received by the Under Secretary to the Home Office, as to what are the intentions of the Government in regard to this matter; that the intentions of the Government are, as a matter of fact, of considerable importance no one is willing to quarrel with. That they have an intention of moving a Bill I am extremely glad to know, and I am glad to hear that they are moving in the matter. But in connection with these reports what puzzled me is that, during the Recess, which lasted some six or seven months, the attention of the Government should not have been directed during that time to the preparation of such a Bill, which might even now have received its Second Reading, and been sent to a Committee. But apparently it required the fortunes of the ballot in order that this question should be brought before the attention of this House. For my part I confess that I should have thought the Government would have introduced legislation for the protection of life and limb, and even have mentioned legislation of that character in the Queen's Speech before mentioning legislation for the protection of the pockets of the spendthrifts. I think that the proceedings of that Report show that the majority who supported the high flash point were consistent throughout in the attitude and line which they took up. We are, in reality, in favour of altering the flash point, and we are not in favour of allowing it to remain at the present point of 73. That brings me to this general statement that the whole of the Report of the Committee—whether you look at it from the point of view of the flash point or of the lamp—is unanimous in one respect, and that is that legislation is required in order to minimise the accidents which take place with paraffin lamps. On that point I maintain that the Committee were unanimously agreed, and it is, therefore, unnecessary to argue the question as to whether legislation is required or not. I notice in one of the reports in the newspapers of a deputation received by the Under Secretary to the Home Office, a statement by the Under Secretary in which he says, dealing with the Memorandum to the Bill—

"A more misleading, more inaccurate statement it would be impossible to make. There was absolutely no difference between the flash point of 1871, which was embodied in the Bill

Mr. Reckitt.

of 1879, and the flash point of the present time. The only difference had been that the method of testing had been altered."

Now I am perfectly willing to join issue with the right honourable Gentleman upon that remark; and so far from my statement being misleading I should have thought that those who have read the Bill would have noticed in the Memorandum that the expression used was, that by repealing the clause in the Act of 1879, and letting the Act of 1871, which fixes the flash point at 100, remain, that that would be carrying out the intentions of the Act of 1871. Now, I will go through the history of the flash point up to the Act of 1879, which is now in operation, and I am perfectly ready to join issue with the right honourable Gentleman who made that statement to a deputation. The question of the flash point was first raised in this country in the year 1862, when Dr. Letheby, the chemical analyst to the City of London, was asked to draw up a report on the question of paraffin oil, and he recommended—

"That petroleum would be perfectly safe for all practical purposes when it does not evolve inflammable vapour at a temperature below 100 degs. Fahrenheit; for there is no ordinary storage place or lamp that could, according to my observation or experiment, reach such a temperature."

Now, those in opposition to the raising of the flash point have often made the statement that the proposal to raise the flash point to 100 degs. in connection with the use of oil in lamps is an entrely new proposal, and I would call the attention of the House to the fact that in his recommendation with regard to the flash point of petroleum lamps were distinctly in the mind of Dr. Letheby in 1862. There was no test then imposed, and yet there we have the fact that that Act intended 100 to be the test in connection with the flash point.

THE UNDER SECRETARY OF STATE FOR THE HOME DEPARTMENT (Mr. COLLINGS, Birmingham, Bordesley): There was the open test.

*MR. RECKITT: There was no test in that Act. We come to 1867, when upon the recommendation of a Committee the suggestion was made for a flash point of 110. But pressure was brought to bear on the Home Office by the trade to reduce the flash point to 100. Here we begin first to trace the baneful influence which seems to have been attached throughout to this question of the safety of the public, when, as a matter of fact, too often the interest of the trader has been preferred. On this three chemists were asked to make a report. These chemists were Dr. Letheby, Dr. Attfield, and Sir Frederick Abel, and in 1868 they made a Report in favour of the flash point being 100, and they laid it down that if it was to be a flash point of 100 it must be with a test which they themselves devised and carried out in the most rigid manner. Now, that test was to be a cup, three inches deep, half-filled with petroleum oil, and the flame was to be passed close to the service of the oil in order to determine the flash point of that oil. That Report was handed in on 4th June 1868, and on the 8th June the Bill carrying out the Report was introduced, but on 15th June the test was altered, the test devised by the three chemists disappeared, and the open test, which apparently is the glory of those who are in favour of low-flash oil, was inserted in that Bill. Now, upon whose authority and recommendation was the test altered? It was by the then Under Secretary to the Home Office referred, after an appeal had been made by the trade, not to the three chemists upon whose Report the Bill of 1868 was introduced, but to one of them only, Sir Frederick Abel, and he was told that he was in no wise to give way upon the rigour of the test. He accepted the test prepared by the trade, and which obviously favoured the trade rather than the public. That test was a three-inch cup, to be filled to the brim, with a wire a quarter of an inch from the surface along which the flame was to pass. Now, the whole question of the test of paraffin oil depends very largely upon what is to be deducted from this test. Now, the vapour of paraffin oil is heavier than the air, and if you have your cup full to the brim, and you raise the temperature of that oil to 73 degs. and so on up to 100, the vapour of the petroleum has a tendency to slip off the surface and over the edge of the cup, and consequently will not come into contact with that flame passing along the wire at a quarter of an inch above the surface. Now, in that way you get a delusive test,

which Professor Abel himself described as being "unreliable and susceptible of manipulation." But if you had taken the test of the three chemists, with a cup half filled, there would have been a considerable tendency to retain the vapour which came off from the surface of the oil, and the instruction to pass the flame close to the surface instead of a quarter of an inch away would give a more accurate test than the one which was adopted upon the recommendation of Sir Frederick Abel. Even Mr. Redwood in 1872, in a report which he prepared at that time, was in favour of keeping the test at 100 on account of the fact that people in this country had got to believe that lamp oil, with a test of 100, was a safe and proper oil to use in connection with lamps. Now, what happened in the legislation which took place in 1879? Sir Frederick Abel discovered the test, which everyone in this controversy has agreed to accept as a perfectly reliable test—that is, the Abel tester, a half-filled cup which is entirely covered in, and the flame allowed to approach the surface of the oil simultaneously with the opening of the aperture in the cover of the cup. He then with his new test, with which nobody quarrels, as against the test which he himself describes as being "unreliable and susceptible of manipulation," discovers that there is a variation of 27 degs. Having come to this conclusion that there is a variation, after a large number of experiments, of 27 degs., the flash point is lowered from 100 to 73 with a safe test, but if you compare Sir Frederick Abel's test closely with the test devised by the three chemists you find a variation of only three degrees. Therefore, in my judgment, the Acts of 1868 and 1871, which inserted the open test, distinctly made a mistake in choosing even at that period the worst of two tests which were open to the Government to make a choice from. But, in dealing with this matter, the important point is that 100 degs. was accepted in 1862, 1868, and 1871, at which it was fixed, and the temperature at which paraffin oil gave off a vapour which would catch fire if a light was applied to it. The question as to by what means you arrive at that test, or what particular apparatus you use, is, in my judgement, immaterial, if you are determined in your own mind to start with what apparently the Legislature thought at that time was a proper flash point at which paraffin oil should be used in this country, and that was 100 degs. If you find that your test is inaccurate and open to manipulation, surely the obvious thing to do is not to lower your standard from 100 to 73, but to use a reliable test to maintain that flash point which you have already come to the conclusion is the one which should be adopted. Now, that is the object of this Bill, and I maintain that I have shown from the remarks which I have made that the Memorandum of the Bill is not a misleading statement, but is a perfectly accurate statement of the history of the flash point of petroleum up to the present date. The Bill which I have the honour of moving might have been drafted in this way: we might have taken the Act of 1871, which fixed the flash point at 100, and eliminated the clause which inserted the open test, and inserted the clause from the Act of 1879, which insists upon the Abel close test; and in that case we should have arrived at precisely the same result as by this Bill, which allows the Act of 1879 to stand with regard to the Abel close test and reverts back to the flash point of 100 instead of 73. That is the object of this Bill, and I think the Memorandum fully bears out the intention of the wording of the Act. Now, the next point I should wish to call the attention of the House to is this: it may be said that it is to some extent ancient history to go back to 1879 and 1868 with regard to this matter, and it may be said that the flash point of 73 has, during the last 30 years, practically been satisfactory to this country, and that there has been little or no complaint. I would at once say that the evidence of a large number of the experts who gave evidence before the Select Committee—men of considerable ability and of undoubted distinction—was in favour of raising the flash point of petroleum oil. I might mention Lord Kelvin, Dr. Attfield, Professor Mendeleef and Sir Henry Roscoe, and a considerable number of others; and if you turn to the evidence either of Mr. Redwood or Sir Frederick Abel you will find that while they, in their evidence in chief, are opposed to the raising of the flash point of petroleum, yet they admit

Mr. Reckitt.

that in their judgment it would be safer to raise the flash point of petroleum oil from 73 to 100, and that there would be a likelihood of the diminution of accidents if the flash point were raised; but that they are afraid that the cost to the public would be so materially raised as to interfere with what is commonly described as "the poor man's light." Then there is the evidence of Professor Chandler, who came over in the interests of the Standard Oil Trust Company, who went very largely in the same direction, and who showed that if you could get an oil at a flash point of 100 which burned as well and as readily as the oil of to-day, and that the price would not be materially raised to the consumer, he said that he believed that for every degree you raised the flash point you added a degree of safety to the oil that was used. Now, as to this point, why it is necessary that the flash point should be above 73 degs. When you are using a paraffin lamp and the oil in the reservoir is feeding the wick and the lamp is alight, it has been found from a large number of experiments made by Mr. Spencer, the chief officer of the Public Control Department of the London County Council, who has devoted a very considerable amount of time during the last five years to research in this matter, that with a glass receiver to a paraffin lamp there is a tendency to add to the temperature of the oil over and above the temperature of the room in which the oil is burned, to the extent of from 10 to 15 degs.; and in the case of a lamp with a metal receiver the temperature of the oil is sometimes added to from 15 degs. up to as much as 25 degs. Now, if the oil flashes at 73 degs., and you raise the temperature of that oil to 85 or 90 degs., you have a vapour given off in that receiver due to the rise of the temperature which, in any case of overturning or sudden draught down the chimney of the lamp, or accident of that character, is likely to produce the ignition of the vapour in the reservoir or cause an explosion. Undoubtedly the evidence showed that explosions of a detonating character in connection with paraffin lamps are few and rare, yet the ignition of the vapour in the reservoir in any receiver is likely to cause a fracture on account of the heat generated in that ignition, and this has given rise to a very large number of the accidents which are recorded, and which have increased during the last few years. Now, in connection with this question, it is obvious that if you have the flash point of your oil raised to 100 degs. —and the oil in the receiver of a lamp when burning in a glass receiver or in a metal receiver seldom rises above 90 degs. temperature—you have the temperature of the oil under the flash point of the oil, and you are not likely to have a large amount of dangerous vapour evolved in the burning of that lamp, and the Abel close test is practically a test of the receiver of a lamp in use. It is a remarkable thing that the attention of Sir Frederick Abel was never drawn to this aspect of the case when he was reporting lately upon the question of the flash point of petroleum oil. In connection with this matter I might point out that Sir Frederick Abel himself was asked to report upon what flash point should be fixed for petroleum used in the Army and Naval depôts of this country, and he recommended that the flash point should not be 73, but that it should be 105 degs., and he said that the reason for this was that in barracks the condition of life was such that it was necessary to take larger precautions than with men who were living an ordinary civilian life. He thought that, with the usual carelessness of soldiers, they might mix up their ammunition with the petroleum, and he thought that generally the condition of barracks, according to his evidence, was an absolute disgrace to the Army of this country. He was asked in cross-examination as to whether he thought the condition of the poor in the East End of London was not considerably worse than the condition of well regulated barracks; and whether, if it was necessary for the safety of the barracks and of our soldiers only to use oil with a flash point of 105, it would not materially add to the safety of the poor people in London and in our large cities to use only oil of a similar flash point? He said, in reply, that he had no knowledge of the East End of London, which, apparently to my mind, is entirely begging the question which was put to him at that time. I might also point out that the flash point of oil used in lighthouses is from 120 to 150, and this is considered necessary where it is essential to protect property

of this character. In the case of railway companies and large dock companies very often you find that the petroleum in use has to be of a higher grade flash point than that in common use at 73 degrees, and, therefore, I say that the deduction to be derived from these facts is that if you raise the flash point of petroleum oil you are increasing the safety of the consumer of that oil. I might point out that the Anglo-American Oil Company themselves some two years ago were advertising a new oil of their own, and it was called the " White Rose Oil." That advertisement described this new oil as being the finest oil on the market, and it stated—

" Its purity adds so greatly to its safety that families can use ' White Rose' with as much confidence as they would use gas."

This is the description given of an oil the flash point of which is 103 degs., which they have put on the market, and which they say is safer and a better oil, and burns brighter than the common oil of 73 degs., which is the ordinary oil of commerce; and they further stated that the price which they were going to charge for it was going to be very small indeed over and above the ordinary oil of commerce. Of course, when the Committee was sitting, the attention of one of the directors of the Anglo-American Oil Company was drawn to this statement, and he said that it was only advertising bunkum, and was done for advertising purposes. I ask them, Are we to accept this statement that it was advertising bunkum, and at the same time not make very large deductions from the argument about the greatly increased cost of the oil in case the flash point was fixed at 100. If on the one hand they are prepared to lie to the public, then it is reasonable to presume that they are prepared to lie in their own interest to the Committee of this House, and the evidence which was given by an expert from America, while it showed that in his opinion it would add a penny per gallon to the cost of the oil, yet I believe that that was a very large exaggeration of the true facts of the case. Now, in this controversy, while we are dealing with the question of America, I will allude to the statement which has often been made that the flash point of the oil used in the United States of

America is low, and that practically it is lower than the flash point at present in use in this country. There have been laid before the Committee three tables upon this matter—there were the tables of Mr. Redwood, Mr. Stewart, and Mr. Gray, all three of them gentlemen of considerable ability in dealing with this matter, and the comparison of these tables shows that dealing with 47 States there was no law in 15, according to Stewart, and that throughout 20 States there was a flash point of 100 degrees and over. According to Mr. Gray, there were 19 States with a flash point of 100 and over, and Mr. Redwood found that there were nine States with a flash point of 94 and over. Both Mr. Stewart and Mr. Gray found that there was no State that had a flash point lower than 73. There were 12 over 80 and under 100, and 13, according to Mr. Gray, over 86 and under 100. Mr. Redwood's figures are by no means so like in parallel as those of Mr. Stewart and Mr. Gray, who differ somewhat from each other in their deductions, but are much more in accord with each other. Now, if we take one State, the State of Iowa, which has a flash point of 105 degs., some of the facts in connection with the history of that State are of interest in connection with this matter. The Anglo-American Oil Company, when that matter was before the American Legislature, used every effort which is open to American politicians and to American wire-pullers to prevent the flash point being raised to 105, but the flash point was eventually raised to that figure, in spite of the fact that the copy of the Bill was abstracted from the possession of the Clerk the day before it should have received the signature and become law. What has been the result? Why, that in a population of 2,000,000 of people during the last 14 years there has been no death from explosions in connection with the use of paraffin lamps.

Mr. COLLINGS: Will the honourable Member state whose evidence that appears in?

*Mr. RECKITT: I do not state that it appeared in the evidence, but, under the circumstances, I think I am entitled to make the statement for what it is worth, although it is not in the evidence. As far as I can make out—and I have made inquiries from sources which I believe to

Mr. Reckitt.

be perfectly reliable—there were no deaths from this cause in Iowa for 14 years. Now, there have been a number of accidents from paraffin lamps in London during the past seven years, and there have been 191 deaths from this cause, with double the population of Iowa. I will leave the House to draw its own inference from this fact. If I turn to Scotland and the North of England, where the use of paraffin oil with a flash point of 103 degs. is common to the people of those districts, you will find that accidents and deaths in connection with the use of paraffin oil are extremely rare, and in many parts of Scotland almost unknown. That, to my mind, speaks largely for the advantage of a high flash oil to be used by the people of this country. But when you turn to England and to London and other districts, you find that accidents and death in connection with the use of paraffin oil have increased, and are upon the increase. If you take the number of fires in London, according to the return of the Metropolitan Fire Brigade, made in 1876, the number of deaths in connection with accidents from the use of paraffin was one, whilst in 1897 it was 21, and the percentage in connection with the number of fires has risen from 3 to 24.1. Now those figures to my mind show, at any rate, that there is a case to meet, and that there is a need for legislation which should, if it is at all possible in any way, try and minimise the number of deaths and the number of people who are injured in connection with lamp accidents. If you take the number of accidents due to petroleum lamps in the city of Glasgow, and in Edinburgh, where the flash point is 105, it is only 1 per cent.; and if you take London it is 13.5 per cent. If you take Amsterdam, where the flash point is 70 degs., the percentage is 37 per cent.

Mr. WEBSTER: (St. Pancras, E.): Does that include manufactories?

*Mr. RECKITT: I believe it also includes those fires in manufactories as well, but if it includes manufactories in one case it includes them in all the others, so that the weight of my statistics is not materially affected by that point. But the question which I would like, in conclusion, to deal with is the question of cost. Now, in arguing the flash point of petroleum oil, the question of cost was one which weighed very largely upon the minds of honourable Members of that Committee who did not vote in favour of raising the flash point to 100, and, for my part, I must confess that it was not until I had satisfied myself that to raise the flash point from 73 to 100 would not materially raise the price of petroleum oil to the general consumers in this country that I myself voted in favour of raising the flash point to 100. The reasons which weighed with us then, and which weigh with us now, are that you can buy Scotch oil at 105 degs. at the same price as you can buy American oil at 73 degs.; and you can buy Russian oil at a flash point of 107 degs. at the same price as the American oil at 73 degs. I have also here with me amongst my papers a copy of a telegram from New York, saying that there is a firm there who are willing to supply and guarantee a flash oil at 100 degs. Abel close test at one-half cent extra cost per gallon over the cost of the 73 degs. oil in use at the present time, which is an increase of one farthing per gallon, and even that increase of one farthing is likely to disappear as regards the consumer on account of the general competition which is likely to go on in this country. Now, seeing that the variation in the price of the American 73 degs. oil in England in the year 1895 was during that period 4½d. per gallon, without even the competition of Russia with the higher grade oil, the extra cost of one farthing taken into consideration with the variation in the market—a variation which in some cases amounted to 4½d. in the year—the extra cost of one farthing is not at all likely to materially increase the market fluctuation of the price of petroleum oil. But the evidence of those who argued that the price would be largely increased depended upon the testimony of an oil refiner from New York, who described to the Committee how he would raise flash oil from 73 to 100, and he said that it would cost him so much more because he would have a residue for which he could not find a market. Then he was asked if he had to manufacture *de novo* from crude oil whether he would adopt the same process as in the case of the 73 degs. oil, and he said if he had to manufacture an oil of 100 degs. he would proceed by a different process, and he

stated that he had forgotten to make any experiments as to what the cost of that process would be, although he had had six months' notice that that was the point upon which we wanted him to give evidence. When he was asked what was the price to be got for naphtha, he declined to state it, but those who turn to the papers and look at the price of American oil and naphtha will see that naphtha is fetching a larger price in the London market than the lamp oil. As to the question of supply, the figures of the expert from the new fields in Java, Sumatra, and Borneo show enormous increases in the imports into both India and Japan, and there is a general decline or a want of proportionate increase in the oil from America and Russia, while the oil from Eastern countries is rapidly, if not supplanting, at any rate is taking the whole of the new supply which is required. These oil fields are new, and have only been partially developed, but I believe that even if it is still maintained, or even shown that it will require the absorption of 30 per cent. more of the crude oil to manufacture oil at a flash point of 100, that even in spite of that fact the enormous oil fields of the world are capable of keeping up the supply, and the competition would be such that the price to the consumer would be regulated by the general competition, and not by the cost of the production of the oil at the present time by the present machinery. I feel I have taken up a large amount of the time of the House, but I have done so because I think that this is a matter of considerable importance. I have done my best to lay before the House some facts in connection with this subject; and I would, in conclusion, remind honourable Members of the remarks so often repeated by the present Under Secretary to the Home Office, that the first consideration of the Government in connection with this matter should be the safety of the public. Are we to put aside this reform on account of what I might describe as a momentary inconvenience to the trader? Are we to put aside this reform on account of a manufactured agitation against this Bill, against the raising of the flash point? If we can, by turning our attention to this question, by means of legislation save a few lives; if we can prevent only a few accidents to poor people; if we can protect somewhat better the property of the people of this country, then I think this Bill deserves well of the consideration of this House. I beg to move, "That this Bill be now read a second time."

MR. A. CROSS (Glasgow, Camlachie): I rise with great satisfaction to support the Second Reading of the Bill brought in by the honourable Member for Brigg. I will endeavour, Sir, in what I desire to say, to be as brief as possible, though I hope the House will bear with me if I recall the fact that I have taken a somewhat prominent part in connection with this Bill. I happen to have been an original member of the Committee which conducted an inquiry into the question, and to have served on the Committee in the last Parliament. Sir, I brought to the deliberations of the Committee an entire ignorance of the subject, but I also brought that quality in which this House boasts—namely, an absolutely unprejudiced mind. I was perfectly disinterested, and if, Mr. Speaker, in the course of five years' inquiry, I have come to hold an earnest opinion, it is because I am earnestly convinced, and when I remember that the question is one which concerns the safety of the people of this country in their homes, I think it is a question with regard to which I do well to be earnest. If I were not earnest I should be almost guilty of a crime. I shall, perhaps, best serve the interests which this Bill seeks to promote if I address myself at once to the crux and essence of the case of those who are opposed to the raising of the flash point. It is alleged that the raising of the flash point will have the effect of making illuminative oil, which is a necessity of the poor, dearer in price. Now, Sir, following in the line of my honourable Friend the Member for Brigg, I traverse that statement. The only two witnesses who were called before the Committee on that matter afforded no information upon the essence of the question, and, as far as those two witnesses were concerned, the Committee remained entirely ignorant on the subject.

MR. COLLINGS: Who sent the two witnesses?

*MR. A. CROSS: You gave the information, I understand.

Mr. Reckitt.

MR. COLLINGS: Certainly not.

MR. A. CROSS: It is within my distinct recollection that an intimation was conveyed, either informally or directly, to the Standard Oil Company that they were expected to furnish witnesses with regard to the question of price if the Committee recommended the raising of the flash point of oil. They had fair warning months before, and the witnesses presented themselves on this footing; but, after they had been examined, we were in precisely the same position as we were at the commencement. If any candid man will read their evidence I venture to say he will be as ignorant of the matter as he was before. I draw attention first of all to the supplies of petroleum now on the market. The Anglo-American Oil Company, which practically possesses the monopoly of the market of this country, sent us last year 2,700,000 gallons; Russia supplied about 900,000 gallons; and the Scottish companies 450,000 gallons. It is true that the Scottish companies started their trade with a high standard of flash oil and stuck to it, not merely from commercial considerations, but also upon humanitarian grounds; but I want to deal with American oil. It is true that the American witness, Mr. Paul Babcock, partner in the Standard Oil Company, gave us no information on the details of this question, but the Committee were in possession of information from other sources. We had the evidence of three distinguished chemists, which went to show that by extracting from the 73 degs. flash oil imported from America 8 per cent. of naphtha, an excellent and safe burning oil at 100 degs. can be obtained without an increase in the present price of oil. In the process of manufacture in America, where 100 gallons of crude oil are treated, the results are that they get 60 gallons of 73 flash oil, 20 gallons of 100 degs. flash fine water-white, and 20 gallons of residue. The loss, therefore, is entirely confined to 8 or 10 per cent. on the 60 gallons of 73 flash oil, which is something like 5 per cent. on the whole of the oil. I have procured the prices from the New York Produce Exchange, and I find that the highest price reached for 73 degs. flash oil, free on board at New York, during the last four years is 5 cents. a gallon in bulk; and the lowest point, which was reached in October, 1897, was 2.90 cents. per gallon. The average price in that period was 4 cents. per gallon, equal to 2d. per gallon. Deducting from this price the cost of transport to New York, and the producer's profit, said to be large, the cost of production at the factory cannot be more than 1½d. per gallon. If enough naphtha is abstracted from the oil to raise the flash point to 100 degs., the cost of production will only be raised 10 per cent. at the very outside—more probably not more than 5 per cent. I rest my whole case on this point, and I challenge the right honourable Gentleman or any honourable Member to upset my figures. If I am reminded that there will also be a loss in making the oil up to 100 degs. flash in heavy oil I differ. There is a " cracking " process, by which it is as easy and practically as cheap to produce oil flashing at 100 degs. as at 73 degs. Fifty per cent. of the oil coming into the market is oil made under the " cracking " process. I have seen a written offer within the last few days from the outside manufacturers of America, undertaking to supply oil flashing at 100 degs. at a rise in price over the oil flashing at 73 degs. of only a farthing a gallon. These manufacturers are willing to contract for a number of years, and I shall be happy to supply the right honourable Gentleman with full particulars—¼d. per gallon is the very outside of it. Now, such an increase of price would scarcely be felt by the consumer. The honourable Member for Brigg has already alluded to the selling prices of oil at which the public gets supplied in this country. I have before me a list of the prices of oil supplied by wholesale dealers in London, and I find that the prices varied from other causes in the course of single years from ⅝d. to 4½d. per gallon, from such causes as freight, cost of distribution, profits to agencies, etc. So much for oils at present on the market. I should like to add a word or two about the oils which are not in the market, but which are rapidly becoming available for the market. The Russian oil fields are hardly touched yet, although they are supplying hundreds of thousands of gallons. In America, while it is notorious that every effort is being made to sup-

press the production in order to keep up the price, there is an enormous production going on. In Canada, the production will still largely increase. In Roumania, large fields are being opened, and in Galicia, Java, Japan, and Borneo, the production is being rapidly developed. The House will realise what is meant by the supply of oil in Borneo when I mention that concessions have been granted to the extent of over 180 square miles of land, and that the flash point of the oil of that country is 150 degs. Now, Sir, the remedy which this House ought to seek in order to prevent a further increase in the price of oil is free competition. Let us welcome oil, whether it comes from Canada, Russia, or anywhere else, but let us at the same time insist as a necessary condition of its purchase that it shall be at a safe flash point. Now, Sir, I should like, if this House will bear with me, to say one word as to why we have brought in this Bill. Having regard to the fact that the Government are going to bring in a Bill in a few days, it has been suggested that we should have waited and seen what they had to say on the subject. It appears to me that there is a complete answer to that suggestion. In the first place there was no mention of petroleum legislation in the Queen's Speech ; and, in the second place, there is reason to believe that the Bill which the Government will bring in will deal with the storage of oil and the regulation of lamps—questions of such complexity and difficulty that I think they might be very well left to the Bill of which the right honourable Gentleman is in charge. The honourable Member for Brigg has dealt with the contention that in this Bill we are introducing a change of great magnitude. As a matter of fact, this Bill only proposes to re-enact that which Parliament did enact in 1861, and intended to enact in 1868, and by subsequent legislation. The principle laid down by Professor Letheby was that the flash-point is the temperature at which the vapour would begin to be freely evolved, and should be higher than the temperature to which the oil under ordinary circumstances would be exposed, whether in store or in lamps. That is the principle on which we proceed. We maintain that it is unsafe to permit an oil to be sold in this country which is of such a nature as to evolve inflammable explosive vapour at any temperature which is lower than that to which it is likely to be exposed in ordinary use. I would remind the House that there is hardly a kitchen in any of our large towns, or drawing-room for that matter, in which there is not a lamp burning, and in which the temperature is higher than 73 degs. On many of our summer days we have a temperature of over 73 degs., and whenever you have a temperature over 73 degs. that oil is giving off a vapour, an invisible vapour, which is as inflammable and combustible as gunpowder itself; and which, if exploded, is certain to carry destruction to all the objects with which it comes in contact. It is urged that explosions do not often happen with petroleum oil. I saw in a leading journal the other day a statement that no explosion ever occurred with petroleum oil; but honourable Members of this House who are curious on these subjects should read an admirable reply to that article by Mr. Spencer, of the County Council, whose labours on this matter deserve the greatest amount of credit, and I am sure they will satisfy themselves that explosions do frequently occur and cause death to the persons in the vicinity of the lamps. But I base my case not on what happens when an explosion occurs, but on what happens under the ordinary conditions of life when a lamp is upset in any man's kitchen, or in any room in the house. If the oil in the lamp is heated to its flash point it gives off all over the room an invisible inflammable vapour, and if the wick touches the vapour floating about the lamp an explosion occurs on a small scale. The oil is scattered in a spray-like form, carrying fire and general destruction with it. But if the oil is of a quality with a flash point of 100 degs., at the time of its discharge from the lamp it would be at a temperature usually of 90 degs. The flame of the lamp instead of exploding the oil would be extinguished by the oil. To put it plainly. If you take two oils, one with a low flash point of 73 degs., or under, and the other of a flash point of 100 degs., and heat them up to 80 degs., if you put a match into one, that oil will blaze and flare, but if you put a match into the high flash oil the match will be extinguished. That is the great advantage

Mr. A. Cross.

of a high flash oil when a lamp is upset. I promised the House not to be tedious, and I trust that I have not gone beyond the limits which my experience of and interest in this question have justified. I apologise to the House for having taken so long, and I thank honourable Members for the patient hearing they have given me.

Amendment proposed—

"To leave out the word 'now,' and at the end of the Question to add the words 'upon this day six months.'"—*(Mr. Kimber.)*

MR. KIMBER (Wandsworth): I am surprised, and I am sure many honourable Members of this House share my surprise, that so large a portion of the speeches of the honourable Members who moved and seconded the Second Reading of this Bill should have dealt with the subject of lamps. Now, let me say at once that whether this Bill passes or whether it does not pass, lamps will not be affected in any way whatever. Lamps will go on burning oil either at a high flash point or at a low flash point just as before. So long as careless people can have access to lamps, accidents will happen to the end of time. That, I think, obviates the necessity of my dealing with arguments such as were used by my honourable Friend who has last spoken, as to what would happen if the oil in the lamp used in the room reached a certain temperature. Lamps have been instrumental in forcing this question on the House and on the public. If serious accidents happened to careless people, or to innocent people who are not careless, they were thrust on the attention of the House, and hence the Committee which has been sitting for some years. I have no doubt that these accidents caused some confusion in the minds of some of the Committee, and some of the witnesses who came before the Committee. I shall not go into the question of lamps at all, or as to the temperature at which, or the conditions under which, the oil in them, if ignited, will explode. I do not know how people can suppose that when a lamp is burning the temperature of it can be as low as 73 degs., or even 100 degs. It is difficult to believe that. If you try the experiment of putting your finger on the metal near the burner you will soon experience a temperature more like 212 degs., which is boiling point. But before dismissing the question of lamps I must say one thing. A large and valuable portion of the Report of the Committee which sat so long on this question, and which included the two honourable Members who have put this Bill before the House, contained recommendations as to what this House should do in the way of legislation in regard to lamps, and that ought, no doubt, to be discussed and considered at the same time that legislation on the other part of the subject is undertaken. That part of the recommendations in the Report of the Committee as to what should be done in regard to lamps is conspicuous by its absence from the Bill now before the House. What is the Bill? It is proposed by the Bill to put a last brick in the edifice of the legislation which for some years has passed through the House on the subject, not of lamps, but simply on the question of storing, handling, and transit of oil—oil not ignited at all, but oil that is as cold as it can be—regulating the conditions under which some of the oils at least ought to be put, in order to render them perfectly free from accidental explosion or ignition. This Bill, then, deals only with the question of handling, storage, and transit of oils. In 1871 a Bill was passed, which the honourable Member for Brigg has correctly, though not very clearly, described as fixing 100 degs. Fahrenheit as the temperature under which if oil gave off inflammable vapour it should be subjected to certain regulations. In the Paper attached to this Bill the honourable Member says he wishes to restore the flash point of oil imported into this country to that point. But he did not tell us, as the fact is, that 100 degs. line was to be ascertained by a certain test, which test was set out in the schedule of the Bill. In 1879 that Bill was continued and made perpetual instead of being annual, but it was altered in one important respect. In the intervening eight years it had been found that the open test, as it was called, of 100 degs. was really only equivalent to the close test, the proper scientific test, of 73 degs. The Act of 1879 did not really alter the temperature at which the line was to be drawn, but it substi-

tuted the more accurate test, and it defined the line to be taken on the Fahrenheit scale, by that test, as at 73 degs. Practically that is admitted in the Report of the Committee 73 degs. under the new test was the equivalent of 100 degs. under the old one. This is taken for granted, it is assumed, all through the Report of the Committee, and the evidence of the witnesses is that that was so. The honourable Member himself says in another part of the Paper he has attached to this Bill, that there was an error of 27 degs. in the Bill of 1879, and that his Bill was intended to rectify that error and to put it right. What the Bill of 1879 enacted was— that all oils which give off a vapour under 73 degs. Fahrenheit under the altered test set out in the schedule of the Bill should be subject to the specific regulations of the Act of 1871. If the honourable Member does not admit that this was the equivalent of the 100 degs. by the open test, I shall venture to ask him why he did not produce the evidence of witnesses to show that it was not so. Evidently he could not, but I take his own admission in this Report in support of my argument. Now, that being so, I want to know the *raison d'être* of this Bill. Is it to go back, is it to ask the House to go back from the legislation of 1879 and restore the legislation of 1871, which is admitted to be defective. What can be the reason of this? Is it to be assumed that the House was less wise in 1879 than it was in 1871? There is nothing in the Report of the Committee to show that we were more ignorant after the large amount of experience which the intervening eight years had given us. Why are we asked in this House in 1899 to repeal the Bill of 1879, which simply corrected a mistake in the Bill of 1871? I hope I shall be able to show the House that there is another reason for introducing the present Bill besides that alleged of rectifying the so-called error in the Bill of 1879. What is the trade in oil in this country? It amounts to 160 million gallons per annum, of which 30 million gallons are below the flash point of 73 degs., and 34 million gallons with a flash point of above 100 degs. For the sake of round figures I shall call them each 30 millions; that is, 60 million gallons are outside the limits of the argument which the honourable Member has used to-day. There remains, therefore, 100 millions of gallons of oil which by this Bill would be put under these onerous conditions which now only apply to the 30 million gallons with a flash point under 73 degs., and would still hold free 30 million gallons that are above 100 degs. flash point. Now, I do not want to touch the honourable Member for Camlachie on a spot in which he is a little tender, by calling him a Scotchman.

MR. A. CROSS: No, not at all.

*MR. KIMBER: I do not want to allude to persons from whom these particular oils with different flash points come; but still, some come from above the Tweed. It so happens that nearly all oil which comes from north of the Tweed is above the flash point of 100 degs. You will therefore see that the oil manufacturers north of the Tweed with their oil of 100 degs. have at present to meet in competition 100 million gallons of oil with a flash point between 73 degs. and 100 degs. And if they can induce Parliament to pass this Bill extending the onerous duties and obligations which are now limited to oil of 73 degs. by putting up the flash point to 100 degs. then some or all of the competitors with these northern traders would be handicapped. The honourable Member did not state it as clearly as that. It was not his business to do so, and I have no fault whatever to find with him for not doing so. He laboured hard to show that it would make no difference in the price. That is the old argument of the protectionist. It is an axiom in trade that duties of any kind, not only pecuniary duties but special obligations, licences, conditions of storage in premises or in transit along the streets—all these mean an increase in price. And it is an axiom in economic language that such duties always fall on the consumer. It is not essentially necessary for me to answer that portion of the honourable Member's argument. It is impossible for this House to consider some of the arguments used by the honourable Member, because the details of facts and figures on which he bases them cannot be tested here. He says his statements can

Mr. Kimber.

be relied on, but whether they can be relied on or not, they are subject to so much controversy and open to so much scientific observation that little consideration can be given to them here. It is sufficient for me to show that his competitors in trade will be seriously handicapped to his advantage. The honourable Member produced to us from the other side of the Atlantic an allegation that oil at a high flash point can be produced without increased cost; and he asked us to accept that as gospel. If the high flash can be produced without increased cost, why in Heaven's name is it not done now, when they could take so much more profit and not be subjected to the onerous obligations to which I have referred. The House will see, therefore, that there is evidence that one part of the trade have a very great interest in having the flash point line drawn differently from what it is now. Whether this interest is the prompting motive of the Bill, or whether it is not, it is not for me to say. I do not want to introduce motives. I do not blame these four Scottish Members for the attitude they took up in the Committee, or are taking up in this House. They have a right to be there, and to maintain the interests of their constituents. But, all the same, it is not an unfair observation to note the interesting coincidence that those gentlemen who took so active a part in the discussion of the flash point, and who secured the passing majority of one in a Committee of 15——

HONOURABLE MEMBERS: No, no!

*MR. KIMBER: I am told by a majority of one.

HONOURABLE MEMBERS: No.

*MR. KIMBER: It was, at any rate a very small majority—a majority of one or two—but I need not labour that point. It was a very curious coincidence, that the very four Gentlemen who are so active and persistent in pressing the raising of the line of flash point are the same Gentlemen who come from the localities in which the great interest to which I have alluded lies, and where a large section of the trade would be benefited at the expense of the remainder of the trade.

This is a Protectionist Measure—a Measure in favour of a portion of the trade —whether Russian, or Scotch, or American I am not going to say—but it is a Bill in favour of that portion of the trade which deals in oil of a flash point above 100 degs. and would enter into trade and meet with less competition than before if the Bill passes. Let us see what will be the effect of this Bill on the great public, because the honourable Gentleman who moved the Bill began by claiming that public interest was the virtuous principle of his Bill. The Mover told us it was not until he came to the conclusion that there would be no rise in price that he resolved to move that the flash point should be raised. But I observe that he put a little qualifying adjective into his statement. He did not venture to say that there would be no rise in price, but that there would be no material rise in price. But any rise in price is to handicap the poor.

Mr. RECKITT: When I said there would be no material rise in price, that was when the Committee was sitting. Now I say that there will be no rise in price at all.

*Mr. KIMBER: The honourable Member says that he has now arrived at the conclusion that there will be no rise in price, but the facts are all against him. He does not require to prove what nobody can prove or what would take place in a given set of circumstances. We have, however, the logic of the past to inform us, and I would quote from the Report of the Committee of which the two honourable Members were members. The Report says—and it confirms my statement—that—

"if the stringent restrictions applied to oil under 73 degs. are applied to petroleum under 100 degs. it would practically have the effect of preventing the use of such petroleum for domestic purposes."

Honourable Members: Hear, hear!

*Mr. KIMBER: That is to say, that there would be probably 100,000,000 of gallons which the poor would not be able to use on account of the price being raised.

Honourable Members: No, no!

Mr. KIMBER: Well, we will see. What does the Report say, "The petroleum oil below 100 degs. close test is 78½ per cent. of the total supply." That is the supply which goes to the poor. One of the witnesses before the Committee, Professor Dewar, stated that there were no less than 10,000,000 lamps burning this oil every night in this country, or 4,000,000,000 lamps a year, and that he considered the average number of accidents from these lamps over six years was only 121 per annum.

Mr. RECKITT: In what area did these accidents take place?

*Mr. KIMBER: I am quoting from the Registrar's Returns, which I have not here.

Mr. A. CROSS: These were figures obtained by the Metropolitan Fire Brigade, and they only refer to fatal accidents in the City of London.

*Mr. KIMBER: I will take the honourable Gentleman's correction. On the question of price, what does the Report say? It says at page 12, "It appears that the difference in price at present" —they are reporting a fact, not an opinion—

" the difference in price at present between the ordinary oil of 73 degs. (Abel close test) and that of 100 degs. (Abel close test) is from 2d. to 4d. per gallon, and that there is, practically, no difference in the illuminating properties of the two grades. . . The difference of the prices is largely affected by the locality in which the oil is sold "—

and in a second paragraph, I find—

" gentlemen of great experience in the petroleum trade stated their full belief that the increase of cost would be only 1d. per gallon or less."

But 1d. per gallon means three-quarters of a million of money to the consumers of this country, who surely ought to be considered. The trade, I maintain, are interested in this matter, although the honourable Member himself disclaims the idea that the trade should have any particular benefit. I am in favour of giving the trade every benefit, and that we should not put too many restrictions on the trade by grandmotherly legislation as to lamps and so forth. I do think that as regards one of the first necessaries of life to consumers, restrictions should not be put in the interest of any section of the trade. I think that the facts entitle me to draw the conclusion that this Bill is not a Bill required in the interest of the general public; in fact, that it is a Bill against the interests of the public. It evidently arises from the different interests of the three great sections of the oil trade. Undoubtedly, in the nature of things, the different classes, all with different flash points, have different qualities, and perhaps, appeal to different markets. But it is not for this House to put on to any section of the trade a handicap by which other portions of the trade may be benefited, and by which the price to the large consuming public will be increased. I think I need not trouble the House any further. I have endeavoured to be as brief as possible. I have not gone into details, but have dealt with general principles. I hope I have so stated my case that the House will feel justified in rejecting the Bill; and I move that the Bill be read a second time this day six months.

On the return of Mr. SPEAKER after the usual interval,

MR. WEBSTER: Mr. Speaker, in rising to second the Amendment for the rejection of this Bill, I do so on precisely the same grounds which actuated the honourable Member for Wandsworth—namely, purely and absolutely on public grounds. I have no interest in this trade other than, as a Metropolitan Member, to prevent, as I believe, the invasion of the rights of a large number of my constituents. The honourable Member for the Brigg Division of Lincolnshire, in moving the Second Reading of this Bill, which I venture to say he did, from his point of view, in a statesmanlike way, pointed out that it was undesirable, and I quite agree with him, that we should in any way raise the question as to our feeling towards the inhabitants of the United States, or Russia, or anywhere else. He rather inferred that the agitation against the Bill which he and some of his Friends had brought forward was purely a manufacturers' agitation. He referred to the fact that a great deal of literature had been sent to Members of this House on the subject,

Mr. Kimber.

and I sometimes wish myself that there was not quite so much literature flying about. But upon this question the literature has not been confined to those who are opposing the Measure. This morning I received two documents, one duly signed by the honourable Member for the Brigg Division and a number of his friends, and the other unsigned. I cannot hold the honourable Member for the Brigg Division or any of his friends responsible for an unsigned document. The document says that to raise the flash point would not be to raise the price. The honourable Member for the Camlachie Division of Glasgow said, on the other hand, that it would increase the price by one farthing per gallon, and I find, on referring to the Blue Book, that it is very distinctly stated that it would probably increase the price by 1d., and perhaps 2d., per gallon. Therefore, we have three different statements. I am not going into any controversial question with regard to the Standard Oil Company, or in regard to Russia, but I do think it is unfair for a document like this to be sent to honourable Members. The document commences, " Shall this Trust dictate to the House of Commons?" That is merely clap-trap. The British House of Commons cannot be dictated to by anybody.

*MR. RECKITT: May I ask my honourable Friend whom he attributes the circular to?

MR. WEBSTER: I do not say who sent it. I simply said that the circular was received by me in the ordinary course. I said also that I received one from the honourable Member as well. We will now come to the question whether or not there has been any agitation. From one point of view I will acknowledge that there has been an agitation to some extent. Newspapers, like other people, change their views. I find that on 16th September 1895, in a newspaper, the name of which I will afterwards announce, it was stated that two more inquests had been held on persons who had been killed by lamp explosions. The newspaper I am referring to was the " Star," and this paper said that it was stated at the inquest that the particular kind of lamp which caused these deaths had been the cause of 300 deaths during the past 12 months. Although the "Star" then acknowledged that the explosions were caused by the bad lamps used, they have since started a low flash campaign. This question is one which affects London very considerably. I will not challenge the accuracy of the figures quoted by the honourable Member as to the number of deaths which have occurred from lamp explosions in London, but I should like to say that the amount of petroleum oil used in manufactures in London is very great. I find, in Appendix No. 1 of the Blue Book, that there are no less than 41 manufactures carried on by means of petroleum. These manufacturers are licensed by the London County Council, and employ a vast number of working men. If the honourable Member succeeded in raising the price of petroleum by even a halfpenny per gallon, it would do considerable injury to many trades in the Metropolis.

*Mr. RECKITT: May I point out to the honourable Member that the Bill does not affect the oil used in manufactures?

Mr. WEBSTER: I am aware that it does not affect that oil to so great an extent, but, at the same time, there is no proposal in the Bill to deal with oil used in manufactures. You cannot prevent oil being used in these manufactures with the lowest flash point. Therefore, your Bill will be absolutely nugatory in those manufactures. In the majority of lamp accidents the explosion is caused by the imperfect kind of lamp used by the working classes— I know that is a fact, for I have served on the Fire Brigade Committee—but there is no provision in this Bill dealing with the manufacture of lamps. The Legislature insists on safety lamps in mines, but ignores the class of lamp used in the poorest dwelling. One of my objections to the Measure is that it does not go far enough. I think the House should wait till they see the Measure which will be brought forward on behalf of the Government by the right honourable Gentleman the Member for Birmingham. The argument drawn from the statistics of accidents caused by petroleum lamps is a mawkish piece of sentimentality. According to the Report of the Registrar-General, the total number of deaths from accidents

from paraffin lamps for the six years from 1888 to 1894 was 736—or an average of 122 each year—whereas in the same period, 4,085 persons met their deaths by falling downstairs. Is the Legislature, therefore, to insist that only one-storey houses should be built, or to prevent people crossing the road at Piccadilly or Charing Cross because a certain number of people lose their lives at those crossings? The honourable Member for the Camlachie Division of Glasgow acknowledged that London was really the open market for this oil. I understand that about 116,000,000 gallons of oil come into this country annually from the United States, whereas only 23,800,000 gallons come from Russia. If the Bill passes into law, there is no doubt that it will divert a great deal of trade that now comes from the United States to the United Kingdom into other channels. I speak with some amount of reserve on this question, because, as a Scotchman, I should not like to do anything to injure a Scottish interest. But I do think the composition of the Committee was one of the most astounding features in the case. I find that on the crucial point as to whether the flash point should be raised from 73 degs. Abel test to 100 degs. Fahr., eight Members voted on one side, and six on the other. The whole of the six represented large urban constituencies in England, while of the majority who carried the resolution four represented districts round Glasgow, where the shale oil industry is carried on. The President of the Committee did not vote, but if he had voted I dare say he would have voted with the minority. The Bill only deals with one recommendation of the Committee, and leaves untouched the question of cheap glass lamps, which are such a frightful source of danger. A vast number of the lamps used by the working classes are very badly manufactured, and I hope that when the Government bring in their Measure they will make provisions for stamping lamps in the way suggested by the Committee. The real object of the Bill now before the House is to encourage the Russian and Scotch oil industries as against the American, and it will make it more difficult and costly for the working man to get an adequate light in his house

2 M

in the evening. Sir Henry Roscoe, while strongly advocating the raising of the present flash point of 73 degs. Abel test for the purpose of storing and handling, is equally strong in his opinion that there should be no prohibition of the use for illuminating purposes of petroleum of low flash point. He says—

" It is, in my opinion, perfectly impossible to legislate to the effect that nobody shall burn a low flash illuminant of any kind, which has a flash point below a certain temperature. For instance, in the streets they burn ordinary naphtha."

Sir Frederick Abel and Mr. Redwood have expressed it as their conviction that the chief danger is in the lamp, and the " Daily News" of 21st September 1886 stated that—

" A lamp containing an oil of high flash power is more liable to become heated than if it contained a comparatively light and volatile oil, in consequence of the much higher temperature developed by the combination, and of the comparative slowness with which the oil is conveyed by the wick to the flame."

I notice with some astonishment that reference has not been made to one of the most important witnesses that the Committee had before them, but who, I am sorry to say, has since passed away. I allude to Col. Sir Vivian Dering Majendie, K.C.B. What did Sir Vivian Dering Majendie say? The Member for Bristol (Sir Edward Hill) put the following question to him—

" May I take it that in your opinion there is not sufficient evidence to cause us to believe that a reduction of the flash point would, at any rate to any very large extent, obviate the accidents enumerated?"

And Sir V. D. Majendie replied—

" The effect of the evidence upon my mind is that that is not the most effective way of approaching the prevention of lamp accidents. Nobody can doubt, I think, that to reduce the flash point would lead to a reduction in the number of accidents; I venture to think that the gain would not be commensurate with the disadvantages which would attend the raising of the flash point."

The honourable Member for Bristol then asked him—

" And I take it that in your opinion a statutory prohibition of the sale of oil, say, at the present flash point, would be attended with inconvenience to sundry industries."

Mr. Webster.

The reply which Sir V. D. Majendie gave to that question was as follows—

" You could not prohibit it, the sale of oil, below a certain flash point, altogether, because there are a great many industries which are absolutely dependent upon a low flash oil."

Sir V. D. Majendie also said he did not see how the use of lower flash point oil could be prevented in lamps. He said that Parliament might lay down that it should not be sold for use in lamps, but he did not see how they were to prevent anybody who had got a low flash oil from using it for any purpose he liked. Unfortunately that distinguished and absolutely impartial witness, who gave this evidence on Friday, 22nd April 1898, and who was to have been re-examined on the following Wednesday, passed away in the meantime. His evidence is evidence which the honourable Member who moved the Second Reading of this Bill will have some difficulty in getting over. I have touched on the question from a Metropolitan point of view and from a scientific point of view, but let me now ask the House of Commons to consider how this Bill will be regarded in the United States if we pass it. We are not entitled to inflict injury upon a nation which at the present time is becoming more and more friendly towards us. As I have already said, if this Bill has any *raison d'être* it is to encourage the Russian oil industry and the Scotch oil industry against American. It will harass trade and commerce, and will put up the price of oil one half-penny per gallon, and make it more difficult for working men to have an adequate light in their homes. Honourable Members laugh, but I ask, Has not the working man as much right as anyone to have a good light in his home?

AN HONOURABLE MEMBER: The flash point is 100 degs. in some of the States of America.

MR. WEBSTER: I believe that is so; but let us look at Germany. There is no country in Europe in which so much is being done for the working classes as in Germany. They have an old age pension scheme, which we do not possess, but their flash point is as low as 70 degs. The class of lamps sold in Germany is better than the rubbish sold here, and I hope that in the Government Bill something will be done to improve the class of lamp which is allowed to be sold in this country. I have much pleasure in seconding the Amendment which has been moved by the honourable Member for Wandsworth.

MR. TULLY (Leitrim, S.): I rise to support the Bill brought in by the honourable Member for the Brigg Division of Lincolnshire. I think the speech we have just listened to is characteristic of what I will describe as the moderate knowledge on this subject, which exists not only amongst the public but also amongst Members of this House. He has stated that the effect of this Bill will be to prohibit all oil being brought into this country which is under 100 degs. flash point.

MR. WEBSTER: I did not say prohibit. I said discourage.

MR. TULLY: The honourable Member said it would prevent oil under 100 degs. being burned by the working classes. That is not the case. The effect of the Bill will be to cause oil under 100 degs. flash point to be placed under the same restrictions as oil which is now under 73 degs. flash point. At present there is a large amount of oil imported into this country under 73 degs. flash point, which is used in manufactures and in naphtha lamps. The raising of the flash point to 100 degs. will not prevent oil being brought into this country under 100 degs., or prevent the use of the lower standard oil in manufactures, or by the working classes. The effect of this Bill will be to enlighten the people as to the dangers of burning oil under 100 degs. flash point. The honourable Member who spoke last has referred to the petitions which have been signed extensively by retail dealers in the oil trade against this particular Bill. Many of the traders in my own constituency have signed these petitions and forwarded them to me, but when I asked them if they really understood the question they replied that they did not. They simply signed these petitions because they were in the position of tied houses. They had either to sign the petitions or were threatened by the Anglo-American Oil Company that they would not get their usual supply of oil. I do not attach any im-

portance to petitions secured in that manner. It has been said that this is a question of Scotch oil against American oil, and that no one spoke in favour of raising the flash point except Members who represent constituencies above the Tweed. I know very little about Scotch oil, but I think anybody who has burned Scotch oil and has experienced its fumes will not be likely to use it again. The question of Scotch oil as against the oil that is brought from all the rest of the world is really a very small one, because the output of Scotch oil is comparatively trifling as compared with the output of oil from America and Russia. I speak as the only Irish Member who sat on this Committee. I have no interest in Scotch oil. I am a large consumer of oil in a particular industry which I carry on, and would be affected by an increase in the price. But what concerns me is the number of accidents that have occurred in my own part of the country from the use of this dangerous American oil. It was I who first raised this question. I was instrumental in getting this Committee appointed, because, within a short distance of where I live, there had been an explosion of paraffin oil at a public rejoicing, by which two boys were burned to death and 14 others were roasted. Honourable Members laugh, but I cannot see where the joke comes in. American oil is nothing else than murder oil. In New York and Brooklyn there were so many persons burned to death by explosions of this murder oil that the American Legislature, in spite of the great influences opposed to the proposal, passed laws prohibiting the sale of any oil under 100 degs. flash point in New York and Brooklyn. The very oil which Mr. Rockefeller's Standard Oil Trust cannot sell in the States of New York and Brooklyn is imported into this country, with the effect that it burns and roasts to death our friends and our own people. That is one of the reasons why I take my stand in supporting this Bill. One honourable Member said the effect of the Bill would be to raise the price of oil by one penny per gallon, which would mean a total increase in the price of this oil of three-quarters of a million sterling. Well, even if it would—and I deny that it would—it would be a very cheap price to pay for the safety of the public. Anybody who reads the frightful list of deaths caused by explosions of this oil will, I am sure, feel himself bound to support a Bill which would prevent this murder oil, which is not allowed to be sold in New York and Brooklyn, from being imported into this country. Lord Kelvin, one of the highest authorities on this subject, is of opinion that the sale of oil for illuminating purposes of a flash point lower than 130 degs. open test '(equal to 103 degs. Abel close test) should be prohibited by law unless there are thoroughly practical reasons to the contrary. He believes that this would greatly diminish the number of lamp accidents, though he is of opinion that 103 degs. is not a safe minimum, and that 120 degs. Abel would not be too high if practicable. Mr. Spencer contends that, though carelessness and neglect are contributory causes, yet lamp accidents are mainly due to burning oil of comparatively low flash point in lamps of unsafe construction. As soon as the American Legislature raised the flash point to 100 degs. the fires in Brooklyn and New York disappeared, and the percentage of deaths from this cause went down as low as the percentage in the city of Glasgow, where they use a safe oil—namely, Scotch oil This fact alone makes a sufficient case why this House should pass this Bill. We have been told that the passing of the Bill would increase the price of oil. I am able to controvert that from the information I obtained on the Committee, and from the answers I obtained to the questions put to the expert witnesses who came before us. I asked one of the American witnesses what the price of the oil was in New York and Brooklyn before the flash point was increased, and what it had been since, but I could get no answer. Another American witness who came up gave us most elaborate statistics, with the object of showing that we should raise the price if we raised the flash point, but when I asked him the same question which I put to the other witness he was in the same state of ignorance, and said that that was not in his department. I take it, from the way in which they evaded the question, that there has been no increase at all, and that this oil is sold at the same price as it was before the flash point was increased to a safe figure.

Mr. Tully.

I remember, when I first called attention to this matter, being informed by a gentleman engaged in the oil trade that a ship load of oil was allowed to leave New York for Ireland without being sufficiently tested. It landed in Ireland, and around a small circle in the West of Ireland there were a number of explosions and deaths in an incredibly short time, all of which were traced to this oil. The lives and the safety of the public of this country should not depend on such indifferent supervision on the part of the American authorities, but we should insist that the oil which is allowed to come into this country should be raised to a flash point of 100 degs. It is quite true that a man may use naphtha for purposes of business, but if we raise the flash point of oil we prevent people having more than a small quantity at a time. We do not keep out 73 degs. flashing point oil altogether. The public and the oil dealers will have to choose, if this Bill passes, whether they will sell oil which will be subject to these restrictions, or sell oil at 100 degs. flash point, which will not be subject to these restrictions. By an extra distillation America can produce a safe oil. I deny that by raising the flash point we shall increase the price of oil. Competition will insure that the price is not raised. I think it is the duty of the Members of this House to support the Bill, in order to safeguard the lives of the people of this country.

*Sir E. HILL (Bristol, S.): I venture briefly to address the House on the Bill now under discussion—firstly, because I have the honour to represent one of the Divisions of Bristol, a city which occupies no less than the third place of importance in connection with the Petroleum Trade, importing 381,343 barrels of petroleum every year; and, secondly, because I was a member of the Petroleum Committee, which sat for four years, giving the subject exhaustive and careful attention. Sir, I took my seat upon that Committee with a thoroughly open mind. I had no knowledge of petroleum except that which may be gained by a fairly considerable household use. I had no interest in American, Russian, or Scotch oils to bias my votes either way. I was naturally most desirous of ascertaining the cause of accidents, and of discovering in what way they might be prevented or seriously reduced. At the same time, I was strongly impressed with the fact that petroleum was the poor man's illuminant—brightening his home where the expensive gloom of a candle had previously prevailed, and enabling his long winter hours of leisure to be agreeably and profitably employed—and that, therefore, nothing must be done which would tend to make his illuminant dearer, unless very strong reasons could be shown for such an interference. Sir, I do not hesitate to express my opinion that the Bill now before the House possesses two defects, each one of sufficient importance to justify its rejection. In the first place, it would fail to eliminate or even seriously to reduce accidents; and, secondly, it would cause great inconvenience to the trade and to private individuals, which would certainly raise the price. The Bill seeks to raise the flash point from 73 degs. Abel close test to 100 degs. Abel close test. By so doing, all oil below 100 degs. would be placed upon the same footing as oil under 73 degs. is at present, i.e., it would be deemed spirit, and subject to the very needful regulations as to storage for spirit now in force. And here I cannot help expressing my astonishment at the suggestion made by the promoters of the Bill in the explanatory Memorandum, that to raise the flash point as proposed would only be reverting to the original point of 100 degs. The flash point of 1871 was ascertained by what was called the "open test," which was soon found to be inaccurate. Sir Frederick Abel invented a more accurate test, which has been received all over the world as practically accurate, and is called the "Abel close test." When this test was applied to the flash point of 1871 it was found that the 100 degs. open test was only equal to 73 degs. Abel close test. All that was done in 1879 was to call the flash point of 1871 by its proper name— 73 degs. Abel close test. If to raise the flash point to 100 degs., as the Bill proposes, or even higher, would mean an immunity from accidents, I should then feel that it would become a subject of grave consideration whether the inconvenience and cost would practically admit of its being done. But I could not come to such a conclusion from the evidence given before the Committee. Lord Kelvin stated that he deemed 103 degs. dangerous, and named 120 degs. or 130 degs. as the flash point, if practicable. Considering the accidents that have happened with high flash oil it seems impossible for a moment to contend that low flash oil can be deemed responsible for all accidents. And this is the opinion of most of the eminent men who gave evidence. Sir Frederick Abel, Professor Dewar, Mr. Redwood, and Mr. Spencer saw no practical advantage in altering the flash point from 73 degs., and Sir Vivian Dering Majendie, K.C.B., whose sad death we all deplore, did not recommend any alteration, and I know was of opinion that safety must be sought in other directions, especially in the direction of lamps, of which the Bill takes no notice. If honourable Members will make an experiment for themselves, by saturating a cloth with 73 degs. flash point oil, and another with 100 degs. flash point oil, and will apply a light to each, they will find that while in theory 73 degs. flash point oil should ignite quicker than 100 degs, flash point, there is practically no appreciable difference. All illuminants in careless or dissipated hands are dangerous, and although I believe proper supervision of lamps (not contemplated in this Bill) would do much good, if a lamp upset with oil heated far beyond any flash point suggested, be brought into contact with fire, ignition must take place, whatever may have been the original flash point. If we turn to foreign countries we find that in Holland, Belgium, Sweden, and Italy the flash point is 72 degs.; Germany, with its paternal Government, is satisfied with a flash point of 70 degs.; in China and Japan, with their inflammable wooden houses, it is only 70 degs. to 72 degs.; while in India, where the thermometer often stands from 100 degs. to 110 degs., and sometimes even 120 degs., the flash point is only from 70 degs. to 72 degs. It appears from Returns, which arrived too late for the use of the Committee, that in America the flash point is from 63 degs. to 73 degs. in 11 States, from 73 degs. to 100 degs. in seven, over 100 degs. in four, while in 10 States there are no regulations at all. In face of these facts, it is difficult for the House to come to a conclusion that the mere altering of the flash point will make any appreciable difference whatever in the number of accidents. Then, Sir, as to the inconvenience of the raising of the price of the oil. I had the honour of introducing to my right honourable Friend the Under Secretary for the Home Department a deputation which, with one exception, represented the whole of the distributing trade in Bristol, the West of England, and South Wales. These gentlemen, who had been engaged in the trade since its commencement, and whose opinion ought to be considered valuable, were loud in their condemnation of this Bill as needless and useless, and one which would certainly increase the cost. I have had a very large number of signatures from retail traders all in the same sense. I am aware that this controversy has assumed somewhat of a national aspect, and efforts have been made to excite the public by sensational leaflets, pamphlets, and newspaper articles against what is styled "Murder Oil." But such literature only serves to fill the waste-paper basket, and can have no effect upon those who give the matter calm consideration, and attach the importance they deserve to the opinions of the great authorities I have named. Sir, it is because I believe that the raising of the flash point from 73 degs. is not needful nor desirable for the prevention of accidents, because I believe great and needless disturbance would arise to an important trade (by means of which 10,000,000 lamps are lighted every night), because I do not wish to see the poor man's illuminant needlessly raised in price for the benefit of a comparatively small section, and because I rely upon a Bill being brought in by Her Majesty's Government which will deal comprehensively with the whole subject, that I shall vote against this Bill.

*Mr. URE (Linlithgow): Sir, no one who, like the right honourable Gentleman opposite, or like myself, has tried his hand at a Report, gathering up the conclusions to be drawn, and marshalling the evidence in support of them, will be likely to underrate the difficulties connected with the questions involved in this discussion. But I think

Sir E. Hill.

it is possible to extract from its 1,200 pages of evidence the salient facts upon which the House must rest its conclusion, and to trace with some confidence the path upon which legislation, to be successful, must necessarily proceed. The frequency of accidents arising from lamp explosions was the main point which induced the House to appoint the Petroleum Committee. Everyone will agree that, if practicable, the House should take some means to prevent the deplorable loss of life arising from these accidents. This could be done by either preventing the light being brought into contact with the inflammable vapour arising from the oil—by means of a proper lamp, carefully attended to and kept in proper order; or by preventing the creation of the inflammable vapour altogether—by ensuring that oil in the lamp could not be brought to that temperature at which it would give out this inflammable vapour. One guards against the danger; the other removes the danger altogether. The latter is the method of the Bill. The Under Secretary for the Home Department has characterised as "inaccurate and misleading" the Memorandum of the Bill. I acknowledge responsibility for the substance and form of that Memorandum, and I hope to be able to demonstrate to the House that its accuracy is unimpeachable. I stand by every line and syllable in the Memorandum. The Memorandum sets out that the object of the Bill is to give effect to the intentions of the Legislature as expressed in the very Act of Parliament passed with regard to petroleum except the last; and to cure the blunder which is to be found in the last Act of Parliament. I think that accurately summarises the language of the Memorandum. The demonstration of its accuracy is easy, and, happily, can be made within a brief compass. Our first attempt at legislation was in 1862, when we laid restrictions upon all petroleum which gives off an inflammable temperature under 100 degs. Fahr. Did Parliament intend what it said when it imposed that restriction? No mode of ascertaining the flash point is laid down in the Act; but it is an incontrovertible proposition that there were methods known and in constant use by which it was possible to ascertain the flash point of oil with as great certainty as can be done to-day by the method prescribed in the statute of 1879. It is certain that in the hands of intelligent and honest operators this method ascertained with scientific accuracy the flash point of oil, and it is equally certain that the man who then advised the Government was in the habit of constantly using a test by which the flash point could be ascertained with as much certainty as by the Abel test. Now did Parliament mean 100 degs. or some other temperature? Was it intended to prescribe an inaccurate and misleading method dishonestly applied? No, Parliament meant what it said, that the flash point should be ascertained by the best known methods then in use, honestly and intelligently applied. The reasoning upon which the Act of 1862 proceeded was that the temperature in the lamp would never, under ordinary conditions, reach 100 degs., and that, therefore, that limit might safely be fixed. The condition of oil in a lamp is the condition of oil in a close space, and not an open space. The conclusion is inevitable. Parliament meant what it said when it laid down that 100 degs. should be the flash point. I now pass to the statute of 1868, which prescribed a method of testing. At that time no one suggested that the flash point was too high, or that the temperature of oil in the reservoir of a lamp under ordinary conditions did not reach nearly 100 degs. When the Bill was brought before Parliament the flash point was 110 degs. The Government of the day took the advice of three chemists, and, on their report, they fixed the flash point at 100 degs. They further prescribed a test, and insisted that it should be rigidly adhered to. It was in constant use for a long period of years, and was known to ascertain the flash point with very great accuracy. Undoubtedly, when the three chemists' fixed upon 100 degs., they really intended what they said. Subsequently, I admit, an open test was substituted, but it turned out to be fallacious and misleading. The question is, did Parliament intend that the flash point should be lowered to 73 degs.? The right honourable Baronet the Member for Manchester, N.E., who, as repre-

senting the Government of the day, was responsible for the insertion of the new test, surely will not say that he intended that the flash point should fall something short of 100 degs., for when he remitted the question to Sir Frederick Abel, he straightly enjoined him not to give way on any question affecting the efficiency of the test. Sir Frederick, when before the Committee in 1896, was asked questions with regard to the test which was substituted for the three chemists' tests. The question was put to him whether the substituted test was a more satisfactory one, and he replied that it yielded a more generally satisfactory result. In answer to further questions, he said he made experiments for the purpose of ascertaining the difference between the results arrived at, and in the end he came to the conclusion that the test prescribed by the Act of 1868 was the more reliable. After that, I venture to assert that Sir Frederick Abel, when he substituted the open for the chemists' test, thought it at the time a better, more reliable, and more accurate test, and it is now certain that the Parliament and Government of the day, together with their chief adviser, intended, whatever else they might have done, to fix the flash point at 100 degs., and nothing short of it. Then we come to the Act of 1871, which, while repealing all prior legislation, re-enacted the main provisions, and retained the open test in the schedule of the Act of 1868. Will the right honourable Gentleman say that when the Act of 1871 was passed Parliament intended to lower the flash point to something less than 100 degs. It is impossible to say that, and for this reason. In 1871, the discovery had not been made that the open test substituted by Sir Frederick Abel was an inaccurate and misleading test. As the right honourable Gentleman knows, it was not till July 1875, four years after the Act of 1871 was passed, that a letter was writen to Sir Frederick Abel, asking him to make full inquiry into this question of tests, so that for four years, at any rate, after 1871, the Government had not their eyes open to the fact that a blunder had been made in 1868. And it was not until August 1876, when Sir Frederick Abel's Report was issued, that everyone knew that the test which had been inserted in the 1868 Act, and re-enacted in the 1871 Act, was fallacious, misleading, and inaccurate, and that the public safety had been sacrificed. If I am right in this, and I know of no flaw in the argument, I think the right honourable Gentleman opposite will agree with me in the statement that the Memorandum of the Bill is rigidly accurate, and that this Short Bill is intended simply to correct a mistake, and to give effect to the intentions of the Legislature as expressed in all these Acts of Parliament. I come last to the Act of 1879. By that time an accurate, scientific test was known to all the world; and in that Act a correct test was substituted for that which had been discovered to be an erroneous test. If that had been all, and ordinary minds thinking in the ordinary way would say that that was all that should have been done, there would have been no Petroleum Committee, no vast mass of evidence collected, and no discussion to-day upon this Bill. And, what is more to the purpose, we should not, I believe, have had to deplore the long list of fatal accidents and serious injuries which have had to be chronicled during these intervening years. The Act of 1879, however, not only corrected the test, but it also lowered the flash point. No man, at that date, suggested that 100 degs. was too high a flash point, and everybody agreed that it was the right one How, therefore, it came about that, having corrected the test, you should have lowered the flash point by exactly 27 degs., has never yet been explained, and no one ever made the smallest attempt to defend the Act of Parliament. It was wrong-headed in the extreme, or perhaps I should say heedless in the extreme; there was absolutely no justification for it.

*MR. COLLINGS: Do I understand the honourable Member to say that the flash point was lowered in 1879 by 27 degs.?

Mr. Ure.

*MR. URE: Most undoubtedly.

*MR. COLLINGS: And also in 1868 by 27 degs.?

*MR. URE: Certainly not. The right honourable Gentleman has wholly misunderstood my argument. He very well knows that in the hands of an extremely careful, skilful, and honest operator, the test will yield an exact and accurate flash point, and it was only in the hands of a man who performed it unskillfully, heedlessly, and dishonestly that a lower temperature was declared. In 1879 the gross mistake was made of lowering the flash point 27 degs., contrary altogether to the intention which the Legislature had expressed in all these prior Acts of Parliament. It was exactly as if a man had come every day 27 minutes late for an appointment, had then discovered that his watch was wrong, and that you had given him the correct time, but bid him at the same time to always come 27 minutes behind time. I summarise the petroleum legislation thus. It is divided into three stages. In the first you have a correct flash point, but with no means of finding it out; in the second you have a correct flash point with a wrong means of finding it out, and in the last stage you have a correct means of finding out the wrong flash point. The object of this Bill is to fix a correct flash point with a correct means of finding it out. It is, in other words, to restore a correct flash point and to retain the accurate means of finding it out. The effect of the Act of 1879 has been to exclude altogether from domestic use oil with a flash point under 73 degs., and the supporters of this Bill maintain that the effect of it, if it is passed, will be to exclude from domestic use all oil with a flash point under 100 degs. Such restrictions are put upon oil under 100 degs. as are now imposed upon oil under 73 degs., and exclude it from use for burning in lamps. That, we firmly believe, will be the effect of passing this Bill. I candidly admit it, and if I believed it would not be the effect I say it would not be worth while troubling about the Bill. If the Measure becomes law there will be no oil used with a flash point under 100 degs., and we believe that by this and this only can you secure safe oil for the lamps of the people. That view proceeds upon past experience. We are encouraged further by all the evidence which has been taken before the Committee, and by all the experience which has been gained during the past 30 years. Time is too short, and I do not propose in my speech to deal with any of the expert evidence given before the Select Committee. But by far the most valuable testimony was that of Mr. Alfred Spencer, of the Public Control Office of the City of London, who made certain investigations at the request of the Committee. He made in all 95 experiments with burning lamps in order to ascertain the temperature of the oil in the reservoir after the lamp had been burning for from three to five hours. He used various kinds of oil and various kinds of lamps, including metal with metal wick tubes. Dr. Stevenson McAdam made 66 experiments of a similar kind, giving a total of 161 experiments, and the results may thus be briefly summarised. In 10 cases the oil in the reservoir, after the lamp had been burning from three to five hours, was found to be under 73 degs. That means, in plain language, that out of 161 cases 151, if the flash point were at 73 degs., would have had their oil in a dangerous condition, because the reservoir would be filled with inflammable vapour. Then they found in 13 cases that the oil, after burning for from three to five hours, was above 100 degs., and in each instance the high temperature was explained by the fact that the lamps were of an unusual description, having metal reservoirs and metal wick tubes, which tended to increase the heat. And, what is most important of all, having in view what we are told is to be the proposal of the Government, in 96 cases out of the 161 the oil was found to be above 85 degs. Fahr. In other words, if the flash point were fixed at 85 degs, then in these 96 cases it would have been in a dangerous condition. Indeed, the evidence was overwhelming in favour of raising the flash point to 100 degs. if complete safety were to be attained. And if we

had all been quite satisfied that this would not have resulted in an increase of price to the consumer, we should have unanimously recommended it. It is obvious that the question of price was therefore of first importance. That was not a question which the Petroleum Committee left out of view. We were almost unanimous in thinking that if there was to be no increased cost to the consumer by raising the flash point of oil we would do well to raise it. We might differ with regard to the extent of the benefit, and I readily concede that we did not agree as to the amount of benefit which might be gained. Still, we all thought that if it could be done without increasing the cost to the consumer it would be well to take that preliminary step. Obviously, all the elements which enter into the question of cost are not susceptible of definite ascertainment. But there are, I think, two elements which are susceptible of ascertainment— one, the cost of manufacturing, from the crude, oil with a flash point of 100 degs., and the second, the prospect of disposing of the increased residue so gained. Briefly, but quite accurately stated, the method of raising the flash point is to drive off so much more of the lighter vapour and to retain so much more of the heavier vapour. If you raise the flash point of oil you will have more naphtha and somewhat less of burning oil. The House will, therefore, see that the crux of the case is, would the manufacturers be able to dispose of the naphtha? The increased cost is infinitesimal. We have definite and clear evidence from no fewer than seven witnesses with regard to the cost of manufacture, and the net result was that if the flash point was raised to 100 degs. the cost would be about 1-10th more than the present cost, or about 2 cents per gallon. That was the nett result of the evidence. In addition to that, we had the clearest testimony from those who had actually made experiments, that the oil would be of unimpaired quality and a good burning oil. The nett increase of the cost, assuming that the naphtha was unmarketable, would be something like from $\frac{1}{8}$d. to $\frac{3}{4}$d. per gallon.

But the House will see that we did not propose to rely solely on the evidence of experimentors on this side of the ocean. After all, this is a question which the Americans themselves are best able to solve, and from them we expected to receive the most valuable evidence. At any rate, so thought the Committee, and at an early stage of our deliberations we suggested that American witnesses of skill and experience should be invited to come over and enlighten us upon this question of increased cost. After waiting for a period of three months the long-looked-for witness at length appeared on the 22nd July 1896, in the person of a Mr. Paul Babcock. He was the only witness of practical experience sent by the Americans to give us light upon what turned out to be the most controverted topic of all. It seems well worth our while, therefore, to ascertain what was the nett result of his evidence. He came to us with very high credentials. In answer to a question by the Chairman, he said he appeared before us in the capacity of a willing witness, and he turned out to be a very willing witness indeed. He also said he was a practical refiner, that he was a general manager of the King's Company Oil Works, where 10,000 barrels of crude petroleum are distilled every day of the year, that he was also a member of the Committee of Practical Experts, who were consulted by all the large manufacturing interests, and that he was a director of the Standard Oil Company. He added that he was not a scientist, but he had a practical knowledge of the daily work of oil refiners. He said that he understood that Committee desired to be furnished with prac tical testimony, and that he was there to give it. Now, I think, the House will admit that his credentials were adequate. Let us see how he supported them. In the first place this practical refiner detailed to us at great length an experiment by which he proposed to convert the 73 degs. flash oil, which could not be sent over to this country if this Bill passed, into 100 degs. flash oil. He stated with great circumstantiality the nature of the experiment, and then added that it was a dismal

Mr. Ure.

failure, as any man of practical intelligence could have told him beforehead, and as Mr. Babcock and his manager knew very well before the experiment was made. He made haste to add, after spending fully half an hour of our valuable time in detailing an absolutely useless experiment, that he desired it to be distinctly understood he would never think of making it that way. It was quite obvious to us that there was a deliberate attempt made to throw dust in the eyes of the Committee. I therefore ventured to ask Mr. Paul Babcock if he would be good enough to tell us how he would go to work if he had to raise the flash point to 100 degs. to-morrow. He then explained to us a totally different process which he would at once set into operation. But when I asked him the innocent question what increased cost to the consumer would be entailed, he answered, "I certainly cannot tell you that." Yet that was the only question he had come to us to answer; it was the only question upon which his evidence would be of the smallest value to the Committee. At the end of an absolutely ineffective examination, he wound up with the oracular sentence—

"If the laws of Great Britain should be so altered as to prevent the importation of refined petroleum for illuminating purposes which did not stand 100 degs. Abel flash test, I think the effect on the price would be very great."

There was not a member of the Committee who could not have done as well. I would back the right honourable Gentleman opposite to do a great deal better. This is flabby indeed, compared to the trenchant rhetoric in his famous letter to "The Times" of the 14th July 1898. But rhetoric is somewhat misplaced when devoted to ascertaining the price, the fraction of a penny per gallon which the consumer will be required to pay if the two and a half million barrels of 73 degs. oil which are sent over to this country every year come across as 100 degs. oil. My objection to Mr. Paul Babcock's evidence is that from the beginning to the end of it there is not a single fact, nor a single figure, nor a single incident of his experience which could have enabled the Committee to form any judgment upon that question. I do him, perhaps, injustice when I say that he left the witness chair without throwing some light upon the important controversy that he came to elucidate. There was put into his hands an advertisement which he himself admitted had been circulated by the Anglo-American Oil Company, advertising an oil of Standard Oil Company manufacture. It was not low-flash—it was 104 deg. oil, and it was offered to the public in these alluring terms—

"'White Rose' is the finest grade lamp oil ever produced from petroleum, and is a desirable and valuable substitute for the slightly cheaper, but vastly inferior, oils sold by many dealers. 'White Rose' burns in the ordinary lamps, and affords a flame of great brilliancy and power, and without incrustation of the wick. It is entirely free from objectionable odour, and its fire test is so high as to make it the safest petroleum lamp oil in the world. Explosion is guarded against, and families can burn 'White Rose' oil with the same assurance of safety as they can gas. Its original cost is only a trifle more per gallon than the ordinary grades of lamp oil."

Well, Sir, the House will be anxious to know what, in the opinion of Mr. Paul Babcock, is a comparatively trifling price. I was curious to know, and I ascertained the fact that it was exactly one penny per gallon, so that any member of the public may at any time buy oil at the flash point of 104 degs.—the most pure, most economical, most brilliant in the world—for exactly one penny per gallon above the price of the 73 degs. flash point! That, Sir, speaks volumes. That, Sir, really solves an immense mass of conflicting testimony. Depend upon it, if this is the best the Americans can do there can be no substance in this case presented by the American oil trade in favour of the view that if we raise the price of oil we shall increase the price and deteriorate the quality. A more complete and hopeless breakdown I have never, in all my experience, seen, than this attempt of the Americans to show that an increase in our safety would be accompanied by a deterioration in quality and an increase in price. They themselves did their best; and the House may take it

from me—I have read every syllable of the evidence—that this was the best they could do. If this is their best, we can see how hollow and flimsy their case must necessarily be. Let me say, in conclusion, that I have heard it said in some quarters that this is a Scotch Bill, and that the sole and simple object of this Bill is to give some encouragement to the Scottish oil trade. A greater mistake than that it would be impossible to make. It is a national question. It is a question which affects the lives and limbs of Her Majesty's subjects throughout the whole of these realms; and, if I am to discriminate among the various nationalities which make up the United Kingdom, I would say that Scotland had the least interest of all in this question, because Scotland consumes a smaller proportion of this dangerous oil than any other of the countries composing the United Kingdom. There is an enormous demand in London, more than in any other part of the country, for this dangerous oil. Sir, it is a London question rather than a Scottish question. I heard one honourable Gentleman say it was to benefit the Scottish oil trade, because they would then be able to supply the 100 degs. flash point to the whole of the consumers in the United Kingdom. That honourable Gentleman can hardly be aware that it would tax to the utmost all the refineries in Scotland, and it would very soon exhaust their resources, if they were to supply for a single year the consumption of burning oil required in the City of London alone. We cannot supply the United Kingdom with 100 degs. flash point oil. It was an open secret, I think the right honourable Gentleman will agree with me, if it be a secret at all, that very early we saw that the trade interests were excited about the question which we were investigating. It was quite obvious to him, as it is quite obvious to me, that the American oil industry believed that their interests would be promoted if the flash point were left unchanged; and it was equally plain to us all that the Scottish oil industries believed that their interests would be furthered if the flash point of burning oil

2 N 2

were raised; but I challenge the right honourable Gentleman to point to a single allusion, to a single sentence, in this vast mass of evidence which is calculated to throw a single direct ray of light upon that question which he, in that famous letter to " The Times," said had occupied by far the most prominent place in our inquiry, whilst the question of public safety receded into very modest proportions. On this question I have a perfectly open mind. I have not given any consideration to it. We were assured, Sir, from many sides, that our investigations and deliberations ' were being carefully watched by every country in the civilised world whose people used burning oils in their lamps, and we were further assured that whatever conclusion we came to they would probably accept—that whatever course we adopted they would probably follow. If that be true—and I have no reason, for my part, to doubt it, for nowhere else in the world has so prolonged, so anxious, so minutely detailed an investigation been made—then I venture to express a confident hope that before many years have passed, and, perhaps, as the result of this day's discussion, no civilised country in the world will tolerate by its law the use of unsafe oil in the lamps of its people.

*MR. COLLINGS: Mr. Speaker, I agree with the honourable Member who opened this Debate in his statement that this is a most important question, and I will add to that that I believe there are few questions more important than the one which has been raised by him this afternoon. Now, I must ask the indulgence of the House for a longer time than I should have liked to occupy in replying to the many points which have been raised by honourable Members who are in favour of this Bill. I can, for the second time, congratulate my honourable Friend opposite on the skill with which he has raised the structure of this question on one of the smallest and most obscure bases that can be found. The "Three Chemists" were his invention—the term "Three Chemists" he has again brought forward,

Mr. Ure.

—a matter that happened 30 years ago, as the basis and the reason of all the difficulties we have encountered, and he again asserted that the flash point was then lowered 27 degs. Well, Sir, the term "27 degs." was never invented until 11 years after the period which my honourable Friend has referred to, and how he can apply it to 1868 is difficult to imagine. But, Sir, I think we can let that ancient history alone. I will refer to one or two points which my honourable Friend stated, while they are in my mind. He said that there were trade interests occupying that Committee, and at the same time he took us to task for saying that the public safety had taken a back seat. Well, Sir, no one who reads the proceedings of that Committee can come to any other conclusion than that, from first to last, it was a Committee which was mainly an arena of trade interests. When we consider the thousands and tens of thousands of pounds which were spent in sending men from the Black Sea, St. Petersburg, Scotland, from America, all supporting their various interests—if that were all done because certain poor people met with lamp accidents, then philanthropy has got to a higher pitch than I thought it had. There was one other matter the honourable Member stated—that we cannot find a remedy for the present state of things through dealing with the lamps. Well, Sir, we had but one point, I think, upon which the witnesses, without exception, were unanimous, and that one point was as to the lamps. I believe it was the only point upon which those who gave evidence had anything in common. Another point he made was that you can remove the existence of accidents by removing inflammable vapours from the lamps. Now here comes in my complaint respecting this Memorandum. A Memorandum outside a Bill is of the utmost importance to inform those who may not be acquainted with the technicalities of the subject and the wording employed, but there is one condition to its usefulness, and that is, it should be correct. I am going to sustain what I say—that it is absolutely incorrect in this instance. The honourable Member says: Remove the cause of accident by removing the inflammable vapour. Well, Sir, he forgot that every lamp is filled with either air or vapour, and that all vapour is inflammable. Now, this Memorandum states that the flash point of petroleum is the lowest temperature at which it begins to give off inflammable vapour. That is absolutely incorrect. Every kind of petroleum, whatever the flash point, whether it be zero or it be 200 degs., is ever giving off vapour, and to give the idea to the public or to the House that that is the meaning of the flash point is to mislead. The flash point is not the lowest point at which it gives off vapour, as the Memorandum says.

SEVERAL HONOURABLE MEMBERS: Inflammable vapour.

*MR. COLLINGS: All vapour is inflammable. There is vapour given off from water (" Oh! oh!" and laughter). What I mean to say is that all vapour given off by petroleum——

AN HONOURABLE MEMBER: No!

*MR. COLLINGS: I used the word petroleum—is inflammable. Therefore, what is meant really by the flash point is, when you heat the oil sufficiently that it gives off vapour enough when a light is applied to give forth a flash.

*MR. RECKITT: Might I ask the right honourable Gentleman if he will explain the difference between his statement and that in the Memorandum?

*MR. COLLINGS: The Memorandum says the flash point—I will read it " is the lowest temperature at which it begins to give off inflammable vapour."

SEVERAL HONOURABLE MEMBERS: Hear, hear!

*MR. COLLINGS: That is not the flash point. The flash point means when these inflammable vapours have come to combine, and have increased sufficiently to give a flash when a light is applied to them—a wide difference. Now, Sir, my honourable Friend re-

ferred to the Government Bill, and the Mover of the Second Reading of this Bill took credit to himself that the Government had only decided to bring in the Bill after the fortune of the ballot had enabled him to introduce his Bill. It is nothing of the kind, I can assure him. The Government decided to deal with this question long before even Parliament met, and, in consequence, before he could have given notice to introduce his Bill. Our Bill has long been in preparation, and it is in a forward state. We cannot very well deal with the question in a one-clause Bill. It is an intricate question. It has to do with the lamp itself; it has to do with handling and storing the oil, with the wholesale part of the trade and the retail part of the trade—all questions following one upon another, and inter-dependent; and after the settlement and consideration of these questions we hope to introduce a Bill that shall, and I believe will, settle this very important matter. It will deal with most of the recommendations by the Committee. Those recommendations were passed either unanimously or by very large majorities, with the exception of one. That one was passed by a bare majority, and is the only one dealt with in the Bill before us. Now, the Government cannot, even if they wish, deal in this piecemeal fashion, and to adopt this Bill would be simply to tie their hands and to prevent them from doing what I believe they will do.

AN HONOURABLE MEMBER: Why?

*MR. COLLINGS: Because it is very simple on paper to raise the flash point to 100 degs., but the ramifications of the present law are very great, and it w'u'd upset the whole conditions of the present law. I would ask the House for a moment to consider the article we are dealing with. Years ago, when this petroleum was a luxury for rich people—we may remember it, many of us—its price was 3s. 6d., and 3s., and 2s. 6d. per gallon; but the competition of American petroleum has brought down the price to 6d. and 8d., or whatever the price may be—at any rate, has brought it within the reach of the poorest classes of this country, and it is therefore constantly called the poor man's light. At the time my honourable Friend refers to—namely, 1868—there was a merely insignificant amount imported. I think it was about 5,000,000 gallons; and at the present time it is about 185,000,000 gallons. Now, there is one particular point I wish the House to consider, that of this vast total, this vast quantity of 185,000,000 gallons, the Bill of the honourable Member, if passed, will put no less than 78 per cent. of it out of the market. That is an important consideration. If that Bill passes—and I acknowledge the candour of the honourable Member in admitting that that will be the effect of it—it will put 78 per cent. of oil out of the market, because there is 78 per cent. of it that is under 100 degree flash point. But that is not all. The ordinary petroleum is something between 73 degs. and 75 degs., and that almost entirely is used and burnt by the working classes and the poorer classes of this country. Now, that has been admitted by my honourable Friend to be the object of the Bill. It would not only do that, but it would prevent the trader from using it. There are vast quantities used by railway and other companies, farmers, gardeners, and people in the country. All of them will have their supplies put out of the market, and they will be compelled to buy oil at above 100 degs. flash point. I think the House will agree that this is a vast change, affecting, as it does, the trade and commerce of the country, and the House will agree that this change should not be made without good cause. Now, what are the arguments brought forward in favour of raising the flash point? I believe the one which has had the greatest effect outside the House is the assertion, repeated and repeated, that England has been made the dumping ground of oil that the Americans will not use at home, and which they are unable to export to other countries but ours. If that were the case, I, for one, would not be here opposing this Bill. But it is the very opposite to the fact. The honourable Gentleman who introduced this Bill quoted certain statistics in the Report. He knows well that at the instance of a member of that Com-

Mr. Collings.

mittee I have secured, through the Foreign Office, an official Report from America. I agree that it did not come in time to be used by the Committee, but I think it is important, and copies of it have been sent to each honourable Member who was a member of the Committee. And according to that Report, what do we find? I venture to think that the official Report acquired through the Foreign Office is far more accurate than any other can be. Now we find, first of all, that there are ten States that have no law at all on the subject; they burn anything or use anything, and there is no regulation of any kind. Ten did not reply, but in answer to what the honourable Member said—I think he said there was hardly any State that used the 73 deg. or lower-flash point oil—I find that there are five States that have got 63 degs. as their flash point.

MR. CROSS: By what test?

*MR. COLLINGS: Oh, by the Abel test.

MR. CROSS: Might I say it is that point I desire the right honourable Gentleman to notice; we do not at all agree with him as to the comparisons of the American test and the Abel test.

*MR. COLLINGS: It must be a scientific man who can reduce the figures and get the equivalent from one to another, and the equivalent is given in the Report.

MR. CROSS: May I ask the right honourable Gentleman to explain exactly how it is obtained?

*MR. COLLINGS: I am not a scientific man, and I take it that the honourable Member is not either. Therefore, the best we can do is to submit it to those who are scientific men. There are five States who have the 63 degs. flash point, and seven who have a flash point of 73 degs., six who have various degrees from 73 to 100, and only six States who have a flash point of 100 degs. and above. Then we have abundant evidence to the effect that it is very doubtful to what extent the law is put in operation. For instance, my honourable Friend, I think, opposite, instanced New York State. Yes, but a witness said, there is the 100 flash point law there, but the State has refused to carry it into effect. Besides that he adds—

"With regard to New York, it makes but little difference. There were 350 to 500 fires in the State attributed to petroleum "

So much for America. Go to Australia, Victoria, New Zealand, and most of our Colonies. Go to Germany, who followed our Bill, immediately we had passed it, in 1879, and adopted the Abel test, but thought our flash point was too high and put their flash point no less than 3½ degs. below ours. Germany was followed by Austria, Italy, and most of the countries of Europe, and the Reports practically say that the whole of Europe has nothing up to or above 100 degs., and most of the countries have the 73 degs. flash point, the same flash point as ourselves. If we go to the East: In China the flash point is 70 degs., in Japan the flash point is 71 degs., Switzerland has 73 degs. to 75 degs. And there is our great dependency of India, which I suppose honourable Members will pay some attention to, and which I would like, seeing the right honourable Gentleman the Member for Wolverhampton present, to draw attention to for a moment. I forget the date exactly, but Lord Kimberley, when he was in office, sent out a request that the Indian Government would inquire into the question with a view of stating if there was any necessity for altering the flash point. The Government of India took 15 months or more to make that inquiry, and on the 24th April 1895, they sent their Report to my right honourable Friend, who was then Secretary of State. It contained most interesting reports, which are all published in the Report of the Committee from Bombay, Calcutta, and all parts of India. I will not trouble the House with reading what conclusions are contained in the Report to my right honourable Friend sent by Lord Elgin and the Members of the Government. This is the answer sent by Lord Elgin. After reporting the steps that were taken, he winds up by saying—

"The returns which we have now received show that there have been few lamp accidents,

and that their occurrence does not appear to us to justify the raising of the present legal minimum flash point, and we see no reason for modifying the opinion previously formed by us in regard to this matter."

Well, I think that counts for something, at any rate as far as the experience of other countries goes. It upsets the contention completely that England is made a dumping ground for this oil. The fact is, the quantity imported into these islands, vast as it is, is a mere bagatelle to the quantities consumed in other parts of the world. Now, the second contention is the one of the "Three Chemists" —that there was a test recommended by the "Three Chemists," and that that was intended to be embodied in the Act of 1868, but that in the course of a week from the introduction of the Bill Sir Frederick Abel, after conference with some of the oil trade representatives, altered the test. Well, that is absolutely denied by Sir Frederick Abel. Can my honourable Friend say that Sir Frederick Abel, after having been notified that the Government wanted the test not reduced —can my honourable Friend say that he was got at?

*MR. URE: Certainly not. Sir Frederick Abel said, and believed, that he had substituted a better and more accurate test than the one first proposed in the Bill of 1868.

*MR. COLLINGS: Then it is an error on the part of Sir Frederick Abel. I do not know that a man of Sir Frederick Abel's eminence might not, if he were measuring the distance from the earth to the stars, make an error of a few feet, but to suppose that a scientific man would make an error of 27 degs. in a total of 100 degs., is to put him down to a very low scale as regards ability. And, therefore, I think we must pass that over—that Sir Frederick Abel made a mistake of 27 degs. Now, I pass from that point, because it is absolutely of no importance what took place during 1868. What was done was repeated in 1871 and 1879. If there is an error, the error by admission has existed for 30 years, and there was as much reason for raising the flash point 30 years ago as there is at the present day. Now, Sir, I say that what took place then is of no importance, and I would ask the House, Is it right that a great revolutionary change should be based upon the disputes of two experts, two professional men, which took place 30 years ago over the relative merits of two tests, and over a commodity which at that time very few people knew much about? Now, Sir, we have facts and experience, and they form the best basis of all for legislation —we have the facts and experience arrived at for the last 30 years, not only in Great Britain, but in all the countries of the world. I wish to speak for one moment as to the suddenness of this question of the flash point. The question was never raised till 1891 which gave rise to the appointment of this Committee. During the whole of the time in which Colonel Majendie and Mr. Redwood were preparing a Bill, they came in contact with the whole trade, and with the interests represented by Scottish Members and Irish and English Members, the question of the flash point was never raised at all. I am reluctant to keep the House so long, but there have been many points brought forward. For instance, the honourable Member mentioned the coroners. Well, the chairman of the Coroners' Society of Great Britain gave his evidence, and he said—

"I know nothing at all about flash points. I think the construction of the lamps is the only thing to account for these fatal accidents."

And I think that that disposes of any weight to be placed on the coroners' evidence with regard to the flash point at all. It has also been said that a high test was recommended for the War Office and the lighthouses, but if the honourable Member had read a question or two further on, he would have seen that Sir Frederick Abel distinctly declared that these recommendations had no reference whatever to light, but to storage only.

MR. CROSS: May I ask what the regulations in the lighthouses are?

*MR. COLLINGS: Yes, there is the 120 degs. flash point in lighthouses, but

Mr. Collings.

that did not prevent the terrible accident last year in the Crosby lighthouse, where three people were burnt, though they had seven gallons of oil only to feed five lamps. It did not prevent accidents with Scotch oil, for instance, in my honourable Friend's own constituency, at Broxholme, where there were 11,000 gallons of oil burnt, and one person lost her life—that with the best Scotch oil. That does not mean that that oil is not safe. You may sum it up in this—that all petroleum is safe with ordinary care, and none of it is safe unless ordinary care is used. We have had an interesting speech from an Irish Member. I would beg him to read the evidence of the Irish witnesses. Every one opposed the idea of raising the flash point. Sir Charles Cameron, Officer of Health in Dublin, who was certainly one of the most practical witnesses we had, said that in three years there had been 36 lamp accidents in the metropolitan area of Dublin, with a population of 350,000 persons, and he goes on to say that he should be sorry to interfere. He says—

"It is a great blessing to a poor family to have a good light instead of the miserable candle of olden times."

Honourable Members spoke of Mr. Spencer. Mr. Spencer gave the greatest assistance to the Committee, but they must remember that he carefully guarded himself; he said what is worth my while to quote. He said—

"The experience gained from lamp accidents has brought me to the conclusion that all, or nearly all, would have been impossible with properly constructed lamps." .

Now, I ask the House to consider whether it is the fact that there has been an increase in the number of fatal lamp accidents? Taking the Registrar General's Returns, I find that for the past eight years there have been varying numbers, making an average of 129 per annum, and when you remember that we have 10 millions of lamps burning not only on a single night, but ten millions every night, making 365 times 10 millions of separate lights, I say it is a proof of the great safety of this illuminant when we have such a comparatively small number of fatal accidents. The wonder is, when we read the Committee's Report as to the kind of lamp commonly used, as to the miserable character of these lamps, many of them penny lamps, that instead of 100˙ accidents there are not 100,000. Now, Mr. Speaker, I will not detain the House for more than a few minutes longer, but there is one thing that I want to point out. Are honourable Members convinced in their own minds that these accidents are caused by the low flash? I know there are thrilling stories about "the deadly 73 degs.," and none of us can compute such statements as we have read in the papers. But, Sir, a week or two ago a certain paper was indiscreet enough to give the places and dates where these inquests were held. I thought, "Now, here is an opportunity for investigation," and I wrote to the coroners of each of these places, and they courteously sent me the sworn depositions connected with each one of those accidents. I have them here. I am not going to read them; but this I will say, and say as a matter of certainty, that there is not a single case in all these depositions, and 60 of them I have here out of a total of 120—not a single case in which you can ascribe the accident to the quality of the oil; not one. The majority of them are abundantly explained, I am sorry to say, by drunkenness, violence, and recklessness, but there is not one that bears out this description of "the deadly 73 degs." And these are the misstatements that have been so industriously circulated in order to rouse public feeling! I take up the coroners' depositions. Here is one: "Dropping a lighted lamp." Here is another accident: "A glass lamp carried by a little girl; she fell; a man in the room was drunk, and the child was left helpless." Here was an imbecile girl with a lamp—(some laughter)—I do not know that this is a laughing matter—here was a cheap lamp dropped by the deceased.

Here is another case: "Deceased was lighting the fire by pouring oil upon it, and thereby set herself on fire." Another lamp was upset by a drunken man. Here is another accident caused by a dog, which the people tied to an old ricketty table and then left the house, and the dog, of course, upset the table and so burnt the house. These are the harrowing tales—and so you might go on. They are all of the same kind, except one, and in that I notice that the County Council sent their inspector—it was described as a very bad case—and he reported that the oil which caused the accident was 103 degs. flash. I do not attach any importance to its being 103 degs. If it had been 100 degs., and an accident had happened, it would have been the same, as in the case of Lord Romilly, who sustained two accidents, by the second of which he lost his life, while burning 110 degs. oil. I have no time to deal with the question of cost; but I simply ask honourable Members, as business men, in this House, whether or no you can dislocate a trade to the extent of 78 per cent., whether it be oil or cotton, or anything else, without interfering with the cost of the article? The honourable Members—both of them—have proved too much. The survival of the fittest we all know is an inexorable law in trade, and if this Russian or Scotch oil be so much better than the low flash, be so much cheaper, or as cheap, then it is bound to put the inferior article out of the market. On these grounds, I would ask that this Bill be rejected; but there is another ground. The Government have a Bill to deal with lamps and with the whole question, which we hope to introduce. There can be Amendments moved to it. I have no hesitation in saying that the Bill now before the House would sacrifice the best interests of the working classes of this country, as it would lay a tax on them, not for the benefit of the country, but for the benefit of certain people who are at the bottom of the agitation, in order to create a monopoly for their kind of oil. (Cries of "Withdraw.") I repeat that the object of this agitation is to create a monopoly, and that the tendency of that monopoly would be to increase the price that the poorer classes have to pay for their oil. On these grounds I ask the House to reject the Second Reading of the Bill.

*Mr. GRAY (West Ham, N.): I wish to offer a personal explanation. I find, to my surprise, that my name has been attached to the Whip issued in support of the Second Reading of this Bill this afternoon. Perhaps I may be allowed to make a short statement thereon. When the Bill was first projected I had no knowledge whatever that the Government were at all likely to deal with this question, and I certainly did express my desire to support this Bill. Unfortunately, the honourable Member in charge of the Bill has been absent from the House through illness, and I regret I have been prevented from holding any communication on the subject with the honourable Member from that time to the present. But I can hardly conceive that the statement I made to him on the occasion referred to was a sufficient justification for attaching my name to the Whip without my knowledge. I beg to say this much, because I propose voting against the Bill, in order that, before a final conclusion on the subject is arrived at, I may have the proposals of the Government in my hand. I should have been strongly disposed to have voted for the Second Reading of this Bill had it not been that I do not think it would be right, in view of the fact that we are likely to have proposals of a more wide-reaching character laid before us before the close of this Session on the authority of the Minister responsible for the work, to advance a Bill of a private character on a subject on which there is such diversity of opinion. I thought it only due to myself to offer this short explanation, as otherwise my vote in the Division Lobby would not have been understood.

Mr. Colling.

*Mr. COMPTON RICKETT (Scarborough): It appears to me that the arguments which have been put forward to-day resolve themselves into three classes. First, if we raise the flash point of oil we shall not prevent accidents. Again, if we raise the flash point of oil we shall increase the price of that oil; and, finally we are told that if we raise the flash point we shall be taking a step in a wrong direction—the direction of protection. But I do not think that to interfere with the use, or to put a limitation on the use, of oil could be a greater interference with trade than is a Factory Act. Therefore, I do not think it is necessary to labour that point. One of the strongest arguments advanced by the right honourable Gentleman the Under Secretary for the Home Office had reference to the increased cost which must follow the raising of the flash point to 100 degs. I think he said it would mean withdrawing from the market 78 per cent. of the American oil. But in my opinion that is quite a mistake. We do not withdraw 78 per cent. of American oil; we only induce the American refiner to withdraw a small percentage of that quantity, and he will, of course, place the rest on the market. The American refiner is not likely to lose the British market. The extra cost in refining is very small; there will be no additional cost for transport, and, therefore, the percentage of increase upon the gallon sold to the consumer must be quite infinitesimal. Then, again, the question of refining does not in itself determine the price of the oil. No doubt there would be a fight for the English market on the part of the American oil, but there is a sufficient margin of profit, and a sufficient amount of enterprise amongst American oil refiners to insure that they would not lose the English market. They will undoubtedly place a sufficient amount of oil flashing at 100 degs. to maintain their present position in that market. The important matter of concern is to avoid accidents. We know that accidents are bound to occur. The gentleman who desires to give a hint to his wife will still throw a lamp at her, and the oil will take fire when the lamp is overset; but if there is no vapour there will be no explosion, and ignition will take place much more slowly. There will be fewer accidents, and few fatal ones. This is a matter for compromise. Already we have heard rumours that the Government are prepared to consider a flash point of 85 degs. If they are going to raise the question at all, it is hardly worth while to disturb the trade for the sake of 12 degs. The heat of oil in a burning lamp in this country does not exceed 95 degs., but frequently goes beyond 85 degs. To secure an absolutely safe oil you must reach from 110 to 120 degs. But why not accept the compromise of 100 degs., which gives a practical amount of safety without diminishing the illuminating quality. If the Government are once prepared to give up 73 degs. the sacredness of that standard is gone. We on this side of the House are not desirous of making this a Party question. We have more at heart the interest of the community, and we do urge the Government to reconsider their point and give us some indication that if they cannot accept this Bill they will embody a standard flash of 100 degs. in their own Measure.

MAJOR RASCH (Essex, S.E.): As the representative of an agricultural constituency I am bound to say I think I ought to be allowed to say just half a dozen words, on behalf of the agricultural labourer, upon a question that interests him so much. I am surprised that the honourable Member should bring in a Bill to raise the price and restrict the production of an article so much in use. It is said by honourable Gentlemen on the other side of the House that this Bill will not raise prices, but when we come to understand that something like 70 per cent. of the oils now used in this country would be thrown out of the market, and when we know that the prices have gone up in the North of England, I do not think much attention will be paid to such statements. Now, it really is extraordinary that honourable Gentlemen opposite, who are always accusing this side of the House of bringing in Bills which raise prices and create monopolies, should have brought in such a Bill as this. Some honourable Gentlemen remember, perhaps, the dismal dulness of the agricultural labourers' cottages years ago, before these cheap oils came in. Now, we do not want that state of things to recur, or to compel these poor men to give a larger price. When a Bill is brought in for the purpose of excluding adulterated produce such as milk and so forth, honourable Gentlemen opposite always scent protection, but when they bring in a Bill which raises the price and restricts the production of an article, it is quite another matter. It is the old story, that one man may steal a horse, and another may not look over the hedge. As an agricultural Member, I should like to diagnose these differences, but, in the interests of those whom I represent, I shall certainly vote against the Bill.

MR. TIMOTHY HEALY (Louth, N.): there is just one question which I should like to ask the right honourable Gentleman the First Lord of the Treasury. The Committee which sat to consider this question was formed through a Debate raised by an honourable Member for Scotland in 1896. I was very much interested in the formation of the Committee, and I watched it closely. It was formed on the 19th of March 1896, and consisted of 12 Members. Now, when the House remits a question of this importance to a Committee, it is most important that the jury should not be packed. But in this case a very remarkable thing happened, upon which I shall ask the right honourable Gentleman the First Lord of the Treasury a question. A month after the Committee was appointed—that is to say, in the month of April—the Committee, having been originally constituted of 12 members, two other members were added to the jury. It is said that the Scotch Members had no special interest in the matter, and had no special rights with regard to it, but the two Members who were added were the honourable Member for Linlithgowshire and the honourable Member for Stirlingshire, and I want to know why this preponderance of Scotch Members was placed upon the Committee. These honourable Gentlemen were added to the Committee at the instance of a Scotch Whip. Now, having seen the names of these Gentlemen down for this Committee, I, being anxious to have some explanation of their being added, and knowing it was the practice to take this business at a particular time, immediately after Questions, watched the matter very carefully; but, strange to say, these Gentlemen were added to the Committee immediately after the unopposed business—directly you had done Prayers. Now, is that the way to do a thing of this sort, which is of the greatest interest to millions of people? Now, I received a letter to-day from the Paris house of Rothschild. It is the first time that the Paris house of Rothschild have ever honoured me with a letter. I opened the letter with fear and trembling. I thought perhaps my account was overdrawn, or that perhaps some unusual form of benevo-

lence was about to take place; but nothing of the kind. It was only a notification from this eminent Paris house of Rothschild that they would be enabled to compete with America if this House only passed this Bill. It is unusual to find the House in the temper it is in at the present moment, and it is unusual to see a Minister dealing with a Bill which affects persons of every shade of politics in the country as this Measure is being treated by the honourable Member the Under Secretary for the Home Office. Is all this benevolence? If it is, it is the most oleaginous form of benevolence that I have ever known. And I have come to the conclusion that this is simply a struggle for the coppers of the poor between Rockefeller of New York and Rothschild of Paris, and there is not a pin's point to choose between them. I prefer, in a matter of this kind, affecting the general interests of the country, irrespective of politics, to be guided by the scientists who have the good of the country at heart, and by the Department most immediately concerned in the question, and I think the House of Commons would do far better to follow the efficient guidance that we have had than follow the Paris house of Rothschild.

Question put—

"That the word 'now' stand part of the Question."

The House divided:—Ayes 159; Noes 244.—(Division List No. 43.)

AYES.

Allan, William (Gateshead)	Birrell, Augustine	Cawley, Frederick
Allen, Wm.(Newc.under Lyme)	Blake, Edward	Clough, Walter Owen
Arrol, Sir William	Bond, Edward	Coghill, Douglas Harry
Ashton, Thomas Gair	Bowles,T.Gibson(King's Lyun)	Colville, John
Asquith, Rt. Hn. Herbert H.	Bryce, Rt. Hon. James	Corbett, A. Cameron(Glasgow)
Atherley-Jones, L.	Burns, John	Crombie, John William
Baird, John George Alexander	Burt, Thomas	Cross, Alexander (Glasgow)
Baker, Sir John	Buxton, Sydney Charles	Dalkeith, Earl of
Barlow, John Emmott	Caldwell, James	Dalrymple, Sir Charles
Bartley, George C. T.	Cameron, Sir Charles (Glasgow)	Dalziel, James Henry
Beaumont, Wentworth C. B.	Cameron, Robert (Durham)	Davies, M.Vaughan-(Cardigan)
Begg, Ferdinand Faithfull	Campbell-Bannerman, Sir H.	Denny, Colonel
Bethell, Commander	Carlile, William Walter	Drucker, A.
Billson, Alfred	Causton,Richard Knight	Dunn, Sir William

Mr. Timothy Healy.

Ellis, Thos. Ed. (Merionethsh.)
Farquharson, Dr. Robert
Fenwick, Charles
Ferguson, R. C. Munro (Leith)
Ffrench, Peter
Fitzmaurice Lord Edmond
Foster, Sir Walter (Derby Co.)
Goddard, Daniel Ford
Gold, Charles
Gourley, Sir Edwd. Temperley
Harwood, George
Hatch, Ernest Frederick Geo.
Hayne, Rt. Hon. Charles Seale-
Hazell, Walter
Healy, Maurice (Cork)
Hedderwick, Thomas Chas H.
Hill,Rt.Hn.A.Staveley(Staffs.)
Holden, Sir Angus
Holland, Hn. Lionel R. (Bow)
Hozier, Hn. James Henry Cecil
Humphreys-Owen, Arthur C.
Jacoby, James Alfred
Jones, David Brynmor (S'nsea)
Kay-Shuttleworth,Rt Hn SirU.
Kearley, Hudson E.
Kilbride, Denis
Kinloch, Sir John Geo. Smyth
Kitson, Sir James
Langley, Batty
Leng, Sir John
Lewis, John Herbert
Lloyd-George, David
Lorne, Marquess of
Lough, Thomas
Macaleese, Daniel
MacDonnell,Dr.M.A.(Qn's.Co.)
Maclean, James Mackenzie
MacNeill, John Gordon Swift
M'Arthur, Charles (Liverpool)
M'Arthur, William (Cornwall)
M'Ewan, William

M'Kenna, Reginald
M'Killop, James
Maddison, Fred.
Maden, John Henry
Malcolm, Ian
Marks, Henry Hananel
Mendl, Sigismund Ferdinand
Milbank, Sir Powlett Chas. J.
Molloy, Bernard Charles
Montagu, Sir S. (Whitechapel)
Morley, Charles (Breconshire)
Morrison, Walter
Norton, Capt. Cecil William
Nussey, Thomas Willans
O'Brien, James F. X. (Cork)
O'Connor, T. P. (Liverpool)
Oldroyd, Mark
Palmer, Geo. Wm. (Reading)
Paulton, James Mellor
Philipps, John Wynford
Pickard, Benjamin
Pickersgill, Edward Hare
Pirie, Duncan V.
Priestley, Briggs (Yorks)
Provand, Andrew Dryburgh
Reid, Sir Robert Threshie
Richardson, J. (Durham)
Ricketts, J. Compton
Roberts, John H. (Denbighs.)
Robertson, Edmund (Dundee)
Rothschild, Hon. Lionel Walter
Samuel, Harry S. (Limehouse)
Samuel, J. (Stockton-on-Tees)
Schwann, Charles E.
Scott, Chas. Prestwich (Leigh)
Shaw, Charles Ed. (Stafford)
Sinclair, Capt. J. (Forfarshire)
Sinclair, Louis (Romford)
Smith, Samuel (Flint)
Souttar, Robinson
Spicer, Albert

Stevenson, Francis S.
Stowart, Sir M. J. M'Taggart
Stirling-Maxwell, Sir John M.
Stone, Sir Benjamin
Stuart, James (Shoreditch)
Sullivan, Donal (Westmeath)
Tanner, Charles Kearns
Tennant, Harold John
Tomlinson,Wm.Edw.Murray
Trevelyan, Charles Philips
Tritton, Charles Ernest
Tully, Jasper
Ure, Alexander
Vincent,Col. Sir C.E.Howard
Wallace, Robert (Perth)
Walton,Jno.Lawson(Leeds,S.)
Walton, Joseph (Barnsley)
Warner, Thos. Courtenay T.
Wedderburn, Sir William
Weir, James Galloway
Welby, Lieut.-Col. A. C. E.
Whittaker, Thomas Palmer
Williams, Jno. Carvell (Notts.)
Wills, Sir William Henry
Wilson, Henry J.(York,W.R.)
Wilson, John (Durham, Mid.)
Wilson, John (Govan)
Wilson,J.W.(Worcestersh.,N.)
Wilson, Jos. H. (Middlesbro')
Woodhouse,Sir J.T.(Hud'fd.)
Woods, Samuel
Wylie, Alexander
Wyndham-Quin, Maj. W. H.
Young, Samuel (Cavan, East)
Yoxall, James Henry

TELLERS FOR THE AYES—Mr.
Harold Reckitt and Mr.
Duncombe.

NOES

Abraham,William (Cork, N.E.)
Acland-Hood, Capt. Sir A. F.
Aird, John
Allhusen, Augustus Henry E.
Allison, Robert Andrew
Allsopp, Hon. George
Ambrose, William (Middlesex)
Anstruther, H. T.
Arnold-Forster, Hugh O.
Ascroft, Robert
Atkinson, Rt. Hon. John
Austin, Sir John (Yorkshire)
Bagot, Capt.Josceline FitzRoy
Balfour,Rt.Hn.A.J.(Manch'r)
Balfour,RtHnGeraldW.(Leeds)
Banbury, Frederick George
Barry, Sir Francis T.(Windsor)
Barton, Dunbar Plunket
Bathurst, Hn. Allen Benjamin
Beach,Rt.Hn.SirM.H.(Bristol)
Beach,W.W.Bramston (Hants)
Beckett, Ernest William
Bentinck, Lord Henry C.
Bhownaggree, Sir M. M.
Biddulph, Michael
Bigwood, James
Blundell, Colonel Henry
Bolton, Thomas Dolling

Bonsor, Henry Cosmo Orme
Bousfield, William Robert
Bowles, Capt. H. F.(Middlesex)
Brassey, Albert
Brown, Alexander H.
Butcher, John George
Cavendish, R. F. (N. Lancs.)
Cavendish, V. C W.(Derbysh.)
Cecil, Evelyn (Hertford, East)
Chamberlain, Rt.Hn.J.(Birm.)
Chamberlain, J. Austen (Wor.)
Chaplin, Rt. Hon. Henry
Charrington, Spencer
Clarke, Sir Edwd. (Plymouth)
Cochrane, Hn. Thos. H. A E.
Cohen, Benjamin Louis
Collings, Rt. Hon. Jesse
Cook, Fred. Lucas (Lambeth)
Cooke, W.Radcliffe (Heref'd)
Cotton-Jodrell, Col. Ed. T. D.
Courtney, Rt. Hn Leonard H.
Crilly, Daniel
Cripps, Charles Alfred
Cross, Herb. Shepherd(Bolton)
Cruddas, William Donaldson
Cubitt, Hon. Henry
Curran, Thomas (Sligo, S.)
Currie, Sir Donald

Curzon, Viscount
Dalbiac, Colonel Philip Hugh
Davenport, W. Bromley-
Dickson-Poynder, Sir John P.
Donkin, Richard Sim
Dorington, Sir John Edward
Douglas, Rt. Hon A. Akers-
Doxford, William Theodore
Dyke, Rt Hn.Sir William Hart
Egerton, Hon. A. de Tatton
Elliot, Hon. A. Ralph Douglas
Fardell, Sir T. George
Fergusson,Rt Hn SirJ (Manc'r)
Field,Admiral (Eastbourne)
Field, William (Dublin)
Finch, George H.
Finlay, Sir Robert Bannatyne
Fisher, Sir William Hayes
FitzWygram, General Sir F.
Fletcher, Sir Henry
Flower, Ernest
Folkestone, Viscount
Forster, Henry William
Foster, Colonel (Lancaster)
Fry, Lewis
Galloway, William Johnson
Garfit, William
Gedge, Sydney

Gibbons, J. Lloyd
Gibbs,HnA.G.H.(City of Lond)
Giles, Charles Tyrrell
Gilliat, John Saunders
Godson, Sir Augustus Fredk.
Goldsworthy, Major-General
Gordon, Hon. John Edward
Gorst, Rt. Hn. Sir John Eldon
Goschen, George J. (Sussex)
Goulding, Edward Alfred
Graham, Henry Robert
Gray, Ernest (West Ham)
Green,Walford D. (Wednsbry.)
Greene, Hnry. D) (Shrewsbury)
Gretton, John
Greville, Hon. Ronald
Gull, Sir Cameron
Gunter, Colonel
Halsey, Thomas Fredarick
Hamilton, Rt. Hon. Lord Geo.
Hanbury, Rt. Hn. Robert Wm.
Hanson, Sir Reginald
Hardy, Laurence
Healy, Thomas J. (Wexford)
Healy, Timothy M. (Louth,N.)
Heath, James
Helder, Augustus
Hermon-Hodge, Robt. Trotter
Hill, Sir Edwd. Stock (Bristol)
Hoare, Ed. Brodie (Hampst'd)
Hobhouse, Henry
Hornby, Sir William Henry
Howard, Joseph
Hubbard, Hon. Evelyn
Hudson, George Bickersteth
Hutchinson, Capt. G.W. Grice-
Jackson, Rt. Hn. Wm. Lawies
Jebb, Richard Claverhouse
Jeffreys, Arthur Frederick
Jessel, Capt. Herbert Merton
Johnston, William (Belfast)
Johnstone, Heywood (Sussex)
Jolliffe, Hon. H. George
Kemp, George
Kennaway, Rt.Hn. Sir John H.
Kenyon, James
Kenyon-Slancy, Col. William
King, Sir Henry Seymour
Knowles, Lees
Lafone, Alfred
Lawrence,SirE.Durning-(Corn)
Lawrence, Wm. F. (Liverpool)
Lawson, SirWilfrid(Cumbrlnd.)
Lea, Sir Thos. (Londonderry)
Lees, Sir Elliott (Birkenhead)

Leigh-Bennett, Henry Currie
Leighton, Stanley
Llewellyn, Evan H.(Somerset)
Lockwood, Lt.-Col. A. R.
Long, Col. Chas.W.(Evesham)
Long, Rt. Hn. Walter(L'pool.)
Loyd, Archie Kirkman
Lubbock, Rt. Hon. Sir John
Macartney, W. G. Ellison
Macdona, John Cumming
MacIver, David (Liverpool)
M'Calmont, H. L. B. (Cambs.)
M'Iver, Sir Lewis (Edin., W.)
Maple, Sir John Blundell
Martin, Richard Biddulph
Massey-Mainwaring,Hn.W.F.
Maxwell, Rt.Hon. Sir Herb. E.
Middlemore,Jno.Throgmorton
Mildmay, Francis Bingham
Milward, Colonel Victor
Monk, Charles James
Montagu, Hn. J. Scott (Hants)
Moon, Edward Robert Pacy
More, Robt. Jasper (Shropsh.)
Morrell, George Herbert
Morris, Samuel
Morton,Arthur H.A.(Deptf'd.)
Mount, William George
Murray, Rt.Hon. A. G. (Bute)
Murray, Chas. J. (Coventry)
Murray, Col. Wyndham (Bath)
Myers, William Henry
Newdigate, Francis Alexander
Nicholson, William Graham
Nicol, Donald Ninian
O'Brien, Patrick (Kilkenny)
O'Connor, J. (Wicklow, W.)
O'Neill, Hn. Robert Torrens
Orr-Ewing, Charles Lindsay
Palmer, Sir Chas. M.(Durham)
Parkes, Ebenezer
Pease, Herb. Pike (Darlington)
Percy, Earl
Phillpotts, Captain Arthur
Pilkington, Richard
Platt-Higgins, Frederick
Pollock, Harry Frederick
Pretyman, Ernest George
Priestley,Sir W.Overend(Edin.
Pryce-Jones, Lt.-Col. Edward
Purvis, Robert
Pym, C. Guy
Rankin, Sir James
Rasch, Major Frederic Carne

Rentoul, James Alexander
Richardson,Sir Thos.(Hart'pl.)
Ritchie,Rt.Hn.Chas.Thomson
Robinson, Brooke
Roche, Hn. Jas. (East Kerry)
Royds, Clement Molyneux
Russell,Gen.F.S.(Chelt'ham.)
Russell, T. W. (Tyrone)
Ryder, John Herbert Dudley
Sandys, Lt.-Col. Thos. Myles
Sassoon, Sir Edward Albert
Savory, Sir Joseph
Scoble, Sir Andrew Richard
Scott, Sir S. (Marylebone,W)
Seely, Charles Hilton
Sharpe, William Edward T.
Sidebotham, J. W. (Cheshire)
Simeon, Sir Barrington
Smith, Abel H. (Christchurch)
Smith, Hn. W. F. D. (Strand)
Stanhope, Hon. Philip J.
Stanley,Hn.Arthur(Ormskirk)
Stanley, Edw. Jas.(Somerset)
Stanley, Henry M. (Lambeth)
Stanley, Lord (Lancs.)
Stock, James Henry
Strauss, Arthur
Strutt, Hon. Charles Hedley
Sturt, Hn. Humphry Napier
Talbot, Lord E. (Chichester)
Talbot,Rt.Hn.J.G.(Oxf'd.Univ)
Thorburn, Walter
Thornton, Percy M.
Tollemache, Henry James
Usborne, Thomas
Valentia, Viscount
Walrond, Rt. Hn. Sir Wm. H.
Wanklyn, James Leslie
Ward, Hn. Robt. A. (Crewe)
Warde, Lt.-Col. C. E. (Kent)
Warr, Augustus Frederick
Webster, Sir R. E. (I. of W.)
Whiteley, George (Stockport)
Whitmore, Charles Algernon
Williams, Jos. Powell-(Birm.)
Willox, Sir John Archibald
Wilson-Todd, Wm. H.(Yorks.)
Wortley, Rt. Hn. C. B. Stuart-
Wyndham, George
Wyvill, Marmaduke D'Arcy

TELLERS FOR THE NOES—Mr.
    Kimber and Mr. R. G.
    Webster.

Main Question, as amended, put, and agreed to. Second Reading put off for six months.

TWELVE O'CLOCK RULE.

THE FIRST LORD OF THE TREASURY (Mr. A. J. BALFOUR, Manchester, E.): I beg to move that the House do now adjourn, and in making that Motion I would propose to give formal notice of what I intimated yesterday—that I shall have to ask the House to suspend the Twelve o'clock Rule.

EXPLOSION ON THE TERRIBLE.

*MR. ALLAN (Gateshead): I beg to ask the honourable Gentleman the Secretary to the Admiralty a question, of which I have given him private notice, namely, whether he can state the extent of the loss of life that has occurred on board H.M.S. "Terrible," in consequence of an explosion in her water-tube boilers, and whether he can give any information as to the injuries to the firemen, and also as to why so much reticence has been displayed in giving information to the public.

THE SECRETARY TO THE ADMIRALTY (Mr. MACARTNEY, Antrim, S.): The only telegram that we have received is one we have received from the Commander-in-Chief at Devonport this morning, stating that on her arrival at Devonport the "Terrible" reported that a tube in one of her boilers had burst, the consequence of which was that one stoker was killed.

*MR. ALLAN: How many were scalded?

MR. MACARTNEY: There are no particulars in the telegram beyond what I have stated. The ship has proceeded to Portsmouth, or I should have caused inquiries to be made.

BILLS DEFERRED.

UNIVERSITY DEGREES BILL.
Second Reading deferred till To-morrow.

COLONIAL MARRIAGES BILL.
Second Reading deferred till Wednesday next.

DISTRESS ABOLITION AND SUBSTITUTION BILL.
Second Reading deferred till Wednesday 12th April.

LIQUOR TRAFFIC LOCAL VETO BILL.
Second Reading deferred till Wednesday 3rd May.

LOCAL AUTHORITIES' SERVANTS' SUPERANNUATION BILL.
Second Reading deferred till Wednesday next.

TOWN TENANTS IRELAND BILL.
Second Reading deferred till Wednesday 19th April.

AGRICULTURAL HOLDINGS BILL.
Second Reading deferred till Tuesday next.

COURT OF CRIMINAL APPEAL BILL.
Second Reading deferred till Monday next.

SUMMARY JURISDICTION ACT (1879) AMENDMENT (No. 2) BILL.
Second Reading deferred till Wednesday next.

WORKMEN'S HOUSES TENURE BILL.
Second Reading deferred till Wednesday next.

CONSTRUCTIVE MURDER LAW AMENDMENT BILL.
Second Reading deferred till Wednesday next.

MERCHANDISE MARKS ACT (1887) AMENDMENT BILL.
Second Reading deferred till Wednesday next.

WORKING MEN'S DWELLINGS BILL.
Second Reading deferred till Wednesday 3rd May.

WAYS AND MEANS.
Committee deferred till Friday.

CORONERS' INQUESTS (RAILWAY
FATALITIES) BILL
Second Reading deferred till Thursday
23rd March.

SCHOOL BOARD ELECTORATE (SCOT-
LAND) BILL.
Second Reading deferred till Wednesday next.

SUPPLY.
Committee deferred till To-morrow.

BUILDING FEUS AND LEASES (SCOT-
LAND) BILL.
Second Reading deferred till Wednesday next.

POOR LAW ACTS AMENDMENT BILL.
Second Reading deferred till Wednesday next.

FINE OR IMPRISONMENT (SCOTLAND
AND IRELAND) BILL.
Second Reading deferred till Wednesday next.

WINE AND BEERHOUSE ACTS AMEND-
MENT BILL.
Second Reading deferred till Wednesday 19th April.

RIVERS POLLUTION PREVENTION
BILL.
Adjourned Debate on Amendment to
Second Reading [8th March] further
adjourned till Thursday 13th April.

PUBLIC LIBRARIES (SCOTLAND) ACTS
AMENDMENT BILL.
Read the third time, and passed.

BILLS REPORTED.

OTLEY URBAN DISTRICT COUNCIL
WATER BILL.
Reported; Report to lie upon the
Table.

LANCASHIRE AND YORKSHIRE RAIL-
WAY (VARIOUS POWERS) BILL.
Reported; Report to lie upon the
Table, and to be printed.

NEW BILLS.

INCEST (PUNISHMENT) BILL.
"For the Punishment of Incest," presented, and read the first time; to be
read a second time upon Wednesday
19th April, and to be printed. (Bill 127.)

COUNTY COUNCILLORS (QUALIFICA-
TION OF WOMEN) (SCOTLAND) BILL.
"To enable Women to be elected and
to act as County Councillors in Scot-
land," presented, and read the first
time; to be read a second time upon
Friday 21st April, and to be printed.
(Bill 128.)

SMALL TENANTS (SCOTLAND) BILL.
"To amend the Law relating to the
Tenure of Land in Scotland by Small
Tenants," presented, and read the first
time; to be read a second time upon
Friday 21st April, and to be printed.
(Bill 129.)

House adjourned at forty-five minutes
after Five of the clock.

An Asterisk (*) at the commencement of a Speech indicates revision by the Member.

HOUSE OF LORDS.

Thursday, 16th March 1899.

THE LORD CHANCELLOR took his seat upon the Woolsack at Four of the clock.

PRIVATE BILL BUSINESS.

BUENOS AYRES AND PACIFIC RAIL-WAY BILL [H.L.]

To be read the second time on the second sitting day after the Recess at Easter.

GREAT YARMOUTH CORPORATION BILL [H.L.]

Report from the Select Committee, That the Committee had not proceeded with the consideration of the Bill, no parties having appeared in opposition thereto; read, and ordered to lie on the Table: The orders made on the 27th of February last and the 7th instant discharged; and Bill committed.

PERTH WATER, POLICE, AND GAS BILL [H.L.]

Report from the Select Committee, That the Committee had not proceeded with the consideration of the Bill, no parties having appeared in opposition thereto; read, and ordered to lie on the Table: The orders made on the 27th of February, the 6th instant, and Friday and Monday last discharged; and Bill committed for To-morrow.

PUBLIC LIBRARIES (SCOTLAND) ACTS AMENDMENT BILL.

Brought from the Commons.

CROWBOROUGH DISTRICT GAS BILL.

Brought from the Commons; read the first time; and referred to the Examiners.

VOL. LXVIII.   [FOURTH SERIES.]

ST. DAVID'S WATER AND GAS BILL.

Brought from the Commons; read the first time; and referred to the Examiners.

RETURNS, REPORTS, ETC.

TREATY SERIES, No. 6 (1899).

Additional Convention to the Convention of 1st December 1897, between the United Kingdom and France, for the exchange of postal parcels between Australia and France.

Presented (by Command), and ordered to lie on the Table.

WEST INDIES.

Correspondence relating to the hurricane of 10th-12th September 1898, and the relief of distress caused thereby.

Presented (by Command), and ordered to lie on the Table.

JUDICIAL STATISTICS (ENGLAND AND WALES), 1897.

Part II. Civil Judicial Statistics: Statistics relating to the Judicial Committe of the Privy Council, the House of Lords, the Supreme Court of Judicature, county courts, and other civil courts, for the year 1897; edited by John Macdonell, esquire, LL.D., Master of the Supreme Court.

Presented (by Command), and ordered to lie on the Table.

BENEFICES ACT, 1898.

Rules made under the Act.

PAWNBROKERS' RETURNS (IRELAND).

Returns from the City Marshal of Dublin, for the year ended 31st December 1898.

SUPERANNUATION.

Treasury Minutes declaring—

I. That Louis Pedreschi, porter, National Gallery, Ireland, was appointed without a civil service certificate through inadvertence on the part of the head of his department, dated 4th March 1899 :

II. That professional or other peculiar qualifications not ordinarily to be acquired in the public service are required for the due and efficient discharge of the duties of the office of Assistant for Chancery and Charity in the department of the Treasury Solicitor, dated 7th March 1899 :

Laid before the House (pursuant to Act), and ordered to lie on the Table.

BRIDLINGTON PIERS AND HARBOUR.

Abstract of the annual general account for the year ended 26th July 1898.

Delivered (pursuant to Act), and ordered to lie on the Table.

SIR JOHN SOANE'S MUSEUM.

Statement of the funds, 5th January 1899.

Delivered (pursuant to Act), and ordered to lie on the Table.

ENDOWED SCHOOLS ACT, 1869, AND AMENDING ACTS.

Scheme for the management of St. Paul's School, in London, now regulated by a scheme made under the Endowed Schools Acts of 1876, as altered by a scheme of the Charity Commissioners 1879 : Laid before the House (pursuant to Act), and to be printed. (No. 26.)

PETITIONS.

MONEY-LENDING BILL [H.L.]

Petitions for amendment of; of Clarendon Financial Association, Limited —City of Liverpool Banking Association, Limited—Liverpool Loan Company, Limited—South Lancashire Loan and Discount and Investment Company, Lmited—Birkenhead Joint Stock Discount Company, Limited — Trustees of the General Loan Association, Limited —Read, and ordered to lie on the Table.

BILLS ADVANCED.

TROUT FISHING ANNUAL CLOSE TIME (SCOTLAND) BILL [H.L.]

To be read a second time on Tuesday next.

PARISH CHURCHES (SCOTLAND) BILL [H.L.]

House to be in Committee on Tuesday next.

PUBLIC LIBRARIES (SCOTLAND) ACTS AMENDMENT BILL.

Read the first time; and to be printed. (No. 29.)

METROPOLIS MANAGEMENT ACTS AMENDMENT (BYELAWS) BILL [H.L.]

Amendments reported (according to order), and Bill to be read third time To-morrow.

NEW BILLS.

SUPREME COURT (APPEALS) BILL [H.L.]

A Bill to amend the law with respect to the hearing of appeals and motions by the Court of Appeal—Was presented by the Lord Chancellor; read the first time; and to be printed. (No. 27.)

ST. ANDREW'S BURGH PROVISIONAL ORDER CONFIRMATION BILL [H.L.]

A Bill to confirm a Provisional Order under the Burgh Police (Scotland) Act, 1892, reducing the number of magistrates and councillors in the Royal Burgh of St. Andrew's—Was presented by the Lord Balfour; read the first time; and referred to the Examiners. (No. 28.)

———

PUBLIC BUSINESS.

———

MONEY-LENDING BILL [H.L.]

SECOND READING.

Order of the Day for the Second Reading, read:

Motion made, and Question proposed—

"That this Bill be read a second time."— *(Lord James of Hereford.)*

THE EARL OF KIMBERLEY: My Lords, I desire to make a few remarks on this Bill. I quite recognise, as I suppose we all do, the manifest evils which arise from the practices at all events of that class of money-lenders who, I observe, were called by Sir G. Lewis, in his evidence, by the very appropriate names of "touts" and "thieves." Of course, the most important clause in the Bill is the one which enables the court to reopen a case of money-lending, and if the amount of interest charged exceeds 10 per cent. to take an account as between the parties, and make an order as to the amount due. No doubt, upon the face of it, this is a very strong Measure. This is, I believe, although I am not a lawyer, a precedent in the action of the Court of Chancery, which was referred to by the noble Lord in moving the First Reading of this Bill, in reopening hard and unconscionable contracts of a money-lending character made against an expectant heir. However that may be, I think that the evils of this system of money-lending are so great that Parliament is justified, at all events, in attempting to mitigate them—I say to mitigate them, because I feel convinced that neither this nor any other legislation will really put an end to these evils, for the reason that in a large number of cases the money-lender trades upon not only the need of the borrower, but also his dread of coming into open court and making public his position and the cause which led him to have recourse to these money-lenders. I do not believe that any legislation, even legislation more stringent than this, would entirely destroy the evils of money-lending. However that may be, it does not, in my opinion, afford sufficient reason for not making such an attempt as is made by the noble Lord in this Bill for the diminution of the evils. There are certain provisions in the Bill which I think will not meet with anything but approval—those, for instance, which require that there should be a register kept of money-lenders, and also those which require that he shall give to the borrower a full and complete statement of all the conditions on which the loan is advanced. Mr. Justice Matthews, in his evidence, said—

"It is, in the case of the borrower, his money or his life. The borrower will do anything, as a general rule, to conceal from those about him, and those who know him, what his position is, and the money-lender may do with him what he pleases."

I feel, even after this Bill passes, that that description will apply to a great many borrowers. They will be at the mercy of the money-lenders, because they will be prepared to do anything which will save them from appearing in a court. Although I am afraid the Bill will not have all the effect the promoters of the Bill hope for, yet I trust it will have some effect, and, therefore, I shall support the Second Reading. Everyone must approve of the provision requiring a money-lender to register himself, and that he should give to the borrower a full and complete statement of all the conditions upon which the loan is obtained.

*LORD JAMES OF HEREFORD: My Lords, I have to thank the noble Earl for the support he has given the Bill. If my only duty was to secure the Second Reading of this Bill by your Lordships' House, I should not have a very difficult task to accomplish. But since the Measure was introduced it has, as was to be expected, attracted a great deal of criticism, and from different classes of the public there

2 O 2

have been many suggestions for its improvement, while from the particular class which will be affected by the proposed legislation the criticism has been in some cases, in a moderate and business-like spirit, and in others in an intemperate manner. I have been unable to deal with all the correspondence on the subject, and I am seeking, therefore, this opportunity of making a somewhat general reply. There has been one class of criticism, that which has proceeded from the Duke of Argyll, which, I am sure, will meet with the respect and consideration of your Lordships. I speak most sincerely when I say that everything that falls from the noble Duke, either from his tongue or pen, will be treated by me with full respect. The criticism of the noble Duke is of a general character, but he admits, and eloquently states, the evils of money-lending, and thinks that the Legislature ought to deal with them. The Duke of Argyll bids this House and the Legislature to take some steps to correct these evils; he approves of the effort made in the Bill, and, if he were here, would, I presume, vote for the Second Reading. But my noble Friend, among many political virtues, includes that of consistency, and takes exception to the clause enabling the Court to revive a hard and unconscionable bargain made by the leader. I deeply regret that this clause has met with such criticism, and I think my noble Friend has overlooked that this second clause contains the whole pith of the Bill, and without it the Bill would be worth very little—indeed, I am pretty sure that it would add to the power of the money-lender, who would be able to say his proceedings had Parliamentary sanction. Therefore, my view is that the Bill stands or falls by virtue of that second clause. The noble Duke says that a contract made by a sane adult who knows the nature of the contract he is making should be sacred, and should not be touched—the Legislature should not interfere with it. Well, as I said just now, the consistency of my noble Friend has been proved, and those who read his letter will now find in it an echo of a speech he delivered here in August 1881. He used almost the same phraseology when speaking in opposition to the Irish Land Bill. He

Lord James of Hereford.

then objected to interference with contracts made between man and man; but, my Lords, you were not influenced by his arguments then, you passed the Irish Land Bill, and, more than that, after years of experience, you extended the principle of it to the leaseholders and improved the Act in other directions, thus admitting the principle that contracts made under the conditions mentioned by the noble Duke may be, and ought to be, from certain economic considerations, subject to review by a court. That was a much stronger case than this we have before us, because you had to deal with the bargains made by a not unmeritorious class of men—Irish landlords—who made practically fair bargains: they were not unconscionable and were freely made, but circumstances had arisen causing them to become oppressive to the tenants, and the Legislature said—

"We will review these contracts made by sane adults, and the Court shall say if the terms shall be changed or not."

So the noble Duke's argument was not accepted 18 years ago, yet still he asserts contracts should not be interfered with. It is certainly a very strange result that the name of the noble Duke, who is a friend of this Bill and a bitter opponent to the class of money-lenders with whom we are endeavouring to deal, should be employed as the champion of the money-lending fraternity, and that appeals should be made to them to enrol themselves under the banner of the Duke of Argyll to support the sanctity of contracts entered into with money-lenders. I do not think for a moment such considerations should prevail. The noble Duke treats the principle with which we are dealing as a novel principle in law, but that is a misapprehension. The Noble Earl opposite has referred to a principle which is the foundation of this Bill, and by which the Courts have long intervened in hard and unconscionable bargains where an expectant heir has had dealings with a money-lender. The sale of reversionary interests has always been within the review of a Court of Equity. In 1880 the principle was applied by Mr. Justice Denman to a case where a person lent money to one who had no means, in the hope that he could obtain the money from his family, and the contract was set aside as a hard and unconscionable bargain. My noble Friend Lord Aldenham, who is unable to be here to-day, has written to me referring to a class of cases affecting clerks in commercial firms. He referred especially to clerks in the Bank of England. It seems that a rule exists at that Bank that any clerk who borrows money shall be immediately dismissed. A certain money-lender having discovered this, lent money to a clerk who borrowed from him, and brought pressure to bear upon him to borrow a second time by threatening to inform the Bank authorities. This represents one of many cases showing how money-lenders obtain power over their unfortunate clients. As will be seen from the evidence taken before the Committee in 1897, a witness, who was a money-lender was called before the Committee, and the following letter addressed by him to a clerk in the Bank of England was placed in his hands—

"As you will probably be taking your holiday before long, it may be convenient to anticipate your salary for a short time. I am prepared to advance you £10 or £20, or more, according to your position and requirements, on your post-dated cheques, at the moderate interest of 2s. 6d. per month for each £5. I do not think you will meet with easier terms. Having already a connection amongst gentlemen in the Bank of England, I am perfectly acquainted with the rules and regulations. Your transactions will be known only to myself, as I keep my own books, and am not a professional money-lender."

The witness admitted that he knew the clerks were liable to instant dismissal if they borrowed money, and that he had in one case threatened to inform the Bank directors, but had never done so. Now, my Lords, would it not be fair for a Court of Equity to say that where pressure of this kind is brought to bear it is a hard and unconscionable bargain? Can anyone object to a Court saying that a man shall be relieved from the terms of a contract which he had no power to refuse to enter into? It is on such a principle that this Bill has been drawn. These are the general principles under which this interference with contract is placed before you; it is not a new, but an old doctrine. It is only slightly advanced in its operation, but it deals with an evil greater, I believe,

than any evil of a like kind that has ever been dealt with by similar legislation. Years ago one of the most astute of our judges, writing on the subject of money-lenders, said that most cruel actions were constantly brought to enforce extortionate demands—actions in which the law, instead of being the handmaid of justice, was really prostituted and made an accomplice in the perpetration of a most iniquitous and cruel robbery. That was written by Mr. Justice Byles 50 years ago, and since then this system of money-lending which he thus described has increased to an enormous extent. The House may not be aware that this country is mapped out into different areas, in which the members of the money-lending fraternity are in the habit of dealing. They make inquiries as to the circumstances of an intending borrower; if he has any expectancy, and what means his family have to save him from disgrace. Then comes an appeal to a person who perhaps does not really wish to borrow; then the yielding to the temptation to borrow thus offered; and so the borrower is led on to his certain ruin. It is said there are cases in which borrowing money has been beneficial to the borrower. But such cases are few compared with the cases in which the borrowers have been ruined. Sir George Lewis, a solicitor of great experience, says that for 40 years he has been acting for men who lent and borrowed money, and he has never known a single instance in which the borrower has benefited. One of our most experienced county court judges says that a borrower who has little necessity to borrow often yields to temptations held out to him by a money-lender; he cannot meet the first demand; has to borrow again; then comes an aggregation of claims upon him; and, to meet these claims, betting and Stock Exchange gambling is resorted to, which only ends in failure, and, as a last resort, comes embezzlement or theft, and perfect ruin ensues. There may be some inconvenience to men in not obtaining the loan they desire. It may drive them to the extremity of the bankruptcy court, but much better begin in the bankruptcy court than end in gaol. There are one or two other matters of general interest to those affected by the

Bill. I admit we ought to be careful in this legislation not to inconvenience the public who may wish to borrow legitimately, or to interfere with that portion of the trade of the country which is carried on by passing money from hand to hand. I have had a good many suggestions made to me by those who support the Bill. They ask that the Bill shall go further and deal with bills of sale. I cannot agree to that. Bills of sale are of general interest apart from professional money-lending. The alteration as to bills of sale may be desirable, but it must be done by another Bill. Now, there are those who think a good many people will be deterred from availing themselves of the benefit of the Act by fear of exposure. It is suggested that application to set aside "hard and unconscionable" bargains by money-lenders should be heard *in camera*. But all that is deterrent in the Bill can only be obtained by publicity. The very principle of the Bill requires that proceedings under it should be in public. If we allowed the proceedings to be in private—a practice never allowed by our law except in the interests of public decency—we should deprive the law of half its force, and establish an objectionable precedent. My noble and learned Friend on the Woolsack, the Lord Chancellor, authorises me to say that in the interests of justice he could not consent to the cases under the Bill being heard in private. If they were heard in that way the public would never know what the law, as laid down in the courts, was. Then, there are certain persons and institutions lending money to whose interest I think we ought to be careful. I should call them legitimate money-lenders, and I do not wish that they should be interfered with in carrying on a business which may be beneficial to the community. It is said that the Bill, as drawn, is retrospective in its character, and that contracts entered into before the Bill was passed will, by the Bill, be subjected to a new condition of things. There is some force in that, and I am inclined to suggest that the Bill should not be retrospective in its character, and should only apply to contracts made after it has been passed. As to clause 2, there are a class of money-lenders who object to the limit of 10 per cent. I put in that limit, not for the purpose of deal-

Lord James of Hereford.

ing with the objectionable money-lender, but for the purpose of protecting the legitimate trader. I thought that would give security to men who were carrying on a fair commercial business by putting some limitation upon the jurisdiction of our courts. On reflection I do not think it would be advisable to leave out some limit, but at the same time I am disposed to consider fully the position of the objectors who think that the courts would take 10 per cent. as a guide that borrowers should pay no more. That is not the intention of those who are promoting the Bill. I think that in many cases 10 per cent. is not sufficient. In the cases of many of the mutual societies who carry on the business of lenders in good faith, and some of the traders who form federated societies, 10 per cent. would scarcely be a sufficient return. Suppose £1 or £2 was lent for a month, that rate of percentage per annum would amount to so little that it would not compensate a man for carrying on his business. The risk for lending for one month and six months is very much the same, and, therefore, the question of permitting the charging of a larger amount of interest is a fair one for consideration by your Lordships. An argument used against the Bill is that we are allowing professional money-lenders to take a sum which may be 10 per cent. only, whilst we allow pawnbrokers to take 25 per cent. In one sense that is correct, and in another sense it is not. It may not be known to all your Lordships that a pawnbroker is not a pawnbroker if he deals with loans beyond £10. The Statute of 1872 allows a pawnbroker on small sums to take a percentage of 25 per cent., but if he lends £20, for instance, he is like any other money-lender except that he has in his possession a certain pledge, and he will not take it into his possession unless it is worth more than the loan. In that respect he is in a better position than the ordinary money-lender. The Bill provides that if a pawnbroker chooses to become a money-lender he must be subject to the law, whatever it is, and I cannot, for the moment, see any reason for drawing any distinction in favour of the pawnbroker. There are a great number of very small matters with which I do not wish to deal now. The Bill has been drawn, not in mere caprice or to satisfy any mere popular demand, but upon evidence given by experienced judges who have themselves asserted that this principle is the only remedy they know of for the evils which have constantly been brought before them. The result of what we wish to do is in force now in an illogical manner. The money-lender presents his case before the county court judge. There is no defence, and the judge administers the law by saying, "Here is a claim for, say, £40 or £50; I give judgment for the plaintiff, and order payment at the rate of 6d. per month." This would mean that it would take 120 years before the debt was paid. A course forced on the judges is to refuse to become the agents of enforcing contracts which are harsh and unconscionable; and they apply a scarcely logical remedy in order that they may arrive at an end which they have in mind. It is because there is no proper remedy now in force under our law for the evils which exist that the Bill has been introduced, and I trust it will pass through both Houses of Parliament.

*VISCOUNT KNUTSFORD: My Lords, the noble and learned Lord has stated that his desire is to aim at harsh and unconscionable bargains, and to have only such contracts reopened. I suggest that some words to that effect should be inserted in clause 2. I am aware that the preamble states that—

"Whereas certain persons trading as, and known by the name of, money-lenders carry on their business of lending money by deceptive methods, and inflict by harsh and unconscionable bargains great injury upon those who borrow from them;"

but the preamble is not binding on the judges or those who administer the law. It is, as has been said, only the door to the Act. As the Bill now stands, if the interest charged exceeds 10 per cent., the contract can be reopened whether the bargain is harsh and unconscionable or not. This law is to be administered not only by judges of the High Court, but by County Court judges also, and it is to be feared, unless words are inserted in section 2 to confine the power of reopening contracts to hard and unconscionable bargains, that that power may be used wrongfully in cases where a judge has

a strong, though not unnatural, bias against money-lenders. I think some words should be inserted in the operative part of the Bill.

Question put, and agreed to.

Bill read a second time, and committed to a Committee of the Whole House.

SCIENCE AND ART DEPARTMENT.

THE LORD PRESIDENT OF THE COUNCIL (The Duke of DEVONSHIRE): My Lords, I rise to call attention to the Report of the Select Committee of the House of Commons on the Museums of the Science and Art Department, with reference to the termination of the engagement of Mr. Weale, late Keeper of the Art Library. I have no intention of calling attention generally to that Report, which is, in some respects, a somewhat remarkable document. I have taken steps to challenge the accuracy of some of its statements by causing a Minute of Council to be laid on the Table of both Houses. That Minute calls in question the accuracy of a good many of the statements found in the Report of the Select Committee. I have not yet observed that any Member of this or the other House has taken up the challenge of the Department, but, of course, there is ample time within the limits of the present Session in which some reference may be made to the contradiction which has thus been given. The only paragraph in the Report to which I desire to call your Lordships' attention to-day is a very short one. The Committee state, on page 36 of their Report—

"Your Committee desire to record their opinion that the termination of the engagement of Mr. Weale, late Keeper of the Art Library, immediately after the rising of the House in 1897, and subsequent to the giving of evidence by Mr. Weale, in which errors and abuses of administration in the Museum were freely exposed, very much resembles a breach of privilege and an infringement of the immunity usually enjoyed by witnesses before Committees of the House of Commons."

I think your Lordships will agree that that is a charge of a character which it is impossible for those who are responsible for the termination of Mr. Weale's engagement to leave unnoticed. The first complaint I have to make is that such a charge should have been made without giving me an opportunity of stating the facts of the case, knowing, as the Committee did, or as they might or ought to have known, that I was myself personally responsible for the decision which put an end to the tenure of office of Mr. Weale. This paragraph, I find on reference to the proceedings, was inserted on the Motion of Lord Balcarres by a majority of four to two in a Committee of seven, the original number of which had been 15, and it was inserted in the unavoidable absence of the Vice-President of the Council, who was occupied at the time in a Grand Committee of the House of Commons on the discussion of the London University Bill. This throws an additional light on the fairness or unfairness of the proceeding, and the charge becomes still more serious on reference to the draft Report submitted to the Committee by Lord Balcarres. In that draft Report this matter is referred to at great length, but I will only quote the first paragraph—

" It is now our duty to refer to a grave public scandal—namely, the dismissal of Mr. Weale, Keeper of the Art Library. Mr. Weale is a man of the highest distinction, being, in fact, the only living man out of the large staff of the Science and Art Department who had international reputation. He gave evidence on several occasions. We admit that this evidence must have been distasteful to the authorities, because he ruthlessly exposed the folly and abuses of the present system; in fact, when asked a question, he answered it fully and without reserve. At the same time, his work in the Library has been of the utmost value, having reduced it from chaos to order. He has had official recognition of the diligence and fidelity with which the work has been carried out."

In fact, the determination of Mr. Weale's engagement is repeatedly referred to as his dismissal. The Committee have not endorsed the whole of the statement of Lord Balcarres, but they have endorsed substantially the charge which he made against the Department in the paragraph I have read to your Lordships. It is, therefore, my duty to give to your Lordships the account of the facts of the case which I should have given to the Committee if they had thought fit to call me before them, and which I think would very shortly have disposed of the imputations which have been made. The case of Mr. Weale came before me in

Lord President of the Council.

February 1897. Mr. Weale's term of office would have expired on 7th March the next month, under the operation of the 65 years' rule, and as the exact terms of that rule are important with reference to this case, I will read them to your Lordships. The terms of the rule are—

" Retirement is compulsory for every officer on attaining 65 years of age. But in special cases, the Commissioners may, at the instance of a Department, extend the officer's employment for a further period, in no case exceeding five years, on being satisfied that such officer's retirement at 65 would be detrimental to the interests of the public service."

The retention of Mr. Weale beyond the age of 65 was not recommended by his Departmental superiors, and his case came before me in the ordinary manner. I was aware, however, at the time that a Select Committee of the House of Commons was going to be appointed to inquire into the administration of the museums of the Department, and as I knew that some friction had taken place between Mr. Weale and the other officials, I therefore put a question to the Vice-President to this effect—

" Do you think that there might be any advantage in retaining Mr. Weale until the Committee of the House of Commons, which is to be appointed, has inquired into this part of the subject ? "

On that question of mine a letter was sent to the Treasury, the terms of which I did not see until it had been sent, and which did not exactly follow the terms of my question. The letter was as follows—

" I am directed to request that you will be so good as to inform the Lords Commissioners of Her Majesty's Treasury that the Lords of the Committee of Council on Education are of opinion that the services of Mr. Weale, one of the Keepers of the South Kensington Museum, in charge of the Art Library, who would, under the 65 years of age rule, be retired on 8th March next, should be retained until after the Committee of the House of Commons, which it is proposed to appoint in regard to the Sout. Kensington Museum, has reported."

This letter was answered by the Treasury in almost the same terms, sanctioning the extension of Mr. Weale's services to such period, not exceeding one year from 8th March 1897, as might elapse before the Report of the Committee. As I have said, the letter was written and replied to without my having seen its exact terms. If I had seen them, I do not know that I should have taken any notice of the alteration which was made in my suggestion that the services of Mr. Weale should be retained until the Committee had inquired into that part of the case; but it is on the terms of these letters that all this controversy has taken place, and that the Committee thought it necessary to go into an elaborate consideration of the question whether our request referred to the final Report of the Committee or any previous Report which might be made by them. However, from the terms of the letter of the Treasury, it became necessary that at the conclusion of the Sitting of the Committee in 1897, when they made a Report recommending their reappointment in the following Session, the case of Mr. Weale should again be brought under my consideration. I then found that Mr. Weale had given his evidence, and that the extension of his services was not considered necessary by the heads of his Department, and, therefore, without the smallest hesitation, I expressed my opinion that there was no reason why his services should be longer extended. I did not know, and I did not make any inquiry, as to what was the nature of the evidence given by Mr. Weale. If I had known that it was adverse to the administration of the Department, certainly it would never have occurred to me that the fact that he had given such evidence would have brought his case under the terms of the Order in Council, and that his retirement on that account would have been detrimental to the public service. A good deal has been made by the Committee in the Draft Report of Lord Balcarres of a further letter which was written by the Treasury in November, 1897, after Mr. Weale had ceased to be a member of the Service. Some correspondence has been going on about the gratuity to be granted to Mr. Weale, and in one of his letters the Secretary to the Treasury wrote—

"With reference to the date fixed for Mr. Weale's retirement, I am to point out that, in compliance with the request of the Lords of the Committee, my Lords had sanctioned the continuance of his services for such period, not later than the 8th of March next, as may elapse before the Report of the Committee, on the South Kensington Museum. It is, of course, for the Lords of the Committee to decide as to the date at which Mr. Weale's services should be dispensed with, but, having reference to the fact that the Committee, after making a first Report, have recommended that they should be reappointed, their Lordships desire me to state that they will be ready to consider favourably any recommendation of their Lordships of the Committee for the further continuation of Mr. Weale's services if they shall think that course will be for the convenience of the Committee and the Public Department of Science and Art."

That letter has been referred to by Lord Balcarres as showing that the Treasury were ready to review the case; but the fact is, that this letter was written under a complete misapprehension on the part of the Treasury. The Treasury had been led to believe by the terms of the first letter that there was some connection between Mr. Weale's retirement and the date of the Committee's Report, and this letter was written apparently in entire forgetfulness that the question had been already decided, and that they had been informed that Mr. Weale's services had been already dispensed with. I quite admit that it was within the competence of the Committee to differ from the officials of the Department and myself as to the question whether the extension of Mr. Weale's services was in the public interests or not; but I do deny that it was within the competence of the Committee either to suggest that something in the nature of a grave scandal had taken place, or that anything like a breach of the privileges of the House of Commons had been committed through what they choose to term the dismissal of Mr. Weale. I cannot think but that the making of such charges, without giving the person chiefly implicated in them—namely, myself, any opportunity of defending himself, manifests a degree of reckless prejudice which I find it extremely difficult to understand.

House adjourned at Half-past Five of the clock.

HOUSE OF COMMONS.

Thursday, 16th March 1899.

Mr. SPEAKER took the Chair at Three of the clock.

PRIVATE BILL BUSINESS.

LONDON WATER (PURCHASE) BILL.
(By Order.) Second Reading deferred till Thursday 13th April.

LONDON WATER (FINANCE) BILL.
(By Order.) Second Reading deferred till Thursday 13th April.

EAST LONDON WATER BILL.
(By Order.) Second Reading deferred till Tuesday next.

EAST LONDON WATER (TEMPORARY SUPPLY BILL.
(By Order.) Second Reading deferred till Tuesday next.

METROPOLITAN WATER COMPANIES BILL.
(By Order.) Second Reading deferred till Tuesday next.

WEST MIDDLESEX WATER BILL.
(By Order.) Second Reading deferred till Tuesday next.

WOKING WATER AND GAS BILL.
(By Order.) Second Reading deferred till Thursday next.

SOUTH EASTERN AND LONDON, CHATHAM, AND DOVER RAILWAY COMPANIES BILL.

Motion made, and Question proposed—

" That it be an Instruction to the Committee that they consider the terms and conditions proper to be imposed upon the said Railway Companies on the occasion of their amalgamation, in respect of reductions of fares, rates, tolls, and charges leviable by them on their local and continental traffic, and in respect of the provision of any such further and better facilities for the conveyance of passengers and goods as may be properly required from them."
—*(Mr. Woods.)*

MR. WOODS (Essex, Walthamstow): I think, after the long Debate on this Bill on Tuesday, that the promoters of the Measure, and the right honourable Gentleman at the head of the Department affected by it, will not require any arguments from me to commend to them the Instruction which I have put down on the Paper. It is so plain, practical, and just, that I hope the promoters of the Bill and the right honourable Gentleman will see their way to accept it.

MR. COSMO BONSOR (Surrey, Wimbledon): I oppose the Motion on the ground that a very strong Committee is to be appointed with a very wide reference, and practically all the subjects referred to in the Instruction can be dealt with by that Committee on the clauses of the Bill. I do not think it is at all necessary that the Committee should be instructed as to the course of procedure which they are going to take, and as a matter of principle, I must ask the House to refuse the Instruction.

THE PRESIDENT OF THE BOARD OF TRADE (Mr. C. T. RITCHIE, Croydon): Mr. Speaker, I hope the honourable Member will not press his Instruction. He is well aware that the Committee may consider these questions, if they think fit, without any Instruction at all. They have full power to consider this matter, and I think that to give the Committee an Instruction with regard to one particular point, and that a point in reference to which these two railway companies are doing more at the present time than any other railway company in the metropolis, would be casting a reflection on the action of those railway companies. The Instruction is not at all necessary.

MR. WOODS: Do I understand from the statement of the right honourable Gentleman the President of the Board of Trade that there will be no limitation on the kind of evidence which can be brought before the Committee? If so, I am perfecty willing to withdraw my Instruction.

MR. COSMO BONSOR: The evidence will be regulated by the Rules of the House.

THE PRESIDENT OF THE BOARD OF TRADE: It is quite clear that anyone who has a *locus standi* under the Rules of the House will be able to give evidence before the Committee.

MR. J. ELLIS (Nottingham, Rushcliffe): When I saw this Instruction on the Paper it struck me that the subjects mentioned were the very points which the Committee would inquire into. Under the circumstances, I think the honourabe Member for Walthamstow should be content with the assurance which has come from the other side, and withdraw the Instruction.

MR. WOODS: After the explanation that has been given, I beg to withdraw my Motion.

Motion, by leave, withdrawn.

PRIVATE BILLS.

Ordered, That the Chairman of Ways and Means be discharged from attendance on the Committees on the Nuneaton and Chilvers Coton Urban District Council Water Bill, and the Cardiff Railway Bill, and that Mr. Arthur O'Connor be appointed Chairman of the Committees on the said Bills.—*(Dr. Farquharson.)*

MIDLAND AND SOUTH WESTERN JUNCTION RAILWAY (NORTHERN SECTION) BILL.

Order [27th February] that the Bill be committed, read, and discharged. Bill withdrawn.—*(Dr. Farquharson.)*

PETITIONS.

LOCAL AUTHORITIES SERVANTS' SUPERANNUATION BILL.

Petition from Fordingbridge, in favour; to lie upon the Table.

OLD AGE PENSION SCHEME.

Petitions for adoption;—From Leeds; —and, Bradford; to lie upon the Table.

PARLIAMENTARY FRANCHISE.

Petition from Liverpool, for extension to women; to lie upon the Table.

PUBLIC HEALTH ACTS AMENDMENT BILL.

Petition from Woking, in favour; to lie upon the Table.

SALE OF INTOXICATING LIQUORS ON SUNDAY BILL.

Petitions in favour;—From Chelmsford; — Totternhoe; — and, Dursley; to lie upon the Table.

RETURNS, REPORTS, ETC.

ARMY (ORDNANCE FACTORIES ESTIMATE, 1899-1900).

Estimate presented,—of Charge for the year 1899-1900 (by Command); Referred to the Committee of Supply, and to be printed. (No. 110.)

WAR OFFICE.

Copies presented,—of Orders in Council defining the duties of the principal officers charged with the Administration of the Army: (1) Order in Council, dated 21st November 1895; (2) Order in Council, dated 7th March 1899, revoking the Order in Council dated 21st November 1895 (by Act); to lie upon the Table.

SCHOOLS (SCOTLAND) (NUMBER OF SCHOLARS, ETC,)

Return presented,—relative thereo [ordered 7th March; *Captain Sinclair*]; to lie upon the Table, and to be printed. (No. 111.)

SCHOOL BOARD (LONDON).

Return presented,—relative thereto [ordered 28th February; *Mr. Charles Morley*]; to lie upon the Table.

WEST INDIES.

Copy presented,—of Correspondence relating to the Hurricane of the 10th-12th September 1898, and the Relief of Distress caused thereby (by Command); to lie upon the Table.

INDUSTRIAL SCHOOLS (IRELAND) (CIRCULARS).

Return presented,—relative thereto [ordered 9th March; *Mr. Dillon*]; to lie upon the Table.

ENDOWED SCHOOLS ACT, 1869, AND AMENDING ACTS.

Copy presented,—of Scheme for the Management of the Foundation, called or known as St. Paul's School, in London, founded by Dean Colet, now regulated by a Scheme made under the Endowed Schools Acts on the 24th March 1876, as altered by a Scheme of the Charity Commissioners of the 4th July 1879 (by Act); to lie upon the Table, and to be printed. (No. 112.)

———

PAPER LAID UPON THE TABLE BY THE CLERK OF THE HOUSE.

———

BENEFICES ACT, 1898.

Copy of Rules dated 15th March 1899, and entitled the Benefices Rules, 1899 (by Act).

VAGRANT CHILDREN RELIEVED.

Return ordered—

" Of the number of Children who received Casual Relief in the several Poor Law Unions of England and Wales on the nights of 1st July 1895, and 1st January and 1st July 1896, 1897, and 1898, distinguishing those under two years of age from those between two years and seven years, and over seven years respectively."—*(Mr. Maddison.)*

NEW MILLS URBAN DISTRICT COUNCIL (WATER) BILL.

Reported [Preamble not proved]; Report to lie upon the Table.

———

CATHCART'S DIVORCE BILL—MESSAGE FROM THE LORDS.

That they have passed a Bill, intituled, " An Act to dissolve the marriage of Thomas Charles Duffin Cathcart, of Ruperta House, Newtownards Road, in that part of the City of Belfast which is situate in County Down, Medical Practitioner, with Emily Jane Cathcart, his now wife, and to enable him to marry again; and for other purposes." [Cathcart's Divorce Bill [H.L.]

Bill read the first time; to be read a second time.

QUESTIONS.

———

WORKMEN'S DWELLINGS AT BERMONDSEY.

MR. A. MORTON (Deptford): I beg to ask the Secretary of State for the Home Department, if he can state whether the South Eastern Railway Company, previous to pulling down 96 houses, and closing 24 other houses, in the parish of Bermondsey and in the contiguous parishes, for the extension and widening of their railway, have provided to his satisfaction other and suitable homes in the immediate vicinity for the labouring classes so displaced; and, if so, whether he will state in what localities such accommodation has been provided, and will give the number of persons for whom accommodation has been found; whether, in view of the further contemplated extensions, widenings, and improvements already entered upon by the South Eastern Railway Company in that immediate district, and which will displace large numbers of the labouring classes, he will state whether, and, if so, in what locality, the company has already provided the requisite accommodation for their re-housing, as required by their Act, 60 and 61 Vic. c. 227; and, if such provision has not been already made, will he state the date by which the necessary accommodation will be provided, the locality in which the buildings will be situated, and the number of persons who will be provided for?

THE UNDER SECRETARY of STATE FOR THE HOME DEPARTMENT (Mr. JESSE COLLINGS, Birmingham, Bordesley): The liability of the railway company to re-house the persons of the labouring class displaced by their operations under the Act referred to is modified by a provision in the further Bill which the company promoted and which received the approval of Parliament last Session. This provision enables the company to submit, and the Secretary of State to approve, a scheme for the temporary re-housing of the persons displaced, pending the erection of new buildings for their permanent accommodation. Under this provision temporary accommodation has been provided for 542 persons in Blocks A, B, and L, of the Guinness Trust Buildings, lately erected in Snowsfields, Bermondsey, and further temporary accommodation is provided in Blocks C, D, and K, of the same buildings, which are in the vicinity of the scene of the widenings, while other persons have been removed at their own request to other dwellings. The blocks referred to contain accommodation for a larger number of persons than has been actually displaced. The question of the permanent re-housing of all these persons is now under the consideration of the Secretary of State, and as he is well aware of the great scarcity of artisans' dwellings in the neighbourhood in question, he will take care that the provision made by the company is adequate.

SCOTCH UNIVERSITIES.

DR. CLARK (Caithness): I beg to ask the Lord Advocate whether he is aware that the abstract of accounts and annual statistical reports of the Universities of Aberdeen, Glasgow, and St. Andrews made to the Secretary for Scotland, in accordance with the provisions of the Universities (Scotland) Act, 1889, contains a statement of the emoluments of the professors in the various faculties from endowments, fees, and other sources; whether the reports sent in by Lord Balfour of Burleigh, on behalf of the University of Edinburgh, do not contain this information; and, whether the Secretary for Scotland will communicate with the Lord Rector of Edinburgh University, with the view of having the returns from the University as full and complete as those of the other Universities?

*THE LORD ADVOCATE (Mr. A. GRAHAM MURRAY, Buteshire): I am informed by the Lord Rector of Edinburgh University that the annual statistical reports of that University from 1889 to 1893 comprised similar details in respect of the emoluments of professors to those contained in the reports of the other Universities, but when the University Commissioners' Financial Ordinance No. 27 came into operation fixing normal salaries for all the Chairs with the exception practically of the three Divinity Chairs, the University authorities considered that there was no longer the same necessity for reporting these details from year to year. But they have no objection to furnish them in future, and that will be done.

EDINBURGH UNIVERSITY.

Dr. CLARK: I beg to ask the Lord Advocate if he could state to the House what proportion of the salaries paid to the theological professors in the University of Edinburgh is defrayed from Parliamentary grant, endowments, and fees paid by students; and, from what funds are the salaries of the assistant professors and the additional examiners of divinity paid?

MR. GRAHAM MURRAY: As regards the first portion of the honourable

Member's Question, I have arranged to furnish him with a written explanatory statement, as the details are too long to trouble the House with. As regards the second portion, the reply is, that the salary of the University Assistant in Hebrew and of the University Assistant in Divinity is paid from the General University Fund.

BRITISH SAILORS IN THE MERCANTILE MARINE.

SIR F. EVANS (Southampton): I beg to ask the President of the Board of Trade whether, having regard to the gradual decrease in the number of British seamen employed in the British mercantile marine, he will recommend to Her Majesty the appointment of a Royal Commission to inquire into the question.

THE PRESIDENT OF THE BOARD OF TRADE (Mr. C. T. RITCHIE, Croydon): No, Sir; I hardly think this is a matter for a Royal Commission. It seems to me it is rather a matter for shipowners themselves to inquire into. Should such an inquiry be instituted, the Government will give consideration to any suggestions which may result.

DISTURBANCES AT ST. CLEMENT'S CHURCH, BELFAST.

MR. DILLON (Mayo, E.): I beg to ask the Chief Secretary to the Lord Lieutenant of Ireland whether he is aware that the man Trew, speaking at the Custom House, Belfast, on recent Sundays, inflamed the mind of the mob against certain churches in Belfast, and stated that as soon as they had finished with St. Clement's they would attack those also; and whether, as the same laws against intimidation and incitement to riot are in force in the North and South of Ireland, he will cause them to be enforced in Belfast as in the South?

THE CHIEF SECRETARY TO THE LORD LIEUTENANT OF IRELAND (Mr. GERALD BALFOUR, Leeds, Central): The strongest words used by Mr. Trew

in the direction suggested in the first paragraph were those spoken on the 8th January, when he said that—

"As soon as things are finally arranged at St. Clement's Church, we will tackle St. George's; we will carry on no tom-foolery outside the church; we will just walk in in a body and bring out everything that ought not to be there."

On the 22nd January, he used similar language about the same church, and also alluded to St. Peter's Church, and to the churches at Bushmills and Hillsboro'. It has hitherto been the practice of successive Governments in Ireland to abstain from prosecuting for incitements in connection with religious disputes, which, unfortunately, are by no means confined to the North of Ireland, and the Government do not consider it desirable to depart from this practice in the present instance. The law with respect to intimidation, and to incitements to riot, is the same all over Ireland, and the attitude of the Government in the present case has been identical with that observed in other parts of Ireland in other cases of a similar kind. The policy of the Government has been to stand neutral between the parties to such disputes, and the police only interfere so far as is necessary to preserve the public peace.

IMPORTS OF BUTTER AND EGGS.

SIR J. LENG (Dundee): I beg to ask the President of the Board of Agriculture if he can explain why the extensive imports of butter and eggs from foreign countries increased in the first two months of this year by 14 per cent. in the case of butter, and 36 per cent. in that of eggs; whether the Board have directed the attention of British farmers to the continued increase in the demand for Danish and other foreign butter; whether the methods adopted abroad to secure high standards of quality and packages of merchantable quantities are being adopted to any appreciable extent by agriculturists in this country; and whether there is a prospect of the native supplies of butter and eggs being so improved as to render unnecessary the present large importations from abroad?

The PRESIDENT OF THE BOARD OF AGRICULTURE (Mr. W. H. LONG, Liverpool, West Derby): I am not aware of the cause of increase to which the honourable Member refers, and, in any case, it would be dangerous to draw conclusions from the figures for two months only. Thus, taking the figures for the whole year 1898, there was a slight diminution in our imports of butter as compared with 1897, and the increase in the case of eggs was 2.8 per cent. only. The facts as to the imports of butter are constantly brought to the notice of British farmers in the "Journal of the Board of Agriculture" and elsewhere, and we have reason to believe that the educational facilities which have been provided in recent years have resulted in a considerable improvement of the methods of butter-making at home. But I cannot anticipate that we shall ever be self-supporting in the matter of butter or eggs or of any items of food supply in such enormous demand.

GREAT EASTERN RAILWAY EMPLOYEES.

Mr. SINCLAIR (Essex, Romford): I beg to ask the President of the Board of Trade whether he is aware that the Great Eastern Railway Company require their firemen and engine drivers to pass an examination before engaging them, and that in each case this certificate is withheld from the man unless he is going on foreign service, and then only given to the office through which he has obtained foreign employment; and whether he can use his influence to secure that the certificate may be handed to and be the property of the man immediately he has earned it?

The PRESIDENT OF THE BOARD OF TRADE: No, Sir, I cannot interfere in a matter of this description, which appears to involve the conditions upon which a railway company chooses to select its servants.

POISON ON AGRICULTURAL LANDS.

Dr. AMBROSE (Mayo, W.): I beg to ask Mr. Attorney-General for Ireland if he is aware that the agent of the Marquess of Sligo has published

notices that various townlands on his lordship's estate have been poisoned, with the result that dogs and poultry straying on the land are subject to destruction, and that the poison is conveyed by birds to the adjoining lands; is such action legal; and could he state in what way the owners of poisoned animals can recover compensation?

The ATTORNEY-GENERAL FOR IRELAND (Mr. ATKINSON, Londonderry, N.): I understand that notices signed by Lord Sligo's agent have been posted up in conspicuous places in the locality referred to intimating that it is intended to lay down poison for the destruction of foxes and other vermin. Neither Lord Sligo nor his agent has in this done anything for which they can be called to account or interfered with by the Executive Government. Though the answer to this Question is obvious, I must respectfully decline to express any opinion on the respective rights of the owners of land and the owners of dogs or poultry which may trespass upon these lands under the circumstances mentioned in the question.

CAPTAIN DONELAN (Cork C., N.): Are foxes correctly described as "vermin"?

Mr. ATKINSON: Yes, Sir.

THE "TOURMALINE."

Mr. HEDDERWICK (Wick Burghs): I beg to ask the Under Secretary of State for Foreign Affairs, in view of the terms of the Treaty of 1856, and the fact that certain subjects of Her Majesty, recently tried upon a charge of introducing in the "Tourmaline" arms and ammunition into Morocco, were confined for 100 days before they were handed over to the British authorities at Tangier; whether any and what punishment has been meted out to Kaid Giluli and the other subjects of the Sultan who were responsible for their detention; whether he is aware that the application of Her Majesty's Vice-Consul for the custody of the prisoners was refused, and the prisoners lodged in a house in Mogador under a guard of Moorish soldiers; whether he is aware that, in sentencing the prisoners at Tangier, Chief Justice Gatty, said "I do not take into consideration the hardships you have suffered at the hands of the Moors, as that may form the basis of a claim for compensation against the Moorish Government"; and whether Her Majesty's Government, having regard to this judicial expression, have taken or mean to take any steps to obtain compensation from the Sultan?

THE UNDER SECRETARY OF STATE FOR FOREIGN AFFAIRS (Mr. ST. JOHN BRODRICK, Surrey, Guildford): Her Majesty's Government have had all the circumstances of this case before them, and, having given them careful consideration, have arrived at the conclusion that these persons who landed arms in the Sus country from the steam yacht "Tourmaline" were implicated in a deliberate attempt to raise a rebellion against the Sultan of Morocco. In these circumstances, they have decided to abstain from demanding pecuniary compensation from the Moorish Government on their behalf. The question of the action taken by Kaid Giluli in this matter is still under discussion between Her Majesty's Minister at Tangier and the Moorish Government.

DESTRUCTION OF THE MADHI'S TOMB.

MR. SWIFT MACNEILL (Donegal, S.): I beg to ask the Under Secretary of State for Foreign Affairs whether the Report for which he telegraphed four weeks ago to Lord Cromer of the destruction of the Mahdi's tomb and the mutilation of his dead body has been yet received; if it has been received when will it, in accordance with the promise of the Government, be printed and circulated among Members of the House of Commons; and, if the Report has not been received, what is the reason of the delay?

MR. BRODRICK: An Official Report was despatched from Cairo on the 13th inst. It will be communicated to the House in due course. There has been no undue delay, allowing for necessary communications between Lord Cromer and Lord Kitchener.

MR. SWIFT MACNEILL: Shall we have the communications *in extenso*, or only selections from them?

[No Reply.]

LOANS FUND (IRELAND) BILL.

MR. SWIFT MACNEILL: I beg to ask the Chief Secretary to the Lord Lieutenant of Ireland whether he is prepared to give an undertaking that reasonable notice will be given of the day to be fixed for the Second Reading of the Loans Fund (Ireland) Bill?

MR. GERALD BALFOUR: I have no wish to spring the Second Reading of this Bill on honourable Members, but I cannot give an undertaking that it will not be proceeded with in the ordinary course on any day for which it may be set down.

CLOGHER GUARDIANS.

MR. SWIFT MACNEILL: I beg to ask the Chief Secretary to the Lord Lieutenant of Ireland whether the Irish Local Government Board dissolved the Board of Guardians of the Clogher Union for their action in the appointment of a lady (Miss Magill) as a rate collector, and their refusal to annul that appointment; whether the Irish Local Government Board found fault with Miss Magill's appointment on the sole ground that under the 152nd section of the Irish Grand Jury Act (6 and 7 Will. IV., c. 116) distress warrants cannot be issued to any other person than the rate collector, who must execute the decree in person, and that a woman is unfitted for the work; whether he is aware that it has been decided by a full court over which the Lord Chief Baron presided in 1888, in the case R. (Jones) v. Rony (23 I. L. T. R., p. 28), that the 152nd section of the Irish Grand Jury Act is inconsistent with the provisions of the Irish Petty Sessions Act, and repealed by that Act, which provides that the execution of the warrant is cast on the police and not on the rate collector; and whether the Local Government Board will sanction the appointment of Miss Magill to a poor rate collectorship in accordance with the practice in England, where several women are poor rate collectors?

MR. GERALD BALFOUR: The Board of Guardians of the Clogher Union was not dissolved for the reasons stated in the first paragraph, but because the Guardians refused to sign the warrants of Collector Cuthbertson. The inquiries in the other paragraphs of the question have already been answered by me in replying to previous questions on the same subject. I would particularly refer the honourable and learned Member to my replies of the 9th and 10th February last.

MR. TREW'S SPEECHES IN BELFAST.

MR. DILLON: I beg to ask the Chief Secretary to the Lord Lieutenant of Ireland whether he is aware that on Sunday, 5th March last, Mr. Trew, speaking from the Custom House steps in Belfast, advised the people to persevere in the conduct for which Johnson was imprisoned, and said that if they did so for three months longer they would starve Mr. Peoples out of Belfast, and that four policemen, numbered 363, 732, 592, and 329 were listening to this language; and whether the Government propose to prosecute Mr. Trew for such language?

MR. GERALD BALFOUR: The facts are substantially as stated in the first paragraph. The reply to the second paragraph is the same as that already given to the first Question put to me by the honourable Member, namely, that it has not been the practice of successive Governments to prosecute for incitements of this kind.

MR. DILLON: I beg to ask the Chief Secretary to the Lord Lieutenant of Ireland whether he is aware that Mr. Trew, on the 1st of January last, publicly declared that he would never stop till he had hounded out Mr. Peoples, and that "he hoped he would live to see him roasted alive," "that he deserved to be cut in pieces"; and why the police, who were present on the occasion, have taken no notice of such language publicly uttered? In putting this Question may I say that the language has been altered. No doubt it was un-Parliamentary, but

VOL. LXVIII.   [FOURTH SERIES]

it was necessary to show the point of the Question, namely, did Mr. Trew say he "would never rest until he had hounded. Mr. Peoples to hell?" Did he use that horrible language?

MR. GERALD BALFOUR: The police were present at the meetings addressed by Mr. Trew on the 1st of January, and carefully noted the language used by him, but their notes contain no evidence that he made use of the words attributed to him, or of words to the effect quoted in the Question.

ST. CLEMENT'S CHURCH, BELFAST.

MR. DILLON: I beg to ask the Chief Secretary to the Lord Lieutenant of Ireland whether he is aware that last November the Lord Mayor of Belfast issued a proclamation against the holding of anti-ritualist demonstrations in the vicinity of St. Clement's Church, and that this proclamation was openly defied by some of the ringleaders, and the police made no attempt to put the proclamation in force; and whether, as meetings for the purpose of agitation are held almost nightly at the east end of St. Clement's Church, adequate measures will be taken to put an end to the present disturbances?

MR. GERALD BALFOUR: The honourable Member seems to be in error as to the nature of the Lord Mayor's proclamation, which did not prohibit any meeting, but merely recited certain instructions that the police had received, and which they afterwards carried out, and in addition exhorted law-abiding citizens to absent themselves from the locality on Sunday evenings, and to assist the authorities in the preservation of the peace. As to the second paragraph, crowds assembled in the neighbourhood of the church and obstructing the thoroughfare, are moved on by the police.

CHINESE SOLDIERS IN BRITISH SERVICE.

MR. DILLON: I beg to ask the Under Secretary of State for Foreign Affairs whether Chinese subjects are being enlisted in the British Service at Wei-hai-

2 P

Wei; and, if so, whether such a proceeding is legal?

MR. BRODRICK: A battalion of Chinese is being enlisted at Wei-hai-Wei for the British service. As regards the legality of this step Her Majesty's Government are not aware of any legal objection to the voluntary enlistment of the subjects of a foreign Power.

LISTOWEL LAND CASES.

MR. DILLON: I beg to ask the Chief Secretary to the Lord Lieutenant of Ireland why no Sub-Commission has sat in Listowel for 15 months, seeing that there are over 150 cases waiting trial, and some of those cases are second term cases on estates which are in the Land Judge's Court.

MR. GERALD BALFOUR: I am informed by the Land Commissioners that it was not possible, having regard to the claims of other districts, to arrange a sitting for the district referred to during the period mentioned. It is probable, however, that a list containing cases from the Union of Listowel will be issued before the end of next month, though no definite arrangements have as yet been made. The Commissioners have no information which would enable them to distinguish between cases situate upon estates in the Land Judge's Court and others not in that Court.

ATTEMPTED TRAIN WRECKING AT LAMBEG.

MR. MACALEESE (Monaghan, N.): I beg to ask the Chief Secretary to the Lord Lieutenant of Ireland if his attention has been called to a desperate attempt made to wreck the 6.50 passenger train from Belfast to Bankbridge, at a point some yards from Lambeg Station, by placing a sleeper across the line; and have the police succeeded in finding any clue to the perpetrators of this crime?

MR. GERALD BALFOUR: I am informed that on the 5th instant the engine of the passenger train referred to came in contact with a sleeper placed on the rails, but that beyond slight injury to the protecting guards of the engine no damage was done to the train or the line. The police have not yet found a clue to the perpetrators of the crime.

AUCKLAND HARBOUR BOARD.

MR. W. M'ARTHUR (Cornwall, St. Austell): I beg to ask the Civil Lord of the Admiralty whether any decision has been come to in regard to the negotiations between the Admiralty and the Auckland Harbour Board; and, if not, what is the reason of the delay?

THE CIVIL LORD OF THE ADMIRALTY (Mr. AUSTEN CHAMBERLAIN, Worcestershire, E.): No decision has yet been come to. The Secretary of the Harbour Board has, however, made a definite proposal to the Admiralty on behalf of his Board, and this offer is now under consideration by the Admiralty and Treasury. I hope that a final decision may be given shortly.

IRISH RESIDENT MAGISTRATES.

CAPTAIN DONELAN: I beg to ask the Chief Secretary to the Lord Lieutenant of Ireland if he can say how many resident magistrates are at present serving who have been promoted from the Royal Irish Constabulary, and how many of that number are Roman Catholics; nd whether such appointments are made by seniority or by selection?

MR. GERALD BALFOUR: The number of resident magistrates now serving who have been promoted from the rank of district inspector in the Constabulary is 26, of whom four were Roman Catholics. Such appointments are made by selection; but seniority has always been one element, though, of course, not the only element in making the selection since the present Government has held office. I cannot speak for the practice of my predecessors.

CONSTRUCTION OF THE KHARTOUM RAILWAY.

MR. SCOTT (Lancashire, Leigh) : I beg to ask the Under Secretary of State for Foreign Affairs whether his attention has been called to the statement made in the public Press to the effect that, under the name of the Railway Brigade, large numbers of artisans and labourers from Egypt have been compelled to construct the railway to Khartoum at a nominal rate of wages and are still employed on similar work ; and whether, if the facts be as stated, steps will be taken by Her Majesty's Government to put an end to a system of forced labour, under cover of military service, which is now illegal ?

MR. BRODRICK : We have heard nothing of the compulsory employment on the railway of artisans and labourers, The Soudan Railways, including that to Khartoum, were constructed primarily for military purposes, and, so far, entirely by military labour ; the employees are soldiers.

TELEGRAPHS (TELEPHONIC COMMUNICATION) BILL.

MR. FAITHFULL BEGG (Glasgow, St. Rollox) : I beg to ask the Secretary to the Treasury whether he will give the House more particular information, by means of a Treasury Minute or otherwise, previous to the Second Reading of the Telegraphs (Telephonic Communication) Bill, as to the precise intentions of the Government regarding conditions to be imposed upon municipalities in connection with licences to be granted to them.

THE FINANCIAL SECRETARY TO THE TREASURY (Mr. R. W. HANBURY, Preston) : I stated on Tuesday that probably the best method of giving the House the required information will be by a Treasury Minute.

TAXATION AT ST. KITTS.

SIR J. WILLOX (Liverpool, Everton) : I beg to ask the Secretary of State for the Colonies whether he is aware that an ordinance has been published imposing on the islands of St. Kitts, Nevis, and Anguilla new taxes, including an income tax on all incomes

from £75 to £150 per annum of two and a half per cent., and over £150 per annum of three per cent., also what is called a mercantile and huckster's licence, costing from £20 to 25s. per annum, without which no person can sell goods, wares, merchandise, provisions, or any other commodities, and a wheel tax on vehicles ; and whether, considering the impoverishment of the Colony, an equilibrium between expenditure and revenue could be established by a reduction in the cost of the administration of the islands ?

THE SECRETARY OF STATE FOR THE COLONIES (Mr. J. CHAMBERLAIN, Birmingham, W.) : I am aware and have approved of the imposition of the taxes referred to, which I consider to be fair and reasonable ; on the other hand, there has been considerable remission of taxation, which bore heavily upon the sugar industry. Every effort has been and will be made to reduce expenditure in these islands.

ADMINISTRATOR OF ST. KITTS.

SIR J. WILLOX : I beg to ask the Secretary of State for the Colonies under what circumstances the Administrator of the Colony has left St. Kitts ; whether he will return to duty in the island ; and, if not, whether the present opportunity will be utilised for reducing the cost of the administrative staff and so lightening the taxes upon the Colonists ?

THE SECRETARY OF STATE FOR THE COLONIES : An Inquiry has been held by a Commission appointed by the Governor of the Leeward Islands into certain charges which have been made against the Administrator of St. Kitts-Nevis ; at the close of the Inquiry the Administrator had leave of absence pending my decision in the matter. The Report of the Commission has been received, and is under consideration. At present it would be premature to say what changes, if any, can be made in the Administrative staff.

CLOGHER RATE COLLECTORSHIP.

MR. JOHNSTON (Belfast, S.): I beg to ask the Chief Secretary to the Lord Lieutenant of Ireland whether his attention has been called to the complaint made at the meeting of the Clogher Board of Guardians, on the 4th March, by Mary M'Elmeel, that Rate-collector Cuthbertson never called or demanded rates from her until he appeared, accompanied by "grippers," and assaulted her, seized her cow, and charged her £2 12s. 9d. rates, and 5s. costs; what notice has been taken of the conduct of this rate collector; and will any compensation be granted to M'Elmeel?

MR. GERALD BALFOUR: It appears that the collector called on Mrs. M'Elmeel without notice, and demanded the rates due by her. As payment was not made, he succeeded, after meeting with some resistance, in seizing a cow and driving it away. The following day Mrs. M'Elmeel appears to have thought better of her refusal, and paid the rates and costs, getting back her cow. Her complaint to the Guardians on the subject was marked read. No notice will be taken of Collector Cuthbertson's action by the Local Government Board, as he appears to have acted strictly in accordance with the law, which in Ireland empowers a collector, on refusal of payment of rates, to distrain forthwith any goods found on the premises of the person in default, without serving any notice whatever. No compensation will be granted to Mrs. M'Elmeel, or to any other ratepayer, who incurs costs by withholding payment of rates. The Guardians have called attention to the unsatisfactory state of the collection in this district, and as the collection must be closed by the appointed day, Mr. Cuthbertson is acting properly in enforcing payment by seizure in all cases where the rates are refused.

MR. SWIFT MacNEILL: Are not these distraints to be levied by the respectable members of the Royal Irish Constabulary, and not by "grippers"? What are "grippers"?

[No Reply.]

CYCLISTS IN PHŒNIX PARK.

MR. TIMOTHY HEALY (Louth, N.): I beg to ask the Secretary to the Treasury why nothing has been done to make the turnstile of Chapelizod Gate, Phœnix Park, more convenient for cyclists; and what has resulted from the Inquiry promised last year?

MR. HANBURY: An attempt was made in the direction indicated by the honourable Member, but, as the park gate was left open and the deer escaped, it was necessary to discontinue it. No Inquiry was promised last year.

MR. TIMOTHY HEALY: Surely, something could be done. The gate has never been unchained, and no attempt has been made to improve it.

DUBLIN EXCISE OFFICERS.

MR. TIMOTHY HEALY: I beg to ask Mr. Chancellor of the Exchequer if the Board of Inland Revenue intend further reducing the number of first-class officers at present in Dublin collection, and if they propose to replace any first-class officers in Excise warehouses in Dublin by assistants, considering the great hardship to officers caused by checking promotion, and reversing the previous policy of the Board?

THE CHANCELLOR OF THE EXCHEQUER (Sir M. HICKS BEACH, Bristol, W.): The Board of Inland Revenue have no intention of replacing first-class officers employed in Excise warehouses in Dublin by assistants.

FRAUDS IN THE DUBLIN EXCISE WAREHOUSE.

MR. TIMOTHY HEALY: I beg to ask Mr. Chancellor of the Exchequer if he is aware that owing to the want of adequate supervision in Excise warehouses in Dublin some years ago a great fraud was perpetrated, over 10,000 gallons of spirits being abstracted, and that lately there have been two cases in bonded warehouses in England of fraudulent abstractions of spirits; and, in view of those frauds, will he represent to the Board of Inland Revenue the inadvisability of reducing the number of first class officers at present in charge of Excise warehouses in Dublin?

THE CHANCELLOR OF THE EXCHEQUER: I am aware that some considerable frauds of the nature described in the Question occurred in an Excise warehouse in Dublin in 1888. The matter was fully dealt with at the time, and the staff was increased, and no fraud of this sort is known to have taken place since. The two cases in England to which I think the honourable Member alludes occurred not in Excise but in Customs warehouses. I do not see any necessity for making such representations to the Board of Inland Revenue as are suggested by the honourable Member.

BELLEVILLE BOILERS.

MR. PATRICK O'BRIEN (Kilkenny): On behalf of the honourable Member for the St. Patrick Division of Dublin, I beg to ask the First Lord of the Admiralty whether he can state the exact amount paid to the French Belleville Company for each set of Belleville boilers placed in or ordered for the ships of Her Majesty's Navy, and also the total amount of royalty paid by the Admiralty or the contractors to the Admiralty to the French Belleville Company for Belleville boilers supplied to or ordered for Her Majesty's ships?

THE SECRETARY TO THE ADMIRALTY (Mr. W. E. MACARTNEY, Antrim, N.): The total amount of the royalties paid to or to be paid to the Belleville Company is £146,690. I cannot state within the limits of an answer to a Question across the floor of the House the exact amount paid on each set of Belleville boilers.

MR. ALLAN (Gateshead): Is the right honourable Gentleman aware that the money paid for these boilers far exceeds what it would cost to make ordinary boilers?

[No Reply.]

RAILWAY ENTERPRISE IN WEST AFRICA.

MR. PATRICK O'BRIEN: On behalf of the honourable Member for the St. Patrick Division of Dublin, I beg to ask the Secretary of State for the Colonies whether he can state the number of railways actually constructed in the British, French, German, Belgian, Spanish, and Portuguese possessions in West Africa, and the places connected by these railways, and the mileage in each case, also the number of proposed railways for which surveys have been made, and the districts over which the surveys have been made; and, whether the railway lines actually constructed in West Africa belong to the State or private companies?

THE SECRETARY OF STATE FOR THE COLONIES: In Sierra Leone, a railway has been laid from Freetown to Songo Town, a distance of 32 miles, and is being continued to Rotofunki; from this place a survey is being made to Mano, the distance of which from Freetown is 97 miles. Surveys have also been made to Bumban and Sulymah. On the Gold Coast a railway is being laid from Skondi to Tarkwa, a distance of 40 miles; and a flying survey has been made from Tarkwa to Kumassi; surveys have also been made from Accra direct, and *via* Apam, to Insuain, and from ¡nsuain to Kumassi; and another is being made from Accra to Kpong on the Volta River. The railway from Lagos to Ibadan, 120 miles, is in course of construction. The first section to Abeokuta, 64 miles, is expected to be opened for public traffic in May, and both construction and survey work are in progress on the Abeokuta-Ibadan section. The railways in the British West African Colonies belong to the State. I must refer the honourable Member to the Foreign Office as to railways in Foreign Possessions in West Africa.

HOLYHEAD AND KINGSTOWN PIERS.

MR. PATRICK O'BRIEN: I beg to ask the Secretary to the Treasury whether he has any objection to grant a Return of the Amounts expended respectively on the Admiralty Pier at Holyhead, and on the Carlisle Pier,

Kingstown, in connection with the last and present Holyhead and Kingstown mail contracts?

MR. HANBURY: I will give the honourable Member the particulars now. The amounts expended, so far as it is possible to distinguish them, have been —upon the Admiralty Pier at Holyhead, £49,187, on the Carlisle Pier at Kingstown, £16,461. The annual expenditure on dredging Kingstown Harbour amounts in addition to £1,000 or £1,200.

GOVERNMENT CONTRACTS IN INDIA.

SIR W. WEDDERBURN (Banffshire): I beg to ask the Secretary of State for India whether his attention has been drawn to a resolution of the Government of India in the Finance and Commerce Department, No. 2587, of 9th June last, under which certain firms have been selected as qualified to tender for Government contracts in articles of steel and iron; whether he will state what public benefit is obtained by limiting the competition to these firms, and upon what evidence of special qualification the selection has been made; whether he is aware that among these selected firms not a single native firm is included; and, will he explain how this exclusion of native enterprise is held to be in accordance with the Standing Orders of the Government of India, published in 1883, which direct that, unless prices or quality compel another course, the preference shall invariably be given to Indian over European manufactures?

THE SECRETARY OF STATE FOR INDIA (Lord GEORGE HAMILTON, Middlesex, Ealing): The Resolution of the Government of India of the 9th June 1898, regarding the receipt of tenders in India for Government contracts for articles of steel and iron, was approved by me before its issue. It is a common practice for Government Departments to invite tenders only from firms as to whose competence and resources they have some reason to be satisfied; and the advantages of this course must, I think, be obvious. But in this case it is only for the present that the competition is limited to the firms specified, as it is expressly mentioned that the list is subject to revision from time to time. The Local Government were consulted as to the firms who were qualified to be placed on the list. I am unable to say whether any of the selected firms are composed wholly or partially of natives of India, but no racial disqualification of any kind has been imposed, and if there are native firms willing and competent to tender, there is nothing whatever to prevent them from being added to the list. The object of the Government is to purchase from producers direct, not to encourage middlemen. The policy of the Orders of 1883, in favour of the purchase of stores of local manufacturers when practicable, remains in full force, and has reference, not to any question of race distinctions, but to the capacity and location of the manufactories at which the required articles are produced.

DOG MUZZLING IN YORKSHIRE.

COLONEL GUNTER (York, W. R., Barkstone Ash): I beg to ask the President of the Board of Agriculture if he is aware of the great discontent that prevails in the agricultural parts of the West Riding of Yorkshire at the prolonged continuation of the Muzzling Order, the muzzle interfering with the work of the dog; and if he can now relax the Order, or say when the Order will be withdrawn?

THE PRESIDENT OF THE BOARD OF AGRICULTURE: I have no doubt that the owners of dogs both in the West Riding and the other districts in which Muzzling Orders still remain in force would welcome the withdrawal of the Orders, but, at the same time, there is, I think, a general opinion that, in view of the stage which our operations have reached, 'it will be better that they should remain in force so long as any appreciable risk exists of our having to re-impose them. I could not with safety indicate a date for the withdrawal of the Orders, but my honourable Friend may be sure that I shall be very glad to find myself able to announce the completion of the task which we have thought it our duty to undertake.

STATE RAILWAYS IN INDIA.

MR. STANHOPE (Burnley): I beg to ask the Secretary of State for India whether offers have been entertained by the authorities from certain capitalists for purchase of State railways in India, in particular the Eastern Bengal Railway; can some statement be made by presentation to Parliament of correspondence or other documents that may serve to explain the principle on which such proposals proceed, or the object with which such transfer of State property and assets is considered expedient; also a statement of the terms offered by capitalists who propose such purchase; in framing such terms, will care be taken to include consideration for interest payments that have been drawn from current revenues of India from time to time, and which stand as debits to the various Indian railways; and, before any purchase or sale of Indian railway property has been agreed upon, will a report be called for from the auditor of the accounts of the Secretary of State in Council, stating his approval or disapproval of the disposal of such property, such report to be laid before Parliament previous to any definite sanction being given to such transaction?

THE SECRETARY OF STATE FOR INDIA: I am not aware that any offer for the purchase of any State line in India has been entertained. Should any such offer be received, the terms of purchase to be entertained would only be arrived at after consideration of all the interests concerned, and would be fixed after consultation with the financial advisers of the Secretary of State; but among these the auditor is not included.

INDIAN NATIVE ARMIES.

MR. STANHOPE: I beg to ask the Secretary of State for India how far and in what direction during the last dozen years have the Indian Military authorities, in the methods of recruiting and organising their native armies, extended the policy of forming regiments or companies of special races, castes, or communities; and can any correspondence be presented, or other form of consecutive statement be made that will serve to explain to Parliament the objects of these sectional organisations and show what authorities have advised these changes in recruiting and in classifying the rank and file of the Indian armies; such statement to include copies of any dissents recorded or objections made either in the Council of the Governor-General or in that of the Secretary of State?

THE SECRETARY OF STATE FOR INDIA: The whole of the Native Army in India is now organised either in class regiments or in class squadron and class company regiments, the general principles as regards the latter being that no class should consist of less than two troops or two companies, and that as a rule there should not be more than three classes in a regiment, and never more than four classes. The composition of each regiment is detailed in the Indian Army list. The change was recommended by the Government of India, with the concurrence of the Commander-in Chief and of the Governments of Madras and Bombay. One member of the Viceroy's Council dissented from the proposal to form class company regiments in Bombay, but did not record any written dissent. There were no dissents recorded in the Council of India. I do not think the subject is one upon which it would be advisable to publish the correspondence, though I could have a Memorandum prepared which, without entering into the reasons for the changes, would show the changes which have been made of late years.

LORD LECONFIELD'S TENANTRY.

MR. PATRICK O'BRIEN: On behalf of the honourable Member for West Clare, I beg to ask the Chief Secretary to the Lord Lieutenant of Ireland if he could state how many civil bill decrees did Lord Leconfield's agent, Mr. Scott, obtain against his tenants at the last January sessions at Ennis and Kilrush; in how many cases are ejectment decrees running concurrently with civil bill decrees on this particular estate; and is there any means of preventing the costs of both decrees falling on poor tenants?

MR. GERALD BALFOUR: There were 11 ejectment decrees and 12 decrees for rent granted at Kilrush Sessions held in January last, and 15 ejectment decrees and 38 decrees for rent granted at Ennis Sessions in January last at the suit of Lord Leconfield. It does not appear that ejectment decrees are running concurrently with civil bill decrees, as none of the parties decreed in ejectments were decreed in civil bills for rent. There is no means, I believe, of preventing the granting of costs in ejectment and civil bill proceedings at the same Sessions if actions are brought, though it is a remedy rarely, I understand, availed of.

SCOTCH CHURCH IN MADEIRA.

MR. E. ROBERTSON (Dundee): On behalf of the honourable Member for the Hawick Burghs, I beg to ask the Under Secretary of State for Foreign Affairs whether his attention has been called to the case of the Reverend A. D. Paterson, M.A., minister of the Scotch Church in Madeira, who has been arrested, and against whom a criminal information has been laid for propagating doctrines contrary to the religion of the State; whether he is aware that the so-called evidence consists in hearsay and conjecture, the witnesses being unable to testify to any act or word on the part of Mr. Paterson insulting to the Roman Catholic religion; and that the religious service or teaching complained of is conducted in Mr. Paterson's own church and the school attached thereto, and the only fact proved against him beyond this is that he has distributed copies of the New Testament; whether an exception to the proceedings has been taken, and an appeal to the authorities at Lisbon has been made; and whether Her Majesty's Government propose to take any steps or use any influence so as to prevent the conviction and banishment from the island of Mr. Paterson, and to protect the Protestant congregations in Madeira?

MR. BRODRICK: This matter is engaging the attention of Her Majesty's Government, who will take all necessary steps for the protection of British subjects in Madeira, but cannot, of course,

interfere with judicial proceedings. Her Majesty's Minister at Lisbon has reported by telegraph that the appeal which Mr. Paterson has made from the decision of the court at Madeira to that of Second Instance in Lisbon has been granted. He thinks it doubtful whether the case will be proceeded with. Further details are promised, and their arrival must be awaited.

OLD AGE PENSIONS IN NEW ZEALAND.

MR. HOGAN (Tipperary, Mid): I beg to ask the Secretary of State for the Colonies whether it would be possible to procure a full and authentic report of the practical working of the State system of Old Age Pensions in New Zealand, in view of prospective legislation on the same subject in this country?

THE SECRETARY OF STATE FOR THE COLONIES: The New Zealand Act providing for Old Age Pensions was passed on 1st November last, and the machinery for receiving claims was not completed till the 9th of December. Any Report on the working of the Act at this early stage would, therefore, be worthless.

GERMANY AND THE CAROLINE ISLANDS.

MR. HOGAN: I beg to ask the Under Secretary of State for Foreign Affairs whether he has any information to impart in reference to the reported acquisition of the Caroline Islands by Germany by purchase from Spain; and whether the interests of Australia and New Zealand, as affected by the extension and consolidation of German power in the Pacific, are receiving the attention they deserve at the hands of Her Majesty's Government?

MR. BRODRICK: Her Majesty's Government are not in possession of any information on the subject referred to in the first paragraph. The interests of Australia and New Zealand in the Pacific will receive due attention at the hands of Her Majesty's Government.

SAMOA.

MR. HOGAN: I beg to ask the Under Secretary of State for Foreign Affairs whether any definite results have yet accrued from the deliberations of the Berlin Treaty Powers in reference to the situation in Samoa and the Kingship of Mataafa?

MR. BRODRICK: The questions referred to are still under consideration, and further Reports with regard to recent events in Samoa are expected.

WORKMEN'S COMPENSATION ACT INSURANCES.

MR. THORBURN (Peebles and Selkirk): I beg to ask the Secretary to the Treasury if he can explain why policies of insurance in connection with the Workmen's Compensation Act require to have a 6d. stamp, while policies in connection with the Employers' Liability Act have hitherto only required a 1d. stamp; and if he can see his way to reduce the stamp for insurance policies in connection with the Workmen's Compensation Act to a penny?

THE CHANCELLOR OF THE EXCHEQUER: The law requires that policies of insurance by employers against their liability under the Workmen's Compensation Act shall bear a 6d. stamp. It seems to me a very moderate charge as compared with the stamp duties on some other kinds of insurance, but proposals have been made to me for the change suggested by the honourable Member, and the matter will be examined.

"ADMIRAL" CLASS OF BATTLESHIPS.

MR. ARNOLD-FORSTER (Belfast, W.): I beg to ask the First Lord of the Admiralty whether it is intended to modify the present armament of the seven first-class battleships, "Anson," "Benbow," "Camperdown," "Collingwood," "Howe," "Rodney," and "Sanspareil," and to provide their secondary batteries with adequate protection against the projectiles of quick-firing guns?

MR. MACARTNEY: Plans have been prepared for the reconstruction and re-armament of the vessels of the "Admiral" class, and the question is kept constantly in view; but there are many considerations which render it inadvisable to undertake these alterations at the present time.

IRISH GRAND JURY CONTRACTS.

MR. TULLY (Leitrim, S.): I beg to ask the Chief Secretary to the Lord Lieutenant of Ireland whether the Local Government Board are aware that the grand juries at the spring assizes have presented for sums due to contractors and others, and, although there are funds and balances on hand sufficient to discharge these liabilities, yet owing to an order of the Local Government Board the contractors and others to whom the money is due cannot be paid; and whether he can state what steps will be taken to have this order modified, and these liabilities paid off by the county officials?

*MR. GERALD BALFOUR: The Local Government Board have not issued any Order of the nature indicated in the Question. The Transitory Provisions Order in Council requires Grand Juries to liquidate from balances in hand all sums legally due at the date of the Assizes, and they are also authorised to make presentments for certain specified services in respect of the period ending the 30th September next, but payments on foot of these presentments will be made by the County Council. If the honourable Member will furnish me with particulars of any case in which he considers the provisions of the Order in Council have not been complied with, I will have further inquiry made into the matter.

SALES UNDER SECTION 40 OF THE LAND LAW (IRELAND) ACT, 1896.

MR. FFRENCH (Wexford, S.): I beg to ask the Chief Secretary to the Lord Lieutenant of Ireland whether he can grant a Return showing the amount of sales that have taken place in the Land Judges Court in Dublin, under the 40th

Section of the Land Act of 1896, also showing the number of cases in which the proceedings have proved inoperative and the sales abortive owing to the fact that the Land Judge and the Land Commission and the tenants have not agreed upon the terms of purchase, also a list showing the number of estates remaining in the Land Judges Court to which the 40th Section will probably be applicable, with the dates that these estates were put into the Land Courts respectively?

*MR. GERALD BALFOUR: On the 10th February, in replying to a Question of the honourable Member for Cork, I gave certain detailed information as to the extent of the operations already carried out under Section 40 of the Act of 1896, and I would ask the honourable Member to refer to my reply to that question. It would obviously be impossible to give a list of the cases of estates to which the 40th Section may hereafter be applied, as the Land Judge cannot say in anticipation what decision he may arrive at in a particular case.

WEXFORD LAND APPEALS.

MR. FFRENCH: I beg to ask the Chief Secretary to the Lord Lieutenant of Ireland whether he is aware that there are over 100 appeal cases on the Ely estate and other estates in the south of the county Wexford which have been pending for the last three months; whether he will inquire about what time the Land Commission will fix a sitting especially to hear those cases; and if the sitting will be held in New Ross or Waterford in order to prevent the expense and inconvenience of going to Dublin, especially as the tenants may be delayed three or four days for the hearing of their cases?

MR. GERALD BALFOUR: There are at present 111 fair rent appeals pending from the Unions of New Ross and Wexford, which represent the southern portion of the county Wexford. No arrangements have as yet been made for a sitting of the Land Commission for the hearing of these cases. The sitting, when arranged for, will probably be held in the town of Wexford, but nothing definite has as yet been settled.

IRISH TEACHERS' EXAMINATIONS.

MR. MACALEESE: I beg to ask the Chief Secretary to the Lord Lieutenant of Ireland whether he is aware that the Commissioners of National Education (Ireland) allowed their examiners on the geometry paper to outstep the requirements of the old programme for second class candidates at the Teachers' Examinations, July 1897, whereby the candidates were deprived of 20 marks owing to the insertion of one of the questions on this paper being selected from the exercises of the third Book of Euclid, which the candidates were not required to know; whether he will provide that those candidates who failed to attain the necessary percentage entitling them to promotion (owing to the fault of the examiner on this subject) be immediately promoted; and whether he will call upon the Commissioners of National Education to make a similar ruling as regards the July examinations of 1898, the examiners on the geometry paper of that year having outstepped the programme in setting questions 1 and 7 to second class candidates; or will the Commissioners make this a 60 instead of 100 marks paper, and order a thorough revision of all the answer papers of those candidates who failed on the geometry paper?

MR. GERALD BALFOUR: The paper set in geometry to candidates for second class at the examination on the old programme in 1897 did not outstep the requirements of the programme for that class. In the geometry paper set for the same class of candidates in 1898, two of the questions might be considered outside the strict limits of the course laid down, but the remaining eight questions (five only being allowed to be attempted) afforded ample scope for the exhibition of the necessary knowledge. In fact, only two teachers failed in geometry on the latter, as on the former occasion, and a careful revision of those teachers' exercises showed their almost complete ignorance of the subject. No further action is considered necessary by the Commissioners in this matter.

VACCINATION BLUE BOOKS.

MR. M'LAREN (Leicester, Bosworth): I beg to ask the President of the Local Government Board whether he is aware that the Blue Books containing the evidence given before and the Report of the Royal Commission on Vaccination are now out of print; and whether, having regard to the great interest taken at present by the public and especially by Boards of Guardians in the Vaccination question, he will give orders for these to be reprinted?

THE PRESIDENT OF THE LOCAL GOVERNMENT BOARD (Mr. H. CHAPLIN, Lincolnshire, Sleaford): I am informed that none of these Blue Books are out of print, but as there is only a small stock of copies of the Final Report of the Royal Commission on Vaccination directions have been given to have more printed.

TOURIST TRAFFIC ON THE WEST COAST OF IRELAND.

MR. O'KEEFFE (Limerick): I beg to ask the Chief Secretary to the Lord Lieutenant of Ireland if he will bring before the Board of Works the desirability of making the subsidised steamers on the River Shannon run from Foynes in connection with the train from Limerick, viâ Tarbert, to Kilrush, and vice versâ, in order to develop the tourist traffic to Kilkee and the West coast of Ireland?

MR. GERALD BALFOUR: The proposal contained in the Question has already engaged attention. The Board of Works have been in communication with the Waterford and Limerick Railway Company and the West Clare Railway Company on the subject, and if effect is given to the recommendations made to these companies the extended service will come into operation this summer.

FRIENDLY SOCIETIES AND THE LAND TAX.

SIR J. RANKIN (Herefordshire, Leominster): I beg to ask Mr. Chancellor of the Exchequer whether, in the case of a friendly society whose income was under £160 per annum and which was in possession of land as mortgagee in possession, the land tax on such land ought to be remitted under section 12 of Finance Act, 1898.

THE CHANCELLOR OF THE EXCHEQUER: I am advised that a friendly society which in any financial year establishes a claim to exemption from income tax by reason of its income not exceeding £160 is entitled, under section 12 of the Finance Act, 1898, to claim that land tax shall not be collected in that year on land of which it is in possession as mortgagee in possession.

ARMENIAN ORPHANAGES.

MR. PLATT-HIGGINS (Salford, N.): I beg to ask the Under Secretary of State for Foreign Affairs whether he is aware that, according to trustworthy information which has reached this country, there are computed to be 25,000 orphan Armenian children now homeless and destitute in the districts of Kharput, Bitlis, Van, and Hedjin; and whether he will take further steps through our Ambassador at Constantinople, to procure the re-opening of the orphanages at Palu, Koorkush, the neighbourhood of Diarbehr and elsewhere, which have been recently closed by order of the Turkish authorities, and give every encouragement to those who desire to alleviate the misery of these children?

MR. BRODRICK: We have no information as to the exact numbers of destitute Armenian orphans in the districts named. Her Majesty's Ambassador has made further representations to the Grand Vizier, and has urged the dispatch of immediate instructions to the Valis not to interfere with the orphanages. His Excellency may be relied upon to press the matter at the Porte.

GALWAY VOTERS' LISTS.

MR. KILBRIDE (Galway, N.): On behalf of the honourable Member for East Galway, I beg to ask the Chief Secretary to the Lord Lieutenant of Ireland whether his attention has been directed to the condition of the voters' lists in the electoral division of the county of Galway; whether in the Barnavilla, Kilconnell, district the Poor Law Guardian of the division and the honorary secretary of the dispensary committee have been deprived of their votes, both resident in the district, and having their rates paid; whether the names of minors have been put on the list; whether the names of men who have been on for many years, and are still entitled, have been expunged; whether these changes were made after the lists passed through the hands of the clerk of the union; whether in the county of Galway the number of voters on the register do not equal or exceed the number of inhabited houses in the county; whether he is aware that the utmost dissatisfaction prevails in the district owing to the present state of the register; and whether the Local Government Board will investigate the matter and ascertain who is responsible?

MR. GERALD BALFOUR: My attention has not been directed to the condition of the voters' lists referred to, and it has not been found possible in the short interval since this Question was placed on the Paper to ascertain whether the facts are as stated. If the honourable Member will postpone the Question for a week, I will endeavour to procure the information he desires, but I may add that the Local Government Board have no responsibility in connection with the preparation of registers of voters.

CLIFDEN PETTY SESSIONS CLERK.

MR. ABRAHAM (Cork Co., N.E.): On behalf of the honourable Member for Connemara, I beg to ask Mr. Attorney-General for Ireland whether he is aware that the petty sessions clerk of Clifden, Mr. Hazel, is most actively supporting and canvassing on behalf of Mr. Henry Robinson, J.P., who is a candidate for the county councillorship of the Clifden district; and whether his action in this respect is contrary to the provisions of the Order in Council; and, if so, whether he will state what steps will be taken to compel Mr. Hazel to comply with the Order?

MR. ATKINSON: Mr. Hazel, who is himself a large ratepayer, appears only to have advised some of his fellow ratepayers who asked for his advice, for whom, in his opinion, they ought to vote. This, no doubt, was a technical violation of the Order in Council recently made, and on Mr. Hazel's attention being called to the matter, he has undertaken to take no further part in the election.

MR. KILBRIDE: Did he go out canvassing for Mr. Robinson?

MR. ATKINSON: I am informed he did not.

SECOND DIVISION CLERKS.

MR. LOWLES (Shoreditch, Haggerston): I beg to ask the Secretary to the Treasury whether he is aware that, in some of the recent promotions of assistant clerks to the Second Division under clause 15 of the Order in Council of 29th November, 1898, the Treasury is adjusting the commencing salary in such a manner as to inflict an immediate pecuniary loss on such clerks which will occupy some time in recovery; and whether, in view of the statement made by him last Session, that this grievance —that is, loss of pay on promotion, had been entirely swept away, this action is still held to be consistent with the terms of such Order in Council?

MR. HANBURY: The facts stated by the honourable Member are correct. The decision is not inconsistent with the terms of the Order in Council; but I think that the existing practice does not fully carry out the promise I made that no loss of pay should occur on promotion, and I will see that it is altered accordingly.

NAVAL MEDICAL OFFICERS.

CAPTAIN NORTON (Newington, W.): I beg to ask the First Lord of the Admiralty whether it has been brought to his notice that certain medical officers, who entered the Royal Navy in 1878, and went through the 128 days' course of

Naval and Military hygiene at Netley (at that time compulsory) on half-pay, have not been allowed to count that time for promotion, while others who joined the service some months later, and were given direct commissions afloat, in consequence of what was then known as the Russian war scare, the hygiene course in their case being dispensed with for the time, have been promoted over the heads of the former, through the latter having more full pay time; and whether, in order to remedy this, he will consider the advisability of altering the rules of the Service, so that the period of training at Netley Hospital may reckon as Naval service for all purposes, and so that the prospects of these senior officers for promotion from the rank of Fleet Surgeon to that of Deputy Inspector-General may not be prejudiced?

MR. MACARTNEY: Certain medical officers were entered for immediate service in 1878, and did not go through the usual course at Netley. One of these officers, after serving afloat, applied to be allowed to go through the course, and his time was allowed to count as a special case, as his application was a voluntary act, and made under the impression that it would count. It is not considered desirable to alter the rules, but directions have been given that when the time approaches for the promotion of the officers entered in 1878 to the rank of Deputy-Inspector-General, their positions on the list shall be considered.

CAPTAIN NORTON: May we take it for granted that these officers will not be prejudiced as regards promotion?

MR. MACARTNEY: Yes, I think that that may be inferred for the answer.

POLLING ON ARRAN ISLANDS.

MR. DILLON: I beg to ask the Chief Secretary to the Lord Lieutenant of Ireland whether, in view of the fact that the South and Middle Islands of Arran are several miles from Kilronan on the North Island, and the people living on those two islands have no means of transit except by small canoes to Kil-

ronan to record their votes at the Local Government elections, and that the passage is dangerous except in fine weather, he will ask the Local Government Board to allow a polling station in a large school house on the Middle Island, or convey the voters free by the s.s. "Duras," a subsidised steamer running to and from Galway?

MR. GERALD BALFOUR: The Returning Officer has not yet made his final arrangements as to the polling stations, and I am not, therefore, in a position to state where the polling for the Arran Islands will take place. The Returning Officer has full discretion as to the number and location of the polling stations in each district electoral division, and I will cause the suggestion contained in the honourable Member's Question to be transmitted to him for consideration.

IRISH TITHE RENT CHARGE BILL.

MR. DILLON: I beg to ask the Chief Secretary to the Lord Lieutenant of Ireland when he proposes to introduce the Irish Tithe Rent-Charge Bill?

MR. GERALD BALFOUR: I am not yet in a position to assign a date for the introduction of this Bill.

PUNISHMENT FOR TRAIN WRECKING.

MR. ASCROFT (Oldham): I beg to ask the Secretary of State for the Home Department whether his attention has been called to the attempt made on Saturday last to wreck the Folkestone express by placing obstructions upon the line, and to the other similar attempts recently made on other railway lines in the United Kingdom; and whether, considering that the crimes of garotting and robbery with violence were checked by the power given to the courts by the Act of 1863 of ordering prisoners convicted of such offences to be flogged, he will, with a view to securing the safety of passengers and railway employees, consider the advisability of at once introducing a Bill giving similar powers to the court where a prisoner has been convicted of an attempt to wreck a railway train?

MR. COLLINGS: The Secretary of State is fully alive to the dastardly nature of these outrages, and to the importance of doing all that can be done to prevent their recurrence; but in view of the fact that penal servitude for life may be (and was in a recent case) the sentence imposed for such crimes he does not think that the present punishment can be considered inadequate, nor does he think it would be desirable to adopt the honourable Member's suggestion?

ROYAL NAVAL RESERVE.

MR. WEIR (Ross and Cromarty): I beg to ask the First Lord of the Admiralty, having regard to the fact that under the expenses of the Royal Naval Reserves in this year's Estimates an increase of £8,300 is set down for pay for men embarked for a period of six months' training on board Her Majesty's ships, will he state whether any of the Stornoway Naval Reserve men will participate in this training?

MR. MACARTNEY: The Stornoway men have participated to a larger extent than any other district in the past, 219 having been embarked for six months' training during the year 1898, and there is no intention to prevent them from continuing to volunteer for this service.

HEALTH OF NATIVE TROOPS IN THE SOUDAN.

MR. PIRIE (Aberdeen, N.): I beg to ask the Under Secretary of State for Foreign Affairs whether the Government have any information as to the state of health of the native troops quartered at the present moment in the Soudan; whether it is the case that they are suffering to a great extent from cerebral fever, from which, even if the attack does not end fatally, the patient never permanently recovers; what has been the mortality amongst those troops since our

taking possession of the Soudan; and what is the percentage of deaths among those attacked by the cerebral fever?

MR. BRODRICK: We have received no detailed report as to the state of health of the native troops at present in the Soudan, but such Reports would naturally be addressed to the Egyptian and not to Her Majesty's Government. It is known that the troops operating on the Blue Nile have suffered severely from the climate there, and the Egyptian Army generally has been subjected to considerable strain during the last 12 months. Statistics as to mortality and sickness will be called for.

EXPENDITURE UNDER THE NAVAL WORKS ACT.

MR. PIRIE: I beg to ask the First Lord of the Admiralty with reference to the Naval Works Act, 1897, if he would state the expenditure during each of the years since the passing of the Act in England, Scotland, and Ireland respectively, and the estimated expenditure in each of the three countries for the coming year under that Act?

MR. AUSTEN CHAMBERLAIN: No, Sir, I am unable to give this information, as the Navy Accounts are not kept in such a form as to show it.

FRANCE AND THE NILE VALLEY.

SIR E. ASHMEAD-BARTLETT (Sheffield, Ecclesall): I beg to ask the Under Secretary of State for Foreign Affairs whether he can give the House any information as to the negotiations with France regarding the Nile Valley, and especially as to the delimitation of the Western Soudan?

MR. BRODRICK: I am unable to say more than that the negotiations are progressing.

IRISH LOCAL GOVERNMENT ORDERS.

MR. M. HEALY (Cork): I beg to ask the Chief Secretary to the Lord Lieutenant of Ireland whether he is aware that considerable difficulty exists at present in obtaining copies of some of the Orders and Rules made under the Local Government Bill; and whether he will arrange to have published at an early date an official collection of all Orders in Council, Rules of Court, and sealed Orders and Rules of all kinds of the Local Government Board made under or in consequence of the Local Government (Ireland) Act?

MR. GERALD BALFOUR: I. believe there has been delay in the issue of some of the Orders in Council and Rules for sale by the Stationery Office, owing, no doubt, to the very unusual pressure on the printers in connection with the Local Government Act. I have no doubt that an official publication of the Rules and Orders under the Act, such as the honourable Member suggests, would be of much advantage to the local authorities and to the public generally, but I do not consider that such a publication should be issued until the Act is in operation, and all the Orders, including the Registration Orders, are made.

MR. M. HEALY: Are not Orders issued from day to day dealing with questions which arise as the clauses come in force, and are they not inaccessible to us?

MR. DILLON: May I suggest that arrangements might be made to circulate them to Members of the House as soon as they are issued?

MR. GERALD BALFOUR: I will inquire into that.

BISHOPRIC OF MADAGASCAR.

MR. S. SMITH (Flintshire): I beg to ask the First Lord of the Treasury whether the Rev. G. L. King, Vicar of St. Mary's, South Shields, has been nominated by the Archbishop of Canterbury to be Bishop of Madagascar; whether he is aware that the new Bishop is a member of the English Church Union, and wears in his present church illegal Romish vestments, and burns altar lights in the daytime; and whether this nomination will be sanctioned?

THE FIRST LORD OF THE TREASURY (MR. A. J. BALFOUR, Manchester, E.): The Bishop of Madagascar, as I understand, has been appointed by the Archbishop of Canterbury on behalf of the Society for the Propagation of the Gospel. He does not receive anything from any public source, nor have the Government any title to interfere in the matter.

MR. TIMOTHY HEALY: With reference to the Question just put, may I ask whether it is in order to introduce into it the words "Romish vestments," seeing that their use is offensive to a great mass of the community? If Irish Members put Questions on the Paper, they are always most severely edited.

MR. SPEAKER: I think it would have been better to have left out the word Romish.

IRISH JUDICATURE ACT.

MR. TIMOTHY HEALY: I beg to ask the First Lord of the Treasury if he is aware that after the passing of the Irish Judicature Act, between 1879 and 1895 the sum of £91,525, being the amount of the unclaimed dividends of Irish bankrupts, was transferred to London from Dublin; what has become of this money, and is it available for expenditure on purely British purposes; is there a further sum of £5,000, now awaiting transfer to England, in the Irish Bankruptcy Court; what will be done with this money; and would he devise a scheme to allow purely Irish funds to remain in or be spent on an Irish account, considering that the stamps payable in bankruptcy in Ireland in 1898 amount to £2,856, all of which went to the Imperial Revenue?

THE FIRST LORD OF THE TREASURY: Subject to the correction of the figure £91,525 for £19,000, the first part of the Question is correct. By Statute all the unclaimed dividends on stock accrue, not for British purposes, but for the reduction of the National Debt, which concerns the United Kingdom. As regards the last part, the Bankruptcy Court is a branch of the High Court, and the fees of the High Court fall far short of the administrative expenses.

FEES ON PRIVATE BILLS.

SIR J. LENG: I beg to ask the First Lord of the Treasury whether, considering that 35 years have elapsed since, on the initiative of the Government of the day, the fees of the two Houses of Parliament on Private Bills were reduced, and that a surplus of more than £30,000 per annum has since accrued, he will, in connection with the Private Legislation (Scotland) Bill, give effect to the recommendation of the Select Committee of last Session by moving the appointment of a Joint Committee of both Houses to revise the scale of fees on Private Bills?

THE FIRST LORD OF THE TREASURY: There is no surplus of £30,000. The honourable Member does not appear to be aware that this £30,000 so received is much less than the expenditure on administration. The mere cost, however, does not settle the question, which awaits further consideration.

NORTH SEAS FISHERY COMMISSION.

MR. HEDDERWICK: I beg to ask the First Lord of the Treasury whether the composition of the International Scientific North Seas Fishery Commission has been fixed, the propositions to be submitted to the Commissioners have been agreed upon, and, if so, could he state who are to represent this country; and, what are the terms defining the scope of the Commission?

THE FIRST LORD OF THE TREASURY: The exact composition of the Commission has not yet been fixed, nor yet have the British delegates been selected. The terms defining the scope of the inquiry are also still under consideration. The Commission is expected to meet early in June.

MR. HEDDERWICK: Where?

THE FIRST LORD OF THE TREASURY: That I cannot say.

WAIMA INCIDENT.

MR. HEDDERWICK: I beg to ask the First Lord of the Treasury whether Her Majesty's Government have abandoned the claim for compensation from France in respect of the British Officers killed by French troops at Waima; and, if not, whether he will state what steps Her Majesty's Government are taking, and what stage the negotiations have reached?

THE FIRST LORD OF THE TREASURY: I regret that I can add nothing to the answer given by the Under Secretary for Foreign Affairs on the 2nd inst. —namely, that communications were addressed to the French Government on 14th July 1898, and that no reply has been received. It is proposed to deal with the claims in question in connection with others arising out of affairs in West Africa now under consideration.

SIR E. ASHMEAD-BARTLETT: May I ask whether a similar answer was not given to me in 1893, and in every succeeding year since that date?

THE FIRST LORD OF THE TREASURY: I do not think a precisely similar answer could have been given, as the answer I read refers to communications in 1898.

MR. HEDDERWICK: Do I understand the Government have taken no further steps?

THE FIRST LORD OF THE TREASURY: They are taking further steps.

INDIA AND BOUNTY-FED SUGAR.

MR. MACLEAN (Cardiff): I beg to ask the First Lord of the Treasury whether, in view of the deep interest taken by Members on both sides of the House in the Bill to impose a countervailing duty on sugar, which has been introduced, with the express authority of the Secretary of State for India, into the Calcutta Legislative Council, and also considering the novelty and importance of the commercial policy embodied in the Bill, he will give a day for its discussion before it receives the Royal Assent?

THE FIRST LORD OF THE TREASURY: I fear that in the present condition of public business it would be quite impossible to afford my honourable Friend the facilities he asks for.

Mr. MACLEAN: Then I beg to give notice that I will raise the question on the Motion for the adjournment over Easter.

Mr. SWIFT MacNEILL: Will the First Lord not ask his honourable Friend the Member for the Central Division of Sheffield to take off his blocking notice?

[No Reply.]

VOLUNTEER RIFLE RANGES.

Mr. MONK (Gloucester): I beg to ask the Under Secretary of State for War whether any grants have been made, under the Military Works Act, 1897, towards providing rifle ranges for Volunteer companies; and, whether, the War Office is prepared to recommend loans from the Public Works Commissioners, on favourable terms, for acquiring rifle ranges for Volunteer companies whose headquarters are not within reasonable distance from any Army range?

The UNDER SECRETARY OF STATE FOR WAR (Mr. G. WYNDHAM, Dover): No special grants have been made under the Military Works Act, 1897, towards providing rifle ranges for Volunteer corps, but ranges are being constructed under that Act in various parts of Great Britain which will, it is anticipated, be available for use by Volunteers on payment of the usual rents. The Military Lands Act of 1892 gave the Secretary of State power to recommend loans by the Public Loan Commissioners to Volunteer corps for the purchase of land, and since that Act was passed, about 40 loans have been made under its provisions, to the amount of about £112,000.

MONMOUTH ASSIZES.

Mr. M'KENNA (Monmouth, N.): I beg to ask the Secretary of State for the Home Department whether his attention has been called to the grave inconveniences suffered by a large number of jurors who were summoned to attend the Assizes held at Monmouth on 20th

February, and were informed in Court that their services would not be required, as there was only one case to be tried; and whether any steps can be taken to prevent as far as possible the useless summoning of jurors?

Mr. JESSE COLLINGS: The Secretary of State is aware of the inconvenience sometimes caused to jurors by their being summoned when no occasion arises for their services; but he does not see his way to propose legislation to prevent this.

AMERICA AND WEST INDIAN SUGAR INDUSTRY.

Mr. LLEWELLYN (Somerset, N.): I beg to ask the Under Secretary of State for Foreign Affairs whether Her Majesty's Government have any information as to the terms on which the United States of America will permit the import of sugar from their new dependencies in the West Indies and the Philippines?

Mr. BRODRICK: No information has been received as to any change in the existing arrangements, but Her Majesty's Ambassador at Washington has been requested to inquire and report.

BRITISH AND FRENCH TRADE.

Sir J. LENG: I beg to ask Mr. Chancellor of the Exchequer whether he has observed the statement made by a member of the British Chamber of Commerce in Paris that for the last 25 years French exports to England have been regularly increasing, while British exports to France have been decreasing, and that not only has the trade between the two countries ceased to increase, but is on the downward grade; and whether, in consideration of the commercial attitude of France to Great Britain, he will consider the advisability of meeting the anticipated deficit in the revenue of this country by bringing under taxation for revenue purposes luxuries imported from France, such as wines, silks, and millinery?

THE CHANCELLOR OF THE EXCHEQUER: I do not think that the statement referred to in the first paragraph of the Question is entirely accurate; but it is the fact that there has been some falling off in recent years in the value of British exports to France, mainly in the re-exports. With regard to the second paragraph of the Question, I must remind the honourable Member that our tariff is drawn up with a view of obtaining revenue and not with the object of reprisals.

BRITISH MUSEUM ATTENDANTS.

CAPTAIN JESSEL (St. Pancras, S.): I beg to ask the Secretary to the Treasury whether he is aware that the attendants at the British Museum are the only class whose minimum and maximum salaries have not been raised since 1857; and that they are the only class who do not participate in the Saturday half-holiday; and whether, considering that all attendants who have entered the service of the trustees since 1887 are liable to serve an hour longer, and that the assistants, in addition to the increase of salary last year, have since 1857 received two rises in response to petitions based on the greater cost of living, the claims of attendants for like favourable treatment will now be taken into consideration?

MR. HANBURY: The attendants at the British Museum are the only class whose minimum and maximum salaries have not been raised since 1857; but appreciable improvements have been made in their position during that period by converting three classes into two, by reducing the number of the lower class, and by the grant of special allowances to 23 out of 155 attendants. It is, of course, not desirable to interfere with the convenience of the public, who visit the Museum in large number on Saturday afternoons. But, on ordinary weekdays, the younger attendants are frequently not required to give the full attendance for which they are liable; and the older attendants receive overtime pay if required to attend after 4 p.m. or 5 p.m (according to the season

of the year). When the staff of attendants are on duty for the full time during summer months they are allowed four Saturday half-holidays. The hours of duty for attendants appointed since 1887 are from 9 to 6 (instead of from 9 to 4, 5, or 6 according to season). In practice, however, the attendants at the Natural History Museum always leave at the old hours; and those at Bloomsbury are frequently allowed to do so. There is, of course, great dissimilarity between the position of the assistants and that of the attendants. The assistants carry on the literary and scientific work of the Museum and correspond to the upper Division of the Civil Service. The attendants are recruited either from the ranks of gentlemen's servants or from boys who have served an apprenticeship as boy attendants. The subjects for entrance examination are elementary, and there is no competition. The increased cost of living was only one of the many reasons put forward by the assistants for an increase in salary.

ACCIDENT ON THE "TERRIBLE."

COMMANDER BETHELL (York, E. R., Holderness): I beg to ask the Secretary to the Admiralty if he can give the House any particulars of the accident on board the "Terrible."

MR. MACARTNEY: The letter received from the captain of the "Terrible" reports the death of Edward Sullivan, stoker, which occurred at 6.43 p.m. on the 13th instant from injuries received in the stokehold, due to the bursting of one of the boiler tubes. Three other men were injured, but are progressing favourably. The accident occurred at about 11 a.m. The cause of the accident will be made the subject of an official inquiry.

MR. ALLAN: Arising out of this answer, may I ask whether it is not advisable to reconsider the making of these boilers for Her Majesty's yacht?

[No Reply.]

BUSINESS OF THE HOUSE.

MR. BUCHANAN (Aberdeenshire, E.): As the right honourable Gentleman has given notice of his intention to suspend the Twelve o'clock Rule to-night, may I ask that Vote 10 in the Navy Estimates, which contain for the first time a demand for money for Wei-hai-Wei, should not be taken after, say, half-past ten?

SIR H. CAMPBELL-BANNERMAN (Stirling Burghs): Is this the proper time to ask as to the course of business and as to the Adjournment for Easter. Also how long the Adjournment will be for?

THE FIRST LORD OF THE TREA-SURY: As regards the question put to me by the honourable Member for Aberdeenshire, I beg to say that it is perfectly true that Vote 10 contains an item for Wei-hai-Wei, but that has nothing to do with the fortification of Wei-hai-Wei. It is a Vote merely for a coal-pier and a coal-shed, as I understand it. I think that a more fitting opportunity for discussing the question will be when the Vote for expenditure on fortifications arises, and that must come on during the present Session. Perhaps the House will consent to the discussion taking place on that Vote rather than upon this Vote, seeing that quite apart from the special exigencies of Supply, which are pressing at the moment, the discussion would then come in more appropriately. I hope we shall not have a late sitting to-night, but I think the House is aware of the reasons why I am making this extra demand on its time. What we have to get before Easter in the way of Supply are Navy Votes A, 1, and 10, and, I should hope, some non-effective Votes, and Army Votes 1, 14, 15, and 16, and the Vote on Account. I propose to take the Vote on Account on Monday, unless such progress is made with Supply to-night that that Vote can be taken to-morrow. On Tuesday I propose to take the Report of Supply, and on Thursday we ought to make some progress with the Second Reading of the Private Bill Procedure (Scotland) Bill, and on Friday I propose to get the Speaker out of the Chair on the Civil Service Estimates. That must

be done on Friday in order that we may proceed regularly with our Friday work of Supply. I do not know what time the right honourable Gentleman desires for the Second Reading of the London Government Bill, but I propose to take it on Monday week, and go on with it until it is finished, and to adjourn for the holidays immediately afterwards. I hope that that will be convenient to the House.

SIR H. CAMPBELL-BANNERMAN: The right honourable Gentleman has made a proposal which I do not think will be acceptable to any part of the House. The idea of the House commencing discussion on the Second Reading of the London Government Bill on the Monday in Passion week, and going on with it until it is finished, I can hardly believe to be a conception of business which is seriously put forward by the right honourable Gentleman. If the Second Reading of the Bill is to be taken before Easter, then I would respectfully suggest that the Debate should be commenced not later than Thursday in next week, so that there may be adequate opportunity for the discussion of a Bill of such immense importance.

THE FIRST LORD OF THE TREA-SURY: No doubt the right honourable Gentleman will assist the Government on Tuesday in getting through the business, and, of course, I shall be glad to meet his views on the London Government Bill. But I think that we ought to get the Second Reading of the Scotch Bill and of the London Bill before Easter.

*MR. WEIR: Will the right honourable Gentleman reconsider his decision, and not take Vote 14 at a late hour?

SIR H. FOWLER (Wolverhampton, E.): I wish to ask the First Lord of the Treasury what is the reason that for the first time it is necessary to take more than one Vote for the Army and Navy for the Appropriation Bill presented before March 31? It has hitherto been usual to take Vote A, which settles the number of men for the year, and Vote 1, which gives enough money to go on with until after Easter It is an entirely new practice to put down other

Votes, and, as a matter of fact, it is not necessary to have the Vote for money at all.

THE FIRST LORD OF THE TREASURY: I do not think that the practice is as new as the right honourable Gentleman supposes. We have now only one Vote on Account, and in order to get sufficient money to go on with to the end of Supply it is necessary to take other Votes besides Vote 1.

SIR H. FOWLER: But the Government are going to ask for the largest Vote on Account which has ever been presented before Easter, and the whole of the Army and Navy wages.

THE FIRST LORD OF THE TREASURY: The right honourable Gentleman is casting his mind back to the period before the new practice obtained. Formerly Votes on Account were taken for two months; but under the new Rules we have only one Vote on Account to carry us on till August. Otherwise one of the counting days of Supply, which might be devoted to a special matter of policy, is occupied with the miscellaneous discussion of a Vote on Account.

SIR H. CAMPBELL-BANNERMAN: If the right honourable gentleman takes so large a sum for the Army and the Navy as is represented by the Votes which he now proposes to take—one-fifth of the whole expenditure of the year— I hope he will at least put himself under some explicit obligation not to huddle the remaining Votes on to the end of the Session. The right honourable Gentleman will see that by giving so large a sum as that the House parts with its control over the discussion of the Army and Navy Votes.

THE FIRST LORD OF THE TREASURY: I do not think that the House does part with its control. The appeal of the right honourable Gentleman to me not to huddle the remaining Votes to the end of the Session hardly does justice to the effort which I have constantly made to allocate Fridays exactly as the right honourable Gentleman desires. What I was reproached for by the right honourable Member for Wolverhampton, when the Order was under discussion, was giving too much

Sir H. Fowler.

weight to the opinion of the Leader of the Opposition in the allocation of Fridays. I am only too anxious to take the advice (which I regard as of the highest value) of the right honourable Gentleman in the distribution of the Estimates; and any appeal he makes for a particular subject to be discussed on a particular Friday will always meet with favourable consideration, as it did in the days of his predecessor.

SIR H. FOWLER: The right honourable Gentleman has not answered my Question as to why it is necessary before 31st March to take more than the two first Votes for the Army and Navy.

MR. HANBURY: If the right honourable Gentleman will allow me I will explain. We want to avoid a second Consolidated Fund Bill, and the amount we shall require to carry us on until August 12th is £29,000,000. By the Vote on Account we take about £15,000,000. Vote 1 of the Army and Vote 1 of the Navy give us only another £12,000,000. That is about £2,000,000 short, and we propose to make it up by taking the other Votes.

SIR H. FOWLER: That is on the assumption that no Votes will be taken between now and 29th March. There is, moreover, power with Army and Navy Votes to transfer money from one Vote to another, and yet the right honourable Gentleman is going to put the House to this great trouble just to avoid the inconvenience to the Treasury of a second Consolidated Fund Bill.

THE FIRST LORD OF THE TREASURY: What trouble am I putting the House to?

SIR H. FOWLER: These long sittings.

THE FIRST LORD OF THE TREASURY: These Army Votes 14, 15, and 16 are not controversial Votes. With regard to Vote 10, that stands on a different footing, and we do not ask for that from the point of view of money. From that point of view, I would rather get the Navy non-effective votes. But I am informed by the Admiralty that it is very important for them to begin all the new works belonging to the year, and unless they get Parliamentary sanction by this Vote they cannot begin. Therefore Vote 10 is asked for on different grounds from Votes 14, 15, and 16, which are uncontroversial.

MR. GIBSON BOWLES (Lynn Regis): The right honourable Gentleman has suggested that the policy of converting Wei-hai-Wei into a naval station might better be discussed on the Army Votes for fortifications instead of on Vote 10. Can the right honourable Gentleman undertake that honourable Members will not be precluded from discussing the question on the Army Votes?

THE FIRST LORD OF THE TREASURY: I am reluctant to answer a question which trespasses on the domain of order, of which I am not the judge. But if what the honourable Member wishes to discuss is the fortification of Wei-hai-Wei as a military base, the Vote for fortifications and not the Vote for a coalshed would form the more appropriate occasion for such a discussion.

SIR H. CAMPBELL-BANNERMAN: In the midst of this anxious series of interrogatories, the right honourable Gentleman has forgotten to answer what was, perhaps, the most important of all the questions—that relating to the holidays.

THE FIRST LORD OF THE TREASURY: I hope that in any case we shall not have to meet before the Monday week after Easter.

MR. SWIFT MacNEILL: Will the right honourable Gentleman undertake not to take Vote 1 of the Army Estimates after midnight if it is not reached before midnight?

THE FIRST LORD OF THE TREASURY: The House will see that to-day and to-morrow are allocated to business which ought very easily to be got into the compass of those two days, especially if the Twelve o'clock Rule is suspended, so that the honourable Member will probably have an opportunity of bringing on the subject early.

SUSPENSION OF THE TWELVE O'CLOCK RULE.

Motion made, and Question put—

"That the Proceedings of the Committee of Supply, if under discussion at Twelve o'clock this night, be not interrupted under Standing Order Sittings of the House."—*(First Lord of the Treasury.)*

The House divided:—Ayes 221; Noes 124.—(Division List No. 44.)

AYES.

Aird, John	Blundell, Colonel Henry	Cross, Herb. Shepherd (Bolton)
Allhusen.Augustus HenryEden	Bonsor, Henry Cosmo Orme	Cruddas, William Donaldson
Allsopp, Hon. George	Boscawen, Arthur Griffith-	Cubitt, Hon. Henry
Arnold, Alfred	Boulnois, Edmund	Currie, Sir Donald
Arnold-Forster, Hugh O.	Bowles, Capt. H.F.(Middlesex)	Curzon, Viscount
Arrol, Sir William	Bowles,T.Gibson(King's Lynn	Dalkeith, Earl of
Ashmead-Bartlett, Sir Ellis	Brodrick, Rt. Hon. St. John	Dalrymple, Sir Charles
Atkinson, Rt. Hon. John	Carlile, William Walter	Denny, Colonel
Bagot, Capt.Josceline FitzRoy	Cavendish, R. F. (N. Lancs.)	Dickson-Poynder, Sir John P.
Baillie, James E. B. (Inverness)	Cavendish, V. C.W. (Derbysh.)	Dorington, Sir John Edward
Baird, John George Alexander	Cecil, Evelyn (Hertford, East)	Douglas, Rt. Hon. A. Akers-
Baldwin, Alfred	Chaloner, Capt. R. G. W.	Doxford, William Theodore
Balfour, Rt. Hn.A. J. (Manc'r)	Chamberlain, Rt.Hn.J. (Birm.)	Drucker, A.
Balfour,RtHnGeraldW.(Leeds)	Chamberlain, J. Austen (Wor.)	Duncombe, Hon. Hubert V.
Banbury, Frederick George	Chaplin, Rt. Hon. Henry	Dyke, Rt.Hn.Sir William Hart
Barry, Sir Francis T.(Windsor)	Charrington, Spencer	Elliot, Hon. A. Ralph Douglas
Bartley, George C. T.	Clare, Octavius Leigh	Fardell, Sir T. George
Barton, Dunbar Plunket	Cochrane, Hon. Thos. H. A. E.	Fergusson,RtHn SirJ.(Manc'r)
Bathurst, Hon. Allen Benjamin	Coddington, Sir William	Field, Admiral (Eastbourne)
Beach,Rt.Hn.Sir M.H.(Bristol)	Coghill, Douglas Harry	Finlay, Sir Robert Bannatyne
Beach,W.W.Bramston (Hants)	Cohen, Benjamin Louis	Fisher, William Hayes
Beckett, Ernest William	Collings, Rt. Hon. Jesse	Fison, Frederick William
Begg, Ferdinand Faithfull	Cooke, C.W.Radcliffe (Heref'd)	FitzWygram, General Sir F.
Bentinck, Lord Henry C.	Cornwallis, Fiennes Stanley W.	Fletcher, Sir Henry
Bethell, Commander	Courtney, Rt. Hn. Leonard·H.	Forster, Henry William
Bhownaggree, Sir M. M.	Cripps, Charles Alfred	Foster, Colonel (Lancaster)
Biddulph, Michael	Cross, Alexander (Glasgow)	Fry, Lewis

Garfit, William
Gibbons, J. Lloyd
Gibbs,HnA.G.H.(City of Lon.
Giles, Charles Tyrrell
Godson,Sir Augustus Frederick
Goldsworthy, Major-General
Gordon, Hon. John Edward
Gorst, Rt. Hn. Sir John Eldon
Goschen, George J. (Sussex)
Goulding, Edward Alfred
Graham, Henry Robert
Gray, Ernest (West Ham)
Green,WalfordD.(Wednesbury)
Greville, Hon. Ronald
Gull, Sir Cameron
Gunter, Colonel
Halsey, Thomas Frederick
Hamilton, Rt. Hn. Lord George
Hanbury, Rt. Hn. Robert Wm.
Hanson, Sir Reginald
Hardy, Laurence
Hare, Thomas Leigh
Heath, James
Heaton, John Henniker
Helder, Augustus
Hill,Rt.Hn.A.Staveley(Staffs.)
Hill, Sir Edwd. Stock (Bristol)
Hoare, Ed. Brodie (Hampst'd)
Hobhouse, Henry
Holland, Hon. Lionel R. (Bow)
Houston, R. P.
Howard, Joseph
Hozier, Hn. James Henry Cecil
Hubbard, Hon. Evelyn
Hudson, George Bickersteth
Jebb, Richa 'd Claverhouse
Jeffreys, Arthur Frederick
Jenkins, Sir John Jones
Jessel, Capt. Herbert Merton
Johnston (William (Belfast)
Jolliffe, Hon. H. George
Kemp, George
Kenyon-Slaney, Col. William
Kimber, Henry
Knowles, Lees
Lafone, Alfred
Lees, Sir Elliott (Birkenhead)
Leigh-Bennett, Henry Currie

Leighton, Stanley
Lockwood, Lt.-Col. A. R.
Loder, Gerald Walter Erskine
Long, Col. Chas. W. (Evesham)
Long, Rt. Hn. Walter (L'pool)
Lorne, Marquess of
Lowles, John
Macartney, W. G. Ellison
Macdona, John Cumming
MacIver, David (Liverpool)
Maclean, James Mackenzie
M'Arthur, Charles (Liverpool)
M'Iver, Sir Lewis (Edin-, W.)
Malcolm, Ian
Maple, Sir John Blundell
Marks, Henry Hananel
Middlemore,John Throgmorton
Milbank, Sir Powlett Chas. J.
Monk, Charles James
Morrell, George Herbert
Morton, Arthur H. A.(Deptf'd)
Mount, William George
Murray,RtHnA.Graham(Bute)
Murray, Charles J. (Coventry)
Myers, William Henry
Nicol, Donald Ninian
Orr-Ewing, Charles Lindsay
Pease, Herbert Pike (Drlngtn.)
Percy, Earl
Philpotts, Captain Arthur
Pilkington, Richard
Platt-Higgins, Frederick
Pretyman, Ernest George
Priestley,SirW.Overend(Edin.)
Pryce-Jones, Lt.-Col. Edward
Purvis, Robert
Rankin, Sir James
Rentoul, James Alexander
Richardson, Sir T. (Hartlepool)
Ritchie, Rt. Hn. Chas.Thomson
Roche, Hn. James (East Kerry)
Rothschild, Hn. Lionel Walter
Round, James
Russell, Gen. F.S.(Cheltenham)
Russell, T. W. (Tyrone)
Rutherford, John
Samuel, Harry S. (Limehouse)
Savory, Sir Joseph

Scoble, Sir Andrew Richard
Seely, Charles Hilton
Sharpe, William Edward T.
Sidebotham, J. W. (Cheshire)
Simeon, Sir Barrington
Sinclair, Louis (Romford)
Smith,Abel H. (Christchurch)
Smith, Jas. Parker (Lanarks.)
Smith, Hon. W. F. D. (Strand)
Stanley, Hn.Arthur (Ormskirk)
Stanley, Edwd. Jas. (Somerset)
Stanley, Henry M. (Lambeth)
Stanley, Lord (Lancs.)
Stewart. Sir M. J. M'Taggart
Stirling-Maxwell, Sir John M.
Stone, Sir Benjamin
Strutt, Hon. Charles Hedley
Talbot,RtHnG.J.(Oxf'd Univ.)
Thorburn, Walter
Thornton, Percy M.
Tomlinson, Wm. Ed. Murray
Tritton, Charles Ernest
Usborne, Thomas
Valentia, Viscount
Vincent, Col. Sir C. E. Howard
Wanklyn, James Leslie
Warr, Augustus Frederick
Webster, R. G. (St. Pancras)
Webster, Sir R. E. (I. of W.)
Welby, Lieut.-Col. A. C. E.
Wentworth, Bruce C. Vernon-
Whiteley, George (Stockport)
Whitmore, Charles Algernon
Williams, Jos. Powell (Birm.)
Willoughby de Eresby, Lord
Willox, Sir John Archibald
Wilson, John (Falkirk)
Wilson-Todd, Wm. H. (Yorks)
Wortley, Rt. Hn. C. B.(Stuart-
Wylie, Alexander
Wyndham, George
Yerburgh, Robert Armstrong
Young, Commander (Berks, E.)

TELLERS FOR THE AYES—
Sir William Walrond and
Mr. Anstruther.

NOES.

Abraham, Wm. (Cork, N.E.)
Allan, William (Gateshead)
Ashton, Thomas Gair
Asquith, Rt. Hon. Herbert H
Austin, Sir John (Yorkshire)
Austin, M. (Limerick, W.)
Bainbridge, Emerson
Baker, Sir John
Barlow, John Emmott
Bayley, Thomas (Derbyshire)
Beaumont, Wentworth C. B.
Billson, Alfred
Blake, Edward
Bryce, Rt. Hon. James
Buchanan, Thomas Ryburn
Burt, Thomas
Buxton, Sydney Charles
Caldwell, James
Cameron, Sir Charles (Glasgow)
Cameron, Robert (Durham)
Campbell-Bannerman, Sir H.

Causton, Sir Richard Knight
Clark, Dr. G. B. (Caithness-sh.)
Clough, Walter Owen
Colville, John
Crombie, John William
Curran, Thomas (Sligo, S.)
Dalziel, James Henry
Davies, M.Vaughan- (Cardigan)
Dilke, Rt. Hon. Sir Charles
Dillon, John
Donelan, Captain A.
Douglas, Charles M. (Lanark)
Duckworth, James
Dunn, Sir William
Ellis, John Edward (Notts)
Ellis, Thos. Ed. (Merionethsh.)
Evans, Sir Fras. H. (South'ton)
Farquharson, Dr. Robert
Fenwick, Charles
Ferguson, R. C. Munro (Leith)
Ffrench, Peter

Fowler, Rt. Hon. Sir Henry
Gladstone, Rt. Hn. Herbert J.
Goddard, Daniel Ford
Gold, Charles
Gourley, Sir Edwd. Temperley
Hammond, John (Carlow)
Hayne, Rt. Hn. Charles Seale-
Hazell, Walter
Healy, Maurice (Cork)
Healy, Timothy M. (N. Louth)
Hogan, James Francis
Holland, Wm. H. (York, W.R.)
Humphreys-Owen, Arthur C.
Hutton, Alfred E. (Morley)
Jacoby, James Alfred
Kay-Shuttleworth,RtHnSir U.
Kearley, Hudson E.
Kilbride, Denis
Kinloch, Sir Jno. Geo. Smyth
Lawson,SirWilfrid(Cumb'land)
Leng, Sir John

L...

Lloyd-George, David
Lough, Thomas
Macaleese, Daniel
M'Ewan, William
M'Kenna, Reginald
M'Killop, James
M'Laren, Charles Benjamin
Maddison, Fred
Maden, John Henry
Montague, Sir S.(Whitechapel)
Moore, Arthur (Londonderry)
Morgan, J. Lloyd(Carmarthen)
Morgan, W.Pritchard(Merthyr
Moulton, John Fletcher
Norton, Capt. Cecil William
Nussey, Thomas Willans
O'Brien, Patrick (Kilkenny)
O'Connor, James(Wicklow, W.)
O'Connor, T. P. (Liverpool)
O'Keeffe, Francis Arthur
O'Kelly, James
Oldroyd, Mark

Palmer, Sir Chas. M. (Durham)
Perks, Robert William
Pickersgill, Edward Hare
Pirie, Duncan V.
Price, Robert John
Priestley, Briggs (Yorks.)
Reckitt, Harold James
Richardson, J. (Durham)
Roberts, John H. (Denbighs.)
Robertson, Edmund (Dundee)
Samuel, J. (Stockton-on-Tees)
Schwann, Charles E.
Scott,Chas. Prestwich (Leigh)
Shaw, Charles Edw.(Stafford)
Sinclair, Capt. Jno.(Forfarshire
Smith, Samuel (Flint)
Soutter, Robinson
Stanhope, Hon. Philip J.
Stevenson, Francis S.
Strachey, Edward
Sullivan, Donal (Westmeath)
Thomas, Alf. (Glamorgan, E.)

Thomas, David Alf.(Merthyr)
Trevelyan, Charles Philips
Tully, Jasper
Wallace, Robert (Perth)
Walton,Jno.Lawson(Leeds,S.)
Walton, Joseph (Barnsley)
Warner, Thomas Courtenay T.
Wedderburn, Sir William
Weir, James Galloway
Williams,Jno.Carvell(Notts.)
Wills, Sir William Henry
Wilson, Henry J.(York,W.R.)
Wilson, John (Govan)
Wilson, Jos. H.(Middlesbro')
Woodhouse,SirJ.T.(Hudder'fd)
Woods, Samuel
Young, Samuel (Cavan, East)

Tellers for the Noes—
Mr. Edward Morton and
Mr. Hedderwick.

Ordered, That the Proceedings of the Committee of Supply, if under discussion at Twelve o'clock this night, be not interrupted under Standing Order Sittings of the House.

ORDERS OF THE DAY.

SUPPLY (NAVY ESTIMATES) [3rd Allotted Day].

Considered in Committee.

[Mr. Arthur O'Connor (Donegal, E.) in the Chair.]

(In the Committee.)

Navy Estimates, 1899-1900.

Debate resumed on Question [13th March]—

"That 110,640 men and boys be employed for the Sea and Coast Guard Services for the year ending on the 31st March 1900; including 18,505 Royal Marines."

*Mr. ALLAN (Gateshead): In reviewing the Navy Estimates this year, and also the statement made by the First Lord of the Admiralty, I will, with the leave of the House, take a short review, in the first place, of how the Estimates are submitted to Members of this House. I have complained repeatedly of the mode of getting up these Estimates, which is very unbusiness-like, so much so that I have great difficulty in following the figures which are put into these statistics as to the names of the ships and the amount of money spent upon them. For instance, I find on page 102 an item for repairs and alterations to ships amounting to £1,463,150. But this statement does not cover all the repairs, for I am brought face to face again with another total for repairs to ships. Here, again, under sub-head B, page 134, we have a sum put down for repairs of £647,330. Now, why is it that these items for repairs are put down in this way? Now, I draw the attention of the House to these figures, for when you add these two amounts together, what are you brought face to face with? Together these two amounts make a gross total of £1,800,000 put down in these Estimates for repairs to Her Majesty's ships. That means that nearly one-fifteenth of the total Navy Vote appears in these Estimates as repairs, and I want to know where all that money has gone? There is nothing mentioned here to show how it has been spent, and I want to know what ships have been repaired, and what has been the cost of the repairs of every ship. I vote the money for the Navy most willingly, but I do want to know where this money has gone to for repairs, and why you have put it down like this and lumped all these amounts together? The Admiralty is asking us to vote the sum of nearly £2,000,000 for repairs. I wish to direct the right honourable Gentleman's attention to the confused manner in which these Estimates are submitted to us in this House; for every vessel the repairs ought to be put down opposite the name of that particular ship, the same as any other great mercantile company would do, so that we should know where we are with regard to the cost of the repairs of Her Majesty's ships. I now come to another point of greater importance in point of fact than even the money. The First Lord of the Admiralty, in his statement, gives us what he purposes doing, and the kind of vessels he proposes to build. We have here a very elaborate and a very nicely-worded account and particulars of the vessels which are to be built, and the draught, displacement, and indicated horse-power are given. They are to have nearly 30,000 indicated horse-power, and are to go at 23 knots. I wonder how long these vessels can steam at that speed, and what they would be able to do in time of war, if taken out to sea. I am afraid that these ships which are put down on this paper are peace vessels and not war vessels. Here you have 30,000 indicated horse-power and you are content to go 23 knots; but judging from the amount of coal which they will attempt to carry they can only have about three days' steaming. Why, such ships are no good. What is the use of building a vessel to go 23 knots with 30,000 indicated horse-power when she cannot go to sea for a longer period than three days? I find also that all these vessels are to be fitted with Belleville boilers. I have stood up in this House now for a number of years, and I have spoken against the sudden and wholesale adoption of these water-tube boilers in the Navy. I am not prejudiced in this matter; I have been too long at engineering to be prejudiced against any improvements in engineering, for I have done a little bit myself at improvements in this respect, and I speak as one who desires to see the best article obtained for our money. But what is the picture presented to us to-day? It is this—you have got these boilers in one of your cruisers, and in consequence of an explosion these poor men have been lying there parboiled. In the Navy we have the best of ships, the best of guns, and the best of men, but down in the engine-room the boilers are all wrong, and you are now finding it out, and my words are unfortunately coming true to-day. What have been the results of your trial trips lately? One of your ships has been six months under trial, and has not yet joined the Fleet; and I ask, is there a shipowner in this House who would have a boat that could not run its trial trip under six months? We have voted the money for the "Niobe," and I am afraid she will turn out to be

Mr. Allan.

another "Terrible." Some of your ships cannot steam from Gibraltar to this country without having a couple of explosions and returning home a cripple. Where is your "Terrible"? It is no use the Admiralty attempting to minimise that disaster, for the public will not have it. We have been gulled too long in these matters, and the Admiralty love darkness rather than light in these things. They are afraid of criticism, and they hush everything up. You come down here to this House with fine, smooth, honeyed statements and with nice stories about the Navy, and we have voted millions for the Fleet, and yet there are numbers of our vessels like the "Terrible" ruined by boiler explosions and fit only for scrap iron. (Laughter.) I see from that laugh that the right honourable Gentleman's responsibilities lie very lightly upon him. I cannot laugh under such circumstances, and I cannot smile while the British sailors are lying in the stoke-hole parboiled. I am rather inclined to shed tears than to smile at statements presented to us from the great "Department of defects." Of course, they tell us that everything will be put all right after the next trial, and that is how the nation is gulled. Now, I want to know what has been the cost of all this when you come down here for £2,370,000 more money? What has been the cost of these trips and these repairs, and why don't you show it? The cost of the repairs to that vessel, the "Terrible," ought to be in that Estimate, but you are afraid to put it there. What a satire it is upon the whole position to read in connection with the Institute of Civil Engineers statements the night before the accident lauding these boilers up to the skies, and the next morning we have a great explosion. I come down and stand on practical ground, and I say that if you want to steam 22 knots your ships are not right, and none of your vessels have done it yet. I speak now of vessels which are well known to the right honourable Gentleman, in which the Admiralty officials have seen fit to adopt a boiler which, as I have often said before, is not a boiler at all, but is one of those combinations of pipes which are commonly known in the North as heaters of conservatories. (Laughter.) I want to impress upon this House the seriousness of this question. It is no laughing matter, for it is a national question. The Navy is our first line of defence, and our first line should be the best line, and on these grounds I appeal to this House to listen to the facts. Why is it that your officials at the Admiralty permit these vessels to carry 280 and 300 pounds of steam in these boilers, and do not use it on the engines, while we in our ordinary daily work can work up to 160 and 180 pounds and put it on the engine. I will enlighten the right honourable Gentleman on this question, for he is not an engineer. The reason of it is this—you are forced to carry 260, 280, and 300 pounds of steam, because when you attempt to do with less the whole of the water in the boilers will come right away into the engine, and what is the result, supposing anything happens with the tubes? They say that in this accident it was only one of the tubes, but we shall see. We will take it at one tube, and what has happened? The whole of the fires are put out, the men are surrounded with flames, and there is an enormous pressure behind in the boiler. The engineering is false, and there is no engineer would pass such a thing. You cannot help yourself by the adoption of such generators. I will just show what can be done, and what really ought to have been done. There was a cruiser built at Elswick for Japan, and it was called the "Asama," and I wish to direct the right honourable Gentleman's attention to this boat. She was put on her trial trip, and she ran with 13,000 indicated horse-power 19 knots an hour, and she did this with ordinary boilers and 150 pounds pressure as against your 280 and 300 pounds. What is more, this vessel at her highest speed of 22 knots can steam for six days. Now, take the "Terrible." What has she done? By your own statement, the "Terrible" at 19,000 indicated horse-power, cannot go more than 20 knots. Then, again, the consumption of coal on the "Terrible" is about 400 tons a day, and her limit of steaming about four days, as against 260 tons of coal by the "Asama,"which can steam six days. Now I want to impress upon the right honourable Gentleman these facts. Why cannot you build ships like that? In adopting these Belleville boilers the Admiralty went against their own Boiler Committee's recommendations, and they heedlessly, foolishly, and hurriedly did so, without giving them a fair trial, and the consequence is that the whole Fleet has got into this mess. I will ask the right honourable Gentleman to-day a very pertinent question. You are now fitting such boilers as these in the new yacht which is being built for Her Majesty. Supposing such an explosion had taken place with Her Majesty on board, what would the country have said? And what is there to prevent such an explosion taking place when she has once been put to sea, because the boilers in Her Majesty's yacht have never been fairly tested. I have challenged the Admiralty to send one of the cruisers fitted with these boilers across the Atlantic, and I have offered to go out with it myself to see what it was like, and I would go at full speed if they like, but they have never done that. I am very sorry that the Fleet for which I have voted so much money should be in this crippled condition, for I do not hesitate to say that our ships are practically ruined by these boilers. I will not weary the House by the letters which I have received from these poor men down in the engine-rooms of the vessels fitted with these boilers. Their nerves are in a state of tension, for they are afraid at every moment that the boilers are going to burst and blow them to bits. Just look at the future, supposing we had a war. Think of these poor men down in the engine-room, with their minds in such a state of anxiety, afraid every moment that something is going to happen to the boilers. The men on the "Terrible" were panic-stricken, and if that accident had occurred in time of war she could have been captured by a gunboat. Is that the condition which the British Navy should be in? I have another name for it, and I say that it is a squandering of the public money heedlessly and recklessly, and not any amount of talk and smoothing over on the Front Bench in trying to whitewash it can take away the facts. I stand on facts, and I am an advocate always of every improvement in engineering, and this is a retrograde action on the part of the Admiralty, for water-tube boilers were played out before some of the officials of the Admiralty were born. They were tried and found wanting 50 years ago, and you now inform the House that you have paid £146,000 for royalties on them. I will show you what that means. Fancy Great Britain, the country of engineers, having to pay £146,000 to a French company! For that sum of money you could have got 5,000 tons of ordinary boilers, such as those with which the "Asama" is fitted, and such as those in use on the White Star, the Cunard, and other boats, which do the work regularly and well. We shall be told that this is a patent; but where is that patent, and who proved to the Admiralty that the so-called patent was a valid one?

THE DEPUTY CHAIRMAN: Order, order! I am very reluctant to interrupt the honourable Gentleman, but it appears to me that he is discussing a question which is very far from the subject under consideration.

*MR. ALLAN: Very well, Sir, I withdraw that statement, and will confine myself to utter condemnation of the Admiralty. I think that the boilers that have been put into these vessels will render these beautiful ships for which we are voting the money nothing less than useless, helpless tubs. Therefore, I bring my remarks to a close by urging the right honourable Gentleman to take this matter in hand. It is time that this House appointed a Committee to inquire into the whole Naval administration of the country. The money, as I have shown, has been squandered by hundreds of thousands—nay, by millions, and we have no statement of how it has been spent; we know nothing. We are kept in the dark, and then those who sit upon that Bench come down here and act as barristers on behalf of a department whose actions have been tried and found wanting. I speak upon this matter with sorrow. Many of our ships are good ships, and I regret that I have been obliged to make use of the words that I have. And I say, without fear of contradiction from any quarters, that our beautiful Fleet is absolutely ruined by the boilers that have been put into her by the honourable Gentlemen sitting opposite.

MR. ARNOLD-FORSTER (Belfast, W.): Upon a point of order, Sir, I desire to know if a general discussion can take place upon this Vote, or whether it

Mr. Allan.

must be confined to matters directly affecting this Vote?

THE DEPUTY CHAIRMAN : This is Vote A—a Vote for men—and any discussion can be allowed which is reasonably connected with that Vote.

*SIR U. KAY-SHUTTLEWORTH (Lancashire, Clitheroe): We were informed by the Leader of the Opposition that the usual discussion upon Vote A would be allowed, as in previous years.

THE DEPUTY CHAIRMAN : The condition in which the Committee is placed is one of great difficulty. But I must do the best I can, and, under the circumstances, I think there should be a general discussion upon this Vote.

MR. E. ROBERTSON (Dundee): I will not anticipate the answer that the Admiralty will have to make to my honourable Friend, nor do I propose to follow him into the details as to the "Belleville" boilers which he has addressed to the Committee; but I will just remind the House, without going into the details, that, beyond the unfortunate accident that took place on board the "Terrible"—which I am sure no one deplores more than the honourable Gentleman himself—my honourable Friend has not added one single iota to the numerous arguments which he has addressed to the House of Commons for five successive Sessions, and which have been rejected by five successive meetings of the Committee.

*MR. ALLAN: The more is the pity.

MR. E. ROBERTSON: I deeply regret the continued absence of the right honourable Gentleman the First Lord of the Admiralty from this Debate, and his absence is all the more to be regretted because, in my opinion, several questions have arisen upon which it would have been most satisfactory to have had additional explanations from the right honourable Gentleman at first hand. But I have no doubt that the honourable Gentleman who takes the place of the right honourable Gentleman upon this occasion comes fully prepared to give all the explanations there are necessary. I do not know that it is of much advantage to say anything more at this stage about the unusual and eccentric course which has been taken by the Admiralty upon this occasion—I mean, of course, of withholding all information about the Navy Estimates, and withholding the Estimates themselves and the explanatory statement until after the speech of the First Lord of the Admiralty in this House. I could not understand myself what was the possible reason for this procedure. But the First Lord of the Treasury told us some 10 days ago that it was dictated by profound reasons of public policy, and I waited to hear from the First Lord of the Admiralty's speech what those reasons were. I confess, if I am right in putting my finger, as I believe I did, upon the reasons to which the First Lord of the Treasury alluded, that those reasons are perfectly satisfactory, and are sufficiently important to my mind to remove all cause of complaint as to the course adopted by the Admiralty this year. What was the reason that the First Lord of the Admiralty gave for the course pursued of withholding the Estimates? Was it not this: that he did not wish these enormous Estimates to go forth to the world unaccompanied by the explanation that he was going to make? In that explanation he said they were not Estimates of aggression—that was his phrase—but that they were in the nature of additional Estimates. Now I take it that the meaning of the First Lord, and what he wanted to declare to the country and to the world, was, that if France or Russia, or either of them, reduced its shipbuilding programme, we on our side would do the same. That is the meaning which I put upon the statement of the right honourable Gentleman, and I find that it is satisfactory, and that all cause of complaint with respect to the course taken this year in connection with the withholding of the Navy Estimates is removed by that statement. But the matter has been entirely altered by the speech of the honourable Gentleman the Secretary to the Admiralty. I had not the good fortune to hear that speech, and therefore I am dependent upon a report in "The Times" as to what he said. Replying to the honourable and gallant Member for Eastbourne, who had protested against the line of policy which had been taken by the Admi-

ralty, the Secretary to the Admiralty used these words. What the First Lord had said was this: "that, if Europe did not agree,"—that is with reference to the proposed conference on the subject of disarmament—"the programme must stand." The honourable and gallant Gentleman inferred from that that the converse of the proposition followed. But the First Lord did not mean for one moment that such a converse should be drawn from his statement. That leaves the meaning of the Government in such obscurity that I must, in justice to the importance of the Question, recall to the House what the right honourable Gentleman the First Lord of the Admiralty really did say. He passes by the case of France with the remark that there is no increase in shipbuilding there; but he says in the case of Russia it is different; and, having called attention to the increase in the amount spent on shipbuilding by Russia, he comes to the declaration which is the real reason for withholding these Estimates from the House. He says—

"We have been compelled to increase our expenditure, as other nations have increased theirs, not taking a lead, nor pressing on more than they. As they have increased, we have increased. I have now to state on behalf of Her Majesty's Government that, similarly, if the other great Naval Powers should be prepared to diminish their programme of ship-building, we should, on our side, be prepared to meet such procedure by modifying ours."

Now, Mr. O'Connor, I cannot reconcile that statement with the statement made subsequently by the honourable Gentleman the Secretary to the Admiralty, because not only did the First Lord of the Admiralty mean the converse to be inferred, as the Secretary to the Admiralty puts it, but he declared it himself—

"Similarly, if the other great Naval Powers should be prepared to diminish their programmes of shipbuilding, we should, on our side, be prepared to meet such procedure by modifying ours."

Now, I think we ought to have this made perfectly clear by some definite statement from the Secretary to the Admiralty to-night. I have no doubt that the honourable Gentleman has consulted his Chief upon the subject, and what we want to get now is a definite statement of what it was that the First Lord of the Admiralty wished to go forth to the world, as qualifying these Estimates, and qualifying them in such a material manner that he would not risk the danger that would otherwise be incurred if these naked Estimates went forth without his explanation. May I point out this to the House: the Secretary to the Admiralty says that the converse was not meant to be inferred. If the honourable Gentleman is right, then what becomes of the reasons of public policy in deference to which the Estimates were withheld from the knowledge of this House until the right honourable Gentleman the First Lord has made his speech? It seems to me that the House and the country are entitled to know exactly what is the reason for the course taken in withholding the Naval Estimates from this House. It appears to me that the message whittled down by the Secretary to the Admiralty as it has been, is a message which is not worth sending out to any country as to the policy of the Government, and much less sending to the Conference which has been summoned on the Question of disarmament. Now, passing from that, what I want to point out is, that if this should be taken as true—and the statement of the First Lord of the Admiralty, as I interpret it, is not the true reason—I am unable to find any other, because, after all, the Estimates when disclosed revealed very little that we did not know before. They revealed nothing, or•next to nothing, which any newspaper gifted with the power of intelligently anticipating events might not have discovered for itself. I shall be quite willing to accept from the "Times," or any other newspaper concerned, that, as an explanation of previous knowledge, they had guessed the result, that there must be something like £3,000,000 in addition to expenses in the year. What is that increase due to? It is due mainly to what is called the Supplemental Programme of 1898. The burden of liability falling upon next year's Estimates in respect to that Supplemental Programme is £2,000,000. The burden of liability in respect of the closing year was 10 or 11 thousand pounds. The whole burden is discussed in the new Estimates, and the effect of that is that before they leave the House at all in the

Mr. E. Robertson.

next year's Estimates, the entire burden of liability, which amounts now to half a million, and the new expenditure of two millions, is given away. That is no secret to anybody. With regard to the Supplemental Programme, I have to remind the House that there, again, a remarkably eccentric and unusual course was taken by the First Lord of the Admiralty, and I do not think that the Question should pass without something more being said about it. The First Lord of the Admiralty last week, when he made a statement, spoke of the Supplemental Programme of last year as having been sanctioned by the House. I deny that it has been sanctioned by the House: it is up for sanction now. I must also remind the Committee as to what took place last year; then, as now, we were mystified by the course which the right honourable Gentleman announced beforehand he was going to take. We all expected that this Supplemental Programme would be submitted in the form of an Estimate, but, in the same same way as this year, no Estimate was forthcoming, or laid before the House. On that occasion a statement was made, and my right honourable Friend the Member for Monmouth with myself opposed the Admiralty upon these two points. And on these two points I desire to draw the attention of the House for a few moments to this fact. There were two specific questions addressed to the First Lord of the Admiralty last year. Those questions were not answered by him; and, after the Debate was over, I repeated those two questions in a letter to the "Times." The questions asked were these: first, "whether the Admiralty intended to put the new programme in execution before submitting a Supplementary Estimate?" And, second, "whether they could cite any precedent for that course of action?" The first question is answered now. They have assumed authority, because they have given orders for the whole of the items practically of the Supplemental Programme of 1898. The question which the Admiralty refused to answer directly they have answered indirectly by what they have done. They assume, from the little discussion which has taken place in this House, that there is no Vote before the House on which the issue can be raised that they had authority to do what they had done; that is the effect of the mere statement dropped by the First Lord to the Committee generally. The other question, the second question, is not answered. That question is, what precedent have you for executing a programme of this magnitude, or any magnitude, without getting direct authority from the House of Commons? And I put that question to the Secretary to the Admiralty now, and I shall expect him to say whether there are any precedents for the course which the Admiralty has adopted; and, in such a case, to tell us what the precedent is. I hope the honourable Gentleman has some explanation to give us of what I consider is the most unconstitutional method which the Admiralty have adopted. There is one thing to which I once more wish to call the attention of the House, and that is, that the aggregate expenditure now submitted to us for our sanction is perfectly appalling. It is only six years ago since this question was under discussion on the first set of Navy Estimates, for which my right honourable Friend the Member for Clitheroe and myself were responsible. The amount we asked the country to spend upon the Navy was a little over 14 millions. That is just about the amount that was asked for in the last year of our management, and that included the expenditure under Vote 10. The amount required has increased each year until this year it is £26,000,000 and a-half upon the ordinary expenditure in the Estimates, to which you must add one million and a-half, taken on the Supplementary Estimates, and the total of that is more than £28,000,000 sterling, or nearly double that amount which both sides of this House agreed to in their discussions six years ago. Now, that is not the thing upon which I base my objection, but upon other matters. Let me turn to another point of comparison. Six years ago the numbers asked for were 76,000; the numbers asked for this year are 110,000, an increase of nearly 34,000. That is a very great increase, but this great increase does not appear to me to show its full proportions. The expenditure, as I have shown, is doubled, but the number of men is not doubled, although they have increased. In his speech the

other night, looking over all the dockyards of the world, he informed us that there were 685,000 tons of shipbuilding going on in the yards of the six most powerful nations, but I wish that the honourable Gentleman had gone on to tell us what was the tonnage of our own yards and the yards of the contractors. I think the figures would have surprised this House, even in the face of these enormous Estimates. I find, excluding all unwarlike vessels, but including small men-of-war, the figures are these. The tonnage of ships building in the dockyards, as revealed by the Estimates for next year, is 200,000, and in the private yards it is 320,000, which gives a total of 520,000 of new warlike shipbuilding in this country alone, against 1,685,000 tons in all the rest of the world practically put together. I do not state that in any way as a matter of complaint, I simply state it as a fact to illustrate the enormous efforts which we are being called upon to make for the strengthening of the Navy of this country. Now, what is the question practically before the House? The main question which the House has to decide is whether it approves of the new programme of construction now laid before us. Now, what is the new programme which we are now being asked to sanction? It really amounts to six battleships, six first-class cruisers, three smaller, 12 torpedo-boat destroyers, and two sloops. That is the existing programme, and it is certainly a matter for us to consider whether we should sanction it or not. Now I am going to consider the question from the same point of view as my honourable Friend the Member for Clitheroe, and I take it that the present Admiralty stands by the obligations of the late Admiralty. Hitherto the principle which has governed the Admiralty has been that the Navy of this country ought to be equal to the combined navies of any two foreign Powers. I never contended that it should not be so; in my opinion it should. I think that should be the minimum strength, but hitherto the Admiralty has been extremely reticent as to naming the two Powers concerned. But that reticence has been entirely given up by the right honourable Gentleman the First Lord of the Admiralty. Now, I am not in the least complaining. but for years past he has been much more frank than any of his predecessors thought it prudent to be. Instead of vaguely referring to "any two Powers," he has dotted his "i's" and stroked his "t's," and boldly asserted on the floor of this House that the two Powers in question are France and Russia. This year we have apparently to deal with Russia, but France and Russia are both named as Powers which we shall have to take into consideration in making our Fleet equal to the combined strength of the fleets of any two other countries. As regards France, the First Lord made reference to the Fashoda incident of last Session in its bearings upon the state of our Navy. It was, in fact, entirely in reference to its bearing on the Navy that the First Lord mentioned the incident, and it is of that somewhat limited reference that I ask leave to speak. Sir, I disagree most profoundly with the inference which the First Lord drew from what took place last year in connection with the Fashoda incident. I do not agree with him that the country was unanimous in supporting the line taken by the Government. The unanimity was apparent only. It was a newspaper unanimity for the most part, and I, who have been all over the country since, know well that vast sections of public opinion were not in agreement with the line taken by the Government on that occasion. In my belief, and in the belief of many more, the Government of this country violently, unnecessarily, and harshly refused to France an opportunity of stating her case.

COMMANDER BETHELL (York, E.R., Holderness): On a point of order, Sir, shall we be allowed to follow the right honourable Gentleman in the discussion he is now raising?

THE DEPUTY CHAIRMAN: I accepted the statement of the honourable Gentleman that he would confine himself to the ground already traversed by a Minister of the Crown. I think he is now going beyond it.

MR. E. ROBERTSON: I will try to keep myself strictly within that reference. I will content myself with contradicting the statement of the First Lord. But contradicting that, and proceeding also to contradict the inference which he drew respecting the Navy, I go on to say that, in my opinion, the action taken by

Mr. E. Robertson.

the Government in reference to the Fashoda incident was, and I believe still is, likely to lead to a still further increase in the Navy. The right honourable Gentleman said, what all people in this country knew, and what the people in France knew—namely, that it was in reliance on our naval strength that we took the line we did; and it was because the French knew of our naval superiority that they submitted to a wrong which they would otherwise not have tolerated.

AN HONOURABLE MEMBER: No!

MR. E. ROBERTSON: I am repeating what they said; I am giving the French view. The use which we made of our naval supremacy on that occasion is one which may have unfortunate results in leading the French nation to listen, as I sincerely hope they will not, to advisers who certainly have told them that they had to submit to England because our Navy was overpoweringly strong, and that the only way to protect themselves was by strengthening their fleet. I am glad that my anticipations have not yet been realised. I hope they will not be realised, because what would be the consequence? The consequence would be that for every ship which France puts down we should be compelled, by the principle which both parties in the State have adopted, to put down a further number of ships. That is all I desire to say about the incident at Fashoda, which, in its bearings on naval policy, appears to me to suggest quite different possibilities from those suggested by the First Lord of the Admiralty. Now, Sir, passing from that, I have already indicated what, in my belief, is the main feature of these new Estimates—namely, this large increase, and the fact that that large increase is based, not upon anything that has been done, or is going to be done, by France —we know nothing about that—but upon what, in the opinion of the First Lord of the Admiralty, is going to be done by Russia. For the first time in the naval history of this country, so far as I know, have we had proposals directed openly, frankly, and expressly against a single Power—and that Power Russia. Where should we be if France also had an increased Estimate? But in France, we are told, as yet, the new construction is inconsiderable, and, therefore, we are left to deal with Russia. And now the question for the House is whether, having regard to the serious statement made by the First Lord of the Admiralty, we are to sanction these new proposals for armaments. Well, for my part, it would take a great deal to induce me to refuse my consent to the application made by the responsible naval authorities of the day, but the reasons which were frankly given by the First Lord of the Admiralty lead me to say that there are some conditions which we might reasonably impose upon the assent which I regard as inevitable. The First Lord, as I said, has told us about Russia. He has gone beyond anything that any of his predecessors have ever said in naming Russia as the one Power against which this new increase of the Navy is to be directed. Having gone so far, the right honourable Gentleman is bound to go farther. Any mischief that may be done from the mention of any particular Power cannot now be undone. Therefore we need have no hesitation in pressing now for information which in former years most probably would not have transpired. I would ask the Secretary to the Admiralty to kindly take note of two conditions which I shall have to make in assenting, as I shall undoubtedly do, to the new proposals before the Committee. I want him to promise, which I suppose he cannot do until he has consulted his chief, as a condition to our assenting to this vast increase in the naval programme, to take the House fully into his confidence with regard to Russia, and give us all the information the naval authorities have in their possession about Russia, and the evidence upon which they base their conclusions. The First Lord may be imperfectly informed. He believes himself that he did not understand one item in the Russian programme put down to wages, and there may be other points on which the Admiralty may be only too glad to be better informed than -they are. At all events, I do think that the Committee, which is now being asked to vote this enormous increase as an answer to the naval policy of Russia, and of Russia alone, is entitled to say, "Give us all the information you have about Russia." I feel certain that that reasonable request will not be refused by the right honourable Gentleman. Sir, the second condition which I should

like to mention is one which I make without much encouragement, for I am bound to say it has not once been laid before the Committee. We never hear in Naval Debates, much less in Army Debates, any question about the possibility of reducing expenditure. I do not mean in curtailing the programme, or in stopping the building of battleships, but in overhauling an ancient Service, which has not been overhauled for a great many years, to see whether we are not spending more than is absolutely necessary. I, for my part, while determined to keep up the Navy to a point that may, in the judgment of the Admiralty of the day, be necessary—because I should always go as far as that—am equally determined, as far as I can, that every penny that this House spends upon the Navy shall go to increase the fighting strength of the Navy. If there are any items in the Votes which can be dispensed with as ones which do not help your fighting strength, I should like to have those Votes explained. There are ratings, for example, which I have naval authority for saying do not conduce to the fighting efficiency of the Fleet, and there may be many more than those which have been mentioned to me. All these items should be overhauled. I think there is a possibility that we are paying too much for armaments. I am, however, aware that we shall be able to discuss that question at a later period. Our main object now is to induce the Admiralty and the Committee to recognise the fact that we are dealing with a very old fighting Service which has not been reformed for many years. Sir, I thank the House for having listened to me so long. I will say once more that I have no hesitation in supporting the new programme which the Admiralty has introduced, but I do entreat them to keep in mind two things—namely, to first give us all the relevant information they can with regard to the policy of Russia, and, in the second place, to encourage ;in every possible way the exercise of economy.

Commander BETHELL: With reference to the concluding suggestion of the honourable Gentleman who has just sat down, I would venture to point out that since he and I have had the honour of sitting in this House a Royal Commission and a Select Committee have both inquired into the question, and it is astounding how few were the recommendations made tending towards economy in the Navy. I sincerely hope that the new Supplementary Estimates may be considered purely as abnormal expenditure not likely to occur again. For my part, I am one of those who believe that our strength, in comparison with other Powers, is ample, and I believe it was last year. There has since been a considerable increase made by one Power, which no doubt ought to be taken into consideration. As far as I understand, all parties last year, excluding my right honourable Friend the Member for the Forest of Dean (Sir Charles Dilke), but including my noble Friend the Member for York (Lord Charles Beresford), were of opinion that our strength in reference to other countries was ample. Certainly, as far as I am concerned, taking as close and accurate a survey as I can of the ships that exist, and of those that are laid down by other countries, I believe that our comparative strength is sufficient. Now, I do not agree with my honourable Friend opposite (Mr. E. Robertson) that the *personnel* of the Navy is not equal to the ships we have completed or have in preparation.

Mr. E. ROBERTSON : I merely pointed out the fact that there was not the same proportionate increase.

COMMANDER BETHELL : I think it is quite right that there should not be. I am not at all of opinion that the country should be expected to support on active service so large a number of officers and men as to man the whole of the ships which we shall have in the hands of the dockyards for any given time. It would be asking the country to undertake an expenditure we ought not to require, because that involves a very important question raised by the honourable Member for Devonport a day or two ago, on which I have often spoken before, but with which I do not propose to trouble the House on the present occasion ; and that is the question of the Reserves. My humble opinion is that the question of the Reserves has not been properly dealt with by the Admiralty. I have said so for many years, and I shall not gain anything by repeating what I have said on other occasions. The honourable

Commander Bethell.

Member for Gateshead · (Mr. Allan) raised again the very technical and difficult question of the Belleville boilers. I cannot enter into that question to discuss it. All I would remind the Admiralty of is what they have been told before, that this question is still in suspense. I do not imagine the Committee, any more than myself, are able to form a definite opinion on this question.

*Mr. ALLAN : The "Terrible."

COMMANDER BETHELL : Never mind the "Terrible." It is absurd to contend that the whole system ought to be condemned because a single boiler has been blown up. I submit to the Committee and my honourable Friend opposite that the question of the Belleville boilers, as against other boilers, so far as the Committee of the House of Commons is concerned, is, and must remain, in suspense. We inexpert persons have not got the material upon which we can form a definite opinion, nor shall we ever have material on which to form such a definite opinion until such a lapse of time has occurred that we can see whether the ships fitted with Belleville boilers are able to perform the duties they are called upon to perform. Most of us, I suppose, are obliged to be guided largely by the official opinion of the Admiralty, who have the means of obtaining the best advice. It has been pointed out over and over again to the Committee that not only the expert opinion of the Admiralty, but of the engineers also, has all along all been in favour of this particular class of boiler. What, however, all most devoutly hope is, as my honourable Friend says, that this splendid Fleet of ours shall not be jeopardised by the introduction of these boilers. I have great faith in the adviser to the Admiralty, and in the skilled engineering opinions which were found in favour of it ; and, acting upon that judgment, with no opinion of my own, I have hitherto, and shall again support the Admiralty in their views upon this question. Sir, my honourable Friend who addressed the House immediately before me took some exception to the manner in which the Supplementary programme was introduced last year. I do not think he takes exception to the nature of the programme, but rather to the method in which it was presented ; but I am bold enough to say that I do not recollect any very severe criticisms as to the way in which it was introduced, either from my honourable Friend or from his Leader.

MR. E. ROBERTSON: On the 2nd of July it was discussed.

COMMANDER BETHELL: I looked it up, and I recollect the general agreement upon the subject. I do not propose to follow my honourable Friend opposite over the very dangerous and debatable ground on which he entered, and which seemed likely to disturb the peaceful calm in which the Naval Estimates are usually discussed. I rose more especially to draw the attention of the Committee to the subject on which my honourable Friend the Member for Gateshead has spoken so ably. That question is still in suspense. And I also think with regard to the question of the *personnel*, that it ought not to be raised to a larger number than would at any given time be necessary to meet the need of the ships.

*MR. KEARLEY (Devonport): I am unable to agree with my honourable Friend the Member for Dundee in his contention that there was no unanimity of opinion among the people of the country in respect to the Fashoda incident. The overwhelming expression of unanimity on that occasion was really the governing factor of the situation. No Government dared disregard it. My honourable Friend thinks, too, that France was badly treated in not being allowed to state her case. There was no case to state. I find myself also in disagreement with my right honourable Friend the Member for Clitheroe with regard to the criticisms he made the other evening in replying to the speech of the First Lord of the Admiralty. He advocated that the time had arrived when the brake should be applied, and that we should pursue a policy of watching and waiting. He gave two sets of reasons for that course, neither of which agreed with the other. The first reason he gave was that we should get great advantages if we followed this watching and waiting policy, because we should be able to profit by any scientific development which might improve our methods with regard to construction or

VOL. LXVIII.   [FOURTH SERIES.]

armaments. He also claimed that owing to our rapidity of construction we were in a position to make up the leeway very rapidly when we decided to resume operations. Well, Mr. O'Connor, I think this watching and waiting policy has been pursued before, and the right honourable Gentleman has had some experience of it. I remember in 1893 a great conflict in this House about the waiting and watching policy in connection with the construction of the "Majestic" and the "Magnificent," and that policy was strenuously opposed and vigorously denounced by the then Opposition. I hope the Government, at all events until something tangible happens in connection with the Peace Conference, will pay no heed whatever to the watching and waiting policy. Well, Sir, the second point of the right honourable Gentleman was, that he objected to the two new battleships being built, because he thought we were entitled to more exact information as to the ground that necessitated these ships being built. He did not, however, follow the courageous course of the honourable Member for Northampton. When the honourable Member for Northampton, for whose methods I have great admiration, takes exception to a given course, he acts up to his conviction and takes a Vote on the question; for instance, he moves the reduction of the number of men. Well, now, the right honourable Gentleman has objected to the number of ships——

*SIR U. KAY-SHUTTLEWORTH: What I stated was that the House was entitled to more information. That is not finally expressing an objection.

*MR. KEARLEY: The words of the right honourable Gentleman were—

"He did not think that the First Lord had given the House sufficient arguments that would justify the building of two more battleships."

Well, the most effective way of protesting against the programme would be to vote against it. An opportunity was afforded the right honourable Gentleman to make his protest effective, but when the occasion arose he did not take advantage of it. I think the criticism of the right honourable Gentleman was of a captious character. But, passing from that aspect of the question, I am glad to see that the right honourable Gentleman the First Lord of the Admiralty in his statement has recognised the good and economic way in which the work had been turned out of the Government dockyards. He might have paid an additional tribute to the work—that it was not only satisfactory and economical, but that it was expeditiously carried out. There has been a record made at Devonport which has never been equalled in any other dockyard. The other day the "Implacable" was launched, under eight months from the day on which it was laid down. That is a very creditable performance, and I would suggest that some recognition should be given to the employees in the dockyards in addition to the tributes of admiration which had been paid. I would remind the honourable Gentleman the Secretary to the Admiralty that we are still continuing to pay very low wages in this dockyard, and, seeing the high character of the work carried out, I hope he will be able to tell us to-night what steps the Admiralty intend to take in regard to the representations made last year to him by the representatives of the dockyards who waited upon him. The point raised by the right honourable Baronet the Member for the Forest of Dean in regard to additional building-slips at Devonport is important. Owing to the increase of slip accommodation that yard has been able to participate in the building of battleships which has been going on; but owing to the insufficiency of the slip accommodation a new ship, the "Bulwark," has been started, not on a slip, but on a temporary staging. A great amount of building material had been put into her which must be pulled down when the ship is finally laid down. I understand the Government now intend to build another slip, and do away with the existing covered sheds Nos. 1 and 2. I would suggest that when they are making the new slip it should be made long enough on which to build first-class cruisers. We have never yet had an opportunity in Devonport Dockyard of building a first-class cruiser, and I hope the Government will give us the opportunity of showing what we can do with large cruisers, as we have done in building large battleships. A few weeks ago I had the opportunity of inspecting the Keyham extension works. Last year,

when I went over the works, I found them in a somewhat backward state, but I was glad to see the other week the enormous amount of work which had been accomplished during the past 12 months. Everything now is plain sailing, and with the large increase of labour contemplated, there should be no room for adverse criticism on the conduct of that great undertaking. I wish to make two references to matters which I think of some importance, and which were noticed in the statement of the First Lord. The first is in regard to the increase of pay to the Royal Marines. That increase has at last been conceded. It is a very tardy concession. I started the agitation in 1893; since which we have fought for it every year, and I am much gratified that at length we have wrung this concession from the Admiralty. I am sure that it will be much appreciated by the Royal Marines; but there is still room for more consideration to be shown to the claims of these men. I will give an illustration. A Marine, prior to embarkation, is compelled to qualify as a "trained" man, for which he draws extra pay. When embarked he has to take his place with the other members of the crew for gunnery work, but is deprived altogether of the chance of qualifying for a seaman's gunner rating. As the seamen are entitled to qualify for gunners' rating, for which, when they are qualified, they get extra pay, this is a hardship to the Royal Marines, and I hope it will receive some attention. The other matter in the First Lord's statement to which I wish to refer, is the scarcity of shipwrights' ratings. The Admiralty have devised a plan, under which they propose to train naval shipwrights in their own yards, and they offer, as an inducement, that on the completion of their training they will be drafted to sea-going ships, and after serving afloat for a certain number of years they will be eligible to be taken on the establishment of the dockyard. I do not think myself the plan will succeed. I do not like to say I hope it won't succeed, for that perhaps might be misconstrued. It would be far better, I think, in my judgment, if the Admiralty were to face the difficulty boldly. It has arisen solely and wholly because the pay and the status of the naval shipwrights are not good enough. My honourable and gallant Friend says that the

Mr. Kearley.

difficulty has arisen from trade unionism, but I do not think trade unionism has anything to do with it. If the naval shipwrights' claim was an unjust one no one would argue in its favour. But these men who go into the Navy as shipwrights are picked out from among the best men in the yards, and have to pass a strict examination, and it seems altogether wrong that there should not be more fitting recognition accorded to them while they are in the Navy. I prophesy that this scheme of the Admiralty will not succeed. Two years ago warrant rank was offered to 50 engine room artificers, but there appears to be some injustice in the qualifying conditions imposed on the men who take warrant rank. It is laid down that no man can take warrant rank unless he is 35 years of age and has had 10 years' continuous service. It is obvious that if a man enters at 21 years of age, and is not permitted to gain warrant rank until he is 35 years of age, that gives him 14 years' continuous service. I suggest that that is an oversight, and that it would satisfy all the requirements of the Service if a man has 10 years' qualified time, irrespective of his age. He should then be eligible for warrant rank. Last year the First Lord said that he would give the matter of the chief petty officers' pensions his serious consideration, and it will be some satisfaction if we are able to learn to-night what the decision of the Admiralty is in regard to this important question. Then there is the question of the stokers which was referred to the other night. These men are the hardest worked and worst paid in the whole Navy; and, as was pointed out by the honourable Member for Gateshead, they are exposed to great danger. Not only is their pay bad, but the privileges accorded to others are denied to them altogether. For example, they are denied the re-engagement money given to the seamen branch. Why should the petty officers, too, not be entitled to progressive pay. the same as in the case of other ratings? Another important body of naval mechanics I would mention which are entitled to an increase of pay, viz., the plumbers and plumbers' mates. Their pay to-day stands at the same rate as it did 30 years ago, as during the entire period they have received no recognition

whatsoever. That practically covers all I desire to say just now. We shall have plenty of opportunity of discussing details when the separate Votes come on. I hope the honourable Member the Secretary to the Admiralty will reply to the questions which have been put this afternoon and the other night. We are entitled to some reply, especially as to what are the possibilities of the Colonies falling in with the views of the First Lord in regard to obtaining men there for the Reserve.

*ADMIRAL FIELD (Sussex, Eastbourne): I am glad to follow the honourable Member for Devonport, and to thank him for the support which he has given us on some points in which he and I feel very strongly. We are grateful to the Admiralty for the concession that has been made in regard to the rations of the Royal Marines when employed on duty on shore. But I do not think that either of us is satisfied with that concession. There are other grievances to be dealt with, and I reserve myself on these points till the reply of the Secretary of the Admiralty is made. I also thank the honourable Member, on behalf of my brother officers, for the slight castigation he gave to the right honourable Gentleman the Member for Clitheroe. It was delightful to witness the disapproval of the honourable Member for Devonport at the cold water thrown on the programme of the Admiralty by the right honourable Gentleman the Member for Clitheroe. It was evident that he thought the right honourable Gentleman should have spoken in a different sense; but I suppose he felt, in common with me, that the right honourable Gentleman conceived it to be his duty to leave his supporters in the country to think that he and his friends were advocating economic principles, though they did not see any way of carrying them out. The honourable Member for Dundee, from the position he holds in this House, and the position he held in the last Government, will pardon me for challenging some of his observations. He finds fault—though he did not propose for a moment to carry his opinion to a Vote—with the programme of the Admiralty on the ground of extravagance. Now, if the Naval Vote were analysed, and the reasons for its increase understood, the view taken by honourable Members on the other side that it is extravagant might be modified, or they would, at any rate, be received with less respect. No one knows better than he that the main cause of the present expenditure is the deplorable way in which past Admiralties —I make no distinction between one Government and another—had lost sight of the necessity for keeping in an efficient state our docks, dockyard works, dredging, and other appliances, and coaling stations. All Governments had allowed these matters to drop out of sight for many a year. The present Government have felt it to be their bounden duty to make large demands on this House and the country, this year and last year, in order to bring up the arrears of work in this direction. That is one cause of the increased Estimates. For this year alone £806,000 is asked for these special works. That is a large sum, but it does not include other large sums of money which will be demanded from the House under the Loans Act for Naval Barracks. These sums are asked for for work that is not directly reproductive, but it adds enormously to the efficiency of our Fleet, although it is not apparent on the high seas. Such work was not thought of 12 years ago. But if war came at a short notice it is evident that we must be prepared for it, and be ready to send the Fleet to sea in a week's time. Therefore, we must have sailors, marines and firemen all prepared, and this cannot be done without a large expenditure. Everyone knows that we cannot draw a comparison between the expenditure on the Navy 15 or 20 years ago, and the present expenditure. Everybody knows, in this scientific age, how enormously the cost of building ships has increased. Again, armour has increased in price since that period, for new methods have been invented of hardening iron. Then, as to guns, you have gone from muzzleloaders to breech-loaders, and from breech-loaders to quick-firing breech-loaders, and to wire guns. All this adds enormously to the expense. Another point I wish to impress upon the House. In olden times—at any rate, up to 13 years ago—the Naval Gun Vote did not appear in the Naval Estimates, but in the Army Estimates. That Vote was then a million and a quarter, but now it has been transferred from the Army

Admiral Field.

Vote to its proper place in the Navy Vote, and that tends to swell the Navy Vote. People have short memories nowa-days, and they forget all this. The Gun Vote since these days has increased from one and a quarter million to £2,800,000, so that in this one direction alone the Navy Vote, which was formerly a modest one, is swelled by nearly three millions of money. People do not understand how the Navy Vote has grown, but it has grown by taking off a large slice of the Army Vote, and adding it to the Navy Vote. The House will also remember that there is a large non-effective Vote amounting to £2,300,000. That means pensions, retired pay, gratuities, and also civil pensions. When you add all these together you have a sum of neary six millions, which formerly never appeared in the Navy Estimates at all. As I have said, if you come to analyse the Navy Votes and explain the reasons for their increase, I am sure the fears of honourable Members will disappear, that we are running into extravagance. In drawing any comparison between the present Naval expenditure and that of 15 or 20 years ago, all this must be taken into account. My honourable and gallant Friend behind me (the Member for Holderness)—an old and distinguished Member of this House—says that in his opinion—and he held that opinion last year—that the condition of the Navy as it stands, so far as sea power on the high seas is concerned, is amply sufficient. I do not agree with him; and I do not think that that view was held last year by the noble Lord the Member for York, except in as far as battleships are concerned. I do not believe that that view is held largely by Naval men. We have never admitted that the number of our cruisers is sufficient to guard efficiently our commerce; and I do not believe that there is any Naval man who would not warmly support the Admiralty if they can see their way to add still more cruisers to the Fleet. It is not for me to indicate what that number should be. Take some of our most distinguished men—for example, the late Admiral Geoffrey Hornby—he held very strong opinions in regard to this question, that the number of the cruisers was still wholly inadequate. These views are held by responsible men who are competent to form a judgment and advise on this question. I now turn to one or two points which specially interest myself; and I hope I shall not trespass too long on the attention of the Committee. I trust the honourable Gentleman the Secretary to the Admiralty or the Civil Lord may see their way to explain the points to which I am going to refer. I notice under the head of Royal Marines on page 5 of the First Lord's Memorandum that the rifle ranges at Plymouth are still not available. They are just as they were last year; and the musketry practice of the Plymouth division is being carried out at Gosport. I remember raising this question last year, and I was told that new land was required at Plymouth for the ranges, and that the matter was under the consideration of the War Office. And now a similar statement is made this year. Is there any justification for this? Why does not the Civil Lord badger somebody and put an end to this miserable state of things? We spend a large amount of money in bringing marines and officers by railway to the Browndown range to carry out their musketry practice. The thing is too preposterous, and ought to be put an end to. It is a waste of public money. The War Office moves more slowly than the Admiralty, and I should like those who know more of the War Office than I do to give us their views on this question. It amounts to a scandal that 12 months should have been wasted without a step having been taken in providing the rifle range, and that we are still no forwarder than we were. I note with great pleasure the paragraph regarding the Naval Reserve, and that the men of the new seamen class are being drawn largely from the fishing population of the United Kingdom. I hope the Scotch fishermen especially will enrol in as large numbers as you can provide training for them. They are a fine hardy set of men, and could be most easily drilled. On page 7 of the First Lord's Memorandum it is said that the drill ships' armaments are being completed in accordance with a plan arranged some years ago. We had that statement made last year; but I inspected one of these ships last year—the "Dædalus"—and found a 6-inch gun lying on the deck, and a 4.7-inch gun lying on the deck unmounted. I asked why the guns were unmounted, and was told in answer that they did not mount them because they were going to be supplied with a new ship, which had been promised. I should like to ask whether that new ship has been provided. I see from another paragraph that you are going to send a gun boat to Portishead to take firing parties to sea. There was a gunboat there in my time, but it was worn out. Are you going to send another? Under the head of mobilisation, I see nothing whatever to indicate that the Admiralty intend to mobilise the Fleet. I hope the House will press on the Admiralty to carry out a mobilisation this year. There is nothing more important. Crews are able to shake down in their places, and many faults are found to exist which, without mobilisation, would most probably not be detected. If you were suddenly to mobilise for war you would not be in a position to rectify these defects. I hope the Admiralty will see their way to carry out some summer manœuvres this year. I rejoice there is to be so much new construction as the Memorandum indicates, and that a new type of cruisers is to be built. Although they are not to carry 9.2-inch guns, they are to carry 2.6-inch quick-firing guns forward and two aft in turrets. That is a very valuable improvement, no matter to whom we are indebted for it—whether to the Comptroller or to the Chief Constructor of the Navy—both very able men, and well adapted for their posts. We are grateful for that change, for some of us think that some of the former cruisers were not adequately armed—especially the cruisers of the "Diadem" class. I see no provision is made for the construction of 8-inch guns, and I ask the attention of the honourable Member for West Belfast, who has paid great attention to these matters, to this. It is very strange that our naval advisers do not see their way to adopt the 8-inch gun. I do not see why they should not. We have tied ourselves to 6-inch, and 9.2-inch guns. The Americans have adopted the 8-inch gun, and so have the Japanese. We saw them at the Naval Review on board the "Brooklyn," and also on board the Japanese warship in Portsmouth Harbour. I was very much struck with these guns, and I should like to see some of our cruisers carrying 8-inch guns forward and aft. The matter should receive more attention than it has yet received. It is stated that a new 12-inch breech-loading wire gun has been approved of. If rumour speaks correctly this 12-inch gun is not a success; that five tons is added to the weight; and that you get very little increased velocity or penetrating power. If that is so, I think something is wrong with the design, and that it is not worth the extra weight you have put on board ship. I am not confident in the matter, for it is only a rumour which has reached me, and I hope it will be contradicted. In the old 12-inch gun we have a most efficient gun to accomplish all our objects. I have heard still worse rumours about the primers. That is a most important matter. Unless the primers are reliable, the gun will not go off at the proper time, and the enemy's ship will not be hit. Those primers want looking into. Rumours have reached me of a very ugly character. I will not tell the House what I have heard, because I hope the mischief may be remedied, but I am sure it calls for searching inquiry, and a large expenditure and loss will be involved if the facts are such as I have heard by these rumours. I have another question to put to my honourable Friend, and that is as to this great increase in ammunition. It is very large, and it will involve a large addition of some kind in some place or other, or more places than one, to our magazines and stores. What are you going to do? Have you a programme for enlarging magazines? The Toulon disaster will have taught you caution in the placing of your magazines in the vicinity of large dockyard towns, or any other towns elsewhere. I have an idea that it is in contemplation to bring a large increase of this new cordite ammunition, and probably melinite and lyddite ammunition, to Priddy's Hard. Everyone who knows Portsmouth knows Priddy's Hard. If that is so, I will use every effort to oppose the Admiralty in this design. It has been a very important magazine for many years, and it has been used with efficiency for storing ordinary gunpowder and shell. This new kind of powder, although everybody has confidence in it, is of recent introduction, and I think in whatever magazines you have to receive this new

Admiral Field.

ammunition, above all melinite and lyddite, each ought to have a magazine to itself, and ought not be mixed up with the old kind of ammunition. Where you are to place it I do not know. It is a very difficult question, and I think you ought to have a Committee to consider it. To bring in a large increase of ammunition right opposite Portsmouth Dockyard after the Toulon experience is a matter which requires very grave consideration. If it is done, it will be the duty of some of us to oppose it with all our energy. I am rather inclined to think that it would be well to try floating magazines. If you like to excavate in the Portsmouth mud, you might find a site not easily approached for a magazine until you have more experience in the character of this ammunition when stored in large quantities. I pass away from that, because I am satisfied that the matter will be considered. I come rapidly on to the Works Vote. I am glad to see there is a sum of money to be expended in adapting our new naval base at Wei-hai-Wei. I commend the Admiralty's decision in losing no time in sending out their dredger. As far as I can gather, good progress has been made in Gibraltar, with the exception of the docks. I should like to know what progress has been made with the dock. My honourable Friend on my right says that we were promised that the two things should go on together; the excavation of the rock for the dock would be necessary, in order that the material might be used in helping to construct the mole. I have no doubt the Civil Lord will give us some information. I will not dwell upon that. Then I see in the Memorandum that there is a sum of money—£2,500—put down for other works in which the Navy is greatly interested. I presume, and hope, that he will be able to tell me that this is really a grant-in-aid for the works in connection with the Auckland Dock. We agitated that question last Session. I understand that a Commissioner of the Harbour Board of Auckland is in England now, and in association with the Admiralty. I am very glad to see that grant down for £2,500, and a grant of £2,000 for the Halifax Dock. We cannot have too many docks, and when they are built for us by the Colonial authorities, it is our duty to accept them gratefully ; and this House will never grudge a grant-in-aid for the building of docks where required. I think with these remarks I may bring my speech to a conclusion, except to say that I regret to see the reduction in ammunition, which I do not quite understand. I do not know how a decrease of £27,850 in projectiles can be justified. There is a large increase in the Gun Vote. For guns there is an increase practically of £272,000, yet there is this decrease for projectiles. Well, guns are useless without projectiles, but I daresay some explanation may be forthcoming, therefore I will not press the matter.

MR. ARNOLD-FORSTER: I think the speech of the late Civil Lord was not particularly appropriate. The impression he left was that of being "willing to wound, but yet afraid to strike." I think it would have been a great deal better that the honourable Member should have spoken definitely. I can quite understand the view that we ought to have no increase in the Navy Estimates, but I cannot understand the particular utility of throwing doubt on the wisdom of this increase and that increase, or the general total, yet not vouchsafing one single suggestion as to what particular Estimates ought to be diminished and what ought to be left out of the programme. I do not see the utility of that course of action. I do not believe the Committee or the country will be particularly impressed by a series of conundrums which were set to the Committee with regard to the particular form in which the Estimates were presented this year and last year. I think we have a Committee of Public Accounts which, if any gross irregularity is committed, will inform the House of the fact. I think that the main facts are perfectly well known, that, as the honourable Member for Devonport has said, the Government stated that an emergency had arisen, and they asked for a free hand, and they obtained it. I think nearly everybody in the House will appreciate the situation, and will be content that it should be acted upon in the way in which it was acted upon. But there was a part of the honourable Member's speech which I confess I wish he had pursued, because it would have been very fruitful indeed. I did not quite understand

whether his suggestion as to economy was to be considered merely as a platitude, or whether it was going to end in a proposal. I suppose no honourable Member of the House is more competent, in the first place by his own knowledge and ability, and in the second place by his vast experience, to put his finger upon these points and tell the Committee where it is that these reductions are to be made. For several years the honourable Member was familiar with the whole interior economy of the Admiralty. I think it would have been a great deal more satisfactory at the present time, when it is of importance to make the public understand the reason why the Navy is necessary, and why a large expenditure is legitimate, if he had pointed out definitely those points in which we might, without detriment to efficiency, have made a reduction, instead of favouring the Committee with these general views which, I am sure, we are all agreed upon—that useless expenditure is undesirable, and that it is a pity to spend too much money if you do not get a return. I think it would have been helpful if the honourable Member had been a little more definite. In regard to the other matter dealt with by the honourable Member for Gateshead, I do not know that it is very profitable for us, who are unacquainted with technical matters, to discuss it, but as an outside student of these matters I think that it is worthy of more attention than was given to it by the honourable Member the late Civil Lord. We cannot quite afford to dismiss it in the summary fashion that he suggested. I have never been able to convince myself that the honourable Member for Gateshead had the best of the argument. I have always felt that there is this enormous amount of testimony in favour of the Belville boiler, of which myself I am not a great admirer, and that we are bound to take cognisance of that testimony, and of the fact that the United States Admiralty, which is exceedingly alive to its best interests, is deliberately, after the experience of the war, adopting the Belville boiler, that the French Admiralty is continuing the use of the Belville boiler, and that we have great bodies such as the Institute of Engineers giving practically unanimous testimony in favour of the Belville boiler. These are facts which I do not think we are justified in disregarding. On the other hand, I know how strongly the honourable Member for Gateshead feels, and I think he is not altogether singular in that. He has, at any rate, this justification in his demand for an inquiry, that the whole of the ships, almost without exception, that have been fitted with Belville boilers have been unfortunate in one way or another. Now, I know a great deal too much about this question to attribute all these misfortunes to the boilers, and I think it is a weak part of the honourable Member's case that he has not been able to give us specific instances of breakdowns of ships which have been directly attributed to the boilers.

MR. ALLAN: The "Niobe."

MR. ARNOLD-FORSTER: The "Terrible" is, of course, a case in point, and I think I can point to similar cases in other ships; but still, it is a weak point that he has not been able to specifically connect the failure of the boilers with the breakdown of ships which undoubtedly has taken place. This fact does remain, that almost all the ships to which he has alluded have been so unfortunate in their trials that there has been practically very little test of their steaming capacities at all. I know there have been exceptions—one or two of the "Circe" class, which have been thoroughly satisfactory from beginning to end, and no doubt one or two of the "Diadem" class—but, speaking generally, it is true. Whether you take the "Powerful" and the "Terrible," or the "Niobe," or three or four other ships of the second-class, or the "Vindictive" class, you will find there have been innumerable accidents upon these ships which have interfered with their trials, and which have prevented us from getting a real estimate of what their capacities at sea would be under service conditions. One also knows this fact, which is undoubted, that the expenditure of coal on these ships is perfectly colossal. And though we are told, and I am sure I hope it is true, that the use of the economiser will greatly reduce this expenditure, there is no doubt that the expenditure of coal on vessels of the "Vindictive" class is altogether out of

Mr. Arnold-Forster.

proportion to the result obtained. I would suggest that it would be greatly to the advantage of the House and the country if something could be done similar to what is being done in the United States, and we could have a report containing a fair and clear account of what has been the history of all these ships. It is an unfortunate remark that was made by the honourable Member opposite, that we were still in the experimental stage in regard to this Belville boiler. We ought not to be in the experimental stage now that we have so many ships and so much money involved. Our judgment can only be in suspense, because the facts are not very clear. A very considerable number of these ships are already in commission, and a very large number of ships are being built, and will be put into commission, and it is unfortunate that it should still be open to any honourable Member to say that we have not yet got the facts before us for judgment. It does seem to be a reasonable thing that we should have the facts before us before the money is voted. There ought to have been a series of explanations which would have made it impossible for the honourable Member for Holderness to make the remark he made this evening. I wish the Government could give us some document such as is given by the Bureau of Navigation in Washington, wherein we could have the life history of these ships, the whole of the three classes, and could learn what has happened to these ships. I am perfectly prepared to find this result, that all the accidents which have happened to these ships have been accidents to machinery, and nothing whatever to do with the boilers. But the excessive coal consumption is a thing which may be remedied; and I think it is only due to my honourable Friend opposite, and to all persons who are interested, that this thing should not be kept in the dark, but that we should have almost an unusual amount of information given to us with regard to what is on all hands admitted to be a most important matter. I have only one thing more to say, and that on a totally different topic. I have some hesitation in pressing my remarks on my honourable Friend the Secretary to the Admiralty, because it might seem that I was pressing him in his capacity as an Irish Member, and not in his capacity as a Member of the Government. I am sure he will dismiss that idea from his mind, and will follow my remarks as they should be followed by reason of their connection with the best interests of the Navy. But I cannot refrain from saying that I do believe it would have been a fair and a just and a right thing that some attempt should at least be made by the Admiralty to allow Ireland to participate in the enormous expenditure which we are making. I am not one of those, and I do not think anyone would make that charge against me, who desire to support any local interest against the interest of the Navy at large. But when I see £26,000,000 sterling spent on the Navy, and when I reflect that as far as Ireland is concerned practically speaking, that expense might as well not be incurred at all, I say there is room for some change. And I say this, not only on the ground of expenditure, which, of course, is very valuable, but on another ground. I put it on the ground that it is desirable in the public interest to engage the attention of all parts of the United Kingdom in this great service of the Navy, and, as far as Ireland is concerned, and especially that part which I represent, there might not be a British Navy at all. We have once or twice in the last few years seen a ship, but we have no English ships in our waters, and no prospect of English ships, or anything of the kind. We have not got even a gun-boat station in our waters. We have no training ships; the whole of the training ships, with one single exception, are spread over the coasts of England and Scotland. My right honourable and gallant Friend reminds me that we have a training ship in Ireland. Where? At Cork. Why? Well, Sir, that is a question which I do not think I am called upon to give an answer to. I come with bad credentials in this matter. I cannot press my claims in the way which is calculated to enforce attention. Those whom I represent are perfectly loyal. They have no desire to see any misfortune happen to the Navy. They are not prepared to interrupt and interfere in the Debates of this House. They have always been too loyal, if I may express myself so, to receive that attention which has been so amply afforded to persons who are more fortunate than I and my colleagues in the North of Ireland. Sir, we do not desire that this unfortunate position should be maintained any longer. We think that there has been enough disappointment and enough discouragement thrown upon those who are only very loyal, and we firmly believe—I know, at any rate, that a very large number of those whom I represent believe—that if we were to change our method, and to join ourselves to the Party with which we cannot join ourselves, we should, at any rate, receive a little more respectful attention in the demand we make, and in which we have never yet got more than a mere put-off—not even a reasoned argument; we have merely been told that it is incompatible with the interests of the Navy that it should be done. Now, Sir, it is not for me to make suggestions. I have made them, and have had very scant attention. But I say it is incumbent upon the Government to give some little attention to this claim by the North of Ireland, and to see whether they cannot, without interfering with the legitimate interests of the Navy committed to their charge, allow the North of Ireland—I do not say the North of Ireland only; I will say, if you like, the whole of Ireland—to participate in some measure in the expenditure on the Navy, and what is to me even far more important, to become participators in the life and work and interests which the Navy excites in England and Scotland, and which, I believe, it would excite, if given a chance, in Ireland, and I am certain it would excite in Ulster. I commend this matter to my honourable Friend the Secretary to the Admiralty, and I do hope that at least we may get something more than one of these perfunctory replies, of which, I am bound to say, some of us are very tired indeed, and that we may get from him a promise that something will be done.

MR. STEADMAN (Tower Hamlets, Stepney): It is not my intention, Mr. O'Connor, to criticise the action of Her Majesty's Government in reference to our Navy, because, although a man of peace myself, I believe the most practical way of ensuring peace is to have a strong Navy, much stronger than any other European Power has, at any rate, at the present moment. But, Sir, with your permission, I should like to say one or two words to the Committee in reference to the manner in which the men are treated in Her Majesty's Navy. It is one thing to build ships, but it is altogether a different thing to man the ships. The First Lord of the Admiralty told the House a few days back that he was going to increase the Navy by men and boys to the number of something like four thousand odd. Now, Sir, there is one class of men employed in Her Majesty's Navy in which I am particularly interested—the shipwrights, and I think there is no body of men, no body of mechanics, who are treated worse than are the shipwrights to-day in Her Majesty's Navy. I was down at Portsmouth Dockyard myself on Saturday last, and I went over some of the ships, and I found that some mechanics had got good messrooms, somewhere to put their food, and some-one to wait upon them. Even the stokers had good messrooms and some-one to cook their food. What is the position of the shipwright? The poor shipwright—the man who, after all, is the most important, if any mechanic is important, because unless you get the hull of a ship constructed you cannot put engines and boilers into her; there-fore, I maintain the shipwright is the most important, if there is any dis-tinction, among the whole of the mechanics employed in Her Majesty's Navy—the shipwright, instead of having a decent messroom, instead of having someone to wait upon him and cook his food, has got to act the menial's part by having his food where he can get it between the decks, and not only to do that, but to cook his own food himself, to clean his own utensils, and to scrub decks. The honourable and gallant Member for Eastbourne on Monday evening stated in this House that the reason Her Majestys' Government were not able to secure sufficient shipwrights to man the Navy was in consequence of the tyranny of the trades unions. I deny that statement. I say, in the first place, it is not a true statement, and in the second place, the reason why Her Majesty's Government are not able to secure sufficient shipwrights is the manner in which the men are treated. Why, if shipwrights are treated pro-perly, or any other body of men are treated properly, by Her Majesty's

Mr. Steadman.

Government, they will have no need to fear the trades unions or any other organisation. No trades union in existence can prevent a man from going to get a job where he can get the highest price; but while the Government to-day pays shipwrights the low rate of wages they do, 4s. a day, whilst an engineer gets 5s. 6d., whilst they also pay 15 per cent. less than the current rate around the coast, it stands to reason that while work is busy in private and commercial shipbuilding yards, men will go and work there in preference to going into the Navy or working in the dockyards. Well, the honourable and gallant Mem-ber for Eastbourne congratulated the Government upon their new departure. What is their new departure? Their new departure is to get lads, apprentice them for four years in the dockyard, and after they have served four years in the dock-yard they are going to put them on board Her Majesty's ships as full-flown shipwrights. They are not to take the place of shipwrights, but to fill up the gaps which the Government are unable to fill up at the present moment. I maintain that, instead of that being one of the best methods ever adopted by Her Majesty's Government, it is going to be one of the worst. Why is it going to be one of the worst? I myself served seven years to learn my trade, and it takes seven years for a mechanic to properly learn his trade. And in most cases he learns more of his trade in the first 12 months after he has gone out of his apprenticeship, because he is then on his own beat, as it were. Whilst, as an apprentice, he is not responsible for any work he spoils, when he becomes a journeyman mechanic he is responsible for his work, and he takes a greater interest in it, and learns more in these first 12 months than he got out of his ap-prenticeship over the whole seven years before. And it stands to reason, there-fore, that these lads will not learn sufficient—nothing near sufficient—in the four years of their work in the dock-yards. It is true they will learn a bit, they will get a smattering more when they get on board ship, but in the four years in the dockyard, and in the time they are in the Navy, they will never become efficient mechanics, able to per-form the work that they should perform as shipwrights. My own father was a shipwright, and he took a fit into his head one day to join Her Majesty's Navy, but he was not in it more than a very few weeks before he wanted to get out of it quicker than he had wanted to get into it, so well was he treated. My own brother has been a carpenter for years in the Merchant Service. Last year he joined the American Navy. He did not go into the American Navy as a menial, as a man to scrub decks, etc., nor join at a carpenter's screw at the rate of 2s. 8d. per day. When he joined the American Navy he was made a full-flown officer at once, and then as soon as he joined the navy his wages were 90 dollars per month. That is the way to treat a man; and my brother is only one of a number of English seamen to-day who prefer the American Navy because they are treated far better than they are treated in the English Navy, and they leave our service when they have an opportunity and join the American Navy. Now, Mr. O'Connor, if we want to get men, and we have not got the men—it is all very well for the First Lord to tell the House that he has got the men; as a matter of fact, you are working short-handed to-day in Portsmouth Dockyard, and in other dockyards, because you cannot get the men—if you want men to man the ships, you have got to treat them as men, and not as menials, the same as you are doing at the present moment. And when you are prepared to treat them as men, and not as menials, and pay them a higher rate of pay than you are paying them at the present time, then you will get all the men that are necessary to man Her Majesty's Navy in times of need and anxiety.

Sir E. LEES (Birkenhead): I would ask my honourable Friend the Under Secretary a question which, I think, can be dealt with very briefly, but which is, nevertheless, one of great importance to the Empire. I refer to the question of armour. When the First Lord was framing Estimates to maintain our command of the sea, he necessarily took into account rapidity of construction. That rapidity is a very serious affair, and is hindered by a deficient supply of armour. I myself have seen Her Majesty's ship "Mars" lying for months waiting for the necessary armour to complete her construc-

tion. Attention has been called to the extraordinary rapidity with which the "Glory" has been floated, but I believe that ship would have been commissioned months ago had the armour been ready to be built in when the structure was ready to receive it. I was asked by the late Mr. John Laird, whose great authority is admitted by all connected with the Admiralty, to bring this point before the attention of the House and the country. It was unnecessary to do so last year, because it was fully dealt with by the First Lord himself, but it has not been dealt with during the present Debate, and I should be pleased if my honourable Friend will say a few words on the matter when he replies. I note the statement of the First Lord that there was a short supply of 8,000 tons of armour during the past year, and that the Admiralty hoped that this will be partially remedied in the future, and that a sufficient supply for the ensuing year will be obtained. I should like to know on what ground my right honourable Friend bases that hope. I am well aware that some of this armour is supplied by firms which have very lately been reconstructed, and I hope he will be able to reassure the House in the matter. I should be glad if my honourable Friend will tell us also how many firms are able to supply this armour, and what is done abroad as regards the supply of armour. France, Germany, and probably Italy, supply their own armour, but I should like to know if some of the great Powers are not partially dependent on this country for their supply. I am sure my honourable Friend will be able in a few words to deal with this very important matter. On the general question it seems to me that the very large Estimates which we have to face this year are not likely to diminish for some years to come. I think foreign nations and statesmen are awakening to the immense power given by the command of the sea. I think it is evident they cannot pursue a policy of colonisation without placing themselves to some extent in the power of the nation which commands the sea. They are beginning to realise that every colony they found and every port they open, and every railway which depends for its traffic on sea-borne trade, is a hostage and a pledge for their good behaviour given into the hands of the greatest sea Power in the world, and, as they realise that more and more, they are more and more likely to resent it, and to endeavour to equalise their own strength. But for us it is absolutely vital, for them it is not, to control the sea. I hope that all parties in this House and in the country will continue to realise how vital that is, not only to our position as an Empire, but to our existence as a country. If the same feeling continues which we have seen during the last few years there is no doubt we shall be able to maintain our position, but I think it is well that it should be constantly borne in mind that we are undertaking these sacrifices for some years to come in order to maintain our position in command of the sea.

*Sir C. DILKE (Gloucester, Forest of Dean): I only intend to make a few remarks which grow out of the Debate of this evening. The matter mentioned by the honourable Member for Birkenhead is one which, as he will remember, has been brought before the House year after year. Just as we used to blame former Governments for having allowed ships to be delayed by having to wait for guns, sufficient provision not having been made, so we have for the past few years blamed the present Government for not having sufficiently foreseen in advance the necessary supply of armour; and I think we must consider the necessity for widening the area of that supply, either by constructing armour ourselves, or by giving engagements to other firms to induce them to put up proper plant. It is not right that ships should be delayed for want of armour or by the absence of slips on which to build them. On the question of slips, I should like to ask the Secretary to the Admiralty to make a clearer explanation than he did the other night with regard to what is to occur at Devonport. A year ago the deficiency of slips as well as of armour was pointed out to the First Lord, and he gave as a reason for postponing that portion of his programme, when he was pressed last year, that he was making an inquiry at Devonport with regard to the possibility of increasing the number of slips. That inquiry was made a year ago, but no reference to it appears either in the Memorandum or the speech

Sir E. Lees.

of the First Lord. When I asked the Secretary to the Admiralty a Question on the matter, he used a very curious phrase, to the effect that some Estimates were being made for the purpose of considering the erection of other slips.

THE CIVIL LORD OF THE ADMIRALTY (Mr. AUSTEN CHAMBERLAIN, Worcestershire, E.): Preparing.

*Sir C. DILKE: What does that mean? Does it mean that they are to be put off until the Estimates for 1900–1?

Mr. AUSTEN CHAMBERLAIN: The present Estimate is to clear and prepare the sites for the slips. That is as much as we can do this year.

*Sir C. DILKE: The only other remark I wish to make arises out of the speech of the honourable Member for Dundee. We must be thankful for small mercies. At the present moment we all know there is an uneasy feeling in the constituencies with reference to our increasing expenditure, and it is incumbent on every Member of this House to search out means of economy. We were all pleased at the references he made at the close of his speech to the chances of future means of economy in the working of the Navy itself. My honourable Friend the Member for Belfast did attack him, although in courteous language, for only making that suggestion of economy now. That is not fair, for he was not in a position of great power when he was at the Admiralty, but he did point out certainly in this House where economy might be effected. But, as I have said, we must be thankful for small mercies, especially those of us who imagine that it is the greatest mistake from the national point of view that we should economise on the Navy. I notice a certain difference in the tone of the Debate to-night from that of a few days ago. The late Secretary to the Admiralty, in his speech the other night, used words which were repeated to-night by the honourable Member for Devonport. I do not want to hold the right honourable Gentleman to the particular words which he used to clothe his thoughts, but it now appears that there was not that deliberate intention which we imagined was conveyed by the words he uttered in the presence of the Leader of the Opposition, that the present programme was to be opposed. We learn to-night that the right honourable Gentleman only intended to ask for information with regard to the Russian programme, a request which the honourable Member for Dundee has also addressed to the House. That is a fair demand. I do not think that the honourable Member for Belfast distinguished sufficiently in his criticism of the speech of the honourable Member for Dundee what was said last year as to the form and what as to the actual merits of the Government proposals. Some of us were strongly in favour of the Government programme of last July. We pressed for it in advance, and we thought it absolutely necessary and barely sufficient. We held that view as strongly as it was possible to hold it, yet we, nevertheless, agreed with the strictures on form made by the Opposition. That question of form is of enormous importance from the point of Parliamentary procedure, but from the point of view of the Navy it is a trifling matter. The programme of last July was generally supported in this House, and the opposition to it by the then Leader of the Opposition was on a point of form, not of substance. The honourable Member for Dundee has alluded to what he said last year, and although some of us would be glad to see a more confident tone in support of the Government proposals as a whole, we must be satisfied at the way he put the matter before us, especially after what occurred the other day. In February 1898 the honourable Member for Dundee pointed out the enormous deficiency in the shipbuilding programme. That was admitted. There was no contest as to the actual fact of that deficiency, and the Government were pressed regarding it from all sides. With reference to the larger programme proposed last July, the honourable Member for Dundee said it was proposed in such a form that it was not sanctioned by the House. There was strong opposition to the form in which the proposals were put forward, but the honourable Member for Belfast is right in saying that substantially that programme was sanctioned by both sides. As regards this year's programme all opposition appears for the moment to be withdrawn, and there is now only a demand for information on the Russian programme. I am glad we remain in the same position as last year, as the honourable Member for Dundee has said that on the merits he was disposed to agree with the programme before the House. On the question as to whether the Government have shown a sufficient case as regards the proposals of Russia we are absolutely in the hands of the Government. As far as they are concerned the facts are not within the knowledge of the public. For my own part I can only repeat what I have said in this House before, that I am so convinced of the weight which is given to this country by the efficiency of the Fleet that I shall support the policy of the Government on this subject. I hope, if economies are necessary, they will be made in other quarters. One other word: it is with reference to a question put by the honourable Member for Devonport to the Government. He asked in the begining of his speech that some statement might be made in the speech of the First Lord or in the Memorandum as to the effects produced by the conference of certain Colonies with regard to the proposal on men that was made last year. The difficulties which were pointed out in two former years appear to be far less strong now. We know the matter was dealt with and considered in the case of Newfoundland, but we have not heard that any definite proposal was made. It was not, I think, stated in the House, and if the Secretary to the Admiralty can give any information I am sure it will receive attention.

*MR. MENDL (Plymouth): Like my right honourable Friend who has just sat down, I have not risen for the purpose of criticising the amount of the Estimates, or suggesting any economy in the naval strength of this country. I find myself in complete agreement with my right honourable Friend the Member for Birkenhead, that it is absolutely vital for us that we should maintain the naval supremacy we now have over other nations, and if economy is to be practised this year—and it is necessary that economy should be practised—the very last direction in which it should be practised is in the direction of our naval supremacy.

These are days when it is not expedient that a righteous man should go about unarmed. But I have not risen for the purpose of proclaiming what I hope has become a truism. The observations which I intended to make have been largely dealt with by my honourable Friend the Member for Devonport. The question of shipwrights and the scheme by which the Admiralty propose to supplement them is one which, to my knowledge, is exciting great interest in the Service. I do not believe that under that scheme the Admiralty will get the best value for their money. I don't think it is a question of trade combination. It is a question of efficiency. I desire to associate myself with the views expressed by the Member for Stepney as to the extreme skill this branch requires. As regards the stokers, it is sometimes forgotten that they have received less increase in pay during the last 30 years than any other branch of the Service. They have been performing duties of greater complexity and difficulty, owing to the advance in marine engineering, than at any other time. Their pay was fixed over 30 years ago; they have to perform their duties under very hard conditions. They have to spend a considerable amount of their lives without seeing the sun, and I think their case ought to be taken into consideration. Again, with regard to the engine-room artificers, they have also, I think, a very strong case, both with regard to the new Admiralty warrants, and also with regard to their messing and other accommodation, which, they complain, is in a dilapidated and inadequate condition. One of the matters to which I desire the attention of the Committee is the question of warrant officers. The warrant officers of the Royal Navy have for many years past asked that they should get a further step, and have Fleet rank, corresponding with the quartermaster or riding-master rank in the Army, and special rates of pay for boatswains and carpenters. Those privileges are enjoyed by all other commissioned and warrant officer ranks in the Service, and I see no reason why this exceedingly reasonable desire should not be considered. They have also a grievance with regard to their promotion to the rank of chief warrant officer.

Mr. Mendl.

Some get it at 18 years' seniority, and others after 24 years. There is no reason, as far as I know, why all should not get it after 18 years' seniority, and thus remedy a block to promotion. These are all the observations I wish to make at this stage of the discussion, and I shall not detain the Committee longer.

*Mr. JOHNSTON (Belfast, S.): I should like to join in the request made by my honourable Friend the Member for West Belfast, that a training ship should be placed in Belfast Lough. It is a source of great annoyance to the inhabitants of Belfast and adjoining districts that the Government has hitherto ignored the reasonable request that a training ship should be placed in the Lough in order that they should be given the opportunity of seeing the vessel themselves, and also of joining Her Majesty's Navy. I do not wish in the least degree to advocate the claims of Belfast against any other portion of Ireland. I rejoice to see anything done for any part of Ireland, and I am not in the least jealous of anything that has been done for Queenstown. I earnestly urge upon the First Lord of the Admiralty and my honourable Friend the Secretary to the Admiralty the expediency of complying with this very earnest request from Belfast. As my honourable Friend the Member for West Belfast has said, we are not likely to kick up a row in Belfast if we don't get what we want, but some Members of Her Majesty's Government are threatened with opposition because this and other demands from Belfast are not listened to. We feel that a firm like Harland and Wolff, that was able to launch the "Oceanic," would be well worthy of supplying material for Her Majesty's Navy. I said I would not occupy more than a few minutes, and I only rise to join in the complaint of my honourable Friend the Member for West Belfast on this subject. He seems to think that, because he is importunate, the Government will probably not listen to him. However, great weight is given to his words, and his labours are appreciated, not only by his own constituency, but also by others.

Sir E. ASHMEAD-BARTLETT (Sheffield, Ecclesall): The right honourable Baronet the Member for the Forest of Dean has just told the House that he cordially supports the naval programme of the Government, especially for the increased Vote for new construction, and the support which this programme—large as it is—has received from all sides of the House makes it perfectly clear to those who attempt to criticise it that the support of such criticism will be small, and that the country is distinctly in favour of this programme. The right honourable Baronet speaks of the feeling of uneasiness which, he thinks, exists in certain portions of the country with regard to our growing Navy. I do not think that this nervousness exists to any great extent. I think it is perfectly easy for any Member who wishes to make out a good case to his constituency for this naval expenditure, and a satisfactory defence which would induce them to support him again as a supporter of the Government which has brought forward this Naval Programme. I was very glad to hear the honourable Member for Stepney also support this naval expenditure. I think it is very significant that a gentleman who is closely connected with trade organisations and with a large section of the working classes should cordially give his support to the programme of the Government. After all, this naval expenditure is nothing more or less than a national insurance. That is almost a hackneyed phrase, but great naval and military expenditure is nothing but a national insurance. I would suggest to those who wish to advance this policy that the question to put before the electorate is this—that this is a national insurance, and to point out how this national insurance compares with similar national insurances of other countries. I understand that the right honourable Gentleman the Member for Clitheroe said the other night that he did not see sufficient reasons for the two new battleships. If I am not misinterpreting him in what he said, he might have found a sufficient reason if he looked at the tremendous menaces to which this country is exposed. He might have seen the great conspiracy worked against this country in many quarters of the globe, which is now at last being dissipated, and which has been dissipated by the fact that we have an overwhelming Navy. Two great rivals, and perhaps enemies, who were engaged in this conspiracy, and who certainly were, to a certain extent, successful, are at last being thoroughly convinced of the naval preponderance of this country, and have been compelled to withdraw from their conspiracy and their aggressive attitude. It is due to our great naval expenditure and our naval supremacy that the carefully planned and carried out conspiracies of our two great rivals against the interests of this country have been practically foiled. I spoke just now of our national insurance, as to how it contrasted with that of other countries. Perhaps the House will allow me to trouble it with a few figures on this point. The national rate per cent. of our naval insurance, as compared with our Imperial commerce, is only 1.8 per cent., our naval expenditure this year being 26½ millions. The total military expenditure of this country, represented by our Navy and Army Votes, represents 3.7 per cent. of our Imperial commerce. In the case of France, her naval expenditure represents 3.4 per cent. of her Imperial commerce, and her total military expenditure no less than 11.1 per cent. Thus France is expending nearly three times as much on her Imperial defences in proportion as we are. Then again, the Russian expenditure on naval defence is 4.3 per cent. The total Russian military and naval expenditure together represent, as compared with her Imperial commerce, no less than 25 per cent., as against our 3.7 per cent. Next I come to Germany. That is the only one among the Great Powers of Europe that spends a smaller proportion on her Navy defence, as compared with her Imperial commerce, than we do. She spends only 1.5 per cent.; but if you add her military expenditure, you get 8.7 per cent. In every case, therefore, we have a good defence to put before the electors of this country. Another point is, as pointed out by the honourable Member for Stepney, that practically the whole of the money is expended in this country, and in giving employment to our own working men. And when you come to consider that it is upon the Navy that this country must rely, not only for the defence of its Imperial commerce, but also of its Imperial strength, and the protection of its Colonies and defences, I do not think that any elector of this country, however prejudiced he might be by misrepresentations and ideas that have been wrongly inculcated in the past, would fail to support the Government in their present naval proposals.

CAPTAIN YOUNG (Berks, Wokingham): I will not detain the House many minutes. I wish to congratulate the Admiralty on the methods they have suggested of getting youngsters to be trained as naval shipwrights. If a youngster has to go to sea, the sooner he goes the better, for there he learns habits of discipline. I cannot, however, congratulate them so freely on their course on the question of leave for officers. They have no doubt done something this year, but still, what they have done is very far behind what these officers deserve, seeing that they have to serve in every climate and in all parts of the world for a period of three or four years. I sincerely hope they will use their exertions to see whether the leave of officers on the paying off of a ship cannot be increased. I also wish to support the case put forward by the honourable Member for Devonport, on behalf of the warrant officers. Senior officers in the Navy very much wish that these men should have their deserts recognised by the Admiralty. I believe them to be the backbone of the Navy, and if the Admiralty can see their way to grant their very small requirements, they will gain the thanks, not only of these officers themselves, but of every man in the Navy.

VISCOUNT CRANBORNE (Rochester): I wish to say a word in support of my honourable Friend's appeal on behalf of the warrant officers, and I would like particularly to impress on the Government the really modest character of their demands. It is an extraordinary thing that among the officers of the Royal Navy there is no corresponding position for warrant officers to that of the quartermaster or riding master in the sister Service. They have no opportunity of rising to commissioned rank. I reduce my request to the very smallest possible dimensions, and I suggest to the Government that the chief warrant officer in a dockyard might at least be granted commissioned rank. He is an officer of importance, and holds a position of great responsibility, and it does not

seem unreasonable that the distinction should be granted in a limited number of cases. There is one other point in connection with warrant officers that I should like to place before the Government. When a chief petty officer is promoted to be a warrant officer, I am informed that in many cases the increment of pay is very small indeed—that it is not sufficient to support his status, and hardly enough to provide him with a uniform suitable to his rank. I would suggest, therefore, that in these cases—it is not in every one that the increment is so small—it might be slightly increased. There is another class in the public service at the dockyard, many of whom I have the honour of representing, who also have a grievance that I wish to mention. I refer to the writers, who for many years have done practically the whole of the work. Recently there have been imported a certain superior kind of accountant officers, who have taken a position of superiority to the writers. The latter do not complain of that, but they do ask that where the writers are particularly deserving, they shall have the opportunity of rising to the superior rank. Then I have once more to draw attention to the position of the riggers of the Royal Navy and of the dockyards. The point I wish to impress upon the Government is the superannuation allowance system. As the honourable Gentleman knows, in the dockyards there are always a certain number of hired men, who, not being entitled to pensions—as the established men are—get rather higher pay during the period of their service. It would be imagined that the difference had some kind of relation to the pension which the established man becomes entitled to at the end of his service. There are some who pay 1s. 6d. and who do not receive a higher pension, but sometimes even a lower pension than others, who only pay to the extent of 1s. My honourable Friend shakes his head, but I think if he makes inquiries he will find that it is so. There is also the case of the riggers and the joiners which ought to be inquired into. There is a great difference of opinion between dockyard men as to what should be done. It is very undesirable and disadvantageous that a rule should exist which admits such apparent injustice as that. It may be that under the conditions in dockyard engagement no injustice is done. On that I pronounce no opinion, but an apparent injustice does as much harm as a real injustice, for the men think that they are cheated, and do not receive as much pension as they are entitled to, compared with men in other departments. The Government ought to reconsider the whole pension system. I think there is something to be said for giving some kind of pension in the cases of hired labour. They have received a certain improvement in their position, but it is not complete. If a hired man becomes a staff man he is paid half-pension; but if he never becomes a staff man he has no claim for a pension at all. I know of a case of a man who is a son of a gentleman in a very high position in the public service. That man served 35 years as a hired man, and had risen to a position by merit, having a salary attached to it of £365 per annum, and a free house. One day he was suddenly dismissed, through no fault of his own, but simply because the Government thought they could reduce the amount of expenditure in his particular department. He received no compensation whatever, although he had served Her Majesty for 35 years, except a small gratuity of something under £300, the income of which would only amount to £11 or £12 per annum. The result was that he fell, as it were, in a month from the position of £365 per annum to £11. I do not say it was unjust, for undoubtedly he knew when he engaged in the public service the conditions under which he would serve; but I think if any private employer had had a servant for 35 years · who had risen to that position without a blemish on his character, he would be treated with more generosity than the Admiralty treated this man. I have no doubt if my honourable Friend the Secretary to the Admiralty takes any notice of the remarks I have made that he will say that it is the fault of the law as it at present stands, and that the law cannot be altered without an Act of Parliament. What I say is, that in these pension matters the Admiralty ought, to some extent, to reconsider their scheme, and if it be necessary to come to Parliament for power to over-awe the Treasury, by all means let them do so.

On the return of the Deputy Chairman after the usual interval,

Sir E. GOURLEY (Sunderland): Mr. O'Connor, I adopt, to a large extent, the views of the honourable Member for Gateshead in regard to the Belleville boilers. The Admiralty ought to institute some drastic trials with that type of boiler. If they were really possessed of all the advantages urged on their behalf, I feel sure that they would have long ere this been adopted by the shipowners of the Mercantile Marine. The very fact of these boilers not having been adopted for general use in the Mercantile Marine proves, to my mind, that they are not adapted for all purposes and for all classes of vessels in Her Majesty's Navy. My belief is that before entering into contracts for boilers of this type for the new vessels we are constructing in accordance with our future programme, the Admiralty ought to make some further inquiry. More especially is this so in regard to the new yacht which is being built for Her Majesty. It is very desirable that Her Majesty should not be placed on board a vessel fitted with experimental boilers. The very fact of Her Majesty being on board a vessel fitted with experimental boilers must create a certain amount of fear and timidity. I hope, therefore, that in place of furnishing the Belleville type of boilers, or any other type of boilers, for that matter, for Her Majesty's yacht, the matter ought to receive the very serious consideration of the Admiralty. In regard to the new ships under construction, unless other contracts have been entered into for these vessels, I am in favour of their being furnished with triple expansion engines. We have had a very large amount of experience with these triple expansion engines in the Mercantile Marine, and that proves that they are in every way suited for propulsion as well as for economy in fuel. It is said on behalf of Belleville boilers that there would be economy in fuel. Nothing of the kind. Experiments that have been made prove that the Belleville type of boiler burns much more coal than any other. I urge the honourable Gentleman the Secretary to the Admiralty to reconsider the question of the Belleville boilers, and also that of triple expansion engines. We have had very satisfactory experience in the Mercantile Marine with the triple expansion engines, and also in our own Navy, and in the other navies f the world. The large war vessel recently dispatched from Armstrong's Works in Newcastle—one of the most powerful vessels afloat—is furnished with triple expansion engines. The Japanese are always in the lead, and are a very knowing people. ʹHad they been advised by Messrs. Armstrong, Whitworth, and Company to fit that vessel with the Belleville type of boiler they would have done so. That proves to us that builders of the wide experience of Armstrong, Whitworth, and Company are not in favour of this type of boiler. The honourable Member for Dundee to-night alluded to the question of expenditure, and considered that the expenditure, using the words of the First Lord, was colossal. He did not enter into details, but he endeavoured to point out that there might be some exercise of economy in regard to the increase in the number of men for the Navy. When the Naval Defence Act was introduced it was said in this House, and Lord Spencer when he introduced it into the House of Lords likewise alleged, that it was not intended that the new ships should be maintained on a war footing in times of peace—that the policy to which the Admiralty was committed was that the new ships should only be provided with a sufficient number of men to keep them in order. But the present Board of Admiralty has departed from that policy, and has determined to maintain these vessels of the Fleet on a war footing. I hold that this is an exceedingly extravagant policy. During the last 10 years the number of permanent men in the Navy has been increased by something like 40,000 men, and we find that 4,250 are this year about to be added to the permanent force. We have thus within the last 10 years a direct increase in the cost of the Navy of something like 3½ to 4 millions of money. That is the direct additional cost; but there are the indirect charges, such as pensions to be given to the additional men, which will swell the pension list that has already attained colossal proportions. I hold that it was never intended that the Reserve ships should be furnished with more than a sufficient number of men to keep them in order, and that the Admiralty ought to utilise the Naval Reserve more than they do. Well, the Admiralty have increased the perma-

Sir E. Gourley.

nent men something over 40,000 within the last 10 years, but they have only increased the number of Reserve men by some 7,000. The question will probably be asked, can we obtain a sufficient number of men for the purpose of increasing our Naval Reserve? I for one hold that we can. It is perfectly true that the number of British seamen in the Mercantile Marine has decreased very considerably during the last few years, especially since the introduction of steam. But still the Board of Trade Returns show that there are 65,000 men who are serving on board the British Mercantile Marine as A.B.'s. But, in addition to these 65,000 serving as A.B.'s in the Mercantile Marine, we have an enormous number of men engaged in the fishing industry. We have at the present moment the flower of the fishing population engaged in the line fishing around our coast, numbering from 80,000 to 100,000, from whom the Navy could be largely recruited in time of war. These men who are trained in our fishing craft are neither more nor less than the class of men who were formerly employed in the sailing collier fleet, and from whom the Navy was largely recruited during the Napoleonic wars. If, then, the Admiralty were to increase the number of the Naval Reserve forces by recruits from the A.B.'s in the Mercantile Marine, and from our fishermen, by offering them a sufficient inducement, I feel bound to say that they could in a very short time increase the Reserve with British seamen and fishermen to the extent of 70,000 or 80,000 men. All that the Reserve men at present get is a retaining fee of £4 per year for 2nd class Reserve, and £6 per year for the 1st class, and when they reach the age of 60 they get a permanent pension of £12 per year. One grievance of the Naval Reserve men is, that they have to serve five years longer for pension than the permanent men in the Royal Navy. I hold that this is a real grievance, and that the pension age of the Naval Reserve ought to be the same as the men in the Royal Navy. Before going further with this continuous increase of the permanent men, I think the Admiralty ought to increase the Naval Reserve by something like 70,000 men, whom you could get for something like £12 to £15 per head per annum, while the cost per man of the permanent service is something like £110 per year. But there is another source from which the Admiralty may obtain, and could if it pleased have obtained, an increase in the Reserve, and that is from the men in the Royal Navy who declined to serve a second term. A Return was made last year of the number of men who joined for a second term in the Royal Navy, and they numbered only something like 10 or 15 per cent. A Return obtained from the Admiralty in 1893 showed that there were only 870 men over 45 years of age serving on board our men-of-war, 5,000 between 35 and 45 years of age, 17,000 between 25 and 30, and the balance under 20 years of age; while there were also 9,000 boys. What I should like to ask is, what is the real percentage of the men who decline to join for a second term? I find that the number of men in receipt of pensions is 22,864, but that includes the men who have passed the period of 55 years. But how many men, I should like to ask, have the Admiralty on the pension list who have served a second time, and who are liable to serve again until they reach the age of 55? If the Admiralty can furnish this information we may be able to ascertain in some shape or form the number of men who decline to join for a second term of service. There must be reasons why many men decline to join for a second term. I believe one reason is this—that the highest position which a bluejacket can attain to in the Navy is that of a warrant officer. Well, you have in the Navy two classes of men—Marines and bluejackets. These two classes of men work side by side. In the case of the Marines, a man in the ranks has the prospect of reaching the commission rank of major; but a bluejacket, working side by side and day by day with the marines, has nothing whatever to look forward to beyond the warrant rank. I was very glad to hear the noble Lord advocate an alteration in the policy of the Admiralty in regard to this matter. The men themselves have presented memorials asking that they may be so situated, so educated, that they may eventually reach the rank of officer, and so be placed in the same position as regards the commissioned ranks as men are in the Marines. It is a very serious question, and except something of this kind is done we shall have difficulty in obtaining men to join the rank and file of the Navy, and we shall have a still larger number of men who decline to rejoin after their first term of service is expired. I think those men whom we find rejoining might find proper inducements on the part of the Admiralty in the first-class Reserve. This is not a question of rank, it is a question of construction. The right honourable Gentleman the First Lord of the Admiralty said in his speech that the naval policy of this country was a question of Foreign Policy, but he omitted to tell us whether he meant that it was the Foreign Policy of the country or the Government, or the Foreign Policy of other Powers. The only Foreign Policy to which he alluded was his fear of Russia. But I fail to understand why the First Lord of the Admiralty should stickle at Russia, because he has told us she has spent only a small sum compared to our annual expenditure on her navy; and yet the First Lord of the Admiralty actually tells us that he is afraid of Russia. I deprecate this mode of placing the Naval Estimates before Parliament and the country. I hold that it is not only impolitic, but it is unwise on the part of the Admiralty that they should be always directing their attention antagonistically to Russia and France. Ever since I came into this House I have been in the habit of listening to the honourable Member's saying Russia was going to do this and Russia was going to do that—so much so, that you might expect to wake up any morning and find a headline in the newspapers to the effect that Russia had invaded India. But just, as the Admiralty knows, all Russia is doing, though it is not disclosed here——

The DEPUTY CHAIRMAN: Order, order! The honourable Gentleman is now travelling rather wide of the matter before Committee. He must confine himself to the question before the House.

Sir E. GOURLEY: I bow to your ruling, Sir, and come at once to the question of construction. There is one point to which I should like to call the attention of the Admiralty, and that is with regard to torpedo catchers. We are building an immense number of torpedo catchers, and those torpedo catchers, according to the information we have, are very weak in point of structure ; they are far too weak, and if they encountered very heavy weather, they would collapse. Now I contend that there ought to be a new torpedo catcher altogether in place of these cockle-shells—for that is really what they are, liable to be sunk by the first shot by which they are hit. We ought to have torpedo catchers with thick armour and protected decks. I am quite sure that the policy of the Government in this matter is an erroneous one. In future warfare a considerable amount of fighting will take place on the ocean, and will not be confined to smooth water, but where you will encounter heavy weather ; and from the reports that we have read, and from that experience we have had with regard to the construction of these torpedo catchers, boats of this class are far too weak for hard work or hard weather. Before I sit down, there is another important matter mentioned in this statement to which I should like to call the attention of the Admiralty. We have building operations under the Naval Defence Act, and notwithstanding the fact that we have a building programme under the Naval Defence Act, the Admiralty are asking for £700,000 or £800,000 for new works, and so forth, under Vote 8. Now, it strikes me that with the amount of money at the disposal of the Admiralty under the Naval Defence Act, there ought to be some saving with regard to the other work. For example, it is proposed to spend £20,000 this year on new works connected with the Coastguard Service. Now, on that Service you must spend annually £25,000 in order to ensure perfection. Now, as the Coastguard Service costs annually something like two millions of money, it does strike me that in connection with this Service there is no necessity for this continual annual increase of £20,000 in connection with works.

Mr. AUSTEN CHAMBERLAIN : I beg the honourable Gentleman's pardon, but do I understand him to say that there is an increase of £25,000 ? Because that is not so. It was the same last year.

Sir E. Gourley.

Sir E. GOURLEY : My contention is this, that inasmuch as it is intended to spend this money on the Coastguard Service, is it necessary ? Now, I should like to ask a question as to how the value of the dockyard stocks is arrived at. These are valued in the Estimates at £2,700,000, and, on the other hand, there is put down a sum of £551,678 as being expended on articles over and above the details in the Estimate laid before Parliament, and a sum of £447,547 also for articles included in the Parliamentary Estimate. Now what I want to arrive at is, how is the value of these things arrived at ? And in order to obtain a correct answer, I would ask, at what valuation do the anchors now in stock stand in the stock valuation as compared with the price they originally cost ? Anchors which cost another £200,000, do they stand in the stock valuation at £200,000, or do they stand at £100,000 ? This is a matter which I should like to sift very carefully, and a question which I think the Secretary to the Admiralty ought to answer.

*Captain PHILLPOTTS (Devon, Torquay) : Before the honourable Gentleman the Secretary to the Admiralty rises to reply, I should like to ask him one or two other questions. In the first place, I should like him to say whether the new cruisers which are to be built are to be fitted with armoured belts on the water-line, and non-inflammable decks and internal fittings. The question of submarine boats is attracting attention in foreign countries at the present time. I should like to know whether anything has been done by the Admiralty in this matter. Do they propose to make any experiments in that direction, or are they satisfied with what has been done by foreign nations ? The honourable Member for Stepney criticised the Admiralty with regard to the action which they have taken with respect to the shipwrights. Now, the Admiralty propose to enter and train young men as shipwrights themselves. In my opinion, that is a very excellent plan, and for this reason : men who join the Service after they are grown up seldom take kindly to a seafaring life, and I can quite understand it. Duties that appear menial and irksome to mechanics trained in workshops on shore are performed as a matter of course by men trained afloat. They see no degradation in doing work on board a ship that their wives and mothers are doing in their own homes. Turning to the statement made by the First Lord of the Admiralty, I am glad to see that certain concessions asked for on behalf of the executive officers are about to be considered. I refer to harbour time, full pay leave, and sick leave. As regards the warrant officers, I do wish that the concession we ask for, namely, of giving them commission rank, could have been granted this year. Unfortunately, it is not so. I should also have been glad to have seen an increase of pension for chief petty officers. As regards the Naval Reserve, I notice that classes are being organised for the instruction of the engineers. It seems to me that very few of them will have an opportunity of joining the classes, and I hope before long the classes will be extended. The regulations for the seaman class in the Naval Reserve appear to work very well, and I am perfectly certain that the year's or six months' training that these men get on board a man-of-war will be invaluable to them. The increase of the clothing allowance will also tend to remove a grievance and source of dissatisfaction. There is another point that I wish the Admiralty would take into consideration, which I believe would effect economy in the Service, and therefore, I think, ought not to be very much objected to by them. It is with reference to the correspondence. I should like the Admiralty to consider whether it is not possible to reduce the amount of correspondence in the Navy. I know, for a fact, that all the senior officers on board our ships spend a considerable portion of their time in signing their names. Many of the documents are quite of a formal character. Now it is quite impossible for the officers to make themselves acquainted with the contents of all the documents which are placed before them for signature, and therefore they entrust that part of the duty to their clerks and secretaries. I do not say a word against these officers— they are thoroughly reliable men, well up to their duties, and absolutely trustworthy; but I hold that

no officer should put his signature to a document with the contents of which he is unacquainted. And I am quite sure that no officer can carefully look into and examine every document that he is expected to sign. I believe if the amount of correspondence was reduced a considerable economy would be effected; and it would enable these officers to devote more time to their more important duties than is possible for them under the present conditions. Various suggestions have been thrown out with regard to this matter. I heard it suggested the other day that it would be a good plan if the clerical staff of the Admiralty had to pay for all the stationery and printing; they would not see it quite in that light, but there certainly does appear to be room for economy in that direction. Another suggestion that has been made with regard to this matter is that at all the important stations, such as Portsmouth and Plymouth, an officer should be appointed as chief of the staff—either a junior flag officer or a captain—who should take over some portion of this work. I would remind the House that there was one admiral in command at these ports when the Fleet was only half its present size, and there is only one admiral now. I think something might be done in this direction, and I certainly do hope that the honourable Gentleman the Secretary to the Admiralty will be able to say something on these points when he rises to reply.

*MR. J. ELLIS (Notts, Rushcliffe): The honourable Gentleman who has just sat down has dealt with this matter from precisely the point of view with which he was so able to deal with it—that is to say, the technical point of view. The view I take is rather different. I do not speak upon that subject as having any technical knowledge of naval establishments, nor am I a Member for a dockyard constituency. I speak solely on behalf of my own constituents, who are interested when they find such an alarming and appalling— I use the word which was used by the honourable Member for Dundee, who spoke earlier in the evening—increase in the demands upon public money. I desire to associate myself entirely with the remarks of the honourable Gentleman the Member for Dundee as to the extreme regret which this House feels at the absence of the First Lord of the Admiralty, and I still further regret the reason which is the cause of it. The right honourable Gentleman, when he made his statement, made use of the expression—

" The Navy Estimates have never, perhaps, been introduced in more singular circumstances in some respects than to-day."

That is so, and he gave a reason for that circumstance; but there were other circumstances to which attention has been called which are also very remarkable. The main facts of the Navy Estimates were communicated to one of our newspapers, by what the First Lord of the Admiralty characterised as a gross breach of trust; but they were withheld from this House till the last moment for reasons given by the First Lord. Not only were they withheld for the reasons which were given to us, but they were withheld in absolute violation of one of the Resolutions of this House —a Resolution of very ancient date. I am not going to dwell upon the breach of trust to which the First Lord of the Admiralty alluded in reply to the question I put to him on the subject, because, as I understand, he wishes the matter to stand over until his return. I accept, of course, fully the statement of the First Lord of the Admiralty and his expression of regret that he has pursued the course this year that is being pursued, and note his intimation that the course pursued in 1896 would not have been pursued if any objection had been raised. I take it for granted that as objection is now being raised in the very strongest manner possible that we shall have no more withholding of the Estimates till the last moment. I say that no Minister coming down to this House and asking for money out of the public taxation has any right to judge in his own person whether he shall reserve or not from the representatives of the taxpayer, or whether he shall give, the data for that taxation or not. The Resolution to which I have alluded runs as follows:—

" That this House considers it essentially useful to the exact performance of its duties as guardians of the public purse that such Estimates should be presented within 10 days after the opening of the Committee of Supply."

Mr. J. Ellis.

And the day in my opinion is coming when that guardianship will be much needed. The Estimates have not been presented within 10 days after the opening of the Committee of Supply for the last year or two. Now, passing from what some may consider a mere matter of procedure, though I am quite sure that the Committee will appreciate the fact that our forms of procedure with regard to the imposing of taxation and the appropriation of public funds are so drawn as to be of the utmost importance, and that they shall be carried out to the utmost letter, I wish to dwell for a moment on the position of extreme gravity in which we find ourselves with regard to the position of the public purse. We have a demand made upon us this year for £28,000,000 sterling for naval works and Estimates. Now, I always think that in these matters of finance it is useless to pick out any particular year, because in that particular year there may be something that vitiates the comparison with another; but when you take a series of years from which to draw your comparison you are on very much safer and sounder ground. Now, I have taken the trouble to work out a few figures, which I think will be found to be of some little value in this respect. During the six years ending March 1887 the annual average expenditure for Navy Estimates was £11,300,000 sterling. For the six years ending March 1893 the average annual expenditure was £13,600,000 sterling, showing an increase of £2,300,000. Members of Parliament who sat during those periods will appreciate the reason that I have for taking those years, because during those years both political parties were responsible for this expenditure. Now, during the three years ending March 1896 the average annual expenditure for Naval Estimates was £17,100,000, showing an increase of £3,500,000, and during the three years ending March 1899 the annual average has risen to £22,300,000, showing an increase of £5,200,000, and this year, as we all know, we have Navy Estimates to the tune of £26,600,000, which is an increase of the three previous years' average of £4,300,000. Therefore, as we stand now our Estimates for Naval purposes exceed by £15,300,000 the amount of the average sum spent during the six years ending 1887. That is in 13 years. Well, the figure stands large enough in itself in all conscience; but what alarms me is, not so much the figure, but the rate of increase that is shown. That is the point which we have to fix in our minds. The rate of increase is such that, as everyone knows, this kind of thing cannot go on. Now, I have only spoken up to the present of the Navy, but when we come to the question of armaments we find that we are spending in three financial years ending March 1899 more than 10s. out of every £1 of our national expenditure on armaments, as against something like 8s. out of every £1 for the six years ending 1887. I think that surely is rather a striking commentary upon what we are pleased to call the civilisation at the end of the 19th century. It is impossible that it can go on, and if anyone doubts this he has only to live a few years longer to realise that he has been very much mistaken. New taxes will most assuredly be needful to meet the increased expenditure. In this matter of the Navy men, ships, and guns hang together. If you wish to increase your Navy you must increase your men, you must increase your guns, and so on through the whole gamut of naval requirements and paraphernalia. I noticed that there was one continuous thread of apology running through the speech of the First Lord, and it came to this—" We are doing this because other Powers are doing it; otherwise we should not do it at all." I must say I thought there was a certain sense of hesitation perceptible in the utterance of the First Lord when he said—

" I do not wish to make any comparison with foreign ships, but I may say we have selected these ships after a careful review of the new designs of other Powers, and we hope that these designs will secure to us that we shall have stronger ships than any which are now building by any country."

Surely that is a comparison of other nations and of other ships, and I cannot help thinking that it has in it a certain provocative element which was unwise. We all know our strength, we all know our capacity, we all know our enormous financial means. But is it worth while

for the First Lord to rise at that Table, and, in the face of Europe, to flaunt these things so publicly? The words " I do not wish to make any comparison" seem to suggest an apology, but I do not see why that which gave rise to such an apology should be necessary, having regard to the fact that the First Lord devoted much time in the earlier part of his speech to proving how entirely satisfactory our naval condition was in what he called the " precarious" state of foreign affairs last autumn. He went on to say that we were able to put the whole of the gigantic machinery of the Navy in motion at a cost of £13,000. That being so, the natural corollary and inference seems to be that you are in a position to pause and to leave well alone. Turning for a moment to what I might call the other-Power argument, I wish to pay my humble tribute of thanks to my right honourable Friend the Member for Clitheroe (Sir U. Kay-Shuttleworth) for the admirable speech he made the other night. I only wish he had had a better audience to listen to it, because that most luminous speech contained some extremely valuable and interesting information. He demonstrated to my mind most conclusively two facts, which have not been contradicted by any succeeding speaker, namely, that in naval construction the French are tardy while the English are expeditious. But he showed also a more important fact still, namely, that for very good reasons the French have definitely abandoned the naval race with England, while within a comparatively few days it has been announced that it is not expedient any longer on the part of France to continue the military race with Germany. But this is by no means all. We all know of the step which I venture to say will be chronicled as one of the most remarkable steps in Europe at the end of the nineteenth century, namely, the issue of the Rescript by the Tsar. I think there must have been a certain amount of misgiving in the minds of the Cabinet when they instructed the First Lord to put forward his remarkable offer. As I understand these Estimates, a certain amount will, in certain eventualities, be cut off. Well, I really doubt the wisdom of such a proposal. I much regret that the Cabinet, in the presence of this remarkable offer of the Tsar of all the Russias, did not say—" We have gladly signified our willingness to take part in those deliberations, and we will pause. We have plenty of time to overtake France or any other nation, and we will suspend our operations." I believe that the Government would have been supported by all that is best and noblest in the country on both sides of politics. I am sure there are many Members opposite who sympathise with the Tsar's proposal. I do not for one moment desire to make this a Party matter, but I think the Cabinet might have adopted a much bolder attitude. But, after all, it is not what other nations of Europe are doing or are likely to do; it is our own general policy which must inspire the magnitude or otherwise of our naval expenditure. Now, I am going to read to the Committee a few words on the subject—

"For the last 20 years, still more for the last 12, you have been laying your hands with almost frantic eagerness on every tract of territory adjacent to your own, or desirable from any point of view, you thought it desirable to take. That has had two results. The first result is this, that you have excited to an almost intolerable degree the envy of other colonising nations, and that in the case of many countries, or several countries rather, that were friendly to you you can reckon in consequence of your colonial policy not on their active benevolence, but on their active malevolence."

These are the words of Lord Rosebery, who was *particeps criminis*, if I may use such an expression with regard to so distinguished a man, in the creation of this particular policy. I agree with Lord Rosebery that we cannot be grabbing territory, forming protectorates, and acquiring spheres of influence without it having an effect upon naval expenditure and armaments generally, and we are reaping the result at this moment of the policy we have hitherto been pursuing. You have been laying upon the Foreign and Colonial Offices and other great Departments duties which they were never created for, and that they cannot properly perform. Sometimes you try to perform them through chartered companies, always with the disastrous result of being made responsible for something that you ought not to be, and sometimes pursuing a will-o'-the-wisp of trade, with the undoubted result that you add intolerably to the burdens of the people, and, above all, distract

Mr. J. Ellis.

the attention of Parliament from those great questions of social amelioration which really lie at the root of the happiness and welfare of the people. " I am all for concentration." to use the words of Mr. Disraeli, which in this connection have singular application. The minds of the people and the attention of Parliament should be given to great measures of social amelioration. There are, it has been said, two schools—

" With the one Party England's duty is held to be the care of her own children within her own shores, redress of wrongs, the supply of needs, the improvement of laws and of institutions. Against this home-spun doctrine the other Party sets up territorial aggrandisement, large establishments, and accumulation of a multitude of fictitious interests abroad."

The great man who uttered these words left us now nearly a year ago, but there are many of us still faithful to the lessons he taught us, and I venture to say that this territorial aggrandisement, with the consequent enormous increase of naval armaments, is on all hands to be deplored.

*THE SECRETARY TO THE ADMIRALTY (Mr. MACARTNEY, Antrim, S.): I am not quite certain whether the speech to which the Committee has just listened expresses more than a note of regret at the size of the Estimates which have been laid before Parliament, or whether the feeling underlying the honourable Gentleman's remarks was that the increased Estimates are unnecessary. If the speech is based on the first motive I, for one, and I think the Government, cordially agree with that sentiment—that it is a matter of regret that circumstances have compelled those who are responsible for the administration of the Admiralty to present Estimates of this kind to the country. If, on the other hand, his objection to the Estimates is that they are unnecessary, then I join issue with him. If that is the motive which underlies his observations to the House, I think that he ought, at all events, to support them by challenging the verdict of the Committee. Sir, it is not any question of foreign policy or of Colonial expansion which has dictated the figures which are now laid before Parliament. They are based upon a policy of Admiralty administration which has been accepted by previous administrations. Parliament has over and over again, and the country also, I take it, have acquiesced in the principle of the Admiralty administration that the naval forces of this country should be at least equivalent to those of two first-class leading Naval Powers. Sir, it has been that principle alone upon which these Estimates have been framed, and not with regard to any accidental circumstances of foreign or colonial policy. Now, the honourable Gentleman alluded to the Estimates of 1887. I have no desire on this occasion to revive any question of Party disputes or Party politics with regard to the administration of the Navy, and I can only say this, that if the cost of maintaining the naval forces of this country have increased, as they have since 1887 under all Administrations, it has, in my opinion, been the result of the inattention of Parliament and of both Parties to the requisite requirements of the Service previous to 1887. Sir, if there is one thing which I think is gratifying to anyone who has anything to do with the administration of the Navy, it is that in recent years the administration of that great Department of the State has been almost entirely removed from Party conflict. Certainly I do not desire tonight to say one word which in the slightest degree should arouse amongst certain Members of the Committee any feeling either on this side of the House or on the other that whatever differences of opinion may divide us it is a question of Party politics. I suppose no Member of this Committee regrets more than do those who are responsible for the administration of the Admiralty that the unavoidable necessities of the times and period have obliged us to present these figures which stand in the Estimates for this year. Now, Sir, the honourable Member for Dundee earlier in the evening drew attention to a statement with regard to the policy of these Estimates which has been made by the First Lord of the Admiralty, and he placed an interpretation on the statement of the right honourable Gentleman which produced a conflict of opinion and of meaning in his speech, and also in the words which he quoted from "The Times" of a speech of my own later on. Sir, the honourable Member was not in the House on the occasion when I spoke, and I think he had not the opportunity of listening to the remarks which were made by my honourable and gallant Friend the Member for Yarmouth (Sir John Colomb), to whom I specially replied. My honourable and gallant Friend said the First Lord of the Admiralty had stated that if the Conference that had been summoned under the auspices of the Tsar did not agree, the programme must stand, and the honourable Member placed upon it a further interpretation that the naval expenditure of this country was placed in the hands of the European Conference. Against that he said he protested with all · is might. It was in regard to that special interpretation of my honourable and gallant Friend's proposition, which he based upon the First Lord's statement, that I protested. I have not the slightest intention of in any way diminishing the statement of the First Lord, namely, that if the Peace Conference does carry out the object which we all believe his Majesty the Tsar sincerely has at heart, an opportunity will probably be afforded to all European Naval Powers of in important elements diminishing their programmes of naval construction. But I pointed out to the Committee on that occasion that the Navy of this country has many responsibilities and many duties to perform which do not naturally. fall within the purview of the duties of any other country in Europe, and, therefore, it was an extraordinary deduction to make from my right honourable Friend's statement that we were prepared to assent to the naval expenditure of the country being placed within the control of a European Conference. Within these limits, going neither beyond them nor less than them, is the natural meaning of my words. I hope I have made myself clear to the honourable Gentleman. Sir, the honourable Member then called attention to the fact, which I do not for a moment dispute, that the Estimates that are presented to the House this year are in reality Estimates which contain an additional programme f r the current year; and he complained, as he did last year I think, of the course we followed with reference to providing the finance without obtaining the assent of the House in the usual manner. He asked me if I could point out any precedent for the fact that we had proceeded to give certain orders in relation to this additional programme without obtaining the consent of the House in the ordinary manner. Sir, I at once admit that I am not aware of any precedent. I do not think for a moment the First Lord of the Admiralty, when he introduced the additional programme in July last, said that there was a precedent, but at the same time he certainly in no way whatever misled the Committee as to what his intention was. He said—

"I have consulted the Chancellor of the Exchequer, and he agrees with me, looking to the uncertainty of the amount which may be earned, and also to the fact that in the large shipbuilding programme that we have in hand outside this new programme there must always be an uncertainty whether the contractors, either for materials or for ships, will be able to earn the whole amount provided in the Estimate, it will be best to introduce the necessary Supplementary Estimate early next Session rather than now, when it would be no guide to the House as to the amount which it will be actually necessary to spend. We consider that this is a business-like proceeding, and I hope the House will approve of it."

It is perfectly true that on that occasion complaints were made to the Committee, not only by the honourable Gentleman opposite, but by the right honourable Gentleman who was then the Leader of the Opposition; but the Committee, as a matter of fact, brushed them aside. There were, no doubt, questions and objections on a point of order, but I think, without the slightest offence to the honourable Gentleman, I may say that neither Parliament nor the country were in a humour then to pay any great attention to points of pedantry. Well, now, the honourable Gentleman asked me why we had not produced a Supplementary Estimate. My right honourable Friend said on that occasion that he carried away with him, or would carry away with him, in that Debate the conviction that the House of Commons had practically authorised him to give orders as he saw fit for the additional programme. But the question remains about the Supplementary Estimate. I admit that if in the current year our contractors had earned the whole amount on the shipbuilding programme which we had expected them to earn, it would probably be necessary to introduce a Supplementary Estimate, but, as a matter of fact, the earnings of the contractors fell far short of what had been anticipated, and there has been no necessity. There has been practically no money earned within this financial year upon

the Supplementary Programme introduced in July, though orders had been given; therefore, I submit to the Committee that there has been no serious infringement of the rights of honourable Gentlemen as representing the taxpayers of this country, and that, interesting as the objections of the honourable Gentleman may be on a point of Parliamentary procedure, they really are not of such a weighty character as to justify any member of this Committee feeling that he has been deprived of any very material portion of his rights and privileges. Sir, the honourable Gentleman has spoken of the "appalling" aggregate of the Naval Vote, and he has been followed this evening in a speech by the honourable Member for Rushcliffe (Mr. John Ellis), who has also used the adjective. For myself I should say that though the Vote is very large it is absolutely necessary. The honourable Gentleman also said that it would be necessary, if the Estimates are accepted, for the Admiralty to take the Committee into its fullest confidence. Well, Sir, I do not know whether the honourable Gentleman wishes to press for every detail of the knowledge that the Admiralty possesses. I do not think myself that it is desirable that everything that is within the knowledge of the Admiralty should be divulged to the Committee at the present moment, having regard especially to this very Conference upon which so much stress has been laid by honourable Gentlemen opposite. The honourable Gentleman, however, may be prepared to take this general statement from me, that we have, neither in regard to the battleships of 1899-1900 nor in regard to the cruisers, drawn that programme up without as full a knowledge as we could obtain of the intentions of other Powers, but, of course, as my honourable Friend says, there, again, we come to the point whether the action of other Powers, consequent upon what may occur at this Conference, will be seriously modified. But the principle which underlies this programme is that which has been consistently acted upon by Admiralty administrators for many years past, and it is that we believe the country expects the Admiralty to maintain our Navy on an equality with those of the two leading Naval Powers in Europe. Then the honourable Gentleman asked me to assent to a second condition, and one which is much easier for me to assent to. I think the honourable Gentleman's experience of the Admiralty must have convinced him that there is nobody more likely to give an ungrudging assent to that proposition than one in the position which he himself occupied.

MR. E. ROBERTSON: I have omitted what I really intended to say, which was that the Admiralty ought to make some attempt to induce the Colonial Governments to make a suitable contribution to the Navy, the increase of which is as much a benefit to them as it is to us.

*MR. MACARTNEY: I think that on the whole the most desirable way to arrive at the conclusion which the honourable Member desires is to leave it to the action of those Colonial Governments themselves. Already we have had one admirable example set by the Government of Cape Colony, which, I hope, will be followed in the near future by other Colonial Governments. My honourable Friend the Member for Gateshead alluded once again to the familiar subject of water-tube boilers, and I am sure the honourable Gentleman will forgive me if I decline on this occasion to fight over again the battle which has been fought so often on the floor of this House. It is perfectly true that a lamentable accident has occurred on board the "Terrible," but that accident would certainly not justify the Admiralty in retracing their action in regard to the construction of water-tube boilers. If the Admiralty, on account of one single accident of this character, were to throw overboard the policy of water-tube boiler construction, then, indeed, the honourable Gentleman, or anybody else, might charge the Admiralty with having arrived at their decision in regard to those boilers upon insufficient grounds.

*MR. ALLAN: Why is it that all your trial trips are failures? What about the "Perseus," "Pactolus," "Pylades," "Argonaut," and others?

*MR. MACARTNEY: I do not know what better knowledge my honourable Friend has, but this is the first accident, so far as I am aware, which has occurred with the water-tube boilers. Vessels, however, fitted with these boilers have developed several defects connected with their engines, and my honourable Friend alleged this defect in reference to the "Blenheim" and other vessels, but the "Blenheim" has cylindrical boilers.

*MR. ALLAN: I did not mention that.

*MR. MACARTNEY: When the honourable Member talks about the "Terrible" being a dismal failure, let me ask the Committee to remember that the "Terrible" has done what no other warship in the world has ever done—she has run for 60 hours at a continuous speed of 20 knots.

*MR. ALLAN: It is nothing to say that she went 20 knots for such a short time, when she was designed to steam 22½ knots.

*MR. MACARTNEY: There are several other ships in Her Majesty's Service fitted with water-tube boilers, about which we have heard little or no complaints. It is perfectly true that the "Niobe" had some defects connected with her machinery, but I have just been informed that she has run successfully a 60 hours' trial, and she is now going to join the Channel Squadron. I think it would be hopeless for me to attempt to convert my honourable Friend to water-tube boilers, for he is their very determined foe, and I am sure that no facts which I could put forward would convince him. My honourable Friend has spoken of the case of the "Asama," which is one of a group of five or six Japanese cruisers fitted with cylindrical boilers, and he has instanced this as an example of the rejection of water-tube boilers. I take it, therefore, that my honourable Friend has the highest opinion of the Japanese naval advisers, because, contrary to our advisers, they have put in cylindrical boilers.

*MR. ALLAN: I must take the vessel as she is, and compare her with your ships.

*MR. MACARTNEY: But the honourable Member thinks their advisers are better than ours.

*MR. ALLAN: I never even hinted such a thing.

*Mr. MACARTNEY: The "Asama" is one of a group of six Japanese cruisers in which cylindrical boilers were to be put, and in the first three these boilers were fitted; but in the last three of the same group they have substituted water-tube boilers, and, therefore, if our advisers are wrong the Japanese advisers are wrong as well. Go where you will, every single Power is now substituting water-tube boilers for cylindrical. The honourable Gentleman also criticised the Admiralty Estimates, and said that he could not find any account in detail of the repairs. I must, however, remind the Committee that these Estimates are the Estimates for the coming year, and if my honourable Friend referred to a certain portion of those Estimates, he would find a detailed statement of every ship which is estimated to come in for repairs during the year, but we cannot state beforehand what the amount will be. When a ship comes in, the repairs which are necessary are reported; they are then inspected by the dockyard and other officials, and the amount which is considered proper is then allowed for those repairs. Of course, my honourable Friend will find a year or two hence in the Expense Accounts of the Navy the exact amount of money spent upon every ship repaired in 1899.

*Mr. ALLAN: I am sorry to interrupt the right honourable Gentleman, but I am aware of the existence of this Suspense Account. My complaint is this, that your Estimate is the expenditure of last year, and I think these ought to be bound together so that Members of this House could compare them.

*Mr. MACARTNEY: But they have no relation the one with the other, and binding them up would be only placing a heavier burden on my honourable Friend than he bears already. The honourable Member for Devonport has referred to the position of the naval shipwrights, and this question has also been alluded to by the honourable Member for Stepney. I do not wish to detain the House upon this matter, but I may say that we have no intention whatever—and this had better be understood at once—of altering the conditions under which naval shipwrights enter the Service. The Admiralty do not look upon these men, as the honour-

able Member for Stepney does, as the highest class of mechanic on board ship. Their qualifications are inferior to others, and it is quite immaterial whether the ship goes to sea either with or without them. If we can get them on certain conditions we are glad to have them, but we have no intention whatever of altering their conditions of service. The honourable Gentleman the Member for Devonport put a question to me with regard to the chief petty officers, which is a subject in which many honourable Members take an interest. Last year, in July, towards the end of the Session, in reply to a Question, I expressed the hope that we should be able to lay before Parliament on this occasion a scheme for meeting some of the grievances complained of at that time, but there were two conditions with which I surrounded that offer. One of those conditions was that no addition should be made to the non-effective Vote of the Service, which is already very large, and which is growing every year, and which, in all probability, in future years, will be larger still. The other condition was that some advantage should accrue to the Service. Now, when my scheme came to be examined, it was found that while it did meet the particular demand for an increase of pensions for the chief petty officers on their own conditions; yet, in order to meet the two conditions I laid down, we had to impose other conditions in connection with our Service on board ship which would make it unpalatable, and would certainly have had a slight effect in retarding promotion. Therefore, I had to give way to the balance of opinion against me at the Admiralty; and, therefore, we are not able to present any scheme such as we hoped at one time to have been able to present in relation to this particular question. Then there is also the question of the Reserves, which was raised by the honourable Member for Devonport. It appears to me, however, that the scheme which the honourable Member laid before the Committee is essentially one for the Board of Trade. It is perfectly true that the Admiralty are interested indirectly in the condition of the Mercantile Marine. As far as I understand the honourable Gentleman, this proposal is one which certainly ought to be considered by those directly interested in the

Mercantile Marine, and when it has been thoroughly discussed and formulated, then it would be a scheme which might be presented for the consideration of the Admiralty; and all I can say is, that when the scheme is presented, and has been fully considered by those interested in the Mercantile Marine, and when it has also been considered by the Board of Trade, the Admiralty are quite ready to consider any proposal that may be made to it in relation to any assistance which it can give. My honourable Friend the Member for Birkenhead asked me a question about the supply of armour, and I can quite understand the great interest which my honourable Friend takes in this matter. I do not think that I could amplify very largely what I said the other day in reply to the right honourable Baronet. It is true that the supply of armour has disappointed the expectations of the Admiralty this year, but we have good reason to believe that early in the financial year the supply of armour plate will be considerably in excess of the amount which has been supplied in the previous year, and that there will not be that delay in private yards which has been alluded to.

MR. COURTENAY WARNER (Stafford, Lichfield): But was not a similar assurance given to us last year?

*MR. MACARTNEY; I think, if the honourable Member will carry his memory back to the discussion which took place last year, he will recollect that the Admiralty were told that we were under-estimating the quantity that would be produced, but the view of the Admiralty has now turned out to be more correct.

MR. COURTENAY WARNER: I think the manufacturers gave assurances that they would supply the Admiralty with a larger amount of armour?

*MR. MACARTNEY; There is no doubt that they hoped to do so.

MR. COURTENAY WARNER: But there is no penalty clause.

*MR. MACARTNEY: That is so, for there is no penalty clause. My honourable Friend asked me a question with regard to the proportion of foreign orders given by the Admiralty. I am hardly in a position to speak at the present moment of the proportion, but I know that it is not very large, and it

does not in any way interfere materially with the supply to our Service, and it cannot be looked upon in any way as an element which would materially diminish the supply expected by the Admiralty. Then my honourable Friend the Member for West Belfast brought up a question which has excited a considerable amount of local interest, when he advocated the claims of Belfast to a training-ship, and he was supported in this by my honourable Friend the Member for South Belfast. The Member for West Belfast had stated that neither he nor anyone else had received from the Admiralty any reason for refusing this training-ship at Belfast. Now, when my honourable Friend complains of a refusal having been given without any reasons, he can hardly be cognisant of what has passed between the Admiralty and certain public bodies in Belfast on this question. The Admiralty has laid down a rule that it is inexpedient to place training-ships for boys in the neighbourhood of large towns, and there is not in the whole of the United Kingdom any training-ship so placed. The general reasons on which that principle is laid down must commend themselves to every Member of the Committee. But besides this, Belfast Lough is not a suitable place, for no training-ship could possibly remain there during the season, because it is such an exposed place, and the boys for a considerable portion of the year would not be able to land. If the training-ship were moored at the head of the Lough, there would have to be a special dredging in the mud, and all our authorities agree that to have a training-ship at that point would be most undesirable from the point of view of health. No one is more anxious than I am to have a question of this sort decided in favour of Belfast, but, looking at it from a purely practical standpoint, I am constrained to say that there are no reasons why the decision which has been arrived at by the Admiralty should be reversed. My honourable Friend the Member for South Belfast has asked me why the great firms of the city of Belfast have had no share in the orders for ship-building from the Admiralty. I may say, in reply to that question, that it is entirely the fault, if fault there be, of the shipbuilding firms in Belfast. Year after year we asked for tenders from Messrs. Harland and Wolff, and year after year they declined to tender. They have a high reputation, and possibly for the reason that they have the cream of the mercantile shipbuilding they find this more profitable than Admiralty contracts. The honourable Member for Torquay has asked me a question about our new protected cruisers, and he has asked me to state whether they will have any side armour. They will have, I understand, about 11ft. of side armour. The honourable Member has also asked me a question with regard to submarine boats, and I may say, in reply, that nothing has occurred, as far as we know, in recent years to alter the views of the Admiralty as to the desirability of building these boats. There are one or two other questions which have been asked me, but I think they will come better on another Vote, and I think I have now attempted to answer all the questions raised during the discussion.

MR. COURTENAY WARNER: There is the question of the warrant officers.

*MR. MACARTNEY: With reference to the warrant officers, I may dispose of that by saying that the Government do not propose to make any alteration in the position of warrant officers at present. With regard to other questions of detail, there will be an opportunity upon the Dockyards Vote of raising the special questions in which honourable Gentlemen are interested, and I have refrained specially from alluding to one or two questions which bore distinctly upon the question of the dockyards. I must apologise to the Committee for having detained them so long.

MR. FENWICK (Northumberland, Wansbeck): I must express my regret that after the extremely favourable statement made last year with regard to the pensions, that we have not had a more sympathetic statement from that question. He has referred to the the honourable Gentleman in relation to chief petty officers, and what he has said I presume also has reference to warrant officers. With regard to the position of the engine-room artificers, I think it is about two years since the Government made a concession to these men, which was received with great satisfaction by them, on the demand that they made for an opportunity of rising to a higher position than that which they occupied as engine-room artificers. The Govern-

ment then fulfilled their promise, and in the regulations for the examination it is stipulated that each candidate must be 35 years of age, and must have had at least 10 years' confirmed service. Now, the question I want to put is this: I presume that it is the object and desire of the Government to attract men into the Service as soon as they reach the years of maturity, and even before that if they possibly can. I think the honourable Gentleman will see that it is quite possible, under those regulations, for a man to have 13 years' confirmed service in the service of the Navy, assuming that he enters the Navy when he is 21 years of age, without being permitted to sit for his examination in order to take up the position of a warrant officer; and, on the other hand, a man who keeps out of the Service until he is 23 or 24 years of age may have his confirmed period of service, and be eligible to sit for examination for that position, whereas the other man who has gone into the Service very much earlier, and has more years of confirmed service than the other, is not eligible to acquire that promotion. What I want to know is, whether some alteration cannot be made so as to permit a man who has the confirmed period of service of 10 years, when he has reached the period of qualification, that he should have some opportunity of becoming a candidate for the post of a warrant officer? I think that is a very reasonable request, and I hope the honourable Gentleman will see his way to grant it.

MR. MACLEAN (Cardiff): I have the deepest respect for the honourable Gentleman the Secretary' to the Admiralty and the honourable Member for Gateshead, but I sometimes wish that they would carry on their quarrel about water-tube boilers outside the precincts of this House. I think if they went to sea, and tried conclusions somewhere beyond the Nore, the House would be free from these interminable controversies, and would be able to devote itself to questions of general policy, which are now almost lost in a perfect wilderness of detail. I do not think anyone can accuse this House of being indifferent to the wants of the Navy. Whenever a responsible Minister comes down to this House and says that more money is wanted to maintain the Navy in a more perfect state of efficiency in order to defend the interests of this country, and in case of any emergency that may arise, this House always gives them that money with a generous and even with a lavish hand. I think anyone who has been a member of the Board of Admiralty will acknowledge that this is the case, but sometimes, I confess, some misgivings arise in my mind as to whether we are not carrying this policy too far. I am sure that we all deeply regret the absence of the right honourable Gentleman the First Lord of the Admiralty this evening, for I wish that he could have given us more substantial reasons than have yet been placed before the Committee to justify the very great increase in the expenditure and in the armaments of this country which the Government are now meditating. There was a very significant passage in the speech of the right honourable Gentleman the First Lord of the Admiralty when he introduced these Estimates, for he said that it was a remarkable fact that the Russians were spending very little money indeed upon the manning of the Navy, and he could not account for the Estimate being so small. The reason, however, is perfectly plain, for it is simply because the Russians are not spending large sums of money upon the manning of their Navy.

AN HONOURABLE MEMBER: No, no!

MR. MACLEAN: All this question of the increase of our armaments and the expenditure upon the Navy is one of degree. We have been going on gaily with full flowing sails for a great many years without having taken in a reef, and now we are face to face with the necessity of finding money for the expenditure which is going on. You may depend upon it that the country, though willing to do everything in its power to maintain such a Navy as we require, will demand from this House of Commons a strict account of any money that it has paid for the service of the country. Is it not the case that our Navy is at the present moment overwhelmingly and irresistibly strong? Since I was last in this House I have travelled over a great part of the world, and I have watched this matter, and wherever I went I conferred with everybody I met, and they laughed at the very idea that there is any real competition between foreign navies and our own. We are so strong that at the present time all the navies of the world put together dare not assail us at any point on the surface of the globe. That is no doubt due to the excellent and intelligent policy which has been pursued for a great many years in this country, and we are now in a position which we never before held, to survey what we have done, and to ask whether it is really necessary for us to do any more. The fact is, that a great many of the foreign navies exist only for the most part on paper; that is to say, they have very few ships fit to compete in actual warfare with an enemy's ships. We are not in such a position; and I ask whether we are required to spend more money on our Navy? My honourable Friend the Under Secretary to the Admiralty says that the Estimates are absolutely necessary, but I should like to ask the First Lord if he will prove to us that these Estimates are necessary. If he can, then I would be the first to say, "Let us vote them with all our hearts." I say that while we should never neglect the improvement of the quality of the Navy, the quantity at the present moment is quite equal to all the requirements that can possibly be put upon it.

*ADMIRAL FIELD: No, no!

MR. MACLEAN: I knew that my honourable and gallant Friend would dissent. We all know that our honourable and gallant Friend will not be happy until every British householder is able to go to sea in his own ironclad. I think that is unreasonable. He takes as his motto that "there is nothing like leather," and he would like to see every penny subscribed by the unhappy taxpayers of this country devoted to increasing the strength of the Navy. I do not blame him for that. That is his *métier*. He is for his own trade—that fighting trade which is always most anxious for war and armaments. But there are other trades besides the trade devoted to the production of armaments. The people of the country are beginning to ask themselves, why should this excessive expenditure go on from year to year. I believe the Government themselves have taken this feeling into consideration. There was a most remarkable passage in the speech of the First Lord of the Admiralty when introducing the Estimates. He spoke of the Conference called by the Tsar of Russia, and which is soon going to assemble; and he made this extraordinary declaration. He said—

"We shall go there and say to the assembled representatives of the various States of the world, 'Well, if you reduce your armaments, we will reduce our programme.'"

Was ever a more fatuous proposal made to a Conference than that? For, of course, the representatives of the other Powers would say, "Tell us what reductions you are going to make, and we will see what reductions we can make." And the whole Conference would end in nothing. And what is the use of reductions of that kind? You cannot see what the other nations are doing. Armaments may be reduced to-day, and increased again to-morrow without your knowing anything about it. It is not by observations of that sort that we can advance the great project of general peace throughout the world. Instead of accepting the invitation of the Tsar in a spirit of benevolent cynicism, we should go to the Conference in a serious spirit—prepared to discuss the matter in a formal and proper way, and in a spirit due to the noble aspirations of the Emperor who has given this proposal to the world. I am not in the confidence of the Government. I do not know what they propose; but I rejoice to see that their spirit is pacific, and that they are calmer than the irresponsible newspapers in the West End of London. I rejoice that the Government is directed by men who are sagacious and far-seeing, and have kept their heads cool during the last two or three years. The Government are anxious, as I understand it, to meet the Emperor of Russia in a fair spirit, and to try and see if they cannot do something for the general good of the world. What are they to do, it may be asked? Well, they ought not to go into that Conference with hypothetical propositions, or to haggle over the cutting down of a line of battleship or two, on one side or the other. You must remove the permanent causes of ill-feeling amongst the nations of the world, and then you can hope for the permanent peace and retrenchment which we all desire. I say if the Government, instead of bringing forward these new Estimates, which I do not think they themselves in their hearts believe are really wanted, had gone into the Conference with definite and concrete

Mr. Maclean.

proposals—if they had said to the Tsar—"We are here with a programme which we pledge ourselves to accept if you do so "—if they were to raise the great questions of general policy throughout the world which divide Russia fro mus, and divide France from us—if they were to try to come to a general agreement on these topics, and to submit a definite and positive programme to the Conference—then I say the statesmen at the head of the Government would have done a thing which would redound to the glory of England, and be a benefit not only to this country but to all the nations of the earth.

*Mr. WEIR (Ross and Cromarty): I wish to ask the Secretary to the Admiralty if he will give the boys of the Highlands and Islands of Scotland a chance of entering the Navy by sending a training ship to the West Highlands. Three years ago I assured the First Lord of the Admiralty that he could get plenty of boys if he did so. There would be no difficulty in the matter. The First Lord in his statement referred to the fact that very few of the boys secured in other parts of the country could swim. In the Island of Lewis alone there is a population of 30,000 people. Hardy industrious men, who are accustomed to the sea and are inured to it; and every one of the boys can swim like a duck. The Admiralty would get plenty of boys in the West Highlands who would gladly join the Navy, and who would make splendid seamen. If I could get the attention of the honourable Gentleman the Secretary to the Admiralty for a minute, I wish to refer to a remark which he made—that it was the policy of the Admiralty to send no training-ships to the neighbourhood of large towns. Here is a chance. Send these training-ships up to the West Highlands, where you will get plenty of boys far removed from the evil surroundings of large towns. But he has made a mistake in saying there are no training-ships in the neighbourhood of large towns. There is the "Mars" at Dundee, which is a large town ; and there is the "Wellesley" in the Tyne, which is in the immediate neighbourhood of many large towns. I do hope I shall get a satisfactory reply from the honourable Gentleman the Secretary to the Admiralty, and that he will take some steps to send a training-ship to the West Highlands—if not to Stornoway, then to the West Coast of the Mainland, Portree or Oban.

SIR J. BAKER (Portsmouth): The honourable Gentleman the Secretary to the Admiralty has done an amount of mischief by the observations he has made to-night, the effects of which will be felt many a month hence. These observations relate to the chief and warrant officers. This is a very serious question, for, next to the commanders, these men are the most important to the whole of our Fleet. And to have dealt with them in the spirit in which the Secretary to the Admiralty has dealt with that class is full of disaster. Then there is the manner in which he also treated the grievances of the petty officers. That was equally disastrous in the interests of the Navy. The remarks which the honourable Gentleman the Secretary to the Admiralty also made in regard to the duties of shipwrights on board ship was a most unqualified mistake—the most fatal mistake ever made in the House of Commons, and one which he will hear more about, and which will be remembered. If the Committee go to a Division, I shall be obliged to vote against the Government, owing to the reply of the Secretary to the Admiralty.

MR. GIBSON BOWLES (Lynn Regis): I regret I am altogether unable to agree with the vigorous speech of the honourable Member for Cardiff; at any rate with the reasons which he gave for saying that the Navy Estimates are too large. I do not think that any honourable Member in this House would be prepared to diminish by one ship, or one man, Her Majesty's Navy, because a Northern despot of amiable intentions has called together a Conference for disarmament, while he himself is arming to the teeth, and while he is increasing his forces from Europe to Asia, from Finland to Port Arthur. I have already suggested that, in my opinion, there must be some ground for the belief that these Estimates are—I will not say excessive, but very, very large. Sir, I listened, and I am sure many honourable Members in this House listened, with care to the right honourable Baronet the Member for the Forest of Dean. He will be satisfied apparently with nothing. His appetite is gigantean. He swallows and digests ironclads, guns and sailors, and everything connected with the Navy with the greatest ease and readiness. I cannot compete with that extraordinary appetite. I notice that even a very large number of the Members on his own side of the House entirely agree with him; some of them, in fact, are trying to go beyond him, and saying that these Navy Estimates are not sufficient. I only hope that these honourable Members, when they come to the Committee of Ways and Means, will not have any objection to the new taxes which undoubtedly will be imposed in consequence partly of the Naval Estimates. I hope they will remember, when they come to the discussion of the Budget, they are pledged to the opinion that these Estimates are not large enough. I hope that will not be forgotten. Well, there is unquestionably at present a feeling of uneasiness throughout the world, from Europe to China, and through the whole Pacific. One of the strongest symptoms that there is danger in the future is the symptom which moved the honourable Member for Cardiff to argue in favour of reduction of the Navy—that symptom that the Navy Estimates are too excessive. What they indicate beyond the fact that there is a large increase over last year's Estimates we cannot tell; but we do know that Her Majesty's Government, having considered the matter with a desire to present the Estimates as small as possible, and having, of course, consulted the Defence Committee of the Cabinet—Her Majesty's Government must have come to the conclusion that there is a danger of approximate war, that there is a danger that the peace of the world is about to be broken at no distant period. That, I am convinced, is the reason why they think it necessary to come down to the House and ask for this very considerable increase in the Navy Estimates. My mind misgives me, because, although I observe that the Government and the people of England always pretend to be particularly calm, to be the most phlegmatic and dispassionate people on the face of the earth, my experience of the Government and the people of England is that there are no people so impulsive and so passionate. For years, up till 1893, many of us were complaining that the Navy Estimates were too small, and that the Navy was not strong enough. But not the slightest attention was paid to us. Now that the Navy Estimates have run up within the last six years from 14½ millions to 28 millions some of us are inclined to think that they go too far in the other direction, and that the impulsive character of the people of the country has been not without its effect. There is the question of armaments. The right honourable Baronet the Member for the Forest of Dean complains that we are not sufficiently rapid with our supply of armour. There, again, the same considerations should be kept in view as in regard to ships. The improvements in armour have been enormous, and are taking place every day. There is the Harvey system, which has introduced great improvements respecting the resisting powers of the plates. And then there is the Nickel system, and between the two systems enormous improvements have taken place in the quality of the armour. Well, if you had ordered your armour a few years ago and had a stock of it in hand, as the right honourable Baronet seems to suggest you should do now, you would have had a large stock of armour without these Harvey and Nickel improvements. The very armour which you are making to-day will be obsolete in the near future, when still further improvements will undoubtedly be made. Therefore I think the Admiralty exercised a sound discretion in not keeping in hand more armour than they actually need or can be put into the ships at present building. My belief is that for the present situation—I speak not of the future, nor of the further increases made by foreign countries, and which the Admiralty conceive are serious increases, although in my opinion a great deal of them will be found only on paper—my belief is that we have ships enough to handle and to give a good account, not only of the fleets of two Powers, but of the fleets of all the Powers of Europe put together. I think, therefore, that the Admiralty ought to delay as long as possible the building of the new ships, and I will give one reason for that opinion. Take the case of the ram, for instance. Our vessels are made for the most part with thin plates, with top hamper, and with partial armour, and are fitted with a ram—an instrument of warfare which has hitherto only proved dangerous in time of peace, and which I am convinced would prove useless in time of war. The doubt as to the use of the ram in war is one that is making rapid progress, and I believe that it will permeate into the Board of Admiralty in a shorter time than any suppose. As soon as that conviction has arrived at the Board of Admiralty and crept up to the first floor we shall have our battleships designed without a ram, and that will be, in my opinion, a stupendous improvement. For you will save the weight of the ram, which you will be able to put into guns and ammunition, and save also a number of defects incident to and inseparable from the ram. My belief is that the next great improvement in battleships will be the absence of the ram, and that the best thing to do with the ram is to get rid of it. Then as to slips. The right honourable Baronet the Member for the Forest of Dean is most anxious to have more slips. My view is that the Admiralty have gone a little too far as it is in the brick and mortar line. I do not think that their methods of dealing with bricks and mortar have been a success. I am informed that the coffer-dam at Keyham is anything but a success, and we shall have someone coming to the Admiralty for more works at Keyham, and the Admiralty coming to the House for further sums of money for these works. The same thing is happening at Gibraltar. My belief is that we are proceeding on a wrong plan there, and that the contract is being carried out under such mistaken conditions that you will have to pay the contractors a much larger sum than the present contract price. I hope I may be mistaken, but both at Keyham and Gibraltar the works will involve a very much larger expense than was originally intended. I think some further explanation is required from the Admiralty as to the methods in which they are making the contracts. One word as to the warrant officers. My own belief is that it is not for the good of the service or for the good of the warrant officers themselves that a special rank should be made for them. But what I do believe is this—that there is a great grievance on the part of the warrant officers, and that there is great mischief in the Article in the Queen's Regulations which prevents the Admiralty promoting warrant officers to commission rank except only for gallantry in

Mr. Gibson Bowles.

action. Gallantry in action is a quality which can only be shown by chance. There are other qualities than gallantry in action which are extremely valuable in the Navy. The Government should amend the Article in the Queen's Regulations, and should open the water-tight door which prevents a man rising from the lower deck to the upper deck, and give any warrant officer commissioned rank who shows himself worthy of the distinction. My belief is that that would satisfy the warrant officers and remove all their grievances. You must hold out at every point the possibility of rising to the highest grades in the Service. That would be an enormous advantage. I am convinced you would soon have boys of a very superior quality joining the Navy; that you would get them to do superior work in the training ships, especially in the higher classes, and that you would give inducements and incitements to action to the warrant officers, who are the backbone of the Navy, such as they never had before. There are two other points on which I want to say a few words. In June last I called the attention of the First Lord of the Admiralty to the question of marksmanship in the Navy, and I ventured to make the suggestion that the Admiral's inspection should always include an inspection of marksmanship, and a test by firing of the actual merits of the gunnery on board ships. I believe the suggestion was entirely new, and I was rejoiced to notice that three or four months afterwards that Admiral Harris at the Cape had, if he had not accepted my suggestion, at least coincided with me in the same idea, and did do exactly what I ventured to suggest. The Admiral in the course of his inspection put the men through target practice from day to day. The same has been done in the Pacific by Admiral Palliser. That is the only way to secure good gunnery. The result is that the officers on board feel that good gunnery is an important factor in the reputation of the ship, and in their own reputation, and that their promotion will depend upon it. The consequence will be that instead of devoting all their attention to paint and brass work—I don't despise paint and brass work; they mean a great deal more than appears on the surface—and they will give a large part of their attention to what is the most important thing in the Navy—actual marksmanship. You can have the best ships, and the best guns, and the best men in the world, but if the men at the end of the guns cannot hit the mark the whole of the Navy is useless. I never did believe in torpedoes or in rams, but I do believe in big guns. I rejoice to see two distinguished Admirals have taken up this method of actual inspection of marksmanship, and I hope to hear from the Secretary to the Admiralty that the Admiralty is increasing the power of the Admirals in this respect. I hope, indeed, that they will go beyond leaving it to the initiative of individual Admirals, and that they will issue an order directing that the practice shall be pursued on all stations. There is only one last point I wish to make, and that is in reference to the officers who have been admitted into the Royal Navy from the Royal Naval Reserve. There are 150 of them. I think the original number was 100; but 50 have been added. They do the work of lieutenants. They were brought into the Navy under special conditions, with a special messing allowance of 2s. per day, so that on the point of pay they have an advantage over the ordinary lieutenants who have passed through all the grades for the "Britannia." There is a strong feeling of suspicion amongst the ordinary lieutenants in the Navy that these gentlemen, introduced over their heads as it were, will be continued over their heads, and will be promoted from lieutenants to commanders, and from commanders to captains. I do not believe any such intention exists at the Admiralty, and I shall be glad if that opinion is confirmed by the honourable Member the Secretary to the Admiralty. Therefore, they have advantages in this way, and they have special retiring allowances. This is the point of the whole thing, for they were specially engaged under the special condition that they were not to advance to the rank of warrant officers. They were taken in under these special conditions, and they thoroughly understood them. What I suggest now is this: that the rest of the Service are beginning to doubt whether those conditions will be carried out. I suggest that it would be a satisfaction to the rest of the Service if the Admiralty would make a specific re-declaration of the conditions under which these gentlemen joined, and give some reassurance that those conditions will not be departed from. It will be seen that it is a very great discouragement to those who join at 13 and work up to 20 years of age, and pass good examinations, to find that some others who have not the same length of service should be promoted over their heads, without having had any of the preliminary training which those who joined at 13 years of age have undergone. I do not mind so much if this is to be only a temporary arrangement, but I do hope that something will be done to satisfy the rest of the Service that this is only a temporary arrangement.

Mr. YOXALL (Nottingham, W.): The honourable Gentleman the Under Secretary referred in a somewhat vague manner to a certain scheme for facilitating the re-manning of the Navy and for strengthening the Naval Reserve, and he referred to that scheme as being embryonic. I should like to point out, however, that that scheme is far more advanced than embryonic, for it is very complete, and it only requires the co-operation of the Admiralty to bring it into full development, and I wish to impress upon the Admiralty the great desirability that this should be done. If the Admiralty would only provide a certain number of training ships, then the cost of training more boys of good parentage and surroundings for the Royal Naval Reserve would be met from other sources. There are a great number of charities in this country, and there are many large bodies like the county councils who would be willing to spend money in giving these young men the necessary training. As I said before, all we want for the full development of this scheme is the co-operation of the Admiralty. This scheme was fully explained in an article in the "Nineteenth Century" for January of this year.

Mr. COLVILLE (Lanark, N.E.): When the honourable Member for King's Lynn addresses this House we always expect to be interested and entertained, but when he speaks on the subject of armour plate he appears to get slightly mixed as to the different processes by which it is manufactured. I may inform him that the processes which he has alluded to are one and the same. I rise for the purpose of calling attention to the fact that the process which our Admiralty exclusively insist upon limits the supply of armour plate very much in this country. The monopoly for providing this class of armour is still in the hands of three large firms, whereas in France, with a very much smaller Navy, they have no less than six firms able to provide them with armour plate. There is another process which has recently been adopted, and that also is a monopoly of those three large firms in this country. Now, if the Admiralty have to complain, as they did last year, of difficulty in obtaining their supplies of armour plate, they have only themselves to blame, because they have insisted upon having only that one class for which those particular firms hold the monopoly. I think the House should know that not only does this cause a great delay in the making of armour plate, but it also means the infliction of an enormous penalty in the cost. Not long ago one of the largest armour plate manufacturers in America undertook to supply the Russian Government at a price of from £50 to £60 per ton. Now, our own Admiralty are paying from £80 to £100 per ton, and I have no doubt that if the door was opened a little wider we should have no difficulty as regards the supply of armour, and the Government would be able to economise very considerably in the cost if they would not insist upon the exclusive supply of these patent processes. I wish to make another remark with respect to the treatment of Scotland with regard to the expenditure of these large sums of money in the Naval Programme. We have no slips, and there are no dockyards or arsenals in the whole kingdom of Scotland, notwithstanding the fact that a large proportion of the 28 millions voted for the Navy comes from that part of the United Kingdom, and while our shipbuilders on the Clyde share the contracts, we are shown no special favours. We hear of certain contracts having gone to certain firms on the Thames and to Belfast, not at the lower prices, and they have gone to those firms for reasons which are well-known to the Admiralty, and the Clyde shipbuilders have only been able to secure those contracts when they were able to accept the finest prices. If new land works are to be undertaken by the Admiralty there ought to be no difficulty in finding suitable sites in the kingdom of Scotland, which offers exceptional facilities for docks that would be suitable for the Navy, where the dockyards would be much nearer to the supply of raw material, and where cheap labour could be got to make the ships of the United Kingdom, where they could be provided on better terms than at Devonport. I lift my voice in this Debate to insist that Scotland is entitled to some consideration on the part of the Admiralty when they are proposing to lay down fresh slips and spend more money in what the honourable Member has referred to as "bricks and mortar." If they propose to go in for schemes of that kind they ought to look out for some suitable sites in Scotland where they could put down slips and dockyards.

*Mr. MACARTNEY: The honourable Member for King's Lynn has asked me a question in reference to the officers of the Royal Naval Reserve. I may say that there is no intention on the part of the Admiralty of departing from the plain conditions laid down in the Order in Council under which officers of the Royal Naval Reserve join the Navy. They cannot be promoted from lieutenancies to be commanders except for one special reason, and that is gallantry in action. The honourable Member for Wansbeck has asked me a question with regard to the engine-room artificers, which was also alluded to by the honourable Member for Devonport. I fully appreciate the importance of the question which the honourable Gentleman has raised, and I think it is worthy of consideration. I cannot, however, give him any specific declaration upon that point, but I can assure him that it will be taken into careful consideration. With regard to the question of my honourable and gallant Friend the Member for Eastbourne, I am afraid that I cannot give any specific information at present about the 4.7-inch gun in drill ships, nor can I give him any specific statement as to mobilisation, and perhaps he will be good enough to wait until I have got further information. With regard to the new 12-inch gun, I have no specific information to give on the point.

*ADMIRAL FIELD: But you promised to answer my question about rations for the Marines.

*Mr. MACARTNEY: And so I will if the honourable and gallant Gentleman will wait until we get to Vote 2. As to the question of the honourable Member for Ross and Cromarty, I cannot give him any assurance with regard to the dispatch of training ships round the coast, but he must recollect that Scotland, as well as every other portion of the United Kingdom, has had, in the past, a fair share of these training ships.

*Mr. WEIR: Not for six years.

*Mr. MACARTNEY: I can assure the honourable Gentleman that he is entirely mistaken about that. The Highlands and Islands of Scotland have had due consideration in this matter.

Dr. CLARK (Caithness): My honourable Friend during the last six or seven years has pressed this case upon the Admiralty, and I regret to say that nothing has been done in the matter, although we have always had the usual statement and dust thrown in our eyes by a promise that it will be considered.

*Mr. MACARTNEY: But the training ships have been there.

Dr. CLARK: Yes, the ships have been all round the Indies, and there is no portion of the United Kingdom where our ships have not been. What has been suggested, not only by my honourable Friend, but by the Select Committee, is, that you should utilise the raw material which you would find in Scotland and Ireland—which is the best possible material you can get—and yet this Government has refused, like the previous Government, to do anything for Scotland in this matter. This is merely on a par with the rest of the treatment which Scotland receives as far as the Admiralty is concerned. Year after year they are spending millions of money, and you have got all your eggs in one basket in the South of England, far away from your supply of iron and skilled labour, and you are still remaining there. There are one or two places which have been proposed on several occasions to the House. The Irish Members have impressed upon the Admiralty the advisability of constructing a dockyard at Cork, which is one of the finest natural harbours in the world. Instead of sending so many millions down to the South of England to carry on shipbuilding under bad physical conditions, where you have to make everything at great expense, you should utilise what nature has made in the harbours of Cork and Scotland, into which harbours you could run your ships quickly in case of accidents. But not a single penny of this money has been spent in Scotland, where you have got the iron and the coal. You ought to have a dockyard on the Clyde and another one on the Forth, and if those rivers were in England you would soon have dockyards there. You have the Clyde and the Forth, and by a little enterprise you could easily carry your ships from the German Ocean into the Atlantic Ocean, and if those rivers were in either France or England this would be done, but because they are in Scotland you don't do it. In Scotland you have got the natural ironfields and coalfields, and you have also got skilled labour which is unequalled anywhere in the world, and Scotland is quite as fit to turn you out as good cruisers for the Navy as she turns out ships for the Merchant Service. We have all the facilities, and you ought not to persist, as you do persist, in having all your arsenals and dockyards in the Southern portion of this kingdom. As a matter of fairness, you ought to utilise the natural resources of Scotland. I, myself, and my honourable Friends, have raised this question on previous occasions, and we have done so again in a few short words. We utter our protest against our country being ignored, and against the natural facilities which she has got not being utilised as they ought to be for the benefit of the country.

MR. E. J. C. MORTON (Devonport): I regret that the honourable Member for King's Lynn is not in his place, because a more extraordinary speech than he has delivered I have never heard in this House. He referred to coffer-dams at Gibraltar, but anyone who knows anything about Naval works throughout the British Empire would laugh at talking about coffer-dams at Gibraltar. However, as he is not here, I will not allude to his remarks further. I am extremely anxious to avoid wasting the time of this House, and I am not going on this particular Vote to refer to what certainly might be referred to, and to which other Members of this House have alluded, but which come more properly under Vote 1. I will deal with the most important, to my mind, in regard to all these Votes dealing with the Navy, namely, the question of the warrant officers, which, inasmuch as they are the top of the Navy, do really concern the whole of the Navy below them. I do want unquestionably to refer, and to refer with some amount of emphasis, to one part of the speech of the Secretary to the Admiralty, and I allude to that

part in which he referred to the naval shipwrights. Now, the honourable Gentleman said that the shipwrights in the Navy were an inferior class of workmen. Now, that word "inferior" was used.

*MR. MACARTNEY: The honourable Gentleman is entirely misquoting me. What I said was that they were inferior to the other classes of mechanics on board ship.

MR. E. J. C. MORTON: That was the statement made, but I will accept this explanation. He says the shipwrights are inferior to the other mechanics on board ship. When we are talking about wanting the Government to treat the naval shipwrights better than they do, and when we get a reply of this character it is a curious fact that while the trades unions of this country will always recommend their members to go as shipwrights into the dockyards, the same trades unions recommend their members never to go as naval shipwrights on board ship, and that to my mind is a very remarkable distinction, showing what the working men of this country think. And while that is the case, we have also to remember the fact that in the dockyards we have a dispute between fitters and shipwrights, and we find that the fitters complain that the shipwrights are employed on fitters' work, and, in fact, that the Government regard the shipwright as a handy man, who can turn his hand to anything, and so they starve the fitters in order to get more shipwrights. But when you get into the Navy you find the treatment of the naval shipwright is so bad that the Government cannot get them, and what I have to say on the point is this, and it is most important, because it does not deal primarily with my own constituency, and it does not deal with the particular class whose interests I am advocating, but it deals with the Government, and the efficiency of the Navy, and it is this: that at the present moment in order to get more naval shipwrights— and they are absolutely essential to the efficiency of the Navy—you have issued a new Admiralty order whereby you are going to get boys trained to be naval shipwrights, and trained under conditions under which you are certain to get a worse article than you have at present. Well, now, it seems to me that it is a matter of absolutely national importance that we should see that we have all our men in the Navy efficient to the very uttermost. I think sometimes in the discussion about the Navy we are apt to forget that really the whole strength of the Navy ultimately depends upon the men, for it is the men we have to look to who are the real strength, and now you are encouraging by a sort of Dutch auction in this matter an inferior sample of naval shipwrights by the Admiralty order you have issued. I say that it is a matter of national importance, and one which ought to be really seriously considered by this House. I submit to this Committee that the whole condition and the treatment of naval shipwrights is one which ought to be altered in the sense of attracting a better class of workman than you have at present, instead of embarking upon the line upon which you are embarking now, namely, that of lowering the standard of men you take by the Admiralty order. It seems to me that that part of the policy of the Government is one which is most disappointing to those who have the welfare of the Navy at heart, and it is only to point out that particular matter that I have risen.

MR. MADDISON (Sheffield, Brightside): I wish to emphasise the point raised by the honourable Member for Devonport, and I should not have risen if it had been merely a question of shipwrights, because that point has been dealt exhaustively with. My point is this, that the case mentioned by the honourable Member for Devonport is not an isolated instance at all, but it is part of a retrograde policy on the part of the Admiralty which is resulting in a lowering of the standard of efficiency among the men who serve on Her Majesty's battleships. We have been told to-night that this question of the shipwrights is the only one that has to do with the trades unions, and the honourable Member who has just spoken has said that while the trades unions endeavour to do all they can to get men for the dockyards they do not recommend men to go in the Navy. Now, that is not quite a correct statement, and I speak impartially, as I have no shipwrights in my constituency at all, and I don't think that any honourable Members will believe that we have any shipwrights at Sheffield. The fact is that these shipwrights have not got their proper ratings on these battleships, and it is not a question of being menials at

all. Surely, it is no degradation for them to do what their wives do. These men are perfectly aware that being on board ship is not the same as being on shore, and many things must be done there which are not done on shore. But the honourable and gallant Member surely will agree with me that a mechanic ought to have a rating worthy of his skill, and that is their complaint. which is not that they consider it menial to do this, that, or the other, but because they do think that they ought to have a proper rating. But in this matter we get no consolation at all, because the Secretary to the Admiralty has gone one worse than the first Lord of the Admiralty did last year, for he has actually gone to the trouble of comparing them with other mechanics on board warships, to whom he says they are inferior. The Secretary to the Admiralty said, in a light sort of way, "Oh, it does not matter what they do, for we can take the ships to sea without any shipwrights." But in spite of that you are altering your regulations to the extent of getting boys to go for four years and spend part of their time at sea, so it seems, after all, that there is some idea in the minds of the Admiralty that the shipwright is needed. But I only mention the shipwrights to lead me to another point. On the 24th of February of this year the Admiralty issued an order, a part of which, with the permission of the Committee, I will quote. Now, this does not refer to shipwrights, but to the engine-room artificers, and the order goes on to say—

"With a view to obtaining more candidates for this rating their Lordships have decided to reduce the qualifications required for recruits. When sufficient candidates present themselves, preference should be given to those who are fully qualified as required by the regulations."

Now, what is the plain meaning of that, if it is not that the Government has failed to get hold of competent mechanics for engine-room artificers? And why is this? Simply because the Admiralty refuse from time to time to listen to the appeals that are made in this House on behalf of these men not to give them some pampered position, but to put them on something like a proper status. Honourable Members plead on behalf of the officers, but when skilled mechanics, who, in the majority of cases, have been seven years learning their trade, ask that they shall have common decency on board our warships they are ignored altogether. Private employers are able to get qualified men by paying them a proper wage, but the nation suffers as a result of the treatment which these men receive on board our warships. We cannot get good men owing to that treatment, and are compelled to take men who are not qualified. That the nation is suffering through this blundering policy on the part of the Admiralty is beyond question. The Admiralty should pay some regard to the fact that a mechanic has a *status* of which he is proud, and that there is some dignity in labour. I am confident that if the great employers of labour in this country were to treat their workmen as the Admiralty do, half the trade of this country would soon disappear. The Admiralty ignore altogether the just demands that are made, and the representative of the Admiralty here to-night has placed a badge of inferiority upon a class of workmen whose skill is as high as that of any mechanic in the country, and upon whom the construction of our ships in their initial stage depends. This is a policy for which the First Lord of the Admiralty is primarily responsible. It began when he helped the employers in the engineers' lockout, and it has been continued, the object being to snub the working men of this country. I submit to the right honourable Gentleman that he will find that the best and the most skilled work of this country is invariably done by trade unionists, whom honourable and gallant Members—especially the gallant Members on the other side of the House—condemn, and at whom they hurl the worst epithets they possess. I appeal to the Admiralty to again take into consideration the modest appeals that are made on behalf of skilled artificers. This is really a National question, and is not brought up by a dockyard Member who is desirous of getting votes. It goes far deeper than honourable Members may think. I do not agree with hardly a single word uttered by the right honourable Baronet the Member for the Forest of Dean, who seems to be a general alarmist and the leader of the Jingo Party, who imagine that Parliament exists for one purpose only, and that to build new battleships and to raise a few more battalions. The right honourable Baronet told us what

the Front Bench believed. It is always difficult to know what either Front Bench believe for some time, but from what the right honourable Baronet said, one would think that the armour plate makers of this country were woefully behind, that there was a great amount of arrears, and that the nation was in danger. On this subject the language of the First Lord last year was most explicit. He declared that the supply of armour plates was well in hand, that what delay had occurred had been the result of circumstances which were not normal, and that he was satisfied. I take it that the Secretary to the Admiralty has endorsed that view, but I do not think he sufficiently enlarged upon it. I do not wish to waste the time of the Committee, but I desire to press upon the honourable Gentleman who represents the Admiralty to-night the fact that, unless something is done, we shall find ourselves, should the Navy be called into action, very deficient of the men upon whom, I think, the success of naval fights largely depends.

SIR E. CLARKE (Plymouth): There is one definite statement which has been made by the honourable Member who represents the Admiralty, on which I should like to say one word. I refer to the special terms of promotion for officers who have joined from the Royal Naval Reserve. The honourable Gentleman said there was no intention of departing from the Order in Council under which, as I understand, these officers are only to have promotion hereafter in consequence of gallantry in action. I am not going to suggest to the Committee that if these officers have accepted commissions on distinct terms they have any claim to be allowed to depart from those terms, but I think it would be desirable to say that those terms are to be very much regretted. The consequence of the enforcement of these terms is to make two classes of lieutenants in Her Majesty's Navy, one class being able only to obtain promotion as the result of gallantry in action, and being passed over from time to time by their juniors simply because they have not had an opportunity of showing that gallantry. It has been suggested that the coming into the navy of officers from the Royal Naval Reserve would be an injustice to those already in the Navy if they were allowed to meet them on equal terms. I cannot see that there would be any injustice at all. The Royal Naval Reserve officers are taken into the Navy because they are experienced and capable seamen, and I think it is an extremely bad thing for the whole tone of the Navy that these Naval Reserve officers, who are brought into the Navy because there is a great National requirement for their services, and because they are known to be capable men, should be specified as a class who should be disqualified for advancement except in instances which it is hoped will seldom, if ever, be offered to them. I think the sooner these special terms are abolished the better it will be for the Navy, and I am sure if this country desires to have men in the Merchant Service who are looking forward to employment in Her Majesty's Navy, and who are prepared to give experienced service to this country in time of need, they had better not advertise that the condition of these men when they become officers will be a condition of disqualification for promotion.

MR. HAVELOCK WILSON (Middlesbrough): I desire to say a word or two on behalf of the men in the Royal Naval Reserve. Last year, during the discussion on the Navy Estimates, I ventured to suggest to the Financial Secretary to the Treasury that the time had come when the Government should treat the men in the Royal Naval Reserve a little more generously than they had been in the habit of doing in the past. These men are supposed to get a pension when they arrive at the age of 60, after doing 20 or 25 years' service in the Royal Naval Reserve. The great question with the merchant firemen to-day is how to live until they arrive at the age of 60. I know that at the present time very few of the men who have served their full term in the Royal Naval Reserve are receiving this pension. The men of the Royal Naval Reserve have been for years petitioning successive Governments, asking that they might have this pension of £12 per annum at the age of 50 instead of 60, but they have received no satisfaction whatever. I do not think it would cost the Government or the country a large sum of money if this pension was given at the age of 50, and I trust that the Government will take this matter into their serious considera-

tion. The total number of stokers in the Royal Naval Reserve is 3,500, but at the rapid rate at which we are building warships, I am satisfied that if all these ships were put into commission to-morrow, it would be impossible to man them with their full complement of men. No doubt you could put skeleton crews on board, but we should be short of 10,000 men if we wanted to man them thoroughly and efficiently. That is a very serious condition, indeed, for this country to be in, and there is no necessity whatever why this state of things should continue to exist. We have the largest Mercantile Marine in the world, and I think if the seamen had a fair opportunity on board our British merchantships, we could have a Reserve, not of 25,000 men, but of over 60,000 men. The number could be increased to this extent if things were managed as they ought to be. What is the Government doing at the present time with regard to finding employment for the men in the Royal Naval Reserve? I have seen a large number of them apply for engagements on board British ships, and I have heard them told that they were not wanted, as the ship was carrying foreigners. These men, who had served their 10 or 15 years at sea, who had good characters, and against whom not a word could be said, were told that they were not required simply because they chose to demand a living wage. I know the Government cannot compel ordinary shipowners to carry British seamen if they do not want to, but I will tell the Government what they could do. There is no reason why the P. and O. Company, who get over £400,000 a year from this country, should not be compelled to carry a certain number of British seamen, both sailors and firemen. The Government has power to do this, for they could stipulate it in their Mail Contract.

THE DEPUTY CHAIRMAN: I should like to remind the honourable Member that the Mail Contract is not before the Committee.

MR. HAVELOCK WILSON: I am not dealing with the Mail Contract, Mr. O'Connor. I am merely endeavouring to show how the Government could find employment for the men who are in the Royal Naval Reserve. It may be a little outside the question, but it certainly has to do with the Royal Naval Reserve. What is the use of men being members of the Reserve, being liable to be called upon in time of war, if they are not able to obtain employment in time of peace? Under the regulations of the Royal Naval Reserve, a seaman is compelled to put in a certain amount of time at sea every year before he can have performed his drill. How can they put in this drill if they cannot find employment? I have been told that outside some British ships they place a notice, " No British seamen need apply."

AN HONOURABLE MEMBER: Where?

MR. HAVELOCK WILSON: I did not say I had seen it. I said I had heard that it had been done, and, what is more, I believe the statement to be true, and that the notices have been put up in the port of London.

THE DEPUTY-CHAIRMAN: I must again draw the attention of the honourable Member to the fact that he is getting wide of the Vote now before the Committee.

MR. HAVELOCK WILSON: I will endeavour, Mr. O'Connor, to keep a little closer to the matter under discussion. I contend that it is time the Government endeavoured to increase the number of firemen in the Royal Naval Reserve. The number at present is 3,500, which is not sufficient. Personally, I think I am entitled to a vote of thanks from the Government, because, in November and December of last year, I encouraged about 300 firemen to join the Royal Naval Reserve, but although I did that, I still have to complain of the treatment these men receive. I am surprised that the Royal Naval Reserve men do not get more support in this House. The statement of the honourable Gentleman the Secretary to the Admiralty with regard to the inferiority of the shipwrights will cause a great deal of discontent throughout the country, because I know, as a matter of fact, that the Admiralty have been continually pestering the Associated Shipwrights to encourage their members to work in the Government dockyards. After doing that, I think it is certainly out of place for the honourable Gentleman to make the statement he did.

*MR. MACARTNEY: I was not speaking of the dockyard shipwrights.

MR WILSON: But it is all the same. The man who goes to sea in a merchant ship as a shipwright is able to work in the dockyards as well as the other men, and the statement of the honourable Gentleman that the men on board ship have not an equal amount of skill to those in the dockyards is one which will be challenged very much in the country. The Admiralty do not appear to give much consideration to the grievances of these men. The warrant officers have also grievances, but no steps have been taken by the Government to remedy them. If there is a Division, I shall, in consequence of my dissatisfaction with the statement that has been made by the Admiralty, vote against the Government.

VISCOUNT CRANBORNE: There is one matter of some importance that has been raised in this Debate, and which has been referred to by myself and other more distinguished Members of this House year after year, which has not received any reply from the Government. I refer to the question of the position of warrant officers and their promotion to commission rank. This is a matter on which, I think, the Committee are entitled to have some statement from the Government. If the honourable Gentleman would desire that I should raise it on another Vote, I shall be willing to do so, but I think it would save time if we had a reply now.

Amendment proposed—

"That 110,140 men and boys, etc., be employed for the said Service."—(*Mr. Steadman.*)

MR. STEADMAN: I move to reduce the Vote for men by 500, as a protest against the remarks of the Secretary to the Admiralty with respect both to the shipwrights and the warrant and petty officers.

Question put—

"That 110,140 men and boys, etc., be employed for the said Service."—(*Mr. Steadman.*)

The Committee divided:—Ayes 49; Noes 153. (Division List No. 45.)

AYES

Allen,Wm.(Newc.-under-Lyme
Austin, Sir John (Yorkshire)
Baker, Sir John
Beaumont, Wentworth C. B.
Billson, Alfred
Caldwell, James
Clark,Dr.G.B.(Caithness-sh.)
Clough, Walter Owen
Colville, John
Davies,M.Vaughan-(Cardigan)
Douglas, Charles M. (Lanark)
Duckworth, James
Fenwick, Charles
Goddard, Daniel Ford
Hayne, Rt. Hn.Charles Seale-
Holland,Wm.H.(York,W.R.)
Jones, Wm. (Carnarvonshire)
Kearley, Hudson E.

Kilbride, Denis
Lawson,Sir Wilfrid(Cumb'lnd)
Lough, Thomas
Macaleese, Daniel
MacNeill, John Gordon Swift
M'Ewan, William
M'Kenna, Reginald
Maddison, Fred.
Mendl, Sigismund Ferdinand
Moss, Samuel
Moulton, John Fletcher
O'Brien, Patrick (Kilkenny)
Oldroyd, Mark
Price, Robert John
Reckitt, Harold James
Richardson, J. (Durham)
Roberts, John H. (Denbigh)
Samuel, J. (Stockton-on-Tees)

Shaw, Chas. Edw. (Stafford)
Sinclair,Capt.Jno.(Forfarshire
Souttar, Robinson
Sullivan, Donal (Westmeath)
Trevelyan, Charles Philips
Walton, Joseph (Barnsley)
Warner, Thos. Courtenay T.
Weir, James Galloway
Whittaker, Thomas Palmer
Williams,John Carvell(Notts.)
Wilson,Henry J.(York,W.R.)
Wilson, John (Durham, Mid)
Wilson, Jos. H. (Middlesbro')

TELLERS FOR THE AYES—
Mr. Steadman and Mr.
Edward Morton.

NOES

Arnold, Alfred
Arnold-Forster, Hugh O.
Arrol, Sir William
Ashmead-Bartlett, Sir Ellis
Atkinson, Rt. Hon. John
Bagot,Capt.Josceline FitzRoy
Balfour,Rt.Hn.A.J.(Manch'r)
Balfour,RtHnGeraldW(Leeds)
Banbury, Frederick George
Barton, Dunbar Plunkett
Bathurst,Hn.Allen Benjamin
Beach,RtHnSir M.H.(Bristol)
Beckett, Ernest William
Bemrose, Sir Henry Howe
Bentinck, Lord Henry C.
Bethell, Commander
Bill, Charles
Blundell, Colonel Henry
Bowles,T.Gibson(King'sLynn)
Brodrick, Rt. Hn. St. John
Butcher, John George
Carlile, William Walter
Cavendish,V.C.W.(Derbysh.)
Cecil, Lord Hugh (Greenwich
Chaloner, Capt. R. G. W.
Chamberlain,Rt.Hn.J.(Birm.)
Chamberlain,J.Austen(Worc'r)
Chaplin, Rt. Hn. Henry
Cochrane, Hn. Thos. H. A. E
Coghill, Douglas Harry
Collings, Rt. Hon. Jesse
Compton, Lord Alwyne
Cook, Fred. Lucas (Lambeth)
Cooke,C.W.Radcliffe(Heref'd)
Cornwallis,Fiennes StanleyW.
Cranbourne, Viscount
Cripps, Charles Alfred
Cubitt, Hon. Henry
Curzon, Viscount
Dalkeith, Earl of
Dalrymple, Sir Charles
Denny, Colonel
Dorington, Sir John Edwd.
Douglas, Rt. Hon. A. Akers-
Doxford, William Theodore
Duncombe, Hn. Hubert V.
Dyke, Rt. Hn. Sir Wm. Hart-
Ferguson, R. C. Munro (Leith)
Field, Admiral (Eastbourne)
Finch, George H.
Finlay, Sir Robert Bannatyne
Fisher, William Hayes
Fison, Frederick William

Fletcher, Sir Henry
Folkestone, Viscount
Forster, Henry William
Foster, Colonel (Lancaster)
Gedge, Sydney
Gibbons, J. Lloyd
Godson, Sir Augustus Fredk.
Goldsworthy, Major-General
Gordon, Hon. John Edward
Gorst, Rt. Hn. Sir John Eldon
Goschen, George J. (Sussex)
Goulding, Edward Alfred
Graham, Henry Robert
Gray, Ernest (West Ham)
Green,WalfordD.(Wednesbury
Gretton, John
Greville, Hon. Ronald
Gull, Sir Cameron
Hamilton,Rt.Hn.Lord George
Hanbury, Rt. Hn. Robert Wm.
Hardy, Laurence
Hare, Thomas Leigh
Helder, Augustus-
Hobhouse, Henry
Holland, Hn. Lionel L. (Bow)
Jebb, Richard Claverhouse
Johnston, William (Belfast)
Joliffe, Hon. H. George
Kay-Shuttleworth,RtHnSirU.
Kemp, George
Kenyon, James
Keswick, William
King, Sir Henry Seymour
Lafone, Alfred
Lees, Sir Elliott (Birkenhead)
Leigh-Bennett, Henry Currie
Long, Col.-Chas. W.(Evesham)
Long, Rt. Hn.Walter(L'pool.)
Lorne, Marquess of
Loyd, Archie Kirkman
Lyttelton, Hon. Alfred
Macartney, W. G. Ellison
Macdona, John Cumming
MacIver, David (Liverpool)
M'Iver,SirLewis(Edinb'h,W.)
Malcolm, Ian
Massey-Mainwaring,Hn.W.F.
Middlemore,Jno.Throgmorton
More,Robt.Jasper(Shropshire
Morley, Charles (Breconshire)
Morrell, George Herbert
Morton,Arth.H.A.(Deptford)
Murray,RtHnA.Graham(Bute

Nicol, Donald Ninian
Nussey, Thomas Willans
Orr-Ewing, Charles Lindsay
Pease,Herb.Pike(Darlington)
Phillpotts, Captain Arthur
Pollock, Harry Frederick
Pretyman, Ernest George
Pryce-Jones, Lt.-Col.Edward
Purvis, Robert
Pym, C. Guy
Rankin, Sir James
Rasch, Major Frederic Carne
Rentoul, James Alexander
Richards, Henry Charles
Richardson, Sir Thos.(Hart'pl)
Ritchie, Rt.Hn.Chas.Thomson
Round, James
Russell, T. W. (Tyrone)
Ryder,John Herbert Dudley
Sassoon, Sir Edward Albert
Seely, Charles Hilton
Sidebotham, J. W. (Cheshire)
Simeon, Sir Barrington
Smith, Abel H. (Christchurch)
Smith,James Parker(Lanarks.)
Smith, Hn. W. F. D. (Strand)
Stanley, Hn. Arth.(Ormskirk)
Stanley, Edw. Jas. (Somerset)
Stanley, Lord (Lancs.)
Strutt, Hn. Charles Hedley
Talbot, Lord E. (Chichester)
Talbot,RtHnJ.G.(Oxf'dUniv.)
Thornton, Percy M.
Valentia, Viscount
Wanklyn, James Leslie
Webster, Sir R. E. (I. of.W.)
Welby, Lieut.-Col. A. C. E.
Wentworth, Bruce C.Vernon-
Williams, Jos. Powell (Birm.)
Willoughby de Eresby, Lord
Willox, Sir John Archibald
Wilson, John (Falkirk)
Wodehouse,RtHn E.R.(Bath)
Wortley, Rt.Hn.C.B.Stuart-
Wylie, Alexander
Wyndham, George
Young,Commander(Berks,E.)

TELLERS FOR THE NOES—
Sir William Walrond and
Mr. Anstruther.

Original Question put, and agreed to.

Motion made, and Question proposed—

" That a sum, not exceeding £5,242,700, be granted to Her Majesty, to defray the Expenses of Wages, etc., to Officers, Seamen and Boys, Coast Guard, and Royal Marines, which will come in course of payment during the year ending on the 31st day of March 1900."

THE FIRST LORD OF THE TREASURY: If the Committee will give the Government this Vote we might adjourn. There will then be for to-morrow the remaining discussion upon Vote 1 of the Army and the uncontentious Vote for the Army, and probably that will be sufficient for to-morrow.

*MR. KEARLEY: I understand that no more Naval Estimates will be taken if this goes through this side of Easter?

THE FIRST LORD OF THE TREASURY: No.

VISCOUNT CRANBORNE: I am sure that the Leader of the House does not wish that we should finish off these Votes until we have dealt with the subject which has been raised with regard to the promotion of warrant officers I know he did not really deal with the subject, and there are other honourable Gentlemen behind me who desire that the subject should be dealt with.

MR. E. J. C. MORTON: The point which has been put is this: I do not want to underrate the private soldier, but I do say that the British sailor is not inferior to him, and yet the British sailor has no career offered him in the way in which the British soldier has. I will not use the old argument over again, but from the point of view of the efficiency of the Navy this is important. You offer no career to the British sailor which is at all analogous to what you offer to the British soldier. I have never been able to understand why there is any objection to giving a similar line of promotion into the commission ranks in the case of the Navy as you have done all along in the case of the Army. I have tried to find where the objection comes from, for every single naval officer in this House has been in favour of opening such a line of promotion, and the great majority have been in ...

Horse, and ...
have ...
discover the ...
is ...
... of ...

opportunity of getting some explanation out of the Admiralty as to why we cannot open certain positions, and give these men commission rank. We have not had an answer to that question yet, although the honourable Gentleman knows the argument perfectly well. I put the question again now in the hope that we shall get some satisfactory answer out of the Government upon · is point.

MR. PARKER SMITH (Lanark, Partick): There is one question which I should like to allude to if the House will permit me, and I will not say a word more than is necessary. As one who has been connected with some of the largest and swiftest ships in the Navy, I think I may say one word in connection with the position of the engineer officers. I think that is a matter of immense importance, and I put it forward not in any narrow sense, but as a question affecting the welfare of our Navy. There was circulated among honourable Members a few days ago a pamphlet—and I received one myself—which shows the necessity of dealing with the matter. I think that pamphlet is a refreshing contrast to the ordinary statements made with regard to persons in the employment of the Government, for it puts very fully and most moderately what the position of the engineers is, and what is required to put that service on a proper footing. A I have to say is, that you have splendid ships and machinery, and if you want justice done to those ships and machines you must take more care than you do at present to attract the best men in the engineering profession. It is a serious responsibility that you put upon these men, and anyone who has not been down in the engine-room does not know what that responsibility is. You must, if you are to have these engines properly treated, and if you want to get out of the ships what you are spending millions of money for, have a proper system, under which you make sure the engineering branch of the service receives due recognition at the hands of the Admiralty. The ...
... work has gr...
... growth of m...
... from ...

important that the man you have at the head, and upon whom the responsibility of the engine is placed, should be a man as good as you can possibly get. I do hope the Admiralty will consider the necessity of making the position sufficiently attractive so that the very best men in the engineering profession may be obtained.

Motion made, and Question proposed—

"That Item A (Wages), be reduced by £100."—*(Mr. Havelock Wilson.)*

MR. HAVELOCK WILSON: I beg leave to move the reduction of Vote 1 by £100, and my reason for doing so is to call attention to the very unsatisfactory payment of seamen in the Royal Navy. I am told by men in the Royal Navy that the food supplied by the Admiralty is not sufficient; and, secondly, that a large portion of the men's wages go to the canteen to provide them with food. It is a very unsatisfactory state of affairs that men have to provide themselves with food on board Her Majesty's ships. I venture to say that it ought to be the duty of the Government to provide the men with sufficient food without having to spend their wages at the canteen for that purpose. Then, with regard to clothing, I am told that they have to purchase a pair of coats out of their own wages, and a large number of naval officers have different ideas as to uniform.

THE DEPUTY CHAIRMAN: The subject which the honourable Member is discussing is more germane to Vote 2.

MR. HAVELOCK WILSON: Then I will not depart from the rule. I venture to say that the wages received by the men in the Royal Navy are not sufficient, more especially for married men, who receive £2 10s. and £2 15s. per week, which I consider is not sufficient. I, therefore, move to reduce this Vote by £100.

Amendment negatived without a Division.

*MR. MACARTNEY: The noble Lord complains that there is no promotion to commissions from the lower ranks, but he is entirely in error, because so far from that being the case at the present moment, upwards of 100 officers hold such commissions. With regard to the question of further promotions I have nothing to add to what I have already said.

VISCOUNT CRANBORNE: There is the difference in the pay between the petty officer and the warrant officer.

*MR. MACARTNEY: We do not propose to make the two alike.

VISCOUNT CRANBORNE: There is a complaint that there is hardly any difference between the two, and not sufficient to support the rank.

*MR. MACARTNEY: I can only say that we do not propose to make any alteration.

Original Question put, and agreed to.

Resolutions to be reported this day; Committee to sit again this day.

BUSINESS OF THE HOUSE.

THE FIRST LORD OF THE TREASURY: I beg leave to move—

"That this House do now adjourn."

I can only repeat that in consequence of the backward state of Supply I shall again to-morrow move the suspension of the Twelve o'clock Rule, because Votes 1, 14, and 15 of the Army Estimates must be obtained, if not more.

*MR. WEIR: Does the right honourable Gentleman intend to move for a Saturday Sitting to-morrow?

THE FIRST LORD OF THE TREASURY: That depends upon whether we get the Votes which I have just mentioned. If we do not get them we must have a Saturday Sitting.

MR. J. SAMUEL (Stockton): I should like to know if the Second Reading of the Workmen's Dwellings (Acquisition of Holdings) Bill will be taken before Easter?

THE FIRST LORD OF THE TREASURY: No, Sir.

Motion agreed to.

SALE OF FOOD AND DRUGS BILL.

Adjourned Debate on Motion for Committal to Standing Committee on Trade, etc. [9th March] further adjourned till Monday next.

SUPPLY [3RD MARCH].

Resolution reported:—

ARMY ESTIMATES, 1899-1900.

"That a number of Land Forces, not exceeding 184,853, all ranks, be maintained for the Service of the United Kingdom of Great Britain and Ireland at Home and Abroad, excluding Her Majesty's Indian Possessions, during the year ending on the 31st day of March 1900."

Resolution agreed to.

UNIVERSITIES (SCOTLAND) ACTS AMENDMENT BILL.

Adjourned Debate on Second Reading [9th March] further adjourned till Monday next.

LICENSING EXEMPTION (HOUSES OF PARLIAMENT) BILL.

Adjourned Debate on Second Reading [23rd February] further adjourned till Monday next.

METROPOLITAN GAS COMPANIES.

The Select Committee on Metropolitan Gas Companies was nominated of,— Mr. William Abraham, Mr. Baldwin, Mr. Banbury, Mr. Cohen, Sir Frederick Dixon-Hartland, Mr. Gilliat, Mr. Brynmor Jones, Mr. Lough, Mr. Lowles, Mr. Nicol, Mr. Pickersgill, Mr. Pirie, Sir James Rankin, Sir Andrew Scoble, and Mr. Steadman.

Ordered, That the Committee have power to send for persons, papers, and records.

Ordered, That Five be the quorum.— *(Sir William Walrond.)*

COLONIAL LOANS FUND BILL.

Second Reading deferred till Monday next.

TELEGRAPHS (TELEPHONIC COMMUNICATION, ETC.) BILL.

Second Reading deferred till Monday next.

LONDON GOVERNMENT BILL.

Second Reading deferred till Monday next.

CHARITABLE LOANS (IRELAND) BILL.

Second Reading deferred till Monday next.

INEBRIATES ACT (1898) AMENDMENT BILL.

Second Reading deferred till Monday next.

IMPROVEMENT OF LAND BILL.

Second Reading deferred till Monday next.

PALATINE COURT OF DURHAM BILL [LORDS].

Second Reading deferred till Monday next.

SOLICITORS BILL [LORDS].

Second Reading deferred till Monday next.

TELEGRAPH (CHANNEL ISLANDS) BILL [LORDS.]

Second Reading deferred till Monday next.

ELECTRIC LIGHTING (CLAUSES) BILL.

Second Reading deferred till Monday next.

ANCHORS AND CHAIN CABLES BILL.

Second Reading deferred till Monday next.

PRIVATE LEGISLATION PROCEDURE (SCOTLAND) BILL.

Second Reading deferred till Monday next.

TOWN COUNCILS (SCOTLAND) BILL.

Second Reading deferred till Wednesday next.

EXECUTORS (SCOTLAND) AMENDMENT BILL.

Second Reading deferred till Thursday next.

CHEAP TRAINS BILL.

Second Reading deferred till Tuesday next.

CROFTERS' HOLDINGS (SCOTLAND) ACT (1886) AMENDMENT BILL.

Second Reading deferred till Wednesday next.

SCHOOL BOARD CONFERENCES (SCOTLAND) BILL.

Second Reading deferred till Thursday 13th April.

PARISH COUNCILLORS (TENURE OF OFFICE) BILL.

Committee deferred till this day.

UNIVERSITY DEGREES BILL

Second Reading deferred till Thursday next.

House adjourned at half-past Twelve of the clock.

HOUSE OF LORDS.

Friday, 17th March 1899.

THE LORD CHANCELLOR took his seat upon the Woolsack at Four of the clock.

PRIVATE BILL BUSINESS.

AIRDRIE AND COATBRIDGE WATER BILL [H.L.]

A witness ordered to attend the Select Committee.

INVERNESS HARBOUR BILL [H.L.]

Committee to meet on Tuesday next.

NORTHERN ASSURANCE COMPANY BILL [H.L.]

Committee to meet on Tuesday next.

MID-KENT GAS BILL [H.L.]

The Chairman of Committees informed the House that the opposition to the Bill was withdrawn: The order made on the 27th of February last discharged; and Bill committed.

WATERMEN'S AND LIGHTERMEN'S ACTS AMENDMENT BILL [H.L.]

To be read second time on the second sitting day after the Recess at Easter.

Coalville Urban District Gas Bill [H.L.]
Bristol Floods Prevention Bill [H.L.]
Dumbarton Burgh Bill [H.L.]
Lanarkshire (Middle Ward District) Water Bill [H.L.]
Perth Water, Police, and Gas Bill [H.L.]

Reported with amendments.

ABERDEEN CORPORATION BILL [H.L.]

Queen's consent signified; and Bill reported from the Select Committee with amendments.

VOL. LXVIII.　　[FOURTH SERIES.]

ABERDEEN HARBOUR BILL [H.L.]

Read third time, and passed, and sent to the Commons.

PUBLIC BUSINESS.

BODIES CORPORATE (JOINT TENANCY) BILL [H.L.]

House in Committee (according to order): Bill reported without amendment; and re-committed to Standing Committee.

PARTRIDGE SHOOTING (IRELAND BILL.

House in Committee (according to order): Bill reported without amendment: Standing Committee negatived; and Bill to be read third time on Monday next.

METROPOLIS MANAGEMENT ACTS AMENDMENT (BY-LAWS) BILL [H.L.]

Read third time (according to order), and sent to the Commons.

BOARD OF EDUCATION BILL [H.L.]

To be read a second time on Friday the 21st of April next.

POOR LAW ADMINISTRATION.

*EARL WEMYSS: My Lords, I rise to move—

"That it is expedient that a Royal Commission be appointed to inquire into the administration and working of the Poor Law."

There is a story told of a French cook who was very extravagant in the matter of meat, and his master sent for him and reproved him. He said: "You ask for more meat; what has become of the ox that was brought into the larder two days ago?" The French *chef* was equal to the occasion, for, putting his forefinger and thumb into his waistcoat pocket, he pulled out a meat lozenge and said, "Voila le bœuf, de Monsieur." I wish I had the condensing power of that French *chef*, but, unfortunately, I have not. The subject which I have to treat is a vast and vital one, and I

2 Y

am sorry to say that though I shall endeavour to compress my remarks as far as possible, I may have to claim your Lordships' indulgence for a longer time than I would desire. I feel that any opinions I may personally give on such a question are worthless, and I shall therefore quote from authorities before whom, I am sure, your Lordships will have to bow on this vital question. I need not take your Lordships far back into the history of the Poor Law legislation of this country, but I would point out that there is one feature which runs through the whole of it, and that is a very marked distinction between those who are able by their thrift and their industry to maintain themselves, and those who through want of thrift and through want of industry have been unable to maintain themselves, and have to be maintained through the thrift and industry of others. So much so was this felt in olden times that "sturdy vagabonds" and "valiant beggars" were kept to continual labour in such wise that they may get their own living by the continual labour of their hands. A sturdy beggar was whipped for the first offence, in some cases his right ear was cropped for the second offence, and, if again offending, he was tried at sessions for loitering and idleness, and, if convicted, executed as a felon and enemy to the commonwealth. Other Acts contained provisions, if possible, more stringent in the first instance, against sturdy beggars and able-bodied vagabonds, who were branded with the letter V on the shoulder and adjudged slaves for two years; and if they ran away they were branded with the letter S on the cheek, and adjudged slaves for life. You find this principle in a modified form in the Act 43rd Elizabeth. This Act was so loosely administered that abuses of the strongest possible kind grew up, and the labouring population was pauperised and demoralised. This ultimately led to the appointment of a Royal Commission, and I venture to think—65 years having elapsed since then—there are causes sufficient now to justify the reissue of a Royal Commission to inquire into the whole of this vast subject of the treatment of the poor. The Commission of 1832 included amongst its members two bishops and Mr. Nassau W. Senior and Mr. Edwin Chadwick, men

Earl Wemyss.

thoroughly acquainted with this subject. The inquiry lasted two years, and after going thoroughly and diligently into the administration and general working of the Poor Law the Royal Commission in 1834 came to the following conclusion—

"It is our painful duty to report that in the greater part of the districts which we have been enabled to examine, the Fund which the 43rd Elizabeth directed to be employed in setting to work children and persons capable of labour, but using no daily trade, and in the necessary relief of the impotent, is applied to purposes opposed to the letter and still more to the spirit of the law, and destructive to the morals of the most numerous class and to the welfare of all."

I do not think that any of your Lordships, except those who have had their attention specially drawn to this subject, and have gone through the Report of the Royal Commission, have the least idea or any conception of the extent to which demoralisation through lax administration had run at that time. I will read to your Lordships a few extracts from the evidence and statements of fact on which the Commissioners formed their conclusions—

In North Wales—a district of comparatively good administration—the payment of rent out of rates is nearly universal. In many parishes it is extended to nearly all married labourers. Paupers thus become a very desirable class of tenants, more so than the independent labourers, whose rent at the same time this mode of relief enhances. There is a consequent rise in value of apartments from £1 to £2, e.g.:—

A baker, in Suffolk, with a family of eight, had his rent, £13 a year, paid by the parish—plus 2s. 6d. a week for his children.

Able-bodied relief, in money, without labour, was common. Relief from the parish in aid of wages was called "Allowance"—sometimes "Bread money."

At Yardley, Hastings, all unemployed were put up for sale weekly. The clergyman of the parish had seen 10 knocked down one week to one of the farmers for 5s. About 70 men were let out in that way out of 170. In the Vale of Taunton all farm labourers during the whole or part of the year received a portion of their wages out of the poor rate.

"Parish Employment."—A man, if he did not like his work, would say, "I can have 12s. a week by going on the roads, and doing as little as I like."

In some agricultural districts mismanagement had led paupers to the notion that they had a right to be exempted from the same labour as independent labourers.

The position of pauper was so much better that the wives of independent labourers regretted their husbands were not paupers.

The overseer of Kettering said the men's remark is, "You must have your 12s. a week, or 10s., whether you work or not. I would not be such a fool as to work—blast work—damn me if I work, etc."

In the parish of Sidford Gore poor rates were £650 per annum, of which £114 were paid in six months to men who did not do one stroke of work for it.

Labourers much deteriorated.—They do not care for regular work, prefer idle work on the roads. At Burnash, in East Suffolk, labourers were put up to auction—hired as low as 2d. or 3d. a day—the rest of their maintenance made up by the parish. The consequence was that farmers turned off regular hands in order to hire them by auction when wanted.

Labour Rate System.—Ratepayers agreed to employ each a certain number of labourers having settlements, not according to the employer's wants, but according to his rental or contribution to the rates.

The evidence taken by the Poor Law Commissioners teems with cases such as I have quoted as samples, showing the utter demoralisation that a lax and injudicious administration of the Poor Law had brought about, and which led to the conclusion already quoted, to which the Commissioners had, after a most full, patient, and searching inquiry unanimously come. The Commissioners recommended that there should be a discontinuance of outdoor relief to the able-bodied, who should be relieved only in the workhouse. The 4th and 5th William IV. was passed on the basis of the Report of the Commissioners, and those who had profited by the lax administration, and found that they could no longer get relief except in the workhouse, where they would have to work, became discontented, with the result that a Committee of the House of Commons was appointed in 1838. That Committee reported as follows—

"The evidence shows the practice of confining relief to able-bodied male paupers in the workhouse has been established in many districts of guardians. The Committee are convinced that the utmost benefit has resulted from the general adoption of this system of relief. They strongly recommend that it should in future be adhered to, subject to such occasional departure from the ordinary rule as it appears local boards have been ready to adopt, and the Commissioners to sanction in cases of real necessity."

What were the results of this change in the law? Industry took the place of idleness, the people became more independent, and thrift increased among the working classes. I will not trouble your Lordships with figures to prove this, but the statement rests on absolutely incontrovertible facts. The Poor Rate, which in 1851 was 4.5 per cent. of the whole population, was, in 1891, 2.4 cent. As regards thrift, it was stated the other day in a Return—I forget where it was issued—that there were 18 million investors in building societies, friendly societies, etc., and the total sum invested was 300 millions sterling. That was the state of things up to recent time, and it is the result, I venture to say without fear of contradiction, of a just administration of the Poor Law as laid down in its principle by the Royal Commission of 1834, and confirmed, as I have read to your Lordships, by the conclusions come to by the Committee of the House of Commons in 1838. But, my Lords, we have come now to a different state of things. The evils we had to complain of 65 years ago were evils and abuses in the administration of the law. We have now to complain not of the abuses in the administration of the Poor Law, but of abuse of the Poor Law root and branch, its principles and everything else. I do not think your Lordships have any idea of the sort of language which is being used with reference to the Poor Law at the present time, especially against what is called the workhouse, which is the test of a man's ability to maintain himself or not. Here are some flowers that I have gathered from the flowery path of abuse with which the road to the poor house is strewn. I have culled them from the Press in various places, and they are as follows—

"Down with the workhouse," "that bastille," "prison," "penal hospital," "place of banishment and disgrace, where existence is intolerable and indefensible." "Down with vile laws and worse administration." "A general gaol delivery may not be feasible all at once—it is a question of time." "They should not be imprisoned in their old age and deprived of their civil rights, i.e., votes."

Aye, votes! There's the rub. This is the tone and language used with reference to the Poor Law and workhouses by irresponsible speakers and writers. But even otherwise wise and prudent men seem to have lost their mental balance in this matter. I have here a quotation from a speech of a very distinguished Member of the Government (Sir M. Hicks Beach), who, speaking at Newport, said—

"The Government intended to reform the Poor Law, and to give to the deserving"—

(that is to say, the Government are going to separate the sheep from the goats)—"comfortable quarters—something they would not look upon, as he feared they now looked upon the workhouse, with loathing and pain."

My feeling when I read this was—Where was Mr. Long, that he did not muzzle his colleague? I cannot conceive it possible that in the Cabinet he showed signs of this "Poor Law phobia"—a fit that probably subsequently came on as the result of having been bitten on his way from Downing Street by "General" Booth, set on perchance by a Cabinet colleague. Nothing could be more demoralising than such language. Now, my Lords, I am a very plain, simple-minded Scotsman, and do not see anything but what is put before me, or listen to anything but what I am plainly told. Therefore, I do not for one moment say or believe that there is anything beyond all these speeches or writings than the purest and most unmitigated philanthropy; but there are other people who take a different view, and who think they see something political behind this. I will take the Leader of the Opposition in another place. He takes the view that there is something more than pure philanthropy in all this, for when he was appointed to his present position he referred to the question of Old Age Pensions, and said it was almost scandalous that Her Majesty's Government had brought in no Bill dealing with this subject, inasmuch as it was in the belief that they would get Old Age Pensions that so many people had voted for the present Government at the last General Election. He quoted from documents and bills that were circulated in Birmingham and elsewhere at the General Election, which led one to believe that behind all this philanthropy there is a political and vote-catching object. "General" Booth has asserted that the people have been deceived, and that they had been promised Old Age Pensions by the present Government. I read in a newspaper the other day that there were 100 Liberal Unionist Members in the House of Commons who had pledged themselves to Old Age Pensions at the election, and who were most indignant that nothing had been done by the Government, and had memorialised Mr. Balfour to that effect, apropos to which there was a very sensible letter in the

Earl Wemyss.

"Times" the other day from Major Rasch, who said he was not going to whistle for a wind to keep floating in the air the kites which these gentlemen had flown at the General Election. As I have said, there are people who think that there is in all this something in the nature of politics and vote-catching. Happily, there are people who take a sound non-political view of this question. The subject of Old Age Pensions has been fully and fairly considered by a Committee, of which Lord Rothschild—than whom there is no better man on finance—was a member, and that Committee presented the following Report—

"The Committee have been forced to the conclusion that none of the schemes submitted to us would attain the objects which the Government had in view, and that we ourselves are unable, after repeated attempts, to devise any proposal free from grave and inherent disadvantages."

I have here some independent views. There are many from which I could quote, all objecting to this Old Age Pension scheme, including many friendly societies. I will take a very independent opinion. The Cambridge Debating Society at its last meeting, which was presided over by Mr. Campken, unanimously passed the following resolution—

"That a general system of Old Age Pensions provided by the State would be subversive of voluntary thrift, antagonistic to the friendly societies' system, and detrimental to the welfare of the community."

I own that as far as I am concerned that resolution absolutely expresses what I feel on the subject. And as regards pauperisation in the case of a man who cannot provide for and keep himself, and has to be kept through the thrift and industry of others, I cannot see what difference there is between that man receiving 2s. 6d. from the rates and his receiving 2s. 6d. from the State. I should be glad if anyone could logically show me that there is any difference in principle between the two, and how a man who is pauperised by receiving from the rates ceases to be pauperised by receiving from the State. I said I would endeavour not to give my own opinion, but to quote the views of men before whom I think your Lordships will have to bow on a question like this. I will give you the opinion of Mr. Loch, the able and energetic Secretary of the Charity Organisation Society, who knows more about the poor, I believe, than any other man. In a letter he wrote to me some time ago, Mr. Loch said—

"They are the worst friends of the people who, with such a past before them"—

by that he means, of course, the success that attended the strict administration of relief in accordance with the rules laid down by the Royal Commission of 1834—

"now preach laxity of administration, using other words, no doubt, to represent their meaning, or propose to re-establish Poor Law employment."

Within the last two hours I have received another letter from him, the substance of which is that he thinks, looking to the change which has been made in the candidature for the post of guardian of the poor and of the electorate, and the effect that this Old Age Pension scheme might have, if put into practice, upon friendly and other societies, that it is desirable that there should be a Commission of Inquiry into the whole subject. Mr. Mackay, whose name is well known to anyone familiar with the subject, and who has been engaged for the last two or three years in writing a history of the Poor Law, says—

"The best statement, perhaps the very best extant, of the principles of public relief is that in the Report of the Commissioners on the continuance of the Poor Law Commission, dated December 31st, 1839."

The opinion of that Commission is that—

"The condition of the pauper should be less eligible than that of the independent, and that relief at home—namely, out-door relief—is inconsistent with this. The only test of destitution is to be found in the pauper's willingness to give up his own resources for a maintenance offered in a Poor Law establishment."

That is the opinion he quotes as the best he knows, and this writer on this great question adds—

"It has always seemed to me there is no escape from the cogency of this argument."

Mr. Mackay says that the diminution of pauperism has fully justified the wisdom of the founders of the Amending Act of 1834, and he favours the appointment of a Royal Commission. I have only to add that the late, Lord Lyttelton, in the year 1875 brought a Motion before this House to the effect—

"That it is expedient, in the administration of the Poor Law, to revert more nearly to the principles laid down in the Report of the Commission of Inquiry of 1833."

This Motion was, by leave, withdrawn, but I am glad to say that the present Leader of the Opposition (the Earl of Kimberley) on that occasion expressed his approval of this resolution. I hope my Motion will also receive the support of my noble Friend, my object being rather in the direction pointed out by Lord Lyttelton, and approved by my noble Friend, than in the direction of these vague, humanitarian, economic, political schemes of Old Age Pensions. You may, perhaps, ask how it is that I have brought this matter before your Lordships, and why I should presume to put myself forward and speak to your Lordships as I have ventured to do, but I hope you will observe that I have given quotations from experts on the subject, and not merely my own views. At the Vestry of St. James's, Westminster, the question of the administration of the Poor Law cropped up a few years ago, and I proposed that the vestry clerk and myself should draw up a Memorandum on the subject. This we did, and in doing so we were necessarily obliged to go thoroughly into the question, and the conclusion we came to was that—

"It is respectfully admitted that while under the operation of this Act (the Poor Law Act) during all these sixty years abuses have been checked, the well-being of the poor has been duly cared for, and provision exceptionally made for cases of emergency. All, then, that is needed at the present time is no new Poor Law, or change in principle or system of relief, but simply a wise, judicious, discriminating, and kindly administration and exercise of the powers conferred by the existing law upon those entrusted with the care and relief of poor persons permanently or temporarily unable to maintain themselves."

The view I held then I hold now, and I am anxious that a Royal Commission should be issued. If there is anything political in all this, if vote-catching has anything to do with the philanthropy of the times and these philanthropic measures which are in the air floating about like cork on the Thames, a Committee of the House of Commons is not the body to whom such a matter should he entrusted. A Commission of a purely judicial character, accustomed to sift evidence and to give their opinion without fear and without favour, is the proper body to deal with this question. A Commission of this character, my Lords, is what we want to see appointed. I believe myself that it is a great mistake to think that any good can come of these philanthropic, political measures. I do not care where they come from. I do not care whether they are imported from Germany or whether they are the political product of a Birmingham workshop. I look at them all in the same light, and with the same view, and I think we want full inquiry into this matter. I hope it will be understood by those who favour these schemes, whatever they may be, that they are not the sole persons in the world who have any sympathy and feeling for their suffering fellow-men; but that there are many others who know much about the subject, and who feel as deeply as any one of those gentlemen to whom I have referred, and who are as anxious as they are to hold out a helping hand to those who have fallen in the battle and in the race of life. I thank your Lordships for having listened to me so long, and I now move the Motion standing in my name on the Paper.

LORD MONKSWELL: My Lords, as I have taken a considerable part in the administration of the Poor Law in London and have sat for many years as a working Member of the Chelsea Board of Guardians, I should like to be allowed, with your Lordships' kind permission, to say a few words with regard to this subject. I do not quite understand how the speech of the noble Earl tallies with the proposition that he has put before your Lordships' House, because it appears to me that the noble Earl has already got exactly what he wants, and that is a condemnation of the system of indiscriminate out-door relief, and a condemnation by a strong Royal Commission which has only just concluded its labours. Not only does that Commission condemn out-door relief, but it finds itself quite unable to suggest any means whatever of satisfactorily solving the question of Old Age Pensions, which we know has been represented by some authorities to be the simplest thing in the world. It appears to me that what

Earl Wemyss.

would logically follow from the speech of the noble Earl is this, that the noble Earl should ask this House to express its agreement with the Report of the Royal Commission on Old Age Pensions. It has been suggested to me that there is one other function that the noble Earl might ask this House to discharge, and that is to suggest that some sort of Committee of Inquiry might be instituted with a view of finding out what are the opinions of Her Majesty's Government on this question of Old Age Pensions. My Lords, I confess that I am not altogether in agreement with the speech of the noble Earl. My experience has taught me that although in the vast majority of cases it is either want of thrift or want of industry that drives persons into the workhouse, still there is a residuum of cases, and I venture to think a considerable percentage of cases, in which it is unavoidable illness or misfortune which has driven people to the shelter of the workhouse. I am not prepared to go so far as to agree with the noble Earl in saying that it is in all cases either want of thrift or industry that drives people into the workhouse.

*EARL WEMYSS: I did not say that it was so in all cases.

LORD MONKSWELL: The noble Earl said a strong division ought to be made between the persons in the workhouse, or supported by the rates, and persons not supported by the rates. I think there are many persons, in the workhouse and in receipt of relief outside the workhouse, who are just as worthy of the consideration of the State as the persons who have managed to keep their heads above water. But I principally rise to call your Lordships' attention to the very curious state of things which exists in London, and in London alone, I believe, with regard to the question of indoor and out-door pauperism. In London four-fifths of the money expended on the Poor Law is expended in in-door pauperism, and only one-fifth in out-door pauperism; whereas, if we take the rural districts in Wales, for instance, we find that the exact opposite is the case, and that four-fifths of the total sum spent on the Poor Law is spent on out-door relief, and only one-fifth on in-door relief. Now, there is a simple explanation of that fact—namely, that in-

London we have a Metropolitan Common Poor Fund which every union subscribes to and draws upon. Originally, when that Common Poor Fund was set up, one of the contributions that was made from that fund was a sum of 5d. a day in respect of every in-door pauper. That, my Lords, was, in my opinion, a wise and judicious proceeding. It was perfectly right, I think, that that 5d. a day should be paid. This sum did not quite cover the expenses of a pauper in the workhouse—that is to say, the cost of a pauper outside the administration expenses, but it very nearly covered it. The cost of feeding and clothing the inmates was computed at 3s. 3d. a week, or somewhere between 5d. and 6d. a day when I was on the Chelsea Board of Guardians, and I think it was quite right that that charge should be thrown on the Metropolitan Common Poor Fund. But 10 years ago a further sum of 4d. a day was paid, and is now paid, out of the Common Poor Fund, making a total of 9d. a day for every pauper in the metropolitan workhouses. The result is that it absolutely pays the unions of London to have their workhouses full. They would gain money if they paid a pauper a shilling a week to come into the workhouse. Ninepence a day more than covers the cost of feeding and clothing the inmates, and the administration expenses, of course, are the same whether a workhouse is full or only three parts full. I think it is right that the expenses of in-door pauperism should be thrown on the Common Poor Fund, and that the Common Poor Fund should continue to contribute as much as it does towards the poorer districts in the way of equalisation of rates, but I am not perfectly certain that it is desirable that you should put a premium on every man and woman who seeks the shelter of the workhouse. It appears to me that that is a matter that might well be considered by the Local Government Board. I do not share the view of the noble Earl that it is necessary at the present moment to have a Commission to inquire into the whole operation of the Poor Law, because it certainly does seem to me that things are moving in the right direction. Pauperism is decreasing throughout the country, and the noble Earl will be perhaps even more glad than I am to find that the decrease is principally in out-door paupers. Consequently it appears to me that outside the question of Old Age Pensions, which, so far from being solved by the Commission, is still in a very fluid state, I do not think the question of the administration of the Poor Law calls for any special action on the part of the Government at the present moment. Of course, I admit that there is between Old Age Pensions and the Poor Law a very considerable connection, because, after all, the Poor Law is one of the means of distributing Old Age Pensions. It may or may not be the best means. There may be another means to be devised, but until another means is devised I should be very sorry to see out-door relief entirely stopped, and I think the best way of dealing with out-door relief is for the boards of guardians to look into every case as far as possible themselves, and if they cannot do that to employ the very best people they can to look carefully into every case. It is a question of administration and not so much a question of the Poor Law. As far as the Poor Law itself is concerned it appears to me we are moving in the right direction, and I doubt very much whether a Royal Commission will be able to do more than to suggest what almost every Poor Law reformer does suggest is necessary—namely, that there should be a further classification of inmates in the workhouse, and that you should not take that rough and ready test of a man being a pauper and say that because he is a pauper he must have been thriftless and idle, but that they should be put into different categories by persons who have investigated every case on its own merits. That appears to me to be the great reform of the Poor Law that is desirable.

Lord HARRIS: My Lords, I only rise in consequence of what my noble Friend opposite (Lord Monkswell) said as regards the Measures which might be taken by executive action to improve the present position of the inmates of our workhouses. May I remind your Lordships that only as late as 1893 a Commission was appointed to inquire into the Poor Law, and that Committee presented in 1895 a very exhaustive Report, not upon all subjects included in the Poor Law, but upon all that portion which deals with the provision made for the poor, and particularly the aged poor.

In the House of Commons the other day, in a discussion upon the subject of cottage homes, the President of the Local Government Board, in his speech, called attention to what the Local Government Board had been doing by executive action. Mr. Chaplin said that shortly after the present Government came into office it was his duty to examine into this question, and his colleagues and himself came to the conclusion that it was desirable to call the attention of all the different boards of guardians in the country to the desirability of trying, by means of improved administration, to do something in the nature of drawing a greater distinction between the treatment of the poor who are deserving and the poor who cannot be included in that category. As long ago as July 1896 the Government addressed a Circular to all the different boards of guardians, drawing their attention to the desirability of classifying more strictly the aged and deserving poor in the workhouses. In connection with that, the Board called the attention of the guardians to what is called the General Consolidated Order, which was passed many years ago, and which provides that guardians shall, so far as circumstances may permit, divide and further sub-divide the inmates, having regard to their moral character and previous habits, upon any other grounds that might seem to be important. And the Local Government Board asked them to give special attention to this matter, so that all those whose circumstances had become so reduced as to force them into the workhouse, but who had been up to the time of their going there leading decent and respectable lives, should be separated from others who, from their habits or speech, or for any other reason, were likely to cause them any discomfort. A separate Circular was issued drawing attention to the fact that there should be special facilities given for their friends to visit them, and for them to visit their friends, and that they might be permitted out for that and other purposes, and when they desired it they should also be permitted to attend their own places of worship on Sunday. And further, it was suggested that, whenever

Lord Harris.

it might be possible, further arrangements might be made for the improvement of their condition. Some time after that Circular was issued the Local Government Board caused inquiries to be made as to what attention had been given to their suggestions and instructions, and very satisfactory replies were received. I only mention this, my Lords, to show that it is in the power of a Department, by executive action, and without the necessity of appointing a body like a Royal Commission, to introduce improvements into the administration of the law in consonance with the views of more advanced opinion; and it is desirable, I suggest, that before anything of the kind is done we should be perfectly sure what are the schemes that may be put forward, having the very proper object in view of securing an administration of the law as generous as possible in spirit, whilst at the same time, of course, not losing sight of the intention of the framers of the Poor Law, that those who provided the funds should be carefully guarded. I believe that is the intention of the Government so far as the Select Committee to which the Cottage Homes Bill has been referred is concerned, and any Bill of a similar character that may be brought before the House. Therefore, there is inquiry going on at the present time in many different directions, and I think it would be wise to wait for some result of these various inquiries before coming to a decision such as that suggested by the noble Earl.

*Earl WEMYSS: My Lords, I shall not press my Motion; but in reference to what my noble Friend has stated I should like to point out that what I said was wanted was a wise, judicious, discriminating, and kindly administration and exercise of the powers conferred by the existing law upon the various authorities. I beg leave to withdraw my Motion.

Motion, by leave, withdrawn.

House adjourned at twenty-five minutes after Five of the clock.

HOUSE OF COMMONS.

Friday, 17th March 1899.

———

MR. SPEAKER took the Chair at Twelve of the clock.

———

PRIVATE BILL BUSINESS.

———

PRIVATE BILLS (STANDING ORDER 62 COMPLIED WITH).

MR. SPEAKER laid upon the Table Report from one of the Examiners of Petitions for Private Bills, That in the case of the following Bill, referred on the First Reading thereof, Standing Order No. 62 has been complied with, viz. : —

West Gloucestershire Water Bill.

Ordered, That the Bill be read a second time.

CROWBOROUGH DISTRICT WATER BILL.

As amended, considered ; to be read the third time.

FISHGUARD WATER AND GAS BILL.

As amended, considered ; to be read the third time.

MENSTONE WATER BILL.

To be read a second time upon Thursday next.

SOUTH EASTERN AND LONDON, CHATHAM, AND DOVER RAILWAY COMPANIES BILL.

Motion made, and Question proposed—

" That all Petitions against the Bill presented six clear days before the meeting of the Committee be referred to the Committee ; that the Petitioners praying to be heard by themselves, their counsel, or agents, be heard against the Bill, and counsel heard in support of the Bill."—(*Mr. Bryce.*)

MR. BRYCE (Aberdeen, S.): Mr. Speaker, I rise to move the Motion which

stands in my name on the Paper ; and as I understand this Motion is agreed to, I will direct my attention, in the two or three words which I have to say, to the question of the Amendment that stands in the name of my right honourable Friend the President of the Board of Trade. My object in moving this Motion is to secure not only that this Bill, which involves large questions of public policy, and which has excited unusual interest in the country, should be taken to a strong Committee, but that that Committee should not be unnecessarily fettered by the purely technical rules of the House. It has, however, been represented to me that the width of the words in which my Motion is drawn might have the effect of exposing the promoters to great worry and expense in defending the Bill against persons having really no particular interest in the matter, and of exposing the Committee to the possibility of their time being taken up and their patience exhausted by the interposition of importunate busy-bodies and of persons with perfectly good intentions but ill-regulated minds, who are commonly called " cranks." Nothing is further from my intention than to impose that additional labour on the Committee, or that additional cost on the promoters, and therefore I am prepared, if the promoters will give an assurance to the House that they will not take any technical objection, on the ground of *locus standi*, to any person who may have substantial interest or view which the Committee itself shall consider ought to be heard, to accept the Amendment put on the Paper by the President of the Board of Trade, to insert the words, " Subject to the Rules, Orders, and Proceedings of this House." I hope that assurance will be given, and that it will be possible to ensure that the inquiry shall be complete, and that the Committee shall not be debarred from hearing anyone whom they think ought to be heard.

MR. COSMO BONSOR (Surrey, Wimbledon): Mr. Speaker, I have listened with great attention to the speech of the right honourable Gentleman, and I rise at once to accept the proposal which he has made. I think we are absolutely at one in wishing that this Bill should be discussed as openly as possible before a strong Committee of this House. I understand that the right honourable Gentleman is now willing that the forms of the House should exclude all persons who have no substantial interest in the South Eastern and London, Chatham, and Dover systems. My original opposition to the honourable Gentleman's proposal was based on the fact that I could not ask my shareholders to go to the great expense of defending their Bill against petitioners coming from all over the Kingdom. I will undertake that no objection will be made on the ground of want of *locus standi* against anybody interested in the South Eastern and London, Chatham, and Dover systems if the Committee consider they have substantial interests or views which deserve to be heard. We wish, however, to exclude blackmailers and "Daily Mailers" from this inquiry.

MR. PICKERSGILL (Bethnal Green, S.W.): Mr. Speaker, I should like to point out to the House that there are many precedents for the omission of these words which the President of the Board of Trade desires to insert. They were omitted in the case of the Birmingham Water Bill of 1892. It may be said that that was not a railway Bill, but the words were also omitted in the case of the Metropolitan Railway Bill, in, I think, the same year, or the year before. I shall not venture to take the responsibility of dividing the House on this question, but I do not think that the assurance of the honourable Gentleman opposite quite meets the case, or that I fully understand it. In the ordinary course, according to the Rules of the House, the Court of Referees would have to decide the question of *locus standi*. That would, I think, be very objectionable in this case, because the Referees are governed by the practice of the House, and would have to decide strictly as a court of law decides—in accordance with precedent. Therefore I think we should have an assurance that the question of *locus standi* in regard to this Bill shall not be decided by the Court of Referees, but that it shall be at the discretion of the Committee whether or not petitioners should be heard.

Amendment proposed—

Mr. Cosmo Bonsor.

"To insert, after the first word 'That,' the words 'subject to the Rules, Orders, and Proceedings of the House.'—(*The President of the Board of Trade.*)

THE PRESIDENT OF THE BOARD OF TRADE (Mr. C. T. RITCHIE, Croydon): Mr. Speaker, I understand from my honourable Friend that that is practically what he has undertaken to do. Where petitioners have a substantial interest and view, which it is desirable should be put before the Committee, they shall not be governed or controlled by the ordinary *locus standi*, but may call witnesses, and the promoters will not object. That is, I understand, the view of my honourable Friend.

MR. COSMO BONSOR assented.

THE PRESIDENT OF THE BOARD OF TRADE: I think that will be satisfactory to my right honourable Friend opposite, and under those circumstances I move the insertion of the words, "Subject to the Rules, Orders, and proceedings of this House."

MR. BRYCE: I accept the Amendment.

Main Question, as amended, put, and agreed to.

Ordered, That, subject to the Rules, Orders, and Proceedings of this House, all Petitions against the Bill presented Six clear days before the meeting of the Committee be referred to the Committee; that the Petitioners praying to be heard by themselves, Counsel, or Agents, be heard against the Bill, and Counsel heard in support of the Bill.

Ordered, That the Committee have power to send for persons, papers, and records.

Ordered, That Five be the quorum.—(*Mr. Bryce.*)

PETITIONS.

EDUCATION OF CHILDREN BILL.

Petition from Southend-on-Sea, in favour; to lie upon the Table.

PARLIAMENTARY FRANCHISE.

Petition from Leicester, for extension to women; to lie upon the Table.

1129   *Returns,*   {17 MARCH 1899}   *Reports, etc.*   1130

LOCAL AUTHORITIES SERVANTS' SUPERANNUATION BILL.

Petitions in favour;—From Epsom ;—and, Hetton ; to lie upon the Table.

PRIVATE LEGISLATION PROCEDURE (SCOTLAND) BILL.

Petitions in favour ;—From Dunfermline ;—Dunbar ;—and, Lanark ; to lie upon the Table.

PUBLIC HEALTH ACTS AMENDMENT BILL.

Petitions in favour;—From Wolverhampton ; —Willenhall ; —Warrington ; —and, Walsall ; to lie upon the Table.

SALE OF INTOXICATING LIQUORS ON SUNDAY BILL.

Petitions in favour ;—From Walton ; — Slymbridge ; — Bedford (five) ; — Wane ; — Spennymoor (five) ; — Uley ; Great Moulton ; — Penzance ; — Wilton ; — Salisbury (thirteen) ; — Fisherton ; — Broadchalke ; — Sadberge ;—Sacriston ; — New Harrington ; — Rookhope ; — Quebec and Hamsteels ; —Ouston ; — Windy Nook ; — Bearpark ; — Todhills ; — Wrekenton ; — Swalwell ; — Westgate ; — Stockton ; —Quarrington Hill ; — Wearhead ; — Blaydon ; — Gainford ; — Binchester ; —Tanfield Lea ; — Ryhope ; — Bowden Close ; — Broom Park (two) ; — Boldon ; — Cotherston ; — Hetton Downs ; —Hunwick ; — Shildon ; — Medomsley ; — Close House ; — Littletown ; — Easington Lane ; — New Seaham ; — Page Bank ; — South Durham ; — Jarrow ; — Wolviston ; — Tow Law ; — Sunderland (two) ; — Durham ; — Pelton Fell ; — Monkwearmouth ; — Birtley ; — New Washington ; — Croxdale ; —Tudhoe Colliery ; — West Hartlepool (two) ; — Brougham Hall ; — Kelloe ; — Wingate ; — Wheatley Hall ; — Castle Eden ; — Trimdon ; — Hartlepool (four) ; — Heighington ; — Willington ; — Darlington ; — Middleton ; —Murton ; — Waterhouses ; — Cornsay (two) ; — Stockton-on-Tees ; — Stainton ; — Evenwood , — Edmonsley ; — Middleton-in-Teesdale ; — Byers Green ; —Langley Moor ; —Ferryhill (two) ; New Brancepeth ; — Coundon ; — West Cornforth ; — Bradbury ; — Brandon ; —Seaham Harbour ; — Lezant ; — and, Westow Hill ; to lie upon the Table.

RETURNS, REPORTS, ETC.

WAR OFFICE.

Paper [presented 16th March] to be printed. (No. 113.)

INDUSTRIAL SCHOOLS (IRELAND) (CIRCULARS).

Return [presented 16th March] to be printed. (No. 114.)

NAVY (VICTUALLING YARD MANUFACTURING ACCOUNTS, 1897-8).

Annual Accounts presented,—of the Cost of Manufacturing, Provisions, Victualling Stores, etc., at the Home Victualling Yards and Malta Yard for 1897-8, etc., with the Report of the Comptroller and Auditor-General thereon (by Act) ; to lie upon the Table, and to be printed. (No. 115.)

UNIVERSITY OF LONDON COMMISSIONERS (NOTIFICATION OF APPOINTMENT).

Copy presented,—of Notification of the Appointment, on the 10th March 1899, of Mr. Thomas Barlow, M.D., F.R.C.P., to fill a vacancy in the body of Commissioners for the University of London, caused by the resignation of Sir William Roberts, M.D. (by Act) ; to lie upon the Table.

RAILWAY, ETC., BILLS.

Copy ordered—

" Of Report by the Board of Trade upon all the Railway, Canal, Tramway, Harbour, and Tidal Waters, Gas, Electricity, and Water Bills, and Provisional Orders, of Session 1899." —(Mr. Ritchie.)

Copy presented accordingly ; to lie upon the Table, and to be printed. (No. 116.)

POST OFFICE (SUB-POSTMASTERSHIPS HELD BY TRADERS).

Return ordered—

" Showing the number of Sub-Postmasterships held by private Traders in which the Salaries and Emoluments exceed £80 per year."—(Mr. Steadman.)

DEER FORESTS, HIGHLAND CROFTING COUNTIES (ARGYLLSHIRE, INVER-NESS-CHIRE, ROSS AND CROMARTY, SUTHERLAND, CAITHNESS, AND ORKNEY AND SHETLAND.

Return ordered—

"Giving the name of each Deer Forest in the six Highland Crofting Counties, amount of its assessment, and the increase or decrease in the acreage of each Forest as compared with 1883."—(*Mr. Weir.*)

CARDIFF RAILWAY BILL.

Reported; Report to lie upon the Table, and to be printed.

NUNEATON AND CHILVERS COTON URBAN DISTRICT COUNCIL WATER BILL.

Reported; Report to lie upon the Table, and to be printed.

PRIVATE BILLS (GROUP A).

Mr. Baldwin reported from the Committee on Group A of Private Bills, That the parties promoting the Horsforth Water Bill had stated that the evidence of E. A. Riley, Land Agent, Horsforth, near Leeds, was essential to their case; and it having been proved that his attendance could not be procured without the intervention of the House, he had been instructed to move that the said E. A. Riley do attend the said Committee upon Tuesday next, at half-past Eleven of the clock, and for as long as the said Bill shall be under the consideration of the Committee.

Ordered, That E. A. Riley do attend the Committee on Group A of Private Bills upon Tuesday next, at half-past Eleven of the clock, and for as long as the said Bill shall be under the consideration of the Committee.

PRIVATE BILLS (GROUP A).

Mr. Baldwin reported from the Committee on Group A of Private Bills, That the parties promoting the Horsforth Urban District Council (Water) Bill had stated that the evidence of Alfred Tomalin, Outfitter, of Nowlay Wood, Horsforth; of Timothy Newby, Fish Mer-

chant, of Newlay Wood, Horsforth; of John Henry Wilkinson, Insurance Manager, of Villa Rosa, Calverley Lane, Horsforth; of Walter Nathaniel Walker, of Bank House, Horsforth; of Henry Doughty, Farmer, of White House Farm, Far Headingley, near Leeds; of John Nightingale, Surgeon, of Horsforth; and of George Robinson, Book-keeper, of Leeds, was essential to their case; and it having been proved that their attendance could not be procured without the intervention of the House, he had been instructed to move that the said Alfred Tomalin, Timothy Nawby, John Henry Wilkinson, Walter Nathaniel Walker, Henry Doughty, John Nightingale, and George Robinson do attend the said Committee upon Tuesday next, at half-past Eleven of the clock, and for as long as the said Bill shall be under the consideration of the Committee, and that the said John Nightingale do produce his books, papers, and memoranda whist Medical Officer to the Horsforth Urban District Council.

Ordered, That Alfred Tomalin, Timothy Newby, John Henry Wilkinson, Walter Nathaniel Walker, Henry Doughty, John Nightingale, and George Robinson do attend the Committee on Group A of Private Bills upon Tuesday next, at half-past Eleven of the clock, and for as long as the said Bill shall be under the consideration of the Committee, and that the said John Nightingale do produce the documents aforesaid.

LANCASHIRE AND YORKSHIRE RAILWAY (NEW RAILWAYS) BILL.

Reported, with Amendments; Report to lie upon the Table, and to be printed.

RAILWAY BILLS (GROUP 1).

Mr. Hobhouse reported from the Committee on Group 1 of Railway Bills, That the parties promoting the Leicester, Groby, and Bradgate Park Railway Bill had stated that the evidence of Frederick Griffiths, of the Town Hall, Leicester, was essential to their case; and it having been proved that his attendance could not be procured without the intervention of the House, he had been instructed to move that the said Frederick Griffiths do attend the said Committee upon Monday next, the 20th March, at Twelve of the clock.

Ordered, That Frederick Griffiths do attend the Committee on Group 1 of Railway Bills upon Monday next, at Twelve of the clock.

NEW BILLS.

WATERMEN'S CERTIFICATES BILL.

"To grant Certificates to Watermen," presented, and read the first time ; to be read a second time upon Monday 15th May, and to be printed. (Bill 130.)

EMPLOYERS AND WORKMEN LAW AMENDMENT BILL.

"To amend the Law relating to the employment of Waiters and Waitresses," presented, and read the first time ; to be read a second time upon Monday 29th May, and to be printed. (Bill 131.)

OLD AGE PENSIONS (FRIENDLY SOCIETIES) BILL.

"To provide for the payment of Old Age Pensions to members of Friendly Societies," presented, and read the first time ; to be read a second time upon Wednesday next, and to be printed. (Bill 132.)

HIGHWAYS AND BRIDGES ACT (1891) AMENDMENT BILL.

"To amend the Highways and Bridges Act, 1891," presented, and read the first time ; to be read a second time upon Wednesday next, and to be printed. (Bill 133.)

QUESTIONS.

FREIGHT RATES ON THE CORK AND BANDON RAILWAY.

MR. GILHOOLY (Cork Co., W.): I beg to ask the President of the Board of Trade whether his attention has been called to the rates for freight on the Cork and Bandon Railway between Bantry and Skibbereen and between Bantry and Dunmanway ; whether he is aware that a Bantry merchant has offered a guarantee to the Cork and Bandon Railway Company to treble the goods traffic between the towns above mentioned provided a reasonable freight be accepted ; and whether, considering that a baronial guarantee is in existence on a portion of the railway line between Bantry and Skibbereen and Dunmanway, he will take steps to compel the Railway Company to accept a reasonable freight, and thereby increase their traffic and relieve the cesspayers of their liability?

THE PRESIDENT OF THE BOARD OF TRADE (Mr. C. T. RITCHIE, Croydon):. The Board of Trade have a complaint: before them as regards certain rates charged by this railway company, and they are dealing with the case under section 31 of the Railway and Canal Traffic Act, 1888. The Board have no power to compel companies to accept rates. Railway companies are entitled to fix their rates within the maximum powers given them by Parliament.

DISTILLERY WORKMEN.

SIR W. LAWSON (Cumberland, Cockermouth): I beg to ask the Secretary to the Treasury whether the whisky which the Board of Inland Revenue permits to be supplied to the workmen in distilleries by their employers is so supplied duty free?

THE FINANCIAL SECRETARY TO THE TREASURY (Mr. R. W. HANBURY, Preston): Yes, Sir.

SIR W. LAWSON: Can the right honourable Gentleman say how much whisky is thus supplied duty free?

MR. HANBURY: No, Sir; I have not the information here.

NAVAL CHAPLAINS.

Mr. CARVELL WILLIAMS (Notts., Mansfield): I beg to ask the Secretary to the Admiralty if he will state to what religious denominations the chaplains to the Royal Navy severally belong; naming the total belonging to each denomination?

THE SECRETARY TO THE ADMIRALTY (Mr. W. E. MACARTNEY, Antrim, S.): There are 106 chaplains of the Church of England in the Royal Navy, and also two Roman Catholic chaplains employed at Portsmouth and Devonport. In addition to the above there are three Church of England, 18 Roman Catholic, seven Wesleyan, and four Presbyterian clergymen, who receive fixed annual allowances, but are not designated chaplains. Various other allowances, based on a capitation scale, are made to clergy of the Church of England and Episcopal Churches of Ireland and Scotland, to Roman Catholic clergymen, and to Wesleyan, Presbyterian, Baptist, and Congregationalist ministers for spiritual ministrations to officers and men of the Navy. Such services are more or less of a casual nature, and the number of clergymen receiving these allowances necessarily fluctuates.

CORK CORPORATION BY-LAWS.

Mr. W. JOHNSTON (Belfast, S.): I beg to ask the Chief Secretary to the Lord Lieutenant of Ireland whether he is aware that the Local Government Board advised the town clerk of Cork that the by-laws of the old Corporation would remain in force till rescinded, but that the Mayor of Cork subsequently declared that all the old rules and by-laws were swept away by the Local Government Act; whether the Council exceeded their powers by expending certain sums of money belonging to the ratepayers; whether the town clerk was prevented from answering certain questions put to him by Sir John Scott, ex-Mayor of Cork, concerning the correspondence with the Local Government Board; and whether the Local Government Board will take any action in consequence of the conduct of the Cork Council?

THE CHIEF SECRETARY TO THE LORD LIEUTENANT OF IRELAND (Mr. GERALD W. BALFOUR, Leeds, Central): The Local Government Board are in communication with the town clerk of Cork in reference to this Question, and if my honourable Friend will repeat it on Tuesday next, I hope to be in a position to give him a reply.

CAPTAIN DONELAN (Cork County, N.E.): Will the Mayor of Cork, who is also a Member of this House, be communicated with in reference to this matter?

Mr. GERALD BALFOUR: I can hardly say until I get the Report.

ROSCOMMON LOCAL GOVERNMENT ELECTIONS.

Mr. DILLON (Mayo, E.): I beg to ask the Chief Secretary to the Lord Lieutenant of Ireland whether he is aware that in the county division of Ballaghaderrin and Edmondstown, in County Roscommon, only two polling stations have been arranged for 1,405 voters, and that these have been so fixed that some voters will be obliged to travel nearly 10 miles to record their votes; and whether he will use his influence to secure the appointment of two more polling stations in this district?

Mr. GERALD BALFOUR: The honourable Member's suggestion will be communicated to the Returning Officer for his consideration.

SOLDIERS' WIDOWS' PENSIONS.

Mr. TREVELYAN (York, W.R., Elland): On behalf of the honourable Member for North Manchester I beg to ask the Under Secretary of State for War whether his attention has been directed to the case of the widow of Samuel Mulholland, once a trooper in the 5th Dragoon Guards, who retired in 1873 on a pension of 8d. a day; whether he is aware that Mrs. Mulholland, on the death of her husband at Manchester last year, applied to the Patriotic Fund for the Widows and Orphans of Soldiers who served in the Russian War, and was refused relief on the plea that 450 widows stand before her on the list of candidates for relief in order of date of marriage, although Mrs. Mulholland married her late husband in 1853 (27th March), and is now 70 years of age; and, considering that the Patriotic Fund has accumulated funds, by last return amounting to about three-quarters of a million sterling, he can do anything for this widow?

THE FINANCIAL SECRETARY TO THE WAR OFFICE (Mr. J. POWELL WILLIAMS, Birmingham, S.): The widow referred to would not be entitled to receive assistance from the Patriotic Fund under the terms of the original trust, inasmuch as that fund was subscribed for the benefit of widows and other dependents of soldiers and sailors who fell in the Crimea Campaign, or who died of wounds or disease consequent upon service in that campaign. In 1897, under a Supplementary Commission, surplus moneys of the Patriotic Fund were placed in a new general fund, to be appropriated to the widows of all men, without restriction, who had served in the Crimea Campaign. No less than 1,400 of such widows applied for relief from the new general fund, but only 400 could be granted life annuities out of the funds available. It is the case that there are 450 applicants senior to Mrs. Mulholland on the list, and some of them were married as far back as 1829.

ISLAND OF LEWIS FISHERIES.

MR. WEIR (Ross and Cromarty): I beg to ask the Lord Advocate, having regard to the fact that the Atlantic sea-board of the Island of Lewis is not included in the limits of the North Sea Convention, 1882, will he state whether the Secretary for Scotland has yet decided to consider the advisability of amending the tenth section of the Sea Fisheries Regulations (Scotland) Act, 1895, so that it may be unnecessary to obtain the sanction of the States Signatories of the Convention in regard to the making of by-laws rendering beam and otter trawling illegal within 13 miles of those parts of the Scottish coasts which are not included in the limits of the North Sea?

THE LORD ADVOCATE (Mr. A. GRAHAM MURRAY, Buteshire): The Government have no intention of proposing legislation in the direction indicated in the Question of the honourable Member at the present time.

MR. WEIR: Is the right honourable Gentleman aware that a similar answer was given a year ago?

MR. GRAHAM MURRAY: Yes, Sir. I am perfectly aware of that fact.

FISHERY BOARD CRUISER "BRENDA."

MR. WEIR: I beg to ask the Lord Advocate whether it has been found practicable to render the Fishery Board cruiser "Brenda" again fit for service; and, if so, at what cost; and will he state how the duties of the "Brenda" are now provided for, and by what date she will again be ready for sea?

MR. GRAHAM MURRAY: I am informed by the Fishery Board that it has been found practicable to render the "Brenda" again fit for service, but it is not yet known at what cost. There is no other vessel to take her place at the Board's disposal, but they expect the "Brenda" will resume duty in four or five weeks.

CATTLE MARKET RETURNS.

MR. WEIR: I beg to ask the President of the Board of Agriculture whether he has yet been able to arrange for the official Returns of prices received under the Markets and Fairs (Weighing of Cattle) Act, 1891, to be published weekly instead of quarterly?

THE PRESIDENT OF THE BOARD OF AGRICULTURE (Mr. W. LONG, Liverpool, West Derby): The suggestion of the honourable Member has not been lost sight of, but for the reasons which I explained last year, we do not feel able to give effect to it at the present time.

POULTRY BREEDING IN SCOTLAND.

MR. WEIR: I beg to ask the Lord Advocate if he will state what steps have been taken by the Congested Districts Board to encourage and improve the breed of poultry in the congested areas?

MR. GRAHAM MURRAY: I am informed by the Congested Districts Board that the subject referred to by the honourable Member was recently considered by a Committee of the Board with the view to distributing eggs of suitable breeds of poultry in certain selected districts. If the honourable Member will repeat his Question after the Easter Recess, it will be possible to give more definite information.

MOY AND CHARLEMONT PETTY SESSIONS CLERKS.

MR. MACALEESE (Monaghan, N.): I beg to ask the Chief Secretary to the Lord Lieutenant of Ireland if, notwithstanding section 7 of the Petty Sessions Clerks Act, which provides that a vacancy in the office of petty sessions clerk serving two districts shall be filled by one person, the Government propose to sanction the appointment of two clerks for Moy and Charlemont districts previously held by one person; and, if so, why is the statute to be contravened?

MR. GERALD BALFOUR: The provisions of section 7 of the Act referred to are applicable only to two or more petty sessional districts which have been amalgamated under section 6 of the Act. Where such an amalgamation exists the districts are served by one and the same clerk of petty sessions. But the districts mentioned in the Question have not been amalgamated, nor is it legally possible to do so, inasmuch as they are in different counties. There is consequently no contravention of the provisions of the Act. It is, of course, in the power of the justices of the districts of Moy and Charlemont to elect the same person to fill the office of clerk for each district.

COUNTERVAILING SUGAR DUTIES IN INDIA.

MR. McKENNA (Monmouth, N.): I beg to ask the Secretary of State for India whether the proposal of the Indian Government to impose countervailing import duties on bounty-fed sugar is made with a view to stimulating the Indian sugar refining industry; and whether the bulk of coarse unrefined sugar now exported from India is refined in England?

THE SECRETARY OF STATE FOR INDIA (Lord GEORGE HAMILTON, Middlesex, Ealing): · The honourable Gentleman asks me what is the object of the Indian Government in imposing countervailing duties in India upon bounty-fed sugar. The object is to prevent a vast indigenous trade in India, based on free enterprise and industry, from being undermined by the subsidised products of foreign countries. The average yearly export of unrefined sugar from India for the past three years was 45,000 tons a year, of which about three-fourths are consigned to the United Kingdom. I have not precise information, but I understand that this Indian sugar is used in the United Kingdom partly by refineries, partly by breweries, and partly for fattening cattle.

SIR H. FOWLER (Wolverhampton, E.): I wish to ask the noble Lord if it is convenient for him to answer the Question now, whether he will postpone his decision as to allowing or disallowing any Act which may be passed by the Legislative Council in reference to the countervailing duties until the papers, including the reports of the Debates in the Legislative Council, be laid on the Table of the House?

THE SECRETARY OF STATE FOR INDIA: If I am in order in answering the Question, perhaps I may be permitted to state what the law is as regards Bills which have passed their final stage through the Indian Legislative Councils. As soon as the Viceroy has given his assent to the Bill it at once comes into legal operation. It is then sent home to the Secretary of State, who can through the Crown intimate at any time afterwards his disapproval of the Act, in which case it ceases to be law. It is the practice, but not legally necessary, for the Secretary of State to officially intimate his intention to leave the Act to its operation. If it be the wish of the right honourable Gentleman that I should abstain from publicly expressing my approval until there has been a discussion on this subject I am quite ready to act on the suggestion.

Mr. COURTNEY (Cornwall, Bodmin): Does the Bill contain within itself any clause fixing a time for it to come into operation?

The SECRETARY of STATE for INDIA: It will come into operation directly—on Monday.

Sir H. FOWLER: I presume the noble Lord will lay the Papers on the Table?

The SECRETARY of STATE for INDIA: As soon as I get the Bill I will take care that it and the correspondence in reference to it, as well as the Report of the Debate in the Legislative Council, shall be laid on the Table of the House.

SHANNON DEVELOPMENT COMPANY.

Mr. PATRICK O'BRIEN (Kilkenny): On behalf of the honourable Member for East Clare, I beg to ask the Chief Secretary to the Lord Lieutenant of Ireland whether his attention has been called to a resolution recently passed by the Grand Jury of the county of Clare, in which they state that, whereas they have already presented a sum of £625 in aid of the Shannon Development Company by way of subsidy, without receiving any tangible advantage in respect of the expenditure, and request that the Board of Works do establish a coach service between Scariff (in connection with the Shannon steamers) and Ennis (in connection with the West Clare Railway), from the months of April to October daily each way; and whether the request contained in this resolution can be granted?

Mr. GERALD BALFOUR: The request contained in the resolution referred to cannot be granted, as the entire amount made available under the Railways Act of 1896 has already been hypothecated.

VOL. LXVIII.   [Fourth Series.]

QUESTIONS ON FOREIGN AFFAIRS.

Mr. CUMMING MACDONA (Southwark, Rotherhithe): On behalf of the honourable Member for the Central Division of Sheffield I beg to ask the Under Secretary of State for Foreign Affairs if he is aware that the popularly elected Legislatures of other countries impose close restrictions upon Parliamentary interrogation upon Foreign Affairs and pending negotiations with other Governments; and whether, having regard to the international difficulties and misunderstandings which may be produced by public questionings without adequate consideration on matters in progress, the Secretary of State will consider the desirability of proposing a Standing Order providing that a Question upon Foreign Affairs shall not be put without six days' notice, and that if the Secretary of State for Foreign Affairs intimate in writing to the Speaker that a particular Question upon Foreign Affairs is prejudicial to the interests of the Empire, it shall be removed from the Order Book?

The UNDER SECRETARY of STATE for FOREIGN AFFAIRS (Mr. St. John Brodrick, Surrey, Guildford): I believe that very close restrictions are imposed in Foreign Legislatures on Parliamentary interrogations on Foreign Affairs. In this country greater latitude has been given, but the Government, while satisfied that the recent decision to demand notice of all Foreign Office Questions is necessary in the public interest, do not deem it necessary to ask the House for further restrictions.

CEYLON ORDINANCES.

Mr. WEIR: I beg to ask the Secretary of State for the Colonies whether he is aware that the Supreme Court of Ceylon, when dealing recently with several cases affecting the land, ruled that the acts of the Government agents in the administration of the Governor's Ordinance, No. 1 of 1897, were illegal and invalid; but that the Governor, Sir West Ridgway, instead of accepting this ruling, is endeavouring to enact an amending Ordinance affecting the rights and liberties of Her Majesty's subjects

2 Z

in the Colony; and if he will consider the expediency of taking such steps as may be necessary to prevent the amending Ordinance being passed into law?

THE SECRETARY OF STATE FOR THE COLONIES (Mr. J. CHAMBERLAIN, Birmingham, W.): The Supreme Court of Ceylon held that certain proceedings of the Government agents under the Ordinance, No. 1 of 1897, did not comply with the provisions of the Ordinance and were consequently invalid. As to the amending Ordinance, I may refer the honourable Member to my answer to the Question of the Member for North Manchester on the 10th instant.

CROFTERS AND THE DOG TAX.

MR. WEIR: I beg to ask the Secretary to the Treasury if he will state under what section of the Customs and Inland Revenue Act, 1878, officers of the Board of Inland Revenue, when applied to by a crofter for a certificate of exemption from dog tax for a dog used on a croft, are entitled to determine on the qualities of the dog for its work; do these officers apply any, and, if any, what tests as to the capabilities of the animal; and will he direct that the judgment and declaration of the crofter that the dog is of service in tending sheep or cattle on the croft shall be accepted as a sufficient guarantee?

MR. HANBURY: The right to exemption is dependent under section 22 of the Act upon the question whether the dog is kept and used solely for " the purpose of tending sheep or cattle on a farm." This is a question of fact upon which the Board of Inland Revenue are bound to form the best opinion they can, founded upon a Report from their officers upon the circumstances of each case. They would not be justified in granting a certificate of exemption upon the mere statement of the dog owner.

LEAD POISONING AT THE ENFIELD FACTORY.

MR. WEIR: I beg to ask the Under Secretary of State for War whether he is aware that Charles George Bassett, who contracted lead poisoning while employed at the Royal Small Arms Fac-

tory at Enfield, and who was discharged for absenting himself from duty while suffering from illness on the 1st November, was examined by two civilian medical officers, Dr. Ridge and Dr. Burns, of Enfield, in December last, and pronounced to be still suffering from the effects of lead poisoning; and will he, in view of this testimony, reconsider Bassett's case?

MR. POWELL WILLIAMS: The honourable Member does not appear to be aware that, since the date of the certificates to which he refers, Bassett has been specifically examined by three medical men, who certify that there are now no evidences of lead poisoning present in his case, and that he is fit for the light work to which he was put, and at which he could earn good wages, but which he refused to do.

MR. WEIR: Was not this man, in the first instance, suffering from lead poisoning?

MR. POWELL WILIAMS: No doubt he was. He was upon recovery put to light work, which the medical man certified he was fit for. He refused to do it, and in consequence lost his situation.

MR. WEIR: Will the honourable Gentleman arrange for a further examination of this man?

MR. POWELL WILLIAMS: He has already been examined by three medical men within the last fortnight, with the result I have given the House.

MR. WEIR: Will he be allowed to return to his job?

MR. POWELL WILLIAMS: I think if he made application to be allowed to return to the job which he refused the Secretary of State would be prepared to let him resume work.

GOVERNMENT GRANTS FOR LOCAL EXPENDITURE.

MR. GIBSON BOWLES (Lynn Regis): I beg to ask the President of the Board of Trade whether he can explain how the sum of £11,464,569, which is stated on page 47 of the Statistical Abstract for the United Kingdom, 1883 to 1897 (under the head of receipts for the purposes of local expenditure in the United Kingdom for the year 1895-6) to be Government contributions for that year, was arrived at; whether he will state in detail the items of which that sum is composed; and whether he will give the reference to the sources of information whence his Department extracted the items in question?

THE PRESIDENT OF THE BOARD OF TRADE: As in previous years, the total is mainly based on the Local Taxation Returns for England, Scotland and Ireland. A list of the items and the sources from whence they are extracted would be too lengthy to read to the House, but they are at the disposal of the honourable Member if he asks to see them.

CLIFDEN PETTY SESSIONS CLERK.

MR. O'MALLEY (Galway, Connemara): I beg to ask Mr. Attorney-General for Ireland whether he is aware of the proceedings of Mr. Hazell, Petty Sessions Clerk of Clifden, who, when canvassing his tenants and others over whom he is agent, on behalf of Mr. Henry Robinson, J.P., candidate for the County Council of Galway, has informed them that he will be present in the booth and will see how those of them who are illiterate will record their votes; and whether he will take steps for the protection of those electors?

THE ATTORNEY-GENERAL FOR IRELAND (Mr. ATKINSON, Londonderry, N.): I informed the honourable Member yesterday that the attention of Mr. Hazell, Petty Sessions Clerk of Carna (not Clifden), had been directed to this matter, and that he had undertaken to take no further part in the election in question. No further action on my part is called for unless Mr. Hazell again violates the Rules of the Department.

MALLOW UNION.

MR. ABRAHAM (Cork Co., N.E.): I beg to ask the Chief Secretary to the Lord Lieutenant of Ireland whether he can state on what date the sworn Inquiry (already consented to by the Local Government Board) will be held at the Mallow Union, and the name of the gentleman who will preside; if he is aware that much local interest is taken by the ratepayers and the public in the matters to be inquired into; and whether representatives of the Press will be permitted to be present, so that those concerned may be able to see a full report of the proceedings?

MR. GERALD BALFOUR: The inquiry referred to will be held by Mr. Lynch Staunton, one of the Board's inspectors, and the Board will communicate with him as to the date upon which he can arrange to open it. I believe the fact is as stated in the second paragraph. The question whether representatives of the Press shall be admitted to these Inquiries is one which is invariably left to the discretion of the inspector holding the Inquiry, though, as a matter of fact, it is not the practice to exclude the Press except in very exceptional circumstances.

MR. ABRAHAM (Cork Co., N.E.): Will the right honourable Gentleman suggest to the inspector that the Press should be admitted.

MR. GERALD BALFOUR: No, Sir. This must be left to the discretion of the inspector.

CEYLON.

MR. SCHWANN (Manchester, N.): I beg to ask the Secretary of State for the Colonies whether his attention has been drawn to a statement made by Mr. Justice Lawrie at the Colombo Criminal Sessions on 24th January 1899, as to the issue of circulars by the Colonial Secretary of Ceylon to magistrates and others, which the Judge held to be more often than not irregular and illegal; and whether he will take measures to prevent interference of the executive of the Government of Ceylon with the judicial establishment of the island and the working of its criminal code?

THE SECRETARY OF STATE FOR THE COLONIES: I have seen the report of the statement made by Mr. Justice Lawrie, but have no information beyond it. The Governor of Ceylon will shortly be in this country, and I will make inquiry from him on the subject.

MR. SCHWANN: I beg to ask the Secretary of State for the Colonies whether the Draft Ordinance printed in the "Ceylon Government Gazette" of 18th November 1898, and proposed as an amendment of the Ceylon Ordinance No. 1, 1897, has yet been submitted to Her Majesty's Government for approval; and whether, before the amending Ordinance receives the Royal sanction, it will be referred to the Law Officers of the Crown for their opinion?

THE SECRETARY OF STATE FOR THE COLONIES: The answer to the first question is "Yes"; and to the second that, as at present advised, I do not anticipate that it will be necessary to refer the Ordinance to the Law Officers.

SALISBURY PLAIN.

MR. BAYLEY (Derbyshire, Chesterfield): I beg to ask the Under Secretary of State for War when the Return, ordered by the House on the 21st February, of further information on the purchase of land on Salisbury Plain by the Government, will be in the hands of Members?

THE UNDER SECRETARY OF STATE FOR WAR (Mr. G. WYNDHAM, Dover): The Return involves the collection of many details, and, therefore, requires time for completion. It is hoped, however, that it will be ready shortly.

MR. BAYLEY: Shall we have it before Easter?

MR. WYNDHAM: I have telegraphed to the agents, asking them to expedite matters. I should think the Return will be ready in 10 days or a fortnight.

AUTOMATIC COUPLINGS.

MR. MADDISON (Sheffield, Brightside): I beg to ask the President of the Board of Trade if he has stated to a deputation representing private waggon owners that he is willing to omit the clauses dealing with automatic couplings from the Railway Regulation Bill; and

whether it is still his intention to proceed with the Bill in its present form?

THE PRESIDENT OF THE BOARD OF TRADE: No, Sir, I did not say to the deputation that these clauses would be omitted, but that the matter would receive consideration. The suggestion made at the deputation was that a Bill omitting the clauses dealing with automatic couplings and confined to the other safety appliances should be passed, and that an inquiry should without delay be instituted into the disputed points connected with automatic couplings. This suggestion I promised should be considered.

MR. COGHILL (Stoke-upon-Trent): Is the right honourable Gentleman aware that the number of accidents in coupling operations in 1897 was 19 on British railways and 214 on American lines?

MR. SPEAKER: Order, order! Notice should be given of that Question.

COST OF PRIVATE BILL LEGISLATION.

MR. D. A. THOMAS (Merthyr Tydvil): I beg to ask the Secretary of State for the Home Department if he can state the amount of expenses incurred by local authorities and railway and other companies in promoting and opposing Private Bills before Parliament for each year from 1892 to 1898, both inclusive, for England, Scotland, Ireland, and Wales (including Monmouthshire) respectively; whether, before the Second Reading of the Private Legislation Procedure (Scotland) Bill is taken, he will give a Return (in continuation of Parliamentary Paper, No. 98, of Session 1893-4); and if he can state whether any material change has taken place since that Return was issued in the proportionate cost of Welsh Private Bill Legislation relatively to that of Scotland?

THE UNDER SECRETARY OF STATE FOR THE HOME DEPARTMENT (Mr. J. COLLINGS, Birmingham, Bordesley): The Secretary of State is unable to give the information asked for in the first and third paragraphs in the absence of a Return on the subject for the years mentioned for the whole kingdom. He will, however, consider whether such a Return can be granted; but it could not, of course, be made even for Wales before the Second Reading of the Private Legislation Procedure (Scotland) Bill.

In answer to a further Question, which was quite inaudible,

MR. COLLINGS said the Return would take months to prepare.

the first paragraph. The reply to the second paragraph is in the affirmative; no complaint has been made that the public are inconvenienced by the transaction of petty sessions business in the office of the Gas Company. He has been permitted to do so by the magistrates. As regards the third paragraph, Mr. Barratt, the clerk of petty sessions, denies he has taken part at any election on behalf of either of the candidates for the county councillorship of Holywood.

HOLYWOOD PETTY SESSIONS CLERK.

MR. MACALEESE: I beg to ask the Chief Secretary to the Lord Lieutenant of Ireland whether, having regard to the fact that Mr. Barratt holds the position of petty sessions clerk for the districts of Holywood, Bangor, and Newtownbreda, which are widely apart; the position of secretary to the School Board Committee of Holywood; the position of clerk of the Holywood Gas Company, which is a private company, and other positions in the town of Holywood, it is consistent with his duties of petty sessions clerk to hold the office of town clerk, in view of section 35 of the Petty Sessions Act, 14 and 15 Vic. c. 90, and sub-section 2 of section 8 of the Petty Sessions Clerk Act, 21 and 22 Vic. c. 100, or to identify himself with local Party business; whether he is aware that Mr. Barratt holds the office of petty sessions clerk in the private office of the Holywood Gas Company, which is a private company; and, if so, is it consistent with the rules with regard to this office; whether he is also aware that Mr. Barratt has identified himself with the candidature of Sir Daniel Dixon, a candidate for the position of county councillor for the Holywood division of the county of Down, and whether any, and what, steps will be taken to prevent a recurrence of the matters complained of; and whether any, and what, steps, will be taken in connection with the intended application of Mr. Barratt for the position of the town clerk of Holywood?

MR. GERALD BALFOUR: A clerk of petty sessions is not prohibited either by statute or departmental rule from holding the appointments specified in

BIGAMY TRIAL AT THE CORK ASSIZES.

MR. T. M. HEALY (Louth, N.): I beg to ask the Chief Secretary to the Lord Lieutenant of Ireland. is he aware that the policeman convicted of bigamy at the last Cork Assizes and sentenced severely by Mr. Justice Kenny, was released in a fortnight; also, that the soldier convicted of bigamy at a previous Cork Assizes and sentenced by Mr. Justice O'Brien, was released within a week; and, are such remissions of sentences usual?

MR. GERALD BALFOUR: I am informed that Constable Quane was convicted of bigamy at the last Cork Winter Assizes, and sentenced by Mr. Justice Kenny to 15 months' imprisonment. Acting on the recommendation of the learned Judge, the Lord Lieutenant ordered the discharge from prison of Quane when he had served one month of his sentence. The prisoner, I understand, had been four months in prison before the Assizes awaiting his trial. His conviction resulted also in his dismissal from the Constabulary Force, in which he had completed 24 years' service, and the loss of a pension to which another year's service would have entitled him. The soldier convicted of bigamy at a previous Assizes at Cork was released on the recommendation of Mr. Justice O'Brien. I am not in a position to say to what extent similar remissions of sentences have occurred, but of course every case is considered on its merits.

RENTS IN EAST LONDON.

MR. STEADMAN (Tower Hamlets, Stepney): I beg to ask the First Lord of the Treasury whether he is aware of the increase of rents in London, amounting in some cases to 30 and 40 per cent.; if his attention has been drawn to the practice of extracting key money on the renewal of tenancies prevailing in the poorer districts; and whether he is prepared to consider the feasibility of appointing a Select Committee to consider the whole question?

THE FIRST LORD OF THE TREASURY (Mr. A. J. BALFOUR, Manchester, E.): I have no information on the point with respect to which the honourable Gentleman asks me the Question, nor have I any means of obtaining it. In any case I do not think it is a subject with which the Government could interfere.

MR. STEADMAN: Then am I to understand that the landlords in East London are to rob workmen——

MR. SPEAKER: Order, order!

WEST INDIAN COLONIES.

MR. CUMMING MACDONA: On behalf of the Member for Central Sheffield, I beg to ask the Secretary of State for the Colonies if he can give any information to the House with respect to the effect of the pecuniary assistance granted last Session by the House of Commons to certain of the West Indian Colonies, and more especially as to the rehabilitation of the sugar industry on which they are so largely dependent; and what hopes he can hold out of the early termination of foreign bounties upon beet sugar?

THE SECRETARY OF STATE FOR THE COLONIES: It is not possible for me to answer the first Question within the limits of a Question, but I may say generally that the sums granted have been, and are being, expended in accordance with my statement made upon the Vote. I am not in a position to express any definite opinion as to the prospect of an early termination of the bounties.

MR. MACLEAN (Cardiff): With regard to that answer, may I ask the right honourable Gentleman whether he agrees with the opinion expressed yesterday by the Under Secretary for the Colonies on this question of the taxation of beet sugar?

MR. SPEAKER: Order, order! A Question stating that an opinion has been expressed by someone else and asking the right honourable Gentleman whether he agrees with it is out of order. If the honourable Gentleman will frame his Question differently and put it on the Paper, possibly he will be able to obtain the information he desires.

MR. MACLEAN: Perhaps I used the wrong word. It should not have been opinion, but policy.

WHITE ESTATE, BANTRY.

MR. GILHOOLY: I beg to ask the Chief Secretary to the Lord Lieutenant of Ireland whether, in view of the decision that Doctor Bird, J.P. (brother to Mr. William S. Bird, J.P., Receiver on the White Estate, near Bantry), is entitled to have the lands of Beach considered (for the purpose of sale) an agricultural holding, and that a valuation of them has been ordered, the land will be disposed of to Doctor Bird before the other tenants on the White Estate, who have already sent in proposals to purchase their holdings, will get an opportunity of doing so?

MR. GERALD BALFOUR: I am informed by the Registrar of the Land Judge's Court that all persons interested in the estate consented to Doctor Bird's holding being put into a separate lot for the purpose of a sale. As regards the other tenants, no such consent was given, and the question whether the 40th section will ever be applied, and when, depends on the exercise of the Court's discretion on facts not ascertained.

ALLOWANCES TO RURAL POSTMEN.

MR. STEADMAN: I beg to ask the Secretary to the Treasury, as representing the Postmaster-General, whether he is prepared to take into consideration the weekly allowance made for providing a horse and conveyance to do the work of rural postmen, with a view to its augmentation, considering that two stables are required, the wear and tear of harness is very great, and remounts have to be provided for?

MR. HANBURY: There is no fixed weekly allowance to rural postmen for providing a horse and cart. The amount of the allowance varies according to the circumstances. The price of forage in the neighbourhood, the cost of stabling, any private earnings from the carriage of passengers, or of parcels above the weight for which the Parcel Post is available, are all elements which affect the Question. The allowances also take some account of the necessity for replacing capital, with a view to obtaining remounts and to renewing harness, etc. If periodical relief to the horse is needed, special provision for such relief is made. The allowances are constantly under revision, and the Department endeavours to see that the postmen do not suffer loss in providing for the Post Office work. It is right to say that in a certain number of cases the postmen have, for reasons personal to themselves, applied for permission to use a horse and cart, although the post has been laid out as a foot post, and the work has been quite within the power of a man on foot. In some such cases no allowance for horse keep whatever is given; in others a small allowance-in-aid has been granted, in view of some slight improvement resulting to the service.

CONSTANTINOPLE RIOTS.

COLONEL DENNY (Kilmarnock Burghs): I beg to ask the Under Secretary of State for Foreign Affairs whether he is aware that the revised claims of British subjects resident in Constantinople for losses incurred by pillage and looting of their warehouses and premises during the Armenian massacres of August 1896 amount to £35,000, for which no indemnity has yet been received by the victims of these outrages, and that two at least of the claimants have had to succumb in consequence of the losses sustained, and that others are on the verge of bankruptcy; whether, since the British Government controls the Cyprus tribute, claims could be made good from

that fund; and would he state what steps have been taken to urge the justice of these claims upon the Sublime Porte for immediate settlement?

MR. BRODRICK: The amount of the British claims as sent in to the Porte is £32,980. The particulars of hardships mentioned have not been reported to the Foreign Office, but the long delay is regrettable. There would be difficulties in the way of obtaining a settlement by the method suggested in the second paragraph of the Question. Her Majesty's Government have concerted with other Powers as to securing payment, and Her Majesty's Ambassador has again brought the matter earnestly to the notice of the Turkish Foreign Minister in addition.

FOREIGN OFFICE QUESTIONS.

MR. D. A. THOMAS: I beg to ask the Under Secretary of State for Foreign Affairs, with reference to his statement that he was often forced in the House of Commons to observe a reticence which he would be glad to discard, whether there is any immediate prospect that the discretion allowed to his predecessors in the Foreign Office of replying to Supplementary Questions will be extended to himself; and whether he is aware of the grave inconvenience caused to honourable Members by reason of the Secretary for Foreign Affairs not being a Member of the House of Commons, and of the Under Secretary not being permitted to supplement his information?

MR. BRODRICK: I believe my observations at Cambridge were correctly reported, but they had reference to the general reticence imposed on the Foreign Office when important negotiations are proceeding, and not to Supplementary Questions. I have endeavoured in reply to Questions to supply the House with the fullest information in my power, and I am confident that all information has been given which could be afforded consistently with the interests of the public service.

MR. D. A. THOMAS: May I venture to point out that the right honourable Gentleman has not answered the last paragraph of the question?

MR. BRODRICK: I think my answer that the fullest possible information has been afforded to the House is an answer to the suggestion of the honourable Gentleman that grave inconvenience has been caused by Supplementary Questions not being answered.

WAIMA.

MR. BRYNMOR JONES (Swansea District): I beg to ask the Under Secretary of State for Foreign Affairs whether the legal aspects of the Waima incident are still under the consideration of the Foreign Office; and whether he is now in a position to give his conclusion on the matter; and, if not, when does he expect to be able to give his conclusion on the legal questions involved?

MR. BRODRICK: The legal questions involved are now before the Law Officers of the Crown. The delay in settlement is, as I have explained, not due to any want of insistence on the part of this country.

PETROLEUM LEGISLATION.

MR. DUNCOMBE (Cumberland, Egremont): I beg to ask the Under Secretary of State for the Home Department if he can state when the Government Bill dealing with the Report of the Royal Commission on Petroleum will be introduced?

MR. COLLINGS: The Government Bill on the subject will be introduced as soon after Easter as possible, but no precise date can be given.

INDIAN SUGAR BOUNTIES BILL.

MR. MACLEAN: I beg to ask the Secretary of State for India whether his attention has been called to a statement made yesterday by Lord Selborne, speaking on behalf of the Colonial Office, that, assuming countervailing duties to be expedient—

"it was idle for the West Indian sugar planters to contend that they had yet converted public opinion, as a whole, to their views, for many who supported the present Government would not accept the principle of countervailing

duties. It was no good of them living in a fool's paradise, and that was why he had laid stress on the fact that they could not deal with the Question unless they had public opinion entirely behind them";

and whether, in face of the declaration that the Colonial Secretary intends to bow to public opinion in this matter, he still means to persevere with the Indian Countervailing Duties Bill?

THE SECRETARY OF STATE FOR INDIA: My honourable Friend will observe that Lord Selborne's observations apply solely to the imposition of countervailing duties in this country. But he did not say (as the Question implies) that public opinion was against the imposition of countervailing duties in this country, but that public opinion, as a whole, was not yet on that side. The conditions surrounding the sugar trade in Great Britain are the reverse of those existing in India, and in India, where the countervailing duties are about to be imposed, public opinion is, I believe, unanimous in their favour.

MR. MACLEAN: I should like to ask the noble Lord if he really assumes that India is governed without any regard to the public opinion of the country?

MR. SPEAKER: Order, order! The honourable Member is trying to raise a Debate.

MR. MACLEAN: It is so difficult to raise a Debate in this House.

MR. BRYN ROBERTS (Carnarvonshire, Eifion): As the noble Lord has stated that the conditions in India are the reverse of those existing in this country, I desire to ask whether there is any difference between here and India excepting that the consumers are not represented there, while they are represented here?

MR. SPEAKER: Order, order! That Question is open to the same objection.

SIR W. LAWSON: I beg to ask the noble Lord how he arrives at the public opinion of India?

THE SECRETARY OF STATE FOR INDIA: Through the recognised channels of public opinion.

LONDON GOVERNMENT BILL.

SIR H. CAMPBELL-BANNERMAN (Stirling Burghs): Perhaps the right honourable Gentleman can now state what the definite course of public business next week will be?

THE FIRST LORD OF THE TREASURY: I have done my best to consider the appeal made to me by the right honourable Gentleman that the discussion upon the Second Reading of the London Government Bill should not begin at a period so late in our labours before Easter, as Monday week, which had been my original proposition. I feel the force of what the right honourable Gentleman said, especially as I learn from such sources of information as are open to me that it is possible, or even probable, that honourable Gentlemen opposite, and perhaps I ought to say honourable Gentlemen on both sides of the House, may desire more than two days for the discussion of the Bill. Under these circumstances, as I am afraid it is impossible, consistently with the due conduct of public business, to postpone the Second Reading until after Easter, there is no choice open to me but to ask the House to fix Tuesday for the beginning of the Debate, which will be continued on Thursday, and, if it be necessary, on the Monday. The Friday will be devoted to getting the Speaker out of the Chair on the Civil Service Estimates.

SIR H. CAMPBELL-BANNERMAN: The right honourable Gentleman will not be surprised to know that there will be considerable objection to the taking of Tuesday, and the sacrifice of another private Members' night. I would also say that there would be great inconvenience in the discussion of a Bill of this kind being taken piecemeal, and I would suggest that if the Debate is not finished on Thursday it might be continued on Friday instead of being postponed until Monday.

THE FIRST LORD OF THE TREASURY: As the House knows, I am unwilling to interfere with the Friday rule unless it is necessary. There is, of course, provision in the Standing Order for other business than Supply being taken on the Friday, and for that Motion being put and decided without Debate. No doubt there are reasons why it would be convenient to finish the Debate on Friday, and, if the appeal is made to me, I will gladly accede to it. In that case, Monday will be devoted to getting the Speaker out of the Chair.

DR. FARQUHARSON (Aberdeenshire, W.): Will the Private Bill Procedure (Scotland) Bill be taken before Easter?

THE FIRST LORD OF THE TREASURY: If honourable Gentlemen will co-operate with the Government, we might take it on the Tuesday before we separate.

SUSPENSION OF TWELVE O'CLOCK RULE.

Motion made, and Question put—

"That the Business of Supply, if under discussion at Twelve o'clock this night, be not interrupted under Standing Order Sittings of the House."—*(First Lord of the Treasury.)*

The House divided:—Ayes 159 ; Noes 96.—(Division List No. 46.)

AYES.

Aird, John
Allsopp, Hon. George
Arnold, Alfred
Arrol, Sir William
Atkinson, Rt. Hon. John
Bagot, Capt. Josceline FitzRoy
Baillie, James E. B. (Inverness)
Baldwin, Alfred
Balfour, Rt. Hn. A. J. (Manch'r)
Balfour, RtHnGeraldW. (Leeds)
Banbury, Frederick George
Barry, Sir Francis T. (Windsor)
Barton, Dunbar Plunket

Bathurst, Hn. Allen Benjamin
Beach, Rt. Hn. SirM.H. (Bristol)
Beckett, Ernest William
Bentinck, Lord Henry C.
Bethell, Commander
Bill, Charles
Blundell, Colonel Henry
Boulnois, Edmund
Bowles, Capt. H. F. (Middlesex
Bowles, T. Gibson (King's Lynn)
Brodrick, Rt. Hon. St. John
Carlile, William Walter
Cavendish, R. F. (N. Lancs.)

Cavendish, V. C. W. (Derbysh.)
Cecil, Evelyn (Hertford, East)
Chaloner, Capt. R. G W.
Chamberlain, Rt. Hn. J. (Birm.)
Chamberlain, J. Austen (Wor.)
Chaplin, Rt. Hon. Henry
Cochrane, Hon. Thos. H. A. E.
Coghill, Douglas Harry
Cohen, Benjamin Louis
Collings, Rt. Hon. Jesse
Colomb, Sir John Chas. Ready
Courtney, Rt. Hn. Leonard H.
Cripps, Charles Alfred

Cross, Herb. Shepherd (Bolton)
Cruddas, William Donaldson
Cubitt, Hon. Henry
Currie, Sir Donald
Curson, Viscount
Dalkeith, Earl of
Dalrymple, Sir Charles
Denny, Colonel
Dixon-Hartland, Sir F. Dixon
Douglas, Rt. Hon. A. Akers
Doxford, William Theodore
Duncombe, Hon. Hubert V.
Dyke, Rt.Hn.Sir William Hart
Elliot, Hon. A. Ralph Douglas
Fardell, Sir T. George
Fergusson, Rt HnSirJ.(Manc'r)
Finlay, Sir Robert Bannatyne
Fisher, William Hayes
FitzWygram, General Sir F.
Fletcher, Sir Henry
Folkestone, Viscount
Garfit, William
Giles, Charles Tyrrell
Goldsworthy, Major-General
Gordon, Hon. John Edward
Gorst, Rt. Hn. Sir John Eldon
Goschen, George J. (Sussex)
Graham, Henry Robert
Gray, Ernest (West Ham)
Green, Walford).(Wednesbury)
Greville, Hon. Ronald
Gull, Sir Cameron
Gunter, Colonel
Halsey, Thomas Frederick
Hamilton, Rt. Hn. Lord George
Hanbury, Rt. Hn. Robert Wm.
Hanson, Sir Reginald
Hardy, Laurence
Hare, Thomas Leigh
Heaton, John Henniker
Helder, Augustus
Hickman, Sir Alfred

Hill,Rt.Hn.A.Staveley(Staffs.)
Hobhouse, Henry
Howard, Joseph
Hozier,Hn. James Henry Cecil
Hubbard, Hon. Evelyn
Jeffreys, Arthur Frederick
Johnston, William (Belfast)
Jolliffe, Hon. H. George
Kemp, George
Lafone, Alfred
Lawrence,SirE.Durning-(Corn)
Leigh-Bennett, Henry Currie
Leighton, Stanley
Lockwood, Lt.-Col. A. R.
Long, Col Chas. W. (Evesham)
Long, Rt. Hn. Walter (L'pool)
Lorne, Marquess of
Lowles, John
Loyd, Archie Kirkman
Macartney, W. G. Ellison
Macdona, John Cumming
MacIver, David (Liverpool)
M'Iver, Sir Lewis (Edin., W.)
M'Killop, James
Malcolm, Ian
Maple, Sir John Blundell
Marks, Henry Hananel
Maxwell,Rt.Hu SirHerbertE.
Monk, Charles James
Moon, Edward Robert Pacy
More, Robt. Jasper (Shropsh.)
Morrell, George Herbert
Morton, Arthur H. A. (Deptf'd)
Mount, William George
Murray,RtHnA.Graham(Bute)
Murray, Charles J. (Coventry)
Nicol, Donald Ninian
Northcote, Hn. Sir H. Stafford
Orr-Ewing, Charles Lindsay
Pease, Herbert Pike (Drlngtn.)
Percy, Earl
Phillpotts, Captain Arthur

Pryce-Jones, Lt.-Col. Edward
Purvis, Robert
Rasch, Major Frederic Carne
Ritchie, Rt. Hn Chas.Thomson
Russell, Gen.F.S. (Cheltenham)
Russell, T. W. (Tyrone)
Ryder, John Herbert Dudley
Samuel, Harry S.(Limehouse)
Saunderson, Rt. Hn. Col. E. J.
Savory, Sir Joseph
Seely, Charles Hilton
Seton-Karr, Henry
Sharpe, William Edward T.
Simeon, Sir Barrington
Smith, Jas. Parker (Lanarks.)
Stanley,Hn.Arthur (Ormskirk)
Stanley, Edwd. Jas. (Somerset)
Stanley, Henry M.(Lambeth)
Stanley, Lord (Lancs.)
Stewart, Sir M. J. M'Taggart
Strutt, Hon. Charles Hedley
Thorburn, Walter
Thornton, Percy M.
Tritton, Charles Ernest
Valentia, Viscount
Ward, Hon. Robert A. (Crewe)
Webster, Sir R. E. (I. of W.)
Whitmore, Charles Algernon
Williams, Jos. Powell (Birm.)
Wilson, John (Falkirk)
Wilson-Todd,Wm. H (Yorks.)
Wodehouse, Rt.Hn.E.R.(Bath)
Wortley, Rt. Hn. C. B. Stuart-
Wylie, Alexander
Wyndham, George
Young, Commander (Berks,E.)

TELLERS FOR THE AYES—
  Sir William Walrond and
  Mr. Anstruther.

NOES.

Allen, W. (Newc.-under-Lyme)
Ashton, Thomas Gair
Asquith, Rt. Hn. Herbert H.
Austin, Sir John (Yorkshire)
Austin, M. (Limerick, W.)
Baker, Sir John
Bayley, Thomas (Derbyshire)
Blake, Edward
Bryce, Rt. Hon. James
Buchanan, Thomas Ryburn
Burt, Thomas
Buxton, Sydney Charles
Caldwell, James
Cameron, Sir Charles (Glasgow)
Cameron, Robert (Durham)
Campbell-Bannerman, Sir H.
Carew, James Laurence
Causton, Richard Knight
Clough, Walter Owen
Colville, John
Davies,M.Vaughan-(Cardigan)
Dilke, Rt. Hon. Sir Charles
Dillon, John
Donelan, Captain A.
Duckworth, James
Ellis, John Edward (Notts)

Ellis, Thos. Ed. (Merionethsh.)
Farquharson, Dr. Robert
Fenwick, Charles
Ferguson, R. C. Munro (Leith)
Foster, Sir Walter (Derby Co.)
Fowler, Rt. Hon. Sir Henry
Goddard, Daniel Ford
Gourley, Sir Edwd. Temperley
Haldane, Richard Burdon
Hammond, John (Carlow)
Hayne, Rt Hon. Charles Seale-
Hazell, Walter
Holland, Wm. H. (York, W.R.)
Humphreys-Owen, Arthur C.
Hutton, Alfred E. (Morley)
Jacoby, James Alfred
Jones, David Brynmor (S'nsea)
Kay-Shuttleworth,RtHnSirU.
Kinloch, Sir John Geo. Smyth
Lawson,SirWilfrid(Cumbrlnd.)
Leng, Sir John
Lowther, Rt. Hon. Jas. (Kent)
Macaleese, Daniel
MacNeill, John Gordon Swift
M'Kenna, Reginald
Maddison, Fred.

Moore, Arthur (Londonderry)
Morgan,J.Lloyd (Carmarthen
Morris, Samuel
Morton, Ed. J. C. (Devonport)
Nussey, Thomas Willans
O'Brien, James F. X. (Cork)
O'Brien, Patrick (Kilkenny)
O'Connor, Jas. (Wicklow, W.)
O'Connor, T. P. (Liverpool)
O'Kelly, James
Oldroyd, Mark
Palmer, Sir Chas. M. (Durham)
Philipps, John Wynford
Pickard, Benjamin
Pirie, Duncan V.
Price, Robert John
Reckitt, Harold James
Richardson, J. (Durham)
Roberts, John Bryn (Eifion)
Robertson, Edmund (Dundee)
Roche, Hn. James (East Kerry)
Samuel, J. (Stockton-on-Tees)
Schwann, Charles E.
Soames, Arthur Wellesley
Stanhope, Hon. Philip J.
Steadman, William Charles

Stevenson, Francis S.	Warner, Thomas Courtenay T.	Young, Samuel (Cavan, East)
Strachey, Edward	Wedderburn, Sir William	Yoxall, James Henry
Sullivan, Donal (Westmeath)	Weir, James Galloway	
Thomas, Alfd. (Glamorgan, E.)	Williams, John Carvell (Notts.)	TELLERS FOR THE NOES—
Trevelyan, Charles Philips	Wills, Sir William Henry	Mr. David Thomas and
Wallace, Robert (Perth)	Wilson, Henry J. (York, W.R.)	Captain Sinclair.
Walton, John Lawson(Leeds,S.	Wilson, John (Govan)	
Walton, Joseph (Barnsley)	Woods, Samuel	

ORDERS OF THE DAY.

SUPPLY (FOURTH ALLOTTED DAY).

Considered in Committee.

[Mr. A. O'CONNOR (Donegal, E.) in the Chair.]

(In the Committee.)

ARMY ESTIMATES, 1899-1900.

Motion made, and Question proposed—

"That a sum not exceeding £6,509,000 be granted to Her Majesty to defray the charge for the Pay, Allowances, and other charges, of Her Majesty's Army at Home and Abroad (exclusive of India) (General Staff, Regiments, Reserve and Departments), which will come in the course of payment during the year ending 31st day of March, 1900."

Motion made—

"That a sum, not exceeding £6,508,800, be granted for the said Service."—(*Mr. Courtenay Warner.*)

MR. COURTENAY WARNER (Stafford, Lichfield): This is the first money Vote on the whole of the Army Estimates, and I think it is the first opportunity that we have had of complaining of the extravagant system on which the Army is carried on at present. The War Office, we all know, are unsatisfactory in their answers to questions, and also in regard to their general management of the Army, and the extravagance of the work which they carry on. On this Vote I do not propose to discuss the administration of the War Office. That will come better later on. There is one thing, at the outset, that we have to make a protest against, and that is, the whole system of expenditure in connection with the Army. We contend that that system might be very much improved, and effect greater results than at present, for less money. I do not speak as an expert, but as an onlooker. I mean that I have tried to understand these Estimates, complicated as they are, in the most serious way, and I do think that I understand, to a certain extent, that there are a

great many things in the administration of the Army in which economy can be practised. My friends on this side of the House are not in any way wedded to any particular form of economy; but we recognise this fact, those of us who are anxious to see the Army really kept up to its present high standard—those of us who like to see the Army kept up to its present numbers and efficiency—we realise that, the Estimates having reached above 21 millions, the country will not stand any more expenditure, and the day will come when a very serious reduction in the Army and its efficiency will be demanded unless something is done to manage the Army on a more economical system than we have at the present moment. There are necessary increases; we do not, any of us, object to necessary increases, either for extension or efficiency. Most of us regret that the Army will have to be increased in the future, in order to occupy the large tracts of territory which have been added to the Empire, and which additions are very unlikely to pay for many years to come. But, once these large tracts of territory have been acquired, we foresee that, unless something is done to modify the present expensive system, the expenditure will go on increasing by leaps and bounds. The public will insist on economy, and the only way that that will be possible will be to reduce the strength and the efficiency of the whole Army. None of us object to the first line of defence, the Navy. When any responsible Government says we must have a strong Navy, that is accepted as a matter of course. But when the Government comes forward, and says "we must increase our Army," there are many people too short-sighted to see that the whole Empire depends on scattered garrisons being maintained. Anybody who has read recent books of travel, and people who know the Colonies well, recognise that it is absolutely necessary wherever we have these Crown Colonies or Territories they must be occupied by troops, and whether we put these troops now under the Colonial Office or the Foreign Office, eventually they must be put on the Army Vote as a part of our Army. I wish to move the reduction of this Vote by the formal sum of £100, as a protest against the large expenditure. I do not wish to dispute the fact that the Army is necessary in the present circumstances, nor that under the system we have got we must spend these 21 millions of money. But I feel that something must be done as a protest to compel the War Office officials to realise that they must come to an economic solution of our existing difficulties. I know that the honourable Gentleman the Under Secretary for War will get up and say that every possible economy is exercised, and that he and his predecessors have tried to exercise this economy. We always hear this, but it is a well-known fact that those who are cognisant of the working of the War Department acknowledge that there are a great many evils which might be remedied, but which we from the outside cannot touch at all. It is quite true that those who do not know the internal iniquities of the War Office say that nothing can be done in the way of reduction in the expense of the War Office; but I wish to make it perfectly clear that a reduction of the expense might be made without reducing the Army by one man, or its efficiency in any degree. In this year's Estimates there is absolutely no attempt at any economy. I believe that in the whole of the Votes there is no sign that the War Office has tried to economise in any way. You may read quite through the Votes, and you find that one or two men have been cut off here, and two or three men put on there, and that in many places there seems to be a large increase in the number of men. There is no doubt about it that the increase is necessary in some cases. We have got more to do, and must pay for it. But, in spite of that, the Returns show that over all there has been no great increase in the number of men, and apparently very little increase in the efficiency of the Army. I want to test the reasons for this huge expenditure for small results. I will go back 33 years, to the Army Estimates of 1866. I find that whereas in 1866 there were

Mr. *Courtenay Warner.*

141,000 men, there are now 180,000 odd. That is not a very material increase, but the Army Estimates have in that period doubled. These figures do not include the Militia, the Volunteers, or the Indian Army, and yet we have nearly doubled the expenditure. It is true that on this particular Vote the increase does not seem to be very large, because the Votes were put down on a very different system in those days from now, and it is very hard to get at the special points where the extravagance comes in. It is quite true that the men get better pay now, and that last year they were granted free groceries. But 1d. or 1½d. per day would account for what they have got in this direction. The men get better food, but I hold that that does not account for the increase of expenditure. It arose from agitation from the outside, which compelled the officers to look after the men's food, instead of leaving it to the quarter-masters and the sergeant, as in the old days. The better food, then, has been given without any increased expenditure. It is also true that there is a good deal more clothing; but that is an item which ought not to be put against this increased Vote. Clothing is very much cheaper now, and certain parts of the clothing have been done away with, including a great deal of ornamentation. I do not say that there is any difference in the durability or the wearing, but there is less expense in the ornamentation and things of that kind. It has been said that Lord Lansdowne has introduced many reforms into the War Office. I believe he is a very able man, and has done a great deal in various ways in the way of reform. But there is one way in which he has not attempted to carry out reform, and that is in a more economic system of administration. We must have something done to introduce a more economic system, while all that his Lordship has done has been to make the system more expensive. Take, for instance, recruiting. Recruiting costs much more than ever, while the results are worse, both in point of numbers and quality. It is true that this year on paper you make the recruiting as good as last year; but it is an absolute fact that the recruits are smaller in numbers. I do not count the Reserve men, who are brought in to strengthen the regular battalions. That is not a fair way of comparison. You have got a few more men by taking on undersized youths. You can always get many recruits at any time by reducing the standards. You have done worse this year than in previous years in securing real good men, and the quality of the recruits is not so good. You have reduced the standard of physique in the Guards, and the unfortunate effect of sending a second battalion of the Guards to Gibraltar has been that the men are not of such good quality as before, or of the same social standing. I know it will be urged that on paper they are the same, but I have information as to the battalions at home and abroad, and it is a well-known fact among the officers of the Guards that the recruits now got are not as good men, independent of physique, as the men who were got before. I know that statistics may be produced to show that so many men can read and write, but absolute credence cannot be put on these statistics as to the quality of the men. I do not want to go into the administration of the War Office itself. That sink of iniquity can only be thoroughly thrashed out by those who are completely cognisant of it. I will only state one difficulty in dealing with the War Office, which, unfortunately, the Under Secretary and myself suffered from. I asked a question in regard to the provision of rifle ranges, and I hoped we should get some trustworthy information on the point. But all the answer the War Office gave was, that arrangements were being made for these ranges. Subsequent inquiry showed that all that had been done was that somebody had been sent down to look at certain land, and that he had reported that the land was a suitable place for a range. Absolutely no contract had been entered into to secure the land, and nothing had been done to erect the ranges. The fact is that the War Office always gives evasive answers to questions, and it is very difficult to get the truth out of it at all. I come now to the actual Army. That is a thing we can all see. Outsiders are better able to obtain some idea of what can be done. I take the Artillery. There is a great increase in the Artillery on paper, but I believe that up to the present time we have not got an in-

crease of a single efficient gun, horse, or man. We are going to increase the guns at the expense of the waggons. That is not a real increase, and there is nothing to show that we are getting more for the money we are spending in the real efficiency of the Artillery. Take the Cavalry, again. There is a belief that we have got more Cavalry than before, but I do not believe that the regiments are much more efficient than they were. The fact is that the home regiments are practically deficient in men and horses, and that the strain on them in sending men from one regiment to another is very great. I come now to another serious question, that of the Staff, an item that in fighting power counts a great deal. We keep on increasing all over the world our Staff officers. There is absolutely no economy exercised at all on this branch of the Service. Our Staff is enormously larger in proportion to the men in the Army than any other Staff in the world. Take Germany, for instance, or any other Continental Army, where they have real divisions, brigades, and army corps. The number of Staff officers is very much smaller than with us. It is a *tour de force* for us to produce an army corps; it is only occasionally that we can produce a division at all, and yet we have an enormous number of field-marshals, lieutenant-generals, and major-generals, who have really no troops to command. Surely these are rather expensive luxuries. Surely we might dispense with these field-marshals and people of that kind, who are rather expensive to keep, and we might reduce the Army expenditure by having fewer generals. It is not only the enormous number of Staff officers, but the number of officers under them, brigade majors, aides de camp, which I am sure we can reduce to a very large extent. I think at the present moment the Staff numbers 1,866 officers, a larger number than was in the grand army which Napoleon took to Moscow, and which was noted for the splendour of its Staff and the splendour of its uniforms. Take the case of Bermuda. The Staff there consists of 55 persons, over and above the regular battalion and battery officers.

Attention having been called to the fact that there were not 40 Members present, the House was counted, when 40 Members being present—

Mr. COURTENAY WARNER (continuing): I was going to refer to the case of Bermuda. Including the Militia and Volunteers there is a very small garrison there. I think the total of all ranks reaches the vast number of 2,000, and for this number, besides regimental officers, they have 55 officers and sergeants to look after them. That seems to me to be rather a larger proportion than is necessary. What we want to have on the Army Estimates is a statement of the real cost of the Army. It is said that we must have distinguished officers to act as Governors in our Colonies, but why should we transfer soldiers from their own proper work to do civilian work? That is a very extravagant process. Let soldiers do soldiers' work, and civilians do civilian work. The result of putting soldiers to do civilian work is often very disastrous. The same excess of Staff officers is observable at other stations. Take the case of Malta. There we have one lieutenant-general, two major-generals, one deputy-adjutant-general, one assistant-adjutant-general, one district inspector of musketry, four brigade-majors, two senior aides-de-camp, one military secretary, three ordinary aides-de-camp, and various other officers and sergeants. This enormous number of Staff officers are actually put in command of only 5,500 men. I believe in most armies you do not require a major-general until you have got a division. A brigadier may be a general, but very often is only a full colonel; but here in Malta you have got three generals for 5,000 men, which I think is a rather extravagant proceeding. It is the same throughout all the Crown Colonies, where we have far too many Staff officers. I would not object to them if they were ordinary battalion or company officers, but these Staff officers are employed simply in working red tape for the War Office. Three parts of their time these Staff officers are occupied in answering memoranda for the War Office. That is a system that has got to be reduced in some way, for the country will not continue to stand it. These men are no doubt highly ornamental, but only partially useful. Then, again, the Line battalions might be

worked cheaper. I admit that the officers of these Line battalions do better work than any other part of the Army, but even there there is great possibility of reducing the expenditure. Now, the extraordinary thing in regard to the Line battalions is that we use the same number of officers to command and instruct a battalion when it is at home, at its weakest strength of something between 300 and 400 men, as when it is abroad, when it is supposed to be about 1,000 strong. Some years ago, when it was suggested to create a number of new battalions, I asked whether it would not be better to fill up the existing battalions before asking for recruits in order to make up these new battalions. But no response was given to my suggestion. The fact is, that all our home battalions are vastly below their strength. According to the War Office system, a home battalion is supposed to be 800 strong, but if you put down the number at 500, it would answer the real purpose. It is only in the case of a battalion having to go very soon abroad that the War Office ever thinks of raising it above 500 men. Now, the number of officers in a home battalion is 24, whereas the number of officers in the Colonies is 28, and in India 29. But a battalion in India has got at least 940 men on its establishment. These are real regiments. We are frequently told that if we want to see the English Army, we must go to India to see it, and the reason is that it is only in India that we have real regiments, and not skeleton regiments. We never see a real cavalry regiment or a real battery of artillery in England. When you bring a battalion home from the Colonies you reduce the number of officers by four, and when you bring a battalion home from India, you reduce the number of officers by five. Well, you reduce the number of the rank and file from 940 to 300 or 400 men. The result is, that the whole establishment of the regiment, which is the expensive part of the regiment, has very little to do. Companies with half their proper strength cannot be properly drilled. You have sometimes companies of only 12 or 13 files, and they have been known to be only eight files. With such skeleton companies you can, no doubt, teach them the ordinary rudiments of company drill and extension motions, but it is hardly necessary for that to have a full complement of officers. And when you come to battalion or brigade drill, it is perfect nonsense to try and teach them in that way. Of course, it is said that the companies are amalgamated for battalion and brigade drill; but when that is done, you have a whole list of officers with nothing to do—five officers to each company, while three are quite ample. I know there are objections to clubbing two companies into one, but these are comparatively slight. I would suggest that the home battalions might be reduced to four companies, with four captains and a major, instead of eight captains and two majors as at the present moment. In asking for the reduction of these officers, I am not asking for anything extraordinary. In the French army a battalion is supposed to be of the strength of 1,000 rank and file, and they have only 14 officers, while at home our battalions never exceed a strength of 400 rank and file, and we have 24 officers, or nearly twice as many as are required in the French army. In the same way you will find that in the German army they have got a very much smaller proportion of officers to men than we have. The officers in foreign armies, moreover, do a great deal of the work that is done by our sergeants. I do not want to alter our system. I have a great affection for it, but I do want that something should be done to do away with the present extravagance. I come to another point, namely, the depôts. There the proportion of officers and sergeants to the number of men is perfectly appalling. You have sometimes five officers to 50 rank and file. Of course, there are occasionally recruits, even as many as 100, but these recruits do not give the officers very much trouble. The only person who has to deal with them is not included in the number of regimental officers—namely, the adjutant. Besides that, you have two adjutants, and two quartermasters, Militia officers, three-fourths of whose time is occupied with depôt work, except when the Militia is called up for training. There are a large number of sergeants at these depôts, only a few of whom are engaged in training the Militia recruits for a month in the year, and a few are also used for recruiting purposes. But a great propor-

tion of them have nothing to do. In short, at the ordinary Line depôts there are four times as many sergeants and three times as many officers as are necessary. If many of these smaller depôts were amalgamated, a large number of sergeants and of higher officers could be done away with altogether, and an enormous amount could be saved, while the efficiency of the recruits and of the Militia battalions would be increased. There is no doubt that in these small depôts both officers and sergeants have so little to do that they become idle, while the Militia only get half a training, and are not much use when called out for permanent drill. I do not want to press any particular plan for the reduction of expenditure. I only suggest one or two points in which it might be made. The country is beginning to feel the enormous burden we are putting on it, and unless something is done, honourable Members on this side of the House and on that will receive from their constituents an absolute mandate to reduce the Army Estimates.

AN HONOURABLE MEMBER: No.

MR. COURTENAY WARNER: An honourable Gentleman says "No"; but I say that the feeling is pretty prevalent in the country that we are spending far too much money on the Army. That feeling is growing stronger day by day, and if you go on increasing these Army Estimates a panic reaction will come, and the Government and this House will be forced to take millions off these Army Estimates all at once. That will be a very serious and a dangerous thing for the Army and for the country. It is true that since the Reserve system was instituted we can fill up the battalions to a certain extent. But though we can do this, and though the Army Reserve is increasing, we are losing ground in another direction. The Militia is growing smaller and smaller year by year. I am not surprised at it, because the Militia gets very little encouragement. The fact remains that while the Army Reserve is increasing it is doing so by very little more than the decrease in the Militia. It is also true that the Volunteers are becoming more and more efficient, and that we are able to rely more completely on them than formerly.

But in case of serious danger there would be a period before the Volunteers would be ready to take the field, and although they are comparatively efficient, it would be a very dangerous thing to bring Volunteers with only a week or ten days' drilling into the field against regular troops. It is apparent to any one who goes about the country and hears what is being said as to the vast expenditure on the Army that the day is not far off when the country will say that these increases of expenditure must go no further. And you will be compelled, in a sort of panic, to reduce your Army very considerably, and be thus landed in a very dangerous position. I hope, therefore, that the Government will be forced into impressing upon the War Office that some reform is necessary, and to reduce the cost of the Army as it stands at present. The War Office must be made to feel that they have got to find out where the money is leaking away, and to put some check on the expenditure, while at the same time it keeps up the efficiency of the Army as in the past. Nobody has a greater admiration of the efficient work done by the Army than I have, but I recognise the fact that there are always in this country a number of people who are ready to make reductions in the Army, and who are calling out loudly against the extravagant expenditure of the Army. Their numbers are increasing, and something must be done to reduce that expenditure. I know that it can be done in many ways without hurting the efficiency of the Army in any manner, and I have, therefore, to move the reduction of the Vote by £100 as a protest against the extravagant conduct of the War Office.

MR. BUCHANAN (Aberdeenshire, E.): I do not think that the honourable Member who has just sat down has by any means, in the speech he has delivered, exaggerated the importance of the questions raised by the increases asked for in the Army Estimates. I should like to ask the Under Secretary for War if he can put before the Committee information as to the true amount of money which is to be spent on the military forces of the Empire from the Army Estimates and other sources. On the first night on which the Army Estimates were discussed I endeavoured to

elicit some information from the Under Secretary for War on this point, and I do not think that he was able entirely to answer the questions I put to him. Speaking generally, I think we have had this information given us in regard to the Navy by the First Lord of the Admiralty, and, so far as I know, there is no reason why we should not have it also given in a similar form in regard to the Army. In the first week of the Session the First Lord stated what the Loan expenditure would be for the current year, and the estimated expenditure for the year to come. And since that time a paper was put in our hands which gave us a rough estimate of what would be expended under the Naval Loans Act for the year ending 31st March 1899. I think we ought to have a similar paper, giving us similar information in regard to the Army, laid before us early in the Session and before the Army Estimates come on. During the discussion the other night as to the expenditure during the current year under the Barracks Loan Act of 1890, the Financial Secretary said that the whole of the balance of £493,000 had been expended. So that we have to add, roughly speaking, half a million to the military expenditure for the year. Then we pass on to the Military Works Act of 1897. There we find at the beginning of the financial year an unexpended balance of £4,800,000. The Under Secretary for War, in answer to a question, said that during the present year there would be expended £800,000. Roughly speaking, therefore, there is an unexpended balance on which you can draw under the Loans Act of 1897 of no less than four millions. On the other hand, we have here, under the Barracks Loan Act of 1890 and the Military Works Act of 1897, an expenditure during the current year of a little over a million and a quarter. Now, in his statement which he issued with the War Office Estimates, Lord Lansdowne told us that a new Loan Bill will be introduced to raise money to be applied to barracks and other military works. But we have not been told, as we ought to have been, what is the amount of money the Government propose to borrow under the new Barracks and Military Works Bill. The Bill has not yet been introduced, and will not be introduced until after Easter, but I think on an occasion like this, when the Army Estimates are under discussion, and when we are reviewing the expenditure of the current year and the prospective military expenditure of the year to come, we have a fair claim to get from the Government a statement of the amount of money that is to be devoted to these purposes. When I asked the Under Secretary for War a question in regard to the matter, he answered a question which I did not put. He told me that he could not give me full and detailed information as to the purposes of the Loan Bill. I did not ask for that. I asked that we should be informed as to the amount of money that it is proposed to borrow under the Bill when it becomes law. I think that we may fairly claim that we should be told that, and on another ground. In Lord Lansdowne's statement in regard to the proposed Loan Bill he tells us that it will be paid off by means of a terminable annuity charged on the Army Estimates. But I can find no terminable annuity for any purpose whatever on the Estimates for this year. In regard to the purposes of the Loan, these are stated in the Memorandum of Lord Lansdowne to be practically twofold. The one is the erection of barracks for a considerable body of troops on Salisbury Plain, and the other is the completion of other large camps, for adding to and improving existing barrack accommodation at home, and for increasing the barracks abroad at those stations where it has been decided to augment the garrisons.

THE DUPUTY CHAIRMAN: I beg to draw the attention of the honourable Member to the fact that there is a Vote for barracks on page 90 of the Estimates, and that he cannot raise the question of the new Loans Bill under Vote 1.

MR. BUCHANAN: That refers to the Barracks Loan Act of 1890, and that an annuity has been asked for to pay off the Barracks Loan of 1890. But I was alluding to the future Loan that the Government are going to introduce this year.

THE DEPUTY CHAIRMAN: No annuity for such a purpose can come under Vote 1, at any rate.

MR. BUCHANAN: I will not trespass further on this subject except to

VOL. LXVIII.   [FOURTH SERIES.]

say that, apart from the Loan Bill altogether, the Memorandum of the Secretary for War states that there is in the Estimates this year a sum of £431,000 which is to bear half of the expense of the new scheme of armaments at our various stations. I do not propose to ask the Under Secretary for War to give us any of the details of the Scheme of Armaments, where the places are, or what the stations are, but I think we ought to get from him within what period of time this scheme of arming those stations may be expected to be carried through, and what it is to cost. This is a new scheme, and it is plain this is only the initial cost, and, therefore, we should like to know what future liabilities it will entail on the Exchequer. Well, there are other military charges to come upon the taxpayers of the country which are not included in the Estimates. The honourable Member the Under Secretary for War, in his statement the other night, when speaking of the new regiments that are to be raised—the Chinese Regiment, the Central Africa Regiment—told us that these would bring up the number of coloured troops, not under the War Office, but under the Colonial Office and the Foreign Office, to 10,000 men, and that they would cost a million of money. Well, of course that million is included in the Army Estimates. He also stated that there were about 25,000 coloured troops not under the War Office control, but under that of the Colonial Office and the Foreign Office. I cannot ask him what cost will be put on the taxpayers for those troops, but I do think that that is an important item in the military expenditure, when we consider the military expenditure which is put upon the country. I think that we shall be well within the mark if we put that expenditure at three-quarters of a million more. And I should like to ask whether it would not be possible for the War Office in the future to enter into the Army Estimates the amount that is put upon the taxpayers of this country for these purposes. We have on page 9 of the Army Estimates a statement of some items of Army charges which do not come into the Army Estimates, but into other charges. I think that you ought to be able to put in that paragraph the amount of the Army charges such as I have alluded to for the coloured troops

3 A

under the Colonial and Foreign Office, which have to be borne by the taxpayers of this country. Then, Sir, besides those expenses that come from outside the Army Estimates, I venture to say that the Army Estimates themselves do not, on the face of them, give actually the proper charge which is put upon the taxpayer under the Army Estimates. On the face of them, the Estimates for the coming year amount to £20,600,000, which represents an increase of £1,396,000. Lord Lansdowne tells us in his Memorandum that they are not the correct figures. He observes that if you want to get the correct figures for the year you must add to those figures certain Supplementary Estimates of the previous year. If honourable Members refer to the bottom of page 5 and the top of page 6, they will see exactly what I refer to. Lord Lansdowne states there that the real Estimate for the ensuing year is not £20,600,000, but £20,978,000. Therefore I think we can take it that about 21 millions of money is the real Estimate for the ensuing year. The Estimate of the previous year amounts to 20 millions of money, and the true increase is £1,107,000. I see at once how liable honourable Members are to make a mistake with regard to this matter, because my honourable Friend just now accepted the figure that the Estimates were £22,000,000; but Lord Lansdowne points out that they come to within £25,000 of £21,000,000. But to this must be added the amounts provided in the Supplementary Estimates, and if those are added, the amount is £20,978,000, which is the proper total. Therefore I was justified in stating that the true amount of the Army Estimates for 1899-1900 is practically £21,000,000. Now, I point out that this practice which has grown up in the War Office of late years of voting money in the Supplementary Estimates of each year for the Army Estimates of the ensuing year is an irregularity, and is liable to cause great inconvenience to honourable Gentlemen or anybody who wishes to compare the Estimates for a series of years, when they have got not merely to look at the expenses of the Army Estimates and the Supplementary Estimates of a given year, but also the Supplementary Estimates of the preceding year, and pick out items from them. I

Mr. Buchanan.

ask the honourable Gentleman whether he can give us any assurance that this practice, of a very recent growth, shall be discontinued in the future. Now, the principal question which I wish to ask the honourable Member first of all is, as to the practice of using the Supplementary Estimates of a previous year for the following year for which they are voted. The second question is, whether the honourable Gentleman could not give a statement early in the Session of the Estimates proposed, similar to that given us by the Admiralty of borrowed money spent in the current year. And I would also like to ask him, if I might do so, what is the amount of these new Colonial troops? I should also like to ask him, before the existing Estimates are produced, whether some statement could be added as to that to the figures given in page 9, to which I have referred, giving the amount of the military moneys required for all the Foreign Office and Colonial Office coloured troops? If we could get that we should get at something like the real military expenditure of the country, and it comes to a very much larger figure than any honourable Member supposes, and a very much larger figure than my honourable Friend gave us in his speech. In the first place, you have £21,000,000 and £1,500,000 for borrowed money, and one million for the coloured troops, which amount altogether to something like £23,000,000 for Army purposes for the current year. Now, I certainly do think with the honourable Member for Lichfield that £23,000,000 is an enormous amount of money. Even if you take it at the lower figure of £21,000,000, it is, I think, an enormous figure to ask for military purposes; but it is a figure which is increasing, and has been increasing at great lengths during the past year. I will not trouble the House with the figures, but I will just look back three years. In 1896-1897—during the period the present Government has been in office—the Army Vote amounted to £18,100,000. It has now gone up in three years—the Army Vote alone is £21,000,000—an increase of £3,000,000 in three years, or at no less a rate than £1,000,000 per annum. Now, in dealing with the items of this increase in the Army Estimates, we have this public question to deal with: that these annual increases are becoming automatic, and all that the authorities consider that they have to do is to administer them. Now, I do not think that we ought to accept that view, looking at the matter from the point of view of the taxpayers of this country. Why should the War Department be automatic? I remember the right honourable Gentleman the Member for Monmouthshire, when this was put forward last year, pointing out that if you once adopt that principle you might just as well have an automaton for the Chancellor of the Exchequer. We must look at the various items in degrees, and not take them in bulk. Then I take the other point, that half of it is attributable to policy and half to administration, and in respect of that I urge upon the House what has been urged by either side of the House for years, that if you want to oppose the policy, you must oppose the money which is asked for it, whatever the policy may be. Not only that, but I believe it is a point of duty on the part of Members of this House to see that criticisms are brought to bear upon the conduct of the great Departments of the State, and that we should be entitled to say that certain large crops of Estimates and large plans of expenditure ought to be reduced, and it is not right on the part of the Administration to say that you must point out a particular item in the Votes upon which you wish to make any reduction. It is an old argument, Mr. O'Connor, and if anybody wishes to reduce anything in these days they will always find that is the first excuse that is applied by the Minister who desires to reduce nothing. Now, I have been here listening to the Debates for the last few nights for the purpose of making my speech, which I should like to have made three nights ago, but which I had no opportunity of doing, owing to the Motion which had been moved, and I was very much struck, particularly during the discussion of the Naval Estimates, by hearing my right honourable Friend the late Secretary to the Admiralty and the Member for Clitheroe suggest that we must call a halt, from both sides of the House. I do not think we in this House represent the opinion of the country in this matter, and if that is so, that, in the case of the Navy Estimates, which are more popular than any Army Estimates in this country, we must call

a halt, I am perfectly certain it is the case in the Army Estimates. I am absolutely sure that all the people in this country will back me up when I say that £21,000,000 for Army Estimates is an excessive sum to ask for; that the increase of one million per annum is too large an increase for the exigencies of the political situation, or for the value we get for our money. Now, I recollect the Chancellor of the Exchequer stating last year that, when speaking of economy, it was like preaching a sermon—that nobody ever listened to him. I believe that during these years of prosperity we have been somewhat apathetic on this question of economy—that we have been too silent on this great question of economy. But where the sermon is wanted most is not inside this House, but inside the Cabinet itself. Both the War Minister and the Naval Minister will always ask for more money, and so long as they get it they will be always able to spend it, and the only safety and defence that we taxpayers have against the ambitious Measures of these men rests with the Chancellor of the Exchequer. I hope he will be able to make both ends meet this year. But, beyond all question, the Debates we have had in this House during the last few days point to the fact that the country has become alive, and honourable Members also, to the fact that this vast increase of expenditure on behalf of these Departments is too big, and ought to be reduced, and they will blame, and are entitled to blame, the Government for this policy with regard to the Colonies, and also for not having stronger and closer guard upon the public purse.

GENERAL GOLDSWORTHY (Hammersmith): With increased responsibilities we must have an increase of strength in the Army and the Navy. There is no doubt about that. But what the country wants, and what I have always heard in this House, is that no money should be spent unless we get full value for it. There has been a Committee sitting on the subject of the War Office for a very long time, for the purpose of seeing whether the Army could not be centralised, and, therefore, have more efficiency and economy. We have rather suffered, in my opinion, by the late Under Secretary having been promoted to the Foreign Office, but at the same time I may say that his place has been filled by a Gentleman who we have no doubt will look after this work, and will not have any pre-conceived ideas as to the War Office. I should like to ask the honourable Gentleman when we are likely to have any report from this Committee sitting on this question of centralisation. Of course, I know it is a difficult thing that the honourable Gentleman has to do in taking up the running, as it were, but at the same time I think something ought to be done, and the general officers ought to have more power than they have had in the past, and that the War Office should have less. There are many duties which the general officers can do much better than those clerks of the War Office, and I trust we may have some Report from this Committee which has been sitting so long upon this subject. There is one fact that should not be lost sight of, and that is, that the military is one of the most expensive forces that we have, and that everything should be done that can be done to popularise the military with the people from whom the rank and file are drawn; and not only with them, but also with the class from which the officers are drawn. I see that it is suggested that officers of the Army after retirement should serve in the Militia, and up to a point that is a good thing. But, of course, we all know that the Army has been under obligations to the Militia, and to get recruits from the Militia would popularise it a great deal, and will also make people acquainted with the military service. There is one thing also that I should like to see, and that is that where any request has been put forward by the masters of schools in the country for the drilling of their pupils an instructor should be sent to them. Many Board school masters and others have told me that they have found very great benefit from the drilling of the children in their schools. General Havelock Allen said some time ago that he had no objection to it whatever.

*THE UNDER SECRETARY OF STATE FOR WAR (Mr. G. WYNDHAM, Dover): The honourable Member for Lichfield, I think, himself has said that he could not put his finger on this or that economy which he thought ought

General Goldsworthy.

to be carried out. He indulges in a general view of the system, and says he sees the necessity for reducing a number of items in the expenditure. Now, of course, it is very difficult to meet a broad attack of that character. We do not treat it in any controversial spirit, but I would point out that when we fight a battle of economy we do not always receive support from those quarters where we might be expected to look mostly for it. It is not so many nights ago, when I was rather hardly pushed for it, when I was fighting the battle of economy that I appealed for that support. But what was my surprise upon the Division taking place to find a great many of the champions of economy walk into the Lobby against me.

MR. COURTENAY WARNER: That was a question of Cavalry, and it was a special point.

*MR. WYNDHAM: It may be a special point, but I notice that many honourable Members coming from Ireland who had insisted that economy would be insisted on voted with the honourable and gallant Member. I feel that I should be hardly justified in following the honourable Member for Lichfield throughout his speech, but I must beg him to reconsider this point. The honourable Member for Lichfield excluded India in the comparison which he made, but India cannot be excluded from any comparison, because, whether the honourable Member likes it or not, the Army of this country is our great training school for the Army in India, and if you have to maintain a higher standard of troops to send to India it stands to reason that the expense will be greater. Then, my honourable Friend made an almost personal attack upon me, and charged me with having given him an answer which was evasive in respect to a range in the neighbourhood of Lichfield. I admit that that answer was evasive. It was intended to be evasive, because when we are going to expend large sums of money, and want to get the land at a low figure which we want to purchase, we find it necessary to be evasive, and as the champion of economy I would ask him to condone such evasive reply. The honourable Member could not have followed very closely the many speeches which I have made when he said that there was no increase in the Artillery. I have explained more than once that during this year we have raised the guns, horses, and men for five batteries of Artillery, and that that has been done without trenching on the horses, guns, or men of any of the existing batteries. We have raised 8 out of 11 companies of Garrison Artillery, and the honourable Member will hardly deny that we have added a material number of trained Cavalry soldiers to the Army. He then dwelt upon the fact that we had a great many Staff officers in the Service. We have a great many Staff officers, and that is one point in the comparison of expense and economy with other nations. We must have at Cape Town and Malta and Gibraltar and other stations of importance officers of a higher standard of experience than would be necessary for the number of men over whom they were placed. They represent us abroad. They are confronted with questions from time to time of a difficult and almost diplomatic character, and apart from that, regarding their purely military duties alone, in providing for the transference of troops from one part of the Empire to another they have many greater difficulties to cope with than an officer who commands an army corps in the district in which it is raised. The honourable Member developed his attack as against our Line battalions. Now, I agree with him in one thing he said; I think our Line battalions are cheap. A private of a British Line regiment costs the country about £45 5s. 3d. a year for his training, his clothing, his housing, feeding, and also his travelling, and his pension. That, I submit, is not at all an excessive charge. The honourable Member admitted that to a certain extent, but he went on to say that we used as many officers at home, save five, as we did in India; that the home battalions were very weak; that they purported to number 800 men, whereas very few of them number 500. I traverse almost every one of these statements. It is true that we have but five fewer officers at home than in India, but far from the battalions being only 500 instead of 800, we only claim 750. Eight hundred is the number at which we are aiming when our increase has been completed. I find that in the 66 battalions at home we have

14 which have over 700 men; we have between 600 and 700 in 33, and in 19 we have between 500 and 600. There is not one battalion with less than 500 men in it. But that is not the point; the point is, that necessarily under our system there are a great number of our men in the depôt. The men go into the depôts for training, and when trained they go into the home battalions; but no one pretends for a moment that we have the whole 750 men in the battalions at every period of the year. The battalions are a training school for the soldier abroad, and that is what we intend; and if you add to the battalions the number of men in the depôts we had 146 over the establishment on the 1st February. That brings me to this point: Have we too many officers at home in comparison with the number abroad? I say certainly not. Surely honourable Members will admit that it requires more time and attention on the part of the officers where they are training this enormous number of young recruits in order to get this great increase of 25,000 men in a period of three years. Our Army is on an altogether different footing, in respect of cost, from Continental armies upon many grounds. We have expensive Staffs all the world over; we have to maintain coaling stations all the world over; we have to take our men at a lower age than Foreign Powers; and we have to train them very much longer. Then the standard of comfort and our rate of wages are higher than abroad. We have to transport many of our men to distant stations. We have to build our barracks and our works at a higher rate than prevails throughout the Continent. Then we have to remember that an enormous amount of capital has been sunk in foreign armies which does not appear in Continental Budgets. In reply to the first great attack upon the Army expenditure in this country—I mean the attack led by Lord Randolph Churchill in 1888—Mr. Stanhope stated that Germany had sunk in 16 years 212 millions sterling in her army which had not appeared in the annual Budgets of that country. Sir, I will now attempt to answer some of the arguments put forward by the honourable Member for Aberdeenshire. He expressed the opinion that we should publish every

year an estimate of the amount of money that we were likely to expend under the current loans. Sir, I cannot give an absolute pledge, but I believe we shall be able to do that, and I think it would be very proper information to lay before the Committee. Then, Sir, with regard to the new loan, it will cover barracks at home and emplacements for guns. It is a loan founded upon the general policy that we wish to let the old insanitary barracks, placed where they are, of no great military value, die out by degrees. Such as are wholly insanitary are condemned, and others will not have much money spent upon them in the future. The policy underlying this loan is that barracks shall be placed where they will best tend to the proper training of the soldiers of the British Army. I do not feel at this moment prepared to go into further details, but I think I may inform the honourable Member that the Vote will be something over £5,000,000. Then, Sir, the honourable Member asked me what we were spending on our new armaments policy, to which I referred in my statement. In addition to what has been spent in armaments in former years, we are spending an increase this year, because of that policy, of £189,000, and the total of this year's instalment will be about £400,000. We know exactly what guns are wanted, and where they are to be placed; but the pace at which that policy will be carried out is not a matter on which I can give the House accurate information. It has been decided to spend so much this year, and this fact will enable the House to refuse or sanction the policy from year to year—a course, I think, which has often found favour with honourable Members. Then, I have been asked whether we could give in the Estimates in future some additional information showing how much money is devoted in Foreign and Colonial Office Votes for Colonial forces not under the War Office. I am glad of this opportunity of correcting an impression that the whole of the 21,000 men are Regular soldiers. They are all men with rifles, but the greater number of them might more properly be termed police or *gendarmes*. Then, an honourable Member referred to the charge over the amount which was set down this year and last year in the Supplementary

Mr. Wyndham.

Estimates. I think he will recollect that when we were debating that point on the Supplementary Estimates, about a fortnight ago, the Chancellor of the Exchequer informed the Committee that he intended to look into the matter, and that he would have something further to say at some future date. Sir, I do not think I can add anything to that statement made by the Chancellor of the Exchequer, but I do not understand the honourable Member that he has found any difficulty in following the policy of the Government as set forth in the Memorandum of my noble Friend. I now come to the speech of my honourable and gallant Friend the Member for Hammersmith, who asked what progress had been made with the policy of decentralisation. My right honourable Friend the present Under Secretary for Foreign Affairs presided over a Committee which inquired very closely into these matters, and published a Report, with which, no doubt, the honourable and gallant Member is familiar. Sir, we have been acting upon the recommendations of that Report, but I should be misleading the Committee if I were to lead them to think it would be easy to make rapid progress in that direction. It may be stated that many communications pass between many officers before a duty can be performed, and it may be added that this involves very great expense. Well, Sir, you may abolish all these methods, and yet you will not advance very far towards reducing the cost of the Army. In fact, I think there is a fundamental error underlying the assumption that decentralisation of necessity spells economy. It certainly is very difficult to make economy and decentralisation march together in this country when we are required, and I think rightly required, by this Committee to give an account of every sixpence we spend. You cannot allow each general to have his own Budget unless you have a very elaborate and expensive staff to check all these accounts—a more elaborate and expensive machinery than that by which we are now able to account to the House for the moneys it authorises the Department to spend. I can assure my honourable and gallant Friend that I listened with great attention to his recommendation with reference to the provision of drill instructors for schools, and it shall have every consideration.

Mr. COURTENAY WARNER: I have one or two words to say as to why we are in favour of economy. I do not understand that there is much economy in the training of the regiments. As far as I understand, the Cavalry were very much more efficient when they were trained at a depôt than they are under the new system, and I think that was the view which the House took of it in the Debate the other night. I do not think the economy side of the question was put forward very strongly by the Under Secretary on that occasion. The Under Secretary evaded the case where I gave a sample of War Office expenditure, and it was not the only evasive answer which we find he has given. If it were a case of economy, I should be quite willing to overlook an evasive answer at once, but the unfortunate fact is that the War Office authorities always give an evasive answer. Well, the Under Secretary said I made a statement about the Artillery not being increased. It is true that there are to be five batteries' increase in future, but I think I am right in saying that there has been a corresponding decrease in the number of the guns, these having been reduced from six to four. Then we further complain

that there are too many generals in various parts of the world. Malta and Gibraltar have been cited. We quite agree that there ought to be responsible officers at those ports, but we say there are too many of them. We think one general is enough even at Gibraltar. The Under Secretary has also stated that our Staff has necessarily to be much more expensive than a foreign Staff. That is quite true, but our Staff need not be so expensive as it is. I agree that our Line battalions at home are cheap, when a private only costs the country £45 a year, but the rest of the Line regiments are rather expensive. When the figures were given last year the average standard of the home battalions was 480. In less than two months, therefore, there has been a big reduction. I do not know how that has happened if the Army has had such a very large increase. I really do not think our case has been shaken in the least. Our Army is being carried on in a very extravagant way, and I shall certainly take a Division as a protest.

Question put—

" That a sum, not exceeding £6,508,800, be granted for the said Service."—*(Mr. Warner.)*

The Committee divided:—Ayes 79; Noes 170.—(Division List No. 47.)

AYES.

Abraham, Wm. (Cork, N.E.)
Allen, Wm.(Newc.underLyme)
Ashton, Thomas Gair
Austin, Sir John (Yorkshire)
Austin, M. (Limerick, W.)
Barlow, John Emmott
Bayley, Thos. (Derbyshire)
Buchanan, Thomas Ryburn
Burt, Thomas
Caldwell, James
Cameron, Robert (Durham)
Clark, Dr.G.B.(Caithness-sh.)
Colville, John
Dalziel, James Henry
Davies, M.Vaughan-(Cardigan)
Dillon, John
Duckworth, James
Farquharson, Dr. Robert
Fenwick, Charles
Foster, Sir Walter (Derby Co.)
Goddard, Daniel Ford
Gourley, Sir Edwd.Temperley
Haldane, Richard Burdon
Hammond, John (Carlow)
Hayne, Rt. Hn. Chas. Seale-
Hutton, Alfred E. (Morley)
Jones, Wm. (Carnarvonshire)
Kay-Shuttleworth,RtHnSirU.

Kearley, Hudson E.
Kinloch, Sir Jno. Geo. Smyth
Lawson,SirWilfrid(Cumb'land
Leng, Sir John
Lewis, John Herbert
Macaleese, Daniel
MacNeill, John Gordon Swift
M'Ewan, William
M'Laren, Charles Benjamin
Maddison, Fred.
Mendl, Sigismund Ferdinand
Morgan,J.Lloyd(Carmarthen)
Morgan,W.Pritchard(Merthyr
Morton, Edw.J.C.(Devonport)
Moss, Samuel
Moulton, John Fletcher
Norton, Capt. Cecil William
Nussey, Thomas Willans
O'Brien, James F. X. (Cork)
O'Brien, Patrick (Kilkenny)
O'Connor, Jas. (Wicklow, W.)
Oldroyd, Mark
Palmer, Sir Chas. M.(Durham)
Perks, Robert William
Reckitt, Harold James
Reid, Sir Robert Threshie
Richardson, J. (Durham)
Robertson, E. (Dundee)

Roche,Hn.James(East Kerry)
Samuel, J. (Stockton-on-Tees)
Smith, Samuel (Flint)
Souttar, Robinson
Stanhope, Hon. Philip J.
Steadman, William Charles
Strachey, Edward
Sullivan, Doral (Westmeath)
Tanner, Charles Kearns
Tennant, Harold John
Thomas, Alf. (Glamorgan, E.)
Trevelyan, Charles Philips
Wallace, Robert (Perth)
Walton, Joseph (Barnsley)
Weir, James Galloway
Whittaker, Thomas Palmer
Williams, Jno.Carvell(Notts.)
Wills, Sir William Henry
Wilson, Henry J.(York,W.R.)
Wilson, John (Govan)
Wilson, Jos. H. (Middlesbro')
Woods, Samuel
Yoxall, James Henry

TELLERS FOR THE AYES—
Mr. Warner and Mr. Pirie.

NOES.

Aird, John
Arnold, Alfred
Arrol, Sir William
Ashmead-Bartlett, Sir Ellis
Atkinson, Rt. Hon. John
Bagot, Capt. JoscelineFitzRoy
Baillie, James E. B. (Inverness)
Baldwin, Alfred
Balfour, Rt. Hn. A. J. (Manch'r)
Balfour, RtHnGeraldW(Leeds)
Banbury, Frederick George
Barry, Sir Francis T. (Windsor)
Barton, Dunbar Plunket
Bathurst, Hn. Allen Benjamin
Beckett, Ernest William
Begg, Ferdinand Faithfull
Bemrose, Sir Henry Howe
Bentinck, Lord Henry C.
Bethell, Commander
Bhownaggree, Sir M. M.
Bill, Charles
Blundell, Colonel Henry
Boulnois, Edmund
Bowles, Capt. H. F. (Middlesex)
Bowles, T. Gibson(King'sLynn)
Brodrick, Rt. Hn. St. John
Carlile, William Walter
Carson, Rt. Hon. Edward
Cavendish, R. F. (N. Lancs.)
Cavendish, V. C. W. (Derbyshire
Cecil, Evelyn (Hertford, E.)
Chaloner, Captain R. G. W.
Chamberlain, Rt. Hn. J. (Birm.)
Chamberlain, J. Austen(Worc'r)
Chaplin, Rt. Hon. Henry
Clare, Octavius Leigh
Clarke, Sir Edw. (Plymouth)
Cochrane, Hn. Thos. H. A. E.
Coghill, Douglas Harry
Cohen, Benjamin Louis
Collings, Rt. Hn. Jesse
Colomb, Sir John Chas. Ready
Compton, Lord Alwyne
Cook, Fred. Lucas (Lambeth)
Corbett, A. Cameron(Glasgow)
Cranborne, Viscount
Cripps, Chas. Alfred
Cross, A. (Glasgow)
Cross, Herb.Shepherd(Bolton)
Cruddas, William Donaldson
Cubitt, Hon. Henry
Curzon, Viscount
Dalkeith, Earl of
Dalrymple, Sir Charles
Dixon-Hartland, SirFredDixon
Douglas, Rt. Hn. A. Akers-
Douglas, Charles M. (Lanark)
Doxford, William Theodore
Drucker, A.

Duncombe, Hon. Hubert V.
Fardell, Sir T. George
Fergusson, RtHnSirJ. (Manc'r)
Finlay, Sir Robert Bannatyne
Fisher, William Hayes
FitzWygram, General Sir F.
Fletcher, Sir Henry
Folkestone, Viscount
Foster, Colonel (Lancaster)
Garfit, William
Gedge, Sydney
Gibbs, Hn. A. G. H. (C. of Lond.)
Goldsworthy, Major-General
Giles, Charles Tyrrell
Gordon, Hon. John Edward
Gorst, Rt. Hn. Sir John Eldon
Goschen, George J. (Sussex)
Greville, Hon. Ronald
Gull, Sir Cameron
Gunter, Colonel
Halsey, Thomas Frederick
Hamilton, Rt. Hn. Lord George
Hanbury, Rt. Hn. Robert Wm.
Hare, Thomas Leigh
Heaton, John Henniker
Hozier, Hn. Jas. Henry Cecil
Hubbard, Hon. Evelyn
Jebb, Richard Claverhouse
Jeffreys, Arthur Frederick
Jessel, Captain Herbert Merton
Johnston, William (Belfast)
Jolliffe, Hon. H. George
Kemp, George
Kennaway, Rt. Hn. Sir John H.
Kimber, Henry
Lafone, Alfred
Lawrence, SirE. Durning-(Corn
Leigh-Bennett, Henry Currie
Leighton, Stanley
Lloyd-George, David
Lockwood, Lieut.-Col. A. R.
Long, Col. Chas. W. (Evesham)
Long, Rt. Hn. Walter(L'pool.)
Lowles, John
Loyd, Archie Kirkman
Lyttelton, Hon. Alfred
Macartney, W. G. Ellison
Macdona, John Cumming
M'Arthur, Charles (Liverpool)
M'Iver, Sir Lewis (Edin., W.)
M'Killop, James
Malcolm, Ian
Maple, Sir John Blundell
Martin, Richard Biddulph
Maxwell, Rt. Hn. Sir Herb. E.
Monckton, Edward Philip
Monk, Charles James
Moon, Edward Robert Pacy
Morrell, George Herbert

Morton, Arth. H. A. (Deptford)
Mount, William George
Murray, RtHnA. Graham(Bute)
Murray, Charles J. (Coventry)
Nicol, Donald Ninian
Orr-Ewing, Charles Lindsay
Phillpotts, Captain Arthur
Pierpoint, Robert
Pollock, Harry Frederick
Priestley, Briggs (Yorks.)
Pryce-Jones, Lt.-Col. Edward
Purvis, Robert
Rentoul, James Alexander
Ritchie, Rt. Hn. Chas. Thomson
Round, James
Russell, Gen. F. S. (Cheltenham)
Russell, T. W. (Tyrone)
Rutherford, John
Ryder, John Herbert Dudley
Samuel, Harry S. (Limehouse)
Savory, Sir Joseph
Seely, Charles Hilton
Sharpe, William Edward T.
Simeon, Sir Barrington
Smith, Jas. Parker (Lanarks.)
Smith, Hn. W. F. D. (Strand)
Spencer, Ernest
Stanley, Edw. Jas.(Somerset)
Stanley, Henry M. (Lambeth)
Stanley, Lord (Lancs.)
Stewart, Sir Mark J. M'Taggart
Strauss, Arthur
Talbot, Lord E. (Chichester)
Thorburn, Walter
Thornton, Percy M.
Tritton, Charles Ernest
Valentia, Viscount
Wanklyn, James Leslie
Ward, Hn. Robert A. (Crewe)
Warr, Augustus Frederick
Webster, R. G. (St. Pancras)
Webster, Sir R. E. (I. of W.)
Welby, Lieut.-Col. A. C. E.
Williams, Jos. Powell (Birm.)
Willoughby de Eresby, Lord
Willox, Sir John Archibald
Wilson, John (Falkirk)
Wilson-Todd, Wm.H. (Yorks.)
Wodehouse, Rt. Hn. E. R. (Bath)
Wylie, Alexander
Wyndham, George
Wyndham-Quin, Major W. H.
Young, Commander(Berks, E.)

TELLERS FOR THE NOES—
Sir William Walrond and
Mr. Anstruther.

MR. SWIFT MACNEILL (Donegal, S.): I wish to draw the attention of this Committee as far as I can, and the attention of the country at large, to the circumstances attending the death of a young man named John Lorrimer, a trooper in the 17th Lancers, who was found dead on the 27th of December last in a punishment cell, in which he had been confined on a diet of bread and water since the 23rd of December, and from which he had only been allowed out an hour a day to do shot drill. Now, this case appeals very strongly to the working men representatives in this House, and through them to the working men themselves. In this discussion on the Army Estimates, to which

I have listened, statistics have been produced by the right honourable Gentleman the Under Secretary of State for War, which have shown that about 90 per cent. of the Army are drawn from the labouring and mechanical classes. If that be so, the facts I am about to state will appeal to every labouring man, and likewise to the taxpayers who pay for the Army—an Army which is exploited by the rich and supported by the poor. What the taxpayers who pay for the Army have a right to demand is this, that their sons who go into the Army should, of course, be subject to the necessary amount of discipline, but should be treated also with kindness and consideration; that they should be carefully treated in sickness; and that barracks should be something in the nature of homes, and not almost prisons. I suppose it will be rather a surprise to honourable Gentlemen in this House to know what has occurred, not to a highly placed man, well born and well bred, but to a poor son of the people, when he comes into the force, for within the last few weeks, in Christmas time, horrors have been enacted in the dungeon cells attached to British barracks which can scarcely find their equal in the history of the Tower of London or the Bastille, or in any chapter of the slavery depicted in "Uncle Tom's Cabin." [Laughter.] The honourable Gentleman laughs, but I do not think he will laugh at the end of my speech, and he will not be delighted with what I am about to say. The honourable Gentleman the Under Secretary of State for War will, I think, do me the justice to say that I have not sprung this upon him, for I have given him full notice and information, and I am only here stating what has been stated in public, and I shall be delighted if the War Office has any explanation which will in the slightest degree palliate this awful outrage on a young man who has been done to death in the dungeon cell of the Ballincollig Barracks. I derive my proof in this case not from civil but from military sources, and I will mention the name of the officer who has presented to me the document which I will cite—he is one of the most distinguished men in the Service; but before I proceed to this document, which may not be perfectly apparent to

the House, I will endeavour, to the utmost of my ability, to summarise that document, and I will just state very briefly the circumstances of the case. This young man, George Lorrimer, is a Scotch lad, and he was, as Scotch lads generally are, inclined for a military life. I hope the Scotch Members here will see that when Scotch lads enlist in the Army they are treated like human beings. He was apprenticed as an iron moulder, and he had always an ambition to go into the Army. He had good testimonials from his employer, and likewise from the commander of the Boys' Brigade, which is a force, as I understand it, which is a semi-military and semi-religious organisation. This poor boy was colour-sergeant in this brigade, and he was proficient in drill, and won the medal for three years. His parents tried to prevent him enlisting, but his passion for military life was very strong. He enlisted, and when he took this step, although his family were not surprised at it, they were very much grieved. He enlisted in the 17th Lancers, which were then stationed in Ireland, and this was in June. He went through his drill with extreme satisfaction to his commanding officer, and everything seemed to go right until he was stricken down with fever on the 27th of last September. He was sent to the hospital, where he was attended by the military doctors until the 7th of November. He came out of the hospital to all appearances convalescent, and we know nothing more of him until Friday, the 23rd of December. On that Friday, it appears that he felt ill, and he stepped out of the ranks, which was a breach of discipline. The fact was that he was ill, and he was suffering at that time from English cholera and intense diarrhœa. This breach of discipline in stepping out of the ranks on the Friday before Christmas Day was reported, and he was brought before the commanding officer, Major Fortescue, and sentenced to 72 hours in the cells for disobeying orders. That was not an extreme sentence, for I recollect perfectly well that this day two years some troopers were sentenced to 14 days'· bread and water. Well, this poor lad retired to spend his Christmas holidays in the cell, and his parents did not know what was going on in the barracks. Of course, the commanding officer spent his Christmas in his own happy home, or possibly with some country gentleman, and he did not appear on the scene, and did not know what was going on in the barracks until he returned on the Tuesday after Christmas Day. Of course, when he returned, he set himself to business, for he had to maintain good discipline. This boy was brought before him again on Tuesday, and he died at eight o'clock that evening. Now let us consider what Major Fortescue did. This lad was brought up before the commanding officer upon a charge of shamming illness, then the charge of disobedience to orders, and afterwards he was charged with committing a nuisance in the cell. Shamming illness is the first charge, and for that he was sentenced to 48 hours' imprisonment; but long before that 48 hours had expired, he had gone, I hope, to a place where he would be received more gently than he was in the Army barracks. Now, what occurred on the first occasion was this: this unfortunate boy was brought to this prison cell. There was no fire in it, of course; and he was stripped naked, and had cans of cold water thrown on him, although it was cold wintry weather, and he was placed in a damp cell. This treatment, be it remembered, was meted out to a boy who had only come out of the hospital a few weeks before. He was given back his clothes, and he was so weak that he was scarcely able to put them on, and he was placed for that evening in a damp cell on a plank bed, which is a plank without any bedding or bed clothes whatever. On the Saturday, the doctor, about whom I shall have to say a good deal, visited this boy, who made no complaint, but he did not get anything all that day except bread and water. Then on the Sunday—which was Christmas Day in the Queen's service—in comes the doctor to know how he was. The boy complained of illness and sickness, but the doctor makes him go through his exercises, and leaves him. That day he had to do these exercises, although he had complained of illness, and he was brought out and made to do shot drill. This is an abominable and barbarous punishment, and it is utterly unproductive of any good whatsoever, and does nothing except disturb and destroy the muscular system of the man who does this exercise. It is a punish-

ment so barbarous that it has been abolished for some years in civil prisons, but, of course, it is allowed in the Army. This boy, who had a weak heart, and who had been kept on a diet of bread and water, and, I believe, some porridge and potatoes, was driven out to this punishment. I myself have seen shot drill, and I shall never forget it, although 30 years have elapsed since then. The shot is two stone in weight, and consists of cannon balls, which are placed in sockets or holes. At the word of command they are taken up and moved three or four paces to another socket, and it would be a gross breach of discipline to bend one knee, for one must stretch down without bending a knee. This punishment is productive of no good, and this barbarous, malignant drill is to be continued for one hour. This boy, in his debilitated and dying state, was put to this drill the day before he actually died. He did his best to move the cannon ball, and he went on for some time, and then he stopped. Of course, this was again a breach of discipline and disobedience to orders, and he was immediately conveyed back to the cells, and then intense diarrhœa and dysentery ensued, and created a nuisance; and then was preferred the charge of shamming illness, for which he was sentenced to an additional 48 hours' imprisonment. Then the commanding officer came to see this boy, whom he had consigned to a hell upon earth. I have stated the case in its barest outline, and I must now, if the House will bear with me, go through some of the documentary evidence on which I support this case. First of all, I would ask every feeling man in this House, and every man who has been in the Service, to help us to destroy shot drill in military life, which is a disgraceful and a barbarous practice. I would ask the Under Secretary for War, who is a gentleman with a military training, and who is a kindly-hearted man, to give me some account of the absence of the commanding officer; and I would ask him further to give us some information why the commanding officer did not inquire as to the state of this boy's health. Then I should also like to know something about the doctor. This doctor, whose evidence I can quote from his own words, was not in the Service at all, but was some person who was brought in for some occasional job.

Mr. Swift MacNeill.

We in this House, who contribute some thousands of pounds distinctly for medical service, are surprised to learn that here is a man brought in to inspect this boy and to say whether he is fit for punishment. I have not stated the way in which this boy died, for I would rather read it. He was sent back to the cell at half-past six in the evening, and his first term of imprisonment expired on the Tuesday morning, and then his second term commenced. The iron door was slammed on him at half-past six, and no one came to see him until eight o'clock, when he was found lying across his plank bed with his head over the side, dead. What an encouragement to recruiting! What a prospect to the Queen's Service is held out to every young man when tragedies of this kind are allowed to be perpetrated! Now, a very eminent friend of mine, the late Lord Chancellor, when he sat on the Treasury Bench once said he was very much amused at the procedure, and he could not understand so many statements being made without any affidavits, but I have plenty of affidavits and proofs. But first of all, I will tell who is my informant. His name is Colonel Patrick Robertson, who has been for years second in command of the 92nd Highlanders, and I have a letter from him, and I have his permission to read it to the House.

AN HONOURABLE MEMBER: Is the honourable Member aware that Colonel Robertson was not considered fit to be in command of the 92nd Highlanders?

MR. SWIFT MACNEILL: That remark only shows the difficulty that any man has to face who brings charges against a great system, and has determined to rake up the iniquities of it, when here an honourable and gallant Gentleman will use his Parliamentary position to throw a taunt at any man. I say that a man who brings charges against another officer in this House uses a coward's castle. This was a case of gross cruelty, for this unfortunate lad was done to death in this cell, and Colonel Robertson writes to me as follows—

"I send you the whole particulars to give you an opportunity of bringing this cruel case before the House on the Army Estimates. Please read my letter to the House. It is the opinion of a military man who has had a long experience in visiting military prisons. Shot drill is a brutal punishment, which makes every nerve and muscle in the whole body ache, and then there is the torture of a whole night upon a plank bed. It is most unnatural to give recruits this punishment in the cells before they have been able to understand what a breach of discipline really means. The whole business from first to last is bad, and no wonder there is a difficulty in getting respectable youths to join the Army. Will you try and get a promise that shot drill will be abolished. You may read this letter to the House."

Now I come to some of the documents which Colonel Robertson has forwarded me. As is well known, there is a rule in this House which makes it contrary to practice to quote from newspapers, and I could easily have avoided this by taking the extracts which I will read from the coroner's inquest. This is the only document which the unfortunate father has, and with the permission of the House I will read some very short extracts from it. Every word of it is reported, and I will hand the document over to the Under Secretary of State for War for his perusal. The inquest on this boy's death was held on Thursday, the 29th of December, in Ballincollig barracks. A curious feature about this inquest is that the next-of-kin were wholly unrepresented, and the poor father and mother knew nothing at all of the inquest until they saw it reported in the Press. Of course, the police were represented, for they represent the town, and every constable represents the town in Ireland; and the officers of the regiment, who knew they were in a close fix, were represented by a very able Cork solicitor. The first person examined was the officer in command, Major Henry Fortescue. I am quoting these details in order to try to protect the living from the outrages to which this unfortunate Scotch lad was subjected. I will read one or two extracts from his evidence. He said—

"The deceased was in the regiment six months. It was the Friday evening before Christmas. On his return at 6.30 he committed him for 72 hours for refusing to obey an order. This expired on Tuesday morning, when he would have been released, but on that day he had been before witness for saying he was sick without due cause."

That night he died to prove that he had due cause.

"Witness was away when he was found dead. He was away on the Sunday and Monday after Christmas."

Probably he was being entertained by some country gentleman and enjoying his hospitality while this poor boy was dying in the cell to which he had been consigned. Then here is another expression in the evidence—

"I was told"—

and this was on the occasion of his second visit—

"that this boy was shamming illness, and he was sent before me because the doctor said he was malingering, and he acted upon the doctor's advice."

Then this doctor, whom I know nothing of, comes in. He gives his evidence, and it turns out that he is not in the Army at all, but is only brought in to do some odd job. Then the report proceeds—

"The Coroner: Was he then undergoing deprivation of ordinary food? Witness: He was in cells and getting punishment diet. The Coroner: If he complained of pains in the loins must there not have been something wrong? Witness: I found nothing wrong. I thought he might be subject to rheumatism. The Coroner: If he were suffering from rheumatism would he not require extra care?"

I am only giving the barest summary of the evidence. Then the doctor proceeded to state that he had made a *post mortem* examination as directed by the coroner, and that he found a clot of blood leading to the heart. The coroner asked, "Would the treatment in the cells have caused that?" and the witness replied "I do not know." A juror asked, "Would you like to send a cold man in that condition to the cells?" Witness replied, "I asked him if he were warm enough, and I ordered him an extra blanket." "Are they heated cells?" Witness, "No, they are not." "So all you gave the dying man was an extra blanket?" Witness, "Yes." "That is nice treatment to give a dying man." The Coroner asked "Had he a bed?" and the witness replied, "Well, he had not an actual bed, but he had a stretcher and blankets." Then the witness was asked, "Did he get a cold bath?"—and here is an observation which, coming from a physician, is abhorrent in the extreme—"I ordered him to be washed,

Mr. Swift MacNeill.

as he was in a filthy condition." That was the way in which this doctor described the condition of a man suffering from intense diarrhœa. Further on he was asked, "Did he only get bread and water on the Tuesday?" and he replied, "The first day prisoners get bread and water, and the next day they get better food," the better food being porridge and a few potatoes. Another doctor was called in—the corroborative doctor—you must have him—and he said, "Lorrimer was leaning across the bed." Then I come to the corporal who had charge of him in prison, and he was asked how often Lorrimer was visited during the night, and he said he was not visited at all. Dr. Dorgan, recalled, stated in reply to the coroner that the stooping to carry the shot might account for the clot of blood. Lorrimer was put to that drill when he was better fitted for hospital, and he died from its effect, combined with bad food, misery, and fever. I have now almost exhausted the case, and I would not dream, except in a matter of life and death, of occupying the time of the Committee so long, and I thank honourable Members for their kind consideration. But I have not yet told the whole story. I have now to deal with the way in which every effort was made that could be made to hush this matter up. Here is a letter from this boy's father to Colonel Robertson, dated 12th January, 1899—

"My Dear Sir,—I am extremely thankful to you for the interest you have taken in my unfortunate son's death, and I shall be pleased to give you any particulars as to the cause of his death. The first news I received of my son's death was a telegram dated 28th December—'Regret to inform you that your son died here last night. Am writing you. Adjutant, 17th Lancers.' I sent back a telegram saying I would like the remains sent to Glasgow, and I received the following reply, 'Will make arrangements to meet your wishes.'"

The poor remains were, in fact, sent from Ballincollig to Glasgow. I have never heard of a private soldier's remains being conveyed to his home before. Why was it done in this case? Was it because the authorities thought that the dead man was the victim of ill-treatment, carelessness and mismanagement? It was not until 31st December that Lorrimer's father received a letter from the adjutant telling him that the doctor said that nothing could have saved his son's life, and, forsooth, conveying the sympathy of the regimental officers. That sympathy would have been better expressed in looking after this dying boy during his life. Then here is another letter from the father, in which he writes—

"I have discovered from the newspapers that the jury were dissatisfied at the treatment he received, and, Sir, I ask you if it is true that he was ordered a cold bath?"

He then writes very indignantly of the shocking allegation that his son was shamming illness, and that he was filthy. He proceeds, " My son was a strong lad, and had always a strong desire to be a soldier," and he winds up by saying that his boy would not have died in vain if the abominable punishment of shot drill were now to be abolished. If Lorrimer had not been a working man's son he certainly would not have been dealt with in the way he was. I have also another letter from the father, which gives the only description I have been able to find supplied by an eye witness as to the cold bath given to this young man in his dying condition—

" Dear Sir,—In one letter you asked me if it was a cold bath my son got, and from what I heard from a Lancer the other night he was so weak he was unable to take his clothes off, and they took the vessels and poured the water over him. It is enough to make one's blood boil. This Lancer said my son only took strong drink once, and could not be persuaded to take it again, and that his only amusement was swimming."

And this is justifiable in a parent who has lost his son—

" I think the persons who are to blame are a disgrace to the British Army, and I hope it may not be long before they are out of it."

I thank the Committee for the kindly attention with which they have heard me. I have placed every document in my possession within the purview of the Under Secretary. I was passing down Whitehall the other day and I was thinking of this case. I looked at one of the posters which are displayed as an inducement and incitement to young men to enlist. I saw soldiers of various regiments in the Queen's Service in full uniform, and I thought that side by side with it should be a picture showing Lorrimer at shot drill and dying in the cells in order that recruits for the Army might

have an idea of what to expect. Does the honourable Gentleman consider that this would be an inducement to young men to enlist in the Queen's Service? Having regard to the treatment meted out to this boy, there is one law in the Army for the rich and another for the poor. The poor men are simply hewers of wood and drawers of water, and the whole thing is an institution for the support of the rich.

HONOURABLE MEMBERS: Oh, Oh!

MR. SWIFT MacNEILL: My honourable Friends do not like that.

COLONEL LOCKWOOD (Essex, Epping): The whole accusation is entirely false.

MR. SWIFT MacNEILL: I am speaking on behalf of the men who should be treated as human flesh and blood. I am speaking in the cause of humanity. These men should not be used as mere fuel for a State machine. Their weaknesses and their illness should be respected, or the people who pay for the Army may take the matter into their own hands.

*MR. WYNDHAM: I thank the honourable Member for having given notice of his intention to bring this subject before the Committee. I thank him also for the offer of the documentary evidence on which he has based his charge, but Colonel Robertson also wrote to the adjutant-general on 4th January, giving the same particulars, and placing the same interpretation upon them as he seems to have given in a letter to the honourable Member. On the receipt of that letter a searching inquiry was instituted into all the circumstances attending Private Lorrimer's death, and, therefore, I think it will be my fault if I am not able to convince the honourable Member that the case is not so sad as he believes. Of course, it is a sad case. The sudden death of any young man within a few months of entering on an honourable calling must always be a sad case, but it was sadder still in this, because a young life was suddenly cut short while under a temporary cloud which would have been quite forgotten in the light of good service rendered in after years. But we must not allow ourselves to be carried away by the very moving periods in which the honourable Member has placed this case before us. It was quite right that our interest in such matters should be quickened, but we must, I trust, turn that quickened interest to some practical account. I submit there are, and can be, only two practical questions before this Committee which must be approached in a judicial frame of mind. The first practical question is, were the existing rules and regulations which govern the enforcement of discipline in the Army and the infliction of penalties observed in this case by all the officers, military and medical, concerned? If they were, no shadow of reproach attached to them, but to the system which they were called on to administer—if blame there was. If they were not, of course the officers were to blame, but on that first question I think I can claim that neither Colonel Fortescue nor any of the other officers were guilty of any dereliction of duty. But I quite agree that there in another question, perhaps not so obvious, before us, one which perhaps we are not bound to search out, but still a question which might quite naturally arise. It is whether the present system is all it should be, or whether it should not be amended? In dealing with the first question, whether Major Fortescue and the other officers are to blame, I think my best plan would be to follow events in their chronological order. I prefer to do that—to give my own account of these events based on contemporary documents, and what took place at the inquest. I prefer it rather than to enter into controversy with the honourable Member who, through no fault of his own, has not given a perfectly accurate account of these events. His information is based very largely on the report of the inquest, but there are some errors. The honourable Member has stated that Private Lorrimer was in hospital from the end of September to the 2nd of November. The true date on which he left hospital was the 2nd of October; it was an illness of only five days' duration, and his medical sheet shows that he was in the enjoyment of general good health during the whole of last autumn, with the exception of these five days. I have said that Lorrimer might, and probably would, have become a soldier of whom

Mr. Wyndham.

everybody would be proud. There was nothing imputed to him of a serious character from an ordinary standpoint, but from a military standpoint there was no doubt that this young soldier had not yet learned soldiers' ways or the necessity for discipline. I find that on the 22nd December he was brought up before the commanding officer for an offence, not in itself very grave, but serious in a young recruit. He was reported for continued idleness and dirtiness. Dirtiness in that sense does not mean habits of personal uncleanliness, but laxity in burnishing and in appearance on parade. Idleness and untidiness are military offences, which have to be taken into account, and he was given a punishment, which cannot be called vindictive, of being confined to barracks for eight days. His squadron officer reported very badly of him, and stated he was not doing well. On the Friday the whole regiment went out, under Major Fortescue, for a long field day. Lorrimer was not out with the regiment on that day. He was one of the men who stayed in barracks, charged with the performance of the routine duties of regimental life. Foremost among those duties is what is called "Stables." Every officer on duty has to attend "Stables," and any officer who, when ordered, refused, would be cashiered, and drummed out of the British Army. On this day, when the bulk of the regiment were on the march, Lorrimer absented himself from "Stables," and when he was found sitting by a fire, he refused to attend. I hope honourable Members will see that that is a very grave military offence, for the whole purpose for which an Army exists falls to the ground if we do not take very serious notice of gross disobedience.

Mr. DILLON (Mayo, E.): Did he allege any cause for refusing?

*Mr. WYNDHAM: He alleged no cause. The regiment came back at half-past five in the afternoon, after a hard day's work. That was why Lorrimer was brought up at half-past six on that day charged with this grave military offence. His commanding officer, Major Fortescue, inflicted a penalty of 72 hours' imprisonment, and I am sure any honourable and gallant Member in this House must know that many commanding officers would have given seven days. I think that would have been quite the natural punishment for insubordination, and the fact that Major Fortescue only gave three days shows that he must have taken into account the youth of this young man emerging from the status of a recruit. That sentence having been inflicted on Friday, the 23rd, it took effect at 2 p.m. on Saturday, and would have lasted until 2 p.m. on Tuesday, the 27th. The honourable Member spoke of a dungeon cell, and of the prisoner being given nothing but bread and water during three days. I do not quite admit that; when a prisoner goes in in the afternoon he would only have supper for the first day, but the prison diet is laid down in black and white in the Queen's Regulations, and if it is cruel or insufficient, then it is for this House to take the question up. The diet is as follows:— Breakfast, 6 oz. of bread and a pint of gruel; dinner, 8 oz. of bread and ½ lb. of potatoes; supper, 6 oz. of bread and a pint of gruel. That was the diet Lorrimer had during the three days. The form of exercise a prisoner may take is also laid down. It may take the form of shot drill, which the honourable Member condemns, but the amount of such drill and the alternatives for it are all laid down. It is not for one hour's exercise a day, but four hours' punishment drill. It may take the form of exercise or of punishment prescribed in the form of exercise, but prisoners must have the exercise that is laid down in the Regulations. But as Lorrimer only went into prison on Saturday afternoon, and as there is no punishment drill on Sunday, his first punishment drill commenced on Monday, the 26th. Lorrimer lifted his shot four times, and then refused to lift any more. He was also reported as having committed a nuisance in his cell. The third charge was that of reporting himself sick without cause. He was brought before Major Fortescue at one o'clock on Tuesday the 27th, and sentenced to a further two days' imprisonment with bread and water for one day—the punishment diet, which is also laid down in the regulations, and is only inflicted under certain restrictions. This unfortunate man, however, never went on that diet, because he was sentenced to it at one o'clock on Tuesday afternoon and died that even-

ing. Now, we have to consider whether Major Fortescue, Dr. Dorgan, the orderly officer, the provost sergeant, and the assistant provost sergeant, did or did not perform their duties scrupulously and with intelligence and zeal. I have read the whole of the evidence, and I cannot find that any one of the officers I have named was remiss in the discharge of his duty.

MR. DILLON: Will the honourable Member tell us whether, on the occasion of the second punishment, the complaint of sickness had been investigated?

*MR. WYNDHAM: That is the point to which I am coming. Major Fortescue acted on the medical reports which had been furnished him, and there was no evidence that the medical officer's diagnosis was incorrect. The prisoner was examined for heart disease with the stethoscope on three days when paraded before the doctor, and Dr. Dorgan gave it as his opinion that the pain of which the prisoner complained could not be anything but rheumatism, if it existed at all. The evidence disclosed at the *post mortem* examination showed that the young man died from a clot of blood in the aortic orifice, which had been formed in the left ventricle—a thing which had nothing whatever to do with the symptoms of which he complained. I will now turn to the point at which I was interrupted by the honourable Member for East Mayo. Did Major Fortescue do all that in him lay to ascertain whether the examination of the doctor was made with sufficient care? If Major Fortescue had taken the medical Report, which said that this man was fit to be punished, and had given him further punishment, I should not say we had any reason to complain; but Major Fortescue seemed so anxious to prevent an accident that he went beyond ordinary zeal, and sent, on the morning of Tuesday, 27th December, in writing, the following letter to Dr. Dorgan—

" From Officer Commanding 17th Lancers.
" To Medical Officer, Ballincollig.
" Dec. 27th, 1898.
" Will you be good enough to forward me a Report in writing on your inspection of a cell prisoner this morning, Private Lorrimer?

(Signed) H. FORTESCUE, Major,
Commanding 17th Lancers."

Major Fortescue received the following note from Dr. Dorgan in reply to his letter—

"From Medical Officer, Ballincollig.
"To Officer Commanding 17th Lancers.
"Dec. 27th, 1898.

"Private Lorrimer, cell prisoner, was brought to me 'sick' this morning, and on yesterday morning, complaining of pain in the back. In my opinion he is malingering, and I would consider him fit to undergo any further imprisonment or punishment.

"(Signed) JAMES DORGAN,
"Medical Officer."

I claim that Major Fortescue did everything in his power to prevent an accident, and that this sad tragedy reveals the fact that in Major Fortescue we have an officer who discharges his duty with great zeal and great discretion. Dr. Dorgan was corroborated in his diagnosis by the other doctor who took part in the *post mortem* examination. The Casualty Report says that Lorrimer's general health had been good, that he was admitted to the hospital on the 27th of September, 1898, with simple continuous fever, and discharged on the 2nd of October, 1898. It was a mild attack. The Casualty Report says that on being examined on 24th December, before imprisonment, there was no evidence of cardiac disease. The following day he complained, on being paraded to hospital with other prisoners, of a pain in the back. On the 26th he still had the pain in the back—in the lumbar region. He was examined stethoscopically, but there was no evidence of cardiac disease. He still said he had some pain on the 27th, but on being asked said he complained of nothing else. He was found dead in his cell at 7.50 p.m. on that day—the 27th—having been last seen alive at 6.20 p.m. Doctor Dorgan says he cannot regard the pain in the back as having any connection with the cause of death. Its existence at all was doubted by him, and he could find no sign of the prisoner having any pain from his behaviour. Dr. Dorgan gives the following brief medical history of the case—

"24.12.98.—Examined prior to imprisonment and found fit. No cardiac disease. Asked if he had any complaints, he said, 'No.' Asked if he felt all right, he said, 'Yes.'

Mr. Wyndham.

"25.12.98.—Paraded to hospital with other prisoners for my inspection. He complained of pain in his back in the lower lumbar region. I asked him if he felt cold. He said, 'Yes.' He said he was all right in other respects. I ordered liniment of turpentine and an extra blanket, after stripping his clothes, etc.

"26.12.98.—Paraded with other prisoners as usual. He said he still had some pain, but that was all he complained of. I examined him again stethoscopically, including his heart, and found no evidence of disease. Put him through several motions of bending his back, etc. He had quite free movement. I asked him if he now felt sufficiently warm. He said he did, and was all right otherwise.

"27.12.98.—Paraded with other prisoners as usual to hospital. Still complained of the pain. Again examined him. Felt his pulse, which was good, and took his temperature—98.2 degs. He complained of nothing else but the lumbar pain. The sergeant of the provost said he did not eat much the day before, but enough. I came to the conclusion, from the absence of all physical signs and the behaviour of the man, and from the word of the guard who watched him unobserved, that he had no cause for the pain, and that he was malingering. I cannot trace any association between the lumbar pain and the subsequent cause of death. The lumbar pain was all he complained of even when I asked him if he had anything else wrong. He was found dead in his cell that night at 7.50. Last seen at 6.20 p.m., when the corporal of the provost considered him all right. I was afterwards informed that he ate nothing at all on Tuesday.

"27.12.98.—He had done no work while in cells except a few minutes of shot drill on Monday.

"26.12.98.—As he would not do any more this was reported afterwards. He gave no reason for not doing so, nor made any complaint. He was ordered further imprisonment for disobedience and committing a nuisance in his cell, and I reported that he was fit to do it on Tuesday, December 27th, 1898, on being asked. I never found myself justified in recommending any change of dieting or punishment in this case, as he only complained of the lumbar pain, and that I doubted."

In the face of this Report I claim that Major Fortescue discharged his duty with zeal and discretion, and there is nothing to make me think that Dr. Dorgan did not act with acumen. Dr. Harding, who was called in for the inquest, agreed with Dr. Dorgan that the lumbar pain, if it existed, had nothing to do with the clot; and that in all probability the shot drill had nothing to do with the clot. It is not true that the jury, as a body, added anything to their verdict in the way of censure, though some of them may have spoken to that effect. I admit that it might be asked whether our treatment of military prisoners is as good as it should be, but this is a question which has not arisen in anyone's mind in connection with this case. The House will remember that we were occupied last year in considering the question of discipline in civil prisons. Discipline in military prisons has also been considered, and questions in connection with it are now being canvassed. The views of Sir Redvers Buller have been invited, and he has urged that a marked distinction should be drawn between civil and military offences in the soldier. A soldier who commits a felony should be, he said, treated as a felon and discharged from the Army, which should have no room for him, his presence in it being inimical to the best interests of the Service. A young soldier who, through thoughtlessness, is absent without leave ought to be encouraged to return and expiate his offence, and ought not to be punished as if he had committed one of the gravest offences against the civil law.

MR. DILLON: I think the honourable Gentleman did well to divide this into two questions—first, whether the officers and the doctor who were responsible in this particular case did their duty in a humane and proper manner; and, secondly, whether the present system of treating military prisoners which resulted in the death of this young soldier ought to be maintained. The honourable Gentleman practically said that provided the rules and regulations had been strictly observed by the officials the latter were entirely free from blame. I do not accept the truthfulness of that maxim without reserve. You may, in dealing with prisoners, observe the rules and regulations of the prison with absolute and most scrupulous fidelity, and yet turn the prison into a hell upon earth. In order to secure decent and fair treatment for these unfortunate persons who find their way into prisons you require something far more than a martinet spirit of strict observance of rules and regulations. Prison rules in the hands of inexperienced men are liable to be interpreted in a harsh way. They should be tempered by a large measure of human sympathy, and it has always seemed to me that one of the great evils in our military prison system is that the military prisons are placed in the hands of men who have no special training in dealing with

prisoners, and consequently the rules are interpreted in a cruel spirit. My honourable Friend the Member for South Donegal did not say that the officer in charge of the prison and the doctor deliberately inflicted punishment on a man who was unable to bear it; but, in spite of what the right honourable Gentleman the Under Secretary has said, I do not admit that he has shown that Lorrimer was sufficiently examined. In this case Lorrimer, who complained of weakness and ill-health, ought to have had the benefit of the doubt. While I make no charge against either the officer or the doctor that they inflicted punishment knowing that they were risking the man's life, I do believe, from the evidence brought forward by my honourable Friend, that there was carelessness and not sufficient sympathy in estimating the true condition of the prisoner. The doctor contented himself with examining the man on the one complaint—that he had a pain in the lumbar region, and he put this down as rheumatism. Speaking as a man with some medical knowledge, I say this was preposterous. I think the doctor has shown himself to be extremely incapable in making such a statement. A clot in the heart has direct connection with weakness, and there is a *prima facie* case that this man's health was not good. We have the statement of the man who was in the cell with him, that he was hardly able to sit up or take off his clothes, but these complaints were overlooked by the doctor, and put down as malingering. I think any medical man will agree with me that physical weakness coming from such extraordinary punishment as shot drill has a direct connection with the formation of a clot in the heart. The doctor at the inquest swore that in his opinion this punishment—this barbarous, unreasonable, and utterly foolish and cruel punishment—alone might cause a clot in the heart, and, of course, it is much more reasonable to suppose that it would do so in a man who was in a weak state of health. Therefore, I do maintain that in this very serious case both the commanding officer, but in a much less degree, and the doctor, in a much greater degree, were to blame for want of sympathy in working these prison rules. I want to ask the honourable Gentleman the

3 B

Under Secretary what became of the military doctor?

*Mr. WYNDHAM: There was no military doctor. Dr. Dorgan was the doctor in charge for the whole year.

Mr. DILLON: Is that not a very serious matter?

*Mr. WYNDHAM: I think the honourable Gentleman will remember that we have asked for money in these Estimates in order to have more Army doctors. I think it is a matter of common knowledge that we are deficient of doctors.

Mr. DILLON: That is because you treat the doctors so badly in the Army. It is a very serious thing to say that in a great town like Cork, where you have a considerable garrison, you have no Army doctor at all. It is a most extraordinary state of things. I could quite understand that in a small place where only a small portion of a regiment was stationed an outside doctor should be called in, but it is most extraordinary that in a large garrison town like Cork, with two large barracks, these troops should be in the hands of a doctor about whose qualifications we know nothing. In dealing with peculiar cases, such as the effect of this shot drill on a man, we ought to have the security of knowing that an experienced doctor had examined the prisoner. Who is Dr. Dorgan? He may be competent, or he may not be competent. We have no proof either way. We do not know who he is, what his qualifications are, or what his practice may be; but of this we may be sure, that he has no prolonged military experience and no special training for deciding these delicate questions. It is one of the most reckless and cruel things that any person in authority can be guilty of, to leave a question of malingering—one of the most difficult medical questions that doctors have to deal with unless they have special instruction in the art of dealing with it— to an inexperienced man. In questions of malingering, where people's lives are at stake, and where great cruelty may be inflicted, it is a gross outrage to leave the decision to inexperienced doctors. The Under Secretary has given us no statement as to the qualifications of Dr. Dorgan or as to his previous medical

Mr. Dillon.

experience, and the ground upon which he was appointed to this prison. I do not think it is fair, and I trust the War Office will abandon the practice, to leave the health of soldiers and questions of this kind in the hands of temporary doctors engaged for six months.

*Mr. WYNDHAM: They are engaged for the whole year.

Mr. DILLON: His appointment, however, depends on the goodwill of the officers, and, therefore, he is not in the independent position of a regular Army doctor, who is an all-important man in the regiment, and has no need to be afraid of the officers, because he stands on an equal footing with them. I do not for a moment say that the punishment was excessive, with the exception of shot drill, but it was for an offence committed by a young recruit whose character was excellent until he came into the Army, and who might have been reasonably expected to make a good soldier. It seems to me peculiarly inhuman to send in a recruit on Christmas Day to punishment. Would it not have shown more kindly spirit in the officer to have deferred his punishment until after Christmas Day? This fact alone gives me the idea that the officer was rather harsh in his treatment of this prisoner. Now I come to the question of shot drill. We have been told that great reform is contemplated in our military prisons. If I recollect aright, when we were discussing the treatment of civil prisoners last year, more horrible statistics were produced about flogging. We obtained the abolition of that punishment in civil prisons, and I hope that before long the right honourable Gentleman will bring before the House a scheme of reform for military prisoners. I hold that all those barbarous punishments, which make a man do painful and excessive work, with no object in view, are a disgrace to humanity. If you want to punish a man, put him into gaol, lock him up in his cell, and place him on a low diet if you like, but do not compel him to do work which would break down a man on full diet when he is in a half-starved condition. It breaks his mind, turns him into an animal, and exercises an evil influence on his whole nature. Let this serve as an occasion to get rid of the system of shot drill, which is a system of torture, for, after an unfortunate man has been at it a short time, every muscle and bone in his body so aches and becomes so sore that he is hardly able to sit or lie down. That, of course, is the object of shot drill; but I would ask those who support it, would it not be just as well to put a man on a rack, or screw his thumbs, or beat him with sticks, if your object is to inflict physical pain and suffering on the man without doing any good in any conceivable way? That system of punishment ought to be abolished, especially in military prisons, where the offence for which the prisoner is confined is generally one which involves no moral guilt. That is a point we intend to press strongly on the honourable Gentleman. I have noticed with satisfaction in the "Army and Navy Gazette" of the 28th July last an article stating "that, so far as shot drill is concerned, there is a general feeling that it ought to be discontinued." Again, one who visits military prisons describes it as "a cruel and clumsy punishment, well known to be dangerous in the case of a man whose heart's action is weak." Further, the writer says there are plenty of fatigue duties that would serve the purpose. We know that it is a degrading and dangerous punishment. We succeeded, in spite of the opposition of every officer in the British Army, in abolishing the lash, and I should like to know if there is now one officer who would like to go back to it. On the very same principle we intend to oppose these degrading punishments being applied to soldiers while they are in prison. I have a most complete contempt and utter disbelief in those men who say you cannot maintain discipline without inflicting these degrading punishments, and I hope that this most melancholy case will be made the occasion for finally sweeping away from the military prisons of the country punishments which are entirely inconsistent with the spirit of the age.

COLONEL LOCKWOOD: I have to apologise for an interruption I made during the speech of the honourable Member for South Donegal, but it was studded with such offensive remarks regarding the officers of Her Majesty's Service that my usually calm temper became for the moment slightly ruffled. The whole case for Major Fortescue and the doctor has been so well put by the Under Secretary that I have nothing to add. I am certain that there is not a Member of the House who, having heard the honourable Gentleman's exposition of the facts, can fail to believe that the authorities not only did their duty in this case, but event went beyond it in their care for this man. The honourable Member for South Donegal said that this young man had been "done to death," and he went on in strained terms to condemn the general conduct of the officers towards their men as not only inhuman, but as animated by a wish to make a difference between classes, which do not exist in the Army.

MR. SWIFT MacNEILL rose, but Colonel Lockwood declined to give way.

MR. SWIFT MacNEILL: The honourable Gentleman must give way?

COLONEL LOCKWOOD: I decline to give way to the honourable Member. I did not interrupt him except on the occasion I have alluded to. The whole speech of the honourable Member was an attempt to prove that there is a difference in the treatment of the rich and poor in the Army, that the officers have no care for the welfare of their men, and that their punishments are brutal in the extreme. The honourable Member said that when the men were in prison they were not properly looked after, and he went on to say that this young man was hurried off to a dungeon and done to death.

MR. SWIFT MacNEILL: Hear, hear!

COLONEL LOCKWOOD: A more untrue picture of what really did happen could not have been put before the House. It has been proved with what care Major Fortescue acted, seeing that he called for a second medical report, not being satisfied with the first one. It is easy enough to be wise after the event. I do not think that the Members for South Donegal and East Mayo even attempted to prove any possible connection between the pains which the man suffered from at the back of his head and the clot of blood which was found at the *post mortem* examination. The only marvel is how few mistakes doctors make when one thinks of the numerous classes of disease they have to deal with. Of course, after the *post mortem* it became known what the man died of. I cannot say the doctor was to blame, and it has been proved that the commanding officer was not only not to blame, but that he went as far as possible in every way to ensure that justice was done. The man's general health was not bad: he had only been in hospital from the 1st to the 5th October with a slight fever. I do not regret that this case has been brought before the House, but I do regret that the honourable Member for South Donegal—humane and kind-hearted man that he is—should have gone out of his way to insinuate that the British officer has no care for the health of his men and that differences are made in the treatment of rich and poor in the Army.

MR. T. P. O'CONNOR (Liverpool, Scotland): My honourable Friend altogether disclaims having made any such accusation. What he did say was that this man was so punished as to die from the effects of the punishment. In that sense, he meant the man was done to death; and in that sense, also, I say he was done to death. I have listened with great attention to what has been said in this Debate, and I think the public will feel indebted to my honourable Friend for having brought forward this case, which is eminently one for consideration by the House of Commons. Nobody could find fault with a single word in the speech of the Under Secretary for War. He treated the case considerately and humanely. But the facts remain, and what are they? This man was declared by the doctor to be malingering—to be without disease, and yet he dies of the disease. That fact has not been controverted or explained by the statement of the Under Secretary. I have been looking over the facts, and I find another fact—perhaps a comparatively trifling one in a tragedy like this. This unfortunate creature actually was allowed to die in the dark: there was no light in his cell! What possible defence is there for the doctor? Let me first say one word about

Colonel Lockwood.

the action of the major in command. The Under Secretary has called attention to the fact that the major called for a written Report. I think two interpretations can be placed on that act. It surely showed anxiety and mental doubt as to whether this officer had adopted a proper course as to that man. Did not the mere fact of asking for a written Report conclusively prove that in his own mind there was grave and painful uncertainty as to whether he was treating this unfortunate man properly or not? As to the doctor, while I am not a medical man, I should say that disease of the character from which the man died could have been diagnosed. Now I come to the phrase that this boy was "done to death." He was only a boy, and the Under Secretary in his speech did not lay sufficient stress on the fact that he was young in years, and that the offence charged against him was a thoughtless, inadvertent act, which all of us—having been young ourselves—should be disposed to charitably consider. The boy died of disease of the heart, and he must have had disease of the heart when the punishment was inflicted upon him. Let us see what happened. This boy was suffering from disease of the heart, he was put into a dark cell, he was fed on bread and water, and in addition to all that, one of the severest and cruellest forms of physical punishment—shot drill—was inflicted upon him. Was not that boy killed by the punishment and the dieting? I challenge the Under Secretary for War to deny that. The Under Secretary for War shakes his head. What did the boy die of, then? What produced the fatal stage of the heart disease? It was produced unquestionably by the shot drill, by confinement to the dark cell, and by bread and water diet. The Under Secretary for War has himself confirmed the statement that this boy was done to death, for he admitted that the shot drill may have contributed to the result. Surely that is a case which ought to have been anticipated by the War Department; but as I interpret the statement of the Under Secretary no notice was taken of the matter. I think the case is too strong for anything to be added to it by exaggeration. I go on from this particular case to the general principle. Last year we had a Committee investigating the whole question of prison treatment. I am afraid, from what the Under Secretary for War says, that a considerable time may elapse before the prison treatment is reformed. I hope, however, that the result of the Debate will be that the question of shot drill will be carefully investigated, and that, above all, proper means will be taken to give soldiers proper medical attendance, and that in future other victims will not follow this poor unfortunate young man who, I believe, was done to death.

CAPTAIN JESSEL (St. Pancras, S.): My excuse for intervening in this Debate is that I was a good many years in the 17th Lancers. In spite of what has been said that the character of the commanding officer has not been aspersed, I think very scant justice has been done to him by honourable Gentlemen opposite. Some general accusations have been made against him, because he was away on leave for two days. All I can say is, that according to the military regulations he was perfectly justified in going on leave at that time. He left the command of the regiment in the hands of the next officer in command—an officer who had seen considerable service. He was only doing what was customary in a commanding officer, and I can see no reason why accusations should be laid against him for being away on Christmas Day, and the Monday following. An honourable Member has said that sometimes the men are dealt with severely by officers who have no experience of active service. I can assure honourable Gentlemen opposite that Major Fortescue has served his country faithfully and well. He has the war medal for the Zulu campaign, and he has served in India, Canada, and other parts of the world. Another thing I can assure the Committee and those honourable Gentlemen opposite, that Major Fortescue has always been known for the extreme care and kindness he has manifested towards his officers and men. I myself had the honour of serving under him, and I can say that he treated all the officers and men in the squadron in the most satisfactory way; in fact, he took more than the usual interest in the welfare of those under him. Then there is another point in Major Fortescue's conduct as commanding officer. The honourable

Member who spoke last, said that somehow there were two reasons which led him to call for a special report on this case. One of these reasons might have been his care and consideration for those under him, and the other reason may have been because he had some doubt in his mind. If the Committee will allow me, I shall quote from a letter received from Major Fortescue on the subject—

"The particular reason," he says, "why I called for the special report was in consequence of his behaviour before me on this occasion—refusing to answer questions, and pretending to be idiotic. I sent for the doctor to make a report on the case, which I enclose."

It is not necessary for me to say anything more about that, as you have got the report of the doctor. I come to the question of the medical officer. I would point out to the House that the medical officer has a very good degree, with the letters M.B. after his name, and it is necessary that he should be very highly educated before he could get such a degree.

DR. CLARK (Caithness): What is his name?

CAPTAIN JESSEL: Dr. Dorgan.

DR. CLARK: I cannot find him in the Medical Register or in the Medical Directory.

CAPTAIN JESSEL: He is a man of some standing and had been attending the corps for a year. The honourable Member for East Mayo referred to military doctors and asked why there was no military doctor near at hand. He seems to be of opinion that this man's troop was at Cork. It was not at Cork, but at Ballincollig—a station for two squadrons. The military authorities could not find a military doctor to do the work at Ballincollig, and therefore they employed a civilian medical man. I can agree in one respect with the honourable Gentleman opposite. I think it would be a very good thing for the Army if we reverted to the old system of having military doctors attached to regiments, for a civilian doctor cannot be so well acquainted with the men as the military doctors who, under the old system, were attached to the regiments. They knew every man in the regiment, and everything about him. Under new regulations of the War Office doctors are called station doctors, and are appointed to look after several regiments. Regiments come and regiments go, but the doctor remains on at the station. We were told that the reason why these new regulations were instituted was that it would cost a great deal of money to appoint 60 more doctors to the Army. It would be a real good thing to go back to the old regimental system. Under the old system there was less chance of malingering, because the regimental doctor knew every man in the regiment and his constitution. Malingering is one of the most difficult things to deal with. It is constantly cropping up in regiments, on board ship, and in prisons; and it is a constant practice in some men when they wish to avoid certain duties. Therefore, Army and Navy officers have to be extremely careful and to be on their guard—much more so than men placed in similar positions in civil life. I cannot help thinking that the honourable Gentleman opposite has been a little hard on the doctor. It was not his fault, and, after all, doctors are human and liable to make mistakes. I am told that a case of clotting of blood is one in which the symptoms arise very quickly, and that it is very difficult to diagnose.

Mr. DILLON: That is quite true, but then it is likely to arise from weakness, and you can generally tell from the condition of the man if there is a predisposition to it.

Captain JESSEL: Well, I cannot see why the doctor was to blame. I come to the question of shot drill. I maintain that in keeping up the punishment of shot drill in the British Army we are 50 years behind the times. I remember when I first went into the Army there were many very severe punishments. A few years after regulations were laid down by which the punishments were not to be so severe as formerly. I knew of a man who had been sent to prison with hard labour for 42 days for some offence. That is reduced now to 30 days, which shows the tendency to a more lenient treatment nowadays. I am sure the Under Secretary

Captain Jessel.

for War will bear me out when I say that this more lenient administration of military justice has greatly improved the Army, and I am perfectly sure that there is a great deal less crime. I am sorry for the death of this young man; we must all regret it, but it was through no fault of the officer commanding or the doctor. All I can say is that it will be a very great thing if from evil comes good, and if the result of this Debate should be that shot drill and other similar punishments are done away with altogether.

On the return of the Deputy Chairman after the usual interval—

Dr. CLARK: Sir, I would congratulate the honourable and gallant Member for St Pancras, South, on the impartiality with which he has treated this question. I regret that there has been some heat exhibited on both sides of the House, perhaps initiated by my honourable and learned Friend who opened the question. The honourable and learned Gentleman has apologised for the heat he displayed, and everybody is pleased that he has done so. But I must say that the honourable and gallant Member for Epping has made insinuations against a brother officer, and has not yet apologised for them. I hope before the Debate is at an end that we shall have some facts bearing on the capacity of the medical officer who reported on the subject. I regret that the Under Secretary for War is not here just now, for I want some information about this Dr. Horgan, or Dorgan, or Dugan. I have examined the Medical Register and I can find there no such name as Horgan, or Dorgan, or Dugan. I have also been to the Library and consulted the Medical Directory, but cannot find there either the name Horgan, or Dorgan, or Dugan. I know that there are some gentlemen who are qualified whose names are not on the Medical Register, for they do not register. But it seems to me that this man is both unqualified and is not registered, and I should like to hear something more about it before the Debate ends. As to the facts of the case, I think the Under Secretary rather minimised the facts, and I am rather sorry that he did so, because otherwise he pretended to be fair and impartial——

Attention having been called to the fact that there were not 40 Members present, the House was counted, when 40 Members being present—

DR. CLARK (continuing): I was saying that I regret the absence of the Under Secretary for War, because we might have got the information we desire. Otherwise, I must come to the conclusion that things are worse in the Medical Department of the Army than I thought they were. I remember 10 years ago pressing on the late Mr. Stanhope, who was then Under Secretary for War—I am glad to see the honourable the Under Secretary for War now in his place, for I want to know if he can give me the name of the medical officer who gave the report on the dead soldier. I have looked in the Medical Register, and in the Medical Directory, and I can find no person of the name of Dorgan, or Horgan, or Dugan.

*MR. WYNDHAM : James Dorgan, M.B.

DR. CLARK: Well, as I have said, I have looked very carefully in the Medical Register, and I found there is no such name in it. If a man is qualified, but is not registered, he can practise, but he cannot sue for fees. I am astonished at the Army Department employing any man who is not on the Medical Register, because some gentlemen have been knocked off the Register for various faults, although they still remain members of a college of physicians or surgeons. If the Under Secretary for War is right as to the name, and if the man is unregistered, the probability is that he is unqualified.

*MR. WYNDHAM : The honourable Member knows that all qualified medical practitioners are not registered. This doctor is a Bachelor of Medicine.

DR. CLARK: Can you give me any further information: whether he took his degree at the Royal University of Ireland, or at Trinity College, or at a Scotch University?

*MR. WYNDHAM: No, I don't know where he took his degree.

DR. CLARK: Well, the Army Medical Department have sunk so low that they are compelled to employ an unregistered practitioner. The honourable and gallant Gentleman is perfectly right; it is quite true that there are medical men who are qualified, but not registered. The honourable and gallant Gentleman who spoke last says that this man is very highly qualified, but I have asked the Under Secretary for War, and have consulted the usual sources, but can get no satisfactory information on the point. I agree with the honourable and gallant Member for South St. Pancras that no accusation can be made against Major Fortescue, and I cannot understand why any accusation should have been made against him. He seems to me to have acted very wisely, and in a calm and judicial spirit, and to have even gone further, and to have done more than might have been required of him. After sentencing the man to the usual punishment, as he observed the peculiarities of the individual, he asked for further information and a special report on his condition. The commanding officer could not have done more than he did. But the further information which he got from the medical officer seems to me to be very unsatisfactory. Where I think the Under Secretary minimised the statement of the facts of the case was this. This man had committed a first offence. He was left behind for the purpose of doing dirty work, cleaning out the stables and so forth. Then he complained of illness and did not do his work, and for that he was sentenced to three days' imprisonment. No one can say that that was too much. Then it was said that he had suffered, or claimed to have suffered, from continued fever a short time before, but in spite of that he was sent to do his work. And what is the second offence. I have only the evidence given before the coroner's jury, and these are the words of Sergeant Hobbs. The deceased was very slow, and he ordered him to increase his speed, which he did not do, that is to say, he was doing shot drill and was not going fast enough. He ordered him a second time, but he did not do it. This witness did not ask him for his reason for not doing it faster, but marched him off to the hospital to be medically examined. The coroner asked what did the doctor say, to which the witness replied that the doctor said he was all right, and that he then marched him to the cells. They only had an idea, for here it is recorded that the doctor said, "I had an idea that the man was shamming." I have had some experience of malingering. So far as the facts go, this young man claimed that he was ill, and suffering from diarrhœa, which is a very weakening disease. He was accused of not taking proper care of himself, and making a mess of his room, and under these circumstances a charge is made against him that he was not doing his work properly, either from inability or from laziness, and he is brought up before the colonel, and he gets two days' more punishment. It you analyse that, you find that the young man complains of being ill, that he was still suffering, that he was sent to a disagreeable work, and that, instead of doing his work in the stable, he went to his room, and was found sitting over the fire. Surely he would have given some reason for that.

*Mr. WYNDHAM: I think the honourable Gentleman has misapprehended the statement which was made in respect to this matter. Everyone who is in barracks has to be present at stable parade. It is a very essential parade, and this man did not attend the stable parade, and, when found, he refused to do so.

Dr. CLARK: What I want to get at is, what this matter is. So far as the evidence is concerned, I have it here in the evidence of Sergeant E. Hobbs; but do I understand that this young man refused to come to work?

*Mr. WYNDHAM: He was found in his room sitting by the fire when he ought to have been standing at attention by his horse. When found sitting by the fire and ordered to the stables, he refused to go, and throughout two days gave no reason.

Dr. CLARK: It seems to me that this young man was not only suffering from physical disease, but mental disease as well.

Dr. Clark.

*Mr. WYNDHAM: That was one of the things which he was thought to be shamming.

Dr. CLARK: But he was shamming everything, or thought to be; but, unfortunately, he died, and we are inquiring into the matter in this House. Now, we know what old soldiers are, and we know that they are very smart in malingering; but you do not expect a young man of 16 or 17, who has only been six months in the Army, to do so. It seems to me that, outside Colonel Fortescue, there does not seem to have been very much inquiry into the matter. It seems to me very hard to talk of a professional colleague who is not here to defend himself, but after listening to everything that has been said, and reading very closely and studying very closely, as closely as I can, the evidence given before the coroner's inquest, I think he has been very much to blame. The system seems to be a bad one—the sergeant did not ask him a question, he simply ordered him to do it quicker, and when he saw that he did not do it quicker he gave him a second order to do it quicker. He did not ask him why he did not do it; that was not his function. His evidence is that he ordered·him to increase his speed, and finding that he did not do so he marched him to the hospital. You do not expect a sergeant to be well up in medical diagnosis. When you get a man to the hospital, you do expect him to be brought before a specially trained man. Now this doctor was only a civil man, and had not had the special training you give to the military man. Naturally, he ought to know something about malingering; but in general practice, though you may find hysterical girls and hypochondriacal men, you never find malingering. I say that the special thing in the Army and Navy that you have to teach the medical man is malingering; because you have got old sailors and old soldiers who dodge their work in many ways by the taking of soap pills and things of that kind, and that is a thing which the medical man ought to be able to detect. When a question comes of this kind, the sergeant takes the man off to the hospital, and he comes before a medical man. The old unfortunate state of things evidently still obtains. At last the Secretary to the War Office has undone a great deal of the evil done by his predecessors, and I think, on the whole, the boycott with regard to the medical part of the Army is ceasing. Of course, in all the medical schools a short time ago the students were being taught to avoid the Army. You had been making many changes, and depriving the medical service of their titular rank, and, in consequence, you could not get the best men from the schools; but at last a change has been made, and, on the whole, the medical men are content, and the boycott will cease, and you will be able to get as good medical men in the Army as we get in civil life. You have been boycotted; you have not only not got the refuse of the profession, for you could not even get that, and you have had to take a number of men from the outside, and this is the result. I think that we can examine this in a fair spirit, I do not think that the Secretary to the War Office is to blame, I do not think that the Under Secretary is to blame, the blame seems to culminate really in one professional gentleman who ought to know better. Now, the man died from syncope, the very last thing upon earth that you would find a young man of 20 years of age dying from. There are two things required in order that he should do so, either he had disease of the heart, which the medical gentleman was unable to diagnose—but I do not think that there was anything of the kind; I think that this poor fellow was done to death. Dr. Dorgan admits that shot drill under the condition that this man was in might bring it about. Here is a young man up to 12 o'clock of the day of his death reported to be malingering, and he dies from syncope, and the jury on the coroner's inquest state that they could find no disease to account for it, that they could only find the fact that the lad had died from syncope. And syncope could only be caused, by nervous causes, by doing him to death; partly by starvation and partly by this extra labour. When he went before the commanding officer his mind was affected as well as his body. I do not, after looking at it very fully, think that anybody is to blame except the medical officer; and if the statement can be true that you are appointing and have been appointing for your purposes men who

are unregistered, I can easily understand it. You do not allow such a man to come before the coroner's jury, and he cannot, if he is an unregistered medical man, claim his fees. I do not find this gentleman's name in any permanent register, and I think that is a very bad story. The honourable and gallant Gentleman said that shot drill was a very bad thing, and acts upon a weak heart. I do not say that moving 28 pounds could not be done, but so far as this man was concerned, he was suffering from a very weakening disease. Now the pains that he complained were of comparative unimportance; they might have been due to rheumatism, or they might have been due to his ricking himself in doing this work. The doctor has been led off the scent by these secondary symptoms. I must say that I never expected that the stupid policy in the War Office would have brought you so low as in this case it evidently has.

*COLONEL BLUNDELL (Lancashire, Ince): My impression is that this poor man had a severe disease of the heart and nothing could have saved him, but I think that had there been a medical officer attached to the regiment, he would have known perfectly well whether this young man, who, they say, was a good man, was malingering or not. He would say, to himself, "My medical skill would lead me to believe that this young man is malingering, but from what I know of his general character I do not think he is" And then he would have taken him into hospital under observation, and this unfortunate accident would never have happened. I recollect years ago, when a change was made in the position of medical officers in the Army, speaking to a great authority on the subject, urging him to attach medical officers to a regiment for a year or other period. He replied, The War Department have taken the plunge they have, but have never come up again. Unless you attach the medical officers to the regiments, and give them the prejudice of soldiers, they remain civilians still, and the old knowledge of the men by the medical officer ceases. A medical officer, I venture to say, ought to be attached to a regiment for a period of time so that he might acquire its prejudices, and so that he may become acquainted with all the men that he will have charge over, and then, from his knowledge of their habits and from the knowledge of their behaviour in the regiment, he will know whether these men are malingering or not.

CAPTAIN NORTON (Newington, W.): I think it will be admitted by every Member of this House that this is a most painful case to have been brought before this House. It seems to have a tendency to divide the Debate upon one subject, to exonerate the officers on the one hand, and to inculpate them on the other. If you come to look at the facts of the case such as the public see them, they appear in this light. A young man, a recruit of 18 years of age, joins the Service; previous to joining the Service he bears a good character, and we are given to understand he does not bear a bad character during the time he is in the regiment. That is a point which I should like to elucidate. But after he has been six months in the Service, he dies in prison, practically after having suffered some slight punishment, and dies, undoubtedly, in consequence of the punishment he has passed through. It will be very well understood that I, as an officer, wish to bring no accusation whatever against any officer in the regiment. My anxiety is to show that I am extremely glad that it has come before the Committee, because it is of the very first importance that matters of this kind should be thoroughly thrashed out, and that the public should not take their views and form their opinions from the reports which they read in the newspapers, where the case is very often stated in a one-sided manner. There is no doubt that everyone concerned attempted to do their duty; whether they did it with any great consideration is quite another question. My view is that it is not the officers who are to blame, but the system. The officer commanding a regiment has no desire but to keep up discipline; that is one of the reasons why I have been wishing to know the character of this man. The man in question appears to be what one would call "a dirty soldier." Now, I am very well aware that it is the custom of the regiment to give men of that class, men who are supposed to be able to do their work, but who will not do it, very scant

Colonel Blundell.

courtesy. Well, it is said that there has been no dereliction of duty. Now I appeal to the right honourable Gentleman, and I ask him whether it is not distinctly laid down in the Queen's regulations that it is the certainty and not the severity of the punishment which acts as a deterrent to crime. Every officer should bear that in mind when dealing out punishment, especially to the recruit. I do not say that the officers did not bear it in mind. But I do say that the whole system is not on a par with the general advance of the civilisation of this country, and the general advance that has been made as regards the humane treatment of those who have to bear the punishment which is inflicted upon them. I am prepared to admit that the issue in the end was unfortunate, but I think every excuse should be made for the honourable Member for Donegal. He is of a passionate nature; he argues with a degree of warmth that is natural to him, and his feeling carried him away because this man was undoubtedly, though accidentally, done to death. There is another person to whom I should like to refer. I notice that the corporal who was in charge of the guard-room does not appear to have visited this man. Now, I may be wrong, but I understand it is his duty to visit the men in the cells every hour.

*MR. WYNDHAM: He visited him three times.

CAPTAIN NORTON: I am very glad to hear that, because it clearly exonerates all the officers concerned. But I now come to a question of much greater importance— the question of the doctor. Now I have been, ever since I entered this House, complaining with reference to the status and treatment of the medical officers of the Army. I have brought case after case before the House, and it cannot be denied that, ever since the abolition of the system of attaching medical men to the regiments, there has been a spirit of discontent on the part of the medical officers of the Army. We shall be told that that is purely because the medical officers do not take the stand which they ought to take, and that they do not take a pride in their profession. They do not do so because you do not get the right class of medical officers. You only get the sweepings of the medical schools. I am glad to hear that you are going to make some improvement, and that the boycott is about to be removed by the medical schools. I agree with these titles being given to the medical officers. They have a separate corps of their own in almost every Continental army in Europe, and it has led to very beneficial results. They have obtained thoroughly competent men, a thing which we have not been able to do. But what is the real idea in reference to the Army Medical Department? It was stated in this House last year that we were capable of putting two Army Corps into the field, and that we were not short of medical officers. I knew at that time for a fact that, without denuding the troops in Egypt, that was absolutely impossible. Now we are told that there is an intention to increase the number of medical men. In the meantime, I consider that the Government are to blame for not employing fully qualified men. Such a man as this should not have the care of Her Majesty's troops. Now, I ask, was there such a man in the regiment as a fully qualified man, and, if there was, why was he not employed? I come now to the question of malingering. My experience teaches me that in a cavalry regiment there is very little malingering indeed, and I should be glad to know whether there is any evidence to show that this man had on any previous occasion attempted to shirk his duty or not. And when the man was sentenced a second time, when he was complaining of being ill—he was either ill or well. If he was well, he ought to be sent to his duty, and forced to do it. If the medical officer had any doubt whether he was able to do his duty, was it not the duty of the medical officer to send the man to the hospital in order that he might be given every care? Instead of that, owing to the fact that this man was not a trained medical officer, he takes the man across, he gives him some liniment and an extra blanket, and allows him to lay on a plank bed in the guard-room. I think that every honourable Gentleman will admit that, so far as that medical officer was concerned, there was dereliction of duty, but if there was no dereliction of duty, there was great misjudgment and incompetence. The honourable Gentleman

shakes his head; but if this man was malingering, he ought to have been punished, and ought not to have been given an extra blanket and this liniment for the pain which he was suffering. But if there was any chance of his being ill, he should have been treated as a person in a civil prison, and sent to the hospital ward. There was either a gross dereliction of duty, or gross incompetence and culpability. Now, I come to prison diet and prison punishment. Last year we passed a Bill through this House for the purpose of humanising and mitigating punishments in our civil prisons. Surely, with our present recruits, and our desire to attract the best men to the Service, this is a question in which the Army ought to immediately follow suit, and place prison diet and prison punishment on a better basis. This is a question which ought to have immediately engaged the attention of the Department, but a whole year has gone by, and they have done nothing. Shot drill is the very worst drill to which any man can be subjected. Did the honourable Gentleman ask me what shot drill was?

THE FINANCIAL SECRETARY TO THE WAR OFFICE (Mr. J. POWELL WILLIAMS, Birmingham, S.): No.

CAPTAIN NORTON: Then I must request the honourable Gentleman not to interrupt me in my observations unless he does so with a pertinent remark.

MR. POWELL WILLIAMS: Mr. O'Connor, I made no observation to the honourable Member at all.

CAPTAIN NORTON: Then I must request the honourable Gentleman to refrain from making observations to himself which have the effect of interrupting me in my argument. I was stating just now that shot drill was one of the worst forms of punishment to which a man could be subjected, inasmuch as it is unremunerative labour, and it has the very worst effect on the man physically, and not only that, but it has a very deleterious effect upon his mind. There is nothing that takes the heart out of a man so much as to be forced to unremunerative labour, and it is very well known that a man would prefer work four times harder if it were of such a character as would lead that man to think he was not throwing his time away. Now the carrying of a weight from one corner of a square to another is one of the most irritating forms of labour both to body and mind, and I hope we shall have some assurance from the honourable and gallant Gentleman that with the least possible delay this useless form of punishment will, so far as soldiers are concerned, be done away with, and that more generous treatment with reference to the diet for soldiers undergoing punishment will shortly be introduced.

*MR. PIRIE : Sir, I am glad the Under Secretary has divided this Question into two parts. I only, however, propose to deal with the second part in the few observations I propose to make, because I do not think it is in any way necessary for anyone who has heard the facts of the case to even attempt a defence of Major Fortescue, for the simple reason that he does not require defence. No one who knows anything about the case, or of the circumstances surrounding such cases in military life, will imagine for a moment that he was in any way to blame ; the blame emphatically lies on the system by which this young man met his death. But perhaps his life will not have been lost in vain if, by his case being brought before the Committee, some very radical changes take place in the system. There are two points in particular which I would like to bring before the Committee, but before doing so I would touch on the case with reference to a matter I have frequently orought before the House, viz., the youth of the victim, and the injustice, both to the soldier himself and to the officer who has to deal with him, of the present system by which a man's given age in the Service may be two or more years less than his real age ; the injustice to the soldier consisting, that while still possibly only a boy, he is required to do man's work and be punished according to a scale settled for a man ; and, as regards the officer, from his being placed in a false position in having to appor- tion punishment while having no reli- able data to go on as to the age of the offender. Now, Sir, what a great re- sponsibility would be placed on this country if it had happened that this young soldier had enlisted as three

Captain Norton.

years older than his actual age, and the commanding officer had had to judge him upon the age written down on the paper. I think the present sys- tem is absolutely wrong, and ought not to be continued. We take our recruits three or four years younger than any Continental army, and it is scarcely pos- sible that these boys can always resist temptations and avoid the punishments we often have to mete out to them. I therefore impute the grossest blame to the system which allows these recruits to enter in many cases under entirely false conditions. My two points, how- ever, directly connected with this case are, first, that the present system of pun- ishments for military offences should have been allowed to continue for so long, and I would hope that the recom- mendations of Sir Redvers Buller will be adopted without delay ; and, secondly, that in this, as in so many other cases, no court of inquiry was held by the mili- tary authorities. It is directly due to their reluctance to hold such courts, from what seems to be a false hope of avoid- ing publicity, that much harm is done, and that such cases have to be brought before this House.

MR. CALDWELL (Lanark, Mid.): As this is a case of a Glasgow lad, whose father has communicated with me on the subject, I desire to say a very few words. No one will regret that this matter has been brought before the House of Com- mons. I think it is desirable that this House should take a watchful care over the comfort of the ordinary soldier in the Army, and to that extent this dis- cussion should be productive of much public good. In this case we start with the important fact that the boy was a son of very respectable parents, and a member of the Boys' Brigade, which. I may mention, is the most highly re- spectable brigade in Glasgow, none but practically the best boys being admitted to membership. However, he was not merely a member of the Boys' Brigade, but for three years was a colour-sergeant, which testifies to the fact that he had military aspirations. He enlisted un- doubtedly against the wishes of his parents, who would have preferred that he should live at home, but he went into the Army with a determination to follow a military profession, and that is impor- tant when we come to consider the question of malingering. For six months he was in the Army in Ireland, but I do not gather from the statement of the Under Secretary for War that there had been any complaint against the boy until five days before his death. On the 27th September to the end of October he was in the hospital suffering from fever, and he had obviously not got the better of its weakening and depressing effects when the first charge, which the Under Secretary described as one of un-tidiness and idleness, was made against him. I think we may assume that having gone into the Army by choice it is not likely that he would try and excuse himself from a position he was evidently anxious to fill. Now, the charge made against him is absolutely incompatible with the character of the disease from which he was suffering. The charge was untidiness. We know quite well that want of cleanliness is meant, and we also know that the disease from which he was suffering was diarrhœa, and that is probably the untidiness charged against him. Now, it has been shown that when the boy was in Glasgow, where there are plenty of opportunities for swimming, he was very fond of swimming, so that if he had got into untidy habits within four or five days of his death it was the result of the disease which was hanging about him at that particular time. Then, again, with regard to the idleness, it is obvious that the lad felt himself weak and unfit. He had suffered from fever. He had been in the hospital, and there is no possible doubt that it was disease, and disease alone, which caused the complaint to be made against him, complaint which only ended at his death. Now we come to the question with regard to the doctor who attended him. A very important question has been put to the Under Secretary: Is this man a registered practitioner? We certainly are entitled to know. As has been pointed out, I think he was not a medical practitioner who had the same knowledge of recruits, or of the way to handle men in the Army, as an Army medical man. We find also that the surgeon who gave evidence evidently conceived the idea that this lad was malingering, but, of course, he had no immediate knowledge of any of the surrounding circumstances. It is all very well for the Under Secretary to make the ap-

pearance of a case against this lad of malingering, when he is dead, and when what he said is filtered through the medical authorities, who, of course, will take very good care to filter nothing that will tell against themselves or against those in the Service. It is all very well to come forward with a medical report and the statements made by witnesses that the lad made no complaint, gave no reason for his being idle, and simply acted the part of a dumb showman. It goes too far. On the other hand, the lad's lips are closed, and you have not one single word except the statement of a fellow officer that the lad appeared to be ill. Then we come to the post-mortem examination. Now, here, again, I ask by whom was the post-mortem examination undertaken? A post-mortem examination, to be of any use whatever, ought to be undertaken by an absolutely independent party.

THE DEPUTY CHAIRMAN: Order, order! The responsibility for the post-mortem examination rests with the coroner, and cannot be discussed here.

MR. CALDWELL: I was only going to point out that it was the same doctor who attended this lad who held the post-mortem examination. That is, of course, the relevancy of my mentioning this matter. If it had been an independent doctor we should have had an independent report as to not merely the cause of death, but as to whether any other circumstances facilitated it. I may also mention that the Under Secretary did not state that in the course of the inquest it was brought out even from the doctor who conducted the post-mortem examination that his death might have been the result of shot drill. It is an unfortunate circumstance that death should take place either in a military or a civil prison. With regard to the shot drill, I disapprove of it being given alike to strong and weak prisoners. In the case of those who are strong shot drill is no punishment whatever, but in the case of one who is weak it may be a very severe punishment indeed. In the letter which the father sent to me he said he knew perfectly well that nothing could be done now so far as his son's death was concerned, but he expressed the hope that the matter might be brought before the·

House of Commons, so that what he regarded as a barbarous system of punishment might, in the interests of those who join the Army, be done away with. The Under Secretary will perhaps remember that when the question of prison life and punishment was being considered in the House of Commons the right honourable Gentleman who was at that time representing the War Office said that if the House of Commons passed the Bill modifying the system of punishment in civil prisons the War Office authorities would be prepared to follow in like manner with regard to military prisons. Well, we are entitled to ask what steps are being taken by the military authorities with a view of revising the punishments inflicted in military prisons, so as to make them conform with the more humane practice now pursued in civil prisons.

MR. CARSON (Dublin University): Mr. O'Connor, I do not think anyone can say that the honourable and learned Member was in any way at variance with his duty towards those who serve in Ireland in bringing this matter before the House of Commons. The discussion has been a valuable one, and the incident is, of course, regretted by every section of this House. I think those who take an interest in the Army will agree with me in saying that we have no reason to complain of any want of sympathy by my honourable Friend the Under Secretary for War. The incident is, of course, a lamentable one, and having listened to the Debate almost from the very commencement I must say that it did strike me that there were some grounds for inquiry as to how it came about that a young man of apparently good character was sentenced to severe military punishment on the very day he met his death. Sir, I have listened to the statement by the honourable and learned Member who introduced this subject to the House, and I must say that until I heard my honourable Friend the Under Secretary give his explanation I felt that there was a serious case against the military authorities in Ireland. But, Sir, so far as the circumstances are connected with the military authorities in command of this regiment, or squadron, I cannot help confessing that I think an entirely different complexion was given by the statement put forward

Mr. Caldwell.

by the Under Secretary. I have asked myself over and over again what omission of duty the officer in command has been guilty of, or what he had done that he ought not to have done. After considering the facts, I must honestly say that I do not think, after what my honourable Friend the Under Secretary has stated, that anyone can say that the officer in command did not act with the greatest possible discretion, discrimination, and humanity. Sir, he acted upon the report of the doctor. Not only did he do that, but apparently seeing that it was a case which required specific investigation, before he acted at all he demanded a written report from the doctor to satisfy himself. I cannot see what more a commanding officer could do, and I cannot see how he could have acted otherwise, having regard to the report of the doctor. Therefore, Sir, I think this House ought to be particularly careful in dealing with those who have to enforce discipline in our Services, not to allow a serious charge to be made against them if it is proved they are absolutely guiltless of that charge. But, Sir, having said so much, I also at the same time state that I am not satisfied with the medical aspect of the case. I do not know that the House ought to be satisfied with the statement that this particular doctor was called in upon that occasion. We have a right to know as to why there was no military doctor, and when I am told that that arose from a scarcity of doctors in the Army I have a right to ask further, why is there a scarcity of doctors in the Army? Because, after all, if we are not to have a proper system, we can hardly expect respectable, well-behaved young men, such as this young man evidently was, to enter our Service at all. Surely it is cold comfort for those who are left behind him to tell them that we could not do more than we did because we had a scarcity of doctors in our military Service. Sir, to discuss that matter at any length would be going very far beyond the question raised, but I think it is a deplorable fact, whoever is accountable for it, that the medical service in our Army has now become so unpopular in our medical schools that you cannot get sufficient candidates to fill up the vacancies which occur in the Army. I do hope before this Debate is concluded we shall have some assurance from my honourable Friend that some means are being taken to get rid of this great blot on our system.

DR. CLARK: The medical profession are perfectly content with the changes that were made last year, and, as far as I know, the boycott has been removed, especially in Ireland.

MR. CARSON: I am exceedingly glad to have that assurance from a medical Member of this House. I was going to observe that it is one of the reasons why I rise at all to speak in this discussion. I am aware that in my own constituency, Dublin University, at all events till very recently, in consequence of the dissatisfaction that prevailed with reference to the Army medical system, the Medical School of Trinity College, which I believe is one of the finest medical schools in the world, absolutely refused to allow any students to prepare themselves for medical service in Her Majesty's Army. Sir, I am told now by the honourable Member that these grievances are removed, and if that is the case probably the school to which I have referred will in the future contribute a quota of doctors to the Army. But certainly we ought to have the very earliest opportunities of filling up those vacancies which have occurred. I must say that for my own part I entirely endorse the views which have been put forward this evening, and if we can only get a return to the old system under which the doctor was the doctor of the regiment, and the soldiers were the life-long patients of the same doctor, I believe you would not have such unfortunate incidents as this occurring. I am aware that one of the most difficult things with which a doctor has to contend is malingering, but the old system minimises that difficulty. Now, Sir, the question which arises with reference to this specific matter may. I think, be entirely reduced to the conduct of the doctor upon this particular occasion. Sir, I could not help noticing that in the medical reports of this particular soldier's death which were read out by my honourable Friend, that doctor seems to have paid particular attention to the cardiac symptoms—the symptoms of affection that caused the death of this unfortunate young man. Well, all I can say is that it is very extraordinary if he paid particular attention to those symp-

toms he was not able to ascertain the complaint from which this private was suffering. I should be very much surprised if the matter were fully investigated if it did not turn out that the examination made by this doctor were of a very perfunctory character. Who is this doctor? What is he? What is his position in the profession? How did he come to be appointed, and what other duties had he to perform? Is a doctor to the Poor Law to be allowed to be called in like this, because I think his hands are quite full enough? Has this doctor any other appointments, and what are his particular qualifications? I cannot but think, when we have a young man of this kind ordered off at one hour of the day to undergo a severe punishment of this character, and he is found a few hours after lying dead on a plank bed in a military prison, I cannot help thinking that this state of things has arisen in consequence of the dearth of doctors in the Military Service. I cannot but think, also, that the conduct of this doctor calls for the most serious and minute investigation. I am not going into the question of what the coroner has ordered, for he has done the best he could under the circumstances; but I do submit to my honourable Friend who represents the War Department in this House that the matter can hardly be left to rest where it is upon the statements that have been made, and I say this with all due deference, because I think that people outside this House who have not the knowledge of these affairs, and who form their opinions of our Service not upon minute details but upon general outlines of fact, I think they ought to be assured and ought to know that when such matters as these occur they may be certain that the whole strength of the Department concerned will be employed to see that there has been no miscarriage of justice in the conduct of the persons in authority. For my part, I should feel very much satisfied, and very much more gratified, if my honourable Friend representing the military authorities in this House could assure us that he would take care that there shall be a further investigation into the cause of the death of this man. At the same time, I desire, at the end of my few observations, to say what I said at the start, that I am absolutely convinced upon the facts as they have been stated that there is no blame to be attached to the military authorities, and I feel that the officer in command has not only acted in strict compliance with the regulations as laid down—regulations that are to guide him in such cases—but that he has interpreted them, as I hope every officer will always do upon such an occasion, not only in accordance with the spirit of those regulations, but as they would be interpreted by a humane and Christian man.

Sɪʀ H. CAMPBELL-BANNERMAN (Stirling Burghs) : I join with all those who have preceded me in the one opinion to which they have given expression—namely, that we are under an obligation to my honourable Friend the Member for South Donegal for bringing this matter forward. I must say that I think the honourable Member who has brought this matter before the Committee has put his case with great warmth of feeling, but in a tone to which no exception can be taken, and no fault is to be found with the manner in which the honourable Gentleman the Under Secretary of State for War has dealt with the question in his reply from the official point of view. One thing is quite clear—and this the honourable Gentleman opposite established completely—that so far as the military officers are concerned, as the right honourable and learned Gentleman who has just sat down has said, they could not have acted with greater discretion or with greater humanity than they have displayed in these trying circumstances. This deplorable incident does not appear to have been due to any lack of precaution or any harshness of conduct or want of attention on their part, or to any failure to carry out the instructions contained in the Queen's regulations. Therefore, the question reduces itself to a somewhat narrow issue. Now, the right honourable and learned Gentleman who has just sat down throws a great deal of blame upon the doctor, and he assumes incompetence or error on his part.

Mʀ. CARSON : I should not like the right honourable Gentleman to be under that impression. I stated that I was not satisfied, and that I thought it was

Mr. Carson.

a matter for further investigation. I do not wish to throw any slur upon the doctor, but I think his conduct ought to be inquired into.

Sɪʀ H. CAMPBELL-BANNERMAN : I think there is one fallacy which underlies a good deal of what has been said about this doctor, about whom I know nothing whatever. It is assumed that it was a disadvantage that this unfortunate soldier was treated by a civilian doctor. On the contrary, surely it tells the other way. If he had been treated by a military surgeon, one can well understand that some people would have a suspicion that a military doctor, who was accustomed to malingering, and well up to the tricks of soldiers, would have taken a harsh professional view of the condition of this unfortunate man. But, on the contrary, here is a fresh doctor brought in from the outside, with no prejudices and no past experience tending to make him exaggerate the chances of malingering taking place, and this doctor, with a perfectly unbiassed judgment, comes to the conclusion that this man's complaints of illness are not substantially existent or well founded. So that this question that we have heard so much talk about, as to the great misfortune of having a civilian doctor, really seems to me to tell directly in the opposite way from that which is supposed. The right honourable and learned Gentleman and some other honourable Members have touched upon a larger question, upon which we can hardly enter in this discussion—the question of the dearth of military doctors, and the possibility of reviving the old regimental medical system. Now, let me tell the right honourable and learned Gentleman—and I address myself to him· because he is the most recent Member who has taken that view—that there is a great deal to be said on the other side of this question. The evils of the old regimental system were glaring and notorious. I know this, because I was a very subordinate official in the War Office myself at the time the change took place, some 26 or 27 years ago, and I know that all the best opinions and experiences in the medical service were then in favour of the adoption of the general hospital organisation as superseding the whole regimental organisation. Everyone can see the advantage—and I will not dwell upon it—of this regimental system, both to the officers and in some cases to the men themselves, of having a medical officer in the regiment living among them all the time, who takes a fatherly or a brotherly interest in the men. Of course, I do not consider the experience that this doctor obtains in the course of his professional life is of much value, because he sees nothing beyond one or two classes of diseases all that time, and he loses some of that tone and fibre which ought to be possessed by an experienced medical officer. But that is not a question upon which we need enter to-day, although it is one of the arguments that might be used. I only wish to warn those who are inclined to jump at the conclusion that a return to an antiquated and discarded system would prevent accidents like this, and I assure the right honourable and learned Gentleman that it would probably have the very opposite effect, and make them more likely to occur. The right honourable and learned Gentleman has referred to the dearth of medical officers in the Army. We know what that arises from, but it has been to a large extent, as my honourable Friend below the Gangway pointed out, let us hope, remedied, and the cause has been largely removed—namely, the jealousy and the distrust upon the part of certain medical schools of the Army as a career for medical officers, and this has been, at all events, mitigated. It will readily be seen that there are very many cases in which civilian officers must be employed, and it would be a waste of money and power, and presumably of skill, to employ an Army medical officer in every case where there are troops stationed when you have, perhaps, civilian medical men at your call in the immediate neighbourhood. But, apart from that, excepting the right honourable and learned Gentleman who has just sat down, most of those I have heard speak in this Debate have admitted that even this medical officer cannot be judged upon what we have heard, for we have no means of judging of his conduct. Now I come to what is, after all, to my mind, the most important part of the whole question, and that is, whether the regulations on the subject of the punishment of prisoners have been brought up to date. There

is no doubt whatever that there has been a great advance in public feeling on this question within recent years. I listened with great sympathy and agreement to the honourable Member for Mayo, when he spoke of this senseless punishment to which men are sometimes condemned—punishments which are not only severe in their effect upon the human system, but are also degrading and discrediting to the man who is subjected to them. We have given up, surely, in these days the idea of having anything vindictive in our punishment, and, although we ought to employ such methods as may have some deterrent effect, yet we do not want, as my honourable Friend has said, to have any even distant flavour of the thumbscrew and the rack in the punishment to which men are subjected; and I think it is very doubtful whether shot drill does not come within that category. But, unfortunately, I am not aware what the honourable Gentleman the Under Secretary for War said upon this point, because I was not in the House at the time, and I do not know whether the honourable Gentleman promised that this matter of soldiers' punishments would be inquired into.

*Mr. WYNDHAM : I said an inquiry was being held, and it commenced last autumn.

Sir H. CAMPBELL-BANNERMAN: That is entirely satisfactory, and if the inquiry is carried out in the spirit which is prevalent at the present time, and which is exhibited in the legislation of last year with reference to civil prisons, I hope the honourable Gentleman will be in a position, when that inquiry has been completed, and the necessary alterations made which the House has sanctioned, to make certain that in a deplorable case like this, where death occurs under such lamentable circumstances, at all events, it will not have been due to the conduct of any of our officers or to defects in the system which we ourselves have authorised.

Mr. DILLON: I only desire to intervene for a few minutes, and, after wha. has been stated, I would ask my honour-able Friend to withdraw his Amendment.

3 C

THE DEPUTY CHAIRMAN: The honourable Member did not move an Amendment.

MR. SWIFT MACNEILL: I intended to move an Amendment, and I thought I had done so.

MR. DILLON: I must confess that, like the right honourable Gentleman the Member for Dublin University, I am not satisfied with the medical aspect of this case. I differ from the Leader of the Opposition in one particular. He said it was an advantage to have the services of a civilian doctor. To that I say yes, if he were an independent doctor of standing. I do not think my right honourable Friend was in the House when we raised this medical question.

SIR H. CAMPBELL-BANNERMAN: Allow me to say that I do not quite accept the words which the honourable Gentleman has put into my mouth. I do not wish to convey that it was necessarily an advantage to have a civilian doctor, because that would be a slur upon the Army medical doctors. What I said was that to have a civilian doctor was an answer to many of the suspicions that might be attached to having an Army doctor in this case.

MR. DILLON: I admit that if the civilian doctor was a doctor of standing that would be so. Of course, I do not know anything about him, and he might have been a competent man, but what I wish to observe is that he was only temporarily employed, and the tenure of his employment was determined by the local military authorities. He was retained for a year, and he did not know whether he would get a renewal of his appointment at the end of the year; therefore he was not an ordinary independent civilian doctor, nor had he the advantage and status, or the weight of a military doctor attached to the Service. I shall not dwell any further on this point except to say one word. It is a point which I passed over when I spoke before, because it is an unpleasant one. There was one step which was taken by this doctor which, as a medical man myself, shocked me. This doctor admits in his evidence that he went into the cell to this poor soldier, and he states that he found him in a state so

Mr. Dillon.

filthy that he could not examine him. I say that any medical man with a heart in his breast, when he finds a young man, as in this case, of respectable up-bringing in this very serious ‚ condition; when he finds a young man of cleanly habits and good character in this state, and does not attribute it to illness, I must confess that I entertain the gravest doubts as to the fitness of this doctor for the duty he is called upon to discharge, and my doubts on this point have been raised by that statement alone. I will say no more upon that question, but I have risen for the purpose of asking that the Debate should be brought to an end, for this reason: that the Under Secretary of State for War made a large and important concession in his statement, and I do not think that we could reasonably ask the Committee to divide after we have obtained from the honourable Gentlemen a promise, or a statement, that a large field of review in the treatment of medical officers is under consideration. All I ask is, that as soon as this question has been settled, the result will be communicated to the House.

Original Question again proposed.

Motion made—

“That a sum not exceeding £6,508,950 be granted for the said Service.”—(*Mr. Pirie.*)

*MR. PIRIE: I desire to bring before the Committee, I am sorry to say, a case which has somewhat the same features as the one which has just been discussed, and one upon which I desire to put myself in order. I move “That this Vote be reduced by £50” and I desire to call the attention of this Committee to a case with which the House, to a certain extent, is familiar on account of questions which I have already put to the Under Secretary of State for War. It is the case of the late Veterinary-Inspector Finlayson. I desire that a discussion should be carried on in this case, in order to see whether it has been adequately dealt with, and whether the way in which this officer was treated can be satisfactorily answered. The case is a very simple one. Veterinary-Captain Finlayson joined the Service as a veterinary lieutenant in 1883. He was employed in the Service in South Africa, and for some time filled very responsible positions, and while in South Africa he suffered very much from sunstroke, and eventually was invalided home, suffering from rheumatism. After recovery from the illness from which he was invalided home, he was dispatched to Egypt, where he was employed on special service, and his professional qualifications, from all accounts, were of the highest order. After his appointment in Egypt he was for some time employed in Ireland in a responsible position. While in Ireland last year the military authorities came to the decision that it was necessary for this officer to retire from the Army and they issued instructions under the Royal warrant for his retirement. I should be the last person to dispute that it is necessary to maintain discipline. Discipline has always to be maintained, although it has sometimes to do very harsh things, and I do not dispute the right of the authorities as to the way they acted upon this occasion, for I must bring to the notice of the House the fact that a month previously to his retirement this officer had been charged with a civil offence, in which there were several very discreditable surroundings, which, without doubt, gave quite sufficient justification for the military authorities acting in the way they did. I feel bound to point out, however, in justice to the memory of this officer, that as far as regards the civil charge which was brought against him, it was dismissed by the magistrate before whom it was brought, and a dismissal from a legal point of view, I am told, is to be considered as if the offence had not been committed, and as if the charge had never been made. That is the case, so far as the legal point of view is concerned. However, my point is that there was not a sufficient opportunity given to this officer—an opportunity which I think ought to have been given him—to defend himself, however small a defence he might have had. It was, without doubt, a question of character upon which he was told he would have to resign the Service. The military law lays down that in' any charge affecting the character of a soldier, a full opportunity must be afforded that soldier of being present throughout the inquiry, and of making any statement which he desires

to make; and also that he shall have the full opportunity of cross-examining any witnesses who gives evidence affecting his character, and of producing any witness in defence of his own character. Now, as far as I can gather from the information I have been able to obtain, this opportunity was not given to him, however little advantage it might have been to him to have had that opportunity, and it is on this point, that no military court of inquiry was held, 'that my point rests, and that the case resembles the last case the Committee has just dealt with, from the fact that the same desire to avoid publicity is manifest, a desire which reacts injuriously on the welfare of the Army. This officer complied with the instruction he had received, as the House will note from the Question answered yesterday, and in a letter of the 6th of January of last year he writes—

"In accordance with instructions received, I have this day sent in an application to be allowed to resign my commission in accordance with the Royal Warrant, although I do not know wherein it applies. I would also beg for leave of absence."

That application for leave was not granted, but the letter resigning his commission was received in the Orderly Room, sent up through the proper channels, and was received by the Field-Marshal commanding in Ireland on the 29th of January. On the 7th of February this unfortunate officer, whose mind must have become quite unhinged, committed suicide. Only a month before his health had entirely given way, and the presumption is that the sunstroke from which he had suffered was the cause of his suicide. Now, the fact of his having sent in his papers entitled him, on account of the length of service which he had to his credit, to a gratuity of £800 upon his retirement after 10 years' service. I cannot help thinking that, although the Government, perhaps rightly, thought that the fact of his becoming entitled to this gratuity did not form an essential element in their decision that he should retire, certainly this was taken into account by the officer himself. He must have known all through the service that his gratuity would become due to him on his retirement, and to him it is immaterial whether this money was given as a reward for service, for it was a condition of an agreement which led him to join the Service; and, as far as he was concerned, he carried out the order to resign, which is all he could do under the circumstances. Of course, there has to be a fixed rule as to date of retirement, but there are two exceptional circumstances connected with this case that differentiate it entirely from ordinary cases of the kind. First of all, it was a case of compulsory retirement, and, secondly, the man who retired was insane. The inquest which was held showed that he was of unsound mind, and the presumption is that a month previous to his death he had been insane. I say, therefore, that this case needs exceptional treatment; that the retirement was not voluntary, but compulsory, and that insanity was present. The three points which I would bring before the Committee are as follows: First of all, I think that, in justice to his memory, we ought to say that his relatives are entitled to the gratuity which, if he had not committed suicide, he would have been entitled to. His parents are very old people in poor circumstances—one is 80 and the other 70 years of age. Captain Finlayson had always done his duty in the way of providing for them, and only just a week before his death he sent a cheque to them towards their support. Although it was stated at the inquest that he was in monetary difficulties, it was not proved that he was so in any way, nor was it the case. Well, Sir, the treatment which has been meted out to the family of this unfortunate man was that instead of their getting the £800 to which, I think, they are entitled they received in May last £20 as a compassionate allowance. In December they received a further £10, and in February another £20. This latter was due as I think to the courtesy and attention of the Secretary to the War Office, and I thank him for what he has done so far as that is concerned. But I do say that that is far from doing full justice to the case, and I think that regulations which permit of such a case as this happening require some amendment. I think it is absolutely necessary that such a hard case should be reconsidered. The Government, no doubt, are strictly within the letter of the law in what they have

done, but I do think that when these hard cases come up from time to time they should be treated with more justice and generosity. The treatment which is meted out to these men by a rich nation like this is, I submit, treatment which no private employer would mete out to his employees. Secondly, I think the actual date in the Gazette should not be taken as the date of the retirement. The date of retirement is the date when the papers are written out and received from the officer retiring by his superior officer, and any claim for a gratuity or a pension ought to be based on the fact itself, and not upon the evidence of the fact, this latter being all that the Gazette amounts to. The fact takes place when the resignation papers are written out, and appearing in the Gazette is merely evidence of it. The third point is—and this again enables the Army and this House to profit by the lesson which it teaches—that it would have been much more desirable when this officer was told to retire, that the information should have been conveyed to him after some court of inquiry before which he had defended himself, however little defence the officer might have had, by his superior officers. Important decisions such as this was should be conveyed to officers in all cases not merely by the commanding officer but by the senior officer available, and where possible by the actual officer by whom the decision was come to, in this case the Field Marshal Commanding in Ireland, and then there would have been less chance of this officer taking it so much to heart; and possibly even the sense of having been harshly treated would in this case not have been so great, and the desperate act by which a life was brought to a tragic end not have taken place. It is unfortunate that these cases come before the House, but I do not think anyone is to be blamed for bringing them up. So long as these cases occur, and there is a feeling of injustice—that justice has not been done to those who suffer—these cases must be brought up to this House as to a higher tribunal. They will only cease to be brought up when they cease to take place. I do not think that the interests of the Army are served by smothering this sort of thing and covering it up; and that is why I appeal for more liberal treatment in this particular case, and for some other regulation more liberal with regard to retiring than that which exists at present, as well as for a greater readiness to hold courts of inquiry.

*MR. WYNDHAM: The honourable Gentleman at the beginning of his speech admitted very frankly and very kindly that the military authorities were justified in calling upon this officer to resign. I do not propose to say another word upon that point. We are agreed that the military authorities were, under the painful circumstances of this case, justified in taking the step which they did take. Later on in his speech the honourable Member stated that he was desirous of having some court of inquiry to deal with the matter; but if the military authorities were justified, as the honourable Member has already admitted, in calling upon this officer to resign, we may take it that their action was merciful; because if an officer prefers to resign rather than to stand a court of inquiry, that is a more merciful way of dealing with the case. I think there can be no allegation as to the hard treatment of this officer. It is true that he was entitled if he had resigned and his resignation had been completed by the Royal signature giving consent to his resigning, to a gratuity of £800; but here I must invite the Committee once more to consider the nature of these gratuities. They are not analogous to the deferred pay of soldiers. The combatant officer who gets a gratuity, gets it to assist the flow of promotion in the Army. Nobody who has joined the Army since 1887 is entitled to a gratuity at all. In the case of veterinary surgeons the case is not so strong; they are given in order to get veterinary surgeons of good standing to enter the Service. In the case of this veterinary surgeon, had he committed suicide, or met with an accident in the street, or even died on active service, he would not have been entitled to this £800 gratuity. When a resignation is completed by receiving the Royal signature, this gratuity is given. Now, I am sorry that any such disappointment should occur, but the honourable Gentleman must remember that in this case there is no legal right. Then, again, he says a distinction ought to be drawn because when this

unhappy man committed suicide the coroner's jury found that he was insane, and the honourable Member urges that he was not accountable for his actions some time before. I had another case in my mind much more harsh than this which the honourable Member has urged—that of Captain Stewart, who was hopelessly insane; he was a distinguished officer about whom there was not the least breath of reproach. When he resigned he was unhappily not in a fit state of mind to complete the necessary documents for his case. A committee should have been appointed in order to complete the documents, but owing to the vacation of the Irish Law Courts, this committee could not be appointed, and this unhappy man did not receive his gratuity. That was a hard case. But in all these cases the Secretary of State finds that he cannot alter the date of the resignation, which is the date when it receives the Royal assent, and it is that which sometimes causes hardship. Now, I think that that disposes of this case; but the honourable Member argued that this case was exceptional, and that it should be given exceptional treatment, not on account of this officer's services, because no one will urge that his services were distinguished beyond others. He did nothing to deserve exceptional treatment on that account. What can we do? The honourable Member knows perfectly well that under the Non-EffectiveVote we have only a certain sum of money at our disposal. We can give pensions to widows of officers, and we can give compensation to the aged mothers of those who leave no widows; but we have only £1,250 in all out of which doles may be given in hard cases. In this case it was proposed that in view of the age and destitution and disappointment of this officer's father and mother, to give them £20. I personally intervened and got it increased to £40, and although it was impossible to renew the grant for three years, when that time elapsed a further amount was given. Beyond that we cannot go, and no case has been made out here for altering the law which may have caused disappointment in this case, and which, no doubt, has caused a great deal of disappointment.

CAPTAIN NORTON: May I appeal to the honourable Member that he will give some guarantee to endeavour to carry out what he is asked. This seems to be a specially hard case. With regard to the veterinary surgeons, when these grants or pensions were revived they were revived for the express purpose of getting a better class of men into the service. This man performed good service both in South Africa and India, and the misconduct of which he was accused, which took place about two weeks after he came home, and his subsequent death, were in all probability brought about by the sunstroke by which he was attacked in South Africa. There is also this point, that if his death had been delayed a few days longer his parents would have been entitled to £800. They are aged people, both between 70 and 80 years of age, and I think that it is a very small thing for the Department to guarantee that so long as they live it will give them some relief out of the Compensation Fund.

MR. COURTENAY WARNER: I do not wish to delay the Committee, but I should like to point out that this relief fund of £1,250 is very small indeed.

THE DEPUTY CHAIRMAN: The honourable Member cannot deal with that fund now. He must wait for the Vote.

MR. COURTENAY WARNER: But the reason adduced for not giving a further grant from the relief fund is that it is so small.

THE DEPUTY CHAIRMAN: But the relief fund does not come in on this Vote.

MR. COURTENAY WARNER: I can only say, I hope that in such cases as this, in the future, there will be a larger grant made.

*MR. PIRIE: I wish rather to emphasise my point that, in a hard case such as this more should be done than is actually done. I do not think it is quite just that a certain date should be chosen as the date of approval, which is merely used from a legal point of view. The date should be that when the officer signs his resignation paper and sends it in. Whether the sum due be large or small we ought to do what is right. As the right honourable Gentleman has kindly stated, that in three years' time this case may be taken again into con-

sideration by the authorities, I will not press the matter further, but will ask leave to withdraw my Amendment.

Amendment, by leave, withdrawn.

Original question again proposed.

SIR W. LAWSON: I wish to know on what authority we enlist Chinese troops. Are they enlisted voluntarily or not? Will it be necessary to enlist any more of them? I should also be glad to know how it is that while £21,000 is asked for the cost of these Chinese troops £33,000 is required for the same number of West African troops. What is the reason for the difference in the cost? And what have you done about barracks for these troops?

*MR. WYNDHAM: We only put down £21,000 for the Chinese troops because when the Estimates were drawn up we only expected to raise five out of eight companies of the Chinese in the course of the year, and, therefore, we only asked for what money we should spend in that period. With regard to the question of barrack accommodation for this regiment, it is not on the Estimate, and, therefore, I should not be in order in discussing it. As to whether we mean to enlist more Chinese, I can only say that sufficient unto the year is the policy thereof. So far as I know there is to be only one battalion of Chinese troops, and the policy is based upon the not unreasonable view that the inhabitants of Wei-hai-Wei should do something for the defence of that place.

MR. CALDWELL: The Committee will see that a very important departure is being made on this question. It may seem a small sum in itself, but there is a very important principle involved, and this is an occasion on which we should gain information as to the policy we are going to adopt in China with regard to the introduction of Chinese soldiers in the British Army. We want to know more about it. Are the subjects of China to be enlisted as subjects of China, or are they to take the oath as British soldiers and be under the military laws of this country? It is all very well for us to begin this policy of enlisting Chinese soldiers, but we may find that Russia and other nations may follow our example, and we shall have all sorts of nations enlisting Chinese soldiers. Further, I should like to ask: Are these Chinese soldiers to be brought here to London, are they to go backwards and forwards like the regular British Army, and are you going to pay them in the same way as you do British soldiers? I think we ought to know. Are you going to differentiate the rates of pay of soldiers in the British Army? Are you going to pay a lesser sum to your soldiers in one place than you do to soldiers in another place? I venture to say that if your are going to introduce a policy of that kind it will have a certain unsettling effect on the Army, because while your men will all be subjected to one discipline you will have them receiving two rates of pay. Then, I think, we are further entitled to ask if there is a deliberate intention to go on with this policy, and to increase the number of Chinese soldiers enlisted. When we first sent our troops into the Soudan we were told they were not going beyond Dongola, and we know that they have gone considerably beyond that now. We are told in the same way that we are only to have just one regiment of Chinese soldiers, and that it will be sufficient for our purposes, but what assurance have we that in the future it may not be found necessary to enlist more regiments? Remember, we are starting a fresh policy, and we are quite entitled to consider how far it may be carried. It is, perhaps, but a small beginning, but it may have a very serious ending, and it must have an effect, not only on the British Army, but on our Imperial relations with China and Russia and other Powers, for you may thoroughly depend upon it that in a matter like this we cannot compete successfully with Russia. We may have absolute command of the sea, but if you once begin to enroll Chinamen in the service of this country, as a matter of course Russia, which is already in China, will follow our example. I contend that a policy of this kind should not be embarked upon without very full consideration, and I venture to assert that it is the duty of the House to insist on having a full definition of it, seeing what a serious effect it must have so far as the British Army is concerned.

SIR W. LAWSON (Cumberland, Cockermouth): The honourable Gentleman has not stated under what authority we enlist these Chinese troops.

DR. CLARK: I wish to raise that point also. We now have a Chinese Army in Hong Kong, and I wish to know whether we are to put another Asiatic Artillery Regiment in India. We have Asiatic Artillery at Singapore. Are we now going to have a third Chinese Army? I should like to ask why these new forces are being raised when you already have in existence the Hong Kong Regiment and your Asiatic Artillery? We ought to have a reason for this new departure. Why are we not developing our existing colonial forces instead of creating new ones?

*MR. WEIR (Ross and Cromarty): There are two items on this Vote as to which I should like an explanation. First, there is the sum of £3,000 for expenses attending the training of Army artificers. That is an increase of £1,000, and I should like to know how it is accounted for? Then, again, there is an increase of £500 in the item for deserters. Is there any idea that during the coming year the number of deserters will be increased? I hope the honourable Gentleman will be able to furnish me with some explanation as to those two items. There is another matter on page 35 of the same Vote upon which I should like to ask a question. I want to know why Nonconformist clergymen are paid much less than clergymen of the Church of England. Many of the Presbyterian ministers are Scotsmen, and there is a tendency to expect Scotsmen to live on less money than Englishmen. That remark, however, does not apply to Scotsmen on the Treasury Bench, who take good care that they get a sufficient sum for themselves. I contend that there should be equality of pay, and not the great difference which at present exists. Nonconformist ministers receive only half the amount paid to clergymen of the Church of England. I do not desire to move a reduction on this Vote, but I hope to get a satisfactory assurance from the honourable Gentleman the Under Secretary of State for War that in future Nonconformist ministers, be they Presbyterians, Wesleyans, or Baptists, shall be paid at the same rate as Episcopalian clergymen.

*MR. WYNDHAM: The honourable Member has asked me for an explanation as to the increases in the Votes for training Army artificers. We under-estimated the sum required for this Service last year, and expect a greater number for training during this year. The honourable Member next asks why Presbyterian chaplains are paid less than clergymen of the Anglican or Episcopalian Church. I think the honourable Gentleman is under a misapprehension. All clergymen in the Army, except chaplains, are paid on the same principle—namely, by capitation grant; payment depends on the number belonging to the particular denominations of which clergymen are the ministers. In reply to the other question put by the honourable Member, increased provision is necessary for the apprehension of deserters in view of the great number of recruits, and it is in proportion to the increase in the Army. In answer to the honourable Baronet as to the policy to be pursued in respect of Wei-hai-Wei, I will explain that, for reasons of State, and at the dictation of naval strategy, the Government are occupying a naval base at Wei-hai-Wei with the assent of the Emperor of China. That being so, we must make some provision for the defence of that place, and to preserve order; and in view of the number of British battalions abroad, we hold that it is not altogether unreasonable that the inhabitants of Wei-hai-Wei should bear a certain proportion of the burden of defence. These men will, I believe, serve under the Mutiny Act. Privates will receive 27 cents a day, or 96 dollars per annum. I doubt whether they will come to this country except on such an auspicious occasion as the Jubilee. The Government, however, are initiating no new policy.

Sir W. LAWSON: I should like to ask the honourable Gentleman whether the authority of the Emperor of China has been obtained for enlisting these people?

*Mr. WYNDHAM: Everything has been done in accordance with law and order, and after long correspondence with the Chinese Government.

Dr. CLARK: You have a Chinese regiment at Hong-Kong, and now you are creating another regiment at Wei-hai-Wei. Why do you not add a few more men to the regiment at Hong-Kong?

Mr. Weir.

*Mr. WYNHAM: That question has been considered, but I am informed that the people who live at Hong-Kong are different from the people at Wei-hai-Wei, and speak a different dialect.

Dr. CLARK: That difficulty has been overcome in India, where the difference in the dialects is greater than in China. With regard to the pay of Nonconformist clergymen as compared with the pay of clergymen of the Church of England, this is a question upon which we Presbyterians feel very strongly. We claim for our church by law established the same status as you claim for the Anglican Church. The clergymen of the Church of England are not paid according to the number to whom they minister. They are paid £600, £500, £400, or £300 a year, according to whether they are first, second, third, or fourth-class chaplains. I want to know why, when you employ ministers of the Established Church of Scotland, you do no place them on an equality, so far as the pay and position are concerned, with the clergymen of the Established Church of England. The present Under Secretary's predecessors have had this nut to crack before, and we have never had a satisfactory answer.

Motion made—

"That a sum, not exceeding £6,508,700, be granted for the said Service."—*(Mr. Caldwell.)*

Mr. CALDWELL: I rise to move a reduction of £300 in respect of the Vote for the Chinese regiment. I submit that the Under Secretary has given no reason whatever why we should call upon these people to defend Wei-hai-Wei, in which they are in no way interested. I do not suppose these people had anything to do with the transference of authority to this Government. Probably they are anxious that Wei-haiWei should remain part of the Chinese Empire, and I do not think we are justified in placing this obligation upon them.

*Mr. PIRIE: am sure the Committee will agree that some explanation should be given as to the enormous salaries paid to the officers of these Chinese troops in comparison with the salaries paid to military officers in less healthy parts of the Empire. I should like to draw the attention of the Committee to the fact that the 28 officers of the

Chinese regiment draw £10,000 a year, while the 27 officers of the West African regiment draw only £7,960 per annum. Whereas in the Indian regiment lieutenant-colonels get £328 a year, they receive £800 a year in the Chinese regiment. In view of the enormously increasing Estimates, I think it behoves everyone, and especially Members on this side of the House, to study economy in every way, and I refuse to accept this enormous and extravagant expenditure without understanding it.

*MR. WYNDHAM: To go out to a place like Wei-hai-Wei, where some

knowledge of the Chinese language is necessary, is a very different thing to taking command of regiments in Africa. Larger salaries are paid to the officers of the Chinese regiment because they are engaged on what is called "Special employment."

Question put—

"That a sum, not exceeding £6,508,700, be granted for the said Service."—*(Mr. Caldwell.)*

The Committee divided:—Ayes 41; Noes 123.—(Division List No. 48.)

AYES.

Allen,Wm.(Newc.underLyme)
Austin, Sir John (Yorkshire)
Barlow, John Emmott
Birrell, Augustine
Bolton, Thomas Dolling
Buchanan, Thomas Ryburn
Burt, Thomas
Causton, Richard Knight
Clark,Dr.G.B.(Caithness-sh.)
Colville, John
Davies,M.Vaughan-(Cardigan)
Fenwick, Charles
Foster, Sir Walter(Derby Co.)
Goddard, Daniel Ford
Hayne, Rt. Hn. Chas. Seale-

Hazell, Walter
Jones, Wm. (Carnarvonshire)
Kinloch, Sir Jno. Geo. Smyth
Lawson,SirWilfrid(Cumb'land)
Macaleese, Daniel
M'Kenna, Reginald
Maddison, Fred.
Morton,Edw.J.C.(Devonport)
Moulton, John Fletcher
Nussey, Thomas Willans
Oldroyd, Mark
Pearson, Sir Weetman D.
Pirie, Duncan V.
Price, Robert John
Provand, Andrew Dryburgh

Rickett, J. Compton
Samuel, J. (Stockton-on-Tees)
Sinclair,Capt.Jno.(Forfarshire
Souttar, Robinson
Steadman, William Charles
Sullivan, Donal (Westmeath)
Warner, Thos. Courtenay T.
Weir, James Galloway
Williams,JohnCarvell(Notts.)
Wilson, John (Govan)
Woods, Samuel

TELLERS FOR THE AYES—
Mr. Caldwell and Mr. Bryn Roberts.

NOES.

Arnold, Alfred
Ashmead-Bartlett, Sir Ellis
Atkinson, Rt. Hon. John
Bagot,Capt.Josceline FitzRoy
Balfour,Rt.Hn.A.J.(Manch'r)
Balfour,RtHnGeraldW.(Leeds)
Banbury, Frederick George
Barton, Dunbar Plunket
Beckett, Ernest William
Bemrose, Sir Henry Howe
Bentinck, Lord Henry C.
Bethell, Commander
Bigwood, James
Blundell, Colonel Henry
Bonsor, Henry Cosmo Orme
Brodrick, Rt. Hn. St. John
Butcher, John George
Carlile, William Walter
Carson, Rt. Hn. Edward
Cavendish,V.C.W.(Derbyshire
Chaloner, Captain R. G. W.
Chamberlain,Rt.Hn.J.(Birm.)
Chamberlain,J.Austen(Worc'r
Chaplin, Rt. Hon. Henry
Clare, Octavius Leigh
Clough, Walter Owen
Cochrane, Hn. Thos. H. A. E.
Coghill, Douglas Harry
Collings, Rt. Hn. Jesse
Colomb, Sir John Chas. Ready
Compton, Lord Alwyne

Corbett,A.Cameron(Glasgow)
Cross, Herb.Shepherd(Bolton)
Curzon, Viscount
Dalkeith, Earl of
Dalrymple, Sir Charles
Douglas, Rt. Hn. A. Akers-
Doxford, William Theodore
Duncombe, Hon. Hubert V.
Fergusson,Rt.Hn.SirJ.(Manc'r
Finch, George H.
Finlay, Sir Robt. Bannatyne
Fisher, William Hayes
FitzWygram, Gen. Sir F.
Fletcher, Sir Henry
Folkestone, Viscount
Foster, Colonel (Lancaster)
Gedge, Sydney
Goldsworthy, Major-General
Gordon, Hon. John Edward
Gorst,Rt.Hn.Sir John Eldon
Goschen, George J. (Sussex)
Gray, Ernest (West Ham)
Greene,Henry D.(Shrewsbury)
Greville, Hon. Ronald
Gull, Sir Cameron
Gunter, Colonel
Hamilton,Rt.Hn Lord George
Hanbury, Rt. Hn. Robt. Wm.
Hardy, Laurence
Hare, Thomas Leigh
Hubbard, Hon. Evelyn

Hutchinson,Capt.W.G.Grice-
Jebb, Richard Claverhouse
Johnston, William (Belfast)
Joliffe, Hon. H. George
Kemp, George
Kennaway, Rt Hn Sir John H.
Keswick, William
Lawrence,SirE.Durning-(Corn
Leighton, Stanley.
Lockwood, Lt.-Col. A. R.
Long,Col.Chas.W.(Evesham)
Long,Rt.Hn.Walter(Liverpool
Lowles, John
Macartney, W. G. Ellison
Macdona, John Cumming
Maclean, James Mackenzie
Malcolm, Ian
Monckton, Edward Philip
More,Robt.Jasper(Shropshire)
Morrell, George Herbert
Morton,Arthur H.A.(Deptford
Murray,RtHnA.Graham(Bute
Murray, Chas. J. (Coventry)
Nicol, Donald Ninian
Orr-Ewing, Charles Lindsay
Phillpotts, Captain Arthur
Platt-Higgins, Frederick
Pollock, Harry Frederick
Pryce-Jones,Lt.-Col.Edward
Purvis, Robert
Ritchie,Rt.Hn.Chas.Thomson

Round, James
Russell, T. W (Tyrone)
Simeon, Sir Barrington
Smith, Abel H.(Christchurch)
Smith, Hn. W. F. D. (Strand)
Stanley,Hn.Arthur(Ormskirk)
Stanley, Lord (Lancs.)
Stewart, Sir MarkJ.M'Taggart
Strauss, Arthur
Talbot, Lord E. (Chichester)
Talbot,Rt.Hn.J.G.(Oxf'dUniv)
Thorburn, Walter

Thornton, Percy M.
Valentia, Viscount
Wanklyn, James Leslie
Webster, Sir R.E. (I. of W.)
Welby, Lieut.-Col. A. C. E.
Wentworth, Bruce C. Vernon
Whitmore, Charles Algernon
Williams,Joseph Powell(Birm.
Willoughby de Eresby, Lord
Willox, Sir John Archibald
Wilson, John (Falkirk)
Wilson,J.W.(Worcestersh. N.)

Wodehouse,Rt.Hn.E.R.(Bath)
Wortley, Rt.Hn. C. B. Stuart-
Wylie, Alexander
Wyndham, George
Wyndham-Quin,Major W.H.
Young, Commander(Berks,E.)

TELLERS FOR THE NOES—
Sir William Walrond and
Mr. Anstruther.

Original Question again proposed.

MR. E. J. C. MORTON (Devonport): This gives me an opportunity of raising a point, which I will raise very briefly, which has been raised before during this Parliament, but not of course this Session. A promise was given on one occasion, nearly two years ago, that the Government would give their attention to it, and I think that on this Vote there is a peculiar reason why I have a right to ask what inquiries the Government have made into the matter, because we have an enormous increase on this Vote in the Estimates, and yet it still remains the fact that the labourers under the War Office are paid a perfectly disgraceful rate of wages, for we have labourers receiving——

THE DEPUTY CHAIRMAN: The honourable Member is discussing a matter which hardly comes under this Vote.

MR. E. J. C. MORTON: I understood that this was the only Vote upon which I could raise the question.

*MR. BRYN ROBERTS (Carnarvonshire, Eifion): There is one point in connection with the capitation grant to which I should like to draw the right honourable Gentleman's attention. The Welsh Calvinistic Methodists are Presbyterians, and in Wales the term Methodist always means the Welsh Presbyterian body, and not the Wesleyan Methodists, who are called Wesleyans only. Welsh Calvinistic Methodist recruits are, however, for the purposes of the capitation grant, classified as Wesleyan Methodists, because they return themselves as Methodists, they understanding the term in the Welsh sense, whereas the Army authorities interpret it in the English sense. The result is that the Presbyterian chaplains minister to these recruits but the capitation grant is credited to the Wesleyan Methodist chaplains. I do not expect any answer from the right honourable Gentleman

now, because I have sprung the matter upon him without any notice whatever, but if he would inquire and ascertain whether the case is as I have suggested I shall be satisfied.

MR. WYNDHAM: I will attend to it.

Motion made—

"That a sum not exceeding £6,508,900 be granted for the said Service."—(*Mr. Weir.*)

*MR. WEIR: The reply of the honourable Gentleman upon this point is extremely unsatisfactory. We are told that these ministers are paid by capitation grant, and that it is the fault of the ministers that there is such a small proportion, but I say that it is the fault of the War Office in not finding more of these men to serve in the Army. It is not the fault of the ministers, for they are prepared to look after the spiritual welfare of larger numbers, but they are prevented from doing so by the rules of the War Office, which are of a hard and fast character. I suggest that these rules should be altered, and as a protest against this, I beg to move that this Vote be reduced by £100.

DR. CLARK: I hope my honourable Friend will not confine this to one section, but raise the question upon the broader ground that all chaplains ought to be placed in the same position, and thus raise it for Roman Catholics as well as for Presbyterians, because the priests ought to be paid as well as the Presbyterian or the Anglican clergy. The present state of things seems to me to be very unsatisfactory. There may be some Scotch regiment or some Welsh regiment where you ought to have somebody else, but it seems to me that the only wise course is that the same rate of pay which you give to the Wesleyan and the priest should be paid to the clergy. You should certainly adopt one principle, and pay them all at the same rate. You pay the capitation grant to all Dissenters, whether they be Presbyterian ministers or Roman Catholic priests, and I know that, as far as this question is concerned, there is a general Nonconformist grievance that the members of the Anglican clergy are taken on as State servants, and that they have large salaries and pensions, while the dissenting ministers are placed upon quite a different footing. It seems to me that justice demands that you should place them all on the same footing, and either pay them all upon a percentage or pay them all fixed salaries. In this respect it seems to me that the Catholics and the Nonconformists at the present time have a serious grievance to complain of. I do not know whether this is the proper time to raise it, but it is one of the grievances which I think ought to be got rid of by placing them all in an equal position by paying all Anglican clergy so much per head. I do not know whether the right honourable Gentleman will say anything in the matter, but I take this opportunity of pressing upon the War Office that this is a grievance, and that they ought either to level up the Nonconformist to the Anglican standard, or level down the Anglican standard to the Nonconformist standard. Now, some good churchmen do not care about the Catholics, and they prefer to be Nonconformists, and I think greater latitude should be allowed in matters of this kind. Upon this subject it should either be a case of levelling up or levelling down.

*MR. WYNDHAM: I may have misled the honourable Member in my first reply. The facts are as follows: There are four recognised denominations— the Church of England, the Roman Catholic, the Presbyterians, and the Wesleyans. In the first three denominations the chaplains are appointed and established without any difference being made between them. To the Wesleyan the same rates of pay are given, but it is impossible to give them the same permanency of character, because it is not the practice of this denomination to give a permanency of station to any one minister. So far as the emoluments and status are concerned, they are treated on all fours, and are treated in exactly the same way. In cases where the men of any particular denomination are not numerous, then

the spiritual wants of the minority are met by officiating clergymen who are paid upon uniform capitation rates.

CAPTAIN SINCLAIR (Forfar): I do appeal to my honourable Friend to withdraw his Motion, for I hardly think that we have sufficient grounds, for we have no evidence of any strong Nonconformist grievance in the matter. If there were, I should be only too glad to support any effort he might make in this House. On that ground, I appeal to him to withdraw this Motion.

*MR. WEIR: I think these ministers should be paid the same rates as the Church of England clergy.

*MR. WYNDHAM: They are.

*MR. WEIR: That is not the result of my experience.

DR. CLARK: Of the 22 first-class chaplains drawing salaries, do any of them belong to the Wesleyans, the Presbyterians, or the Roman Catholics?

*MR. WYNDHAM: Certainly. I cannot give you the exact proportion, but certainly there are some belonging to those denominations.

THE DEPUTY CHAIRMAN: Does the honourable Member withdraw his Motion?

*MR. WEIR: I will withdraw my Motion.

Motion, by leave, withdrawn.

Original Question again proposed.

Motion made—

" That a sum not exceeding £6,508,750 be granted for the said Service."—*(Mr. Warner.)*

MR. COURTENAY WARNER: With regard to the item for miscellaneous expenses in connection with the apprehension and conviction of deserters and other offenders I desire to draw the attention of the Committee to a great increase in the amount. There is an increase to the extent of 20 per cent., and it is apparently expected that there will be a great increase in the number of deserters. The answer given by the honourable Gentleman to a question the

3 E

other day was read right off the paper, because I am sure that the Secretary of State would not have given such an answer as to say that this was in proportion to the increase of recruits. The increase in the Army was just 2½ per cent., but the increase in this item is 20 per cent., therefore there must be something wrong about that answer. I quite understand that if the Army is increased there may be a few more deserters, but an increase of 20 per cent.— £500—is too much, and I shall move that this Vote be reduced by £250. This Vote for miscellaneous expenses includes the deserters and other offenders. I think that one reason for this increase is that we are getting a worse class of recruits in some of the regiments, the class of recruits is not as good as it used to be in the Guards; and I think that possibly the lower standard that we have accepted will render it likely that we shall have more offenders and more deserters, and you may have a considerable amount more to spend in catching your deserters than you did before. At the same time, I think that an increase of 20 per cent. to catch deserters is a little too much, and I think the House will agree with me that it is too much, and this Motion is in favour of economy this time.

*MR. PIRIE: As regards improvements in the Army, it is rather remarkable that we have to increase the fund for the capture of deserters. This is a most melancholy fact, following upon the report of the Inspector-General of Recruiting. The only result of our effort seems to have been to obtain a worse standard of recruit who is not so well educated, and therefore there is a tendency more and more to desert. We know that the number of men who purchase their discharges is increasing instead of diminishing, and this is proof positive that the result of the present state of affairs instead of improving, is deteriorating our Army. How honourable Members can say—as they did on the last occasion when a discussion upon this Vote took place—that they are satisfied with this state of affairs I cannot understand. To me it is most melancholy to think that this country spends this enormous amount of extra money, and that this is the result. I hope the Under Secretary will give some explanation of this enormous increase of expenditure on page 7. I should also like the Under Secretary to explain to me why this item is not given in the same way as all the other items of expenditure are given. The item for chaplains shows a decrease, but in this particular item on page 7 there is no explanation given at all.

Question put—

"That a sum, not exceeding £6,508,750, be granted for the said Service."—(*Mr. Warner.*)

The Committee divided:—Ayes 38; Noes 118.—(Division List No. 49.)

AYES.

Allen, Wm.(Newc. underLyme)
Austin, Sir John (Yorkshire)
Buchanan, Thomas Ryburn
Caldwell, James
Campbell-Bannerman, Sir H.
Clark, Dr.G.B.(Caithness-sh.)
Colville, John
Davies,M.Vaughan-(Cardigan)
Fenwick, Charles
Foster, Sir Walter(Derby Co.)
Goddard, Daniel Ford
Hayne, Rt. Hn. Charles Seale-
Hazell, Walter
Jones, Wm. (Carnarvonshire)

Lawson,SirWilfrid(Cumb'land)
Macaleese, Daniel
M'Kenna, Reginald
Maddison, Fred.
Morton,Edw.J.C.(Devonport)
Moulton, John Fletcher
Nussey, Thomas Willans
Oldroyd, Mark
Pearson, Sir Weetman D.
Price, Robert John
Provand, Andrew Dryburgh
Reckitt, Harold James
Rickett, J. Compton
Roberts, John Bryn (Eifion)

Samuel, J. (Stockton-on-Tees)
Sinclair,Capt.Jno.(Forfarshire)
Souttar, Robinson
Steadman, William Charles
Sullivan, Donal (Westmeath.)
Trevelyan, Charles Philips
Walton, Joseph (Barnsley)
Weir, James Galloway
Williams,John Carvell(Notts.)
Wilson, John (Govan)

TELLERS FOR THE AYES—
Mr. Warner and Mr. Pirie.

NOES.

Arnold, Alfred
Ashmead-Bartlett, Sir Ellis
Atkinson, Rt. Hn. John
Bagot, Capt.JoscelineFitzRoy
Balfour,Rt.Hn.A.J.(Manch'r.)
Balfour,RtHnGeraldW.(Leeds)

Banbury, Frederick George
Barton, Dunbar Plunkett
Beckett, Ernest William
Bemrose, Sir Henry Howe
Bentinck, Lord Henry C.
Bethell, Commander

Blundell, Colonel Henry
Bonsor, Henry Cosmo Orme
Brodrick, Rt. Hn. St. John
Butcher, John George
Carlile, William Walter
Carson, Rt. Hn. Edward

Cavendish,V.C.W.(Derbyshire
Chaloner, Captain R. G. W.
Chamberlain,Rt.Hn.J.(Birm.)
Chamberlain,J.Austen(Worc'r)
Chaplin, Rt. Hn. Henry
Clare, Octavius Leigh
Cochrane, Hn. Thos. H. A. E.
Coghill, Douglas Harry
Collings, Rt. Hon. Jesse
Colomb, Sir Jno. Chas. Ready
Compton, Lord Alwyne
Corbett,A.Cameron(Glasgow)
Cross, Herb.Shepherd(Bolton)
Curzon, Viscount
Dalkeith, Earl of
Dalrymple, Sir Charles
Douglas, Rt. Hn. A. Akers-
Duncombe, Hon. Hubert V.
Fergusson,RtHnSirJ.(Manc'r)
Finch, George H.
Finlay, Sir Robert Bannatyne
Fisher, William Hayes
FitzWygram, General Sir F.
Fletcher, Sir Henry
Folkestone, Viscount
Foster, Colonel (Lancaster)
Gedge, Sydney
Goldsworthy, Major-General
Gordon, Hon. John Edward
Gorst, Rt. Hn. Sir John Eldon
Goschen, George J. (Sussex)
Gray, Ernest (West Ham)
Greene,Henry D.(Shrewsbury)
Greville, Hn. Ronald
Gull, Sir Cameron

Hamilton, Rt.Hn. Lord George
Hanbury, Rt. Hn. Robt. Wm.
Hardy, Laurence
Hare, Thomas Leigh
Hutchinson, Capt. G.W.Grice-
Jebb, Richard Claverhouse
Johnston, William (Belfast)
Joliffe, Hon. H. George
Kemp, George
Kennaway, Rt.Hn.Sir John H.
Lawrence,Sir E.Durning-(Corn
Leigh-Bennett, Henry Currie
Leighton, Stanley
Lockwood, Lieut.-Col. A. R.
Long, Col. Chas. W.(Evesham)
Long, Rt. Hn.Walter (L'pooi.)
Lowles, John
Macartney, W. G. Ellison
Macdona, John Cumming
Maclean, James Mackenzie
M'Calmont, H. L. B. (Camba.)
Malcolm, Ian
Monckton, Edward Philip
More, Robt.Jasper(Shropshire)
Morrell, George Herbert
Morton,Arth.H.A.(Deptford)
Murray,RtHnA.Graham(Bute)
Murray, Charles J.(Coventry)
Nicol, Donald Ninian
Orr-Ewing, Charles Lindsay
Phillpotts, Captain Arthur
Platt-Higgins, Frederick
Pollock, Harry Frederick
Pryce-Jones, Lt.-Col. Edward
Purvis, Robert

Richards, Henry Charles
Ritchie,Rt.Hn.Chas.Thomson
Round, ames
Russell,T. W. (Tyrone)
Simeon, Sir Barrington
Smith,James Parker(Lanarks.)
Smith, Hn. W. F. D. (Strand)
Stanley,Hn.Arthur(Ormskirk)
Stanley, Lord (Lancs.)
Stewart,Sir Mark J.M'Taggart
Strauss, Arthur
Talbot, Lord E. (Chichester)
Talbot,RtHn J.G.(Oxf'dUniv.)
Thornton, Percy M.
Valentia, Viscount
Wanklyn, James Leslie
Webster, Sir R. E. (I. of W.)
Welby, Lieut.-Col. A. C. E.
Wentworth,Bruce C.Vernon-
Whitmore, Charles Algernon
Williams,Joseph Powell(Birm)
Willox, Sir John Archibald
Wilson, John (Falkirk)
Wilson,J.W.(Worcestersh.N.)
Wodehouse, Rt.Hn.E.R.(Bath
Wortley, Rt. Hn. C. B.Stuart-
Wylie, Alexander
Wyndham, George
Wyndham-Quin, Major W.H.
Young, Commander(Berks,E.)

TELLERS FOR THE NOES—
    Sir William Walrond and
    Mr. Anstruther.

Original Question again proposed.

MR. CALDWELL: I wish to ask the Under Secretary of State a question. If the honourable Gentleman will refer to page 27, I think he will find, as regards the Army, that the amount is £1,207,000 for the officers out of a total of £3,900,000. So far as I can see the great cost of the British Army is in the officers, for the pay of the men is only just about three times that of the officers. If you look down the page you will find that as regards regimental extras, the pay to the officers is £141,000, while the amount paid to the men is only £284,000. That is to say, it is the officers who have one-half of the whole total. In the ordinary pay, the men have three-and-a-half times the amount of the officers, but when we are dealing with regimental extra pay we find that the men only get double the amount of the officers. I think we ought to have some explanation, because I suppose that the extra regimental pay should follow very much in the same proportion as the ordinary pay, and the men should have three-and-a-half times as much of the extra pay as the officers, in the same way as with the ordinary

pay. I wish to ask the Under Secretary, in the first place, how he makes out in regard to this extra pay the enormous cost in regard to the officers. You have only 5,000 officers in the case of the Cavalry, Engineers, and Infantry, and these officers get a million of money; on the other hand, you have about 150,000 men who only get about 3½ millions amongst them. I venture to say that the great cost of the British Army is not so much what the men get as the amount which you give to the officers. When you come to the non-effective Votes the disparity is even greater, and the matter is even worse when we are dealing with extra pay, because the officers get £125,000 as against £235,000 for the men. Some explanation, I think, is needed there as well. The extra pay should be fixed upon certain definite lines, but I do not know upon what principle it is fixed in this case. I want to know how it is that in a matter of this kind the men do not get the same proportion of extra pay as is given to the officers?

*MR. WYNDHAM: The extra pay is given for special service to the men, mainly for good conduct and for prizes.

3 E 2

MR. CALDWELL: But so far the officers get the largest proportion. When you come to deal with good conduct pay and the regimental extra pay the officers get one-half as compared with the men, and the proportion is utterly different to what it is in the case of the ordinary pay. It is all very well to say that you give it to the men for good conduct and under the prize scale, but I have got the whole of the sums here, and they are not in proportion to their relative share if you are going to give them in proportion to their respective cost. But in this particular case what you do is this: you give your money away to the officers, and you give 5,000 officers one-half as much as you pay to 150,000 men.

*MR. PIRIE: I think it is lamentable that an increase in the amount of fines for drunkenness should be estimated. I think the Committee should know that in the United States an Act has been passed abolishing all the regimental canteens in the United States Army. I am convinced that if something on the same lines could be done here it would be a great inducement to parents to allow their sons to join the Army. I submit that suggestion for consideration in the hope that it will be laid before the Committee which is sitting in Aldershot at the present moment inquiring into the canteen system generally, so that it may further report upon whether such a step would be an advantage to the Army. In my opinion the total abolition of the regimental canteen system in the British Army would be a most beneficial reform.

Original Question put.

Vote agreed to.

Motion made, and Question proposed—

"That a sum not exceeding £1,555,000 be granted to Her Majesty, to defray the Charge for Retired Pay, Half-Pay, and other non-effective Charges for Officers and others, which will come in course of payment during the year ending on the 31st day of March 1900."

SIR H. CAMPBELL-BANNERMAN: I venture to appeal at this stage to the right honourable Gentleman the Leader of the House to be content on this occasion with having obtained Vote 1. There is, I submit, no necessity for breaking through the universal rule of former days. If the Government take the non-effective Votes now they will be inde-

pendent of the House of Commons as far as the Army Estimates are concerned until the middle of August, and that is a very undesirable state of things. Another day might be devoted in the Session to Army Estimates and of raising points on other Votes. The money would be obtained without difficulty sufficient to carry the Department on to a later month of the Session. But by this new departure on the part of the Government the House is left without any power in the matter. The right honourable Gentleman stated with the greatest courtesy and kindness that in making this criticism I had forgotten the fact that he was always willing to put down the Army Votes for any particular Friday I name, with the general assent of the House. That, however, is putting a little too much responsibility upon me and on the Opposition, however kindly it may be meant. The right honourable Gentleman is himself really responsible, and I do not think it is desirable in the interests of the general order and regularity of our proceedings that we should go out of our way to vote so large a sum for the purpose of the Army. I have known a year when the whole Votes of the Army were taken on the first night that the Army Estimates were introduced, but that was in the old antediluvian times before honourable Members showed so lively an interest in these matters. But in recent years the invariable practice has been that when this huge Vote 1 was obtained then there was peace between the House and the Government on the subject of the Army Votes until another large sum was wanted. I think it would be a graceful concession on the part of the right honourable Gentleman, and the proper course for him to adopt, to be content with this large Vote just obtained.

THE FIRST LORD OF THE TREASURY (Mr. A. J. BALFOUR, Manchester, E.): Mr. O'Connor, I confess I have listened with some surprise to the speech of the right honourable Gentleman. The form of it was courtesy itself, but the substance of it struck me as being most extraordinary in view of the right honourable Gentleman's previous utterances. If I understood what fell from the right honourable Gentleman on Tuesday, the protest then made was against taking Vote 10, and, in answer to that protest

I abandoned Vote 10. I certainly understood the right honourable Gentleman to suggest that he would have no objection to that course.

SIR H. CAMPBELL-BANNERMAN: I beg the right honourable Gentleman's pardon. I explicitly raised the question of the non-effective Votes.

THE FIRST LORD OF THE TREASURY: I quite agree that the right honourable Gentleman did yesterday or to-day raise this question, but I confess I thought on a previous occasion the right honourable Gentleman had taken the course which I have described. I will not argue with the Committee as to whether we have or have not taken an undue period in getting Vote A and Vote 1 of the Army. I will only say that the period was much longer than we have been in the habit of taking in recent years, and, unless I am mistaken, we would, in different circumstances, have got them in somewhat less time than has actually elapsed. Now, what has been the plan proposed by the the Government, what has been the alternative plan suggested by the right honourable Gentleman, and what are the objections he has raised against the plan of the Government? The plan the Government propose is that we should take sufficient money now, at a time when it could be embodied in the Consolidated Fund Bill about to be introduced. The result of that would be that we would not require to ask the House for another Vote on Account, before the end of the Session, and that we should not ask the House to pass the other Consolidated Fund Bill before the end of the Session. Unquestionably, when the new Supply Rule was introduced, it was distinctly contemplated, both by the Government and the House, that the old system of Votes on Account and of Consolidated Fund Bills introduced at intervals through the Session should be abandoned, and that we should substitute for that antiquated and clumsy system a single Consolidated Fund Bill at the end of the financial year and an Appropriation Bill at the end of the Session. That plan is, in my opinion, more convenient, and will have to be abandoned if the right honourable Gentleman carries his point to night. The result of his carrying his point would be that at some later stage

of the Session, and perhaps at a most inconvenient period for discussion, the Government would have to ask the House to pass somewhat large Army and Navy Votes—large in point of money, through perhaps unimportant in point of substance—in order to found upon those Votes another Consolidated Fund Bill, which would have to be got through its various stages before the Appropriation Bill. That, I think, is not a good plan, but I will not labour the inconvenience attached to it. The right honourable Gentleman's objection to the plan of the Government is that it would be in the power of the Government, if they got this money, not to bring Army Estimates on again until the end of the Session, until an inconvenient period, about 1st August, or even later. The fears of the right honourable Gentleman are altogether illusory, because under the Supply Rule Friday in every week must be devoted to Supply, and because the particular Supply to be taken depends upon the general wish of the House, but chiefly upon the wish of the Opposition, and most of all upon the wish of the Leader of the Opposition. Under the practice that has been established since the Supply Rule was adopted a request from the Leader of the Opposition that such an cuch a Friday should be given up ao such and such Supply has never yet been refused by the leader of the House, and I venture to say will never be refused while the Supply Rule is in operation. I appeal to the Members of the Opposition present whether I made any undue claim upon their credulity when I told them that my one desire when arranging Supply was to meet the wishes of the House, and, above all, to meet the wishes of the Opposition. Therefore, the fears of the right honourable Gentleman are illusory, and, that being so, I appeal to the right honourable Gentleman to allow me to get the Votes for which, in the interest of public business, I ask.

Motion made—

"That the Chairman do report Progress; and ask leave to sit again."—(*Mr. Buchanan.*)

MR. BUCHANAN: I venture to think this interpretation of the Supply Rule is a new interpretation. The right honourable Gentleman must be aware that in past years, with the exception of 1897, there has not been a single occasion when there has not been a second Consolidated Fund Bill. I have gone back 12 years.

AN HONOURABLE MEMBER: The Rule was only passed in 1896.

MR. BUCHANAN: I am quite aware of that, but the right honourable Gentleman has appealed to the practice of the House as well as to what he conceives to be the interpretation of the new Rule. I have looked back for the past 12 years, and in no case, except in the year 1897, has there been a year in which there was not a second Consolidated Fund Bill. The House will practically lose all control over Army affairs if we are to vote as the Leader of the House asks us to do, the money for the whole period of the Session. There is no real difficulty in adhering to the previous practice of the House. I think the right honourable Gentleman is under a misapprehension when he says that these Votes are not proper subjects of discussion. They amount to nearly three millions of money, and we all know very well that in Appropriation Accounts, constantly, points connected with the very Vote we are coming to, Vote 13, matters of irregularity in the way this part of servants arise in the way this half-pay is distributed. If we agree to the Motion of the right honourable Gentleman, and accept it as a precedent as he desires, we part for ever, for ourselves and successors, with the power of control over these important Votes, and in order to emphasise the opinion which is felt very strongly on this side of the House, I beg to move " That we now re-

MR. COURTENAY WARNER: The right honourable Gentleman the Leader of the House has stated that he would put down any Votes he liked, but he need not put down contentious Votes, and it would be very unfair if he were to take such advantage of his powers as to avoid dangerous subjects. I think on the Consolidated Fund Bill——

THE DEPUTY CHAIRMAN: I would remind the honourable Member that the subject before the House is reporting progress.

Mr. Buchanan.

MR. COURTENAY WARNER: There is one important reason why we should oppose the right honourable Gentleman's proposal. In many of the non-effective charges there is no increase, and although they look non-contentious, they are really very contentious subjects. Now, one of the first items is half-pay for the Field-Marshals, and that is not the sort of Vote which goes through, as a rule, without some remarks, and I think it is very certain to be contested on the first item. There are other items which are likely to be contested, and, therefore, I hope we shall be allowed to go to bed to-night without these Votes, which are absolutely unnecessary to carry on the business of the country, and which have only been taken at this period on one occasion during the last six years, and there is no possible object in keeping the whole House here to a late hour.

CAPTAIN SINCLAIR: I should like to ask the right honourable Gentleman why in this year he is treating the Army Votes differently to all other years? He reminded us that the Army Votes did not take so much time previously, but the right honourable Gentleman must remember that great changes have been made, and many of them are only in the experimental stages. When such huge increases are proposed, we naturally expect more time to discuss them, and I for one, without any desire to obstruct, candidly confess that there are points in the Votes which have already been taken which I desired to discuss, but which I refrained from in order that the business should go on. In the case of the Navy, the right honourable Gentleman has been content to take Vote 1, and by taking this Vote he precludes us from criticising these matters, and practically takes them from the control of the House.

MR. CALDWELL: We are now asked to vote three millions of money, but, on the other hand, what is the position of matters with regard to the discussion of Votes in Supply? The First Lord knows perfectly well that our time for discussion in Supply is limited to 20 or 23 days. It is obvious, therefore, that if we take up more time in discussing the Army Estimates it comes off the time at our disposal to discuss the other Votes at the end of the Session, and not one moment of the time of the Government will be wasted if the Estimates are continued on another Friday. It is only a question of convenience, and I venture to say that it is a matter for the Opposition more than the Government that they should regulate the time devoted to Supply. It is all very well for the right honourable Gentleman to say that in certain circumstances he could have had his Vote. I do not know why he should claim the right, as it were, when he has got the general closure, to hold out a threat of this kind to this side. We are the critics of the Government, and I think the First Lord of the Treasury will admit that hitherto we have acted upon the principle of devoting the time according to the importance of the Votes. This has worked very well in the past, and I do not see, supposing that you were to pass these Votes to-night, that you will gain anything practical in the operation. The mere saying that they would not ask for a second Consolidated Fund Bill before the end of the Session makes no difference, for, as has been said by my honourable Friend the Member for Aberdeen, I do not know of any discussions having taken place upon the Second Consolidated Fund Bills, so that it does not apply. I venture to think that the Government have hitherto always succeeded best by a mutual arrangement instead of trying to force matters through the House. You are entitled to Vote 1 of the Navy and the Army, and so far as it is absolutely necessary for you to have the Votes, we are quite willing to give them before Easter. But supposing you postpone this Vote, there is nothing to hinder you taking it up again three weeks after Easter. You can put it down any time you want, and if we take that Vote a month or six weeks hence, the Government suffer nothing by it. It is a question of arrangement with the Opposition,

and the First Lord must always remember that whatever rule is established when you are in power applies to you when you are in opposition. [Cries of "Divide, Divide!"] Honourable Members need not think that they are going to force anything down us, for if you are trying to do that, you will find you are mistaken.

THE DEPUTY CHAIRMAN: Order, order!

MR. CALDWELL: Supposing the Government do succeed in forcing on Supply by sitting on till to-morrow night, I do not suppose that they will have made a single hour of advance, and I question very much whether they will not have found that their attempt has had a backward result. It has been the experience of the past that instead of gaining anything, you actually lose by attempting to force matters in this way. It is very well known that if we are to go on with these non-effective Votes, it is perfectly evident that we can go on for a very indefinite period. But there is no reason why we should do that. If the Government can show us that it is absolutely necessary that they should have these Votes, as they have done in the case of Vote 1, then by all means let them have the Vote. But as it is not absolutely necessary, and as it can be done by a Second Consolidated Fund Bill, and will not deprive the Government of one hour's time, I think they might agree, looking to the importance of the Army Votes this year, to leave these matters over for discussion, and not insist that we should vote this money without discussion.

Question put—

"That the Chairman do report Progress; and ask leave to sit again."—(*Mr. Buchanan.*)

The Committee divided:—Ayes 32; Noes 107.—(Division List No. 50.)

AYES.

Allen, Wm. (Newc. under Lyme)	Lawson, Sir Wilfrid (Cumb'land)	Sinclair, Capt. Jno. (Forfarshire
Buchanan, Thomas Ryburn	Macaleese, Daniel	Souttar, Robinson
Caldwell, James	Maddison, Fred	Sullivan, Donal (Westmeath)
Campbell-Bannerman, Sir H.	Morton, Edw. J. C. (Devonport)	Trevelyan, Charles Philips
Clark, Dr. G. B. (Caithness-sh.)	Moulton, John Fletcher	Walton, Joseph (Barnsley)
Colville, John	Nussey, Thomas Willans	Warner, Thos. Courtenay T.
Douglas, Charles M. (Lanark)	Oldroyd, Mark	Weir, James Galloway
Fenwick, Charles	Pearson, Sir Weetman D.	Williams, John Carvell (Notts.)
Goddard, Daniel Ford	Pirie, Duncan V.	
Hayne, Rt. Hn. Chas. Seale-	Price, Robert John	TELLERS FOR THE AYES—
Hazell, Walter	Reckitt, Harold James	Mr. Causton and Mr. Munro
Jones, Wm. (Carnarvonshire)	Samuel, J. (Stockton-on-Tees)	Ferguson.

NOES.

Arnold, Alfred
Ashmead-Bartlett, Sir Ellis
Atkinson, Rt. Hn. John
Bagot,Capt.JoscelineFitzRoy
Balfour,Rt.Hn.A.J.(Manch'r)
Balfour,RtHnGerald W(Leeds)
Banbury, Frederick George
Barton, Dunbar Plunket
Beckett, Ernest William
Bemrose, Sir Henry Howe
Bentinck, Lord Henry C.
Bethell, Commander
Blundell, Colonel Henry
Brodrick, Rt. Hon. St. John
Carlile, William Walter
Cavendish,V.C.W(Derbyshire)
Chaloner, Captain R. G. W.
Chamberlain, Rt.Hn.J.(Birm.)
Chamberlain,J.Austen(Worc'r.
Chaplin, Rt. Hn. Henry
Clare, Octavius Leigh
Cochrane, Hn. Thos. H. A. E.
Coghill, Douglas Harry
Collings, Rt. Hn. Jesse
Colomb,Sir John Chas. Ready
Compton, Lord Alwyne
Corbett, A. Cameron(Glasgow)
Cross, Herb.Shepherd(Bolton)
Curzon, Viscount
Dalkeith, Earl of
Dalrymple, Sir Charles
Douglas, Rt. Hn. A. Akers-
Duncombe, Hon. Hubert V.
Finch, George H.
Finlay, Sir Robert Bannatyne
Fisher, William Hayes
Fletcher, Sir Henry

Folkestone, Viscount
Foster, Colonel (Lancaster)
Gedge, Sydney
Goldsworthy, Major-General
Gordon, Hon. John Edward
Goschen, George J. (Sussex)
Gray, Ernest (West Ham)
Greville, Hon. Ronald
Gull, Sir Cameron
Hamilton,Rt.Hn.Lord George
Hanbury, Rt. Hn. Robert Wm.
Hardy, Laurence
Hare, Thomas Leigh
Hutchinson,Capt.G.W.Grice-
Jebb, Richard Claverhouse
Johnston, William (Belfast)
Jolliffe, Hon. H. George
Kemp, George
Kennaway,Rt.Hn.Sir John H.
Lawrence,SirE.Durning-(Corn.
Leigh-Bennett, Henry Currie
Lockwood, Lt.-Col. A. R.
Long,Col. Chas.W.(Evesham)
Long,RtHnWalter(Liverpool)
Lowles, John
Macartney, W. G. Ellison
Macdona, John Cumming
M'Calmont, H. L. B. (Cambs.)
Malcolm, Ian
Monckton, Edward Philip
More,Robt.Jasper(Shropshire)
Morrell, George Herbert
Morton,ArthurH.A.(Deptford)
Murray,RtHnA.Graham(Bute)
Murray, Charles J.(Coventry)
Nicol, Donald Ninian
Orr-Ewing, Charles Lindsay

Phillpotts, Captain Arthur
Platt-Higgins, Frederick
Pollock, Harry Frederick
Pryce-Jones, Lt.-Col. Edward
Purvis, Robert
Richards, Henry Charles
Ritchie,Rt.Hn.Chas.Thomson
Roberts, John Bryn (Eifion)
Round, James
Russell, T. W. (Tyrone)
Simeon, Sir Barrington
Smith,James Parker(Lanarks.)
Smith,Hn. W. F. D. (Strand)
Stanley,Hn.Arthur(Ormskirk)
Stanley, Lord (Lancs.)
Strauss, Arthur
Talbot, Lord E. (Chichester)
Talbot,RtHnJ.G.(Oxf'dUniv.)
Thornton, Percy M.
Valentia, Viscount
Wanklyn, James Leslie
Webster, R. G. (St. Pancras)
Welby, Lieut.-Col. A. C. E.
Wentworth, Bruce C. Vernon-
Williams,JosephPowell(Birm.)
Willox, Sir John Archibald
Wodehouse,Rt.Hn.E.R.(Bath)
Wortley, Rt.Hn. C. B. Stuart-
Wylie, Alexander
Wyndham, George
Wyndham-Quin, Major W.H.
Young, Commander (Berks,E.)

TELLERS FOR THE NOES—
　Sir William Walrond and
　Mr. Anstruther.

Original Question again proposed.

DR. CLARK : I should like some information with regard to Vote 14. It is quite satisfactory to find that some of the non-effective, Votes are decreasing as far as warrant and non-commissioned officers and men are concerned, but on Vote 14 there is a considerable increase, and I think we ought to have some explanation. The first of these increases is an increase upon the half-pay of field-marshals and generals. Now, under the new regulations, we have fixed the number of our generals during the time of peace. We have six field-marshals, 10 generals, 20 lieutenant-generals, and 70 major-generals for our small Army, and that is a very fair list. There were a number of general officers who were beyond this scheme, and they were to remain, but gradually they were to be wiped out year by year, and were to be a constantly decreasing factor in our Army. Unfortunately, the first of these increases is £4,500, and this cannot be for field-marshals, because we have not increased them. I do not think it is for generals, but I think there has been a large number of major-generals created. Surely, in time of peace, the number fixed by the War Office was quite sufficient, especially when you remember that in regard to a number of these you are employing them in the Colonies, and so, to a certain extent, you are saving expense. But this year, for some reason or other, it has been found necessary to have a larger number of major-generals, and I suppose the way you have done it is that you have made this increase by promotions from the rank of colonel. You must have increased the number of colonels, and made them major-generals, and so you have brought them under this list. I think we ought to have some explanation as to this increase, for this is a question which was fought out and settled, and now, instead of finding, as we all expected, that these general officers were more than were supposed to be required for the Army during the time of peace, this year we find that there has been a very considerable increase. I think we ought to have some explanation from the Under Secretary as to what has been the cause of this increase.

MR. POWELL WILLIAMS: This increase is due to the fact that colonels have been employed in certain commands instead of major-generals. The consequence is that a larger number of major-generals remained upon the half-pay list to which this item refers. In the course of time, as vacancies occur, they will be absorbed, and the list of major-generals and colonels will be reduced to the numbers indicated in the warrant to which the honourable Member for Caithness has referred. In the meantime the list remains practically where it was, although it is found, in certain cases, that this causes a larger number of major-generals to be on the half-pay list, which causes this increase, but it is quite a temporary increase in the amount taken.

MR. BUCHANAN: I am glad the First Lord of the Treasury has returned to the House, because I wish to point out, in two or three words, how important questions that arise under this Vote, which deserve discussion, can get through without due consideration. We had a discussion last year in this House as to the reinstatement of those officers who were concerned in the Jameson Raid, and five of them were reinstated. During the course of the past year Colonel Rhodes, who was not reinstated, was allowed to be put back into the Army, and is now on half-pay, and his half-pay is contained in this Vote. Now, if we want to challenge the executive action of the Government, there is no Vote on which we can challenge it upon this question. If you look at the Appropriation Accounts and the Reports of the Comptroller and Auditor-General, you will find that year after year he calls the attention to the way in which pay-warrants are issued, and to the fact that the present Secretary of State for War, at any rate, is very lax in his interpretation of pay-warrants, and is also

lax in the way undue charges are put on the public Exchequer on this Vote. Now, in this very year there are two cases—there is the case of a colonel of a regiment who made false statements in the regimental acounts. He was hauled over the coals, and he stated that he closed the account in 1888, but, on proceeding further, it turned out that he had invested the money in his wife's name. Very naturally he was dismissed the Service, but subsequently he was allowed to retire. He was removed from the Army, and the only deduction made from his retiring allowance was the lowest minimum deduction possible.

MR. POWELL WILLIAMS: No, no!

MR. BUCHANAN: That only increases the force of my argument, for the evidence we have in the Report of the Comptroller and Auditor-General reveals this very serious state of matters as to the way in which the Secretary of State for War deals with these questions. A commanding officer of one regiment had been compelled to retire because of gross and continued intemperance. He was called upon to retire, and then the matter was compromised by allowing him to go on half-pay for a period of two years. He then applied to be allowed to retire, and he was rewarded at the full rate of his pension, and the Comptroller and Auditor-General calls attention to the fact that this is the first occasion upon which the Secretary of State for War had so interpreted the pay-warrant as to include and state that intemperance was not misconduct under the pay-warrant. These are three cases which I have given, and they might be multiplied, which I have laid before the House to show that the present Secretary of State has been very lax in his interpretation of pay-warrants, and the charges he puts upon the public Exchequer under this Vote. I ask this Committee what chance and opportunity is there of discussing matters of this character? What possibility is there of any public attention being drawn to these questions if we are compelled—not merely this year, but, according to the statement of the First Lord of the

Treasury, and according to the rule he wants to lay down, this year and all succeeding years—to withdraw from the consideration of the House these Votes which are to be taken as non-contentious Votes?

THE FIRST LORD OF THE TREASURY: I must correct this view of my policy which has been suggested by my honourable Friend. What I said was that before the 31st of March we should get enough money to save us from having to ask for another Consolidated Fund Bill. I do not raise any complaint at the lengthy discussion of Vote 1, but the honourable Member must be aware that had we taken the same length of time as was taken last year or the year before there would have been no difficulty in discussing these Votes.

MR. BUCHANAN: The contention of the right honourable Gentleman both to-night and last night, when the matter was discussed across the floor of the House, was this—that these Votes were really non-contentious, and did not need discussion, and what he has said to-night is that what he wants the House of Commons to do this year is what he wants the House to do in succeeding years, and that is, to vote practically as a matter of course these non-effective Votes as a Supplementary Vote, in order to enable the Government of the day to get enough money for the Army to go on during the whole of the Session.

THE FIRST LORD OF THE TREASURY: The honourable Gentleman misunderstands me most distinctly. The word "non-contentious" is perfectly understood in Parliamentary language, and it does not mean a Vote on which nothing is to be said, but it means that they are non-contentious in the sense that they raise no great principle. These Votes certainly come under that category, and if the honourable Gentleman will look at the time which has been taken up in the past he will see that I am not exaggerating in the sense in which I used the word, and that they are not contentious Votes. If they were postponed now, and brought up again at a later period of the Session, there would be really no additional opportunity given for the discussion of the Army Estimates, and all that would happen

Mr. Buchanan.

would be that the House would be put to the trouble of passing a Second Consolidated Fund Bill. All the time that has been taken could have been avoided if the honourable Gentleman had seconded the efforts of the Government to obtain these Votes earlier.

SIR H. CAMPBELL-BANNERMAN: I must make a little additional protest against the misuse of the word "non-contentious." There was a time when these Votes, above all others, were contentious. In the old days, when purchase in the Army existed, we know that these non-effective Votes were the most contentious of all the Army Estimates, and therefore we must not be led to class this Vote or that Vote as being a perfectly harmless and non-contentious Vote which is to be passed without any observations.

*MR. PIRIE: I desire to lay before the right honourable Gentleman the First Lord of the Treasury the fact that I think he is mistaken in imagining that the discussion on the Army Estimates can go on year after year in the same way as they have done in the past, when year after year they are increasing in so great an amount.

THE DEPUTY CHAIRMAN: I would draw the honourable Member's attention to the fact that the question is the granting of half-pay.

Motion made—

"That a sum, not exceeding £1,551,000, be granted for the said Service."—(*Mr. Courtenay Warner.*)

MR. COURTENAY WARNER: I wish to draw the attention of the Committee to item B in this Vote, which, I think, contains an amount of extravagance which ought not to be allowed. This increase amounts to £4,500 a year, and I beg to move that item B on page 14 be reduced by £4,500.

MR. CALDWELL: I merely want to point out that Vote 14, which relates to the non-effective Service, and Vote 15 contain some matters of great importance. So far as regards the emoluments to the officers in Vote 14, it will be seen that it is more than the amount paid to the whole body of men. That is certainly a matter which is deserving of consideration when the Army Estimates are discussed. The officers have representatives in this House who look after their interests, whereas the men have very few representatives here. I simply wish to point to the fact that the officers in retirement get a million and a half of money, which is more than is paid to the whole body of warrant and non-commissioned officers and men in like circumstances.

Dr. CLARK: This is a very important question. I see we have 70 major-generals on the staff. Ought not the War Office to be content with its 16 field-marshals, its 10 generals, and its 70 major-generals? Yet this list of half-pay officers is continually increasing, and this year we are asked to Vote an extra £4,500. Why is it necessary to increase the number of major-generals? As my honourable Friend has pointed out, as far as the other branches of the non-effective Services are concerned these retiring allowances are a constantly increasing factor. But this only applies to the higher ranks, and not to the lower ones. I think my honourable Friend is perfectly right in moving a reduction on this Vote, and I do appeal to the honourable Gentleman to give us some explanation of the facts.

*Mr. PIRIE: I think the country will be grateful to-morrow when it reads what has gone on in this House. We know there are men here who are constantly advocating an increase of the Army year by year, but the most serious point of view is to be found in the fact that the expenses for the higher ranks are on the increase, whereas those of the lower ranks are positively decreasing. We want the country to realise the present state of affairs. I believe the Commander-in-Chief can, if he likes, do a good deal more to ensure economy. It is all very well to talk about patriotism and the wants of the country, but we in this House are responsible to the taxpayers, and for that reason I think it is our bounden duty to resist these enormous increases year by year, until we are convinced that the country gets the full value for its ever-

increasing expenditure. The more we resist them the more we shall have the country at our back. I do not wish to exaggerate the importance of this question, but in the interests of the Army itself it is surely desirable to have more economical administration. The House of Commons may be quite willing to Vote the money now, but the time will come when it will be much more economically disposed.

The DEPUTY CHAIRMAN: Order, order! The honourable Member must confine himself to the Question before the Committee.

*Mr. PIRIE : The higher officers in the Army are, to a great extent, responsible for this great expenditure, and I think that if they will realise that there is a limit to the amount of money to be voted to the Army, they will see the desirability of reducing these retiring allowances and salaries.

Mr. MADDISON (Sheffield, Brightside) : I agree with my honourable Friend that we ought to have some explanation of this increase in the Vote for half-pay officers. The Financial Secretary for War has given a certain explanation, but there are discrepancies which still want to be cleared up. Many of us believe that the Army is chiefly valuable to the officers. We are often told that the officers serve the Army and the nation out of pure patriotism, but it does not look quite as if that patriotism is undiluted, for it carries with it very heavy pay. I appeal to the Under Secretary for War to show us if he can that, in respect to this increase, there is to be some extra work done in some way or other, and, unless he does so, I for one shall be obliged to vote with the mover of the reduction. It is a serious thing when you see as much as £4,500 increase in the Vote for half-pay field-marshals and general officers eligible for employment. But why should they be paid when they are not employed? A workman when he is out of employment gets no pay. Honourable Members may interrupt me by making unearthly noises, and one who is doing so belongs to the very class with which I am dealing. I will ask him, is it unreasonable on our part to demand some explanation of the reason why this large sum of £4,500 is to be given to officers of the highest rank, who usually are men of very considerable wealth? Of course, I live at a very remote distance from these high officials, and I may be wrong as to their financial position. But I do venture to say that there are not many poor men among them. I only wish to appeal to the honourable Gentleman, to tell us in simple words, which we can easily understand, why this increase is taking place; and, if he does not tell us, the impression will be left on the minds of many of us that he has diplomatic reasons for witholding the explanation.

MR. COURTENAY WARNER : As no answer has been given to my question, I must point out that the increase is directly contrary to what appears in the Royal Warrant, which allows 10 full generals, whereas there are 12; 20 lieutenant-generals, whereas there are 24; and 70 major-generals, whereas there are 84. How is it this increase has been brought about? Why should we have this plethora of general officers? Is it not time to demand a reduction in this extravagant item? Remember, you are reducing the amount of half-pay to the men; they are costing you less, whereas your general officers are costing you more. I do hope that some explanation will be given.

MR. FENWICK (Northumberland, Wansbeck): I, too, think we are entitled to some explanation on this point. The Question has been brought before the House again and again during the last 14 years. May I point out that there are Gentlemen, Members of this House, coming here as political partisans, who are on the retired list, and in receipt of half-pay.

COLONEL LOCKWOOD: If the honourable Member is alluding to me as a half-pay officer he is entirely wrong.

MR. FENWICK: I never for a moment had the honourable and gallant Member in my mind. I know there are such Members to be found in both political Parties. We find that the half-

Mr. Maddison.

pay staff is increasing year by year, and I repeat that Gentlemen who are on the retired list and are in receipt of half-pay ought not to be allowed to come to this House as political partisans, and to take part in Debates the object of which is to increase the expenditure of the country, which comes out of the tax-payers' pockets. I think we are entitled to ask that the Government shall not sit in silence and refuse an explanation of the alarming increase in this Estimate.

MR. POWELL WILLIAMS: I can only repeat the explanation I gave half an hour ago. When the honourable Member speaks of the increase in this Vote, he alludes, no doubt, to the increase in this one item, for he must bear in mind that the Vote itself shows a decrease of no less than £16,000. With regard to the increase for half-pay, I have already explained it is due to the fact that in certain cases, instead of employing general officers for particular services requiring particular qualifications, colonels have been employed, and the result is that a larger number of general officers remain on the half-pay list than otherwise would be the case. That is the explanation of the increase in this particular item. There has been no increase in the total number of general officers, and the list of officers, including colonels, is being worked down to the number stated in the Royal Warrant, which in future is to be the establishment.

MR. COURTENAY WARNER : We complain there has been no decrease. We do not say there has been an increase, but there are two full generals, four lieutenant-generals, and 14 major-generals over and above the proper number.

Question put—

"That a sum, not exceeding £1,551,000, be granted for the said Service."—(*Mr. Courtenay Warner.*)

The Committee divided:—Ayes 27; Noes 99.—(Division List No. 51.)

AYES.

Allen,Wm.(Newc.underLyme)
Buchanan, Thomas Ryburn
Caldwell, James
Clark,Dr.G.B.(Caithness-sh.)
Colville, John
Fenwick, Charles
Goddard, Daniel Ford
Hayne, Rt. Hn. Chas. Seale-
Hazell, Walter
Jones, Wm. (Carnarvonshire)

Lawson,SirWilfrid(Cumb'land)
Macaleese, Daniel
Maddison, Fred.
Morton,Edw.J.C.(Devonport)
Moulton, John Fletcher
Nussey, Thomas Willans
Oldroyd, Mark
Pearson, Sir Weetman D.
Price, Robert John
Reckitt, Harold James

Samuel, J.(Stockton-on-Tees)
Sinclair,Capt.Jno.(Forfarshire
Souttar, Robinson
Sullivan, Donal (Westmeath)
Walton, Joseph (Barnsley)
Weir, James Galloway
Williams, John Carvell(Notts.

TELLERS FOR THE AYES—
Mr. Warner and Mr. Pirie.

NOES.

Arnold, Alfred
Ashmead-Bartlett, Sir Ellis
Atkinson, Rt. Hon. John
Bagot,Capt.JoscelineFitzRoy
Balfour,Rt.Hn.A.J.(Manch'r)
Balfour,RtHnGeraldW.(Leeds)
Banbury, Frederick George
Barton, Dunbar Plunket
Beckett, Ernest William
Bemrose, Sir Henry Howe
Bentinck, Lord Henry C.
Bethell, Commander
Blundell, Colonel Henry
Brodrick, Rt. Hn. St. John
Carlile, William Walter
Cavendish,V.C.W.(Derbyshire)
Chaloner, Captain R. G. W.
Chamberlain,Rt.Hn.J.(Birm.)
Chamberlain,J.Austen(Worc'r.
Chaplin, Rt. Hon. Henry
Clare, Octavius Leigh
Cochrane, Hn. Thos. H. A. E.
Coghill, Douglas Harry
Collings, Rt. Hon. Jesse
Colomb, Sir John Chas. Ready
Compton, Lord Alwyne
Corbett, A. Cameron(Glasgow)
Cross, Herb.Shepherd(Bolton)
Curzon, Viscount
Dalkeith, Earl of
Dalrymple, Sir Charles
Douglas, Rt. Hn. A. Akers-
Duncombe, Hon. Hubert V.
Finch, George H.
Finlay, Sir Robert Bannatyne

Fisher, William Hayes
Folkestone, Viscount
Foster, Colonel (Lancaster)
Gedge, Sydney
Goldsworthy, Major-General
Gordon, Hon. John Edward
Goschen, George J. (Sussex)
Gray, Ernest (West Ham)
Greville, Hon. Ronald
Gull, Sir Cameron
Hamilton,Rt.Hn.Lord George
Hanbury, Rt.Hn. Robert Wm.
Hardy, Laurence
Hare, Thomas Leigh
Hutchinson, Capt. G.W.Grice-
Jebb, Richard Claverhouse
Johnston, William (Belfast)
Kemp, George
Lawrence,Sir E.Durning-(Corn
Leigh-Bennett, Henry Currie
Lockwood, Lieut.-Col. A. R.
Long, Col. Chas.W.(Evesham)
Long,RtHnWalter(Liverpool)
Lowles, John
Macartney, W. G. Ellison
Macdona, John Cumming
McCalmont, H. L. B. (Cambs.)
Malcolm, Ian
More, Robt.Jasper(Shropshire)
Morrell, George Herbert
Morton,Arthur H.A.(Deptf'd)
Murray,RtHnA.Graham(Bute
Murray, Charles J. (Coventry)
Nicol, Donald Ninian
Orr-Ewing, Charles Lindsay

Phillpotts, Captain Arthur
Platt-Higgins, Frederick
Pollock, Harry Frederick
Pryce-Jones, Lt.-Col. Edward
Purvis, Robert
Richards, Henry Charles
Ritchie,Rt.Hn.Chas.Thomson
Round, James
Russell, T. W. (Tyrone)
Simeon, Sir Barrington
Smith, James Parker(Lanarks)
Smith, Hn. W. F. D. (Strand)
Stanley,Hn.Arthur(Ormskirk)
Stanley, Lord (Lancs.)
Talbot, Lord E. (Chichester)
Thornton, Percy M.
Valentia, Viscount
Wanklyn, James Leslie
Webster, Sir R. E. (I. of W.)
Welby, Lt.-Col. A. C. E.
Wentworth, Bruce C. Vernon
Williams,Joseph Powell(Birm)
Willox, Sir John Archibald
Wilson, John (Falkirk)
Wortley, Rt.Hn. C. B. Stuart-
Wylie, Alexander
Wyndham, George
Wyndham-Quin, Major W. H.
Young, Commander(Berks,E.)

TELLERS FOR THE NOES—
Sir William Walrond and
Mr. Anstruther.

Original Question again proposed.

DR. CLARK: There is one very important matter already alluded to as to which we have had no explanation from the Financial Secretary. A serious statement is made by the Comptroller-General, in his Report on the Army Appropriation Account, to the effect that the country has to pay £800 a year to two lieutenant-colonels, one of whom had been turned out for mis-appropriating £100, and the other for drunkenness, but had been reinstated. In the case of one colonel, which was discussed last year, considerable sympathy was expressed on both sides of the House, but the principle then adopted has been carried still further this year, and I think we have a right to know what action has been taken on this accusation by the Comptroller-General, that the Royal Warrant is being evaded by the Secretary for War by putting an absolutely new construction on the offence of misdemeanour. In the case of the colonel who misappropriated the £100 the money was taken from a regimental fund and invested in his wife's name. Surely, the misappropriation and investment of regimental funds in a man's wife's name was an offence for which he should have been dismissed the Service, yet it was held it was not sufficiently serious to justify that step. You have one law for the rich and another for the poor. If a soldier had appropriated a comrade's money he would have been imprisoned, but the officer you treated quite differently. I suppose an officer may steal or get drunk, and do exactly as he pleases. Under the circumstances I propose to move to reduce the Vote by £800.

THE FIRST LORD OF THE TREASURY: Before we put that Motion, I understand, from what has fallen from the honourable Gentleman, that his complaint is in regard to a case brought before the Public Accounts Committee by the Comptroller-General, in which two pensions under this Vote are called in question. In order to save further trouble, I will give an undertaking on the part of the Government that no money shall be paid to either of these two officers until the Public Accounts Committee have had the matter under their consideration.

DR. CLARK: Under those circumstances I beg to withdraw my Amendment.

MR. WEIR: I should like an assurance that the Government will look into the question of the pensions of widows of deceased officers.

THE FIRST LORD OF THE TREASURY: There is a general pledge to deal with all these questions.

Motion made—

" That the Chairman do report Progress, and ask leave to sit again."—(*Mr. Allen.)*

MR. ALLEN (Newcastle-under-Lyme): It is now nearly an hour and a half beyond the usual time at which the House adjourns, and an hour since I made an appeal to the First Lord to allow us to adjourn. I therefore beg now to move to report progress.

THE DEPUTY CHAIRMAN: The House has by Resolution suspended the Twelve o'clock Rule for the express purpose of considering Supply, and the Committee has itself decided since Twelve o'clock not to report progress. Out of respect for the honourable Gentleman I will not decline altogether to put the Question from the Chair, but I will put it without Debate.

Question put—

" That the Chairman do report Progress, and ask leave to sit again."—(*Mr. Allen.)*

The Committee divided:—Ayes 22; Noes 97.—(Division List No. 52.)

AYES.

Caldwell, James	Maddison, Fred.	Samuel, J.(Stockton-on-Tees)
Clark,Dr.G.B.(Caithness-sh.)	Morton,Edw.J.C.(Devonport)	Sullivan, Donal (Westmeath)
Fenwick, Charles	Moulton, John Fletcher	Weir, James Galloway
Goddard, Daniel Ford	Nussey, Thomas Willans	Williams, John Carvell(Notts.
Hayne, Rt. Hn. Chas. Seale-	Oldroyd, Mark	
Hazell, Walter	Pearson, Sir Weetman D.	TELLERS FOR THE AYES—
Jones, Wm. (Carnarvonshire)	Pirie, Duncan V.	Mr. Warner and Mr.
Lawson,SirWilfrid(Cumb'land)	Price, Robert John	William Allen.
Macaleese, Daniel	Reckitt, Harold James	

NOES.

Arnold, Alfred	Brodrick, Rt. Hn. St. John	Corbett, A. Cameron(Glasgow)
Ashmead-Bartlett, Sir Ellis	Carlile, William Walter	Cross, Herb.Shepherd(Bolton)
Atkinson, Rt. Hon. John	Cavendish,V.C.W.(Derbyshire)	Curzon, Viscount
Bagot,Capt.JoscelineFitzRoy	Chaloner, Captain R. G. W.	Dalkeith, Earl of
Balfour,Rt.Hn.A.J.(Manch'r)	Chamberlain,Rt.Hn.J.(Birm.)	Dalrymple, Sir Charles
Balfour,RtHnGeraldW.(Leeds)	Chamberlain,J.Austen(Worc'r.	Douglas, Rt. Hn. A. Akers
Banbury, Frederick George	Chaplin, Rt. Hon. Henry	Duncombe, Hon. Hubert V.
Barton, Dunbar Plunket	Clare, Octavius Leigh	Finch, George H.
Beckett, Ernest William	Cochrane, Hn. Thos. H. A. E.	Finlay, Sir Robert Bannatyne
Bemrose, Sir Henry Howe	Coghill, Douglas Harry	Fisher, William Hayes
Bentinck, Lord Henry C.	Collings, Rt. Hon. Jesse	Folkestone, Viscount
Bethell, Commander	Colomb, Sir John Chas. Ready	Foster, Colonel (Lancaster)
Blundell, Colonel Henry	Compton, Lord Alwyne	Gedge, Sydney

Dr. Clark.

Goldsworthy, Major-General
Gordon, Hon. John Edward
Goschen, George J. (Sussex)
Gray, Ernest (West Ham)
Greville, Hon. Ronald
Gull, Sir Cameron
Hamilton,Rt.Hn.Lord George
Hanbury, Rt.Hn. Robert Wm.
Hardy, Laurence
Hare, Thomas Leigh
Hutchinson, Capt. G.W.Grice-
Jebb, Richard Claverhouse
Johnston, William (Belfast)
Kemp, George
Lawrence,Sir E.Durning-(Corn
Leigh-Bennett, Henry Currie
Lockwood, Lieut.-Col. A.,R.
Long, Col. Chas.W.(Evesham)
Long,RtHnWalter(Liverpool)
Lowles, John
Macartney, W. G. Ellison

Macdona, John Cumming
McCalmont, H. L. B.(Cambs.)
More, Robt.Jasper(Shropshire)
Morrell, George Herbert
Murray,RtHnA.Graham(Bute
Murray, Charles J. (Coventry)
Nicol, Donald Ninian
Orr-Ewing, Charles Lindsay
Phillpotts, Captain Arthur
Platt-Higgins, Frederick
Pollock, Harry Frederick
Pryce-Jones, Lt.-Col. Edward
Purvis, Robert
Richards, Henry Charles
Ritchie,Rt.Hn.Chas.Thomson
Round, James
Russell, T. W. (Tyrone)
Simeon, Sir Barrington
Smith, James Parker(Lanarks)
Smith, Hn. W. F. D. (Strand)
Stanley,Hn.Arthur(Ormskirk)

Stanley, Lord (Lancs.)
Talbot, Lord E. (Chichester)
Thornton, Percy M.
Valentia, Viscount
Wanklyn, James Leslie
Webster, Sir R. E. (I. of W.)
Welby, Lt.-Col. A. C. E.
Wentworth, Bruce C. Vernon
Williams,Joseph Powell(Birm)
Willox, Sir John Archibald
Wilson, John (Falkirk)
Wortley, Rt.Hn. C. B. Stuart-
Wylie, Alexander
Wyndham, George
Wyndham-Quin, Major W. H.
Young, Commander(Berks,E.)

TELLERS FOR THE NOES—
Sir William Walrond and
Mr. Anstruther.

Original Question put.

Vote agreed to.

Motion made, and Question proposed—

"That a sum not exceeding £1,325,500 be granted to Her Majesty to defray the Charge for Chelsea and Kilmainham Hospitals and the In-Pensioners thereof, of Out-Pensions, of the Maintenance of Lunatics for whom Pensions are not drawn, and of Gratuities awarded in Commutation or in lieu of Pensions, of Rewards for Meritorious Services, of Victoria Cross Pensions, and of Pensions to the Widows and Children of Warrant Officers, etc., which will come in course of payment during the year ending on the 31st day of March 1900."

Motion made—

"That a sum not exceeding £1,313,500 be granted for the said Service."—(*Mr. Caldwell.*)

MR. CALDWELL: I wish to point out that this Vote shows a decrease. We have just passed the Officers' Vote, in which there is a considerable increase, and I should like to know what is the reason for it?

MR. POWELL WILLIAMS: To what item is the honourable Member referring?

MR. CALDWELL: Item " C " on page 117. What we want to know is, how it comes about that, while there is an increase in the number of men in the Army, there is not a corresponding increase in the number of pensioners. If I cannot get an explanation on this

point, I shall have to move a reduction in order to emphasise our opinion that there is no reason whatever for reducing the amount paid to the men while the sum for the officers is increased. I shall move to reduce the Vote by £12,000.

MR. MADDISON: Is it necessary to put us to the trouble of a Division when a few words of explanation would save it.

MR. W. JOHNSTON (Belfast): It is no trouble at all.

MR. MADDISON: Is there any necessity to waste the time simply because the Financial Secretary will not answer the Question put to him.

MR. POWELL WILLIAMS: It is due to the increase in the number of men upon the pension list, but I cannot say what that decrease is exactly at the present moment. The long service men who are entitled to pensions are dying off, and their places are being taken by short service men who are not entitled to pensions, so that there will, of course, be a decrease from time to time.

Motion, by leave, withdrawn.

DR. CLARK: I should like to call the attention of the Financial Secretary to the fact that in the item for Chelsea Hospital we find the field-marshal drawing a salary of £500 a year, and holding what is practically a sinecure. I hope the House will use its pruning knife in matters such as this.

MR. POWELL WILLIAMS: May I trouble the Committee for a moment. I see that the numbers for which I was asked a few minutes ago are given on page 121 of the Estimates, and if the honourable Member will look at that he will see that the number has fallen from 79,529 to 78,393, so that will account for the reduction.

Original Question put.

Vote agreed to.

4. £183,700, Superannuation, Compensation, Compassionate Allowances and Gratuities.

Vote agreed to.

Resolutions to be reported upon Monday next; Committee to sit again upon Monday next.

REPORT OF SUPPLY.

SUPPLY [16TH MARCH].

Resolutions reported—

NAVY ESTIMATES, 1899-1900.

" 1. That 110,640 men and boys be employed for the Sea and Coast Guard Services for the year ending on the 31st day of March 1900, including 18,505 Royal Marines."

" 2. That a sum not exceeding £5,242,700 be granted to Her Majesty to defray the Expenses of Wages, etc , to Officers, Seamen, and Boys, Coast Guard, and Royal Marines, which will come in course of payment during the year ending on the 31st day of March 1900."

Resolutions agreed to.

Dr. Clark.

Ordered, That the Resolution which, upon the 16th instant, was adopted from the Committee of Supply, and which was then agreed to by the House, be now read;

"That a number of Land Forces not exceeding 184,853 all ranks be maintained for the Service of the United Kingdom of Great Britain and Ireland at Home and Abroad, excluding Her Majesty's Indian Possessions, during the year ending on the 31st day of March 1900."

ARMY (ANNUAL) BILL.

Ordered, that leave be given to bring in a Bill to provide, during Twelve Months, for the Discipline and Regulation of the Army; and that Mr. Wyndham, Mr. Goschen, and Mr. Powell Williams do prepare and bring it in. Bill presented accordingly, and read the first time; to be read a second time upon Monday next, and to be printed. (Bill 134.)

WAYS AND MEANS.

Committee deferred till Monday next.

SUMMARY JURISDICTION ACT (1879) AMENDMENT BILL.

Third Reading deferred till Monday next.

PARISH COUNCILLORS (TENURE OF OFFICE) BILL.

Committee deferred till Monday next.

House adjourned at Two of the clock till Monday next.

An Asterisk (*) at the commencement of a Speech indicates revision by the Member.

HOUSE OF LORDS.

Monday, 20th March 1899.

———

THE LORD CHANCELLOR took his seat upon the Woolsack at a quarter past Four of the clock.

———

PRIVATE BILL BUSINESS.

———

THE LORD CHANCELLOR acquainted the House that the Clerk of the Parliaments had laid upon the Table the Certificates from the Examiners that the further Standing Orders applicable to the following Bills have been complied with :—

Crowborough District Gas.

St. David's Water and Gas.

And the Certificate that no Standing Orders are applicable to the following Bill—

Broughty Ferry Gas and Paving Order [H.L.]

The same were ordered to lie on the Table.

STANDING ORDERS COMMITTEE.

Report from, That the Standing Orders not complied with in respect of the Petition for additional provision in the Mersey Docks and Harbour Board (Pilotage) Bill [H.L.] ought to be dispensed with, and leave given to the Committee on the Bill to insert the additional provision.

That the Standing Orders not complied with in respect of the Petition for additional provision in the Gainsborough Urban District Council (Gas) Bill [H.L.] ought to be dispensed with, and leave given to the Committee on the Bill to insert the additional provision.

That the Standing Orders not complied with in respect of the London Water (Welsh Reservoirs and Works) Bill ought to be dispensed with.

That the Standing Orders not complied with in respect of the Belfast Corporation Bill ought to be dispensed with, provided clause 41 be struck out of the Bill.

That the Standing Orders not complied with in respect of the National Telephone Company (No. 1) Bill ought to be dispensed with, provided clause 94 be struck out of the Bill.

That the Standing Orders not complied with in respect of the National Telephone Company (No. 2) Bill ought to be dispensed with, provided clause 16 be struck out of the Bill.

Read, and agreed to.

WORKINGTON CORPORATION WATER BILL [H.L.]

Petition for additional provision; of the Corporation of Workington; together with proposed clauses and amendments annexed thereto; read, and referred to the Examiners.

DUNDEE GAS, TRAMWAYS, AND EXTENSION BILL [H.L.]

A Petition of Messrs. Grahames, Currey, and Spens, of 30, Great George Street, Westminster, Parliamentary agents, praying for leave to present a petition of Captain Clayhills Henderson, praying to be heard by counsel against the Bill, although the time limited by Standing Order No. 92 for presenting such Petition has expired; read, and ordered to lie on the Table; and Standing Order No. 92 to be considered To-morrow in order to its being dispensed with in respect of the said Petition.

ARBROATH CORPORATION GAS BILL
[H.L.]
Committee to meet on Friday next.

KIRKCALDY CORPORATION AND
TRAMWAYS BILL [H.L.]
Committee to meet on Friday next.

CROMER PROTECTION BILL [H.L.]
The Queen's consent signified; and
Bill reported from the Select Committee
with amendments.

BIRKENHEAD CORPORATION BILL
[H.L.]
Reported from the Select Committee
with amendments.

WALLASEY TRAMWAYS AND IM-
PROVEMENTS BILL [H.L.]
The Queen's consent signified; and
Bill reported from the Select Committee
with amendments.

LOUGHBOROUGH AND SHEEPSHED
RAILWAY BILL [H.L.]
Reported from the Select Committee
with amendments.

AIRDRIE AND COATBRIDGE WATER
BILL [H.L.]
Report from the Committee of Selection that the Lord Fermanagh (E. Erne)
be proposed to the House as a member
of the Select Committee in the place of
the Earl of Northbrook; and that the
Lord Fermanagh (E. Erne) be Chairman of the said Committee; read, and
agreed to.

CAMBRIDGE UNIVERSITY AND TOWN
GAS BILL [H.L.]
THE CHAIRMAN OF COMMITTEES
informed the House that the opposition
to the Bill was withdrawn: The order
made on Tuesday the 7th instant discharged; and Bill committed.

TOTLAND WATER BILL [H.L.]
THE CHAIRMAN OF COMMITTEES
informed the House that the opposition
to the Bill was withdrawn: The order
made on Friday the 10th instant discharged; and Bill committed.

EDUCATION DEPARTMENT PROVI-
SIONAL ORDER CONFIRMATION
(SWANSEA) BILL [H.L.]
Committed to a Committee of the
Whole House on Thursday next.

TRANSVAAL MORTGAGE LOAN AND
FINANCE COMPANY BILL [H.L.]
Committed: The Committee to be
proposed by the Committee of Selection.

SURREY COMMERCIAL DOCKS BILL
[H.L.]
Committed.

GLASGOW DISTRICT SUBWAY BILL
[H.L.]
Read third time, and passed, and sent
to the Commons.

RUSHDEN AND HIGHAM FERRERS
DISTRICT GAS BILL [H.L.]
Read third time, and passed, and sent
to the Commons.

GREAT YARMOUTH PIER BILL [H.L.]
The Queen's consent signified; and
Bill reported from the Select Committee,
with amendments.

———

RETURNS, REPORTS, ETC.

———

TRADE REPORTS, 1899.
I. Annual Series: No. 2211. Trade of
Ancona for the year 1898;

II. Miscellaneous Series: No. 500.
Commercial Education in Austria:

Presented (by Command), and ordered
to lie on the Table.

WAR OFFICE.

Two Orders in Council defining the duties of the principal officers charged with the administration of the Army—

1. Dated 21st November 1895;

2. Dated 7th March 1899, revoking the Order in Council dated 21st November 1895.

UNIVERSITY OF LONDON COMMISSIONERS.

Notification of appointment on the 10th March 1899 of Mr. Thomas Barlow, M.D., F.R.C.P., to fill a vacancy in the body of Commissioners for the University of London caused by the resignation of Sir William Roberts, M.D.

Laid before the House (pursuant to Act), and ordered to lie on the Table.

RAILWAY COMPANIES POWERS ACT, 1864 (EALING AND SOUTH HARROW RAILWAY COMPANY).

Draft Certificate of the Board of Trade for authority to raise additional capital.

Laid before the House (pursuant to Act), and ordered to lie on the Table.

———

PETITION.

———

VIVISECTION.

Petition for the suppression of the practice of; of Meeting in London; read, and ordered to lie on the Table.

———

BILLS ADVANCED.

———

BROUGHTY FERRY GAS AND PAVING ORDER BILL [H.L.]

To be read second time To-morrow.

LINCOLNSHIRE CORONERS BILL.

Motion made and Question proposed—
"That this Bill be read a second time."—
(Lord Heneage.)

LORD HENEAGE: My Lords, this is a very simple Bill, and a very local Bill, but I think I should be wanting in courtesy to your Lordships if in moving that it be read a second time I did not say why the Bill is necessary for the county of Lincolnshire and not for the rest of England. The Bill is drawn on the same lines as the Yorkshire Bill, and its object is to abolish the anomalous state of things existing with regard to coroners in the county of Lincolnshire. The Yorkshire Bill became law last year, and this Bill is introduced, under the advice of the Home Office, by the Lincolnshire County Committee, which was constituted under the Act of 1888 for the three divisions of Lincolnshire. The divisions of Lindsey, Kesteven, and Holland are represented on that Committee. I do not propose to enter fully into this Bill, which is really of a very technical character. Under the Statute Law Revision Act, 1891, the latter part of section 38 of the Coroners Act of 1844 relating to the counties of Lincoln and York was repealed. These are the only two counties in which there are three different divisions which are separate administrative counties. Under the Coroners Act of 1887 it is provided by section 38 that the whole of Lincolnshire shall be a county for the purposes of that Act, and section 41 constitutes the justices in gaol sessions the "local authority." But in direct contradiction to that it is enacted under the Local Government Act of 1888 that the divisions of Lincolnshire shall respectively be separate administrative counties, and that the business of gaol sessions in regard to coroners shall be transacted by the joint committee of the three county councils of Lindsey, Kesteven, and Holland. The exact effect of that is not clear even to lawyers, much less to laymen, but in practice coroners whose districts are situate wholly in one division of Lincolnshire are appointed and their salaries paid by the county council of that division, whilst their disbursements are rendered to and paid by another body, formerly the gaol sessions, but now the joint committee of the county

3 F 2

councils of the three divisions. To remove this anomaly, it is desirable to provide that each division of Lincolnshire shall be a separate administrative county for all the purposes of the Coroners Acts. It is also desirable to remove the doubt at present existing as to the proper authority to arrange for any alteration of the coroners' districts which are situate wholly within one administrative county, and to provide that such alteration may be made by the respective county councils. That is, in short, the purport of this Bill, and I have now to ask your Lordships to give it a Second Reading.

THE LORD CHANCELLOR (The Earl of HALSBURY): I am afraid I cannot ask your Lordships to take this Bill so shortly as my noble Friend has done. The Bill seems to me to raise very important and serious questions which are in the highest degree technical. I have not seen the Bill before now, and I am of opinion that its provisions might be attended with serious consequences. It repeals two sections of an Act of Parliament which was passed with very great care and after considerable discussion, and I would ask the noble Lord whether it would not be proper to adjourn this matter in order that the Bill might be carefully examined. I do not think any of your Lordships, except the noble Lord himself, has had any notice of it, and the light and airy fashion, if I may say so, with which he has dealt with the Bill is likely to mislead the House as to the effect of it. The Bill seems to me to raise very serious and important questions, and I think the Second Reading should be adjourned.

LORD HENEAGE: My Lords, I do not know whether I am in order in replying to the remarks of the noble and learned Earl on the Woolsack, but I should like to say that this Bill is on exactly the same lines as the Bill which was passed last year for Yorkshire, and in which the Home Office invited Lincolnshire to join. Unfortunately, however, through some delay in the meeting of the county authority, Lincolnshire was unable to be included in the Bill. The Bill which I am now asking your Lordships to read a second time is brought in not only by the advice, but at the request of the Home

Lord Heneage.

Office, and I am authorised to say that they support the Bill in every respect, but they thought it would be better that it should be brought in by the local authority. If the noble and learned Earl on the Woolsack thinks I was wanting in courtesy to the House in not going more fully into the provisions of this Bill, I apologise to the House, but I spoke briefly on the subject because the Bill is a highly technical one, and because an explanaion would involve reference to such a lot of statutes. I thought it would be for the convenience of the House that I should not go into them, especially as this Bill is on exactly the same lines as the Yorkshire Bill which was passed last year.

*THE PRIME MINISTER AND SECRETARY OF STATE FOR FOREIGN AFFAIRS (The MARQUESS of SALISBURY): My Lords, the noble and learned Earl on the Woolsack is one of your Lordships whose duty it is to look through that number of statutes which I think the noble Lord opposite spoke of with horror, if not with some contempt, and I feel that unless he who is the guardian of the law has properly looked into this matter it would be rather rash on our part to give this Bill a Second Reading to-day, especially when the amount of work is not so pressing as to prevent the Bill being taken up at a later period. Although the noble Lord who represents the Home Office, who is away owing to illness, is, I believe, an assenting party to the introduction of this Bill, I think it would be wiser on the whole to accept the suggestion of the noble and learned Lord on the Woolsack and adjourn it.

THE EARL OF KIMBERLEY: I see the noble and learned Lord the Chancellor of the Duchy of Lancaster in his place, and I think we should be glad to hear his view. Probably he will understand the Bill.

LORD JAMES OF HEREFORD: No doubt I shall understand it when I have had an opportunity of reading it, and I should have that opportunity if the Bill was adjourned.

Second Reading adjourned to Thursday next.

UGANDA.

THE EARL OF CAMPERDOWN: My Lords, I rise to ask, with reference to recent events in Uganda, whether Major Macdonald's expedition has finally terminated; and whether his Report will be presented to Parliament when received. The most recent Papers which have been presented with regard to Uganda carry the history of the expedition of Major Macdonald only so far as the unfortunate fighting which followed upon the mutiny of the Soudanese, and I ask this question in the hope that Her Majesty's Government may be able to give us some later information with regard to the expedition. Your Lordships will remember that Major Macdonald's expedition was a large expedition, fitted out in the year 1897, in the month of June, I think it was, and that the instructions to that expedition were that they were to investigate the sources of the Juba. That expedition, which was a very large and important one, consisted of 600 Swahalis, 50 Sikhs, and five British officers specially detached from this country. There was a Maxim battery, and it was to be joined by a body of 300 Soudanese. Major Macdonald took command of the expedition, and proceeded up country on the 23rd September. The Soudanese who joined him rose in revolt, and from that day—the 23rd September 1897 —to the 3rd May 1898 the expedition was occupied in fighting these Soudanese, and also in resisting other revolts which arose in other parts of Uganda. So far as the official Papers relating to Major Macdonald's expedition are concerned they terminate there. On the 3rd May Major Martyr, an officer who was well acquainted with the Arabic language, and also with the habits of the Soudanese, arrived and took over the command of the troops. My Lords, the expedition was then incited to revert to its original plan, and all information since that date is derived only from newspapers and similar sources. It was believed that Major Martyr left Kampala about the end of May, and marched to Mumias, 150 miles towards the coast, from where he branched off to Save, about 80 miles from Mumias, on the north of Mount Elgon, where the headquarters of the expedition are reported to have remained. Two small flying columns proceeded, one led by himself,

which went to the north-west as far as a place called Tarrangole and subsequently returned to headquarers, the other led by Captain Austin, and proceeding up the west coast of Lako Rudolph. It returned in November to headquarters. Since that date nothing has been heard, but on the 4th March Major (now Colonel) Macdonald arrived at Mombasa, and I believe has since proceeded to Cairo. It was reported in the papers that Colonel Macdonald had returned to Mombasa for the purpose of reorganising the expedition, having left a post somewhere near Save with the intention of returning and proceeding in the north-west. I merely state the report as I read it in the papers. I want to know whether that expedition is finally terminated, and whether the Report of its proceedings since made, which will, of course, be presented to the Foreign Office, will be laid on the Table of this House when it is received?

*THE PRIME MINISTER: My Lords, it is perfectly true that an expedition was sent out under Col. Macdonald, of which the main object was to ascertain more exactly the frontier which had been agreed upon some time before between what was then the Italian sphere of influence and our own, and as the boundary was indicated by the head waters of the river Juba, and our geographical knowledge of the locality was singularly deficient, we thought that it was important that we should be able to exactly indicate how far British influence extended. I may, however, say fairly that that was not the only object of Col. Macdonald's expedition. There were rumours at the time of designs on the Upper Nile, which experience did not altogether falsify, and these made us anxious to establish our military power at some station of the Upper Nile. Unfortunately the mutiny among the Soudanese troops, to which the noble Earl has referred, brought that particular branch of the expedition to an untimely end. It has been thought that it involved special blame to Col. Macdonald that such a mutiny took place, but if the noble Earl will study what has gone on in the neighbouring Free State of the Congo, where they have had larger experience and a fuller establishment, he will see that the difficulty of avoiding a mutiny of coloured troops was one to which they were exposed in quite as great a degree as we were. I believe it was the knowledge of the successful mutiny that was carried on shortly before against Baron Dhanis that incited our Soudanese to rise in their turn. The suppression of the mutiny, as the noble Lord says, occupied several months, but it had a worse effect than that, for it so diminished the force at the command of Col. Macdonald that it was not thought wise to prosecute the original enterprise to its full extent, so certain movements connected with the exploration of Lake Rudulph took place, and the result will be shown when Papers are laid on the Table. A more important point alluded to by the noble Earl is that connected with the name of Major Martyr, a very efficient and gallant officer. A considerable portion of Col. Macdonald's troops, with other troops that were in the Protectorate, made an expedition from the higher water of the Nile down the river bank, and that expedition under Major Martyr has, on the whole, been successful. The first object of it was to deal with the Dervishes, who were at a place on the right bank of the Nile a few miles south of Bor. When Major Martyr arrived at Bedden, which is the extreme point to which steamer navigation from Khartoum is practicable, he entered into communication with the Congolese Commandant at Kero, which is about half-way between that place and Bor. He proceeded in his steamboat to Kero, and after a friendly consultation with the Commandant, who expressed his readiness to co-operate with him, advanced to reconnoitre towards Bor, which he found abandoned, and learnt that the Dervishes, hearing that an English force was en route, had dispersed. The Sudd obstruction, which the Egyptian steamers had been unable to pentrate at the junction of the White Nile with the Bahr Ghazel, was reported to extend southward as far as Shambe, which is midway from that junction to Bedden, and about 200 miles from either point. This 200 miles of Sudd lies therefore at present as an insuperable obstruction to the navigation between Bedden and Khartoum. Perhaps, however, when the Nile is high again—it is now low—a navigable channel may be reopened by natural causes

The Prime Minister.

or by the efforts of steamers, as has happened in the past. Until, however, that takes place, I do not suppose Major Martyr is likely to proceed much further down the Nile, and, under these circumstances, I should imagine that after establishing a post at Bedden, which, as I have said, will be the eventual head of navigation, he would return to the Protectorate. But the noble Earl will bear in mind we have no direct means of communication. The telegraph only extends 300 miles from the coast, and there are 500 miles above that which can only be reached by runners. Our information, therefore, is very imperfect. We hope Col. Macdonald's Report will be soon in our hands, and, when we have the Papers, we shall have great pleasure in laying them upon the Table. If we have not given information up to the present, it is simply because up to now it has only reached us in a fragmentary form, and could hardly afford any information to the House.

THE EARL OF CAMPERDOWN: I am much obliged to the noble Marquess for the information he has given. I suppose we may assume that Colonel Macdonald's own command has now terminated.

*THE PRIME MINISTER: I think that is the case unless any other circumstances arise, but I must not be understood to be pledged on the subject.

POLICE IN CEYLON.

The following Notice stood on the Paper in the name of Lord Stanley of Alderley—

" To call the attention of the House to the inefficient action of the magistrates and police in Ceylon in the cases of the deaths of Mr. Tewson and Mr. Talwattee; to the oppression and extortion taking place there under the Waste Lands Ordinance; and to the persecution of Mr. Le Mesurier; and to move for papers."

*LORD STANLEY OF ALDERLEY: My Lords, I regret to say that I heard to-day from Lord Stanmore, who wrote to me yesterday, and has telegraphed again to-day, stating that he is confined to his bed through a bad cold or influenza. He has, therefore, requested me to postpone my Notice until Friday.

Motion, by leave, postponed.

PARTRIDGE SHOOTING (IRELAND) BILL.

Motion made—

"That this Bill be read a third time."— *(The Earl of Camperdown.)*

Question put.

Motion agreed to.

Motion made—

"That this Bill do pass."

Question put.

Motion agreed to.

EASTER RECESS.

The Earl of KIMBERLEY: Before the House adjourns, I would ask the noble Marquess if he can tell us at what period he intends to move the adjournment of the House for the Easter holidays, and for how long?

The PRIME MINISTER: I believe the House must sit till Monday for the purpose of receiving money Bills, to which the Royal Assent will be necessary. From Monday, three weeks, I believe, is the usual time, according to precedent.

SUPREME COURT (APPEALS) BILL [H.L.]

To be read second time To-morrow.

Lea Bridge District Gas Bill [H.L.]
Queen's Ferry Bridge Bill [H.L.]
Nene Valley Water Bill [H.L.]
St. Neot's Water Bill [H.L.]

Report from the Committee of Selection, That the Earl of Camperdown be proposed to the House as a member of the Select Committee in the place of the Earl of Derby; and that the Earl of Camperdown be Chairman of the said Committee; read, and agreed to.

House adjourned at fifty-five minutes after Four of the clock.

HOUSE OF COMMONS.

Monday, 20th March 1890.

Mr. SPEAKER took the Chair at Three of the clock.

PRIVATE BILL BUSINESS.

LONDON WATER (WELSH RESERVOIRS AND WORKS) BILL.

To be read a second time To-morrow.

SOUTH EASTERN AND LONDON, CHATHAM, AND DOVER RAILWAY COMPANIES BILL.

Mr. Banbury, Mr. Griffith-Boscawen, Mr. Channing, Lord E. Fitzmaurice, and Lord Stanley nominated members of the Select Committee, with Four to be added by the Committee of Selection.— *(Sir William Walrond.)*

PRIVATE BILLS (GROUP A).

Mr. Baldwin reported from the Committee on Group A of Private Bills, That the parties promoting the Horsforth Water Bill had stated that the evidence of John Wood, of Horsforth, near Leeds, was essential to their case; and it having been proved that his attendance could not be procured without the intervention of the House, he had been instructed to move that the said John Wood do attend the said Committee To-morrow, at Twelve of the Clock, and during such time as the said Bill shall be under the consideration of the said Committee.

Ordered, That John Wood do attend the said Committee To-Morrow, at Twelve of the clock, and during such time as the Horsforth Water Bill shall be under the consideration of the Committee.

LEICESTER, GROBY, AND BRADGATE PARK RAILWAY BILL.

Reported [Preamble not proved]; Report to lie upon the Table, and to be printed.

MESSAGE FROM THE LORDS.

That they have passed a Bill, intituled, "An Act to confer further powers upon the Aberdeen Harbour Commissioners." [Aberdeen Harbour Bill [Lords].

And also a Bill entituled, "An Act to amend the provisions of the Metropolis Management Acts with respect to By-laws." [Metropolis Management Acts Amendment (By-laws) Bill [Lords]

ABERDEEN HARBOUR BILL (LORDS).

Read the first time; and referred to the Examiners of Petitions for Private Bills.

—

NEW WRIT.

For the County of Middlesex (Harrow Division), in the room of William Ambrose, esquire, Q.C., Master in Lunacy.—*(Sir William Walrond.)*

—

PETITIONS.

—

LIQUOR TRAFFIC LOCAL VETO (SCOTLAND) BILL.

Petition from Stair, in favour; to lie upon the Table.

LOCAL AUTHORITIES SERVANTS' SUPERANNUATION BILL.

Petitions in favour;—From Southwark; — Buckhurst Hill; — and, St. Saviour's; to lie upon the Table.

METROPOLIS WATER BILL.

Petition from Wandsworth, in favour; to lie upon the Table.

METROPOLITAN WATER COMPANIES BILL.

Petition from Wandsworth, in favour; to lie upon the Table.

PARLIAMENTARY FRANCHISE.

Petitions for extension to women;—From Norwood; — Fletching Common; —Ashurst Wood; — and, Horsted Keynes; to lie upon the Table.

PRIVATE LEGISLATION PROCEDURE (SCOTLAND) BILL.

Petitions in favour;—From Forfar; —Linlithgow; — Perth;—and, Forres; to lie upon the Table.

PUBLIC HEALTH ACTS AMENDMENT BILL.

Petitions in favour;—From West Bromwich;—Middlesbrough;—Exeter; —and, Eccles; to lie upon the Table.

SALE OF INTOXICATING LIQUORS ON SUNDAY BILL.

Petitions in favour;—From Liskard; —Fordham; — West Kent; — Middlesbrough; — Forest Gate;—Castle Cary; —and, Cricklewood; to lie upon the Table.

SALE OF INTOXICATING LIQUORS TO CHILDREN.

Petition from Samford, for alteration of Law; to lie upon the Table.

STREET NOISES BILL.

Petition from Wandsworth, in favour; to lie upon the Table.

SUPERANNUATION (METROPOLIS) BILL.

Petition from St. Saviour's, in favour; to lie upon the Table.

WORKMEN'S COMPENSATION ACT (1897) AMENDMENT BILL.

Petition from Linlithgow, in favour; to lie upon the Table.

RETURNS, REPORTS, ETC.

LONDON LOCAL GOVERNMENT (RATES)

Return presented,—relative thereto [ordered 2nd March; *Mr. Bartley*]; to lie upon the Table, and to be printed. (No. 117.)

SOUTH AFRICA.

Copy presented,—of Further Correspondence relative to the Affairs of Swaziland (by Command); to lie upon the Table.

RAILWAYS (CERTIFICATES) (EALING AND SOUTH HARROW RAILWAY COMPANY).

Copy presented,—of Draft Certificate of the Board of Trade authorising the Ealing and South Harrow Railway Company to raise additional capital (by Act); to lie upon the Table..

TECHNICAL EDUCATION (SCOTLAND).

Return presented,—relative thereto [ordered 24th June 1898; *The Lord Advocate*]; to lie upon the Table, and to be printed. (No. 118.)

TRADE REPORTS (ANNUAL SERIES).

Copy presented,—of Diplomatic and Consular Reports, Annual Series, No. 2211 (by Command); to lie upon the Table.

TRADE REPORTS (MISCELLANEOUS SERIES).

Copy presented,—of Diplomatic and Consular Reports, Miscellaneous Series, No. 500 (by Command); to lie upon the Table.

PERTH BRANCH MINT.

Copy presented,—of Treasury Minute, dated 11th March 1899, relative to the Audit of the Accounts of Perth Branch Mint (by Act); to lie upon the Table.

RAILWAY BILLS (GROUP 5).

Mr. Jeffreys reported from the Committee on Group 5 of Railway Bills; That, for the convenience of parties, the Committee had adjourned till Wednesday next, at Twelve of the clock.

Report to lie on the Table.

SHOPS BILL.

Adjourned Debate on Second Reading [21st February] further adjourned from To-morrow till Tuesday 11th April.

NEW MEMBER SWORN.

Sir William Brampton Gurdon, K.C.M.G., C.B., for the County of Norfolk (Northern Division).

QUESTIONS.

RECOVERY OF STOLEN PROPERTY IN LONDON.

COLONEL SIR HOWARD VINCENT (Sheffield Central): I beg to ask the Secretary of State for the Home Department if he can state the amount of property reported as stolen and the amount recovered in the Metropolitan and City Police districts between 1st January 1888 and 31st December 1897, and if he is in a position to give this information as to the year 1898?

THE UNDER SECRETARY OF STATE FOR THE HOME DEPARTMENT (Mr. JESSE COLLINGS, Birmingham, Bordesley): As regards the Metropolitan Police, the figures for 1898 cannot be given at present, but figures for the previous 20 years are given on page 49 of the Commissioner's last Annual Report. As regards the City of London, the amount of property reported as stolen in the City Police district between 1st January 1888, and 3rd December, 1897, was valued at £186,270 12s. 10d., of which amount £33,155 6s. 3d. was recovered; the similar figures for 1898 are, respectively, £15,020 5s. 0d. and £2,259 15s. 9d.

COLONEL SIR HOWARD VINCENT: I beg to give notice that at the earliest opportunity I shall call attention to the small proportion property recovered bears to that stolen.

DISCHARGES FROM THE ROYAL GUN FACTORY.

MR. BURNS (Battersea): I beg to ask the Financial Secretary t' the War Office why discharges are taking place in the Royal Gun Factory whilst men of the same trade in the Royal Carriage Department are working from 6 a.m. to 9 p.m. Monday to Friday, 6 a.m. to 6 p.m. Saturday; and if it would be possible for men to be transferred from the Royal Gun Factory to the Royal Carriage Department, and so avoid discharges?

THE FINANCIAL SECRETARY TO THE WAR OFFICE (Mr. J. POWELL WILLIAMS, Birmingham, S.): Before men are finally discharged on reduction, the authorities at the Arsenal are instructed to ascertain whether men of the same trade are likely to be required within a reasonable time in other departments. Some of the men who were not required in the Gun Factory have been given employment elsewhere. The employment of such men on work in another department is not at all times possible. The space and machines in the workshops can only accommodate a certain number of men.

MR. BURNS: May I ask whether, in the event of any men being discharged, the discharges will be carried out with the minimum sacrifice of bonus and sick pay in case the men are taken on again?

MR. POWELL WILLIAMS: The discharge of men, whether temporary or permanent, always takes place in order of seniority.

REFRESHMENT BARS AT THE ROYAL COURTS OF JUSTICE.

MR. MALCOLM (Suffolk, Stowmarket): On behalf of the honourable Member for Dublin University, I beg to ask the Secretary of State for the Home Department by what authority and under what licence intoxicating liquors are sold at bars erected in the corridors of the Royal Courts of Justice, and almost immediately in view of the entrances to the various courts; and whether he will consider the advisability of having the sale of such liquors restricted to the refreshment rooms downstairs?

MR. COLLINGS: The licence under which intoxicating liquors are sold at bars in the Royal Courts of Justice is an ordinary six day early closing publican's licence gran'ed by the magistrates of the three divisions on which the buildings stand, namely, the City of London, St. Clement's Danes, and the Liberty of the Rolls, in the Holborn Division. The second part of the Question does not fall within the Secretary of State's jurisdiction.

MR. MALCOLM: Can the honourable Gentleman say within whose jurisdiction it falls?

MR. COLLINGS: I believe it is under the Lord Chancellor.

CAUM KILLINARDRISH POSTAL DELIVERIES.

MR DONAL SULLIVAN (Westmeath, S.): On behalf of the honourable Member for Cork (Mr. Maurice Healy), I beg to ask the Secretary to the Treasury, as representing the Postmaster-General, whether complaints have been made as to the non-delivery of letters at the house of Mr. Edward M'Cullagh, of Caum Killinardrish, county Cork; whether, notwithstanding that a postman passes within a few hundred yards of his house, Mr. M'Cullagh is obliged to send to the post office over a mile off for his letters; and whether, in view of the promise of a house to house delivery of letters, arrangements will be made to deliver his letters at Mr. Cullagh's house.

THE FINANCIAL SECRETARY TO THE TREASURY (Mr. R. W. HANBURY, Preston): A surveying officer shall be sent to visit the locality very shortly. The extension of the free delivery in the rural districts of Ireland is being carried out as rapidly as possible.

CORK AND BLARNEY MAIL CAR.

MR. DONAL SULLIVAN: On behalf of the honourable Member for Cork (Mr. Maurice Healy), I beg to ask the Secretary to the Treasury, as representing the Postmaster-General, whether he is aware that a mail car leaves Cork for Blarney at 3.30 p.m., and could he explain why there is no parcels delivery by that car?

MR. HANBURY: No mail car now runs from Cork to Blarney at 3.30 p.m. The afternoon mail from Cork to Blarney at that hour is sent by train, which does not stop at Blarney, but drops a bag containing letters only.

WARRANT OFFICERS' GRIEVANCES.

MR. JEFFREYS (Hants, Basingstoke): I beg to ask the Under Secretary of State for War whether he can now state the result of the inquiry of the Committee appointed last year by the Secretary of State for War to inquire into certain alleged grievances of warrant officers?

MR. POWELL WILLIAMS: The Report of the Committee is still under the consideration of the authorities.

COUNTY COURT FEES.

SIR C. DILKE (Gloucester, Forest of Dean): I beg to ask the Secretary to the Treasury whether, having regard to his offer to state the view of the Government on the possible reduction of fees in county courts, on the Vote on Account, and to the fact that the subject may probably not be reached, he will undertake to at once consider the fees in county courts together with the legal authorities, with a view to reduction; and whether it is the case that county court fees in many cases are higher than would be in the same cases the fees in the superior courts?

MR. HANBURY: This subject is already being considered by the Treasury in order to see whether such a reduction of fees can properly be effected. It is no doubt true that in many cases the fees are higher than in the Superior Courts. These are, however, not as a rule the fees levied in actions for small amounts; and in almost all cases the fees charged in the county courts include payment for work which in the superior courts would be done by solicitors at the cost of the litigant.

PRISON TREATMENT OF ANTI-VACCINATIONISTS.

MR. McKENNA (Monmouth, N.): On behalf of the honourable Member for East Northamptonshire, I beg to ask the Under Secretary of State for the Home Department whether his attention has been called to the fact that at Oundle Police Court, on Tuesday 14th instant, a defendant named Wolfe was fined 10s. for an offence under the Vaccination Acts, and in default of payment sent to prison for seven days with hard labour; and whether he will forthwith direct that this prisoner be treated as a first-class misdemeanant as provided in the Vaccination Act, 1898?

MR. COLLINGS: The honourable Member for East Northamptonshire wrote me a letter, and as he is laid up with illness I was going to reply to him by letter. Instructions have been given that such offenders shall in future be treated as first-class misdemeanants. In this case the governor of the prison was telegraphically communicated with on the subject.

DUBLIN CAVALRY BARRACKS.

GENERAL RUSSELL (Cheltenham): I beg to ask the Financial Secretary to the War Office whether it is the intention of the War Office to build another cavalry barracks in Dublin; and, if so, whether the site has yet been selected, and when it is proposed to commence building?

Mr. POWELL WILLIAMS: There is no intention of building another cavalry barracks in Dublin.

BRITISH LOSSES IN THE CONSTANTI-NOPLE RIOTS OF 1896.

Mr. MONK (Gloucester): I beg to ask the Under Secretary of State for Foreign Affairs whether any portion of the claims of British subjects at Constantinople for losses sustained by them during the massacres of August 1896, has been paid by the Turkish Government; if not, whether the Porte still denies its liability to pay those claims; and whether Her Majesty's Government are prepared to take steps to obtain a settlement of them?

THE UNDER SECRETARY OF STATE FOR WAR (Mr. ST. JOHN BRODRICK, Surrey, Guildford): The Turkish Government have not as yet paid any portion of the British claims, and have continued to deny their liability to pay them. As regards the second paragraph of the Question, I can add nothing to the answer given by me on the 17th instant to a similar Question.

ITALY AND CHEKEANG.

Mr. YERBURGH (Chester): I beg to ask the Under Secretary of State for Foreign Affairs whether he can state what the exact nature and extent of the Italian demands are with regard to the province of Chekeang; and whether, seeing that the islands of Chusan are part of the province of Chekeang, they are included in such demands?

Mr. BRODRICK: We have not had the text of the Italian demands, but we understand they do not include the Islands of Chusan, which are the subject of Treaty engagements between England and China, and are limited to the Eastern slope of the province towards the sea, which in no way comes within the Yangtze Basin.

COUNTY ANTRIM POLICE.

Mr. DILLON (Mayo, E.): On behalf of the honourable Member for East Cavan I beg to ask the Chief Secretary to the Lord Lieutenant of Ireland whether he will state the number of sergeants and acting sergeants of the Roman Catholic religion stationed in county Antrim in April 1894, when County Inspector Lennon took charge of the county; the number of Roman Catholic sergeants who retired in the county from then until the death of County Inspector Lennon in 1897; the number of Roman Catholic constables promoted from the seniority list during the same period; the number of Protestants promoted from the same list during the same period; and the number of Roman Catholic constables; will he explain why, since County Inspector Scott took charge of Antrim there have been promoted from the seniority list four Protestants and only one Roman Catholic, and also why members of the Constabulary force in the same county and in the same list, who happen to be Roman Catholics, have been overlooked; and whether similar treatment has been given to Roman Catholics in the county Down branch of the force?

THE CHIEF SECRETARY TO THE LORD LIEUTENANT OF IRELAND (Mr. GERALD W. BALFOUR, Leeds,Central): The number of Roman Catholic sergeants and acting sergeants in the county Antrim in April 1894, was 31. The number of Protestant sergeants and acting sergeants was also 31. The number of Roman Catholic sergeants who retired from April 1894, to January 1897, was 9. The number of Roman Catholic and Protestant constables promoted from the seniority list during the same period was three and six respectively. The number of Roman Catholic constables at present in Antrim is 104. As regards the second paragraph, one Roman Catholic and three Protestant constables have been promoted from the seniority list since Mr. Scott took charge of the county. Promotions are not made with reference to religious considerations, and the claims of all deserving constables for advancement are considered quite irrespective of their religious views. Nor can seniority be regarded as the only, or even the chief qualification for promotion. The general principles upon which promotion is regulated in Down are the same as those existing in other counties.

CAVALRY DRAFTS FOR INDIA.

Captain JESSEL (St. Pancras, S.): I beg to ask the Under Secretary of State for War if he could state how, in view of his recent promise to the effect that regiments of Cavalry on the higher establishment should not be called upon to furnish drafts for regiments serving abroad, drafts will be supplied during the coming year to Lancer regiments in India; and whether he is aware that both Lancer regiments at home are on the higher establishment?

Mr. POWELL WILLIAMS: Drafts for the two Lancer regiments in India will be furnished from the depôt at Canterbury, supplemented by a certain number of men from the 21st Lancers, should that regiment be brought back from Egypt next trooping season.

VOLUNTARY RETIREMENTS OF COMBATANT OFFICERS.

Captain JESSEL: I beg to ask the Under Secretary of State for War whether the instructions as to the voluntary retirement of combatant officers, laid down in Army Orders of February 1899, are retrospective in their application; and, if so, whether he can state to what extent?

Mr. POWELL WILLIAMS: The regulations contained in Army Order 27 of February 1899 have been in the main part in force since 1886. The modifications introduced by this Order are in the nature of a relaxation of the regulations, and came into effect from the 1st February 1899.

QUEEN'S BUCKHOUNDS.

Mr. CARVELL WILLIAMS (Notts, Mansfield): I beg to ask the Under Secretary of State for the Home Department whether he has seen a published statement by the Rev. J. Stratton to the effect that, during a recent hunt of the Queen's Buckhounds, the stag, after injuring itself by jumping into a pigstye, was, though wounded and bleeding, again hunted; and then, on taking refuge in a farmyard, was once more, and in an exhausted condition, hunted for 10 miles; and whether steps can be taken to prevent tame animals being subjected to such treatment?

Mr. COLLINGS: The Secretary of State has seen a newspaper paragraph containing statements made by the Rev. J. Stratton to the effect suggested. On inquiry into the matter it appears that there is no ground for the allegation that the stag was wounded as suggested; in fact, when it was finally taken, the stag was uninjured in any way.

VOLUNTEER ARTILLERY ARMAMENTS.

Mr. WANKLYN (Bradford, Central): I beg to ask the Under Secretary of State for War when it is proposed to issue lighter and more modern guns to the Volunteer Battalions of position now armed with 40-pound rifled breech-loading guns manufactured 35 years ago, and weighing with carriage and packed limber 4½ tons?

Mr. POWELL WILLIAMS: The Volunteer batteries are allocated to defensive positions, and it is not possible at present to make any change in the armament.

LOCAL GOVERNMENT OFFICES IN SCOTLAND.

Mr. KILBRIDE (Galway, N.): I beg to ask the Lord Advocate whether any statutory provision exists making the conjunction of the offices of inspector of the poor and county councillor illegal; and, if not, will the Local Government

Board, either by rule or legislation, make the tenure of these two offices by one gentleman illegal?

THE LORD ADVOCATE (Mr. A. GRAHAM MURRAY, Buteshire): There is no statutory provision making the conjunction of the offices of inspector of poor and county councillor illegal. The Local Government Board for Scotland have more than once expressed the opinion that such a conjunction of offices is inexpedient, and should occasion arise, they are prepared to consider whether a rule on the subject should be made.

BORACIC ACID IN IMPORTED BACON.

MR. KILBRIDE: I beg to ask the President of the Board of Agriculture whether he is aware that foreign bacon imported into this country has been found to contain 0.33 per cent. of boracic acid, and that the French authorities have refused to admit the importation of bacon thus preserved on the ground that it is injurious to health; whether he is aware that the law in Brazil prohibits the use of borax as a food preservative; and whether, in view of the action taken by other Governments, inquiry will be made into the use of borax in the interest of the public health?

THE PRESIDENT OF THE LOCAL GOVERNMENT BOARD (Mr. CHAPLIN, Lincolnshire, Sleaford): I was not aware of the facts alleged in the first two paragraphs of the Question. I have not yet ascertained how far they are accurate, for the Local Government Board have no direct information on the matter. But I am considering the question of such an inquiry as that suggested by the honourable Member, and, if it should appear to be necessary or desirable in the interests of the public health, it will be my duty to direct it to be made.

INLAND REVENUE PROSECUTIONS.

MR. W. REDMOND (Clare, S). I beg to ask the Chief Secretary to the Lord Lieutenant of Ireland whether he has any objection to grant the Return as to the prosecutions by the Inland Revenue Department, which stands on the Paper this day?

MR. GERALD BALFOUR: Yes, a Return will be given, subject to certain alterations.

DISEASE AMONG INDIAN TROOPS.

MAJOR RASCH (Essex, S.E.): I beg to ask the Secretary of State for India whether his attention has been called to the fact that the Returns for 1897 show an increase of secondary syphilis of 8.5 in admission rate per 1,000, of mortality of .17, of constantly sick of 1.18, as compared with previous year: and that the number invalided home was 662 in 1897 as against 479 in 1896, being an increase of 183, or 38 per cent., of venereal disease; whether the information in the hands of the War Office shows that this increased virulence is due to the fact that patients do not undergo early treatment, but are removed from cantonments to spread disease elsewhere; and, if it is the practice to treat men suffering from constitutional syphilis in barracks instead of in hospital, which causes an apparent reduction in the number of admissions and renders the statistics misleading?

THE SECRETARY OF STATE FOR INDIA (Lord GEORGE HAMILTON, Middlesex, Ealing): The figures relating to venereal disease are correctly given by my honourable and gallant Friend, but as regards admissions are applicable to troops in cantonments only. The information available does not admit of any definite conclusion being drawn as to the cause of the increased virulence of secondary syphilis in 1897 as compared with 1896. Treatment of soldiers in barracks, in certain stages of the disease, has doubtless caused some reduction in the admission rate, but as it has been practised for some years, it does not, I think, affect the comparison of one year with another.

TRAINED NURSES IN IRELAND.

MR. DILLON: On behalf of the honourable Member for East Cavan, I beg to ask the Chief Secretary to the Lord Lieutenant of Ireland whether his attention has been directed to a letter by

Edward Thompson, M.D., Omagh, on the question of trained nurses in relation to the late order of the Local Government Board; and whether, in view of the statements contained in that letter, the Local Government Board will reconsider its decision in regard to Miss Widdes, of Bailieboro', and other certified nurses similarly circumstanced?

MR. GERALD BALFOUR: My attention has been directed to the letter referred to. This letter contains several important mis-statements of facts, and inaccuracies. Dr. Thompson is surgeon to the Tyrone County Infirmary, which is believed to have a maximum of 62 beds, but no fever hospital attached. The Local Government Board do not consider it would be expedient to include small provincial hospitals in their list of recognised teaching institutions, and are not prepared to reconsider their decision in regard to Miss Widdes and other nurses similarly situated.

MR. TREW'S MEETINGS IN BELFAST.

MR. DILLON: On behalf of the honourable Member for East Cavan I beg to ask the Chief Secretary to the Lord Lieutenant of Ireland whether, considering the present disturbed state of public feeling, and the likelihood of serious riots in Belfast, he will proclaim Mr. Trew's meetings and gatherings of a like nature in the neighbourhood of 't. Clement's Church?

MR. GERALD BALFOUR: The police, as I have already stated, have full power to suppress meetings calculated to lead directly to a breach of the peace. No formal proclamation is necessary to this end, and no proclamation that might be issued would *per se* make an assemblage illegal if it would otherwise have been legal. The police at Belfast have been instructed to prevent disorder and obstruction of the thoroughfare, and this duty they will continue to discharge as well as to afford every necessary protection to person and property.

PEACE CONFERENCE AT THE HAGUE.

MR. STANHOPE (Burnley): I beg to ask the Under Secretary of State for Foreign Affairs whether he can make any announcement as to the names of the British representatives at the approaching Peace Conference at the Hague; and whether, having regard to the position already taken by this country for the promotion of arbitration, in the case of the Alabama, Behring Straits, and Venezuelan difficulties, and in the proposals made for the conclusion of an Anglo-American Treaty of Arbitration, Her Majesty's Government will take the initiative of laying before the Peace Conference a scheme for establishing a permanent system of international arbitration?

MR. BRODRICK: No announcement can be made as to the choice of the British Plenipotentiaries until the formal invitation to the Conference has been received and the date of the meeting fixed. It would not be convenient to give any undertaking as to proposals to be brought forward in the Conference. But Her Majesty's Government will be ready to use their best efforts to promote the principle of recourse to arbitration and mediation for the prevention of war.

MR. SIMPSON'S DEATH AT MANILA.

MR. STANHOPE: I beg to ask the Under Secretary of State for Foreign Affairs whether he has now received any report upon the recent lamentable occurrence at Manila, when a British subject, Mr. C. F. Simpson, was unfortunately killed; whether he is aware that Mr. Simpson's family was partially dependent upon him for support; and whether, under the circumstances, Her Majesty's Government will endeavour to obtain some pecuniary compensation for Mr. Simpson's family, by friendly representations to the Government of the United States?

MR. BRODRICK: There has not been time to receive a detailed report on the occurrence in question. It was reported by telegraph on 27th February, and the dispatches by mail cannot be expected before April. Without sufficient information it would be useless to make representations to the United States Government as regards compensation.

ITALY AND CHINA.

Mr. DILLON: I beg to ask the Under Secretary of State for Foreign Affairs whether, before making a demand for a coaling station and sphere of influence in China, the Italian Government consulted the British Government; and, if they did, what advice they received from the British Government?

Mr. BRODRICK: The Italian Government informed Her Majesty's Government of their desire to obtain a coaling station and sphere of influence in China previous to addressing their application to the Chinese Government. The advice tendered to Italy by Her Majesty's Government was that the matter should be treated diplomatically, and that there should be no employment of force.

RUSSIA AND THE DUM-DUM BULLET.

Mr. DILLON: I beg to ask the Under Secretary of State for Foreign Affairs whether he has any information as to the statement that Dum-dum bullets have been served out to Russian troops serving in the neighbourhood of the Indian frontier?

Mr. BRODRICK: We have no information with regard to the statement.

Mr. DILLON: Cannot the right honourable Gentleman make inquiry?

[No Reply.]

MR. TREW'S PROCEEDINGS AT BELFAST.

Mr. DILLON: I beg to ask the Chief Secretary to the Lord Lieutenant of Ireland whether he is aware that a man called Trew, with a number of his followers, on Monday, the 2nd of January, broke into a house in Skipton Street, Belfast, in which the Rev. William Peoples had been holding a service, threw the furniture out on the street and smashed it, and that Mr. Trew has openly boasted of this in a paper edited by him; and, if so, what action the Government intend to take in the matter?

Mr. GERALD BALFOUR: On the 11th January last the Rev. Mr. Peoples reported that between the 1st and 3rd of that month a house in Skipton Street, used by him as a mission hall, had been broken into and his property injured. A head constable of police was at once sent to make inquiry into the matter, and was informed by Mr. Peoples that a fanlight, two small oil lamps, and a small seat had been broken. Another house in the same street, and used for similar purposes by the Methodist body, was also damaged at the same time. No suggestion was made by Mr. Peoples that the damage was done by Mr. Trew or his followers, and the police, who have made careful inquiries, have been unable to obtain a clue to the guilty persons. The police have no reason to believe that Mr. Trew, or his party, participated in the occurrence; in their opinion the damage was done by boys. It is a fact that the publication, to which reference is made in the Question, contained an allusion to the destruction of the articles mentioned, but I am not aware that Mr. Trew has boasted that he was the author or instigator of the offence.

ST. CLEMENT'S CHURCH, BELFAST.

Mr. DILLON: I beg to ask the Chief Secretary to the Lord Lieutenant of Ireland whether the town inspector of Belfast called on the Protestant Bishop of Belfast, and advised him to remove the Reverend Mr. Peoples from St. Clement's Church?

Mr. GERALD BALFOUR: It is the fact that the Commissioner of Police recently had an audience with the Bishop of Down and Connor. The proceedings at the interview were of a confidential nature, and I am unable, therefore, to make any statement as to what transpired on the occasion.

Mr. DILLON: I must press the right honourable Gentleman for a definite answer, as this is a serious matter. Did the police official, representing the Government of Belfast, give this advice?

Mr. GERALD BALFOUR: The interview was of a confidential character.

Mr. DILLON: I shall endeavour to raise the question on the Vote on Account.

GREAT BRITAIN AND ITALY'S DEMANDS IN CHINA

Mr. DILLON: I beg to ask the Under Secretary of State for Foreign Affairs whether the British Minister at Pekin is pressing the claims of Italy on the Chinese Government?

Mr. BRODRICK: Her Majesty's Minister at Pekin was instructed on the 25th February to support diplomatically the Italian request for a coaling station off the coast of Chekiang, and for a sphere of influence over the eastern slope of the province towards the sea. The Italian Government have in the last few days withdrawn their representative and requested the British Minister to represent them temporarily. No action has since been taken.

DUM-DUM BULLETS AND THE SOUDAN CAMPAIGN.

Mr. DILLON: I beg to ask the Under Secretary of State for War whether dum-dum bullets were used in the Soudan Campaign?

Mr. POWELL WILLIAMS: No dum-dum bullets were used in the Soudan Campaign.

COMPULSORY PURCHASE OF PROPERTY FOR RAILWAYS.

Sir W. HART DYKE (Kent, Dartford): I beg to ask the President of the Local Government Board whether his attention has been called to the serious loss to ratepayers where property is taken under Parliamentary powers by railways or other companies, and a long interval occurs before the said property comes under rating, the liability for which falls upon the new purchasers; and, whether he can advise such an amendment of the Lands Clauses Consolidation Act, 1845, as shall entitle local authorities to be recouped not only the poor rate, but the whole of the local rates, until the new works come into rating?

VOL. LXVIII. [Fourth Series.]

The PRESIDENT of the LOCAL GOVERNMENT BOARD: I can only refer my right honourable Friend to the reply I gave to a similar Question last week. My right honourable Friend is no doubt aware that a Royal Commission has investigated the whole question.

Sir W. HART DYKE: I suppose the right honourable Gentleman does admit there is a certain amount of grievance when the sale is compulsory?

The PRESIDENT of the LOCAL GOVERNMENT BOARD: On the face of it, yes.

INDIAN CIVIL SERVICE.

Mr. BILL (Staffordshire, Leek): I beg to ask the Secretary of State for India whether, having regard to the importance of a knowledge of Russian in the Indian Civil Service, he will cause that language to be added to the list as an optional subject for candidates in the open annual Civil Service competition?

The SECRETARY of STATE for INDIA: The subjects in which the open competition for the Indian Civil Service is held are chosen with the view of testing the general ability of the candidates, and their proficiency in the studies which usually form part of the higher education of this country. The candidates thus selected have to pass a subsequent examination in languages and other subjects which are likely to be specially useful for work in India; and, if a knowledge of Russian were made an optional subject, it would have to be added at this stage, and an extra language so added would tend to oust some other language more generally useful. The honourable Member is probably aware that the study of Russian among Indian civilians is encouraged by the grant of special facilities and privileges.

3 G

LASCARS ON P. AND O. BOATS.

MR. HAVELOCK WILSON (Middlesbrough): 1 beg to ask the President of the Board of Trade whether he can state the number of lascars employed respectively on board of the Peninsular and Oriental steamships "Himalaya," "Oriental," "Ceylon," and "Japan"; whether he will state how many of the lascars are employed upon the deck department of each ship, and how many in the engine-room and stokehold departments, and how many are employed in the cook and stewards' departments; whether he can state the number of forecastles or berths set apart for the use of the lascars on each vessel; whether he can state how many cubic feet and how many superficial feet is provided in each of such forecastles or berths for each lascar, and the number of lascars located in such forecastles or berths; and whether the crew spaces are kept entirely free as required by Section 210 of the Merchant Shipping Act, 1894, sub-section (2) ?

THE PRESIDENT OF THE BOARD OF TRADE (Mr. C. T. RITCHIE, Croydon): The questions put by the honourable Member number over 40, and are of so complicated a nature and involve so many details, that I fear I cannot satisfactorily reply to them within the limits of an answer in the House, but I shall be happy to furnish the honourable Member with a Memorandum giving the particulars he desires, as far as it is possible to give them.

ELDER, DEMPSTER, AND CO.'S EMPLOYEES.

MR. HAVELOCK WILSON: I beg to ask the President of the Board of Trade whether he is aware that Messrs. Elder, Dempster, and Co., shipowners, of Liverpool, make it a condition of employment on all their ships for sailors and firemen whom they employ that they must insure with the Norwich Union Life Assurance Society, of which Messrs. Elder, Dempster, and Co. are agents; whether he is aware that this firm compelled two firemen named R. Unsworth and Robert Leitch, who served on board their steamship "Calabar," which was wrecked on the 25th of October last, to pay 13s. 4d.

each for insurance premium out of 17s. wages due to them at the time of the wreck, leaving these men only 3s. 8d. balance of their wages; and whether he is aware that in consequence of this these men were landed at Liverpool without clothes, and destitute ?

THE PRESIDENT OF THE BOARD OF TRADE: "I am informed by Messrs. Elder, Dempster, and Co. that for some years they have required their seamen and firemen to insure their lives. This they do in the interests of the men, and to encourage prudence on their part, having regard to the special risks of the African trade, and in many cases the practice has proved a great help to widows and children. The firm add that they do not insist upon insurance in the Norwich Union, many of their men insuring with other companies. As regards the specific cases mentioned in the Question, I am informed that, in Unsworth's case, his wages were £3 10s. per month, making £7 7s. for the voyage. His deductions were one month's advance (£3 10s.), life insurance 13s. 4d., and £3 paid his wife in cash, reducing his balance to 3s. 8d. In Leitch's case, I understand the wages were also £7 7s., being £3 10s. per month. The deductions were one month's advance (£3 10s.), postage 2d., and insurance 10s., leaving a balance of £3 6s. 10d.

MR. HAVELOCK WILSON: Arising out of that Question, I wish to ask whether the insurance policies do not bear the name of Elder, Dempster, and Co., as agents for this particular company ?

THE PRESIDENT OF THE BOARD OF TRADE: I know nothing of that. I am told that the firm did not insist on the insurances being effected with the Norwich Union Company.

CONDITIONS OF LASCAR EMPLOYMENT.

MR. HAVELOCK WILSON: I beg to ask the Secretary of State for India if he can state whether any communications passed between the Board of Trade and the India Office from the 9th of August 1898 up to and including the 9th of January 1899 with regard to the accommodation of lascar seamen on British registered vessels?

THE SECRETARY OF STATE FOR INDIA: No written communication has passed on this subject, but on behalf of the Board of Trade inquiry was made orally, and after reference to the Government of India, I informed the Board that the matter remains under the present law—that is, under the Indian Merchant Shipping Acts of 1857 and 1876.

SUGAR CANE INDUSTRY.

MR. WEIR (Ross and Cromarty): I beg to ask the Secretary of State for the Colonies if he will state under what circumstances the sum of £13,870 has been placed on this year's Estimates, Class 5, Vote 3, Sub-head D (Grants-in-aid of Local Revenues), to make provision, amongst other matters, for the purpose of assisting the Governments of Tobago, Grenada, St. Vincent, St. Lucia, Antigua, Granada, Nevis, Dominica, Barbados, and British Guiana, in the experimental cultivation of sugar cane?

THE SECRETARY OF STATE FOR THE COLONIES (Mr. J. CHAMBERLAIN, Birmingham, W.): This sum has been placed on the Estimates to give effect to the recommendations of the West Indian Royal Commission in connection with the establishment of an Agricultural Department in the West Indies for the purposes stated in the Estimate, which is only partially quoted by the honourable Member.

DINGWALL BARRACKS.

MR. WEIR: I beg to ask the Under Secretary of State for War, having regard to the fact that the War Office states that the character and sanitary surroundings of the buildings at Dingwall, in which a portion of the staff of the Ross-shire Militia are now quartered, are not such as to make it desirable to extend the accommodation, will he consider the expediency of erecting new buildings in or near the town such as will accommodate the whole of the staff?

MR. POWELL WILLIAMS: As detached Militia head-quarters are undesirable, and as there is accommodation at Fort George for recruits for the 3rd Battalion of the Seaforth Highlanders during their drill on enlistment, it would not be right to incur the heavy cost of building barracks at Dingwall.

THE FISHERY CRUISER "BRENDA."

MR. WEIR: I beg to ask the Lord Advocate if he will state under what circumstances the late commander of the Fishery Board cruiser "Brenda" was appointed; and was the appointment advertised as vacant, and was the commander selected from several candidates; if so, from how many, and by whom was the selection made?

MR. GRAHAM MURRAY: I am informed by the Fishery Board that all the vacancies referred to by the honourable Member were duly advertised in the newspapers. There were many applications, which were carefully considered by a Committee of the Board, and their recommendations were afterwards confirmed by the whole Board at their regular meeting.

DELAGOA BAY RAILWAY.

MR. WEIR: I beg to ask the Under Secretary of State for Foreign Affairs whether he is aware that about nine years ago the Portuguese Government took possession of the Delagoa Bay Railway; and that, by the consent of both parties, the matter was referred to certain Swiss arbiters in Berne who over two years ago ceased to take evidence, but have now determined to take evidence which they had previously decided not to take; and whether, in the interests of arbitration, he will communicate with the arbiters with the view of having the questions at issue settled without further delay?

MR. BRODRICK: Her Majesty's Government are aware that certain inquiries with regard to the value of land at Lorenço Marques are being made for the information of the arbiters. They cannot, however—as has already been stated in answers to previous Questions in the House on this subject—interfere in a matter which is under arbitration.

to review his judgment, even if I disagreed with it; and I have always, as he is aware, refused to give purely legal opinions in answer to Questions in this House. I am afraid I cannot depart from my usual practice.

CEYLON ORDINANCES.

MR. WEIR: I beg to ask the Secretary of State for the Colonies, in view of the conflict which has arisen between the Supreme Court of Ceylon and the Agents of the Governor in regard to the working of the Governor's Ordinance, No. 1, of 1897, will he, pending the consideration of the whole question by the Colonial Office, give instructions that the police forces of the Crown shall not be employed for the purpose of evicting people by force from lands to which they claim ownership?

THE SECRETARY OF STATE FOR THE COLONIES: There has been no conflict between the Supreme Court and the Government Agents in Ceylon. I am awaiting the receipt of a Report from the Governor, and pending its receipt I have not seen any reason to give special instructions in the matter.

WORKMEN'S COMPENSATION ACT.

SIR M. STEWART (Kirkcudbright): I beg to ask the Lord Advocate if his attention has been called to a case recently decided by Sheriff Fyfe at Lanark, and reported in the "Glasgow Herald" of 1st instant, as follows: A girl, the servant of an adjoining farmer, was sent by her employer gratuitously to assist his neighbour at a day's threshing by a portable steam mill. Contrary to orders, she moved from her place, was entangled in the machinery, and badly injured; and whether, seeing that Sheriff Fyfe held that a travelling threshing mill was a factory under the Workmen's Compensation Act, and gave damages and maintenance, the Government will be prepared to bring in a Bill to define a factory and a threshing mill?

MR. GRAHAM MURRAY: My honourable Friend invites me to criticise the decision of the Sheriff. I have no power

Mr. Graham Murray.

CHINA AND THE POWERS.

SIR E. ASHMEAD - BARTLETT (Sheffield, Ecclesall): I beg to ask the Under Secretary of State for Foreign Affairs whether he is now in a position to give the House information as to the agreement between the Powers regarding China?

MR. BRODRICK: No general agreement between the Powers interested in China is in contemplation. I am not at present in a position to make a statement.

NEW PUBLIC OFFICES.

MR. MALCOLM: I beg to ask the First Commissioner of Works whether he can now state when and where the plans of the new public offices will be exhibited for the inspection of Members; and whether the Government have given consideration to the suggestion which was urged upon them last year that the remainder of the Great George Street site should be acquired?

THE FIRST COMMISSIONER OF WORKS (Mr. AKERS DOUGLAS, Kent, St. Augustine's): The designs for the new public offices will be placed for the inspection of honourable Members in the Tea Room to-morrow. The plans as prepared for the new buildings on the Great George Street site show them extending back to the Park, and these plans will be laid in their entirety before the House, the portion which cannot at present be proceeded with being distinctly coloured. Having regard to the heavy extra outlay which the extension of the scheme would involve, the Government have not felt themselves to be in a position to apply for the additional funds, and they propose, therefore, to carry out only so much of the building as will cover the site now acquired.

COUNTY COURT JUDGE LEONARD.

Mr. PATRICK O'BRIEN (Kilkenny): I beg to ask Mr. Attorney-General whether Mr. P. M. Leonard, after being for 22 years county court judge of Circuit No. 51, and having attained the age of 75 years, was on the 12th March 1896 invited to tender his resignation, and was informed that in the event of its acceptance the question of pension would be considered by the Lord Chancellor; whether, in consequence of the aforesaid invitation, Mr. Leonard did resign on the 16th March 1896; whether the question of his pension has been so considered; and, has the same been granted; and, if not, on what grounds?

The ATTORNEY-GENERAL (Sir R. Webster, Isle of Wight): It is not possible within the limits of an answer to a Question to deal with the facts of this case. After full consideration, the Lord Chancellor came to the conclusion that it was not possible to recommend the grant of a pension to Mr. Leonard.

FEES TO SPECIAL JURIES.

Mr. LLOYD MORGAN (Carmarthen, W.): I beg to ask Mr. Attorney-General whether his attention has been called to the growing practice of special juries in cases which last over one day applying, with the consent of the presiding judge, to the parties to the action in course of trial before them for increased fees; and whether a common jury is entitled to make similar application for some remuneration for their services?

The ATTORNEY-GENERAL: I am not aware that the practice to which the honourable Member refers has increased, though I know that in long cases it has been customary for the parties to agree that an increased fee shall be allowed. This can only be done by the consent of both parties. There is no precedent for a similar allowance being made in a common jury case.

LASCAR SEAMEN.

Mr. HAVELOCK WILSON: I beg to ask Mr. Attorney-General whether any communications have passed between the Board of Trade and the Law Officers of the Crown from the 9th of August 1898 to the 9th January 1899, with regard to the state of the law as to the accommodation of lascar seamen on board British registered vessels?

Sir R. WEBSTER: The matter referred to in the honourable Member's Question has been submitted by the Board of Trade to the Law Officers of the Crown, and is now under their consideration.

Mr. HAVELOCK WILSON: That is not an answer to my Question. I wished to know if any correspondence had passed between the dates named.

Sir R. WEBSTER: No written communications have passed during the period in question, but certain oral communications took place. I am sorry I missed the point of the honourable Member's Question.

BLOCKING MOTIONS FOR ADJOURNMENT.

Mr. MACLEAN (Cardiff): I beg to ask the First Lord of the Treasury whether his attention has been drawn to the growing practice of blocking Motions for the Adjournment of the House to discuss definite matters of urgent public importance; and whether he will consider the expediency of leaving such Motions to the absolute discretion of the Speaker and the House, with only such limitations on their authority as are already imposed by the terms of Rule 17?

The FIRST LORD of the TREASURY (Mr. A. J. Balfour, Manchester, E.): In answer to my honourable Friend I have to say that no evidence has come before me that would induce me to believe that the practice of blocking Motions for Adjournment has increased.

Mr. J. LOWTHER (Kent, Thanet): May I ask whether my right honourable Friend remembers an episode when I put down a Motion of the character——

Mr. SPEAKER: Order, Order! I think the right honourable Gentleman should give notice of any specific Question of that kind.

Mr. J. LOWTHER: I was only asking my right honourable Friend whether he would refresh his memory.

The FIRST LORD of the TREASURY: It has escaped my memory at this moment, but I shall be glad to refresh it if my right honourable Friend desires.

CLOSURE IN COMMITTEE OF SUPPLY.

Mr. DUNCOMBE (Cumberland, Egremont): I beg to ask the First Lord of the Treasury whether his attention has been called to a Notice now on the Paper respecting the desirability of enabling Mr. Speaker, in the unavoidable absence through illness of the Chairman of Ways and Means, to appoint a temporary Chairman of Ways and Means, who shall for the time being only have the same duties and powers as the Chairman of Ways and Means; and whether, with a view to preventing great public inconvenience and loss of time in the unavoidable absence through illness at the same time of Mr. Speaker and the Chairman of Ways and Means, he is prepared at an early date to propose some Amendment to the Standing Orders on the lines indicated in the Notice in question?

The FIRST LORD of the TREASURY: Undoubtedly the present rules are of such a kind that difficulties may arise in connection with the matter alluded to by my honourable Friend. I think the subject is worthy of consideration, and that consideration the Government is prepared to give to it.

COUNTERVAILING DUTIES.

Mr. McKENNA: I beg to ask the First Lord of the Treasury whether he intends to introduce legislation for the purpose of imposing countervailing duties on bounty-fed sugar, in order to carry out the same policy in Great Britain and Ireland as has been declared to be that of the Government with regard to India, namely, to prevent a vast indigenous trade in Britain, based on enterprise and industry, from being undermined by the subsidised products of foreign countries?

The FIRST LORD of the TREASURY: Without discussing the question of countervailing duties in this country, I must point out to the honourable Gentleman that my noble Friend the Secretary of State for India in his answer referred to the fact that there was in India a great indigenous production of sugar, which under ordinary and natural conditions of trade might largely increase. As the honourable Gentleman knows, there is no indigenous production of sugar in this country.

Mr. O'KELLY (Roscommon, N.) was understood to ask if butter was not an indigenous product?

[No Reply.]

CAVALRY ENLISTMENTS.

Mr. ARNOLD-FORSTER (Belfast, W.): I beg to ask the Under Secretary of State for War if the Secretary of State will obtain the opinion of counsel as to whether the drafting of soldiers from one Cavalry regiment to another, without their consent, and in time of peace, be legal, or whether it be in contravention of the meaning and intention of section 83 of the Army Act of 1881; and whether, in view of the inability of the private soldier actually serving to enforce his rights against the War Office, the Secretary of State will receive a statement of the case of the soldier 'or submission to counsel before any final opinion be given. I beg also at the same time to ask the Under Secretary of State for War whether in the event of it being established that the drafting of Cavalry soldiers from one regiment to another in time of peace and against their will be legal, and that the statutory protection given by section 83 of the Army Act of 1881 can be legally taken away from 17,000 men serving in the Cavalry by means of a Royal Warrant, the War Office can in a similar manner declare the whole of the Infantry of the Line to be a corps within the meaning of the Act, and thereby deprive 136,973 men serving in the Infantry of the right conferred on them by Parliament; and if such a step can be lawfully taken in respect of the Cavalry and not in respect of the Infantry, what is the circumstance which differentiates the two cases?

Mr. POWELL WILLIAMS: The Secretary of State for War sees no occasion for taking counsel's opinion upon this point, as to which legal advice was taken in 1893. Under section 83 of the Army Act, it is laid down that—

"A soldier of the Regular Forces when once appointed to a corps shall serve in that corps for the period of his Army service."

But in section 190 (15) a corps is defined as being—

"Any such military body, whether known as a territorial regiment or by any other name, as may be from time to time declared by Royal Warrant to be a corps for the purpose of this Act."

The Household Cavalry, the Dragoons, the Lancers, and the Hussars were respectively declared to be such corps under the Royal Warrant of February 1893, and there is, therefore, no doubt as to the legality of transfers within those corps, nor do such transfers involve the removal of any statutory protection. In the attestation paper signed by every recruit who enters the Cavalry, it is distinctly stated that he is engaged for service with the corps of Dragoons, Lancers, or Hussars, as the case may be. Every recruit is, however, now permitted to select the regiment in which he wishes to serve, and if he is accepted for that regiment he will be allowed to remain with it unless urgent reasons require his transfer to another regiment. This, too, is set out in the attestation paper. There is, so far as I am aware, nothing in the Army Act to debar the Secretary of State from grouping into corps a larger number of battalions than constitute the present regiments of Infantry. But the fact that the Cavalry has been subdivided into four corps does not justify the inference that it would be a reasonable exercise of the powers conferred by the Act to declare the whole of the Infantry of the Line to be a corps.

Mr. ARNOLD-FORSTER: Was not the section of the Act of 1881 speci-

fically passed to secure linked battalions?

Mr. POWELL WILLIAMS: I believe the answer to that is in the negative, but it is a legal point on which I have no right to give an opinion. If the honourable Member wishes an answer perhaps he will put a Question down.

Mr. ARNOLD-FORSTER: The point cannot be tested by an action at law because soldiers are under the Mutiny Act; therefore a legal decision is necessary.

TELEPHONES.

Sir J. FERGUSSON (Manchester, N.E.): I beg to ask the First Lord of the Treasury whether it is the intention of the Government to take the Telegraphs (Telephonic Communication, etc.) Bill to-night?

The FIRST LORD of the TREASURY: No, we shall not take the Bill to-night.

Sir J. FERGUSSON: Is there any chance of the Bill being taken before Easter?

The FIRST LORD of the TREASURY: No; I think there is no chance of that Bill coming on before Easter.

RAILWAY COUPLINGS.

Mr. TENNANT (Berwickshire): May I ask the President of the Board of Trade if he intends to proceed with the Automatic Railway Couplings Bill, or if he proposes to appoint a Committee to investigate the matter?

The PRESIDENT of the BOARD of TRADE: I think it more convenient that I should say what I have to say on this subject when the Bill is reached without explaining matters now.

SUSPENSION OF TWELVE O'CLOCK RULE.

Motion made, and Question put—

"That the Business of Supply, if under discussion at Twelve o'clock this night, be not interrupted under Standing Order Sittings of the House."—*(First Lord of the Treasury.)*

The House divided:—Ayes 180; Noes 89.—(Division List No. 53.)

AYES

Allhusen,August. Henry Eden
Arnold, Alfred
Arnold-Forster, Hugh O.
Ashmead-Bartlett, Sir Ellis
Atkinson, Rt. Hn. John
Bagot,Capt.JoscelineFitzRoy
Bailey, James (Walworth)
Balcarres, Lord
Baldwin, Alfred
Balfour,Rt.Hn.A.J.(Manch'r)
Balfour,RtHnGeraldW(Leeds)
Banbury, Frederick George
Barry,Sir FrancisT.(Windsor)
Barton, Dunbar Plunket
Bathurst,Hn.Allen Benjamin
Beckett, Ernest William
Bentinck, Lord Henry C.
Bethell, Commander
Bill, Charles
Bonsor, Henry Cosmo Orme
Boulnois, Edmund
Bowles,Capt.H.F.(Middlesex)
Bowles,T.Gibson(King'sLynn)
Brodrick, Rt. Hn. St. John
Butcher, John George
Carlile, William Walter
Cavendish, R. F. (N. Lancs.)
Cavendish,V.C.W.(Derbysh.)
Cecil, Evelyn (Hertford, East)
Chaloner, Captain R. G. W.
Chamberlain,Rt.Hn.J.(Birm.)
Chamberlain,J.Austen(Worc'r)
Chaplin, Rt. Hon. Henry
Charrington, Spencer
Cochrane, Hn. Thos. H. A. E.
Coddington, Sir William
Coghill, Douglas Harry
Cohen, Benjamin Louis
Collings, Rt. Hon. Jesse
Colomb, Sir John Chas. Ready
Courtney, Rt. Hn. Leonard H.
Cripps, Charles Alfred
Cross, Herb.Shepherd(Bolton)
Cruddas, William Donaldson
Cubitt, Hon. Henry
Currie, Sir Donald
Curzon, Viscount
Dalbiac, Colonel Philip Hugh
Dalkeith, Earl of
Davenport, W. Bromley-
Dixon-Hartland,SirFrd.Dixon
Doughty, George
Douglas, Rt. Hn. A. Akers-
Doxford, William Theodore
Drage, Geoffrey
Duncombe, Hn. Hubert V.
Dyke, Rt. Hn. Sir Wm. Hart
Elliot, Hon. A. Ralph Douglas
Fardell, Sir T. George
Fergusson,Rt.Hn.SirJ.(Manc'r
Fisher, William Hayes
Folkestone, Viscount

Forster, Henry William
Garfit, William
Gedge, Sydney
Gibbs,Hn.A.G.H.(C.ofLond.)
Giles, Charles Tyrrell
Goldsworthy, Major-General
Gordon, Hon. John Edward
Gorst, Rt. Hn.Sir John Eldon
Goschen, George J. (Sussex)
Green,WalfordD.(Wednesbury
Greville, Hon. Ronald
Gull, Sir Cameron
Gunter, Colonel
Halsey, Thomas Frederick
Hamilton, Rt. Hn.Lord George
Hanbury, Rt. Hn. Robt. Wm.
Hanson, Sir Reginald
Hare, Thomas Leigh
Helder, Augustus
Hill,Rt.Hn.A.Staveley(Staffs)
Hoare,Edw.Brodie(Hampstead
Hoare, Samuel (Norwich)
Hobhouse, Henry
Howard, Joseph
Hozier, Hn. Jas. Henry Cecil
Hutchinson,Capt.G.W.Grice-
Jebb, Richard Claverhouse
Jeffreys, Arthur Frederick
Jessel, Capt. Herbert Merton
Lafone, Alfred
Lawrence, Wm. F.(Liverpool)
Leigh-Bennett, Henry Currie
Leighton, Stanley
Llewellyn,Evan H.(Somerset)
Lockwood, Lt.-Col. A. R.
Long, Col. Chas.W.(Evesham)
Long,RtHnWalter(Liverpool)
Lerne, Marquess of
Lowe, Francis William
Lowles, John
Lucas-Shadwell, William .
Macartney, W. G. Ellison
Macdona, John Cumming
M'Calmont, H. L. B. (Cambs.)
M'Iver, Sir Lewis (Edin., W.)
Malcolm, Ian
Maple, Sir John Blundell
Mellor, Colonel (Lancashire)
Meysey-Thompson, Sir H. M.
Middlemore,JohnThrogmorton
Milbank,SirPowlettChas.John
Mildmay, Francis Bingham
Monckton, Edward Philip
Monk, Charles James
Morrell, George Herbert
Morton,Arthur H.A.(Deptford
Mount, William George
Murray,RtHnA.Graham(Bute)
Murray, Col.Wyndham(Bath)
Myers, William Henry
Nicol, Daniel Ninian
Northcote, Hn. Sir H. Stafford

Orr-Ewing, Charles Lindsay
Pease, Herb.Pike(Darlington)
Penn, John
Pilkington, Richard
Platt-Higgins, Frederick
Powell, Sir Francis Sharp
Priestley,SirWOverend(Edin.)
Pryce-Jones, Lt.-Col. Edward
Purvis, Robert
Rasch, Major Frederic Carne
Rentoul, James Alexander
Ritchie,Rt.Hn.Chas.Thomson
Rothschild, Hn. Lionel Walter
Royds, Clement Molyneux
Russell, Gen. F.S.(Cheltenham
Russell, T. W. (Tyrone
Rutherford, John
Samuel, Harry S. (Limehouse)
Scoble, Sir Andrew
Scott, Sir S. (Marylebone, W.)
Seton-Karr, Henry
Sharpe, William Edward T.
Sidebottom,William (Derbysh.
Sinclair, Louis (Romford)
Skewes-Cox, Thomas
Smith, Abel H. (Christchurch)
Smith, Hon. W. F. D. (Strand)
Spencer, Ernest
Stanley, Henry M. (Lambeth)
Stanley, Lord (Lancs.)
Stewart, Sir M. J. M'Taggart
Stock, Henry James
Talbot, Lord E. (Chichester)
Talbot,RtHnJ.G.(Oxf'd Univ.)
Thorburn, Walter
Thornton, Percy M.
Tollemache, Henry James
Tritton, Charles Ernest
Usborne, Thomas
Valentia, Viscount
Vincent, Col. Sir C. E. Howard
Wanklyn, James Leslie
Ward, Hon. Robert A. (Crewe)
Warr, Augustus Frederick
Webster, R. G. (St. Pancras)
Webster, Sir R. E. (I. of W.)
Welby, Lieut.-Col. A. C. E.
Wentworth, Bruce C. Vernon-
Wharton, Rt. Hon. John Lloyc
Whiteley, George (Stockport)
Williams, Jos Powell (Birm.)
Wodehouse, Rt.Hn.E.R.(Bath)
Wortley, Rt. Hn. C. B. Stuart-
Wyndham-Quin, Major W. H.
Wyvill, Marmaduke D'Arcy
Yerburgh, Robert Armstrong

TELLERS FOR THE AYES—
Sir William Walrond and
Mr. Anstruther.

NOES.

Abraham, Wm. (Cork, N.E.)
Allen, Wm. (Newc. under Lyme)
Allison, Robert Andrew
Ashton, Thomas Gair
Austin, Sir John (Yorkshire)
Austin, M. (Limerick, W.)
Bainbridge, Emerson
Baker, Sir John
Barlow, John Emmott
Blake, Edward
Bryce, Rt. Hon. James
Buchanan, Thomas Ryburn
Buxton, Sydney Charles
Caldwell, James
Cameron, Sir Charles (Glasgow
Campbell-Bannerman, Sir H.
Carew, James Laurence
Carmichael, Sir T. D. Gibson-
Causton, Richard Knight
Clark, Dr. G. B. (Caithness-sh.)
Clough, Walter Owen
Curran, Thomas (Sligo, S.)
Dilke, Rt. Hon. Sir Charles
Dillon, John
Douglas, Charles M. (Lanark)
Duckworth, James
Ellis, John Edward (Notts)
Farquharson, Dr. Robert
Fenwick, Charles
Ferguson, R. C. Munro (Leith)
Fitzmaurice, Lord Edmond

Gladstone, Rt. Hn. Herbert J.
Goddard, Daniel Ford
Grey, Sir Edward (Berwick)
Gurdon, Sir William Bramptor
Hayne, Rt. Hn. Chas. Seale-
Hedderwick, Thomas Chas. H.
Humphreys-Owen, Arthur C.
Hutton, Alfred E. (Morley)
Jones, William (Carnarvonsh.)
Kinloch, Sir John Geo. Smyth
Lambert, George
Leese, Sir Jos. F. (Accrington)
Lewis, John Herbert
Lloyd-George, David
Logan, John William
Lowther, Rt. Hon. Jas. (Kent)
Macaleese, Daniel
M'Dermott, Patrick
M'Kenna, Reginald
Maddison. Fred
Mappin, Sir Frederick Thorpe
Morgan, J. Lloyd (Carmarthen)
Moulton, John Fletcher
Norton, Capt. Cecil William
O'Brien, James F. X. (Cork)
O'Connor, Arthur (D onegal)
O'Kelly, James
Paulton, James Mellor
Pearson, Sir Weetman D.
Price, Robert John
Richardson, J. (Durham)

Roche, Hn. James (East Kerry)
Samuel, J. (Stockton-on-Tees)
Schwann, Charles E.
Shaw, Charles Edw. (Stafford)
Sinclair, Capt. J. (Forfarshire)
Soames, Arthur Wellesley
Souttar, Robinson
Spicer, Albert
Stanhope, Hon. Philip J.
Stevenson, Francis S.
Strachey, Edward
Sullivan, Donal (Westmeath)
Tanner, Charles Kearns
Tennant, Harold John
Thomas, Alfd. (Glamorgan, E.)
Trevelyan, Charles Philips
Ure, Alexander
Wallace, Robert (Edinburgh)
Wallace, Robert (Perth)
Walton, Joseph (Barnsley)
Wedderburn, Sir William
Weir, James Galloway
Williams, John Carvell (Notts)
Wills, Sir William Henry
Wilson, Frederick W. (Norfolk
Wilson, Jos. H. (Middlesbro')
Yoxall, James Henry

TELLERS FOR THE NOES—
Mr. Hazell and Mr. Lough.

Ordered, That the Business of Supply, if under discussion at Twelve o'clock this night, be not interrupted under Standing Order Sittings of the House.

BUSINESS OF THE HOUSE—(GOVERNMENT BUSINESS).

Motion made, and Question proposed—

"That Government Business have precedence to-morrow."—(*First Lord of the Treasury.*)

THE FIRST LORD OF THE TREASURY (Mr. A. J. BALFOUR, Manchester, E.): I explained to the House on a previous occasion how it was necessary, in order to meet the appeal that has been made to me that the Second Reading of the London Municipal Bill should not be thrust too near the Easter holidays, that we should begin the discussion to-morrow. I think the House acceded to that suggestion, and, therefore, without any further remark, I move the Motion that stands in my name.

MR. BUCHANAN (Aberdeenshire, E.): I think that the right honourable Gentleman has been very sparing in his arguments in support of his Resolution, and I think that the reason why he has been very sparing in his arguments is because there are very few arguments that can be adduced in support of it. Now, I am opposed to the method adopted by the right honourable Gentleman in continually making Motions of this sort for using private Members' time. I oppose it to-night, not only because I have a Motion upon the Paper, but upon other general grounds. With regard to my Motion ever having a fair chance of coming on, I knew perfectly well when I put it down upon the Paper a few weeks ago that its chance of life was somewhat precarious. I know that the right honourable Gentleman is one of the severest enemies of private Members' Motions, and of their being brought forward at all, but I will admit this, that he serves out equal measures to all Motions, whether important or unimportant, whether large or small, those coming from this side of the House and those coming from that—no matter from which side of the House they come. I strongly oppose the Motion of the right honourable Gentleman, not because of my own Motion, but upon general grounds. Now, what is the reason, and is there any reason, for this course being taken? Why should to-morrow be taken? Is there any possible reason, in the urgency of public business at the present moment, why to-morrow night should be taken away from the private Members? The right honourable Gentleman has not had the excuse this evening which he has had so often in the past—that the private Members have not availed themselves of the opportunities given to them. We have only had three nights for the purposes of our discussions, and the right honourable Gentleman cannot in any way deny that important Motions have been brought forward, from his own side of the House and from that of his opponents, and there has not been any time wasted, and there has been no count out. He cannot allege that there has been even the slightest waste of time on the part of the private Members. The only time that has been wasted was wasted last Friday week, not by the private Members, but by the right honourable Gentleman himself—his excuse being there was some mistake on the part of the printer!

THE FIRST LORD OF THE TREASURY: Does the honourable Member imply that I used the printer as a shield?

MR. BUCHANAN: I say that certainly the responsibility was on the right honourable Gentleman himself.

THE FIRST LORD OF THE TREASURY: It is nothing of the kind.

MR. BUCHANAN: The right honourable Gentleman is responsible for the business in this House, and if half a sitting is thrown away, it is the right honourable Gentleman himself who is responsible for it. I could never have imagined that he would endeavour to shirk the responsibility which must remain upon his shoulders. To-night he has no such question in his mind, and I wish to know what possible reason is there for urgency in

Mr. Buchanan.

this matter? If he put down his Motion for financial reasons and Supply I could have understood his doing so,. but he has not done that; he has put down the Motion in perfectly general terms, and has told us to-night that it. is in order to bring forward the London. Municipal Bill. Now, is there really any reason why this London Government. Bill should be taken to-morrow at the expense of the private Members' time? I say that no such reason can be given. We had it fixed, first of all, for next Monday, and then for next Thursday, and now it is fixed for Tuesday, and we are to have one or two days for it. Now, whatever time is necessary for this London Government Bill, I say that that time ought to be found out of Government time, and that the time of private Members ought not to be sacrificed at the hands and by the Motions. of the Government. The right honourable Gentleman has shown us that the only important business to be done in this House, in his idea, is the passing of Government Bills and Measures. That is a very limited view to take of the duties of this House and the Members, and our constituents who send us here send us with the idea that we shall, at. least, have some opportunity of bringing forward some discussions on very important matters in this House in which they and we take considerable interest. And because the right honourable Gentleman has, I consider, been acting improperly, and is ruthlessly trespassing on the rights of the private Members, I shall certainly give this Motion the greatest opposition in my power.

COLONEL SIR HOWARD VINCENT (Sheffield, Central): May I ask my right honourable Friend whether, if he takes to-morrow for Government business, he will, after Easter, give us some equivalent time? It seems rather hard upon us if he does not, as there are several interesting Motions put down upon the Paper for to-morrow for private Members.

MR. LOUGH (Islington, W.): I desire to support my honourable Friend who spoke in opposition to this Motion, and who took exception to it from the standpoint that the exigencies of Parliamentary business did not require it. As a London Member, I should like to take a different point. The only explanation that the right honourable Gentleman gives us is that to-morrow is a very desirable day to take this London Government Bill. I think it is a most undesirable day to take it. I think it is being hurried through with undue haste. Two or three weeks ago the right honourable Gentleman said that he was most anxious to hear the voice of London upon this matter; but he gives no time for the voice of London to be heard upon it—no time whatever. The Bill is of very far-reaching importance, affecting as it does 42 municipal bodies in the metropolis, and it is only right that some time should be given to those bodies to consider a Bill of this character, which affects their welfare so much. Already 17 of those bodies have protested against this Bill, and I have no doubt that it is because of the rapidity with which these protests are coming in that the right honourable Gentleman is pressing on the Bill in this manner. It is an extraordinary state of things; and the fact that 17 of these bodies have used these few days to protest against it shows that London ought to have some further time to consider the matter. The London County Council is considering this question, and as it only meets once a week it must take some time to do so. I doubt if it is not too late already. The right honourable Gentleman, I do think, might see his way to give us more time to consider the Bill; everybody would be glad of it, and if he cannot see his way to allowing us a little further time, I shall be obliged to oppose this Motion.

Question put—

"That Government Business have precedence to-morrow."—(*First Lord of the Treasury.*)

The House divided:—Ayes 196; Noes 96.—(Division List No. 54.)

AYES

Allhusen,August. Henry Eden
Arnold, Alfred
Arnold-Forster, Hugh O.
Ashmead-Bartlett, Sir Ellis
Atkinson, Rt. Hn. John
Bagot,Capt. JoscelineFitzRoy
Bailey, James (Walworth)
Balcarres, Lord
Baldwin, Alfred
Balfour,Rt.Hn.A.J.(Manch'r)
Balfour,RtHnGeraldW(Leeds)
Banbury, Frederick George
Barry,Sir FrancisT.(Windsor)
Barton, Dunbar Plunket
Bathurst,Hn.Allen Benjamin
Beckett, Ernest William
Bentinck, Lord Henry C.
Bill, Charles
Bonsor, Henry Cosmo Orme
Boulnois, Edmund
Bowles,Capt.H.F.(Middlesex)
Bowles,T.Gibson(King'sLynn)
Brodrick, Rt. Hn. St. John
Butcher, John George
Carlile, William Walter
Cavendish, R. F. (N. Lancs.)
Cavendish,V.C.W.(Derbysh.)
Cecil, Evelyn (Hertford, East)
Chaloner, Captain R. G. W.
Chamberlain,Rt.Hn.J.(Birm.)
Chamberlain,J.Austen(Worc'r)
Chaplin, Rt. Hon. Henry

Charrington, Spencer
Cochrane, Hn. Thos. H. A. E.
Coddington, Sir William
Coghill, Douglas Harry
Cohen, Benjamin Louis
Collings, Rt. Hon. Jesse
Colomb, Sir John Chas. Ready
Cook, Fred. Lucas (Lambeth)
Corbett, A. Cameron(Glasgow)
Cripps, Charles Alfred
Cross, Herb.Shepherd(Bolton)
Cruddas, William Donaldson
Cubitt, Hon. Henry
Currie, Sir Donald
Curzon, Viscount
Dalbiac, Colonel Philip Hugh
Dalkeith, Earl of
Dalrymple, Sir Charles
Davenport, W. Bromley-
Dickson-Poynder, Sir John P.
Dixon-Hartland,SirFrd.Dixon
Dorington, Sir John Edward
Doughty, George
Douglas, Rt. Hn. A. Akers-
Doxford, William Theodore
Drage, Geoffrey
Duncombe, Hn. Hubert V.
Dyke, Rt. Hn. Sir Wm. Hart
Elliot, Hon. A. Ralph Douglas
Fardell, Sir T. George
Ferguson,Rt.Hn.SirJ.(Manc'r
Finlay, Sir Robert Bannatyne

Fisher, William Hayes
Folkestone, Viscount
Forster, Henry William
Garfit, William
Gedge, Sydney
Gibbs,Hn.A.G.H.(C.ofLond.)
Giles, Charles Tyrrell
Goldsworthy, Major-General
Gordon, Hon. John Edward
Gorst, Rt. Hn.Sir John Eldon
Goschen, George J. (Sussex)
Gray, Ernest (West Ham)
Green,WalfordD.(Wednesbury
Greville, Hon. Ronald
Gull, Sir Cameron
Gunter, Colonel
Halsey, Thomas Frederick
Hamilton, Rt.Hn.Lord George
Hanbury, Rt. Hn. Robt. Wm.
Hanson, Sir Reginald
Hardy, Laurence
Hare, Thomas Leigh
Helder, Augustus
Hill,Rt.Hn.A.Staveley(Staffs)
Hoare,Edw.Brodie(Hampstead
Hoare, Samuel (Norwich)
Holland, Hon. Lionel R. (Bow)
Howard, Joseph
Hozier, Hn. Jas. Henry Cecil
Hudson, George Bickersteth
Hutchinson,Capt.G.W.Grice-
Jebb, Richard Claverhouse

Jeffreys, Arthur Frederick
Jessel, Capt. Herbert Merton
King, Sir Henry Seymour
Lafone, Alfred
Lawrence, Wm. F.(Liverpool)
Lecky, Rt. Hn. Wm. Edw. H.
Leigh-Bennett, Henry Currie
Leighton, Stanley
Llewellyn,Evan H.(Somerset)
Lockwood, Lt.-Col. A. R.
Long, Col. Chas.W.(Evesham)
Long,RtHnWalter(Liverpool)
Lorne, Marquess of
Lowe, Francis William
Lowles, John
Loyd, Archie Kirkman
Lucas-Shadwell, William
Macartney, W. G. Ellison
Macdona, John Cumming
M'Calmont, H. L. B. (Cambs.)
M'Iver, Sir Lewis (Edin., W.)
Malcolm, Ian
Maple, Sir John Blundell
Martin, Richard Biddulph
Mellor, Colonel (Lancashire)
Meysey-Thompson, Sir H. M.
Middlemore,JohnThrogmorton
Milbank,SirPowlettChas.John
Mildmay, Francis Bingham
Monckton, Edward Philip
Monk, Charles James
More,Robt.Jasper(Shropshire)
Morrell, George Herbert
Morton,Arthur H.A.(Deptford
Mount, William George

Murray,RtHnA.Graham(Bute)
Murray, Col. Wyndham(Bath)
Myers, William Henry
Nicol, Daniel Ninian
Northcote, Hn. Sir H. Stafford
Orr-Ewing, Charles Lindsay
Pease, Herb. Pike(Darlington)
Penn, John
Pilkington, Richard
Platt-Higgins, Frederick
Powell, Sir Francis Sharp
Priestley,SirWOverend(Edin.)
Pryce-Jones, Lt.-Col. Edward
Purvis, Robert
Pym, C. Guy
Rasch, Major Frederic Carne
Rentoul, James Alexander
Ritchie,Rt.Hn.Chas.Thomson
Rothschild, Hn. Lionel Walter
Round, James
Royds, Clement Molyneux
Russell, Gen. F.S.(Cheltenham)
Russell, T. W. (Tyrone
Rutherford, John
Samuel, Harry S. (Limehouse)
Savory, Sir Joseph
Sooble, Sir Andrew
Scott. Sir S. (Marylebone, W.)
Seton-Karr, Henry
Sharpe, William Edward T.
Sidebottom,William (Derbysh.)
Sinclair, Louis (Romford)
Skewes-Cox, Thomas
Smith, Abel H. (Christchurch)
Smith, Hon. W. F. D. (Strand)

Spencer, Ernest
Stanley, Henry M. (Lambeth)
Stanley, Lord (Lancs.)
Stewart. Sir M. J. M'Taggart
Stock, Henry James
Talbot, Lord E. (Chichester)
Talbot,RtHnJ.G.(Oxf'd Univ.)
Thorburn. Walter
Thornton, Percy M.
Tollemache, Henry James
Tomlinson, Wm. Edw. Murray
Tritton, Charles Ernest
Usborne, Thomas
Valentia, Viscount
Wanklyn, James Leslie
Ward, Hon. Robert A. (Crewe)
Warr, Augustus Frederick
Webster, R. G. (St. Pancras)
Webster, Sir R. E. (I. of W.)
Welby, Lieut.-Col. A. C. E.
Wentworth, Bruce C. Vernon-
Wharton, Rt. Hon. John Lloyd
Whiteley, George (Stockport)
Whitmore, Charles Algernon
Williams, Jos. Powell (Birm.)
Wodehouse, Rt.Hn.E.R.(Bath)
Wortley, Rt. Hn. C. B. Stuart-
Wyndham-Quin, Major W H
Wyvill, Marmaduke D'Arcy
Yerburgh, Robert Armstrong

TELLERS FOR THE AYES—
Sir William Walrond and
Mr. Anstruther.

NOES.

Abraham, Wm. (Cork, N.E.)
Allison, Robert Andrew
Ashton, Thomas Gair
Austin, Sir John (Yorkshire)
Austin, M. (Limerick, W.)
Bainbridge, Emerson
Baker, Sir John
Barlow, John Emmott
Blake, Edward
Bryce, Rt. Hon. James
Burt, Thomas
Buxton, Sydney Charles
Caldwell, James
Cameron, Sir Charles (Glasgow)
Campbell-Bannerman, Sir H.
Carmichael, Sir T. D. Gibson-
Causton, Richard Knight
Clark, Dr. G. B.(Caithness-sh.)
Clough, Walter Owen
Courtney, Rt. Hon. Leonard H.
Curran, Thomas (Sigo, S.)
Dilke, Rt. Hon. Sir Charles
Dillon, John
Douglas, Charles M. (Lanark)
Duckworth, James
Ellis, John Edward (Notts)
Farquharson, Dr. Robert
Fenwick, Charles
Ferguson, R. C. Munro (Leith)
Fitzmaurice, Lord Edmond
Gladstone, Rt. Hn. Herbert J.
Goddard, Daniel Ford
Gourley, Sir Edwd. Temperley

Grey, Sir Edward (Berwick)
Gurdon Sir William Brampton
Hayne, Rt. Hon. Charles Seale-
Hazell, Walter
Hedderwick, Thomas Chas. H.
Hobhouse, Henry
Humphreys-Owen, Arthur C.
Hutton, Alfred E. (Morley)
Jones, William (Carnarvonsh.)
Kay-Shuttleworth,RtHnSirU.
Kinloch, Sir John Geo. Smyth
Lambert, George
Leese, Sir Jos. F. (Accrington)
Leng, Sir John
Lewis, John Herbert
Lloyd-George, David
Logan, John William
Lowther, Rt. Hon. Jas. (Kent)
Macaleese, Daniel
M'Dermott, Patrick
M'Ewan, William
M'Kenna, Reginald
Maddison, Fred.
Mappin, Sir Frederick Thorpe
Montagu, Sir S. (Whitechapel)
Morgan,J.Lloyd (Carmarthen)
Moulton, John Fletcher
Norton, Capt. Cecil William
O'Brien, James F. X. (Cork)
O'Connor, Arthur (Donegal)
Paulton, James Mellor
Reid, Sir Robert Threshie

Richardson, J. (Durham)
Roche, Hn. James (East Kerry)
Samual, J. (Stockton-on-Tees)
Shaw, Charles Edw. (Stafford)
Sinclair, Capt. J. (Forfarshire)
Soames, Arthur Wellesley
Souttar, Robinson
Spicer, Albert
Stanhope, Hon. Philip J.
Stevenson, Francis S.
Strachey, Edward
Sullivan, Donal (Westmeath)
Tanner, Charles Kearns
Tennant, Harold John
Thomas, Alfd. (Glamorgan,E.)
Trevelyan, Charles Philips
Ure, Alexander
Vincent, Col. Sir C. E. Howard
Wallace, Robert (Edinburgh)
Wallace, Robert (Perth)
Walton, Joseph (Barnsley)
Wedderburn Sir William
Weir, James Galloway
Whittaker, Thomas Palmer
Williams, John Carvell (Notts)
Wills, Sir William Henry
Wilson, Frederick W. (Norfolk)
Wilson, Henry J. ,York, W.R.)
Wilson, Jos. H. (Middlesbro')
Woods, Samuel

TELLERS FOR THE NOES—
Mr. Buchanan and Mr.
Lough.

Ordered, That Government Business have precedence To-morrow.

ORDERS OF THE DAY.

SUPPLY [5TH ALLOTTED DAY].

Considered in Committee.

[Mr. J. W. LOWTHER (Cumberland, Penrith), CHAIRMAN OF WAYS AND MEANS, in the Chair.]

(In the. Committee.)

CIVIL SERVICES AND REVENUE DEPARTMENTS, 1899-1900 (VOTE ON ACCOUNT).

Motion made, and Question proposed—

"That a sum, not exceeding £14,781,000, be granted to Her Majesty, on account, for or towards defraying the Charges for the following Civil Services and Revenue Departments for the year ending on the 31st day of March 1900, viz. : —

CIVIL SERVICES.

CLASS II.

	£
Colonial Office	17,500

CLASS I.

	£
Royal Palaces and Marlborough House	16,000
Royal Parks and Pleasure Gardens	40,000
Houses of Parliament Buildings ...	12,000
Miscellaneous Legal Buildings, Great Britain	18,000
Art and Science Buildings, Great Britain	10,000
Diplomatic and Consular Buildings	9,000
Revenue Buildings	120,000
Public Buildings, Great Britain ...	100,000
Surveys of the United Kingdom...	80,000
Harbours under the Board of Trade	2,000
Peterhead Harbour...	6,000
Rates on Government Property ...	210,000
Public Works and Buildings, Ireland	70,000
Railways, Ireland	70,000

CLASS II.

United Kingdom and England : —

	£
House of Lords, Offices	4,000
House of Commons, Offices ...	13,000
Treasury and Subordinate Departments	30,000
Home Office	50,000
Foreign Office	25,000
Privy Council Office, etc.... ...	5,000
Board of Trade	60,000
Mercantile Marine Services ...	30,000
Bankruptcy Department of the Board of Trade	3
Board of Agriculture	75,000
Charity Commission	15,000
Civil Service Commission	15,000
Exchequer and Audit Department	22,000
Friendly Societies Registry ...	2,000
Local Government Board	66,000

	£
Lunacy Commission	5,000
Mint (including Coinage)	10
National Debt Office	5,000
Public Record Office	10,000
Public Works Loan Commission ...	10
Registrar General's Office	13,000
Stationery and Printing	250,000
Woods, Forests, etc., Office of ...	7,000
Works and Public Buildings, Office of	19,000
Secret Service	17,000

Scotland : —

	£
Secretary for Scotland	4,500
Fishery Board	8,000
Lunacy Commission	2,000
Registrar General's Office... ...	2,000
Local Government Board	4,000

Ireland : —

	£
Lord Lieutenant's Household ...	2,000
Chief Secretary and Subordinate Departments	15,000
Charitable Donations and Bequests Office	750
Local Government Board	15,000
Public Record Office	2,000
Public Works Office	12,500
Registrar General's Office	6,000
Valuation and Boundary Survey ...	6,000

CLASS III.

United Kingdom and England : —

	£
Law Charges	40,000
Miscellaneous Legal Expenses ...	26,000
Supreme Court of Judicature ...	120,000
Land Registry	7,000
County Courts	10,000
Police, England and Wales ...	14,000
Prisons, England and the Colonies.	200,000
Reformatory and Industrial Schools, Great Britain	140,000
Broadmoor Criminal Lunatic Asylum	10,000

Scotland : —

	£
Law Charges and Courts of Law...	30,000
Register House, Edinburgh ...	15,000
Crofters Commission	2,000
Prisons, Scotland	25,000

Ireland : —

	£
Law Charges and Criminal Prosecutions	30,000
Supreme Court of Judicature, and other Legal Departments ...	38,000
Land Commission	50,000
County Court Officers, etc. ...	36,000
Dublin Metropolitan Police ...	35,000
Constabulary	600,000
Prisons, Ireland	45,000
Reformatory and Industrial Schools	55,500
Dundrum Criminal Lunatic Asylum	2,500

CLASS IV.

United Kingdom and England :—

Public ' Education, England and Wales	3,600,000
Science and Art Department, United Kingdom	200,000
British Museum	64,000
National Gallery	5,000
National Portrait Gallery	2,500
Wallace Gallery	6,000
Scientific Investigation, etc., United Kingdom	15,000
Universities and Colleges, Great Britain, and Intermediate Education, Wales	38,000
London University	5

Scotland :—

Public Education	600,000
National Gallery	1,400

Ireland :—

Public Education	600,000
Endowed Schools Commissioners...	350
National Gallery	1,200
Queen's Colleges	2,500

CLASS V.

Diplomatic and Consular Services	220,000
Uganda, Central and East Africa Protectorates and Uganda Railway	250,000
Colonial Services	180,000
Cyprus, Grant in Aid	12,000
Subsidies to Telegraph Companies	35,000

CLASS VI.

Superannuation and Retired Allowances...	280,000
Merchant Seamen's Fund Pensions, etc.	3,000
Miscellaneous Charitable and other Allowances...	1,000
Hospitals and Charities, Ireland...	10,000

CLASS VII.

Temporary Commissions	8,000
Miscellaneous Expenses	6,572
Congested Districts Board, Scotland	— —

Total for Civil Services ... £9,271,000

REVENUE DEPARTMENTS.

Customs	350,000
Inland Revenue	650,000
Post Office	3,000,000
Post Office Packet Service	210,000
Post Office Telegraphs	1,300,000

Total for Revenue Departments £5,510,000

Grand Total ... £14,781,000

SIR E. ASHMEAD-BARTLETT (Sheffield, Ecclesall): The House is to be congratulated that the Colonial Vote has at last been put in the Paper. In South Africa, or rather in the Transvaal, during the past three' years, the opportunities for discussing South African matters have always been absorbed by the question of Rhodesia and the questions relating to that country. Now, I propose to bring before the House, and for which I ask the attention of the House, an entirely different matter. The non-Boer population of the Transvaal is generally known by the name Uitlanders. These Uitlanders, who comprise the great majority of the non-Boer population of the Transvaal, are something over three-fifths, and something under three-fourths, of the total white population. Of those three-fifths at least two-thirds, and probably three-fourths, consist of English or British subjects; so that it may be fairly said that more than one-half of the entire white population of the Transvaal consists of British subjects. Well, Sir, the right honourable Gentleman who now occupies the position of Colonial Secretary has been continually in office for quite three and one-half years, and it is over three years since that the events occurred which are generally known and referred to as the Jameson Raid. At that time the right honourable Gentleman the Colonial Secretary did declare himself very forcibly in favour of an amelioration, both politically and economically, of the condition of the non-Boer population in the Transvaal. He wrote some very strong dispatches on the subject; he made definite pledges to the Uitlanders—definite and distinct pledges, which I regret to say have not been carried out. Since that time the condition of the non-Boers in the Transvaal, so far from having been ameliorated, has been aggravated. It has been so bad during the last three years as to be absolutely intolerable at the present time. We used to say that under the late administration the Uitlanders were chastised with whips, but under the present administration we may fairly say that they have been scourged with scorpions. This year the government of the Transvaal has become more tyrannical and corrupt, and the condition of the non-Boer population has been injured and made worse.

We are now face to face with a spectacle of a great European population who pay five-sixths of the taxation of the Transvaal, who have, beyond doubt, made its prosperity, and who are deprived of all political rights and most civil rights, and whose privileges are being steadily diminished. What has become of the pledges made by President Kruger to the Uitlanders of Johannesburg? What has become of the pledges of this Government to those Uitlanders?—the pledges under which the Uitlanders were induced to disarm? There has not been one performed, and the result is that the position of the Uitlanders is made intolerable. There has been played in this House with regard to the Transvaal what I may describe as an amusing farce. Each time the Debate has been postponed to the last moment, and then the right honourable Gentleman has made a very clear and decisive speech, in the course of which he suggested certain schemes for the improvement in the condition of the Uitlanders, and then the House adjourned; and directly the House adjourns President Kruger and his myrmidons set to work there and then to flout you. The right honourable Gentleman has made some protests; and there have been some telegrams, mostly inspired by those who control the Press out there, and the net result has been that the position of the Uitlanders has been weakened and made worse. Let me give the right honourable Gentleman and the House two or three incidents of what has happened, in detail, towards worsening the condition of the non-Boer population. In 1896 the right honourable Gentleman made a speech, early in August, of the character of which I have described, a very optimistic speech on the affairs of the Transvaal; directly this House had adjourned, the Volksraad met and proceeded to pass three Bills most injurious to the happiness and the rights of the Uitlander population. They brought in what is known as the Alien Immigration Law, the Alien Exploration Law, and the Press Gag Law. It is quite true that the right honourable Gentleman protested against the Alien Immigration Law, which was the least important to the Uitlanders of the Transvaal; but the other two Acts still remain upon the Statute Book, and the Boer Executive, which consists of President Kruger and six others, have it in their own power to exclude by their own act any Uitlander at present in the Transvaal. Not only do they control the liberty of every Uitlander, but they hold this position as well, that the Press Gag Law is just in the same position, for every writer, editor, and proprietor of a newspaper is at the mercy of the Boer Executive. Again, in July, the right honourable Gentleman made an optimistic speech, and again there was no Debate upon the Transvaal. Directly this House rose, President Kruger formally repudiated the suzerainty of Her Majesty the Queen. The right honourable Gentleman protested against that, but President Kruger and the Volksraad have never withdrawn that repudiation. They refused to relieve the gold industries, and they practically carried out the invasion of Swaziland, and have destroyed the few rights which were retained for these unfortunate people by the Convention made by us in 1894. This is practically what has happened in the Transvaal during the last three years. Of course, there are many other facts which might be given to the House, but it is very well known that the condition of the Uitlander is becoming more and more intolerable; they are being subjected to many acts of tyranny and oppression and extortion, against which, in many cases, they dare not protest. The conduct of the Boer officials is exceedingly oppressive and corrupt, and to the medical and legal class of Uitlanders the oppression and corruption of the Boer Government is becoming intolerable. I am perfectly aware that these oppressions may not apply to the great kings of the gold and diamond industries who spend a great deal of their time in other countries, and who know how to secure for themselves personal immunity from these abuses. But I have always tried in this House to protect, not the great people of South Africa, but the vast majority of British subjects who live in the Boer country—the lawyers, barristers, doctors engineers, mechanics, etc., who have to earn their living there. Their position is unbearable, and it has not been redressed. It operates when the gold industry is flourishing, and they are getting large wages, which are all but taken out of their pockets, and the English and non-Boer population of the Transvaal find it exceedingly hard to get any justice at all under Boer law. A crisis arose in Johannesburg when an Englishman was shot by a Boer policeman in a dispute. I am not prepared to say it was an act of deliberate murder, but it was a very violent act. There may have been some provocation for it, but it is an act that would not be permitted in this country. But what I want to draw the attention of the Committee to is the fact that when this crisis occurred, and the Uitlanders of Johannesburg, especially the Englishmen, endeavoured to hold a meeting, they were threatened in many ways by the Boer police, and the Boer population, some of whom advised the entire destruction of Johannesburg, but at last the Boer Executive consented to allow the meeting to be held. Now, under the law passed in recent years, all rights of public meeting have been taken away from the Uitlanders. They are denied the right of political meetings and every other meeting, and every right can be refused by the Boer Oligarchy and the Boer Executive. Well, this meeting was at last consented to, but the meeting was invaded by a party of armed Boers, most of them engaged by the Boer Government; they behaved with exceeding violence, and broke up the furniture of the meeting, and but for the sound advice that was given to the Uitlanders, because the Chief of the Police was watching the scenes of confusion with gratification, there would have been a very serious riot. The Chief of Police had a large body of armed Boers at his command to bring down, and there is no doubt that this meeting was broken up by armed Boers, who were certainly encouraged by the Boer police. So the House will be able to judge the state of things there. I have details with which it is scarcely worth troubling the House. The policeman who shot this unfortunate man was liberated on bail, which was only one-fifth of the amount required in the case of the leaders of the Raid. The condition of the present taxation in the Transvaal is also worth considering in this House. During the last six or eight years, I am not quite sure whether it is six or eight years, the expenditure of the Transvaal has increased from under £1,000,000 to £4,500,000, and the greater part of that goes in corruption. The total white population of the Transvaal is 245,000, of which only

Sir E. Ashmead-Bartlett.

66,000 are Boers. The Boer population are only taxed to the extent of £6 18s. 6d. per head; the non-Boers have to pay £23 1s. 0d. per head. Out of the £4,589,000 which forms the total revenue of the Transvaal, £1,216,000, or 25 per cent. of the whole, is actually spent in the costs of administration. Of the remainder, £2,985,000 goes in the military service, which is directed against this country; a large portion goes for bribing the Press and general acts of corruption in South Africa, and Europe as well. It is well known what control the Boer Government keep over all communications. All telegrams sent are sent with extreme Boer bias, and they endeavour in every possible way to control the companies. Out of the total money made out of the goldfields 46 per cent. goes for working expenses, 23 per cent. goes to the Transvaal Government, and 31½ per cent. goes to the shareholders of the various companies. I see, by the paper to-day, that President Kruger is reported to have made a conciliatory speech promising certain reforms. It is possible that he was advised of the arrangement come to between Germany and this country, and of the visit of Mr. Rhodes, before he made that speech; but we have had many speeches of a similar kind from him during the last 15 years, and we have had many pledges from both President Kruger and the Boer Executive, in the shape of promises of reforms, but none of those promises have been kept, and I am suspicious of these interminable speeches, and of these verbal promises of President Kruger, unless they are backed up by very strong guarantees of Her Majesty's Government. I see that President Kruger has suggested the reduction of the period of residence qualifying for the franchise of the Uitlanders from 14 to nine years. Now, to get political rights, nine years is a very long time to wait for the franchise; but this reduction is of no value. No reduction would be of the slightest advantage to the Uitlanders unless at the same time two conditions which are attached to the franchise are removed. The first of these conditions is that every application for the franchise on the part of a non-Boer shall have the direct support of the Boer magistrate of the district in which the Uitlander resides; and the second, that it shall receive the consent of the Volksraad. So it is perfectly clear that unless these conditions are removed or modified it does not matter much to the Uitlander population whether the period of residence is reduced from 14 years to nine or five, because the Boer magistrate and the Volksraad will have the power to prevent the Uitlanders having the franchise at all, and they will take care to have it. Now, we have seen that something has been done in South Africa. During the last two years 3,000,000 square miles have been added to the British Empire; our territory has been extended 1,500 miles northward, and there is every reason to believe that it will be connected by telegraph and railroad. This is due to a single man. These great achievements are due to the enterprise of Mr. Rhodes, and I am very much afraid that if the future of this country in the way of administration had been left to the British Government we should have been in a very different position to-day. What the Government has to do is to look after the interests of the British residents in the Transvaal, and in that they have failed. It may be that there have been, and I will not contend for a moment there have not, great difficulties in the way of the right honourable Gentleman. There have been difficulties in South Africa and elsewhere which would be to a certain extent an excuse for the delay that has taken place. I cannot admit that it is so entirely, as I believe that those difficulties have been sometimes due to the action of Her Majesty's Government and the right honourable Gentleman. I am very glad that those difficulties have been removed, and that the interests of this country are established, and that our position is infinitely greater in repute than it was six months ago. But I think if the right honourable Gentleman who is now one of the most devoted supporters of the German alliance had been converted three years ago our business in South Africa would have gone up by leaps and bounds. In a dispatch to Sir Hercules Robinson on the 13th of January 1896 the right honourable Gentleman gave perhaps the most distinct pledge that could be given to the British Uitlanders. He said in that dispatch that there could be no settlement until the questions raised by the Uitlanders were disposed of, and the people of Johannesburg laid down their arms;

and until the reforms were granted or definitely promised by the President the real cause of the trouble would remain, and it was the duty of Sir Hercules Robinson to use firm language. The dispatch constitutes a most definite statement, and the people of Johannesburg laid down their arms at the voice of the High Commissioner, who was acting under the orders of the right honourable Gentleman. They laid down their arms, not only upon the pledges made to them by President Kruger, but that the Government would see that their undoubted grievances would be redressed. In conclusion, I say that none of those grievances have been redressed; for five years this condition of things has gone from bad to worse. They are under more serious obligations than they were before, they are under heavier taxation than they were before, the rule of the Government is more tyrannical and corrupt than it was before. And now that the hands of the Government are clear, and they have more support, and are less isolated in Europe, I appeal to them to do something for the grievances of the Uitlanders in the Transvaal.

*Sir C. DILKE (Gloucester, Forest of Dean) : There is one question with regard to the Colonial Office Vote which the honourable Gentleman the Member for Southampton proposed to raise, with regard to the contract which the Colony of Newfoundland has entered into with Mr. Reid. I am not aware of the reasons upon which my honourable Friend has decided not to raise that question to-night, but it is a matter which many of us looked into, and some of us looked into last Session when it was first heard of; it is a question on which we may not be disposed to blame the Government, but which deserves the attention of the Committee for a moment. Now, the Colonial Secretary said in his dispatch that there was no precedent whatever for such legislation on the part of a Colonial Government, but that the scheme was one which concerned the Colony. He had given the House two reasons which led him not to veto, not to disallow the Reid contract. Now, my honourable Friend the Member for Southampton wished, I suppose, to blame the Colonial Secretary, but that

is not my intention. I should like to try and make clear to the Committee, if I can, what is the position between this country and Newfoundland in dealing with the matter. I have here the contract itself, and that contract is one entered into by the Colony of Newfoundland, by which they have handed over to Mr. Reid, the contractor of the railway, the railway system, the telegraphs, the whole of the coal fields, and mineral mines, and, so far as I can make out, the whole of the best land in the Colony as well. There is a nominal payment in all of 1,350,000 dollars by the contractor, and so far as I am able to discover the charges which he is entitled to make on the postal service contracts which have been made over to him will almost immediately give him back the amount he has paid. On page 15 of the contract we find this—

"From the time when the contractor shall satisfy the Government that he is able to operate his coal mine or mines as to supply not less than 50,000 tons per annum of coal of good quality, and to continue to furnish such supply, the Government agree to procure the imposition of a duty of not less than $1 per ton upon all coal imported into this Colony."

That appears to me to be a contract on the part of the Government with regard to future legislation of a most extensive character, and one which deserves the attention of this Committee. Then, in the last paragraph but one of the contract the Government give a general contract in this form—

"The Government undertake to enact all such legislation as may be necessary to give full effect to the contract and its several clauses and provisions thereof, according to the spirit and intent thereof."

As a condition of the arrangement, the Government also undertook to carry into effect at a future time all such legislation as may be necessary in the interests of the contractor to give full effect to the contract. Now, Sir, the position of Mr. Reid with reference to the railway is this. The original railway of 80 miles, which has been working for nine years, has been working lately under my honourable Friend the Member for Southampton, who is the receiver in the original bankruptcy. I am informed that since the railway has been working under my honourable Friend it has paid its working expenses and interest on debentures. That railway was

Sir C. Dilke.

bought three years ago by the Colony for £350,000. The rest of the line has been built as far as it at present extends by Mr. Reid, who has contracted with the Colony to build it at 15,600 dollars a mile. This undertaking will cost the Colony 12 million dollars. Both these lines, 80 miles of which have been paying their expenses have been handed over to Mr. Reid for one million dollars, and in return for working that railway for 50 years he gets in addition the coal and best land in the Colony. Then, Sir, there is also a dock handed over to Mr. Reid. The dock cost over 600,000 dollars, and that has been handed over for 325,000 dollars. The dock is not, perhaps, worth more than the sum put down for it, but it is at present in the hands of a lessee who is under an agreement to return it to the Colony as good as new. Mr. Reid is under an engagement to carry on the coastal service. The conditions provide for a much longer term of years than those previously stipulated, namely, 30 years, and I am informed that the best judges in the Colony believe that the amount which has been paid Mr. Reid makes the contract a very wasteful one. Now, Sir, I need not, I think, labour these points, because the Colonial Secretary in his dispatches admits the badness of the contract to the Colony. The Governor has conveyed to him that opinion—and the Governor is a very high authority—in the strongest terms, and the Colonial Secretary accepts that opinion, and, therefore, it is not necessary to ask the question as to whether it is wasteful or not. We may assume that it is an absolutely wasteful contract. The whole of the assets of the Colony, which have been handed over to this contractor, were the assets put forward when the money was borrowed by which the 80 miles of railway and the dock were built, the loan being advanced from London. The Colonial Secretary has discussed in his dispatches the question of whether the assets which were handed over to the contractor were already pledged to someone else, and he appears to have rejected that view, and to have been of the opinion that there was no positive breach of faith towards anyone; he therefore concludes that it is impossible to interfere with the discretion of a self-governing Colony. Well, Sir, I do not think anyone could question that judgment. At the same time, if the power of veto is ever to be used, this contract, embodying as it does undertakings involving the sacrifice of the rights of the future inhabitants of the country, forms a fitting instance for the interference of the Colonial Secretary. Those who are opposed to centralisation in local government—those who object to the interference of the Local Government Board, for example, with the rights of districts —have always admitted that where present ratepayers interfere with future ratepayers by putting those who are to come 50 years hence at a great disadvantage, there ought to be governmental interference; and I am bound to say in a case of this sort, where the assets of the Colony as regards railways, telegraphs, mines, etc., are done away with for a small sum of money, such a course has something to recommend it. The matter has been sprung with extraordinary suddenness upon the Colony. It has followed an election, in the course of which it has not been even discussed, and has been rushed through both Houses of Parliament with a speed almost as great as that with which the Explosives Act was once carried through the Houses of Parliament here. The Colony, I say, was undoubtedly taken by surprise, and when we consider that the whole birthright of the Colony, so to speak, appears to have been sold to the contractor for a comparatively small sum of money, I cannot but think that this is a case in which time might have been given to enable the electorate to pronounce its opinion on the subject. There has been no appeal to the electorate at all on the question, and I confess that this does seem to have been a case, not perhaps for veto or refusal, but at all events for fully allowing the intention of the Government to be known. Of course, no Colonial Secretary would dream of interfering with the action of such colonies as those of Australia, Canada, or New Zealand, but the position of Newfoundland is not the same as that of the Colonies I mention. Mr. Lowther, the only other subject connected with this Vote which I should like to mention before I sit down concerns another matter of self-government. When, on the Colonial Office Vote last year, and the year before, we discussed the new grant to the West Indies, and the probable

future financial policy towards these islands, the right honourable Gentleman the Colonial Secretary did not see his way to announce any general change with regard to the administrative and legislative position of these islands. Since that time he has taken steps in respect of one or two Colonies in the direction of getting rid of the oligarchical system——

THE SECRETARY OF STATE FOR THE COLONIES (Mr. J. CHAMBERLAIN, Birmingham, W.): The right honourable Baronet will recollect that the Royal Commission recommended that wherever grants were made from Imperial sources the Crown should have full control over the financial proceedings of the Colonies, and I announced that as our policy.

*SIR C. DILKE : The right honourable Gentleman said two years ago he did not see his way in that direction, but since that time he has taken steps in the direction of giving increased control to the Crown. Now, Sir, the two policies which really seem defensible in the West Indies are the two extremes and not the middle course. The policy which has been followed up to the present time has, except in one exceptional case, been the middle course of giving real power to the Crown in a certain indirect form. In some Colonies there are some members who are elected by the Crown, that is to say, who are selected by the Crown, as well as the regular official members. In other Colonies the whole power is in the hands of the officials. I must confess that if the right honourable Gentleman is unable to admit in any of the islands the experiment of free government resting upon a vote from the mass of the population, then I would sooner myself see him assume the responsibility of sending out persons in a high position who would govern those islands directly —autocratically if you like; because I believe they would have greater regard to the interests of the masses of the population. When we discussed this matter last year, I ventured to mention the case of the French colonies, where they rely upon the votes of the mass of the population. The right honourable Gentleman then said that his impression was that these Colonies were more autocratic than the government of any of the islands by this country. I cannot gather that there is sufficient foundation for the statement of the right honourable Gentleman. But if you are not prepared to trust local opinion, it would be better to get rid of this Government machinery which we possess in these islands, and to substitute direct rule by the head Colonial Government itself; because I am convinced that if you choose the right man —and you generally do—he is more likely to govern the islands according to the real wish of the general population than are those who are selected under the curiously complicated methods which exist at the present time. I think, at all events, the right honourable Gentleman is hardly prepared to dispute that his own man, responsible directly to himself, would be more trustworthy in financial matters and would be more likely to govern the country in the interests of the whole population than many representing the Colonies at the present time.

MR. SCHWANN (Manchester, N.): Mr. Lowther, I regret very much that owing to the prevailing influenza, the Debate upon the question I desire to raise, which was to have taken place this afternoon in another place, has had to be postponed. I find some excuse in bringing this question before the House, because in 1893 I had the honour of taking a very humble part in the abolition of the paddy-tax. That abolition was chiefly due to the efforts of Mr. George Wall, Mr. Le Mesurier, and Sir Henry Havelock, the Governor for the time being. When that abolition took place, it was received with great rejoicing by the natives, who let off fireworks, and expressed in every way their delight at the change. But, Sir, while that impost, which fell heavily on the population, has been removed, other abuses remain. If not literally correct, I believe it is practically correct to say that the Governor in Ceylon is absolute ruler, whilst in the legislative council the official element predominates. There are nine officials, but only five representatives of three millions of Cingalese, and three of the rest of the population. Now, no doubt the right honourable Gentleman will say that Ceylon is in a very flourishing condition. I am delighted to know it. The exports from Ceylon last year were three millions in

Sir C. Dilke.

tea alone, and the whole revenue of the island amounted to £666,000. But it is no reason why, because the island is prosperous, the citizen rights of any individual should be attacked. Now, the question of abuse to which I wish to refer is what may be called the appropriation by the Government of Ceylon of lands which belong to private individuals. I refer chiefly to jungle lands, which lie just by the low-lying rice-fields between the coast and the high ranges of forests. In 1819, the English Government found they could not get on without some taxes being paid, and they claimed as a tithe one-tenth of the produce, and took one-fourth to a half for rent. In 1895, the Surveyor of Forests announced to the Government that there were still remaining two million acres of good forest land, and another two million acres of wilder jungle suitable for the growth of tea. This was at a time when tea lands were very valuable, and I suppose the officials of the Government saw a vista of enormous wealth before them if they took possession of these lands. Now I am coming to a very interesting phase of the question. In 1896, the present ʼGovernor, Sir West Ridgway, arrived in the island. I may remind the Committee that in the very same year Mr. Le Mesurier, who had been an official of the Government of Ceylon, and who had shown that he took a very deep interest in the welfare of the Cingalese, bought some of these lands which the Government claimed, in order to test whether the Crown had really or not a right to them. Well, I may relate to the House that when Mr. Le Mesurier took this step, he was met by a very prompt and summary opposition. He was very severely handled—indeed, it was said that his life even was in danger—and was driven off the lands which he supposed belonged to him by right of purchase. While his case was pending in the courts, the Government thought they had better strengthen the law, and they brought in Ordinance No. 1 of 1897, and passed it through the Ceylon legislature. It was carried by the nine official members against the eight unofficial members, three of whom represented Europeans. That Ordinance was denounced by one of the members of the legislature as a most unprincipled Bill, devoid of all the principles of common honesty. Well, I am going to give the House, if I may be allowed, the latest paragraphs in this Ordinance. It is of no use talking to the House of Ordinance No. 1, 1889, if the House does not know what it contains. I apologise if I seem to be tedious, but I regard it as my duty to bring this matter fully before the House. The first paragraph says—

"That all forest waste, and unoccupied or uncultivated lands, and all lands that can only be cultivated at intervals of several years (these are called Chenas lands) shall be presumed to be the property of the Crown, till the contrary thereof be proved."

The second paragraph runs—

"That the occupation by any person of one or more portions or parcels of land shall not be taken as creating a presumption of ownership against the Crown in his favour for any greater extent of land than that actually occupied by him."

I take it that to an unbiassed mind it must be evident that if a man claims a piece of land as his own, and that land is immediately adjoining the land the surface of which he occupies and cultivates, there is a slight presumption that it belongs to him. The third paragraph says—

"That the term 'unoccupied land' includes uncultivated parts of cultivated lands;"

and the fourth paragraph goes on—

"That all land that has not been in the uninterrupted personal occupation of the claimant for five years before the passing of the Ordinance shall be declared to be Crown land."

I think that is very stiff indeed. I am not a lawyer myself, and I do not profess to understand the whole ramifications of this clause; but my learned Friends will perhaps be able to point out the full force of the iniquity of that clause. The next paragraph sets out—

"that Government Agents have a summary power to declare such land to be Crown land without any right of appeal."

That is pretty stiff, too. I am bound to say that there is a right of appeal in the Act further on, that is to the Governor himself. Well, we all know in this House that some hare-brained individuals send up petitions to the House of Commons. I don't know any more

fatuous or futile proceeding than that of these poor petitioners. The petitions are deposited in some pigeon-hole or cupboard, and nothing more is heard of them. I am sure that it is very much the same thing in Ceylon. If you attack, by petition, the Attorney-General or any very gorgeous person of that character, in all probability the petition or claim to be heard will be refused. The sixth paragraph declares—

"That if a man wrongfully loses his land under the operation of the above provisions, and proves in court that he has suffered pecuniary loss by the eviction, even then he cannot get back his land, but he can only get as compensation what the Government get by the sale of it by public auction, or what the Governor chooses to allow him."

The seventh paragraph sets forth—

"that it is a criminal offence punishable by fine and imprisonment for a man to go on his own land after the Crown has claimed it."

That is the sort of plan they have in Ceylon. If a man looks after his own property he can be forcibly ejected from it. Well, I am glad to think that the course of injustice, like that of true love, does not always run smoothly, as was found when Mr. Le Mesurier appealed to the judge of the Màtara district court. It appears that three months' notice must be given to the occupier when any land is claimed by the Government. But the officers of the Government were so exceedingly anxious to take possession of this land of M. Le Mesurier's that they seized it within two months and six days. They had not the patience to wait for three months. That was a very fortunate circumstance, because the court decided in the plaintiff's favour on 8th June 1898. The judge, Mr. Cassie Chetty, said—

"It is an Ordinance enacted in contravention of the well-established laws of the country."

That is a sort of sly hit at the Ordinance which he evidently does not approve of. That is one for the Governor. But Mr. Cassie Chetty was only the judge in the Màtara district court. What was it that the Chief Justice said when the case was taken on appeal to the Supreme Court before the Chief Justice and Mr. Justice Withers on 2nd September 1898? Chief Justice Bonser "spoke scornfully of the Ordinance as one of 'an extraordinary nature' and one in the enforcement of which ' no irregularity ought to be condoned.' " What a condonation coming from the Chief Justice of the High Court of Colombo! There is a much longer and a still more condemnatory judgment by Mr. Justice Withers, who was the companion on the bench of the Chief Justice. I do not wish to take up the attention of the House longer than necessary, and therefore I will not trouble it by reading Mr. Justice Withers' judgment. But to return to Mr. Cassie Chetty; I am sorry to say that very shortly after having given the bold judgment to which I have referred he was removed to Panadura, a distant part of Ceylon, and promoted to the position of a police magistrate with a much smaller salary. I do not know by whose instructions this was done, but I suppose all these matters came under the care and solicitude of the Governor. And if you are to have absolute Government tempered by the House of Commons it seems to me that it is the Governor who must bear a large responsibiity for any miscarriage of that kind. Whenever anything goes wrong in Russia, where the Tsar is an absolute monarch, we do not care very much for what the Minister of Education or the Home Minister says; we look directly to the Tsar. And, therefore, I may fairly say that it is the Governor who is responsible for this awkward instance of promotion to a lower position and a lower salary. Well, Mr. Cassie Chetty was transferred to Panadura, which means in Spanish "hard bread," and Mr. Cassie Chetty must have found it a case of hard bread with him, and that it is not always best to express an honest opinion on a Government Ordinance. Besides that, I am bound to say that the Government has had various experiences in its attempts to convict Mr. Le Mesurier. Mr. W. H. Moor convicted him for having entered on his own land, and sentenced him to three months' imprisonment—I suppose with hard labour—which would be in harmony with the views of the same judge. But that sentence of three months' imprisonment was afterwards reduced to a fine. Then, I am sorry to say, that a counter charge of murder was brought against Mr. Le Mesurier in another court. That is a very serious charge to be made against anyone in

Mr. Schwann.

this world; but when it was brought against Mr. Le Mesurier, the magistrate dismissed it and described it as " a baseless fabrication." Fortune again varied, for the three men who had attacked him on his own property and beat him on the head a good deal, were convicted and sentenced to three months' imprisonment. When I asked a question on the subject the other day, the right honourable Gentleman the Colonial Secretary admitted that that was the case. I am glad to say that Mr. Le Mesurier has the noble qualities of a generous foe, and he interceded with the Government for these men and got their sentence remitted, because he knew perfectly well that they were only tools and bound to carry out the orders given to them. Not only did he secure the remission of their sentence, but pleaded that they should be restored to the Service, which is about to be done. I think I may draw the right honourable Gentleman's attention to the fact that these conflicts between that judicial part of the Government of Ceylon and the Executive do not tend to edification, and I hope that he will himself see the importance of putting an end to these conflicts by looking into the Ordinance of 1897. The right honourable Gentleman is cute enough tn forming his own judgment, and he can send out instructions for the modification of that Ordinance, which is really of an arbitrary nature. I cannot help mentioning Mr. Le Mesurier's name so frequently, because he is the man who has taken up this question as champion on behalf of the people. Well, Mr. Le Mesurier has claimed 80,000 rupees for the cost of the abortive actions which were brought against him, and for compensation for the charge of murder laid against him. Such a charge is always distressing to the mind, and should be compensated for if it is found by the magistrate who tried it to be " a baseless fabrication." Then he claims compensation for the occupation of his lands by the Government, during which time, of course, the lands went out of cultivation. Then there are the fines imposed on Mr. Le Mesurier, which he demands should be refunded. But Mr. Le Mesurier's is not the only case, although it was typical. There are other cases which I shall mention to the House. There is the case of Don Simon, who rented from a man called Andris, a piece of land with a growing crop of citronella grass upon it. It is quite common in Ceylon, as it is in England, to purchase a standing crop. Andris had held this land for years, and, as I have said, Don Simon made an offer for the crop, which was accepted. But when he went to carry off the crop he found that the land had been claimed by the Government and he was put into the Martara police court on 30th July 1888, where he was fined 50 rupees and sent to prison for a month with hard labour. I am glad to say, however, that this sentence was quashed on appeal after ten days. Judgment was given in his favour, and Don Simon was set at liberty. If I had been the Governor of Ceylon I must say I should have been rather disappointed if all the cases brought before the courts by the Government were overturned. I am sorry to say that Don Simon is still a mournful man, because up to the present he has not received any compensation for his grass, nor any compensation for his imprisonment. Further, if I am not misinformed, that very land which belonged to the original owner, Andris, has been advertised for sale in the "Government Gazette" of 20th January 1899, and that the sale by auction was to take place on the 10th or 11th of this month, although Andris had appealed to the District Court against the appropriation of the land by the Government. The decision of the District Court has not yet been given, and, when given, is subject to review by the Supreme Court in Ceylon. These various opinions having been given by the highest judges against the Ordinance No. 1 of 1897, the Government has begun to think that that Ordinance is pretty nearly unworkable; and quite recently they have drawn another Ordinance, which is to strengthen No. 1, and which will be submitted to Her Majesty for signature. When I read to you the last paragraph of the new Ordinance, you will understand that it is a sort of whitewashing Ordinance—that its object is to whitewash any errors or faults on the part of the Government of Ceylon or their officers which occurred in previous cases. The draft of the new Ordinance was printed in the "Government Gazette" in Colombo on the 18th November, 1898, and I shall

read the concluding paragraph, which is by far the strongest. It says—

"No notice purporting to have been published and advertised under the provisions of section 1 of the principal Ordinance, or Order purporting to have been made under the provisions of sections 2 and 4 of the said Ordinance, prior to the passing of this Ordinance, shall be deemed to be invalid or inoperative by reason of any irregularity in the publishing, advertising, or making of such notice or order."

In other words, whatever errors or legal laches which had been committed by the Government or their officials in administering the original Ordinance are to be condoned, in spite of the Chief Justice having said that " no irregularity ought to be condoned" over such an act. There are many other points to which I might refer in connection with the Government of Ceylon, such as the road tax, and the arrack monopoly. The sale of arrack is a monopoly of the Government. It is one of the strongest spirits known, and it is forced on the inhabitants of the colony; at any rate, if it is not forced on the inhabitants, wonderful facilities are given them for imbibing it, and the income derived from its sale is 3,000,000 rupees per annum. I do not wish to take up too much time of the House, but I desire to concentrate attention on the land Ordinances, actual and prospective. The Act of 1897, No. 1, is, I hold, harsh and unjust. It annexes by the Government

"all lands which at the passing of the Act were not in the actual occupation of any person or persons; and also all lands which shall not have been in the uninterrupted occupation of some persons or person for a period exceeding five years next before notice given by the Government."

It must be noted that many lands are, according to the custom of the country, only cultivated at long intervals. My next point is that the Ordinance of 1897, No. 1, has settled little or nothing. On the 30th November 1898, although 280 notices had been issued referring to 140,000 acres of land and 700 separate parcels of land, down to the present time only 61 parcels of land, covering 318 acres, have been settled. That is to say, only one-twelfth covered by the notices and 1-400th part of the acreage has been settled. That, I think, shows that the judges are obviously against the working of the Act, and that it is productive of conflicts between the judiciary and the executive. There is another case which I think the House ought to be in possession of, because it shows what a gulf is widening between the judiciary and the executive. At Colombo, on 24th January this year, Mr. Justice Lawrie tried a case of alleged fratricide. In that case it was admitted by the magistrate, who enjoys the name of Mr. Rosemalecocq (who appeared himself as a witness), that he had detained certain persons in custody, although no charge had been laid against them. He only said he had very good reasons for detaining them. At an inquiry in the Supreme Court on the 25th January, Mr. Justice Lawrie inquired from Mr. Rosemalecocq how he came to detain people in custody against whom there was no charge. His Lordship observed that . he could not understand how anybody could be kept in custody without a complaint being made against them. Mr. Rosemalecocq answered that, in serious cases, they had instructions from Government to do all they could in the interests of justice. His Lordship, tendering a copy of the Code to the witness, asked him to point out his authority for such a proceeding. The witness admited that there was nothing in the Code permitting him to do so, but that he had instructions from the Government to keep such people in custody. What does Mr. Justice Lawrie say to that? He observed that the Colonial Secretary issued a large number of circulars which did more harm than good, and were, more often than not, quite irregular and illegal. Mr. Rosemalecocq's conduct, Mr. Justice Lawrie continued, was very serious; and he would make a serious report to His Excellency the Governor. It was a very serious thing that Mr. Rosemalecocq had done, and his Lordship would see that the bullying of witnesses bv magistrates in this country would not occur again. That was to say, that if Mr. Rosemalecocq did not cease from crowing he was going to have his comb cut. I trust that the right honourable Gentleman the Colonial Secretary will listen to the petition of Mr. Le Mesurier. I remember that two or three years ago he received petitions from the Zulu chiefs regarding their grievances. I trust that in this

Mr. Schwann.

case the right honourable Gentleman will do all that lies in his power to remove what we consider the very serious and somewhat ridiculous position which the Government have taken up. I believe that, moved by those sentiments of justice common to him and to all of us, he will think it right to take an interest in the poorer inhabitants of Ceylon, the native Cingalese, who have inherited their lands from their forefathers. It is with the greatest confidence that I call upon the right honourable Gentleman to redress what I consider the factious and illegal action of the Governor, Sir West Ridgway. Of course, I know it will be said in this House that it is always necessary to protect our Colonial Governors, but I trust the right honourable Gentleman, while protecting the Governor of Ceylon, will see that abuses are put an end to, and that this internecine strife between the judiciary and the executive shall be terminated.

THE SECRETARY OF STATE FOR THE COLONIES : I think it will be more convenient to the Committee, as the Debate has already travelled over a considerable space, and as several Members have dwelt at great length upon the subjects which they have introduced to the Committee, that I should answer them at once while the matter is fresh in the minds of honourable Members of this House. That, of course, will not prevent my giving any further reply to any other questions which may be brought before the attention of the Committee by any other honourable Members. I will first deal with the statements made to us by the honourable Member for North Manchester. I am sorry, I confess, that the right honourable Gentleman who has given, I think, notice of a Motion on this subject for another stage of the Estimates, should have thought it necessary to bring the subject forward to-day, because he had been informed by me, in answer to a question on these matters, that I have called for a report, and, of course, until I have received that report I am in the position of a person who has only heard one side of the case. I am dealing with an *ex parte* statement, and it is impossible for me to do otherwise than give a perfunctory reply to the numerous charges brought by the honourable Gentleman. If he had only been willing to wait until the time originally contemplated, I think I should have been able to give him a more satisfactory reply than I can possibly give him to-night. I understand the honourable Member puts forward a series of charges, which he considers are well founded, against the Governor of Ceylon, and he expects that I shall take notice of them. Of course, if a Governor does wrong it is quite right that his conduct should come up for review. But at the same time, I may lay down the general rule that charges of this kind affecting the character of a Governor who is in a position of great responsibility, and who cannot by any possibility reply for himself, should only be made upon the most complete evidence, and under circumstances which would thoroughly justify their being brought before the notice of this House. What is the state of affairs on the present occasion? Certainly, it may be that some criticisms may be justly passed upon the Ordinance to which the honourable Member has referred. Upon that I offer no opinion whatever until I have received the reply for which I have called. It may well be that the Legislature of Ceylon, like some other legislatures I know, has passed a faulty Measure; and, if so, on the case being proved, steps may be taken to correct that action. It may be, although, again, I have no knowledge of the subject at the present moment, that certain persons in Ceylon—subordinate officials, I understand from the statement of the honourable Member, or even subordinate magistrates, may have done things which they are not entitled to do and which it would be quite wrong for them to do in their position. But, Sir, there is a great difference between a statement that that is done, and that something has occurred which would involve the condemnation of the Governor. You have to prove, not merely that irregular proceedings have taken place on the part of a subordinate, but that this subordinate has been subsequently upheld by the Governor. Take the only case which has been brought before the Committee in the speech of the honourable Gentleman. He has mentioned the case of Mr. Rosemalecocq, who, he says, wrongfully imprisoned persons without authority. But then we have the state-

ment of the Colonial Secretary of Ceylon, speaking for the Government, that this was a most wrongful act on the part of Mr. Rosemalecocq. But, Sir, surely, if matters of this kind are being dealt with in that spirit by the Governor of Ceylon, it is unnecessary to bring forward charges against the Governor, as if he were responsible for everything done, and of which he had subsequently expressed disapproval. Before charges of this kind can be brought it is of course essential that the honourable Gentleman should be furnished with the necessary brief of the case, and it becomes of the greatest importance to know from whom that brief comes. In the present case the honourable Member has, so far as I can gather, received all his information from Mr. Le Mesurier.

Mr. SCHWANN: I quoted from the papers, and from the Judge's own statement.

The SECRETARY of STATE for the COLONIES: I am speaking on the general question. The brief, as I have said, has been furnished by Mr. Le Mesurier, and the starting point to know is who is Mr. Le Mesurier? The honourable Gentleman, as I understand it, tells us that Mr. Le Mesurier was an officer in the service of the Ceylon Government, and that he was arbitrarily dismissed by Sir West Ridgway.

Mr. SCHWANN: No.

The SECRETARY of STATE for the COLONIES: Well, I have seen that stated in a London newspaper which is taking notice of these charges, all of which I invariably trace to Mr. Le Mesurier. They come from every quarter, and are raised in many places. They were, I understand, to have been raised in another place to-night, and I believe that in every case they are to be traced to the energy and zeal of Mr. Le Mesurier. Mr. Le Mesurier was in the service of the Ceylon Government; he was dismissed by the present Governor, as he says, tyrannically dismissed, and has been subjected to persecution ever since. What was his fault? Mr. Le Mesurier was married to an English wife. He sought a divorce from that wife, and he failed to obtain it. Thereupon he converted himself to Mohammedanism, and married a second English wife under Mohammedan rites.

MR. SCHWANN: What has that got to do with his civil rights?

THE SECRETARY OF STATE FOR THE COLONIES: That was the reason why he was dismissed. In fact, it was by my instructions—because the Governor applied to me for instructions upon the subject—that he was at once dismissed from the Service, because I thought his conduct constituted nothing more nor less than a scandal. Since then what has he done? I am not blaming the honourable Gentleman for undue credulity, but, also on the authority of Mr. Le Mesurier——

MR. SCHWANN: I have given the facts, and I have quoted from official documents.

THE SECRETARY OF STATE FOR THE COLONIES: Also on the authority of Mr. Le Mesurier, the honourable Gentleman has told the Committee that Mr. Le Mesurier has taken the steps he has taken in the interests of the native population—that he is a champion of the natives, and it is as a champion of the natives that he is presented to us. On what ground is he presented to us as the champion of the natives? Is it because this ex-official of the Ceylon Civil Service has been buying up at absolutely insignificant sums from the native population speculative claims against his own Government, and trying to make them good in the Ceylon courts? It appears that many of these lands are valuable only because of certain property which would become vacant, and Mr. Le Mesurier has been taking possession of these lands, to which, after all, there is only a speculative claim, clearing the plumbago out of them, and leaving the natives to make good their claims. It was in consequence of this action, and of the temptation which an example of this kind afforded to others to follow in the same line, that the Governor found it necessary to introduce these ordinances. As to whether those ordinances are all they should be, as to whether they are more arbitrary than necessary, I pronounce no opinion at the present stage; but such conduct had to be promptly dealt with, and I am informed by the Governor that these ordinances are not objected to by the non-official members of the Council, and that the principle of the ordinances has been accepted by them. He says, further, that they are regarded with satisfaction by the vast majority of the natives, and that under them the legitimate, the *bona fide*, claims of the natives are being rapidly settled. They are being confirmed in possession of their lands, and they would be the chief sufferers if everything was thrown into the pot in order merely to enable Mr. Le Mesurier to continue the practices to which I have referred. That is all I can say on the subject to-night. If the honourable Gentleman is not satisfied, I will take care, as soon as I get a full report from the Governor, to present it to the House, or at all events to take steps to enable me to make a further answer on another occasion. Then I come to the speech of my right honourable Friend the Member for the Forest of Dean, who referred to matters of great importance. In the first place, he referred to the Reid Contract. I wish very much he had been a little more distinct in saying what it was that he wished me to do. He rather played with the subject. He pointed out how grave was the injury which this contract might inflict on the Colony, how unusual it was, and how it would affect future interests and rights; but when he came to the point as to whether or not I should have advised Her Majesty to disallow the Act, then he gave an altogether uncertain sound.

*SIR C. DILKE: The Governor has himself, in one of the dispatches published in the last Blue Book, given very powerful reasons which, in his opinion, might tell as against veto, and although in the difficult circumstances I hesitated to express a direct opinion, I intended to suggest that the grounds given by the right honourable Gentleman against veto appear to me to be stronger than those which he has given against delay.

THE SECRETARY OF STATE FOR THE COLONIES: I still fail to understand what the right honourable Gentleman advises me to do, or what he would have done if he had been in my place. Does my right honourable Friend, as a Home Ruler, recommend me to take this line in connection with a self-governing Colony, and to interfere with their legislation because it does not suit my ideas of what is for the benefit of the inhabitants? The arguments with regard to delay are precisely the same with regard to disallowing the Act. In the meantime, the Act was in force, and a considerable sum of money had been paid by the contractor under the Act, and the result either of disallowing the Act or of delaying its operations would have been to plunge the Colony at once into bankruptcy, for which I and the Governor would have been held responsible. My right honourable Friend's argument is a strange one coming from those Benches. He contends, as I understand, that if this had been Canada, for instance, or Australia, I could not have interfered, but he says the politics of this Colony are confessedly on a lower scale. Well, suppose, for example, we had granted Home Rule to Ireland. Would we subsequently have been justified—because we thought, as very likely some of us on this side of the House would have thought, that their politics were on a lower scale—in vetoing their Acts because, forsooth, although they dealt absolutely and exclusively with matters of domestic concern, we considered that for a period of fifty years they were pledging the future of the country? Then the right honourable Gentleman says that he thinks the best people on both sides in the Colony would have supported me. I have heard that " best people " argument very often; but if we were to proceed, either in this country or in any colony, upon what those who considered themselves the best people on either side say upon the matter, I am afraid we should always be supported by a very small minority. It would be a very dangerous principle to set up, and I for one am not at all prepared to set it up in any attempt to deal with those Colonies that have got Home Rule, and, having got Home Rule, must be trusted to act under it. I will only say this as regards the contract itself—that, although I share very largely the opinions which my right honourable Friend has expressed on the subject, still there is another point of view. It may be that we are mistaken, and that the Government of the Colony have done the best for themselves. At all events, what they say is that the property, the assets, they have handed

over were involving them in an annual expenditure they could not well bear, but from which they are now entirely relieved. They admit—I confess it is an extraordinary admission for any Government to make, but they do admit —that as matters are at present, they do not feel as a Government that they are capable of carrying on with efficiency these very large public obligations, and that they prefer handing them over to a contractor as to whom, at all events, I believe there is a general consensus of opinion that he is a very competent and a very honourable man. Then my right honourable Friend went on to discuss the general constitution of the West Indies, and there again I found difficulty in understanding what he was driving at, or what was the change he suggested in our procedure. The fact is, that the Constitutions of the West Indies, especially up to a very recent date, afforded almost every diversity. They varied from a very wide franchise and a very considerable, practically an absolute, control of financial operations, to what my right honourable Friend calls the mixed system, under which the Governor, in the last resort, was supreme, but was assisted by the advice of a consultative council. My right honourable Friend thinks that the mixed system is the worst. I, on the other hand, think it the best. I think it is absolutely impossible to give to these Colonies at the present moment representative government in the sense that we have representative government at home. It would be, in my opinion, perfectly absurd to give household suffrage, or practically universal suffrage, to the native population in some of these islands. I think there is sufficient proof that they do not value it, because in the cases in which the suffrage is very low, and in which a very large number of the coloured population might avail themselves of it, only the very smallest proportion ever go to the poll; and, when they do go to the poll, the gentlemen who are elected under this system have certainly not shown themselves so efficient as to justify any sanguine expectation of advantage from any extension of the system. Take the case of Trinidad. I saw the other day that a deputation from that Colony waited upon certain

Members of this House. I observe that one newspaper stated that the Colonial Office was officially represented. That is a mistake. So far as I can make out, no intimation of the deputation was sent to Members on this side of the House, much less to the Colonial Office. These gentlemen came forward to represent their views—views which they represented before the West India Commis sion, but which, I am happy to say, made no impression upon the Commission. They asked for an extension of the representative Government in Trinidad. They have representative Government in Trinidad in the shape in which, I think, it is the most useful, and which, at all events, is the least dangerous—a municipality. What has been the result? These gentlemen of the municipality of the Port of Spain got the finances into the most hopeless disorder, and then came and demanded that the Imperial Government should go to their assistance, and, still more, that the necessary deficiency should be met by taxation to be levied on the whole of the Colony. I protested against this, as unfair to those who did not live in the municipality, and did not benefit by this expenditure, and I called upon them to make such rates as were necessary to meet the deficit in their finances. They refused absolutely to do that, and under these circumstances it has been necessary to abolish the municipality and to carry on the work by a Commission. That is the experience of the representative Government of which these gentlemen desire an extension—an experience which does not encourage us to go further. As regards the government of the colonies, they are, with the exception of Barbardos, which, as my right honourable Friend says, is altogether an exceptional case, practically under the control of the Colonial Office. I do not mean by that to say that we should use our control on every occasion or on every matter. On the contrary, we should give a very large amount of freedom to the elected and unofficial members, but in matters of finance, in matters where the vital interests of the Colony are concerned, we have in the last resort the power to say what should be done. That system gives us at once the means of knowing what is the opinion of the mass of the population and it gives us the opportunity of consulting and of obtaining suggestions

Secretary of State for the Colonies.

from the representatives of the population, while, at the same time, it leaves the last responsibility in our hands, and is, I think, on the whole, the best system which can be adopted in the West Indies in their present state of civilisation. Then, Sir, I come to the speech of my honourable Friend the Member for Sheffield. It was an interesting speech, and my interest in it is not diminished by the fact that I heard it once or twice during the present Parliament. Of course, the details are altered, but the substance is always the same. My honourable Friend makes statements as to what he considers the grievances of the Uitlanders, but he will not expect me to accept these *ex parte* statements as being absolutely correct without some allowance to what may be said on the other side. Now, I ask myself when my honourable Friend speaks what is the object, granting that everything that he states is true, what does he wish us to do? Does he wish this Government to send an ultimatum to the Transvaal Government on these matters? Does he wish us to insist upon the reforms which my honourable Friend brings before us, and, failing satisfaction, does he expect us to go to war with the Transvaal? I believe he does. It appears to me that my honourable Friend would not be continually making these speeches unless he had a definite policy of the kind to impress upon us. If, however, that is his view, the first question I should like to ask him is, whom does he represent? Of course, he does not represent the Transvaal Government. But does he represent Uitlanders? My honourable Friend comes here as if he had authority to speak in their name, but I am very much inclined to think that if we were to adopt his advice the Uitlanders themselves would be the first to quarrel with us on that subject, and they might ask why we had interfered when they had not asked us. They might say that we had interfered in the wrong way. Let me quote from a gentleman who represents the principal industry, that of gold-mining, in the Transvaal, and who is President of the Chamber of Mines at Johannesburg. He said that, on one side, he deprecated this perpetual criticism of every act at Pretoria, even if the facts could be constructed so as to justify it. He says that this constant nagging is undignified, and does not tend to the advantage of anyone; and that they should not apply the microscope to magnify every incident into an event of colossal magnitude. " We have given the Transvaal Government credit when credit was due." I do not think that my honourable Friend has ever done that. Then the President of the Chamber adds that it will not be a party to a policy of pinpricks, which is unworthy of them. That is the opinion of the representative of those on whose behalf my honourable Friend makes these strong suggestions. I am not inclined to adopt his policy, even at his suggestion. I am going to admit a good deal of what he has said. It is perfectly true that, at the time of the Raid, three years ago or more, President Kruger made certain promises. He promised to forgive and forget. He promised to listen attentively and favourably to representations made to him as grievances. I think he promised to deal with several of the leading grievances, and I am sorry to say it is true that, up to the present time, not one of those promises has been fulfilled, and that up to the present time those grievances have been rather increased than diminished. In the matter of education, nothing has been done to satisfy the natural demands of the English - speaking people to allow their children that education which they have a proper right to claim, and that they should have some proportionate help from the State. Nothing has been done in the way of giving a municipality to Johannesburg. Even in such a question as the disposal of sewage, that is taken out of the hands of the people, and it is made a monopoly—to their great disadvantage, and possibly to the danger of their health. Nothing has been done as to the dynamite monopoly, and nothing has been done in regard to the franchise. It is true that to-day, as on previous occasions, we have what I hope I may call an advance towards the representation of the Uitlanders grievances; but after reading the telegram which professes to give an account of what President Kruger has lately promised, I confess that, so far as I can see, these promises are entirely illusory. I do not think that what he suggests as to the franchise is of the slightest advantage. I observe, as to the dynamite monopoly, that, though it is to be in

the hands of the Government, it is still to be a monopoly, and I see no advance towards the remedy of other grievances. There would be an easy way, in my opinion, of remedying these grievances—at least the most important of them—without derogating from the interests of the Transvaal, or from the dignity of the Transvaal Government, or any interference with its national dependence, and that would be to give to the people of Johannesburg, where the Uitlanders mostly congregate, a municipality—a real municipality, in the sense in which we understand the word in the United Kingdom. That would give them the control of their own sanitary business—the control of their education and the control of the civil police, which would not be an armed police; and this one step would remove nine out of ten of the grievances put forward by the Uitlander population. Though, as I think, a grant of this kind might be made without any possible injury to anything which President Kruger might think of importance, still I am assured that there is no chance of such a concession at the present time. That being so, what are we to do? My honourable Friend says that I make pledges and promises three years ago which I have not fulfilled, and he read out a number of them. Well, what he refers to were not pledges or promises at all. It was a statement of fact, and not a promise at all, which in no way binds the Government. It was a statement to the effect that the people of Johannesburg had laid down their arms in the belief and expectation that Sir Hercules Robinson would make representations on their behalf, which representations he did accordingly proceed to make. It was communicated to President Kruger from Her Majesty's Government that, in the opinion of the Government, so long as those grievances continued so long would there be more or less unrest and so long would the situation be unhappy, and even perhaps disastrous. I adhere to every word of that. But what more can we do? There are certain clear cases where we can intervene, and rightly intervene. in the Transvaal, In the first place, we may intervene if there is any breach in the Convention; but it is not contended, so far as I know, that any of these things to which my honourable Friend refers are breaches.

Then no doubt we should have the usual right of interference if the comity of nations is not observed—that is to say, that the treatment of British subjects in the Transvaal was of such a nature as would give us the right to interfere as to the treatment of British subjects in France or Germany. When we have been asked to interfere, and when we have not interfered, it has been because we have been advised that no such case has arisen for interference. We interfered in the case of the Alien Law, and subject to our intervention the Alien Law has been repealed. I say subject to our interference, but not in consequence of it; other reasons dictated their action. The Transvaal was anxious that we should understand that it was not because of our interference. We have interfered in the case of the Cape boys, and we have interfered with good results. We have complained of the harsh conduct shown to some of these Cape boys, natives of the Cape Colony; and we complained of the action of a certain field cornet. He was, at least temporarily, removed from his position, though I have heard that he has since been re-appointed. That is, no doubt, bad, but other Powers have acted in precisely a similar way, particularly one Power, in which my honourable Friend takes more than ordinary interest. We have heard of similar things happening in Turkey, and yet my honourable Friend does not advise us immediately to go to war with the Sultan. Then there is only one other case—the third case—in which we can intervene, and it is this—we can undoubtedly, having regard to our predominant position in South Africa, make friendly recommendations to the Transvaal for the benefit of South Africa generally and in the interest of peace. That we can do; but I do not know that my honourable Friend would suggest that this would be a particularly suitable time to take such action. We did do it at the time of the Raid, because we believed that President Kruger was inclined to make some concession to the non-Boer population. But nothing has occurred since, and nothing has reached me since as to the tone and temper of the Transvaal Government which would lead me to believe that friendly suggestions of that kind would be for a moment effective. Therefore, under the cir-

Secretary of State for the Colonies.

cumstances, I do not think that it would be dignified or expedient to make a representation which would receive no consideration. I would say, in conclusion, that I think the condition of the Transvaal must be to every friend of the Transvaal, as well as to every friend of South Africa, unsatisfactory. It must be unsatisfactory to see that the Transvaal cannot come to any kind of terms with the great majority of the white population, who contribute so largely to the prosperity of the State. As long as that condition of things continues it constitutes a real danger; and I can only say that we are watching the situation most carefully. Sir Alfred Milner is on the spot, and I have every confidence in his tact and discretion; but I do not feel at the moment that any case has arisen which would justify me in taking the very strong action which seems, at all events, to have been suggested by my honourable Friend.

MR. BUXTON (Tower Hamlets, Poplar): In reference to the last remarks made by the right honourable Gentleman, with regard to the Transvaal, we have had many friendly representations, and I hope from the tone of the recent speech made by President Kruger that the President will be able to meet our views and the position taken up by the Colonial Secretary. It is perfectly true that President Kruger has made promises before which have not been fulfilled, such as on the question of the franchise and taxation, but he has now met the right honourable Gentleman half way. That is a matter of very great regret, I am quite sure, to everyone who takes an interest in South Africa, and it is a very serious danger to South Africa itself. I trust that the speech of President Kruger, the other day, will be considered as an approach to the position taken up by the right honourable Gentleman, because I understand that the President not only proposes to deal with the question of the franchise and taxation, but he is also going to reduce the enormous burden under which the franchise is obtained There is no doubt that the real matter which rests at the bottom of all this agitation is the question of the impossibility of obtaining a Vote in the country in which they dwell. I trust that what President Kruger said yesterday may be a step in the right direction, and the only difficulty that I feel in regard to the matter is that, unfortunately, President Kruger has, as the right honourable Gentleman has stated, made previous promises which have not been fulfilled. In regard to what fell from the honourable Member for Sheffield, I can only say that he made no suggestion or proposition which would lead to the carrying out of the policy which he advocated. We all agree that, as a general proposition, if the existing oath of allegiance is enforced, it will be almost impossible for a British subject to become a subject of the Transvaal, and it is an absolute injustice in regard to all those British subjects who are living in that country. He has no real suggestion to make, and I can only again say that, with regard to the future of the Transvaal, the only policy we can pursue since the Raid has been a policy of friendly advice and giving advice where it is likely to be taken, but not forcing it where it is certain to be refused. The position as regards this country and the Transvaal was placed on a totally different basis after the Raid, for we are getting more reforms carried out in a more satisfactory way before the Transvaal Raid took place, when our relations were steadily improving, but that Raid caused the Transvaal Government to look upon us with absolute suspicion. With regard to other matters discussed this evening, I may say, in reference to the Newfoundland question, which has been raised, that I think the only course for the Secretary of State to have taken was to refuse all responsibility. My right honourable Friend suggested that he might have undertaken the responsibility of delaying this contract, but to have insisted on delaying its completion would have been as great a responsibility as to have disallowed it. It seems to me that in this matter you must have one rule and one rule alone. You have the varied interests of the country to consider, and the only justification for intervention in a self-governing Colony is the protection of Imperial interests. In regard to this legal contract, it may be possibly absolute ruination, and the most extraordinary financial transaction that any Colony has ever undertaken; but it is, after all, purely a financial and local matter, whatever

else may be said about it, and it cannot interfere with Imperial matters. Therefore, I think the Secretary of State had only one possible course open to him in connection with this matter, and that was to wash his hands of all responsibility, and to say that, whatever might be the result of this contract being carried out, he declined to accept any responsibility at all as representing the Imperial Government. With regard to the Ordinance of the Government of Ceylon, I think my honourable Friend the Member for Sheffield was quite entitled to bring this matter forward, because it is, as it were, the only occasion, and he would not have another opportunity of doing so.

THE SECRETARY OF STATE FOR THE COLONIES: No, no!

MR. BUXTON: The right honourable Gentleman has asked for Reports with regard to this matter, and, when they come, I suppose he will lay Papers on the Table with regard to this matter?

THE SECRETARY OF STATE FOR THE COLONIES: Yes, if it is desirable.

MR. BUXTON: I think my right honourable Friend should bring this matter forward in the House. I have no information in regard to the matter, but I have some knowledge as to whom the right honourable Gentleman referred as possibly being at the bottom of this agitation. I think my right honourable Friend, after reading the official Papers as he does, is perfectly entitled to lay the matter before the House and give his version of the matter. The right honourable Gentleman has asked for a Report, and, until that Report is received, we must, of course, reserve our opinion in regard to this matter. I think those are all the points raised by the different honourable Gentlemen who have spoken already in the Debate, and I will only conclude by again saying that, in regard to the question of the Transvaal, that we on this side of the House do not feel at the present moment that any special or extra pressure should be brought to bear with regard to internal affairs of the Transvaal on the Transvaal Government. I do not believe that the honourable Gentleman the Member for Sheffield is correct in saying that matters are worse now than they were before. We do not think that the Government ought to go beyond the Convention either in regard to foreign or local affairs, and I for one shall certainly support the right honourable Gentleman in the attitude which he has taken up.

DR. CLARK (Caithness): There are one or two statements which I much regret that the right honourable Gentleman has made. After reading the telegram in this morning's paper, he has proceeded to criticise some remarks made by President Kruger, and he has offered an opinion, after reading this abstract and very condensed telegram, that if those changes were carried out they would not be of the slightest value to anyone in the country. Well, surely, on a matter of this kind, if the right honourable Gentleman had made a speech of an hour's duration, and it was condensed into a telegram to South Africa—and misrepresented, as is often the case—it would not be very creditable for somebody out in Africa to discuss his remarks in the way the right honourable Gentleman has treated this telegram to-night. I am very much inclined to think that he has not tended to bring about the reforms desired by the course he has taken, and I believe that, in consequence of the attitude taken up by the Press, both in England and Johannesburg, reforms have been delayed by the course which has been taken. Now, President Kruger has been in London, and he knows the condition of things here, and, when he hears the right honourable Gentleman pleading that Pretoria should have a municipality and the right to control the police, the President knows that in London you refuse to give the local ·uthority control of the police. Therefore, you are asking President Kruger to give to foreigners the right which you refuse to your own people in London. The President also knows that the police in Ireland are under the control of the Imperial Government, and therefore you are asking him to give to foreigners a right which you will not give to your own countrymen in Ireland. I do not think—and I say it advisedly—that there is very much to complain of as far as the franchise is concerned. It is perfectly true that under the present

Mr. Buxton.

law you have to wait 14 years before you can have a voice in the election of the representatives to the First Chamber. But you can live in this country a whole lifetime and you never have the right to vote for anybody who sits in the First Chamber in this country, and yet you complain that you have to wait 14 years in the Transvaal. After two years you do get a vote for the Second Chamber. I remember when my honourable Friend the Member for one of the Divisions of Perthshire and myself were in Pretoria when this scheme was brought out, we impressed upon President Kruger the desirability of giving further powers in this respect, and he told us that he would increase those powers later on. This has not been very long in operation. Now, I know that one of the most important reforms is to give the control of the purse strings to the Second Chamber, the same as we have in England. If they had that, then I think nearly all the grievances complained of would be met, for that seems to me, looking at the facts of the case, to be the only real grievance. Then, again, as far as taxation is concerned, I do not see why there should be any complaint, because the rate of taxation in the Transvaal is lower than it is in the neighbouring Colony. In our own Colony everything that we say is wrong in the Transvaal is still worse there, because the rates are still higher. As far as education is concerned, I think that you have no ground at all to say a single word, and if you want French, German, and Russian taught in your schools you must pay for it yourselves. The State control of education has not a very long history, and we cannot look upon ourselves as being very far advanced in educational matters, and it is really preposterous, because foreigners go into State schools in the Transvaal, that you should demand that they should be taught various languages there, and if you once begin to give a special teaching to one particular class you will eventually have to give it to the others. Lastly, with regard to the dynamite concession, the right honourable Gentleman thinks the changes proposed will not be very beneficial, because there will still remain a monopoly. This is, then, monopoly, and it will always remain a monopoly. And why are they so strongly in favour of this monopoly? Why, simply because of the past action of the British Government. When the Boers have been fighting native wars you have stopped their supplies on several occasions and have left them at the mercy of the tribes. You stopped their importation of explosives, and because of that they have determined upon this policy of having explosives manufactured in their own country. This monopoly will always remain, because it is now the settled policy of the Transvaal to have all explosives under the control of the State, and I think the policy is a very wise one. Then, with reference to the policy of indirect taxation and protection, if you are having a policy of protection in India in regard to sugar, surely they cannot be far wrong to have protection in the Transvaal. These grievances have been magnified by the right honourable Gentleman, and the result is that reforms which otherwise would have been granted if different tactics had been adopted both in London and Johannesburg, have not been passed because the Transvaal Government is much more easily led than driven. In the Transvaal, as in this country, there are reforms required, but I do not think the speech of the right honourable Gentleman to-day will tend to make President Kruger do more to persuade his Volksraad to pass those Measures. There is a powerful Conservative Party in the Transvaal, and it is like our own Conservative Party, very difficult to move when it has got cherished ideas, and they think some of your changes in the Transvaal may do what was done before when the gold industry was first discovered and developed, namely, bring a lot of foreigners who will try and overturn their independence. With regard to the oath of allegiance which has caused so much trouble, it is only analogous to the oath of allegiance in the United States, and it is absolutely word for word the same as the American system, the only difference being that you have the South African Republic instead of the United States. That is the character of some of the bogus grievances mentioned in this House, and which have prevented some of the real grievances being removed.

Mr. CLOUGH (Portsmouth): I desire to point out that in the Legislature of Cape Colony there has been passed an Act imposing an additional tax on companies which very seriously affects limited companies trading in that Colony. It is entitled, "An Act to amend the law relating to Licenses and Stamps," and by this Act a tax of one shilling per cent. on the paid-up capital of a company has been imposed. This tax is in addition to the taxes which already exist. For instance, there is the dealers' tax of £3, the importers' tax of £12; and then the limited companies trading in Cape Colony who have offices and warehouses have the usual expenses of rent, rates, and taxes, which are very heavy indeed, especially in Port Elizabeth. My point is this, that this is a tax not upon the volume of trade which limited companies may do with Cape Colony, but it is a tax upon the entire paid-up capital of the companies doing trade with that Colony. In round figures it works out as representing about 1½ per cent. upon the trade done, and it constitutes almost a prohibitive tax with many Cape merchants. Take, for instance, a company with £150,000 capital, the tax would be £75; assuming the year's trading to be £5,500, it would mean 1½ per cent. of a charge upon the direct trade done with the Colony.

The SECRETARY of STATE for the COLONIES: May I ask the honourable Gentleman when this Act was passed.?

Mr. CLOUGH: Quite recently.

The SECRETARY of STATE for the COLONIES: In what way is it suggested that we should interfere with that Act?

Mr. CLOUGH: My intention is to call the attention of the right honourable Gentleman to these facts, which are very seriously affecting trade in London, with a view to the Colonial Secretary taking some steps in the way of remedying this state of things, and with a view to getting him to bring his influence to bear upon the Cape Legislature.

The SECRETARY of STATE for the COLONIES: I have no influence whatever, and I would not interfere on any account, because it is a matter which concerns the Cape Parliament solely.

3 I

MR. CLOUGH: I will, nevertheless, finish my statement.

THE CHAIRMAN OF WAYS AND MEANS: Order, order! Unless the honourable Member can show that the Secretary of State for the Colonies can forbid the passing of the Act or withhold his assent from it I do not see how the honourable Member can raise the subject here. He ought to raise the question in the Cape Parliament.

MR. CLOUGH: Not having a seat in the Cape Colony Legislative Assembly, and as it affects a very large number of merchants who trade in London, and who have approached me on this matter, and whose business as English traders is going to be very much affected, I deemed it to be my duty to bring this matter forward in this House, but after the answer of the right honourable Gentleman I do not think it is any use pursuing the subject further.

MR. BRYCE (Aberdeen, S.): Before this House proceeds to take a vote upon this question there are two or three words which I should like to say. I think most of us on this side of the House will entirely agree with the decision at which the Colonial Secretary has arrived with regard to Newfoundland. The temptation in this case to overrule the action of the local Legislature was, no doubt, a very strong one, because it would appear that the contract was not only highly objectionable, but, in some circumstances, it was very improper, and there was evidence that the local Legislature had exceeded its powers. Nevertheless, I think the Colonial Secretary arrived at a right decision when he said that we ought not to give self-government by halves, and that if you once concede self-government to a Colony you ought to allow that Colony to take the result of its own action, and you ought not to bring in the Imperial Government unless some large Imperial interests are at stake. To the reasons stated by him and by other honourable Members who have spoken, I would like to add others. I understand from what has been said by my honourable friend the Member for Southampton, that it will be in the power of a future Legislature to repeal this Act, and, of course, there will be

no moral obligation upon the Colonial Office in the future to interfere with the local Legislature in using any power it may have. My other argument is this, that if any of our self-governing Colonies —even such a small one as Newfoundland—begin to expect the Home Government to deliver them from the consequences of their own improvidence and want of care in the selection of legislators or ministers their case will go from bad to worse. These Colonies must learn that their future is entirely in their own hands. With regard to South Africa, if we were now reviewing the whole policy of the present Government as regards the Transvaal, I should have some observations to make with regard to that policy as a whole, and I should criticise a good deal the conduct of the present Government in its earlier stages, believing that that conduct has had something to do with the unfortunate results which have followed. But all that I have to add on this occasion is to express the satisfaction with which I heard from the right honourable Gentleman the Colonial Secretary that he does not intend to listen to the inducements which come to him from many quarters, and adopt a policy of aggression against the South African Republic; that he intends to adhere strictly to the lines of the Convention of 1884, that he will enforce that Convention clearly and firmly, without interfering in matters where the Convention does not authorise interference with the internal affairs of the Transvaal. I believe that the right honourable Gentleman is acting in a way which will open up a prospect of an early settlement of the difficulty. Of course, we do not agree with the honourable Member for the Ecclesall Division of Sheffield, that this state of things is worse now than it was three or four years ago, but I am bound to say that I agree with him to this extent—that I do not think it is substantially better. I think there is a great deal of mis-government in the Transvaal, and I am sure President Kruger lost a very valuable, and what I may call a golden, opportunity of trying to unite the people of the Transvaal after the events of 1895-96. Reforms would then have been accepted with thankfulness, the position of the country would have been much better, and his

own government would have been
stronger. Unfortunately that opportunity was lost, and it is impossible to
acquit President Kruger from the blame
of losing it, because, in spite of what
has been said to the contrary, no one
can doubt that his opinion is paramount
there, and that if he were to tell his
Conservative friends that they might
safely accept—and I think they might
very safely accept—these reforms, his
Government would accept them. Therefore the fault is to be laid on President
Kruger himself. No doubt President
Kruger has a tenacity which belongs
to an old man who has had a troublesome life, and who wishes to keep things
quiet as long as he lives. Still there is
unrest, and so long as these grievances
last, that unrest will remain. But the
real reason why I feel glad that the
Government appear to have determined
not to listen to those who ask them to
embark on a policy of aggression is, that
the real difficulty in South Africa for
many years past has been the tendency
everywhere to take sides in politics according to racial divisions. Ever since
1826 there has been a tendency on the
part of Englishmen to take one side,
and men of Dutch blood and speech to
take the other, and that has been a
constant trouble in the way of all
Governments which have had to.deal
with South Africa. The latent dissension
between the Dutch and the English
elements has been always present, ready
to burst into flame whenever that feeling
is stimulated by events. It appeared
to have nearly died out until it was revived in 1877. When we annexed the
Transvaal it was revived so much by
that annexation that it very nearly led
to a civil war in the Transvaal in 1881,
and that, I suppose, was the principal
reason that the British Cabinet of
that day determined to make
terms with the Transvaal and
give them back the qualified authority which they enjoyed under the Convention of 1881. Between 1881 and
1895 this feeling of animosity between
Dutchmen and Englishmen had again
almost ceased, but unfortunately it was
revived by the events of 1895, and since
then it has been, and is now, a very
powerful factor in South African politics.
I suppose there can be no doubt that
at the present moment the feeling runs
as high in South Africa as it has ever

run before, but, fortunately, in Cape
Colony there is no disloyalty towards
Her Majesty or the British. The Dutchmen are just as loyal to the British connection as the Englishmen. At the same
time, it is extremely desirable that the
home Government and the Cape Government should avoid any new cause for
disquiet or hostility which would arouse
racial passions in South Africa, and set
Englishmen and Dutchmen against one
another, and we know that to enter
upon a policy of aggression against the
Transvaal would have this result. For
this reason I am extremely glad that a
policy of patience and quiet is being
adopted by Her Majesty's Government,
and I hope the right honourable Gentleman will persevere in that policy, and
that the result will be that those reforms
will be instituted which are so necessary
for the well-being of the country.

Captain SINCLAIR (Forfar): I
should like to call the attention of
the Committee to the evils resulting
from the importation of strong drink
into semi-civilised countries under
British protection. I will do so briefly,
not by way of complaint against what
has been done by the right honourable
Gentleman, but in.order to urge upon
him the desirability of using his influence with the Government to get them
to do something more than has already
been done. We should administer our
Colonies in such a way as would be for
the best advantage of the natives themselves, and only in a secondary degree
for our own advantage and our own
profit. This question is a very important one from a business point of
view, because these natives are customers of ours. It is amongst them that
we hope to increase the sale of our
merchandise which is exported to these
countries. I know this is a very difficult
question, because what we do is very
often counteracted by what is done by
other nations, and with a Revenue very
largely depending on this source, we are
always confronted with the danger that
if we in any way diminish that revenue
we should be doing so at our own loss
and to the profit of the traders of other
nations. But the fact still stares us in
the face that, in spite of what has been
done, the importation of strong drink

into these Colonies and Protectorates is a trade which is very largely on the increase, and which is doing serious injury to the native population. In Lagos, over £23,000 worth of spirits and rum were imported in 1883, and in 1895 this amount had increased to £38,000, but has now diminished to £32,000. In the Gold Coast there has been a gradual increase in the importation of strong drink generally. The import has increased relatively in a larger degree in British Central Africa. These are, I think, sufficient grounds for considerable apprehension, alarm, and great regret on the part of a considerable body in this country. The evil is very difficult to deal with, because it has been shown by the Papers which have been presented to the House that where there is trade in liquor there is trade in other goods, and if we were to entirely prohibit the trade in liquor we should probably strangle our trade in other goods. Various methods of controlling the drink traffic have been considered, but none of them seem entirely to meet the difficulty. Prohibition might lead to smuggling and illicit manufacture. One must not forget that these native races have their own special brands of strong drinks, but still I cannot help thinking that the present is not an inopportune time to draw the attention of the Committee to this question, because the regulations made under the Brussels Act will come up for revision this year. Both the right honourable Gentleman and the noble Marquess at the head of the Government are agreed that a conference, with a view of getting other European Powers to raise their duties to the same rate as ours, is very desirable in order to prevent the present demoralisation. The other part of the world to which I will direct attention is the New Hebrides. The right honourable Gentleman was good enough to answer a question I put to him the other day on that subject, but there is a very strong feeling on the part of those who are interested in the New Hebrides that the influence of this Government might now be exerted very beneficially to prevent any relaxation of the present restrictions which are placed upon the importation by British traders of spirits into the New Hebrides. Perhaps I may, in one or two words, explain what has

Captain Sinclair

arisen in the last two months. The Federal Council in Australasia has had the matter under consideration, as traders under the British flag taking spirits to the New Hebrides have found that, in consequence of the restrictions placed upon them, they are, in selling these goods to the natives, at a disadvantage with French and German traders. Reports in the newspapers go to show that the Federal Council addressed a communication to the right honourable Gentleman the Secretary for the Colonies, urging the view that if the French and German Governments could not be persuaded to raise their restrictions to the same level as those which are imposed on British traders, it would be necessary that the British restrictions should be levelled down. Unfortunately, a report got into the Australian papers that the right honourable Gentleman had expressed himself as being favourable to the view of the Federal Council, a report which the right honourable Gentleman contradicted the other day in answer to a question put to him. Those who have taken the matter up are still extremely apprehensive lest the Federal Council, or the honourable Gentleman, or both, should be committed to any action in this matter by any expression that has been given, and for that reason I should like to ask the right honourable Gentleman whether it is in his power to give us any further and fresh information on the subject. There are other instances which could be given of this trade in alcohol and strong drink in other parts. In regard to East Africa, I hope it will be possible for the Government to use even stronger and more energetic efforts to obtain joint action on the part of the civilised Powers in regard to the importation of spirits.

THE SECRETARY OF STATE FOR THE COLONIES: I gather that the honourable Gentleman has read the Blue Book published on this subject, which contains a very full account of the matter, and that he has also read the speeches which he himself has repeated again and again in this House. I think, under the circumstances, that a great part of the honourable Gentleman's speech was entirely a work of supererogation. What can we say more than we have said? I have told the honourable Gentleman, and I tell him now, that whatever interest I take in this matter, it is not greater than that which the Government have taken and are taking. They are doing everything they possibly can, and more than that is impossible. The honourable Member has referred to statements which have been made, and with regard to that I think myself it is a disgraceful thing that after the contradiction I gave to the statement which had been made it should now form the subject of a pamphlet which is being passed round the House and in other directions, and which is supposed to be in aid of the temperance cause. Anyone who knows what has passed in this House knows that it is absolutely unfounded. We are most anxious to stop the sale of spirits, and the only difficulty arises from the unwillingness of other Powers to join us in the arrangements we propose.

• CAPTAIN SINCLAIR: As to the right honourable Gentleman's condemnation of the pamphlet he has referred to, I should like to say that I am in no way responsible for it. I am sorry that the right honourable Gentleman does not take the view that I have endeavoured to do him a service in enabling him to again contradict the statement which appeared in the Australian paper.

Motion made, and Question proposed—

"That Item 5, Class 2 (Foreign Office), be reduced by £100."—*(Mr. Joseph Walton.)*

*MR. JOSEPH WALTON (York, W.R., Barnsley): The correspondence respecting the affairs of China, the presentation of which to the House has so long been delayed, makes it necessary to ask the Government for certain information, in order to enable the Committee to understand more clearly what is the present actual situation in China. It is hardly necessary to remind the Committee that the announced policy of the Government at the beginning of the last Session was the upholding of the rights which the Treaty of Tien-tsin conferred upon Great Britain; and the Foreign Secretary declared that there was no sacrifice which the Government were not prepared to make rather than allow those rights to be destroyed. The question is, how far has that announced policy, as revealed by the Blue Book, been successfully pursued? In order to show how far the policy of Her Majesty's Government has failed, it is necessary to recapitulate some of the principal events which have taken place in China during the last 18 months. First, with regard to Germany, when she took possession of Kiao-chau and a limited area of territory around it, Her Majesty's Government very properly sought to obtain from the German Government a satisfactory assurance that British Treaty rights would in no way be interfered with. It was, indeed, startling to learn, however, that instead of adhering to this position, the Government almost immediately afterwards declared spontaneously to Germany that in establishing herself at Wei-hai-Wei, England had no intention of injuring or contesting the rights and interests of Germany in the Province of Shan-tung, or of creating difficulties for her in that Province, and that it was especially understood that England would not construct any railroad communication from Wei-hai-Wei, and the district leased therewith, into the interior of the Province. The right honourable Gentleman the Under Secretary contended in the Debate on China at the opening of the present Session that our trading rights were not affected, inasmuch as Kiao-chau was a free port, which was better than a Treaty port. But I would remind the right honourable Gentleman that, though the port of Kiao-chau is at present a free port, yet it is equally true that Herr von Bülow had distinctly stated in the Reichstag that, whilst he believed that the best way to serve the commercial interests of Germany would be to put Kiao-chau on the footing of a free port, he would not like to pledge himself beforehand, especially to foreign nations, for he believed it was better to hold themselves free to do what they liked, as he believed the English had done and were doing at Hong-Kong. Therefore, whether in the matter of the construction of railways, the acquisition of mining rights, or equal opportunities for trading in Shan-tung, British rights under the Treaty of Tien-tsin have been disregarded, and there is no guarantee whatever that they will not ultimately be destroyed. By annexation Germany is now in a position to extinguish at any moment the rights which Great Britain have hitherto · enjoyed in the great Province of Shantung, with its 37 millions of people. Therefore, I think I have a right to say that though Kiao-chau may now be open as a free port, yet it has been put into the power of Germany, when she thinks fit, to practically extinguish the rights we have hitherto enjoyed in the Province under the Treaty of Tien-tsin. Now, I ask what *quid pro quo* has this country got from Germany in return for the encroachments upon our Treaty rights which Her Majesty's Government have suffered her to make? I know of none; on the contrary, there is the extraordinary declaration to Lord Salisbury made by the German Ambassador on the 11th of May last, that Germany, by her occupation of Kiao-chau and her agreement with China respecting Shantung, has acquired a special position in that Province, which consequently is not unreservedly open to British enterprise; whereas Great Britain, not having occupied any place in the Yang-tsze region, that region is still unreservedly open to German enterprise. Lord Salisbury, no doubt, has said that he is unable to assent to that. As matters, however, stand at present, the contention of the German Ambassador cannot be gainsaid. It is with the greatest satisfaction that I find from the Blue Book that the British and German Governments have come to the conclusion—in September last—that it is desirable to agree about the sphere of influence of the two countries regarding railway construction in China, and to mutually support the interest of either country, the Germans undertaking not to compete in the English sphere, or the English in the German sphere. And I may point out to the Committee that in the arrangement concluded the British sphere of interest and the German sphere of interest in the matter of railway construction is actually defined between the contracting parties. This certainly involves a practical adoption of a "sphere of concessions" policy in place of the policy of upholding unimpaired the rights we enjoy under the Treaty of Tien-tsin, which states that we are to enjoy—

"Free and equal participation in all privileges, immunities, and advantages which may

Mr. Joseph Walton.

have been given, or which may hereafter be given, by the Emperor of China to the nationals or Government of any other nation."

This undoubtedly conferred upon us not only an equal right with other nations to trade, but also an equal right to undertake commercial enterprises throughout the Chinese Empire. The agreement, however, for the construction of the Tien-tsin and Chin-kiang Railway jointly by Germany and England on equal terms and conditions, constitutes a friendly co-operation in favour of which there is much to be said. With regard to Russia, I do not wish to take up the time of the Committee by referring again in detail to the series of diplomatic defeats which Her Majesty's Government have sustained at the hands of the Russian Government. I will deal only with the present situation as created by accomplished facts. Russia is practically in military occupation of the whole of the North of China. The "open-door" has been actually closed; so far the undertaking of commercial enterprises by British capitalists on equal terms and conditions to those obtained by the Russians is conclusively shown by Her Majesty's Government having allowed Russia to impose terms and conditions, in connection with the Niu-chwang Railway Extension loan, of a much less favourable character than those which they themselves obtained for their Manchurian Railway system. I will draw the attention of the Committee to what the Tsung-li-Yamen consider a fair view of the question of terms and conditions for railway concessions. They state in their communication to Sir Claude Macdonald, of the 14th August last, in defending the terms and conditions of the Pekin-Han-kau concession, which confers enormous powers on the concessionaires that—

"In borrowing funds for the construction of a railway, if the lenders of the money or their representatives were not allowed to have anything to do with the concerns of the line (prior to the repayment of the loan with interest) would your Excellency so permit your merchants to commit themselves to such a wild cat undertaking? What you would not permit your own merchants to do you can hardly require the merchants of other nations to undertake."

And yet those are precisely the terms and conditions which Her

Majesty's Government have allowed the Russian Government to impose upon British capitalists who are providing money to construct 250 miles of railway north of the Great Wall to Niu-chwang. They have permitted our merchants to commit themselves to what the Tsung-li-Yamen in their wisdom declared would be "a wild cat undertaking." The fact that the public subscribed £12,000,000 sterling for the Niu-chwang Extension Loan, as against £2,300,000 required, shows that British capitalists are quite prepared to take part in the development of China even on somewhat disadvantageous terms. But the shock which has been given to the confidence of the investing public by the renewed, though fortunately unsuccessful, opposition to the part of Russia to the amended Niu-chwang Loan contract has probably created such a sense of insecurity in the minds of British investors that, unless some clear and definite understanding be come to, as between the various Powers interested in China, as to spheres of concessions, our commercial interests in that country will seriously suffer. By their acquiescence in the demands of Russia Her Majesty's Government have surrendered the principle of equal treatment in commercial enterprises for British traders north of the Great Wall. The Government will no doubt contend that the open door is still open in Manchuria for general trade, but they are bound to admit that Russia has placed herself in a position to absolutely close the open door by annexation, whenever she considers the moment opportune. Not only has Russia been allowed to acquire, however, exclusive and preferential rights in Manchuria, but, as clearly shown in the Blue Book, the Governments of Russia and France are at the back of the Belgian Syndicate which has obtained the concession for the railway from Pekin right down into the heart of our supposed sphere of trade and commercial enterprise in the Yang-tsze Valley at Han-kau. Her Majesty's Government, in their dispatches, recognise the serious danger to British interests that the giving of this concession by the Chinese Government to foreign nations constitutes. The terms and conditions upon which the concession is granted are clearly a contravention of the agreement on the part of the Chinese Government that they

will never alienate any territory in the provinces adjoining the Yang-tsze to any other Power, whether under lease, mortgage, or any other designation. The fact that Russia and France are both interested in this railway is further proved by the steps they have taken to secure large concessions of land at Han-kau, and, further, by the fact that not only has money been found by the Russo-Chinese Bank for the construction of the northern end of the railway from Pekin to Pao-ting, but they have also taken steps to secure a concession for a line from Tai-yuen-fu which will connect with the Pekin and Han-kau line at Shan-tung. It appears, therefore, that Russia has no intention whatever of confining her operations to the portion of China north of the Great Wall, but is making strenuous efforts to place herself in a position, in the not remote future, to dominate the very heart of China, the Yang-tsze Valley. I am convinced that the question of the Pekin and Han-kau concession ought to have been made the Fashoda of China. There seems to be little doubt that Russia has been enormously encouraged in her aggressive action by the series of humiliating surrenders made by Her Majesty's Government, just as France was encouraged by the surrenders made to her prior to the Fashoda incident. Her Majesty's Government should have absolutely declined, on the ground of infringement of their Treaty rights by the Chinese Government, to allow the Pekin and Han-kau railway contract to be ratified, and they ought at the same time to have entered into negotiations with Russia and the other Powers interested, with the view of defining, by friendly arrangement the spheres of concessions to be reserved to the respective countries. I venture to suggest that Her Majesty's Government might, with great advantage to the interests of this country, learn a lesson from the policy so unflinchingly and successfully pursued by Lord Palmerston, who, when Lord Granville had advised a concession being made to France, replied—

"What France may want is either just or not—it is either right or wrong. If it is just and right, it ought, therefore, to be done; and if it is unjust and wrong, it ought. therefore, not to be done; and I never can admit that it can be wise to give way to the unjust pretensions of France. Depend upon it, no good is gained by such concessions; you only whet the appetite, instead of satisfying it. We should betray our weakness and encourage fresh demands."

This applies equally to Russia. Again, in 1841, in commenting upon the policy of Lord Aberdeen, Lord Palmerston said—

"As to our foreign affairs, they go on as usual; we yield to every foreign State and Power all they ask, and then make it our boast that they are all in good humour with us. This is an easy way of making friends, but in the end a somewhat costly one."

I am afraid that to a large extent it may be truly said that history has repeated itself in this respect under the present Tory Administration. I am aware that Her Majesty's Government claimed that they had sought and obtained compensation for the breach of faith on the part of the Chinese Government in the granting of the Pekin and Han-kau Concession over our heads; but I am bound to say that, in my opinion, we ought to regard the concessions obtained not as compensation, but as merely our just and equitable right, apart from all idea of compensation. In any case, valuable though some of the concessions undoubtedly are, they in no sense give adequate compensation for our consenting to leave under the control of foreign Powers an undertaking like the Pekin and Han-kau Railway; which may in the future be fraught with such serious consequences to British interests in the Yang-tsze region. Further, Japan also has acquired a sphere of concessions in China by obtaining an assurance that no territory in the province of Fu-kien shall be alienated to any nation but Japan. Italy likewise is seeking as a naval base and coaling station, Sammun Bay, and will no doubt look to having its hinterland as a sphere of concessions. With regard to the action of France in Southern China—and I must remind the Committee that the densely populated regions of Southern China are of much more value commercially than Northern China—I have more than once drawn the attention of the House to the Agreement of January 1896 between the French Government and the British Government, in which it is provided that

"all commercial and other privileges and advantages conceded in the two Chinese Provinces of Yun-nan and Szu-chan either to

Mr. Joseph Walton.

Great Britain or France shall, as far as rests with them, be extended and rendered common to both Powers and to their nationals and dependents, and they engage to use their influence and good offices with the Chinese Government for this purpose."

The Papers on China presented to the House last Session disclose, however, the fact that the French Government have contravened both the spirit and the letter of this agreement, in opposing our efforts to get a concession for a railway from British Burmah to the Upper Yang-tsze, and in putting pressure upon the Chinese Government to prevent the opening of Nan-ning on the West River. Whilst the Blue Book, just issued, shows a further contravention of that treaty, inasmuch as France has compelled China. not only in regard to the Province of Yun-nan, but also the Provinces of Kwang-si and Kwang-tung, to enter into a similar agreement as to non-alienation, ceding and leasing to that which we have obtained from the Chinese Government in respect of the Yang-tsze Valley. In the course of a Debate last Session Mr. Curzon stated that this country had obtained an agreement precisely similar to that which the French had got; but from the Blue Book, so far as it gives light on the subject, it appears that our Representative has applied for such an undertaking, in writing, only in regard to the Provinces of Yun-nan and Kwang-tung; thus apparently sanctioning the claim of France to preferential rights in the Province of Kwang-si. Perhaps the right honourable Gentleman the Under Secretary will inform the Committee whether this be so or not. But, so far as can be gathered from the Blue Book, the pledge in writing demanded by Her Majesty's Government has not been obtained, the Yamen merely stating verbally that they have no great objection to giving England the same pledge: but that France will ask for a similar pledge in regard to the Yang-tsze. More than once last Session it was stated in the House that the correspondence relating to affairs in Southern China could not be published, because it was still proceeding. But, though I have carefully searched the Blue Book just published, I have not found any dispatches whatever addressed to the French Government with regard to their attempted encroachments upon our Treaty rights in Southern China, and especially in reference to the action they have taken in contravention of the Agreement of January 1896; and I will therefore be glad if the Under Secretary will make a statement to the Committee on the subject, and also say whether a special effort will be made to come to a friendly understanding with France respecting affairs in China generally in connection with the negotiations now proceeding for the settlement of outstanding difficulties between the two countries. A question of the greatest importance to the trading interests of this and other nations is that of the opening of the inland waterways of China, in accordance with the understanding announced in the House last year, namely, that an arrangement had been arrived at, under which the waterways of China were to be opened so that British goods in British ships could be taken to every riverside town and station throughout the Chinese Empire. I gather from the Blue Book that this agreement has not yet by any means been fully carried out; and I should like to have some assurance from the Government that this subject is engaging their earnest attention. I understand that the waterways of China have up to the present been but partially opened, that only the treaty ports can be traded with and the intervening riverside towns and stations are not opened to trade. I shall be glad to know from the Under Secretary whether this is so or not, and whether Her Majesty's Government are determined to insist that the arrangement shall be given effect to in its entirety, with the least possible delay. Her Majesty's Government are to be congratulated on the firm stand which they took, jointly with America, in making and successfully maintaining their protest against France obtaining an exclusive settlement at Shanghai, where the total French tonnage visiting the port in 1896 was only 115,000 tons out of a total of nearly 4 millions, and where she has already an equal right with other nations to use the international settlement for trading purposes. This shows how powerful united action on the part of England and America is; and I trust that a similar line will be taken whenever necessary. To sum up the situation, it is clear that Germany, Russia, Japan, Italy, and France have secured, or are taking steps to secure,

special spheres of interest in China, where they will enjoy preferential, if not exclusive, rights to concessions. Yet England, notwithstanding the fact that she was the pioneer in opening up China to trade, and has waged more than one war, at heavy cost, to keep that market open, and though at present about two-thirds of the whole foreign trade in China is in British hands, has no special sphere of concessions in which she will have any right of priority. I have quoted the express statement of the German Ambassador to show that, in consequence of our non-occupation, in any form, of the Yang-tzse Valley, they regard that region as being unreservedly open to German enterprise; and the fact that Russia, France, and Belgium have secured the Pekin and Han-kau Railway concession on the one hand, and the Americans the Canton and Han-kau concession on the other, shows that we alone among the nations interested in the trade of China have no sphere in which we have any preference in the matter of concessions for railways or for mining enterprises. This condition of affairs, involving, as it necessarily must, the sacrifice of British interests, ought not to be allowed to continue, and I must press the Under Secretary for some definite statement of what Her Majesty's Government really intend to do. I do not overlook the fact that latterly Her Majesty's Government have been more successful in securing railway concessions, but I notice a discrepancy between the statement of the right honourable Gentleman the Under Secretary, in the Debate on the 8th of February, when he gave the mileage for which concessions up to that time had been "granted" to British investors as 2,800 miles, and his statement in reply to a question I subsequently addressed to the right honourable Gentleman, when he referred to the concessions as those to which a preference had been "secured" or "promised" to British enterprise, and I may remark that, in dealing with a bad life like that of the Chinese Government, there is a vital difference between a concession granted and one merely promised. The right honourable Gentleman added that he could not give the particulars of the concessions comprised in the total of 2,800 miles. I am glad that what was then declared to be impossible has since become possible, as a full detailed statement of the various concessions obtained appears in the Blue Book recently issued. Under these circumstances, I hope the right honourable Gentleman will now be prepared to inform the Committee in respect of which concessions comprised in the 2,800 miles agreements have been finally ratified by the Chinese Government. I am glad to observe that included in the list of British railway concessions is the right to extend the Burmah railway system into China as far as the Yang-taze; and I trust that this indicates that Her Majesty's Government no longer consider the construction of the railway a physical impossibility. I have no wish to depreciate the success of the Government in the matter of gaining railway concessions, but I would point out that the Canton to Han-kau line, having been granted to an American syndicate, and the Tien-tsin to Chin-kiang Railway having been secured by the joint efforts of Germany and England; also, the Pekin, Tien-tsin and Shanghai-Kwan line being already constructed, these can hardly be regarded as achievements to be placed to the credit of British diplomacy alone. It is, however, not the less essential, if the future commercial interests of this country in China are to be upheld, that the special sphere in which we are to have a preference in regard to the construction of railways and the working of mines on at any rate equally favourable terms to those enjoyed by the Germans in the Province of Shantung, should be clearly defined and embodied in an agreement with the Chinese Government, and subsequently notified to other Powers. It should be borne in mind that the fact that other Powers can rely upon the British special sphere of concessions remaining open on equal terms to the trade of all nations leaves no ground for objection to our having a sphere commensurate with our trade in China reserved to us in the way I have indicated. In order to facilitate such an arrangement, it seems to me that the proper course would be for Her Majesty's Government to frankly admit the right of Russia to regard that portion of China to the North of the Great Wall as her sphere of concessions, and endeavour to come to an arrangement with her to take

Mr. Joseph Walton.

over the Niu-chwang Extension line contract in exchange for the Pekin to Han-kau concession, and thus obviate any interference in our respective spheres. The policy I have indicated as regards spheres of concessions does not necessarily conflict with the "open-door" theory, and I submit that an agreement ought to be earnestly sought by Her Majesty's Government with the various Powers interested in the trade of China, under which the right to carry on general trade throughout that Empire would be equally enjoyed by all nations.

On the Return of the CHAIRMAN, after the usual interval—

MR. MOON (St. Pancras, N.): It appears to me that in this matter Russia occupies a special position in her sphere of influence in Manchuria, and that we have recognised this special sphere of influence in a very marked manner. We have recognised the special character of it, because we have compelled people of our own nationality, British subjects, to recede from contracts which, but for the special nature of the position which Russia holds, would have been reasonable and proper contracts. I hope that the honourable Gentleman the Secretary to the Foreign Office will be able to give some assurance to the Committee that our sphere of influence in the Yang-taze Valley has also received a similar degree of special recognition. But there are, unfortunately, causes for apprehension that this is not the case, because we have very strong reasons for believing that the Belgian syndicate which obtained the concession for the railway from Pekin to Han-kau is in reality a Franco-Russian syndicate. I believe in the contract that the French Minister is to be made arbitrator in the event of any conflict on this agreement arising between the syndicate and the Chinese authorities, and that the Russo-Chinese Bank is financing it. Prince Uchtomsky, the President of the Russo-Chinese Bank, is an intimate friend of the Tsar's—that is a matter of pretty general knowledge —and he is credited with having the support of the Government. Therefore, the Russo-Chinese Bank can hardly be regarded as a private concern, especially if, as is believed to be the case, the contract contains a clause giving the syndicate a right to call for a mortgage on the line, and to enter into possession if default is made either in the repayment of the principal or interest. I do not think that our position in connection with the railways in the Yang-tsze Valley is equal to that of Russia in Manchuria. The honourable Member for Barnsley has made a suggestion that we should effect an exchange with Russia. Whether that is possible or not, I cannot say; but there are many of us who see that other Powers are endeavouring to acquire and carry out railways in our sphere of influence, and we should be very glad if some arrangement could be come to with Russia upon this very subject.

*Mr. DRAGE (Derby): I rise to give all the support in my power to what we understand to be the policy which the Government is now carrying out in China, which is mainly a case of coming to some understanding with Russia as to the questions at issue between the two countries. I have never believed myself that it was possible for the Peace Conference, which is now about to assemble, to produce any scheme of disarmament which would prove feasible; but it seems to me that it was always possible that out of the Conference we might obtain some scheme of settling our difficulties with Russia in China, or such as are likely to arise in Persia, and in other parts of the world where we are likely to come in conflict. That seems to me a practical method of dealing with the Peace Conference. I should like to point out to the Committee that the present moment is, perhaps, one of the most opportune for arriving at some settlement of the outstanding questions between this country and Russia. We stand in a very favourable position for entering into this Peace Conference. The Russian Army on a peace footing is placed at about 1,000,000 men ; our standing army is not half that number. As regards the Russian Navy, whether we take the country which it has to protect, or the amount of commerce it has to safeguard, it is several times as large as ours; and, after the statement to this House by the right honourable Gentleman the First Lord of the Admiralty, it cannot be said that we do not enter into this

Peace Conference under the most favourable circumstances. But I should like to point out to the Committee that, earnest as the Tsar's desire is for disarmament, it is not always in the power of the Tsar to conduct the foreign policy of the Russian Government. This is no new fact. Twenty years ago, in 1879, Count Andrassy writing to Prince Bismarck, after the Russo-Turkish war, used the following remarkable words—

"I entertain no doubt as to the personal intentions of the Emperor Alexander. I am convinced that he does not wish for war at present, but as the Minister of a neighbouring State I cannot forget that he had no desire for the war just concluded, and that from the beginning he was trying to master the movement which originated in his immediate entourage. I consider it a European necessity to provide in some way against this danger."

Now, what is the entourage of the present Tsar at the moment. It consists of four very remarkable men, all of whom are imbued with Slavophile ideas, and believe that Russia has a great political, social, and religious mission to carry out, and it may be that in the future the Tsar may not be able to control his entourage, autocrat though he be, as he has in the past. A few days after he sent out the Peace Rescript he sent out another most remarkable rescript to the Admiral of the Russian Fleet in the Black Sea, in which he said he rejoiced in the results obtained, because in the strong fleet assembled at Sebastopol he saw a sound guarantee for the further peaceful development of Southern Russia, and expressed the confident hope that the Black Sea Fleet would ever maintain the famous traditions of its predecessors, the heroes of Sinope and the bastions of Sebastopol. Who are the councillors of the Tsar, and what are the views that they have expressed in no unmistakable terms? First and foremost comes Count Mouravieff, who is familiar to this House after the negotiations described in the China Blue Book of last year, and I should like to call attention to some remarks made by him before he was in his present responsible position. They show the policy he favours, although he may not be in a position to carry it out. While a diplomatist at Stockholm he said, in an interview published in a Swedish newspaper—

"Russia is the silent Power, and is growing stronger in geometrical proportion than any other Power. She is able and ready to wait. One must howl with the wolves while one is among them."

This is an interesting observation, if one compares the action of Russia just now all over the world with her peace proposals. He went on to say—

"I am a Slavophile, as all Russians are in their inmost hearts. I believe that Russia has a civilising mission, not only in Asia, but also in Europe. We come to relieve the tired men."

Honourable Members who have read that extremely remarkable story by Mr. Rudyard Kipling, the story of "The Man Who Was," will observe the remarkable coincidence between the views put into the mouth of the Russian agent Dirkovitch, and those which were expressed by the gentleman who now occupies the highest post in the Russian service. But perhaps it is better to pass from Count Mouravieff to another extremely gifted Russian public man, who occupies a position of a different character. I refer to Prince Uchtomsky. My honourable Friend on my left (Mr. Moon) referred to him just now. Prince Uchtomsky is an intimate friend of the Tsar. He was at the head of the last special mission to Pekin; he is also the head of the Russo-Chinese Bank, and the editor of the "Petersburgskiya Viedomosti." Now, the Committee is aware that in Russia newspapers have far more influence and far more latitude on subjects connected with foreign policy than on subjects connected with internal policy, and the influence that Prince Uchtomsky undoubtedly has is directed, as I desire to show the Committee, on very definite lines. Prince Uchtomsky, in words which I quoted in this House last year, has laid down the policy he desires to see carried out in Russia. He desires to see an alliance with Germany against England to destroy her commerce. He also desired the absorption of China under the ægis of her present dynasty, and the last of his remarkable observations was that any opposition on the part of Great Britain would be met by the invasion of India. With regard to this, honourable Members who have read the recent Blue Book will recollect the context in which the invasion of India is there mentioned. There remain, however, two more great and important men, with an equally thorough belief in the mission of Russia in the direction

Mr. Drage.

in which they desired her to advance, but more inclined to peace at the present time—M. de Witte and M. Pobyedonostseff. M. de Witte is the Finance Minister, who has had to cope with some of the most difficult problems, at any rate within the last 20 years, that have fallen to the lot of any Minister. He has had to find money to make the grants to meet railway advances, to meet famine and agricultural depression; he has had to effect the transition to a gold standard, and he has to deal with the demands now made on the Russian Central Government by Poland. Those honourable Members who have read the recent Report of Prince Tmeritinsky are well aware how deep is the discontent of Poland, and how much the Russian Government has to do to cope with it. M. de Witte has been a railway man to start with, and is a railway man still; and he is the author of that network of railways stretching throughout the whole of the Empire, and to him has been attributed the remark that Russia will conquer China by railways. I point this out to the Committee, and I ask the Committee to bear in mind that not only are these extensions of Russian railways in northern Europe, but we have the project of a railway projected from Alexandropol in Transcaucasia to Tabriz in Persia. We have the new railway which has been pushed on from Merv as far as Kushk, in the direction of Herat; and we have the project of a railway through Saistan to Benduabbas on the Persian Gulf. Last of the four great statesmen is M. Pobyedonostseff, who desires to see the orthodox Greek Church supreme in Russia before moving further forward. He has already made his hand felt on the Protestants in Livonia and the Roman Catholics in Poland. It is due to him that our missionaries have been driven from Persia. He has absorbed the Nestorian Church, and will in time absorb the Armenian Church. He is behind the movement against Protestant Finland as much as the military authorities. He disbelieves in liberty and Parliamentary government, which he has called the greatest falsehood of our time. It is he, too, turn to Africa, who desires Russian interference in Abyssinia on religious grounds. Well, the Committee will see what are the points of difference with reference to which we should ask the Government to try and come to an understanding in the Conference which is to take place at the Hague. Sir, I do not think it is always remembered in this country upon how many points at the present time we come in contact with Russia, nor how many guarantees this country has given that are likely to conflict with Russian interests. In the first place, there is the Treaty of 1855 with regard to the integrity of Sweden and Norway; then the Treaty by which we guaranteed Turkey in Asia; then there are treaties with regard to Abyssinia; treaties in a recent Blue Book with regard to the integrity of Persia; agreements with Afghanistan; and, last of all, the agreements we have undertaken with regard to China. It appears to me that in looking at the policy of Her Majesty's Government, which we understand they have undertaken, and which the honourable Baronet the Member for Northumberland has so often pressed upon the Committee, we must take into consideration the points of possible difference in future, and ask the Government whether, even supposing the Peace Conference fails to achieve the object which the Tsar of Russia has in view, it would not be possible on these points to obtain some firm and stated understanding between Russia and this country. One word before I sit down, and one word only, with regard to the policy which we desire to forward in China. Of course, there was a guarantee, by a Resolution of this House last year, with reference to the integrity of China, but it is no longer possible to go back. We must recognise that, and, looking at the future, I cannot help expressing the belief that the only sound policy in China now is the delimitation of our sphere of interest; because I, for one, feel convinced that in that sphere, and in that sphere alone, will be found what is called the "open-door" for all nations. That is a point which some of us pressed on the Government last year. There are three other points, not less important, which I desire again to urge on the Government. First, that we should patrol the Yang-tzse with our gunboats to insure the safety of our shipping; secondly, that we should reorganise the judicial system of the local Yamens, for our commerce

will require trustworthy law courts; and lastly, I believe, in order to secure order and justice in the interior, we shall have to organise the local military forces within our sphere. If I have ventured to detain the Committee on these points, it is because I believe that there is now before us a chance of incalculable value; because, although we are in no sense afraid of Russia—and the more one knows of Russia, the less is one likely to be afraid of her—still, the one great interest of England is peace. I would therefore venture to press upon the Government the desirability of coming to an understanding with Russia on one and all of these points.

*MR. PROVAND (Glasgow, Blackfriars): Mr. Lowther, I think what has fallen from the last speaker is a very useful contribution to this Debate. According to recognised authorities, not only in this House, but outside, until we can arrive at some definite arrangement with Russia, all our trouble in China, and all our anxieties and doubts as to the future of that country, must remain as they are, and fresh difficulties at regular intervals must be created. At the same time, I can hardly see how we can divert the attention of representatives of the Peace Conference from the Tsar's Rescript—the one matter we are called together to discuss—in order to consider our relations with China. Though the replies of every European country to the Tsar's invitation have no doubt been couched in the language of strict diplomatic courtesy, I think there is not much general faith in any practical diminution of the risk of war, or even of a decrease of naval and military armaments. At the same time, I hope some understanding will be arrived at to enable us to conduct the business we have in China, which is entirely commercial, alongside, not only with Russia, but with all other countries, with equal advantage to ourselves, to them, and to China. The last speaker referred to our special sphere in China, but what part of the country have we any right to at all? At the present time there are at least three leading European countries—Russia, Germany, and France —and all have carved out a portion of the country to themselves. They say "We have prior rights in this province for our own people with regard to railways, trade, mines, and every sort of commerce." Against the claims set up by all these countries—claims which, I venture to say, China will not nor ever will be able to dispute—we have nothing but the valley of the Yang-tsze. Of what value is the promise of China to this country? She is prepared to promise anything to any country to keep peace for the day. There is no love of war amongst the Chinese. I have lived amongst the Chinese people, and speak from experience. In dealing with mandarins, there is no doubt whatever that we are under a great disqualification, inasmuch as we cannot bribe anybody. We have no money for the purpose. There is in this country an enormous amount of bribery and corruption. No one has lived in China of any authority—missionary or merchant—who has not expressed himself in the plainest language to that effect. There is no secrecy about it, and there is no attempt to conceal it. Well, Sir, as to the delimitation of our sphere, I think the Government should look to that point as soon as possible. I should like the right honourable Gentleman the Under Secretary to inform the House what is being done to obtain some delimitation of our geographical position in the future. There may hereafter be some variations proposed which are not indicated in the Blue Book. The right honourable Gentleman the Under Secretary of State for Foreign Affairs has spoken of the railway concessions that have been made to us by China. I attach very little importance to them. Apart from a few short lines near the Eastern seaboard, I do not believe more than 10 per cent. of the 2,800 miles of railway has in the early future the least chance of being constructed. For my part, I should be sorry to see the Government find a shilling for any such purpose, and I hope it has no intention of doing so. Germany may find money for railroads, but unless the German Government either find money or guarantee the payment of a dividend, capitalists are not likely to interest themselves in such enterprises. The concessionaires do not expect to make their money out of railway building, but out of the concessions themselves. Therefore, I hope the right honourable

Mr. Provand.

Gentleman will not expect the House to be satisfied when he tells us that concessions have been made for so many hundreds or thousands of miles of railroad in China. Well, Sir, when the China Papers were issued last year, we had to read one of the most humiliating documents ever placed on the Table of this House—it was in reference to the taking of Wei-hai-Wei—and before we read the first three pages of the new Blue Book, just issued, we shall find as humiliating a dispatch as was ever writen by a person in authority in this country. We took Wei-hai-Wei as a counterpoise for Russia taking Port Arthur and Talienwan. They have Talienwan and Port Arthur, with the whole of Russia at its back, soon to be connected by a complete railway system with the extreme east of Russia. What have we got at Wei-hai-Wei? Now the Government have decided to make it a naval base. Well, it would be an advantage to a naval base to be able to obtain coals from Shan-tung, where there are many coal beds; but we have expressly barred ourselves from doing so, because no railway is to be constructed to connect Wei-hai-Wei with the rest of Shan-tung. It is said that it was impossible to make a railway from Wei-hai-Wei to the Hinterland. I should like to know on whose authority that statement was made. We have heard of many impossible railways in different parts of the world, which were, however, all ultimately made. I question if there is any place at all in which a railway cannot be made. Most certainly, hills do not stop engineers from making a railway. All over South America you have many instances where huge mountains have been negotiated by engineers. There is no difficulty about making a railway from Wei-hai-Wei, but we have deliberately shut ourselves out from the trade of the Hinterland, which should have gone to the port of Wei-hai-Wei. In the very first page of the Blue Book the First Lord of the Treasury said it was impossible to make Wei-hai-Wei into a commercial port, and that it would be foolish to try to do so. There is no doubt the Government have done their best to prevent its being made a commercial port. They have shut out railway communication, and whatever goes into Wei-hai-Wei must, therefore, be taken into it by water. A naval base must have a very large stock of coal, and now we must take it over sea. There are ample coal deposits, as I have said, in Shang-tung, and I want to know why it was that the renunciation of our rights there was made. The right honourable Gentleman told us the last time the Chinese question was discussed that no door had been closed. But this door has been closed by themselves. We want to know the reason why that dispatch voluntarily renouncing our rights was written. Germany never asked for anything of the kind, but we calmly said we will not build a railway into the Hinterland, and we will not make Wei-hai-Wei a commercial port. I would like to know what policy the right honourable Gentleman thought he was carrying out when he renounced all those rights which we possessed under the treaty of Tien-tsin. It is impossible to say that that renunciation does not fly in the face of the 54th article of the treaty of Tien-tsin. It was not only that this was given in this way without being asked for by Germany, but we allowed the German Government afterwards to actually dictate the very words in which the Government agreed to make the renunciation. It is the most extraordinary case of the kind in the foreign policy of our country. I believe it is without precedent, and that no Foreign Minister of this country ever did such a thing as to voluntarily renounce the rights we possessed in that place. And yet we cannot get a full and complete explanation for it from our Foreign Office authorities. What reasons they had at the time I expect were merely panic reasons. So far as we know just now, there is only one country we have any difficulty with in regard to China. and that is Russia. There is one thing which should be impressed on the Front Bench, and that is that it is idle for us to make any arrangement with the Tsung-li-Yamen. There is nothing they will not promise to us, and there is nothing they can possibly perform if any other European country interferes. Anything promised us might hereafter conflict with the interests of France, or Russia, or Germany, or even any small Power, and it is perfectly certain that the Chinese Government would be ready at any time to renounce and to promise to agree to any terms these other countries may demand. That has been shown in years past, and it will be shown in the future. The Chinese Government is willing to do it because they cannot help doing it. I am astonished that no one connected with the foreign policy of the country is at the present moment in his place on the Front Benches; but I would ask that some account should be given to-night of what it was that dictated the policy of renouncing our rights in the Shang-tung peninsula. I would also like that the general policy of the Government in China should be clearly announced, because notwithstanding the 400 pages of the Blue Book, we are as much in doubt about it as we were last year.

MR. GIBSON BOWLES (Lynn Regis): The honourable Member who has just sat down has discussed the reason which had actuated Her Majesty's Government in spontaneously making the declaration to Germany that England would not interfere with the German position in Chang-tung. and in Kiao-chau, and that they would not make a railway from Wei-hai-Wei into the interior of the province of Chang-tung. The reason lies on the surface. It was that we were then about to occupy Wei-hai-Wei, and the Foreign Minister naturally foresaw the possibility of an objection being made to that occupation by Germany. And consequently, in order to forestall and stave off Germany he favoured Germany spontaneously with this concession of very enormous value. That is really the history of the transaction. I think that neither the honourable Gentleman nor anybody else who has read the Blue Books and considered the real aspects of the case can have any doubt whatever that that concession was a concession intended to buy off any possible objection by Germany to the British occupation of Wei-hai-Wei.

*MR. PROVAND: It is because of the enormous value of the concession that I fail to understand why the Government voluntarily made it.

MR. GIBSON BOWLES: No doubt it was most enormous. By the 54th article, not the 9th as the honourable Member said, of the treaty of Tien-tsin, it is expressly stipulated that the British Government and British subjects should always have free and equal participation in all privileges and advantages with all other nations in China. We renounced that 54th article by the spontaneous declaration we made to Germany, and consequently, I say, the declaration to Germany involved enormous concessions in the whole of the province of Wei-hai-Wei, and in the whole of the territory occupied by Germany. I think that is undoubtedly the true and the only explanation of that concession. I have painfully toiled through this conflicting Blue Book. A more conflicting one I have never read, for it is full of useless details and astounding mistakes. Mistranslations we expect, of course, from the Foreign Office. But here is simply a farago of nonsense, and some of the most execrable English. But that is a small matter. I have read the Blue Book with some sense of shame. I have seen the British Minister going day after day to the mild diplomatists of the Tsung-li-Yamen—those wretched people who are being pestered by every nation from every quarter of the globe. I have seen him bluffing them—I can scarcely find another word for it—and squeezing them with the most pitiless pressure, menacing them with English Fleets, and threatening them with war the next day. But I was more ashamed to find that Her Majesty's Government have published in this Blue Book documents strictly confidential—confidential communications from the Minister and from the Tsung-li-Yamen—which I cannot conceive were published with the consent of the Chinese Government. I hope the right honourable Gentleman in the course of his reply will tell us that he received the consent of the Chinese Government to their publication. It is unusual for such confidential documents to be published without the assent of the Foreign Government, and if the Chinese Government gave that assent I shall receive the information with the greatest surprise. Well, what is the policy of England in regard to China? It is the integrity and independence of China, and the maintenance of the "open-door" into China itself. I am sorry to see these smiles and to hear these laughs, because it is the declared policy of this House made by a solemn Resolution against which no Member protested. No honourable Member denies that that Resolution was passed unanimously, and therefore it does not lie with any honourable Member to laugh, or any honourable Member to wreathe his face in smiles. If my honourable Friend dissents, then why did he not challenge a division. Sir, that is the policy of England, and I am warranted in saying that England is capable of maintaining that policy now, as she was capable of maintaining it before the annexation of Port Arthur by Russia. It has been declared many times by Ministers that England is stronger and that Russia is weaker since the annexation of Port Arthur by Russia. It has been declared by Ministers in this House and in the other House, not only by an Under Secretary, but by the Chief Arbiter of the Ministry—the Colonial Secretary. He knows, whoever else fails to know, what England can do. He has told us that strategically and commercially England is far stronger to-day than before Russia had got Port Arthur; therefore I say that we have got a policy, and the strength to maintain that policy, which is the integrity and the independence of China, and the maintenance of the "open-door" into China—not, mark you, into Russia, or into Germany, or Italy, or some other country, but into China itself. I come to the modification that has been made in the situation by the introduction of spheres of influence and spheres of interest. We were told by that eminent person who surveys mankind from China to Peru—I need not say I allude to Lord Curzon—on 25th January 1899—

"It seemed to be thought in some quarters that any foreign Power might, by establishing what is called 'a sphere of influence' in China or elsewhere, succeed in introducing its own tariff, and in establishing exclusive commercial control."

That is precisely what Lord Salisbury said in one of his dispatches a year back. But I shall show that Lord Salisbury did not know the real effect of spheres of influence, because Lord Curzon said—

"He was certain, however, that no sphere of influence which stopped short of actual annexation could possibly give to any Government the right to abrogate or curtail Treaty rights possessed by other Powers. Under our Treaty rights with China we en oyed precisely the same right of entry to overy port under the same conditions and the same tariff as any other Power. The Treaty rights of Great Britain rendered the operation of spheres of influence impossible, "and these were rights which every British Government might be relied upon to assert, and which no British Government could afford to see extinguished."

Here there , were loud cheers. Well, that is what we were told by the great authority about spheres of influence. It is now suggested that the policy of the integrity and independence of China and the "open-door" is to be in some way modified by spheres of influence. Well, no doubt, in a sense, spheres of influence might be held not to be inconsistent with "open-door," and if there is to be merely spheres of concession, this might not be inconsistent with the integrity of the country. If these are to be held as spheres of territory, wherein are to be granted railway concessions, which, in my opinion, are almost valueless— if we except the railway from Shanghai to Canton—if there are to be spheres for the construction of railways, which may or may not pay, and probably won't, and spheres of concessions for mines, which probably won't pay either—then I think that they may perfectly well consist with the integrity of China and the "open-door" into China. If, therefore, spheres of concession mean wholly and solely and exclusively spheres of concession, then I don't know that there would be any reason to quarrel with them. But what is the thing in practice? Germany has a sphere of influence. It is Kiao-chau. In this territory she has a complete sovereignty. It is not a question merely of a railway concession or a mining concession; she has a complete sovereignty.

Mr. BRODRICK apparently gave a sign of dissent.

Mr. GIBSON BOWLES: Oh, yes, China has formally renounced sovereignty. Do you doubt that?

Mr. BRODRICK dissented.

Mr. GIBSON BOWLES: You do; then I shall have to quote. Here is Article III. of the Treaty between the German Empire and China respecting the lease of Kiao-chau, on page 70 of the Blue Book—

"In order to avoid the possibility of conflicts, the Imperial Chinese Government will

abstain from exercising rights of sovereignty in the ceded territory during the term of the lease, and leaves the exercise of the same to Germany."

Does the right honourable Gentleman the Under Secretary for Foreign Affairs doubt it now? No, he does not. Sir, that is what has occurred in the sphere of concessions of Germany. Germany has obtained absolute sovereign rights from the Chinese Government, and from England the spontaneous declaration that she will respect the rights of Germany, and that she will not run a railway into the Hinterland. That is a complete renunciation on the part of England in regard to Kiao-chau of the 54th Article of the Treaty of Tien-tsin, because it is a renunciation of the article which provides for equal rights and privileges to England as to any other foreign Power. Take the case of Port Arthur. We have renounced our rights there in connection with the 54th Article of the Treaty of Tien-tsin, and it will be found on page 128 of the Blue Book. Russia has absolutely prohibited the entry of British men-of-war into Port Arthur, and that is a renunciation of the 52nd Article of the Treaty of Tien-tsin, which says that British ships of war coming for no hostile purpose, or being engaged in pursuit of pirates, shall be at liberty to visit all parts of the dominion of China, and shall receive every facility for the purchase of provisions, water, etc. Is that a mere concession for facilitating the building of railways or opening mines? It is far more. Well, take the French sphere of influence. I have been very much struck by the fact that in the whole of this Blue Book, which is very much concerned in French concessions, there is not a single hint given that Her Majesty's Minister at Pekin, or our Government in London, were cognisant of the distinguishing feature of that French concession. First of all, the Chinese Government agreed not to alienate the three provinces in the neighbourhood of Ton-king—the provinces of Konang-tong, of Konang-si, and of Yunnan. But in addition to that we find, on page 48 of the French Yellow Book, published in October last—of which I have taken the precaution to obtain a copy, knowing that I could not rely wholly and exclusively on the British

Blue Book—in that Yellow Book there is a dispatch, in which the Minister describes, in his own words, the concessions that have been made by China to France. Now, in our Blue Books we have a general notion conveyed to us that China has conceded to France a railway from Ton-king to Penang. But we are not told, as in the French Yellow Book, the conditions—the extraordinarily favourable and altogether unusual conditions which accompany that concession. Not only has the Chinese Government given to the French Government the right to make this railway, but they have undertaken to give to the French Government, *pro forma*, all the lands required for the railway and its dependencies. The French Charge d'Affaires says it is the first time this concession has been made by the Chinese Government in any concession. I will read the words of the Chinese concession—

"The right to construct a railway from the frontier of Ton-king to the capital of Yun-nan is conceded to the French Government, or to a French company which it will designate, the Chinese Government having no other charge than to furnish the necessary land for the railroad track and its dependencies. That is the first time that a concession has been given under this form by the Chinese authorities."

I think that is a very remarkable thing. I have heard nothing in our concessions of the land being given—not only for the line, but for all that belongs to the line, the stations, sidings, etc. I do not know, and I do not believe that the English concessions imply any such grant as this, which is a very important one. Furthermore, the Russian sphere of influence is defined, the German sphere of influence is defined, and the French sphere of influence is defined, but who shall define the English sphere of influence? The very words are chosen with the most subtle ambiguity. No one can tell what it means. At one time it speaks of a region, at another time it is a territory. All we know is that it is some part of the earth's surface through which the Yang-tsze flows. It may extend from the North Pole to the South Pole; it may extend for a breadth of a quarter of a mile or for hundreds of miles. But its real extent no human being can know. It is a region, it is a territory, but nothing more. Then, again, having entered

Mr. Gibson Bowles.

into a policy of a suggested sphere of influence, nobody knows what it is, although we know what the foreign spheres of influence are. And in these foreign spheres you are admittedly deprived of your Treaty rights by your voluntary renunciations, although the infinite mind of Lord Curzon had declared that—

"Great Britain had a right to demand compensatory advantages, and to demand that the privileges given to others should not be inconsistent with our Treaty rights."

You find that while your sphere of influence is entirely uncertain, and unaccompanied by certain advantages, the foreign spheres of influence are well defined, and carry with them decided advantages to your detriment. Another point I want to notice is a certain hesitation on the part of Lord Salisbury himself, and a certain doubt as to the effects of the concessions to foreign countries of these so-called spheres of influence. In one of his dispatches he says—but I must not vulgarise his language. He first of all remarks that we are getting the worst of it in the race for concessions, and on page 164 he says—

"It does not seem that the battle of concessions is going well for us, and that the mass of Chinese railways, if they are ever built, will be in foreign hands is a possibility that we must face. That we cannot help."

Now mark—

"One evil of this is, that no orders for materials will come to this country. That we cannot help."

But observe, Lord Salisbury goes on—

"The other evil is, that by differential rates and privileges the managers of the railways may strangle our trade. This we ought to be able to prevent, by pressing that proper provisions for equal treatment be inserted in every concession."

Now mark, that eminent statesman, Lord Curzon, showed us that nothing in the spheres of influence could touch us. Lord Salisbury says—

"Oh, yes! The evil is that by differential privileges the managers of these railways may strangle our trade, and that we ought to be able to prevent it."

How are you going to prevent it? Take the assumption that you have a sphere of influence, which you have not, handed over to France and Germany. In that sphere of influence China chooses to give a concession to make a railway to France or Germany, and, of course, the managers of these railways will put on differential rates on British goods and strangle your trade in your own sphere of influence. Lord Salisbury says you ought to be able to prevent that, but there is no suggestion how you are to be able to prevent it. The railway is a foreign railway, conceded to a foreigner with rights to make his own tariff. With what sort of a face can you go and say that these rates are such as will strangle your trade? When you agree to an exclusive sphere of influence you agree, as in the case of Madagascar, to all its consequences, and consequently you must have also agreed in advance to that strangling of your trade which is one of its necessary concomitants. Now, I have said that we present rather a humiliating spectacle in the attitude we are adopting towards China. Chinn, from the beginning, has been ready to do whatever England wished her. She applied to England for support against those who would dismember her, and use her as a lever against England and English trade. She was most anxious for our support, and perfectly ready to do what we wished, and it is singular that on the only occasion on which we professed ourselves ready to give her assistance, when the French wished to extend their territory at Shanghai, France withdrew her claim, where Great Britain objected. Here is the dispatch dated 29th December 1898—

"Under instructions from the Tsung-li-Yamen the Chinese Minister called here on the 28th inst., and stated that as the French Minister is pressing the Government at Pekin for a settlement of the question of the land proposed to be leased to France at Shanghai, he was to request that the matter might be settled by direct negotiation between England and France, so as not to place the Chinese Government in a difficult position. In reply I have informed him that this suggestion was not one on which I could undertake to act."

Now mark this—

"Further he inquired as to what amount of support in resisting French pressure Her Majesty's Government would give to China. Her Majesty's Government will, I have informed him, support China materially in refusing to give France rights over British owned property."

On that particular occasion Great Britain offered China the support which she had been asking for for months and months, and Great Britain succeeded in averting the evil which China feared, and France, as I have said, withdrew her claim, and I believe it was owing to the action of Great Britain that the French demand fell through. One thing I would say—I am still on the spheres of concession. I think I have shown that if spheres of concession are to mean in practice, which in theory they are supposed to mean, in theory they are supposed to mean, they will amount to little. If they continue to mean what we say they mean— that is special privileges to strangle British trade, and the exclusion of England from equal opportunities, then I say it is a very deadly policy for China and for England. In the meantime, China is being gnawed away. Every beast of the field is taking a bite; not only the bear and the lion, but the jackal and the mongrel terrier are all snapping. At first it was Russia, Germany, and England; now it is Italy and Belgium. To-morrow it may be Holland and Monte Carlo. I confess I view this with great misgiving. I believe that if we are to agree, if we are to stand by while the ports and naval stations of China are thrown away one by one—and we are bound to agree because we cannot now resist, after having set the example and encouraged Germany—but if this course of action is to be continued, there will be very little of the integrity of China left, and there will not be much value in your sphere of influence when you have got it delimitated and marked out, which you have not done yet. These infringements upon China, these violations of her integrity, are perpetrated against the policy of England, and in spite of the fact that England still retains preponderating strength in China and the Chinese Sea. Do let me affirm once again that, certainly during this generation, until the Russian railway is built, and for years afterwards, whoever may be strong in China, Great Britain will be stronger. It matters not that there will be a railway from St. Petersburg to Talienwan and Port Arthur. Railways for transporting large masses of troops with their supplies are not to be compared with fleets, and for every man and gun that Russia could send by railway Great

3 K 2

Britain could send 10. Therefore, both now and for many years Great Britain will remain the strongest of all Powers in China. Nay, even in Pekin, we could put a larger body of troops into it, taking into account our resources, than even Russia herself could. Therefore, we are still masters of the situation in China, and can dictate our own policy. Of course, I admit that the situation is very much altered from what it was. There is no doubt that on that fatal day in January 1898, when the Fleet was ordered away from Port Arthur—I have never been able to get the First Lord of the Admiralty to avow that he did it—on that fatal day we did practically give up, not only the integrity of Manchuria, but the integrity of the whole of China. We were never in a stronger position to negotiate in pursuance of our policy to maintain the integrity of China, but when we sent our force away we practically gave up the whole fight. I confess I look with much misgiving to the future of China, and to our future in that country. I cannot read the Blue Book without seeing that when other countries make aggressions on China, it is not to them we complain, but to poor weak China herself. We visit on China the sins of those who are trying to dismember her. If we have reason to complain of the action of European Powers as to their conduct in China, it is to them we ought to complain, not to the miserable Chinese victims of their aggression. I do hope a better spirit will animate the Government, and that they will carry out the policy they have adopted and avowed—the policy of maintaining the integrity and independence of China, coupled with it, if you like, spheres of influence, so far as they are merely spheres of concession, but no sphere of influence should include the partition of China, or the exclusion of Great Britain from those spheres by the imposition of special regulations which would injuriously affect our trade.

Mr. BECKETT (York, N.R. Whitby): I think that if we compare the aspect of the House now with reference to China with the aspect last year, we will see that more confidence is felt in Her Majesty's Government. I think the sense of alarm which pervaded the House last year has given way to a sense of security. I think anyone who will

Mr. Gibson Bowles.

study the Blue Book just issued, and compare it with the Blue Book last year, will be inclined to agree with me on that point. At the same time, I think we are still somewhat in doubt as to the policy to be pursued by Her Majesty's Government, and a little information would be acceptable on both sides of the House. It may be that the policy of the "open-door" is still their policy, but I venture to say that the most dangerous of all policies in China is the policy of the open mind. That, I hope, is a policy which the Government will repudiate. I think that if we knew exactly what we want, and what is the end of our policy, it would relieve the tension of the present situation. We know what we are not prepared to do. The Under Secretary for Foreign Affairs has stated that the Government refused to guarantee the integrity of the Chinese Empire against any or all of the Powers. With the exception of the honourable Member for Sheffield, I suppose everybody will agree that that is a sound policy, but does the Government realise what that commits them to? It means that there are certain portions of China where other Powers may secure a footing without any protest from us, and having secured a footing, it means they will exercise administrative power there, first of all by interference, then by direct control, and finally the whole government of that particular portion will inevitably pass into their hands. My right honourable Friend said we might spend half an hour in defining spheres of influence. A sphere of influence sooner or later becomes a sphere of interest or concession, and then develops into a protectorate. In any part of Europe, Asia, Africa, or America you always find that is the inevitable result. You cannot resist the march of events. You may say that the integrity of China should be maintained, but what I have pointed out will inevitably happen. It was certain from the day that Germany occupied Kiao-Chau that China would be parcelled out into spheres of influence. We can only maintain our policy of the "open-door" by maintaining the integrity of China, but how are you going to maintain that integrity? The noble Lord the Member for York, speaking with the fullest information, told us that the only means of maintaining the integrity of China was to form an alliance between England, Germany, the United States, and Japan, as against Russia. I do not think that people in this country would be inclined to adopt that policy, even if the other three nations would be prepared to agree to it. Our policy at the present moment is the "open-door" and the equality of opportunity. It may be the best policy from an ideal point of view, but, however, the best is no better than the worst if it cannot be carried out. What effective action can be taken if it is resisted, and if other Powers refuse to keep the "open-door" in their spheres of influence in Manchuria and elsewhere? What are you going to do? Are you going to comp-l them? If not, they will inevitably establish a protectorate, and we will be unable to prevent them from doing what they will. It seems to me rather unfortunate that we should be trying to shut our eyes against facts recognised by all other Powers. My honourable Friend who has just spoken has certainly changed very much from the views he expressed in his speech delivered a month ago. He then entirely repudiated the idea of spheres of influence or concession; now he practically admits that they exist, and he has told us that China is being gnawed away by Russia, Germany, and Italy. Spheres of influence have practically been established in China—we cannot back out of that, and it is folly to be feeding ourselves on a form of words when facts will not fit in. We are running serious risk by clinging to an antiquated form of words, and by discrediting spheres of influence we are certain to lose a valuable opportunity for consolidating our position in the Yang-tsze Valley. That is the object to which we should direct our policy if we wish to get something out of the scramble for China. My right honourable Friend said that the pledges given by the Chinese with regard to the Yang-tsze Valley are of the highest possible value. The pledges may be, but they certainly will not be of any value to us if we repudiate spheres of influence and do nothing to consolidate our position. Other countries, at all events, have recognised the policy of spheres of influence. I saw the other day a quotation from "The Times" with reference to the railways which Germany proposes to build. It said that the

building of those railways would inevitably lead to the occupation of a sphere of interest towards which the whole tendency of German policy in China seems to be now directed. We also know that Italy has recently demanded what practically amounts to a sphere of influence, with the approval of our Government. I have said enough to prove that whatever the Government may say, the policy of spheres of influence has undoubtedly taken a practical hold of other European nations. We may repudiate the idea as much as we will, but I think that policy will remain. My right honourable Friend spoke about the realisation of our aspirations in China. What are our aspirations? He defined them very well indeed. One of our aspirations is to see transport on every river in China, and the country studded with railways. I do not think we can secure that by the policy of the "open-door." It can only be secured through concessions and by the investment of capital in China. You will not attract capital to China without security, and the only possible security that will attract capital is when capitalists know that when pledges are given by the Government they will be maintained. How are you going to maintain the pledges which you give? If you repudiate spheres of influence, those pledges will be of no value, certainly in the East, and unless people believe that an effective force will be employed to maintain the rights given by these pledges, it is no use giving them a local habitation and a name. They must be practical and tangible, and in the sight of all men. That could be done if we establish spheres of influence. On this point it is evident that the Government will be forced to adopt a policy of spheres of influence, and they will be drawn, in spite of themselves, into that policy. There is just one question I would like to ask my right honourable Friend. At the beginning of the Session, I urged him to let the House and the country know whether the reports as to the possibility of an arrangement with Russia were sound and substantial, and whether he could hold out to us any hope of an understanding with Russia, which would enable us to avoid those alarms which certainly of late have exercised the mind of the country very considerably. It was only a short time ago that we seemed to be on the brink of a serious breach with Russia. That would not happen, however, if we had an understanding with Russia. It was said last year by those who urged the Government to adopt a more vigorous line of policy in the Far East, that they were Russophobes. I do not think that at all. Years ago I advocated a friendly understanding with Russia, and everything that has happened since confirms me in that view. But you cannot come to an arrangement with a country by weak concessions on every point. If you want to negotiate with Russia you must negotiate direct with St. Petersburg, but until we have arrived at an understanding with Russia with regard to our policy in the Far East, any other understanding would not rest on a sure foundation, and would be certain to be disturbed by alarms and excursions, very injurious to our trade and to our interest in the Far East. I think last year, as my honourable Friend pointed out, we had a unique opportunity of arriving at an understanding with Russia. It may not occur again, but if we had maintained our ships at Port Arthur, Russia would have been forced into the open, and obliged to show her hand, and having shown her hand we should have known how to have dealt with her. Unfortunately, through an inadvertence, we lost that opportunity. It is true that the Government has made up a good deal of lost ground. The Government stands in a very strong position in the Far East, far too strong to be beaten off by Russia, and the present moment, when the heart of the Tsar is settled on peace, is a great opportunity, and it would be unfortunate if we were to throw it away again. If the Government are well advised, they would put in the forefront of their policy the necessity of coming to a sound and friendly understanding with Russia.

*Sir C. DILKE: There are two questions I wish to put before the right honourable Gentleman replies to the Debate. One is in reference to China and the other another subject also connected with the salary of the Secretary of State. I should like to ask whether I ought to put that other question now or upon another occasion?

Mr. Beckett.

THE CHAIRMAN of WAYS AND MEANS: It will probably be most convenient to continue the discussion which is now going on.

*Sir C. DILKE: The only question I will put, then, is one which concerns the spheres of influence of which we have heard so much in the course of this Debate to-night. My honourable Friend who moved this reduction alluded to the Chinese promise to France not to alienate territory in three provinces of which Yun-nan is one. That matter is one which is left by the Blue Book in a most unsatisfactory position, and the question I wish to put concerns it. It is stated in the Blue Book that the French received from China a pledge with regard to three provinces of which Yun-nan was one, and one given in the same terms as the pledge given to ourselves in regard to the Yang-tsze Valley. The honourable Member for King's Lynn in his speech a few minutes ago, alluded to what the French had obtained by quoting a statement contained in their own Yellow Book. All we have before us in our own Blue Book is the French demand which has been accepted by the Chinese, and which gives them the province of Yun-nan as one of the three. provinces which they state border on the French frontier. This promise was given in the same terms as it was given in the case of the Yangtsze Valley, and that promise has been stated by the Under Secretary to be " of the highest possible value to ourselves." This province of Yun-nan is said to be conterminous with Tonking, but it is also conterminous with British Burmah, along a much longer frontier than that which is connected with Ton-king the French possession. It is within 20 miles of the British station at Bhamo, and within 110 miles of British India proper in Assam. This French demand was granted by the Chinese in the same terms in which the grant was made to us in what we sometimes call rather loosely our Yang-tsze sphere. This French demand was followed by a demand from ourselves with regard to the same province. I shall not go into the point which was raised by my honourable Friend in opening this Debate as to whether the promise to France was a violation of the agreement with ourselves. What has now become of the demand by ourselves that the province of Yun-nan should not be alienated? As far as I can gather, the Chinese having made this promise to the French as regards the district which so greatly concerns British Burmah, we asked for a similar undertaking which would have given us an equally privileged position with the French in this province behind British Burmah. But as far as I can gather from the Chinese Blúe Book the Chinese made the greatest difficulty about giving a promise to us in the same terms as that given to the French. We are not finally told in this Blue Book what comes to us with regard to the province of Yun-nan. There is some talk of a verbal statement which the Chinese are willing to make as to Yun-nan, but there is no written undertaking similar to that with regard to the Yang-tsze Valley, or similar to that given to the French with regard to Yun-nan, and the French claim that this province is within their sphere of influence. The Committee, I think, will feel that this is not a matter which ought to be left in this vague position, for it is one of those questions above all others, from which disputes and difficulties are likely to occur. I want to know whether there has been any negotiation between ourselves and France with regard to anything like a division of our respective spheres of influence in Yun-nan, or whether it is the view of the Government that being mainly on the waters of the Yang-tsze, it is included in our Yang-tsze sphere. If so, I confess that I fail to see why the Government did not make that statement and not ask for a further engagement on the part of China not to alienate this particular province. However that may be, I feel convinced that the matter ought not to be left in this absolutely vague condition. Here is a province bordering on British Burmah to a larger extent than it borders on Ton-king, which is claimed as being in the Yang-tsze sphere, but which, if so, is now affected by the promise given to France which the honourable Member for King's Lynn has read to the House from the French Blue Book, and which gives the concession of a railway. I am sure the matter ought not to stand in the absolutely vague condition in which the Blue Book leaves it, and I trust the Under

Secretary will give us some further explanation.

MR. JAMES LOWTHER (Kent, Thanet): I think it is very desirable before the right honourable Gentleman replies that he should make a note of the various opinions expressed with a view to clearing up the doubts which exist in the minds of some honourable Members upon this subject. Several questions have been specifically addressed to my right honourable Friend with regard to the concessions to the French, and the conditions attached to the various engagements into which China has entered. Now, we have heard a good deal about various rival policies, and we have heard about spheres of influence and spheres of interest, and we have heard one or two references even to that defunct institution the "open-door." It is desirable, I think, to have these terms defined. As regards the "open-door," I confess that I do not like open doors, because you are apt to get your fingers jammed in them under certain conditions. As regards spheres of influence and spheres of interest, I must say that I associate myelf completely with my honourable Friend behind me in thinking that this policy of spheres of influence is a policy which all persons who are authorities on China—with one exception—appear to advocate, and that is a clear delimitation of one section of China over which British influence is to be supreme. I do not mean that we should annex it, or administer it, but at any rate we should ear-mark it so that when the inevitable partition takes place it will naturally be a clearly defined sphere of British influence. The one exception which I allude to is that of my noble and gallant Friend the Member for York, who is now occupied in the preparation of a valuable historical document which, when it appears, will be one of the most marvellous productions of our time. I believe, according to what my noble and gallant Friend is reported to have said in speeches outside this country, that he is prepared to advocate the deliberate assumption by this country of the guardianship of China. I believe my noble and gallant Friend is quite prepared to advocate the officering of the Chinese army, and the commanding of the Chinese fleet by British officers, and

I imagine whenever a ruler of China is relieved of the cares of State and relegated to the more genial functions of tending goats and monkeys, or when any domestic incident occurs in China, my noble Friend will ask in the House of Commons if the British Government are prepared to intervene. That is not a prospect which Members of this Committee will view with great satisfaction, and with which I do not think this country will agree; in fact, I very much doubt whether Her Majesty's Government will be prepared, through my right honourable Friend to-night, to announce that the policy of my noble and gallant Friend the Member for York is their policy. It is believed in some quarters that my noble Friend held some authoritative position as the representative of the Government, and this was the view entertained by the Leader of the Opposition. Now, I do hope that my right honourable Friend will be prepared to assure the Committee that Her Majesty's Government entertain no sympathy whatever with any policy of this kind, and that this country intends solely to devote its attention to securing British interests in that particular sphere in China which we have marked out as peculiarly our own. We have heard a great deal about the Treaty of Tien-tsin, and I am afraid that some Members of Her Majesty's Government have committed themselves to the doctrine that all our rights and commercial privileges under existing treaties were to be adhered to, even when the territory had passed into the hands of other Powers. According to that, we could insist upon the Treaty of Tien-tsin being executed within the limits of Manchuria. Now, do Her Majesty's Government contemplate insisting upon their privileges in the Treaty of Tien-tsin within the limits of Manchuria? Some of the language of Ministers might be capable of that interpretation, but it is an absurdity. As we have seen, Russia has invested an enormous amount of capital in Manchuria, and railway lines have been and are being constructed there with Russian capital and with Russian supervision, and I think we can hardly expect that when Russia has assumed those responsibilities she is going to allow any more interference with her jurisdiction there than we should allow in the Valley of the Nile. At any rate, Russia is, for

Mr. J. Lowther.

all practical purposes, in effective occupation of Manchuria, just as much as we are in the effective occupation of the Valley of the Nile, and any attempt to vamp up obsolete privileges extorted at the cannon's mouth when China was a very different locality than it is now, I think, will only lead to mischief and disaster. Therefore, I hope we shall be assured that Her Majesty's Government realise that any idea of appealing to obsolete Treaties like the Tien-tsin Treaty—which is as obsolete as the Treaty of Tilsit—with regard to territories over which European Powers have deliberately assumed control will not be for a moment considered by them. I do not wish to detain the Committee at this hour, and I merely rise to ask my right honourable Friend where the limit is going to be placed in this race for concessions in China? We have already been told that we have obtained railway concessions, and I for one should be very glad to see railway systems constructed in China, but it is scarcely the right thing for the influence of this country to be thrown into the scale in order to encourage and bribe mandarins with a view to promoting concessions for the purpose of their being exploited on the Stock Exchange. I would especially apply that remark to concessions which extend, either wholly or in part, to the spheres which have been declared already to be within the special province of foreign States. Now, what power in the world have we of guaranteeing the money of those who are foolish enough to invest their capital · in enterprises in Manchuria? Doubtless the Russian Government, until they have got their railways completed and their preparations made, will not take any active part in deterring people from investing capital in Manchuria. But what a prospect in time to come if the British Government are to be called upon to compel the Russian Government to allow persons who have been foolish enough to embark in those enterprises to have their money back! Is that a nice prospect for this country? The Russian Government will be in a position to say that they have given full and due notice that the whole of Northern China from the Great Wall was within her exclusive sphere, and that nobody could say that they had not been fully apprised of that fact before they invested a shilling. Consequently, any person who loses his money in this absurd way which my noble Friend the Member for York practically advises them to embark in, any person who puts his money in such investments, deserves to lose it. I hope that by my right honourable Friend's statement we shall have the mist cleared away from our eyes as to this lingering doubt whether the "open-door" has been taken off its hinges and broken up for firewood or not. If there is any idea that this country is going to interfere hereafter within the spheres of foreign States as to commercial privileges, I think we are embarking in a policy which we cannot too soon repudiate, and I venture to hope that we shall stick to our own sphere of influence in China, and not attempt to interfere with those spheres which have been acquired by others.

MR. KESWICK (Surrey, Epsom): I cannot allow this opportunity to pass without making some remarks upon this subject. The statement made by the French Government I regard as meaning what was entered in the Blue Book, and I do not find that it assumes for one moment to set aside a single provision of the Treaty of Tien-tsin. We have in Shan-tung a Treaty port, and it is not stated that from that port there shall be no railway into Shan-tung, or that there shall be no trading in the country of which Chefoo is the outlet. It has been remarked with regard to this railway which France has obtained into Yun-nan, that for the first time in connection with these concessions the land has been given by China. Allow me to say that of all the concessions with which I am acquainted, the same rule has been made that land will be given by China for the construction of her railways. There is one other point that I think we should very carefully bear in mind in connection with the naval station of Port Arthur. I regard—as I have very little doubt the majority of the Members of this House regard—our withdrawal from that port with great regret. But we did withdraw, and I think the moment the mistake was discovered the best remedy was applied to it: and allow me to say that, acquainted as I am with that part of China, and knowing something of Chinese ports, if those two ports were available for us the one

that I should say our country should choose is Wei-hai-Wei, and not Port Arthur. Wei-hai-Wei occupies a position on the point of a promontory, and as a naval station, and if due care be taken to convert it into a stronghold, we shall be able to defy the fleets of the world. With regard to the sphere of influence or interest in the Yang-tsze Valley, I think that the whole subject comes back to the fact that China is unable to take care of herself. It is no use bolstering up or attempting to maintain a Government which will not be maintained. Its corruption, its weakness, its childishness, and the almost imbecility of its rulers must inevitably lead to those spheres of influence which have been mapped out becoming spheres of annexation. In connection with these spheres of annexation those territories within which we have at present Treaty ports, with which Great Britain has had intercourse since they were opened, and which, through her influence, were acquired, we should endeavour at all hazards to maintain all the privileges which we enjoy at those ports, and see that those privileges shall never be alienated. I do not for a moment imagine that this country is to stand up and maintain, in the face of a united Europe, and dictate and maintain her position in China to the exclusion of other nations. That is not possible. Therefore, what is practical has to be considered, and not what is chimerical and impossible. What is practical, is that in the Yang-tsze Valley and the adjacent country connected with it, including the group of islands and the Hinterland of that district—which is the wealthiest part of the whole of China, and the very garden of the country—we should maintain as our sphere of influence until we meet our own dominion in India. I have seen in to-day's newspapers a telegram that the Belgians want a concession at Han-kau. Now Han-kau is in our sphere of influence on the Yang-tsze, and any concessions granted to any Power when we look forward to what is inevitable—that it will be our territory—will be a thorn in the side of the position we desire. I quite recognise that Belgium ought to have a place there, but that concession should be granted by England, and the right given to Belgium to build upon it; but it should not be given to Belgium, nor should there be any concession whatever, from my point of view, allowed to any foreign nation within that sphere which is exclusively our own. It is to be remembered that when we acquire territory, such as we obtain on the Yang-tsze, that it is not for ourselves alone. We are the only nation which throws open the whole of our territory to the commerce of the world, and that we deny, in taking up such a position in the Yang-tsze, no nation a right, because we give them the same rights which we possess ourselves; but the jurisdiction and the absolute territorial power we should possess, and with that we admit of no interference, and no possible alienation of a single inch of that territory. There are other places in China where we enjoy treaty rights, and we cannot, surely, allow that the treaty rights which we possess shall ever deprive us of the privileges which we at present enjoy there, which are of the greatest possible importance to our trade. And, whilst regarding it as impossible that we can maintain our influence over the whole area of China, still we should regard it as an impossible thing that we should ever be deprived of that priority of position and of influence, and that priority in everything that has been connected with China which we have bought, and bought dearly, with blood and treasure, and we cannot allow that those privileges which we have obtained shall ever go from our hands. There is much that I could say in connection with other matters, but it would be, perhaps, going somewhat beyond what I have the exact data for, because I was not aware that this Debate would take place, and I have come to the House, in a measure, unprepared for it. I thank the House for listening to me so patiently.

*The UNDER SECRETARY OF STATE FOR FOREIGN AFFAIRS (Mr. BRODRICK): My honourable Friend, who has just spoken for the first time, was certainly entitled, in the short time he has taken to give us his views, and I confess that, while I feel sure the cheers which greeted his speech must have assured him that the Committee welcomed his interposition in this Debate, I have welcomed it from another point of view— that, at all events, to use his own words,

Mr. Keswick.

he has addressed the House from the point of view of what is practical and not what is impossible with regard to China. In that respect his speech differed from some of the speeches that preceded it. I have been struck by the extraordinary unanimity which the House appears to present during these Chinese Debates—unanimity in favour of an ultra-forward policy, which does not appear on the surface in any other Debates on Foreign Policy in which the House is engaged. It is specially absent in some cases in which our interposition is even more natural than in China, and which, coinciding as it does with the extreme silence of honourable Gentlemen opposite who usually do not agree with the forward policy, leaves on the Member of the Government who has the honour to reply the task of throwing cold water on many ambitious schemes, and of appearing unsympathetic in many matters on which the House is entirely set. This evening we have had extreme progress suggested. We have had it suggested not merely that we ought to exercise a sphere of influence of our own, equal in the Yang-tsze Valley to many rights described by the honourable Member for King's Lynn as rights of Sovereignty, and equal to those enjoyed by any foreign nation, and to keep the door open in the spheres of interest of others, but that we ought to maintain the independence of China. But I ask the Committee to consider rather more closely what it has been possible to accomplish and what the Government have accomplished. The honourable Member for Barnsley was very much exercised at any other Power getting a share of China at all.

MR. JOSEPH WALTON: I must interrupt the right honourable Gentleman. I distinctly advocated spheres of concessions for all Powers interested in trading with China as regards railway construction and mining enterprises, and the "open-door" in regard to general trade throughout the whole of China by an agreement between the Powers.

*Mr. BRODRICK: But each case in which a foreign nation had obtained any one of these advantages the honourable Gentleman subjected to the severest criticism.

MR. JOSEPH WALTON: What I said was that the terms and conditions on which these concessions had been gained by the various foreign Powers were an infringement of the treaty rights of Tientsin.

*MR. BRODRICK: In other words, they ought not to have been given, and we ought to have protested against them. I was greatly struck, not merely by the honourable Member's arguments, but by the manner in which, by a summary process, he proposed to make adjustments in these concessions already obtained. He objected to the Pekin and Han-kau Railway concession having gone to another Power. We objected also. The honourable Member in a variety of well-chosen periods explained to the Committee the extraordinary weakness which Her Majesty's Government have shown. He maintained that the moment they heard that the Pekin and Han-kau concessions had been given to another Power they ought to have gone to the Yamen and claimed that the concession should be cancelled. He went further; he contended that this country ought to have addressed an ultimatum to France, Russia, and Belgium.

MR. JOSEPH WALTON: I cannot be misrepresented in this way. I said that they ought to have compelled the Chinese Government to respect our treaty rights in regard to the Yangtsze Valley.

*MR. BRODRICK: And in doing so they ought to have forced the Chinese Government to cancel the concession. It is absolutely impossible in all these affairs in China to carry on business in the style which the honourable Member prefers. We, on our side, have had some regard for international amenities, and we have also considered that our first object should be not to show a vehement jealousy, which the honourable Gentleman shows, of other Powers, but to show a studied regard for the commercial and political advantages which they may obtain and which it is necessary we should obtain in the spheres in China to which we are specially addicted. What I cannot understand is why honourable Members assume that all these pledges of the Chinese Government to foreign nations are valid with regard to the spheres they have obtained, and why they should assume that the pledges they have given us with regard to the Yang-tsze Valley are null and void and waste paper. The right honourable Baronet the Member for the Forest of Dean argued that we should clear up the question of the pledge given to the French Government with regard to Yunnan. There are several allusions to it in the Blue Book. I do not see why we should object in any way, or that those who are so anxious for the integrity of China need object in the least, to any pledge being given to any foreign Power that there will be no alienation or concession of any particular province. The fact that the Chinese Government pledged themselves to France not to alienate the Province of Yun-nan, while at the same time they have pledged themselves to us not to alienate any province bordering on the Yang-tsze Valley, cannot stultify that pledge, but only rather fortifies it. But honourable Members made a great point of the fact that in the single case of a particular railway the French Government had received a pledge that there would be given with the railway the land on which to make it. That has been disposed of by the Member for Epsom. He told us that the same condition had been put into other concessions. The provision which affects us most is this, not that in giving a commercial concession it is made easier for one Power to carry it out than for another —although this great number of concessions has been obtained, there is considerable doubt whether they will all be acted on—but what is far more important is that the Yamen has declared that no exclusive concessions have been granted to France. My honourable Friend the Member for King's Lynn said he could not read this Blue Book without a sense of shame, and his shame consisted in what he called our ungenerous dealings with the Yamen. What I want to know is, with whom is it our duty to deal so long as there is an established Government in China? Are we not bound to go to the Yamen, a body of men eminently alive to their own interest, with an uncommon perception of the advantages of China on one side or the other, and a faculty of weighing one Power against another, and, as far as I can see, of playing off one Power against another. We are

bound to go to them. We all know
that in the East you are exposed to
pleasing talk which is not always conducive to action. On 1st January 1898
the President of the Yamen, in welcoming the foreign representatives at a
banquet, expressed the hope, in proposing their health, that all of them would
receive, in the course of the year, every
advantage or privilege they might ask,
a suggestion which it has been pointed
out would have left China very little
jurisdiction in her own dominions at
the end of the year if it had been
realised. But even my honourable Friend
will admit that there is some advantage
in having the Yamen to deal with as a
buffer at all events against Foreign
Powers competing in China at the
present moment. What my honourable
Friend asked was that we should go
direct and attack the European Powers
on this subject, and not China, and that
we should show spirit by defending the
integrity of China against all comers.
I noticed some cheers at that statement,
but I do not believe they represent the
deliberate opinion of the House of Commons. I believe this policy of asking
China to concede everything to ourselves
and to refuse everything to everybody
else is an untenable one in the present
condition of affairs. It has been said
that it would be most dangerous for the
Government to appear to preserve an
open mind. I do not believe this Blue
Book, properly considered, indicates that
the Government have faltered in a
single instance. You will not find a
sentence in the Blue Book to show that
we accept the idea of closing a single
port to commerce of the world, including
our own. You will not find a single sentence
in which we recognise the right of any
other Power to interfere exclusively in
the Valley of the Yang-tsze or to place
itself in a position in which they can
interfere with our trade. It is true
that, by the old treaties with China,
whose inland ports are open to the navigation of steamers as well as boats,
trade can only be through the treaty
ports. I hope some day the Chinese
may be wise enough to see the desirability of enabling us to distribute goods
as well as to bring them in, but at
present that has not been done. But
we have succeeded in getting all the
treaty ports named last year open. All
that was then asked for has been carried

Mr. Brodrick.

out, with the single exception of
opening Talienwan as a treaty port.
Nan-ning has been opened on the West
River, an object upon which British
diplomacy has been long engaged. An
undertaking with regard to the Yang-
tsze has been given, and has been acted
upon. A demand we had not even then
put forward with regard to Hong Kong
has been conceded, and our protection
there is assured. And Wei-hai-Wei has
been taken in the north. All these are
solid advantages. When we are asked
to compare what we have obtained with
what other nations have obtained, I
venture to repeat what I said on the
second night of the Session, that there
is not a nation in the world which, standing in our place, would not be satisfied
with what has been achieved in the last
year on our behalf. When concessions
are weighed, I think there is considerable force in the statement made in the
course of the Debate that of the 2,800
miles of railway for which concessions
have been granted it is doubtful whether
more than 10 per cent. will be made. I
do not give that as my opinion, but
there is every reason to believe that
what we are waiting for in China now is
not concessions, but concessionaires—
not merely men who have gone there to
get concessions which they can sell to
the public, but men who have got money
at their back to enable them to carry
them out. My predecessor, Lord
Curzon, recently referred to the unequalled field, as he believed, presented by railways in India for capital.
At this moment we have not got the
evidence as regards a single line of railway, except that to the north, as to the
possible traffic, or even the possible expenditure. Of the majority of railway
concessions which have been applied for
by foreign nations as much as by our
own people, the concessions have been obtained even before the surveys have been
carried out. I gather from that this fact
—that when we are attacked for not
having secured all the concessions that
might be demanded, I think we may be
perfectly certain that in connection with
concessions in China British capitalists
will not have the slightest difficulty in
finding persons ready to take their
money. After all, what we have at
heart is not that these lines of railway
should be laid by British capital, but
that they should be open to the com-

merce of all nations. We must not regard these questions from a narrow standpoint; we must look at the broad facts of what has been achieved during the past year. But let the Committee understand that we are not prepared to proceed with our eyes shut in regard to these concessions and other questions. My honourable Friend the Member for Derby asked that we should not forget the organisation of the military and naval forces of the Chinese Empire. That has been a strong point also in the speeches of my noble Friend the Member for York, whose views, I have been asked to assure the Committee, have not obtained the support of the Government. The noble Lord represents himself. I believe he also represents a certain number of commercial individuals who were interested in his expedition; but from first to last the noble Lord has told the public, what must have been evident to all, that he in no sense represented the views of the Government. But I cannot help feeling that we ought to be very careful in listening to the extreme views which have been expressed to-night, such as that we should undertake the reorganisation of the Chinese army and navy, for the end of all these steps—the end, indeed, which those who advocate them have in view—would be that which we have no intention of undertaking, namely, the taking upon ourselves of the whole responsibility of the Government of the Chinese Empire. The progress we have achieved during the past year can only be appreciated by looking back upon the past history of China. I doubt whether, if we go back for 50 years, we will find so great a change made on paper as that which has been in fact made during the last 12 months towards the opening up of China. In that we have obtained our share. We have been asked to-night to define our position in regard to Russia. The Blue Book before the Committee does not contain any allusion to the particular point of the railway in Manchuria in which Russia is interested. We have been obliged to exclude it because the negotiations with Russia in regard to it are not absolutely completed, and until we are able to put our case before the House necessarily we must stand condemned. But when we are in a position to tell our story we shall be able to show that we have thoroughly safeguarded our interests; that we are thoroughly aware of the importance to our trade of keeping open the north of China; and also that we are impressed with the extreme desirability of coming to an understanding with the Russian Government. We are not without hope that such an understanding may be come to. There is, so far, a perfectly conciliatory and friendly disposition on both sides; and I think the House will be prepared to leave the matter there, seeing that, as the negotiations are still proceeding, it is absolutely impossible to say more without trenching in some degree upon the reticence imposed upon us. Our desire is at the earliest possible moment to lay Papers before the House to show what has been accomplished in this matter. But, in the meantime, we stand by the policy we have proclaimed in regard to China. We stand by the necessity for safeguarding to the utmost of our power the particular sphere in which we are interested—I do not call it a sphere of interest, but the particular part to which our trade mainly goes. We also, in all our operations, desire to preserve freedom of trade, freedom of commerce, for the products of other nations as well as for our own, which we believe to be the best policy for China, as well as being the policy upon which our own fiscal system is based. But when we are asked to lay down a hard and fast rule as to what we must have ourselves, and as to the limits we must lay down in respect to other nations, we are obliged to stand back. It is impossible for us to map out China according to our own desires; and we cannot lay down a law to the whole world in regard to it. But, so far as our own interests are concerned, we propose to continue the course we have taken in the past year—a course which, so far as we can see, will prove to be advantageous to China, and which will certainly secure, with due regard to the rights of other nations, a considerable and proper share of benefits to the British nation, and which, in the minds of those who are best qualified to judge —those whose interests in China are the largest—entitle the Government to their gratitude and their confidence.

SIR E. GREY (Northumberland, Berwick): The right honourable Gentleman at the opening of his speech complained that there had been a general consensus of opinion in the House in favour of an ultra-forward policy, and he selected as an instance in proof of that contention the speech of my honourable Friend the Member for Barnsley. I think my honourable Friend's criticisms were perfectly legitimate, as appeared in the explanation he made when the right honourable Gentleman the Under Secretary was speaking. What he was doing was to examine the policy of the Government, judged by its results, and to see whether or not that policy had admitted of any infractions of the Treaty of Tien-tsin. The upholding of the Treaty of Tien-tsin, Lord Salisbury told us last year, was the test of the policy of the Government. I think the best way to test that is not to push forward uninvited an ultra-forward policy, but to apply to that policy exactly that test which it had been asked should be applied to it. I think if there has been an ultra-forward policy, I should say it was to be found in the speeches which have been made on behalf of the Government on such occasions as that of the moving of the resolution last year by the honourable Member for Sheffield, when we were told that the first point in the policy of the Government was the maintenance of the independence and integrity of China. I do not know whether those words are still adhered to, but if so, they are construed in a different sense to that of a year ago. I think the true genesis of the ultra-forward policy is to be found in those speeches much more than in that of my honourable Friend behind me. It is exceedingly difficult to deal with the Blue Book in Debate, because, although the Blue Book is interesting to us, it does not deal with the large issues of policy involved, but with a succession of miscellaneous incidents— many interesting, some of them important, but which do not take us very much further forward in our judgment as to how matters have been going on in China regarding our policy as a whole. There is a list of concessions, and some of these are valuable, but they do not justify the assurance quoted this evening, and attributed, I believe,

to the Colonial Secretary, that the result of these transactions is to leave England far stronger in the East than she ever was before. If she is stronger, we can only say that strength is a relative strength, and that she is stronger compared with what might have been expected at one time, considering the drift taken. No list of concessions as a whole compensates us for the disturbances of the balance of naval power and the disturbances of territorial ascendancy which have taken place in various parts of China. I suppose we all recognise willingly and gladly that there is a certain brisk tone about Sir Claude Macdonald's diplomacy, the very reading of which has contributed to the interest of the Blue Book; and we recognise also that, in pressing various matters upon Chinese Ministers, he has met with a considerable amount of success. I am sure the Government feel they have been exceedingly well served by him, and I am sure the Committee feel that British interests have been guarded by him with energy and activity. I do not wish to depreciate the value of some of the concessions gained. Take, for instance, some of the railway concessions given to British concessionaires. It is true that some of these railways may either be long in making or never be made at all. But this we are sure of—that when a concession has been given to British capitalists for the making of a railway in any part of China, that railway has, at least, as good a chance of being made as if granted to any other Power; and we may be sure that, when made, on the ground occupied by that railway there will be no differential duties. The general impression produced on me by reading the Blue Book was one of discomfort all round. It is the record of a continued struggle at Pekin of one Power against the concessions given to another, and the discomfort is greatest of all, of course, in the unhappy Chinese Government itself. The Under Secretary said the Chinese Government had a great deal of perception. Yes, I think they have a great deal of perception of the evils to which they are exposed. I wish we could say that their perceptions of the remedies to be applied were equally clear. At present they seem to realise most thoroughly the position in which they are placed. At one part there is a pathetic appeal that Lord Salisbury will cease to press at Pekin and deal with the French direct about some questions in which the two Governments were interested. The Chinese Ministers, in regard to concessions, do not object to grant them simply because they dislike particular concessions, but they are afraid to grant anything because of the demands consequent on the granting of it from other quarters. The real difficulty is not a lack of perception on the part of the Chinese Government, but their weakness. The question we ask is: Is that Government growing weaker or stronger? If it is growing weaker, all these concessions which have been granted, and the very extension of trade, will be apt to lead to further trouble in China. Wherever trade goes, there goes a natural desire on the part of the Government to whom the traders belong that that trade should be protected. Wherever a railway is made, if that railway is interfered with, if it is not allowed fair play in the working, there will at once come demands to the Government to whose subjects the concession was granted that their Government should interfere and protect the interests of their own subjects. The more China is pierced by railways, the more trade is spread, the more important should it become that the Chinese Government should, at any rate, be in a position to keep order in its own territories. We all have an interest in maintaining the strength of China, not merely for resisting outside aggression, but in order that she may prevent those provocations to interference which are certain to arise in the working of the railways and the extension of trade if she is not supreme in her own house. I will pass lightly over some of the concessions. The concession with regard to the opening of river-side towns is, I have no doubt, beneficial, but not so beneficial as we were led to suppose when it was first announced. The last information about it is that it will not be so important a concession because of the regulations which have been made in regard to it. Then take the concession of Nan-ning. That we all welcome; but we are told again here that the area of settlement is to be so narrow, and the likin duties outside the area are likely to be so heavy, that the opening of Nan-ning will not lead to any extension of trade. This question of likin is far more important with regard to the development of trade than the opening of any number of ports. In one part of the Blue Book there is an expression of opinion that it would not be difficult to place the collection of likin in the same hands as the collection of the Customs duties themselves. If that be carried out, if the collection of likin be placed on some respectable basis judged by Western ideas, more would have been done, I believe, to facilitate the progress of trade in China than by the opening of any number of ports or the opening of waterways. Now I come to the question of preferential rates on railways. The right honourable Gentleman opposite asked that we should mention something definite that the Government might have done. I should like to see these preferential rates guarded against on the railways, and the suggestion I would make is, that Lord Salisbury's own suggestion should be carried out. His suggestion is that we ought to be able to provide for proper provisions for equal treatment being inserted in every concession. I should like to know whether provisions against differential treatment have been inserted in concessions such as the Pekin-Han-kau concession. That is a definite question of fact on which we may some time get an answer. Then with regard to the Yang-tsze. I cannot say that the right honourable Gentleman's speech has taken us into a much more definite sphere of thought with regard to the concession in the Yang-tsze. The concession given to Germany in Shan-tung is definiteness itself compared with our concession in the Yang-tsze. We have given them a promise that we will not construct any railway from Wei-hai-Wei to the interior of their sphere of interest, and I think the right honourable Gentleman the First Lord of the Treasury cheered the suggestion that we were still at liberty to construct a railway from any other place. But then why did we give the pledge about Wei-hai-Wei at all? We were told that its very commercial future depended upon having a railway constructed, and I do think that we ought to recognise that the giving of the pledge was a concession, and we ought to expect that there is some mutual recognition of our sphere of interest. As far as our information goes at present, we have a request from the China Association, or a statement made by them, that no doubt explicit communications have been made to other Governments as to our sphere of interest in the Yang-tsze region which safeguard it. We have the statement that such communications really have been made, and we have the statement that the Germans themselves do not at all accept our view with regard to the Yang-tsze. We know that the region is pierced by the Pekin-Han-kau Railway, and we now hear that the Belgians are asking for a concession themselves at Han-kau. All these things increase our doubt as to what is meant by our sphere of interest in the Yang-tsze region. It clearly does not mean that no other railways can be made into it, as is the German view with regard to Shan-tung, and we should like to hear a little more about the Belgian concession at Han-kau. I recognise that in the case of the Italians there were reasons why the Government could not possibly stand aloof, and that their support of Italy may rather have modified than have exaggerated what would have taken place if they had stood aside altogether. We defend the policy of the "open-door," but we do not want the "open-door" to be understood in the sense that everybody is entitled to press for territorial acquisitions in the Yang-tsze region, and before we welcome the support given to the Belgian concession I think we should like to know what its conditions are.* I think it would be interesting to know what has been the result of the struggle about the settlement of Shanghai. That also is in the Yang-tsze region. But I pass from these small points, and I take the larger issues, which we hope will be dealt with in a subsequent Blue Book—the larger issues which can only be settled by direct discussions between the British Government and the other European Governments interested. What we really want to be assured of is that there is some direct understanding between the different European Governments interested. What is that understanding to be upon? What is to be the base of that agreement? The base of that agreement undoubtedly must be the recognition of spheres of interest. We have got so far that it is no good ignoring the fact that

Sir E. Grey.

spheres of interest must be the base of whatever settlement takes place. I do not see why the "open-door" should not go with spheres of interest. There is nothing in this book, there is nothing in the 11 format.on before us, to show that the sphere of influence as at present arranged is through the "open-door." I hope, however, it may be possible to come to some arrangement, and that an agreement may be arrived at which will safeguard us from two dangers. The first is that two Powers should fall out, and the second is that all or any of them may be led on to annex large tracts of country, and, above all, it is surely a thing on which we are most in doubt as to what progress we are making in getting an understanding with the Russian Government. Our last cause of anxiety is as to the extension of the railway to Niu-chwang, and about that we have very little in the Papers before us. We did hear this—that Lord Salisbury proposed to exchange that railway to Niu-chwang for the Pekin and Han-kau Railway. That would have been a legitimate and consistent step to have taken if it were possible, but, as it has not been carried out, I presume that it has not been found possible. Then there occurred a further hitch, about which we are still in the dark, and which we were glad to hear, from the answer given to a question, has now been removed. It must be quite clear that, with Russia especially, if we are to come to an understanding, our negotiations must be with her direct, for it cannot be done at Pekin. On the contrary, we have had a most unpleasant incident displayed in these Papers, which is a deliberate attempt on the part of the Chinese Minister to make trouble between us and the Russian Government, by misrepresenting the words of the Russian representative. That emphasises the necessity for direct negotiations between the British and the Russian Governments. We have consistently advocated that, because we believe them to be not only reasonable, but possible. I do not know whether any such view is held in this country now, to the effect that difference of opinion is so inevitable between ourselves and Russia, that there never can be an understanding between us. But that is not the view which we hold, and it is not the view, which I am glad to hear from the right honourable Gentleman the Under Secretary for War—which we always supposed to be the case —which Her Majesty's Government hold. They hold, as we all hold, that there is room in Asia for both ourselves and Russia, provided there is a reasonable amount of moderation and common sense on either side. And the only obstacle I can conceive as a reason why it should be at all impracticable. to come to an understanding with the Russian Government is that, in the course of these transactions in the Far East there have been instances of inconsistency in Russian policy which may have shaken people's hopes as to how far it was possible to get a binding agreement. Of course, frankness and good faith must be the essential elements of an understanding between the two countries, but we ought not to forget, when we criticise what seem to be the inconsistencies of Russian policy in the Far East, we ought not to forget that, just as here we have two schools—one in favour of a Russian understanding and one against it—so there have been two schools of different political thought in Russia; and that distrust which Russia has displayed to us in the Far East has not arisen in the course of these transactions, but it has its roots in what our declared policy was a few years ago. When a distrust has grown up like that with a past policy it creates in the country a school of politicians who believe that it is only by opposition, outwitting, and circumventing that they can get the way of their country. Suspicions have existed for the last few years, ever since we declared this ancient policy to be the diplomacy, and we have tried to get rid of that distrust, but it does need energy and initiation to overthrow what has been the growth of years, and to show how far the Government has displayed that energy and initiation in this vital policy of the country. The Blue Book told us nothing last year except that a great opportunity had been lost, but I will not labour that point at length. Can anybody believe that if we had departed so far from our policy of past years as to willingly admit the occupation by Russia of a commercial and naval port in Chinese waters; and. further, if we had been also prepared

to admit the extension of a railway from Siberian territory to that port with a considerable amount of political ascendancy in the province through which that railway passed; could anybody, if they had believed that, say that we could not have been able to get an excellent understanding with Russia? But that opportunity has passed. Russia was not prepared, and we were not prepared, to make this concession. The Government, in the autumn, in some of their speeches, claimed credit for having refused to be driven into a war over this question of Port Arthur. But, if they meant to yield, why did they not say so sooner? Instead of doing that, they first put forward a demand about Talienwan, that it should be made an open port. Then Russia, construing that as an attempt on the part of the British Government to forestall her plans in Manchuria—though I am not sure that it was not—Russia resists the British demand, and then the British Government submits or allows the Chinese Government to withdraw its promise under pressure. Then comes the episode of the withdrawal of the ships at Port Arthur, and Russia occupies Port Arthur, and finally there is a belated attempt on the part of Her Majesty's Government to get Russia to forego the advantage of her occupation. Now, that is not the way to take advantage of the opportunity of removing distrust and coming to an understanding; that was not the way to make Russia feel that we were either cordial in support of what we might consider to be her legitimate interests, or that our friendship was worth having. We did not show in the earlier stages either that clearness of view or that strength of purpose which was necessary to promote an understanding with Russia. Now, I welcome most cordially the statement from the right honourable Gentleman that, since the information given us last year, some fresh information is contained in the recent Blue Book, and since that time some progress has been made. We shall welcome that progress, and we most sincerely trust that it will lead to the favourable conclusion which the right honourable Gentleman opposite anticipates. The Peace Conference at Brussels was adduced earlier in the Debate as a reason why this should be a specially favourable moment for an understanding. That Conference, I take it, is to deal purely with international questions. Its conditions will not be such as to permit that two Powers will be able to avail themselves of it, for special understandings, as far as that problem is concerned. It is clear that it is a matter in which all the Powers must be engaged, and I have always felt that, whatever the direct result of that Conference internationally might be, the indirect results may be still greater. The result of the proposal of that Conference has been to make it felt—and we have made no secret of it —that we believe that proposal to be genuine and sincere, and that the motive of that Conference is a real desire for peace. Now, a desire for peace on the part of a great Power is a strong asset on the side of peace, and I hope that this year a more peaceful atmosphere has been introduced into the Councils of Europe by the European Powers which will entirely get rid of this friction that has existed between us and Russia, and, perhaps, between some other Powers as well.

*Mr. JOSEPH WALTON: My object was to have a discussion. I beg leave, with the consent of the Committee, to withdraw my Motion.

Amendment, by leave, withdrawn.

Original Question again proposed—

*Sir C. DILKE: I will now put a Question in relation to the United States and the recent Conference. I believe that by an understanding with both parties it was decided to keep the proceedings secret until the Conference meetings were resumed in August next. That, I understand, was the opinion of the delegates on both sides. But, unfortunately, statements have been made very widely in the United States bearing the complexion of authority with regard to what has passed in that Conference. It has been said with regard to a matter which, at any moment, may become a very dangerous one—I allude to the Alaskan Boundary Question—that it was agreed to refer the matter to arbitration, but that the proposal had broken down upon the stipulation by America that the ultimate arbitrator, in the event of a difference between the two sides. should

Sir E. Grey.

be chosen from Central or South America. I can hardly believe in a matter so dangerous as the Alaskan frontier, that the arbitration would have been allowed to break down upon the mere question whether a referee arbitrator chosen for the event of a difference between the arbitrators selected by the two sides should come from Mexico or from Chili, or some other States of South or Central America, which are well able to provide an impartial referee. I cannot help but think, Sir, from what I have gathered, that matters had not reached such an advanced state, and that if a breakdown occurred it was not after we had reached a point of being completely satisfied with all the conditions which were to be submitted to arbitration. But the Government must be aware that such statements have been made in the United States, which profess to be on very high authority indeed, and if the right honourable Gentleman can reassure us with regard to this matter, I am sure it will be a very wise thing to do.

*Mr. BRODRICK: The right honourable Gentleman has rightly said that there was an agreement among the members of the Commission on both sides that absolute secrecy should be preserved as to the proceedings of the Commission. But, as constantly happens on such occasions, some sort of accounts have crept out, which are more or less authentic, no doubt. With regard to the statement made by the right honourable Baronet, I am sure he will see that it will be extremely undesirable for me to give, either by contradiction or assertion, any partial account of what took place. But so far, I can say at this moment, the accounts which have crept out have not been exact, and must be accepted with considerable reservation. I will say, however, that the one desire and hope of the late Lord Herschell and of the other Commissioners, was that an agreement would be arrived at when the Commission met again.

Sir W. WEDDERBURN (Banffshire): I should like to know if the right honourable Gentleman can give us some information regarding the North Sea Fisheries Conference. I do not wish to make any complaint against

Her Majesty's Government, but I desire to know how the Conference will be constituted, and it is extremely desirable that this matter should be disposed of, so that the Committee can get to work. I should, therefore, like to ask him whether he can tell us when this Conference will really go to business? At the same time, perhaps, he can give the Committee some information with regard to the constitution of this proposed Conference, and what instructions will be given to it. I am aware, of course, that the initiative in this matter comes from the Government of Sweden. I recently had an opportunity of visiting Sweden, and making the acquaintance of the eminent scientific gentleman who initiated this proposal. My point is this: I am aware that the object of the original proposal was a scientific one, but at the same time the ultimate object, as set down by Sweden, was that there should be some international regulations as to fisheries, and what I wish to point out is that if this matter is laid too much on a scientific basis, hope of a business settlement would be delayed. We know that when scientific gentlemen start on a commission their investigations will spread in various directions, and we can hardly expect them to voluntarily come to an end with their investigations. Therefore, what I wish to put to the Foreign Office is that they should put this matter rather in the hands of practical administrators. There are two interests concerned, namely, the practical administrators, and the scientific experts. What I wish is that the matter should be commenced by the appointment of practical administrators for the Conference who would be able to settle something like a practical basis, and they could decide what sort of regulations were practicable. Then a reference might be made to a Committee of scientific experts who could give their opinion as to the best scientific methods to be followed in order to guide the drawing up of these regulations. I would also point out that the present condition of affairs, as has been often stated in this House is very anomalous, and it is extremely desirable that some *modus vivendi* amongst the fishermen should be established as soon as possible, and I take it that if this Conference of practical men is not to meet soon they might find

some temporary and provisional arrangement which would prevent the antagonism now existing between fishermen of different nationalities and between the different classes of fishermen in our own country. We know that there is considerable antagonism between the trawling interest on the one side, and the line fishermen on the other. The object we have in view is not to favour one class of fishermen or another. The two main objects, as I understand it, of this Conference will be to make international regulations which will maintain and increase the supply of fish, and also make such international regulations as will prevent conflict and antagonism either between the fishermen of different nations, or between the different classes of fishermen among our own people. This matter is a very urgent one, for there is a very large population in Scotland, estimated at about 400,000 individuals, more or less dependent upon this industry, and they are extremely anxious that this matter should be settled. I should, therefore, be very glad if the right honourable Gentleman can give us some information as to what is being done, and will assure the Committee that efforts will be made to come to a speedy settlement.

*MR. BRODRICK: The Foreign Office are quite aware of the urgency of this question to which the honourable Baronet called attention in the last Session of Parliament, and the Swedish Government are on the point of issuing invitations to a Conference. We have urged the Swedish Government to hurry on the assembling of the Conference, which will probably meet in the month of May, and delegates will be sent to it by the various Powers concerned. This question will be fully considered by experts and by practical men. Practical considerations will be put forward first, and a reference will be made to a Committee of experts who, we hope, will sit together. The proposal for the programme of the Conference is now before He Majesty's Government.

THE FIRST LORD OF THE TREASURY: I do appeal to the House now to bring this Debate to a close. The Twelve o'clock Rule was not suspended with a view to a very long Debate on the Vote on Account, but in order to enable the Government to bring in the Resolution in Committee of Ways and Means, without which we cannot comply with the law.

Dr. CLARK: I will not take up the time of the House more than a couple of minutes, but I trust that one aspect will not be forgotten, and that is, that British fishermen are prevented from fishing at certain times or from selling their fish in this country, while the foreigners are allowed to fish in our own waters and to come and sell their fish in this country. Either you must abolish the regulations and permit British fishermen to trawl where Swedish and German trawlers are trawling, or you must prevent the landing of this fish by foreign vessels in this country. I do hope that something will be done in this matter by legislation. There are two or three points which we shall require to discuss when the Vote comes on, but I hope something will be done under which our own fishermen on our own coast will be enabled to fish as well as foreign fishermen, and that they will be able to come and sell their fish in our own country, as the foreigners do at present. I also desire very briefly to ask for some further information with regard to a question raised by my honourable Friend the Member for Canterbury with regard to the people who invested money in a foreign railway. The Portuguese Government took charge of the railway from Delagoa Bay to the Transvaal frontier. On pressure being brought to bear by the Portuguese and American Governments, it was agreed that the questions in dispute should be referred to Swiss arbitrators, and that was nine years ago. These gentlemen took evidence up to about three years ago, when they ceased to take evidence, and they sent two or three experts out to Delagoa Bay to view the railway, and estimate the value of some of the property, but towards the end of last year they began to take evidence again. They received evidence from the Transvaal Government, from the Transvaal standpoint, evidence which three or four years ago they refused to receive at all, for they then considered it quite outside their jurisdiction and quite outside the case. They have been again hearing evidence, and in the worst days of the Chancery Court things were not as bad

First Lord of the Treasury.

as that. If this kind of thing is to go on; if these matters are to be considered, and nine years afterwards we are to be told that something is being done in the matter, then the principle of international arbitration receives a deadly blow. After receiving evidence year after year, and sending out experts to get information, they again opened the evidence, and it looks as though it will be another nine or 10 years more before they arrive at any decision. We ask the right honourable Gentleman to-day if, in the interests of international arbitration, he will communicate with the arbitrators on the Delagoa Bay Railway question, with a view to having it settled without further delay. Surely it is time for the British and American Governments to bring pressure to bear upon these Swiss gentlemen, who have taken too long already, and it is time that the British Government—because it is a question in which Britain is just as interested as other countries—should bring some pressure to bear to get these gentlemen to give their decision. The company is practically bankrupt, the bondholders having had no interest for the last 10 years. I do not think we ought to be put off in this evasive fashion as we were by a reply given by the Under Secretary to a Question. We do ask the right honourable Gentleman to say whether the Government are going to allow this state of things to continue, or whether they are going to bring legitimate pressure to bear to see that these gentlemen carry out their duty. I think during the last five or six years four or five Questions have been put by various Members on both sides of the House upon this question, and we are always told that we are to have the decision in the autumn, but now we seem to be as far off as ever we were. I think the Government ought to do something under this condition of things, and not give us the usual official reply that they are making some inquiries about the value of this property.

*MR. BRODRICK: The honourable Member puts to me this Question, but I may say that it is not a matter for which the Government are responsible, and the honourable Member puts the Question as if we had some control over it. If it were in our power we should do so, but, as is perfectly well known, Her

Majesty's Government desire that the matter should be concluded, and that a decision should be come to as quickly as possible. We have, however, no power in the matter, and we have no power in any way either to withdraw the question from arbitration or to bring pressure to bear upon the arbitrators.

Dr. CLARK: Why not?

*Mr. BRODRICK: All that we can do is to wait for their decision. We have made it perfectly clear that the sooner the decision is given the better it will be, and we can go no further. When you refer a matter like that to arbitration, you place it in that way out of your own hands, and we cannot withdraw it now. The other question which the right honourable Gentleman asked me the Government do not propose to deal with, and do not intend to take any steps with regard to the fishery laws, as they exist at present, as it is obvious that the matters alluded to will come on at the Conference. Therefore the Government are not prepared to take any steps pending the sitting of that Conference to make any alteration of the law, but when the Conference has reported, the whole matter will be open for consideration.

The subject then dropped.

Mr. LOUGH (Islington, W.): There is a question with regard to the printing and stationery which I want to put to the right honourable Gentleman. The Secretary to the Treasury has very kindly carried out the promise he gave at the beginning of this Session that he would distribute the "Parliamentary Debates," but that promise has been carried out more in the letter than in the spirit, for it is a very troublesome thing now for the Members who desire to get the "Debates" in consequence of the unsatisfactory arrangements made, which are also, I understand, giving a great deal of trouble at the Paper Office. When the right honourable Gentleman was asked a question on this matter he said the subject was in an experimental stage, and, therefore, he could not make any change until he had had some experi-

ence of how it was working. I understand that some 175 Members of the House have applied for copies of the "Debates" daily, and yet every one of these 175 Members, including some right honourable Gentlemen on the Government Bench, have to fill up their pink paper, which I think is a useless bit of red-tapeism. Why are we not allowed to write out an order at once that these "Debates" may be sent to us direct? I do not think this is a very handsome way of carrying out the promise made by the right honourable Gentleman, even if we admit that the proposal was a considerate one. It is well known now that a very large section of the House want these "Debates," and I believe there are only 130 orders for the whole of the papers. I hope the right honourable Gentleman will be able to give us some assurance of a more satisfactory arrangement, for he has got now some evidence that a good deal of interest is taken in the matter, and I would like to ask if he has been able to make arrangements that those Members who desire to have the "Debates" may be able to fill up an order at once and order them direct.

THE FINANCIAL SECRETARY TO THE TREASURY (Mr. HANBURY, Preston): I have not been able to make a convenient arrangement yet. I agree, to some extent, that the present arrangement is not a satisfactory one. I think it is unsatisfactory, not only as regards signing for the "Debates," but with regard to the great length at which the Debates are printed at the present time. Even from the point of view of expense, if we could get the House to agree that these reports should be printed at a more reasonable length than they are at the present moment——

HONOURABLE MEMBERS: No, no!

Mr. HANBURY: And if we were content with something like the eight or nine volumes we used to have, instead of everybody's speech being printed verbatim—I think it would be much more convenient to the business of the House. If that were done, the expense would be considerably reduced, and it would be quite possible for the Treasury to make arrangement by which the reports would be so short that we should be able to supply them to every Member of the House who might require them. I know a great number of Members who have subscribed who have complained very much of the great length to which the reports run at the present moment. There is a great deal in the reports of what I should call "padding," which I think might very well be avoided, and, if they were condensed, I am quite certain that we should have a very much more satisfactory report, and one which would be much more valuable as a record of the real þusiness of the House if they were cut down a little more, and we went back to the old state of things when the speeches were reported, instead of verbatim, at about two-thirds of their actual length.

HONOURABLE MEMBERS: No, no!

MR. HANBURY: I think that on most subjects that would be a sufficient record, and I believe that the great majority of the House would be quite content if all the speeches—except perhaps their own—were condensed to that extent.

MR. LOUGH: Do I understand, from the reply of the right honourable Gentleman, that we shall be able to give one order for about a month or for some period longer than a day?

MR. HANBURY: I do not want to answer right off, but I do see my way to doing something of that sort, and I shall have to make some such arrangement.

MR. GODDARD (Ipswich): There is one other point with regard to this subject which I think might easily be rectified. Under the present regulation it is absolutely impossible to get the back numbers. I do ask the right honourable Gentleman if he cannot, in some way, by sending a letter to the Vote Office, make arrangements so that we shall be able to get the back numbers of the "Debates."

The subject then dropped.

THE SCOTTISH FISHERY BOARD
CRUISER "BRENDA."

*MR. WEIR: I sincerely trust that the Lord Advocate will reply to the question

Mr. Hanbury.

I am about to put to him. My honourable Friend the Member for Banffshire did not touch upon this question. There are two points I wish to impress upon the Lord Advocate. One is, that the new fishery cruiser, which was wrecked a short time ago, has not been replaced by another boat, and, up to the present, no substitute has been found to perform her duties. I understand that it will be five or six weeks, or probably longer, before the "Brenda" is ready for sea. What I want to ask the Lord Advocate to do is to press upon the Secretary for Scotland or upon the Admiralty the importance of having another cruiser to watch the trawlers on the North-West Coast of Scotland. The other point refers to the Scottish Office Vote, in which a sum of £200 is taken from the Congested Districts Board Fund, to pay an inspector engaged by the Scottish Office. Now, the money set aside for the Congested Districts Board is for the purpose of relieving certain districts, and not to pay the salaries of gentlemen in the Scottish Office. I hope the Lord Advocate will be able to arrange that this £200 will be utilised for the benefit of the people in the congested districts, and not given to this inspector, who is already receiving £420 per annum. I do not know whether he is to have that £200 in addition to his salary paid by the Scottish Office. I do hope the Lord Advocate will be able to give a satisfactory reply to these questions, as I have no desire at this late hour to put the House to the necessity of going to a Division.

THE LORD ADVOCATE (Mr. A. GRAHAM MURRAY, Buteshire): I can reply to the honourable Member best by referring him to the answers which I gave to the two questions put by him within the last two weeks, which really answer what he asks for. I can only practically repeat what I said in answer to those questions now. As regards the "Brenda," which has been temporarily withdrawn from the duty of protecting the North Sea Fisheries, she will be ready for sea again in four or five weeks. The honourable Member is quite well aware that there are not other vessels—though the Admiralty have many vessels—available for mere police service, which is not a service which ought to be thrown upon the Admiralty.

As the honourable Member is aware, when this extra sum for sea policing was given, it was arranged that the policing should be done by the Scotch Office directly, and not by the Admiralty. I think it is scarcely reasonable to put upon the Admiralty any policing duties whilst this ship is being repaired. I can only hope that it will not be found that the temporary absence of this vessel has caused any material inconvenience. With regard to the salary of the official alluded to, there seems to be some cross-purposes, but, if there has been a mistake, I shall be glad to confer with the honourable Member privately about it. As to the duties, it is perfectly right and proper that work of this sort should be done, and it is absolutely necessary that the Govern-

ment should have an officer to see that the work is properly carried out.

MR. LEWIS (Flint Boroughs): I wish to draw attention very briefly to a case which has arisen in my own constituency of a child whose parents had asked that he might be withdrawn from denominational instruction in the Flint National School. The rector, who is correspondent and manager of the Flint school, wrote in reply—

THE FIRST LORD OF THE TREASURY: I beg to move—

"That the original Question be now put."

Question put—

"That the Original Question be now put."

The Committee divided:—Ayes 136; Noes 33.—(Division List No. 55.)

AYES.

Arnold, Alfred
Atkinson, Rt. Hon. John
Bagot, Capt.Josceline FitzRoy
Balfour, Rt. Hn. A. J. (Manc'r)
Balfour,RtHn(;erldW.(Leeds)
Banbury, Frederick George
Barton, Dunbar Plunket
Bathurst, Hn. Allen Benjamin
Beach,Rt.Hn.SirM.H.(Bristol)
Beckett, Ernest William
Bemrose, Sir Henry Howe
Bentinck, Lord Henry C.
Bethell, Commander
Bhownaggree, Sir M. M.
Bill, Charles
Bond, Edward
Bowles, Capt.H.F. (Middlesex)
Brodrick, Rt. Hon. St. John
Butcher, John George
Cavendish,V. C.W. (Derbvsh.)
Cecil, Evelyn (Hertford, East)
Cecil, Lord Hugh (Greenwich)
Chaloner, Captain R. G. W.
Chamberlain, Rt.Hn.J. (Birm.)
Chamberlain,J.Austen(Worc'r)
Chaplin, Rt. Hon. Henry
Charrington, Spencer
Cochrane, Hn. Thos. H. A. E.
Coghill, Douglas Harry
Collings, Rt. Hon. Jesse
Colomb, Sir John Chas. Ready
Compton, Lord Alwyne
Corbett, A. Cameron (Glasgow)
Cranborne, Viscount
Cubitt, Hon. Henry
Curzon, Viscount
Dalrymple, Sir Charles
Davenport, W. Bromley-
Denny, Colonel
Dorington, Sir John Edward
Douglas, Rt. Hon. A. Akers-
Duncombe, Hon. Hubert V.
Elliot, Hn. A Ralph Douglas
Finlay, Sir Robert Bannatyne
Fisher, William Hayes
Folkestone, Viscount
Foster, Harry S. (Suffolk)

Gedge, Sydney
Godson,Sir Augustus Frederick
Goldsworthy, Major-General
Gordon, Hon. John Edward
Gorst, Rt. Hn. Sir John Eldon
Goulding, Edward Alfred
Gray, Ernest (West Ham)
Green, WalfordD.(Wednesbury)
Gretton, John
Greville, Hon. Ronald
Gull, Sir Cameron
Hamilton, Rt.Hn. Lord George
Hanbury, Rt. Hn. Robert Wm.
Hardy, Laurence
Hare, Thomas Leigh
Heaton, John Henniker
Helder, Augustus
Henderson, Alexander
Hoare, Samuel (Norwich)
Jebb, Richard Claverhouse
Kemp, George
Kenyon, James
Lafone, Alfred
Lea, Sir Thos. (Londonderry)
Lecky, Rt. Hn. William E. H.
Leigh-Bennett, Henry Currie
Lockwood, Lieut.-Col. A. R.
Long, Rt. Hn. Walter (L'pool)
Lopes, Henry Yarde Buller
Lowles, John
Loyd, Archie Kirkman
Lyttelton, Hon. Alfred
Macartney, W. G. Ellison
Macdona, John Cumming
Malcolm, Ian
Massey-Mainwaring, Hn.W.F.
Meysey-Thompson, Sir H. M.
Middlemore,John Throgmorton
Mildmay, Francis Bingham
More, Robt. Jasper (Shropsh.)
Morrell, George Herbert
Morton, Arthur H. A.(Deptf'd)
Muntz, Philip A.
Murray,RtHnA.Graham(Bute)
Myers, William Henry
Nicholson, William Graham
Nicol, Donald Ninian

Northcote, Hn. Sir H. Stafford
Pease, Herbert Pike (Drlngtn.)
Penn, John
Pierpoint, Robert
Pilkington, Richard
Pollock, Harry Frederick
Powell, Sir Francis Sharp
Pryce-Jones, Lt.-Col. Edward
Purvis, Robert
Rasch, Major Frederic Carne
Ritchie, Rt.Hn. Chas.Thomson
Robinson, Brooke
Royds, Clement Molyneux
Russell, T. W. (Tyrone)
Ryder, John Herbert Dudley
Sassoon, Sir Edward Albert
Scott, Sir S. (Marylebone, W.)
Seton-Karr, Henry
Sharpe, William Edward T.
Sidebottom, Wm. (Derbyshire)
Simeon, Sir Barrington
Smith, Abel H. (Christchurch)
Smith, Hn. W. F. D. (Strand)
Stanley, Lord (Lancs.)
Stock, James Henry
Strauss, Arthur
Strutt, Hon. Charles Hedley
Talbot, Lord E. (Chichester)
Thornton, Percy M.
Tollemache, Henry James
Valentia, Viscount
Webster, R. G. (St. Pancras)
Webster, Sir R. E. (I. of W.)
Welby, Lieut.-Col. A. C. E.
Wentworth, Bruce C. Vernon-
Williams,JosephPowell(Birm.)
Willox, Sir John Archibald
Wilson, John (Falkirk)
Wodehouse,RtHn.E.R.(Bath)
Wylie, Alexander
Wyndham-Quin, Major W. H.
Wyvill, Marmaduke D'Arcy

TELLERS FOR THE AYES—
  Sir William Walrond and
  Mr. Anstruther.

NOES.

Allen,Wm.(Newc.underLyme)
Ashton, Thomas Gair
Billson, Alfred
Caldwell, James
Clark, Dr. G. B. (Caithness-sh)
Colville, John
Douglas, Charles M. (Lana·k)
Ellis,Thos.Edw.(Merionethsh.)
Goddard, Daniel Ford
Grey, Sir Edward (Berwick)
Gurdon, Sir William Brampton
Hayne, Rt. Hn. Charles Seale-·
Horniman, Frederick John

Jones, Wm. (Carnarvonshire)
Lambert. George
Lough, Thomas
Macaleese, Daniel
Morton, Edw.J.C.(Devonport)
O'Brien, Patrick (Kilkenny)
Pearson, Sir Weetman D.
Provand, Andrew Dryburgh
Richardson, J. (Durham)
Roberts, John Bryn (Eifion)
Roberts, John H. (Denbighs.)
Samuel, J. (Stockton-on-Tees)
Shaw, Chas. Edw. (Stafford)

Sullivan, Donal (Westmeath)
Trevelyan, Charles Philips
Ure, Alexander
Walton, Joseph (Barnsley)
Weir, James Galloway
Williams,John Carvell(Notts.)
Wilson, Jos. H. (Middlesbro')

TELLERS FOR THE NOES—
Mr. Herbert Lewis and Mr.
Lloyd-George.

Original Question put.

The Committee divided:—Ayes 136; Noes 32.—(Division List No. 56.)

AYES.

Arnold, Alfred
Atkinson, Rt. Hon. Jchn
Bagot, Capt.Josceline FitzRoy
Balfour, Rt Hn. A. J. (Manc'r)
Balfour,RtHnGeraldW.(Leeds)
Banbury, Frederick George
Barton, Dunbar Plunket
Bathurst, Hn. Allen Benjamin
Beach,Rt.Hn.SirM H.(Bristol)
Beckett, Ernest William
Bemrose, Sir Henry Howe
Bentinck. Lord Henry C.
Bethell, Commander
Bhownaggree, Sir M. M.
Bill, Charles
Bond, Edward
Bowles, Capt.H F. (Middlesex)
Brodrick, Rt. Hon. St. John
Butcher, John George
Cavendish,V. C.W. (Derbysh.)
Cecil, Evelyn (Hertford, East)
Cecil, Lord Hugh (Greenwich)
Chaloner, Captain R. G. W.
Chamberlain, Rt.Hn.J. (Birm.)
Chamberlain,J.Austen(Worc'r)
Chaplin, Rt. Hon. Henry
Charrington, Spencer
Cochrane, Hn. Thos. H. A. E.
Coghill, Douglas Harry
Collings, Rt. Hon. Jesse
Colomb, Sir John Chas. Ready
Compton, Lord Alwyne
Corbett, A. Cameron (Glasgow)
Cranborne, Viscount
Cubitt, Hon. Henry
Curzon, Viscount
Dalrymple, Sir Charles
Davenport, W. Bromley-
Denny, Colonel
Dorington, Sir John Edward
Douglas. Rt. Hon. A. Akers-
Duncombe, Hon. Hubert V.
Elliot, Hn. A. Ralph Douglas
Finlay, Sir Robert Bannatyne
Fisher, William Hayes
Folkestone, Viscount
Foster, Harry S. (Suffolk)

Gedge, Sydney
Godson,Sir Augustus Frederick
Goldsworthy, Major-General
Gordon, Hon. John Edward
Gorst, Rt. Hn. Sir John Eldon
Goulding, Edward Alfred
Gray, Ernest (West Ham)
Green,WalfordD.(Wednesbury)
Gretton, John
Greville, Hon. Ronald
Gull, Sir Cameron
Hamilton, Rt.Hn. Lord George
Hanbury, Rt. Hn. Robert Wm.
Hardy, Laurence
Hare, Thomas Leigh
Heaton, John Henniker
Helder, Augustus
Henderson, Alexander
Hoare, Samuel (Norwich)
Jebb, Richard Claverhouse
Kemp, George
Kenyon, James
Lafone, Alfred
Lea, Sir Thos. (Londonderry)
Lecky, Rt. Hn. William E. H.
Leigh-Bennett, Henry Currie
Lockwood, Lieut.-Col. A. R.
Long, Rt. Hn. Walter (L'pool)
Lopes, Henry Yarde Buller
Lowles, John
Loyd, Archie Kirkman
Lyttelton. Hon. Alfred
Macartney, W. G. Ellison
Macdona, John Cumming
Malcolm, Ian
Massey-Mainwaring, Hn.W.F.
Meysey-Thompson, Sir H. M.
Middlemore,John Throgmorton
Mildmay, Francis Bingham
More, Robt. Jasper (Shropsh.)
Morrell, George Herbert
Morton, Arthur H. A.(Deptf'd)
Muntz, Philip A.
Murray,RtHnA.Graham(Bute)
Myers, William Henry
Nicholson, William Graham
Nicol, Donald Ninian

Northcote, Hn. Sir H. Stafford
Pease, Herbert Pike (Drlngtn.)
Penn, John
Pierpoint, Robert
Pilkington, Richard
Pollock, Harry Frederick
Powell, Sir Francis Sharp
Pryce-Jones, Lt.-Col. Edward
Purvis, Robert
Rasch, Major Frederic Carne
Ritchie, Rt.Hn. Chas.Thomson
Robinson, Brooke
Royds, Clement Molyneux
Russell, T. W. (Tyrone)
Ryder, John Herbert Dudley
Sassoon, Sir Edward Albert
Scott, Sir S. (Marylebone, W.)
Seton-Karr, Henry
Sharpe, William Edward T.
Sidebottom, Wm. (Derbyshire)
Simeon, Sir Barrington
Smith, Abel H. (Christchurch)
Smith, Hn. W. F. D. (Strand)
Stanley, Lord (Lancs.)
Stock, James Henry
Strauss, Arthur
Strutt, Hon. Charles Hedley
Talbot, Lord E. (Chichester)
Thornton, Percy M.
Tollemache, Henry James
Valentia, Viscount
Webster, R. G. (St. Pancras)
Webster, Sir R. E. (I. of W.)
Welby, Lieut.-Col. A. C. E.
Wentworth, Bruce C. Vernon-
Williams,JosephPowell(Birm.)
Willox, Sir John Archibald
Wilson, John (Falkirk)
Wodehouse,RtHn.E.R.(Bath)
Wylie, Alexander
Wyndham-Quin, Major W. H.
Wyvill, Marmaduke D'Arcy

TELLERS FOR THE AYES—
Sir William Walrond and
Mr. Anstruther.

NOES.

Allen,Wm.(Newc.underLyme)	Jones, Wm. (Carnarvonshire)	Shaw, Chas. Edw. (Stafford)
Ashton, Thomas Gair	Lambert, George	Sullivan, Donal (Westmeath)
Billson, Alfred	Lough, Thomas	Trevelyan, Charles Philips
Caldwell, James	Macaleese, Daniel	Ure, Alexander
Clark, Dr. G. B. (Caithness-sh)	Morton, Edw.J.C.(Devonport)	Walton, Joseph (Barnsley)
Colville, John	O'Brien, Patrick (Kilkenny)	Weir, James Galloway
Douglas, Charles M. (Lanark)	Pearson, Sir Weetman D.	Williams,John Carvell(Notts.)
Ellis,Thos.Edw.(Merionethsh.)	Provand, Andrew Dryburgh	Wilson, Jos. H. (Middlesbro')
Goddard, Daniel Ford	Richardson, J. (Durham)	
Gurdon, Sir William Brampton	Roberts, John Bryn (Eifion)	TELLERS FOR THE NOES—
Hayne, Rt. Hn. Charles Seale-	Roberts, John H. (Denbighs.)	Mr. Herbert Lewis and Mr.
Horniman, Frederick John	Samuel, J. (Stockton-ôn-Tees)	Lloyd-George.

Resolution to be reported this day; Committee to sit again on Wednesday.

WAYS AND MEANS.

Considered in Committee.

[Mr. J. W. LOWTHER (Cumberland, Penrith), CHAIRMAN of WAYS and MEANS, in the Chair.]

(In the Committee.)

Motion made, and Question proposed—

" That towards making good the Supply granted to Her Majesty for the service of the years ending on the 31st day of March, 1898 and 1899, the sum of £1,860,115 5s. 1d. be granted out of the Consolidated Fund of the United Kingdom."—*(Mr. Hanbury.)*

MR. LEWIS: I understand, Mr. Lowther, that upon this, the first stage of a Consolidated Fund Bill, Members have the opportunity of raising questions of an administrative character.

THE CHAIRMAN OF WAYS AND MEANS: No question can be raised on this proposal, the House having already decided to appropriate this money to particular Votes.

Question put.

The Committee divided:—Ayes 136; Noes 27.—(Division List No. 57.)

AYES.

Arnold, Alfred	Charrington, Spencer	Gray, Ernest (West Ham)
Atkinson, Rt. Hon. John	Cochrane, Hn. Thos. H. A. E.	Green,WalfordD.(Wednesbury)
Bagot, Capt.Josceline FitzRoy	Coghill, Douglas Harry	Gretton, John
Balfour, Rt Hn. A. J. (Manc'r)	Collings, Rt. Hon. Jesse	Greville, Hon. Ronald
Balfour,RtHnGeraldW.(Leeds)	Colomb, Sir John Chas. Ready	Gull, Sir Cameron
Banbury, Frederick George	Compton, Lord Alwyne	Hamilton, Rt.Hn.'Lord George
Barton, Dunbar Plunket	Corbett, A. Cameron (Glasgow)	Hanbury, Rt. Hn. Robert Wm.
Bathurst, Hn. Allen Benjamin	Cranborne, Viscount	Hardy, Laurence
Beach,Rt.Hn.SirM.H.(Bristol)	Cubitt, Hon. Henry	Hare, Thomas Leigh
Beckett, Ernest William	Curzon, Viscount	Hayne, Rt. Hn. Charles Seale-
Bemrose, Sir Henry Howe	Dalrymple, Sir Charles	Heaton, John Henniker
Bentinck, Lord Henry C.	Davenport, W. Bromley-	Helder, Augustus
Bethell, Commander	Denny, Colonel	Henderson, Alexander
Bhownaggree, Sir M. M.	Douglas, Rt. Hon. A Akers-	Hoare, Samuel (Norwich)
Bill, Charles	Duncombe, Hon. Hubert V.	Jebb, Richard Claverhouse
Bond, Edward	Elliot, Hn. A. Ralph Douglas	Kemp, George
Bowles, Capt.H.F. (Middlesex)	Finlay, Sir Robert Bannatyne	Kenyon, James
Brodrick, Rt. Hon. St. John	Fisher, William Hayes	Lafone, Alfred
Butcher, John George	Folkestone, Viscount	Lea, Sir Thos. (Londonderry)
Cavendish,V. C.W. (Derbysh.)	Foster, Harry S. (Suffolk)	Lecky, Rt. Hn. William E. H.
Cecil, Evelyn (Hertford, East)	Gedge, Sydney	Leigh-Bennett, Henry Currie
Cecil, Lord Hugh (Greenwich)	Godson,Sir Augustus Frederick	Lockwood, Lieut.-Col. A. R.
Chaloner, Captain R. G. W.	Goldsworthy, Major-General	Long, Rt. Hn. Walter (L'pool)
Chamberlain, Rt.Hn.J. (Birm.)	Gordon, Hon. John Edward	Lopes, Henry Yarde Buller
Chamberlain, J. Austen (Wor.)	Gorst, Rt. Hn. Sir John Eldon	Lowles, John
Chaplin, Rt. Hon. Henry	Goulding, Edward Alfred	Loyd, Archie Kirkman

VOL. LXVIII.   [FOURTH SERIES.]   3 M

Lyttelton, Hon. Alfred
Macartney, W. G. Ellison
Macdona, John Cumming
Malcolm, Ian
Massey-Mainwaring, Hn.W.F.
Meysey-Thompson, Sir H. M.
Middlemore, John Throgmorton
Mildmay, Francis Bingham
More, Robt. Jasper (Shropsh.)
Morrell, George Herbert
Morton, Arthur H. A.(Deptf'd)
Muntz, Philip A.
Murray,RtHnA.Graham(Bute)
Myers, William Henry
Nicholson, William Graham
Nicol, Donald Ninian
Northcote, Hn. Sir H. Stafford
Pease, Herbert Pike (Drlngtn.)
Penn, John
Pierpoint, Robert
Pilkington, Richard

Pollock, Harry Frederick
Powell, Sir Francis Sharp
Pryce-Jones, Lt.-Col. Edward
Purvis, Robert
Rasch, Major Frederic Carne
Ritchie, Rt.Hn. Chas.Thomson
Robinson, Brooke
Royds, Clement Molyneux
Russell, T. W. (Tyrone)
Ryder, John Herbert Dudley
Sassoon, Sir Edward Albert
Scott, Sir S. (Marylebone, W.)
Seton-Karr, Henry
Sharpe, William Edward T.
Sidebottom, Wm. (Derbyshire)
Simeon, Sir Barrington
Smith, Abel H. (Christchurch)
Smith, Hn. W. F. D. (Strand)
Stanley, Lord (Lancs.)
Stock, James Henry
Strauss, Arthur

Strutt, Hon. Charles Hedley
Talbot, Lord E. (Chichester)
Thornton, Percy M.
Tollemache, Henry James
Valentia, Viscount
Webster, R. G. (St. Pancras)
Webster, Sir R. E. (I. of W.)
Welby, Lieut.-Col. A. C. E.
Wentworth, Bruce C. Vernon-
Williams,JosephPowell(Birm.)
Willox, Sir John Archibald
Wilson, John (Falkirk)
Wodehouse,RtHn.E.R.(Bath)
Wylie, Alexander
Wyndham-Quin, Major W. H.
Wyvill, Marmaduke D'Arcy

TELLERS FOR THE AYES—
Sir William Walrond and
Mr. Anstruther.

NOES.

Allen,Wm.(Newc.underLyme)
Ashton, Thomas Gair
Billson, Alfred
Clark, Dr. G. B. (Caithness-sh)
Colville, John
Goddard, Daniel Ford
Horniman, Frederick John
Jones, Wm. (Carnarvonshire)
Lambert, George
Lloyd-George, David
Lough, Thomas

Macaleese, Daniel
Morton, Edw.J.C.(Devonport)
O'Brien, Patrick (Kilkenny)
Pearson, Sir Weetman D.
Provand, Andrew Dryburgh
Richardson, J. (Durham)
Roberts, John Bryn (Eifion)
Roberts, John H. (Denbighs.)
Samuel, J. (Stockton-on-Tees)
Shaw, Chas. Edw. (Stafford)
Sullivan, Donal (Westmeath)

Ure, Alexander
Walton, Joseph (Barnsley)
Weir, James Galloway
Williams,John Carvell(Notts.)
Wilson, Jos. H. (Middlesbro')

TELLERS FOR THE NOES—
Mr. Herbert Lewis and
Mr. Caldwell.

Resolved, That towards making good the Supply granted to Her Majesty for the service of the years ending on the 31st day of March 1898 and 1899, the sum of £1,860,115 5s. 1d. be granted out of the Consolidated Fund of the United Kingdom.

Motion made and Question put—

"That towards making good the Supply granted to Her Majesty for the service of the year ending on the 31st day of March 1900, the sum of £29,596,900 be granted out of the Consolidated Fund of the United Kingdom."—(*Mr. Hanbury.*)

The Committee divided:—Ayes 135; Noes 27.—(Division List No. 58.)

AYES.

Arnold, Alfred
Atkinson, Rt. Hon. John
Bagot,Capt Josceline Fitzroy
Balfour, Rt Hn. A. J. (Manc'r)
Balfour.RtHnGeraldW.(Leeds)
Banbury, Frederick George
Barton, Dunbar Plunket
Bathurst, Hn Allen Benjamin

Beach,Rt.Hn.SirM.H.(Bristol)
Beckett, Ernest William
Bemrose, Sir Henry Howe
Bentinck, Lord Henry C.
Bethell, Commander
Bhownaggree, Sir M. M.
Bill, Charles
Bond, Edward

Bowles, Capt.H.F. (Middlesex)
Brodrick, Rt. Hon. St. John
Cavendish, V. C. W. (Derbysh.)
Cecil, Evelyn (Hertford, East)
Cecil, Lord Hugh (Greenwich)
Chaloner, Captain R. G. W.
Chamberlain, Rt.Hn.J. (Birm.)
Chamberlain. J. Austen (Wor.)

Chaplin, Rt. Hon. Henry
Charrington, Spencer
Cochrane, Hn. Thos. H. A. E.
Coghill, Douglas Harry
Collings, Rt. Hon. Jesse
Colomb, Sir John Chas. Ready
Compton, Lord Alwyne
Corbett, A. Cameron (Glasgow)
Cranborne, Viscount
Cubitt, Hon. Henry
Curzon, Viscount
Dalrymple, Sir Charles
Davenport, W. Bromley-
Denny, Colonel
Douglas, Rt. Hon. A. Akers
Duncombe, Hon. Hubert V.
Elliot, Hn. A. Ralph Douglas
Finlay Sir Robert Bannatyne
Fisher, William Hayes
Folkestone, Viscount
Foster, Harry S. (Suffolk)
Gedge, Sydney
Godson, Sir Augustus Frederick
Goldsworthy, Major-General
Gordon, Hon. John Edward
Gorst, Rt. Hn. Sir John Eldon
Goulding, Edward Alfred
Gray, Ernest (West Ham)
Green, WalfordD.(Wednesbury)
Gretton, John
Greville, Hon. Ronald
Gull, Sir Cameron
Hamilton, Rt.Hn. Lord George
Hanbury. Rt. Hn Robert Wm.
Hardy, Laurence
Hare, Thomas Leigh
Hayne, Rt. Hn. Charles Seale-
Heaton, John Henniker
Helder, Augustus

Henderson, Alexander
Hoare, Samuel (Norwich)
Jebb, Richard Claverhouse
Kemp, George
Kenyon, James
Lafone, Alfred
Lea, Sir Thos. (Londonderry)
Lecky, Rt. Hn. William E. H.
Leigh-Bennett, Henry Currie
Lockwood, Lieut.-Col. A. R.
Long, Rt. Hn. Walter (L'pool)
Lopes, Henry Yarde Buller
Lowles, John
Loyd, Archie Kirkman
Lyttelton, Hon. Alfred
Macartney, W. G. Ellison
Macdona, John Cumming
Malcolm, Ian
Massey-Mainwaring, Hn.W.F.
Meysey-Thompson, Sir H. M.
Middlemore,John Throgmorton
Mildmay, Francis Bingham
More, Robt. Jasper (Shropsh.)
Morrell, George Herbert
Morton, Arthur H. A.(Deptf'd)
Muntz, Philip A
Murray,RtHnA.Graham(Bute)
Myers, William Henry
Nicholson, William Graham
Nicol, Donald Ninian
Northcote, Hn. Sir H. Stafford
Pease, Herbert Pike (Drlngtn.)
Penn, John
Pierpoint, Robert
Pilkington, Richard
Pollock, Harry Frederick
Powell, Sir Francis Sharp
Pryce-Jones, Lt.-Col. Edward
Purvis, Robert

Rasch, Major Frederic Carne
Ritchie, Rt.Hn. Chas.Thomson
Robinson, Brooke
Royds, Clement Molyr.eux
Russell, T. W. (Tyrone)
Ryder, John Herbert Dudley
Sassoon, Sir Edward Albert
Scott, Sir S. (Marylebone, W.)
Seton-Karr, Henry
Sharpe, William Edward T.
Sidebottom, Wm. (Derbyshire)
Simeon, Sir Barrington
Smith, Abel H. (Christchurch)
Smith, Hn. W. F. D. (Strand)
Stanley, Lord (Lancs.)
Stock, James Henry
Strauss, Arthur
Strutt, Hon. Charles Hedley
Talbot, Lord E. (Chichester)
Thornton, Percy M.
Tollemache, Henry James
Valentia, Viscount
Webster, R. G. (St. Pancras)
Webster, Sir R. E. (I. of W.)
Welby, Lieut.-Col. A. C. E.
Wentworth, Bruce C. Vernon-
Williams,JosephPowell(Birm.)
Willox, Sir John Archibald
Wilson, John (Falkirk)
Wodehouse,RtHn.E.R.(Bath)
Wylie, Alexander
Wyndham-Quin, Major W. H.
Wyvill, Marmaduke D'Arcy

TELLERS FOR THE AYES—
Sir William Walrond and
Mr. Anstruther.

NOES.

Allen,Wm.(Newc.underLyme)
Ashton, Thomas Gair
Billson, Alfred
Caldwell, James
Clark, Dr. G. B. (Caithness-sh)
Colville, John
Goddard, Daniel Ford
Horniman, Frederick John
Lambert, George
Lewis, John Herbert
Lloyd-George, David

Lough, Thomas
Macaleese, Daniel
Morton, Edw.J.C.(Devonport)
O'Brien, Patrick (Kilkenny)
Pearson, Sir Weetman D.
Provand, Andrew Dryburgh
Richardson, J. (Durham)
Roberts, John Bryn (Eifion)
Roberts, John H. (Denbighs.)
Samuel, J. (Stockton-on-Tees)
Shaw, Chas. Edw. (Stafford)

Sullivan, Donal (Westmeath)
Ure, Alexander
Walton, Joseph (Barnsley)
Weir, James Galloway
Williams,John Carvell(Notts.)

TELLERS FOR THE NOES—
Mr. Havelock Wilson and
Mr. William Jones.

Resolved, That towards making good the Supply granted to Her Majesty for the service of the year ending on the 31st day of March 1900, the sum of £29,596,900 be granted out of the Consolidated Fund of the United Kingdom.

Resolutions to be reported this day; Committee to sit again upon Wednesday.

House resumed.

REPORT OF SUPPLY.

SUPPLY [MARCH 17.]

Resolutions reported—

ARMY ESTIMATES, 1899-1900.

1. "That a sum, not exceeding £6,509,000, be granted to Her Majesty, to defray the Charge for the Pay, Allowances, and other Charges of Her Majesty's Army at Home and Abroad (exclusive of India) (General Staff, Regiments, Reserve, and Departments), which will come in course of payment during the year ending on the 31st day of March 1900."

3 M 2

2. "That a sum, not exceeding £1,555,000, be granted to Her Majesty, to defray the Charge for Retired-Pay, Half-Pay, and other Non-Effective Charges for Officers and others, which will come in course of payment during the year ending on the 31st day of March 1900."

3. "That a sum, not exceeding £1,325,500, be granted to Her Majesty, to defray the Charge for Chelsea and Kilmainham Hospitals and the In-Pensioners thereof, of Out-Pensions, for the Maintenance of Lunatics for whom Pensions are not drawn, and of Gratuities awarded in Commutation and in lieu of Pensions, of Rewards for Meritorious Services, of Victoria Cross Pensions, and of Pensions to the Widows and Children of Warrant Officers, etc., which will come in course of payment during the year ending on the 31st day of March 1900."

4. "That a sum, not exceeding £185,700, be granted to Her Majesty, to defray the Charge for Superannuation, Compensation, and Compassionate Allowances and Gratuities, which will come in course of payment during the year ending on the 31st day of March 1900."

Resolutions read a second time.

Amendment proposed—

"In First Resolution, leave out '£6,509,000,' and insert '£6,508,900' instead thereof."— *(Mr. Weir.)*

*Mr. WEIR: I beg to move that this Vote be reduced by £100, and I do so as a protest against the system of recruiting in the Highlands of Scotland. I object—and I believe I have honourable Members on this side of the House with me—to the recruiting which has been carried on at such an extravagant cost in the Highlands, where the recruiting officers have been marching through the lonely glens of Scotland instead of seeking men in the towns and populous country districts. It is simply madness to send recruiting officers to those lonely parts of the country, and the results show that after spending about £250 in one march, one recruit only was secured. I represent a constituency where there are many poor fishermen, crofters, and cottars, and it is my duty to protest against this extravagance.

Mr. LEWIS: I rise to support this Motion upon other grounds than those which have been given by the honourable Member who has just sat down. I consider the expenditure upon the Army in this country is most extravagant and disproportionate to the needs of this country. This expenditure is the outcome of the Jingo policy of which we have heard so much in the country during the past year. I hope in the future that Her Majesty's Government, instead of stimulating this policy, will do their utmost to keep it down, and that they will provide for the country and the Army at a more moderate and reasonable cost, which will be sufficient, and not more than sufficient, in order to defend the possessions of our Empire. The increase of our armaments in every direction has become one of the most grave and pressing problems we have to meet. Attempts are being made in different countries of Europe to decrease those armaments, and the olive branch has been held out to us, and I think we ought to show a good example. I shall vote for my honourable Friend's Motion, as a protest against taxation in this respect, for there is a point beyond which taxation should not go. I see the Chancellor of the Exchequer in his place, and I wonder what sort of a statement he will be able to lay on the Table of this House. I imagine, owing to the great expenditure on our armaments and the increase in the Army which they entail, that the right honourable Gentleman will find himself probably in a position of considerable difficulty, and this notwithstanding the great prosperity of this country. There is a very serious aspect to this question, and honourable Members opposite must not treat it as a jest. If honourable Members on this side have not had opportunities of speaking their minds on this question, there is no reason why at this eleventh hour—or rather at this hour of the morning—some protest should not be made against the enormous and excessive expenditure of this country upon armaments. I can say that so far as the people outside this House are concerned, honourable Members have no idea of the intensity of the feeling that prevails on this subject in many quarters. Have honourable Members not heard of the enthusiastic meetings that have been held and attended, not only by partisans, but by bishops and ministers of religion and those whose business it is in life to promote the principles of peace in this country? I say again that the feeling that has been evoked in this country has been intense, and I only hope that Her Majesty's Government will definitely abandon these enormous schemes for increasing the Army. We hear sometimes—and not from irresponsible persons either—that this country is rapidly approaching the necessity for a system of conscription, and we ought not to give any countenance whatever to that state of things, and I sincerely hope that we shall never see conscription adopted in this country. With reference to this increase in the Army, I can only say that it takes some steps along the road to conscription, and I shall oppose this increase as a matter of principle, believing that the charges sought to be imposed upon the taxpayer of this country are, unhappily, in excess of the burdens which they ought to be called upon to bear.

Question put—

"That £6,509,000 stand part of the said Resolution."

The House divided:—Ayes 133; Noes 28.—(Division List No. 59.)

AYES.

Arnold, Alfred
Atkinson, Rt. Hon. John
Bagot, Capt. Josceline FitzRoy
Balfour, Rt. Hn. A. J. (Manc'r)
Balfour, Rt Hn Gerald W.(Leeds)
Banbury, Frederick George
Barton, Dunbar Plunket
Bathurst, Hn. Allen Benjamin
Beach, Rt.Hn. Sir M.H.(Bristol)
Beckett, Ernest William
Bemrose, Sir Henry Howe
Bentinck, Lord Henry C.
Bethell, Commander
Bhownaggree, Sir M. M.
Bill, Charles
Bond, Edward
Bowles, Capt.H.F. (Middlesex)
Brodrick, Rt. Hon. St. John
Cavendish, V. C.W. (Derbysh.)
Cecil, Evelyn (Hertford, East)
Cecil, Lord Hugh (Greenwich)
Chaloner, Captain R. G. W.
Chamberlain. Rt Hn J. (Birm.)
Chamberlain, J. Austen (Wor.)
Chaplin, Rt. Hon. Henry
Charrington, Spencer
Cochrane, Hn. Thos. H. A. E.
Coghill, Douglas Harry
Collings, Rt. Hon. Jesse
Colomb, Sir John Chas. Ready
Compton, Lord Alwyne
Corbett, A. Cameron (Glasgow)
Cubitt, Hon. Henry
Curzon, Viscount
Dalrymple, Sir Charles
Davenport, W. Bromley-
Denny, Colonel
Douglas, Rt. Hon. A. Akers-
Duncombe, Hon. Hubert V
Elliot, Hn. A. Ralph Douglas
Finlay, Sir Robert Bannatyne

Fisher, William Hayes
Folkestone, Viscount
Foster, Harry S. (Suffolk)
Gedge, Sydney
Godson, Sir Augustus Frederick
Goldsworthy, Major-General
Gordon, Hon. John Edward
Gorst, Rt. Hn. Sir John Eldon
Goulding, Edward Alfred
Gray, Ernest (West Ham)
Green, WalfordD.(Wednesbury)
Gretton, John
Greville, Hon. Ronald
Gull, Sir Cameron
Hamilton, Rt.Hn. Lord George
Hanbury, Rt. Hn. Robert Wm.
Hardy, Laurence
Hare, Thomas Leigh
Heaton, John Henniker
Helder, Augustus
Henderson, Alexander
Hoare, Samuel (Norwich)
Jebb, Richard Claverhouse
Kemp, George
Kenyon, James
Lafone, Alfred
Lea, Sir Thos. (Londonderry)
Lecky, Rt. Hn. William E. H.
Leigh-Bennett, Henry Currie
Lockwood, Lieut.-Col. A. R.
Long, Rt. Hn. Walter (L'pool)
Lopes, Henry Yarde Buller
Lowles, John
Loyd, Archie Kirkman
Lyttelton, Hon. Alfred
Macartney, W. G. Ellison
Macdona, John Cumming
Malcolm, Ian
Massey-Mainwaring, Hn.W.F.
Meysey-Thompson, Sir H. M.
Middlemore,John Throgmorton

Mildmay, Francis Bingham
More, Robt. Jasper (Shropsh.)
Morrell, George Herbert
Morton, Arthur H. A.(Deptf'd)
Muntz, Philip A.
Murray,RtHnA.Graham(Bute)
Myers, William Henry
Nicholson, William Graham
Nicol, Donald Ninian
Northcote, Hn. Sir H. Stafford
Pease, Herbert Pike (Drlngtn.)
Penn, John
Pierpoint, Robert
Pilkington, Richard
Pollock, Harry Frederick
Powell, Sir Francis Sharp
Pryce-Jones, Lt.-Col. Edward
Purvis, Robert
Rasch, Major Frederic Carne
Ritchie, Rt.Hn. Chas.Thomson
Robinson, Brooke
Royds, Clement Molyneux
Russell, T. W. (Tyrone)
Ryder, John Herbert Dudley
Sassoon, Sir Edward Albert
Scott, Sir S. (Marylebone, W.)
Seton-Karr, Henry
Sharpe, William Edward T.
Sidebottom, Wm. (Derbyshire)
Simeon, Sir Barrington
Smith, Abel H. (Christchurch)
Smith, Hn. W. F. D. (Strand)
Stanley, Lord (Lancs.)
Stock, James Henry
Strauss, Arthur
Strutt, Hon. Charles Hedley
Talbot, Lord E. (Chichester)
Thornton, Percy M.
Tollemache, Henry James
Valentia, Viscount
Webster, R. G. (St. Pancras)

Webster, Sir R. E. (I. of W.)
Welby, Lieut.-Col. A. C. E.
Wentworth, Bruce C. Vernon-
Williams, JosephPowell(Birm.)
Willox, Sir John Archibald

Wilson, John (Falkirk)
Wodehouse, Rt Hn. E. R. (Bath)
Wylie, Alexander
Wyndham-Quin, Major W. H.
Wyvill, Marmaduke D'Arcy

TELLERS FOR THE AYES—
Sir William Walrond and
Mr. Anstruther.

`NOES.

Allen, Wm.(Newc.underLyme)
Ashton, Thomas Gair
Billson, Alfred
Caldwell, James
Clark, Dr. G. B. (Caithness-sh)
Colville, John
Goddard, Daniel Ford
Hayne, Rt. Hn. Charles Seale-
Horniman, Frederick John
Jones, Wm. (Carnarvonshire)
Lambert, George

Lewis, John Herbert
Lloyd-George, David
Lough, Thomas
Macaleese, Daniel
Morton, Edw. J.C.(Devonport)
O'Brien, Patrick (Kilkenny)
Pearson, Sir Weetman D.
Provand, Andrew Dryburgh
Richardson, J. (Durham)
Roberts, John Bryn (Eifion)
Samuel, J. (Stockton-on-Tees)

Shaw, Chas. Edw. (Stafford)
Sullivan, Donal (Westmeath)
Ure, Alexander
Walton, Joseph (Barnsley)
Williams, John Carvell(Notts.)
Wilson, Jos. H. (Middlesbro')

TELLERS FOR THE NOES—
Mr. Weir and Mr. Herbert
Roberts.

Question put—

"That this House doth agree with the Committee in the said Resolution."

The House divided:—Ayes 133; Noes 28.—(Division List No. 60.)

AYES.

Arnold, Alfred
Atkinson, Rt. Hon. John
Bagot, Capt.Josceline FitzRoy
Balfour, Rt. Hon. A. J. (Manc'r)
Balfour, RtHnGeraldW.(Leeds)
Banbury, Frederick George
Barton, Dunbar Plunket
Bathurst, Hn Allen Benjamin
Beach, Rt. Hn. SirM.H.(Bristol)
Beckett, Ernest William
Bemrose, Sir Henry Howe
Bentinck, Lord Henry C.
Bethell, Commander
Bhownaggree, Sir M M.
Bill, Charles
Bond, Edward
Bowles, Capt.H.F. (Middlesex
Brodrick, Rt. Hon. St. John
Cavendish, V. C. W. (Derbysh.)
Cecil, Evelyn (Hertford, East)
Cecil, Lord Hugh (Greenwich)
Chaloner, Captain R. G. W.
Chamberlain, RtHn J (Birm)
Chamberlain, J. Austen (Wcr.)
Chaplin, Rt. Hon. Henry
Charrington, Spencer
Cochrane, Hn. Thos. H. A. E.
Coghill, Douglas Harry
Collings, Rt. Hon. Jesse
Colomb, Sir John Chas. Ready
Compton, Lord Alwyne
Corbett, A. Cameron (Glasgow)
Cubitt, Hon Henry
Curzon, Viscount
Dalrymple, Sir Charles
Davenport, W. Bromley-
Denny, Colonel
Douglas, Rt. Hon. A. Akers-
Duncombe, Hon. Hubert V.

Elliot Hn A. Ralph Douglas
Finlay, Sir Robert Bannatyne
Fisher, William Hayes
Folkestone, Viscount
Gedge, Sydney
Godson, Sir Augustus Frederick
Goldsworthy, Major-General
Gordon, Hon. John Edward
Gorst, Rt. Hn. Sir John Eldon
Goulding, Edward Alfred
Gray, Ernest (West Ham)
Green, WalfordD.(Wednesbury)
Gretton, John
Greville, Hon. Ronald
Gull, Sir Cameron
Hamilton, Rt.Hn. Lord George
Hanbury, Rt. Hn. Robert Wm.
Hardy, Laurence
Hare, Thomas Leigh
Heaton, John Henniker
Helder, Augustus
Henderson, Alexander
Hoare, Samuel (Norwich)
Jebb, Richard Claverhouse
Kemp, George
Kenyon, James
Lea, Sir Thos. (Londonderry)
Lecky, Rt. Hn. William E. H.
Leigh-Bennett, Henry Currie
Lockwood, Lieut.-Col. A. R.
Long, Rt. Hn. Walter (L'pool)
Lopes, Henry Yarde Buller
Lowles, John
Loyd, Archie Kirkman
Lyttelton, Hon. Alfred
Macartney, W. G. Ellison
Macdona, John Cumming
Malcolm, Ian
Massey-Mainwaring, Hn.W.F.

Meysey-Thompson, Sir H. M.
Middlemore, John Throgmorton
Mildmay, Francis Bingham
More, Robt. Jasper (Shropsh.)
Morrell, George Herbert
Morton, Arthur H. A. (Deptf'd)
Muntz, Philip A.
Murray, RtHnA.Graham(Bute)
Myers, William Henry
Nicholson, William Graham
Nicol, Donald Ninian
Northcote, Hn. Sir H. Stafford
Pease, Herbert Pike (Drlngtn.)
Penn, John
Pierpoint, Robert
Pilkington, Richard
Pollock, Harry Frederick
Powell, Sir Francis Sharp
Pryce-Jones, Lt.-Col. Edward
Purvis, Robert
Rasch, Major Frederic Carne
Ritchie, Rt.Hn. Chas.Thomson
Robinson, Brooke
Royds, Clement Molyneux
Russell, T. W. (Tyrone)
Ryder, John Herbert Dudley
Sassoon, Sir Edward Albert
Scott, Sir S. (Marylebone, W.)
Seton-Karr, Henry
Sharpe, William Edward T.
Sidebottom, Wm. (Derbyshire)
Simeon, Sir Barrington
Smith, Abel H. (Christchurch)
Smith, Hn. W. F. D. (Strand)
Stanley, Lord (Lancs.)
Stock, James Henry
Strauss, Arthur
Strutt, Hon. Charles Hedley
Talbot, Lord E. (Chichester)

Thornton, Percy M.
Tollemache, Henry James
Valentia, Viscount
Webster, R. G. (St. Pancras)
Webster, Sir R. E. (I. of W.)
Welby, Lieut.-Col. A. C. E.

Wentworth, Bruce C. Vernon-
Williams, Joseph Powell (Birm.)
Willox, Sir John Archibald
Wilson, John (Falkirk)
Wodehouse, Rt.Hn. E. R. (Bath)
Wylie, Alexander

Wyndham-Quin, Major W. H.
Wyvill, Marmaduke D'Arcy

TELLERS FOR THE AYES—
Sir William Walrond and
Mr. Anstruther.

NOES.

Allen, Wm.(Newc.underLyme)
Ashton, Thomas Gair
Billson, Alfred
Caldwell, James
Colville, John
Goddard, Daniel Ford
Hayne, Rt. Hn. Charles Seale-
Horniman, Frederick John
Jones, Wm. (Carnarvonshire)
Lambert, George
Lewis, John Herbert

Lloyd-George, David
Lough, Thomas
Macaleese, Daniel
Morton, Edw.'J.C.(Devonport)
O'Brien, Patrick (Kilkenny)
Pearson, Sir Weetman D.
Provand, Andrew Dryburgh
Richardson, J. (Durham)
Roberts, John Bryn (Eifion)
Roberts, John H. (Denbighs.)
Samuel, J. (Stockton-on-Tees)

Shaw, Chas. Edw. (Stafford)
Sullivan, Donal (Westmeath)
Ure, Alexander
Walton, Joseph (Barnsley)
Williams, John Carvell(Notts.)
Wilson, Jos. H. (Middlesbro')

TELLERS FOR THE NOES—
Mr. Weir and Dr. Clark.

Resolution agreed to.

Amendment proposed—

"In Second Resolution, leave out '£1,555,000," and insert '£1,550,500' instead thereof."—(*Dr. Clark.*)

DR. CLARK: I beg to move a reduction of £4,500 in this Vote. This question came up in Committee about this time on Saturday morning, and I tried to get some information from the War Department of this extra increase of £4,500 for half-pay to general officers, but I could get no satisfactory reply. There is a Warrant by which the number of general officers in the Army is determined. That Warrant determines that there shall be six field-marshals, 10 generals, 20 lieutenant-generals, and 70 major-generals. One would think that that large Staff would be quite sufficient to do all the work of the Army. Whether 70 major-generals are sufficient or not, this is the number which the Warrant allows. When the Warrant was passed in 1891 there were more than 70 major-generals, but they were allowed to remain, and it was agreed that as by age they retired their places should not be filled up. But this year we have got an increase in this one Estimate of £4,500, which means nine extra major-generals, so that instead of the War Office carrying out the Warrant both in spirit and in letter, they are breaking it

both in spirit and in letter, and are increasing the number of officers. I can understand you increasing the number of your men, because at the present time, and in comparison with European armies, you cannot call your Army an Army. It is merely a division; but you have more officers, and you spend more money on officers, than Germany and France put together. What has been done has been to promote nine colonels beyond the number determined by the War Office. Honourable Gentlemen on the other side used to be fond of the name "Constitutionalist," but I am glad to say that the new Unionist Party does not call itself constitutional, because it is revolutionary in many respects, and this is one of the revolutionary things it has done. You ought not to have made those promotions until you had weeded out some of the older major-generals. As it is, you are spending £4,500 in adding more officers to an already over-officered Army, and I think it is the duty of the House of Commons not to vote this money without some information.

MR. CALDWELL (Lanark, Mid.): I rise to support this reduction not only for the reasons stated, but for other reasons, which I shall give. Vote No. 4 deals with non-effective Services, and the Vote which follows deals with the men, and includes the warrant officers, non-commissioned officers, men, and others. I think it is important to look at the sum total of these two Estimates. I find that the officers take amongst them more in pensions and retired pay than the whole of the men. I venture to say that is a state of affairs which should not exist. The pay of the men amounts to 3¼ times more than the pay of the officers, and I contend that the pensions and rewards should be in a corresponding proportion. It is curious that you should be pensioning off so many officers at a time when you are anxious to increase the Army, and when there is work to be done. The sum of £27,900 is provided extra, owing to officers who are expected to retire this year, as compared with last year, and last year was an advance on the year before; and I think we are entitled to some explanation. How is it, when you are doing everything you can to recruit your Army, that your officers are allowed to go out on retiring pensions and half-pay? I hope, before this Vote is taken, we shall have an explanation.

MR. LLOYD - GEORGE (Carnarvon, etc.): I think we ought to have an explanation on the point which has been raised by my honourable Friend the Member for Caith-

ness. As he has already stated, he called attention to this matter on Saturday morning last, but the reply which he received was of the summary character of all the explanations which were given at that early hour of the morning. I think these large Army Votes require some explanation, especially when there is a suggestion of something in the nature of a "job." There has been an increase of £7,000 caused by the handing over to colonels work which ought to have been performed by major-generals; and if that is contrary to the rules of the Army and to precedent, I think we ought to have some explanation. Although we are unable to provide funds for the establishment of an old-age pension scheme for pensioning civilians who are doing quite as effective service to the State, still we are able to find £1,550,000 to pension off these officers. In common courtesy to honourable Members the Government should give some explanation of the great increase that has taken place in this Vote.

Question put—

"That £1,555,000 stand part of the said Resolution."

The House divided:—Ayes 133; Noes 28.—(Division List No. 61.)

AYES.

Arnold, Alfred
Atkinson, Rt Hon. John
Bagot, Capt.Josceline FitzRoy
Balfour. Rt. Hn. A. J. (Manc'r)
Balfour,RtHnGeraldW.(Leeds)
Banbury, Frederick George
Barton, Dunbar Plunket
Bathurst. Hn Allen Benjamin
Beach,Rt.Hn.SirM.H.(Bristol)
Beckett, Ernest William
Bemrose, Sir Henry Howe
Bentinck, Lord Henry C.
Bethell, Commander
Bhownaggree, Sir M. M.
Bill, Charles
Bond, Edward
Bowles, Capt.H.F. (Middlesex)
Brodrick. Rt. Hon. St John
Cavendish,V. C.W. (Derbysh.)
Cecil, Evelyn (Hertford, East)

Cecil, Lord Hugh (Greenwich)
Chaloner, Captain R. G. W.
Chamberlain, Rt Hn.J (Birm.)
Chamberlain, J. Austen (Wor.)
Chaplin, Rt. Hon. Henry
Charrington, Spencer
Cochrane, Hn. Thos. H. A. E.
Coghill, Douglas Harry
Collings, Rt. Hon. Jesse
Colomb, Sir John Chas. Ready
Compton, Lord Alwyne
Corbett, A. Cameron (Glasgow)
Cubitt, Hon. Henry
Curzon, Viscount
Dalrymple, Sir Charles
Davenport, W. Bromley-
Denny, Colonel
Douglas, Rt. Hon. A. Akers-
Duncombe, Hon. Hubert V.
Elliot, Hn. A Ralph Douglas

Finlay, Sir Robert Bannatyne
Fisher, William Hayes
Folkestone, Viscount
Foster, Harry S. (Suffolk)
Gedge, Sydney
Godson,Sir Augustus Frederick
Goldsworthy, Major-General
Gordon, Hon. John Edward
Gorst, Rt. Hn. Sir John Eldon
Goulding, Edward Alfred
Gray, Ernest (West Ham)
Green, WalfordD.(Wednesbury)
Gretton, John
Greville, Hon. Ronald
Gull, Sir Cameron
Hamilton, Rt.Hn. Lord George
Hanbury, Rt. Hn. Robert Wm.
Hardy, Laurence
Hare, Thomas Leigh
Heaton, John Henniker

Mr. Caldwell.

Helder, Augustus
Henderson, Alexander
Hoare, Samuel (Norwich)
Jebb, Richard Claverhouse
Kemp, George
Kenyon, James
Lafone, Alfred
Lea, Sir Thos. (Londonderry)
Lecky, Rt. Hn. William E. H.
Leigh-Bennett, Henry Currie
Lockwood, Lieut.-Col. A. R.
Long, Rt. Hn. Walter (L'pool)
Lopes, Hency Yarde Buller
Lowles, John
Loyd, Archie Kirkman
Macartney, W. G. Ellison
Macdona, John Cumming
Malcolm, Ian
Massey-Mainwaring, Hn.W.F.
Meysey-Thompson, Sir H. M.
Middlemore, John Throgmorton
Mildmay, Francis Bingham
More, Robt. Jasper (Shropsh.)
Morrell, George Herbert
Morton, Arthur H. A.(Deptf'd)
Muntz, Philip A.

Murray,RtHnA.Graham(Bute)
Myers, William Henry
Nicholson, William Graham
Nicol, Donald Ninian
Northcote, Hn. Sir H. Stafford
Pease, Herbert Pike (Drlngtn.)
Penn, John
Pierpoint, Robert
Pilkington, Richard
Pollock, Harry Frederick
Powell, Sir Francis Sharp
Pryce-Jones, Lt.-Col. Edward
Purvis, Robert
Rasch, Major Frederic Carne
Ritchie, Rt.Hn. Chas.Thomson
Robinson, Brooke
Royds, Clement Molyneux
Russell, T W. (Tyrone)
Ryder, John Herbert Dudley
Sassoon, Sir Edward Albert
Scott, Sir S. (Marylebone, W.)
Seton-Karr, Henry
Sharpe, William Edward T.
Sidebottom, Wm. (Derbyshire)
Simeon, Sir Barrington
Sinclair, Louis (Romford)

Smith, Abel H. (Christchurch)
Smith, Hn. W. F. D. (Strand)
Stanley, Lord (Lancs.)
Stock, James Henry
Strauss, Arthur
Strutt, Hon. Charles Hedley
Talbot, Lord E. (Chichester)
Thornton, Percy M.
Tollemache, Henry James
Valentia, Viscount
Webster, R. G. (St. Pancras)
Webster, Sir R. E. (I. of W.)
Welby, Lieut.-Col. A. C. E.
Wentworth, Bruce C. Vernon-
Williams,JosephPowell(Birm.)
Willox, Sir John Archibald
Wilson, John (Falkirk)
Wodehouse,RtHn.E.R.(Bath)
Wylie, Alexander
Wyndham-Quin, Major W. H.
Wyvill, Marmaduke D'Arcy

TELLERS FOR THE AYES—
Sir William Walrond and
Mr. Anstruther.

NOES.

Allen,Wm.(Newc.underLyme)
Ashton, Thomas Gair
Billson, Alfred
Caldwell, James
Colville, John
Goddard, Daniel Ford
Hayne, Rt. Hn. Charles Seale-
Horniman, Frederick John
Jones, Wm. (Carnarvonshire)
Lambert, George
Lewis, John Herbert

Lough, Thomas
Macaleese, Daniel
Morton, Edw.J.C.(Devonport)
O'Brien, Patrick (Kilkenny)
Pearson, Sir Weetman D.
Provand, Andrew Dryburgh
Richardson, J. (Durham)
Roberts, John Bryn (Eifion)
Roberts, John H. (Denbighs.)
Samuel, J. (Stockton-on-Tees)
Shaw, Chas. Edw. (Stafford)

Sullivan, Donal (Westmeath)
Ure, Alexander
Walton, Joseph (Barnsley)
Weir, James Galloway
Williams,John Carvell(Notts.)
Wilson, Jos. H. (Middlesbro')

TELLERS FOR THE NOES—
Dr. Clark and Mr. Lloyd-
George.

Question put—

"That this House doth agree with the Committee in the said Resolution."

The House divided:—Ayes 133; Noes 28.—Division List No. 62.)

AYES.

Atkinson, Rt. Hon. John
Bagot, Capt. Josceline FitzRoy
Balfour, Rt. Hn. A. J.(Manc'r)
Balfour,RtHnGeraldW.(Leeds)
Banbury, Frederick George
Barton, Dunbar Plunket
Bathurst, Hn. Allen Benjamin
Beach,Rt.Hn.SirM.H.(Bristol)
Beckett, Ernest William
Bemrose, Sir Henry Howe
Bentinck, Lord Henry C.
Bethell, Commander
Bhownaggree, Sir M. M.
Bill, Charles
Bond, Edward
Bowles, Capt.H.F. (Middlesex)
Brodrick, Rt. Hon. St. John
Cavendish,V. C.W. (Derbysh.)

Cecil, Evelyn (Hertford, East)
Cecil, Lord Hugh (Greenwich)
Chaloner, Captain R. G. W.
Chamberlain, Rt.Hn.J. (Birm.)
Chamberlain,J.Austen(Worc'r)
Chaplin, Rt Hou Henry
Charrington, Spencer
Cochrane, Hn. Thos. H. A. E.
Coghill, Douglas Harry
Collings, Rt. Hon. Jesse
Colomb, Sir John Chas. Ready
Compton, Lord Alwyne
Corbett, A. Cameron (Glasgow)
Cubitt, Hon. Henry
Curzon, Viscount
Dalrymple, Sir Charles
Davenport, W. Bromley-
Denny, Colonel

Douglas. Rt Hon A Akers-
Duncombe, Hon. Hubert V.
Elliot, Hon. A. Ralph Douglas
Finlay, Sir Robert Bannatyne
Fisher, William Hayes
Folkestone, Viscount
Foster, Harry S. (Suffolk)
Gedge, Sydney
Godson,Sir Augustus Frederick
Goldsworthy, Major-General
Gordon, Hon. John Edward
Gorst, Rt. Hn. Sir John Eldon
Goulding, Edward Alfred
Gray, Ernest (West Ham)
Green,WalfordD.(Wednesbury)
Gretton, John
Greville, Hon. Ronald
Gull, Sir Cameron

Hamilton, Rt.Hn. Lord George
Hanbury, Rt. Hn. Robert Wm.
Hardy, Laurence
Hare, Thomas Leigh
Heaton, John Henniker
Helder, Augustus
Henderson, Alexander
Hoare, Samuel (Norwich)
Jebb, Richard Claverhouse
Kemp, George
Konyon, James
Lafone, Alfred
Lea, Sir Thos. (Londonderry)
Lecky, Rt. Hn. William E. H.
Leigh-Bennett, Henry Currie
Lockwood, Lieut.-Col. A. R.
Long, Rt. Hn. Walter (L'pool)
Lopes, Henry Yarde Buller
Lowles, John
Loyd, Archie Kirkman
Macartney, W. G. Ellison
Macdona, John Cumming
Malcolm, Ian
Massey-Mainwaring, Hn.W.F.
Meysey-Thompson, Sir H. M.
Middlemore,John Throgmorton
Mildmay, Francis Bingham
More, Robt. Jasper (Shropsh.)

Morrell, George Herbert
Morton, Arthur H. A.(Deptf'd)
Muntz, Philip A.
Murray,RtHnA.Graham(Bute)
Myers, William Henry
Nicholson, William Graham
Nicol, Donald Ninian
Northcote, Hn. Sir H. Stafford
Pease, Herbert Pike (Drlngtn.)
Penn, John
Pierpoint, Robert
Pilkington, Richard
Pollock, Harry Froderick
Powell, Sir Francis Sharp
Pryce-Jones, Lt.-Col. Edward
Purvis, Robert
Rasch, Major Frederic Carne
Ritchie, Rt. Hn. Chas.Thomson
Robinson, Brooke
Royds, Clement Molyneux
Russell, T. W (Tyrone)
Ryder, John Herbert Dudley
Sassoon, Sir Edward Albert
Scott, Sir S. (Marylebone, W.)
Seton-Karr, Henry
Sharpe, William Edward T.
Sidebottom, Wm. (Derbyshire)
Simeon, Sir Barrington

Sinclair, Louis (Romford)
Smith, Abel H. (Christchurch)
Smith, Hn. W. F. D. (Strand)
Stanley, Lord (Lancs.)
Stock, James Henry
Strauss, Arthur
Strutt, Hon. Charles Hedley
Talbot, Lord E. (Chichester)
Thornton, Percy M.
Tollemache, Henry James
Valentia, Viscount
Webster, R. G. (St. Pancras)
Webster, Sir R. E. (I. of W.)
Welby, Lieut.-Col. A. C. E.
Wentworth, Bruce C. Vernon-
Williams,JosephPowell(Birm.)
Willox, Sir John Archibald
Wilson, John (Falkirk)
Wodehouse,RtHn.E.R.(Bath)
Wylie, Alexander
Wyndham-Quin, Major W. H.
Wyvill, Marmaduke D'Arcy

TELLERS FOR THE AYES—
   Sir William Walrond and
   Mr. Anstruther.

NOES.

Allen,Wm.(Newc.underLyme)
Ashton, Thomas Gair
Billson, Alfred
Colville, John
Goddard, Daniel Ford
Hayne, Rt. Hn. Charles Seale-
Horniman, Frederick John
Jones, Wm. (Carnarvonshire)
Lambert, George
Lewis, John Herbert
Lloyd-George, David

Lough, Thomas
Macaleese, Daniel
Morton, Edw.J.C.(Devonport)
O'Brien, Patrick (Kilkenny)
Pearson, Sir Weetman D.
Provand, Andrew Dryburgh
Richardson, J. (Durham)
Roberts, John Bryn (Eifion)
Roberts, John H. (Denbighs.)
Samuel, J. (Stockton-on-Tees)
Shaw, Chas. Edw. (Stafford)

Sullivan, Donal (Westmeath)
Ure, Alexander
Walton, Joseph (Barnsley)
Weir, James Galloway
Williams,John Carvell(Notts.)
Wilson, Jos. H. (Middlesbro')

TELLERS FOR THE NOES—
   Dr. Clark and Mr. Caldwell.

Resolution agreed to.

Amendment proposed—

" In Third Resolution, leave out
' £1,325,500,' and insert ' £1,325,100 ' instead
thereof."—(*Mr. Weir.*)

*Mr. WEIR: I move this reduction on account of the large salary which is paid to the Governor of the Chelsea Hospital, who receives £500 per year simply for the honour and glory of being Governor of that hospital. I think that with £1,300 a year as a field-marshal pension he should be satisfied with £100 for acting as the Governor of Chelsea Hospital. I hope that the Gentleman on the Front Bench who represents the War Office will not remain silent, and I trust that he will get up and explain matters, and inform the House whether he can see his way to reduce this remuneration by at least £400. I have no desire at this time of the night, having regard to the appeal made by the First Lord of the Treasury, to occupy the time of the House further, although there are other matters on which I should like to speak.

Mr. CALDWELL: I rise to second this Motion, because I understand that there will be no other opportunity of moving any other reduction. In this Vote No. 15 I do not think that the Government need complain of the little time which has been devoted to its discussion, because a sum of £1,325,000 is involved. Why, there are Votes amounting to three or four millions which have taken an hour and a half, and I don't think we are taking an undue amount of time in discussing a matter of this kind. Of course, if we are taking an undue amount of time, then the First Lord of the Treasury knows the remedy. The Twelve o'clock Rule was suspended, and what is the use of suspending that Rule if we are not——

*Mr. SPEAKER: Will the honourable Member confine himself to criticising this Vote?

Mr. CALDWELL: I would point out that in the Vote which we passed for the officers we paid £175,000 for widows' pensions, but the corresponding Vote with regard to the men is only about £6,000 for widows' pensions. Now, there is another point. When you are dealing with the officers the rewards for distinguished or meritorious service amount to £12,200 in the Vote we have passed, but when we turn to the case of the men we find that they get about £6,500. I venture to say——

Mr. BANBURY (Peckham): Mr. Speaker, I rise to a point of order. The honourable Member is alluding to a Vote that has already been passed.

Mr. CALDWELL: I was only drawing a contrast. Here you have got two classes of people, the officers and the men, and it is perfectly fair criticism to say that in regard to your treatment you deal with the officers in a more handsome manner than you do the men, and that is the point of my observation. You find, for instance, with regard to the pensioners in Chelsea, that the amount is going rapidly down. There is a reduction of £12,000 on the Vote this year compared with the year before, and we are getting out of the giving of pensions to the men, and although we are increasing enormously Vote 14 you find that the Vote to the officers is in-

creased by £12,800, while in the case of this Vote there is an increase of £10,000. I venture to say that now we are increasing the number of the Army we ought to be increasing the pay of the rank and file, and their allowances ought to be all the more, as they have the hard work to do. For these reasons I support the reduction which has been moved; and I am inclined to vote against the whole Vote, if we are treated as we were on the last Vote without any reply from the Government.

The FINANCIAL SECRETARY to the WAR OFFICE (Mr. J. Powell Williams, Birmingham, S.): The field-marshal, as Governor of Chelsea Hospital is entitled, under the Queen's Regulations, to half-pay, amounting to £1,300 per year, and he is also entitled to £500 a year as the Governor of Chelsea Hospital. It is an important appointment, to which is attached much responsibility; and it is impossible to put duties of that kind upon a retired officer without giving due remuneration for the performance of those duties. With regard to the additional salary of the Lieutenant-Governor and Secretary, that is a matter personal to the present holder of the office. The present holder of the office at the time of his appointment was Governor of Hong Kong, and he accepted this appointment which was offered him. In the meantime, representations were made that the salary might be reduced, but he had accepted the appointment on the original terms, and it was not felt to be fair under these circumstances to insist upon a reduction. When his term of office expires, and a new Lieutenant-Governor is appointed, the reduction will be made.

Dr. CLARK: I cannot allow this discussion to end without calling attention to this important question of holding plural offices. If there is one thing which honourable Members of this House have been strong and eloquent in, it is in denouncing this system of pluralism. The salaries of these officers are very high, and everybody admits that they are more than they ought to be. This officer gets his half-pay, and he has earned it, and no one can say anything against it, but in most of these appointments it is a case of, "What are you doing, Bill?" And the reply is, "Nothing." Then the question is asked, "What are you doing, Jack?" And the answer is, "Helping Bill." I only hope that before another Estimate comes before us the Government will abolish these sinecures. This is one of the things which they ought to look into, and they will find plenty of room for doing so.

Question put—

"That £1,325,500 stand part of the Resolution."

The House divided:—Ayes 133; Noes 27.—(Division List No. 63.)

AYES.

Arnold, Alfred
Atkinson, Rt. Hon. John
Bagot, Capt Josceline FitzRoy
Balfour, Rt. Hn A. J. (Manc'r)
Balfour, RtHnGeraldW.(Leeds)
Banbury, Frederick George
Barton, Dunbar Plunket
Bathurst, Hn Allen Benjamin
Beach, Rt Hn.SirM.H.(Bristol)
Beckett, Ernest William
Bemrose, Sir Henry Howe
Bentinck, Lord Henry C.
Bethell, Commander
Bhownaggree, Sir M. M.
Bill, Charles
Bond, Edward
Bowles, Capt.H.F. (Middlesex)
Brodrick, Rt. Hon St. John
Cavendish, V. C.W. (Derbysh.)
Cecil, Evelyn (Hertford, East)
Cecil, Lord Hugh (Greenwich)
Chaloner, Captain R. G. W.
Chamberlain, Rt.Hn.J (Birm.)
Chamberlain, J.Austen(Worc'r)
Chaplin, Rt. Hon Henry
Charrington, Spencer
Cochrane, Hn. Thos. H. A. E.
Coghill, Douglas Harry
Collings, Rt. Hon. Jesse
Colomb, Sir John Chas. Ready
Compton, Lord Alwyne
Corbett, A. Cameron (Glasgow)
Cubitt, Hon. Henry
Curzon, Viscount
Dalrymple, Sir Charles
Davenport, W. Bromley-
Denny, Colonel
Douglas, Rt. Hon A Akers
Duncombe, Hon. Hubert V.
Elliot, Hn. A. Ralph Douglas
Finlay, Sir Robert Bannatyne
Fisher, William Hayes
Folkestone, Viscount
Foster, Harry S. (Suffolk)
Gedge, Sydney
Godson, Sir Augustus Frederick
Dr. Clark.

Goldsworthy, Major-General
Gordon, Hon. John Edward
Gorst, Rt. Hn. Sir John Eldon
Goulding, Edward Alfred
Gray, Ernest (West Ham)
Green, WalfordD.(Wednesbury)
Gretton, John
Greville, Hon. Ronald
Gull, Sir Cameron
Hamilton, Rt.Hn. Lord George
Hanbury, Rt. Hn. Robert Wm.
Hardy, Laurence
Hare, Thomas Leigh
Heaton, John Henniker
Helder, Augustus
Henderson, Alexander
Hoare, Samuel (Norwich)
Jebb, Richard Claverhouse
Kemp, George
Kenyon, James
Lafone, Alfred
Lea, Sir Thos. (Londonderry)
Lecky, Rt. Hn. William E. H.
Leigh-Bennett, Henry Currie
Lockwood, Lieut.-Col. A. R.
Long, Rt. Hn. Walter (L'pool)
Lopes, Henry Yarde Buller
Lowles, John
Loyd, Archie Kirkman
Macartney, W. G. Ellison
Macdona, John Cumming
Malcolm, Ian
Massey-Mainwaring, Hn.W.F.
Meysey-Thompson, Sir H. M.
Middlemore, John Throgmorton
Mildmay, Francis Bingham
More, Robt. Jasper (Shropsh.)
Morrell, George Herbert
Morton, Arthur H. A.(Deptf'd)
Muntz, Philip A.
Murray, RtHnA.Graham(Bute)
Myers, William Henry
Nicholson, William Graham
Nicol, Donald Ninian
Northcote, Hn. Sir H. Stafford
Pease, Herbert Pike (Darlngtn.)

Penn, John
Pierpoint, Robert
Pilkington, Richard
Pollock, Harry Frederick
Powell, Sir Francis Sharp
Pryce-Jones, Lt.-Col. Edward
Purvis, Robert
Rasch, Major Frederic Carne
Ritchie, Rt.Hn. Chas.Thomson
Robinson, Brooke
Royds, Clement Molyneux
Russell, T. W. (Tyrone)
Ryder, John Herbert Dudley
Sassoon, Sir Edward Albert
Scott, Sir S. (Marylebone, W.)
Seton-Karr, Henry
Sharpe, William Edward T.
Sidebottom, Wm. (Derbyshire)
Simeon, Sir Barrington
Sinclair, Louis (Romford)
Smith, Abel H. (Christchurch)
Smith, Hn. W. F. D. (Strand)
Stanley, Lord (Lancs.)
Stock, James Henry
Strauss, Arthur
Strutt, Hon. Charles Hedley
Talbot, Lord E. (Chichester)
Thornton, Percy M.
Tollemache, Henry James
Valentia, Viscount
Webster, R. G. (St. Pancras)
Webster, Sir R. E. (I. of W.)
Welby, Lieut.-Col. A. C. E.
Wentworth, Bruce C. Vernon-
Williams, JosephPowell(Birm.)
Willox, Sir John Archibald
Wilson, John (Falkirk)
Wodehouse,RtHn.E.R.(Bath)
Wylie, Alexander
Wyndham-Quin, Major W. H.
Wyvill, Marmaduke D'Arcy

TELLERS FOR THE AYES—
Sir William Walrond and
Mr. Anstruther.

NOES.

Allen,Wm.(Newc.underLyme)	Lloyd-George, David	Sullivan, Donal (Westmeath).
Ashton, Thomas Gair	Macaleese, Daniel	Ure, Alexander
Billson, Alfred	Morton, Edw.J.C.(Devonport)	Walton, Joseph (Barnsley)
Caldwell, James	O'Brien, Patrick (Kilkenny)	Williams,John Carvell(Notts.)
Clark, Dr. G. B. (Caithness-sh)	Pearson, Sir Weetman D.	Wilson, Jos. H. (Middlesbro')
Colville, John	Provand, Andrew Dryburgh	
Goddard, Daniel.Ford	Richardson, J. (Durham)	TELLERS FOR THE NOES—
Hayne, Rt. Hn. Charles Seale-	Roberts, John Bryn (Eifion)	Mr. Weir and Mr. William
Horniman, Frederick John	Roberts, John H. (Denbighs.)	Jones.
Lambert, George	Samuel, J. (Stockton-on-Tees)	
Lewis, John Herbert	Shaw, Chas. Edw. (Stafford)	

Question proposed—

"That this House doth agree with the Committee in the said Resolution."

MR. LEWIS: There is one rather important question which I wish to raise before this Vote is finally put. An item of £2,500 for the Royal Commissioners of the Patriotic Fund appears in the Estimates for the first time. It is extremely important that the House should watch, and watch closely, any items of new expenditure of this kind. I do not suppose there is a Member on either side of the House who would disapprove of the object to which this £2,500 is to be applied—namely, in pensions to widows, compassionate allowances, and so forth; but the Commissioners of the Patriotic Fund have not had, I venture to say, a very brilliant history, and they have at various periods not very far distant from each other been severely criticised by the Press of this country. Perhaps it would be going too far to say there had been extravagance and mismanagement, but at the same time it has been found necessary to make very careful inquiries into the way in which the Royal Commissioners of the Patriotic Fund have performed their work. I contend that some of this money should be devoted to the soldiers who have been awarded the Victoria Cross for meritorious service in the field. Piper Findlater, for instance, when he left the Army had to maintain himself, and in order to do so was practically compelled to hire himself out to enter-

tainers. Honourable Members know very well that this resulted in a very painful exposure of the way in which we treat the men who have risked their lives for their country. I hope the right honourable Gentleman will be able to give the House some satisfactory assurance in regard to this point, and also some explanation with reference to the item for the Royal Commissioners of the Patriotic Fund which appears in the Estimates for the first time.

MR. HAVELOCK WILSON (Middlesbrough): In consequence of the noise which honourabe Members are making on the other side of the House, and the fact that we cannot get satisfactory explanations to our questions, I beg to move—

"That the Debate be now adjourned."

*MR. SPEAKER: I cannot accept that Motion.

MR. POWELL WILLIAMS: The soldiers who receive the Victoria Cross may, by a recent regulation, if their circumstances require it, receive a payment not exceeding £50 a year for life, supposing, as I say, that they are not able to earn sufficient to keep them in the position which men who receive that distinction ought to occupy. With regard to the other question, the Patriotic Fund is not an annual payment. A little time ago an acute eye at the War Office discovered a fund which had been accumulating for a good many years,.

and which was originally derived from the sale of old stores. This had been administered by the Quartermaster-General in the interest of persons who are benefitted by the Patriotic Fund, but it has now been transferred to the Patriotic Fund Commissioners.

Question put and agreed to.

Resolution agreed to.

Amendment proposed—

"In Fourth Resolution, leave out '£183,700,' and insert '£179,000' instead thereof."—(*Mr. Caldwell.*)

MR. CALDWELL: I rise to move this reduction in order to call attention to the superanuation allowance of members of the Metropolitan Police. We have

always maintained that the cost of the Metropolitan Police should be a charge on the metropolitan funds.

MR. POWELL WILLIAMS: I do not think the honourable Member who has raised this question quite understands what the charge is. The members of the Metropolitan Police are allowed to count their Army Service in respect of their pension, and the War Office have undertaken to pay so much of their pension as applies to their service in the Army. That accounts for this charge.

Question put—

"That £183,700 stand part of the said Resolution."

The House divided:—Ayes 134 ; Noes 26.—(Division List No. 64.)

AYES.

Arnold, Alfred	Dalrymple, Sir Charles	Lecky, Rt. Hn. William E. H.
Atkinson, Rt. Hon. John	Davenport, W. Bromley-	Leigh-Bennett, Henry Currie
Bagot, Capt. Josceline FitzRoy	Denny, Colonel	Lockwood, Lieut.-Col. A. R.
Balfour. Rt Hn. A. J (Manc'r)	Douglas, Rt Hon A. Akers	Long, Rt. Hn. Walter (L'pool)
Balfour, Rt Hn Geral J W.(Leeds)	Duncombe, Hon. Hubert V.	Lopes, Henry Yarde Buller
Banbury, Frederick George	Elliot, Hn. A. Ralph Douglas	Lowles, John
Barton, Dunbar Plunket	Finlay, Sir Robert Bannatyne	Loyd, Archie Kirkman
Bathurst, Hn. Allen Benjamin	Fisher, William Hayes	Macartney, W. G. Ellison
Beach,Rt.Hn.SirM.H.(Bristol)	Folkestone, Viscount	Macdona, John Cumming
Beckett, Ernest William	Foster, Harry S. (Suffolk)	Malcolm Ian
Bemrose, Sir Henry Howe	Gedge, Sydney	Massey-Mainwaring, Hn.W.F.
Bentinck, Lord Henry C.	Godson, Sir Augustus Frederick	Meysey-Thompson, Sir H. M.
Bethell, Commander	Goldsworthy, Major-General	Middlemore, John Throgmorton
Bhownaggree, Sir M. M.	Gordon, Hon. John Edward	Mildmay, Francis Bingham
Bill, Charles	Gorst, Rt. Hn. Sir John Eldon	More, Robt. Jasper (Shropsh.)
Bond, Edward	Goulding, Edward Alfred	Morrell, George Herbert
Bowles, Capt.H.F. (Middlesex)	Gray, Ernest (West Ham)	Morton, Arthur H. A.(Deptf'd)
Brodrick, Rt. Hon. St. John	Green, WalfordD.(Wednesbury)	Muntz, Philip A.
Cavendish,V. C.W. (Derbysh.)	Gretton, John	Murray,RtHnA.Graham(Bute)
Cecil, Evelyn (Hertford, East)	Greville, Hon. Ronald	Myers, William Henry
Cecil, Lord Hugh (Greenwich)	Gull, Sir Cameron	Nicholson, William Graham
Chaloner, Captain R. G. W.	Hamilton, Rt.Hn. Lord George	Nicol, Donald Ninian
Chamberlain, Rt Hn.J. (Birm.	Hanbury, Rt. Hu. Robert Wm.	Northcote, Hn. Sir H. Stafford
Chamberlain, J. Austen (Wor.)	Hardy, Laurence	Pease, Herbert Pike (Drlngtn.)
Chaplin, Rt. Hon. Henry	Hare, Thomas Leigh	Penn. John
Charrington, Spencer	Heaton, John Henniker	Pierpoint, Robert
Cochrane, Thos. H. A. E.	Helder, Augustus	Pilkington, Richard
Coghill, Douglas Harry	Henderson, Alexander	Pollock, Harry Frederick
Collings, Rt. Hon. Jesse	Hoare, Samuel (Norwich)	Powell, Sir Francis Sharp
Colomb, Sir John Chas. Ready	Jebb, Richard Claverhouse	Pryce-Jones, Lt.-Col. Edward
Compton, Lord Alwyne	Kemp, George	Purvis, Robert
Corbett, A. Cameron (Glasgow)	Kenyon, James	Rasch, Major Frederic Carne
Cubitt, Hon Henry	Lafone, Alfred	Ritchie, Rt. Hn. Chas.Thomson
Curzon, Viscount	Lea, Sir Thos. (Londonderry)	Robinson, Brooke

Mr. Powell Williams.

Royds, Clement Molyneux
Russell, T. W. (Tyrone)
Ryder, John Herbert Dudley
Sassoon, Sir Edward Albert
Scott, Sir S. (Marylebone, W.)
Seton-Karr, Henry
Sharpe, William Edward T.
Shaw, Chas. Edw. (Stafford)
Sidebottom, Wm. (Derbyshire)
Simeon, Sir Barrington
Sinclair, Louis (Romford)
Smith, Abel H. (Christchurch)

Smith, Hn. W. F. D. (Strand)
Stanley, Lord (Lancs.)
Stock, James Henry
Strauss, Arthur
Strutt, Hon. Charles Hedley
Talbot, Lord E. (Chichester)
Thornton, Percy M.
Tollemache, Henry James
Valentia, Viscount
Webster, R. G. (St. Pancras)
Webster, Sir R. E. (I. of W.)
Welby, Lieut.-Col. A. C. E.

Wentworth, Bruce C. Vernon-
Williams,JosephPowell(Birm.)
Willox, Sir John Archibald
Wilson, John (Falkirk)
Wodehouse,RtHn.E.R.(Bath)
Wylie, Alexander
Wyndham-Quin, Major W. H.
Wyvill, Marmaduke D'Arcy

TELLERS FOR THE AYES—
Sir William Walrond and
Mr. Anstruther.

NOES.

Allen,Wm.(Newc.underLyme)
Ashton, Thomas Gair
Billson, Alfred
Clark, Dr. G. B. (Caithness-sh)
Colville, John
Goddard, Daniel Ford
Hayne, Rt. Hn. Charles Seale-
Horniman, Frederick John
Jones, Wm. (Carnarvonshire)
Lambert, George

Lewis, John Herbert
Lloyd-George, David
Macaleese, Daniel
Morton, Edw.J.C.(Devonport)
O'Brien, Patrick (Kilkenny)
Pearson, Sir Weetman D.
Provand, Andrew Dryburgh
Richardson, J. (Durham)
Roberts, John Bryn (Eifion)
Roberts, John H. (Denbighs.)

Sullivan, Donal (Westmeath)
Ure, Alexander
Walton, Joseph (Barnsley)
Weir, James Galloway
Williams,John Carvell(Notts.)
Wilson, Jos. H. (Middlesbro')

TELLERS FOR THE NOES—
Mr. Caldwell and Mr.
Jonathan Samuel.

Question put—

"That this House doth agree with the Committee in the said Resolution."

The House divided:—Ayes 129; Noes 27.—(Division List No. 65.)

AYES.

Arnold, Alfred
Atkinson, Rt. Hon. John
Bagot, Capt Josceline FitzRoy
Balfour, Rt. Hn. A J. (Manc'r)
Balfour,RtHnGeraldW.(Leeds)
Banbury, Frederick George
Barton, Dunbar Plunket
Bathurst, Hon. Allen Benjam
Beach,Rt Hn.SirM.H.(Bristol)
Beckett, Ernest William
Bemrose, Sir Henry Howe
Bentinck, Lord Henry C.
Bethell, Commander
Bhownaggree, Sir M. M.
Bond, Edward
Bowles, Capt.H.F. (Middlesex)
Brodrick, Rt. Hon. St. John
Cavendish,V. C.W. (Derbysh.)
Cecil, Evelyn (Hertford, East)
Cecil, Lord Hugh (Greenwich)
Chaloner, Captain R. G. W.
Chamberlain, Rt Hn.J. (Birm.)
Chamberlain, J. Austen (Wor.)
Chaplin, Rt. Hon. Henry
Charrington, Spencer
Cochrane, Hn. Thos. H. A. E.
Coghill, Douglas Harry
Collings, Rt. Hon. Jesse
Compton, Lord Alwyne
Corbett, A. Cameron (Glasgow)
Cubitt, Hon. Henry

Curzon, Viscount
Dalrymple, Sir Charles
Davenport, W Bromley-
Denny, Colonel
Douglas, Rt. Hon. A. Akers
Duncombe, Hon. Hubert V.
Elliot, Hn. A. Ralph Douglas
Finlay, Sir Robert Bannatyne
Fisher, William Hayes
Folkestone, Viscount
Foster, Harry S. (Suffolk)
Gedge, Sydney
Godson,Sir Augustus Frederick
Goldsworthy, Major-General
Gordon, Hon. John Edward
Gorst, Rt. Hn. Sir John Eldon
Goulding, Edward Alfred
Gray, Ernest (West Ham)
Green,WalfordD.(Wednesbury)
Gretton, John
Greville, Hon. Ronald
Gull, Sir Cameron
Hamilton, Rt.Hn, Lord George
Hanbury, Rt. Hn. Robert Wm.
Hardy, Laurence
Hare, Thomas Leigh
Heaton, John Henniker
Helder, Augustus
Henderson, Alexander
Hoare, Samuel (Norwich)
Jebb, Richard Claverhouse

Kemp, George
Kenyon, James
Lafone, Alfred
Lea, Sir Thos. (Londonderry)
Lecky, Rt. Hn. William E. H.
Leigh-Bennett, Henry Currie
Lockwood, Lieut.-Col. A. R.
Long, Rt. Hn. Walter (L'pool)
Lopes, Henry Yarde Buller
Lowles, John
Loyd, Archie Kirkman
Macartney, W. G. Ellison
Macdona, John Cumming
Malcolm, Ian
Massey-Mainwaring, Hn.W.F.
Meysey-Thompson, Sir H. M.
Middlemore,John Throgmorton
Mildmay, Francis Bingham
More, Robt. Jasper (Shropsh.)
Morrell, George Herbert
Muntz, Philip A.
Murray,RtHnA.Graham(Bute
Myers, William Henry
Nicholson, William Graham
Nicol, Donald Ninian
Northcote, Hn. Sir H. Stafford
Pease, Herbert Pike (Drlngtn.)
Penn, John
Pierpoint, Robert
Pilkington, Richard
Pollock, Harry Frederick

Powell, Sir Francis Sharp
Pryce-Jones, Lt.-Col. Edward
Purvis, Robert
Rasch, Major Frederic Carne
Ritchie, Rt.Hn. Chas.Thomson
Robinson, Brooke
Royds, Clement Molyneux
Russell, T. W. (Tyrone)
Ryder, John Herbert Dudley
Sassoon, Sir Edward Albert
Scott, Sir S. (Marylebone, W.)
Seton-Karr, Henry
Sharpe, William Edward T.
Sidebottom, Wm. (Derbyshire)

Simeon, Sir Barrington
Sinclair, Louis (Romford)
Smith, Abel H. (Christchurch)
Smith, Hn. W. F. D. (Strand)
Stanley, Lord (Lancs.)
Stock, James Henry
Strauss, Arthur
Strutt, Hon. Charles Hedley
Talbot, Lord E. (Chichester)
Thornton, Percy M.
Tollemache, Henry James
Valentia, Viscount
Webster, R. G. (St. Pancras)
Webster, Sir R. E. (I. of W.)

Welby, Lieut.-Col. A. C. E.
Wentworth, Bruce C. Vernon-
Williams,JosephPowell(Birm.)
Willox, Sir John Archibald
Wilson, John (Falkirk)
Wylie, Alexander
Wyndham-Quin, Major W. H.
Wyvill, Marmaduke D'Arcy

TELLERS FOR THE AYES—
Sir William Walrond and
Mr. Anstruther.

NOES.

Allen,Wm.(Newc.underLyme)
Ashton, Thomas Gair
Billson, Alfred
Caldwell, James
Clark, Dr. G. B. (Caithness-sh)
Colville, John
Goddard, Daniel Ford
Hayne, Rt. Hn. Charles Seale-
Horniman, Frederick John
Jones, Wm. (Carnarvonshire)
Lambert, George

Lewis, John Herbert
Lloyd-George, David
Macaleese, Daniel
Morton, Edw. J.C.(Devonport)
O'Brien, Patrick (Kilkenny)
Pearson, Sir Weetman D.
Provand, Andrew Dryburgh
Richardson, J. (Durham)
Roberts, John Bryn (Eifion)
Roberts, John H. (Denbighs.)
Shaw, Chas. Edw. (Stafford)

Sullivan, Donal (Westmeath)
Ure, Alexander
Walton, Joseph (Barnsley)
Williams,John Carvell(Notts.)
Wilson, Jos. H. (Middlesbro')

TELLERS FOR THE NOES—
Mr. Weir and Mr. Jonathan
Samuel.

Motion made and Question proposed— "That this House do now adjourn."—*(The First Lord of the Treasury.)*

MR. LEWIS: Mr. Speaker, I have one word to say on the Motion for adjournment. There has been a certain feeling of irritation aroused on this side of the House by the action of the right honourable Gentleman, who generally gets on so admirably with us, in moving the Closure when the oppor-

tunity arrived for bringing forward a case, the statement of which would only have occupied five minutes.

*MR. SPEAKER: The remarks of the honourable Member are out of order.

Motion agreed to.

House adjourned at fifty-five minutes after Two of the clock.

ERRATA.

HOUSE OF LORDS.

Tuesday, 21st March 1899.

———

THE LORD CHANCELLOR took his seat on the Woolsack at fifteen minutes after Four of the clock.

———

REPRESENTATIVE PEERS FOR IRELAND.

———

EARL OF WICKLOW.

Report made from the Lord Chancellor, that the right of Ralph Francis Earl of Wicklow to vote at the elections of Representative Peers for Ireland has been established to the satisfaction of the Lord Chancellor; read, and ordered to lie on the Table.

———

PRIVATE BILL BUSINESS.

———

HERNE BAY WATER BILL [H.L.]

Committee to meet on Thursday next.

WALTON-ON-THAMES AND WEYBRIDGE GAS BILL [H.L.]

Committee to meet on Thursday next.

CAMBRIDGE UNIVERSITY AND TOWN GAS BILL [H.L.]

Committee to meet on Friday next.

YEADON AND GUISELEY GAS BILL [H.L.]

Reported from the Select Committee with amendments.

NORTHERN ASSURANCE COMPANY BILL [H.L.]

Reported with amendments.

VOL. LXVIII.   [FOURTH SERIES.]

OYSTERMOUTH RAILWAY OR TRAMROAD BILL [H.L.]

Read third time, and passed, and sent to the Commons.

DUNDEE GAS, TRAMWAYS, AND EXTENSION BILL [H.L.]

Standing Order No. 92 considered (according to order), and dispensed with, with respect to a petition of Captain Clayhills Henderson: Leave given to present the said petition.

———

RETURNS, REPORTS, ETC.

———

EDUCATION (ENGLAND AND WALES).

Return showing—

1. The expenditure from the grant for public education in England and Wales in the year 1898, upon annual grants to elementary schools;

2. The actual number of public elementary day schools on the Annual Grant List, on the 31st August 1898; the accommodation and number of scholars in those schools;

3. Detailed statistics of inspected schools, 1897-98: Public elementary day schools, evening continuation schools, and certified efficient schools; the accommodation, number of scholars, teachers employed, particulars of grant earned, income, expenditure, etc.;

4. Summary tables of educational statistics; and

5. Number of school boards under various heads of population.

SOUTH AFRICA.

Further correspondence relative to the affairs of Swaziland.

BOARD OF AGRICULTURE.

Annual Reports of Proceedings for the year 1898, under—

1. The Diseases of Animals Acts, the Markets and Fairs (Weighing of Cattle) Acts, etc., etc.;

2. The Tithe Acts, the Copyhold Act, 1894, the Inclosure Acts, the Metropolitan Commons Acts, the Drainage and Improvement of Land Acts, the Universities and College Estates Acts, the Glebe Lands Act, 1888, etc., etc.

LIGHT RAILWAYS ACT, 1896

Orders made by the Light Railway Commissioners and modified and confirmed by the Board of Trade authorising the construction of—

I. A light railway in the county of Lincoln from Grimsby to Saltfleetby, with a branch to Cleethorpes;

II. Light railways between Barking Town and the Beckton Gas Works, in the county of Essex;

III. Light railways in the county of Lincoln and the West Riding of the county of York, from Haxey to Crowle and Marshlands, with branches;

IV. A light railway in the county of Lancaster from Liverpool to Prescot;

V. A light railway from the Esplanade to the Isle of Wight Railway Company's Station, Ventnor;

VI. Light railways in the townships of Chirton, North Shields, Tynemouth, and Cullercoats, and the Urban District of Whitley and Monkseaton, in the county of Northumberland;

VII. Light railways in the county of Stafford from Cheddleton Junction on the North Staffordshire Railway to Caldon Low and Hulme End;

VIII. A light railway between Didcot in the county of Berks and Watlington in the county of Oxford;

IX. A light railway from Trowse in the county of Norfolk to Beccles in the county of Suffolk;

X. Light railways from Stourbridge to Kinver in the counties of Worcester and Stafford.

Presented (by command), and ordered to lie on the Table.

UNIVERSITIES (SCOTLAND) ACT, 1889.

I. Abstract of accounts of the University of St. Andrews, for the year ended 30th September 1898, being the annual report on the state of the finances of the University under the provisions of section 30 of the Universities (Scotland) Act, 1889.

II. Abstract of accounts of the University of Glasgow, for the year ended 30th September 1898, being the annual report on the state of the finances of the University under the provisions of section 30 of the Universities (Scotland) Act, 1889.

Laid before the House (pursuant to Act), and ordered to lie on the Table.

BROUGHTY FERRY GAS AND PAVING ORDER BILL [H.L.]

Read second time (according to order).

PUBLIC BUSINESS.

TROUT FISHING ANNUAL CLOSE TIME (SCOTLAND) BILL [H.L.]

Second Reading (which stands appointed for this day) put off to Tuesday the 18th of April next.

PARISH CHURCHES (SCOTLAND) BILL.

THE SECRETARY FOR SCOTLAND (Lord BALFOUR of BURLEIGH): My Lords, I move that the House do now resolve itself into Committee on this Bill.

Question put.

Motion agreed to.

Question proposed—

"That Clause 1 stand part of the Bill."

Question put.

Motion agreed to.

On Clause 2—

Amendment proposed—

"Page 1, line 10, after 'of' insert 'the heritors and Kirk Session of the parish and.'"—(Lord Tweedmouth.)

LORD TWEEDMOUTH: My Lords, my object in moving this Amendment is to secure that all the interests in any particular church or manse which it is proposed to deal with under this Bill should be thoroughly considered, and that all parties interested should give their consent to any proposal under the Bill. It is an important and serious thing to pull down an old church, or manse, to sell that old church or manse, and the site of it, and the churchyard that may surround it, in order to apply the money so obtained to other purposes. I admit there are cases where it is desirable to do so, but I think in every case all the interests concerned should be most carefully considered, and that their consent should be obtained. The Bill only requires the consent of the Presbytery in which the particular church is situated. The Presbytery, your Lordships well know, consists only of the ministers of the churches in that particular district. In Scotland the lay element has a very strong interest in the Established Church. The whole of the property of the church, whether it be teinds, or fabrics, or land, is vested in the heritors, and this Bill provides in no way for the consent of the heritors being obtained. The church has only a sort of life interest in the funds, the sites, and the fabrics, whereas the reversionary interests are vested entirely with the heritors. If a church becomes vacant permanently, they can dispose of the church and its site. It seems to me that it is only fair that their consent should be required to any proposal under this Bill. The noble Lord the Secretary for Scotland appeared last Session to be of this opinion, because when this Bill was brought before your Lordships' House last year I moved an exactly similar Amendment to the effect that the consent of the heritors should be required as well as that of the Presbytery, and the noble Lord was good enough to consent to my Amendment, and the Bill passed through in that amended form. I have this year gone one step further, and I ask the House to support me in requiring the consent also of the representatives of the congregation—that is to say, the Kirk Session, consisting of the ministers and the elders of the church, the latter being on an equal footing in Scotland with the minister of the church, and being the direct representatives of the congre-

gation. Last year it was rather hinted that the congregations in the churches that were likely to be affected by this Bill were not large, and that their interests were not great; but only the other day, so far as the nine city churches in Edinburgh are concerned, the noble Lord the Secretary for Scotland admitted that the average number of communicants in those churches were 800. There are five churches, I believe, which would be affected by the Bill in Glasgow, and there again the number of communicants is considerable, averaging, I believe, something like 700. I do really think it will commend itself to your Lordships that the consent of the congregation should in some way be obtained before a proposal under this Bill is accepted. My object, then, is not in any way to contravene the principle of the Bill. I only am anxious that all the parties interested, who have by law an interest in a particular church, shall in some way give their consent before a scheme under this Bill receives sanction. My Amendment, therefore, would run in this way—

"Where, from changes of population, it is expedient to change the site of a parish church in a city or town, and any person shall undertake to provide a new church in a suitable situation in the same city or town, any person interested, with the consent of the heritors and Kirk Session of the parish and the Presbytery of the Bounds, may apply to the Court of Teinds to sanction the change of site of such church, and the Court may dispose of the application as may seem just."

I beg to move the Amendment standing in my name.

THE SECRETARY FOR SCOTLAND: My Lords, I am sure the noble Lord will allow me to put him right upon one matter of fact in which he made an erroneous statement, I am perfectly certain, by inadvertence. He said the Presbytery in Scotland consisted only of ministers, but, as a matter of fact, there are as many elders in the Presbytery as there are ministers, because every Kirk Session has a right to send an elder. I am afraid I cannot accept this Amendment, on the ground that I think there is no real occasion for it. The proper body to represent the interests of the church is the Presbytery, and while the Presbytery should legitimately have a veto on any proposal of this kind, I do not think it would be right to give the Kirk Session an absolute veto, which would be the effect obtained by putting in the noble Lord's Amendment. I think it is quite right that both heritors and the Kirk Session should be consulted, and that they should both have an opportunity of being heard, but that will be done as a matter of course under the procedure which is adopted by the Court of Teinds. There is no doubt whatever that the Court of Teinds will take care that notice is given both to the heritors and the Kirk Session, and I think that is a sufficient safeguard of their interests. It is no doubt the case that the heritors have a large interest in the fabric of the church, but I am afraid I must say that the heritors are not in all cases members of the church, and I am also obliged to add that I am afraid if they were given in all cases a veto there would be some amongst them who would use that veto not for the purpose of protecting their interests, but for hindering the procedure under this Bill. No heritor under this Bill can be put to increased pecuniary charges, and I think the best course will be that provided in the Bill as it now stands—namely, that while the heritors and Kirk Session may be heard in their own interests they may not have an absolute veto. Therefore I am unable to accept the Amendment of the noble Lord.

LORD TWEEDMOUTH: May I ask the Secretary for Scotland why, if he takes this view now with regard to the heritors, he consented to my Amendment last year?

THE SECRETARY FOR SCOTLAND: The construction of the clause was different last year, and now the initiative is placed upon all persons interested. I accepted the Amendment last year over the Table without consultation with others. After consideration and consultation with others, I have come to the conclusion that I was too hasty in accepting the Amendment at that time, and that what I now say is the right view to take—namely, that while heritors and Kirk Sessions are entitled to appear in their own interests, it is

Secretary for Scotland.

going too far to give them absolute veto over all the changes proposed.

Question put.

Amendment negatived.

Question put—

"That Clause 2 stand part of the Bill."

Motion agreed to.

New clause proposed—

"Page 2, after line 11, insert new Clause 3—

"3. The Court of Teinds, before making any order under this Act for the sale of any old church or site thereof, and manse, shall satisfy itself whether there are any objects of historical or architectural interest in connection with such church, site, or manse which are worthy of being preserved and maintained, and, on being satisfied that such objects exist, to direct that such church, site, or manse shall be disposed of subject to such stipulations and conditions as the Court shall consider appropriate and sufficient to secure the proper preservation and maintenance of such objects.

"The Court of Teinds, before making any order to change the site of a parish church in a city or town, shall satisfy itself that reasonable provision is made for the care and support of the poor of the district from which said church is proposed to be removed.

"Should the Court of Teinds be of opinion that any locality from which a church or manse is proposed to be removed is in need of an open space, it may, in its discretion, sanction the removal of such church or manse on condition only that the old church or manse shall be demolished, and that the site thereof shall be cleared and left as an open space in all time coming.—
(*Lord Tweedmouth.*)

LORD TWEEDMOUTH: I hope the noble Lord will look upon my new clause with better favour than he regarded the Amendment I moved to clause 2. The object of this clause is to give directions to the Court of Teinds with regard to the manner in which they are to make alterations under the Act. It does seem to me that very great care should be taken as to the method in which these sites of old churches are dealt with under this Bill. My Amendment asks, in the first place, that the Court of Teinds shall be directed to consider carefully all matters of historical or architectural interest, and that they should make provision for the safeguarding of any such objects. The second point raised by my Amendment is that reasonable provision should be made for the care of the poor of the parish. It has always been recognised in Scotland that the care of the poor of the parish, whether they belong to the Established Church congregation or not, is essentially a duty of the Established Church of the parish, and of the ministers and elders of that church. John Knox himself laid down that one-third of the Church revenue should go to the Church, one-third to the poor, and one-third to education. I am afraid very little now goes from the Church funds in Scotland to either the poor or to education, but that the ministers take the whole. On these grounds it is all the more necessary, I think, that real provision is made for the poor of the parish, especially in the city districts where, however much the population may have been depleted, there will be a residuum of poor, who will require to have their interests looked after. The third point which this new clause raises is the question of open spaces within the particular district in which the old church is to be abolished. I think, my Lords, and I hope your Lordships will agree with me, that when it is proposed to pull down a church or manse in a densely-populated district one of the subjects which should be carefully considered is whether the site of the church is suitable, as such sites have often been found to be in London, for an open space. I therefore propose that the Court of Teinds should specially inquire into that subject when they are dealing with applications under this Bill, and that they should, if necessary, in making the Order, lay down that the site of the church or manse or churchyard should be applied to this purpose when it is thought desirable. These are the objects of my Amendment, and they are objects which, I think, are very clear and which want very little argument to support them. I know we on this side of the House are in the hands of your Lordships on the other side, and I move this Amendment, therefore, *ad misericordiam.* I am sure my view is the right one, whatever view may be taken by the noble Lord the Secretary for Scotland.

THE SECRETARY FOR SCOTLAND: The noble Lord has a confident assurance that he is in the right as to which he will not value my opinion. I am quite willing to accept the first of the paragraphs proposed with one or two verbal alterations. I do not see how there can be any architectural interest in connection with the site or the manse. If the noble Lord would confine it to the church, and substitute for the words "*to* direct that such church, site, or manse shall be disposed" the words "*may* direct," which is necessary to make the sentence grammatical, I will accept it. So far as the second and third paragraphs are concerned I am afraid I cannot accept them. With regard to the care and support of the poor, I am not quite sure that I fairly understand the object which the noble Lord has in view. I should think he would have known, so far as the pecuniary support of the poor is concerned, that that has now very largely been transferred from the Kirk Sessions to the parish councils. To accept the Amendment in the form in which it is placed on the Paper would clearly be to presume an interference with the duty of the parish councils. The noble Lord let fall a sort of *obiter dictum,* if I may so call it, that very little money now went to the poor. I think he underestimates the amount that is done for the poor, but, of course, there is ambiguity in the term "poor." I admit that very little money collected at the church door goes to the poor who are paupers, but a great deal is done for the poor who are not upon the paupers' roll. Of course, I am not able to say whether the proportion so spent is a third or not, but I know from my own experience that a considerable portion is expended in that direction. I object to the Court of Teinds being brought in to look after the spiritual condition of the poor. That is entirely beyond their function, and a function which they could not possibly discharge. The proper court for taking charge of these interests is the Presbytery, and under it the Kirk Sessions. The

Presbytery is as fully a court of Scotland as the Court of Teinds, and it is to the Presbytery that the spiritual affairs of the district under its charge are committed. The noble Lord may say he has not the same confidence in the Presbytery that I have——

LORD TWEEDMOUTH: Hear, hear.

THE SECRETARY FOR SCOTLAND: But I believe no Presbytery will consent to the removing of a church if by its removal the spiritual needs and interests of the poor of the district will be prejudiced, and therefore, on that ground, I cannot accept the second paragraph of this Amendment. The third paragraph, of course, opens up a subject which appeals very much to the sympathy of your Lordships. I do not think I can accept it in the form in which it stands, because it seems to imply that if the Court of Teinds so decrees, the whole value of the site and the fabric may be devoted to making an open space for the district. I do not think that is a fair burden to lay on the fund which would be set free, and I am sure the town councils of Edinburgh and Glasgow would take that view. I admit that it is an element, however, which ought to be considered, and if it was put in a form less peremptory than it is I should be glad to consider it. I propose not to accept the second and third paragraphs, but as regards the third paragraph I will postpone the Standing Committee until after Easter to see if I can devise a paragraph which would go somewhat in the direction of meeting the views of the noble Lord.

LORD TWEEDMOUTH: I beg to thank the noble Lord for the modicum of concession he has made to me, but I think what he said as to the amount of the funds which go to the benefit of the poor has gone somewhat in the direction of proving my case. Funds are given to the poor in these parishes now. That is the very thing I want to secure that the poor shall have in the future. I hope the noble Lord may see his way in the Standing Committee to meet that *Secretary for Scotland.*

point also. I am glad to accept for what it is worth—and I hope it may be of great worth—the Amendment as the noble Lord proposes to alter it.

Question put—

"That this clause, as amended, be here inserted."

Motion agreed to.

Question put—

"That clause 3 stand part of the Bill."

Motion agreed to.

Question put—

"That clause 4 stand part of the Bill."

Motion agreed to.

Bill re-committed to the Standing Committee; and to be printed. (No. 30.)

SUPREME COURT (APPEALS) BILL.

Motion made, and Question proposed—

"That this Bill be read a second time."—*(The Lord Chancellor.)*

THE LORD CHANCELLOR (The Earl of HALSBURY): My Lords, I beg to move the Second Reading of this Bill, which is urgently needed, and which enacts that notwithstanding anything in section 12 of the Supreme Court of Judicature Act, 1875, or in section 1 of the Supreme Court of Judicature Act, 1890, if all parties to an appeal or Motion consent to the Appeal or Motion being heard and determined before two Judges of the Court of Appeal, the Appeal or Motion may be heard and determined accordingly, subject, nevertheless, to the same right, if any, of appeal to the House of Lords as if the hearing and determination had been before three judges.

Question put.

Bill read a second time, and committed to a Committee of the Whole House.

HOUSE OF COMMONS.

Tuesday, 21st March 1899.

———

Mr. SPEAKER took the Chair at Three of the clock.

PRIVATE BILL BUSINESS.

———

PRIVATE BILLS (STANDING ORDER 63 COMPLIED WITH.

Mr. SPEAKER laid upon the Table Report from one of the Examiners of Petitions for Private Bills, That in the case of the following Bill, referred on the First Reading thereof, Standing Order No. 63 has been complied with, viz :—

Kensington and Notting Hill Electric Lighting Bill.

Ordered, That the Bill be read a second time.

PRIVATE BILLS (PETITION FOR ADDITIONAL PROVISION) (STANDING ORDERS NOT COMPLIED WITH).

Mr. SPEAKER laid upon the Table Report from one of the Examiners of Petitions for Private Bills, That, in the case of the Petition for additional Provision in the following Bill, the Standing Orders have not been complied with, viz :—

London and North Western Railway (Additional Powers) Bill.

Ordered, That the Report be referred to the Select Committee on Standing Orders.

CROWBOROUGH DISTRICT WATER BILL.

Read the third time, and passed.

FISHGUARD WATER AND GAS BILL.

Read the third time, and passed.

CATHCARTS' DIVORCE BILL [LORDS].

Read a second time, and committed.

BEXHILL AND ROTHERFIELD RAILWAY BILL (BY ORDER).

Read a second time, and committed.

EAST LONDON WATER BILL.

(By Order.) Order for Second Reading read.

Motion made, and Question proposed—

"That the Bill be now read a second time."

Amendment proposed—

"To leave out the word 'now,' and at the end of the Question to add the words 'upon this day six months."—*(Mr. Stuart.)*

Mr. STUART (Shoreditch, Hoxton): I paused from rising for the moment in the hope that someone in charge of the Bill would give us the reasons for bringing it on just now, and the reasons also for the particular form of the Bill. I would point out that it affects a million and a half of money for impounding the waters of the Lea and supplying them to the inhabitants of London at some distant date when the construction of the reservoirs will be accomplished. It is not one of those Bills that supply the immediate and urgent necessities of London; that was dealt with by the Government, and this Bill does not touch that point. There are other Bills before us to-day that do, but this Bill does not touch what I may call the urgent question. There are some omissions in the Bill—for instance, the sinking fund is not introduced into the Bill. So far as I know, there is no Bill affecting the raising of capital for any London water company for many years that has passed this House without the introduction of a sinking fund, the object of that sinking fund being to make the public, the water consumers of London, and the ratepayers in some way sharers in the proceeds of the capital. There were two Bills of the East London Company—in 1894 and 1897 respectively—which two Bills provided reservoirs for impounding the water of the Lea precisely as this has done, and in both of those, though introduced, if I remember rightly, without a sinking fund clause, the Committee of the House of Commons, and the Committees, in fact, of both Houses, introduced and maintained a sinking fund clause. The companies have sometimes found fault with the London County Council for expending money in appearing upon their Bills, but surely an omission from a Bill like this necessitates the spending of money under any circumstances in connection with this Bill. I hoped and imagined that some explanation at least would have been given from the other side as to the omission of the sinking fund clause. Then there is another clause which has been recently introduced of late in this House, and which was really introduced as arising from the suggestion of the right honourable Gentleman the President of the Local Government Board in 1896. That clause is one which states that the concessions thus granted to the company shall not be taken to increase the value of that company's undertaking in case of purchase within a certain number of years. That clause is omitted from this Bill. I am told that that clause has been introduced into recent Bills which the companies have brought forward; I think it really was introduced to carry out a suggestion, not exactly in that form, but yet an *imprimatur* suggestion, made in 1896, by the right honourable Gentleman the President of the Local Government Board. There are these two clauses omitted from the Bill, and I hoped, as I said, to have heard some explanation as to why they are omitted. Then there is another point in respect to this Bill which I wish to bring before the House. It is a Bill for the future water supply of London, and it is a Bill for gathering that supply from the river Lea, in connection with large reservoirs. Now, I venture to think that the Lea is not a satisfactory source from which to secure more water for London. It was only the other day that we had occasion to refer in this House to the constitution of the Conservancy Board of the river Lea, and largely because of the enormous draws of water from the Lea that there are at the present moment, and greater draws of water from the river Lea will have to be taken before we can serve the increasing needs of

Mr. Stuart.

East London in the manner which this Bill indicates. It has been in evidence before the Royal Commission, in evidence given by Sir Alexander Binnie, Mr. Baldwin Latham, and others, that, in order to supply water adequately all the year round, you will require no less than 6,000 million gallons of storage for the water of the river Lea, and that even that apparently would be insufficient. Now, there has been a good deal said about the deficiency of last year being, as it was, certainly an abnormal one, but it is not nearly so abnormal as at first sight you would suppose. I hold in my hand one of the most recently issued Reports of the present Royal Commission—not Reports, but Notes of Evidence, of the present Royal Commission—and I see that the flow of the river Lea has been continuously diminishing. Here I have the flow given in millions of gallons over King's Weir for 20 years—at least, for 18 years—and in whatever way you group those years (I am merely quoting from the Paper placed before the Royal Commission) you find that the total flow of the river Lea has been very greatly diminished. If you compare the last five of those years with the first five of those years you find that the decrease in the flow of the Lea has been 15 per cent. There has been during that period a certain decrease of the rainfall, but it has only been 10 per cent., and the winter rainfall has hardly decreased at all.

MR. WHITMORE (Chelsea): Will the honourable Gentleman say by whom the evidence was given?

MR. STUART: These tables were given by Mr. Baldwin Latham, who was the last witness examined. And there is another check upon that, that the springs—these natural springs from which the water is got—namely, the Chadwell Springs, have been decreasing in nearly the same ratio, so that the produce of those wells and of the river Lea is distinctly diminishing. Now, I do not know whether the honourable Gentleman who asked me the Question means to dispute the figures, but, whether or not, it is certainly undoubted that that is the main tenour of those figures, which I think he will admit to be true, and that is also clear from the fact that the New River Company, before the Committee on which I sat in 1896, were obliged to admit that, while a certain amount of water could be got from their wells, that amount was deficient now by 10 million gallons.

*SIR F. DIXON-HARTLAND (Middlesex, Uxbridge): A day?

MR. STUART: Yes, a day. In other words, the whole evidence before Lord Balfour of Burleigh's Committee requires to be reconsidered, and, indeed, has been very much under reconsideration. But I point out that to show that this is a very doubtful source of supply from which to secure the future increase of the London water supply for six, eight, or ten years hence, as this Bill intends and purposes to do. You have the Lea river, with a large population on its hands, you have the sources of supply diminishing, and you have enormous reservoirs, and the extensions of those reservoirs. Now, I will venture to tell the House my opinion on this Bill in the manner that I have indicated. It is because the County Council, whom I have the honour of speaking for, and I, believe that a far better source of supply is to be found than in the Thames and the Lea, and that a far better source is to be found in going to Wales. I will not venture to anticipate any argument that I may raise at a later period this afternoon upon the Welsh Bill; but I will only say this: that you have in this East London Bill one of the proposed means of meeting the increase of supply necessary a number of years hence. I ask the House to remember that this is not an urgent question—it is a question of increasing the future supply. You have this Bill giving one means of meeting that—a means which, as I have ventured to show, is at least somewhat doubtful. On the other hand, you have the Welsh scheme of the County Council, and that is undoubtedly a pure supply and abundant in quantity. It will be for me to point that out at a later stage to-day, but the two Bills are brought in, one by the authority for the moment supplying water, and the other by the London County Council, which, under Sir Matthew White Ridley's Report of 1891, was instructed to make full inquiries into the condition of the London water supply, and to bring forward a Measure embodying what should be done.

We bring forward this Measure, which we shall come to at a later stage, carrying out our duty as an authority so constituted. But what I want to point out is this, that, while I shall move that this East London Water Bill be read this day six months before I sit down, in order to obtain from the honourable Gentlemen opposite some light upon their position, and some answer to the question I am going to put, I am not appearing here as opposing this Bill on Second Reading, because I want to have a competent Committee upstairs to consider not only this, but all the opportunities of getting water for London. It may be said that the Welsh scheme is in the air, but I want to point out (and I will not allude to the Welsh Bill except in relation to this Bill that I am now really dealing with) that the two things are perfectly on the same footing. The East London Company asks to bring water here in this way, and it will have to hand over that water to the future water authority for London. On behalf of the London County Council, we take the same attitude about the Welsh Bill; and what we are anxious to secure is the opportunity of obtaining for London a better supply of water. I want to ask the honourable Gentlemen opposite, Are they going to stand in the way of this Committee considering all the means of London getting water? Are they going to prevent this Committee considering not only their own scheme, but also considering the Welsh scheme? There are two separate means of getting water for the future supply of the East End and for any part of London, and they are not compatible with one another, so that we shall prejudge the whole question if we decide on one of these means before they go to a Committee. It would be perfectly different if the two Bills were not now before the House. The two Bills are before the House, and neither of them need to wait for the Report of the Royal Commission. And the reason neither of them need wait for the Report of the Royal Commission is this: the Royal Commission has not been asked to report on this question. It is not in its reference to report on the place from which the future supply of water is to be got. It is true that it has taken incidentally, in order to see the cost, a considerable amount of evidence upon that matter, and that evidence can now be placed before the Committee to which these Bills are referred. I think that Commission's evidence is complete; and I for one shall have no objection that the evidence before that Commission should go before the Committee to which both these Bills should be referred. I therefore must make an appeal to honourable Gentlemen opposite to act by me as I am endeavouring to act by them, and to say: Let us send these two Bills—without any committal of approval on either part—to a Committee, let us place them before the Committee, and let us be able to place the whole facts of the case before the Committee, which we are quite capable of doing. This has nothing to do with the question of purchase, or who should be the future water authority for London. Are they going to say that they are going to stand by only one method of solution to the future water supply when there are two before the House? With these remarks I move that the Bill be read this day six months.

MR. LOUGH (Islington, W.): I beg to second the Amendment.

COLONEL LOCKWOOD (Essex, Epping): I have no intention of not answering the remarks as to the object of the Bill. As to the future supply of water to London from Wales, I must decline to enter into a discussion. The object of the Bill is a very simple one. It is true that it concerns a very large sum of money; but, what is more important, I believe it will place the company of which I am chairman in a position to provide the East End of London with water even during a drought. The object of the Bill, really and shortly, is to provide the company against falling short in future if a recurrence of drought should take place. In order to provide for that object we are asking leave to acquire land upon which to construct two large reservoirs, with the incidental works. These are to complete an instalment of the water scheme of reservoirs laid before Lord Balfour's Commission, and authorised in 1894 and 1897, and, but for the exceptional drought of 1898, I am bound to believe there would not have been any urgency for these reservoirs; but, in view of

Mr. Stuart.

what we suffered last year, I maintain that this Bill is absolutely urgent and necessary, and I press for its Second Reading in order that it may go before a Committee. These two reservoirs will hold 5,000 millions of gallons of water—additional storage capacity—and will cover an area of 462 and 384 acres respectively, and these reservoirs and kindred works will cost us about one million of money. The company also ask power to create debenture stock for 1½ millions. Our engineer maintains that the erection of these reservoirs is absolutely necessary, and but for that we should not have wished to create that large amount of additional stock. We believe, however, that the scheme cannot be postponed; and we also say that it has been sanctioned by a Royal Commission. To wait until the water question is finally settled would be to expose the East End of London to the dangers of another drought. My opponents find fault that we have failed in the past, and yet when these Bills are introduced to provide against these failures in the future. they proceed to oppose them. The honourable Member for Shoreditch (Mr. Stuart) stated his case the other night, making several strong points against the East London Company: I was unable to answer him at the time, but the main point which I now wish to keep to is the urgency of the Bill. If the House rejects the Second Reading, it must take the responsibility, and if any future scarcity of water does arise which might have been remedied by the passing of this Bill, on the House must rest the responsibility, and not on me. With regard to the quality of the River Lea, I may assure the honourable Member that the vintage of 1898 was magnificent, and that the water of the East London Company left nothing to be desired. and it came next to the standard of the New River Company. which I confess is high. That being the case, I ask the honourable Member if he is placing the London County Council in a good position, even from his point of view? I was perfectly aware when I took over the chairmanship of this company that my position would not be a bed of roses; but I may assure the House that my one object. in conjunction with my Board and advisers, is to prevent any recurrence of past troubles. We believe by these Measures which we now place before the House, that scarcity of water will in the future be prevented. We believe that the wells of the Lea are increasing, and did commence to increase, oddly enough, immediately after the drought. I acknowledge with gratitude the fair way in which the honourable Member placed his views before the Committee. Without doubt, should the House reject the Bill, it will mean a very serious thing indeed for the East End. It will shift the responsibility from my shoulders and place it on those who oppose the Measure.

MR. PICKERSGILL (Bethnal Green, S.W.): The Bill has been urged forward in consequence of last year's experience——

COLONEL LOCKWOOD: I said it was an instalment of the system of reservoirs.

MR. PICKERSGILL: The honourable and gallant Member said the Bill was brought forward in consequence of last year's experiences, and that it was intended to provide against similar failure in the future to that which East London suffered from last year. The single point I rise to make is this—the honourable and gallant Member says that if the company is provided with these new reservoirs they will be able to store water to meet such an emergency as arose last year. But, as a matter of fact, if the company had had not these reservoirs alone, but any amount of storage accommodation last year, they would not have met the deficiency. If they had had every particle of water that flowed over the Teddington Weir, they would still have been short of their supply by 2,000 million gallons. Under these circumstances, the very basis upon which the honourable and gallant Gentleman rested this Bill seems to fall to the ground. I quite admit that this is a proper matter for the Committee to consider. The honourable and gallant Member has given no reply to the Question of the honourable Member for Shoreditch (Mr. Stuart), and we have a right to ask that if the Second Reading of this Bill is assented to, honourable Gentlemen on the other side of the

House shall agree that the London County Council Bill, which also provides an alternative method of supplying water for London, shall be referred to the Committee, too.

MR. SINCLAIR (Essex, Romford): I have heard the honourable and gallant Member's reference to the proposed increased storage, and I trust the hopes he has expressed will be realised to the utmost. I must, however, point out that the mains of the East London Water Company are scarcely fitted to carry the supply through a thickly populated district. In East Ham, at any rate, it is essential that the mains should be good. In a case where the population has increased from 5,000 to 80,000 the same mains cannot be expected to do service. There are other points in the Bill that I take exception to. It was said that, in a great measure, the famine which occurred and the depression which occurred was due to the fact that the consumers had done away with their cisterns. That is not quite the fact. The cisterns had to be done away with because the local authorities insisted on their being done away with. And although it has been urged by the Board of Trade that new cisterns could be introduced, and that they would not be detrimental to the consumers, yet I would say that the expenditure of buying these cisterns would fall in a large measure upon a class of people who could not afford to pay for them. Then, I think if these jars supplied by the East London Water Company had not been supplied it might have been better for the consumers at large. Now, there is another matter which I think the House should take cognisance of. At Leyton, I believe, the authorities there manage the whole of their sewage evaporation of every drop of water consumed, and it appears that in normal times the amount of water they evaporate is 2,800,000 gallons per day. During the drought they only evaporated about 900,000 gallons a day, which shows that about one-third of the normal amount was evaporated. Taking the amount which it is supposed the consumer requires at 24 gallons per head per day, it would show that the consumer in this instance only had eight gallons per day, and that they lived on that small total amount. If you deduct the amount consumed for manufacturing purposes, you will find that the eight gallons per day was very much diminished; consequently the eight gallons cannot be held to be an adequate supply in the East London districts. Now, there is another remark I have to make —I do-not want to weary the House on this matter, but what I wish to press upon the House is that the East London Water Company at the present moment have bad mains, and that they are not remedied by this Bill. Now, Sir, I wish to point out also a remark which took place at the meeting of the East London Water Company, in which it was said that a large amount of water was wasted by the consumers. The words the chairman was supposed to have used were these—

"That there is ample proof of a great deal of the quantity supplied to the consumer during the shortened hours was wasted partly by the tenants' neglect, and partly from a desire to serve out the company."

If the company had to resort to such an excuse, it only showed how bad their case must be. But if that is so, I see nothing in the Government Bill by which the people who waste the water in times of drought could be prosecuted. I think anybody watering their gardens, or wilfully leaving their taps on, and so forth, in times of drought, should by some means or other be punished for their careless action. In conclusion, all I have to say is that I in no way desire to see the London County Council, or any other body, take up this enterprise. I think it is absolutely obligatory on this House to say that concessions granted should be maintained to the advantage of the public. Lastly, I think it is a question of supply to the public of an adequate quantity of water first, and that the payment of dividends should be the last consideration; and that if the dividend paid by the East London Water Company had been lessened and the sum devoted to supplying these cisterns, which they think necessary, instead of to supplying jars, which were utterly useless to the conumers at large, the poorer classes would have been the better off.

Mr. BUXTON (Tower Hamlets, Poplar): Mr. Speaker, I want to say a few words about the position as we regard it from this side of the House. I

Mr. Sinclair.

think my honourable Friend the Member for the Epping Division (Colonel Lockwood) has entirely misunderstood the view taken by my honourable Friend sitting behind me. We do not intend to divide against the Second Reading of this Bill, because I recognise that it is very likely that this expenditure by the East London Water Company may be necessary in order to prevent further water famines. The honourable Gentleman said there was no question of urgency; therefore there was no question of the Bill at the present time. I think he has forgotten the Bill introduced by the right honourable Gentleman the President of the Local Government Board, which was intended to provide against any likelihood of urgency during the next few years. If my honourable Friend will read the evidence before the Royal Commission, of Mr. Brian, the engineer to the East London Water Company, he will find that he admitted that this system of connection would enable them to carry on without any fear of water famine, for, at all events, two or three years to come. Therefore, there is no immediate urgency in regard to this House. I fully recognise that it may be right and proper these proposals should be passed in order that they may be in a position to provide for their customers in future years. What we want to impress upon the House is this: as my honourable Friend behind me pointed out to the House, we have before us two alternative proposals for the supply of water—

SEVERAL HONOURABLE MEMBERS: We have no alternative proposals.

MR. BUXTON: There are at the present moment before the House two or three Bills dealing with the London water supply, and they are dealing with the question of the future supply. The point of view we take in regard to this matter is that we do not desire to stand in the way of any proposal made by which we may have an increased and improved supply of water. We contend that these proposals made by a responsible body like the London County Council, as well as those made by the water companies, ought to go before the same Committee, so that the question may be dealt with, not piecemeal, but as a whole. The right honourable Gentleman the President of the

Local Government Board has himself declined to accept proposals in regard to the water question, because he said it prejudiced action subsequently to be taken by the Government when the Royal Commission reported. The Bill involves an expenditure of 1½ millions, but the other Bills, with an expenditure of 4½ millions, did prejudice the question of the future water supply. But, while we do not desire to commit the House at this stage to any definite approval of the system of bringing an alternative supply from Wales rather than from the Lea and the Thames, we do think that if the future is to be prejudiced by this large expenditure on the part of the East London Company, the alternative scheme ought to be placed in the hands of the same Committee. What I want to ask the right honourable Gentleman the President of the Local Government Board is, whether he really intends to take up this position, that, while he will do nothing himself or allow the County Council to do something, he will allow the water companies to prejudice the question of future supply. That is the position which my honourable Friend the Member for Epping (Colonel Lockwood) takes up. I do not wish to prejudice the case or to enter into any inconvenient matter by saying anything in derogation of the East London Water Company. We are quite prepared to allow the company to go to an expenditure to put their mains in a proper condition with a view to, if possible, prevent future water famines. I think everybody admits that some increase in the supply will be necessary before long, and the only alternative is our taking the water from the Lea and the Thames, or going to Wales. It is on that point that I would appeal to the right honourable Gentleman the President of the Local Government Board for justice in the consideration of these Bills.

MR. H. S. SAMUEL (Tower Hamlets, Limehouse): Mr. Speaker, I must confess to very much surprise at the changed attitude of honourable Members opposite on this question since the Debates in 1893 and 1894. It seems to me that the East London Members are far more concerned, if I may say so, with the immediate supply of water in the East of London rather than

in the future supply. I disagree in this case, therefore, with the honourable Member for Poplar. I must confess it is a difficult matter for me to vote for this Bill, though I intend to do so, for the simple reason I think we East London Members have some grave accusations to make against the East London Water Company. I cannot help thinking that if the company charge the consumers large sums of money for the water they do not receive I am entitled to bring that accusation against them. On the other hand, we have considered what are the absolute needs of East London. In 1893 and 1894 honourable Members took upon themselves the responsibility of depriving us of a water inquiry. I notice they are not so ready to do so now. No East London man dare, considering the interest of his constituency, go into the Lobby against the Second Reading of this Bill. An honourable Member has told us that it is absolutely necessary for the supply of water to the East of London that the company should have power to construct these reservoirs. With all due deference to the honourable Gentleman, I think the chairman of the company has greater knowledge of the needs and the water necessities of the company than honourable Gentlemen who have addressed this House this afternoon. I prefer to get the bird in hand offered to us by the East London Water Company rather than the birds in the bush offered to us by the London County Council Bill. Therefore, in the interests of East London, I shall register my vote in favour of the Second Reading of this Bill.

THE PRESIDENT OF THE LOCAL GOVERNMENT BOARD (Mr. H. CHAPLIN, Lincolnshire, Sleaford): I am very glad indeed to hear from honourable Members on that side of the House that they do not propose to oppose the Second Reading of this Bill. After the experiences of 1896 and 1894 they would be taking a very grave responsibility upon themselves had they elected to adopt that course. I have been asked, while I am considering this Bill, not to forget the Bill for bringing water from Wales, which we are to discuss directly, and the honourable Members hold, I understand, that that Bill will in no wise prejudice any of the questions affecting the future water supply of London. My position is this, that I am waiting, and I shall listen with the greatest interest to what honourable Members have to say with regard to the Welsh Bill. But, pending that, I must reserve my opinion with regard to this Bill now before the House, and which itself also may prejudice the future of these questions quite as much as the Bill for bringing water from Wales. I am asked to put before the House some information bearing directly upon the question, and which is of great interest. My honourable Friend the honourable Baronet the Member for Gloucestershire (Sir John Edward Dorington), who is also a member of the Royal Commission, sitting this afternoon, asked me to say on his behalf, as expressing the opinion of the Commission—as he was unable to say it himself—that they have considered this Bill which we are discussing at this moment, and they are of opinion that that Bill and its provisions, being indeed as a matter of security for the water supply of the inhabitants, would not in their judgment or opinion prejudice in any way questions before the Commission. I thought it only right that I should say so. I am very glad that honourable Members are not going to oppose the Second Reading.

MR. BICKERSTETH HUDSON (Hertfordshire, Hitchin): I can only say that, as a matter of fact, the stream which in my boyhood was full of water dries up more and more, and we wish to try and impress upon the Committee upstairs that they should not allow further wells to be sunk; if they do, we shall be absolutely dry of water in Hertfordshire.

Amendment, by leave, withdrawn.

Bill read a second time.

Motion made and Question proposed—

"That it be an Instruction to the Committee to whom the East London Water Bill is referred, having regard to the Resolution of this House of 12th March 1896, they do insert such provisions in the Bill as will insure the acquisition by the local authority of a suitable area of open space in substitution for the common rights proposed to be extinguished under the Bill, the extent and situation of such area of open space to be determined by the Committee."—(*Mr. Paulton.*)

President of Local Government Board.

*MR. PAULTON (Durham, Bishop Auckland): In moving the Instruction which stands in my name, I think I need only say that it is identical with the Instruction which I moved, and which was accepted unanimously, in February 1897, on a similar Bill by the East London Water Company. The object is simply this, to maintain what is now, happily, the settled policy of Parliament with regard to open spaces, and provide that where a public company takes land over which common rights exist, they should give a suitable area of open space to the local authority in substitution. This, I am glad to say, is accepted by the promoters, and I desire to express my satisfaction at the fair and open way they have met my views. I therefore beg to move.

Motion agreed to.

EAST LONDON WATER (TEMPORARY SUPPLY) BILL (BY ORDER).

Motion made, and Question proposed—

"That this Bill be read a second time."

MR. STUART: I only wish to know what is the attitude of the Local Government Board with respect to this Bill. This Bill only covers the same ground as is covered by the Bill of the right honourable Gentleman, with one exception, as far as I can see. The right honourable Gentleman told us that this Bill gives no additional powers for taking water from the Thames, and this Bill does. It says in clause 4 that they shall have power to use; to supply a larger quantity of water than the said company are now authorised to take, and the right honourable Gentleman said that was not in his Bill, and I should like to know what attitude he takes, and whether this Bill is going to the same Committee as the other Bills which are dealt with to-day.

THE PRESIDENT OF THE LOCAL GOVERNMENT BOARD: No, Sir; the Bill will not go to the same

Committee as the Government Bill. That is a Committee already appointed. It is practically true that much the same ground is covered by these two Bills, but in some respects the Bill which we are now discussing goes beyond the Government Bill—that is to say, taking additional supplies of water from the Thames. What I propose to do is to agree to this Bill being read a second time and going to a Committee, and I apprehend that when the Government Bill has passed it will be a matter for consideration as to what clauses are necessary.

MR. BUXTON: Do I understand that we have two Bills dealing with the same points, and that the only difference is whether water shall be allowed to be taken from the Thames? Do I understand that the Government are allowing these two Bills dealing with the same question to go to different Committees, and that it is only after the Government Bill has been agreed to that the difference will be discussed? Shortly, it is not putting the House in a proper position that they should have two Committees sitting for the same object— one dealing with a Bill promoted by a London company, and the other with a Bill promoted by the Local Government Board. I do hope the Government will reconsider their position in regard to this Bill, and do what I cannot help thinking has invariably been done— namely, to send Bills dealing with the same subject to the same Committee, who will come to some general conclusion as to what should be done with regard to them.

*SIR F. DIXON-HARTLAND: This is a question which very largely affects the Thames Conservancy. We are bound by the Act of Parliament under which we work to see that we have sufficient water to navigate the Thames, and when this Bill was produced we looked very carefully into the clause which the honourable Member for Poplar has alluded to, and we objected to it, because we thought that in times of drought we might have the river denuded of its water, and its navigation seriously affected. We had a conference with the London company, and the East London Company has consented to a clause being put in by which they will not take water from the Thames when the overflow is less than 200 million gallons over Teddington Weir, which is settled to be a proper amount. Therefore this clause will be inserted, and put an end to the difficulty alluded to.

Bill read a second time, and committed.

METROPOLITAN WATER COMPANY'S BILL.

Motion made and Question proposed—

"That this Bill be read a second time."

MR. STUART: Does the right honourable Gentleman intend also to send this Bill to a Committee?

THE PRESIDENT OF THE LOCAL GOVERNMENT BOARD: Yes.

*SIR F. DIXON-HARTLAND: The same clause was put into this Bill with regard to water being taken from the Thames.

MR. BUXTON: With reference to this Bill—because the right honourable Gentleman will remember when he introduced his Bill, to which we made objection, because it was founded upon the distinct recommendation of the Royal Commission in regard to this matter—they say there has been no communication between the companies, in order to save any possibility of famine, such as that which occurred last year. But the Royal Commissioners did hedge it about, with certain conditions. They hedged it about with conditions that under temporary circumstances such as those, no further water should be taken from the Thames. They hedged it about with the condition that the capital expended on that Measure should not go to increase the value of the companies when they were purchased, and in regard to the question of the sinking fund, they also introduced that by the Bill. This Bill does not deal with any of those three points satisfactorily, but the honourable Gentleman who represents the

Thames Conservancy says, as I understand, that there will be a certain check upon their taking water from the Thames.

*SIR F. DIXON-HARTLAND: A clause will be inserted the same as in the last Bill, that they are not to take water unless the overflow at Teddington Weir exceeds 200 million gallons.

MR. BUXTON: Quite so; but still they are liable to take more water from the Thames, and that seems to me to be a matter which is going beyond what is our view of the intention and will of the Royal Commission. There is no clause in this Bill dealing with the question of the sinking fund, as to which the Royal Commission made a special Report—namely, that any capital expended on this matter should not go to increase the value of the companies when purchased. Therefore I should really like the right honourable Gentleman to explain to us what is the advantage of this Bill at all. He has the Government Bill to carry out this very object. It is surrounded with certain safeguards which will not prejudice the question of water supply, and on that ground we are willing to support the Bill. We have passed an automatic Bill to enable that very company, which is likely to have large questions of emergency arise, to deal with them, because when discussing the right honourable Gentleman's Bill the other day I ventured to ask him across the House whether he intended that Bill to be of a temporary character, and one which would not prejudice the question of communication in the future, when a fresh supply was taken either from the Thames or elsewhere. The right honourable Gentleman, replying himself across the House, practically agreed to that proposition. This Bill, as it stands, is a much more far-reaching one than that of the Government, and I hope the right honourable Gentleman will see himself that in the shape and way in which it is drawn it will very considerably prejudice, or may prejudice, the question of future supply, because it provides for a large system which may cost £300,000 or £400,000, and when the new system is taken in hand, may be unnecessary, or which may be brought about in a much better or more

Mr. Buxton.

economical way. Therefore I do hope the right honourable Gentleman will take up a different attitude with regard to this Bill than in regard to the last one, and see that it is not a Bill which ought to be passed, taking into account the fact that no emergency can arise, because of the Government Bill, and that we are dealing with a company, for whom special provisions may specially be made.

THE PRESIDENT OF THE LOCAL GOVERNMENT BOARD: The honourable Gentleman asked me what attitude I should take towards this Bill. The answer is that this Bill goes further and contains provisions which the Government Bill does not. Possibly some of these provisions are valuable. I am informed that arrangements have been come to between the Conservancy interests and the company, but that was impossible in the Government Bill, because it was impossible to give the notices required by statute. All the other matters which the honourable Gentleman referred to are matters that can be adjusted in Committee. As to the question he puts, why all these Bills are not to go to the same Committee, the reason is that this matter is one of urgency, works require to be done within a period when we may possibly expect them to be effective. Under these circumstances, though I admit that the matter has not been very simple, I have done the best thing I possibly could. My object has been to get the Bills through as rapidly as possible for the purpose of arranging for these works, and if all the Bills were to go to the same Committee it naturally would lead to very considerable delay.

Bill read a second time, and committed.

WEST MIDDLESEX WATER BILL.

On the Motion for the Second Reading,

MR. STUART: I understand this Bill is purely temporary in connection with what is to be permanently done. There are some things that have been omitted as in the other Bills, such as the sinking fund, and the clause with respect to purchase to which I must call attention; but I think perhaps the honourable Gentleman in charge of the Bill will say if my interpretation of the Bill is correct?

MR. BOULNOIS (Marylebone, E.): The object of this Bill is to provide a main from the intake at Hampton to the reservoirs at Barnes, and to take an additional quantity of water from the Thames by arrangement with the Thames Conservancy, which we should be entitled to take under the Staines Reservoirs Act, say three years hence, when the reservoirs will be completed. It is practically a temporary Measure, and is brought forward to meet not so much an emergency as with a view to prevent anything like a deficiency of water, and especially in view of the arrangements which we have made with the other companies in the metropolis to carry out a communication for the water supply. With regard to the observation of the honourable Member for Shoreditch as to the sinking fund clause being omitted from the provisions of this Bill, I would point out to the House that if the sinking fund clause is inserted in this Bill, whatever is deducted from the company must absolutely come out of the consumers' pockets. It will not come out of the shareholders' dividends in any form or shape; and although, of course, the directors of this company look for their dividends to pay their shareholders, they are equally interested in the consumer. I hear some Gentlemen laugh, but I do assure the House, as far as I am personally concerned, I stand here as the representative of my constituents, and I claim for them that if this clause should be inserted in this Bill they will be the sufferers and not the shareholders of the company. Under these circumstances I hope the clause will not be inserted by the Committee upstairs, but I thought it right that I should supplement the honourable Gentleman's observations to that extent.

The Bill was read a second time, without a division.

VOL. LXVIII.   [FOURTH SERIES.]

LONDON WATER (WELSH RESERVOIRS AND WORKS) BILL.

Order for Second Reading read.

Motion made, and Question proposed—
" That this Bill be now read a second time."

MR. STUART: This Bill is for purchasing land in Wales, by agreement or otherwise, and creating reservoirs there in order to provide for the future water supply of London. It is not intended by this Bill to substitute this water for the water—the most part at any rate—that is at present used in London; but in the opinion of many who are very well acquainted expertly with the subject the demands already sanctioned on the Thames and on the Lea, and on the wells in the neighbourhood—Hertfordshire and the like, are as great as we can well and with safety allow them to be. It may be known to the House that 150 millions of gallons are at present liable to be taken from the Thames, but that by two Bills recently passed, of the Southwark and Vauxhall Company and the Staines Reservoirs, this has been raised to a total amount of 180 million gallons.

SIR F. DIXON-HARTLAND: One hundred and thirty millions.

MR. STUART: The total amount is 185 millions now.

SIR F. DIXON HARTLAND: Yes.

MR. STUART: That is the total figure; probably the honourable Gentleman and I quite agree on the figures—185¼ million gallons is now authorised to be taken from the Thames, although not at present taken and that, with something like 120 million gallons from the Lea and the wells, make up the quantity of water which is authorised to be taken by the various companies permanently from the courses immediately available in the Thames and Lea Valley, making a total, roughly speaking, of 300 million gallons, which water is recognised by those who have given evidence on the matter to be practically sufficient for the requirements of London till the year 1911 or 1912. Therefore some steps had to be

3 O

taken to secure additional supplies before the year 1911 or 1912, that is to say, roughly about a dozen years hence. Those, therefore, who are interested in the water supply of London have been casting about for the source from which that additional supply should be taken, and there have, roughly speaking, been two groups of ideas. One has been that a greater quantity of water may be taken from the Thames, and the other is that that safe limit has now been reached in the numbers that I have stated, and that further water ought to be taken from some other and more distant source, such as Wales. Those who propose to take water from the Thames and Lea propose to do so by a large system of impounding that water at flood, or at any rate when the river is very full, and permitting a certain residue, which has been laid down as sufficient for the river, to flow in each river over certain weirs. Now, that residue is wholly insufficient in the case of the Lea, but that is not before us for the moment. That Bill has now gone to a Committee; we have passed the Second Reading, and that question is no longer before us. But in respect of the Thames, if what is urged by those who oppose taking a larger amount than is already agreed to be taken be correct—and I ask the House always to remember that that is considerably in excess of what is at present taken—those who oppose the taking of a larger quantity of water from the Thames do so on the ground that it cannot be done without very great expense. The enormous expense of the Staines Reservoirs will have to be multiplied very much when they take the greater quantity of water than they now take, because the House will see if you are to fix a certain minimum which is to flow over a certain weir each day, then every multiple of that which you took before and which you use by impounding, creates the necessity of impounding only the surplus, and therefore the getting of large areas of impounding tanks. That practically is the system proposed by the water companies, roughly speaking, and it means an extremely large expenditure, however you like to look at it, upon tanks or impounding reservoirs. And the smaller the flow of the river becomes in any year the more large, far more large in

Mr. Stuart.

proportion, do these impounding reservoirs need to be, because if there was only a very few gallons over the minimum then it would require enormous reservoirs to preserve sufficient to make any adequate daily supply. I apologise to the House for having to deal with such an intricate matter, but it is necessary in order to know where the great expense comes in of these reservoirs. Then there is another matter which we feel a great deal of force in, that is that the Thames is a river which has a large population upon its banks, and if you will look at the recent report laid before the London County Council, in respect of pollution, you will see there is going on, in spite of the praiseworthy efforts of the Thames Conservancy, a large amount of pollution in respect of the river.

Sir F. DIXON-HARTLAND: No.

Mr. STUART: A large amount of pollution, which must increase, and which the honourable Gentleman must admit must take place at the time of flood water; and unless these reservoirs take the water at the time of flood water they will have to reduce the quantity of water that flows over the weirs at the minimum. There comes the exact point of extreme importance in respect of the whole of this great scheme for the supply of London with water in future—that in order to avoid the taking of flood water you must be driven to reduce the minimum flow of the Thames lower than what it is just now; and whereas the minimum flow was held to be, and is well defended by the honourable Gentleman, if he will allow me to compliment him, the minimum flow of the Thames as it has been laid down, yet the evidence that has been given more recently, particularly by the water companies, shows that it is quite obvious that what these companies have in view is that a very much smaller flow over the weir of the Thames is adequate, and that they ought to be allowed to reduce that minimum flow. Now, what I want to point out is this: If you find, by taking water from the Thames only in that way, and not taking it at times of high flood, that you cannot get enough water, then it is inevitable that you will be driven to reducing the minimum flow of the Thames until you get it in much the same condition below the intakes as the River Lea is at present, which, as any honourable Member who chooses to go to the East End of London will see to be a very unsatisfactory condition. Those are some of the points with respect to the inadvisability of taking the future increase of London water to a larger extent than has now been agreed upon from the Thames and the Lea. Now, the London County Council has had this matter under very careful consideration for a long time, and it has not been without a proper authority that we have had to consider this question. We have been instructed to do it. Sir Matthew White Ridley's Committee in 1891 reported that powers should be granted to the London County Council to expend such further sums as may be reasonably necessary in order that they may examine for themselves, as the responsible municipal authority of London, the whole position of the metropolitan water supply, and come to a conclusion as to the policy which, for financial and other reasons, it is desirable to adopt. We have done that. We have done that over a series of years, and we have had two main lines of resolution. The first is that the water companies ought to be purchased by the London County Council, under circumstances laid down in Bills to be introduced, and the second is that the future supply for London ought to be got from a certain district in Wales which is indicated in the Bill to which I am now alluding. That latter part of our programme, so to speak, has taken a longer period to mature because of the great investigations that we required on the rainfall and other matters, and the quality of the water, and so on. But the London County Council—being empowered by Parliament, as it was after this report of Sir Matthew White Ridley's Committee in the direction I have just read—has now, this Session, brought before Parliament a complete scheme—an absolutely complete scheme for the future of the London water supply. You may find fault with the scheme or not, but it is a complete scheme. It is a scheme whereby we propose, in a certain Bill before the House, to purchase the water companies under certain circumstances and under certain terms; the other part is that we should continue to take the

water supply from the Thames and the Lea so far as it is satisfactory and authorised; and that we should go for additional water in the way described in this Bill, bringing it from Wales by an aqueduct, as provided in a subsequent Bill that will be laid before this House. That is our scheme. It is a coherent scheme. It is a scheme that does not deal with the water supply of to-morrow; it deals with the future water supply of London. I think I may point out that had our Purchase Bill been carried we should have been immediately empowered, and we should have been under the obligation to have done the very thing which the right honourable Gentleman the President of the Local Government Board has endeavoured to do by no less than three Bills sent to two different Committees; but, however that may be, we should, if our scheme had been carried out this year, have been able to do all that his scheme proposes. However that may be, his Bill may be regarded as meeting the immediate points, and the future of the London water supply is dealt with in the comprehensive scheme which I have just suggested to the House. The first portion of the scheme comes before the House to-day in the Bill the Second Reading of which I have just moved. That is a Bill, as I have said, for securing the land and for making the reservoirs. I have already stated in the House that the Motion which the honourable Gentleman on the other side (Mr. Whitmore) intends to make against this Bill, that it should be hung up until after the Report of the Royal Commission, is beside the mark, because the Royal Commission has no instruction whatever to report upon the question of getting water from Wales. It has not such reference. It has certainly taken a great deal of evidence about that; but it is obvious you can see why it has done so—to secure some knowledge of what should be the future sum necessary to be expended by whoever should be the water authority for London; and it has seemed that that sum will not be very different in amount one way or the other whichever of the two schemes be carried out. Having got that sum, that is what the Royal Commission needs to know. It has certainly taken evidence on the matter a considerable time ago, but that evidence is finished; and although the Commission has not reported, that evidence can go before the Committee on that Bill; and, therefore, all that need be done, all the effect of the Royal Commission upon the judgment of the House upon this Bill is such that it neither influences whether this Bill should be read a second time or not on this occasion. If you postpone this Bill till after the Report of the Royal Commission, you are practically preventing the Committee, which has before it one system of dealing with the future supply of London, from considering another system for dealing with the supply of London. There is no ground whatever for postponing this Bill until the Royal Commission has reported; and therefore what we do is to ask the House to read it now, inasmuch as it is a Bill seriously affecting the future method of dealing with the water supply of London. You can see that this Bill should go forward at this time, and, anxious as we are, we realise that it might be said that the passing of this Bill would prejudge the question of the future water authority of London, because it may be said that the London County Council are securing an area for the supply of water, and that in that way they are in some surreptitious manner becoming the authority for the water supply of London. All I can say is this: having investigated this matter for many years, having gone into it very fully, we are so impressed with the terrible evil of going along the Thames line only to supply London—the Thames and the Lea lines—and not adopting a Welsh system, such as this, that we feel it is necessary to proceed with it now in the face of these Bills, and we are perfectly prepared, if this Bill is granted to us, to hold the area in trust for whoever should be the future responsible water authority for London. If that is so, where is the ground for throwing out this Bill because the Royal Commission has not reported? There is no ground, and I ask the Government, who are extremely anxious, as I can imagine, that there should be a reasonable opportunity of securing a good future supply to London, are they or are they not to allow this Bill to pass now? Because they can allow it to pass if the right honourable Gentleman the President of the Local Government Board will stand up and say he is prepared to do so. Are

Mr. Stuart.

they or are they not going to allow this Bill to pass now? If they pass the Bill which is to secure water by enormous reservoirs from the already exhausted and unsanitary sources of the river Lea—— ("No!") Whatever may be your view upon that, at any rate they passed a Bill which involves the expenditure of 1½ millions of money by the other method of supplying water for London than that from Wales. That is passed by the assistance and with the approval of the Government, and, I say, are they now going to throw out this particular Bill that I bring before the House, and thereby allow the Committee only to consider the one method and not to consider the two methods? We should be committed to the one method of necessity, probably because the argument may be urged that London requires more water within five or six years. If that is so, I do not think we should be committed to this particular method of dealing with the matter, and it will be a whole year before we can bring up this Welsh scheme again, which will then be rendered practically impossible, having passed the other Bill which we have passed to-day. I do appeal to the right honourable Gentleman to be fair all round in this matter—to let these two Bills go before the Committee, and if he does not, on behalf of the Government and on behalf of himself, he takes a very serious and a very heavy responsibility.

Amendment proposed—

"To leave out from the word 'That' to the end of the Question, in order to add the words, 'it is inexpedient that the Bill be read a second time before the Royal Commission on London Water Supply has presented its Report,' instead thereof."—*(Mr. Whitmore.)*

MR. WHITMORE : I beg, Sir, to move the Amendment which stands in my name. The honourable Gentleman the Member for Shoreditch has made a very interesting, but not, I think, a very convincing speech. The whole burden of it is that there are two alternative methods of meeting the demand of London with regard to water. That is not so. As regards the immediate future, we must go to the Thames, and the water companies, by the Bills we have just read a second time, will give us every security that London will be safe in the immediate future from any danger whatever of a recurrence of a water famine. When you come to the larger future and the more distant future, I think there is much to be said for the view of the honourable Gentleman. Certainly, in moving this Amendment, I do not wish to be understood for a moment as committing myself to the proposition that some other source of supply than the Thames may not at some future time be required for London. I think that is very likely the case. It may be the case that these particular sources of supply in Wales are about the best that can be obtained, and for my part I do not think that London ought to be slow to secure some such site—not perhaps immediately to construct aqueducts and connections between those new sources of supply and London. But without doubt, there will be a race between all the great populations of England to secure for themselves an ample supply in the future, and it will be well that London should not be behind-hand in that competition. But what we have got to face to-day is the statement of the honourable Gentleman himself. He says that the London County Council has got a complete, a coherent scheme, which is brought before Parliament. The essential part of that scheme is its Purchase Bill—the Purchase Bill by which the County Council proposes to acquire the water companies, and to become itself the water authority for London. That is part of the coherent and complete scheme. But the honourable Gentleman himself has postponed the second reading of that Bill in the hope that the Royal Commission may report on this matter before he brings the Second Reading before the House. If this scheme is a complete and coherent scheme, surely it is necessary also to postpone this component part of the whole scheme.

Mr. STUART: It does not follow that part of a coherent scheme is itself bad.

*Mr. WHITMORE: Not bad, but what applies to one part of a coherent scheme applies to another part of it. I am not arguing that it is bad, but as part of the scheme has been, at the instigation of the honourable Gentleman himself, postponed, it would be wise also

to have this part postponed until the Committee has reported. I cannot conceive myself how any honourable Gentleman really thinks that a Select Committee of this House could give its sanction to the acquisition of a great tract of country and the construction of reservoirs without being certain that the body which undertakes this great task was certain to be the water authority for London. How would the Select Committee know whether that is to be the case with regard to London? It may be so, or it may not be so—we do not know. Surely it is only right, it is only reasonable, that the authority which is to be created after the Report of the Royal Commission, without doubt by the Government, or by Parliament, should have the responsibility from the very beginning for the future water supply of London. In my judgment it is just as futile to ask a Select Committee of this House at the present moment to pass an opinion as to the wisdom of the London County Council in acquiring these new sources of supply, as it is, on the admission of the honourable Gentleman himself, to ask the Committee to sanction the purchase of the water supply. I don't for a moment wish to put off the question of this great water problem of London. The present uncertainty is hard upon the water companies. It is demoralising the County Council and——

Mr. STUART: The Motion to bring forward the Bill was passed unanimously.

*Mr. WHITMORE: This uncertainty is expensive to the ratepayers of London, and unfair to the consumers. But we cannot remove the uncertainty, we cannot obtain the desired settlement, until the Royal Commission has presented its Report. I beg to move the Amendment.

Mr. COHEN (Islington, E.) formally seconded the Amendment.

Mr. BUXTON: I agree to a very large extent with the views expressed by the honourable Member for Chelsea (Mr. Whitmore). The whole question of the future supply must be considered at an early date. The honourable Member also thinks it is very important that some area of a possible future supply ought to be secured at as early a date as possible. He said he did not wish to urge a dilatory plea, but it seemed to me that his argument tended that way. It is quite certain that whatever the Report of the Royal Commission is, Parliament will not be able to deal with the matter for some time to come. Then the authority will have to be stated, and it is quite certain that it will be at least two or three years before the question of purchase has been carried to such completion as to satisfy my honourable Friend. He also submitted that it was necessary, for fear of it getting into other hands, for London to get a good source of supply, and that he would like to see the question settled, because it gave rise to disputes. At all events, we are not sure these disputes will not continue for another three or four years. Now, what I want to ask the President of the Local Government Board is this— whether he is going to treat the question of this supply in a different way to what he has treated the question of supplies in other quarters, as discussed earlier in the afternoon? Already large sums of money have been spent in increasing the supply, and it will certainly take 10 or 11 years to bring this new supply to London. As regards the question of purchase, that does not come in one way or the other in this Bill. I hope the right honourable Gentleman will take into account the points raised, which are of such serious moment to the metropolis at large.

*SIR F. ˙ DIXON - HARTLAND: We do not think that if this Bill is passed it will bring up the question of the full scheme. We ought to have the Welsh supply and this all brought up together, because if the matter is prejudiced by allowing the London County Council to obtain the Welsh supply they will then have the power, if they please, to make an alternative system of water supply to that provided by the water companies, and that would interfere with the counties at present supplied by these companies, which are not at all under the control of the county councils. In Middlesex we object to the London County Council having any rights within our borders, and we should not be prepared to go for a supply in that county from the London County Council. I am told that every other county round London objects in exactly the same way. The honourable

Mr. Buxton.

Member for Shoreditch (Mr. Stuart) spoke of the action of the Thames Conservancy. I can assure the House that they have taken a good deal of trouble. A report which was presented only last week shows that only 113 cases of pollution at the present moment exist, and that water has been purified to such an extent that 500,000 people who in 1884 had polluted water have now pure water. We do hope that the salmon trout which we propose to put into the river this year will have the effect of making the Thames a salmon-producing river. If that is done, it will show that the Thames water is as good a water as people can have to drink.

*MR. A. C. HUMPHREYS-OWEN (Montgomery): I desire to say a few words with reference to the case of the small Welsh farmers whose lands will be submerged by the operation of this Bill. Although the valleys are sparsely populated, they still contain many inhabitants who will be compelled to seek other habitations. Now, the class of people who hold these farms are for the most part small holders, who generally work their farms with only the labour of their own families. Well, now, we know it is a certain fact that the demand for farms in Welsh speaking districts is exceedingly great. I do not suppose that in the whole of these counties there is a single farm vacant for want of tenants. What then is to become of the farmers who are in this position? It might be contended that the clause which provides for the rehousing of persons of the working classes which appears in the Bill would be sufficient to provide for them. I think, however, that looking at the definition part of the clause, it will be seen that this definition does not cover the case of the small farmers working their own land. It meets the case of the town artizan. No doubt this clause was framed with the view of meeting the case of persons of the artizan classes who are ejected in consequence of railways being made or other clearances in the suburbs of large towns. Now, Sir, I think the ideal way of dealing with this would be to alter the definition clause so as to make it clear that it should be the duty of the Council to provide other farms for those whose holdings are thus taken from them. I understand, however, that as

this is what is known as a Model Clause there will be considerable difficulty with the authorities in the House in getting such an alteration as that. Then there is the other alternative, of course—that of compensation. Now, here is another difficulty. These tenant farmers have been on their farms from generation to generation; yet legally they only hold their tenancy from year to year. They have, therefore, if they go for compensation under the Land Clauses Acts, next to no claim. I think this raises a very strong claim upon the London County Council to take a generous view of the position of these small farmers. I believe they are ready to do so. I am bound to say that, though I am glad there is a possibility of that being done, yet I cannot regard that as really satisfactory. I do not wish to oppose the Bill on this ground. The Bill is of far too great importance to the metropolis of London for us to obstruct it and oppose it. Indeed, we shall be, for many reasons, glad to welcome the London County Council in Wales. At the same time, I hope I may be able to receive from my honourable Friend the Member for Shoreditch (Mr. Stuart) some statement as to the intention of the Council to provide as fully as they possibly can, for the small Welsh farmers whom their operations will displace.

MR. W. JONES (Carnarvon): Mr. Speaker, I understand that this Welsh scheme will affect two or three schools in this neighbourhood which are to come down, and I hope my honourable Friend the Member for Shoreditch (Mr. Stuart) will be able to give us an assurance that the London County Council is prepared to replace them in the interests both of scholars and teachers.

MR. LLOYD MORGAN (Carmarthen, W.): Mr. Speaker, I won't trouble the House with more than two or three observations in support of the case put forward by my honourable Friend the honourable Member for Montgomeryshire. I quite agree with the observations he has made as to the unfortunate position in which a very considerable number of small Welsh farmers on the hills will be placed when the London County Council proceed to construct reservoirs, if this Bill becomes law. It seems to me, as far as I can gather, that

this Bill would have been petitioned against but for the very short time given for the presentation of petitions, because it was thought that the Bill would have been thrown out owing to non-compliance with the Standing Orders. The Bill, as it stands, so far as small farms are concerned, seems to me to be unsatisfactory, because—unless we have some distinct understanding as to the manner in which they will be dealt with when the honourable Gentleman the Member for Shoreditch replies to the questions put to him by my honourable Friend—this clause deals with various classes of people, but it does not deal with the small occupying tenant-farmer. The landowner will receive very substantial compensation; the leaseholder will also receive substantial, and, perhaps, very great compensation; the small shopkeeper will be looked after, but there is one class which, under this Bill, will receive no consideration at all, and that is the class entitled to the most consideration, in my opinion, and that is the small occupying farmer in the Welsh counties. Unless we have from my honourable Friend the Member for Shoreditch some satisfaction that they will receive not only fair, but reasonable and liberal compensation, I shall have to consider the attitude which I take in reference to the Bill. But I feel sure that my honourable Friend will make a statement which will give us satisfaction, and make it impossible for us to oppose this Bill.

MR. STUART: Mr. Speaker, with the leave of the House, I will just answer that question as to the clause with respect to the displacement of persons. The labouring clause is, of course, the ordinary model clause which would refer to all agricultural labourers, but not to the occupiers of small farms, who have no lease whatever, but which they hold entirely at the word of the landlord or landlady. Many of these small occupying tenants had not only held their farms for many years, but their ancestors for many years had held the same farms. They do not come under the labour clause. On the question of compensation, the London County Council has met some representatives of these bodies, and, having heard the circumstances from them— one member of the deputation said he would rather have the word of Mrs. So-and-So than the mention of his landlord and a written document from anybody else—all I have got to say is, that the London County Council has given them assurances, and I give the assurance to the House, that the fact that it is the customary condition in the country that they have no lease will not be regarded as a bar to their receiving compensation. We shall deal with each case on its merits. As to the schools, if it is quite clear that a population is moved, the schools must be created again.

THE PRESIDENT OF THE LOCAL GOVERNMENT BOARD: Mr. Speaker, I hope it will be possible for me to follow the example of those who have aready spoken, and to delay the House for only a few moments. My honourable Friend opposite asked me why a distinction should be made between the two Bills dealing with this subject. The answer, I think, is an extremely simple one. The House has already heard something which I said a few moments ago on the other Bill—that it was not calculated to prejudice in any way the number of precedents which have been submitted to the Royal Commission. The present Bill prejudices nearly all the questions which are at this moment before the consideration of the Royal Commission. The House must remember that the Bill raises a number of questions of the first importance. One is, whether the present sources of water supply to the East of London are so insufficient and so precarious as to render it absolutely necessary in the interests of London to acquire others within the shortest possible space of time. The second question is, whether that necessity has been proved, and whether the urgency is pressing. The honourable Member said—

"Why wait for the decision of the Royal Commission on this point? They have nothing whatever in their reference entitling them to inquire into the question as to the supply from Wales."

They have no direct reference, that is true; but unquestionably, under one aspect of the case, it must come within their consideration. The very first thing they would require to know was whether, having regard to financial considerations, the present and prospective requirements with regard to water supply could be in the interests of the

Mr. Stuart.

ratepayers. Incidentally, also, the Bill refers to other questions. It raises the question who is to be the new authority, and it also raises the whole question of the policy of purchase. But, as everybody knows, these are questions which are before the Royal Commission at the present moment. I am quite aware that my honourable Friend said the County Council, if this Bill was carried, are quite prepared to hold the new property in trust. Yet I think everybody will agree with me in this, if the London County Council acquire the property they are seeking to acquire that practically settles the question of who is to be the new authority, and whether purchase is to be undertaken or not, because it is perfectly obvious that the two systems could not run in competition side by side. Well, then, the only ground that the honourable Member is pressing the Bill is the ground of extreme urgency. He says there is not a moment to lose, and this question must be dealt with during the present Session, and he entered into an elaborate argument to show that although there would be within a certain number of years a provision of 300 million gallons a day for the use of the inhalbitants of London, still he said that by the year 1912 the population of London would have assumed such enormous proportions that it was absolutely necessary to proceed without a moment's delay, because the works necessary to be carried out by the County Council to bring water from Wales would occupy practically the whole of the intervening time. The honourable Member has made a mistake in his calculations. Unless I am totally misinformed, and I am entitled to think I am correctly informed, it will not be until the year 1917 that the population will reach the extent which will require more than that amount of water for their consumption. I am very sorry indeed that it unfortunately appears always to be falling to my lot, speaking as the representative of the Local Government Board, to oppose the Bills and wishes of this great authority, but I feel that in a case of this kind I have no alternative. The Government made themselves responsible for this Commission and the questions submitted to them, and a number of those questions they have already reported upon, and I have every reason to believe that they are now at this moment entering upon the completion of their labours. The honourable Member has practically admitted there is great force in these contentions, and that he and his friends have adopted a very unusual and very exceptional, if not unprecedented, course in endeavouring to seek the decision of Parliament upon questions which in a very few weeks the Commission must report. It will be remembered that the honourable Member himself put down a Motion postponing the Second Reading of the Council's Purchase Bill in order that the Commission might have reported before the House assents to the Second Reading.

Mr. STUART: I did not propose to postpone the Bill in order that the Commission might report, but that it might have an opportunity of reporting.

The PRESIDENT of the LOCAL GOVERNMENT BOARD: I don't see the distinction. I suppose the honourable Member took that course because he thought it would be a great advantage to have the views of the Commission before us. The honourable Gentleman, therefore, does admit the force of the contention I am submitting to the House. I don't think it is necessary to say anything further upon this point. There is a very great volume of opinion in the House that the County C^{o}uncil is ill-advised in pressing further this Motion just at the present time, and, much as I regret being in constant opposition to that body, I have no alternative.

Question put—

"That the words proposed to be left out stand part of the Question."

The House divided:—Ayes 130; Noes 206.—(Division List No. 66.)

AYES.

Abraham, Wm. (Cork, N.E.)
Abraham, William (Rhondda)
Allen, W. (Newc.-under-Lyme)
Allison, Robert Andrew
Ambrose, Robert
Ashton, Thomas Gair
Austin, Sir J. (Yorkshire)
Austin, M. (Limerick, W.)
Baker, Sir John
Barlow, John Emmott
Bayley, Thomas (Derbyshire)
Billson, Alfred
Birrell, Augustine
Blake, Edward
Broadhurst, henry
Bryce, Rt. Hon. James
Buchanan, T. Ryburn
Burns, John
Burt, Thomas
Buxton, Sydney Charles
Caldwell, James
Cameron, Sir C. (Glasgow)
Campbell-Bannerman, SirH.
Carmichael, Sir T.D.Gibson-
Causton, Richard Knight
Cawley, Frederick
Clark, Dr. G. B. (Caithness-sh)
Colville, John
Corbett, A. C. (Glasgow)
Crombie, John William
Cross, H. Shepherd (Bolton)
Curran, T. B. (Donegal)
Curran, Thomas (Sligo, S.)
Dillon, John
Donelan, Captain A.
Douglas, C. M. (Lanark)
Duncombe, Hon. Hubert V.
Elliot, Hon. A. R. Douglas
Ellis, T. W. (Merionethsh.)
Farquharson, Dr. Robert

Fenwick, Charles
Fergusson, R. C. Munro (Leith)
Fitzmaurice, Lord Edmond
Flynn, Jas. Christopher
Gladstone, Rt. Hon. Herbt. J
Goddard, Daniel Ford
Gold, Charles
Gordon, Hon. J. Edw.
Grey, Sir Edw. (Berwick)
Gurdon, Sir William Brampton
Haldane, Richard Burdon
Hayne, Rt. hon. C. Seale-
Hazell, Walter
Hedderwick, T. C. H.
Hoare, Samuel (Northwich)
Holland, W. H.(York,W.R.)
Horriman, Frederick J.
Humphreys-Owen, A. C.
Hutton, Alfred E. (Morley)
Jacoby, James Alfred
Jameson, Major J. Eustace
Jones, Wm. (Carnarvonshire)
Kay-Shuttleworth,RtHnSirU.
Kearley, Hudson E.
Kilbride, Denis
Kitson, Sir James
Lambert, George
Langley, Batty
Lawson, Sir W. (Cumberland)
Leese, Sir J. F. (Accrington)
Leng, Sir John
Lewis, John Herbert
Lloyd-George, David
Logan, John William
Lough, Thomas
Lowles, John
Macaleese, Daniel
MacDonell,Dr.M.A.(Queen'sC
M'Laren, Chas. Benjamin
M'Leod, John

Maddison, Fred.
Mappin, Sir Frederick T.
Mendl, Sigismund Ferdinand
Montagu, Sir S. (Whitechapel)
Morgan, J. L. (Carmarthen)
Morley, Chas. (Breconshire)
Moulton, John Fletcher
Norton, Capt. Cecil Wm.
O'Brien, J. F. X. (Cork)
O'Connor, T. P. (Liverpool)
Paulton, James Mellor
Pearson, Sir Weetman D.
Pickard, Benjamin
Pirie, Duncan V.
Priestley, Briggs (Yorks.)
Pryce-Jones, Lt.-Col. Edw.
Reid, Sir Robert Threshie
Rickett, J. Compton
Roberts, J. H. (Denbighs.)
Robertson, Edmund (Dundee)
Roche, Hon. J. (East Kerry)
Samuel, J. (Stockton-on-Tees)
Schwann, Charles E.
Scott, C. Prestwich (Leigh)
Shaw, Chas. E. (Stafford)
Shaw, Thos. (Hawick B.)
Sinclair, Capt. J. (Forfarshire)
Smith, Samuel (Flint)
Soames, Arthur Wellesley
Souttar, Robinson
Spicer, Albert
Steadman, William Charles
Strachey, Edward
Sullivan, D. (Westmeath)
Tennant, Harold John
Thomas, A. (Glamorgan, E.)
Trevelyan, Charles Philips
Ure, Alexander
Wallace, Robert (Edinburgh)
Wallace, Robert (Perth)

1547   London Water (*Welsh*   {COMMONS}   *Reservoirs and Works) Bill.* 1548

Walton, J. Lawson (Leeds,S.)
Wedderburn, Sir William
Weir, James Galloway
Williams, J. Carvell (Notts.)
Wills, Sir William Henry

Wilson, Fredk. W. (Norfolk)
Wilson, John (Durham, Mid.)
Wilson, John (Govan)
Woods, Samuel
Yoxall, James Henry

NOES.

Aird, John
Allhusen, Augustus H. Eden
Anstruther, H. T.
Arnold-Forster, Hugh O.
Atkinson, Rt. Hon. John
Bailey, James (Walworth)
Baird, J. G. A.
Baldwin, Alfred
BalfourRt.Hn.A.J.(Manch'r
Balfour,Rt.Hh.G. W.(Leeds)
Banbury, Fredk. George
Barry, Sir F. T. (Windsor)
Barton, Dunbar Plunket
Bathurst, Hon. Allen Benj.
Beach,RtHnSirM.H.(Bristol)
Beckett, Ernest William
Begg, Ferdinand Faithful
Bemrose, Sir Henry Howe
Bethell, Commander
Bhownaggree, Sir M. M.
Biddulph, Michael
Bigwood, James
Bill, Charles
Blundell, Colonel Henry
Bond Edward
Boulnois, Edmund
Bowles, Capt.H.F.(Middlesex)
Bowles, T. G. (King's Lynn)
Brodrick, Rt. Hon. St. John
Brown, Alexander H.
Burdett-Coutts, W.
Butcher, John George
Carson, Rt. Hon. Edw.
Cavendish, R. F. (N. Lancs.)
Cavendish, V.C.W.(Derbysh.
Cecil, E. (Hertford, E.)
Cecil, Lord H. (Greenwich)
Chaloner, Captain R. G. W.
Chamberlain, J. A. (Worc'r)
Chaplin, Rt. Hon. Henry
Charrington, Spencer
Clarke, Sir E. (Plymouth)
Clough, Walter Owen
Cochrane, Hon. T. H. A. E.
Coddington, Sir William
Coghill, Douglas Harry
Collings, Rt. Hon. Jesse
Colomb, Sir John Chas. Ready
Cooke, C. W. R. (Hereford)
Cornwallis, Fiennes S. W.
Cripps, Charles Alfred
Cruddas, Wm. Donaldson
Cubitt, Hon. Henry
Curzon, Viscount
Dalbiac, Colonel Philip Hugh
Dalrymple, Sir Charles
Davenport, W. Bromley-
Denny, Colonel
Dixon-Hartland, Sir F. Dixon
Doughty, George
Douglas, Rt. Hon. A. Akers-
Doxford, William Theodore
Drage, Geoffrey
Dyke, Rt. Hon. Sir W. Hart
Egerton, Hon. A. de Tatton
Fardell, Sir T. George

Fergusson,RtHnSirJ.(Manc'r
Finlay, Sir Robt. Bannatyne
Fisher, William Hayes
Fison, Frederick William
FitzGerald, Sir R. Penrose-
Flower, Ernest
Folkestone, Viscount
Fry, Lewis
Garfit, William
Gedge, Sydney
Gibbs, Hn.A.G.H.(City Lond.)
Goldsworthy, Major-General
Gorst, Rt. Hon. Sir J. Eldon
Goulding, Edward Alfred
Graham, Henry Robert
Gray, Ernest (West Ham)
Green, W. D. (Wednesbury)
Gretton, John
Greville, Hon. Ronald
Gull, Sir Cameron
Gunter, Colonel
Halsey, Thomas Frederick
Hamilton, Rt. Hon. Lord G.
Hanbury, Rt. Hon. Robert W.
Hanson, Sir Reginald
Hare, Thomas Leigh
Heath James
Heaton, John Henniker
Helder, Augustus
Henderson, Alexander
Hill, Rt. Hon. A. S. (Staffs.)
Hill, Sir Edw. Stock (Bristol)
Hoare, E. Brodie (Hampstead)
Holland, Hon. L. R. (Bow)
Hornby, Sir Wm. Henry
Houldsworth, Sir W. Henry
Howard, Joseph
Hozier, Hon. J. Henry Cecil
Hubbard, Hon. Evelyn
Hudson, George Bickersteth
Hughes, Colonel Edwin
Hutchinson,Capt.G.W.Grice-
Jessel, Capt. Herbt. Merton
Kenyon, James
Kimber, Henry
Lafone, Alfred
Lawrence, W. F. (Liverpool)
Lea, Sir T. (Londonderry)
Lees, Sir Elliott (Birkenhead)
Llewellyn, E. H. (Somerset)
Lockwood, Lt.-Col. A. R.
Long, Col. Chas. W. (Evesham
Long, Rt.Hn.W. (Liverpool)
Lopes, Henry Yarde Buller
Lowe, Francis William
Lowther, Rt. Hon. J. (Kent)
Lloyd, Archie Kirkman
Lucas-Shadwell, William
Macartney, W. G. Ellison
Macdona, John Cumming
Maclure, Sir John William
M'Iver, Sir L. (Edinburgh, W.)
Malcolm, Ian
Maple, Sir John Blundell
Maxwell, Rt. Hon. Sir H. F.
Mellor, Col. (Lancashire)

Meysey-Thompson, Sir H. H.
Middlemore, J. Throgmorton
Milbank, Sir Powlett C. J.
Milward, Colonel Victor
Monckton, Edward Philip
Monk, Charles James
Moon, Edward Robert Pacy
More, R. Jasper (Shropshire)
Morrell, George Herbert
Morton, Arthur H. A.(Deptf'd)
Mount, William George
Muntz, Philip A.
Murray, Rt. Hn. A. G. (Bute)
Myers, William Henry
Nicholson, William Graham
Nicol, Donald Ninian
O'Connor, Arthur (Donegal)
Orr-Ewing, Chas. Lindsay
Pease, H. Pike (Darlington)
Penn, John
Percy, Earl
Pierpoint, Robert
Pilkington, Richard
Platt-Higgins, Frederick
Powell, Sir Francis Sharpe
Priestley, Sir W. O. (Edin.)
Purvis, Robert
Rankin, Sir James
Ritchie, Rt. Hon. C. Thomson
Robertson, Herbert (Hackney)
Rothschild, Hn. Lionel W.
Royds, Clement Molyneux
Russell, Gen.F.S. (Chelt'ham)
Russell, T. W. (Tyrone)
Samuel, H. S. (Limehouse)
Sassoon, Sir Ed. Albert
Savory, Sir Joseph
Scott, Sir S. (Marylebone,W.)
Sharpe, William Ed. T.
Sidebottom, Wm. (Derbyshire)
Sinclair, Louis (Romford)
Skewes-Cox, Thomas
Smith, Abel H. (Christch.)
Smith, Hn. W.F.D. (Strand)
Spencer, Ernest
Stanley, Hon. A. (Ormskirk)
Stanley, H. M. (Lambeth)
Stanley, Lord (Lancs.)
Stewart, Sir Mark J.M'Taggart
Stock, James Henry
Stone, Sir Benjamin
Strutt, Hon. C. Hedley
Talbot, Lord E. (Chichester)
Thornton, Percy M.
Tomlinson, W. E. Murray
Tritton, Charles Ernest
Valentia, Viscount
Vincent, Col. Sir C. E. H.
Walrond,Rt Hn Sir Wm. H.
Wanklyn, James Leslie
Warr, Augustus Frederick
Webster, R.G. (St. Pancras)
Webster, SirR.E.(Isle of Wight
Welby, Lieut.-Col. A.C.E.
Wharton, Rt. Hn.J. Lloyd

Whiteley, Geo. (Stockport)	Wodehouse,Itt Hn.E R (Bath)	Yerburgh, Robert Armstrong
Williams, J. Powell (Birm.)	Wortley,Rt.Hn. C.B.Stuart	
Willox, Sir J Archibald	Wylie, Alexander	TELLERS FOR THE NOES—
Wilson, John (Falkirk)	Wyvil, Marmaduke D'Arcy	Mr.Whitmore and Mr. Cohen

Words added.

Main Question, as amended, put, and agreed to.

Resolved, That it is inexpedient that the Bill be read a second time before the Royal Commission on London Water Supply has presented its Report.

_____

PETITIONS.

_____

EDUCATION OF CHILDREN BILL.

Petition from London, in favour; to lie upon the Table.

LOCAL AUTHORITIES SERVANTS' SUPERANNUATION BILL.

Petitions in favour;—From Woking; —Petersfield;—Croydon;—and Hammersmith; to lie upon the Table.

LONDON GOVERNMENT BILL.

Petition of the District Surveyors' Association, against; to lie upon the Table.

PARLIAMENTARY FRANCHISE.

Petitions for extension to women;— From Edinburgh;—and Saffron Walden (two); to lie upon the Table.

POOR LAW OFFICERS' SUPERANNUATION (SCOTLAND) BILL.

Petition from Edinburgh, in favour; to lie upon the Table.

PUBLIC HEALTH ACTS AMENDMENT BILL.

Petition from Wednesbury, in favour; to lie upon the Table.

SALE OF INTOXICATING LIQUORS ON SUNDAY BILL.

Petitions in favour;—From Rainham; — Sunderland; — Norwich (two); — Stone;—Thomas Guthrie Lodge of Good Templars; — March; — Nottingham;— Gaisgill; — Nateby; — Milburn; — Soulby;—Crosby Garrett;—Bolton;— Appleby (two);—Great Strickland;— King's Meaburn; — Kirkby Stephen (two); — Kendal; — Westmorland;— Fell End; — Beck Foot; — Preston Patric;—Mallerstang;—Hollin Crag; Sowerby; — Old Hutton; — Asby; — Burnside;— Winton;— Greenholme; — Warcop; — Kirkby Lonsdale; — Grayrigg;— Whinfell;— Crook;— Staveley; —Great Musgrave;—and Manchester; to lie upon the Table.

VACCINATION ACT, 1898.

Petition from Rotherham, for appeal; to lie upon the Table

_____

RETURNS, REPORTS, ETC.

_____

FACTORY AND WORKSHOP (LEAD COMPOUNDS IN POTTERY).

Copy presented,—of Report to the Secretary of State for the Home Department by Professor T. E. Thorpe, LL.D., F.R.S., Principal of the Government Laboratory, and Professor Thomas Oliver, M.D., F.R.C.P., Physician to the Royal Infirmary, Newcastle-upon-Tyne, on the employment of Compounds of Lead in the Manufacture of Pottery, their influence upon the health of the workpeople, with suggestions as to the means which might be adopted to counteract their evil effects (by Command); to lie upon the Table.

POLLING DISTRICTS (MIDDLESEX).

Copy presented,—of Order made by the County Council of Middlesex, altering the Highgate and Muswell Hill Polling Districts in the Parliamentary Division of Hornsey (by Act); to lie upon the Table.

UNIVERSITY OF GLASGOW.

Copy presented,—of Abstract of Accounts of the University of Glasgow for the year ending 30th September 1898 (by Act); to lie upon the Table, and to be printed. (No. 119.)

UNIVERSITY OF SAINT ANDREW'S.

Copy presented,—of Abstract of Accounts of the University for the year ended 30th September 1898 (by Act); to lie upon the Table, and to be printed. (No. 120.)

BOARD OF AGRICULTURE.

Copy presented,—of Annual Report of Proceedings under the Tithe Acts, Copyhold Act, 1894, Inclosure Acts, and other Acts for the year 1898 (by Command); to lie upon the Table.

Of Annual Reports of Proceedings under the Diseases of Animals Acts, the Markets and Fairs (Weighing of Cattle) Acts, etc., for the year 1898 (by Command); to lie upon the Table.

LIGHT RAILWAYS ACT, 1896.

Copy presented,—of Order made by the Light Railway Commissioners, and modified and confirmed by the Board of Trade, authorising the construction of Light Railways between Barking Town and the Beckton Gas Works in the County of Essex (Barking and Beckton Light Railways Order, 1898) (by Command); to lie upon the Table.

Copy presented,—of Order made by the Light Railway Commissioners, and modified and confirmed by the Board of Trade, authorising the construction of a Light Railway between Didcot, in the county of Berks, and Watlington, in the county of Oxford (Didcot and Watlington Li t Railway Order, 1898) (by Com- ; to lie upon the Table.

Copy presented,—of Order made by the Light Railway Commissioners, and modified and confirmed by the Board of Trade, authorising the construction of a Light Railway in the county of Lincoln from Grimsby to Saltfleetby, with a branch to Cleethorpes (Grimsby and Saltfleetby Light Railway Order, 1898) (by Command); to lie upon the Table.

Copy presented,—of Order made by the Light Railway Commissioners, and modified and confirmed by the Board of Trade, authorising the construction of Light Railways in the county of Lincoln and the West Riding of the county of York from Haxey to Crowle and Marsh- lands with branches (Isle of Axholme Light Railways Order, 1898) (by Com- mand); to lie upon the Table.

Copy presented,—of Order made by the Light Railway Commissioners, and modified and confirmed by the Board of Trade, authorising the construction of Light Railways from Stourbridge to Kinver, in the counties of Worcester and Stafford (Kinver Light Railway Order, 1898) (by Command); to lie upon the Table.

Copy presented,—of Order made by the Light Railway Commissioners, and modified and confirmed by the Board of Trade, authorising the construction of Light Railways in the county of Staf- ford between Cheddleton Junction, on the North Staffordshire Railway, to Caldon Low and Hulme End (Leek, Caldon Low, and Hartington Light Rail- ways Order, 1898) (by Command); to lie upon the Table.

Copy presented,—of Order made by the Light Railway Commissioners, and modified and confirmed by the Board of Trade, authorising the construction of a Light Railway in the county of Lan- caster from Liverpool to Prescot (Liverpool and Prescot Light Railway Order, 1898) (by Command): to lie upon the Table.

Copy presented,—of Order made by the Light Railway Commissioners, and modified and confirmed by the Board of Trade, authorising the construction of Light Railways in the townships of Chirton, North Shields, Tynemouth, and Cullercoats, and the urban district of Whitley and Monkseaton, in the county of Northumberland (North Shields, Tynemouth, and District Light Rail- ways Order, 1898) (by Command); to lie upon the Table.

Copy presented,—of Order made by the Light Railway Commissioners, and modified and confirmed by the Board of Trade, authorising the construction of a Light Railway from Trowse, in the county of Norfolk, to Beccles, in the county of Suffolk (South Norfolk Light Railway Order, 1898) (by Command); to lie upon the Table.

Copy presented,—of Order made by the Light Railway Commissioners, and modified and confirmed by the Board of Trade, authorising the construction of a Light Railway from the Esplanade to the Isle of Wight Railway Company's Station, Ventnor (Ventnor Inclined Light Railway Order, 1898) (by Command); to lie upon the Table.

EGYPT (No. 1, 1899).

Copy presented,—of Despatches from Her Majesty's Agent and Consul-General in Egypt respecting the conduct of the British and Egyptian Troops after the Battle of Omdurman (by Command); to lie upon the Table.

EDUCATION (ENGLAND AND WALES).

Copy presented,—of Statement showing (1) the Expenditure from the Grant for Public Education in England and Wales in the year 1898 upon Annual Grants to Elementary Schools; (2) the number of Public Elementary Day Schools on the Annual Grant List on the 31st August 1898; (3) Detailed Statistics of Inspected Schools, 1897-8, Public Elementary Day Schools, Evening Continuation Schools, and Certified Efficient Schools, etc.; (4) Tables of Educational Statistics; and (5) Number of School Boards under various Heads of Population (by Command); to lie upon the Table.

INEBRIATE REFORMATORIES (IRELAND) (RULES).

Copy presented,—of Rules for the Management of State Reformatories in Ireland (by Act); to lie upon the Table.

COAL EXPORTS, ETC.

Return ordered,

"giving, for the year 1898, the export of coal from each port in the United Kingdom to each country abroad, together with a summary statement showing the export of coal from the principal districts of the United Kingdom to the principal groups of foreign countries; and also showing the quantity of coal shipped at each port in the United Kingdom for ships' use on foreign voyages during the same period (in continuation of Parliamentary Paper No. 352, Session 1898)."—(Mr. D. A. Thomas.)

NAVAL EXPENDITURE AND MERCANTILE MARINE (GREAT BRITAIN, ETC.).

Return ordered, "Showing Aggregate Naval Expenditure on Seagoing Force; Aggregate Revenue; Aggregate Tonnage of Mercantile Marine; Annual Clearances of Shipping in the Foreign Trade; Annual Clearances of Shipping in the Coasting Trade; Annual Value of Imports by Sea, including Bullion and Specie; and Annual Value of Exports by Sea, including Bullion and Specie, of various Countries, exclusive of China and South American Republics, but including British Self-governing Colonies, for the year 1898 (in continuation of Parliamentary Paper, No. 362, of Session 1898)."—(Sir John Colomb.)

BILLS ADVANCED.

BRYNMAWR AND WESTERN VALLEYS RAILWAY BILL.

Reported, with Amendments; Report to lie upon the Table, and to be printed.

STOCKPORT CORPORATION WATER BILL.

Reported; Reports to lie upon the Table, and to be printed.

WETHERBY DISTRICT WATER BILL.

Reported; Reports to lie upon the Table, and to be printed.

STOCKPORT DISTRICT WATER BILL.
Reported; Report to lie upon the Table.

GLASGOW DISTRICT SUBWAY BILL [H.L.]

Read the first time; and referred to the Examiners of Petitions for Private Bills.

RUSHDEN AND HIGHAM FERRERS DISTRICT GAS BILL [H.L.]
Read the first time; and referred to the Examiners of Petitions for Private Bills.

CENTRAL ELECTRIC SUPPLY BILL.
Reported; Report to lie upon the Table, and to be printed.

ST. JAMES'S AND PALL MALL ELECTRIC LIGHT BILL.
Reported; Report to lie upon the Table, and to be printed.

STANDING ORDERS.
Resolution reported from the Committee—

"That, in the case of the Lowestoft Promenade Pier, Petition for leave to deposit a Petition for Bill, the Standing Orders ought to be dispensed with :—That the parties be permitted to deposit their Petition for a Bill."

Resolution agreed to.

MESSAGE FROM THE LORDS.
That they have agreed to—

Partridge Shooting (Ireland) Bill, without amendment.

That they have passed a Bill, intituled, "An Act to authorise the Glasgow District Subway Company to raise additional capital; and for other purposes." (Glasgow District Subway Bill [H.L.].)

And, also, a Bill, intituled, "An Act for incorporating and conferring powers on the Rushden and Higham Ferrers District Gas Company." (Rushden and Higham Ferrers District Gas Bill [H.L.].)

_____

EGYPT (FINANCIAL AID).

Address for—

"Return showing (so far as may be possible) all expenditure charged in any one year on the public revenues of the United Kingdom in connection with military operations in the Soudan since January 1883."—*(Mr. Scott.)*

_____

NEW BILLS.

_____

PARLIAMENTARY DEPOSITS BILL.

" To amend the Law relating to Parliamentary Deposits in certain cases," presented, and read the first time; to be read a second time upon Tuesday next, and to be printed. (Bill 136.)

METROPOLITAN COMMON SCHEME (HARROW WEALD).

" To confirm a scheme relating to Harrow Weald Common,. in the parish of Harrow Weald in the county of Middlesex," presented accordingly, and read the first time; to be referred to the Examiners of Petitions for Private Bills,. and to be printed. (Bill 135.)

QUESTIONS.

SMALL HOLDINGS ACT, 1892.

MR. BILLSON (Halifax): I beg to ask the President of the Local Government Board if he will state the number ber of 'small holdings acqired under the Small Holdings Act, 1892, during the year 1898, and the number and area of holdings acquired since the Act came into operation.

THE PRESIDENT OF THE BOARD OF AGRICULTURE (Mr. W. H. LONG, Liverpool, West Derby): Perhaps I may be allowed to answer this question. Full information as to the operations of local authorities under the Small Holdings Act, 1892, to the 24th June 1897, will be found in the Returns No. 407 of 1895 (Session 2) and 17 of 1898. Any later details would require to be specially collected and tabulated.

STORNAWAY MAILS.

MR. WEIR (Ross and Cromarty): I beg to ask the Secretary to the Treasury, as representing the Postmaster-General, if he will state how often during the months of December, January, and February last the steamer carrying Her Majesty's mails between Stornoway and Kyle of Lochalsh was late in her arrival at Stornaway and Kyle of Lochalsh respectively, and how often the delay exceeded half an hour at each place; and will he state the maximum delay on any one occasion?

THE FINANCIAL SECRETARY TO THE TREASURY (Mr. R. W. HANBURY, Preston): The mail steamers arrived late 57 times at Stornoway and 13 times at Kyle. The delay exceeded half an hour on 19 and 12 occasions respectively. The late arrivals at Stornoway of the outward mails were due, in part, to loss of time on the railway. The maximum delay, four hours, occurred on two occasions, namely, on the voyages from Stornoway to Kyle on the nights of the 22nd December and 20th January, the cause in each being the severity of the weather.

RAILWAY LEVEL CROSSINGS IN SCOTLAND.

MR. WEIR: I beg to ask the Lord Advocate if he will state how many railway level-crossings there are in Scotland which pass over public thoroughfares, and which, being private property, do not come under the jurisdiction of the Board of Trade or any Government Department?

THE LORD ADVOCATE (Mr. A. GRAHAM MURRAY, Buteshire): I am not in possession of the information for which the honourable Member asks. Inasmuch as all such crossings are within the jurisdiction of the county councils and burgh councils, who are, as the case may be, the road authority, and as there is no reason to suppose that the road authorities fail in their duty to provide for public safety, I can see no useful purpose in obtaining the information desired, even if it were possible to do so.

PROTECTION OF WATER SUPPLIES.

MR. CORNWALLIS (Maidstone): I beg to ask the President of the Local Government Board whether he will introduce a Bill dealing with the protection of water supplies before Easter; and, if not before Easter, at an early date after the holidays?

THE PRESIDENT OF THE LOCAL GOVERNMENT BOARD (Mr. H. CHAPLIN, Lincolnshire, Sleaford): I answered a similar Question only a few days ago. I cannot undertake to introduce a Bill dealing with the protection of water supplies before Easter, but I shall be quite ready to do so afterwards as soon as I see any reasonable hope of making progress with it.

LONDON AND DUBLIN ROYAL PARKS.

MR. DONAL SULLIVAN (Westmeath, S.): On behalf of the honourable Member for North Louth I beg to ask the Secretary to the Treasury if he could state the number of miles of road per square mile in the London and Dublin Royal parks, the comparative cost of maintenance per mile, and the number of men employed in each case on road work?

Mr. HANBURY: The number of miles of carriage road per mile in London Royal Parks (including Hyde Park, Kensington Gardens, St. James's Park, Green Park, Regent's Park, and Primrose Hill) is a little over six; in Phœnix Park, Dublin, it is a little under six. The annual cost of maintenance per mile is £697 in London and £124 in Dublin. The difference is due partly to the far heavier traffic in the London parks and partly to the greater width of the roads. The cost per square yard of road is, in Dublin 2¼d. per annum; in London 10½d.—or, if Greenwich, Richmond, and Bushey Parks are included, 5½d. per annum. The number of men daily employed by the Department is 30 in London and 27 in Dublin; but in London there is also a good deal of work done by contract. The figure in the latter case includes men employed on stone-breaking.

WORKMEN'S TRAINS ON THE SOUTHERN RAILWAYS.

Mr. WOODS (Walthamstow): I beg to ask the President of the Board of Trade if his attention has been called to the great need of an increased service of workmen's trains on the South Eastern and the London, Chatham, and Dover Railways; whether he is aware that the fares on some portions of these companies' lines are very high; also that no workmen's trains are run by these companies from a number of important places, such as Croydon, Bromley, Bickley, Beckenham, Catford, Lee, etc.; and whether he will use his influence to cause a provision to be made in the Bill for the amalgamation of these railways, to compel them to run cheap trains for workmen and women between their central stations and these suburbs up to eight o'clock in the morning?

THE PRESIDENT OF THE BOARD OF TRADE (Mr. C. T. RITCHIE, Croydon): My attention has been called to this matter. There are, I understand, proceedings pending before the Railway Commissioners affecting most of the places referred to. I am not aware that the ordinary law is insufficient to meet this case, or that any special provisions are desirable. It is, however, open to the Committee on the Bill to consider that question if they are moved to do so by petition. The companies suffer a great deal from congested traffic in the early morning, but they are dealing with the workmen's trains question in a conciliatory spirit, and I shall be happy to supply the honourable Member with a copy of the correspondence the Board of Trade have had with the companies on the subject.

DOCKYARD EXPENDITURE.

Mr. WOODS: I beg to ask the First Lord of the Admiralty whether he could state to what class of workmen in the dockyard the amount of £199,000, the increased cost under the heading of Shipbuilding Vote, would be appropriated?

THE SECRETARY TO THE ADMIRALTY (Mr. W. E. MACARTNEY, Antrim, S.): The increased amount taken for wages will be distributed over all classes of workmen employed in the Naval Dockyards.

LOANS UNDER THE SMALL HOLDINGS ACT.

Mr. LLOYD MORGAN (Carmarthen, W.): I beg to ask the President of the Local Government Board whether he can state the amount of money borrowed by county councils up to the end of 1898 from the Public Works Loan Commissioners for the purpose of advancing money under the provisions of the Small Holdings Act, 1892; and whether there are any cases of county councils having borrowed money for the purpose from any source other than from the Public Works Loan Commissioners?

THE PRESIDENT OF THE LOCAL GOVERNMENT BOARD: County councils in England and Wales have been authorised to borrow up to the end of 1898, the amount being £9,150, and I understand the whole of this has been obtained from the Public Works Loan Commissioners.

RUNAWAY SLAVES AT MOMBASA.

Sir C. DILKE (Gloucester, Forest of Dean): On behalf of the honourable Member for the Middleton Division of Lancashire, I beg to ask the Under Secretary of State for Foreign Affairs, with reference to the case to which the attention of the Foreign Office was directed on the 31st August last—namely, the surrender, on 15th June last, to their former owner, one Salehe bin Hussein, of three slaves, named respectively Kazibeni, Kombo, and Mamekombo (a father, mother, and daughter), who had been resident for the previous 10 years at Ribe, whether his attention has been called to the decision of the Court at Mombasa, presided over by Mr. Edward Loyd, the Acting District Officer, which affirmed the legality of that surrender, and declared that the slaves had no plea wherewith to claim their freedom, as Ribe is within the Sultan's dominions, and that he was of opinion that they had always been in slavery, and ordered them to return to their master; what action the Government propose to take in this case, in view of the opinion of Mr. Attorney General, that a British subject taking any part in returning a runaway slave to his master against his will is guilty of a breach of British law; whether he is aware that the daughter, having first been detained by her former owner, the presence of her father and mother at Mombasa, where the surrender was made, was due to a summons from the court, issued by a British official, but for which their freedom would not have been endangered; whether the missionaries in the districts of the East Africa Protectorate have intimated their determination to intercept all similar summonses for the future, and to do their utmost, regardless of the consequences to themselves, to protect the runaway slaves who take refuge at their missions; and whether he can explain why no reply, beyond a statement on 10th October that instructions for inquiry had been given, has been received from the Foreign Office since 31st August last?

The UNDER SECRETARY of STATE for FOREIGN AFFAIRS (Mr. St. John Brodrick, Surrey, Guildford): The Papers with respect to this case have now reached the Foreign Office.

VOL. LXVIII. [Fourth Series.]

They have been delayed by the fact that when the Foreign Office inquiries reached Mombasa in November last Mr. Lloyd had been appointed to a station up country. There is considerable conflict of statement as to this case. As against the suggestions in the Question, Mr. Lloyd states that famine existed at Ribe at the time, and that the three slaves were brought before him by their master solely to get a formal declaration of his right to their services in return for the subsistence he was willing to afford them, and that, although Mr. Lloyd closely questioned them as to whether they had any cause of complaint, they made no objection to returning, and would take no legal action to secure manumission. The opinion of the Attorney General applied to the detention of a slave by force, of which no question arose in this instance. It is believed that since the conclusion of the famine at Ribe these slaves have now left their master again. It is not known what action the missionaries propose to take, but Her Majesty's Government, having laid it down that British officials shall not take part in returning escaped slaves to their masters, see no reason for taking further action in this case.

Mr. T. BAYLEY (Derbyshire, Chesterfield): When shall we have the Papers mentioned by the right honourable Gentleman?

[No Reply.]

INDIAN SECTION OF THE IMPERIAL INSTITUTE.

Sir MANCHERJEE BHOWNAGGREE (Bethnal Green, N.E.): I beg to ask the Secretary of State for India whether, in the contemplated transfer of a part of the Imperial Institute to another body, such portions thereof are included as have been heretofore devoted to the purposes for which money grants have been made by the Government of India, and also such other parts of the Institute as have been built at the expense of donations received from India; and, if so, will he state if any and what measures are being adopted to reserve the portions in question for the special

3 P

purposes for which they were originally intended or set apart?

THE SECRETARY OF STATE FOR INDIA (Lord GEORGE HAMILTON, Middlesex, 'Ealing): In behalf of India, whence very liberal gifts were contributed to the Imperial Institute, I have taken steps to secure the objects contemplated in the honourable Member's Question. It has been arranged that, in the event of any transfer such as is suggested in the Question, the Imperial Institute buildings now devoted to Indian purposes, and the parts of the buildings constructed from Indian contributions, shall be reserved for Indian objects. I shall be happy to give to my honourable Friend, if he wishes it, a copy of a Memorandum showing the arrangement that has been made.

POSTMASTERS AND IRISH LOCAL GOVERNMENT.

MAJOR JAMESON (Clare, W.): I beg to ask the Chief Secretary to the Lord Lieutenant of Ireland whether postmasters and sub-postmasters are eligible for election to the new county and district councils?

THE CHIEF SECRETARY TO THE LORD LIEUTENANT OF IRELAND (Mr. GERALD W. BALFOUR, Leeds, Central): There is nothing in the Local Government Act disqualifying the officers named from being elected county or district councillors. This disqualification will depend on the regulations of the Post Office Service. As already stated by me, in answer to a Question of my honourable and gallant Friend the Member for North Armagh, I have been informed that it would be contrary to the regulations issued by the Postmaster-General for postmasters to take any part in such elections except to record their votes.

MR. MACALEESE (Monaghan, N.): I beg to ask Mr. Attorney-General for Ireland, could a sub-postmaster, if elected to the position of district councillor, legally take his seat and share in transacting the business of the Board?

THE ATTORNEY-GENERAL FOR IRELAND (Mr. ATKINSON, Londonderry, N.): I have nothing to add to the reply just given by my right honourable Friend to the similar Question put to him by the honourable Member for West Clare.

CITY OF CORK BY-LAWS.

MR. W. JOHNSTON (Belfast, S): I beg to ask the Chief Secretary to the Lord Lieutenant of Ireland whether he is aware that the Local Government Board advised the town clerk of Cork that the by-laws of the old Corporation would remain in force till rescinded, but that the Mayor of Cork subsequently declared that all the old rules and by-laws were swept away by the Local Government Act; whether the council exceeded their powers by expending certain sums of money belonging to the ratepayers; whether he is aware that the town clerk was prevented from answering certain questions put to him by Sir John Scott, ex-Mayor of Cork, concerning the correspondence with the Local Government Board; and whether the Local Government Board will take any action in consequence of the conduct of the Cork Council?

MR. CREAN (Queen's County, Ossory): Before that Question is answered, may I say that no intimation was given to me that it was to be put, and, as a portion of it referring to me is altogether inaccurate——

*MR. SPEAKER: Order, order! The honourable Member is not entitled to comment on the Question.

MR. GERALD BALFOUR: I am informed that the town clerk of Cork stated that the by-laws of the old Corporation would remain in force till rescinded. This is provided for by Article 44 of the Application of Enactments Order in Council, dated the 22nd December last, and the Local Government Board did not address the Corporation on the subject. The statement made by the Mayor appears to have been to the effect quoted in the first paragraph. The Local Government

Board have no knowledge of any proceedings of the nature indicated in the second paragraph. If, however, the council have exceeded their powers, their action will be subject to review by the auditor. The questions put to the town clerk by Sir John Scott were, it appears, for the purpose of testing the validity of the Mayor's ruling, which Sir John Scott contended was not in accordance with the Standing Orders. The town clerk obeyed the order of the Mayor as chairman, and did not answer Sir John Scott's interrogatories. The only action which it is competent for the Local Government Board to take in the matter is to inform Sir John Scott of the bearing of the new Act upon the points raised by him at the meeting of the Corporation.

MR. CREAN: May I make a personal explanation, Sir? The statement I made was not as suggested in the Question, but that the new Act kills the old Corporation, and any resolution of that body could be set aside by the new body constituted by the new Act. The resolution which we complained of as set aside——

MR. SPEAKER: Order, order! This hardly comes within the rule applying to personal explanations.

MR. FLYNN (Cork, N.): Have the Local Government Board, as a matter of law, any power whatever to interfere with the Corporation of Cork?

MR. GERALD BALFOUR: None.

DEATH DUTIES.

MR. GIBSON BOWLES (Lynn Regis): I beg to ask Mr. Chancellor of the Exchequer whether the opportunity, which he understood on 9th February would shortly arise, has yet arisen for testing by the High Court the question whether the Finance Act, 1894, charges estate duty at the death of a life tenant of settled property when that life tenant has surrendered his life interest in such property within twelve months of his death; and, if so, when a decision of the question may be expected?

THE CHANCELLOR OF THE EXCHEQUER (Sir M. HICKS BEACH, Bristol, W.): A case has arisen in which this question can be tested, and the matter will be brought before the High Court of Justice as soon as possible; but when a decision may be expected must depend on the state of business in the Court.

MR. GIBSON BOWLES: I beg to ask Mr. Chancellor of the Exchequer whether he has given attention to the decision of the House of Lords in "Earl Cowley v. Commissioners of Inland Revenue," whereby it was decided that when the tenant for life and the remainderman have disentailed a settled estate, have then charged the estate with a mortgage debt, and have subsequently re-settled the estate, the Finance Act, 1894, does not charge estate duty upon the total principal value of the estate as passing on the death of the life tenant, but only upon what remains of that value after the mortgage debt has been deducted therefrom; whether any estate duty not charged by the Act has actually been demanded by and paid to the Commissioners of Inland Revenue in similar cases, through the refusal of the Commissioners to allow such mortgage debts to be deducted in such cases from the total principal value of the property passing; if so, whether he can state approximately in how many instances such duty has been exacted and paid in, and since, 1894; and whether, in all such cases, the duty so paid will now be returned?

THE CHANCELLOR OF THE EXCHEQUER: I am not prepared to accept the first paragraph of the Question as a complete statement of the Cowley case, the circumstances of which were somewhat peculiar. Nor can I say how many cases there have been which involve the point decided in it. It is believed, however, that the number of such cases is very small. If it is found that in any cases similar to that of Earl Cowley the duty has been paid without allowing for the deduction of the mortgage, the duty erroneously paid will be returned; but in very few, if any, instances has duty been actually paid in such cases.

INLAND REVENUE PROCEDURE IN SCOTLAND.

Mr. THORBURN (Peebles and Selkirk): I beg to ask Mr. Chancellor of the Exchequer whether, in determining the amount of stamp duty payable under an agreement transferring a business to a limited company, it is the case that the Board of Inland Revenue sitting in London insist upon the revenue officials in Edinburgh acting upon the decisions of the English courts, although such decisions conflict with decisions of the Court of Session; and whether instructions will now be given that, in dealing with matters in Scotland, the Inland Revenue authorities will give a full and fair effect to the decisions of the Scotch courts?

THE CHANCELLOR OF THE EXCHEQUER: There is no such general practice on the part of the Board of Inland Revenue as is suggested in the Question. The honourable Member probably has in his mind a recent case in which a decision of the Court of Session was quoted as not being in harmony with decisions of English courts in similar cases. The Scotch adviser of the Board, however, did not consider that the decision of the Court of Session was applicable in the circumstances of the particular case under inquiry, and the Board acted on his advice. I may add that no case is known in which the Board of Inland Revenue have overruled the advice of their Scotch solicitor where a point of Scotch law was involved.

TRAVELLING ALLOWANCES FOR INDIAN OFFICERS.

GENERAL RUSSELL (Cheltenham): I beg to ask the Secretary of State for India whether he is aware that the messing on board ship for officers proceeding out to India on duty was formerly 2s. per diem, and for officers granted an indulgence passage 6s. 6d. per diem; will he explain why these charges have been raised to a uniform rate of 10s. per diem; and into whose pocket does the large profit go which must result from such a high charge?

THE FINANCIAL SECRETARY TO THE WAR OFFICE (Mr. J. POWELL WILLIAMS, Birmingham, S.): Perhaps I may be allowed to answer this Question. There has been no change in the messing charges for officers proceeding out to India on duty. The rate is 2s. a day for officers on duty, and 6s. 6d. for officers granted indulgence passages.

INLAND REVENUE INQUIRIES.

Mr. JOHN WILSON (Govan): I beg to ask Mr. Chancellor of the Exchequer whether he is aware of district surveyors of Inland Revenue asking for returns of anticipated profits of income; and whether, considering the trouble and annoyance in giving such information, which can only be illusionary and unsatisfactory, he will see his way to stay this procedure?

THE CHANCELLOR OF THE EXCHEQUER: The object of these inquiries is to obtain information on which to found the estimate of the Board of Inland Revenue of the produce of the income tax for the coming year. They are made in the month of March, by which time the result of the trading of the year ended 31st December preceding is generally known. They are not pressed on any persons who have any reluctance to answer them; but, as a rule, the information is willingly given, and is of much service to the Department.

IRISH GRAND JURIES.

Mr. O'KEEFFE (Limerick): I beg to ask the Chief Secretary to the Lord Lieutenant of Ireland, inasmuch as the fiscal powers of grand jurors have now ceased under the Local Government Act, if the high sheriffs of Irish counties are bound to observe any property qualification in summoning future grand jurors to discharge the duties of considering Bills on criminal indictment at assizes in Ireland?

Mr. GERALD BALFOUR: No change whatever has been made in the position of grand juries so far as their relation to criminal business is concerned, nor does the Local Government Act affect in any way the obligation otherwise imposed upon high sheriffs, as to the qualifications of persons summoned to serve as grand jurors.

CLARE ISLAND LOCAL GOVERNMENT ELECTIONS.

Dr. R. AMBROSE (Mayo, W.): I beg to ask the Chief Secretary to the Lord Lieutenant of Ireland whether he is aware that there are 137 county council electors in Clare Island; that the island is 17 miles from the mainland; and that it would be very difficult for them to come to the mainland, especially in bad weather, to record their votes; and, under the circumstances, will he use his influence to have a polling station situated at Clare Island for the convenience of the voters?

Mr. GERALD BALFOUR: The facts are as stated in the first paragraph, except that the number of local government electors on Clare Island is, I am informed, 120. The question of the establishment of a polling station on the island has already formed the subject of communications between the Local Government Board and the returning officer, who states he is anxious to make arrangements to facilitate all persons as far as possible, but that he is not prepared to undertake the serious liability involved in carrying out the suggestion contained in the Question. Clare Island, for the purpose of these elections, is in precisely the same position as it is for Parliamentary elections. The returning officer points out that if a poll were arranged to be taken on the island, the election for the entire county electoral division might be invalidated should the presiding officer be unable, owing to bad weather, to reach the island either the day before, or on the day fixed for the poll.

VACCINATION EXEMPTION CERTIFICATES.

Mr. LOGAN (Leicester, Harborough): I beg to ask the President of the Local Government Board if he proposes during the present Session to so amend section 2 of the Vaccination Act, 1898, as to prevent cases of an undue refusal by the magistrates to grant the certificates which are authorised by the Act?

The PRESIDENT of the LOCAL GOVERNMENT BOARD: The Government have already stated that they do not propose to introduce any legislation on that subject during the present Session.

IRISH LICENCE DUTIES.

Major JAMESON: I beg to ask the Secretary to the Treasury whether the amount of duties collected from licensed traders in Ireland will be handed over to the local authorities of the different districts in which such duties are collected; if so, will he state the purposes to which such moneys will be applied by the local authorities?

Mr. GERALD BALFOUR: At the request of my right honourable Friend the Secretary to the Treasury I will answer this Question. The manner of the application of the proceeds of the duties collected in Ireland by the Commissioners of Inland Revenue on the Local Taxation Licences specified in the third schedule to the Local Government (Ireland) Act, 1898, will be found in section 58 of the Act. Under sub-section (1) of that section the equivalent of these duties will be annually paid out of the Consolidated Fund to the Local Taxation (Ireland) Account, and under sub-section (2) will be applied to certain local services specified in that sub-section. The amount of payments made to the local authorities does not depend on the amount of the duties collected in their respective districts.

FINANCIAL AID TO EGYPT.

MR. SCOTT (Lancashire, Leigh): I beg to ask the Under Secretary of State for Foreign Affairs whether he will agree to the Motion for a Return as to financial aid given to Egypt which stands on the Paper this day.

MR. BRODRICK: The Return will be given, but I will ask the honourable Member to substitute for his Motion a form of words which I think will carry it out more completely. •

THE MAHDI'S TOMB.

MR. SCOTT: I beg to ask the Under Secretary of State for Foreign Affairs whether he has yet received the Report which Lord Cromer was requested to furnish as to the statement that, on the day of the battle of Omdurman, the camp followers murdered and plundered wounded dervishes; whether he has received Lord Cromer's Report on the alleged dismemberment of the Mahdi's body before it was thrown into the Nile; and whether these Reports, when received, will be printed and issued to Members?

MR. BRODRICK: I will lay upon the Table to-day Papers containing Reports from Lord Cromer and Lord Kitchener on all these subjects.

THE "BRENDA."

MR. WEIR: I beg to ask the Lord Advocate if the Secretary for Scotland, in selecting a new commander for the Fishery Board cruiser "Brenda," will consider the desirability of giving preference to officers possessing an intimate knowledge of the northern coast of Scotland?

MR. GRAHAM MURRAY: In the event of any vacancies occurring amongst the officers commanding their cruisers, the Fishery Board will no doubt carefully consider the qualifications of those selected to take their places.

LOW FLASH PETROLEUM.

COLONEL DENNY (Kilmarnock Burghs): I beg to ask the Under Secretary of State for the Home Department if he is aware that the Fire Brigade Committee of the London County Council have presented a Report to the Council drawing attention again, as they have on previous occasions, to the dangers arising from the use of low flash oil, and expressing their conviction ·that no oil should be sold in London the flash point of which is less than 100 degrees Abel close test; and whether he will take any action in the matter?

THE UNDER SECRETARY OF STATE FOR THE HOME DEPARTMENT (Mr. COLLINGS, Birmingham, Bordesley): I have seen the Report to which the honourable and gallant Member refers. As he is aware, the Government are preparing a Bill dealing with the question of petroleum.

TREATMENT OF INEBRIATES IN SCOTLAND.

COLONEL DENNY: I beg to ask the Lord Advocate. whether it is the intention of the Government to establish a State Inebriate Reformatory in Scotland; and if any applications have been received for the establishment of certified reformatories?

MR. GRAHAM MURRAY: Her Majesty's Government propose to defer the expenditure required for the establishment in Scotland of a State Inebriate Reformatory until experience has been had of the operation of the new legislation and the permanent demand it is likely that such an institution will have to meet. The Secretary for Scotland has not as yet received any application for the establishment of certified inebriate reformatories. •

PARLIAMENTARY PAPERS.

SIR C. CAMERON (Glasgow, Bridgeton): I beg to ask the First Lord of the Treasury. whether, for the convenience of Members, he would cause to be issued along with the weekly list of Public Bills now distributed, a list of all Codes or Orders lying upon the Table of the House from time to time, with the dates at which they were laid, and the date at which the period expires within which, unless otherwise determined by the House, they acquire the force of law?

THE FIRST LORD OF THE TREASURY (Mr. A. J. BALFOUR, Manchester, E.): I am informed that there is circulated already a Parliamentary Paper which gives the list referred to in the Question, and apparently affords all the information the honourable Member desires.

SIR. C. CAMERON was understood to say that it did not give it in the way he wished.

THE FIRST LORD OF THE TREASURY: If the honourable Member wants it in a different shape, perhaps he will give me a little more information, and then I will consider the Question.

"BOUNTY-FED" BUTTER.

MR. O'KELLY (Roscommon, N.): I beg to ask the First Lord of the Treasury whether he is aware that butter made in the United Kingdom is handicapped in the home markets by the importation of colonial and foreign "bounty-fed" butter; and whether he will afford this home industry the protection of a countervailing duty on the same principle that he has consented to have applied to the importation of "bounty-fed" sugar into India?

THE FIRST LORD OF THE TREASURY: I am not aware that there is any "bounty-fed" butter, as the honourable Member suggests.

BLOCKING NOTICES.

MR. J. LOWTHER (Kent, Thanet): I beg to ask the First Lord of the Treasury whether he is prepared to support some reasonable modification of the existing practice under which Motions of Urgency under Standing Order No. 17 can be ousted by a blocking notice, a condition of things which was described by himself upon 1st March

1897 as leaving the House bound and helpless before the will of one single and irresponsible individual?

THE FIRST LORD OF THE TREASURY: There is no reasonable proposal on this or any other subject which I am not ready to consider, but before I pronounce in favour of any scheme dealing with this matter, which would require a large amount of Parliamentary time to carry it into effect, I think my right honourable Friend should put his proposal in terms on the Paper.

BUSINESS OF THE HOUSE.

SIR H. CAMPBELL-BANNERMAN (Stirling Burghs): I venture to ask the right honourable Gentleman when he proposes to take the Scotch Private Bill Procedure Bill, and to express the hope that it will not be either immediately before or immediately after the Recess. That would be very inconvenient to Scotch Members, who have a long journey to take at this inclement season of the year.

THE FIRST LORD OF THE TREASURY: I recently suggested, as the House will remember, that that Bill might be taken on Tuesday before we separate, but I am quite ready to meet the right honourable Gentleman so far as to put it down on Monday. I would endeavour to meet the general views of the House by putting down nothing for Tuesday, except the Motion for the Adjournment, and I shall take the Question that the Speaker do leave the Chair on the Civil Service Estimates either on the first Monday or the first Friday after we meet.

THE BUDGET.

SIR H. FOWLER (Wolverhampton, E.): Has any day been fixed for the Budget?

THE FIRST LORD OF THE TREASURY: I hope it will be taken on the first Thursday after we return, but that must not be taken as a pledge.

SIR C. DILKE: In the event of Report of Supply being concluded, and the

Consolidated Fund Bill introduced to-night, will it be the first Order to-morrow?

THE FIRST LORD OF THE TREASURY: Yes, Sir.

ORDERS OF THE DAY.

LONDON GOVERNMENT BILL.

Order for Second Reading read.

.Motion made, and Question proposed—

" That the Bill be now read a second time."

Amendment proposed—

"To leave out from the word 'That' to the end of the Question, in order to add the words 'no Bill dealing with the local government of the metropolis will be satisfactory which, while disturbing the existing system, fails to simplify and complete it, and which at the same time renders more difficult the attainment of the unity of London.'"—(*Mr. H. Gladstone.*)

MR. H. GLADSTONE (Leeds, W.): I rise to move the Amendment which stands in my name. The Amendment embodies a principle which is inconsistent, in my judgment, with the Bill. That principle is the unity of London. We who oppose the Bill hold that, excepting in size, London is in no way distinct from other great cities. While it is necessary to adapt the organisation of its government. to the vastness of its population, the structure of that organisation should consist of one central authority for the ·whole metropolis, and subordinate councils amply equipped for the management of local concerns. We stand by the principle of the unity of London, which we hold to be directly challenged by the. Bill. The whole scheme and tendency of the Bill is to weaken the central authority, and to set up under the name and guise of municipal boroughs a number of parishes named in the Bill, and arbitrarily selected on no settled plan, and several others which are to be subsequently fashioned by an authority practically independent of Parliament. I am afraid I must trouble the House, although I will do so as briefly as possible, with a little of the history of this movement. The weight of authority, as shown by the history

of the past 60 years, is against the policy set forth in the Bill. The Commission of 1834 found that the paramount defect of the corporations of England and Wales was that corporate bodies existed independently of the communities among which they were found, and they did not except the City. Three years later, when dealing with the City itself, the Commissioners were unable to discover any circumstances justifying the distinction of the small area within the municipal boundary from the rest, except that it was and had been so distinguished. The Commission thought that the City should be transformed into a great municipality of all London. That was the opinion of Lord John Russell, but the opinion of the City was so strong that nothing was done. Then we come to the Commission of 1854. That Commission made two recommendations. In the first place they said—

" If an attempt were made to give a municipal organisation to the entire metropolis by a wider extension of the boundaries of the City, the utility of the present corporation, as an institution suited to its limited area, would be destroyed."

So it seemed to that Commission that the virtues of the City were such that they could not be extended beyond the limited area of its own authority. In the second place they found that it would be desirable to set up seven independent municipal authorities. Now, Sir, it is significant that these recommendations were ignored by the Government in 1855. They were made practically at the instance of the City, and were founded principally upon the evidence of the Lord Mayor himself. The Government, ignoring the Commission, passed the Metropolis Management Act of 1855, and for the first time we find the germ of the unity of London in the setting up of the Metropolitan Board of Works and the Commissioners of Sewers. In the second place, the Government, rejecting the seven independent municipalities, set up the 37 vestries and district boards which have existed down to the present time as the subordinate local authorities. Now, Sir, what has been the tendency since 1855? For 40 years the tendency has been to add powers to the central authority. The need for a strong central authority was evidently apparent to the Committee of 1861, which sat to consider metropolitan local taxation.

They advised that members of this central body should be directly elected by the ratepayers of the whole metropolis. Then, Sir, we come to the Bill for the better government of London in 1884, and it is interesting to remember that two distinguished members of the present Cabinet were members of the Cabinet which produced that Bill, a Bill which indicates the high-water mark of unification. In 1885 we find the City approaching the present Lord Cross, who was then Home Secretary, and pressing its views upon him. Those views apparently were not accepted, because in 1888 we had the Bill of the right honourable Gentleman the President of the Board of Trade. Now, Sir, I must quote his words when introducing that Bill. He said—

"We do not put this Bill forward as a complete settlement of the great problem of London government. We have our own proposals to make. They are on the lines, not of creating separate municipalities throughout London, but of amalgamating within certain defined areas in London existing vestries and district boards, and constructing in London district councils, having, in the various areas in the county, district councils with large and improved administrative functions."

Now, Sir, it is interesting also to notice that the right honourable Gentleman the Member for Birmingham, speaking in a Debate on the Bill, said—

"If I were able to place my own draft side by side with the present Bill, I think it would be found that in the main principles there was an entire agreement. No doubt there are notable differences on some rather important points of detail, but I am not perfectly certain that the advantage is always on the side of my draft."

Very well, Sir, it is quite clear that right honourable and honourable Gentlemen opposite were in absolute agreement that the local government of London should be settled on the basis, first, of a strong central authority directly elected by the ratepayers, and, secondly, of district councils and municipalities. The right honourable Gentleman expressly declared then that they were not to be municipalities, but that they were to be strictly subordinate local authorities. Now, Sir, the Opposition at that time, as is admitted by the right honourable Gentleman opposite, gave a frank support on the whole to that Bill. It was not all that they wished for. The City was absolutely excluded. No Bill which excludes the City from its operations can be satisfactory to most of my honourable Friends on this side of the House; but apart from that, we recognised that the Bill of the right honourable Gentleman worked in the direction of the unity of London, and, as such, we gave it our hearty support. Now, Sir, since 1888 there has been one Inquiry, namely, the Royal Commission of 1894. That Commission issued a Report, which was brief, lucid, and incontrovertible. It represents the basis on which the ultimate settlement of London government must be made, which has been absolutely ignored by the Government in drafting this Bill. Well, Sir, that, in brief, is the history which is necessary for my purpose, but the whole of it points to the necessity of having one paramount authority over the whole of London, and of the delegation of a mass of important work—all that can properly be separated from the central government—to local authorities, with ample powers for dealing with their own affairs, subordinate to the central authority in all matters touching the higher interests of the metropolis. Now, Sir, I want to deal with this change of view on the part of right honourable and honourable Gentlemen opposite. Since 1888 efforts have been made to revert to the policy recommended by the Commission of 1854, but ignored by the Government of the day. What is the reason of this change of policy? I suspect that the reason is to be found in the City. What is known as "tenification" sprang from the City, and it became after 1888 a commonplace on the political platforms of honourable Gentlemen opposite. Well, this Bill is the outcome of it. Now, what is the explanation of the change? The right honourable Gentleman the Leader of the House did not utter a word in explanation of the change. Why has he gone back from the teaching of experience and from the Debates of 1888, and why has he wholly and entirely ignored the Report of the Commission of 1894? Has he all of a sudden so fallen in love with the municipal system that he must have 25 corporations in London instead of one, or does this change spring from antipathy to the London County Council? I ask the Government for their authority for this proposal. On what Report of Commission or Committee do they base it? Where is their mandate? Sir, I think, in the light of previous utterances, we are entitled to know. Now, Sir, in 1888 the Government gave us a distinct pledge that when the next Bill dealing with London government, designed to complete the Bill of 1888, was brought in, they would consult the London County Council. For this is what happened. Mr. Firth put down a new clause giving power to the London County Council to submit a scheme to rearrange municipal government, after it was created by the Act of 1888, and the right honourable Gentleman the President of the Board of Trade, replying to Mr. Stansfeld, said—

"He did not think that the right honourable Gentleman would wish him to go further than to say when once this body was set up it would be impossible not to give full consideration to the representations which they might make."

Why have they not asked the County Council to make representations? If you said so in 1888, why don't you say so this year? The Government does not seem to have approached the County Council in any way to learn its views, so far as I know, and it has hurried forward the Second Reading of this Bill before it has been physically possible—[Ministerial cries of "Oh, oh!"]—I repeat, physically possible for the London County Council to follow all the ramifications of this most complicated Measure, and to report fully and clearly upon it. Now, Sir, I suppose that this change of policy, which I hope will be explained in the course of the Debate, is due to two considerations. It is due to the fact that the Government have felt that the constitution of the present central authority for London represented the principle of the unity of London government, and in the second place it is due to the fact that the City desire to run on lines against any change in the realisation of that principle. The right honourable Gentleman the Member for Bodmin, referring to the City of London, said—

"Some day the City of London would have to be touched, and when it was touched the Conservative Members of the future would wonder at the reasons which had led to the maintenance of this anomalous institution."

I am glad to see that "The Times" itself seemed to approve of the right honourable Gentleman's language, because, commenting on his speech, it said—

"Upon the whole, Mr. Courtney, in the light of his experience on the Royal Commission, has probably summed up the matter with considerable accuracy."

Now, Sir, for my part, I should like to know how long this stolid indifference on the part of the City is to last? How long will it be content to remain a mere speck in the administrative county of London, luxuriating in its enormous wealth, unburdened, unbalanced, uninspired by any responsible discharge of duties in the least degree adequate to its position? How long will it be content to occupy that position, which every day becomes more of a reproach and an anomaly, neglecting each successive opportunity of once more becoming the great and vitalising centre of the greatest metropolis of the world? I desire to emphasise that change of policy, although that change of policy is not so great as at one time appeared. This Bill is not "tenification," because it proposes to set up, I suppose, at least 20 boroughs instead of 10, but it does make the attainment of the unity of London more difficult. The County Council elections of 1898 imposed a somewhat awkward difficulty on Her Majesty's Government. There was a remarkable change in their attitude after those elections, which resulted in a decisive expression of opinion by London on the question of London government, and practically on no other. That led you to mask your batteries. You have abandoned warfare in the open, but I think it can be shown that your opinions are unchanged. Now, Sir, this Bill depends, to a very considerable extent, on the standpoint from which it is regarded, and, so far as I am concerned, if there were any reason to believe that we had a chance of securing necessary and adequate Amendments, I, for one, and I think I express the views of my right honourable Friends also, would not be responsible for moving an Amendment hostile to the Second Reading of the Bill. But we know that the Government are welded to several of its most objectionable provisions. We are numerically weak, we know we will be out-voted, we know we may be closured as we were on the Education Bill in

Mr. H. Gladstone.

1897, and we prefer, under those circumstances, to have no Bill at all. The Government cannot complain of that. The Bill scarcely settles anything. It leaves to other authorities in the future the carrying out of a large part of its proposals. It puts immense responsibility on the Local Government Board and the Privy Council, and the subsequent arrangements to be made by these authorities are practically removed from the authority of Parliament. There are no instructions even set out in the Bill to the Boundary Commissioners: still less do we know who they are to be. What did the House of Lords and the Conservative Party do in 1885? They hung up the Franchise Bill, and refused to allow the Government of the day to pass it. They did that because they said, without a Redistribution Bill they could not deal with the principle of the Franchise Bill, and they said we were taking a leap in the dark. On that ground they absolutely refused, through their majority in the House of Lords, to let the Franchise Bill pass. Honourable Members cannot complain if we turn this argument against them now. This Bill is a leap in the dark, and we have nothing to expect from the House of Lords. Therefore, that is a reason for moving this Amendment. There is another point to which I will refer before I deal with the Bill itself. I remember the argument honourable Members opposite used with regard to the Home Rule Bills of 1886 and 1893. They told us repeatedly they must examine into the motives of the promoters of those Bills, and by that analysis of motives they would form an idea of how the Bills would be used if passed into law. They made their analysis, and we all know how they gave effect to it. We claim that right now. We claim the right to examine into the motives of honourable Members opposite. We believe the main object of this Bill is to weaken and discredit the central authority of London. What is the evidence? I am only going to briefly refer to it. We all remember Lord Salisbury's speech at the Albert Hall, when he gave advice to the Moderates. What was that advice? He said—

"I earnestly hope that it will be entertained by the County Council—though perhaps it may have a suicidal course to recommend it—in a wise, patriotic, and enlightened spirit, and I earnestly hope that our friends will do their best, even at some inconvenience, to furnish, at this or the next election, a sufficient number of candidates to enable this matter to be impartially considered."

Lord Salisbury advised a policy of enlightened suicide to the County Council. We all know that the right honourable Gentleman the Member for Birmingham went down to Limehouse and Camberwell, and made very long and excellent speeches from the opposite point of view on the question of London government, and put forward, with all the force at his disposal, the advisability of building up independent municipalities in London. He pointed out particularly to Camberwell the advantages of these municipalities, but I think Limehouse and Camberwell rejected the right honourable Gentleman's advice, and showed how absolutely they disregarded it by returning Progressives at the head of the poll. We have it from the speeches of the Prime Minister and the right honourable Gentleman what their views are on this Bill. We have also the evidence of the attack on the London County Council in the County Council elections of March in last year. The whole official force of the Conservative Party was turned on during those elections. I believe every Cabinet Minister made speeches in various parts of London. Well, Sir, the County Council won all along the line.

The FIRST LORD of the TREASURY (Mr. A. J. Balfour, Manchester, E.): Did we make speeches against the London County Council?

Mr. H. GLADSTONE: My opinion is that you did. It is a fair construction to put on those speeches that they involved a most emphatic attack on the County Council. After the defeat of the Moderates and the policy of setting up independent municipal boroughs in London, there was a discreet silence among honourable Gentlemen opposite for a considerable period, but that silence was broken by the Prime Minister, who reaffirmed at Westminster his Albert Hall speech, and said he had nothing to change in it, as it expressed his views very clearly, and he proposed to facilitate the granting of municipalities to communities which obviously in size and importance were designed for them. That is the proposal of this Bill. What is really intended with regard to the future of these bodies? Are they to be set up under the provisions of this Bill, and then left as they are, with the powers to be given to them by the Bill? Now, we have plenty of evidence to show that the design of the Government and of honourable Gentlemen opposite ¡is to arm these bodies with much fuller powers in future. Let me quote Lord Onslow's letter to the Westminster Vestry. He stated, and he spoke with knowledge, and he says—

"It certainly was not that the Government intended by future legislation to transfer further powers from the London County Council to the new municipal boroughs, but that Parliament, when satisfied that they are competent, would no doubt from time to time entrust other and further powers to those municipal boroughs, and that in time the metropolitan boroughs would take rank with their great sister municipalities already existing in the provinces."

[Ministerial cheers.] I am obliged to honourable Gentlemen for cheering that, because it is perfectly clear, if the words of Lord Onslow are true, that if these municipal bodies are to be brought up to the level of Birmingham, Leeds, and Manchester, that the London County Council will be stripped of all the powers it has got. If you do not take powers from the London County Council, where are you to get them from? You may get them from gas and water companies, but if you take them from gas and water companies, you are giving to these local bodies powers which ought certainly to belong to the central authority, and, in any case, you are defrauding the central authority of powers it ought to have. The intentions of the Government are clear. If these municipalities are to be set up and developed, as the cheers of honourable Gentlemen opposite show clearly is their intention, it is perfectly obvious it means the destruction of the central authority. We, therefore, suspect the drift of this Bill, and we are forced, by the evidence before us, taken in conjunction with the character and provisions of the Bill, to oppose its Second Reading. Now, I will proceed to state my main objections to the Bill, and I will summarise them under four heads—(1) The Bill sets up in an imperfect manner independent

Mr. H. Gladstone.

bodies—municipalities only in name—with a ruthless disregard to local feeling, historic boundaries, and the general well-being of the metropolis; (2) it seriously impairs the central governing authority of London, and endangers its future powers for practical good; (3) it proceeds on the faulty and mischievous principle of throwing all responsibility for numberless difficulties on the Local Government Board and Privy Council, and leaving every kind of important question to be settled by Provisional Order, or by scheme; and (4) in defiance of the Royal Commission of 1894, and of the decisive opinion expressed by London in March 1898, the Bill reverses the policy of the Conservative Government in 1888, thus inevitably compromising the whole municipal life of the metropolis by forcing into the political arena large questions relating to the whole form and constitution of London government. I will take those points *seriatim.* We agree that London should be divided into local administrative areas, and that the power of the central authority should be limited to those objects common to the whole of the metropolis. We desire to effect this as recommended by the Royal Commission of 1894. It said—

"London, we repeat, is one large town, which, for convenience of administration as well as from local diversities, comprises within itself several smaller towns, and the application of the principles, and still more of the machinery, of municipal government to these several areas, must be limited by conditions arising from this fact—that is to say, the fact that London is one large town."

We wish to see the efficiency of the present local bodies extended, and to increase as far as possible, both in form and substance, the dignity of their administration. We have no objection to that, and I speak, at any rate, for some of my honourable Friends. We support the intention of the Royal Commission, that these authorities should consist of mayors and district councillors. But this Bill sets up in the fullest panoply in a certain area a form of municipal government. It provides for a full accompaniment of aldermen. Even in the draft Westminster Bill it was not proposed to have aldermen. Aldermen certainly are not wanted on these councils, and I speak with some impartiality, because I am an alderman myself, though perhaps not a very useful one. While I agree that aldermen perform a very useful function on the County Council, I cannot see why London is to have 500 aldermen set up and clothed by this Bill. I suppose they will wear the usual robes, as in provincial boroughs. You cannot invest with the full authority attaching to the great provincial centres districts of London which are merely, and must in the nature of the case be, parts of the whole. They are in their composition divisions of London, and are in every way analogous to the wards of a great provincial town. You propose to set up these municipal authorities with the full dignity of municipal corporations, while they will only possess, and must only possess, the most partial powers. They will not have the police, main drains, gas, water, or tramways. An honourable Member says they will have the tramways. I was under the impression that the tramways were under the authority of the County Council, but, perhaps, the honourable Gentleman knows better. They will not have the parks, or the fire brigade, and they will be debarred from considering all the higher matters which belong to the metropolis as a whole. They will not, in fact, exercise 50 per cent. of the power and authority now exercised by the great municipalities in the provinces. The best illustration I have seen of the Bill was contained in a sentence in a speech of a gentleman who said that the Government were cutting off the legs and arms of a man in order to make a man of each part. Now, I come to the powers to be given to these councils. First of all, I wish to deal with the question of audit. Why have the Government determined to continue the system of elected auditors—a system which has been found to be full of danger and mischief. Other municipalities, I am aware, have that system, but I do not think the right honourable Gentleman will say that it is a system which has worked well in London. If the right honourable Gentleman would say that I would pay great attention to the opinion of such an authority, but he does not make that assertion. It would be far better to have a Local Government Board audit than the proposal in the Bill. The right honourable Gentleman says there is no proposal in the Bill,

but am I not right in assuming that under the Bill the audit authority will be elective. Why is it not possible to follow the precedent of Imperial finance? The change brought about in the auditing of Imperial finance has, as every one knows, worked exceedingly well. What is it? We have an Auditor-General, who is absolutely independent of Government authority. He reports direct to Parliament, and Parliament appoints its Public Accounts Committee. That Committee considers the report of the Auditor-General, and it has the power to call before it any official in the Government whose evidence it thinks necessary to explain any doubtful transaction. That system has undoubtedly worked with most excellent results in the public departments of the Government. Why cannot it be applied to London finance? The right honourable Gentleman says that the system of elected auditors is in force in all our provincial municipalities. But what do we find in London? The County Council, the School Board, boards of guardians, and the Metropolitan Asylums Board have all a Local Government Board audit. I would sooner have that than the audit proposed by the Bill. But why is it necessary to be always throwing important matters relating to the administration of localities on to the shoulders of the Local Government Board? It is a wrong system. Why should it not be possible to set up a central audit board for London, presided over by an official appointed by the Government, who should consider the accounts of all the London authorities, and embody those accounts in a report to be presented to Parliament? I consider if that were done you would have a most perfect public audit for London, and it would give a great stimulus to local administration and would lead to greater efficiency and economy in the conduct of business on the part of the local authorities. Clause 2 of the Bill provides that overseers shall be appointed by the boroughs. That is a good provision as far as it goes. But why does not the Government transfer the whole of the duties of the overseers to the borough councils? The Bill, as it stands, involves a great injustice to some of the existing authorities. For example, there is Shoreditch, which has the power of managing the business usually transacted by overseers. But under the Bill that power will be removed, and handed over to the overseers, who will, I suppose, be a body of officials with separate establishments. I do not understand the reason for this proposal, which; it seems to me, will not simplify the present system, and will, by the duplication of offices, increase the cost of administration. Then I come to the question of assessment. The assessment committees, under clause 13, instead of being appointed by the guardians will be appointed partly by the guardians and partly by the borough councils. I believe everyone will admit that one uniform system of assessment is a great necessity in London, and there appears to be no attempt to achieve this in the Bill. There is no machinery, as a matter of fact, for ensuring uniform action in the assessment of the various burghs, although 10 per cent. of the aggregate rates of London find their way to a common account. The Bill is wholly unsatisfactory in the matter of assessment. Then, why does not the Bill deal with the Poor Law administration of London. This is a very large question, which, no doubt, will be amply enlarged upon in the course of the Debate. The Government are evidently desirous of giving large powers to these local authorities, and as they are limited in the powers they can give, why have they not turned their attention to the question of Poor Law administration, and brought in a Bill giving poor law powers to the local authorities. Then there is the question of annual elections. London is to be disturbed every year by elections to these municipal lodies. Everyone knows that it is a very difficult thing to interest any city in continual local elections, and perhaps it is more difficult to interest London than any other city in the country. Why are Londoners to be harassed by having these local elections every year? The Local Government Act gave the option to boards of guardians to choose between annual and triennial elections, and it gave power to the county councils to meet their wishes in that respect. Every board of guardians has exercised its option in favour of triennial elections. Experience is all in favour of triennial elections, and I cannot see why London is to be burdened by this annual disturb-

Mr. H. Gladstone.

ance. I have spoken about a considerable number of important details, and I will not say any more about them, because many of my honourable Friends can speak on them with infinitely more knowledge and authority than I can. But I must call attention to one more point. That is that the Government, in carrying out the policy of ignoring the Report of the Commission of 1894, have not adopted a most admirable suggestion of the Commission, namely, that the members of the central authority should be ex-officio members of the particular council which represents the constituency for which they sit. That proposal would bring the central authority and the municipal councils into touch with each other, and I fail to see any objection to it. Now, Sir, several of the points which I have indicated can undoubtedly be remedied in Committee, but the chief defect cannot be made good. You can never invest these municipalities with the full powers and dignity of the great provincial boroughs. The deficiency in that respect comes out in sharpest relief in the case of the Greater Westminster which the Bill proposes to constitute. Because the more important your municipal body the more incongruous appears the emasculated powers which you propose to give to it. Now, Greater Westminster has a population of 200,000, with a rateable value of five millions. It is to be composed of four vestries and one district board, rolled into one. It is to have the whole pageantry of a corporation, with its officials, but with only a part of the powers usually attached to municipal boroughs. Now, what is the reason for Greater Westminster? What has it done to be thus set up as a great municipal borough? The right honourable Gentleman the Leader of the House said that Westminster has played a great part in English history. But what part of Westminster? The House of Commons or the House of Lords? I can understand their playing a great part in English history. But does my right honourable Friend mean to say that the Westminster Vestry has played a great part in English history? Now, I was interested to get a Report of the petition which shows the grounds on which the Westminster Vestry base themselves in asking Parliament to confer upon them this enormous power and prestige. What does the Vestry say?

I will quote a paragraph from the petition—

"Your petitioners humbly submit that such an area, comprising within its ample circuit the Royal and national sanctuary which has for centuries enshrined the various memories of your Majesty's august ancestors and the other manifold glories of Her free and famous Kingdom, the Royal Palaces, the Houses of Parliament, the offices of the several Departments of Her Majesty's Government, the Supreme Courts of Law, the Royal Parks, the Albert Memorial, the Imperial Institute, many of the museums and other centres of science and art, and the abodes of many of the great men who have helped to make the name of England famous; an area which has enjoyed the distinction of having been represented in Parliament by some of England's greatest statesmen"

—you observe that that is in the past, not in the present—

"an area instinct with imperishable memories of more than eight centuries; an area the influence of which is acknowledged throughout the civilised world—is entitled to the recognition proposed by the said Bill to be accorded to it."

I say a more grotesque claim for a charter of incorporation I never read in my life. Sir, I do not deny—I am the last man to deny—the great associations which centre in and around Westminster. But these associations are the property of the nation, and they do not constitute any valid reason for bestowing upon Lord Onslow and his vestry the dignity of a great municipal corporation. Sir, it is the pride of Liverpool, of Birmingham, of Leeds, and of Manchester that these great towns have been built up by the energy, the enterprise, and the self sacrifices of the inhabitants. Each town has its own history—a history which belongs to the inhabitants; and the inhabitants know that the greatness of this city is due to the energy of themselves and their forefathers. Each of these great provincial municipalities contains within its boundaries all classes and all sorts and conditions of men. It has the rich and the poor. It has the employed and the employer. It has its own manufacturing, its industrial, and its residential quarters. It has its own municipal buildings, which it has created. It has its own municipal institutions, of which it is proud. Everything which it has got it owes to the energy and enterprise of its own inhabitants. Each city is a

perfect and complete structure of social life and municipal enterprise. And all these conditions, I say, are wanting in this Westminster. Why, Sir, a great city like Birmingham or Leeds keeps its workmen within its boundaries; Westminster gets rid of them. Westminster gets rid of them it is true, but the poorer districts of London have to provide for then. Sir, the chief glories of Westminster belong either to the nation or they are common to all the Empire. All the authority of the Empire centres in this proposed area. The places of amusement, recreation, and the picture galleries, and everything which people swarm to see from all parts of the world —all these must be brought, forsooth, into the area destined to the honour and glory of Lord Onslow and his Westminster Vestry. I am glad the honourable Member for Westminster laughs, and I have no doubt that he will have full opportunity of explaining the paragraph which I have had the honour to submit to this House. The right honourable Gentleman says he is going to reconstitute the City of Westminster. Reconstitute it to what? I do not know what the right honourable Gentleman had in his mind. I do not know to what he refers. The City of Westminster is merely a name. It has never had any corporate municipal existence. It has not a shred of municipal tradition. I quite agree that the Westminster Vestry is a most excellent body; I do not wish to say one word against it. I believe it has very high merit as an administrative body. But to set it up and extend it in the manner proposed by the Bill is another thing. I say that Westminster owes little or nothing of its enormous advantages to its own inhabitants. Sir, there is a great improvement going on in its area. The Government is spending millions of money in the improvement of Parliament Street and neighbourhood, and intends to adorn it with magnificent buildings. Westminster Vestry had no hand in that. Why, I had the honour of initiating that scheme, but they have not asked me to support their petition. The improvement of the thoroughfares of Westminster and its grand public buildings are due partly to the work of the central authority, and carried out by a general rate, and therefore belong to the whole of London. Take, for instance, the Embankment—a large section of which will come into the Greater Westminster area. Or the improvements which have been set up by the Government and paid for by the Government. But all these things will add to the honour and glory of Westminster Vestry. I should like to know why the Westminster Vestry should have a practical monopoly of these things. I sincerely hope that this preposterous municipality will not be set up by this Bill. I pass to the question of areas. There are fifteen areas in the Bill; the remainder are left to a somewhat dark and uncertain future. Our only guidance is in the sub-section of clause 1, which states that the qualification for a borough is a rateable value of not less than £500,000, or a population of between 100,000 and 400,000. Now, I fail to understand on what principle the Government has proceeded in this matter. It has not adopted the Report of the Royal Commission. The Royal Commission specified the number of areas which are perfectly fit at once to be created into district councils. They mentioned St. George's, Westminster, and St. Margaret's coupled together, but these are found in the Bill as a part only of the Greater Westminster. They mentioned Shoreditch and Whitechapel, but these do not appear in the Bill at all. But you do find in the Bill areas not recommended by the Royal Commission, such as Battersea, Camberwell, Lewisham, and Wandsworth. Now, why does not the Government include parishes like Greenwich, Deptford, Woolwich, Whitechapel, Newington, Shoreditch, which are here omitted and left to the tender mercies of the Boundary Committee? There is no principle in the Measure. There seems to be no principle either in regard to the areas which are put in the Bill or in regard to those that are left out. Why should you force St. George's, St. James's, St. Martin's and the Strand into a union with Westminster, which they detest?

HONOURABLE MEMBERS: Oh, oh!

MR. H. GLADSTONE: They seem to detest it, and they say so. I saw a communication from one of these aggrieved vestries bitterly complaining of the proposal to include them in Westminster. Why should these parishes be combined?

Mr. H. Gladstone.

There is no unity of administration between these different areas which this Bill proposes to merge in Greater Westminster. I am aware they are combined for school board purposes, but I also know that they conduct the school board elections with different bodies of electors, with different officials, and with different organisations. In these respects they are all separate one from the other. There is nothing in common between these areas which you propose to join in one. Let us come to Wandsworth. I should like to know from the Government why they set up this huge and unwieldy Wandsworth as a municipal borough. It is not in the centre of London, but in the suburbs. It includes Streatham, Clapham, Tooting, Putney, and Wimbledon, with a total area of 10,000 acres—a most unmanageable size for administrative purposes. Chelsea has only 794 acres. In fact, this proposed district of Wandsworth will be in extent 3,000 acres larger than any other area proposed in the Bill, and double the size of most of them. I really cannot see why the Government propose to set up this great Wandsworth, which is not only unmanageable for municipal purposes, but is a district which is rapidly filling up, and the population is rapidly expanding. In a very short time it will be found that the population is out of all proportion —if we except Westminster—to that of the other bodies to be set up in other parts of London. I am wrong. Westminster is to have a population of only 200,000, while that of Wandsworth is likely to exceed that number before many years are over. Why do you keep wholesome local administration alive in one place and abolish it in another? Why are the rich districts joined together in the Schedule of the Bill, and why are the poor districts almost wholly ignored? I am aware that one of the poorest districts appears in the schedule —namely, Poplar; but the great majority of the poor districts are left to shift for themselves. I do not know why it is so, and I say that the provisions of the Bill in regard to these areas are most unsatisfactory. I come now to the proposal in regard to the Boundary Commission that is to be appointed. I agree that it will be necessary to have a Boundary Commission. That is clear. But the Commission ought to be appointed upon distinct principles and conditions. The names of the Commissioners ought to be in the Bill, and they should be instructed, in considering the question of areas, to bear in mind local traditions, local feeling, administrative efficiency, and the present boundaries of existing areas. But, above all this, provision ought to be made in the Bill that any result arrived at by the Boundary Commissioners should be submitted to Parliament before it passes into law. And now I pass to my second point, the interference by the Bill with the efficiency of this Central Authority. I say that the Central Authority ought to have power over the general finance of London, to watch it, and to keep it within bounds, in the interest of London as a whole. Under the Bill it is proposed to transfer the power for sanctioning loans required by the subordinate councils from the London County Council to the Local Government Board. What is the authority for that proposal? I cannot arrive at it myself. I have never heard that the London County Council had erred on this question of finance. They have had the most eminent men to watch over it— the honourable Member for West London, Lord Farrer, Lord Welby, Lord Lincoln—the greatest financial experts in the country. I fail to know why this attack has been made on their use of the power of sanctioning loans to the local authorities. I believe that that power has worked with great success and advantage to the local authorities. The local authorities have been able to borrow cheaply and quickly, and I think I am right in saying that they have never asked that this power should be transferred from the London County Council to the Local Government Board. I want to know on what ground this transfer is to be made. One objection, amongst others, to the present proposal is, that it will give the local authorities power to mortgage their rates, and to impair the borrowing powers of the London County Council itself. Why should not the London County Council remain as it is, with power to appropriate and consent to these loans? I think the proposed transfer involves distinctly the impairment of the powers of the Central Authority. I come to the question of the equalisation of rates. You are setting up by this Bill a Greater

Westminster, with its enormous rateable value of 1-7th of the rateable value of the whole metropolis, and are going to give it a preponderating power. There are great inequalities at the present time in regard to the rates of different governing areas in London. For instance, in St. James's parish you have a rate of 8s. 7d. in the pound. I should like the House to remember the past, and that equalisation of rates is not a modern cry of fanatical County Councillors, but is suggested by every consideration of justice. The Committee of 1866 appointed to consider Metropolitan local government reported that so heavy had the charges for local taxation become that in the less wealthy districts of the metropolis it had become an intolerable burden, and that the direct taxation of property there had reached its utmost limits. What was the state of things at the date of the sitting of the Committee? Improvements had been carried out in the western part of the metropolis by means of general rates, at a cost of £4,371,000. And further improvements were to be at once taken in hand at a cost of £663,000. Against that sum of five millions spent in the improvement of the Metropolitan district, on the Eastern part of London the humble sum of £329,000 was spent. That shows that there is a great inequality to be redressed. You have had the Act of 1894, and undoubtedly there will be further schemes brought forward in the municipal future. I ask the House, Is it wise, therefore, to set up a body like the Greater Westminster, with its enormous rateable value, which is 1-7th of the rateable value of the metropolis? Such a body will be tempted to throw every difficulty in the way of proposals which are intended for the just benefit of the poorer parts of London. That is one of the greatest and most imminent dangers attaching to this Greater Westminster. At any rate, this subject does involve some distinct modification of the present central authority. I come to clause 6, which proposes to give power to the Committee of the Privy Council to transfer the provisions of the Buildings Act from the London County Council to the local authorities. The local authorities have not asked for that power. The Act of 1894, with its 218 clauses, was long and carefully considered by a Hybrid Committee, and after the fullest consideration its powers were given to the London County Council. Why does the Government override the Committee of this House? Why does it override the action of the Government of that time? It does seem to me that what is required is uniformity in this matter, uniformity to be provided for by one central authority. There is the question of street frontages and of the height and structure of buildings in different localities. These are matters of vital importance, and you will throw them into the greatest confusion if you transfer these powers from the central authority to the subordinate authorities. A builder might come to erect a block of houses on an area controlled by different authorities, one half of the block being in one subordinate municipality, and the other half in another; and the builder would have to evoke the sanction of both for his operations. This clause is a most mischievous clause; it takes away from the central authority power which it is absolutely necessary for it to have. Then there are the Parliamentary powers, which are to be given by clause 7 to the local authorities. I have been told that the Moderate members of the London County Council have protested against these powers being given even to the London County Council itself. Why then, does the Government propose to entrust such powers, which ought not to have been entrusted to the central authority, to no less than 20 or 25 other bodies in London? It seems to me a thoroughly bad proposal which, if carried out, will produce chaotic confusion and heavy and unnecessary expense. At the present moment when local bodies want something they go to the London County Council, and that council includes what they want, if it be necessary, in a General Powers Bill, and the matter is put through Parliament at a minimum of expense. Under this clause of the Bill each locality will have the power of promoting a Bill on its own account, and there will be no limit to the number of separate and conflicting Bills. There again, you are seriously impairing the duties and responsibilities of the Central authority. Then there is the transfer of powers from the London County Council to the subordinate councils. There is no reason why powers should not be transferred from the County

Mr. H. Gladstone.

Council when it is deemed necessary and right; but the proper method of doing that is through Parliament. Let the London County Council bring in a Bill for the purpose, and Parliament, if it sees wise, will transfer the powers. This Bill sets up an automatic process by which once the London County Council part with power to one body, every borough in the metropolis can take it, whether or not the London County Council consents, subject to the consent of the Local Government Board. That will introduce confusion. What is wanted in these matters is uniformity of administration, and that is what you will not get under this Bill. There is not even the power to retransfer such powers from the boroughs to the London County Council. I maintain that if a transfer of power is necessary it ought to be done by a Private Bill in Parliament. It is the obvious intention of the Government to keep on adding to the powers of these municipal boroughs set up by the Bill, and that process must inevitably result in the further curtailment of the power and authority of the Central Authority of London. For these reasons, therefore, I strongly object to the retrograde proposals of the Bill. I pass to the third head of my objection. There is no finality in the Bill. The City is untouched; it is left in its splendid isolation, dead to the higher impulses on behalf of the metropolis as a whole. The administration of the Poor Law is not touched. The Metropolitan Asylums Board is left untouched. The Bill sets up a condition of things in these localities which cannot be permanent, if we are to judge by the language of Lord Salisbury and the Leader of the House. Then, Sir, the principles of the Bill are to be given effect to in various ways. They are to be given effect to through the Local Government Board, through the Privy Council, and partly by Provisional Orders—a most unsatisfactory method of procedure, which may or may not have the attention of the House. Even more unsatisfactory still is the clause which enables the Government to proceed by schemes under the Bill, which will practically be withdrawn from the purview of Parliament. I find that out of 28 clauses no less than 21, either in part or in whole, are to operate in this most unsatisfactory manner. As far as possible, Parliament is not to have have a controlling voice, and, therefore, I say the Bill proceeds on faulty and mischievous principles. I now come to my last head, and I apologise to the House for speaking at such length, and thank honourable Members for the patient hearing they have given me. I agree, to a certain extent, with the Prime Minister when he deplores the harm that follows upon deciding local questions on political principles. I think we all admit that such matters should be dealt with upon their merits apart from general political controversy. Lord Salisbury has himself attacked the London County Council and London government, and has forced my right honourable Friends on this side of the House to enter the political arena. I do not say the fault is more on one side than on the other, but I do say that this Bill is, and must be, an aggravation of the evil. It ignores the Commission of 1894; it ignores the policy to which, at any rate, honourable Members on this side of the House are attached, and for which they have worked and mean to work; it reverses their own policy of 1888, embodying as it did the principle of the unity of London—a policy which obtained from this side of the House very cordial support. Suddenly we find that the Government have gone back in the direction of the old Commission of 1854, and have produced a Bill which must be most distasteful in many of its provisions to all those on this side of the House who have taken great interest in the question of London government. The whole design of it is really to save the City from attack, and to impede the realisation of the idea of the unity of London. These corporations which the Bill proposes to set up are intended to be so many bulwarks between the City and those whom the City look upon as its enemies. None the less, however, shall we stand by what we believe to be best for London, and what London wants. It is the Government who will be responsible if in the future embittered controversies arise over questions concerning the government of London. They have chosen to depart from their own policy, they have chosen to go in the opposite direction to ours. The question of London government

goes far beyond ordinary political lines, and enthusiasts in favour of London unity are to be found in the ranks of the supporters of Her Majesty's Government. The Government have no mandate for this Bill. Let them show their mandate if it exists at all. I assert that they are intending to pass this Bill in the face of opposition deliberately expressed by London last year—expressed with the clearness of a plebiscite. This Bill is to be forced, I suppose, down our throats. I am afraid it will intensify feeling, and make the attainment of the unity of London more difficult. That is your object, and you may achieve it with your big battalions here and with the assistance of your friends in the House of Lords. This Bill spells disintegration in every clause, and, above all, London requires municipal unity. It is a city so vast, so unwieldy, with so little cohesion in its huge districts, that its people have little or no sense of corporate existence, and for that reason London requires the fullest possible development of municipal life with devolution of powers to local councils stronger and more dignified than those that now exist. We consider it of vital importance to the whole that these local councils should work harmoniously together for the good, not only of themselves, but for the whole of London, and to effect this the system of government must centre in one high authority, and that authority must be representative of all London, possessed with a living sense of responsibility for the whole welfare of London, and provided with the power and the influence necessary to bring home to every man of understanding that he owes a duty not only to himself and to his locality, but to the inhabitants in general of that great metropolis of which he is a citizen. Sir, this Bill conflicts with the attainment of this great result, and for that reason I have the honour to move the Amendment which stands in my name.

MR. WHITMORE (Chelsea): Mr. Speaker, I hope the House will not think me presumptuous in rising to speak upon this Bill. I venture to do so because I happen to be a London Member, and also a member of the London County Council, who has for many years taken a great interest in this question. I should like to utter one word of protest against the suspicion which the right honourable Gentleman who has just sat down seems to entertain as to the object of the Government in bringing in this Bill. If I for one moment thought that the Government, by the introduction of this Bill, had in some sinister and ulterior way a design to attack the London County Council, I should not be inclined to support this Measure. The right honourable Gentleman the Leader of the Opposition smiles at that remark. I hope he is not smiling incredulously at what I am saying. The question of London government was fought at the last County Council election, but the question before the electors then was not of the unity of London as understood by the right honourable gentleman the Member for Leeds. The question, no doubt, was whether the Council should remain in its integrity with all its essential powers; but there was no question of amalgamation with the Corporation. The question was also before the electors whether there should not be set up by the side of the County Council authoritative and dignified local authorities, and no man spoke out with greater distinctness in favour of that proposition than the right honourable Gentleman the late Home Secretary. I do not know whether he wishes to be reminded of what he said in 1894, at a meeting held in the Queen's Hall, but he certainly used language which justifies the Government in introducing this Bill. He said the then Government proposed to give the local bodies the stimulus of more attractive titles and of conspicuous positions which would create a more fruitful field for the best energy and the best efforts of the best men of the localities. His phrase was rather rotund, but if it meant anything it meant that these bodies should have the dignity of possessing mayors and councillors.

MR. ASQUITH (Fife, E.): I was speaking at the time in support of the Courtney Commission, and against a scheme for creating municipalities.

*MR. WHITMORE: Then I am afraid the language which the right honourable Gentleman used did not convey that impression. Let me now refer to the speech of the right honourable Gentleman, the Member for Leeds. It is vain

Mr. Whitmore.

for honourable Members on the other side of the House to expect from this Government the amalgamation of the County Council with the City. We hold the view that it is not expedient to make one municipality in London. I think it would be unwise to make the head of the County Council the Lord Mayor of London, and to give to the County Council all the attributes and dignities of the old Corporation. In my opinion London does not want this. No doubt at one time there was a great feeling in favour of unification, because it was supposed that the City was possessed of great wealth, and that if merged into Greater London the ratepayers of London generally would be relieved in consequence. It is now known that if amalgamation took place no relief would accrue to the rates of London. After all, the County Council must always have most important, varied, and difficult duties to perform. The strain on the ordinary county councillor now is great. Why should you add to that the wholly unnecessary ceremonial attributes which attach to the City? As regards the administrative work of London in general, what real practical good would result from the amalgamation of the City with the area of the County Council? I frankly admit that if I were a citizen of London I should like to see the City Corporation reformed, but it has reformed itself in many ways since 1834, notably in the abolition of the old Commissioners of Sewers. That was a real administrative reform. But whether the Corporation requires reforming or not, there is no doubt that it governs admirably the part of London over which it has jurisdiction. So I fail to see that the unification of London in that sense is of any great practical importance to Londoners in general. As the right honourable Gentleman the First Lord of the Treasury pointed out when he introduced this Bill, there have always been two sets of institutions in London for local government purposes. Unlike the great provincial towns, we have always had some kind of institution for central purposes and some kind of institution for local purposes. That principle was acted upon by the legislation of the Metropolis Management Act; it was acted upon by the last Unionist Government in 1888, when that Government deliberately set up the London County Council. When the County Council was established it was the admitted intention of the Government to set up by its side administrative local bodies. I think the real problem with all reformers of London government has been, first of all, to ascertain what are the proper functions of a central authority and local authorities; then to decide what are the proper areas for the local authorities; and, thirdly, to provide and maintain a proper equipoise and relation between the central and local authorities. In London, so far as I can understand, there must always be a central authority—the County Council —exercising far and away the most important and interesting functions of all, and by its side independent and dignified local authorities. I do not see why there should be any subordination of the local authorities to the central authority or superiority of the central authority over the local authorities. In London there should be no inconsistency in theory or practice between patriotism to one's parish and to one's city at large. The necessity for dignifying the local bodies is generally agreed upon, and the method adopted in this Bill does not meet with much real or serious objection. In giving the local authorities mayors and aldermen, the Government have followed the precedent of the Municipal Corporations Act. With regard to the transfer of powers from the County Council to local authorities, the Government have been tender to the feelings of county councillors. The powers to be transferred are "agreed" powers, and no Moderate councillor wishes, or would ever wish, to transfer powers unnecessarily from the Council to local authorities. The members of any municipal body are anxious to make that body powerful, they are slow to get rid of any of their powers and to hand them over to any other body. I am perfectly certain that no Councillor would unnecessarily relieve the London County Council of duties which it is obviously right that that body should retain. With regard to the clause which proposes to give local authorities power to promote and oppose Bills, I am sure it will not be used against the County Council, or in favour of private monopolies. You have only to look at the way in which the Conservative City of London has always co-operated in such matters with the London County Council, to convince you that that will be so. The City has been as warm as the County Council in opposition to private monopolies, to the Water Companies and to the Telephone Company. I must say I was astonished at the way in which the right honourable Gentleman the Member for Leeds has dealt with the manner in which the Government propose to deal with the question of areas. Everybody knows that this question is the crux of any Bill re-constituting local authorities in London. There are two extreme schools of thought which have made themselves apparent on this question. On the one hand, you have those who wish arbitrarily and capriciously to carve London into something like 10 districts; and, on the other extreme, you have those who would preserve the existing areas; and the Bill which was promoted by the honourable Members for Islington and Battersea showed what I call an excessively conservative tendency in that direction. As a matter of fact, they proposed to give municipal dignity to all the existing vestries and district boards. That was the low-water mark of reform in that direction. The report of the Commission presided over by the right honourable Gentleman the Member for Bodmin took a middle course, and on the whole the Government are acting upon the lines of that report as to areas. That report, it will be remembered, selected 19 areas. I do not say that they were all wisely selected, but still the Commission did select certain districts, and declared that the rest of London must be delimited by a Boundary Commission. That is essentially what the Government have done in this Bill. They have selected 15 areas, and have left the rest to be delimited by a Boundary Commission. I cannot pass by in silence the grossly unfair and misleading statement, that in the selection of the 15 areas the Government have chosen out the rich districts as opposed to the poor. Has the right honourable Gentleman the Member for Leeds looked at Schedule A of the Bill? It is really worth examining for one moment. The accusation he has made is a grave one; if it be true he should substantiate it, and if false it should be withdrawn. There are 15 areas in Schedule A. I am afraid that at the present time there is not a much better test of the character of the population of any particular district than the politics of those who are returned to the London County Council. At any rate, I am afraid that that is so. I find, when I look at the way in which the County Council election went at the last contest, in 13 of these areas, which returned in all 54 members, exactly 27 were Progressive councillors, and 27 were Moderates. That is a most significant fact, and it absolutely shows that these districts are not in any way exclusively the districts of the rich. · I would like to ask anybody who knows anything about London if they think that Battersea is a city of the rich?

MR. BURNS (Battersea): In some things it is. We have no monopolies.

*MR. WHITMORE: I should also like to ask whether Camberwell, Fulham, Hammersmith, Islington, Lambeth, and St. Pancras, are cities of the rich? With regard to the delimitation of the rest of London, I cannot help hoping that the Boundary Commission will think not only of the express directions given them•in the Bill, but also somewhat of the kind of districts which have been put in the first schedule. I must thank the Government for having selected Chelsea as one of the areas. I am aware that its population is somewhat smaller than that of the other areas, but no doubt it has been selected, because it has had a vigorous local life and possesses those local traditions, which go to make the success of the municipal boroughs of this country. Surely, the Boundary Commission will take note of that, and in delimiting the rest of London will not think simply of putting together great aggregations of population, but will have due regard to local circumstances, to ancient history, and to present local feeling. And I am bound to say I shall be glad, while this Bill is in Committee, to see two other areas included in the first schedule. Both Shoreditch and Bethnal Green, have all the attributes which the Boundary Commissioners would say would make them worthy of receiving a charter of incor-

Mr. Whitmore.

poration. Therefore, I think it would be wise if this House itself included them in the first schedule, for it would make it still more difficult for imaginative gentlemen who know nothing about London, to rake up the absurd charge that the districts are arranged in favour of the rich, at the expense of the poor. I think it is as well that the Conservatives of London should freely express their minds on some of these points. I pass from the matter of areas to what, perhaps, is, after all, in most men's minds, when they are thinking about this Bill. I have heard cynical friends say—"What, after all, will be the outcome of it? It may be a good enough Bill, but will you get a better class of men to serve on your local authorities?" I do not know. I do not wish to indulge in any prophecy but, at all events, it seems to me that by this Bill, the Government are doing what they can, by legislation, to attract the best kind of men to the service of local government. You are going to invest the local authorities with those titles and dignities which have proved attractive in other parts of the country. Most wisely, you are going to limit the number of your councillors, so that in future each individual councillor shall have a distinct sense of responsibility, and shall feel that he is able to perform some useful work for the body of which he is a member. As regards areas, I hope that on the one hand, they will not be too big, and that, on the other hand, they will be large enough to prevent any little clique or body of tradesmen from bossing their affairs. If the Government do that by this Bill, we must leave the rest to the good feeling and growing sense of responsibility of the citizens of London. It is a curious thing, but I suppose there is no city in the world where so many men and women of leisure and means are giving up their time, their thoughts, their energies, and their money to the service of their fellow-citizens in every other department of life, except that of local government, as in London. I do not suppose that in any other country you can find so glorious a record of self-sacrificing lives. That is the proud boast of London. Its disgrace has been, unfortunately, that the local bodies have not been able to attract to their service the same class of men as are to be found on local bodies in provincial towns. I do think, from the bottom of my heart, that if this Bill does a little something by way of legislation to encourage that which we want to see, and to get rid of that stain on the reputation of Londoners, and to make them as zealous in this branch of public service as they are showing themselves in every other department of public life, it will be a great achievement. And, if that be so, we have a right to be grateful to the Government for introducing this Measure. I believe that it proceeds on the right lines. If we can only purge these local bodies of the curse of excessive Party spirit, it will be a great means by which we can elevate the local life of London. Unlike the right honourable Gentleman who has just spoken, I can assure him that, in my judgment, and in the judgment of many others who are not extreme partisans, this Measure is a sound and sensible instalment of practical administrative reform. We thank the Government for having introduced it, and we will do our best, with, I hope the co-operation of the right honourable and honourable Gentlemen opposite, to make it a really useful Measure, which will add to the prosperity and happiness of this great town, of which we are all so proud.

Mr. STEADMAN (Tower Hamlets, Stepney): The honourable Member, in a very able speech, has done his best to convince the House and London that this Bill is to the interest of the people of London. He also pointed out that at the present time the London County Council is so overworked that the natural consequence is that some of its powers should be transferred to the local authorities. I do not happen to know how long the honourable Member for Chelsea has been a member of the London County Council, but I do know that I have been a member myself for seven years, not like the honourable Member, an alderman, responsible to no constituents for my work or my faults, but elected by the people of the East End of London to represent them upon the Council. I have also been for some years a member of the Mile End Vestry, and, there-

fore, I have some practical knowledge of the matter now before the House. I am one of those who entirely object to Party politics being introduced into municipal affairs. I maintain that we on this side of the House, and the Progressive Party in the London County Council are not responsible for the elections being fought on Party political lines. As a matter of fact, the First Lord of the Treasury himself during one election came down to my constituency to speak in support of the Moderate candidates, and I am pleased to inform the House that, in spite of the right honourable Gentleman's high position and oratory, and the great influence he was able to bring to bear upon a mass meeting, the answer given him was the return of Progressive members in that and in the adjoining constituencies. On a previous occasion, the right honourable Gentleman the Member for Birmingham came down into the constituency to advocate a system of tenification. But the people of East London, having more knowledge of their local affairs than even the right honourable Gentleman, gave him his answer by saying that they wanted unification and not tenification. So far as the remarks of the honourable Member for Chelsea, with regard to the County Council being overworked are concerned, all I have to say is that if he and his friends in the Moderate Party were to do their share equally with the Progressive Party we could do more work than we are undertaking to do even at the present moment. What does this Bill propose to do? In the first place, it proposes to set up a semi-House of Lords in our local bodies by the election of aldermen. What and who is an alderman? He is a gentleman selected by the party who for the time being may be in power. It was the case that in 1895 the Moderates and Progressives returned to the Council were equal in number, and for this fact the honourable Member for Chelsea must thank his lucky stars, because owing to it he was elected an alderman of the Council. I am a democrat myself, and I am opposed to the House of Lords interfering with the legislative machinery of this country. As such, I am opposed to the election of aldermen either on the London County

Council, or on the local bodies. They go there not with any mandate from the constituencies, they are responsible to no one, they do absolutely as they like, and no one can call them to account for their votes. We all know that reform is very much needed in the vestries and district boards of London. Take the case of the overseers. They are elected, it is true, by the vestries; but their election has to be confirmed by a stipendiary magistrate, and when he has done that they have the power of raising the necessary money for local purposes. They also are able to spend what money they choose, they may go down to the seaside at the expense of the ratepayers, and neither the vestry nor anybody else can call them to account. They are responsible to no one for their actions. Yet this Bill will retain them in exactly the same position.

THE FIRST LORD OF THE TREASURY: No, no!

MR. STEADMAN. Can the right honourable Gentleman show me anything in the Bill making the overseers responsible to any local authority for their action in the same way as committees elected by that body are? I can assure him I am prepared to support any reform in that direction. I admit that, so far as the churchwardens are concerned, the Bill abolishes their election by the municipality, and rightly so. I am a Churchman myself and have been so from my infancy, but I have seen cases where men have been elected as churchwardens who have no religious belief at all. Plenty of them go to the church on the Sabbath morning, and when they come out enter a public-house, and stick there until closing time. Such men, in my humble opinion, are not fit to be churchwardens. I have known cases in which a Nonconformist has been elected to the office. That man, too, has no right to be a churchwarden, because he shows by the very fact of his being a Nonconformist that he disbelieves in the principle of an established church. But he has accepted the office, because prior to the Bill brought forward by the Liberal Party in 1894 it carried with it the chairmanship of the vestry, and in order to secure that official po-

Mr. Steadman.

sition he took that inconsistent action. Then there is the question of the transfer of powers. That is a very important matter, for I maintain that every power transferred from the London County Council to these new municipalities will weaken the influence of that council in spite of the eloquence of the honourable Member for Chelsea. What has been our past experience upon our vestries? They have had to carry out the Public Health Act, a most important duty for any administrative body. But, as a rule, our vestries to-day are manipulated by men who are property owners in the district, whose interest it is that the sanitary laws should not be carried out. However much a Sanitary Inspector may desire to carry those laws out, it is very often the case that, owing to the intimidation of Members of the vestry who own property in the district, he is unable to put them in force. Then there is the question of loans. To-day, the London County Council lends money to our local boards at 3½ per cent. interest. It is true that the Local Government Board will lend money at a cheaper rate, but only for short terms; for longer terms they charge a higher rate of interest. You say under this Bill that in the future the Municipalities shall apply to the Local Government Board and not to the London County Council for loans. Yet the great outcry to-day is that municipal enterprise, more especially in the East End of London, is retarded by the fact that they are not able to borrow money re-payable not in 10, 50, or 60 years, but in 100 years. Then there is the question of cow-houses and slaughter-houses. To-day, the London County Council looks after the administration of those places. You propose to transfer these powers to the local authority, and what is happening to-day on our vestries with reference to our Sanitary Laws will happen on these new authorities in regard to cow-houses and slaughter-houses, because the owners of them will aspire to become members of these bodies in order to prevent their interests being interfered with, whereas, at the present moment, the London County Council sees that the regulations on this matter are properly carried out. Next, I come to the question of the main roads. In this subject, I am specially interested, as the representative of the East End of London. The honourable Member for Chelsea stated that the County Council itself was in favour of the transfer, among other things, of the maintenance of our main roads to the new municipalities. There is one main road in the East End of London, the Commercial Road, which runs through four parishes, Poplar, Limehouse, Mile End Old Town, and St. George's in the East. The County Council have to pay part of the cost of maintenance of that road to-day. Now, it must be borne in mind that we have in this district the Albert Docks, the Victoria Docks, the East and West India Docks, and the Millwall Docks, and this road is the thoroughfare along which are carted all the bonded goods · conveyed from the Docks to the City and West End of London. Why should the poor people in the East End of London, who are already over-rated, be still more heavily taxed for the maintenance of this road, which is used in the interests of the City and West End merchants? In the time of Charles II. the hackney carriage licence of £5 per annum was applied towards the cost of sewering and paving our roads, yet at the end of this enlightened nineteenth century we are going back from what was done in those days. The chief item of interest to myself, however, as the representative of the East End of London is the incidence of rates. I find, after carefully going through the last returns, the following facts in regard to the rates. Those of Bow which in 1892 were 7s. 3d. in the £1 are to-day 8s. 1d. In Bromley they have risen from 7s. 5d. to 7s. 8d.; in Limehouse, from 6s. 2d. to 6s. 8d.; in Poplar, from 6s. 3d. to 7s. 4½d.; in Ratcliffe, from 5s. 8d. to 6s. 5d.; in St. George's in the East, from 5s. 5d. to 5s. 11d.; in Shadwell, from 6s 3d. to 6s. 9d.; in Wapping, from 5s. 7½d. to 6s. 5d.; in Whitechapel, from 6s. 1d. to 6s. 6d.; and in Mile End, from 6s. 6d. to 6s. 9d. The reason I give these figures is this: in 1894 the Equalisation of Rates Act came into operation, and, strange to say, every parish I have mentioned, although it has benefited by that Act, has since had its rates increased in spite of the sum it has received under it. Take the hamlet of Mile End Old

Town. We receive £12,288, which is equal to a rate of 8d. in the £1. Yet in spite of that our rates have gone up year by year, and I will attempt to show the House the reason for it. The Poor Rate in Mile End, which includes the School Board, the Police, the County Council, and the Asylums Board Rate, is 4s. 4d. in the £1. In Bow it is 5s. 5d., in Bromley 4s. 10d., in Limehouse 4s. 2d., in Poplar 4s. 6d., in Ratcliff 3s. 11d., in St. George's in the East, 3s. 3d., in Shadwell, 4s. 4d., in Wapping 3s. 8½d., and in Whitechapel 3s. 9d. in the £1. Our Poor Rate in Mile End in 1894, previously to our receiving over £12,000 under the Equalisation of Rates Act, was 3s. 7d. in the £. In 1895 it was 3s. 9d., in 1896 it was 4s., and now it stands at 4s. 4d. in the £. These figures prove conclusively the poverty that exists to-day in the East End of London, and, instead of limiting the evil by means of this Bill, you are going to intensify it by shutting us off from the West End of London. The result is that the Bill will keep us poor. You cannot wonder at the fact that the East End of London, in consequence of this poverty, has always been the happy hunting-ground for philanthropists and political pensioners. Under this Bill the people of the East End are still to stew in their poverty, while the rich are to be eased from their present responsibilities of paying an equal share of the public burdens. It is not because we spend money in waste. We have not even adopted the Free Libraries Act in Mile End, or the Public Baths and Washhouses Act. Our roads to-day, too, are not in that state of repair which they should be; our streets are badly lighted; and yet our rates are 6s. 9d. in the £. The reason is, that our people are getting poorer every day; our poor rate is 4s. 4d. in the £; and in that fact you have proof of the poverty which exists. The result is that we are not able to put into force Acts which were passed for the benefit of the people; we dare not increase our rates even ½d. more in the £, because the working classes are not able to bear any additional burden. Take the parish of the honourable Member for Chelsea. He was very keen in trying to demonstrate to the House that some of the parishes which are scheduled under this Bill are as poor as some of those that are left out. I do not see that, Mr. Speaker. I find that in Kensington the Poor Rate is only 3s. 5¼d. in the £, while the total rate is only 5s. 8½d. In Westminster (St. James's) the rates are 5s. 1d., in St. Martin's-in-the-Fields 5s. 6d., and in Chelsea 5s. 6d. only. And what is the case in the City? The City for years past has been driving the poorer population out of its area to swell the already over-congested districts that surround it, and the result is that the City, instead of bearing its own responsibilities in looking after the working classes that at one time used to reside there, has driven them away to places like Battersea and Mile End, to the great relief of their own rates. Their minimum rate is 2s. 11½d. in the £, and their maximum only 3s. 0½d. in the £, or more than 40 per cent. less than we in the East End of London are paying. Yet these people in the City, whom this Bill does not touch, are better able to bear their burdens and pay their way than those who live in the East End. They, however, are to be let off scot-free by this Bill, and the poor are to go on struggling in the best way they can. I myself am in favour of some reform in our vestries and district boards. Personally I should be satisfied with a simple alteration of the title from the vestry or district board to district council, and instead of the members of our vestries being called vestrymen—they are commonly known as "Bumbles"—I would give them the title of councillors. But you do not propose to do that in this Bill. It is true you do not advocate a system of tenification, but by reducing the number of areas you are going in the right direction to bring that about on some future occasion. Plus the tinsel pomp of Lord Mayors' Shows, you are going to construct certain municipalities, with mayors as chairmen, and with aldermen in their dignified robes and chains of office, which will be the means of swelling their heads to such an extent that the time will not be far distant when the London County Council will be got rid of altogether. Now, I must point out that the secret of the success and popularity of the London County Council is its simplicity. Its chairman, while he is not Lord Mayor, is the real Mayor of London. He does not repre-

Mr. Steadman. ·

sent a city within a city, but he repre-sents the whole of the County of London. He does not preside over the meetings of the Council robed in ermine and wearing a chain of office, and neither do our aldermen attend in their garb of office. On the contrary, they come in all their simplicity, the same as myself and my colleague the Member for Battersea, who are looked upon as belonging to the working classes. I repeat, it is because of that simplicity that the London County Council is so popular to-day with the people of London. Another cause of its popularity is that it attacks interests and privileged monopolies. It is distasteful to the present Government for the very same reasons, and, therefore, they are going to do their level best, not to put it out of existence perhaps, but to deprive it of the more important of its powers. I have called attention to several parishes which are going to be put in what I may term "the melting-pot." If the Government had been wise—or if the honourable Member for Chelsea, who I believe has had a very important finger in advising the Government as to the details of the Measure, had been wise—they would have selected for municipalities all the vestries and district boards, and then there would have been no occasion to have appointed boundary commissioners. But instead of that they have selected only a few, although in order if possible to get the united support of this House they have included even the constituency of my honourable Friend the Member for Battersea. They have included, too, one of the constituencies in the East End of London—Poplar. But Poplar does not want the Bill; it disagrees with it; and others of the large municipalities which are to be created under it—Westminster, for instance, in connection with which several parishes are to be joined together in order to form one municipality—are dissenting from the Bill. My own constituency, which, it is true, comprises only 677 acres, has a population of 111,200 persons, and its rateable value is £401,677. Now, the new municipalities are based upon rateable value, and, as usual, we have a Conservative Government bringing in class legislation, because, while Chelsea has a population of only 97,676, which is less than Mile

End, yet because its rateable value is £787,430, which is more than that of Mile End, it is to be created into a municipality. I maintain that these new authorities should have been based, not upon the rateable value, but on the population of the area. Our population in Mile End is greater than that of Chelsea, but because our rateable value is less—and that is our misfortune, it is not our fault—we are not to be converted into a municipality. I have shown how poor some of these East End parishes are, and what heavy rates they are called upon to pay. Some of them, perhaps—Limehouse, St. George's, and Whitechapel—may be amalgamated into one municipality, but the fact remains that under this Bill you are going to centralise the poor to the poor, and that is the great object of the Bill. I have heard a remark outside that Mile End is to be tacked on to Bethnal Green, but that will not place us in any better position; and in any case, whatever parish you tack us on to in the East End, you join us to poverty instead of relieving our burdens. Now, all these parishes have boards of guardians, and while the members of some of these East End boards believe in the principle of outdoor relief—and when I was a guardian I did my best to administer the law in that direction—others are opposed to the principle. Therefore, in any East End municipality which you may create under this Bill to administer the laws relating to the lighting, maintenance of roads, and other local purposes, you may have three, four, or five boards of guardians varying in their methods of administering the Poor Law, and the result will be a confusion worse than that which prevails even at the present moment. I see no earthly reason why the Bill should not entrust to these new authorities the administration of the Poor Law. My own experience both as a guardian and as a vestryman is that a municipality could well undertake all these powers instead of having two separate boards to deal with them. Now, in the Report of Mr. Courtney's Commission in 1894 it was stated that Mile End had a larger population than Birkenhead, Derby, Halifax, Norwich, or Swansea, while it was more fully assessed than Burnley, Birkenhead, Halifax, or Plymouth, yet because we are poor, and have not got the rateable qualification, we are not to have the same privileges and powers as those smaller towns possess. As a matter of fact, there are only three cities in England—Liverpool, Manchester, and Birmingham—that are larger than any municipality we have in London at the present time. I commenced by saying that, personally, I deprecated politics being introduced into these discussions. At the same time, I maintain that the Party to which I belong are not responsible for Party politics having been introduced. On 16th November 1897 Lord Salisbury, at a public meeting in London, stated that as London was 10 or 12 times as great as any other municipality it ought to be regarded, not as one municipality, but as an aggregation of municipalities, and he appealed to the electors of London to return the Moderates to power. I think that the electors of London, in March 1898, gave Lord Salisbury an answer to that speech, and I would remind the House that at every election I have fought—and I have been returned at the top of the poll in each case—the principle of unification has been in the forefront of our programme, and not tenification. Decentralisation always means weakness, while centralisation always means strength. [Dissent.] Well, honourable Members may not agree with me, but they must admit that I have had some experience. I have not been engaged in the Labour movement for 25 years without realising that fact. I know that the present Bill proceeds upon the line of making impossible any further equalisation of rates, and this is being done in spite of the fact that, under the present system, the East End of London is getting every year poorer, and now you are going to make it impossible for the incidence of taxation to fall upon the shoulders of those best able to bear it; you are, in fact, placing it upon the shoulders of the people who are least able to bear it. In setting up a powerful municipality, as you are doing at Westminster, not on the basis of population, but upon that of rateable value, you are practically creating a second City of London. Not only does the Government Bill proceed upon wrong principles, but it embodies no real local reform. It purports to establish new bodies, but it retains an antiquated system; and instead of working on self-contained areas, it marks out for the boroughs of Westminster and Wandsworth areas that are universally acknowledged to be too large to ensure that minute personal attention which is the very essence of local administration. It erects the paraphernalia of municipalities with their mayors and aldermen, without adding the distinctive duties ordinarily attaching to municipalities, and I am afraid that instead of vivifying it will stifle local life and activity; it will undoubtedly add to the cost of administration. For these reasons I strongly support the Amendment moved by the right honourable Gentleman the Member for Leeds.

Upon the return of Mr. SPEAKER after the usual interval—

*MR. ALBAN GIBBS (London): It is not my intention to trespass for any length of time on the patience of the House, but as Member for the City of London, against which this Amendment, or at any rate the larger half of it, appears to be directed, I feel it to be my duty to say a few words, and I will ask the House to bear with me for a few moments while I do so. I have not myself the honour to be a member of the Corporation, but I think that, as representing the individuals who form the Corporation as their Member in Parliament, and many other constituents in the City who are not members in the Corporation, I may say they thoroughly approve of this Bill. The Corporation in London have long desired to see municipalities about them such as these are, and I was sorry to hear the right honourable Gentleman who moved this Amendment say that it would rob the County Council of its vitality and utility. I am sorry that the right honourable Gentleman has such a low opinion of the vitality of the County Council as to think it would be weakened by having municipalities gathered round it, even if they remove from it some of its less important work. As one who believes it is desirable that London should live an entity, but not be interfered with as honourable Members want it to be, I think I may say that my right honourable Friend the First Lord of the Treasury has made good his claim that this Bill would complete the edifice of London government in the metropolitan area. I know that honourable and right honourable Gentlemen

opposite have made use of expressions which show that they have a very different opinion, but we all know that on the transpontine stage, when one player gets the better of another, that one always has the opportunity of taking his place upon the stage and saying, "No matter; the time will come." I do not think the time will ever come when the County Council will be able to despoil the City of its ancient privileges, and what I hope is, that when the Debate is over and the Bill is passed, the County Council will recognise that fact. I desire to speak of the County Council with the utmost respect; they have some very important duties and some very high duties to perform, and I hope they will now settle down quietly to attend to those duties. If that is the case, I think this Bill will have done a very great and good work for London. Now, the only clause of this Bill that directly affects the City is clause 12. I think—I do not speak with that authority for the Corporation that my honourable colleague would do, but I believe that the City has always been ready to make the arrangements that has been put forward in this Bill; but I think that the County Council has preferred to keep their grievance. Very little money is involved, and I really think myself, if you have a nice grievance, it is foolish to give it up for so small an amount of money. I think I may say, with due deference, that this clause is perhaps rather loosely drawn—I am sure it is not the intention of the clause; but if it by chance does permit the County Council to come into the City and interfere with the county fund and the way it is now being administered by the City, it will have my strong opposition and it will be my duty to put down Amendments and to make that matter perfectly clear. I do not wish to go through a detailed defence of the City at this time; there has not been very many detailed accusations brought against it, but if when the Bill comes to another stage Amendments are put down which challenge the administration of the City in any way I shall be quite prepared to meet them then. One thing that has been said about the City is that there are too many aldermen. I have heard it said a great many times that the number of the common councillors and aldermen was excessive, and I was very much sur-

Mr. Steadman.

prised. I would like to point out that the 26 alderman discharge many great and important duties besides that of sitting in the debates of Common Council. They do all the magisterial work, and certainly they are a very hard-worked body of men. Moreover, I do not suppose that anybody making a new municipality would make it so large as this. In a municipality which has lived for more than a thousand years, and people have been trained to municipal work, there is not the slightest difficulty in finding good men to do that work, and when it is found that there are too many at one time, that the number of them has become inconvenient, the number can be lowered by the City itself. The right honourable Gentleman who moved the Amendment referred to a speech which was made by my right honourable Friend the Member for Bodmin, who I am sorry to see is not here at present. He referred to the great pleasure with which he expressed himself as favourable to the unification of the City. He certainly did say he was favourable, but I do not complain of the rest of his speech. He said the City administered its funds as if they were in trust to the whole of the metropolis, and he instanced several things which the City had done for the benefit of the metropolis, such as the building of the Tower Bridge, and he said they administered their funds and administered them well; but, Sir, to say that they administer their funds and administer them for the benefit of the whole of the metropolis is not sufficient reason for taking away the administration of those funds from them. I had hoped that the right honourable Gentleman the Member for Leeds would have been here to hear my speech, because there is one thing which he said caused me a great deal of surprise. He alluded to the Municipalities Corporation Commission of 1835, and he said it made no exception in the case of the City. I should like to read, if the House will bear with me, just a few lines of that Report, It is on page 36 of the Report, paragraph 78—

"The Common Council of the City of London presents a striking exception to the system of self-election for life, and it affords a remarkable instance of the absence of those evils which we refer to it. The Common Councilmen of the City are annually elected by a numerous constituency, yet changes seldom

happen among them. The important requisites in the experience of the functionary and the power of control in the electors are there effectually united, and produce that efficiency and confidence which are wanting in most other corporate towns. The history of the Common Council of London is that of a body which has watched vigilantly over the interests of its constituents, and for a long series of years has studied to improve the corporate institutions with great earnestness, unremitting caution, and scrupulous justice."

Well, Sir, that is as much as to say that the City is a reformed corporation; therefore I do not think any honourable Members opposite are entitled to say as they invariably say, whenever they do want to say anything at all against the City of London, that it is unreformed. As my honourable Friend the Member for Chelsea said, ever since that date the City of London has gone on reforming itself, and whenever it has had to come to Parliament for reforms, those reforms have been resisted to the best of their ability by honourable Members opposite. The right honourable Gentleman did not make any very specific charges against the City. He did not put forward anything that seems to require any particular answer. He said the City was a reproach and an anomaly. He meant, I suppose, that they were a reproach to other bodies who did not do so well as they. Then, as for their being an anomaly, I do not think that a borough situated in a county can be considered an anomaly. He said they were dead to all the higher influences, over all the City. I suppose he means by that that they did all the business that they had to do, and having administered their own business did not concern themselves officially with the business of other people. I do not suppose that the right honourable Gentleman is ignorant of the amount of charity that is done by the City or individual members of the City; I do not think that he meant to disparage that in any way, so I will leave that question alone. The honourable Member for Stepney also did not make any specific charges against the City, though I cannot say he seemed to have any friendly feelings towards it. The one thing he did say, I have heard said very often, both in the City and the more central parishes of London, and that is that we drove the poor out of the City. It is natural that the poor should go outwards from the centre where they can get cheaper houses and purer air, and the facilities for getting into the City have so increased of late years that it is true that the poor have gone out to places where the value of land and houses is much cheaper than in the City, or at Kensington, or places of that description. But the City poor rate is lower, because each penny in the pound produces so much more. Now, I think that is all the attack that has been brought against the City. I do not wish to follow the right honourable Gentleman through all his attacks upon the Bill, because they were so ably answered by my honourable Friend the Member for Chelsea. I merely say now that I think this Bill merits the hearty support of all people who care for the good government of London, and I do think it will have the hearty support of the Metropolitan- Members on this side of the House, and I thank the Government very much for having introduced it.

Mr. HOLLAND (Tower Hamlets, Bow): The one thing I think which strikes one in this Debate is the difference between the tone of the honourable Members opposite to-night and that of their speeches which they made upon the First Reading of the Bill. The Debate has been raised from a mere philanthropic opposition to the dignity of a Party attack. It is true that this Bill detracts nothing from the powers of the County Council except those powers which were agreed upon at the conference at the County Hall, and the powers with regard to the Building Act. I entirely agree that that is a matter to be discussed in Committee, and I certainly do think that that provision with regard to the Building Act and the power it is proposed to transfer to the local municipalities is unfortunate. So far as the other powers are concerned it detracts nothing from the powers of the County Council except the powers that were, as I have said before, agreed to at the conference at the County Hall. But honourable Members opposite had their prophecies to maintain. They prophesied that evil consequences would come of this Bill, and indeed after their victory at the last County Council election they actually said that no Bill

Mr. Alban Gibbs.

would be introduced at all, but that if a Bill was introduced it would be a retrograde Measure and an attempt to wreck the County Council, so that they are obliged to attempt to justify their prophecy. They fixed chiefly on the provisions of this Bill in regard to Westminster, and they say that this creation of a municipality of Westminster with a rateable value larger, I believe, than any other rateable value in this kingdom, including Liverpool, is a menace to the County Council and an insidious attempt to weaken its prestige and influence, and it is a symptom of the disease of meglomania against which the Prime Minister uttered a well-considered warning in the remarks he made in his speech at the Albert Hall. I confess that I never hoped that this Bill would err from any excess of ambition, and if the present Government have any failing at all—and I am sure that they can be conscious of none—it is not a tendency to meglomania. I think it is a great satisfaction that the Government in this case have resisted any idea to make this Measure an optional Measure, but have resolved that the system established by this Measure shall run throughout London, so that the process of transition from one system to another will be as brief as possible. I say with regard to the question of Westminster that I hope the Government will not endeavour to stay the hostility of any honourable Members opposite by making any concession on any of the material points of this Bill, because that hostility is certain to be accentuated in the exact proportion in which the Bill is thought to require it. The true principle of this Bill is approved by the Party on this side of the House, and I hope that the Government will not minimise the provisions of this Bill so as to escape any local dissatisfaction which may be expressed with regard to it; for this dissatisfaction which is certain to be given expression to is merely temporary, and will all disappear when this Bill, which is a good one, has been in operation for some time. I cannot help thinking it is from some desire to escape from this dissatisfaction to a certain extent that we must attribute the basis of the areas which are scheduled in this Bill.

But whatever criticism may be passed on this side of the House, I think we are unanimous in the view that this Measure is a great advance in the simplification and improvement of London Government, and I think it would have been more valuable if the provisions with regard to Westminster which are so objectionable to honourable Members opposite had struck the keynote of the whole matter. I take it that the restoration of the old borough of Westminster, which is homogeneous and self-contained, and an integral unit for all municipal purposes—an area large enough and important enough to give some dignity and responsibility to the members who serve on the council, to render the position of the mayor a position of some dignity, importance, and standing, and some historical association. The right honourable Gentleman the Member for Leeds suggests that these historical associations were somewhat fabulous, but after all the fables of history are not the least authoritative part of it—I say an area of this character will tend to develop and encourage a spirit of civic patriotism within the boundaries of that area, and tend also to encourage men of leisure and capacity to take part in the municipal work of the borough. I take it that one of the objects of the Bill is to improve the *personnel* of the local governing body. Well, that is an excellent provision in that direction. A provision which would be accepted on both sides of this House is the provision which cuts down the number of members who serve on the local boards. I hope that provision will not be altered by the Government from the minimum of 72, because of any deputation which may wait upon it and which expresses the sad dying notes of dispossessed vestrymen. For instance, the district which I represent at the present moment is governed by a district board in two schedules, by two vestries, one with 102 members and one with 80 or 82. Now, I must say that in this division the operation of this Act with regard to cutting down the number will not, in itself, be sufficient; it may be sufficient in districts which are better to do, but in the poor districts of London it is only by merging several into one administrative area, perhaps of the size of Westminster, that you will be able to obtain actual and real authority. There will be no difficulty, of course, in the district of Westminster, which is a wide and wealthy area, in obtaining 72 councillors of capacity and leisure to attend to the municipal business; but it is more difficult to man the local Board in districts in poor industrial neighbourhoods, and I myself hope that the Government will consider the advisability and possibility of applying the principle that Westminster has accepted, that the administrative area should be the old boundaries of the ancient borough, to the Tower Hamlets. In this case the Government propose to create 32 municipalities under the Bill. Will that very much increase the dignity of the councillors?—he is going to have 3,000 councillors for London, as many councillors as there are 'bus drivers. He is going to have 30 mayors in London, and the dignity of the position must be, to an extent, determined by the duties and responsibilities which devolve upon them, and the duties which devolve on any of the municipal councils must be determined ultimately by the area of population which those councils control. The powers which are transferred, therefore, to the largest and most important municipality in London will be determined in the end by the powers they consent to transfer to the smallest and poorest municipality of London. It will, therefore, be agreed that there is a want of uniformity and similarity in the powers, whether transferred now or later to these bodies, which will be detrimental to the good government of London. I venture to suggest to the Government that some of the areas proposed by this Bill are altogether too small, and may be detrimental to the whole object of this Measure, and will mar and handicap its development, and will prevent the chance of further powers being extended to them in the future. Generally speaking, I think the proposal should be, in these cases, to select as large an area as can be conveniently governed from one centre. Of course, that does not represent the views of the honourable Members opposite; but Members on that side of the House are hostile to the whole principle of the Bill. It is conceded on both sides that there must be a central council, but the honourable Members opposite wish to approximate as nearly as possible to the principal of a central Government for London, and they insist upon the paramount superiority of the County Council. The view of this side is municipal diversity in London, and if that view is to prevail it is better that it should be carried out in an effective manner, and should not be handicapped by half-hearted opinion. It must also be considered that, as every council exercises similar functions and similar powers, there should be as much uniformity as possible in rateable value, population and acreage, without disturbing excessively the local feeling. But the want of uniformity in this Bill is almost astonishing. We find Hampstead with a population of 75,000, Lambeth with a population of 295,000, Islington with a population of 336,000, and then comes Chelsea, which, even with its outer district, Kensal Town, only has a population of 100,000, and without Kensal Town it only has a population of 70,000; yet it is proposed that this district of Kensal Town shall be detached from Chelsea for the purposes of municipal government, but shall be one with Chelsea for the purposes of electing representatives to the County Council. Surely this is a very undesirable arrangement; the whole spirit of municipal government, the whole chance of securing better municipal treatment is imperilled if every area selected is not an integral area for all government purposes. So far as possible, for its Parliamentary and electoral and all other purposes, it should be an integral unit. One of the great merits of this Bill is that it gets rid of the over-lapping of districts to a great extent, but its chief defect is, that it does not get rid of the overlapping altogether. We have, as I have said, the district of Chelsea, where the people of Chelsea and Kensal Town will vote for the same Parliamentary representatives, and for different municipal representatives; and if, as I suppose, part of Kensal Town is taken into Chelsea and part is absorbed by Bayswater, we shall have part of these districts voting as an integral unit for municipal purposes, while for Parliamentary and County Council purposes they will be voting as another

Mr. Holland.

borough. I think the condition should be insisted on that each area should be an integral area, not only for municipal purposes, but for County Council, poor law, and all electoral purposes as well. We have another instance in Hammersmith and Fulham; they are now one for poor-law and rating purposes, but they will be two for municipal purposes. I think the Government would have done better with this question of municipalities if they had reverted to the old Parliamentary boroughs; and what I personally desire to know is, whether it would not be expedient in may cases to follow this precedent of the Municipal Government Act. The provisions of the Municipal Government Act show that areas of the population and size of the municipal boroughs of London can be governed with efficiency and success, and it would be difficult to follow a better precedent than that. Now, in London, parishes have seen such changes that their boundaries have been altered beyond recognition, but the old Parliamentary boroughs offer the most ancient and historical areas that can be selected. Of course, it is impossible to suggest that the boundaries of these historical areas can be followed rigidly in every instance, but there are many districts which are properly so scheduled in this Bill, and which are already forward enough to have municipal councils of their own. It is a matter for consideration whether the areas of these Parliamentary boroughs cannot be followed in more than a single instance, which is the case in this Bill. The Committee of 1884, which was referred to by the right honourable Gentleman the Member for Leeds, laid stress upon the two first conditions for good municipal local government—minute local knowledge and common interest; and, so to carry out these two conditions, suggested that municipalities should be created in certain Parliamentary boroughs of London existing now. The right honourable Gentleman the Member for Leeds, in giving us a brief history of this subject, no doubt for the sake of brevity—after he had suggested that this Committee was influenced by the City, and that its recommendations were influenced by a desire to strengthen that ancient Corporation—omitted to mention the all-important fact that in 1868 one of the most distinguished Members whom London has ever had, Mr. John Stuart Mill, himself strongly recommended the establishment of separate municipalities in the ten municipal boroughs of London. That also is the opinion of another eminent Radical, Mr. Samuel Morley; and, as a matter of fact, at that time that was universally the opinion of honourable Gentlemen opposite, and the Bill which was introduced for the establishment of these ten municipalities in the ten Parliamentary boroughs of London, by Mr. Mill and by Mr. Buxton, and other Members, received the support of the majority in this House, and it was only Lord Elcho, the present Lord Wemyss, who was the advocate of a single municipality for London. Is there any reason why the principle applied to Westminster should not also be applied to the Tower Hamlets? Surely this arrangement in reference to the Tower Hamlets is a most unfortunate one, for one part of the Tower Hamlets has been left to the tender mercies of the Commission which is going to be appointed. Then they have cut out from the Tower Hamlets, to create separate municipalities, the two poorest parts of the district in the whole of the Tower Hamlets, which have the -highest rate and the smallest rateable value in proportion to the population—namely, Bromley and Poplar. Now, what chance of prosperity is there for a municipality of this character? It is perfectly true what the honourable Member for Stepney said, that the separation of the poorer from the richer districts of London is one which may be inevitable, but at any rate it is one of the least desirable outcomes of the development of this great city. And, surely, it is the opposite of true statesmanship to do anything which is likely to increase, instead of diminish, this tendency; and it should be the object of statesmanship to try and remedy this. But what does this Bill do in regard to the Tower Hamlets? The average rate in London is about 5s. 9d. in the pound. Now, the average in the Tower Hamlets is 6s. 8d., and this Bill proposes to take the two poorest districts of the Tower Hamlets with a rate of 8s. in the pound, and, because of their poverty, make them into one municipality, while this district is wholly unsuitable for the purposes of a separate

municipal area. It is a long strip of land, with houses, four miles long and only one mile in width at its broadest part, and the inhabitants of Bow and North Bromley abut on the main thoroughfare of the Tower Hamlets, and are as intimately and closely connected with Stepney and Mile End as they are with Poplar, and it takes them as much time to get to the City as to Poplar Town Hall. I do not suggest that the areas should be altered merely because they meet with disfavour in one or another district, but what I do suggest is, that to create a small municipality of this kind in one of the poorest districts of London must be detrimental to the future operation of this Bill, for it must diminish the powers, or the measure of the powers, which can be given in the future to the largest and most important municipality of London, which is the measure of the powers which you can give in this municipality of Poplar. And we must remember that to create such a limited area in a poor district such as that does not form a proper recruiting ground from which to obtain a strong and authoritative council. And, besides this, in regard to the powers, there are many powers, at any rate, which we on this side of the House believe might be very properly transferred in the future to these municipal councils. But, while it may be said that municipalities controlling a large corporation of an important character may, be safely and economically able to exercise these powers, they cannot with safety nor with economy be transferred to a small municipality in a small area any more than they can be transferred to the existing vestries or district boards, and what this Bill does in regard to Poplar is, that it takes the present district board, calls it a council, and calls its chairman a mayor. It is quite clear that one of the objects of this Bill should be to give a better chance of practising economy in London Government by creating municipalities in areas large enough to allow of economy by the combination of any powers that may be transferred to them under this Bill. Under any powers which may be transferred, they will require officers and inspectors to carry them out. Now, either a small municipality of this kind will have to be content with officers of an inferior character and too small a staff, or they will have to incur an expenditure for officials and inspectors altogether out of proportion to their means or to their population. The Commission which the right honourable Gentleman the Member for Bodmin presided over laid special stress upon the advisability of dissociating local influence from the officers entrusted with the enforcement of penal statutes. Now, the areas settled by this Bill should be wide enough to satisfy that requirement, and they should be wide enough and large enough to avoid any chance of undesirable local influences or jobbery, or of what has been termed "ward politics," or the accentuation of small local interests. While I believe and I hope that the District Board of Poplar is above suspicion in these matters, I think anyone who reads the local papers and the reports of the proceedings of vestries and district boards will get a very unfavourable impression on this subject, and it is clear that these local influences and this accentuation of small interests can only bé avoided by forming bodies representing large areas where these local influences and interests cannot obtain. I have no desire to detain the House further, or to enter into any points which can be properly discussed in Committee. There are such points as the burden of finance, and I think in this matter it is a fair claim that any expenditure thrown upon the local bodies in reference to the transfer of powers, that costs should be revised at fixed periods, for which there is no provision at present made in the Bill, and I agree with honourable Members opposite—and I do not know whether any honourable Member on this side has expressed the same opinion—that one of the reasons which deter people in the metropolis from taking active interest in the government of the various parts of London is the fact that they are bothered by too many elections, and instead of one-third of the Members retiring every year the whole body should retire every three years. I confess that I think it is desirable that some better method of auditing should be adopted than that which is contained in this Bill, but I do not want to enter now into any detailed criticism. Although the dominant note of my remarks may be criticism, yet I do not criticise because I am in any way hostile to the principle of the Bill, but because

Mr. Holland.

I wish to see this Measure have the fullest possible operation. I hope that the development of this Bill will provide that any municipal council created in any part of London will not have too small an area or too small a population. Finally, I congratulate the Government upon their courage for having taken up this question, which has engaged the attention of endless Commissions and Committees, and which hitherto successive Governments have been somewhat afraid to deal with. I think, therefore, that it is a matter of general satisfaction in London that the Measure has at last been taken in hand by the First Lord of the Treasury himself.

*MR. HALDANE (Haddington): The House has listened with interest to the speech of the honourable Member who has just sat down, which was nothing if not moderate. It breathed a spirit of democratic conservatism, and its tone was similar to the sentiments which have come from this side of the House. But the speech of the honourable Member who represents the City, on the other hand, had, if he will allow me to say so, a fine old flavour of crusted Toryism which does credit to his constituents. The honourable Member began his speech by expressing the gratitude of the electors of the City for this Bill. The City, he said, had desired these municipalities; and then he went on to say that when the Bill was passed the County Council would certainly see that they never could any more try to despoil the City of its ancient privileges. This is the inference which the honourable Member has drawn from the provisions of this Bill. To my mind the chief objection to this Bill, as regards that part of it which concerns the City, is not what it does not do—not that it leaves the City, in a sense, intact—but that it makes the work of the reformer almost an impossibility in the future. Therefore, from that point of view, Her Majesty's Ministers may be congratulated, from the point of view of the City, on the creation of these new municipalities, for they will surround the City with a sort of Prætorian guard which cannot easily be broken through by those who wish hereafter to tread the pathway of reform. And when Her Majesty's Ministers next go to the Mansion House —although I am not in the confidence of the City—I think I can promise them

a right Royal welcome from the City, not as far as the affairs of the Empire are concerned—nor as reformers of the great municipality of London—but as men who have rescued the City from all danger of attack upon its ancient privileges as an old and unreformed Corporation. The honourable Member for Bow and Bromley, however, took a different line. He represents a poor and needy part of London, and, if he will allow me to say so, I think he has done very good work in this House. But I noticed that the speech of the honourable Member was conspicuous by its silence upon those very topics which seem to trouble the honourable Member who preceded him in the Debate. There was not one word about privileges there, but, on the contrary, the whole speech of the honourable Member for Bow and Bromley was rather a criticism of the Government for leaving such small areas as the City, with its 600 or 700 acres, instead of creating large areas which would do justice to what he conceived to be the democratic tendencies of this Bill. The honourable Member began his speech by saying that the Bill detracted nothing from the power of the County Council except in such matters as had been agreed upon at conferences, and he went on to say that there was one exception—a very notable exception—that of the Building Acts, of which a great deal will be heard in this Debate. I cannot think that the honourable Member has paid much attention to the deliberations of the County Council, because, as the result of the Conference of 1896, the County Council emphatically protested against the transfer, either exclusively or concurrently, of many of the powers which this Bill proposes to transfer, more particularly the power which municipal corporations now possess, the important power of making by-laws. That power will be exercised for the future concurrently by these new municipalities against the recommendation of the London County Council. Take, again, the power of enforcing the Shops Hours Act, which is an Act in which the honourable Member takes a great interest. That is transferred to these municipal bodies against the wishes of the London County Council. Then, again, there is the regulating and the keeping up to the standard of

common lodging-houses throughout the metropolis, which has hitherto been exercised with great success by the County Council, and which power will be exercised in the different parts of the metropolis by these different boroughs. Passing from these two speeches to the general current of the Debate, the questions which were put by my right honourable Friend who moved this Amendment appeared to have been fairly and clearly answered. My right honourable Friend began by asking by what mandate has this Bill been brought in, and for what motive; and he was followed in the Debate by the honourable Member for Chelsea, who made a speech which was marked not only by ability, but by candour. The honourable Member went on to say that it was perfectly true that at the last election for the London County Council there were issues raised which were germane to the issues raised by this Bill. He said quite truly that the question of the City was, on that occasion, not so prominent as it had been on former occasions. But he admitted that the question of the integrity of the powers of the London County Council and the question of the creation of the new municipalities were clearly before the electors. It was impossible for the honourable Member to have said otherwise in face of the memorable speech made by Lord Salisbury in the Albert Hall in November 1897, and the speech of the First Lord of the Treasury at Stepney, and the speech of the right honourable Gentleman the Member for West Birmingham at Camberwell, for all these speeches dealt with these issues. Of course, they dealt with the subject in different tones. The Prime Minister, who is nothing if not candid, told us that the County Council were affected with a megalomania which they ought to try to check; and then he went on to say that he was bound to admit that the process of checking might involve some kind of suicidal action on the part of the London County Council. The First Lord of the Treasury made a much more moderate speech, and I read that he clearly foreshadowed and gave an outline of the provisions of the Measure now brought forward. But the right honourable Gentleman the Member for West Birmingham took a different tone. He knew more about municipalities and the importance of their unity than did his colleagues, and he took refuge in a different sort of appeal to the electors to return the Moderate candidates at the coming election. He based his case for claiming votes for the Moderates not on the provision of the Bill which he foreshadowed, but rather on the fact that if London supported Her Majesty's Government by returning the Moderates it would be taken by the Government as a testimony of the desire of London to see that those in whose hands the integrity of the Empire was safe should be returned. Then came the elections, and instead of Moderates and Progressives being evenly balanced, there followed a large majority given to the Progressives on the County Council, and the emphatic verdict of the electors was against this system. Then the honourable Member for Chelsea went on to say that after all you make a great deal too much of the changes which this Bill makes, and he says, " Did you not propose something of the kind yourselves?" And he quoted the speech of the Member for East Fife in 1898, in which my right honourable Friend proposed the creation of local bodies in London. But we have always been in favour of creating local bodies, because we have always been in favour of carrying out the recommendations of the Courtney Commission appointed by the late Government, and which resulted in the Report which was framed by the right honourable Gentleman the Member for Bodmin. But the Report of that Commission and the speech of my right honourable Friend the Member for East Fife went upon very different lines from those adopted in this Bill. What is that unity in London which we desire to preserve, and which honourable Members on the other side desire to destroy? (Ministerial cries of " No, no!")' Well, I am going to make that point good, and I am coming to close quarters in a moment. What is the difference between the proposition in this Bill and the propositions advocated in the Courtney Report and the policy put forward from this side of the House? The difference is this: That while you propose to take the administrative county of London and chop it into blocks, and make each block independent, as far as possible, of the other, and are weakening instead of strengthening the powers of the central

Mr. Haldane.

control and co-ordination which exist in an imperfect form under the present system, which we propose to develop, we on the other side recognise what London is in fact, an organic whole which can be no more broken up than any other great city in the world, and which is as much deserving of being treated as one undivided area as either Paris, Vienna, or St. Petersburg. It has its distinct characteristics just as much as Liverpool, Birmingham, and Glasgow, which cannot be broken and parcelled out in the way you suggest without danger to the organic welfare of London. What will be the position of the residents in the different parts of London if this Bill is passed? Why there will be no longer the opportunity for a London resident to say, " I am a citizen of the great municipality of London." He will be a citizen of Fulham, of Hammersmith, of Battersea, or wherever else he may be, and he will be a citizen of a municipality which will have wholly different laws, different traditions, and different local customs and municipal spirit to that which prevails in other parts of the metropolis. When you work out what the propositions of this Bill really are you will see that it does nothing to enable or to encourage the different districts to act together. It proposes as its leading principle the division of the metropolis into so-called boroughs, which will diminish the central control, and that is the general proposition of the Bill. It does nothing to enable the richer parts to come to the assistance of the poorer districts, but it rather tends to separate them, and magnifying the differences and independence of the local bodies, brings in as the controlling influence a Government Department, the Local Government Board, instead of the County Council, which is the unifying influence at the present time. I ask the House not to separate London in this unjust fashion. What is the position of the tradesman in the West End? He serves the necessities of the community by keeping a shop where he sells clothes or other goods, but where do the people who really make those clothes live? It is not only one or two people who keep that shop in . the West End, but the workmen who live in the East End, and who are absolutely essential to the organic life of the metropolis. That tradesman who discharges these functions in the West End will probably go and live in other parts of London because it is cheaper, although he draws his sustenance from the richer parts of the metropolis which he serves by doing this work. The whole tendency of your modern legislation has been in the direction of recognising the different parts of London for many purposes as an integral whole. This Bill contains a clause which declares that the principle of the Equalisation of Rates Act will not be injured, and when you follow out the meaning of that expression "equalisation of rates," what does it mean? It means that the richer parts of London should contribute to the necessities of the poorer parts; that is to say, that the burden should be distributed according to the necessities of the population. Now, you are introducing a new system, the whole tendency of which is not to combine, not to keep as a whole, but to sever into parts, and to make it more difficult than ever to give to London the character of unity which will enable the poorer parts, not to feel that they have interests diverse from the richer parts, but to feel that they are bound up in one common welfare. Well, Sir, the Bill proposes to do this because of the way in which it treats the area upon which London is situated. In order to realise how really extraordinary the character of this Bill is, one has to glance at the circumstances under which London is at present constituted. In 1835, one of the first acts of the Reformed Parliament was to pass the great Municipal Corporations Bill. From that Act the City of London was excluded; the metropolis, in fact, was not touched by it. The scheme of that Act was to deal with municipal corporations throughout the rest of the country. It took every district that was an urban district, an aggregate of houses, and it reformed the old-fashioned unreformed municipal corporations. These corporations had the most varying constitutions. Some were constituted by charter, some apparently without charter, or the charters were in many cases lost; they were subject to local laws and customs, and their franchises and arrangements were most diverse. The Act of 1835 did not touch their powers. It dealt with their constitutions and franchises, and

extended their areas, so that they could take in houses round about where they were situated, and that Act laid the foundations of the modern municipal corporations. The provisions of that Act were altered, improved, and consolidated in the Municipal Corporations Act of 1882. The whole powers of the municipal corporations outside London were conferred by Acts like the Public Health Act, which added the powers which were so necessary for the development of the modern municipality, in the proper sense of the word. London was outside all this, and until 1855 nothing was done which in the least affected the character of London. In 1854 the Commission sat which has been alluded to in the course of these Debates—a Commission of a not very revolutionary character, which was presided over by Mr. Harry Labouchere, a distinguished Statesman, but by no means a man of such advanced principles as the honourable Member for North-ampton. There were serving upon it Mr. Cornwall Lewis, afterwards Sir George Cornwall Lewis, and the third Commissioner was a distinguished judge, Mr. Justice Patterson. That Commission, though a very Conservative Commission, and though it reported in a very retrograde sense compared with the Commission which reported in 1837 specially upon London, still insisted that something extensive must be done, and what it did was to make recommendations, which did not receive effect, but which were followed next year by the Act of 1855, which embodied the policy of the Government of that day. Now, it is most instructive to read that Report, and to read the speech of Sir Benjamin Hall, who introduced the Bill of 1855. He pointed out what the government of London was. The City was unreformed and unextended in its area. Outside that, nothing existed except a series of confused local areas, created by a profusion of special Statutes, and ruled over by Commissioners. Between Charing Cross and Temple Bar, along the Strand, there were no fewer than seven bodies of Commissioners controlling the highway. Regent Street was under the control of two separate sets of Commissioners. One watered one side of the street, and the other watered the other side. Well, one did it in the morning, and the other in the evening, and eventually they quarrelled, and tho result of the quarrel was that Regent Street was not watered properly at all. Sir Benjamin Hall recommended that a central board should be created, which should impart to London the character which he claimed for it—that of being a whole. He did not touch the reform of the City, for the sons of Zeruiah, even in those days, were too strong for him, but for the rest of London he recommended the creation of a central board, which should control and regulate the proceedings of the various district boards. That central board was not directly elected—that was its misfortune, and that, I believe, led to the ultimate failure of the Metropolitan Board of Works. I am not here to' disturb what I fear must be called a dishonoured grave.

SEVERAL HONOURABLE MEMBERS: No, no!

*MR. HALDANE: I am here to go back upon the history of the Metropolitan Board of Works. Honourable Members opposite seem to have forgotten what it was that brought that piece of machinery for the organisation of the metropolis to an end. They have forgotten the attacks made upon it—the just attacks — by Lord Randolph Churchill in this House, which led to the appointment of the Herschell Commission, and the recommendation of the absolute necessity of the Government taking up the problem of London government as a whole. What followed? What followed was, that the Government of the day recognised that they must proceed to the solution of this problem; and they proceeded to its solution upon a basis which certainly was not satisfactory. Instead of following out what had been the· recommendation of the previous Commission, and the policy of previous Governments, instead of taking the City and reforming it on the lines of the Municipal Corporations Act, and extending its areas so as to embrace the whole of London, and creating local bodies—because right through we have been in favour of the creation of these local bodies, to whom local powers should be delegated—in its area, and reforming its constitution so as to make it really representative of London, the Government of 1888 proceeded to treat London as though it was a rural, instead of being, as it certainly is, an urban, district, and did so by taking a piece of

Mr. Haldane.

Surrey, a piece of Middlesex, and a piece of Kent, and so they created the modern county of London. That was a rural county. It was a rural county with peculiar features, but still it was constituted on the model of the county councils, and partook strictly of the nature of a county council. But although the Government of that day had not the time—or it may be that they thought the task too great for them— to constitute the district councils which were necessary to carry out what they intended, they announced most distinctly in the course of the Debate that such was their intention. They recognised what we say ought to be the true policy of this Bill, what we have insisted upon, and what we say was your policy until you departed from it upon this occasion—that London is a whole, and cannot be broken up into separate organisations, and the proper way is to treat it as a whole, with a central government of the same pattern and nature as the various local bodies into which you separate it for local purposes. If the Government had followed out the principle which underlay their legislation, then they would have done one of two things. They would have adhered to one notion consistently; they would have made London either what it was constituted by the Act of 1888, either a rural district with a county council—of a peculiar nature, no doubt, but still having all the powers of a county council, and with district councils —or they would have made it a great municipality with sub-municipalities, with local bodies to whom would be delegated those municipal powers which were properly exercised locally, and in that way they would have proceeded on the footing of consistency. They have done neither the one nor the other. They keep the principle of the county councils, they keep the rural principle, and at the same time they go and dot down on the administrative county so constituted a number of municipalities of a town pattern, belonging more nearly to an urban character, which will exhaust and sub-divide its areas. They seem to desire to ride two horses, and two horses which go in different directions, and apparently they are of opinion that in the Act of 1888 they had been upon the wrong horse, upon this as upon other occasions.

An honourable Member: A lively steed!

*Mr. HALDANE: Well, I presume that this Bill is intended to be final. We know that its motive is finality as regards the City. The City is to be delivered from the reformer, and the reformer is to have his right arm cut off so far as that is concerned. I presume, also, that finality is intended as regards these municipalities. I presume that the Government have not in view any future propositions for the further unification of London, of the creation of any other body from which they are going to carve out districts of administration. If that is so, I think their Bill has some disastrous consequences. Just let us look at it from one or two points of view; and I will try not to repeat what has been said by previous speakers in this Debate. The first point on which I am struck with the difficulties to which this Bill will give rise is on the question of finance. Now, London occupies, to my mind, not only a most remarkable but a most favourable position in respect to borrowing powers, and partly as the result of an accident. Honourable Members know that the County Council of London cannot borrow sixpence except by a Bill which comes before this House after being carefully revised and settled by the Treasury. The result has been that the Treasury has established a system of most complete and minute supervision over the finances of London, very much to the advantage of London. The County Council has as members of its body some of the most distinguished ex-representatives of the Treasury, and it has also the advantage of the control of the present officials of the Treasury. They have been able to give such good advice and to guide the County Council on such good principles that already, by common consent, the County Council is in the most favourable position as to its borrowing powers. The County Council borrows money at present at about 2 per cent. on its short loans, and on its longer loans at 2½ per cent. In other words, the finances of London are almost on as advantageous a footing as the finances of the Government itself. That is a matter which is not only one for sentimental congratulation, but is of the utmost im-

portance to the ratepayers whom we have to consider, because, obviously, if the money which is necessary for improvements can be borrowed at 2½ per cent., and on short loans at 2 per cent., that diminishes the charge upon that already overburdened person who has to contribute to the rates of London. But what does this Bill propose? By, I think, clause 4, the power of consenting to borrowing by the new municipalities, by the vestries as it would be at present, is transferred from the London County Council to the Local Government Board. I ask, Mr. Speaker, why? So far as I know, there is no case in which the London County Council has unreasonably withheld its consent from borrowing by a vestry. There have been one or two small cases where the County Council has interfered to the great advantage of the vestries, but it has never interfered arbitrarily when they have wished to borrow money for public purposes. The result of that working together was this, that instead of the vestries raising their loans themselves, they went to the London County Council and got the advantage of that most solid credit and cheap rate of interest of which I have spoken. Now, what do the Government propose? We are going to have Fulham stock, and Hammersmith stock, and, I suppose, Poplar stock. My honourable Friend who sits below me represents a most admirable constituency, but one not famous for its wealth. I believe that its rates are higher than in any other part of the metropolis, and I should not expect that Poplar was able to borrow money at 2½ per cent. If this is really the new financial arrangement, there are sure to be most disastrous consequences. At all events, in point of finance, what advantage is it to have those matters transferred to the Local Government Board? In the case of municipalities, in the case of various other bodies where the consent of the Local Government Board is necessary to borrowing, the Local Government Board impose terms as to repayment of loans for improvements which are not permanent, which terms are of a very stringent character. Take the Electric Lighting Acts. Under these Acts local authorities have in many cases borrowed, and have borrowed largely in many parts of England, for the purpose of laying down electric lighting plant. Well, the Local Government Board impose as the term in which loans must be repaid either 25 years or 30 years—I forget which. But the London County Council, knowing the people with whom they were dealing, and knowing the necessity for these things, and recognising their control over the finance, have extended the period of these loans to 42 years, and the result is that the municipal bodies when they come under this Bill and desire money for the purpose of developing electric light enterprise, will find that they are borrowing on much more onerous terms, by reason of the shortness of the period in which their loans must be repaid. I have spoken of finance. Now I turn to another topic, and it seems to me to be a very important thing. There is no more important code of legislation in London than the code which is known as the Consolidated Building Act. That is a Private Act of 1894. It was passed after most careful investigation by two Committees, one of this House, and the other of the House of Lords. The Committee of this House, I think, sat for many weeks before they finished their deliberations ; and the result of the Act considered by these two Committees was to make a most careful distribution of powers under the Building Acts between the central and local authorities. It specified what powers the local authority should exercise, and what the County Council should keep in their own hands. Now, this Bill proposes to unrip all that was done then, and to put the distribution of powers under this Act at the mercy of the Privy Council, indicating no principle, no scheme, according to which the London County Council is to proceed, but simply leaving it to the mercy of the administrative body acting upon what principle they choose to lay down. There, again, you have a blow at what I call the real, not merely the sentimental, unity of London. Take another case. I have spoken of equalisation. There is a most glaring case of imperfect safeguard in clause 8. Clause 8 provides that powers may be transferred from the County Council to the local authorities, in the first instance by agreement between the County Council and the particular local authority, followed by a Provisional Order. After

Mr. Haldane.

that is done—the Provisional Order to which I have referred is in clause 5— the Local Government Board may, if they think fit, on the application of any borough council, make an order for transfer. Clause 8 says—

" Where any power or duty is transferred from the London County Council to a borough council by or under this Act, the borough council shall defray as part of their ordinary expenses the expenses of and incidental to the power or duty, and the County Council shall contribute to the borough council in respect of those expenses, such amount, if any (whether capital or annual) as may—

" *(a)* If the transfer is made by this Act, be agreed on between the councils within *six* months after the transfer, or, in default of agreement, be finally determined by the Local Government Board."

What does that mean? Does it mean that the county is to contribute in proportion to the work done? Does it mean that you are to have there the principle of equalisation, that the County Council is not to be bound to have regard to how much money is raised by the locality itself, in a case where they consider that the locality would be overburdened by having to contribute in proportion to its rateable value as distinct from the necessities of its population? Does it mean that the Local Government Board are to act on such a principle as that? If so, all would be well ; but the clause steadily leaves that at large, and you may have the contribution to be made on no fixed principle at all, but upon a purely arbitrary footing, to have no regard whatever to the principle which underlies the equalisation of rates, and leaves the poorer localities at the disadvantage from which they suffer from being poorer localities, without any contribution at the expense of those which are richer. Take another objection to this clause. Look at the enormous irregularity of it. Power is transferred to one local authority for certain purposes in case they ask for it. Perhaps none of the others intervene. The result is that you will have these powers exercised in some places by the County Council, in others by the local authority, and you will have absence of uniformity everywhere. Then, again, take the question of audit. Now, this Bill does not provide for the audit of the accounts of the new borough councils by any Government auditor. In other words, it departs altogether from the principle which the Government applied when they passed the Act of 1888 to the councils which their legislation then constituted. I `ask, why? The London County Council is subject to the strictest audit. Why should not these new borough councils be subject to that audit? I think here again I can throw a little light upon that. These municipalities constitute what I have ventured to describe as a bodyguard to the City. As far as possible, they are likened to the City. If the audit were applied to them, it would be difficult not to apply it to the City. Now, the City is not audited, and would strenuously object to that; and, therefore, I presume the Government have not thought right to subject these new bodies to the audit to which they would naturally be subject but for the fact that the City would inevitably, much against its wishes, have to submit to it. These are small points taken singly, but cumulatively they amount to much. There are many things not only committed in, but omitted from, this Bill. I think that some attempt might have been made to simplify the finances of London in point of rating. True, there is a clause which talks as though there was going to be a single rate, but it only says that one paper is to be issued for sending in a number of different demands. I should have thought it possible to simplify the rating of London, which is already grotesque and complicated enough. London raises some £12,000,000 yearly for its local necessities—School Board Rate, Metropolitan Asylums Rate, and the different rates which are raised by other bodies. Of this the County Council raises about £2,000,000, of which £1,000,000 goes for borrowing purposes, and the other for the expenses of general administration. I should have thought it would have been possible to introduce something like order into that chaos. The citizen should know what he has to contribute to the necessities of the city in which he lives. That is not the policy of this Bill. It introduces municipalities which are not municipalities, not like anything that we are aware of in any other part of the country, not like municipalities which exist under the Municipal Corporations Act, but which are municipalities more in name than in fact. You weaken and belittle the County Council. It will not be so easy in the future as in the past, it will not be possible to get these distinguished

men to serve upon this somewhat attenuated body in the same spirit that they have served hitherto, and destroys the sentimental unity of London as well as the practical unity. No more will a man have the sense that he is the citizen of a great city, one and undivided, with single attributes and a single spirit of government. But worst of all, to my mind, is as to the future. Somehow or another, the people of London will continue to govern themselves under this Bill. They may be hampered, but they will succeed in carrying on the administration of their affairs. But all prospects for the future are shut out. The Bill will stereotype the existing state of things. It makes reform almost impossible in the City, and extremely difficult in the case of the new corporations which the Bill seeks to set up. If you should find it necessary to attempt to strengthen the central organisation of London, you will be confronted by a new set of vested interests which have grown up. We have watched the history of the London County Council. I have never thought of it as a perfect body, but I have thought of it as a body which has effected great and remarkable changes, and, not the least, the conversion of many of the Moderates into Progressives, and some of the Progressives into Moderates. It has shown a singular capacity for continuity of policy in administration; and whatever we may say about fixity of policy in other things, in this kind of administration it is, up to a certain limit, a necessity. We have watched it; we have seen order come out of chaos, purity out of corruption, energy out of listlessness. We have seen it do its work carefully, in such a fashion that London has begun to have something like a common public spirit, and its citizens have begun to wake up to the fact that they have a common city and common interests to defend. This seems to me now to be in jeopardy. I would hope against hope that this Bill may not be pressed by the Government in its present form. I would trust that they may be willing in the course of the discussions which will ensue, not merely in this House, but outside this House—in that great municipality of London, the real municipality, although not so in law, in which we live—I would trust that the discussions which will ensue will convince the Government that in this

Bill they have gone too far, have acted without any mandate, and · on motives which do not commend themselves to the citizens among whom they live. I trust it is not too late. I trust that it will be possible by Amendment in Committee, in the course of the future progress of this Bill, at any rate, to lessen some of the mischiefs which I have endeavoured to indicate to the House, and which, I fear, will constitute a serious barrier to the future welfare of London.

*EARL PERCY (Kensington, S.): A great deal of criticism has been levelled by honourable Members opposite against the provisions of this Bill, to which I wish to add my own quota in a perfectly friendly spirit. I listened very carefully to the very brilliant speech of the honourable and learned Gentleman who last spoke, and I confess that although in regard to many points his arguments were cogent to the details of the Bill, I do not see that there is any single one of those points upon which he laid special stress which might not perfectly well be raised in Committee, or which should in any way be permitted to endanger the principle of the Bill, which is all we are considering on Second Reading. If I may say so without impertinence, I do not think it is possible to imagine an attack upon the principle of a Measure, on the Second Reading of a Bill of this kind, based on grounds more utterly irrelevant than those put forward by the right honourable Gentleman the Member for West Leeds. To give only two instances: he began by stating at the very outset of his speech that he objected to the proposals of the Government on the ground that the transfer which was intended of powers to the local corporations would inflict a serious and almost irreparable blow upon the position of the London County Council. He went on to say that these local corporations, after these powers had been transferred, would never be in possession, in control, of any of the great powers which the great municipalities of Manchester and Liverpool enjoyed. If it be true that the London County Council is such an important body as honourable Members opposite would have us believe—and I think we are quite willing to believe—and if it be true that these powers which are to be transferred to the local corporations are, after all, so very re-

Mr. Haldane.

stricted, then this Bill cannot reasonably be said to be a very grave attack upon the London County Council. Then he asked us why it was that the Government had not approached the London County Council; but he answered that question himself by telling us that at the last London County Council election the electorate had already decided upon the Government programme, and that the Government had no mandate for the Bill. It is quite clear, therefore, that if the electors had already decided on the Government programme, it was no good to ask the London County Council to express an opinion on the Bill. But even supposing that the majority of the London County Council is opposed to the Bill, why are we to ignore the opinion of all those who are favourable to this Measure, and who are elected on a franchise immeasurably wider than that of the London County Council? What is the Amendment that is before the House? As I understand it, it makes two charges against the proposal of the Government. It asserts, in the first place, that the Bill disturbs without simplifying the present system of London Government; and, in the second place, that it will render more difficult, if not impossible, the attainment of the idea of honourable Gentlemen opposite for the future unification of London. It is hardly necessary that we should be assured by honourable Gentlemen opposite that this Bill disturbs the present system. I cannot understand any reform being accomplished which will not disturb the existing system, and I am rather astonished to hear such a very ultra-Tory sentiment coming from honourable Gentlemen opposite. They might have quieted their fears by the recollection that of all the Bills that have been carried through this House this is the one which disturbs the existing municipal arrangements the least. The Bill of 1856 completely revolutionised the whole of London government. It transferred the whole powers of the Commissioners of Sewers to the Metropolitan Board of Works. The Bill of 1888 carried reform still further by substituting the London County Council for the Metropolitan Board of Works. Both of these Bills were deliberate attempts to smash the existing state of things. A little later in history we come to the recommendation of the Royal Commission of 1894. If the recommendation of that Commission had been carried into effect the process of attack on the London County Council would have been carried still further, for it would have altered the franchise. What does this Bill do? It leaves the City practically untouched. It does not affect the London County Council except in so far as it proposes to relieve it of a few powers which it is not excessively anxious to retain. And in regard to the vestries, it does not really propose any change which has not been substantially advocated by all reformers. The argument that we are to reject the Bill because it disturbs the present system is ridiculous. I am inclined to wonder if it was not due to a mistake in drafting the Amendment, that the word "not" was left out before the word "disturbed." The real reason of the opposition to this Bill by honourable Gentlemen opposite is that it does not disturb the existing state of things enough. If the Bill had gone a little farther, and had included the City, and absorbed it into the London County Council, it would not only not have had their opposition, but would have secured their enthusiastic welcome. Then we come to the assertion that this Bill does not simplify the present system of London government. That is not a question of opinion, but of fact. In at least four different directions this Bill must simplify local arrangements. In the first place, whereas you now have the powers under the Adoptive Act exercised by a variety of local bodies, you will in future assign all these powers to the corporation. Instead of the present overlapping of civil and ecclesiastical affairs, you will place the control of secular matters in the hands of the councils, and the control of ecclesiastical matters in the hands of the churchwardens and parishioners. Any conflict of jurisdiction which now exists as between the London County Council and the vestries will cease as between the Council and the new corporations, and, lastly, in the place of a number of different rating authorities through which the spending authority has now to issue its precepts, you will, if the Bill passes, have only one. I admit, however, that the process of simplification is not carried far enough, and that it is a pity that it is not

carried even further than the Bill proposes to do. I will illustrate my meaning by referring to sub-sections 3, 4, and 5 of clause 5. I understand that the Government have come to the conclusion on their own responsibility that a transfer of certain powers from the London County Council to the municipal corporations is desirable on its own merits. These powers may be roughly described under three heads. First, the powers contained in the first portion of the schedule which are to be exercised by the corporations alone; second, the powers under the second part of the schedule which are to be exercised by the municipal corporations concurrently with the London County Council; and, lastly, the powers as to the maintenance of main roads, the enforcement of by-laws, and the power to promote and oppose Bills in Parliament. All these powers will be transferred to the corporations. I believe that at the Westminster Conference a common agreement was come to between every one of the vestries, that all these powers, with the possible exception of the administration of the Act of 1890 relating to the Housing of the Working Classes, should be transferred to, and exercised in the future by the boroughs. In regard to the powers that are not mentioned in the schedule or the clauses of the Bill, the transference of these powers is left to the discretion of the Local Government Board. But that discretion is limited in a rather curious way. Not a single one of the powers can be handed over to the municipal corporations by the Local Government Board without the consent of the London County Council. On the other hand, the moment the London County Council hands over any power to a corporation any other corporation can apply to the Local Government Board, and also get a transfer of these powers. I can hardly conceive machinery more directly calculated to prevent the transfer of these powers. And for this reason, that not only will the vestries be confronted with the natural reluctance of the London County Council to part with a share of its power, but with all the abstract theories exhibited of late years to concentrate in its own hands the powers of the vestries. I submit to the Government that it is a great pity to give the London County Council an absolute veto of that kind. It seems to me that the London County Council is disqualified from exercising that veto on two grounds. In the first instance, it is personally interested in the transfer, and is, therefore, not likely to take an independent and impartial view of the matter any more than the municipal corporations themselves; and, in the second place, the decisions of the London County Council are notoriously influenced by Party considerations. Questions of London local government ought to be kept as far as possible from Party considerations, and should be settled by the House of Commons on broad, impartial lines. I cannot see on what principle we are to say that the Local Government Board is qualified to prevent concessions of this kind, and yet not qualified to confer concessions. What you are practically proposing by the Bill to do is to make the Local Government Board a kind of guardian angel over the London County Council to prevent it from parting with any share of its patrimony in a fit of generosity, while you give the Local Government Board absolutely no power to intervene to further the legitimate aspirations of the smaller municipalities. It does seem to me that, considering one of the main objects of this Bill is to increase interest in local life as far as possible, it is a pity that we cannot call in the Local Government Board to decide on concessions of local autonomy as well as in protecting the London County Council in keeping power in its own hands. I frankly admit that, to a great extent, I share the views of honourable Gentlemen opposite as to the effects of this Bill. I think it would be absurd to represent this Bill, as some honourable Members on our side of the House are inclined to do, as merely a harmless Bill for conferring birthday honours on the general local government staff of the metropolis. On the other hand, it would be equally wrong to represent it as a great and revolutionary change in London municipal life. It will not detract seriously from the powers and authority of the London County Council; and it will not add much to the power and authority of the new corporations. It will create a system under which, in a year's time, after the election of 1900, we shall have in every area of London a body exer-

cising complete authority on every matter distinctly within its own province, and enjoying a certain local dignity in proportion to the size and importance of its rateable area. That may have the effect—we all hope it will—of increasing the amount of individual interest and ambition in the administration of local affairs such as we find displayed in the provinces. Whether it will have that effect or not may depend upon the peculiar position of each part of London. This charge of apathy in local affairs, of which we complain in London, is by no means confined to London. It is shared by every centre of municipal Government on the Continent in which a similar condition of things to that which prevails in this metropolis exists. In Berlin, no doubt, the apathy is due to the concentration of the electoral power in the hands of the propertied classes. In Paris, on the other hand, the apathy is said to be largely due to the splitting up of the electoral areas into small parts, and to the practice of requiring candidates to be resident in the electoral districts for which they stand. It is also said to be largely due to the concentration of the executive powers in a small body. That seems to be the condition of things which obtains in London. I know that the noble Marquess at the head of the Government has expressed the opinion that the apathy of London was mainly due to the political atmosphere which surrounded the elections of the London County Council. That may be so, but it does not explain the fact that the same apathy exists in a more marked degree in connection with the elections of the vestries. I think it is partly due to the fact that the electoral areas are too small, and partly to the fact that the powers vested in the local bodies are not sufficient to attract men of ambition. If that be the case, it will be largely remedied by the present Bill. Apart from that, I would vote for the present Bill, if only on the ground that it removes a stigma that the unremunerated services given to the administration of local affairs in London have never been recognised at a properly high value. The Leader of the Opposition, on the First Reading of the Bill, and the honourable Member for West Leeds, both rather scoffed at what they called the empty boast of Lord Salisbury that he

would smash the London County
Council; and seemed to think that
the mountain had laboured to
produce on this occasion a mouse.
We all know that those words used by
the Prime Minister were not intended
in the sense which has been attributed
to them. I am inclined to think that
what the Prime Minister did intend will
be very effectively carried out by the
Bill. The Bill will not smash the London County Council. If I thought that
it would do so, I would not vote for it,
for I think that, beyond all controversy,
the London County Council has conferred immense benefits on London
municipal life. But the Bill will prevent any tendency on the part of the
London County Council to overstep its
legitimate limits, and to starve the interest in local life by concentrating
public attention entirely on its own proceedings. I wish to note what, in my
opinion, is a grave omission in the
Bill—the only important omission, and
I regret it. The Bill does not make
provision for the representation of the
vestries on the London County Council,
and in doing so, the Government have
rejected the opinion of the westminster
Conference in favour of the opinion of
the small Conference at Islington. If
we are to be guided by the wishes of
the majority of the people of London,
there can be no question which of these
Conferences represents the real sentiment of London. The first Conference
at Westminster represented a population
of 2½ millions, and a rateable value of
over 20 millions. The second Conference at Islington represented a population of only 1½ million, and a rateable
value of scarcely 9 millions sterling.
The first Conference was attended by all
the representatives from the scheduled
areas mentioned in the Report of 1894.
The second Conference was attended
practically by representatives of the
minor areas—not one of which would
have had its status altered even
if the recommendations of that
Commission had been carried out.
Therefore, there can be no doubt that
the Westminster Conference represented
the vast majority of the people of London. I would like to point out that
while it is true that the Royal Commission of 1894 did not propose to give a
representation of the vestries on the
London County Council, they did propose that representatives of the London

County Council should sit on the vestries. The important point to notice is,
that every authority which has spoken,
at all events lately, has been in favour
of some such link between the administrative system of London as that which
I now propose. The Government, however, have decided against it. The First
Lord of the Treasury, in dealing with
this question on the First Reading,
made use of the somewhat theoretic objection that by introducing this system
we should introduce the old anomaly
of indirect representation. That is undoubtedly true, but whatever force the
argument possesses is derived from the
analogy which the First Lord attempted
to draw between what he described as
the failure of the Metropolitan Board of
Works and the future corporations. I
see no such analogy at all.

THE FIRST LORD OF THE TREA-
SURY: All I said was that the
fact that indirect representation
had failed in the case of the Metropolitan Board of Works might create a
prejudice in the minds of the ratepayers
of London against re-establishing a
similar system in the case of the London County Council.

*EARL PERCY: I accept the right hon-
ourable Gentleman's correction; but I
do not think it materially alters my
point. The fact that the Metropolitan
Board of Works was not directly elected
may or may not have been largely responsible for the failure of that Board.
There might have been something in
that argument if you had proposed
under this Bill to adopt the recommendation of the Royal Commission of 1894,
and do away with the presence of aldermen in the London County Council.
But so far from proposing to carry out
that suggestion, you are proposing to
re-introduce the aldermanic element into
the new municipal corporations—for
which, I believe, none of them have
asked—in an even more extended form
than it exists in the present London
County Council. I doubt very much
whether the failure of the Metropolitan
Board of Works was due to the fact of
indirect election. It seems to me to
have been far more largely due to the
fact that they had only a very narrow
area to select from, whereas the new
corporations will practically have an unlimited field to select from. Well, I
will also pass over the argument that if

we gave a representation to the vestries on the London County Council it would actually diminish the influence the vestries already possessed. That does not seem to me likely, considering that although many vestries already possess indirectly a representative on the London County Council, no one proposes at the present moment to pass a law that no man must at the same time have a seat on the vestries and on the London County Council. And no one suggests that such a law would increase the influence of the vestries. In my opinion, the usefulness of the London County Council would be increased if its duties and responsibility were shared by representatives of the municipal corporations. I pass on to the argument that by introducing this indirect element we should be involving the municipal corporations in all the worry and turmoil of political elections such as those which surround the London County Council. I admit at once that if that would really be the effect of such a provision, it would be fatal to my proposal. I am utterly unable, however, to see how that would be the effect. That local elections are likely to be more and more dominated in the future by political considerations, I do not doubt; but how that danger can be accentuated by the present Bill I cannot imagine. Let us suppose that in any particular year some 24 Members presented themselves for election to the local corporation, and that at the moment of election there is a burning question at issue between the local corporation and the London County Council, the election would be determined by political considerations, whatever system might be proposed in the Bill. But supposing there was no such burning question, does anyone believe that an election of that kind would be likely to be determined by general considerations affecting the London County Council rather than by those small matters which are perpetually cropping up, and which come directly within the purview of, and are felt by, every resident in the district? Such an idea runs counter to all experience. We know that even in Parliamentary elections there is the greatest difficulty in keeping to Imperial questions. These considerations are nearly always subordinated to that which affects the electors' own

Earl Percy.

pockets. On every ground, therefore, I really hope that the Government may see their way to consider this question before the Bill reaches the Committee stage. That is the only question of detail which really affects the principle of the Bill. The Prime Minister a short time ago drew a very poetical analogy between the present vestries and the London County Council. He compared the vestries to the limbs of the human body, and the London County Council to the trunk ; and he said that the body was starved when all the life blood was concentrated in the stomach. That is to say, that the London County Council has completely overshadowed local life, and has become the stronger member, and has starved the life of the vestries. From that point of view I hope the Government will reconsider its policy in this matter. I do not regard it as an absolutely vital question ; but it is an important one. I think the Bill is an enormously valuable one in itself, and the stimulus which it will give to local life will, as a matter of fact, render it absolutely impossible to prosecute the policy of honourable Gentlemen opposite. It certainly will not, as some of them have said, prevent them, if ever they have the misfortune to sit on the Ministerial side of the House again— as I suppose they will some day—from altering and revising the powers and the areas ; and it will not prevent them from absorbing the City in the London County Council in the future. But it will absolutely prevent them proposing, as the right honourable Gentleman the Member for Monmouth did in 1884, to smash the remaining vestries, and to concentrate their powers in the hands of the London County Council. That will be impossible, not because we are now creating the vestrymen councillors, and the chairman of vestries mayors, but because the whole trend of pubic opinion is in favour of the Government policy, and antagonistic to that of honourable and right honourable Gentlemen opposite.

MR. BUXTON (Tower Hamlets, Poplar): There was one part of the very interesting and admirable speech of the noble Lord with which I cordially agreed, and that was when he spoke of the unfortunate apathy which no doubt exists to a very large extent with regard to local elections in London. If I thought this Bill, bad or good, would do something to diminish the local apathy of London, I certainly would give it my most hearty support. Now, Mr. Speaker, some of us have been wondering why some responsible Member of the Government has not seen fit to take part in the Debate this evening. We have now had two nights' Debate in regard to this matter—namely, on the First Reading and this evening, and only the First Lord has spoken; and if he will allow me to say so, though his speech was a very interesting one, it did not give that view of the Bill which has come home to many of us since we have had the opportunity of examining its details. I think the speech of my right honourable Friend the Member for Leeds, and the remarks he made in regard to the Bill, are entitled to some reply from some Member of the Government. We have been twitted by one or two honourable Gentlemen with having taken a different attitude than we did on the First Reading of this Bill. The reason is the very simple one, that the more we have looked into the Bill the less we like it. There were points made by my honourable Friend behind me which I do not say cannot be answered, but, until they are answered, give us the impression that the Bill is not exactly what we thought after the speech of the right honourable Gentleman when he first introduced it. Certainly the trend of the speeches this evening, and particularly the speech of the honourable Member for Chelsea, of the noble Lord, and of others, has been in the direction of minimising the importance of this Bill. They have every one of them stated that it is not directed against the London County Council. I am quite willing to admit that there are some very good points in the Bill as it stands. I think every one of us on both sides of the House desires to get rid of the opprobrious name of "vestrymen," and to confer further dignity and power on the local bodies throughout London. I think, at all events, there are two good things in this Bill. In the first place, it reduces the number of those who are managing our local affairs, because I am quite sure if the numbers are reduced we shall get better men ; and, in the second place, it concentrates the power and duties which are at present spread over many bodies. My honourable Friend the Member for

Chelsea quoted the speech of my right honourable Friend the late Home Secretary, in which he spoke of preserving the dignity and power of these local bodies. We are all at one with regard to that matter, but the essential difference between us is this—that we desire to confer these powers in connection with a reform which would have completed the edifice of London government. The right honourable Gentleman the First Lord, in his opening speech, said he thought this was completing the edifice, but he omitted one very important matter—namely, any provision dealing with the City. That, to my mind, makes all the difference in regard to the attitude which we take up in reference to this matter, because if the City had been included, and if there had been no question of creating this larger Westminster, it would have been possible, with one predominant body in the centre, to confer, without any danger, greater powers on local bodies than we can under present circumstances. The City is to remain in existence as an enemy to progress in London, as it always has been. (Ministerial cries of No!) Well, I can only say that it would be difficult to show that it has not been due to the City of London that we are 50 years behind in regard to our municipal privileges and liberties. The City has always been opposed to municipal reform in London for fear the edifice of the City should be attacked. The result has been that, from year to year, London becomes more and more one large metropolis. Unfortunately, one part of London has been getting richer and another part has been getting poorer. From year to year we find a greater division between wealth and poverty, between capital and labour, between those who are employing and those who are employed, between different trades, classes, and sections, and the result is that you get less and less of real local interest in a district and greater need for a general central body. Now, I do not wish at this late hour of the evening, after what has been already said, to go into the question of whether or no it is the object and desire of the Government to attack the London County Council. My honourable Friend the Member for Chelsea repudiated, on his behalf, as a Moderate member of the London County Council, any such intention, and I can only' say that Lord Salisbury and the Members of the Government, a couple of years ago, were very much misunderstood, and ought to be commiserated on that account; but the electors, whatever might have been the intention of right honourable Gentlemen opposite, certainly took their speeches to represent the view that they wished to disintegrate, to a large extent, the London County Council. The effect of the County Council elections was certainly intended to show that they did not desire that the power of the London County Council should be in any way interfered with. I do not wish to go into that again, but I do want to ask the right honourable Gentleman in charge of this Bill to explain one or two points which have been raised in the course of the Debate in regard to the position of the London County Council and these local bodies—a point which seems to some of us to be of great importance. He repudiates any desire to attack the London County Council, and, to my mind, therefore, this is a matter which requires some very considerable explanation before we can accept the statement that the Bill is not intended in any way to weaken the position of the central Metropolitan body. Now, in the first place, I submit that it is a curious thing that these local bodies are to be called municipalities instead of urban district councils, which the Government themselves, many years ago, intended to call them, because it seems to me that it invites them to think that they are separated and isolated bodies, and that they have their own local life and local feeling, when as a matter of fact, they can only use it as a whole. There are three points to which attention has been already drawn. One of the most important, to my mind, is the question of transfer of power. Now, the noble Lord, in the course of his speech, seemed to me to hit upon one or two blots with regard to this Bill which certainly require explanation, and which seem to me to show that the clause is absolutely unworkable as it stands. But the line of opposition which I shall take in regard to this matter is this. The right honourable Gentleman said that we had exaggerated its importance. What we on the Opposition side of the House fear is that the

Mr. Buxton.

clause may be used by those on the Council desiring to play into the hands of those who intend to weaken the Council, to transfer powers from it to the local bodies which ought not to be transferred. Everyone understands that there ought to be power given to the London County Council to transfer such powers when such a step can be taken to the general advantage. But no such transfer ought to take place without publicity. I would specially call the attention of the right honourable Gentleman the Leader of the House to this matter, because I understood him to say we had exaggerated its importance. The importance I attached to it was due to the fact that the powers can be transferred without publicity. I cannot help thinking, when the right honourable Gentleman sets up a most elaborate machinery, under which powers can be transferred and cannot be re-transferred to the County Council, it is desirable to consider whether this clause cannot be so reconstructed that there shall be adequate and proper publicity in regard to these matters. It is shown conclusively that the power of borrowing conferred by this Bill will be a great detriment to the ratepayers of the whole of London and of the locality in particular.

THE FIRST LORD OF THE TREASURY: They can borrow from the County Council.

MR. BUXTON: Yes, but surely the object of this clause is to encourage them to borrow on their own initiative. I think it is important that there should be one central body under proper audit to control the borrowing of money throughout the metropolis. Then, with regard to the question of promoting Bills in Parliament, we have had no explanation as to what is the object of giving the new councils this power. So far as I know, there has never been a complaint on the part of the localities that any proposal they wanted introduced into a London County Council Bill had not been accepted and introduced. We want to protect the ratepayers from the cost which would be incurred by 25 or 30 municipalities promoting their own Bills in Parliament at our expense as ratepayers, and at the expense of our time as Members. When these municipalities are created, the power of promoting and opposing Bills in Parliament may be used in the interest of the great monopolies. The London County Council ought to be the supreme body, and ought not to have their hands tied or forced by the action of the local authorities. There is another matter on which I trust the right honourable Gentleman may be able to see his way to meet us to a certain extent; that is, that all the powers transferred to these bodies should be more specifically scheduled in the Bill. It is very difficult indeed to understand this Bill as it stands. The whole of the Bill is by reference, and how the unfortunate member of the new municipality, when he is elected, is to understand what his duties or his powers are, passes, I think, the wit of man. I think it is unfortunate that three Acts—the Metropolis Management Act, the Municipal Corporations Act, and the Local Government Act of 1888—should have been mixed up for the creation of these new bodies. I should have thought it would have been better to have created them under the Local Government Act of 1888 as district councils. The right honourable Gentleman said, in his speech, that the new councils would be practically identical with the municipalities throughout the country, but I think he can hardly argue that they will have anything like the powers now enjoyed by municipalities outside London. The only three points taken from the Municipal Corporations Act—the audit, the question of aldermen, and annual instead of triennial elections—are all bad : and, in fact, that Act has nothing to do with these bodies. As to boundaries, I think it is to be regretted that the Government have not taken a little more trouble to specify in the Bill a larger number of municipalities which are to be created. They have actually omitted some of those which were named, and very properly named, by the Royal Commission of 1894. The objection we find to the present Bill is that too wide a discretion is left to the Commissioners, only 16 districts being specified in the schedule. We do not even know who these gentlemen will be ; but we think the Government might very well have scheduled at the

least another six or eight districts, leaving comparatively few unscheduled, and thereby making pretty clear the basis on which the Boundaries Commissioners would have to act. At present the unfortunate districts do not know on what basis they will be formed into municipalities. The directions to the Commissioners are very vague, and the Government are in this respect evading a responsibility which they ought to have taken in their own hands. The transference of power from the central to the local authorities will throw greater cost on the poorer districts, and relieve the richer districts of part of the cost they now have to bear, and the richer districts will, in consequence, have a great temptation to go to the County Council and ask for the transfer of powers. There is one point which affects my own constituency. Under this Bill the main roads are to be transferred from the central to the local authority, and this without any pecuniary assistance on the part of the central to the local body. In Poplar there are two great main roads, covering some miles, and I believe the charge for maintaining them is something like £8,000 or £9,000 a year. I should like to know whether, as the Bill now stands, that charge will be taken away from the general fund and thrown upon the very poor district which I represent?

THE FIRST LORD OF THE TREASURY: The cost of maintaining the main roads will not be thrown upon the local authority, but will be borne, as at present, by the central authority.

MR. BUXTON: Then I have no objection to the sub-section. Another serious effect of this transfer of powers will be that in many of the poorer districts the powers, though transferred, will not be carried out as efficiently as they are under the present arrangement. As regards a considerable number of these powers, I think that it is of the utmost importance that those who carry them out should be above any suspicion of local influence, that the inspectors should be absolutely free, and should be the servants not of the locality, but of the central authority. I also fear that when this Bill is passed the richer municipalities will be opposed to any extension of the principle of the equalisation of rates. Therefore, though I admit that this Bill has some good points, I fear that one of its results will be that a greater burden will be thrown on the poorer districts, and the richer districts will be relieved. We all admit that one of the greatest social evils of the metropolis is that the rich live in one part and the poor in another, and I think we also agree that the richer districts, having, to a great extent, got rid of their poor ought to pay for their relief. I do not think the Bill is likely to effect that object. There are a good many other points we shall have to discuss in detail in Committee, but I am afraid I cannot take a very sanguine view of the position of those local bodies in regard to the London County Council. It is said that it is not intended to diminish efficiency or destroy the power of the County Council, but it is curious that any proposal of the County Council for the improvement of the condition of the people is generally opposed by honourable Members opposite. I cannot help thinking that there will be some diminution of the position of the County Council, and therefore I shall vote for the Amendment. We shall, however, endeavour to so improve this Bill in Committee as to make it, if possible, a real step forward in London government.

Sir J. BLUNDELL MAPLE (Camberwell, Dulwich): I have paid a great deal of attention to this particular subject, and I have listened very attentively to the speeches which have been made on the other side of the House, but I have not heard a single speech against the proposal that greater local life and administrative work is required. In fact, I am sure every honourable Member in his heart welcomes some further local government for London. Honourable Members who have spoken have told us that they will accept this Bill, but that it will have to be altered in Committee. I believe a great many alterations will have to be made in the Bill in Committee. I am of the same opinion as the noble Lord below me, the Member for South Kensington, as to the aldermen or members

of municipalities coming on to the County Council. As the clause dealing with this matter stands at present, this Bill seems to be rather an impossible Bill. I am one of them who believe in maintaining the strength of the London County Council as the central authority, and should consider it right and proper that that body should be the custodian of the common county fund. I think also that when any work is to be delegated from the County Council to the new municipalities the money they are to spend should be settled at the same time. It would also be an advantage if there were on the County Council a representative of these new bodies. I must say I cannot see the advantage of having aldermen on the municipalities, but it would be a great advantage if one man were chosen as a representative who should go as alderman to the County Council. In dealing with the delegation of powers, it seems to me that the Government have gone wrong in clause 5, because they do not clearly set out that when work is transferred the County Council should agree as to the amount of money that is to go from the common county fund to pay the expenses of carrying out that work. You cannot expect the new councils to execute the work unless this point is settled. If you do not give them the money the new municipalities will be out of pocket. Our friends on the other side seem to contemplate that these new municipalities are to carry out these works without getting the money to pay for them. That was never anticipated, I am certain, in the Government Bill. Under clause 5 of this Bill if the London County Council were unwilling to transfer further powers there would be no means of forcing them, and in the event of the new municipalities not carrying out the powers which had been transferred to them in a proper manner, there would be no way of getting those powers taken back again. In my Bill I proposed that these powers should be transferred for three years only, to see how they were discharged by the new councils. There are common duties which must remain centralised to a certain extent—those of the fire brigade, of sewerage, and of tramways—but the councils of the new boroughs could assist a great deal by a system of delegation, the new municipalities undertaking work which would relieve the committees of the London County Council. I am of opinion that clause 6 is not desirable. The duties of the Building Acts Committee are very difficult, and the work of the 65 district surveyors would become very complicated. One of these surveyors is at present looking after work which would be in four of these municipalities. Consequently, he would not only have to render an account of each of the four municipalities respecting the different houses in those districts, but he would also have to report to the London County Council.

And, it being Midnight, the Debate stood adjourned.

Debate to be resumed upon Thursday.

REPORT OF SUPPLY.

SUPPLY [20th MARCH].

Resolution Reported.

CIVIL SERVICES AND REVENUE DEPARTMENTS, 1899-1900 (VOTE ON ACCOUNT).

"That a sum, not exceeding £14,781,000, be granted to Her Majesty, on account, for or towards defraying the charges for the Civil Services and Revenue Departments for the year ending on the 31st day of March 1900, viz. :—

CIVIL SERVICES.

CLASS II.

	£
Colonial Office	17,500

CLASS I.

	£
Royal Palaces and Marlborough House	16,400
Royal Parks and Pleasure Gardens	40,000
Miscellaneous Legal Buildings Great Britain	18,000
Houses of Parliament Buildings ...	12,000
Art and Science Buildings, Great Britain	10,000
Diplomatic and Consular Buildings	9,000

	£
Revenue Buildings...	120,000
Public Buildings, Great Britain ...	100,000
Surveys of the United Kingdom ...	80,000
Harbours under the Board of Trade	2,000
Peterhead Harbour	6,000
Rates on Government Property ...	210,000
Public Works and Buildings, Ireland	70,000
Railways, Ireland	70,000

CLASS II.

United Kingdom and England—

	£
House of Lords, Offices	4,000
House of Commons, Offices ...	13,000
Treasury and Subordinate Departments	30,000
Home Office	50,000
Foreign Office	25,000
Privy Council Office, etc.... ...	5,000
Board of Trade	60,000
Mercantile Marine Services ...	30,000
Bankruptcy Department of the Board of Trade	3
Board of Agriculture	75,000
Charity Commission	15,000
Civil Service Commission	15,000
Exchequer and Audit Department .	22,000
Friendly Societies Registry ...	2,200
Local Government Board	66,000
Lunacy Commission	5,000
Mint (including Coinage)	10
National Debt Office	5,000
Public Works Loan Commission ...	10
Public Record Office	10,000
Registrar General's Office	13,000
Stationery and Printing	250,000
Woods, Forests, etc., Office of ...	7,000
Works and Public Buildings Office of	19,000
Secret Service	17,000

Scotland—

	£
Secretary for Scotland	4,500
Fishery Board	8,000
Lunacy Commission...	2,000
Registrar General's Office	2,000
Local Government Board	4,000

Ireland—

	£
Lord Lieutenant's Household ...	2,000
Chief Secretary and Subordinate Departments	15,000
Charitable Donations and Bequests Office	750
Local Government Board	15,000
Public Record Office	2,000
Public Works Office	12,500
Registrar General's Office	6,000
Valuation and Boundary Survey...	6,000

CLASS III.

United Kingdom and England—

	£
Law Charges	40,000
Miscellaneous Legal Expenses ...	26,000
Supreme Court of Judicature ...	120,000
Land Registry	7,000
County Courts	10,000

	£
Police, England and Wales ...	14,000
Prisons, England and the Colonies	200,000
Reformatory and Industrial Schools, Great Britain	140,000
Broadmoor Criminal Lunatic Asylum	10,000

Scotland—

	£
Law Charges and Courts of Law	30,000
Register House, Edinburgh ...	15,000
Crofters Commission	2,000
Prisons, Scotland	25,000

Ireland—

	£
Law Charges and Criminal Prosecutions	30,000
Supreme Court of Judicature, and other Legal Departments ...	38,000
Land Commission	50,000
County Court Officers, etc.	36,000
Dublin Metropolitan Police ...	35,000
Constabulary	600,000
Prisons, Ireland	45,000
Reformatory and Industrial Schools	55,500
Dundrum Criminal Lunatic Asylum	2,500

CLASS IV.

United Kingdom and England—

	£
Public Education, England and Wales	3,600,000
Science and Art Department, United Kingdom	200,000
British Museum	64,000
National Gallery	5,000
National Portrait Gallery	2,500
Wallace Gallery	6,000
Scientific Investigation, etc , United Kingdom	15,000
Universities and Colleges, Great Britain, and Intermediate Education, Wales	38,000
London University	5

Scotland—

	£
Public Education	600,000
National Gallery	1,400

Ireland—

	£
Public Education	600,000
Endowed Schools Commissioners .	350
National Gallery	1,200
Queen's Colleges	2,500

CLASS V.

	£
Diplomatic and Consular Services	220,000
Uganda, Central and East Africa Protectorates and Uganda Railway	250,000
Colonial Services	180,000
Cyprus, Grant in Aid	12,000
Subsidies to Telegraph Companies	35,000

CLASS VI.

	£
Superannuation and Retired Allowances	280,000
Merchant Seamen's Fund Pensions, etc.	3,000
Miscellaneous Charitable and other Allowances	1,000
Hospitals and Charities, Ireland ...	10,000

CLASS VII.

	£
Temporary Commissions	8,000
Miscellaneous Expenses	6,572
Congested Districts Board, Scotland	— —
Total for Civil Services ...	£9,271,000

REVENUE DEPARTMENTS.

	£
Customs	350,000
Inland Revenue	650,000
Post Office	3,000,000
Post Office Packet Service	210,000
Post Office Telegraphs	1,300,000
Total for Revenue Departments	£5,510,000
Grand Total	14,781,000

Resolution read a second time.

Amendment proposed—

"To leave out '£14,781,000,' and insert '£14,780,900' instead thereof."—(*Mr. Havelock Wilson.*)

*MR. HAVELOCK WILSON (Middlesbrough): Mr. Speaker, I move to reduce the Vote for the Board of Trade by £100, in order to call attention to the administration of the Merchant Shipping Act. We are desirous at times to get fresh legislation, but I am very much afraid our hopes of obtaining legislation from the right honourable Gentleman the President of the Board of Trade have little chance of being realised. We have a right, however, to ask that the President of the Board of Trade will at least administer the Merchant Shipping Act in a just and proper spirit. I have called attention repeatedly in this House to the fact that one of the sections of the Merchant Shipping Act, with reference to the accommodation provided for lascar seamen, has been continually broken by a large and important company, which is receiving a considerable subsidy from the Government. In August of last year I was told by the President of the Board of Agriculture, on behalf of his right honourable colleague, the President of the Board of Trade, that the matter was receiving the serious attention of that Board, and had been referred to the Law Officers of the Crown, and that as soon as the law had been ascertained the matter would be dealt with finally.

That was last August, but from that month up till January of this year not a single thing was done by the President of the Board of Trade to inquire into the state of the law on the subject. I have put a number of Questions to the right honourable Gentleman this year, but have received evasive replies each time. We were told that the matter had been referred to the Law Officers of the Crown, and though five or six weeks have gone by we have had no further light upon the subject. I am entitled to complain of the conduct of the right honourable Gentleman in this matter. I claim to have a right, in the interests of British seamen, to expect other than evasive replies when I call attention to these matters. I would be the last Member in this House to obstruct business, but when we cannot get satisfactory answers to respectful Questions addressed to the Board of Trade there is no alternative but to have it out, and to have it out properly, on an occasion like this. I asked the right honourable Gentleman the other day as to the number of men carried on certain vessels belonging to the P. and O. Company, and the accommodation provided for them. The right honourable Gentleman replied that one of the two vessels named carried 65 men, but I found, on inquiry, that the vessel carried 87, which, of course, largely reduced the crew space. In the case of the other ship—the " Caledonia "—the right honourable Gentleman said she was only carrying 157 men, but, according to the list supplied by the company to the Customs officers, 192 men were carried on that vessel. The figures given by the President of the Board of Trade did not correspond with the facts; indeed, I assert that the P. and O. Company have misled the right honourable Gentleman. For this reason I say we have good grounds of complaint. This has been going on for years. The right honourable Gentleman has told us repeatedly that there is some conflict between the Indian law and the Imperial law with reference to the accommodation of lascars. I have maintained all through these discussions that the Indian law only applies to ships registered in India and sailing on the Indian coast. The Imperial Act applies to all vessels registered under the Imperial Act, and belonging to the

United Kingdom. The P. and O. Company's vessels are all registered in the United Kingdom under the Imperial Act, and the men employed on those vessels are entitled to have the 72 cubic feet of space which is provided by that Act. Again, the Board of Trade have, during the last four or five years, given instructions that wherever any company failed to give the proper amount of accommodation to the lascar crews, in accordance with the Act, there was to be a deduction from the tonnage. The Board of Trade have applied that law to small companies, but the Department is evidently afraid of the powerful P. and O. Company, and have neglected to do their duty. The Royal Commission on Labour recommended that seamen should have 120 cubic feet of space. The Board of Trade recognised that by saying they believed all shipowners were giving this amount of accommodation, and they recommended generally that shipowners should be encouraged to give 120 cubic feet, but now we find one large company who are not giving the men more than 50 cubic feet. The company are, therefore, breaking the law, but the President of the Board of Trade and his advisers are evidently afraid to put the law into force. That is one indictment I make against the President of the Board of Trade, but there are others. There was a Manning Committee appointed by the late Liberal Government, which sat for over two years, and recommended that a manning scale should be passed into law, so that every vessel would be provided with a proper crew according to her tonnage and steam power. We expected that the present Government would have brought in legislation to deal with that question in a proper manner. It is true the right honourable Gentleman brought in a Bill to declare that ships undermanned were unseaworthy, but nothing was said as to the scale. The new Act left it in the hands of the Board of Trade to say what the scale should be, but only a leaflet has been issued giving some vague instructions as to the vessels of 700 tons and over, and even this does not include coasting vessels. The right honourable Gentleman proposes in such leaflet that there shall be, independent of the master and two mates, a sufficient number of deck hands available for division into two watches. There is nothing in the leaflet to guide the Board of Trade officer as to whether the available deck hands should be boys or men. If the President of the Board of Trade had been desirous of putting the manning scale into proper form, with the view of safeguarding the men on board our ships, if he meant that vessels of over 700 tons should carry three hands in a watch, he would have declared whether they were to be men or boys. As I have said, this scale is only to apply to vessels going on foreign voyages. If the right honourable Gentleman had consulted anybody connected with the seafaring trade, they would have told him that there was more danger in trading around our coasts than on vessels going on foreign voyages, and yet vessels trading round the coast can carry what hands they like, and the President of the Board of Trade does not interfere. I put a question to him the other day with regard to two vessels which are trading on the coast, and which have only three able seamen and a boatswain. The majority of the ships on the coast have six able seamen, and it has been the rule in all coasting steamers of 700 or 800 tons to carry six able seamen, so as to have three men in each watch. The right honourable Gentleman said the other day that the Board of Trade did not deem vessels to be undermanned when they only had three or four men. From what I know, that is not the opinion of the permanent officials of the Board of Trade. The Manning Committee included amongst its members one of the permanent secretaries of the Board of Trade, and also the nautical adviser to the Board of Trade, and both of these officers signed the Majority Report, which recommended that no vessel under 50 feet in length or 700 tons burden should be allowed to leave any port in the United Kingdom with less than six hands, so as to provide three effective hands in each watch. I can hardly conceive that they would recommend to the right honourable Gentleman that four men would be sufficient, when in their Reports they have declared vessels to be unseaworthy when they have less than six. There have been many Board of Trade inquiries. I have in my hand a list of a number of inquiries as to the cause of the loss of ships that have been held at the direction of the Board of Trade,

and in every case, out of a total of 30, the Court have declared that where these vessels have had less than six able seamen, so as to provide three in each watch, they were unseaworthy. I want the right honourable Gentleman to tell me how he can say that the Board of Trade officials who have held inquiries into the matter have declared this class of vessel to be seaworthy with less than six hands. I think I have some right to complain in this matter. We are not asking for fresh legislation; we are simply asking the President of the Board of Trade to put into force the law, or rather the rule, that he has himself made. I attended an inquest three or four weeks ago on a man who was killed on board a ship entering Tilbury Dock. This vessel was short-handed, and in checking the vessel round the dock head by wire rope, the man's leg caught in the slack of the wire and was cut off. I was able to elicit from one of the witnesses at that inquiry that if there had been another man on the deck to take away the slack of the wire rope the accident would not have happened. Instead of endeavouring to save the lives of our seamen by enforcing the regulations which the Courts have insisted ought to be enforced, the Board of Trade, which costs the country some thousands of pounds every year, take no action in the matter. I hope the right honourable Gentleman will give some satisfactory reply to the effect that he will insist upon shipowners carrying a sufficient number of seamen to render their ships seaworthy, and to prevent accidents of this kind occurring in the future. There is another matter upon which I wish to make a complaint. We have a Department in connection with the Board of Trade which is called the Labour Department. The present Government brought in a Measure entitled the Conciliation Act, in order to prevent, if possible, labour disputes, and wherever they did occur to endeavour to have them settled without any trouble. We had a dispute in Glasgow in October of last year, and the men had very serious grievances in connection with the Shipping Federation. They complained that the officials of this organisation in Glasgow had been levying blackmail on the sailors and firemen who wanted employment, and that the Board of Trade had allowed the Shipping Federation to supply men in contravention of section 111 of the Merchant Shipping Act. Because these men refused to take what is known as the Federation Ticket the Shipping Federation immediately commenced to import hands from other ports, so as to compel the men to take this ticket and submit to be blackmailed by these officials. I wrote to the President of the Board of Trade with regard to this matter, and I explained in detail what the men had to complain of. We sent up to the President of the Board of Trade a number of instances where the men alleged they had been compelled to pay money in order to get employment. We have instances where men belonging to the Royal Naval Reserve, who had been engaged by officers of ships to go on a voyage, had been objected to by the Federation officials when they went to sign on, and subsequently lost their employment. We sent these charges, as I have said, to the President of the Board of Trade, and asked him, under the Conciliation Act, to send down one of the Board's officials to investigate the charges with a view to the matter being settled in a proper manner. Instead of taking these steps the Board of Trade simply sent our charges on to the Shipping Federation, and asked that body what they had to say with regard to them. I think the Shipping Federation denied every statement we made, and I would not have expected that they would have done anything else. I want to know for what reason the Board of Trade sent our charges on to the Shipping Federation. It was the duty, I contend, of the Board of Trade, seeing that it concerned their interests as well as ours, to have held a proper inquiry in regard to the matter. We were told that no inquiry could be held, and although there was a strike in Glasgow, which lasted over three months, causing great suffering to the men, the Board of Trade made no effort whatever to try and bring that dispute to a termination. In this matter we certainly have a right to complain of the conduct of the right honourable Gentleman. Are we to understand that the Conciliation Act of the Board of Trade is only intended for very large industrial disputes where there is a great dislocation of trade? Surely, if there is any body of men in this country who

ought to have the benefit of the Conciliation Act it is the men who are compelled to go down to the sea in ships. We have appealed to the President of the Board of Trade before any strikes have taken place to put the Conciliation Act into force, but on every occasion he has refused to move. I understand the Board of Trade are afraid to take any step which is at all likely to offend the great shipping interest. In March of last year I sent the President of the Board of Trade a lengthy statement with regard to the state of affairs existing in the Consular Shipping Office at New York. In July I put a further question to the right honourable Gentleman as to whether anything had been done to put an end to that state of affairs. He stated in reply that the matter was still under the consideration of the Board of Trade and the Foreign Office. Since that time I have had many complaints from seamen who inform me that the same state of things exists in the Consular Shipping Office in New York as has existed there for years. I sent the right honourable Gentleman a letter which I had received, and which was signed by 18 men connected with a sailing ship, in which they stated that they were compelled to pay crimps £8 each as a shipping fee for getting the chance of employment on this vessel. They were told that the balance of their advance note—60 dollars—would be paid to them when they got on board the ship. No payment was made on board the ship, and they demanded to be taken to the Consul. Instead of that a crowd of crimps and loafers came up to the vessel in a tug-boat and the men were assaulted. I have had many complaints as to this kind of thing. I believe the Consul-General has denied my statement with regard to the matter, but I want to point out to the right honourable Gentleman that the Consul-General's office is not in the same place as the Consular Shipping Office. It is in a different building and a different locality, and the Consul-General himself has no opportunity of witnessing the state of affairs existing in the Shipping Office. Therefore I venture to say, with all respect, that he is not a competent person to form an opinion. The right honourable Gentleman has said that the Government are anxious to do something in the matter, but that there are great difficulties in the way. I should like to know what those difficulties are. I have spent three months at that office, and I know of no insuperable difficulties. The Consul-General in New York has a right to say to the crimps and loafers and the other undesirable persons that they shall not come into the Shipping Office with the sailors. I think the United States Government are prepared and willing to provide police protection in order to prevent them coming into the office. The Consular shipping masters themselves are very much to blame; I find they raise no objection at all to the presence of these persons. When I asked them why these men were there I was told that they were allowed because they represented the sailors and firemen. This, of course, is not the case. The present state of things will go on unless the President of the Board of Trade makes up his mind definitely on the matter. It is only necessary for the Government to give instructions to the Consul-General in New York to the effect that these people shall not be allowed to come into that office, and that instruction would be carried out at once. I desired to call attention to the advance notes that the men receive on signing articles in a ship, and I urged on the President of the Board of Trade the desirability of giving instructions that whenever a man is engaged in a Consular Office in a foreign port he shall receive from the Consul his advance note direct. I was promised that that instruction should be given long ago, but nothing has been done, and when a man signs on in the office he is told to go down to the shipmaster to get his advance note. When he goes the shipping master tells him he intends to deduct 10s. or £1 as a shipping fee. Of course, the man cannot help himself and has to pay. I believe one of the points urged by the right honourable Gentleman with regard to New York was that the United States law says it is illegal to give any advance notes to seamen on board a ship. That is true, but the United States law only says that it is illegal to give advance notes to vessels belonging to the United States. They have no control over our Consular Office. Sailors and firemen are people who have no political influence. If they had votes at their disposal there are plenty of hon-

Mr. Havelock Wilson.

ourable Members in this House who would be ready and willing to run about seeing what could be done. I always find that where men have no political influence very little is done for them in the House of Commons. The right honourable Gentleman, in answer to the honourable Member for St. Pancras the other night, promised, with regard to the number of foreigners in British ships, that the Government would make some inquiry as to the engagement and position of seamen. The right honourable Gentleman was asked by the honourable Member for Southampton as to whether the Government were prepared to appoint a Royal Commission to inquire into the position of seamen on board ship, and he was told in reply that the Government did not intend to do anything in this direction. I am not going to ask the Government to appoint a Royal Commission, because I know it would be a very costly thing to do when a Select Committee of the House of Commons can deal with the question just as effectively and thoroughly. Seeing that the right honourable Gentleman promised that the Government were prepared to inquire into the matter, I am going to ask him whether he is willing to appoint a Select Committee to inquire into the whole of the question. One of the matters which the Committee could consider would be whether the system of continuous discharge would be best. The right honourable Gentleman appears to have made up his mind that a form of continuous discharge would be the best thing seamen could have, and that the captain should have a right to record in that continuous discharge a seaman's character for conduct and ability. I have no objection whatever to a form of continuous discharge giving a record of a man's character for conduct and ability, provided that whenever a captain gives a man a bad discharge the man should have the right to go before some competent court to have the matter tried on its merits. I do not object to a captain giving a man such a character if he has a right to appeal; but to leave it in the hands of the captain to give a bad character for conduct and ability without allowing the man an opportunity for redress would be a most tyrannical proceeding, and that is what we have to complain of now.

Mr. SPEAKER: The question of whether the seamen should have an appeal or not can only be decided by legislation.

*Mr. HAVELOCK WILSON: Yes, Sir, but this is a matter which is in the hands of the Board of Trade. The right honourable Gentleman has power now, if he chooses to exercise it, to issue continuous discharges, and seeing that he has such power I claim to be quite within my right in saying that it would be a most unjust thing for the President of the Board of Trade to issue such certificates without giving a seaman a right to appeal in the event of the captain giving him a bad character for conduct and ability. If such a power was given to captains it would be possible for them to give men who had served a number of years on board a ship, and had hitherto a good record, a bad character, and in such a case, what chance, I ask, would that man stand of getting employment if there were men around who had no stain whatever in their books? Once a bad character, always a bad character. Under the present system the captain has the power to give a man a bad discharge and he has no remedy whatever. This is a state of things which should not exist. The Board of Trade have a large number of outdoor officers who are supposed to watch the crimps and prevent such cases as I have alluded to, but during the months of October, November, and December of last year wholesale crimping was being carried on by agents of the Shipping Federation. I called attention to a case where the agents of the Shipping Federation went on board a Russian steamer in Hull and persuaded a young ordinary seaman to desert his ship. They conveyed him to the railway station without any sea-kit, took him to Greenock, and put him on board the "Duchess of York." This man could not speak a word of English, but he was shipped as a fireman, and sent across the Western Ocean. I want to ask the right honourable Gentleman why the Board of Trade did not undertake a prosecution against the man who persuaded this Russian to desert his ship, and who conveyed him to Greenock, and also what the officials

at Greenock were doing to allow a man to be signed on as a fireman who had never had any experience on an English ship and who could not speak a word of the English language? Was there an interpreter there? This man was persuaded to go down to Greenock on false pretences, and was kept on the "Duchess of York" as a prisoner, and then signed on by the officials of the Board of Trade, and yet we pay over £40,000 a year in order, amongst other things, to prevent such a thing occurring. Are we to understand that the Shipping Federation have full liberty to break the law with impunity? Under another branch of the Board of Trade there are deputy-superintendents who sign on crews. They are provided at considerable cost throughout the country where seamen are engaged. I find that in many cases deputy-superintendents are employed signing on at all hours of the night crews that have been brought on board by the most notorious crimps. I have called the right honourable Gentleman's attention to the case of a railway servant who took a trip to the Isle of Man in a pleasure steamer, and was signed on as an able seaman by one of the Board of Trade officials. I now have to deal with the Surveying Department of the Board of Trade. There has been a tendency in the Board of Trade for a number of years to appoint shipwright surveyors and engineer surveyors, but at the present time there is only one nautical surveyor for the whole of Scotland; and I ask, how can the right honourable Gentleman expect that ships can be thoroughly looked after under such circumstances? Engineer surveyors are quite competent to examine engines and boilers and that kind of work. The shipwright surveyors are perfectly competent to look after the woodwork of the vessel; but the nautical surveyor is the man who is supposed to have knowledge of the loading of the ship, the stowage, the outfit, and the cargo, and yet there is only one nautical surveyor for the whole of Scotland, and his time is fully occupied in Glasgow. There is no nautical surveyor for Aberdeen, Dundee, and Leith. How can the right honourable Gentleman expect that ships can be thoroughly looked after if the Board of Trade continue to appoint engineer and shipwright surveyors. What do they know about getting boats out over the side of the ship, and the gear attached to them? It is a farce. For the north-east coast of England there is only one nautical surveyor stationed at Hull. We need not be surprised about vessels foundering or going to sea unworthy when the Board of Trade are not taking proper measures and precautions to look after vessels before leaving port. I trust, from the point of view of humanity, and in the interest of life and limb, that the right honourable Gentleman will make some promise that his Department will seriously consider the question of appointing a larger number of nautical surveyors in order to look after the ships that leave our ports. There are many other ports where there are no surveyors at all, and we have heard numerous instances of foreign ships overloading in British ports. There is no surveyor, for instance, in the port of Burntisland, Scotland, and foreign ships are allowed to leave in an overloaded state, and these vessels are competing with our British vessels. Is this state of affairs to continue? I come next to the question of provisions. An Act of Parliament was passed a short time ago giving powers to the Board of Trade to inspect all provisions to be consumed on board vessels going through the Suez Canal round the Cape of Good Hope or Cape Horn. I find the Board of Trade inspectors under this Act have in many cases gone on board ships bound on these voyages, and have condemned provisions as unfit for use, but instead of the food being destroyed it has been transferred to vessels going up the Baltic and the Black Sea. I want to ask the right honourable Gentleman if he cannot do something to prevent this, and not allow food condemned as unfit for use in one ship to be put on board another vessel which is outside the limit of the Act to which I have referred. If the right honourable Gentleman will consult his inspectors in regard to this matter, I think he will find that they will bear out my statement. There is only one other matter to which I will refer. There was a dispute in Liverpool a short while ago, and in order to defeat the men one or two of the large companies there resorted to a practice which was entirely

illegal, and which the Board of Trade could have prevented, and ought to have prevented. We called the attention of the Board of Trade to this matter some months ago, but have had no reply yet. A number of the men, desiring to have a better wage, refused to sign on. The Cunard and another company got their men who were employed in port—old and infirm men and shore gangs—to sign on the articles of their vessels, as though they were the crew, in order to get their clearance from the Board of Trade Passenger Surveyor. When the ships got outside, the shore gangs came back and their places were filled by all kinds of incompetent men who pretended to be seamen and firemen, and who were supplied from boarding houses. That was a distinct breach of the Merchant Shipping Act. The deputy-superintendent had no right to sign these men on when it was known that there was no intention on the part of the agents of the owners of sending them to sea. Because one old man refused to sign on, although he was told he would not be required to go to sea, he was discharged, notwithstanding the fact that he had worked for the company for nearly 40 years. The deputy-superintendent who signed these men on knew perfectly well that he was doing wrong, and that he had no right to sign them on, knowing that they were not going to form the crew of the ship. Furthermore, the Board of Trade Surveyor, or the Medical Officer of the Board of Trade, had no right to pass these men as the crew of the vessel when he knew they were not going to sea in the ship. This matter was then brought under the notice of the Board of Trade, but no answer has been given, no doubt for the reason that they do not want to do anything which would offend the shipping interest. All I ask, and all the seamen ask, is that the Board of Trade will administer the law fairly and impartially between employer and man. If we get that we cannot expect any more, but I can assure the right honourable Gentleman that the Board of Trade at the present moment are a long way short of administering the law in an impartial manner. It is administered all on one side at the present moment. The right honourable Gentleman has said that seamen

Mr. Havelock Wilson.

are better off now than they were, and that they are getting higher wages now than they have ever received. The President of the Board of Trade is entirely mistaken on that point. The men are getting wages as low as ever they did, and in many cases they are getting 25 per cent. less than the wages which were paid 30 years ago. I cannot see how, in the face of these facts, the right honourable Gentleman can say that seamen are enjoying a prosperous time. With regard to accommodation, I have no hesitation in saying that there are a large number of cases in which the accommodation provided is contrary to the Board of Trade regulations. It is supposed that a man shall be able to read a newspaper in any part of a forecastle by the light of day, but I have been in many forecastles where I could not see my hand in front of me, and where the ventilation was very imperfect. If the Board of Trade would step out manfully in the right direction this could be remedied. Laws on the subject have been passed, and I contend that it is the duty of the Board of Trade to see that those laws are properly administered. I beg to move to reduce the Vote by £100.

MR. J. SAMUEL (Stockton-on-Tees): Mr. Speaker, I formally second the reduction of the Vote.

THE PRESIDENT OF THE BOARD OF TRADE (Mr. RITCHIE, Croydon): No one can doubt that the honourable Member has taken full advantage of the opportunity afforded him by the forms of the House, but I venture to think that if honourable Members generally who had criticisms to make were to take similar advantage it would be so intolerable as to render it necessary to take some action in the matter. I make no complaint whatever about being asked questions, but I do complain of the honourable Member having, without the slightest notice, challenged the Board of Trade on the whole administration of the Merchant Shipping Act. I decline at such an hour, without the adequate material with which I should have supplied myself if I had received notice, to traverse in detail all the statements and accusations which the honourable Member has put forth; but it must not

be assumed in consequence that I accept any of the figures or statements that have been made by him. The honourable Gentleman has raised questions with regard to the administration of the Merchant Shipping Act, the inspection of provisions, nautical surveyors, advance notes, the Conciliation Act, the manning of ships, and the accommodation of lascars. Surely, that is a Budget which might well afford ample scope for discussion at many sittings, and which cannot be debated in the course of a quarter of an hour, or even half an hour. I can only say that if the honourable Gentleman supplies me with particulars of the cases in which, in his opinion, the administration of the Merchant Shipping Act has fallen short of what he considers necessary, I will inquire into the matter. But I am bound to say, with regard to many statements which have been made by the honourable Member, that I have found in previous inquiries that the honourable Gentleman's accusations have been, if not baseless, grossly exaggerated.

*MR. HAVELOCK WILSON: I have over and over again supplied this information to the Board of Trade, and the right honourable Gentleman has inquired into them by sending them to the very people against whom I made the charges, which were, of course, denied.

THE PRESIDENT OF THE BOARD OF TRADE: The honourable Gentleman has made accusations against shipowners and against officials of the Board of Trade, and he seems to think it extraordinary that we should ask for an explanation from those accused. He desires to be free to make accusations, but he denies the right of those who are charged to answer those accusations. There are one or two matters to which I will refer. We have been in frequent communication with the Consul-General of New York, and only this week I authorised a letter to be sent to the Foreign Office answering in detail the statements made by the Consul-General. If the honourable Gentleman thinks that matters can be dealt with in a week or two he is greatly mistaken. I deprecate just as much as he does the action of crimps at New York, and I can assure him that everything is being done to put an end to the system of which he complains. As to the Board of Trade refusing an inquiry under the Conciliation Act at Glasgow, the Board of Trade have no right, and ought not, to interfere unless they believe that their interference will tend to a peaceful solution of the question in dispute, and what I have to consider is whether any interference on my part will do harm or good. I shall act on my own initiative, and must decline to act on the advice of the honourable Member unless I am satisfied that any action on my part will tend to a peaceful solution. With regard to the manning of ships, the honourable Member knows perfectly well that the only legislation which exists on this subject was passed by myself, and when he says the Manning Scale was issued without any instructions to those interested he is making a statement which is groundless.

*MR. HAVELOCK WILSON: I did not say that. What I did say was that the Scale was not in accordance with the views of the permanent officials of the Board of Trade.

THE PRESIDENT OF THE BOARD OF TRADE: The honourable Member said that if we had consulted anybody connected with the seafaring trade we should not have acted as we did. May I tell the honourable Gentleman that I did consult, not only those connected with the seafaring trade, but shipowners, and also the men.

*MR. HAVELOCK WILSON: The seamen were not consulted.

THE PRESIDENT OF THE BOARD OF TRADE: The seamen were consulted. The honourable Member professes to be the only representative of the sailors, but there are others in this House who know quite as much about them as he does, and there are those who repudiate him and his action. The only other point to which I will refer is the lascar question. Here again the House must not imagine that the honourable Gentleman appears as the representative of the lascars, because, although he no doubt conscientiously professes great interest in the welfare of lascar seamen, the latter are not only very content with their lot, but entirely repudiate the action which the honourable Member is taking on their behalf. They are quite content, and are extremely happy in their employment, and if the honourable Member is moving on their behalf he is doing so without their approval. How-

President of the Board of Trade.

ever, I am bound to acknowledge that, whether they are satisfied or not, the Board of Trade are bound to see that the Act of Parliament with regard to them and to other seamen is properly administered. The honourable Member says he knows the law much better than any official of the Board of Trade.

*MR. HAVELOCK WILSON: I did not say that.

THE PRESIDENT OF THE BOARD OF TRADE: He said I had maintained all along that the Act does not apply. This is purely a legal question, but the honourable Member professes to know exactly what the law is with regard to it. Lascars are dealt with under the Indian Act and the English Act. The Board of Trade have always disallowed tonnage in all ships, whether belonging to the P. and O. Company or not, which have not given the requisite space for the crews. Then comes the question whether we ought to prosecute for penalties. That is another question altogether, and it is an extremely difficult and complicated one. The honourable Gentleman says that my right honourable Friend the Pr'd t f the Board of Agriculture s a len o last year that the matter was under the consideration of the law officers of the Crown. I am sure my right honourable Friend said nothing of the kind. I have not got the volume of "Hansard" here, but if my right honourable Friend said the matter was under the consideration of the legal advisers of the Board of Trade he would have been saying what was incorrect. I have thought the matter so intricate and difficult that it ought to be considered by even higher legal authorities than the legal advisers of the Board of Trade. The matter is now under the consideration of the Attorney-General and the Solicitor-General, and we shall be guided by the opinion given to us by these Gentlemen. If it turns out that in their opinion the P. and O. Company or any other company is liable to penalties because of their action in respect to lascars, the Board of Trade will take action. The honourable Gentleman said that the figures supplied to me do not agree with the figures which have been ascertained by him. I cannot, of course, enter into the question of figures across the Table of the House without notice, but I must say that the figures quoted by the right honourable Gentleman are not at all in accord with the figures which have been supplied to me.

Question put—

"That '£14,781,000' stand part of the said Resolution."

The House divided:—Ayes 139; Noes 31.—(Division List No. 67.)

AYES.

Allhusen, Augustus H. Eden
Arnold, Alfred
Arnold-Forster, Hugh O.
Atkinson, Rt. Hon. John
Bagot, Capt. J. FitzRoy
Baird, John G. Alexander
Balfour, Rt.Hn.A.J. (Man.)
Banbury, Frederick George
Barton, Dunbar Plunket
Bathurst, Hn. Allen Benj.
Beach, Rt.Hn.Sir H.M.(Bris.)
Beckett, Ernest William
Bemrose, Sir Henry Howe
Bigwood, James
Bill, Charles
Bond, Edward
Brodrick, Rt.Hn St. John
Burdett-Coutts, W.
Butcher, John George
Cavendish, V.C.W.(Derbysh.)
Cecil, Lord H (Greenwich)
Chaloner, Capt. R. G. W.
Chamberlain,Rt.Hn J. (Bir.)
Chamberlain, J. A. (Worc'r)
Chaplin, Rt. Hn. Henry
Charrington, Spencer
Cochrane, Hn. T. H. A. E.
Cohen, Benjamin Louis
Collings, Rt. Hon. Jesse
Colomb, Sir John C. Ready
Compton, Lord Alwyne
Cooke, C. W. R. (Heref'd
Cornwallis, Fiennes S. W.
Curzon, Viscount
Dalrymple, Sir Charles
Davenport, W. Bromley-
Denny, Colonel
Dickson-Poynder, Sir J. P.
Disraeli, Coningsby Ralph
Dorington, Sir John Edward
Doughty, George
Douglas, Rt. Hn. A Akers
Doxford, William Theodore
Duncombe, Hn. Hubert V.
Egerton, Hn. A. de Tatton
Fardell, Sir T. George
Fisher, William Hayes
Fison, Frederick William

Fletcher, Sir Henry
Folkestone, Viscount
Fry, Lewis
Gedge, Sydney
Goldsworthy, Major-General
Gordon, Hn. John Edward
Gorst, Rt. Hn. Sir J. Eldon
Goschen, George J. (Sussex)
Gray, Ernest (West Ham)
Greene, H D. (Shrewsbury)
Gretton, John
Greville, Hon. Ronald
Gull, Sir Cameron
Hamilton, Rt. Hn. Lord G.
Hanbury, Rt. Hon. Robert W.
Hanson, Sir Reginald
Hare, Thomas Leigh
Heath, James
Henderson, Alexander
Hill, Sir Ed. Stock (Bristol)
Hobhouse, Henry
Holland, Hn. Lionel R. (Bow)
Jessel, Capt. Herbert Merton
Lafone, Alfred
Lees, Sir Elliott (Birkenhead)
Llewellyn, E. H. (Somerset)
Lockwood, Lt.-Col. A. R
Long, Rt. Hn W. (Liverpool)
Lorne, Marquess of
Lowe, Francis William
Lowles, John
Loyd, Archie Kirkman
Macartney, W. G. Ellison
Macdona, John Cumming
MacIver, David (Liverpool)
Maclure, Sir John Wm.
M'Arthur, Chas (Liverpool)
M'Iver, Sir L.(Edinburg,W)
Massey-Mainwaring,Hn.W.F.
Mellor, Colonel (Lancashire)
Middlemore, J. Throgmorton
Mildmay, Francis Bingham
Milward, Colonel Victor
More, Robt. J. (Shropshire)
Morrell, George Herbert
Murray, Rt. Hn. A. G. (Bute)
Nicholson, William Graham
Nicol, Donald Ninian

Orr-Ewing, Chas. Lindsay
Pease, H. Pike (Darlington)
Penn, John
Percy, Earl
Pilkington, Richard
Platt-Higgins, Frederick
Pollock, Harry Frederick
Pryce-Jones, Lt.-Col Ed.
Purvis, Robert
Pym, C. Guy
Rankin, Sir James
Richardson, Sir T. (Hartlep'l)
Ritchie, Rt.Hn. C. T. Thomson
Royds, Clement Molyneux
Russell, Gen. F.S. (Chelten'm)
Russell, T. W. (Tyrone)
Rutherford, John
Scoble, Sir Andrew Richard
Scott,Sir S.(Marylebone,W.)
Smith, Abel H (Christch.)
Smith, Samuel (Flint)
Smith, Hn.W.F.D. (Strand)
Stanley, Hon. A. (Ormskirk)
Stanley, Lord (Lancs.)
Stewart, Sir M. J. M'Taggart
Stock, James Henry
Stone, Sir Benjamin
Talbot, Lord E. (Chichester)
Thornton, Percy M.
Tollemache, Henry James
Valentia, Viscount
Wanklyn, James Leslie
Warde, Lieut.-Col. C.E.(Kent)
Warr, Augustus Frederick
Webster, R. G. (St. Pancras)
Webster,SirR.E.(Isle ofWight)
Wentworth, Bruce C. Vernon
Williams, Jos. Powell (Birm.)
Willox, Sir John Archibald
Wilson, John (Falkirk)
Wilson, J. W. (Worcester.N.)
Wodehouse,Rt.Hon.E.R.(Bath)
Wylie, Alexander

TELLERS FOR THE AYES—
  Sir William Walrond and
  Mr. Anstruther.

NOES.

Abraham, William (Rhondda)
Austin,Sir John (Yorkshire)
Caldwell, James
Clark, Dr. G. B. (Caithness-sh)
Douglas, Charles M. (Lanark)
Ellis, Thos.Ed. (Merioneth-sh.
Goddard, Daniel Ford
Gurdon, Sir William Brampton
Hayne,Rt. Hon.Charles Seale
Horniman, Frederick John
Jameson, Major J. Eustace
Jones, William (Carnarvonsh.

Kilbride, Denis
Lambert, George
Lawson,SirWilliam(Cumb'land
Lewis, John Herbert
Lloyd-George, David
Macaleese, Daniel
M'Kenna, Reginald
M'Leod, John
Morton, Edw.J.C.(Davenport)
Pirie, Duncan V.
Roberts, J. H. (Denbighs)
Samuel, J. (Stockton-on-Tees)

Shaw, Thomas (Hawick B.)
Stanhope, Hon. Philip J.
Sullivan, Donal (Westmeath)
Thomas, David A. (Merthyr)
Trevelyan, Charles Philips
Weir, James Galloway
Wilson, FrederickW.(Norfolk)

TELLERS FOR THE NOES—
  Mr. Havelock Wilson and
  Mr. John Wilson Durham).

Mr. LEWIS (Flint Boroughs): Mr. Speaker, my only object in intervening in the Debate is to give a practical illustration, drawn from my own constituency, of the injustice with which parents who desire to take the advantage of the Free Education Act or the conscience clause are treated. The circumstances of which I speak have occurred within the last few days. Mr. R. T. Price, a parent, residing in Flint, applied for a free place for his child in one of the National schools, there being no Board or British school in the town. On the 16th of February last he wrote to the rector of the parish, Rev. W. Ll. Nicholas, one of the managers of the Flint National schools, the following letter—

" Rev. Sir,—Having made an application to the head master of the above school for free schooling for my child, he gives me the information that your school is not a free school; therefore, it debars me from the right to free education for my children. I beg to ask you is the information received correct? If so, upon what grounds? An early reply will oblige."

That was a perfectly civil letter, containing no imputation on anyone. The rector replied as follows—

"Flint Rectory, February 17th, 1899.

" Sir,—A letter just reached me. It bears no date, and no address, but is signed by ' R. T. Price.' On inquiry I am led to the conclusion that it is written by you, the agent of one of the most respected of English Insurance Companies, and it is this that increases my wonder. You inform the managers that you wrote to Mr. E. I. H. Williams, the headmaster of our school, asking for certain information, and on receipt of his letter, you at once write to the managers practically accusing Mr. Williams of giving you wrong information. Such a charge against Mr. Williams, who bears the highest character for honesty and truth, reveals a baseness of mind that, in my opinion, unfits the writer for any consideration at the hands of the managers, who respect Mr. Williams as a gentleman, whose conduct has always been marked by straightforwardness.—On behalf of the managers, yours faithfully, W. Ll. Nicholas. To Mr. Price, Agent for the Prudential Society."

This is a strange letter for a clergyman to write to a parishioner who had made no reflection upon anyone. Mr. Price replied to this letter, disclaiming the least intention of reflecting upon Mr. Williams' character, and stating that he had written for an authoritative reply from the managers of the Flint National schools to his question whether it was a free school or not. The rector, writing him on the 20th February, informed him that three of the elementary schools in Flint are free schools, while in two others fees are charged in certain standards. Mr. Price then wrote to the rector asking him to state definitely what were the standards in which the managers could make a charge, and there, I believe, the correspondence ended. On the 25th February, Mr. Price received a letter from the Divisional Superintendent of the Prudential Assurance Company, stating that a complaint had gone up to the head office that Mr. Price had given serious offence in influential quarters by reason of his extreme conduct in political matters, and asking him to meet the superintendent at Flint on the following Monday. Mr. Price accordingly met the inspector on Monday, the 27th February. The subject of the conversation was Mr. Price's action in relation to the school, and the correspondence he had had with the rector of Flint. I do not know who it was who wrote the letter to the Prudential Insurance Company, but whoever wrote it, the House will readily understand the nature of the influences brought to bear against a parent who had dared to request that a free place should be provided for his child, and had asked to be informed of the grounds on which the managers refused a free place. I ask the Vice-President of the Council for a full inquiry into the circumstances connected with this correspondence. There is another point I wish to raise in connection with free education in the same place. Mr. Price's child did not bring the money for stationery, and was caned. I want to ask the right honourable Gentleman whether it is legal for a schoolmaster to inflict corporal punishment on a child because it did not bring twopence to pay for school stationery? Is the obligation on the parent or on the child? I now come to the case of parents who have withdrawn their children from denominational instruction. On the 1st of February last, Mr. John Williams, of Chester Street, Flint, wrote to the managers of the Flint National Schools asking that his boy and girl should be exempted from repeating or learning the Church of England Catechism, but stating that he had no objection to their receiving Scripture lessons. On the same day, the Rev. W. Ll. Nicholas, the rector of Flint, sent him a reply to the effect that his wishes would be strictly carried out. Mr. Nicholas's letter contained the following remarkable passage—

" This is the second letter you have sent to the Rectory, and on its receipt my mind could not help reverting to the time when you wrote your first letter, and I earnestly trust that a similar period of so much misery to your family and numerous friends may not follow the writing of this your second letter."

Subsequently, several parents withdrew their children from denominational instruction, and on the evening of Sunday, 19th February, the names and occupations of four of the parents who had withdrawn their children from denominational instruction were published from the parish pulpit. The publication of names in such a connection from the pulpit of the parish church could only have been intended to terrorise people from claiming their legal rights. It amounted to putting the parents named on a black list, and it was calculated to expose them to annoyance and loss. As a matter of fact, it has since then exposed them to considerable annoyance. In various parts of the country many illegitimate influences have been brought to bear on parents who wish to avail themselves of the protection conferred by the conscience clause. It is perfectly monstrous that the manager of a public elementary school should use his clerical position for the purpose of treating Nonconformist parents, who have acted strictly in accordance with their legal rights, in the way I have described, and I ask the Department to make a full inquiry into the circumstances of this case. I have shown that an attempt has been made by someone to prejudice Mr. R. T. Price in the eyes of his employers. That, unfortunately, does not appear to be the only case of that kind. Mr. S. Catherall, of Gladstone Terrace, Flint, on the 27th February, signed the following statement—

" Being a London and North Western Railway servant, and having requested the managers of the Flint National School not to teach my children any creed or catechism of the Church of England, the Rector, the Rev. W. Ll. Nicholas, interviews my station-master about my doing so, and at the same time stating his intention of writing to the Railway Company's headquarters, pointing out that he has saved the Railway Company many pounds by keeping the Board School out of Flint.—S. Catherall."

Now, that looks very like a case of interference with a workingman's employment, and I wish to know whether the Education Department or any other department, or arm of Government, have the power to protect parents in cases of this kind. If not, it is a state of things that calls for immediate action on the part of the Government. It is bad enough that parents in 7,000 or 8,000 parishes should have no voice in the local management of the public elementary school to which all alike are compelled to send their children, but when it comes to this, that parents can be denounced by name, and that people can be prejudiced in their means of getting a livelihood, it is time to ask what action the Government are going to take to protect parents in the quiet and peaceable enjoyment of their rights as citizens. On behalf of the parents in Flint who wish to take advantage of the conscience clause, I ask that the Government should make a searching and impartial inquiry into all the circumstances attending the withdrawal of the children, and that they should take such action as will enable parents in the future to exercise their legal rights without being subjected to annoyance or oppression.

Sir J. GORST (Cambridge University): When these matters were brought before the House the other day by the Member for Flint I stated that it was the settled policy of the Education Department to keep itself out of these local quarrels, and that I hoped they would do so in Flint. I am happy to say they have done so up to now, and I do not think the honourable Member will be able to draw the Department into taking sides for one party or the other. He asks me whether I think it was right for the rector of Flint to denounce parents from the pulpit because they had withdrawn their children from denominational teaching. That is a question upon which the Committee of Council have no information whatever. If there was any ground for supposing anybody had been intimidated, that would be a different question ; but, as these gentlemen who were denounced from the pulpit were themselves preachers, it is quite plain, however much they were irritated, they were not intimidated. It would be folly for the Education Department to assume episcopal functions, by censuring clergymen of the Church of England or any other church for their ecclesiastical conduct. The London and North Western Railway servant referred to was a man who, having two children at school, aged three and four respectively, desired that they should be withdrawn from religious instruction. I have no doubt the rector ought to have received that request with great meekness and consideration, but he appears to have made a confidant of the station-master, who was not the employer, and had no power to dismiss the man. The clergyman seems to have unbosomed his grief to the station-master, and to have told him how bad he thought the man to be. However, he made no representation to the railway company, the children were duly withdrawn from denominational instruction, and the father is as happy as he can be. The other case was one in which some angry letters seem to have passed. It is impossible for the Education Department to secure that all correspondence that takes place shall be conducted with perfect courtesy, and in the style of the " Perfect Letter-writer." These things do arise, and must settle themselves. It is not for a Department of State to meddle with them. The Education Department will not interfere in these ecclesiastical squabbles, but it will see that the law of the land is carried out. In the particular case referred to there had been a little temper shown on both sides, but nobody has been coerced or intimidated, and, if there had been no outside intervention, the whole squabble would, I believe, have settled itself very quickly. The case of the unfortunate child who was caned for not bringing its twopence for stationery is entirely new to me. I have never heard of it until this moment, and if the honourable Member will get the parent to make a formal complaint to the Education Department the matter will be inquired into.

Sir J. Gorst.

MR. LLOYD-GEORGE (Carnarvon): Mr. Speaker, I must say that, in my opinion, one of the worst features in the whole matter is the speech of the right honourable Gentleman himself. Here is a legal right claimed by citizens of this country, who, unfortunately, happen to be Nonconformists. They claim to have their children exempted from denominational teaching under the conscience clause, and are intimidated by the rector and manager of the school. The right honourable Gentleman says he has nothing whatever to do with that. Surely, it is one of the prime functions of the Education Department to see that the law is carried out in the letter and in the spirit. The right honourable Gentleman says there has been no intimidation. I say that to go to a man's employer in the way in which this rector has done is clearly to intimidate, and I contend that this matter ought to be inquired into by the Education Department. The right honourable Gentleman has evidently had some communication with the rector of the parish. He says it is not the business of the Education Department to take sides, but the right honourable Gentleman himself has taken a side, for he has accepted the statement made by the rector of the parish without any investigation. A working man, although he may be a Nonconformist lay preacher, has as much right to have his word taken as has the rector of the parish, until, at any rate, there is an investigation into the matter. The letters which have been referred to by my honourable Friend prove that the rector has absolutely no control over his feelings or his emotions when excited. When we raised the question of the treatment of Nonconformists in schools the question was asked, " How is it they do not avail themselves of the conscience clause?" This is our answer. Whenever there is a demand made to avail ourselves of the conscience clause there is intimidation on the part of the managers. This Debate has had one good effect. Honourable Members opposite received the support of thousands of Nonconformists in this country at the last election, and we shall not cease to remind Nonconformists throughout the country that when they have legitimate grievances which are not denied as far as the facts are concerned, and when those grievances are brought before the House of Commons, they are met by the laughter and the contempt of the Minister whom they helped to return and place in his present position, and also by the jeers of honourable Members opposite who have been returned to this House largely through the support accorded them by Nonconformists. We do not bring this matter forward because we expect redress, for never has the right honourable Gentleman really attempted to do justice to Nonconformists.

MR. WEIR (Ross and Cromarty): I rise to draw attention to a matter of very great importance to my constituency. It is with reference to a dog licence. I have tried to get information on the subject, and have written numerous letters to the Chairman of the Board of Inland Revenue, but without result. The case is as follows: A spinster who resides in Ross-shire owns a cow and two heifers. The Excise Act of 1878 definitely states that every per-

son who owns cattle or sheep is entitled to keep a dog for the purpose of attending them without paying a licence, but this poor woman is compelled to pay. She signed a sworn information that she kept the dog for the purpose of attending to the cattle, and I have forwarded this to the Secretary of the Board of Inland Revenue. I was told there was no reason why the dog should not be taxed. The next-door neighbour to this woman has obtained exemption from taxation in respect of her dog, and I am told that her dog is not qualified to receive exemption. The question I wish to put is a very natural question—namely, What is the test as to whether a dog is qualified for exemption or not? This is a serious matter to a poor crofter. I want to know how it is the Board of Inland Revenue do not abide by the statute, which distinctly states that a person keeping cattle or sheep is entitled to keep a dog to look after them without paying a licence.

Question put—

"That this House doth agree with the Committee in the said Resolution."

The House divided:—Ayes, 134; Noes, 32.—(Division List No. 68.)

AYES.

Allhusen, Augustus Henry E.
Arnold, Alfred
Arnold-Forster, Hugh O.
Atkinson, Rt. Hon. John
Bagot, Capt. Josceline FitzRoy
Baird, John George Alexander
Balfour, Rt.Hon.A.J.(Manch'r
Banbury, Fredrick George
Barton, Dunbar Plunket
BathurstHon.Allen Benjamin
Beach,Rt.Hn.Sir M.H.(Bristol)
Beckett, Ernest William
Bigwood, James
Bond,Edward
Brodrick,Rt.Hon.St.John
Burdett-Coutts, W.
Butcher, John George
Cavendish,V.C.W.(Derbyshire
Cecil, Lord Hugh (Greenwich)
Chaloner, Captain R.G.W.
Chamberlain Rt.Hon.J.(Birm.)

Chamberlain,J.Austen(Worc'r)
Chaplin, Rt. Hon. Henry
Charrington, Spencer
Cochrane, Hon.Thos. H.A.E.
Cohen, Benjamin Lewis
Collings, Rt. Hon. Jesse
Colomb, Sir John Chas. Ready
Compton, Lord Alwyne
Cooke,C.W.Ratcliffe(Heref'd)
Cornwallis, Fiennes Stanley W
Curzon, Viscount
Dalrymple, Sir Charles
Davenport, W. Bromley-
Denny, Colonel
Dickenson-Poynder, Sir J.P.
Disraeli, Coningsby Ralph
Dorington. Sir John Edward
Doughty, George
Douglas, Rt. Hon. A.Akers-
Doxford, William Theodore
Duncombe, Hon. Hubert V.

Egerton, Hon.A. de Tatton
Fardell, Sir T. George
Fisher, William Hayes
Fison, Frederick Wiliam
Fletcher, Sir Henry
Folkestone, Viscount
Gedge, Sydney
Goldsworthy, Major-General
Gordon, Hon. John Edward
Gorst, Rt. Hon. Sir John Eldon
Goschen, George J. (Sussex)
Gray, Ernest (West Ham)
Greene,Henry D.(Shrewsbury)
Gretton, John
Greville, Hon. Ronald
Gull, Sir Cameron
Hamilton,Rt.Hon.Lord George
Hanbury,Rt.Hon.Robert Wm.
Hanson, Sir Reginald
Hare, Thomas Leigh
Heath, James

Henderson, Alexander
Hill, Sir Edward S. (Bristol)
Hobhouse, Henry
Holland, Hon. Lionel R. (Bow)
Jessel, Captain Herbert Merton
Lafone, Alfred
Lees, Sir Elliott(Birkenhead)
Llewellyn, Evan H. (Somerset)
Lockwood, Lt.-Col. A. R.
Long,Rt.Hon.Walter(Liverp'l)
Lorne, Marquess of
Lowe, Francis William
Lowles, John
Loyd, Archie Kirkman
Macartney, W. G. Ellison
Macdona, John Cumming
MacIver, David (Liverpool)
Maclure, Sir John William
M'Arthur, Charles (Liverpool)
M'Iver,SirLewis(Edinburgh,W
Massey-Mainwaring, H. W.F.
Mellor, Colonel (Lancashire)
Middlemore,John Throgmorton
Mildmay, Francis Bingham
Milward, Colonel Victor

More, Robert J. (Shropshire)
Morrell, George Herbert
Murray,Rt.H.A.Graham(Bute)
Nicholson, William Graham
Nicol, Donald Ninian
Orr-Ewing, Charles Lindsay
Pease,HerbertPike(Darlington)
Penn, John
Percy, Earl
Platt-Higgins, Frederick
Pollock, Harry Frederick
Pryce-Jones, Lt.-Col. Edward
Purvis, Robert
Pym, C. Guy
Rankin, Sir James
Richardson,Sir Thos.(Hartle'l
Ritchie,Rt.Hn.Chas.Thomson
Royds, Cement Molyneux
Russell, Gen. F. S.(Cheltenham
Russell, T W. (Tyrone)
Rutherford, John
Scoble, Sir Andrew Richard
Scott, Sir S. (Marylebone, W.)
Smith, Abel H. (Christchurch)
Smith, Hn. W. F. D. (Strand)

Stanley,Hon.Arthur(Ormskirk
Stanley, Lord (Lancs.)
Stewart,Sir Mark J. M'Taggart
Stock, James Henry
Stone, Sir Benjamin
Talbot, Lord E. (Chichester)
Thornton, Percy M.
Tollemache, Henry James
Valentia, Viscount
Wanklyn, James Leslie
Warde, Lieut.-Col. C. E.(Kent)
Warr, Augustus Frederick
Webster, R. G. (St. Pancras)
Webster,SirR.E.(Isle of Wight
Wentworth, Bruce C. Vernon-
Williams,Joseph Powell-(Birm.
Willox, Sir John Archibald
Wilson, John (Falkirk)
Wilson, J. W. (Worcestersh. N.
Wodehouse,Rt.Hon.E.R.(Bath)
Wylie, Alexander

TELLERS FOR THE AYES—
Sir William Waldrond and
Mr. Anstruther.

NOES.

Abraham, William (Rhondda)
Austin, Sir John (Yorkshire)
Bill, Charles
Caldwell, James
Clark, Dr. G. B. (Caithness-sh)
Douglas, Charles M. (Lanark)
Ellis, Thos. Edw.(Merionethsh-
Goddard, Daniel Ford
Gurdon, Sir William Brampton
Hayne, Rt. Hon. Charles Seale-
Horniman, Frederick John
Kilbride, Denis

Lambert George
Lawson,Sir Wilfrid (Cumb'land
Lloyd-George, David
Macaleese, Daniel
M'Kenna, Reginald
M'Leod, John
Morton, Ed. J. C.(Davenport)
Pilkington, Richard
Pirie, Duncan V.
Roberts, John H. (Denbighs)
Samuel, J. (Stockton-on-Tees)
Shaw, Thomas (Hawick B.)

Stanhope, Hon. Philip J.
Sullivan, Donal (Westmeath)
Thomas, David A. (Merthyr)
Trevelyan, Charles Philips
Weir, James Galloway
Wilson,Frederick W.(Norfolk
Wilson, John (Durham, Mid.)
Wilson,Jos.H.(Middlesboro'

TELLERS FOR THE NOES—
Mr. Herbert Lewis and
Mr. William Jones.

Resolution agreed to.

REPORT OF WAYS AND MEANS.

WAYS AND MEANS [20th MARCH].

Resolutions reported—

"That, towards making good the Supply granted to Her Majesty for the service of the years ending on the 31st day of March 1898 and 1899, the sum of £1,860,115 5s. 1d. be granted out of the Consolidated Fund of the United Kingdom."

"That, towards making good the Supply granted to Her Majesty for the service of the year ending on the 31st day of March 1900, the sum of £29,596,900 be granted out of the Consolidated Fund of the United Kingdom."

Resolutions agreed to.

Bill ordered to be brought in upon the said Resolutions by Mr. James William Lowther, Mr. Chancellor of the Exchequer, and Mr. Hanbury.

CONSOLIDATED FUND (NO. 1) BILL.

" To apply certain sums out of the Consolidated Fund to the service of the years ending on the thirty-first day of March one thousand eight hundred and ninety-eight, one thousand eight hundred and ninety-nine, and one thousand nine hundred." Presented accordingly, and read the first time ; to be read a second time upon this day at Twelve of the clock.

ARMY (ANNUAL) BILL.

Second Reading deferred till this day.

COLONIAL LOANS FUND BILL.

Second Reading deferred till Thursday.

INEBRIATES ACT (1898) AMENDMENT BILL.

Second Reading deferred till Thursday.

METROPOLITAN STREETS ACT (1867) AMENDMENT BILL.

Second Reading deferred till Monday 10th April.

SMALL HOUSES (ACQUISITION OF OWNERSHIP) BILL.

Second Reading deferred till Monday 10th April.

WILD BIRDS PROTECTION BILL.

Second Reading deferred till Monday next.

PLACES OF WORSHIP (LEASEHOLD ENFRANCHISEMENT BILL.

Second Reading deferred till Tuesday next.

SALE OF FOOD AND DRUGS BILL.

Adjourned Debate on Motion for Committal to Standing Committee on Trade, etc. (9th March) further adjourned till Monday next.

TELEGRAPHS (TELEPHONIC COMMUNICATION, ETC.) BILL.

Second Reading deferred till Monday 10th April.

CHARITABLE LOANS (IRELAND) BILL.

Second Reading deferred till Monday next.

IMPROVEMENT OF LAND BILL.

Second Reading deferred till Monday next.

PALATINE COURT OF DURHAM [H.L.]

Second Reading deferred till Thursday.

SOLICITORS BILL [H.L.]

Second Reading deferred till Thursday.

TELEGRAPH (CHANNEL ISLANDS) BILL [H.L.]

Second Reading deferred till Thursday.

UNIVERSITIES (SCOTLAND) ACTS AMENDMENT BILL.

Adjourned Debate on Second Reading (9th March) further adjourned till Thursday.

LICENSING EXEMPTION (HOUSES OF PARLIAMENT) BILL.

Adjourned Debate on Second Reading (23rd February) further adjourned till Thursday.

ELECTRIC LIGHTING (CLAUSES) BILL.

Second Reading deferred till Thursday.

ANCHORS AND CHAIN CABLES BILL.

Second Reading deferred till Thursday.

PRIVATE LEGISLATION PROCEDURE (SCOTLAND) BILL.

Second Reading deferred till Monday next.

POOR LAW OFFICERS' SUPERANNUATION (SCOTLAND) BILL.

Second Reading deferred till Wednesday 26th April.

SUPERANNUATON (METROPOLIS) BILL.
Second Reading deferred till Tuesday 25th April.

SALE OF INTOXICATING LIQUORS ON SUNDAY BILL.
Second Reading deferred till Thursday 13th April.

SEATS FOR SHOP ASSISTANTS (SCOTLAND) BILL.
Second Reading deferred till Thursday.

ADULTERATION (FOOD PRODUCTS) BILL.
Second Reading deferred till Wednesday 12th April.

LOCAL GOVERNMENT ACT (1888) AMENDMENT BILL.
Second Reading deferred till Monday next.

POOR LAW OFFICERS' SUPERANNUATION ACT (1896) AMENDMENT BILL.
Second Reading deferred till Thursday 13th April.

WATER SUPPLY BILL.
Second Reading deferred till Tuesday 18th April.

OYSTERS BILL.
Second Reading deferred till Monday 10th April.

AGRICULTURAL HOLDINGS BILL.
Second Reading deferred till Tuesday 11th April.

INFECTIOUS DISEASE (NOTIFICATON) ACT (1889) EXTENSION BILL.
Second Reading deferred till Friday.

CHEAP TRAINS BILL.
Second Reading deferred till Wednesday 12th April.

COURT OF CRIMINAL APPEAL BILL.
Second Reading deferred till Monday 10th April.

SALE OF NTOXICATING LIQUORS (IRELAND) BILL.
Second Reading deferred till Monday 1st May.

SUMMARY JURISDICTION ACT (1879) AMENDMENT BILL.
Third Reading deferred till this day.

COLONIAL SOLICITORS BILL.
Second Reading deferred till Monday next.

PARISH COUNCILLORS (TENURE OF OFFICE) BILL.
Committee deferred till this day.

House adjourned at twenty-five minutes after Two of the clock.

INDEX

TO

THE PARLIAMENTARY DEBATES

(AUTHORISED EDITION).

THIRD VOLUME OF SESSION 1899.

MARCH 7—MARCH 21.

EXPLANATIONS OF ABBREVIATIONS.

Bills = Read First, Second, or Third Time = 1R., 2R., 3R.   [*c.*] = Commons. [*l.*] = Lords.   Os. = Observations.   Qs. = Questions.   As. = Answers. Com. = Committee. Con. = Consideration. Rep. = Report. Where in the Index * is added to the Reading of a Bill it indicates that no Debate took place upon that stage of the Measure.

VOL. LXVIII.   [FOURTH SERIES.]   3 X

ARMY—cont.
　Volunteer Artillery Armaments
　　Q. Mr. Wanklyn; A. Mr. J. Powell
　　Williams, 1314
　Volunteer Rifle Ranges
　　Q. Mr. Monk; A. Mr. G. Wyndham,
　　985
　Warrant Officers' Grievances
　　Q. Mr. Jeffreys; A. Mr. J. Powell
　　Williams, 1309
　West African Frontier Force, Os. 474
　West Indian Regiment, Os. 473

ARMY (ANNUAL) BILL
　c. 1R* 1288

ARMY ESTIMATES
　1899-1900
　　Com., 1106, 1161
　Qs. Sir C. Dilke; As. Mr. A. J. Balfour.
　　Os. Mr. Deputy Speaker (Mr. J. W.
　　Lowther), Mr. Caldwell, and Mr.
　　Pirie, 449
　Chelsea and Kilmainham Hospitals
　　£1,325,500 — Meritorious Services,
　　　Victoria Cross Pensions, etc.—
　　　Com., 1285; Rep., 1470
　　Motion for Reduction (Mr. Caldwell),
　　　1285
　　Governor's Salary
　　　Motion for Reduction (Mr. Weir),
　　　1483
　Chinese Regiment
　　Motion for Reduction (Mr. Caldwell),
　　　1252
　Miscellaneous Expenses
　　Motion for Reduction (Mr. Courtenay
　　　Warner), 1258
　Ordnance Factories
　　Estimate, 1899-1900
　　　Estimate Presented, 942
　　Excess, 1897-98, copy presented of
　　　Statement, 263
　　Excess Vote—£100—Com., 508;
　　　Rep., 660
　Pay, Allowances, etc.
　　Vote—£6,509,000—Com., 790, 1161;
　　　Rep., 1469
　　Motions for Reduction (Mr. Pirie),
　　　1240; (Mr. Courtenay Warner),
　　　1161; (Mr. Weir), 1256, 1470
　Recruits and Recruiting
　　Motion for Reduction (Mr. Weir), 790;
　　　(Mr. Courtenay Warner), 835
　Retired Pay, Half Pay, and other Non-
　　Effective Charges for Officers and
　　others
　　£1,555,000—Com., 1263; Rep., 1470
　　Motion for Reduction (Dr. Clark),
　　　1475; (Mr. Courtenay Warner),
　　　1276
　Superannuation, Compensation, etc.
　　£183,700—Com., 1287; Rep., 1470
　Vote for Men
　　184,853—Rep., 1106, 1288

ARNOLD-FORSTER, Mr. H. O. [Belfast, W.]
　"Admiral" Class of Battleships, 969
　Cavalry Enlistments, 1332
　Navy Estimates, 628, 655
　Supply
　　Navy Estimates, 1899-1900, 3rd
　　　Allotted Day, Considered in
　　　Committee, 1003
　Telegraph Way-Leaves in Belfast, 271

ARRAN ISLANDS, POLLING ON
　Q. Mr. Dillon; A. Mr. G. Balfour, 977

ARTILLERY, ROYAL, FIELD BATTERIES
　Q. Major Rasch; A. Mr. G. Wyndham.
　　526
　Q. Mr. Wanklyn; A. Mr. J. Powell
　　Williams, 1314

ASCROFT, Mr. R. [Oldham]
　Navigation on Chinese Inland Waters, 772
　Punishment for Train Wrecking, 978
　Sale of Food and Drugs Bill, 383
　Service Franchise Bill, 202
　Water Gas, 444

ASHMEAD-BARTLETT, Sir E. [Sheffield,
　　Ecclesall]
　Alleged Murder of Mr. Edgar, 18
　Barristers in the Transvaal, 19
　Boer Government and the South African
　　League, 28
　China and the Powers, 1328
　Chinese Northern Railway Extension
　　Loan, 445
　Chinese Territory (Demands of Italy)
　　Motion for Adjournment, 543
　Erythrea, 530
　France and the Nile Valley, 980
　Muscat, 291
　Navy Estimates, Os., 644
　Russian Protest at Pekin, 291
　Supply
　　Civil Services and Revenue Depart-
　　　ments (Supplementary Estimates),
　　　1898-99, 453
　　Colonial Vote and South Africa, 1348
　　Navy Estimates, 1899-1900, 3rd
　　　Allotted Day, Considered in
　　　Committee, 1044
　　Supplementary, Colonial Office, 465
　Waima Incident, 984

ASQUITH, Mr. H. H. [Fife, E.]
　London Government Bill, 1599
　Supply
　　Navy Estimates, the First Lord of the
　　　Admiralty's Statement, 325
　The Circulation of the Estimates, 38

ASSAM
　Labour Immigration into
　　Q. Mr. Schwann; A. Lord G. Hamil-
　　ton, 282

[Continued

[Continue·

CHANNING, Mr. F. A. [Northampton, E.]
Business of the House
(Government Business), Precedence,
553, 558
Navy Estimates, 638
Primary Education (England and Wales),
92
St. James's School, Northampton, 30
South Eastern and London, Chatham,
and Dover Railway Companies Bill,
695
Tuberculosis, 837

CHAPLAINS, NAVAL
Q. Mr. Carvell Williams; A. Mr. W. E.
Macartney, 1135

CHAPLIN, Mr. H. [Lincolnshire, Sleaford]—
President of the Local Government
Board
Compulsory Purchase of Property for
Railways, 1322
Contaminated Oysters, 767
Cubic Space in Registered Common Lodg-
ing Houses, 34
East London Water Bill (By Order), 1522
East London Water (Temporary Supply)
Bill (By Order), 1524
Hanwell and Southall Schools, 769
Loans under the Small Holdings Act, 1560
Local Government Audit Districts, 33
Local Rating, 767
London Water (Welsh Reservoirs and
Works) Bill, 1543
Metropolis Water Bill, 31
Metropolitan Water Companies Bill, 406,
1526
Protection of Water Supplies, 1558
Rivers Pollution Prevention Bill, 239
Vaccination Blue Books, 973
Vaccination Exemption Certificates, 1570

CHARITIES, ENDOWED CHARITIES, Etc.
Anglesey
Inquiries Held (Return), 168
Inquiry into Charities (County of Lan-
caster) (Return), 431
London
Return, 168
Norfolk
Return, 168

CHARITY COMMISSIONERS
Reports, and Swansea County Borough
(Inquiry into Charities) and Cardiff
County Borough (Inquiry into Chari-
ties), Return, 168

CHARLEMONT AND MOY PETTY SES-
SIONS CLERKS
Q. Mr. Macaleese; A. Mr. Gerald Bal-
four, 1139

CHEKEANG AND ITALY
Q. Mr. Yerburgh; A. Mr. Brodrick, 1311

CHELSEA HOSPITAL
Supply
Os. 1483

CHILDREN
Juvenile Vagrancy
Petition, 13
Sale of Intoxicating Liquors to
Petition, 14
Vagrant Children Relieved (Return
Ordered), 944

CHINA
Agreements
Q. Mr. Moon; A. Mr. Brodrick, 272
Army Estimates
Os. 807, 813, 1248
Belgium
Q. Mr. Moon; A. Mr. Brodrick, 279
Correspondence respecting Affairs, 512
Eastern Railway Company
Q. Mr. Moon; A. Mr. Brodrick, 273
England and Russia in
Q. Mr. Yerburgh; A. Mr. Brodrick,
41
Great Britain and Italy's Demands
Q. Mr. Dillon; A. Mr. Brodrick,
1321
Great Britain's Pledges
Qs. Mr. Yerburgh and Mr. Gibson
Bowles; A. Mr. Brodrick, 294
Italy and
Qs. Mr. Pritchard Morgan; A. Mr.
Brodrick, 269
Q. Mr. Dillon; A. Mr. Brodrick,
1319
Italy and Chekeang
Q. Mr. Yerburgh; A. Mr. Brodrick,
1311
Navigation on Inland Waters
Q. Mr. Ascroft; A. Mr. Brodrick, 772
Northern Railway Extension Loan
Qs. Sir E. Ashmead-Bartlett; As.
Mr. Brodrick, 445
Papers on
Q. Commander Bethell; A. Mr.
A. J. Balfour, 39
Powers
Q. Sir E. Ashmead-Bartlett; A. Mr.
Brodrick, 1328
Russian Protest at Pekin
Qs. Sir E. Ashmead-Bartlett; As.
Mr. Brodrick, 291
Soldiers in British Service
Q. Mr. Dillon; A. Mr. Brodrick,
954
Supply, 1393
Talienwan
Q. Mr. Provand; A. Mr. Brodrick,
38
Trade Depôts in
Q. Mr. Yerburgh; A. Mr. Brodrick,
769
Troops
Os. Army Estimates, 1248

CHINESE SOLDIERS IN BRITISH
SERVICE
Q. Mr. Dillon; A. Mr. Brodrick, 954

CHINESE TERRITORY
Demands of Italy
Motion for Adjournment, 539

CONTAGIOUS DISEASES

Civil Services (Supplementary Estimates)
Os. 486

Disease among Indian Troops
' Q. Major Rasch; A. Lord G. Hamilton, 1316

East India, Petition, 13

Indian Troops
Q. Major Rasch; A. Lord G. Hamilton, 300

CONTAMINATED OYSTERS
Q. Mr. Loder; A. Mr. H. Chaplin, 767

CONTRACTS
[Government Contracts, see that Title]

CONVICTIONS FOR ILLEGAL TRAWLING IN SCOTTISH WATERS
Qs. Mr. Weir, Mr. Pirie; As. Mr. G. Murray; Os. Mr. Speaker, 522

CORK

Army Doctors, 1207

Bigamy Trial at the Assizes
Q. Mr. T. M. Healy; A. Mr. Gerald Balfour, 1150

Blarney Mail Car
Q. Mr. D. Sullivan; A. Mr. Hanbury, 1309

City By-Law's
Qs. Mr. W. Johnston, Mr. Crean, and Mr. Flynn; As. Mr. Gerald Balfour; Os. Mr. Speaker, 1564

Corporation By-laws
Qs. Mr. W. Johnston and Captain Donelan; As. Mr. Gerald Balfour, 1135

Registration in Ireland
Qs. Dr. Tanner; A. Mr. G. Balfour, 524

CORK   AND   BANDON   RAILWAY, FREIGHT RATES
Q. Mr. Gilhooly; A. Mr. Ritchie, 1134

CORNWALLIS, Mr. F. S. W. [Maidstone]
Protection of Water Supplies, 1558

CORPORATION BY-LAWS, CORK
Qs. Mr. W. Johnston and Captain Donelan; As. Mr. Gerald Balfour, 1135

CORRESPONDENCE RESPECTING AFFAIRS
China No. 1 (1899), 512
West Indies, 322

COST OF PRIVATE BILL LEGISLATION
Qs. Mr. D. A. Thomas; As. Mr. J. Collings, 1148

COUNTERVAILING SUGAR DUTIES IN INDIA
Qs. Mr. McKenna, Sir H. Fowler, and Mr. Courtney; As. Lord George Hamilton, 1140
Qs. Mr. McKenna and Mr. O'Kelly; A. Mr. A. J. Balfour, 1331

COUNTY CESS, IRELAND

Longford Collector
Q. Mr. Kilbride; A. Mr. G. Balfour, 289

COUNTY   COUNCILLORS   (QUALIFICATION OF WOMEN) (SCOTLAND) BILL
c. 1R° 920

COUNTY COURT FEES
Qs. Sir C. Dilke; As. Mr. Hanbury, 16, 1309

COUNTY COURT JUDGE LEONARD
Q. Mr. P. O'Brien; A. Sir R. Webster. 1329

COUPLINGS, AUTOMATIC
Qs. Mr. Maddison and Mr. Coghill; A. Mr. Ritchie; O. Mr. Speaker, 1147
Q. Mr. Tennant; A. Mr. Ritchie, 1334

COURTNEY, Mr. L. H. [Cornwall, Bodmin]
Business of the House (Government Business), Precedence, 564
Chinese Territory (Demands of Italy), Motion for Adjournment, 548
Countervailing Sugar Duties in India, 1141
Supply
Navy Estimates, the First Lord of the Admiralty's Statement, 329

COWDENBEATH, PROVOST MUNGALL, OF
Qs. Mr. Weir; A. Mr. A. G. Murray, 771

CRANBORNE, Viscount [Rochester]
Primary Education (England and Wales), 116
Supply
Navy Estimates, 1899-1900, Third Allotted Day, Considered in Committee, 1047

CREAN, Mr. E. [Queen's County, Ossory]
City of Cork By-Laws, 1564

CRETE
Navy Estimates, 601

◄ ►

GOURLEY, Sir E. [Sunderland]
Apprentices in the Mercantile Marine, 780
Supply
Navy Estimates, 1899-1900, 3rd Allotted Day, Considered in Committee, 1050

GOVERNMENT BUSINESS
Course of
Qs. Mr. E. Robertson and Sir C. Cameron; As. Mr. A. J. Balfour; O. Mr. Speaker, 36

GOVERNMENT CONTRACTS IN INDIA
Q. Sir W. Wedderburn; A. Lord G. Hamilton, 963

GOVERNMENT GRANTS FOR LOCAL EXPENDITURE
Q. Mr. Gibson Bowles; A. Mr. Ritchie, 1144

GRAND JURIES
Q. Mr. O'Keeffe; A. Mr. Gerald Balfour, 1569

GRAND JURY CONTRACTS, IRELAND
Q. Mr. Tully; A. Mr. Gerald Balfour, 970

GRAND JURY PRESENTMENTS (IRELAND)
Copies Presented of Presentments, 14, 248

GRAY, Mr. E. [W   N.]
Petroleum Bil,st Ham,
Primary Educatio20(England and Wales), '90

GREAT BRITAIN AND ITALY'S DEMANDS IN CHINA
Q. Mr. Dillon; A. Mr. Brodrick, 1321

GREAT BRITAIN'S PLEDGES TO CHINA
Qs. Mr. Yerburgh and Mr. Gibson Bowles; A. Mr. Brodrick, 294

GREAT EASTERN RAILWAY EMPLOYEES
Q. Mr. Sinclair; A. Mr. Ritchie, 949

GREAT GRIMSBY STREET TRAMWAYS BILL
Committed: The Committee to be proposed by the Committee of Selection, 426
Opposition withdrawn, and Committed, 510

GREAT SOUTHERN AND WESTERN, AND WATERFORD, LIMERICK, AND WESTERN RAILWAY COMPANIES AMALGAMATION BILL
c. 2R, 723

GREAT SOUTHERN AND WESTERN RAILWAY BILL
c. 2R* 762

GREAT YARMOUTH CORPORATION BILL
Com., 3
Report, 921

GREAT YARMOUTH PIER BILL
Com., 3
Witness ordered to attend Select Committee, 509
The Queen's Consent signified; and Bill reported from the Select Committee with Amendments, 1292

GREEN AND HYDE PARKS
Q. Colonel Welby; A. Mr. Collings, 770

GREENE, Mr. H. D. [Shrewsbury]
Licences on Hearses and Wheel Biers, 289

GREVILLE, Captain R. [Bradford, E.]
Bradford Tramways and Improvement Bill, 681
Rivers Pollution Prevention Bill, 237

GREY, Sir E. [Northumberland, Berwick]
Chinese Territory (Demands of Italy)
Motion for Adjournment, 549
Supply
China, 1443

GROUND RENTS (TAXATION BY LOCAL AUTHORITIES)
Petition, 166

GROUND VALUES (TAXATION) (SCOTLAND) BILL
c. 1R* 16

GUINEA, NEW BRITISH
Q. Mr. Hogan; A. Mr. J. Chamberlain, 21

GULL, Sir CAMERON [Devon, Barnstaple]
Education in Rural Districts, 526

GUNTER, Colonel R. [York, W.R., Barkston Ash]
Dog Muzzling in Yorkshire, 961

HEALY, Mr. T. M. [Louth, N.]
Bigamy Trial at the Cork Assizes, 1150
Bishopric of Madagascar, 982
Cyclists in Phœnix Park, 960
Dublin Excise Officers, 960
Frauds in the Dublin Excise Warehouse, 960
Great Southern and Western, and Waterford, Limerick, and Western Railway Companies Amalgamation Bill, 760
Irish Judicature Act, 982
Petroleum Bill, 910

HEARSES AND WHEEL BIERS, LICENCES ON
Q. Mr. H. D. Greene; A. Sir M. Hicks Beach, 289

HEATON, Mr. J. H. [Canterbury]
Delagoa Railway Arbitration, 284

HEDDERWICK, Mr. T. C. H. [Wick Burghs]
North Sea Fishery Commission, 983
Orkney Land Tax, 267
Service Franchise Bill, 205
Supply
    Civil Services and Revenue Departments (Supplementary Estimates), 1898-99, 465
" Tourmaline," 950
Waima Incident, 983

HENEAGE, Lord
Lincolnshire Coroners Bill, 1294

HEREFORD, Lord JAMES of
Lincolnshire Coroners Bill, 1296
Money Lending Bill, 926

HER MAJESTY'S SHIP " BRENDA," 1459

HICKS BEACH, Sir M. [Bristol, W.]—
    Chancellor of the Exchequer
British and French Trade, 987
Death Duties, 1566
Dublin Excise Officers, 960
Ex-Lord Chancellors' Pensions, 436
Frauds in the Dublin Excise Warehouse, 961
Friendly Societies and the Land Tax, 974
Inland Revenue Inquiries, 1568
Inland Revenue Officials and Irish Local Government, 537
Inland Revenue Procedure in Scotland, 1567
Licences on Hearses and Wheel Biers, 290
Penzance, Lord, 438
Post Office Savings Bank, 17
Workmen's Compensation Act, Insurances, 969

HIGH SHERIFFS' (IRELAND) EXPENSES OF OFFICE
Copy presented of Circular, 167, 248

HIGHLANDS AND ISLANDS OF SCOTLAND
Crofters and the Dog Tax
    Q. Mr. Weir; A. Mr. Hanbury, 1143
Deer Forests
    Q. Mr. Weir; A. Mr. Graham Murray, 779
Island of Lewis, Fisheries
    Qs. Mr. Weir; As. Mr. Graham Murray, 1137

HIGHWAYS AND BRIDGES ACT (1891) AMENDMENT BILL
c. 1R* 1133

HILL, Sir E. [Bristol, S.]
Petroleum Bill, 880

HILLTOWN (CO. DOWN) TELEGRAPH OFFICE
Q. Mr. McCartan; A. Mr. Hanbury, 20

HOBHOUSE, Mr. H. [Somerset, E.]
Business of the House
    (Government Business), Precedence, 560

HOGAN, Mr. J. F. [Tipperary, Mid]
British New Guinea, 21
Germany and the Caroline Islands, 968
Old Age Pensions in New Zealand, 968
Public Road in County Tipperary, 19
Samoa, 969

HOLLAND, Mr. L. R. [Tower Hamlets, Bow]
London Government Bill, 1619

HOLYHEAD AND KINGSTOWN PIERS
Q. Mr. P. O'Brien; A. Mr. Hanbury, 962

HOLYWOOD PETTY SESSIONS CLERK
Q. Mr. Macaleese; A. Mr. G Balfour, 1149

HOSPITALS
St. Bartholomew, Oxford
    Q. Mr. Morrell; A. Mr. Grant Lawson, 23
Workhouse Nurses (Ireland)
    Q. Dr. Tanner; A. Mr. G. Balfour, 777

HOUSES OF PARLIAMENT
Resident Engineer to
    Q. Mr. Hazell; A. Mr. Hanbury, 439

[*Contin··· *

IRELAND—*cont.*

Roman Catholic University Petition, 166

Roscommon Local Government Elections
Q. Mr. Dillon; A. Mr. Gerald Balfour, 1136

Royal Irish Constabulary, Promotion in
Q. Mr. Macaleese; A. Mr. G. Balfour, 285

St. Clement's Church, Belfast
Qs. Mr. Dillon; As. Mr. Gerald Balfour, 26, 299, 954, 1320
Q. Mr. Young; A. Mr. G. Balfour, 529, 775

Sales under Section 40 of the Land Law Act, 1896
Q. Mr. Ffrench; A. Mr. Gerald Balfour, 971

Shannon Development Company
Q. Mr. P. O'Brien; A. Mr. G. Balfour, 1141

Stoney, Mr. Vesey
Q. Dr. Ambrose; A. Mr. G. Balfour, 532

Sub-Postmasters as County Councillors
Qs. Mr. P. O'Brien; As. Mr. Hanbury, 281

Teachers' Examinations
Q. Mr. Macaleese; A. Mr. G. Balfour, 972

Telegraph Facilities at Belfast
Q. Mr. Young; A. Mr. Hanbury, 273

Telegraph Way-Leaves at Belfast
Q. Mr. Arnold-Forster; A. Mr. Hanbury, 271

Tithe Rent Charge Bill
Q. Mr. Dillon; A. Mr. G. Balfour, 978

Tourist Traffic on the West Coast of
Q. Mr. O'Keeffe; A. Mr. G. Balfour, 973

Town Tenants in
Q. Mr. Field; A. Mr. G. Balfour, 776

Townshend, Constable, of Bedragh
Q. Dr. Ambrose; A. Mr. G. Balfour, 33

Trained Nurses
Q. Mr. Dillon; A. Mr. Gerald Balfour, 1316

Training Colleges
Q. Mr. M'Ghee; A. Mr. G. Balfour, 277

Trew, Mr., and the Belfast Church Disturbances
Q. Mr. Young; A. Mr. G. Balfour, 27
Qs. Mr. Dillon; As. Mr. G. Balfour, 953, 1317, 1319

Waterville Post Office
Qs. Mr. Kilbride; As. Mr. Hanbury, 287

Wexford Land Appeals
Q. Mr. Ffrench; A. Mr. G. Balfour, 971

White Estate, Bantry
Q. Mr. Gilhooly; A. Mr. Gerald Balfour, 1152

Workhouse Hospital Nurses
Q. Dr. Tanner; A. Mr. G. Balfour, 777

ISLAND OF LEWIS FISHERIES
Qs. Mr. Weir; As. Mr. Graham Murray, 1137

ITALY
Chekeang
Q. Mr. Yerburgh; A. Mr. Brodrick, 1311

China
Qs. Mr. Pritchard Morgan; A. Mr. Brodrick, 269
Great Britain's Demands in China, and
Q. Mr. Dillon; A. Mr. Brodrick, 1321, 1321

Erythrea
Q. Sir E. Ashmead-Bartlett; A. Mr. St. John Brodrick, 530

JACKSON, Mr. W. L. [Leeds, N.]
Rivers Pollution Prevention Bill, 240

JAMAICA
Civil Service Supplementary Estimates
Os. 493

JAMESON, Major J. E. [Clare, W.]
Irish Licence Duties, 1570
Postmasters and Irish Local Government, 1563

JAPAN
China, 546
Indemnity, 540
Navy Estimates
Os. 590

JEFFREYS, Mr. A. F. [Hants, N.]
Supply
　Army Estimates (1899-1900), 817
　Warrant Officers' Grievances, 1309

JESSEL, Captain H. M. [St. Pancras, S.]
British Museum Attendants, 987
Cavalry Drafts for India, 1313
Service Franchise Bill, 199
Supply
　Army Estimates, 1899-1900, Fourth Allotted Day, Considered in Committee, 1213
　Voluntary Retirements of Combatant Officers, 1313

JOHNSON, GEORGE, CASE OF, AT LIVERPOOL ASSIZES
Q. Mr. M'Ghee; A. Mr. J. Collings, 301

JOHNSTON, Mr. W. [Belfast, S.]
Antrim District Council, 520
City of Cork By-Laws, 1564
Clogher Board of Guardians, 298
Clogher Rate Collectorship, 959
Cork Corporation By-laws, 1135
Supply
　Navy Estimates, 1899-1900, Third Allotted Day, Considered in Committee, 1044

NEW PUBLIC OFFICES
Q. Mr. Malcolm; A. Mr. Akers Douglas, 1328

NEW WRITS ISSUED
Middlesex County (Harrow Division), 1302

NEW ZEALAND, OLD-AGE PENSIONS IN
Q. Mr. Hogan; A. Mr. J. Chamberlain, 968

NICOL, Mr. D. N. [Argyll]
Teachers' Superannuation in Scotland, 265

NILE VALLEY AND FRANCE
Q. Sir E. Ashmead-Bartlett; A. Mr. Brodrick, 980

NORTH EASTERN AND HULL AND BARNSLEY RAILWAYS (JOINT DOCK) BILL
Committed : The Committee to be proposed by the Committee of Selection, 426

NORTH SEA FISHERY COMMISSION
Qs. Mr. Hedderwick; As. Mr. A. J. Balfour, 983

NORTH STAFFORDSHIRE RAILWAY BILL
Com., 3
Order appointing Select Committee to consider Bill discharged, 510

NORTHAMPTON
St. James School
Qs. Mr. Channing; As. Sir J. Gorst, 30

NORTHERN ASSURANCE COMPANY BILL
Com., 2
Reported, with Amendments, 1497

NORTON, Captain C. W. [Newington, W.]
Army Nurses, 534
Compulsory Rotation Sorting Duties, 293
Employees of Parliament, 534
Military Funerals for Volunteers, 279
Naval Medical Officers, 976
Service Francise Bill, 185
Supply
Army Estimates, 1899-1900, Fourth Allotted Day, Considered in Committee, 1223
Civil Services and Revenue Departments (Supplementary Estimates), 1898-99, 455

NORTON, Lord
Board of Education Bill [H.L.], 677

NUNEATON AND CHILVERS COTON URBAN DISTRICT COUNCIL WATER BILL
Reported, 1131

NURSES
Army
Q. Captain Norton; A. Mr. G. Wyndham, 534
Irish Workhouse Hospital
Q. Dr. Tanner; A. Mr. G. Balfour, 777
Trained, in Ireland
Q. Mr. Dillon; A. Mr. Gerald Balfour, 1316

O'BRIEN, Mr. P. [Kilkenny]
Belleville Boilers, 961
Connemara Police Hut, 271
County Court Judge Leonard, 1329
Holyhead and Kingstown Piers, 962
Inland Revenue Officials and Irish Local Government, 537
Irish Militia Trainings, 277
Irish Sub-Postmasters as County Councillors, 281
Leconfield's, Lord, Tenantry, 966
Militia O.R.C.S., 276
Militia Transport, 276
Railway Enterprise in West Africa, 962
Shannon Development Company, 1141

O'CONNOR, Mr. A. [Donegal, E.]
Supply
Army Estimates, 1899-1900, 792
Fourth Allotted Day, Considered in Committee, 1173
Navy Estimates, 1899-1900, Third Allotted Day, Considered in Committee, 1003

O'CONNOR, Mr. J.
Rathfarnham Police Barrack, 523

O'CONNOR, Mr. T. P. [Liverpool, Scotland]
Supply
Army Estimates, 1899-1900, Fourth Allotted Day, Considered in Committee, 1211

OFFICE OF WOODS AND FORESTS
Q. Mr. Weir; A. Mr. R. W. Hanbury, 523

O'KEEFFE, Mr. F. A. [Limerick]
Grand Juries, 1569
Limerick Telephone Service, 771
Tourist Traffic on the West Coast of Ireland, 973

[Contin·

REID, Sir R. [Dumfries Burghs]
Supply
  Civil Services and Revenue Depart-
    ments   (Supplementary   Esti-
    mates), 1889-99, 462

RELIGIOUS INSTRUCTION IN ELEMEN-
TARY SCHOOLS
  Q. Mr. Hubbard ; A. Mr. A. J. Balfour,
    296

RENTS IN EAST LONDON
  Qs. Mr. Steadman ; A. Mr. A. J. Balfour,
    1151

RESIDENT ENGINEER TO THE HOUSES
OF PARLIAMENT
  Q. Mr. Hazell ; A. Mr. Hanbury, 439

RESIDENT MAGISTRATES (IRELAND)
  Q. Captain Donelan ; A. Mr. G. Balfour,
    956

REVENUE
[See Title FINANCE]

REVENUE PROSECUTIONS, INLAND
  Q. Mr. W. Redmond ; A. Mr. Gerald Bal-
    four, 1315

REVISED STATUTES
  Q. Mr. Marks ; A. Sir R. Webster, 782

RICKETT, Mr. J. COMPTON [Scarborough]
  Petroleum Bill, 908

RIFLE RANGES, VOLUNTEER
  Q. Mr. Monk ; A. Mr. G. Wyndham, 985

RIOTS AT CONSTANTINOPLE
  Q. Colonel Denny ; A. Mr. Brodrick,
    1153

RITCHIE, Mr. C. T. [Croydon]—President of
the Board of Trade
  Apprentices in the Mercantile Marine, 781
  Automatic Couplings, 447, 1148, 1334
  British Sailors in the Mercantile Marine,
    947
  Castlewellan Boiler Explosion, 28
  Elder, Dempster and Co.'s Employees,
    1324

RITCHIE, Mr. C. T.—cont.
  Electric Lighting, 440
  "Ellington" and "Springhill," 784
  Freight Rates on the Cork and Bandon
    Railway, 1134
  Government Grants for Local Expendi-
    ture, 1145
  Great Eastern Railway Employees, 949
  Inniskeen Railway Accident, 437
  Lascars on P. and O. Boats, 782, 1323
  London and North Western Railway
    Company's Servants, 435
  Margarine Factories, 771
  Patent Law, 18
  Provost Mungall of Cowdenbeath, 446
  Report of Supply, Merchant Shipping Act,
    1677
  Scotch Railway Station Water Supplies,
    780
  South Eastern, and London, Chatham and
    Dover Railway Companies Bill, 706,
    940, 1128
  Tiumpan Head Lighthouse, 780
  Unclaimed Debtors' Estates, 438
  Workmen's Trains on the Southern Rail-
    ways, 1559

RIVERS   POLLUTION   PREVENTION
BILL, 227

RIVERS POLLUTION PREVENTION (No.
2) BILL
  Bill Withdrawn, 242

ROBERTS, Mr. H. [Denbighshire, W.]
  Bounty-Fed Sugar in India, 528
  Mining in India, 35

ROBERTS, Mr. J. BRYN [Carnarvonshire,
Eifion]
  Chinese Territory (Demands of Italy),
    Motion for Adjournment, 551
  Indian Sugar Bounties Bill, 1156
  Supply
    Army   Estimates,   1899-1900,   4th
      Allotted Day, Considered in Com-
      mittee, 1255
    Civil Services and Revenue Depart-
      ments   (Supplementary   Esti-
      mates), 1898-99, 464

ROBERTSON, Mr. E. [Dundee]
  Course of Business, 36
  Scotch Church in Madeira, 967
  Supply
    Navy   Estimates,   1899-1900,   Third
      Allotted Day, Considered in Com-
      mittee, 1004

ROMAN   CATHOLIC   UNIVERSITY   IN
IRELAND
  Petition, 166

SUPPLY—cont.

Mercantile Marine Services
£30,000—Com., 1345; Rep., 1662
Merchant Seamen's Fund Pensions, etc.
£3,000—Com., 1347; Rep., 1663
Mint (including Coinage)
£10—Com., 1346; Rep., 1662
Miscellaneous, Charitable and other
Allowances
£1,000—Com., 1347; Rep., 1663
Miscellaneous Expenses
£6,572—Com., 1347; Rep., 1664
Miscellaneous Legal Buildings
£18,000—Com., 1345; Rep., 1661
Miscellaneous Legal Expenses
£26,000—Com., 1346; Rep., 1662
National Debt Office
£5,000—Com., 1346; Rep., 1662
National Gallery
£5,000—Com., 1347; Rep., 1663
National Portrait Gallery
£2,500—Com., 1347; Rep., 1663
Peterhead Harbour
£6,000—Com., 1345; Rep., 1662
Police, England and Wales
£14,000—Com., 1346; Rep., 1663
Prisons, England and the Colonies
• £200,000—Com., 1346; Rep., 1663
Privy Council Office, etc.
£5,000—Com., 1345; Rep., 1662
Public Buildings, Great Britain
£100,000—Com., 1345; Rep., 1662
Public Record Office
£10,000—Com., 1346; Rep., 1662
Excess Vote
£1 5s.1d.—Com., 503; Rep., 660
Public Works Loan Commission
£10—Com., 1346; Rep., 1662
Rates on Government Property
£210,000—Com., 1345; Rep., 1662
Reformatory and Industrial Schools, Great
Britain
£140,000—Com., 1346; Rep., 1663
Registrar General's Office
£13,000—Com., 1346; Rep., 1662
Royal Palaces, etc.
£16,000—Com., 1345; Rep., 1661
Royal Parks
£40,000—Com., 1345; Rep., 1661
Science and Art Department, United
Kingdom
£200,000—Com., 1347; Rep., 1663
Scientific Investigation, etc., United King-
dom
£15,000—Com., 1347; Rep., 1663
Secret Service
£17,000—Com., 1346; Rep., 1662
Stationery and Printing
£250,000—Com., 1346; Rep., 1662
Superannuation and Retired Allowances
£280,000—Com., 1347; Rep., 1663
Supreme Court of Judicature
£120,000—Com., 1346; Rep., 1663
Surveys of the United Kingdom
£80,000—Com., 1345; Rep., 1662
Telegraph Companies—Subsidies
£35,000—Com., 1347; Rep., 1663
Temporary Commissions
£8,000—Com., 1347; Rep., 1664
Treasury and Subordinate Departments
£30,000—Com., 1345; Rep., 1662

SUPPLY—cont.

Uganda, Central and East Africa Protectorates, and Uganda Railway
£250,000—Com., 1347; Rep., 1663
Supplementary Vote
£256,000—Com., 450; Rep.,
659
Universities and Colleges (Great Britain)
and Intermediate Education
(Wales)
£38,000—Com., 1347; Rep., 1663
Valuation and Boundary Survey
£6,000—Com., 1346; Rep., 1662
Wallace Gallery
£6,000—Com., 1347; Rep., 1663
Woods, Forests, etc., Offices of
£7,000—Com., 1346; Rep., 1662
Works and Public Buildings, Office of
£19,000—Com., 1346; Rep., 1662

IRISH VOTES.

Charitable Donations and Bequests Office
£750—Com., 1346; Rep., 1662
Chief Secretary and Subordinate Departments
£15,000—Com., 1346; Rep., 1662
Constabulary
£600,000—Com., 1346; Rep., 1663
County Court Offices, etc.
£36,000—Com., 1346; Rep., 1662
Dublin Metropolitan Police
£36,000—Com., 1346; Rep., 1663
Dundrum Criminal Lunatic Asylum
£2,500—Com., 1346; Rep., 1663
Education
£600,000—Com., 1347; Rep., 1663
Endowed Schools Commissioners
£350—Com., 1347; Rep., 1663
Hospitals and Charities
£10,000—Com., 1347; Rep., 1663
Land Commission
£50,000—Com., 1346; Rep., 1663
Law Charges and Criminal Prosecutions
£30,000—Com., 1346; Rep., 1663
Local Government Board
£15,000—Com., 1346; Rep., 1662
Lord Lieutenant's Household
£2,000—Com., 1346; Rep., 1662
National Gallery
£1,200—Com., 1347; Rep., 1663
Pauper Lunatics, Ireland
Supplementary Vote (£517)—Com.,
503; Rep., 659
Prisons
£45,000—Com., 1346; Rep., 1663
Public Record Office
£2,000—Com., 1346; Rep., 1662
Public Works and Buildings
£70,000—Com., 1345; Rep., 1662
Public Works Office
£12,500—Com., 1346; Rep., 1662
Queen's Colleges
£2,500—Com., 1347; Rep., 1663
Railways
£70,000—Com., 1345; Rep., 1662
Reformatory and Industrial Schools
£55,500—Com., 1346; Rep., 1663 •
Registrar-General's Office
£6,000—Com., 1346; Rep., 1662
Supreme Court of Judicature and other
Legal Departments
£38,000—Com., 1346; Rep., 1663

[Continued